# BRITISH ATHLETICS 1996

Compiled by the
National Union of Track Statisticians

Editor: Rob Whittingham
Assistant Editors: Peter Matthews, Ian Hodge,
Liz Sissons

*Published by:*     Umbra Software Limited,
                    Unit 1, Bredbury Business Park,
                    Bredbury Park Way, Bredbury, Stockport SK6 2SN
                    Tel: 0161 406 6320    Fax: 0161 406 6732

*Copyright ©*       Umbra Software Limited/National Union of Track Statisticians
                    All rights reserved

                    ISBN 1 898258 04 X

*Front Cover:*      JONATHAN EDWARDS. British and World Records,
                    World Champion, unbeaten in 1995, best triple jumper ever,
                    OK Jonathan you're on the cover.

*All photos by:*    All photographs provided by Mark Shearman,
                    22 Grovelands Road, Purley, Surrey CR2 4LA
                    Tel: 0181-660 0156    Fax: 0181-660 3437
                    His help is greatly appreciated.

*Distributed by:*   Old Bakehouse Publications,
                    The Old Bakehouse, Church Street,
                    Abertillery, Gwent NP3 1EA
                    Tel: 01495 212600    Fax: 01495 216222

*Printed in*
*Great Britain by:*  J.R. Davies (Printers) Limited,
                     The Old Bakehouse, Church Street, Abertillery, Gwent NP3 1EA
                     Tel: 01495 212600    Fax: 01495 216222

# CONTENTS

# NATIONAL UNION OF TRACK STATISTICIANS AND COMPILERS

Compilation

General Editor - Rob Whittingham

Assistant Editors - Ian Hodge, Peter Matthews, Liz Sissons

Records - Bob Sparks  All Time Lists and Index - Martin Rix, Tony Miller
Results - Rob Whittingham, Ian Hodge

Men's Lists - Ian Hodge (HJ,PV and overall), Joe Barrass  (sprints),
Tim Grose (800m to 10,000m), Steve Mitchell (5000m, 10,000m), John Walsh (Marathon),
Shirley Hitchcock (hurdles), Bill Myers (LJ,TJ),Tony O'Neill (throws).

Under 20 & Under 17 Men - Ian Hodge with above compilers and Melvyn Jones

Under 15 Men - Ian Hodge and Melvyn Jones          Under 13 Men - Roy Waters

Women's Lists - Liz Sissons, Tony Miller (Under 17),
John Brant (Under 15), Bill Green (Under 13), Sally Gandee (Veterans).

Walks - John Powell    Relays - Keith Morbey    Multi-Events - Alan Lindop

Also acknowledgements for specific help to Alan and Brenda Currie (Wales), John Glover and
Alan Keys (Northern Ireland), Arnold Black (Scotland) and various other NUTS members.

# ABBREVIATIONS & NOTES

| | | | |
|---|---|---|---|
| A | - | mark set at altitude over 1000m | |
| a | - | automatic timing only known to one tenth of a second | |
| D | - | performance made in a Decathlon | |
| dh | - | downhill | |
| e | - | estimated time | |
| et | - | extra trial | |
| ex | - | exhibition | |
| h | - | heat | |
| H | - | performance made in a Heptathlon | |
| hc | - | handicap race | |
| i | - | indoor | |
| jo | - | jump off | |
| m | - | position in race when intermediate time taken | |
| mx | - | performance in mixed race | |
| O | - | performance made in an Octathlon | |
| o | - | over age | |
| P | - | performance made in a Pentathlon | |

| | | |
|---|---|---|
| Q | - | qualifying round |
| q | - | quarter final |
| r | - | race number |
| s | - | semi final |
| t | - | track |
| u | - | unofficial time |
| un | - | unconfirmed performance |
| w | - | wind assisted (> 2.0 m/sec) |
| W | - | wind assisted (over 4m/sec in decathlon/heptathlon) |
| x | - | relay team may include outside age-group members |
| + | - | intermediate time |
| * | - | legal performance where best is wind assisted |
| " | - | photo electric cell time |
| # | - | Unratified (may not be ratifiable) |
| & | - | as yet unratified |
| § | - | now competes for another nation |
| ¶ | - | drugs ban |

## AGE GROUP DESIGNATIONS

Men's events:

| | | |
|---|---|---|
| U13 | - Under 13 | (born 1.9.82 or later) |
| U15 | - Under 15 | (born 1.9.80 to 31.8.82) |
| U17 | - Under 17 | (born 1.9.78 to 31.8.80) |
| U20 | - Under 20 | (born 1.1.76 to 31.8.78) |
| V | - Veteran | (age 40 or over) |

Women's events:

| | | |
|---|---|---|
| U13 | - Under 13 | (born 1.9.82 or later) |
| U15 | - Under 15 | (born 1.9.80 to 31.8.82) |
| U17 | - Under 17 | (born 1.9.78 to 31.8.80) |
| U20 | - Under 20 | (born 1.1.76 to 31.8.78) |
| V | - Veteran | (age 35 or over) |

Care must be taken with very young age groups for athletes with an unknown date of birth from Northern Ireland since their age groups differ slightly.

*Italics indicates the athlete competes for a British club but is not eligible to represent Britain.*

## MULTI - EVENTS

Pentathlon, Heptathlon and Decathlon lists show the complete breakdown of individual performances in the following order:

Pentathlon (women) - 100mH, SP, HJ, LJ, 800m; Junior: LJ, SP, 75mH, HJ, 800m
Heptathlon (women) - 100mH, HJ, SP, 200m (1st day); LJ, JT, 800m (2nd day)  (80mH - Inters)
Decathlon (men)    - 100m, LJ, SP, HJ, 400m (1st day); 110mH, DT, PV, JT, 1500m (2nd day)

Totals which include performances made with following winds in excess of 4 m/s are denoted by W.  The date shown is the second day of competition.

## RANKING LISTS:

These show the best performances in each event recorded during the 1995 season.
For each performance the following details are shown:

Performance; wind reading (where appropriate);   name (with, where appropriate, age-group category);
date of birth (DDMMYY);   position in competition;   venue;   date.

The following numbers are used, although strength of performance or lack of information may vary the guidelines -

50 perfomances    100 athletes for each standard event

Age Groups - 40 Under 20, 30 Under 17, 20 Under 15, 10 Under 13

In the junior men, athletes are shown in older age groups if their performances merit this, e.g. an U15 can appear in the U17 list etc. For junior women, athletes are shown in their age group as per womens rules. Although juniors of any age will be shown in the main list on merit.

## INDEX

Club details and previous personal bests, where better than those recorded in 1995, are shown in the index for all athletes in the main lists.

# VENUES

Major venues for athletics - the name by which the stadium is denoted is shown in capitals:

LONDON (xx)

| | | | |
|---|---|---|---|
| BP | Battersea Park | Nh | Terence McMillan, Newham, Plaistow |
| Col | Colindale (Metropolitan Police track) | PH | Parliament Hill Fields, Camden |
| CP | Crystal Palace, Nat. Sports Cen. Norwood | SP | Southwark Park |
| Elt | Sutcliffe Park, Eltham | TB | Tooting Bec |
| EL | East London, Mile End | WC | White City Stadium |
| Ha | New River Sports Centre, Haringey | WF | Waltham Forest, Walthamstow |
| He | Barnet Copthall Stadium, Hendon | WL | West London Stadium |
| Hu | Hurlingham | | |

ABERDEEN, Chris Anderson Stadium, Balgowrie
ALDERSHOT Military Stadium (Army)
ANDOVER, Charlton Sports Centre
ANTRIM Forum
BARKING, Mayesbrook Park
BARRY, Jenner Park
BASILDON, Gloucester Park
BASINGSTOKE, Down Grange
BEBINGTON, The Oval, Wirral
BEDFORD, Newnham  Track, Barkers Lane
BELFAST, Mary Peters Track
BIRMINGHAM, Alexander Stadium, Perry Park
         (Un) University Track, Edgbaston
BLACKBURN, Witton Park
BLACKPOOL, Stanley Park
BOLTON
BOURNEMOUTH, Kings Park
BRACKNELL, John Nike Stadium, Bracknell SC
BRAUNTON, North Devon Athletic Track
BRIERLEY HILL, The Dell, Dudley
BRIGHTON Sports Arena, Withdean
BRISTOL, Whitchurch Stadium
BROMLEY, Norman Park
CAMBRIDGE, Wilberton Road
CANNOCK, Festival Stadium, Pye Green Road
CARLISLE, Sheepmount Stadium
CHELTENHAM, Prince of Wales Stadium
CLECKHEATON, Pr. Mary Pl. Fields, Spenbro
COATBRIDGE
COLWYN BAY, Eirias Park Arena
CORBY, Rockingham Triangle
COSFORD (RAF), Indoor and outdoor arenas
COVENTRY, Warwick Univ., Kirby Corner Rd
CRAWLEY Leisure Centre, Haslett Avenue
CREWE, Cumberland Road Sports Ground
CROYDON Arena
CUDWORTH, Dorothy Hyman Sports Centre
CWMBRAN Sports Centre
DARTFORD, Central Park
DERBY, Moorways Stadium
EDINBURGH, Meadowbank Sports Centre
ENFIELD, Q. Eliz. II Stadium, Carterhatch Lane
GATESHEAD International Stadium
GLASGOW, Crown Point
         Indoors: Kelvin Hall
GRANGEMOUTH Stadium, Falkirk
GRIMSBY, K George V Stadium, Weelsby Rd
HARLOW Sports Centre
HARROW, Bannister Sports Centre, Hatch End
HIGH WYCOMBE, Handy Cross Track
HOO, Deangate Stadium, Rochester
HORNCHURCH Stadium, Havering, Upminster
HORSHAM, Broadbridge Heath Sports Centre
HULL, Costello Stadium
ILFORD, Cricklefields Athletic Ground
IPSWICH, Northgate Sports Centre
ISLEWORTH, Borough Road College
JARROW, Monckton Stadium

JERSEY, Greve D'Azette, Jersey, CI
KINGSTON, K Meadow, Kingston-u-Thames
KIRKBY Sports Centre, Liverpool
LEAMINGTON, Edmonscote Track
LEEDS, Carnegie College
LEICESTER, Saffron Lane Sports Centre
LINCOLN, Yarborough Sports Centre
LIVERPOOL, Wavertree Track
LOUGHBOROUGH, Ashby Rd Stadium (Univ)
LUTON, Stockwood Park
MANCHESTER, Wythenshawe Park
MANSFIELD, Berry Hill Athletcs Track
MELKSHAM, Christie Miller Sports Centre
MIDDLESBROUGH, Clairville Stadium
MOTSPUR PARK
NORWICH, Norfolk Athletics Track, Earlham
NOTTINGHAM, Harvey Hadden Stadium
OXFORD, Iffley Road (University)
PERIVALE Park Tr, Ruislip Rd,Greenford, Mx
PETERBOROUGH, Embankment Track
PITREAVIE Playing Fields, Dunfermline
PLYMOUTH, Brickfields Stad,Devonport(R.N)
PORTSMOUTH, Mountbatten Cen, Alex. Park
        (RN) Stadium, Burnaby Road
READING, Palmer Park
REDDITCH, Abbey Stadium
ROTHERHAM, Herringthorpe Stadium
ST. IVES, St. Ivo Outdoor Centre
SHEFFIELD, Don Valley Stadium
        (W) Woodburn Road, Attercliffe
SOLIHULL, Tudor Grange Park
SOUTHAMPTON, Shirley Sports Centre
SOUTHEND, Southchurch Park Stadium
STOKE, Northwood C,Hanley, Stoke-on-Trent
STRETFORD, Longford Park
SUNDERLAND, Silksworth
SUTTON COLDFIELD,Wyndley Leisure Cent.
SWANSEA, Morfa Stadium, Landore
SWINDON, Thamesdown Tr., County Ground
THURROCK, Blackshots Stadium, Grays
WARLEY, Hadley Playing Fields, Smethwick
WARRINGTON, Victoria Park, Knutsford Rd
WATFORD, Woodside Stadium, Garston
WELWYN, Gosling Stad, Welwyn Garden City
WIGAN, Robin Park
WINDSOR, Vansittart Road Track
WISHAW Stadium
WOKING, Blackmore Crescent, Sheerwater
WOLVERHAMPTON Stadium, Aldersley Road
WOODFORD, Ashton P Fields,Woodford Br.
WORTHING, West Park, Shaftesbury Avenue
WREXHAM, Queensway Sports Complex
YATE, Broadlane Track, Gloucester
YEOVIL Recreation Centre, Chilton Grove

Note also, in Ireland
DUBLIN (B) Belfield
       (M) Morton Stad. (Santry)

6

# INTRODUCTION - by Rob Whittingham

A World Championship year has passed and it is now an Olympic year. No doubt this year's performances will receive an Olympic boost and be better than normal years.

I must always start my introduction with special thanks to the people who have made extraordinary efforts to ensure the accuracy of the book. Peter Matthews and Ian Hodge found time between all their other commitments, to check all the lists and this is always appreciated. This year Tony Miller again provided extra assistance on the women's lists and checked the whole index. We required a late substitute for the mens Under-13 lists and Roy Waters solved this problem admirably. I also received help from Geoff Blamire, Mike Kubiena and Julie Fletcher at Umbra Software and Marty assisted with many areas of the book.

As in previous years, I have tried to expand the contents of the book and the men's all-time lists are now complete. My thanks go to Martin Rix for his help in this and in the other all-time sections. I hope to expand the women's all-time lists next year.

Also next year, I intend to examine those areas which have been overlooked for many years. In particular, I wish to bring the venues up to date and any reader with information on new tracks is invited to write to me. This year I have been much more rigorous in examining the foreign athletes to be included on the lists. This process will be continued next year. Finally, I intend to revise some of the standards for the book. Unfortunately in some junior events, not enough athletes are reaching these traditional levels and I wish to encourage the youngsters by easing some of the standards required.

I have traditionally avoided producing analysis in my introduction but instead leave it to the reader to check the lists and draw his own conclusions on the state of British Athletics. Obviously from the comments above, there is concern in some of the junior events, but I also invite the reader to look at some of the longer distance lists and wonder where have all the athletes gone. Ten years ago, the 1986 annual contained 186 Marathon runners under 2:25.00. However, all is not doom and gloom, the top of the Pole Vault list is the best ever.

For the second year, the TSB Junior Rankings are included along with information on how the calculations are made. Although the purists do not like ranking across events, there is no doubt that this incentive has created great interest amongst the junior athletes.

For readers in the 21st Century, new junior rankings will be posted at http://www.tsb.co.uk.

My thanks to the B.A.F. for their financial assistance.

Any corrections are always welcome.

**Rob Whittingham**
March 1996
7 Birch Green   Glossop   SK13 8PR

# BAF & OTHER ADDRESSES

**British Athletic Federation**
225A Bristol Road
Edgbaston
Birmingham
B5 7UB
Tel: 021 440 5000

**AAA of England**
225A Bristol Road
Edgbaston
Birmingham
B5 7UB
Tel: 021 440 5000

## SCOTLAND
**Scotland A.F.**
Caledonia House
South Gyle
Edinburgh
Tel: 031 317 7320

## WALES
**A.A. of Wales**
Morfa Stadium Landore
Swansea
West Glamorgan SA1 7DF
Tel: 0792 456237

## NORTHERN IRELAND
**Northern Ireland A.A.F.**
Honorary Secretary: J.Allen
House of Sport
Upper Malone Road
Belfast BT9 5LA
Tel: 0232 381222

**Midland Counties A.A.**
**Edgebaston House**
3 Duchess Place
Hagley Road
Birmingham
B16 8NM
Tel: 021 452 1500

**North of Engnd A.A.**
Studio 106, EMCO House
5/7 New York Road
Leeds LS2 7PJ
Tel: 0532 461835

**South of England A.A.**
Suite 36 City of London Fruit Exchange
Brushfield St
London E1 6EU
Tel: 071 247 2963

**Commonwealth Games Councils:**
**England**
General Secretary: Miss A.Hogbin
1 Wandsworth Plain
London SW18 1EH
Tel: 081 871 2677

**Northern Ireland**
Honorary Secretary: R.J.McColgan MBE
22 Mountcoole Park, Cave Hill
Belfast BT14 8JR
Tel: 0232 716558

**Scotland**
Honorary Secretary: G.A.Hunter OBE
139 Old Dalkeith Road
Little France
Edinburgh EH16 4SZ
Tel: 031 664 1070

**Wales**
Honorary Secretary: M.John MBE
Pennant
Blaenau, Ammanford
Dyfed SA18 3BZ
Tel: 0269 850390

**British Athletics League**
Honorary Secretary: M.Ison
7 Green Hill Avenue
Luton
Beds LU2 7DN
Tel: 0582 26283

**National Young Athletes' League**
Honorary Secretary: R.Sales
78 Orchard Road
South Ockendon
Essex RM15 6HH
Tel: 0708 852178

**Supporters Club - British Athletics Club**
Honorary Secretary: Mrs M.Pieri
11 Railway Road
Newbury, Berks RG14 7PE
Tel: 0635 33400

**Sports Council**
The Sports Council
16 Upper Woburn Place
London WC1H OQP
Tel: 071 388 1277

**Athletics Weekly**
Editor: David Clarke
Bretton Court, Bretton
Peterborough PE3 8DZ
Tel: 0733 261144

**National Union of Track Statisticians**
Secretary: Dr. S. Hitchcock
2 Chudleigh Close
Bedford
MK40 3AW

8

# MAJOR OUTDOOR FIXTURES IN 1996

**APRIL**

| | | |
|---|---|---|
| 21 | Flora London Marathon | London |

**MAY**

| | | |
|---|---|---|
| 11-12 | County Championships | Various |
| 11-12 | District Championships (Scotland) | Various |
| 25 | Welsh Games | Cardiff |
| 26-27 | Inter-Counties Championship | Bedford |

**JUNE**

| | | |
|---|---|---|
| 1-2 | European Cup | Madrid, SPA |
| 9 | ENG v EST v FIN v POL v LAT v BEL | Tallinn, EST |
| 14-16 | AAA Championships/Olympic Trials | Birmingham |
| 28-29 | Scottish Championships | Glasgow |
| 30 | BUPA Games | Gateshead |

**JULY**

| | | |
|---|---|---|
| 1 | Welsh Championships | Newport |
| 6 | NI Championships | Antrim |
| 12 | Securicor Games | London (CP) |
| 12-13 | TSB English Schools Championships | Sheffield |
| 14 | GB v RUS v GER (U23) | Hexham |
| 26-4 Aug | Olympic Games | Atlanta, USA |
| 27-28 | AAA Under 20 Championships | Bedford |
| 27-28 | GB v FRA v GER v RUS (Combined Events Senior/U23/U20) | FRA |

**AUGUST**

| | | |
|---|---|---|
| 3 | GB v ITA v FRA v RUS v ESP (U20) | Nembro, ITA |
| 11 | EAA Permit Meeting | London (CP) |
| 17-18 | AAA U17/U15 | Birmingham |
| 19 | BUPA Challenge GB v USA | Gateshead |
| 21-25 | World Junior Championships | Sydney, AUS |
| 24 | GB v ITA v FRA (Field Events) | ITA |
| 25 | McDonalds' Games | Sheffield |
| 31 | Club Cup Final | |

**SEPTEMBER**

| | | |
|---|---|---|
| 9 | GB v HUN | Salgotargan, HUN |
| 29 | World Half Marathon | Palma, SPA |

**DECEMBER**

| | | |
|---|---|---|
| 15 | European Cross Country Championships | Charleroi, FRA |

# BEST AUTHENTIC PERFORMANCES (MEN)

(as at 31 Dec 1995)

W = World,  E = European,  C = Commonwealth,  A = UK All-Comers,  N = UK,  J = Junior

| | | | | | | | |
|---|---|---|---|---|---|---|---|
| **100 m** | W | 9.85 | Leroy Burrell | USA | 6 Jul 94 | Lausanne |
| | E,C,N | 9.87 | Linford Christie | Eng | 15 Aug 93 | Stuttgart |
| | A | 10.03 | Jon Drummond | USA | 15 Jul 94 | London (CP) |
| | WJ | 10.05 # | Davidson Ezinwa | NIG | 3 Jan 90 | Bauchi |
| | | 10.08 A | Obadele Thompson | BAR | 16 Apr 94 | El Paso |
| | EJ | 10.14 | Sven Matthes | GER | 13 Sep 88 | Berlin |
| | NJ | 10.21 | Jamie Henderson | | 6 Aug 87 | Birmingham |
| | | | | | | |
| **200 m** | W,E | 19.72 A | Pietro Mennea | ITA | 12 Sep 79 | Mexico City |
| | C | 19.85 | Frank Fredericks | NAM | 20 Aug 93 | Stuttgart |
| | A | 19.85 | Michael Johnson | USA | 6 Jul 90 | Edinburgh |
| | N | 19.87 A& | John Regis | | 31 Jul 94 | Sestriere |
| | | 19.94 | John Regis | | 20 Aug 93 | Stuttgart |
| | WJ | 20.07 # | Lorenzo Daniel | USA | 18 May 85 | Starkville |
| | | 20.13 | Roy Martin | USA | 16 Jun 85 | Indianapolis |
| | EJ | 20.37 | Jürgen Evers | GER | 28 Aug 83 | Schwechat |
| | NJ | 20.54 | Ade Mafe | | 25 Aug 85 | Cottbus |
| | | | | | | |
| **300 m** | W | 31.48 | Danny Everett | USA | 3 Sep 90 | Jerez de la Frontera |
| | | 31.48 | Roberto Hernández | CUB | 3 Sep 90 | Jerez de la Frontera |
| | E,C,A,N | 31.67 | John Regis | Eng | 17 Jul 92 | Gateshead |
| | WJ | 32.08 | Steve Lewis | USA | 28 Sep 88 | Seoul |
| | EJ,NJ | 32.53 | Mark Richardson | | 14 Jul 91 | London (Ha) |
| | | | | | | |
| **400 m** | W | 43.29 | Butch Reynolds | USA | 17 Aug 88 | Zürich |
| | E | 44.33 | Thomas Schönlebe | GER | 3 Sep 87 | Rome |
| | C | 44.17 | Innocent Egbunike | NIG | 19 Aug 87 | Zürich |
| | A | 43.98 | Michael Johnson | USA | 10 Jul 92 | London (CP) |
| | N | 44.47 | David Grindley | | 3 Aug 92 | Barcelona |
| | WJ | 43.87 | Steve Lewis | USA | 28 Sep 88 | Seoul |
| | EJ | 45.01 | Thomas Schönlebe | GER | 15 Jul 84 | Berlin |
| | NJ | 45.36 | Roger Black | | 24 Aug 85 | Cottbus |
| | | | | | | |
| **600 m** | W | 1:12.81 | Johnny Gray | USA | 24 May 86 | Santa Monica |
| | E,C,A,N | 1:14.95 | Steve Heard | Eng | 14 Jul 91 | London (Ha) |
| | NJ | 1:16.79 | Andrew Lill | | 24 Jul 90 | Mansfield |
| | | | | | | |
| **800 m** | W,E,C,N | 1:41.73 " | Sebastian Coe | Eng | 10 Jun 81 | Florence |
| | A | 1:43.22 | Steve Cram | | 31 Jul 86 | Edinburgh |
| | WJ | 1:44.9 y# | Jim Ryun | USA | 10 Jun 66 | Terre Haute |
| | | 1:44.3 | Joaquim Cruz | BRA | 27 Jun 81 | Rio de Janeiro |
| | EJ | 1:45.45 | Andreas Busse | GER | 7 Jun 78 | Ostrava |
| | NJ | 1:45.64 | David Sharpe | | 5 Sep 86 | Brussels |
| | | | | | | |
| **1000 m** | W,E,C,N | 2:12.18 | Sebastian Coe | Eng | 11 Jul 81 | Oslo |
| | A | 2:12.88 | Steve Cram | | 9 Aug 85 | Gateshead |
| | WJ | 2:16.84 | Ali Hakimi | TUN | 28 Jul 95 | Lindau |
| | EJ | 2:18.31 | Andreas Busse | GER | 7 Aug 77 | Dresden |
| | NJ | 2:18.98 | David Sharpe | | 19 Aug 86 | Birmingham |
| | | | | | | |
| **1500 m** | W | 3:27.37 | Noureddine Morceli | ALG | 12 Jul 95 | Nice |
| | E,C,N | 3:29.67 | Steve Cram | Eng | 16 Jul 85 | Nice |
| | A | 3:30.72 | Noureddine Morceli | ALG | 15 Jul 94 | London (CP) |
| | WJ | 3:34.63 # | Daniel Komen | KEN | 5 Jun 95 | Moscow |
| | | 3:34.92 | Kipkoech Cheruiyot | KEN | 26 Jul 83 | Munich |
| | EJ | 3:35.51 | Reyes Estévez | SPA | 16 Aug 95 | Zürich |
| | NJ | 3:36.6 | Graham Williamson | | 17 Jul 79 | Oslo |

| Event | Cat | Time | | Name | Country | Date | Venue |
|---|---|---|---|---|---|---|---|
| **1 Mile** | W | 3:44.39 | | Noureddine Morceli | ALG | 5 Sep 93 | Rieti |
| | E,C,N | 3:46.32 | | Steve Cram | Eng | 27 Jul 85 | Oslo |
| | A | 3:49.49 | | Steve Cram | | 12 Sep 86 | London (CP) |
| | WJ | 3:51.3 | | Jim Ryun | USA | 17 Jul 66 | Berkeley |
| | EJ,NJ | 3:53.15 | | Graham Williamson | | 17 Jul 79 | Oslo |
| **2000 m** | W | 4:47.88 | | Noureddine Morceli | ALG | 3 Jul 95 | Paris |
| | E,C,N | 4:51.39 | | Steve Cram | Eng | 4 Aug 85 | Budapest |
| | A | 4:55.20 | | Steve Cram | | 28 Aug 88 | London (CP) |
| | WJ | 5:00.6 | +e | Daniel Komen | KEN | 25 Jul 95 | Monaco |
| | EJ | 5:04.4 | | Harald Hudak | GER | 30 Jun 76 | Oslo |
| | NJ | 5:06.56 | | Jon Richards | | 7 Jul 82 | Oslo |
| **3000 m** | W | 7:25.11 | | Noureddine Morceli | ALG | 2 Aug 94 | Monaco |
| | E,A,N | 7:32.79 | | Dave Moorcroft | | 17 Jul 82 | London (CP) |
| | C | 7:27.18 | | Moses Kiptanui | KEN | 25 Jul 95 | Monaco |
| | WJ | 7:37.58 | | Philip Mosima | KEN | 25 Jul 95 | Monaco |
| | EJ | 7:43.20 | | Ari Paunonen | FIN | 22 Jun 77 | Cologne |
| | NJ | 7:48.28 | | Jon Richards | | 9 Jul 83 | Oslo |
| **2 Miles** | W | 8:07.46 | | Haile Gebrselassie | ETH | 27 May 95 | Kerkrade |
| | C | 8:09.01 | | Moses Kiptanui | KEN | 30 Jul 94 | Hechtel |
| | E | 8:13.2 | i | Emiel Puttemans | BEL | 18 Feb 73 | Berlin |
| | E,A,N | 8:13.51 | | Steve Ovett | | 15 Sep 78 | London (CP) |
| | WJ | 8:25.2 | | Jim Ryun | USA | 13 May 66 | Los Angeles |
| | EJ,NJ | 8:28.31 | | Steve Binns | | 31 Aug 79 | London (CP) |
| **5000 m** | W | 12:44.39 | | Haile Gebrselassie | ETH | 16 Aug 95 | Zurich |
| | C | 12:55.30 | | Moses Kiptanui | KEN | 8 Jun 95 | Rome |
| | E,N | 13:00.41 | | Dave Moorcroft | Eng | 7 Jul 82 | Oslo |
| | A | 13:06.72 | | William Sigei | KEN | 15 Jul 94 | London (CP) |
| | WJ | 12:56.15 | | Daniel Komen | KEN | 8 Jun 95 | Rome |
| | EJ,NJ | 13:27.04 | | Steve Binns | | 14 Sep 79 | London (CP) |
| **10 km** | W | 26:43.53 | | Haile Gebrselassie | ETH | 5 Jun 95 | Hengelo |
| | C | 26:52.23 | | William Sigei | KEN | 22 Jul 94 | Stockholm |
| | E | 27:13.81 | | Fernando Mamede | POR | 2 Jul 84 | Stockholm |
| | A | 27:20.38 | | Aloÿs Nizigama | BUR | 7 Jul 95 | London (CP) |
| | N | 27:23.06 | | Eamonn Martin | | 2 Jul 88 | Oslo |
| | WJ | 27:11.18 | | Richard Chelimo | KEN | 25 Jun 91 | Hengelo |
| | EJ | 28:22.48 | | Christian Leuprecht | ITA | 4 Sep 90 | Koblenz |
| | NJ | 29:21.9 | | Jon Brown | | 21 Apr 90 | Walnut |
| **20 km** | W | 56:55.6 | | Arturo Barrios | MEX | 30 Mar 91 | La Flèche |
| | E | 57:18.4 | | Dionisio Castro | POR | 31 Mar 90 | La Flèche |
| | C,N | 57:28.7 | | Carl Thackery | Eng | 31 Mar 90 | La Flèche |
| | A | 58:39.0 | | Ron Hill | | 9 Nov 68 | Leicester |
| **1 Hour** | W | 21,101 m | | Arturo Barrios | MEX | 30 Mar 91 | La Flèche |
| | E | 20,944 m | | Jos Hermens | HOL | 1 May 76 | Papendal |
| | C,N | 20,855 m | | Carl Thackery | Eng | 31 Mar 90 | La Flèche |
| | A | 20,472 m | | Ron Hill | | 9 Nov 68 | Leicester |
| | NJ | 18,221 m | | Eddie Twohig | | 16 Jun 81 | Leamington |
| **25 km** | W | 1:13:55.8 | | Toshihiko Seko | JAP | 22 Mar 81 | Christchurch, NZ |
| | E | 1:14:16.8 | | Pekka Päivärintä | FIN | 15 May 75 | Oulu |
| | C,A,N | 1:15:22.6 | | Ron Hill | Eng | 21 Jul 65 | Bolton |
| **30 km** | W | 1:29:18.78 | | Toshihiko Seko | JAP | 22 Mar 81 | Christchurch, NZ |
| | E,C,A,N | 1:31:30.4 | | Jim Alder | Sco | 5 Sep 70 | London (CP) |
| **Half Marathon** | W,C | 59:47 | | Moses Tanui | KEN | 3 Apr 93 | Milan |
| | A | 60:02 | | Benson Masya | KEN | 18 Sep 94 | Tyneside |
| | E,N | 60:09 | | Paul Evans | | 15 Jan 95 | Marrakesh |
| | WJ | 62:11 | | Melk Mothuli | RSA | 3 Oct 93 | Brussels |
| | NJ | 66:48 | | Alan Wilson | | 29 May 83 | Kirkintilloch |

11

| Event | | Time/Mark | | Athlete | Country | Date | Venue |
|---|---|---|---|---|---|---|---|
| **Marathon** | W | 2:06:50 | | Belayneh Dinsamo | ETH | 17 Apr 88 | Rotterdam |
| | E | 2:07:12 | | Carlos Lopes | POR | 20 Apr 85 | Rotterdam |
| | C | 2:07:02 | | Sammy Lelei | KEN | 24 Sep 95 | Berlin |
| | N | 2:07:13 | | Steve Jones | | 20 Oct 85 | Chicago |
| | A | 2:08:16 | | Steve Jones | | 21 Apr 85 | London |
| | WJ | 2:12:49 | | Negash Dube | ETH | 18 Oct 87 | Beijing |
| | | 2:12:49 | | Tesfayi Dadi | ETH | 9 Oct 88 | Berlin |
| | NJ | 2:23:28 | | Eddie Twohig | | 28 Mar 82 | Wolverhampton |
| **2km St** | W,C | 5:14.43 | | Julius Kariuki | KEN | 21 Aug 90 | Rovereto |
| | E | 5:18.36 | | Alessandro Lambruschini | ITA | 12 Sep 89 | Verona |
| | A | 5:19.68 | | Samson Obwocha | KEN | 19 Jul 86 | Birmingham |
| | N | 5:19.86 | | Mark Rowland | | 28 Aug 88 | London (CP) |
| | WJ,EJ | 5:25.01 | | Arsenios Tsiminos | GRE | 2 Oct 80 | Athens |
| | NJ | 5:29.61 | | Colin Reitz | | 18 Aug 79 | Bydgoszcz |
| **3km St** | W,C | 7:59.18 | | Moses Kiptanui | KEN | 16 Aug 95 | Zürich |
| | E | 8:07.62 | | Joseph Mahmoud | FRA | 24 Aug 84 | Brussels |
| | A | 8:08.11 | | Patrick Sang | KEN | 7 Jul 95 | London (CP) |
| | N | 8:07.96 | | Mark Rowland | | 30 Sep 88 | Seoul |
| | WJ | 8:19.21 | | Daniel Njenga | KEN | 11 Jun 94 | Tokyo |
| | EJ | 8:29.50 | | Ralf Pönitzsch | GER | 19 Aug 76 | Warsaw |
| | NJ | 8:29.85 | | Paul Davies-Hale | | 31 Aug 81 | London (CP) |
| **110m H** | W,E,C,N | 12.91 | | Colin Jackson | Wal | 20 Aug 93 | Stuttgart |
| | A | 13.03 | | Colin Jackson | | 4 Sep 94 | Sheffield |
| | WJ | 13.23 | | Renaldo Nehemiah | USA | 16 Aug 78 | Zürich |
| | EJ,NJ | 13.44 | | Colin Jackson | | 19 Jul 86 | Athens |
| **200m H** | WECAN | 22.63 | | Colin Jackson | Wal | 1 Jun 91 | Cardiff |
| | NJ | 23.2 | | Jon Ridgeon | | 19 Sep 86 | Thurrock |
| | | 24.02 | | Paul Gray | | 13 Sep 87 | London (CP) |
| **400m H** | W | 46.78 | | Kevin Young | USA | 6 Aug 92 | Barcelona |
| | E | 47.37 | | Stéphane Diagana | FRA | 5 Jul 95 | Lausanne |
| | C | 47.10 | | Samuel Matete | ZAM | 7 Aug 91 | Zürich |
| | A | 47.67 | | Kevin Young | USA | 14 Aug 92 | Sheffield |
| | N | 47.82 | | Kriss Akabusi | | 6 Aug 92 | Barcelona |
| | WJ | 48.02 | | Danny Harris | USA | 17 Jun 84 | Los Angeles |
| | EJ | 48.74 | | Vladimir Budko | RUS | 18 Aug 84 | Moscow |
| | NJ | 50.22 | | Martin Briggs | | 28 Aug 83 | Schwechat |
| **High Jump** | W | 2.45 | | Javier Sotomayor | CUB | 27 Jul 93 | Salamanca |
| | E | 2.42 | | Patrik Sjöberg | SWE | 30 Jun 87 | Stockholm |
| | | 2.42 | i# | Carlo Thränhardt | GER | 26 Feb 88 | Berlin |
| | (C,N) | 2.38 | i# | Steve Smith | Eng | 4 Feb 94 | Wuppertal |
| | C | 2.38 | | Troy Kemp | BHM | 12 Jul 95 | Nice |
| | N,WJ,EJ,NJ | 2.37 | | Steve Smith | | 20 Sep 92 | Seoul |
| | N | 2.37 | | Steve Smith | | 22 Aug 93 | Stuttgart |
| | A | 2.41 | | Javier Sotomayor | CUB | 15 Jul 94 | London (CP) |
| | WJ,EJ | 2.37 | | Dragutin Topic | CRO | 12 Aug 90 | Plovdiv |
| **Pole Vault** | W,E | 6.15 | i# | Sergey Bubka | UKR | 21 Feb 93 | Donetsk |
| | | 6.14 | | Sergey Bubka | UKR | 31 Jul 94 | Sestriere |
| | C | 6.03 | | Okkert Brits | RSA | 18 Aug 95 | Cologne |
| | A | 6.05 | | Sergey Bubka | UKR | 10 Sep 93 | London (CP) |
| | N | 5.70 | | Nick Buckfield | | 23 Jul 95 | Sheffield |
| | WJ,EJ | 5.80 | | Maksim Tarasov | RUS | 14 Jul 89 | Bryansk |
| | NJ | 5.50 | | Neil Winter | | 9 Aug 92 | San Giuliano |

| Event | | Mark | | Athlete | Country | Date | | | Venue |
|---|---|---|---|---|---|---|---|---|---|
| **Long** | W | 8.95 | | Mike Powell | USA | 30 | Aug | 91 | Tokyo |
| **Jump** | E | 8.86 | A | Robert Emmiyan | ARM | 22 | May | 87 | Tsakhkadzor |
| | C | 8.45 | | James Beckford | JAM | 18 | Sep | 95 | Oristano |
| | A | 8.54 | | Mike Powell | USA | 10 | Sep | 93 | London (CP) |
| | N | 8.23 | | Lynn Davies | | 30 | Jun | 68 | Berne |
| | WJ | 8.34 | | Randy Williams | USA | 8 | Sep | 72 | Munich |
| | EJ | 8.24 | | Volodymyr Ochkan | UKR | 21 | Jun | 87 | St. Petersburg |
| | NJ | 7.98 | | Stewart Faulkner | | 6 | Aug | 88 | Birmingham |
| | | | | | | | | | |
| **Triple** | W,E,C,N | 18.29 | | Jonathan Edwards | Eng | 7 | Aug | 95 | Gothenburg |
| **Jump** | A | 18.00 | | Jonathan Edwards | | 27 | Aug | 95 | London (CP) |
| | WJ,EJ | 17.50 | | Volker Mai | GER | 23 | Jun | 85 | Erfurt |
| | NJ | 16.58 | | Tosi Fasinro | | 15 | Jun | 91 | Espoo |
| | | | | | | | | | |
| **Shot** | W | 23.12 | | Randy Barnes | USA | 20 | May | 90 | Los Angeles |
| | E | 23.06 | | Ulf Timmermann | GER | 22 | May | 88 | Khaniá |
| | C,N | 21.68 | | Geoff Capes | Eng | 18 | May | 80 | Cwmbrân |
| | A | 22.28 | # | Brian Oldfield | USA | 18 | Jun | 75 | Edinburgh |
| | | 21.72 | | Ulf Timmermann | GER | 5 | Aug | 89 | Gateshead |
| | WJ | 21.05 | i# | Terry Albritton | USA | 22 | Feb | 74 | New York |
| | | 20.65 | # | Mike Carter | USA | 5 | Jul | 79 | Boston |
| | | 20.38 | | Terry Albritton | USA | 27 | Apr | 74 | Walnut |
| | EJ | 20.20 | | Udo Beyer | GER | 6 | Jul | 74 | Leipzig |
| | NJ | 18.21 | i# | Matt Simson | | 3 | Feb | 89 | Cosford |
| | | 18.11 | | Matt Simson | | 27 | Aug | 89 | Varazdin |
| | | | | | | | | | |
| **Discus** | W,E | 74.08 | | Jürgen Schult | GER | 6 | Jun | 86 | Neubrandenburg |
| | C | 67.80 | | Adewale Olukoju | NIG | 11 | May | 91 | Los Angeles |
| | A | 68.32 | | John Powell | USA | 30 | Aug | 82 | London (CP) |
| | N | 65.16 | # | Richard Slaney | | 1 | Jul | 85 | Eugene |
| | | 64.32 | | Bill Tancred | | 10 | Aug | 74 | Woodford |
| | WJ | 65.62 | # | Werner Reiterer | AUS | 15 | Dec | 87 | Melbourne |
| | (WJ),EJ | 63.64 | | Werner Hartmann | GER | 25 | Jun | 78 | Strasbourg |
| | NJ | 55.10 | | Glen Smith | | 31 | Aug | 91 | Brierley Hill |
| | | | | | | | | | |
| **Hammer** | W,E | 86.74 | | Yuriy Sedykh | UKR/RUS | 30 | Aug | 86 | Stuttgart |
| | C | 77.58 | | Sean Carlin | AUS | 11 | Feb | 94 | Adelaide |
| | A | 85.60 | | Yuriy Sedykh | UKR/RUS | 13 | Jul | 84 | London (CP) |
| | N | 77.54 | | Martin Girvan | | 12 | May | 84 | Wolverhampton |
| | WJ,EJ | 78.14 | | Roland Steuk | GER | 30 | Jun | 78 | Leipzig |
| | NJ | 67.48 | | Paul Head | | 16 | Sep | 84 | Karlovac |
| | | | | | | | | | |
| **Javelin** | W,E,A | 95.66 | | Jan Zelezny | CS | 29 | Aug | 93 | Sheffield |
| | C,N | 91.46 | | Steve Backley | Eng | 25 | Jan | 92 | Auckland |
| | WJ,EJ | 80.94 | | Aki Parviainen | FIN | 5 | Jul | 92 | Jyväskylä |
| | NJ | 79.50 | | Steve Backley | | 5 | Jun | 88 | Derby |
| | | | | | | | | | |
| **Pent.** | W,A | 4123 | | Bill Toomey | USA | 16 | Aug | 69 | London (CP) |
| | E | 4079 | | Rein Aun | EST | 17 | Jul | 68 | Tartu |
| | C,N | 3841 | | Barry King | Eng | 20 | May | 70 | Santa Barbara |
| | | | | | | | | | |
| **Dec.** | W, | 8891 | | Dan O'Brien | USA | 5 | Sep | 92 | Talence |
| | E,C,N | 8847 | | Daley Thompson | Eng | 9 | Aug | 84 | Los Angeles |
| | A | 8663 | | Daley Thompson | | 28 | Jul | 86 | Edinburgh |
| | WJ,EJ | 8397 | | Torsten Voss | GER | 7 | Jul | 82 | Erfurt |
| | NJ | 8082 | | Daley Thompson | | 31 | Jul | 77 | Sittard |
| (1986 Javelin) | | | | | | | | | |
| | E,C,N | 8811 | # | Daley Thompson | Eng | 28 | Aug | 86 | Stuttgart |
| | WJ,EJ | 8114 | # | Michael Kohnle | GER | 25 | Aug | 89 | Varazdin |
| | NJ | 7488 | # | David Bigham | | 9 | Aug | 90 | Plovdiv |

| | | | | | | | | |
|---|---|---|---|---|---|---|---|---|
| **4x100m** | W | 37.40 | | United States | | 8 Aug 92 | Barcelona |
| | | 37.40 | | United States | | 21 Aug 93 | Stuttgart |
| | E,N | 37.77 | | UK National Team | | 22 Aug 93 | Stuttgart |
| | C | 37.83 | | Canada | | 22 Aug 93 | Stuttgart |
| | A | 38.39 | | UK National Team | | 5 Aug 89 | Gateshead |
| | WJ | 39.00 | A | United States | | 18 Jul 83 | Colorado Springs |
| | EJ | 39.21 | # | UK National Team | | 20 Sep 92 | Seoul |
| | (EJ) | 39.25 | | West Germany | | 28 Aug 83 | Schwechat |
| | NJ | 39.21 | | UK National Team | | 20 Sep 92 | Seoul |
| | | | | | | | |
| **4x200m** | W | 1:18.68 | | Santa Monica T.C. | USA | 17 Apr 94 | Walnut |
| | E | 1:21.10 | | Italy | | 29 Sep 83 | Cagliari |
| | C | 1:20.79 | | Jamaica | | 24 Apr 88 | Walnut |
| | A,N | 1:21.29 | | UK National Team | | 23 Jun 89 | Birmingham |
| | NJ | 1:27.46 | i | UK National Team | | 28 Jan 89 | Glasgow |
| | | 1:27.6 | | Borough of Enfield | | 13 Jun 82 | London (He) |
| | | | | | | | |
| **4x400m** | W | 2:54.29 | | United States | | 22 Aug 93 | Stuttgart |
| | E,C,N | 2:57.53 | | UK National Team | Eng | 1 Sep 91 | Tokyo |
| | A | 3:00.93 | | UK National Team | | 19 Jun 92 | Edinburgh |
| | WJ | 3:01.90 | | United States | | 20 Jul 86 | Athens |
| | EJ,NJ | 3:03.80 | # | UK National Team | | 12 Aug 90 | Plovdiv |
| | (EJ) | 3:04.58 | | East Germany | | 23 Aug 81 | Utrecht |
| | | | | | | | |
| **4x800m** | WECAN | 7:03.89 | | UK National Team | Eng | 30 Aug 82 | London (CP) |
| | NJ | 7:35.3 | | Liverpool Harriers | | 14 Aug 90 | Leeds |
| | | | | | | | |
| **4x1500m** | W,E | 14:38.8 | | West Germany | | 17 Aug 77 | Cologne |
| | C | 14:40.4 | | New Zealand | | 22 Aug 73 | Oslo |
| | A | 15:04.7 | | Italy | | 5 Jun 92 | Sheffield |
| | N | 14:56.8 | a# | UK National Team | | 23 Jun 79 | Bourges |
| | | 15:04.6 | | UK National Team | | 5 May 76 | Athens |
| | NJ | 16:04.3 | | Blackburn Harriers | | 15 Sep 79 | Luton |
| | | | | | | | |
| **4x1mile** | W,E | 15:49.08 | | Ireland | | 17 Aug 85 | Dublin (B) |
| | C | 15:59.57 | | New Zealand | | 1 Mar 83 | Auckland |
| | A | 16:21.1 | | BMC National Squad | | 10 Jul 93 | Oxford |
| | N | 16:17.4 | | Bristol A.C. | | 24 Apr 75 | Des Moines |
| | WJ,EJ,NJ | 16:56.8 | | BMC Junior Squad | | 10 Jul 93 | Oxford |

## Track Walking

| | | | | | | | | |
|---|---|---|---|---|---|---|---|---|
| **1500 m** | W,E | 5:12.0 | | Algis Grigaliunas | LIT | 12 May 90 | Vilnius |
| | C | 5:19.1 | | Dave Smith | AUS | 7 Feb 83 | Melbourne |
| | N | 5:19.22 | i | Tim Berrett § | | 9 Feb 90 | East Rutherford |
| | | | | | | | |
| **1 mile** | W,E | 5:36.9 | | Algis Grigaliunas | LIT | 12 May 90 | Vilnius |
| | C | 5:54.6 | i | Marcel Jobin | CAN | 16 Feb 80 | Houston |
| | N | 5:56.39 | i | Tim Berrett § | | 2 Feb 90 | New York |
| | (C),A,(N) | 5:59.1 | | Darrell Stone | Eng | 2 Jul 89 | Portsmouth |
| | NJ | 6:09.2 | | Phil Vesty | | 23 Jun 82 | Leicester |
| | | | | | | | |
| **3000 m** | W,E | 10:47.11 | | Giovanni DeBenedictis | ITA | 19 May 90 | S. G. Valdarno |
| | C | 10:56.22 | | Andrew Jachno | AUS | 7 Feb 91 | Melbourne |
| | A | 11:19.00 | i | Axel Noack | GER | 23 Feb 90 | Glasgow |
| | | 11:19.9 | | Tim Berrett | CAN | 20 Apr 92 | Tonbridge |
| | N | 11:24.4 | | Mark Easton | | 10 May 89 | Tonbridge |
| | WJ,EJ | 11:13.2 | | Jozef Pribilinec | SVK | 28 Mar 79 | Banská Bystrica |
| | NJ | 11:54.23 | | Tim Berrett § | | 23 Jun 84 | London (CP) |

| | | | | | | | | |
|---|---|---|---|---|---|---|---|---|
| **5000 m** | W,E | 18:07.08 | i | Mikhail Shchennikov | RUS | 14 Feb 95 | Moscow |
| | | 18:17.22 | | Robert Korzeniowski | POL | 3 Jul 92 | Reims |
| | C | 18:52.20 | i | Dave Smith | AUS | 7 Mar 87 | Indianapolis |
| | | 18:52.87 | | Dave Smith | AUS | 21 Feb 86 | Canberra |
| | A | 18:56.27 | i | Axel Noack | GER | 23 Feb 90 | Glasgow |
| | (A),N | 19:35.0 | | Darrell Stone | | 16 May 89 | Brighton |
| | WJ,EJ | 19:19.3 | | Mikhail Shchennikov | RUS | 9 Aug 86 | Chemnitz |
| | NJ | 20:16.40 | | Philip King | | 26 Jun 93 | Lubeck |
| | | | | | | | |
| **10 km** | W,E | 38:02.60 | | Jozef Pribilinec | SVK | 30 Aug 85 | Banská Bystrica |
| | C | 38:06.6 | | Dave Smith | AUS | 25 Sep 86 | Sydney |
| | A | 39:26.02 | | Guillaume Leblanc | CAN | 29 Jun 90 | Gateshead |
| | N | 40:06.65 | | Ian McCombie | | 4 Jun 89 | Jarrow |
| | WJ,EJ | 38:54.75 | | Ralf Kowalsky | GER | 24 Jun 81 | Cottbus |
| | NJ | 41:52.13 | | Darrell Stone | | 7 Aug 87 | Birmingham |
| (Road ) | NJ | 41:46 | | Darrell Stone | | 26 Sep 87 | Paris |
| | | | | | | | |
| **1 Hour** | W | 15,577 m | | Bernardo Segura | MEX | 7 May 94 | Fana |
| | E | 15,447 m | | Jozef Pribilinec | SVK | 6 Sep 86 | Hildesheim |
| | C | 15,300 m | | Dave Smith | AUS | 6 Sep 86 | Hildesheim |
| | A | 14,383 m | | Anatoliy Solomin | UKR | 26 Aug 77 | Edinburgh |
| | N | 14,324 m | # | Ian McCombie | | 7 Jul 85 | London (SP) |
| | | 14,158 m | | Mark Easton | | 12 Sep 87 | Woodford |
| | NJ | 13,487 m | | Darrell Stone | | 12 Sep 87 | Woodford |
| | | | | | | | |
| **20 km** | W | 1:17:25.6 | | Bernardo Segura | MEX | 7 May 94 | Fana |
| | E | 1:18:35.2 | | Stefan Johansson | SWE | 15 May 92 | Fana |
| | C | 1:20:12.3 | | Nick A'Hern | AUS | 8 May 93 | Fana |
| | A | 1:24:07.6 | # | Phil Vesty | | 1 Dec 84 | Leicester |
| | | 1:24:22.0 | | José Marín | SPA | 28 Jun 81 | Brighton |
| | N | 1:23:26.5 | | Ian McCombie | | 26 May 90 | Fana |
| | WJ,EJ | 1:22:42 | | Andrey Perlov | RUS | 6 Sep 80 | Donetsk |
| | NJ | 1:31:34.4 | | Gordon Vale | | 28 Jun 81 | Brighton |
| | | | | | | | |
| **2 Hours** | W,E | 29,572 m | | Maurizio Damilano | ITA | 4 Oct 92 | Cuneo |
| | C | 28,800 m | # | Guillaume Leblanc | CAN | 16 Jun 90 | Sept Iles |
| | | 27,123 m | | Willi Sawall | AUS | 24 May 80 | Melbourne |
| | A,N | 27,262 m | # | Chris Maddocks | | 31 Dec 89 | Plymouth |
| | (A) | 26,265 m | | Jordi Llopart | SPA | 28 Jun 81 | Brighton |
| | (N) | 26,037 m | | Ron Wallwork | | 31 Jul 71 | Blackburn |
| | | | | | | | |
| **30 km** | W,E | 2:01:44.1 | | Maurizio Damilano | ITA | 4 Oct 92 | Cuneo |
| | C | 2:04:55.7 | | Guillaume Leblanc | CAN | 16 Jun 90 | Sept Iles |
| | A,N | 2:11:54 | # | Chris Maddocks | | 31 Dec 89 | Plymouth |
| | (A) | 2:17:26.4 | | Jordi Llopart | SPA | 28 Jun 81 | Brighton |
| | (N) | 2:19:18 | | Chris Maddocks | | 22 Sep 84 | Birmingham |
| | | | | | | | |
| **50 km** | W,E | 3:41:28.2 | | René Piller | FRA | 7 May 94 | Fana |
| | C | 3:43:50.0 | | Simon Baker | AUS | 9 Sep 90 | Melbourne |
| | A | 4:03:52 | | Gerhard Weidner | GER | 1 Jun 75 | Woodford |
| | N | 4:05:44.6 | | Paul Blagg | | 26 May 90 | Fana |

### Road Walking - Fastest Recorded Times

| | | | | | | | |
|---|---|---|---|---|---|---|---|
| **20 km** | W | 1:17:25.6 | t | Bernardo Segura | MEX | 7 May 94 | Fana |
| | E | 1:18:13 | | Pavol Blazek | SVK | 16 Sep 90 | Hildesheim |
| | C | 1:19:22 | | Dave Smith | AUS | 19 Jul 87 | Hobart |
| | A | 1:21:42 | | José Marin | SPA | 29 Sep 85 | St. John's, IoM |
| | N | 1:22:03 | | Ian McCombie | | 23 Sep 88 | Seoul |
| | WJ | 1:20:41 | | Wang Yinhang | CHN | 24 Oct 95 | Nanjing |
| | EJ | 1:21:40 | | Ralf Kowalsky | GER | 7 Aug 81 | Jena |
| | NJ | 1:26:13 | | Tim Berrett § | | 25 Feb 84 | Dartford |

| 30 km | W,E | 2:01:44.1 t | Maurizio Damilano | ITA | 4 Oct 92 | Cuneo |
|---|---|---|---|---|---|---|
| | C | 2:04:55.7 t | Guillaume Leblanc | CAN | 16 Jun 90 | Sept Iles |
| | A | 2:07:47 | Simon Baker | AUS | 31 Jul 86 | Edinburgh |
| | N | 2:07:56 | Ian McCombie | | 27 Apr 86 | Edinburgh |
| | NJ | 2:30:46 | Phil Vesty | | 31 Jul 82 | London (VP) |
| | | | | | | |
| 50 km | W,E | 3:37:41 | Andrey Perlov | RUS | 5 Aug 89 | St. Petersburg |
| | C | 3:43:13 | Simon Baker | AUS | 28 May 89 | L'Hospitalet |
| | A | 3:47:31 | Hartwig Gauder | GER | 28 Sep 85 | St. John's IoM |
| | N | 3:51:37 | Chris Maddocks | | 28 Oct 90 | Burrator |
| | WJ,EJ | 4:07:23 | Aleksandr Volgin | RUS | 27 Sep 86 | Zhytomyr |
| | NJ | 4:18:18 | Gordon Vale | | 24 Oct 81 | Lassing |

## RECORDS set in 1995

| 1000m | WJ | 2:16.84 | | Ali Hakimi | TUN | 28 Jul 95 | Lindau |
|---|---|---|---|---|---|---|---|
| 1500m | WJ | 3:34.63 | # | Daniel Komen | KEN | 5 Jun 95 | Moscow |
| | W | 3:27.37 | | Noureddine Morceli | ALG | 12 Jul 95 | Nice |
| | EJ | 3:35.51 | | Reyes Estévez | SPA | 16 Aug 95 | Zürich |
| 2000m | W | 4:47.88 | | Noureddine Morceli | ALG | 3 Jul 95 | Paris |
| 3000m | C | 7:27.18 | | Moses Kiptanui | KEN | 25 Jul 95 | Monte Carlo |
| | WJ | 7:37.58 | | Philip Mosima | KEN | 25 Jul 95 | Monte Carlo |
| 2 miles | W | 8:07.46 | | Haile Gebrselassie | ETH | 27 May 95 | Kerkrade |
| 5000m | W, C | 12:55.30 | | Moses Kiptanui | KEN | 8 Jun 95 | Rome |
| | WJ | 12:56.15 | | Daniel Komen | KEN | 8 Jun 95 | Rome |
| | W | 12:44.39 | | Haile Gebrselassie | ETH | 16 Aug 95 | Zürich |
| 10km | W | 26:43.53 | | Haile Gebrselassie | ETH | 5 Jun 95 | Hengelo |
| | A | 27:20.38 | | Aloys Nizigama | BUR | 7 Jul 95 | London (CP) |
| HMAR | E, N | 60:09 | | Paul Evans | | 15 Jan 95 | Marrakesh |
| MAR | C | 2:07:02 | | Sammy Lelei | KEN | 24 Sep 95 | Berlin |
| 400mH | E | 47.37 | | Stéphane Diagana | FRA | 5 Jul 95 | Lausanne |
| 3km St | A | 8:08.11 | | Patrick Sang | KEN | 7 Jul 95 | London (CP) |
| | W, C | 7:59.18 | | Moses Kiptanui | KEN | 16 Aug 95 | Zürich |
| HJ | C | 2.37 | | Troy Kemp | BAH | 9 Jul 95 | Eberstadt |
| | C | 2.38 | | Troy Kemp | BAH | 12 Jul 95 | Nice |
| PV | C | 5.91 | | Okkert Brits | SAF | 3 Mar 95 | Potchefstroom |
| | C | 5.92 | | Okkert Brits | SAF | 25 Mar 95 | Stellenbosch |
| | N | 5.70 | | Nick Buckfield | | 23 Jul 95 | Sheffield |
| | C | 6.00 | | Okkert Brits | SAF | 29 Jul 95 | Sestriere |
| | C | 6.03 | | Okkert Brits | SAF | 18 Aug 95 | Cologne |
| LJ | C | 8.44 | | James Beckford | JAM | 16 Aug 95 | Zürich |
| | C | 8.45 | | James Beckford | JAM | 18 Sep 95 | Oristano |
| TJ | C | 17.62 | ^ | Brian Wellman | BER | 15 Apr 95 | El Paso |
| | C | 17.92 | | James Beckford | JAM | 20 May 95 | Odessa, Tx |
| | N | 17.58 | | Jonathan Edwards | | 11 Jun 95 | Loughborough |
| | N | 17.72 | | Jonathan Edwards | | 25 Jun 95 | Lille |
| | A, N | 17.72 | | Jonathan Edwards | | 2 Jul 95 | Gateshead |
| | A, N | 17.74 | | Jonathan Edwards | | 2 Jul 95 | Gateshead |
| | W, E, C, N | 17.98 | | Jonathan Edwards | Eng | 18 Jul 95 | Salamanca |
| | W, E, C, N | 18.16 | | Jonathan Edwards | Eng | 7 Aug 95 | Gothenburg |
| | W, E, C, N | 18.29 | | Jonathan Edwards | Eng | 7 Aug 95 | Gothenburg |
| | A | 18.00 | | Jonathan Edwards | | 27 Aug 95 | London (CP) |

## Road Walking

| 20km | WJ | 1:21:16 | Yevgeniy Shmalyuk | RUS | 11 Feb 95 | Adler |
|---|---|---|---|---|---|---|
| | WJ | 1:20:41 | Wang Yinhang | CHN | 24 Oct 95 | Nanjing |
| | W,E | 3:41:28.2 | René Piller | FRA | 7 May 94 | Fana |

# WOMEN'S EVENTS

| Event | Cat | Time | Name | Nat | Date | Place |
|---|---|---|---|---|---|---|
| 100 m | W | 10.49 | Florence Griffith Joyner | USA | 16 Jul 88 | Indianapolis |
| | E | 10.77 | Irina Privalova | RUS | 6 Jul 94 | Lausanne |
| | C | 10.78 | Merlene Ottey | JAM | 30 May 90 | Seville |
| | | 10.78 | Merlene Ottey | JAM | 3 Sep 94 | Paris |
| | A | 11.02 | Merlene Ottey | JAM | 14 Jul 89 | London (CP) |
| | N | 11.10 | Kathy Smallwood/Cook | | 5 Sep 81 | Rome |
| | WJ,EJ | 10.88 # | Marlies Oelsner/Göhr | GER | 1 Jul 77 | Dresden |
| | | 10.89 | Kathrin Krabbe | GER | 20 Jul 88 | Berlin |
| | NJ | 11.27 A | Kathy Smallwood/Cook | | 9 Sep 79 | Mexico City |
| 200 m | W | 21.34 | Florence Griffith Joyner | USA | 29 Sep 88 | Seoul |
| | E | 21.71 | Marita Koch | GER | 10 Jun 79 | Chemnitz |
| | | 21.71 # | Marita Koch | GER | 21 Jul 84 | Potsdam |
| | | 21.71 | Heike Drechsler | GER | 29 Jun 86 | ' Jena |
| | | 21.71 # | Heike Drechsler | GER | 29 Aug 86 | Stuttgart |
| | C | 21.64 | Merlene Ottey | JAM | 13 Sep 91 | Brussels |
| | A | 22.23 | Merlene Ottey | JAM | 9 Sep 94 | London (CP) |
| | N | 22.10 | Kathy Cook | | 9 Aug 84 | Los Angeles |
| | WJ,EJ | 22.19 | Natalya Bochina | RUS | 30 Jul 80 | Moscow |
| | NJ | 22.70 A | Kathy Smallwood/Cook | | 12 Sep 79 | Mexico City |
| 300 m | W,E | 34.1 # | Marita Koch | GER | 6 Oct 85 | Canberra |
| | | 34.8 + | Marita Koch | GER | 8 Sep 82 | Athens |
| | | 35.00 + | Marie-José Pérec | FRA | 27 Aug 91 | Tokyo |
| | C,A,N | 35.46 | Kathy Cook | | 18 Aug 84 | London (CP) |
| | (A) | 35.46 | Chandra Cheeseborough | USA | 18 Aug 84 | London (CP) |
| | WJ,EJ,NJ | 36.2 | Donna Murray/Hartley | | 7 Aug 74 | London (CP) |
| | WJ,EJ | 36.24 | Grit Breuer | GER | 29 Aug 90 | Split |
| | NJ | 36.46 | Linsey Macdonald | | 13 Jul 80 | London (CP) |
| 400 m | W,E | 47.60 | Marita Koch | GER | 6 Oct 85 | Canberra |
| | C,N | 49.43 | Kathy Cook | Eng | 6 Aug 84 | Los Angeles |
| | C | 49.43 A | Fatima Yusuf | NIG | 15 Sep 95 | Harare |
| | A | 49.33 | Tatjána Kocembová | CS | 20 Aug 83 | London (CP) |
| | WJ,EJ | 49.42 | Grit Breuer | GER | 27 Aug 91 | Tokyo |
| | NJ | 51.16 | Linsey Macdonald | | 15 Jun 80 | London (CP) |
| 600 m | W,E | 1:23.5 | Doina Melinte | ROM | 27 Jul 86 | Poiana Brasov |
| | C | 1:26.0 | Charlene Rendina | AUS | 12 Mar 79 | Adelaide |
| | A | 1:25.90 | Delisa Walton-Floyd | USA | 28 Aug 88 | London (CP) |
| | N | 1:26.18 | Diane Edwards/Modahl | | 22 Aug 87 | London (CP) |
| | NJ | 1:27.33 | Lorraine Baker | | 13 Jul 80 | London (CP) |
| 800 m | W,E | 1:53.28 | Jarmila Kratochvílová | CS | 26 Jul 83 | Munich |
| | C,N | 1:56.21 | Kelly Holmes | Eng | 9 Sep 95 | Monaco |
| | A | 1:57.14 | Jarmila Kratochvílová | CS | 24 Jun 85 | Belfast |
| | WJ | 1:57.18 | Wang Yuan | CHN | 8 Sep 93 | Beijing |
| | EJ | 1:57.45 # | Hildegard Ullrich | GER | 31 Aug 78 | Prague |
| | (EJ) | 1:59.17 | Birte Bruns | GER | 20 Jul 88 | Berlin |
| | NJ | 2:01.11 | Lynne MacDougall/McIntyre | | 18 Aug 84 | London (CP) |
| 1000 m | W | 2:29.34 | Maria Lurdes Mutola | MOZ | 25 Aug 95 | Brussels |
| | E | 2:30.6 # | Tatyana Providokhina | RUS | 20 Aug 78 | Podolsk |
| | (E) | 2:30.67 | Christine Wachtel | GER | 17 Aug 90 | Berlin |
| | C,A,N | 2:32.82 | Kelly Holmes | Eng | 23 Jul 95 | Sheffield |
| | WJ,EJ | 2:35.4 a | Irina Nikitina | RUS | 5 Aug 79 | Podolsk |
| | NJ | 2:38.58 | Jo White | | 9 Sep 77 | London (CP) |
| 1500 m | W | 3:50.46 | Qu Yunxia | CHN | 11 Sep 93 | Beijing |
| | E | 3:52.47 | Tatyana Kazankina | RUS | 13 Aug 80 | Zürich |
| | C,N,(EJ),NJ | 3:59.96 | Zola Budd/Pieterse | Eng | 30 Aug 85 | Brussels |
| | A | 3:59.31 | Ravilya Agletdinova | BLR | 5 Jun 83 | Birmingham |
| | WJ | 3:59.81 | Wang Yuan | CHN | 11 Sep 93 | Beijing |
| | EJ | 4:04.39 | Zola Budd/Pieterse | | 28 May 84 | Cwmbrân |

| Event | | | | Name | Country | Date | | | Place |
|---|---|---|---|---|---|---|---|---|---|
| **1 Mile** | W,E | 4:15.61 | | Paula Ivan | ROM | 10 | Jul | 89 | Nice |
| | C,N,WJ,EJ,NJ | 4:17.57 | | Zola Budd/Pieterse | Eng | 21 | Aug | 85 | Zürich |
| | A | 4:19.59 | | Mary Slaney | USA | 2 | Aug | 85 | London (CP) |
| **2000 m** | W,E,A | 5:25.36 | | Sonia O'Sullivan | IRE | 8 | Jul | 94 | Edinburgh |
| | C,N | 5:26.93 | | Yvonne Murray | Sco | 8 | Jul | 94 | Edinburgh |
| | WJ,EJ,NJ | 5:33.15 | | Zola Budd/Pieterse | | 13 | Jul | 84 | London (CP) |
| **3000 m** | W | 8:06.11 | | Wang Junxia | CHN | 13 | Sep | 93 | Beijing |
| | E,A | 8:21.64 | | Sonia O'Sullivan | IRE | 15 | Jul | 94 | London (CP) |
| | C,N,NJ | 8:28.83 | | Zola Budd/Pieterse | Eng | 7 | Sep | 85 | Rome |
| | WJ,EJ | 8:28.83 | # | Zola Budd/Pieterse | | 7 | Sep | 85 | Rome |
| | (WJ) | 8:36.45 | | Ma Ningning | CHN | 6 | Jun | 93 | Jinan |
| | (EJ) | 8:40.08 | | Gabriele Szabo | ROM | 10 | Aug | 94 | Helsinki |
| **5000 m** | W,E | 14:36.45 | | Fernanda Ribeiro | POR | 22 | Jul | 95 | Hechtel |
| | A | 14:47.64 | | Sonia O'Sullivan | IRE | 7 | Jul | 95 | London (CP) |
| | C,N,EJ,NJ | 14:48.07 | | Zola Budd/Pieterse | Eng | 26 | Aug | 85 | London (CP) |
| | WJ | 14:45.90 | | Jiang Bo | CHN | 24 | Oct | 95 | Nanjing |
| **10 km** | W | 29:31.78 | | Wang Junxia | CHN | 8 | Sep | 93 | Beijing |
| | E | 30:13.74 | | Ingrid Kristiansen | NOR | 5 | Jul | 86 | Oslo |
| | C,A | 30:52.51 | | Elana Meyer | RSA | 10 | Sep | 94 | London (CP) |
| | N | 30:57.07 | | Liz McColgan | | 25 | Jun | 91 | Hengelo |
| | WJ | 31:15.38 | # | Sally Barsosio | KEN | 21 | Aug | 93 | Stuttgart |
| | | 31:40.56 | | Delilah Asiago | KEN | 16 | Jun | 91 | Tokyo |
| | EJ | 31:54.29 | | Annemari Sandell | FIN | 9 | Aug | 95 | Gothenburg |
| **1 Hour** | W,E | 18,084 m | | Silvana Cruciata | ITA | 4 | May | 81 | Rome |
| | C,A,N | 16,460 m | i | Bronwen Cardy-Wise | Wal | 8 | Mar | 92 | Birmingham |
| | | 16,272 m | | Zina Marchant | Eng | 30 | Mar | 88 | London (TB) |
| **20 km** | W | 1:06:48.8 | | Izumi Maki | JAP | 19 | Sep | 93 | Amagasaki |
| | E | 1:06:55.5 | # | Rosa Mota | POR | 14 | May | 83 | Lisbon |
| | C,A,N | 1:21:43.0 | # | Eleanor Adams/Robinson | Eng | 16 | Oct | 82 | London (He) |
| **25 km** | W,E | 1:29:29.2 | | Karolina Szabó | HUN | 22 | Apr | 88 | Budapest |
| | C,A,N | 1:42:36.9 | # | Eleanor Adams/Robinson | Eng | 16 | Oct | 82 | London (He) |
| **30 km** | W,E | 1:47:05.6 | | Karolina Szabó | HUN | 22 | Apr | 88 | Budapest |
| | C,A,N | 2:03:53.0 | # | Eleanor Adams/Robinson | Eng | 16 | Oct | 82 | London (He) |
| **Half** | W,E | 67:58 | | Uta Pippig | GER | 19 | Mar | 95 | Kyoto |
| **Marathon** | C | 68:21 | | Tegla Loroupe | KEN | 12 | Mar | 95 | Lisbon |
| | A,N | 68:42 | | Liz McColgan | | 11 | Oct | 92 | Dundee |
| Distance unverified | | 66:40 | | Ingrid Kristiansen | NOR | 5 | Apr | 87 | Sandnes |
| Downhill (.16%) | | 67:11 | | Liz McColgan | Sco | 26 | Jan | 92 | Tokyo |
| | WJ | 69:05 | | Delilah Asiago | KEN | 5 | May | 91 | Exeter |
| | NJ | 77:52 | # | Kathy Williams | | 28 | Mar | 82 | Barry |
| | | 78:00 | | Karen Whapshott/Downer | | 4 | Apr | 82 | Fleet |
| **Marathon** | W,E,A | 2:21:06 | | Ingrid Kristiansen | NOR | 21 | Apr | 85 | London |
| | C | 2:23:51 | | Lisa Martin/Ondieki | AUS | 31 | Jan | 88 | Osaka |
| | N | 2:25:56 | | Véronique Marot | | 23 | Apr | 89 | London |
| | WJ | 2:30:15 | | Gu Dongmei | CHN | 4 | Apr | 93 | Tianjin |
| | NJ | 2:58:58 | | Tracy Howard | | 9 | May | 82 | London |
| **2km St** | W,E | 6:11.84 | | Marina Pluzhnikova | RUS | 25 | Jul | 94 | St. Petersburg |
| | C,A,N | 7:04.7mx& | | Sally Young | Eng | 14 | Jul | 93 | Sutton |
| | | 7:13.3 (2'6") | | Sally Young | | 11 | Aug | 93 | Watford |
| | NJ | 7:52.8 (2'6") | | Victoria Wilkinson | | 25 | Sep | 93 | Leeds |
| **100mH** | W,E | 12.21 | | Yordanka Donkova | BUL | 20 | Aug | 88 | Stara Zagora |
| | C | 12.75 | | Michelle Freeman | JAM | 28 | Aug | 92 | Brussels |
| | A | 12.51 | | Ginka Zagorcheva | BUL | 12 | Sep | 86 | London (CP) |
| | N | 12.82 | | Sally Gunnell | | 17 | Aug | 88 | Zürich |
| | WJ | 12.84 | | Aliuska López | CUB | 16 | Jul | 87 | Zagreb |
| | EJ | 12.88 | | Yelena Ovcharova | UKR | 25 | Jun | 95 | Lille |
| | NJ | 13.25 | | Diane Allahgreen | | 21 | Jul | 94 | Lisbon |

18

| Event | | Mark | | Athlete | Nat | Date | Venue |
|---|---|---|---|---|---|---|---|
| **400mH** | W | 52.61 | | Kim Batten | USA | 11 Aug 95 | Gothenburg |
| | E,C,N | 52.74 | | Sally Gunnell | Eng | 19 Aug 93 | Stuttgart |
| | A | 53.69 | | Sandra Farmer-Patrick | USA | 10 Sep 93 | London (CP) |
| | WJ | 55.20 | | Leslie Maxie | USA | 9 Jun 84 | San Jose |
| | EJ | 55.46 | | Ionela Tirlea | ROM | 11 Aug 95 | Gothenburg |
| | NJ | 58.02 | | Vyvyan Rhodes | | 28 Jun 92 | Birmingham |
| **High** | W,E | 2.09 | | Stefka Kostadinova | BUL | 30 Aug 87 | Rome |
| **Jump** | C | 1.99 | i | Debbie Brill | CAN | 23 Jan 82 | Edmonton |
| | | 1.98 | | Debbie Brill | CAN | 2 Sep 84 | Rieti |
| | | 1.98 | | Vanessa Ward | AUS | 12 Feb 89 | Perth |
| | | 1.98 | | Alison Inverarity | AUS | 17 Jul 94 | Ingolstadt |
| | A | 2.03 | | Ulrike Meyfarth | GER | 21 Aug 83 | London (CP) |
| | | 2.03 | | Tamara Bykova | RUS | 21 Aug 83 | London (CP) |
| | N | 1.95 | | Diana Elliott/Davies | | 26 Jun 82 | Oslo |
| | WJ,EJ | 2.01 | # | Olga Turchak | KAZ | 7 Jul 86 | Moscow |
| | | 2.01 | | Heike Balck | GER | 18 Jun 89 | Chemnitz |
| | NJ | 1.91 | | Lea Haggett | | 2 Jun 91 | Khaniá |
| **Pole** | W,C | 4.28 | & | Emma George | AUS | 17 Dec 95 | Perth |
| **Vault** | (W),E | 4.22 | | Daniela Bártová | CZE | 11 Sep 95 | Salgótarján |
| | (C) | 4.16 | | Emma George | AUS | 19 Nov 95 | Melbourne |
| | A | 4.14 | | Daniela Bártová | CZE | 2 Jul 95 | Gateshead |
| | N | 3.80 | | Kate Staples | | 2 Jul 95 | Gateshead |
| | WJ | 4.08 | | Zhong Guiqing | CHN | 18 May 95 | Taiyuan |
| | EJ | 3.90 | | Nicole Rieger | GER | 21 Jul 91 | Berlin |
| | NJ | 3.50 | & | Rhian Clarke | | 20 Jul 95 | Weston, Mass. |
| | | 3.41 | | Clare Ridgley | | 10 Jul 94 | Salisbury |
| **Long** | W,E | 7.52 | | Galina Chistyakova | RUS | 11 Jun 88 | St. Petersburg |
| **Jump** | C,N | 6.90 | | Beverly Kinch | Eng | 14 Aug 83 | Helsinki |
| | A | 7.14 | | Galina Chistyakova | RUS | 24 Jun 89 | Birmingham |
| | WJ,EJ | 7.14 | # | Heike Daute/Drechsler | GER | 4 Jun 83 | Bratislava |
| | | 6.98 | | Heike Daute/Drechsler | GER | 18 Aug 82 | Potsdam |
| | NJ | 6.90 | | Beverly Kinch | | 14 Aug 83 | Helsinki |
| **Triple** | W,E | 15.50 | | Inessa Kravets | UKR | 10 Aug 95 | Gothenburg |
| **Jump** | C,N | 14.66 | | Ashia Hansen | Eng | 21 Aug 95 | Gateshead |
| | A | 14.81 | | Anna Biryukova | RUS | 7 Jul 95 | London (CP) |
| | WJ | 14.36 | | Ren Ruiping | CHN | 1 Jun 94 | Beijing |
| | EJ | 14.32 | | Yelena Lysak | RUS | 18 Jun 94 | Voronezh |
| | NJ | 13.05 | | Michelle Griffith | | 16 Jun 90 | London (CP) |
| **Shot** | W,E | 22.63 | | Natalya Lisovskaya | RUS | 6 Jun 87 | Moscow |
| | C | 19.74 | | Gael Mulhall/Martin | AUS | 14 Jul 84 | Berkeley |
| | A | 21.95 | | Natalya Lisovskaya | RUS | 29 Jul 88 | Edinburgh |
| | N | 19.36 | | Judy Oakes | | 14 Aug 88 | Gateshead |
| | WJ,EJ | 20.54 | | Astrid Kumbernuss | GER | 1 Jul 89 | Orimattila |
| | NJ | 17.10 | | Myrtle Augee | | 16 Jun 84 | London (CP) |
| **Discus** | W,E | 76.80 | | Gabriele Reinsch | GER | 9 Jul 88 | Neubrandenburg |
| | C | 68.72 | | Daniele Costian | AUS | 22 Jan 94 | Auckland |
| | A | 73.04 | | Ilke Wyludda | GER | 5 Aug 89 | Gateshead |
| | N | 67.48 | | Meg Ritchie | | 26 Apr 81 | Walnut |
| | WJ,EJ | 74.40 | | Ilke Wyludda | GER | 13 Sep 88 | Berlin |
| | NJ | 54.78 | | Lynda Whiteley | | 4 Oct 82 | Brisbane |
| **Hammer** | W,E | 68.16 | | Olga Kuzenkova | RUS | 18 Jun 95 | Moscow |
| | C,A | 65.24 | | Debbie Sosimenko | AUS | 15 Jul 95 | Birmingham |
| | N | 64.90 | | Lorraine Shaw | | 10 Jun 95 | Bedford |
| | WJ,EJ | 65.48 | | Mihaela Melinte | ROM | 25 Feb 94 | Bucharest |
| | NJ | 55.44 | # | Lyn Sprules | | 19 Jul 94 | Haslemere |
| | | 54.48 | | Lyn Sprules | | 2 Jul 94 | Bedford |
| **Javelin** | W,E | 80.00 | | Petra Felke | GER | 8 Sep 88 | Potsdam |
| | C,N | 77.44 | | Fatima Whitbread | Eng | 28 Aug 86 | Stuttgart |

| | | | | | | | |
|---|---|---|---|---|---|---|---|
| | A | 75.62 | Fatima Whitbread | | 25 May 87 | Derby |
| | WJ,EJ | 71.88 | Antoaneta Todorova | BUL | 15 Aug 81 | Zagreb |
| | NJ | 60.14 | Fatima Whitbread | | 7 May 80 | Grays |
| **Hept.** | W | 7291 | Jackie Joyner-Kersee | USA | 24 Sep 88 | Seoul |
| | E | 7007 | Larisa Nikitina | RUS | 11 Jun 89 | Bryansk |
| | C | 6695 | Jane Flemming | AUS | 28 Jan 90 | Auckland |
| | A | 6419 | Birgit Clarius | GER | 21 Jul 91 | Sheffield |
| | N | 6623 | Judy Simpson | | 30 Aug 86 | Stuttgart |
| | WJ,EJ | 6465 | Sybille Thiele | GER | 28 Aug 83 | Schwechat |
| | NJ | 5833 | Joanne Mulliner | | 11 Aug 85 | Lons-le-Saunier |
| **4x100m** | W,E | 41.37 | East Germany | | 6 Oct 85 | Canberra |
| | C | 41.94 | Jamaica | | 1 Sep 91 | Tokyo |
| | | 41.94 | Jamaica | | 22 Aug 93 | Stuttgart |
| | A | 41.87 | East Germany | | 5 Aug 89 | Gateshead |
| | N | 42.43 | UK National Team | | 1 Aug 80 | Moscow |
| | WJ,EJ | 43.33 # | East Germany | | 20 Jul 88 | Berlin |
| | | 43.48 | East Germany | | 31 Jul 88 | Sudbury |
| | NJ | 44.16 | UK National Team | | 12 Aug 90 | Plovdiv |
| **4x200m** | W,E | 1:28.15 | East Germany | | 9 Aug 80 | Jena |
| | C,N | 1:31.57 | UK National Team | Eng | 20 Aug 77 | London (CP) |
| | A | 1:31.49 | Russia | | 5 Jun 93 | Portsmouth |
| | NJ | 1:42.2 | London Olympiades AC | | 19 Aug 72 | Bracknell |
| **4x400m** | W,E | 3:15.17 | U.S.S.R. | | 1 Oct 88 | Seoul |
| | C | 3:21.21 | Canada | | 11 Aug 84 | Los Angeles |
| | A | 3:20.79 | Czechoslovakia | | 21 Aug 83 | London (CP) |
| | N | 3:22.01 | UK National Team | | 1 Sep 91 | Tokyo |
| | WJ,EJ | 3:28.39 | East Germany | | 31 Jul 88 | Sudbury |
| | NJ | 3:35.10 | UK National Team | | 25 Aug 85 | Cottbus |
| **4x800m** | W,E | 7:50.17 | U.S.S.R. | | 5 Aug 84 | Moscow |
| | C | 8:20.73 | UK National Team | Eng | 5 Jun 93 | Portsmouth |
| | A | 7:57.08 | Russia | | 5 Jun 93 | Portsmouth |
| | N | 8:19.9 m | UK National Team | | 5 Jun 92 | Sheffield |
| | NJ | 8:53.1 | Havering AC | | 24 May 80 | Birmingham |
| **4x1500m** | W | 17:18.10 # | Villanova Univ | USA/IRE | 27 Apr 90 | Philadelphia |
| | (W),E | 17:22.30 | Providence Univ | IRE | 26 Apr 91 | Philadelphia |
| | N | 18:16.2 | Cambridge & Oxford Univs | | 27 Apr 90 | Philadelphia |
| **4x1mile** | WECAN | 19:17.3 | BMC National Squad | Eng | 10 Jul 93 | Oxford |

## Track Walking

| | | | | | | | |
|---|---|---|---|---|---|---|---|
| **1500 m** | W,C | 5:50.51 | | Kerry Saxby-Junna | AUS | 20 Jun 91 | Sydney |
| | E | 5:53.0 | | Sada Eidikyte | LIT | 12 May 90 | Vilnius |
| | A | 6:04.5 | i | Beate Anders/Gummelt | GER | 4 Mar 90 | Glasgow |
| **1 Mile** | W, E | 6:16.72 | i | Sada Eidikyte | LIT | 12 May 90 | Vilnius |
| | | 6:19.39 | | Ileana Salvador | ITA | 15 Jun 91 | Siderno |
| | C | 6:47.9 | | Sue Cook | AUS | 14 Mar 81 | Canberra |
| | A | 6:30.7 | i | Beate Anders/Gummelt | GER | 4 Mar 90 | Glasgow |
| | (A),N | 7:14.3 | | Carol Tyson | | 17 Sep 77 | London (PH) |
| | NJ | 7:31.6 | | Kate Horwill | | 22 Aug 93 | Solihull |
| **3000 m** | W,E | 11:44.00 | i | Alina Ivanova | RUS | 7 Feb 92 | Moscow |
| | | 11:48.24 | | Ileana Salvador | ITA | 29 Aug 93 | Padua |
| | C | 11:51.26 | | Kerry Saxby-Junna | AUS | 7 Feb 91 | Melbourne |
| | A | 12:32.37 | + | Yelena Nikolayeva | RUS | 19 Jun 88 | Portsmouth |
| | N | 12:49.16 | | Betty Sworowski | | 28 Jul 90 | Wrexham |
| | WJ,EJ | 12:29.98 | i | Susana Feitór | POR | 6 Mar 93 | Braga |
| | WJ | 12:39.1 | | Wang Yan | CHN | 30 Mar 86 | Beijing |
| | EJ | 12:53.61 | + | Oksana Shchastnaya | RUS | 7 Aug 87 | Birmingham |
| | NJ | 13:03.4 | | Vicky Lupton | | 18 May 91 | Sheffield |

| 5000 m | W,E | 20:07.52 # | Beate Anders/Gummelt | GER | 23 Jun 90 | Rostock |
|---|---|---|---|---|---|---|
| | (W),C | 20:17.19 | Kerry Saxby-Junna | AUS | 14 Jan 90 | Sydney |
| | E | 20:21.69 | Anna-Rita Sidoti | ITA | 1 Jul 95 | Cesenatico |
| | A | 21:08.65 | Yelena Nikolayeva | RUS | 19 Jun 88 | Portsmouth |
| | N | 21:52.38 & | Vicky Lupton | | 9 Aug 95 | Sheffield |
| | | 22:02.06 | Betty Sworowski | | 28 Aug 89 | Gateshead |
| (Road) | N | 21:36 | Vicky Lupton | | 18 Jul 92 | Sheffield |
| | WJ | 20:37.7 | Jin Bingjie | CHN | 3 Mar 90 | Hefei |
| | EJ | 21:01.8 | Susana Feitór | POR | 8 May 93 | Fana |
| | NJ | 22:36.81 | Vicky Lupton | | 15 Jun 91 | Espoo |
| 10 km | W,E | 41:56.23 | Nadezhda Ryashkina | UKR | 24 Jul 90 | Seattle |
| | C | 41:57.22 | Kerry Saxby-Junna | AUS | 24 Jul 90 | Seattle |
| | A,N | 45:18.8 | Vicky Lupton | | 2 Sep 95 | Watford |
| | WJ | 42:49.7 | Gao Hongmiao | CHN | 15 Mar 92 | Jinan |
| | EJ | 46:28.6 | Flyura Akhmetzhanova | RUS | 13 Oct 85 | Alushta |
| | NJ | 47:04 | Vicky Lupton | | 30 Mar 91 | Sheffield |
| 1 Hour | W | 12,771 m | Victoria Herazo | USA | 20 Oct 91 | Cambridge, Mass |
| | E | 12,644 m | Giuliana Salce | ITA | 25 Apr 86 | Ostia |
| | C | 12,555 m | Sue Cook | AUS | 29 Jun 85 | Canberra |
| | A,N,NJ | 11,590 m | Lisa Langford | | 13 Sep 86 | Woodford |
| 20 km | W,E | 1:35:29.5 | Madeleine Svensson | SWE | 10 Jul 91 | Borås |
| | C,N | 1:58:37.8 | Margaret Lewis | Eng | 15 Sep 71 | Sotteville |
| | WJ | 1:48:18.6 | Sue Liers/Westerfield | USA | 20 Mar 77 | Kings Point |
| 50 km | W,E | 5:13:49.8 | Zofia Turosz | POL | 13 Oct 85 | Warsaw |
| | C,N | 5:26:59 | Sandra Brown | Eng | 27 Oct 90 | Etrechy |

**Road Walking - Fastest Recorded Times**

| 10 km | W,E | 41:29 | Larissa Ramazanova | RUS | 4 Jun 95 | Izhevsk |
|---|---|---|---|---|---|---|
| | C | 41:30 | Kerry Saxby-Junna | AUS | 27 Aug 88 | Canberra |
| | A | 43:27 | Graciella Mendoza | MEX | 8 Oct 89 | Hull |
| | N | 45:18.8 t | Vicky Lupton | | 2 Sep 95 | Watford |
| | WJ,EJ | 41:55 | Irina Stanika | RUS | 11 Feb 95 | Adler |
| | NJ | 47:30 | Vicky Lupton | | 17 Mar 91 | Sheffield |
| 20 km | W,C | 1:29:40 | Kerry Saxby-Junna | AUS | 13 May 88 | Värnamo |
| | E | 1:30:42 | Olga Kardopoltseva | BLR | 29 Apr 90 | Kaliningrad |
| | A,N | 1:40:45 | Irene Bateman | | 9 Apr 83 | Basildon |
| | WJ,EJ | 1:34:31 | Tatyana Titova | RUS | 4 Oct 87 | Alushta |
| | NJ | 1:52:03 | Vicky Lupton | | 13 Oct 91 | Sheffield |
| 50 km | WECAN | 4:50:51 | Sandra Brown | Eng | 13 Jul 91 | Basildon |

## RECORDS set in 1995

| 400m | C | 49.43 | Fatima Yusuf | NGR | 15 Sep 95 | Harare |
|---|---|---|---|---|---|---|
| 800m | C, N | 1:56.95 | Kelly Holmes | Eng | 13 Aug 95 | Gothenburg |
| | C, N | 1:56.21 | Kelly Holmes | Eng | 9 Sep 95 | Monte Carlo |
| 1000m | C, A, N | 2:32.82 | Kelly Holmes | Eng | 23 Jul 95 | Sheffield |
| | W | 2:29.34 | Ma Lurdes Mutola | MOZ | 25 Aug 95 | Brussels |
| 5km | A | 14:17.64 | Sonia O'Sullivan | IRE | 7 Jul 95 | London (CP) |
| | W, E | 14:36.45 | Fernanda Ribeiro | POR | 22 Jul 95 | Hechtel |
| | WJ | 14:45.90 | Jiang Bo | CHN | 24 Oct 95 | Nanjing |
| 10km | EJ | 32:10.19 | Annemari Sandell | FIN | 11 Jun 95 | Turku |
| | EJ | 31:54.29 | Annemari sandell | FIN | 9 Aug 95 | Gothenburg |
| HMAR | C | 68:21 | Tegla Loroupe | KEN | 12 Mar 95 | Lisbon |
| | W, E | 67:58 | Uta Pippig | GER | 19 Mar 95 | Kyoto |
| 100mh | EJ | 12.98 | Yelena Ovcharova | UKR | 27 May 95 | Kiyev |
| | EJ | 12.88 | Yelena Ovcharova | UKR | 25 Jun 95 | Lille |
| 400mh | EJ | 55.26 | Ionela Tîrlea | ROM | 12 Jul 95 | Nice |
| | W | 52.61 | Kim Batten | USA | 11 Aug 95 | Gothenburg |
| | EJ | 55.46 | Ionela Tîrlea | ROM | 11 Aug 95 | Gothenburg |

| | | | | | | | |
|---|---|---|---|---|---|---|---|
| **PV** | W | 4.06 | Sun Caiyun | CHN | 25 Mar 95 | Gwangzhou |
| | W | 4.07 | Cai Weiyan | CHN | 29 Apr 95 | Hefei |
| | W, WJ | 4.08 | Zhong Guiqing | CHN | 18 May 95 | Taiyuan |
| | W | 4.08 | Sun Caiyun | CHN | 18 May 95 | Taiyuan |
| | W, E | 4.10 | Daniela Bártová | CZR | 21 May 95 | Ljubljana |
| | C, A, N | 3.70 | Kate Staples | Eng | 10 Jun 95 | Bedford |
| | C, A, N | 3.72 | Linda Stanton | Eng | 11 Jun 95 | Loughborough |
| | W, E | 4.12 | Daniela Bártová | CZR | 18 Jun 95 | Duisburg |
| | W, E | 4.13 | Daniela Bártová | CZR | 24 Jun 95 | Wessel |
| | C, A, N | 3.75 | Kate Staples | Eng | 25 Jun 95 | Haringey |
| | A | 3.80 | Daniela Bártová | CZR | 2 Jul 95 | Gateshead |
| | C, A, N | 3.80 | Kate Staples | Eng | 2 Jul 95 | Gateshead |
| | A | 4.00 | Daniela Bártová | CZR | 2 Jul 95 | Gateshead |
| | W, E, A | 4.14 | Daniela Bártová | CZR | 2 Jul 95 | Gateshead |
| | W, E | 4.15 | Daniela Bártová | CZR | 5 Jul 95 | Ostrava |
| | W, E | 4.16 | Daniela Bártová | CZR | 14 Jul 95 | Feldkirk |
| | W, E | 4.17 | Daniela Bártová | CZR | 15 Jul 95 | Gisingen |
| | NJ | 3.50 * | Rhian Clarke | | 20 Jul 95 | Weston, Mass. |
| | W, E | 4.18 | Andrea Müller | GER | 5 Aug 95 | Zittau |
| | W, E | 4.20 | Daniela Bártová | CZR | 18 Aug 95 | Cologne |
| | W, E | 4.21 | Daniela Bártová | CZR | 22 Aug 95 | Linz |
| | W, E | 4.22 | Daniela Bártová | CZR | 11 Sep 95 | Salgótarján |
| | C | 3.85 | Emma George | AUS | 26 Sep 95 | Darwin |
| | C | 4.00 | Emma George | AUS | 14 Oct 95 | |
| | W | 4.23 * | Sun Caiyun | CHN | 5 Nov 95 | Shenzhen |
| | C | 4.15 | Emma George | AUS | 11 Nov 95 | Melbourne |
| | C | 4.16 | Emma George | AUS | 19 Nov 95 | Melbourne |
| | W, C | 4.25 * | Emma George | AUS | 30 Nov 95 | Melbourne |
| | W, C | 4.28 * | Emma George | AUS | 17 Dec 95 | Perth |
| **TJ** | C, N | 14.16 * | Ashia Hansen | Eng | 5 Jun 95 | Moscow |
| | C, N | 14.37 | Ashia Hansen | Eng | 24 Jun 95 | Lille |
| | A | 14.81 | Anna Biryukova | Rus | 7 Jul 95 | London (CP) |
| | W, E | 15.50 | Inessa Kravets | UKR | 10 Aug 95 | Gothenburg |
| | C, N | 14.38 | Ashia Hansen | Eng | 16 Aug 95 | Zürich |
| | C, N | 14.57 | Ashia Hansen | Eng | 21 Aug 95 | Gateshead |
| | C, N | 14.66 | Ashia Hansen | Eng | 21 Aug 95 | Gateshead |
| **HT** | C | 62.66 | Debbie Sosimenko | AUS | 28 Jan 95 | Adelaide |
| | C | 63.04 | Debbie Sosimenko | AUS | 11 Feb 95 | Sydney |
| | C | 63.22 | Debbie Sosimenko | AUS | 3 Mar 95 | Sydney |
| | W, E | 66.86 | Mihaela Melinte | ROM | 4 Mar 95 | Bucharest |
| | C | 63.92 | Debbie Sosimenko | AUS | 21 Mar 95 | Sydney |
| | A, N | 59.74 | Lorraine Shaw | | 22 Apr 95 | London (Co) |
| | A, N | 60.56 | Lorraine Shaw | | 22 Apr 95 | London (Co) |
| | A, N | 61.56 | Lorraine Shaw | | 29 Apr 95 | London (WP) |
| | N | 62.30 | Lorraine Shaw | | 13 May 95 | Halle |
| | W, E | 67.08 | Olga Kuzenkova | RUS | 24 May 95 | Moscow |
| | W, E | 68.14 | Olga Kuzenkova | RUS | 5 Jun 95 | Moscow |
| | N | 62.52 | Lorraine Shaw | | 5 Jun 95 | Rehlingen |
| | N | 63.52 | Lorraine Shaw | | 5 Jun 95 | Rehlingen |
| | N | 63.80 | Lorraine Shaw | | 5 Jun 95 | Rehlingen |
| | C, A, N | 64.90 | Lorraine Shaw | Eng | 10 Jun 95 | Bedford |
| | W, E | 68.16 | Olga Kuzenkova | RUS | 18 Jun 95 | Moscow |
| | C, A | 65.24 | Debbie Sosimenko | AUS | 15 Jul 95 | Birmingham |
| **5kW** | E | 20:21.69 | Anna-Rita Sidoti | ITA | 1 Jul 95 | Cesenatico |
| | N | 21:52.38 | Vicky Lupton | | 9 Aug 95 | Sheffield |
| **10kW** | A, N | 45:18.8 | Vicky Lupton | | 2 Sep 95 | Watford |

**Road Walking**

| | | | | | | | |
|---|---|---|---|---|---|---|---|
| **10kW** | WJ, EJ | 41:55 | Irina Stankina | RUS | 11 Feb 95 | Adler |
| | W, E | 41:29 | Larisa Ramazanova | RUS | 4 Jun 95 | Izhevsk |
| | N | 45:19 | Vicky Lupton | | 2 Sep 95 | Watford |

# NATIONAL RECORDS OF THE UNITED KINGDOM (MEN)

(as at 31 Dec 95)

These are the best authentic performances for the four countries of the U.K.
E = England  S = Scotland  W = Wales  NI = Northern Ireland

| | | | | | |
|---|---|---|---|---|---|
| 100 m | E | 9.87 | | Linford Christie | 15 Aug 93 | Stuttgart, GER |
| | S | 10.11 | | Allan Wells | 24 Jul 80 | Moscow, RUS |
| | W | 10.29 | | Colin Jackson | 28 Jul 90 | Wrexham |
| | NI | 10.46 | | Mark Forsythe | 17 Jun 89 | Tel Aviv, ISR |
| 200 m | E | 19.87 | A& | John Regis | 31 Jul 94 | Sestriere, ITA |
| | | 19.94 | | John Regis | 20 Aug 93 | Stuttgart, GER |
| | S | 20.21 | | Allan Wells | 28 Jul 80 | Moscow, RUS |
| | W | 20.75 | | Doug Turner | 9 Sep 95 | Stoke |
| | NI | 20.81 | | Paul McBurney | 24 Aug 94 | Victoria, CAN |
| 300 m | E | 31.67 | | John Regis | 17 Jul 92 | Gateshead |
| | S | 32.44 | | David Jenkins | 4 Jul 75 | London (CP) |
| | NI | 33.77 | | Simon Baird | 24 Jun 85 | Belfast |
| | W | 34.4 | | Jeff Griffiths | 2 Jul 80 | Cwmbrân |
| | | 34.57 | i | Gareth Davies | 20 Feb 93 | Birmingham |
| 400 m | E | 44.47 | | David Grindley | 3 Aug 92 | Barcelona, SPA |
| | S | 44.93 | | David Jenkins | 21 Jun 75 | Eugene, USA |
| | W | 45.14 | | Jamie Baulch | 23 Aug 95 | Copenhagen, DEN |
| | NI | 46.49 | | Paul McBurney | 22 Aug 94 | Victoria, CAN |
| 600 m | E | 1:14.95 | | Steve Heard | 14 Jul 91 | London (Ha) |
| | S | 1:15.4 | | Tom McKean | 21 Jul 91 | Grangemouth |
| | W | 1:18.02 | | Glen Grant | 2 Aug 78 | Edmonton, CAN |
| | NI | 1:18.3 | i | Joe Chivers | 14 Dec 74 | Cosford |
| | | 1:20.1 | | Kenneth Thompson | 24 May 80 | Belfast |
| 800 m | E | 1:41.73 | " | Sebastian Coe | 10 Jun 81 | Florence, ITA |
| | S | 1:43.88 | | Tom McKean | 28 Jul 89 | London (CP) |
| | W | 1:45.44 | | Neil Horsfield | 28 Jul 90 | Wrexham |
| | NI | 1:46.94 | | Mark Kirk | 20 Jul 87 | Belfast |
| 1000 m | E | 2:12.18 | | Sebastian Coe | 11 Jul 81 | Oslo, NOR |
| | S | 2:16.82 | | Graham Williamson | 17 Jul 84 | Edinburgh |
| | W | 2:17.36 | | Neil Horsfield | 9 Aug 91 | Gateshead |
| | NI | 2:19.05 | | Mark Kirk | 5 Aug 87 | Oslo, NOR |
| 1500 m | E | 3:29.67 | | Steve Cram | 16 Jul 85 | Nice, FRA |
| | S | 3:33.83 | | John Robson | 4 Sep 79 | Brussels, BEL |
| | NI | 3:34.76 | | Gary Lough | 9 Sep 95 | Monaco, MON |
| | W | 3:35.08 | | Neil Horsfield | 10 Aug 90 | Brussels, BEL |
| 1 Mile | E | 3:46.32 | | Steve Cram | 27 Jul 85 | Oslo, NOR |
| | S | 3:50.64 | | Graham Williamson | 13 Jul 82 | Cork, IRE |
| | W | 3:54.29 | | Neil Horsfield | 8 Jul 86 | Cork, IRE |
| | NI | 3:55.0 | | Jim McGuinness | 11 Jul 77 | Dublin (B), IRE |
| 2000 m | E | 4:51.39 | | Steve Cram | 4 Aug 85 | Budapest, HUN |
| | S | 4:58.38 | | Graham Williamson | 29 Aug 83 | London (CP) |
| | NI | 5:02.61 | | Steve Martin | 19 Jun 84 | Belfast |
| | W | 5:05.32 | | Tony Simmons | 4 Jul 75 | London (CP) |
| 3000 m | E | 7:32.79 | | Dave Moorcroft | 17 Jul 82 | London (CP) |
| | S | 7:45.81 | | John Robson | 13 Jul 84 | London (CP) |
| | W | 7:46.40 | | Ian Hamer | 20 Jan 90 | Auckland, NZ |
| | NI | 7:49.1 | | Paul Lawther | 27 Jun 78 | Oslo, NOR |

| Event | Cat | Time | Name | Date | Location |
|---|---|---|---|---|---|
| 2 Miles | E | 8:13.51 | Steve Ovett | 15 Sep 78 | London (CP) |
| | S | 8:19.37 | Nat Muir | 27 Jun 80 | London (CP) |
| | W | 8:20.28 | David James | 27 Jun 80 | London (CP) |
| | NI | 8:30.6 | Paul Lawther | 28 May 77 | Belfast |
| 5000 m | E | 13:00.41 | Dave Moorcroft | 7 Jul 82 | Oslo, NOR |
| | W | 13:09.80 | Ian Hamer | 9 Jun 92 | Rome, ITA |
| | S | 13:17.9 | Nat Muir | 15 Jul 80 | Oslo, NOR |
| | NI | 13:39.11 | Terry Greene | 31 Jul 86 | Edinburgh |
| 10 km | E | 27:23.06 | Eamonn Martin | 2 Jul 88 | Oslo, NOR |
| | W | 27:39.14 | Steve Jones | 9 Jul 83 | Oslo, NOR |
| | S | 27:43.03 | Ian Stewart | 9 Sep 77 | London (CP) |
| | NI | 28:40.03 | John McLaughlin | 29 May 83 | Edinburgh |
| 20 km | E | 57:28.7 | Carl Thackery | 31 Mar 90 | La Flèche, FRA |
| | S | 59:24.0 | Jim Alder | 9 Nov 68 | Leicester |
| 1 Hour | E | 20,855 m | Carl Thackery | 31 Mar 90 | La Flèche, FRA |
| | S | 20,201 m | Jim Alder | 9 Nov 68 | Leicester |
| | W | 18,587 m | Malcolm Edwards | 15 Sep 89 | Westhofen, GER |
| 25 km | E | 1:15:22.6 | Ron Hill | 21 Jul 65 | Bolton |
| | S | 1:15:34.3 | Jim Alder | 5 Sep 70 | London (CP) |
| 30 km | S | 1:31:30.4 | Jim Alder | 5 Sep 70 | London (CP) |
| | E | 1:31:56.4 | Tim Johnston | 5 Sep 70 | London (CP) |
| | W | 1:33:49.0 | Bernie Plain | 1 Dec 73 | Bristol |
| Half Marathon | E | 60:09 | Paul Evans | 15 Jan 95 | Marrakesh, MAR |
| | W | 60:59 | Steve Jones | 8 Jun 86 | Tyneside |
| | NI | 62:16 | Jim Haughey | 20 Sep 87 | Philadelphia, USA |
| | S | 62:19 # | Mike Carroll | 3 Jun 90 | Irvine, USA |
| | | 62:28 | Allister Hutton | 21 Jun 87 | Tyneside |
| Marathon | W | 2:07:13 | Steve Jones | 20 Oct 85 | Chicago, USA |
| | E | 2:08:33 | Charlie Spedding | 21 Apr 85 | London |
| | S | 2:09:18 | Allister Hutton | 21 Apr 85 | London |
| | NI | 2:13:06 | Greg Hannon | 13 May 79 | Coventry |
| 2km St | E | 5:19.86 | Mark Rowland | 28 Aug 88 | London (CP) |
| | S | 5:21.77 | Tom Hanlon | 11 Jun 92 | Caserta, ITA |
| | W | 5:23.6 | Roger Hackney | 10 Jun 82 | Birmingham |
| | NI | 5:31.09 | Peter McColgan | 5 Aug 86 | Gateshead |
| 3km St | E | 8:07.96 | Mark Rowland | 30 Sep 88 | Seoul, SKO |
| | S | 8:12.58 | Tom Hanlon | 3 Aug 91 | Monaco, MON |
| | W | 8:18.91 | Roger Hackney | 31 Jul 88 | Hechtel, BEL |
| | NI | 8:27.93 | Peter McColgan | 25 Jun 91 | Hengelo, HOL |
| 110m H | W | 12.91 | Colin Jackson | 20 Aug 93 | Stuttgart, GER |
| | E | 13.00 | Tony Jarrett | 20 Aug 93 | Stuttgart, GER |
| | S | 13.86 | Kenneth Campbell | 23 Aug 94 | Victoria, CAN |
| | NI | 14.19 | C.J. Kirkpatrick | 16 Jun 73 | Edinburgh |
| 200m H | W | 22.63 | Colin Jackson | 1 Jun 91 | Cardiff |
| | E | 22.79 | John Regis | 1 Jun 91 | Cardiff |
| | S | 23.76 | Angus McKenzie | 22 Aug 81 | Edinburgh |
| | NI | 24.81 | Terry Price | 31 Aug 92 | Belfast |
| 400m H | E | 47.82 | Kriss Akabusi | 6 Aug 92 | Barcelona, SPA |
| | NI | 49.60 | Phil Beattie | 28 Jul 86 | Edinburgh |
| | W | 50.01 | Phil Harries | 5 Jun 88 | Derby |
| | S | 50.79 | Mark Davidson | 18 Jun 89 | Sittard, HOL |

| Event | | Mark | | Athlete | Date | | | Venue |
|---|---|---|---|---|---|---|---|---|
| **High** | E | 2.38 | i | Steve Smith | 4 | Feb | 94 | Wuppertal, GER |
| **Jump** | | 2.37 | | Steve Smith | 20 | Sep | 92 | Seoul, SKO |
| | | 2.37 | | Steve Smith | 22 | Aug | 93 | Stuttgart, GER |
| | S | 2.31 | | Geoff Parsons | 26 | Aug | 94 | Victoria, CAN |
| | W | 2.24 | | John Hill | 23 | Aug | 85 | Cottbus, GER |
| | NI | 2.20 | | Floyd Manderson | 14 | Jul | 85 | London (CP) |
| | | 2.20 | | Floyd Manderson | 21 | Jun | 86 | London (CP) |
| | | 2.20 | | Floyd Manderson | 16 | Aug | 86 | Leiden, HOL |
| **Pole** | E | 5.70 | | Nick Buckfield | 23 | Jul | 95 | Sheffield |
| **Vault** | W | 5.60 | | Neil Winter | 19 | Aug | 95 | Enfield |
| | NI | 5.25 | | Mike Bull | 22 | Sep | 73 | London (CP) |
| | S | 5.21 | | Graham Eggleton | 10 | Jul | 82 | Grangemouth |
| **Long** | W | 8.23 | | Lynn Davies | 30 | Jun | 68 | Berne, SWZ |
| **Jump** | E | 8.15 | | Stewart Faulkner | 16 | Jul | 90 | Belfast |
| | NI | 8.14 | | Mark Forsythe | 7 | Jul | 91 | Rhede, GER |
| | S | 7.67 | | David Walker | 14 | Sep | 68 | Portsmouth |
| **Triple** | E | 18.29 | | Jonathan Edwards | 7 | Aug | 95 | Gothenburg, SWE |
| **Jump** | S | 16.17 | | John Mackenzie | 17 | Sep | 94 | Bedford |
| | W | 15.90 | | David Wood | 16 | Sep | 84 | Karlovac, CRO |
| | NI | 15.78 | | Micky McDonald | 31 | Jul | 94 | Corby |
| **Shot** | E | 21.68 | | Geoff Capes | 18 | May | 80 | Cwmbrân |
| | W | 20.33 | & | Paul Edwards | 9 | Jul | 91 | Roehampton |
| | | 19.85 | | Paul Edwards | 2 | Jul | 89 | Walton |
| | S | 18.93 | | Paul Buxton | 13 | May | 77 | Los Angeles, USA |
| | NI | 16.35 | | Michael Atkinson | 18 | Jul | 81 | Dublin (B), IRE |
| | | 16.35 | | John Reynolds | 16 | Aug | 86 | Leiden, HOL |
| **Discus** | E | 65.16 | # | Richard Slaney | 1 | Jul | 85 | Eugene, USA |
| | | 64.32 | | Bill Tancred | 10 | Aug | 74 | Woodford |
| | S | 59.84 | # | ¶Colin Sutherland | 10 | Jun | 78 | San Jose, USA |
| | | 58.58 | | Darrin Morris | 22 | Jun | 91 | Enfield |
| | W | 57.12 | | Paul Edwards | 10 | Aug | 88 | London (Col) |
| | NI | 51.76 | | John Moreland | 1 | Jul | 95 | Antrim |
| **Hammer** | NI | 77.54 | | Martin Girvan | 12 | May | 84 | Wolverhampton |
| | E | 77.30 | | David Smith | 13 | Jul | 85 | London (CP) |
| | S | 75.40 | | Chris Black | 23 | Jul | 83 | London (CP) |
| | W | 68.64 | | Shaun Pickering | 7 | Apr | 84 | Stanford, USA |
| **Javelin** | E | 91.46 | | Steve Backley | 25 | Jan | 92 | Auckland, NZ |
| | W | 81.70 | | Nigel Bevan | 28 | Jun | 92 | Birmingham |
| | NI | 70.34 | | Damien Crawford | 20 | Jul | 91 | Hayes |
| | S | 69.20 | | Roddy James | 28 | Apr | 89 | Des Moines, USA |
| **Decathlon** | E | 8847 | | Daley Thompson | 9 | Aug | 84 | Los Angeles, USA |
| | S | 7885 | h | Brad McStravick | 6 | May | 84 | Birmingham |
| | | 7856 | | Brad McStravick | 28 | May | 84 | Cwmbrân |
| | NI | 7874 | | Colin Boreham | 23 | May | 82 | Götzis, AUT |
| | W | 7308 | h | Clive Longe | 29 | Jun | 69 | Kassel, GER |
| | | 7268 | | Paul Edwards | 14 | Aug | 83 | Bonn, GER |
| **4x100m** | E | 37.98 | | D. Braithwaite, J. Regis, M. Adam, L. Christie (UK) | 1 | Sep | 90 | Split, CRO |
| | S | 39.24 | | D. Jenkins, A. Wells, C. Sharp, A. McMaster | 12 | Aug | 78 | Edmonton, CAN |
| | W | 40.0 | ay | T. Davies, L. Davies, K. Jones, R. Jones | 13 | Aug | 66 | Kingston, JAM |
| | NI | 40.8 | | M. Bull, G. Carson, J. Chivers, J. Kilpatrick | 13 | Jun | 70 | Edinburgh |
| | | 40.94 | | D. Marrs, S. Baird, N. Watson, M. Forsythe | 19 | Jul | 88 | Tarragona, SPA |

| | | | | | | |
|---|---|---|---|---|---|---|
| **4x400m** | E | 2:57.53 | R. Black, D. Redmond, | | | |
| | | | J. Regis, K. Akabusi (UK) | 1 Sep 91 | Tokyo, JAP |
| | W | 3:03.68 | P. Maitland, J. Baulch, | | | |
| | | | P.Gray, I.Thomas | 27 Aug 94 | Victoria, CAN |
| | S | 3:04.68 | M. Davison, T. McKean, | | | |
| | | | D. Strang, B. Whittle | 3 Feb 90 | Auckland, NZ |
| | NI | 3:11.81 | ??, ??, | | | |
| | | | ??, ?? | 1 Sep 85 | Tel Aviv, ISR |

**Track Walking**

| | | | | | |
|---|---|---|---|---|---|
| **3000 m** | E | 11:24.4 | Mark Easton | 10 May 89 | Tonbridge |
| | W | 11:45.77 | Steve Johnson | 28 Jun 87 | Cwmbrân |
| | S | 11:53.3 | Martin Bell | 9 Aug 95 | Birmingham |
| | NI | 13:35.6 | Arthur Agnew | 18 Jun 77 | Belfast |
| **5000 m** | E | 19:22.29 i | Martin Rush | 8 Feb 92 | Birmingham |
| | | 19:35.0 | Darrell Stone | 16 May 89 | Brighton |
| | W | 20:08.04 i | Steve Barry | 5 Mar 83 | Budapest, HUN |
| | | 20:22.0 | Steve Barry | 20 Mar 82 | London (WL) |
| | S | 20:13.0 | Martin Bell | 2 May 92 | Enfield |
| | NI | 25:06.2 | G. Smyth | 13 Jul 80 | London (He) |
| **10 km** | E | 40:06.65 | Ian McCombie | 4 Jun 89 | Jarrow |
| | W | 41:13.62 | Steve Barry | 19 Jun 82 | London (CP) |
| | S | 41:13.65 | Martin Bell | 22 Jul 95 | Cardiff |
| | NI | 48:42.41 | Stephen Murphy | 31 Jul 83 | Edinburgh |
| **20 km** | E | 1:23:26.5 | Ian McCombie | 26 May 90 | Fana, NOR |
| | W | 1:26:22.0 | Steve Barry | 28 Jun 81 | Brighton |
| | S | 1:44:37.0 | Derek Howie | 19 Aug 78 | Brighton |
| **30 km** | E | 2:11:54 # | Chris Maddocks | 31 Dec 89 | Plymouth |
| | | 2:19:18 | Chris Maddocks | 22 Sep 84 | Birmingham |
| **50 km** | E | 4:05:44.6 | Paul Blagg | 26 May 90 | Fana, NOR |
| **1 Hour** | E | 14,324 m # | Ian McCombie | 7 Jul 85 | London (SP) |
| | | 14,158 m | Mark Easton | 12 Sep 87 | Woodford |
| | W | 13,987 m | Steve Barry | 28 Jun 81 | Brighton |
| | S | 13,393 m | Bill Sutherland | 27 Sep 69 | London (He) |
| **2 Hours** | E | 27,262 m # | Chris Maddocks | 31 Dec 89 | Plymouth |
| | | 26,037 m | Ron Wallwork | 31 Jul 71 | Blackburn |

**Road Walking**

| | | | | | |
|---|---|---|---|---|---|
| **10 km** | E | 40:17 | Chris Maddocks | 30 Apr 89 | Burrator |
| | W | 40:35 | Steve Barry | 14 May 83 | Southport |
| | S | 42:08 | Martin Bell | 4 Mar 89 | Kenilworth |
| | NI | 51:53 | Arthur Agnew | 6 Aug 80 | Helsinki, FIN |
| | | 51:53 | G. Smyth | 6 Aug 80 | Helsinki, FIN |
| **20 km** | E | 1:22:03 | Ian McCombie | 23 Sep 88 | Seoul, SKO |
| | W | 1:22:51 | Steve Barry | 26 Feb 83 | Douglas |
| | S | 1:25:42 | Martin Bell | 9 May 92 | Lancaster |
| | NI | 1:47:49 | Arthur Agnew | 4 Nov 78 | Ashbourne, IRE |
| **30 km** | E | 2:07:56 | Ian McCombie | 27 Apr 86 | Edinburgh |
| | W | 2:10:16 | Steve Barry | 7 Oct 82 | Brisbane, AUS |
| | S | 2:22:21 | Martin Bell | 8 May 94 | Cardiff |
| **50 km** | E | 3:51:37 | Chris Maddocks | 28 Oct 90 | Burrator |
| | W | 4:11:59 | Bob Dobson | 22 Oct 81 | Lassing, AUT |
| | S | 4:14:59 | Graham White | 5 Mar 95 | Burrator |

# NATIONAL RECORDS OF THE UNITED KINGDOM (WOMEN)

| | | | | | |
|---|---|---|---|---|---|
| **100 m** | E | 11.10 | Kathy Smallwood/Cook | 5 Sep 81 | Rome, ITA |
| | W | 11.39 | Sallyanne Short | 12 Jul 92 | Cwmbrân |
| | S | 11.40 | Helen Golden/Hogarth | 20 Jul 74 | London (CP) |
| | NI | 11.91 | Joan Atkinson | 1 Sep 61 | Sofia, BUL |
| **200 m** | E | 22.10 | Kathy Cook | 9 Aug 84 | Los Angeles, USA |
| | W | 22.80 | Michelle Scutt | 12 Jun 82 | Antrim |
| | S | 22.98 | Sandra Whittaker | 8 Aug 84 | Los Angeles, USA |
| | NI | 23.62 | Linda McCurry | 8 Aug 78 | Edmonton, CAN |
| **300 m** | E | 35.46 | Kathy Cook | 18 Aug 84 | London (CP) |
| | W | 36.01 | Michelle Probert/Scutt | 13 Jul 80 | London (CP) |
| | S | 36.46 | Linsey Macdonald | 13 Jul 80 | London (CP) |
| | NI | 38.20 | Linda McCurry | 2 Aug 78 | Edmonton, CAN |
| **400 m** | E | 49.43 | Kathy Cook | 6 Aug 84 | Los Angeles, USA |
| | W | 50.63 | Michelle Scutt | 31 May 82 | Cwmbrân |
| | S | 51.16 | Linsey Macdonald | 15 Jun 80 | London (CP) |
| | NI | 52.4 | Stephanie Llewellyn | 1 Jul 95 | London (He) |
| | | 52.54 | Stephanie Llewellyn | 9 Jul 95 | Cwmbrân |
| **600 m** | E | 1:26.18 | Diane Edwards/Modahl | 22 Aug 87 | London (CP) |
| | W | 1:26.5 | Kirsty McDermott/Wade | 21 Aug 85 | Zürich, SWZ |
| | S | 1:27.4 i | Linsey Macdonald | 12 Dec 81 | Cosford |
| | | 1:29.88 | Anne Clarkson/Purvis | 25 Sep 82 | Brisbane, AUS |
| | NI | 1:29.46 | Joanna Latimer | 19 May 93 | Birmingham |
| **800 m** | E | 1:56.21 | Kelly Holmes | 9 Sep 95 | Monaco, MON |
| | W | 1:57.42 | Kirsty McDermott/Wade | 24 Jun 85 | Belfast |
| | S | 2:00.15 | Rosemary Stirling/Wright | 3 Sep 72 | Munich, GER |
| | NI | 2:03.27 | Joanna Latimer | 29 Jun 94 | Helsinki, FIN |
| **1000 m** | E | 2:32.82 | Kelly Holmes | 23 Jul 95 | Sheffield |
| | W | 2:33.70 | Kirsty McDermott/Wade | 9 Aug 85 | Gateshead |
| | S | 2:37.05 | Chris Whittingham | 27 Jun 86 | Gateshead |
| | NI | 2:48.59 | Jane Ewing | 26 Jun 90 | Antrim |
| **1500 m** | E | 3:59.96 | Zola Budd | 30 Aug 85 | Brussels, BEL |
| | W | 4:00.73 | Kirsty Wade | 26 Jul 87 | Gateshead |
| | S | 4:01.20 | Yvonne Murray | 4 Jul 87 | Oslo, NOR |
| | NI | 4:11.46 | Ursula McKee/McGloin | 20 Jan 90 | Auckland, NZ |
| **1 Mile** | E | 4:17.57 | Zola Budd | 21 Aug 85 | Zürich, SWZ |
| | W | 4:19.41 | Kirsty McDermott/Wade | 27 Jul 85 | Oslo, NOR |
| | S | 4:22.64 | Yvonne Murray | 22 Jul 94 | Oslo, NOR |
| | NI | 4:38.86 | Ursula McKee/McGloin | 7 Jan 90 | Sydney, AUS |
| **2000 m** | S | 5:26.93 | Yvonne Murray | 8 Jul 94 | Edinburgh |
| | E | 5:30.19 | Zola Budd | 11 Jul 86 | London (CP) |
| | W | 5:45.81 i | Kirsty Wade | 13 Mar 87 | Cosford |
| | | 5:50.17 | Susan Tooby/Wightman | 13 Jul 84 | London (CP) |
| | NI | 5:57.24 | Ursula McKee/McGloin | 25 Jun 90 | Antrim |
| **3000 m** | E | 8:28.83 | Zola Budd | 7 Sep 85 | Rome, ITA |
| | S | 8:29.02 | Yvonne Murray | 25 Sep 88 | Seoul, SKO |
| | W | 8:47.59 | Angela Tooby | 5 Jul 88 | Stockholm, SWE |
| | NI | 9:16.25 | Ursula McKee/McGloin | 7 Jun 90 | Helsinki, FIN |
| **5000 m** | E | 14:48.07 | Zola Budd | 26 Aug 85 | London (CP) |
| | S | 14:56.94 | Yvonne Murray | 7 Jul 95 | London (CP) |
| | W | 15:13.22 | Angela Tooby | 5 Aug 87 | Oslo, NOR |
| | NI | 17:27.15 | Angela McCullagh | | |

| Event | | Time/Mark | Athlete | Date | Venue |
|---|---|---|---|---|---|
| **10 km** | S | 30:57.07 | Liz McColgan | 25 Jun 91 | Hengelo, HOL |
| | E | 31:07.88 | Jill Hunter | 30 Jun 91 | Frankfurt, GER |
| | W | 31:55.30 | Angela Tooby | 4 Sep 87 | Rome, ITA |
| | NI | 41:16.4 | Wendy Dyer | Jun 89 | Antrim |
| **Half Marathon** | S | 1:07:11 | Liz McColgan | 26 Jan 92 | Tokyo, JAP |
| | E | 1:09:39 | Andrea Wallace | 21 Mar 93 | Bath |
| | W | 1:09:56 | Susan Tooby/Wightman | 24 Jul 88 | Tyneside |
| | NI | 1:15:57 # | Moira O'Boyle/O'Neill | 23 Mar 86 | Cavan, IRE |
| | | 1:16:23 | Moira O'Neill | 24 Sep 88 | Londonderry |
| **Marathon** | E | 2:25:56 | Véronique Marot | 23 Apr 89 | London |
| | S | 2:27:32 | Liz McColgan | 3 Nov 91 | New York, USA |
| | W | 2:31:33 | Susan Tooby/Wightman | 23 Sep 88 | Seoul, SKO |
| | NI | 2:37:06 | Moira O'Neill | 31 Oct 88 | Dublin, IRE |
| **100m H** | E | 12.82 | Sally Gunnell | 17 Aug 88 | Zürich, SWZ |
| | W | 12.91 | Kay Morley-Brown | 2 Feb 90 | Auckland, NZ |
| | NI | 13.29 | Mary Peters | 2 Sep 72 | Munich, GER |
| | S | 13.35 | Pat Rollo | 30 Jul 83 | London (CP) |
| **400m H** | E | 52.74 | Sally Gunnell | 19 Aug 93 | Stuttgart, GER |
| | NI | 55.91 | Elaine McLaughlin | 26 Sep 88 | Seoul, SKO |
| | S | 57.43 | Liz Sutherland | 6 Jul 78 | Düsseldorf, GER |
| | W | 58.16 | Diane Fryar | 9 Jul 83 | Cwmbrân |
| **High Jump** | E | 1.95 | Diana Elliott/Davies | 26 Jun 82 | Oslo, NOR |
| | NI | 1.92 | Janet Boyle | 29 Sep 88 | Seoul, SKO |
| | S | 1.91 | Jayne Barnetson | 7 Jul 89 | Edinburgh |
| | W | 1.84 | Sarah Rowe | 22 Aug 81 | Utrecht, HOL |
| | | 1.84 | Sarah Rowe | 31 May 82 | Cwmbrân |
| **Pole Vault** | E | 3.80 | Kate Staples | 2 Jul 95 | Gateshead |
| | W | 3.00 | Claudia Filce | 20 May 95 | Birmingham |
| | S | 3.00 | Alison Murray/Jessee | 2 Jul 95 | Juárez, MEX |
| **Long Jump** | E | 6.90 | Beverly Kinch | 14 Aug 83 | Helsinki, FIN |
| | W | 6.52 | Gillian Regan | 29 Aug 82 | Swansea |
| | S | 6.43 | Myra Nimmo/McAskill | 27 May 73 | Edinburgh |
| | NI | 6.11 | Thelma Hopkins | 29 Sep 56 | Budapest, HUN |
| | | 6.11 | Michelle Rea | 11 Aug 90 | Oporto, POR |
| **Triple Jump** | E | 14.66 | Ashia Hansen | 21 Aug 95 | Gateshead |
| | S | 12.89 | Karen Hambrook/Skeggs | 17 May 92 | London (CP) |
| | W | 12.10 | Jane Falconer | 29 Aug 93 | Colchester |
| | NI | 11.79 | Michelle Rea | 16 Jun 91 | Grangemouth |
| **Shot** | E | 19.36 | Judy Oakes | 14 Aug 88 | Gateshead |
| | S | 18.99 | Meg Ritchie | 7 May 83 | Tucson, USA |
| | W | 19.06 i | Venissa Head | 7 Apr 84 | St. Athan |
| | | 18.93 | Venissa Head | 13 May 84 | Haverfordwest |
| | NI | 16.40 i | Mary Peters | 28 Feb 70 | Bucharest, ROM |
| | | 16.31 | Mary Peters | 1 Jun 66 | Belfast |
| **Discus** | S | 67.48 | Meg Ritchie | 26 Apr 81 | Walnut, USA |
| | W | 64.68 | Venissa Head | 18 Jul 83 | Athens, GRE |
| | NI | 60.72 | Jacqui McKernan | 18 Jul 93 | Buffalo, USA |
| | E | 57.32 | Lynda Whiteley/Wright | 16 Jun 84 | London (CP) |
| **Hammer** | E | 64.90 | Lorraine Shaw | 10 Jun 95 | Bedford |
| | W | 53.00 | Sarah Moore | 13 May 95 | Halle, GER |
| | S | 50.12 | Jean Clark | 28 Aug 95 | Welwyn Garden City |
| | NI | 48.56 | Julie Kirkpatrick | 20 Jun 95 | Antrim |

| Event | | Mark | | Athlete(s) | Date | Venue |
|---|---|---|---|---|---|---|
| **Javelin** | E | 77.44 | | Fatima Whitbread | 28 Aug 86 | Stuttgart, GER |
| | S | 62.22 | | Diane Royle | 18 May 85 | Stretford |
| | W | 59.40 | | Karen Hough | 28 Aug 86 | Stuttgart, GER |
| | NI | 47.54 | | Alison Moffitt | 4 Sep 93 | Antrim |
| **Hept.** | E | 6623 | | Judy Simpson | 30 Aug 86 | Stuttgart, GER |
| | S | 5803 | | Jayne Barnetson | 20 Aug 89 | Kiyev, UKR |
| | W | 5642 | | Sarah Rowe | 23 Aug 81 | Utrecht, HOL |
| | NI | 5065 | h | Catherine Scott | 13 Sep 87 | Tullamore, IRE |
| | | 4564 | | Wendy Phillips | 18 Jul 82 | Birmingham |
| **4x100m** | E | 42.43 | | H. Oakes, K. Cook,  (UK) B. Callender, S. Lannaman | 1 Aug 80 | Moscow, RUS |
| | S | 45.2 | | A. Robb, S. Pringle,  (ESH) H. Hogarth, E. Sutherland | 27 Jun 70 | London (CP) |
| | | 45.37 | | J. Booth, K. Hogg, J. Neilson, S. Whittaker | 8 Jun 86 | Lloret de Mar, SPA |
| | W | 45.37 | | H. Miles, S. Lewis, S. Short, C. Smart | 2 Aug 86 | Edinburgh |
| | NI | 46.36 | | K. Graham, H. Gourlay, J. Robinson, R. Gaylor | 31 Aug 85 | Tel Aviv, ISR |
| **4x400m** | E | 3:22.01 | | L. Hanson, P. Smith,  (UK) S. Gunnell, L. Keough | 1 Sep 91 | Tokyo, JAP |
| | S | 3:32.92 | | S. Whittaker, A. Purvis, A. Baxter, L. Macdonald | 9 Oct 82 | Brisbane, AUS |
| | W | 3:35.60 | | C. Smart, K. Wade, D. Fryar, M. Scutt | 4 Jul 82 | Dublin (M), IRE |
| | NI | 3:42.20 | | C. Hill, C. O'Connor, S. McCann, V. Jamieson | 23 Jul 95 | Cardiff |

## Track Walking

| Event | | Mark | | Athlete | Date | Venue |
|---|---|---|---|---|---|---|
| **3000 m** | E | 12:49.16 | | Betty Sworowski | 28 Jul 90 | Wrexham |
| | S | 13:31.32 | i | Verity Larby/Snook | 13 Feb 93 | Birmingham |
| | | 13:31.5 | | Verity Larby/Snook | 16 May 93 | Portsmouth |
| | W | 14:28.2 | | Karen Dunster | 18 May 91 | Portsmouth |
| **5000 m** | E | 21:52.38 | * | Vicky Lupton | 9 Aug 95 | Sheffield |
| | S | 23:22.52 | | Verity Larby/Snook | 18 Jun 94 | Horsham |
| | W | 24:32.92 | | Karen Nipper | 21 Jul 84 | Lyngby, DEN |
| **10 km** | E | 45:18.8 | | Vicky Lupton | 2 Sep 95 | Watford |
| | S | 47:10.07 | | Verity Larby/Snook | 20 Jun 93 | Horsham |
| | W | 50:25.0 | | Lisa Simpson | 1 Apr 87 | Hornchurch |
| **1 Hour** | E | 11,590 m | | Lisa Langford | 13 Sep 86 | Woodford |

## Road Walking

| Event | | Mark | | Athlete | Date | Venue |
|---|---|---|---|---|---|---|
| **5000 m** | E | 21:36 | | Vicky Lupton | 18 Jul 92 | Sheffield |
| | W | 23:35 | | Lisa Simpson | 31 Oct 87 | Cardiff |
| | S | 23:52 | | Verity Larby/Snook | 23 Mar 91 | London (BP) |
| **10 km** | E | 45:18.8 | t | Vicky Lupton | 2 Sep 95 | Watford |
| | S | 46:06 | | Verity Larby/Snook | 25 Aug 94 | Victoria, CAN |
| | W | 49:33 | | Lisa Simpson | 14 Mar 87 | Ham |
| **20 km** | E | 1:40:45 | | Irene Bateman | 9 Apr 83 | Basildon |
| **50 km** | E | 4:50:51 | | Sandra Brown | 13 Jul 91 | Basildon |

# BRITISH INDOOR RECORDS
## as at March 1996

## MEN

| Event | Mark | Athlete | Date | Venue |
|---|---|---|---|---|
| 50 m | 5.76 | Selwyn Clarke | 19 Feb 83 | Dortmund, GER |
| 60 m | 6.47 | Linford Christie | 19 Feb 95 | Lieven, FRA |
| 200 m | 20.25 | Linford Christie | 19 Feb 95 | Lieven, FRA |
| 300 m | 32.90 | Ade Mafe | 31 Jan 92 | Karlsruhe, GER |
| 400 m | 45.56 | Todd Bennett | 3 Mar 85 | Piraeus, GRE |
| 800 m | 1:44.91 | Sebastian Coe | 12 Mar 83 | Cosford |
| 1000 m | 2:17.86 | Matthew Yates | 22 Feb 92 | Birmingham |
| 1500 m | 3:34.20 | Peter Elliott | 27 Feb 90 | Seville, SPA |
| 1 mile | 3:52.02 | Peter Elliott | 9 Feb 90 | East Rutherford, USA |
| 2000 m | 5:05.20 | John Gladwin | 15 Mar 87 | Cosford |
| 3000 m | 7:43.90 | Rob Denmark | 10 Mar 91 | Seville, SPA |
| 5000 m | 13:21.27 | Nick Rose | 12 Feb 82 | New York, USA |
| 50 m Hurdles | 6.48 | Colin Jackson | 14 Mar 92 | Birmingham |
| 60 m Hurdles | 7.30 | Colin Jackson | 6 Mar 94 | Sindelfingen, GER |
| High Jump | 2.38 | Steve Smith | 4 Feb 94 | Wuppertal, GER |
| Pole Vault | 5.61 | Nick Buckfield | 4 Feb 96 | Birmingham |
| Long Jump | 8.05 | Barrington Williams | 11 Feb 89 | Cosford |
| | 8.05 # | Stewart Faulkner | 27 Feb 90 | Seville, SPA |
| Triple Jump | 17.31 | Keith Connor | 13 Mar 81 | Detroit, USA |
| Shot | 20.98 | Geoff Capes | 16 Jan 76 | Los Angeles, USA |
| | 20.98 # | Geoff Capes | 14 Feb 76 | Winnipeg, CAN |
| Heptathlon | 5978 | Alex Kruger | 12 Mar 95 | Barcelona, SPA |

(7.16, 7.23, 14.79, 2.16, 8.36, 4.90, 2:48.66)

| | | | | |
|---|---|---|---|---|
| 5000m Walk | 19:22.29 | Martin Rush | 8 Feb 92 | Birmingham |
| 4 x 200m Relay | 1:22.11 | UK National Team | 3 Mar 91 | Glasgow |

(Linford Christie, Darren Braithwaite, Ade Mafe, John Regis)

| | | | | |
|---|---|---|---|---|
| 4 x 400m Relay | 3:07.04 | England | 13 Mar 87 | Cosford |

(Kermit Bentham, John Regis, Steve Heard, Paul Harmsworth)

## WOMEN

| Event | Mark | Athlete | Date | Venue |
|---|---|---|---|---|
| 50 m | 6.21 | Wendy Hoyte | 22 Feb 81 | Grenoble, FRA |
| 60 m | 7.13 | Beverly Kinch | 23 Feb 86 | Madrid, SPA |
| 200 m | 23.00 | Katharine Merry | 12 Feb 94 | Glasgow |
| 400 m | 51.72 | Sally Gunnell | 6 Mar 94 | Sindelfingen, GER |
| 800 m | 2:01.12 | Jane Colebrook/Finch | 13 Mar 77 | San Sebastian, SPA |
| 1000 m | 2:38.95 | Kirsty Wade | 1 Feb 87 | Stuttgart, GER |
| 1500 m | 4:06.87 | Zola Budd | 25 Jan 86 | Cosford |
| 1 mile | 4:23.86 | Kirsty Wade | 5 Feb 88 | New York, USA |
| 2000 m | 5:40.86 | Yvonne Murray | 20 Feb 93 | Birmingham |
| 3000 m | 8:34.80 | Liz McColgan | 4 Mar 89 | Budapest, HUN |
| 5000 m | 15:03.17 | Liz McColgan | 22 Feb 92 | Birmingham |
| 50 m Hurdles | 7.03 | Yvette Wray/Luker | 21 Feb 81 | Grenoble, FRA |
| 60 m Hurdles | 8.01 | Jacqui Agyepong | 12 Mar 95 | Barcelona, SPA |
| High Jump | 1.94 | Diana Elliott/Davies | 7 Mar 82 | Milan, ITA |
| | 1.94 | Debbie Marti | 3 Feb 91 | Cosford |
| | 1.94 | Jo Jennings | 13 Mar 93 | Toronto, CAN |
| Pole Vault | 3.81 | Kate Staples | 24 Feb 96 | Glasgow |
| Long Jump | 6.70 | Susan Hearnshaw/Telfer | 3 Mar 84 | Göteborg, SWE |
| Triple Jump | 14.29 | Ashia Hansen | 25 Feb 95 | Birmingham |
| Shot | 19.06 | Venissa Head | 7 Apr 84 | St. Athan |
| Pentathlon | 4363 | Kim Hagger | 4 Feb 84 | Vittel, FRA |

(8.44, 1.82, 11.89, 6.31, 2:27.08)

| | | | | |
|---|---|---|---|---|
| 3000m Walk | 13:12.01 | Julie Drake | 12 Mar 93 | Toronto, CAN |
| 4 x 200m Relay | 1:33.96 | UK National Team | 23 Feb 90 | Glasgow |

(Paula Dunn, Jennifer Stoute, Linda Keough, Sally Gunnell)

| | | | | |
|---|---|---|---|---|
| 4 x 400m Relay | 3:35.11 | UK National Team | 3 Mar 91 | Glasgow |

(Sandra Douglas, Sally Gunnell, Janet Levermore, Dawn Kitchen)

# UK ALL TIME LISTS - MEN
## as at 31 December 1995

### 100 METRES

|  |  |  |
|---|---|---|
| 9.87 | Linford Christie | 15 Aug 93 |
| 10.09 | Jason Livingston ¶ | 13 Jun 92 |
| 10.11 | Allan Wells | 24 Jul 80 |
| 10.12 | Darren Braithwaite | 15 Jul 95 |
| 10.15 | Michael Rosswess | 15 Sep 91 |
| 10.15 | John Regis | 29 May 93 |
| 10.20 | Cameron Sharp | 24 Aug 83 |
| 10.20 | Elliot Bunney | 14 Jun 86 |
| 10.21 A | Ainsley Bennett | 8 Sep 79 |
| 10.21 | Jamie Henderson | 6 Aug 87 |
| 10.22 | Mike McFarlane | 20 Jun 86 |
| 10.23 | Marcus Adam | 26 Jul 91 |
| 10.23 | Jason John | 15 Jul 94 |
| 10.23 | Terry Williams | 22 Aug 94 |
| 10.25 | Jason Gardener | 21 Jul 94 |
| 10.26 | Daley Thompson | 27 Aug 86 |
| 10.26 | Ernest Obeng | 1 Aug 87 |
|  | 10.21 for Ghana | 11 Aug 80 |
| 10.29 | Peter Radford (10.31?) | 13 Sep 58 |
| 10.29 | Colin Jackson | 28 Jul 90 |
| 10.30 | Clarence Callender | 26 Jul 91 |
| 10.30 | Julian Golding | 28 Jun 95 |
| 10.32 | Buster Watson | 1 Jul 83 |
| 10.32 | Donovan Reid | 4 Aug 84 |
| 10.32 | Lincoln Asquith | 11 Aug 86 |
| 10.32 | Lenny Paul | 29 May 93 |
| 10.32 | Toby Box | 28 Jun 95 |
| 10.33 | Brian Green | 15 Jul 72 |
| 10.33 | Solomon Wariso | 19 Jun 94 |
| 10.34 | Drew McMaster | 9 Jul 83 |
| 10.34 | Barrington Williams | 5 Aug 88 |
| 10.34 | Darren Campbell | 9 Jul 95 |
| 10.35 A | Barrie Kelly | 13 Oct 68 |
| 10.35 | Brian Taylor | 29 May 93 |
| 10.36 | David Jenkins | 24 Jun 72 |
| 10.37 | Micky Morris | 23 Aug 87 |
| 10.37 | Steve Gookey | 20 Jul 91 |
| 10.39 | Ray Burke | 13 Jun 92 |
| 10.40 | Trevor Hoyte | 11 Aug 79 |
| 10.40 | Jim Evans | 24 Jul 82 |
| 10.40 | Paul White | 31 Aug 95 |
| 10.41 | Dwain Chambers | 28 Jul 95 |
| 10.41 | Jamie Henthorn | 28 Jul 95 |
| 10.42 A | Ron Jones | 13 Oct 68 |
| 10.42 | Peter Maitland | 3 Jun 95 |
| 10.42 | Owusu Dako | 5 Jun 95 |
| 10.43 | Steve Green | 5 Jun 80 |

**hand timing**

|  |  |  |
|---|---|---|
| 10.1 | David Jenkins | 20 May 72 |
| 10.1 | Brian Green | 3 Jun 72 |
| 10.1 | Ernest Obeng (for GHA) | 2 Aug 79 |
| 10.2 | McDonald Bailey | 25 Aug 51 |
| 10.2 | Menzies Campbell | 20 May 67 |
| 10.2 | Drew McMaster | 29 Jun 80 |
| 10.2 | Ed Cutting | 19 May 84 |
| 10.2 | Derek Redmond | 2 May 87 |

### wind assisted

|  |  |  |
|---|---|---|
| 10.02 | Allan Wells | 4 Oct 82 |
| 10.07 | Cameron Sharp | 4 Oct 82 |
| 10.07 | John Regis | 28 Aug 90 |
| 10.07 | Toby Box | 11 Jun 94 |
| 10.07 | Michael Rosswess | 11 Jun 94 |
| 10.08 | Mike McFarlane | 27 May 84 |
| 10.08 | Jason John | 11 Jun 94 |
| 10.10 | Donovan Reid | 26 Jun 83 |
| 10.11 | Drew McMaster | 26 Jun 83 |
| 10.12 | Buster Watson | 27 May 84 |
| 10.14 | Ernest Obeng | 20 Jun 87 |
| 10.14 | Marcus Adam | 28 Jan 90 |
| 10.17 | Terry Williams | 23 Aug 94 |
| 10.20 | Lincoln Asquith | 6 Jul 85 |
| 10.25 | Lenny Paul | 14 Jul 91 |
| 10.26 | Peter Little | 21 May 80 |
| 10.27 | Barrington Williams | 2 Jul 88 |
| 10.27 | Clarence Callender | 22 Jun 91 |
| 10.28 | Darren Campbell | 26 Jul 91 |
| 10.29 | Trevor Cameron | 11 Jun 94 |
| 10.31 | Jim Evans | 22 Aug 81 |
| 10.32 | Brian Green | 16 Jun 72 |
| 10.32 | Harry King | 22 Aug 81 |
| 10.33 | Steve Gookey | 20 Jul 91 |
| 10.33 | Danny Joyce | 10 Jun 95 |
| 10.34 | Phil Davies | 13 Jul 86 |
| 10.34 | Jason Fergus | 5 Jun 94 |
| 10.35 | Nigel Walker | 26 Aug 89 |
| 10.36 | Les Piggot | 15 Jul 72 |
| 10.37 | Earl Tulloch | 22 Aug 81 |
| 10.37 | Courtney Rumbolt | 25 Jun 88 |
| 10.37 | Allyn Condon | 3 Jul 93 |
| 10.38 | Don Halliday | 17 Jul 70 |
| 10.38 | Ian Green | 17 Jul 70 |
| 10.38 | Kevin Mark | 3 Jul 93 |
| 10.38 | Ejike Wodu | 3 Jul 93 |
| 10.39 | Trevor McKenzie | 21 Jul 84 |
| 10.39 | David Kirton | 4 Jun 87 |
| 10.39 | Dave Clark | 3 Jun 90 |
| 10.39 | Andrew Mensah | 15 Jun 94 |
| 10.40 | Steve Green | 3 Jun 78 |
| 10.40 | Gus McKenzie | 25 Aug 81 |
| 10.40 | Simon Baird | 26 Jul 86 |
| 10.41 | Vincent Jones | 27 May 84 |
| 10.41 | Eugene Gilkes | 7 Sep 85 |

**hand timing - wind assisted**

|  |  |  |
|---|---|---|
| 10.0 | Allan Wells | 16 Jun 79 |
| 10.0 | Drew McMaster | 1 Jun 80 |
| 10.1 | David Roberts | 17 Jul 82 |
| 10.2 | Ian Green | 20 May 70 |
| 10.2 | Les Piggot | 19 Aug 72 |
| 10.2 | Eugene Gilkes | 7 Jul 84 |
| 10.2 | Andy Carrott | 5 Jul 88 |
| 10.2 | Dave Clark | 25 Jun 89 |

**200 METRES** (* 220 yards time less 0.12)

| | | | |
|---|---|---|---|
| 19.87 A | John Regis | 31 Jul 94 | |
| 19.94 | | 20 Aug 93 | |
| 20.09 | Linford Christie | 28 Sep 88 | |
| 20.21 | Allan Wells | 28 Jul 80 | |
| 20.36 | Todd Bennett | 28 May 84 | |
| 20.41 | Marcus Adam | 13 Jun 92 | |
| 20.42 A | Ainsley Bennett | 12 Sep 79 | |
| 20.84 | | 31 Aug 80 | |
| 20.43 | Mike McFarlane | 7 Oct 82 | |
| 20.47 | Cameron Sharp | 9 Sep 82 | |
| 20.47 | Darren Braithwaite | 13 May 95 | |
| 20.50 | Terry Williams | 24 Aug 94 | 10 |
| 20.50 | Tony Jarrett | 16 Jul 95 | |
| 20.50 | Solomon Wariso | 16 Jul 95 | |
| 20.51 | Michael Rosswess | 28 Sep 88 | |
| 20.54 | Ade Mafe | 25 Aug 85 | |
| 20.57 | Owusu Dako | 16 Jul 95 | |
| 20.60 | Roger Black | 4 Aug 90 | |
| 20.62 | Buster Watson | 5 Jun 83 | |
| 20.62 | Donovan Reid | 28 May 84 | |
| 20.66 A | Dick Steane | 15 Oct 68 | |
| 20.66 | David Jenkins | 27 Aug 73 | 20 |
| 20.70 | Chris Monk | 20 Aug 73 | |
| 20.71 | Doug Walker | 24 Aug 94 | |
| 20.72 | Toby Box | 24 Aug 94 | |
| 20.73 A | Ralph Banthorpe | 15 Oct 68 | |
| 20.94 | | 3 Aug 68 | |
| 20.75 | Dave Clark | 20 Jan 90 | |
| 20.75 | Julian Golding | 7 Jul 95 | |
| 20.75 | Doug Turner | 9 Sep 95 | |
| 20.76 | Andy Carrott | 5 Jul 88 | |
| 20.76 | Clarence Callender | 24 Jun 91 | |
| 20.77 | Drew McMaster | 9 Jul 83 | 30 |
| 20.79 | Phil Goedluck | 6 Aug 94 | |
| 20.81 | Mike St. Louis | 21 Jun 86 | |
| 20.81 | Paul McBurney | 24 Aug 94 | |
| 20.83 | Martin Reynolds | 22 Jul 70 | |
| 20.83 | Claude Moseley | 23 Aug 81 | |
| 20.84 | Brian Green | 4 Sep 71 | |
| 20.84 | Earl Tulloch | 25 May 81 | |
| 20.84 | Jamie Baulch | 24 Aug 94 | |
| 20.85 | Richard Ashby | 25 Aug 85 | |
| 20.86 | Lincoln Asquith | 28 Aug 83 | 40 |
| 20.86 | Roger Hunter | 5 May 84 | |
| 20.86 | Gus McCuaig | 28 May 84 | |
| 20.86 | Darren Campbell | 4 Aug 93 | |
| 20.86 | Jason John | 1 Jul 95 | |
| 20.87 | Mark Smith | 28 Jul 90 | |
| 20.88 | Daley Thompson | 18 Aug 79 | |
| 20.88 | Phil Brown | 28 May 84 | |
| 20.89 | Mark Forsythe | 12 Aug 90 | |
| 20.90 * | Menzies Campbell | 23 Jun 67 | |
| 20.90 | Glen Cohen | 14 Aug 76 | 50 |
| 20.91 | Trevor Hoyte | 11 Jul 80 | |
| 20.91 | Nigel Will | 27 Aug 89 | |
| 20.91 | Ian Mackie | 23 Jul 94 | |
| 20.92 | Alan Pascoe | 15 Jul 72 | |
| 20.93 | George McCallum | 30 Jun 84 | |
| 20.93 | Mark Richardson | 6 May 92 | |

**wind assisted** (* 220 yards time less 0.12)

| | | | |
|---|---|---|---|
| 20.10 | Marcus Adam | 1 Feb 90 | |
| 20.11 | Allan Wells | 20 Jun 80 | |
| 20.26 | Ade Mafe | 1 Feb 90 | |
| 20.48 | Michael Rosswess | 9 Sep 90 | |
| 20.51 | Jason John | 2 Jul 93 | |
| 20.53 | Doug Walker | 8 May 95 | |
| 20.55 | Buster Watson | 10 Aug 85 | |
| 20.55 | Darren Campbell | 2 Jul 93 | |
| 20.61 | Martin Reynolds | 22 Jul 70 | |
| 20.62 | Adrian Patrick | 10 Jun 95 | 10 |
| 20.64 | Drew McMaster | 23 Aug 80 | |
| 20.68 | Doug Turner | 9 Jul 95 | |
| 20.69 | Julian Golding | 2 Jul 95 | |
| 20.70 * | David Jones | 20 May 61 | |
| 20.70 | Trevor Hoyte | 14 Sep 79 | |
| 20.73 | Phil Goedluck | 22 Apr 95 | |
| 20.84 | Nigel Stickings | 9 Jul 93 | |
| 20.85 | Phil Brown | 28 May 84 | |
| 20.85 | Mark Smith | 1 Jul 90 | |
| 20.88 | Trevor Cameron | 12 Jun 94 | 20 |
| 20.88 | Marlon Devonish | 26 Aug 95 | |
| 20.89 | Tim Bonsor | 10 Aug 78 | |
| 20.89 | David Grindley | 13 Jun 93 | |
| 20.91 | Peter Little | 21 May 80 | |

**hand timing** (* 220 yards time less 0.1)

| | | | |
|---|---|---|---|
| 20.3 | David Jenkins | 19 Aug 72 | |
| 20.4 * | Peter Radford | 28 May 60 | |
| 20.6 | Donovan Reid | 1 Jul 84 | |
| 20.7 * | Menzies Campbell | 10 Jun 67 | |
| 20.7 | Martin Reynolds | 2 Aug 70 | |
| 20.7 | Brian Green | 3 Jun 72 | |
| 20.7 | Drew McMaster | 16 Aug 80 | |
| 20.7 | Claude Moseley | 28 Aug 81 | |
| 20.7 | Julian Golding | 13 May 95 | |

**wind assisted**

| | | | |
|---|---|---|---|
| 20.4 | Buster Watson | 11 Aug 85 | |
| 20.6 | Ainsley Bennett | 22 Jun 74 | |

**300 METRES**

| | | | |
|---|---|---|---|
| 31.67 | John Regis | 17 Jul 92 | |
| 32.08 | Roger Black | 8 Aug 86 | |
| 32.14 | Todd Bennett | 18 Aug 84 | |
| 32.31 | Mark Richardson | 12 Jul 92 | |
| 32.32 | Derek Redmond | 16 Jul 88 | |
| 32.44 | David Jenkins | 4 Jul 75 | |
| 32.45 | David Grindley | 19 Jun 93 | |
| 32.59 | Kriss Akabusi | 14 Jul 91 | |
| 32.61 | Brian Whittle | 16 Jul 88 | |
| 32.73 | Du'aine Ladejo | 4 Sep 94 | 10 |
| 32.75 | Ade Mafe | 16 Jul 88 | |
| 32.79 | Phil Brown | 18 Aug 84 | |
| 32.82 | Solomon Wariso | 21 Jun 91 | |
| 32.9 | Mark Hylton | 21 Aug 94 | |
| 32.91 | Nigel Will | 12 Aug 90 | |

**during 400m**

| | | | |
|---|---|---|---|
| 32.06 + | Roger Black | 29 Aug 91 | |
| 32.26 + | Derek Redmond | 1 Sep 87 | |
| 32.35 + | David Grindley | 26 Jun 93 | |
| 32.4  + | David Jenkins | 13 Aug 71 | |

32

## 400 METRES

| | 44.47 | David Grindley | 3 Aug 92 |
|---|---|---|---|
| | 44.50 | Derek Redmond | 1 Sep 87 |
| | 44.59 | Roger Black | 29 Aug 86 |
| | 44.81 | Mark Richardson | 9 Aug 95 |
| | 44.93 | David Jenkins | 21 Jun 75 |
| | 44.93 | Kriss Akabusi | 7 Aug 88 |
| | 44.94 | Du'aine Ladejo | 2 Aug 94 |
| | 45.14 | Jamie Baulch | 23 Aug 95 |
| | 45.22 | Brian Whittle | 25 Sep 88 |
| 10 | 45.26 | Phil Brown | 26 May 85 |
| | 45.27 | Todd Bennett | 7 Aug 88 |
| | 45.30 | Ade Mafe | 23 Jul 93 |
| | 45.33 | Paul Sanders | 15 Jun 91 |
| | 45.47 | David McKenzie | 12 Jun 94 |
| | 45.48 | John Regis | 17 Apr 93 |
| | 45.49 | Glen Cohen | 21 May 78 |
| | 45.58 | Iwan Thomas | 20 Jun 95 |
| | 45.63 | Adrian Patrick | 5 Jul 95 |
| | 45.64 | Paul Harmsworth | 7 Aug 88 |
| 20 | 45.65 | Alan Bell | 14 Jun 80 |
| | 45.67 | Roger Hunter | 19 May 85 |
| | 45.74 | Steve Heard | 26 May 85 |
| | 45.75 | Robbie Brightwell | 19 Oct 64 |
| | 45.81 | Terry Whitehead | 14 Jun 80 |
| | 45.83 | Mark Hylton | 16 Jul 95 |
| | 45.88 | Wayne McDonald | 17 Aug 91 |
| | 45.91 A | Martin Winbolt-Lewis | 17 Oct 68 |
| | 45.92 | Mark Thomas | 27 Jun 87 |
| | 45.97 | Steve Scutt | 14 Sep 79 |
| 30 | 46.03 | Peter Crampton | 8 Aug 87 |
| | 46.04 | Alan Slack | 27 Jun 85 |
| | 46.08 | Tim Graham | 19 Oct 64 |
| | 46.08 | Rod Milne | 15 Jun 80 |
| | 46.10 | Peter Gabbett | 7 Sep 72 |
| | 46.11 | Martin Reynolds | 4 Sep 72 |
| | 46.13 | Guy Bullock | 31 Jul 93 |
| | 46.15 | Ainsley Bennett | 29 Aug 75 |
| | 46.16 | Gary Armstrong | 15 Jul 72 |
| | 46.16 | Claude Moseley | 1 Jul 83 |
| 40 | 46.18 | Garry Cook | 14 Jun 80 |
| | 46.19 | Roy Dickens | 28 May 84 |
| | 46.24 | Mel Fowell | 15 Jun 80 |
| | 46.27 | Richard Ashton | 6 Aug 78 |
| | 46.31 | Neil Jackson | 14 Jun 80 |
| | 46.31 | Kent Ulyatt | 10 Sep 95 |
| | 46.34 | Tim O'Dell | 19 Aug 95 |
| | 46.35 A | Colin Campbell | 17 Oct 68 |
| | 46.37 | Gary Cadogan | 27 Jun 87 |
| | 46.39 | Danny Laing | 25 Sep 78 |
| 50 | 46.39 | Alex Fugallo | 12 Jun 94 |
| | 46.42 | Nigel Will | 12 Jul 92 |
| | 46.44 A | Mark Smith | 27 May 95 |

### hand timing (* 440 yards time less 0.3)

| 45.6 * | Robbie Brightwell | 14 Jul 62 |
|---|---|---|
| 45.7 | Adrian Metcalfe | 2 Sep 61 |
| 45.9 | Colin Campbell | 2 Jul 68 |
| 46.0 | Garry Cook | 20 May 81 |
| 46.3 | John Wrighton | 21 Aug 58 |
| 46.3 | John Wilson | 30 Jun 73 |

## 600 METRES

| 1:14.95 | Steve Heard | 14 Jul 91 |
|---|---|---|
| 1:15.0 + | Sebastian Coe | 10 Jun 81 |
| 1:15.4 | Garry Cook | 30 Jul 84 |
| 1:15.4 | Tom McKean | 21 Jul 91 |
| 1:15.6 | David Jenkins | 3 Aug 74 |
| 1:15.94 | Brian Whittle | 28 Jul 92 |

## 800 METRES (* 880 yards time less 0.70)

| | 1:41.73" | Sebastian Coe | 10 Jun 81 |
|---|---|---|---|
| | 1:42.88 | Steve Cram | 21 Aug 85 |
| | 1:42.97 | Peter Elliott | 30 May 90 |
| | 1:43.84 | Martin Steele | 10 Jul 93 |
| | 1:43.88 | Tom McKean | 28 Jul 89 |
| | 1:43.98 | David Sharpe | 19 Aug 92 |
| | 1:44.09 | Steve Ovett | 31 Aug 78 |
| | 1:44.55 | Garry Cook | 29 Aug 84 |
| | 1:44.59 | Tony Morrell | 2 Jul 88 |
| 10 | 1:44.65 | Ikem Billy | 21 Jul 84 |
| | 1:44.65 | Steve Heard | 26 Aug 92 |
| | 1:44.92 | Curtis Robb | 15 Aug 93 |
| | 1:45.05 | Matthew Yates | 26 Aug 92 |
| | 1:45.12 | Andy Carter | 14 Jul 73 |
| | 1:45.14 | Chris McGeorge | 28 Jun 83 |
| | 1:45.14 | John Gladwin | 22 Jul 86 |
| | 1:45.31 | Robert Harrison | 21 Jul 84 |
| | 1:45.35 | Kevin McKay | 16 Aug 92 |
| | 1:45.44 | Neil Horsfield | 28 Jul 90 |
| 20 | 1:45.47 | Brian Whittle | 20 Jul 90 |
| | 1:45.6 | Graham Williamson | 12 Jun 83 |
| | 1:45.64 | Paul Herbert | 5 Jun 88 |
| | 1:45.66 | Paul Forbes | 8 Jun 83 |
| | 1:45.69 | Steve Crabb | 17 Aug 88 |
| | 1:45.76 | Frank Clement | 10 Jul 76 |
| | 1:45.85 | David Strang | 13 Jun 92 |
| | 1:46.10 | Gary Marlow | 10 Jul 87 |
| | 1:46.1 | Colin Campbell | 26 Jul 72 |
| | 1:46.16 | Gareth Brown | 2 Jul 84 |
| 30 | 1:46.20 | David Warren | 29 Jun 80 |
| | 1:46.21 | Peter Browne | 14 Jul 73 |
| | 1:46.26 | Phil Lewis | 27 Jan 74 |
| | 1:46.3 | Chris Carter | 4 Sep 66 |
| | 1:46.37 | Andrew Lill | 28 Jun 92 |
| | 1:46.51 | John Boulter | 18 Jun 66 |
| | 1:46.54 | Craig Winrow | 15 Jul 94 |
| | 1:46.6 | Derek Johnson | 9 Aug 57 |
| | 1:46.63 | Peter Hoffman | 11 Jun 78 |
| | 1:46.64 | David Moorcroft | 25 Jul 82 |
| 40 | 1:46.65 | Steve Caldwell | 31 May 82 |
| | 1:46.70 * | John Davies I | 3 Jun 68 |
| | 1:46.70 | Atle Douglas | 9 Jun 88 |
| | 1:46.72 | Mal Edwards | 13 Sep 87 |
| | 1:46.8 | Bob Adams | 9 Aug 69 |
| | 1:46.8 | Dave Cropper | 1 Jul 73 |
| | 1:46.8 | David McMeekin | 6 Jun 74 |
| | 1:46.92 | Colin Szwed | 7 Aug 82 |
| | 1:46.94 | Mark Kirk | 20 Jul 87 |
| | 1:47.0 | Brian Hewson | 13 Sep 58 |
| 50 | 1:47.0 | Mike Rawson | 13 Sep 58 |
| | 1:47.01 | Nick Brooks | 12 Apr 80 |

## 1000 METRES

| | | | |
|---|---|---|---|
| | 2:12.18 | Sebastian Coe | 11 Jul 81 |
| | 2:12.88 | Steve Cram | 9 Aug 85 |
| | 2:15.91 | Steve Ovett | 6 Sep 79 |
| | 2:16.30 | Peter Elliott | 17 Jan 90 |
| | 2:16.34 | Matthew Yates | 6 Jul 90 |
| | 2:16.82 | Graham Williamson | 17 Jul 84 |
| | 2:16.99 | Tony Morrell | 28 Aug 88 |
| | 2:17.14 | John Gladwin | 6 Jul 90 |
| | 2:17.20 | Robert Harrison | 18 Aug 84 |
| 10 | 2:17.36 | Neil Horsfield | 9 Aug 91 |
| | 2:17.43 | Gareth Brown | 18 Aug 84 |
| | 2:17.45 | Chris McGeorge | 20 Aug 84 |
| | 2:17.63 | Kevin McKay | 14 Jul 89 |
| | 2:17.75 | Steve Crabb | 5 Aug 87 |
| | 2:17.79 | David Sharpe | 31 Aug 92 |
| | 2:17.95 | Mark Scruton | 17 Jul 84 |

## 1500 METRES (+ during 1 mile)

| | | | |
|---|---|---|---|
| | 3:29.67 | Steve Cram | 16 Jul 85 |
| | 3:29.77 | Sebastian Coe | 7 Sep 86 |
| | 3:30.77 | Steve Ovett | 4 Sep 83 |
| | 3:32.69 | Peter Elliott | 16 Sep 90 |
| | 3:33.34 | Steve Crabb | 4 Jul 87 |
| | 3:33.79 | Dave Moorcroft | 27 Jul 82 |
| | 3:33.83 | John Robson | 4 Sep 79 |
| | 3:34.00 | Matthew Yates | 13 Sep 91 |
| | 3:34.01 | Graham Williamson | 28 Jun 83 |
| 10 | 3:34.05 | John Mayock | 18 Aug 95 |
| | 3:34.1 + | Tony Morrell | 14 Jul 90 |
| | 3:34.50 | Adrian Passey | 4 Jul 87 |
| | 3:34.53 | Mark Rowland | 27 Jul 88 |
| | 3:34.76 | Gary Lough | 9 Sep 95 |
| | 3:35.08 | Neil Horsfield | 10 Aug 90 |
| | 3:35.26 | John Gladwin | 5 Sep 86 |
| | 3:35.28 | Jack Buckner | 1 Jul 86 |
| | 3:35.66 | Frank Clement | 12 Aug 78 |
| | 3:35.74 | Rob Harrison | 26 May 86 |
| 20 | 3:35.94 | Paul Larkins | 10 Jul 87 |
| · | 3:35.94 | Kevin McKay | 19 Jun 92 |
| | 3:36.53 | David Strang | 15 Jul 94 |
| | 3:36.81 | Mike Kearns | 26 Jul 77 |
| | 3:37.55 | Colin Reitz | 27 Jun 85 |
| | 3:37.64 | Brendan Foster | 2 Feb 74 |
| | 3:37.88 | Jason Dullforce | 17 Jul 92 |
| | 3:37.97 | Rod Finch | 30 Jul 93 |
| | 3:37.99 | Rob Denmark | 5 Jun 95 |
| | 3:38.05 | Glen Grant | 12 Aug 78 |
| 30 | 3:38.06 | Tim Hutchings | 31 Aug 84 |
| | 3:38.08 | Tom Hanlon | 28 Jun 92 |
| | 3:38.1 | Jim McGuinness | 1 Aug 77 |
| | 3:38.2 a | James Espir | 11 Jul 80 |
| | 3:38.22 | Peter Stewart | 15 Jul 72 |
| | 3:38.31 | Matt Barnes | 23 Jul 93 |
| | 3:38.52 | Ray Smedley | 15 Jul 72 |
| | 3:38.56 | Curtis Robb | 26 Jun 93 |
| | 3:38.64 | Simon Fairbrother | 17 Jun 92 |
| | 3:38.65 | Ian Stewart II | 8 Aug 81 |
| 40 | 3:38.68 | John Kirkbride | 15 Jul 72 |
| | 3:38.7 | Jim Douglas | 27 Jun 72 |
| | 3:38.78 | Mark Scruton | 17 Jun 84 |
| | 3:38.8 | Paul Lawther | 12 Jun 77 |
| | 3:38.9 | Ian Hamer | 5 Aug 89 |
| | 3:38.9 | Brian Treacy | 28 Aug 94 |
| | 3:39.0 | David Lewis | 9 Aug 83 |
| | 3:39.06 | Andy Keith | 5 Jun 93 |
| | 3:39.10 | Alan Simpson | 15 Aug 64 |
| | 3:39.12 | Ian Stewart I | 1 Sep 69 |
| | 3:39.19 | Steve Green | 28 Aug 94 | 50 |

## ONE MILE

| | | | |
|---|---|---|---|
| | 3:46.32 | Steve Cram | 27 Jul 85 |
| | 3:47.33 | Sebastian Coe | 28 Aug 81 |
| | 3:48.40 | Steve Ovett | 26 Aug 81 |
| | 3:49.20 | Peter Elliott | 2 Jul 88 |
| | 3:49.34 | Dave Moorcroft | 26 Jun 82 |
| | 3:50.64 | Graham Williamson | 13 Jul 82 |
| | 3:51.02 | John Gladwin | 19 Aug 87 |
| | 3:51.31 | Tony Morrell | 14 Jul 90 |
| | 3:51.57 | Jack Buckner | 29 Aug 84 |
| | 3:51.76hc | Steve Crabb | 14 Aug 87 | 10 |
| | 3:52.20 | | 1 Jul 89 |
| | 3:51.89 | John Mayock | 16 Aug 95 |
| | 3:52.44 | John Robson | 11 Jul 81 |
| | 3:52.75 | Matthew Yates | 10 Jul 93 |
| | 3:52.99 | Mark Rowland | 10 Sep 86 |
| | 3:53.20 | Ian Stewart II | 25 Aug 82 |
| | 3:53.64 | Kevin McKay | 22 Jul 94 |
| | 3:53.82 | Gary Staines | 12 Aug 90 |
| | 3:53.85 | Robert Harrison | 15 Jul 86 |
| | 3:54.2 | Frank Clement | 27 Jun 78 |
| | 3:54.30 | David Strang | 22 Jul 94 | 20 |
| | 3:54.39 | Neil Horsfield | 8 Jul 86 |
| | 3:54.53 | Tim Hutchings | 31 Jul 82 |
| | 3:54.9 | Adrian Passey | 20 Aug 89 |
| | 3:55.0 | Jim McGuinness | 11 Jul 77 |
| | 3:55.3 | Peter Stewart | 10 Jun 72 |
| | 3:55.38 | Rob Denmark | 12 Aug 90 |
| | 3:55.41 | Colin Reitz | 31 Jul 82 |
| | 3:55.68 | Alan Simpson | 30 Aug 65 |
| | 3:55.8 | Geoff Smith | 15 Aug 81 |
| | 3:55.9 | Brendan Foster | 10 Jun 72 | 30 |
| | 3:55.91 | Gary Lough | 27 Aug 95 |
| | 3:55.96 | David Lewis | 23 Aug 83 |
| | 3:56.0 | Jim Douglas | 10 Jun 72 |
| | 3:56.04 | Mike Downes | 25 Aug 82 |
| | 3:56.1 | Neill Duggan | 11 Jun 66 |
| | 3:56.19 | Ian Hamer | 5 Jul 91 |
| | 3:56.29 i | Andy Keith | 22 Jan 94 |
| | 3:56.36 | Steve Martin | 5 Aug 86 |
| | 3:56.38 | Mike McLeod | 31 Aug 79 |
| | 3:56.5 | John Kirkbride | 10 Jun 72 | 40 |
| | 3:56.5 | Paul Davies-Hale | 20 Aug 89 |
| | 3:56.6 | Walter Wilkinson | 31 May 71 |
| | 3:56.65 | Paul Larkins | 17 Jul 87 |
| | 3:56.7 | James Espir | 15 Aug 81 |
| | 3:56.71 | Chris McGeorge | 5 Jul 88 |
| | 3:56.8 | Ian McCafferty | 11 Jun 69 |
| | 3:56.83 | Simon Fairbrother | 17 Aug 90 |
| | 3:56.9 a | Ron Speirs | 30 Apr 77 |
| | 3:56.95 | Sean Cahill | 31 Aug 79 |
| | 3:56.95 | Dave Clarke | 17 Jul 82 | 50 |

## 2000 METRES

| | | |
|---|---|---|
| 4:51.39 | Steve Cram | 4 Aug 85 |
| 4:52.82 | Peter Elliott | 15 Sep 87 |
| 4:53.06 | Jack Buckner | 15 Sep 87 |
| 4:53.69 | Gary Staines | 15 Sep 87 |
| 4:57.71 | Steve Ovett | 7 Jul 82 |
| 4:58.38 | Graham Williamson | 29 Aug 83 |
| 4:58.84 | Sebastian Coe | 5 Jun 82 |
| 4:59.57 | Nick Rose | 3 Jun 78 |
| 5:00.37 | Tim Hutchings | 29 Aug 83 |
| 5:01.09 | Eamonn Martin | 19 Jun 84 |
| 5:01.48 | Paul Larkins | 5 Jun 88 |
| 5:02.35 | Sean Cahill | 4 Aug 85 |
| 5:02.61 | Steve Martin | 19 Jun 84 |
| 5:02.8 a | Frank Clement | 10 Sep 78 |
| 5:02.86 | David Moorcroft | 19 Jul 86 |
| 5:02.93 | Brendan Foster | 4 Jul 75 |
| 5:02.98 | Ian Stewart | 4 Jul 75 |
| 5:03.16 | David Bedford | 8 Jul 72 |
| 5:03.8 | Lawrie Spence | 26 May 78 |
| 5:04.16 | Eddie Wedderburn | 15 Jul 83 |
| 5:04.51 | Steve Harris | 29 Aug 83 |
| 5:04.53 | David Lewis | 26 Jun 83 |
| 5:04.56 | Geoff Smith | 26 Jun 83 |
| 5:04.75 | Dave Clarke | 15 Jul 83 |
| 5:04.85 | Billy Dee | 15 Jul 83 |
| 5:04.86 | Colin Reitz | 7 Aug 82 |
| 5:05.00 | Steve Emson | 18 Aug 79 |

## 3000 METRES (+ during 2 Miles)

| | | |
|---|---|---|
| 7:32.79 | Dave Moorcroft | 17 Jul 82 |
| 7:35.1 | Brendan Foster | 3 Aug 74 |
| 7:39.55 | Rob Denmark | 1 Aug 93 |
| 7:40.4 | Nick Rose | 27 Jun 78 |
| 7:40.43 | Jack Buckner | 5 Jul 86 |
| 7:40.94 | Eamonn Martin | 9 Jul 83 |
| 7:41.3 | Steve Ovett | 23 Sep 77 |
| 7:41.79 | Gary Staines | 14 Jul 90 |
| 7:42.26 | Graeme Fell | 9 Jul 83 |
| 7:42.47 | David Lewis | 9 Jul 83 |
| 7:42.77 | Billy Dee | 18 Jul 92 |
| 7:43.03 | Tim Hutchings | 14 Jul 89 |
| 7:43.1 + | Steve Cram | 29 Aug 83 |
| 7:43.90 | Ian Stewart II | 26 Jun 82 |
| 7:44.40 | Colin Reitz | 9 Jul 83 |
| 7:44.76 | Paul Davies-Hale | 20 Jul 85 |
| 7:45.2 + | Geoff Turnbull | 12 Sep 86 |
| 7:45.29 | Dennis Coates | 9 Sep 77 |
| 7:45.81 | John Robson | 13 Jul 84 |
| 7:46.22 i | Mark Rowland | 27 Feb 90 |
| 7:49.82 | | 28 Jul 89 |
| 7:46.39 | Adrian Royle | 28 Jun 83 |
| 7:46.40 | Ian Hamer | 20 Jan 90 |
| 7:46.4 | David Bedford | 21 Jun 72 |
| 7:46.6 + | Dave Black | 14 Sep 73 |
| 7:46.80 i | John Mayock | 25 Feb 95 |
| 7:47.28 | | 23 Jul 95 |
| 7:46.83 | Ian Stewart I | 26 May 76 |
| 7:46.85 i | Ricky Wilde | 15 Mar 70 |
| 7:46.95 | David James | 26 May 80 |
| 7:47.12 | Simon Mugglestone | 27 Jun 88 |
| 7:47.54 | Paul Larkins | 14 Jul 89 |
| 7:47.56 | Richard Callan | 15 Jul 83 |
| 7:47.6 | Dick Taylor | 6 Sep 69 |
| 7:48.00 | Richard Nerurkar | 15 Jul 92 |
| 7:48.09 | Adrian Passey | 28 Jul 89 |
| 7:48.18 | Mike McLeod | 9 Jul 78 |
| 7:48.28 | Jon Richards | 9 Jul 83 |
| 7:48.59 | John Nuttall | 23 Jul 95 |
| 7:48.6 + | Nat Muir | 27 Jun 80 |
| 7:48.66 | Julian Goater | 26 May 80 |
| 7:48.81 | Tim Redman | 18 Aug 84 |
| 7:49.1 | Paul Lawther | 27 Jun 78 |
| 7:49.45 | Gary Lough | 30 May 95 |
| 7:49.47 | Roger Hackney | 13 Jul 84 |
| 7:49.64 | Barry Smith | 26 Jul 81 |
| 7:49.72 | Ray Smedley | 9 Jul 78 |
| 7:49.80 | Steve Jones | 13 Jul 84 |
| 7:49.83 i | Andy Keith | 6 Feb 94 |
| 7:50.20 | Jon Solly | 8 Aug 86 |
| 7:50.38 | Mark Scrutton | 15 Jul 83 |
| 7:50.69 | Sean Cahill | 23 May 85 |
| 7:50.8 | Ken Newton | 3 Jun 82 |
| 7:50.82 i | Matthew Yates | 4 Mar 93 |
| 7:50.90 | Tom Buckner | 10 Jul 92 |
| 7:51.0 + | Eddie Wedderburn | 16 Jul 88 |
| 7:51.31 | Tom Hanlon | 10 Jul 92 |
| 7:51.53 | Tony Simmons | 23 Aug 78 |
| 7:51.53 | Malcolm Prince | 16 May 79 |
| 7:51.53 | John Hartigan | 14 Jul 89 |
| 7:51.72 | Jon Brown | 1 Aug 93 |

## 2 MILES

| | | |
|---|---|---|
| 8:13.51 | Steve Ovett | 15 Sep 78 |
| 8:13.68 | Brendan Foster | 27 Aug 73 |
| 8:14.93 | Steve Cram | 29 Aug 83 |
| 8:15.53 | Tim Hutchings | 12 Sep 86 |
| 8:15.98 | Geoff Turnbull | 12 Sep 86 |
| 8:16.75 | Dave Moorcroft | 20 Aug 82 |
| 8:17.12 | Jack Buckner | 12 Sep 86 |
| 8:18.4 i | Nick Rose | 17 Feb 78 |
| 8:18.98 | Eamonn Martin | 16 Jul 88 |
| 8:19.37 | Nat Muir | 27 Jun 80 |
| 8:20.28 | David James | 27 Jun 80 |
| 8:20.66 | David Lewis | 7 Sep 84 |
| 8:21.09 | Barry Smith | 27 Jun 80 |
| 8:21.86 | David Black | 14 Sep 73 |
| 8:21.97 | Rob Denmark | 9 Aug 91 |
| 8:22.0 | Ian Stewart I | 14 Aug 72 |
| 8:22.41 | Nick Rose | 15 Sep 78 |
| 8:22.65 | Ian Hamer | 17 Jul 92 |
| 8:22.98 | Geoff Smith | 27 Jun 80 |
| 8:23.16 | Gary Staines | 9 Aug 91 |
| 8:23.80 | Billy Dee | 9 Aug 91 |
| 8:23.92 | Ray Smedley | 6 Aug 76 |
| 8:24.58 | Adrian Royle | 16 May 82 |
| 8:24.82 | Eddie Wedderburn | 16 Jul 88 |
| 8:25.02 | Tony Simmons | 6 Aug 76 |
| 8:25.52 | Colin Reitz | 19 Aug 86 |
| 8:25.6 | Mike McLeod | 26 Jan 80 |

## 5000 METRES

|  |  |  |
|---|---|---|
| 13:00.41 | Dave Moorcroft | 7 Jul 82 |
| 13:09.80 | Ian Hamer | 9 Jun 92 |
| 13:10.15 | Jack Buckner | 31 Aug 86 |
| 13:10.24 | Rob Denmark | 9 Jun 92 |
| 13:11.50 | Tim Hutchings | 11 Aug 84 |
| 13:14.28 | Gary Staines | 15 Aug 90 |
| 13:14.6 a | Brendan Foster | 29 Jan 74 |
| 13:15.59 | Julian Goater | 11 Sep 81 |
| 13:16.70 | John Nuttall | 8 Jun 95 |
| 13:17.21 | David Bedford | 14 Jul 72 |
| 13:17.84 | Eamonn Martin | 14 Jul 89 |
| 13:17.9 | Nat Muir | 15 Jul 80 |
| 13:18.6 | Steve Jones | 10 Jun 82 |
| 13:18.91 | Nick Rose | 28 Jun 84 |
| 13:19.66 | Ian McCafferty | 14 Jul 72 |
| 13:19.78 | Jon Brown | 2 Jul 93 |
| 13:20.06 | Steve Ovett | 30 Jun 86 |
| 13:21.13 | David Lewis | 4 Jul 85 |
| 13:21.14 | Barry Smith | 7 Jun 81 |
| 13:21.2 | Tony Simmons | 23 May 76 |
| 13:21.60 | Paul Davies-Hale | 8 Jul 88 |
| 13:21.73 | Geoff Turnbull | 5 Sep 86 |
| 13:21.83 | Mark Rowland | 1 Jun 88 |
| 13:22.17 i | Geoff Smith | 12 Feb 82 |
| 13:26.33 | | 8 Aug 81 |
| 13:22.39 | Jon Solly | 7 Jul 86 |
| 13:22.54 | Dave Clarke | 28 Jan 83 |
| 13:22.73 | Adrian Passey | 2 Jul 95 |
| 13:22.8 a | Ian Stewart I | 25 Jul 70 |
| 13:23.26 | Mike McLeod | 24 Jun 80 |
| 13:23.36 | Richard Nerurkar | 10 Aug 90 |
| 13:23.48 | John Doherty | 1 Jun 85 |
| 13:23.52 | Dave Black | 29 Jan 74 |
| 13:23.71 | Steve Binns | 1 Jun 88 |
| 13:25.38 | Paul Evans | 28 Jun 95 |
| 13:26.0 | Bernie Ford | 30 Jul 77 |
| 13:26.19 | Adrian Royle | 4 Jul 83 |
| 13:26.2 | Dick Taylor | 13 Jun 70 |
| 13:26.74 | Craig Mochrie | 25 Aug 89 |
| 13:26.97 | John Mayock | 9 Jun 92 |
| 13:27.14 | Richard Callan | 25 Aug 82 |
| 13:27.41 | Billy Dee | 10 Jul 92 |
| 13:28.15 | Malcolm Prince | 14 Sep 79 |
| 13:28.29 | Simon Mugglestone | 8 Jul 88 |
| 13:28.58 | Steve Cram | 3 Jun 89 |
| 13:28.7 a | Charlie Spedding | 13 Aug 78 |
| 13:28.99 | Steve Emson | 4 Sep 79 |
| 13:29.8 a | Allan Rushmer | 25 Jul 70 |
| 13:29.91 | John Downes | 4 Jul 94 |
| 13:29.93 | Mark Roberts | 10 Jun 84 |
| 13:30.79 | Steve Harris | 18 Jun 83 |
| 13:30.8 | Ricky Wilde | 5 Jul 72 |
| 13:30.88 | Tony Milovsorov | 10 Jun 84 |
| 13:31.3 a | Neil Coupland | 21 Jun 77 |
| 13:31.38 | Jon Richards | 13 Aug 87 |
| 13:32.20 | Mark Scrutton | 9 Jun 82 |
| 13:32.71 | Mike Chorlton | 10 Jun 84 |
| 13:33.0 | Mike Wiggs | 30 Jun 65 |
| 13:33.59 | Nick Lees | 14 Sep 79 |

## 10000 METRES

|  |  |  |
|---|---|---|
| 27:23.06 | Eamonn Martin | 2 Jul 88 |
| 27:30.3 | Brendan Foster | 23 Jun 78 |
| 27:30.80 | David Bedford | 13 Jul 73 |
| 27:31.19 | Nick Rose | 9 Jul 83 |
| 27:34.58 | Julian Goater | 26 Jun 82 |
| 27:36.27 | David Black | 29 Aug 78 |
| 27:39.14 | Steve Jones | 9 Jul 83 |
| 27:39.76 | Mike McLeod | 4 Sep 79 |
| 27:40.03 | Richard Nerurkar | 10 Jul 93 |
| 27:43.03 | Ian Stewart I | 9 Sep 77 |
| 27:43.59 | Tony Simmons | 30 Jun 77 |
| 27:43.74 | Bernie Ford | 9 Sep 77 |
| 27:43.76 | Geoff Smith | 13 Jun 81 |
| 27:47.16 | Adrian Royle | 10 Apr 82 |
| 27:47.79 | Paul Evans | 5 Jul 93 |
| 27:48.73 | Gary Staines | 6 Jul 91 |
| 27:51.76 | Jon Solly | 20 Jun 86 |
| 27:55.66 | Steve Binns | 9 Jul 83 |
| 27:55.77 | Dave Clarke | 25 May 82 |
| 27:57.77 | Ian Hamer | 13 Sep 91 |
| 27:59.12 | Allister Hutton | 30 May 86 |
| 27:59.24 | Carl Thackery | 16 Jul 87 |
| 27:59.33 | Steve Harris | 22 Jul 86 |
| 28:00.62 | Jim Brown | 1 Aug 75 |
| 28:00.64 | Billy Dee | 13 Sep 91 |
| 28:03.34 | Rob Denmark | 11 Jun 94 |
| 28:04.04 | Andy Bristow | 17 Aug 90 |
| 28:05.2 | Dave Murphy | 10 Apr 81 |
| 28:06.13 | Barry Smith | 7 Aug 81 |
| 28:06.6 | Dick Taylor | 22 Jun 69 |
| 28:07.43 | John Nuttall | 25 Aug 95 |
| 28:07.57 | Tim Hutchings | 7 Jul 90 |
| 28:08.12 | Charlie Spedding | 23 Jul 83 |
| 28:08.31 | Jon Brown | 25 Aug 95 |
| 28:08.44 | David Lewis | 5 Jun 88 |
| 28:09.39 | Mark Dalloway | 5 Jun 88 |
| 28:11.07 | Karl Harrison | 20 Jun 86 |
| 28:11.71 | Lachie Stewart | 18 Jul 70 |
| 28:11.85 | Lawrie Spence | 29 May 83 |
| 28:13.04 | Gerry Helme | 29 May 83 |
| 28:13.13 | Colin Moore | 29 Jun 90 |
| 28:13.36 | Jack Buckner | 13 Sep 91 |
| 28:14.08 | Jon Richards | 20 Jun 86 |
| 28:14.65 | Mike Tagg | 10 Aug 71 |
| 28:14.89 | Bernie Plain | 1 Aug 75 |
| 28:15.58 | Martin McLoughlin | 20 Jun 86 |
| 28:16.0 | Mike Baxter | 23 May 74 |
| 28:16.73 | Neil Coupland | 11 Jun 77 |
| 28:17.00 | Justin Hobbs | 29 Jun 94 |
| 28:18.6 | John Davies II | 11 Apr 79 |
| 28:18.68 | Terry Thornton | 17 Aug 90 |
| 28:18.8 | Nick Lees | 7 May 79 |
| 28:19.97 | Kevin Forster | 29 May 83 |
| 28:20.29 | Steve Kenyon | 7 Aug 81 |
| 28:21.48 | Roger Matthews | 18 Jul 70 |
| 28:22.48 | Paul Dugdale | 10 Jul 93 |
| 28:22.53 | Tony Staynings | 11 Apr 80 |
| 28:23.02 | Dave Long II | 7 Jun 90 |
| 28:23.04 | Mark Scrutton | 20 Jun 86 |

## MARATHON

| | | |
|---|---|---|
| 2:07:13 | Steve Jones | 20 Oct 85 |
| 2:08:33 | Charlie Spedding | 21 Apr 85 |
| 2:09:08 | Geoff Smith | 23 Oct 83 |
| 2:09:12 | Ian Thompson | 31 Jan 74 |
| 2:09:16 | Allister Hutton | 21 Apr 85 |
| 2:09:24 | Hugh Jones | 9 May 82 |
| 2:09:28 | Ron Hill | 23 Jul 70 |
| 2:09:28 | John Graham | 23 May 81 |
| 2:09:43 | Mike Gratton | 17 Apr 83 |
| 2:09:54 | Tony Milovsorov | 23 Apr 89 |
| 2:10:03 | Richard Nerurkar | 31 Oct 93 |
| 2:10:12 | Gerry Helme | 17 Apr 83 |
| 2:10:30 | Dave Long II | 21 Apr 91 |
| 2:10:31 | Paul Evans | 2 Apr 95 |
| 2:10:39 | Mike O'Reilly | 5 Dec 93 |
| 2:10:48 | Bill Adcocks | 8 Dec 68 |
| 2:10:50 | Eamonn Martin | 18 Apr 93 |
| 2:10:51 | Bernie Ford | 2 Dec 79 |
| 2:10:52 | Kevin Forster | 17 Apr 88 |
| 2:10:55 | Chris Bunyan | 18 Apr 83 |
| 2:10:57 | Steve Brace | 29 Sep 91 |
| 2:11:06 | Dave Buzza | 31 Oct 93 |
| 2:11:18 | Dave Murphy | 12 Jun 83 |
| 2:11:22 | Dave Cannon | 6 Sep 80 |
| 2:11:25 | Paul Davies-Hale | 29 Oct 89 |
| 2:11:35 | Malcolm East | 20 Apr 81 |
| 2:11:36 | Kenny Stuart | 15 Jan 89 |
| 2:11:40 | Steve Kenyon | 13 Jun 82 |
| 2:11:43 | Jimmy Ashworth | 29 Sep 85 |
| 2:11:44 | Jim Dingwall | 17 Apr 83 |
| 2:11:50 | Fraser Clyne | 2 Dec 84 |
| 2:11:54 | Martin McCarthy | 17 Apr 83 |
| 2:11:58 | Mark Hudspith | 2 Apr 95 |
| 2:12:04 | Jim Alder | 23 Jul 70 |
| 2:12:07 | Jon Solly | 14 Oct 90 |
| 2:12:07 | Mark Flint | 17 Apr 94 |
| 2:12:12 | Dennis Fowles | 13 May 84 |
| 2:12:12 | Andy Green | 25 Apr 93 |
| 2:12:13 | John Wheway | 17 Apr 88 |
| 2:12:17 | Dave Long I | 16 Jan 82 |
| 2:12:19 | Don Faircloth | 23 Jul 70 |
| 2:12:23 | Peter Whitehead | 2 Apr 95 |
| 2:12:32 | Trevor Wright | 3 Dec 78 |
| 2:12:33 | Tony Simmons | 7 May 78 |
| 2:12:37 | Carl Thackery | 25 Oct 92 |
| 2:12:41 | Derek Stevens | 16 Jun 84 |
| 2:12:50 | Jeff Norman | 7 May 78 |
| 2:13:06 | Greg Hannon | 13 May 79 |
| 2:13:12 | Chris Stewart | 8 Dec 74 |
| 2:13:15 | Ray Crabb | 17 Apr 83 |

## 2000 METRES STEEPLECHASE

| | | |
|---|---|---|
| 5:19.86 | Mark Rowland | 28 Aug 88 |
| 5:21.77 | Tom Hanlon | 11 Jun 92 |
| 5:23.56 | Tom Buckner | 17 Jul 92 |
| 5:23.6 | Roger Hackney | 10 Jun 82 |
| 5:23.71 | Colin Walker | 28 Aug 88 |
| 5:23.87 | Colin Reitz | 28 Jun 84 |
| 5:24.91 | Eddie Wedderburn | 19 Aug 86 |
| 5:26.24 | Paul Davies-Hale | 26 Aug 85 |
| 5:26.64 | Nick Peach | 19 Aug 86 |
| 5:26.82" | David Lewis | 12 Jun 83 |
| 5:30.6 | Dennis Coates | 23 Apr 78 |
| 5:30.86 | Tony Staynings | 26 May 76 |
| 5:31.04 | John Hartigan | 17 Apr 90 |
| 5:31.09 | Peter McColgan | 5 Aug 86 |
| 5:31.43 | John Bicourt | 26 May 76 |

## 3000 METRES STEEPLECHASE

| | | |
|---|---|---|
| 8:07.96 | Mark Rowland | 30 Sep 88 |
| 8:12.11 | Colin Reitz | 5 Sep 86 |
| 8:12.58 | Tom Hanlon | 3 Aug 91 |
| 8:15.16 | Graeme Fell | 17 Aug 83 |
| 8:18.32 | Eddie Wedderburn | 5 Jul 88 |
| 8:18.91 | Roger Hackney | 30 Jul 88 |
| 8:18.95 | Dennis Coates | 25 Jul 76 |
| 8:20.83 | Paul Davies-Hale | 10 Jun 84 |
| 8:22.48 | John Davies II | 13 Sep 74 |
| 8:22.82 | John Bicourt | 8 Jun 76 |
| 8:23.90 | Justin Chaston | 18 Jul 94 |
| 8:24.64 | Spencer Duval | 16 Jul 95 |
| 8:25.15 | Colin Walker | 28 Jun 92 |
| 8:25.50 | Tom Buckner | 28 Aug 92 |
| 8:26.05 | Keith Cullen | 21 Aug 95 |
| 8:26.4 | Andy Holden | 15 Sep 72 |
| 8:26.6 | Gordon Rimmer | 4 Jun 80 |
| 8:27.21 | Tony Staynings | 15 Jun 80 |
| 8:27.8 | Steve Hollings | 5 Aug 73 |
| 8:27.93 | Peter McColgan | 25 Jun 91 |
| 8:28.6 | David Bedford | 10 Sep 71 |
| 8:29.46 | Julian Marsay | 14 Jul 79 |
| 8:29.72 | David Lewis | 29 May 83 |
| 8:30.6 a | Peter Griffiths | 17 Jul 77 |
| 8:30.8 | Gerry Stevens | 1 Sep 69 |
| 8:31.09 | Ian Gilmour | 16 Jul 78 |
| 8:31.22 | David Lee | 19 Jun 92 |
| 8:32.00 | Steve Jones | 8 Aug 80 |
| 8:32.06 | David Camp | 10 Aug 74 |
| 8:32.13 | Barry Knight | 25 Jul 82 |
| 8:32.4 a | Maurice Herriott | 17 Oct 64 |
| 8:33.0 | John Jackson | 13 Aug 69 |
| 8:33.8 a | Gareth Bryan-Jones | 23 Jul 70 |
| 8:33.8 | Peter Morris | 4 Aug 73 |
| 8:33.83 | Richard Charleston | 24 May 80 |
| 8:33.89 | Nick Peach | 21 Jun 86 |
| 8:33.97 | John Hartigan | 20 Jul 90 |
| 8:34.77 | Kevin Capper | 18 Aug 85 |
| 8:34.83 | Ken Baker | 1 Jul 84 |
| 8:35.49 | Micky Morris | 14 Aug 76 |
| 8:35.52 | Neil Smart | 28 Aug 89 |
| 8:35.8 | Ron McAndrew | 9 Jul 71 |
| 8:35.8 | John Wild | 3 Aug 77 |
| 8:36.18 | Rob Hough | 23 Jul 95 |
| 8:36.2 a | Bernie Hayward | 26 Jan 74 |
| 8:36.55 | Mick Hawkins | 16 Jul 95 |
| 8:37.0 | Ernie Pomfret | 15 Jul 67 |
| 8:37.59 | Dave Baptiste | 28 Aug 89 |
| 8:37.68 | Darren Mead | 26 Jun 93 |
| 8:37.70 | Ken Penney | 19 Jul 91 |

## 110 METRES HURDLES

| |  |  |  |
|---|---|---|---|
| | 12.91 | Colin Jackson | 20 Aug 93 |
| | 13.00 | Tony Jarrett | 20 Aug 93 |
| | 13.29 | Jon Ridgeon | 15 Jul 87 |
| | 13.42 | David Nelson | 27 Aug 91 |
| | 13.43 | Mark Holtom | 4 Oct 82 |
| | 13.44 | Hugh Teape | 14 Aug 92 |
| | 13.51 | Nigel Walker | 3 Aug 90 |
| | 13.52 | Andy Tulloch | 11 Aug 94 |
| | 13.53 | Paul Gray | 22 Aug 94 |
| 10 | 13.60 | Wilbert Greaves | 21 Aug 85 |
| | 13.60 | Neil Owen | 28 Jun 95 |
| | 13.69 | Berwyn Price | 18 Aug 73 |
| | 13.72 | David Hemery | 1 Aug 70 |
| | 13.75 | Lloyd Cowan | 17 Jul 94 |
| | 13.79 | Alan Pascoe | 17 Jun 72 |
| | 13.86 | Ken Campbell | 23 Aug 94 |
| | 13.96 | Steve Buckeridge | 31 May 86 |
| | 14.02 | Mark Lambeth | 9 Jul 95 |
| | 14.03 | Brett St Louis | 27 Jun 87 |
| 20 | 14.04 | Daley Thompson | 28 Aug 86 |
| | 14.08 | Paul Brice | 26 Aug 83 |
| | 14.08 | Brian Taylor | 13 Apr 91 |
| | 14.09 | Colin Hamplett | 11 Aug 90 |
| | 14.10 | Graham Gower | 15 Jul 72 |
| | 14.10 | Bob Danville | 4 Jul 76 |
| | 14.10 | Jamie Quarry | 25 Jun 94 |
| | 14.11 | Neil Fraser | 11 Jul 87 |
| | 14.11 | Ererton Harrison | 31 Jul 91 |
| | 14.14 | Mike Hogan | 5 Sep 63 |
| 30 | 14.14 | Max Robertson | 7 Jun 86 |
| | 14.14 | Martin Nicholson | 12 Jun 94 |
| | 14.16 A | Mike Parker | 16 Oct 68 |
| | 14.26 | | 17 Oct 64 |
| | 14.17 | Colin Bovell | 23 Jul 94 |
| | 14.18 | Chris Breen | 13 Jul 75 |
| | 14.18 | James Archampong | 21 Jul 94 |
| | 14.19 | C. J. Kirkpatrick | 16 Jun 73 |
| | 14.20 A | Stuart Storey | 16 Oct 68 |
| | 14.20 | Kevin Lumsdon | 16 Jul 94 |
| | 14.21 | David Wilson | 15 Jul 72 |
| 40 | 14.21 | Alan Cronin | 13 Jul 75 |
| | 14.21 | Mark Whitby | 14 Jun 85 |
| | 14.23 | Alan Tapp | 14 Jun 86 |
| | 14.24 | Kieran Moore | 7 Jun 86 |
| | 14.24 | Mark Stern | 28 Aug 93 |
| | 14.26 | Peter Hildreth | 14 Sep 58 |
| | 14.26 | Phil Barthropp | 24 Jun 84 |
| | 14.28 | Gus McKenzie | 25 May 80 |
| | 14.28 | Glenn MacDonald | 22 Aug 82 |
| | 14.28 | Nick Dakin | 12 Jun 93 |
| 50 | 14.29 | Greg Dunson | 28 Jun 86 |
| | 14.29 | John Wallace | 17 Sep 89 |
| | 14.29 | Rhys Davies | 25 Jun 90 |
| | 14.29 | Jon Hazel | 4 Jul 92 |
| | 14.32 | Tony James | 27 Jun 81 |
| | 14.34 | Gary Oakes | 5 Jul 80 |
| | 14.34 | Norman Ashman | 26 Jul 91 |
| | 14.34 | Damien Greaves | 16 Jul 95 |
| | 14.35 | Neil Gerrard | 27 Jun 81 |
| | 14.35 | Anthony Brannen | 27 Aug 89 |

### wind assisted

| |  |  |  | |
|---|---|---|---|---|
| | 13.49 | Nigel Walker | 3 Jun 89 | |
| | 13.65 | Berwyn Price | 25 Aug 75 | |
| | 13.66 | David Hemery | 18 Jul 70 | |
| | 13.97 | Brett St Louis | 30 Jul 88 | |
| | 13.99 | Bob Danville | 14 Aug 76 | |
| | 14.06 | Tony James | 22 Aug 81 | |
| | 14.08 | David Wilson | 15 Jul 72 | |
| | 14.11 | Mark Stern | 20 Jun 93 | |
| | 14.16 | Mark Hatton | 14 Jul 79 | |
| | 14.17 | C. J. Kirkpatrick | 13 Jul 74 | 10 |
| | 14.19 | Alan Cronin | 25 Aug 75 | |
| | 14.19 | Norman Ashman | 15 Aug 92 | |
| | 14.22 | Phil Barthropp | 1 Jul 84 | |
| | 14.23 | Gus McKenzie | 21 May 80 | |
| | 14.23 | John Wallace | 26 Jul 86 | |
| | 14.23 | Greg Dunson | 10 Jun 89 | |
| | 14.25 | Stuart Storey | 18 Jul 70 | |
| | 14.25 | Glenn MacDonald | 13 Jun 82 | |
| | 14.25 | Anthony Brannen | 30 Apr 95 | |
| | 14.27 | Richard Harbour | 1 Jul 90 | 20 |
| | 14.30 | David Humphreys | 15 Jul 89 | |
| | 14.33 | Mark Johnson | 10 Aug 85 | |

### hand timing

| |  |  |  | |
|---|---|---|---|---|
| | 13.5 | Berwyn Price | 1 Jul 73 | |
| | 13.6 | David Hemery | 5 Jul 69 | |
| | 13.7 | Alan Pascoe | 5 Jul 69 | |
| | 13.7 | C. J. Kirkpatrick | 29 Jun 74 | |
| | 13.8 | Martin Nicholson | 25 Jun 94 | |
| | 13.9 | Mike Parker | 2 Oct 63 | |
| | 13.9 | David Wilson | 29 Jun 74 | |
| | 13.9 | Brian Taylor | 8 May 93 | |
| | 14.1 | Mike Hogan | 5 Sep 63 | |
| | 14.1 | Stuart Storey | 2 Aug 67 | 10 |
| | 14.1 | Colin Bovell | 17 Jul 94 | |
| | 14.1 y | Laurie Taitt | 5 Sep 63 | |
| | 14.2 | | 2 Oct 63 | |
| | 14.2 | Bob Birrell | 6 Sep 61 | |
| | 14.2 | Andy Todd | 27 Oct 67 | |
| | 14.2 | Mark Whitby | 12 May 84 | |
| | 14.2 | James Hughes | 2 Jul 94 | |
| | 14.2 | Anthony Brannen | 6 May 95 | |
| | 14.2 y | Rodney Morrod | 13 Jun 64 | |

### wind assisted

| |  |  |  | |
|---|---|---|---|---|
| | 12.8 | Colin Jackson | 10 Jan 90 | |
| | 13.4 | Berwyn Price | 7 Jul 76 | |
| | 13.7 | Lloyd Cowan | 27 Apr 95 | |
| | 14.0 | Laurie Taitt | 13 Sep 62 | |
| | 14.0 y | Bob Birrell | 9 Sep 61 | |
| | 14.1 | Donald Finlay | 8 Sep 37 | |
| | 14.1 | Neil Fraser | 30 May 87 | |
| | 14.2 | Jack Morgan | 24 Apr 82 | |
| | 14.2 | Kieran Moore | 1 Jun 85 | |
| | 14.2 | Mark Bishop | 22 Jun 91 | 10 |
| | 14.2 y | Peter Hildreth | 18 Aug 59 | |
| | 14.2 y | Desmond Price | 18 Aug 59 | |
| | 14.2 y | Tony Hogarth | 20 Jul 68 | |
| | 14.2 y | Rupert Legge | 20 Jul 68 | |

## 400 METRES HURDLES

| | | | |
|---|---|---|---|
| | 47.82 | Kriss Akabusi | 6 Aug 92 |
| | 48.12 A | David Hemery | 15 Oct 68 |
| | 48.52 | | 2 Sep 72 |
| | 48.59 | Alan Pascoe | 30 Jun 75 |
| | 48.73 | Jon Ridgeon | 6 Sep 92 |
| | 49.03 A | John Sherwood | 15 Oct 68 |
| | 49.88 | | 13 Aug 69 |
| | 49.07 | Gary Cadogan | 22 Jul 94 |
| | 49.11 | Gary Oakes | 26 Jul 80 |
| | 49.25 | Max Robertson | 28 Aug 90 |
| | 49.26 | Peter Crampton | 8 Aug 94 |
| 10 | 49.49 | Mark Holtom | 20 Jul 85 |
| | 49.60 | Phil Beattie | 28 Jul 86 |
| | 49.65 | Bill Hartley | 2 Aug 75 |
| | 49.82 | Martin Gillingham | 14 Aug 87 |
| | 49.82 | Gary Jennings | 27 Jun 95 |
| | 49.86 | Martin Briggs | 6 Jun 84 |
| | 49.95 | Steve Sole | 24 Jul 83 |
| | 50.01 | Philip Harries | 5 Jun 88 |
| | 50.1 a | John Cooper | 16 Oct 64 |
| | 50.19 | Lawrence Lynch | 27 Jul 91 |
| 20 | 50.19 | Steve Coupland | 12 Jun 94 |
| | 50.31 | Tony Williams | 27 Jun 95 |
| | 50.37 | Bob Danville | 27 Jul 82 |
| | 50.38 | Andy Todd | 18 Sep 69 |
| | 50.58 | Colin O'Neill | 29 Jan 74 |
| | 50.58 | Mike Whittingham | 7 Aug 82 |
| | 50.68 | Peter Warden | 18 Jun 66 |
| | 50.70 | Noel Levy | 8 Jul 94 |
| | 50.71 | Steve Hawkins | 4 Jun 89 |
| | 50.79 | Mark Davidson | 17 Jun 89 |
| 30 | 50.79 | Lloyd Cowan | 3 Jun 95 |
| | 50.82 " | Paul Atherton | 12 Jun 83 |
| | 50.84 | Mark Whitby | 6 Jun 84 |
| | 50.86 | Wilbert Greaves | 18 May 80 |
| | 50.88 | Greg Dunson | 7 Jun 92 |
| | 50.90 | Chris Rawlinson | 16 Jul 95 |
| | 50.91 | Brian Whittle | 5 Jun 93 |
| | 50.94 | Trevor Burton | 17 Jul 87 |
| | 50.98 | Stan Devine | 14 Jul 82 |
| | 51.04 | Peter Kelly | 12 Jun 76 |
| 40 | 51.08 | Tim Gwynne | 30 May 94 |
| | 51.09 | Steve Black | 14 Jul 73 |
| | 51.15 | Eddie Betts | 26 Jun 94 |
| | 51.16 | Keith van Vollenhoven | 8 Aug 81 |
| | 51.17 | Dave Scharer | 21 Jul 70 |
| | 51.21 | Steve James | 23 Jun 78 |
| | 51.22 | Roger Bell | 13 Jul 79 |
| | 51.23 | Paul Beaumont | 17 Jun 89 |
| | 51.28 | Robin Woodland | 18 Jun 66 |
| | 51.28 | Mark Bishop | 11 Aug 89 |
| 50 | 51.29 | Gary Tefler | 27 May 95 |

### hand timing

| | | |
|---|---|---|
| 49.9 | Andy Todd | 9 Oct 69 |
| 50.5 | Wilbert Greaves | 12 Feb 80 |
| 50.7 | Steve Black | 20 Aug 74 |
| 50.7 | Stewart McCallum | 21 Mar 76 |
| 50.8 | Dave Schärer | 26 Jun 71 |

## HIGH JUMP

| | | | |
|---|---|---|---|
| 2.38 i | Steve Smith | 4 Feb 94 | |
| 2.37 | | 20 Sep 92 | |
| 2.37 i | Dalton Grant | 13 Mar 94 | |
| 2.36 | | 1 Sep 91 | |
| 2.32 i | Brendan Reilly | 24 Feb 94 | |
| 2.31 | | 17 Jul 92 | |
| 2.31 | Geoff Parsons | 26 Aug 94 | |
| 2.28 i | John Holman | 28 Jan 89 | |
| 2.24 | | 27 May 89 | |
| 2.25 | Floyd Manderson | 20 Aug 88 | |
| 2.24 | Mark Naylor | 28 Jun 80 | |
| 2.24 | John Hill | 23 Aug 85 | |
| 2.24 | Phil McConnell | 26 Aug 85 | |
| 2.23 | Mark Lakey | 29 Aug 82 | 10 |
| 2.23 i | David Abrahams | 12 Mar 83 | |
| 2.19 | | 7 Oct 82 | |
| 2.21 | Fayyaz Ahmed | 29 Jun 86 | |
| 2.21 | Steve Chapman | 30 Jul 89 | |
| 2.20 | Brian Burgess | 11 Jun 78 | |
| 2.20 | Trevor Llewelyn | 15 Jul 83 | |
| 2.20 | Byron Morrison | 14 Jul 84 | |
| 2.20 i | Henderson Pierre | 10 Jan 87 | |
| 2.18 | | 16 Aug 86 | |
| 2.20 | Alex Kruger | 18 Jun 88 | |
| 2.20 | Ossie Cham | 21 May 89 | |
| 2.20 i | Warren Caswell | 10 Mar 90 | 20 |
| 2.18 | | 2 Sep 90 | |
| 2.19 | David Barnetson | 4 Jul 92 | |
| 2.18 | Tim Foulger | 23 Sep 79 | |
| 2.18 | Rupert Charles | 25 Jul 82 | |
| 2.18 | Steve Ritchie | 15 Jul 89 | |
| 2.18 | Hopeton Lindo | 23 Jul 89 | |
| 2.18 i | James Brierley | 5 Feb 95 | |
| 2.17 | | 28 Jul 95 | |
| 2.18 | Andrew Lynch | 9 Jul 95 | |
| 2.17 | Stuart Ohrland | 27 Aug 94 | |
| 2.17 | Mike Robbins | 5 Aug 95 | |
| 2.16 i | Mike Butterfield | 23 Jan 76 | 30 |
| 2.14 | | 31 May 75 | |
| 2.16 i | Claude Moseley | 13 Apr 80 | |
| 2.16 | | 19 Jul 81 | |
| 2.16 i | David Watson | 13 Mar 82 | |
| 2.15 | | 19 Aug 84 | |
| 2.16 | Andy Hutchinson | 2 Sep 84 | |
| 2.16 | Mike Powell | 3 Sep 88 | |
| 2.16 | John Wallace | 29 Jul 90 | |
| 2.16 | Richard Aspden | 7 Jul 95 | |
| 2.16 | Rob Brocklebank | 7 Jul 95 | |
| 2.15 i | Andrew McIver | 26 Jan 80 | |
| 2.10 | | 4 May 81 | |
| 2.15 | Femi Abejide | 6 Jun 82 | |
| 2.15 | Leroy Lucas | 19 Aug 84 | 40 |
| 2.15 | Paul Jeffs | 14 Jun 85 | |
| 2.15 | Canisus Alcindor | 14 Jul 85 | |
| 2.15 i | John Hopper | 25 Feb 90 | |
| 2.11 | | 12 Jun 88 | |
| 2.15 | Stanley Osuide | 1 Sep 91 | |
| 2.15 | Darran Baker | 19 Jul 92 | |

## POLE VAULT

|  |  |  | |
|---|---|---|---|
| 5.70 | Nick Buckfield | 23 Jul 95 | |
| 5.65 | Keith Stock | 7 Jul 81 | |
| 5.60 | Neil Winter | 19 Aug 95 | |
| 5.59 | Brian Hooper | 6 Sep 80 | |
| 5.52 | Michael Edwards | 13 May 93 | |
| 5.45 i | Andy Ashurst | 16 Feb 92 | |
| 5.40 | | 19 Jun 88 | |
| 5.42 | Mike Barber | 26 Aug 95 | |
| 5.40 A | Jeff Gutteridge ¶ | 23 Apr 80 | |
| 5.40 | | 5 Jun 83 | |
| 5.40 i | Paul Williamson | 18 Feb 95 | |
| 5.40 | | 3 Jun 95 | |
| 5.35 | Matthew Belsham | 26 Jun 93 | [10] |
| 5.30 i | Ian Tullett | 14 Mar 92 | |
| 5.30 | | 7 Jun 92 | |
| 5.30 i | Kevin Hughes | 25 Feb 95 | |
| 5.30 | | 28 Aug 95 | |
| 5.30 | Dean Mellor | 17 Jun 95 | |
| 5.26 | Mark Johnson | 31 Aug 91 | |
| 5.25 | Mike Bull | 22 Sep 73 | |
| 5.25 | Allan Williams | 29 Aug 77 | |
| 5.25 | Daley Thompson | 15 Jun 86 | |
| 5.21 | Graham Eggleton | 10 Jul 82 | |
| 5.20 | Billy Davey | 5 Jun 83 | |
| 5.20 | Warren Siley | 4 Aug 90 | [20] |
| 5.20 ns | Tim Thomas | 16 Jul 94 | |
| 5.10 | | 23 Jul 94 | |
| 5.18 | Steve Chappell | 15 Jun 78 | |
| 5.11 | Andrew Gayle | 10 Aug 91 | |
| 5.10 | Darren Wright | 12 Jun 88 | |
| 5.10 | Paul Phelps | 9 Jul 89 | |
| 5.10 | Mark Grant | 20 May 95 | |
| 5.10 | Mark Hodgkinson | 3 Jun 95 | |
| 5.02 | Bob Kingman | 29 Aug 94 | |
| 5.01 | Paul Hoad | 16 Aug 86 | |
| 5.00 | Richard Gammage | 19 Aug 84 | [30] |
| 5.00 | Brian Taylor | 5 May 91 | |
| 5.00 | Dan Gilby | 20 Jul 91 | |
| 5.00 | Paul Wray | 26 Jul 91 | |
| 5.00 | Alex Greig | 31 May 92 | |
| 5.00 | Barry Thomas | 23 Aug 92 | |
| 5.00 | Mark Davis | 3 Jun 95 | |
| 4.98 A | Richard Williamson | 17 Apr 78 | |
| 4.88 | | 25 Jun 77 | |
| 4.90 | Stuart Tufton | 22 Jul 72 | |
| 4.90 | Tim Anstiss | 28 May 80 | |
| 4.90 | Phil Lovell | 18 May 83 | [40] |
| 4.90 | Gary Jackson | 22 Jun 86 | |
| 4.90 | Steve Leader | 15 Jul 90 | |
| 4.90 | Justin Richards | 3 Aug 91 | |
| 4.90 i | Dylan MacDermott | 11 Mar 92 | |
| 4.85 | | 19 May 90 | |
| 4.90 | Christian North | 11 Jul 92 | |
| 4.90 | Matt Weaver | 14 May 94 | |
| 4.90 | Dominic Shepherd | 11 Sep 94 | |
| 4.90 i | Anthony Brannen | 5 Feb 95 | |
| 4.90 i | Alex Kruger | 12 Mar 95 | |
| 4.90 | | 28 May 95 | |
| 4.90 | Egryn Jones | 14 Jun 95 | [50] |

## LONG JUMP

|  |  |  | |
|---|---|---|---|
| 8.23 | Lynn Davies | 30 Jun 68 | |
| 8.15 | Stewart Faulkner | 16 Jul 90 | |
| 8.14 | Mark Forsythe | 7 Jul 91 | |
| 8.10 | Fred Salle | 9 Sep 94 | |
| 8.08 | Roy Mitchell | 27 Sep 80 | |
| 8.05 i | Barrington Williams | 11 Feb 89 | |
| 8.01 | | 17 Jun 89 | |
| 8.01 | Daley Thompson | 8 Aug 84 | |
| 8.00 | Derrick Brown | 7 Aug 85 | |
| 7.98 | Alan Lerwill | 29 Jun 74 | |
| 7.94 i | Paul Johnson | 10 Mar 89 | [10] |
| 7.85 | | 3 Jun 89 | |
| 7.91 | John King | 26 Sep 87 | |
| 7.91 | Steve Phillips | 10 Aug 91 | |
| 7.90 | Ian Simpson | 3 Jun 89 | |
| 7.89 | John Morbey | 8 Aug 66 | |
| 7.87 | Keith Fleming | 7 Jun 87 | |
| 7.84 | Wayne Griffith | 25 Aug 89 | |
| 7.79 | Geoff Hignett | 31 May 71 | |
| 7.79 | Don Porter | 13 Jul 75 | |
| 7.77 | Len Tyson | 25 Jul 82 | |
| 7.76 | Carl Howard | 31 Jul 93 | [20] |
| 7.75 | Ken Cocks | 2 Jul 78 | |
| 7.75 | Trevor Hoyte | 6 May 84 | |
| 7.75 | Michael Morgan | 30 Jul 94 | |
| 7.74 | Fred Alsop | 6 Jun 64 | |
| 7.74 i | Phil Scott | 17 Feb 73 | |
| 7.68 | | 27 May 73 | |
| 7.74 i | Aston Moore | 10 Jan 81 | |
| 7.61 | | 3 Jun 78 | |
| 7.74 | John Herbert | 14 Jul 85 | |
| 7.74 | David Burgess | 4 Jul 87 | |
| 7.73 | Jason Canning | 20 Apr 88 | |
| 7.72 | Femi Abejide | 20 Jun 86 | [30] |
| 7.71 | Billy Kirkpatrick | 2 Jun 78 | |
| 7.71 i | Keith Connor | 20 Feb 81 | |
| 7.61 | | 14 May 82 | |
| 7.70 | Kevin Liddington | 27 Aug 88 | |
| 7.68 | Garry Slade | 1 Aug 92 | |

### wind assisted

|  |  |  | |
|---|---|---|---|
| 8.17 | Mark Forsythe | 11 Jun 89 | |
| 8.16 | Roy Mitchell | 26 Jun 76 | |
| 8.15 | Alan Lerwill | 29 May 72 | |
| 8.12 | Derrick Brown | 14 Jun 86 | |
| 8.11 | Daley Thompson | 7 Aug 78 | |
| 8.04 | Ian Simpson | 3 Jun 89 | |
| 7.96 | Colin Jackson | 17 May 86 | |
| 7.94 | John Herbert | 25 Jul 82 | |
| 7.94 | John King | 20 Jun 86 | |
| 7.93 | David Burgess | 15 Jun 86 | [10] |
| 7.91 | Steve Ingram | 18 Jun 94 | |
| 7.89 | John Shepherd | 20 Jun 86 | |
| 7.87 | Paul Johnson | 15 May 88 | |
| 7.82 | Peter Reed | 20 Jul 68 | |
| 7.82 | Femi Abejide | 20 Jun 86 | |
| 7.82 | Kevin Liddington | 25 Jun 89 | |
| 7.81 | Onochie Onuorah | 21 Aug 95 | |
| 7.76 | Aston Moore | 7 Aug 77 | |

## TRIPLE JUMP

| | | | |
|---|---|---|---|
| | 18.29 | Jonathon Edwards | 7 Aug 95 |
| | 17.57 A | Keith Connor | 5 Jun 82 |
| | 17.30 | | 9 Jun 82 |
| | 17.41 | John Herbert | 2 Sep 85 |
| | 17.21 | Tosi Fasinro | 27 Jul 93 |
| | 17.18 | Francis Agyepong | 7 Jul 95 |
| | 17.06 | Julian Golley | 10 Sep 94 |
| | 17.01 | Eric McCalla | 3 Aug 84 |
| | 16.87 | Mike Makin | 2 Aug 86 |
| | 16.86 | Aston Moore | 16 Aug 81 |
| 10 | 16.75 | Vernon Samuels | 7 Aug 88 |
| | 16.53 | Larry Achike | 24 Jul 94 |
| | 16.46 | Fred Alsop | 16 Oct 64 |
| | 16.32 | Tayo Erogbogbo | 21 Aug 95 |
| | 16.30 | Femi Abejide | 27 Jun 85 |
| | 16.29 i | David Johnson | 1 Mar 78 |
| | 16.18 | | 22 Jun 75 |
| | 16.26 | Joe Sweeney | 3 Aug 91 |
| | 16.22 | Derek Boosey | 15 Jun 68 |
| | 16.20 | Rez Cameron | 5 Jun 88 |
| | 16.18 | Tony Wadhams | 6 Jul 69 |
| 20 | 16.17 | John Mackenzie | 17 Sep 94 |
| | 16.16 | Conroy Brown | 19 Sep 81 |
| | 16.15 | Wayne Green | 10 Jul 88 |
| | 16.15 | Michael Brown | 23 Jul 89 |
| | 16.13 | Steven Anderson | 11 Jun 83 |
| | 16.10 | Alan Lerwill | 28 Aug 71 |
| | 16.09 | Courtney Charles | 17 Jun 90 |
| | 16.08 | Craig Duncan | 21 Jun 86 |
| | 16.03 | Femi Akinsanya | 18 Jun 95 |
| | 16.02 | Peter Akwaboah | 15 Jun 89 |
| 30 | 15.98 | Frank Attoh | 5 Sep 80 |
| | 15.97 | Mike Ralph | 23 Jul 64 |
| | 15.97 | Carl Howard | 6 May 95 |
| | 15.95 | Derek Browne | 12 Jun 93 |
| | 15.92 | John Slaney | 15 Oct 77 |
| | 15.92 | Lawrence Lynch | 13 Jul 85 |

**wind assisted**

| | | | |
|---|---|---|---|
| | 18.43 | Jonathon Edwards | 25 Jun 95 |
| | 17.81 | Keith Connor | 9 Oct 82 |
| | 17.30 | Tosi Fasinro | 12 Jun 93 |
| | 17.29 A | Francis Agyepong | 29 Jul 95 |
| | 17.24 | | 2 Jul 95 |
| | 17.02 | Aston Moore | 14 Jun 81 |
| | 16.82 | Vernon Samuels | 24 Jun 89 |
| | 16.67 | Larry Achike | 24 Jul 94 |
| | 16.65 | Fred Alsop | 13 Aug 65 |
| | 16.49 | Tony Wadhams | 16 Sep 69 |
| 10 | 16.38 | Femi Abejide | 10 Jun 89 |
| | 16.38 | Courtney Charles | 22 Jul 90 |
| | 16.33 | David Johnson | 28 May 78 |
| | 16.32 | Craig Duncan | 20 Jun 87 |
| | 16.32 | Rez Cameron | 21 May 89 |
| | 16.21 | Alan Lerwill | 28 Aug 71 |
| | 16.17 | Chris Colman | 15 Jul 78 |
| | 16.12 | Donovan Perkins | 21 Sep 80 |
| | 16.00 | Frank Attoh | 14 Jun 80 |
| | 15.96 | Paul Johnson | 27 Jun 87 |

## SHOT

| | | | |
|---|---|---|---|
| | 21.68 | Geoff Capes | 18 May 80 |
| | 20.43 | Mike Winch | 22 May 74 |
| | 20.33 | Paul Edwards ¶ | 9 Jul 91 |
| | 19.56 | Arthur Rowe | 7 Aug 61 |
| | 19.49 | Matt Simson | 28 Aug 94 |
| | 19.44 i | Simon Williams | 28 Jan 89 |
| | 19.17 | | 18 May 91 |
| | 19.43 | Bill Tancred | 18 May 74 |
| | 19.37 | Mark Proctor | 21 Jul 95 |
| | 19.18 | Jeff Teale ¶ | 7 Aug 68 |
| 10 | 19.01 | Billy Cole | 21 Jun 86 |
| | 18.94 | Bob Dale | 12 Jun 76 |
| | 18.94 | Shaun Pickering | 19 Aug 95 |
| | 18.93 | Paul Buxton | 13 May 77 |
| | 18.62 | Martyn Lucking | 2 Oct 62 |
| | 18.59 i | Alan Carter | 11 Apr 65 |
| | 18.26 | | 1 May 65 |
| | 18.50 | Mike Lindsay | 2 Jul 63 |
| | 18.46 | Roger Kennedy | 22 May 77 |
| | 18.46 i | Simon Rodhouse | 20 Feb 82 |
| | 18.20 | | 25 Jul 82 |
| | 18.46 | Lee Newman | 9 Jul 95 |
| 20 | 18.35 | Peter Tancred | 9 Jul 74 |
| | 18.34 | Richard Slaney | 3 Jul 83 |
| | 18.14 i | Neal Brunning ¶ | 26 Jan 92 |
| | 17.45 | | 17 Aug 91 |
| | 18.05 | John Watts | 19 Aug 72 |
| | 18.04 | Andy Vince | 30 Apr 83 |
| | 17.96 | Nigel Spratley | 28 Aug 94 |
| | 17.95 | Graham Savory | 4 Jun 88 |
| | 17.92 | Nick Tabor | 9 Apr 83 |
| | 17.87 | Bill Fuller | 15 Jul 72 |
| | 17.87 i | Ian Lindley | 15 Mar 81 |
| | 17.58 | | 25 May 81 |
| | 17.87 i | Antony Zaidman | 22 Jan 83 |
| 30 | 17.22 | | 4 Jul 81 |
| | 17.79 | John Alderson | 31 Jul 74 |
| | 17.78 | Steve Whyte | 11 Feb 89 |
| | 17.62 | Neil Gray | 7 Jun 89 |
| | 17.55 | David Callaway | 1 Aug 93 |
| | 17.54 | Eric Irvine | 16 Aug 86 |
| | 17.47 | Carl Jennings | 13 Sep 87 |
| | 17.45 | Abi Ekoku | 3 Feb 90 |
| | 17.44 | Hamish Davidson | 3 Jun 78 |
| | 17.41 | Lee Wiltshire | 1 May 94 |
| 40 | 17.40 | Barry King | 11 Apr 70 |
| | 17.40 | Allan Seatory | 27 Apr 75 |
| | 17.36 i | Chris Ellis | 8 Dec 84 |
| | 17.26 | | 10 Sep 86 |
| | 17.30 | Mark Aldridge | 19 Sep 82 |
| | 17.25 | Tony Satchwell | 2 Jun 84 |
| | 17.13 | John Turton | 29 Apr 77 |
| | 17.04 | Paul Reed | 14 May 88 |
| | 16.95 | Nick Morgan | 23 Sep 61 |
| | 16.94 | Tony Elvin | 14 Aug 66 |
| | 16.94 | Paul Mardle | 16 May 84 |
| | 16.94 | Gary Sollitt | 11 Jun 95 |
| 50 | 16.91 | Barclay Palmer | 10 Oct 56 |
| | 16.89 | Andy Drzewiecki | 20 Jul 75 |

| | DISCUS | | | | HAMMER | |
|---|---|---|---|---|---|---|
| | 65.16 | Richard Slaney | 1 Jul 85 | 77.54 | Martin Girvan | 12 May 84 |
| | 64.94 | Bill Tancred | 21 Jul 74 | 77.30 | Dave Smith I | 13 Jul 85 |
| | 63.56 | Bob Weir | 10 Jun 95 | 77.02 | Matt Mileham | 11 May 84 |
| | 62.36 | Peter Tancred | 8 May 80 | 75.40 | Chris Black | 23 Jul 83 |
| | 61.86 | Paul Mardle | 13 Jun 84 | 75.08 | Bob Weir | 3 Oct 82 |
| | 61.62 | Peter Gordon | 15 Jun 91 | 74.02 | Paul Head | 30 Aug 90 |
| | 61.14 | Simon Williams | 18 Apr 92 | 73.86 | Barry Williams | 1 Jul 76 |
| | 61.00 | Allan Seatory | 6 Oct 74 | 73.80 | Jason Byrne | 19 Sep 92 |
| | 60.92 | Graham Savory | 10 May 86 | 73.20 | Paul Dickenson | 22 May 76 |
| 10 | 60.42 | Mike Cushion | 16 Aug 75 | 72.10 | Mick Jones | 28 Aug 88 | 10 |
| | 60.08 | Abi Ekoku | 16 May 90 | 71.60 | Shane Peacock | 24 Jun 90 |
| | 59.84 | Colin Sutherland ¶ | 10 Jun 78 | 71.52 | Dave Smith II | 22 Jul 95 |
| | 59.78 | Glen Smith | 5 Jun 94 | 71.28 | Peter Vivian | 25 Jun 95 |
| | 59.76 | John Hillier | 27 Jul 74 | 71.00 | Ian Chipchase | 17 Aug 74 |
| | 59.70 | John Watts | 14 Jul 72 | 70.88 | Howard Payne | 29 Jun 74 |
| | 59.50 | Kevin Brown | 9 Sep 95 | 70.30 | Stewart Rogerson | 14 Aug 88 |
| | 58.64 | Steve Casey | 19 May 91 | 70.28 | Paul Buxton | 19 May 79 |
| | 58.58 | Darrin Morris | 22 Jun 91 | 69.52 | Jim Whitehead | 23 Sep 79 |
| | 58.34 | Geoff Capes | 29 Sep 73 | 68.64 | Shaun Pickering | 7 Apr 84 |
| 20 | 58.34 | Lee Newman | 9 Jun 94 | 68.18 | Ron James | 2 Jun 82 | 20 |
| | 58.08 | Mike Winch | 7 Sep 75 | 67.82 | Steve Whyte | 15 Apr 89 |
| | 57.58 | Arthur McKenzie | 17 Aug 69 | 67.32 | Gareth Cook | 1 Jun 91 |
| | 57.12 | Paul Edwards ¶ | 10 Aug 88 | 66.54 | John Pearson | 14 May 94 |
| | 57.10 | Dennis Roscoe | 3 May 80 | 65.36 | Russell Devine | 23 Apr 94 |
| | 57.00 | Gerry Carr | 17 Jul 65 | 65.30 | Karl Andrews | 2 Jul 94 |
| | 56.70 | Roy Hollingsworth | 14 Sep 63 | 65.24 | Steve Pearson | 19 Jul 94 |
| | 56.42 | Paul Buxton | 6 Aug 76 | 64.96 | Mike Ellis | 4 Jun 59 |
| | 56.40 | Guy Dirkin | 1 Aug 75 | 64.80 | Bruce Fraser | 30 Sep 73 |
| | 56.32 | Gary Herrington | 17 Jun 95 | 64.54 | Michael Petra | 30 May 79 |
| 30 | 55.68 | Neville Thompson | 12 Jun 93 | 64.36 | Andrew Tolputt | 27 Jun 87 | 30 |
| | 55.60 | Jeff Clare | 25 Jul 88 | 63.74 | Mark Sterling | 18 Jul 84 |
| | 55.52 | Jamie Murphy | 29 Jul 95 | 63.74 | Chris Howe | 15 Aug 90 |
| | 55.42 | Geoff Tyler | 3 May 80 | 63.20 | Peter Gordon | 17 Sep 82 |
| | 55.38 | Leith Marar | 24 Jun 95 | 63.16 | Graham Callow | 29 May 89 |
| | 55.34 | Nick Woolcott | 27 Jul 88 | 62.92 | Bill Beauchamp | 23 Aug 95 |
| | 55.32 | Mike Lindsay | 4 May 60 | 62.70 | Paul Barnard | 19 Jul 95 |
| | 55.04 | Denzil McDonald | 28 Aug 95 | 62.60 | Peter Weir | 2 Aug 87 |
| | 54.78 | Colin Bastien | 29 Mar 87 | 62.60 | Rob Earle | 1 Aug 95 |
| | 54.50 | Paul Reed | 13 Jul 94 | 62.56 | Adrian Palmer | 6 Aug 94 |
| 40 | 54.38 | Shaun Pickering | 26 Aug 89 | 62.54 | Tony Elvin | 25 May 70 | 40 |
| | 54.36 | Matt Symonds | 24 Jun 95 | 62.42 | Malcolm Fenton | 16 May 82 |
| | 54.28 | Mark Proctor | 7 Aug 93 | 62.40 | Lawrie Nisbet | 5 Jul 86 |
| | 54.26 | Mark Pharoah | 27 Nov 56 | 62.32 | Peter Aston | 6 Sep 75 |
| | 54.00 | Eric Cleaver | 21 Oct 62 | 62.28 | Lawrie Bryce | 13 Oct 73 |
| | 53.80 | Perris Wilkins | 23 Jul 94 | 62.24 | Phil Scott | 16 Jun 76 |
| | 53.76 | John Turton | 18 May 79 | 62.24 | Tony Kenneally | 18 May 85 |
| | 53.64 A | Barry King | 7 May 66 | 62.16 | Geoff Whaley | 30 Apr 80 |
| | 53.54 | Tony Satchwell | 30 Sep 73 | 62.10 | Chris Melluish | 7 Sep 74 |
| | 53.48 | George Patience | 11 Jul 87 | 62.00 | Eric Berry | 26 Aug 74 |
| 50 | 53.46 | Neal Brunning ¶ | 1 May 91 | 61.76 | Steve Minnikin | 11 Jul 93 | 50 |
| | 53.24 | Andy Drzewiecki | 8 Aug 76 | 61.72 | Peter Seddon | 10 May 67 |
| | 53.06 | Mark Davies | 20 Jun 92 | 61.38 | Russell Tolputt | 7 Aug 85 |
| | 53.02 | Nick Tabor | 3 May 80 | 61.22 | Malcolm Croad | 25 Aug 92 |
| | 52.80 | Peter Nimmo | 3 Apr 65 | 61.10 | Vaughan Cooper | 5 May 84 |
| | 52.38 | Michael Jemi-Alade | 30 Jun 87 | 60.96 | Stuart Spratley | 19 Jul 92 |
| | 52.34 | Ted Kelland | 30 Jun 73 | 60.54 | Niall McDonald | 6 Jun 70 |
| | 52.26 | Scott Hayes | 24 Jun 95 | 60.42 | Tom Campbell | 31 May 75 |
| | 52.14 | Robert Russell | 4 Jul 93 | 60.12 | David Allan | 7 May 95 |
| | 52.06 | Danny Maloney | 10 Aug 74 | 59.84 | Sandy Sandu | 16 Jun 82 |

| JAVELIN (1986 model) | | | DECATHLON (1985 Tables) | | |
|---|---|---|---|---|---|
| 91.46 | Steve Backley | 25 Jan 92 | 8847 | Daley Thompson | 9 Aug 84 |
| 86.94 | Mike Hill | 13 Jun 93 | 8131 | Alex Kruger | 2 Jul 95 |
| 83.84 | Roald Bradstock | 2 May 87 | 7980 | Simon Shirley | 24 Aug 94 |
| 82.38 | Colin Mackenzie | 7 Aug 93 | 8036 for AUS | | 29 Sep 88 |
| 81.70 | Nigel Bevan | 28 Jun 92 | 7922 w | Brad McStravick | 28 May 84 |
| 80.98 | Dave Ottley | 24 Sep 88 | 7885 h | | 6 May 84 |
| 80.92 | Mark Roberson | 12 Jun 88 | 7904 | David Bigham | 28 Jun 92 |
| 78.54 | Gary Jenson | 17 Sep 89 | 7901 h | Peter Gabbett | 22 May 72 |
| 77.84 | Peter Yates | 21 Feb 87 | 7889 | Eugene Gilkes | 18 May 86 |
| 10 76.30 | Nick Nieland | 3 Jun 95 | 7874 | Colin Boreham | 23 May 82 |
| 75.52 | Marcus Humphries | 25 Jul 87 | 7861 | Anthony Brannen | 30 Apr 95 |
| 75.32 | Steve Harrison | 9 Jul 95 | 7787 | Brian Taylor | 30 May 93  10 |
| 75.28 | Nigel Stainton | 5 Aug 89 | 7766 | Barry Thomas | 2 Sep 95 |
| 74.90 | Darryl Brand | 27 Jun 86 | 7748 | Eric Hollingsworth | 30 May 93 |
| 74.72 | Chris Crutchley | 13 Jul 86 | 7740 | Greg Richards | 7 Jun 87 |
| 74.70 | Myles Cottrell | 16 May 92 | 7713 | James Stevenson | 5 Jun 93 |
| 74.24 | Stuart Faben | 29 Jul 95 | 7708 | Fidelis Obikwu | 28 May 84 |
| 73.88 | Keith Beard | 12 May 90 | 7663 | Rafer Joseph | 24 Aug 94 |
| 73.26 | David Messom | 25 Apr 87 | 7643 w | Tom Leeson | 8 Sep 85 |
| 20 72.92 | Stefan Baldwin | 8 May 93 | 7565 | | 11 Aug 85 |
| 71.86 | Tony Hatton | 3 May 93 | 7610 | Jamie Quarry | 24 Aug 94 |
| 70.30 | Tim Newenham | 11 Jun 89 | 7596 h | Mike Corden | 27 Jun 76 |
| 70.12 | Paul Morgan | 12 Sep 87 | 7594 | Mark Bishop | 3 Sep 89  20 |
| 70.10 | Richard Hooper | 21 May 89 | 7579 h | Mark Luscombe | 8 May 88 |
| 70.00 | Paul Bushnell | 22 Jul 90 | 7535 | Duncan Mathieson | 24 Jun 90 |
| 70.00 | Phil Parry | 2 Jul 94 | 7515 | Ken Hayford | 9 Jun 85 |
| 69.90 | Ken Hayford | 5 Jul 87 | 7500 h | Barry King | 22 May 72 |
| 69.68 | Shane Lewis | 23 Apr 94 | 7500 | Pan Zeniou | 2 Aug 81 |
| 69.20 | Roddy James | 28 Apr 89 | 7439 | Kevan Lobb | 19 Aug 84 |
| 30 69.18 | Tony Smith | 11 Jul 92 | 7431 | Alan Drayton | 8 Aug 78 |
| 69.02 | Kevin Murch | 3 Sep 89 | 7425 w | Paul Field | 21 May 95 |
| 68.84 | James Hurrion | 12 Jul 91 | 7295 | | 2 Jul 95 |
| 68.74 | Jon Clarke | 14 Jun 86 | 7367 h | John Garner | 8 May 88 |
| 68.74 | Tony Norman | 23 May 87 | 7363 | Mike Bull | 27 Jan 74  30 |
| 68.38 | James Drennen | 12 Jul 91 | 7363 h | Nick Phipps | 27 Jun 76 |
| 68.30 | Mark Lawrence | 31 Jul 88 | 7335 | Stewart McCallum | 19 Aug 73 |
| 68.10 | Paul Edgington | 12 Oct 86 | 7308 h | Clive Longe | 29 Jun 69 |
| 67.62 | Allan Holloway | 25 Jun 89 | 7295 | Stephen Rogers | 4 Jun 95 |
| 67.60 | Dean Smahon | 9 Jul 94 | 7275 | Buster Watson | 18 Jun 78 |
| 40 67.48 | Rob Laing | 31 May 87 | 7268 | Paul Edwards ¶ | 14 Aug 83 |
| 67.44 | John Guthrie | 17 May 89 | 7240 | Paul Allan | 25 Aug 91 |
| 67.22 | Richard Atkinson | 14 Aug 93 | 7221 | Andy Lewis | 19 Jun 94 |
| 67.16 | Damien Crawford | 12 Jul 92 | 7198 | Robert Betts | 7 Aug 83 |
| 66.92 | Demetrio Barros | 7 Aug 93 | 7172 h | Dave Kidner | 20 Aug 72  40 |
| 66.60 | Kevin Hill | 23 Aug 94 | 7147 h | Justin Whitfield | 12 May 85 |
| 65.96 | Duncan MacDonald | 15 Jul 95 | 7136 | Billy Jewers | 3 Sep 89 |
| 65.80 | David Bigham | 4 Jun 94 | 7112 | Gavin Sunshine | 30 Jul 93 |
| 65.74 | Mark Pinner | 19 May 93 | 7094 | Paul Howard | 31 May 92 |
| 65.68 | Scott MacHardie | 7 Jun 92 | 7089 w | John Howell | 18 Jun 78 |
| 50 65.42 | Jeremy Adadom | 15 Mar 92 | 7062 h | | 2 Jul 78 |
| | | | 7078 | Steve Leader | 19 Jun 94 |
| **rough tailed model** | | | 7076 | Rob Laing | 30 Jul 89 |
| 82.60 | Colin Mackenzie | 1 Jun 91 | 7076 w | Trevor Sloman | 22 Aug 93 |
| 79.54 | Gary Jenson | 19 Jun 91 | 6905 | | 2 Jun 91 |
| 76.10 | Keith Beard | 18 May 91 | 7075 h | Tony Southward | 27 Aug 95 |
| 70.34 | Damien Crawford | 20 Jul 91 | 7061 | Graham Flood | 12 Jun 83  50 |
| 70.16 | James Hurrion | 19 Jul 91 | 7061 | Gary James | 20 Aug 89 |
| 69.94 | Tony Smith | 22 Jun 91 | 7053 | George Robertson | 18 May 86 |
| 67.92 | Bruce Craven | 7 Sep 91 | 7047 | Steve Gutteridge | 14 Apr 94 |

## 3000 METRES TRACK WALK

| | | | |
|---|---|---|---|
| | 11:24.4 | Mark Easton | 10 May 89 |
| | 11:28.4 | Phil Vesty | 9 May 84 |
| | 11:29.6 i | Tim Berrett | 21 Jan 90 |
| | 11:54.23 | | 23 Jun 84 |
| | 11:31.0 | Andi Drake | 22 Jul 90 |
| | 11:32.2 | Ian McCombie | 20 Jul 88 |
| | 11:33.4 | Steve Partington | 12 Jul 95 |
| | 11:39.0 i+ | Martin Rush | 8 Feb 92 |
| | 11:49.48 | | 1 Jul 84 |
| | 11:39.54 | Andy Penn | 22 May 91 |
| | 11:44.68 | Roger Mills | 7 Aug 81 |
| 10 | 11:45.1 | Chris Maddocks | 9 Aug 87 |
| | 11:45.77 | Steve Johnston | 20 Jun 87 |
| | 11:47.12 i | Philip King | 26 Feb 95 |
| | 11:49.64 | | 29 May 95 |
| | 11:49.0 | Darrell Stone | 10 Jul 90 |
| | 11:51.1 | Paul Nihill | 5 Jun 71 |
| | 11:52.51 | Sean Martindale | 28 Jul 90 |
| | 11:53.3 | Martin Bell | 9 Aus 95 |
| | 11:53.46 | Steve Barry | 21 Aug 82 |
| | 11:54.7 | Mike Parker | 20 Apr 82 |
| | 11:55.0 | Phil Embleton | 24 May 71 |

## 10000 METRES TRACK WALK

| | | | |
|---|---|---|---|
| | 40:06.65 | Ian McCombie | 4 Jun 89 |
| | 40:53.60 | Phil Vesty | 28 May 84 |
| | 40:55.6 | Martin Rush | 14 Sep 91 |
| | 41:06.57 | Chris Maddocks | 20 Jun 87 |
| | 41:10.11 | Darrell Stone | 16 Jul 95 |
| | 41:13.62 | Steve Barry | 19 Jun 82 |
| | 41:13.65 | Martin Bell | 22 Jul 95 |
| | 41:14.3 | Mark Easton | 5 Feb 89 |
| | 41:14.61 | Steve Partington | 16 Jul 95 |
| 10 | 41:18.64 | Andi Drake | 5 Jun 88 |
| | 41:49.06 | Sean Martindale | 26 Jun 90 |
| | 41:55.5 | Phil Embleton | 14 Apr 71 |
| | 41:59.10 | Andy Penn | 27 Jul 91 |
| | 42:06.35 | Gordon Vale | 2 Aug 81 |
| | 42:08.57 | Paul Blagg | 28 Aug 89 |
| | 42:23.0 | Mike Parker | 2 Feb 86 |
| | 42:28.0 | Kieron Butler | 22 Jun 93 |
| | 42:28.0 | Philip King | 17 May 95 |
| | 42:34.6 | Paul Nihill | 28 May 72 |
| 20 | 42:35.6 | Ken Matthews | 1 Aug 60 |

**track short**

| 40:54.7 | Steve Barry | 19 Mar 83 |
|---|---|---|

## 20 KILOMETRES ROAD WALK

| | | | |
|---|---|---|---|
| | 1:22:03 | Ian McCombie | 23 Sep 88 |
| | 1:22:12 | Chris Maddocks | 3 May 92 |
| | 1:22:51 | Steve Barry | 26 Feb 83 |
| | 1:23:34 | Andy Penn | 29 Feb 92 |
| | 1:23:34 | Martin Rush | 29 Feb 92 |
| | 1:24:04 | Mark Easton | 25 Feb 89 |
| | 1:24:04.0t | Andi Drake | 26 May 90 |
| | 1:24:07.6t | Phil Vesty | 1 Dec 84 |
| | 1:24:18 | Steve Partington | 12 Dec 90 |
| 10 | 1:24:25 | Tim Berrett | 21 Apr 90 |
| | 1:24:49 | Darrell Stone | 29 Apr 95 |
| | 1:24:50 | Paul Nihill | 30 Jul 72 |
| | 1:25:42 | Martin Bell | 9 May 92 |
| | 1:25:53.6t | Sean Martindale | 28 Apr 89 |
| | 1:27:00 | Roger Mills | 30 Jun 80 |
| | 1:27:16 | Les Morton | 25 Feb 89 |
| | 1:27:35 | Olly Flynn | 3 Oct 76 |
| | 1:27:46 | Brian Adams | 11 Oct 75 |
| | 1:27:59 | Phil Embleton | 3 Apr 71 |
| 20 | 1:28:02 | Paul Blagg | 27 Feb 82 |
| | 1:28:15 | Ken Matthews | 23 Jul 60 |
| | 1:28:26 | Chris Harvey | 29 Sep 79 |
| | 1:28:30 | Allan King | 11 May 85 |
| | 1:28:34 | Chris Smith | 11 May 85 |
| | 1:28:37 | Dave Jarman | 30 Jun 80 |
| | 1:28:46 | Jimmy Ball | 4 Apr 87 |
| | 1:28:46 | Steve Taylor | 20 Dec 92 |
| | 1:28:50 | Amos Seddon | 3 Aug 74 |
| | 1:29:07 | Philip King | 20 Aug 95 |
| 30 | 1:29:11 | Chris Cheeseman | 21 May 94 |
| | 1:29:19 | Stuart Phillips | 31 May 92 |
| | 1:29:24 | George Nibre | 6 Apr 80 |
| | 1:29:29 + | Steve Johnson | 16 Apr 89 |
| | 1:29:37 | John Warhurst | 28 Jul 73 |
| | 1:29:42 | Dennis Jackson | 10 May 86 |
| | 1:29:48 | Mike Parker | 8 May 82 |
| | 1:29:49 | Peter Marlow | 3 Aug 74 |
| | 1:30:00 | John Webb | 18 May 68 |

## 50 KILOMETRES ROAD WALK

| | | | |
|---|---|---|---|
| | 3:51:37 | Chris Maddocks | 28 Oct 90 |
| | 3:57:48 | Les Morton | 30 Apr 89 |
| | 3:59:55 | Paul Blagg | 5 Sep 87 |
| | 4:03:08 | Dennis Jackson | 16 Mar 86 |
| | 4:06:01 | Mark Easton | 30 Apr 95 |
| | 4:06:14 | Barry Graham | 20 Apr 85 |
| | 4:07:23 | Bob Dobson | 21 Oct 79 |
| | 4:07:57 | Ian Richards | 20 Apr 80 |
| | 4:08:41 | Adrian James | 12 Apr 80 |
| 10 | 4:09:15 | Don Thompson | 10 Oct 65 |
| | 4:09:22 | Mike Smith | 27 Mar 89 |
| | 4:10:23 | Darrell Stone | 6 May 90 |
| | 4:10:42 | Amos Seddon | 9 Mar 80 |
| | 4:11:31 | Paul Nihill | 18 Oct 64 |
| | 4:12:00 | Sean Martindale | 16 Oct 93 |
| | 4:12:02 | Martin Rush | 28 Jul 91 |
| | 4:12:37 | John Warhurst | 27 May 72 |
| | 4:12:50 | Darren Thorn | 6 May 90 |
| | 4:13:25 | Allan King | 16 Apr 83 |
| 20 | 4:14:03 | Tom Misson | 20 Jun 59 |
| | 4:14:25 | Dave Cotton | 15 Jul 78 |
| | 4:14:59 | Graham White | 5 Mar 95 |
| | 4:15:14 | Shaun Lightman | 13 Oct 73 |
| | 4:15:22 | Brian Adams | 17 Sep 78 |
| | 4:15:52 | Ray Middleton | 27 May 72 |
| | 4:16:47 | George Nibre | 9 Mar 80 |
| | 4:17:24 | Andi Drake | 18 Oct 87 |
| | 4:17:34 | Gordon Vale | 9 Oct 83 |
| | 4:17:52 | Stuart Elms | 17 Apr 76 |
| | 4:18:30 | Peter Ryan | 10 Apr 82 |

## 4 x 100 METRES RELAY

37.77 UK 22 Aug 93
Jackson, Jarrett, Regis, Christie
37.98 UK 1 Sep 90
Braithwaite, Regis, Adam, Christie
38.05 UK 21 Aug 93
John, Jarrett, Braithwaite, Christie
38.08 UK 8 Aug 92
Adam, Jarrett, Regis, Christie
38.09 UK 1 Sep 91
Jarrett, Regis, Braithwaite, Christie
38.28 UK 1 Oct 88
Bunney, Regis, McFarlane, Christie
38.34 UK 9 Sep 89
Callender, Regis, Adam, Christie
38.36 UK 31 Aug 91
Jarrett, Regis, Braithwaite, Christie
38.39 UK 5 Aug 89
Jarrett, Regis, Adam, Christie
10 38.46 UK 10 Sep 94
Braithwaite, Jarrett, Regis, Christie
38.52 UK 1 Oct 88
Bunney, Regis, McFarlane, Christie
38.53 UK 26 Jun 93
John, Jarrett, Regis, Christie
38.62 UK 1 Aug 80
McFarlane, Wells, Sharp, McMaster
38.64 UK 7 Aug 91
Livingston ¶, Regis, Callender, Rosswess
38.64 UK 7 Aug 92
Jarrett, Regis, Adam, Christie
38.64 UK 15 Jul 94
John, Braithwaite, Regis, Christie
38.67 England 3 Feb 90
Callender, Regis, Adam, Christie
38.68 UK 11 Aug 84
Thompson, Reid, McFarlane, Wells
38.71 UK 31 Aug 86
Bunney, Thompson, McFarlane, Christie
20 38.72 UK 25 Jun 94
John, Wariso, Regis, Christie
38.73 UK 24 Jun 95
Gardener, Jarrett, Braithwaite, Christie
38.75 UK 12 Aug 95
Gardener, Braithwaite, Regis, Wariso
38.80 UK 21 Aug 93
John, Jarrett, Braithwaite, Christie
38.84 G. B. All Stars 17 Jul 92
Livingston ¶, John, Adam, Christie
38.86 UK 19 Jun 88
Jackson, Christie, Regis, Obeng
38.86 UK 16 Jul 88
McFarlane, Christie, Regis, Callender
38.86 UK 5 Jun 93
Adam, Jarrett, Regis, John
38.88 UK 20 Aug 83
Asquith, Reid, McFarlane, Sharp
38.90 UK 31 Aug 90
Braithwaite, Regis, Adam, Christie

## 4 x 400 METRES RELAY

2:57.53 UK 1 Sep 91
Black, Redmond, Regis, Akabusi
2:58.22 UK 1 Sep 90
Sanders, Akabusi, Regis, Black
2:58.86 UK 6 Sep 87
Redmond, Akabusi, Black, Brown
2:59.13 UK 11 Aug 84
Akabusi, Cook, Bennett, Brown
2:59.13 UK 14 Aug 94
McKenzie, Whittle, Black, Ladejo
2:59.49 UK 31 Aug 91
Mafe, Redmond, Richardson, Akabusi
2:59.73 UK 8 Aug 92
Black, Grindley, Akabusi, Regis
2:59.84 UK 31 Aug 86
Redmond, Akabusi, Whittle, Black
3:00.25 UK 27 Jun 93
Ladejo, Akabusi, Regis, Grindley
3:00.34 UK 25 Jun 95 10
Thomas, Patrick, Richardson, Black
3:00.46 UK 10 Sep 72
Reynolds, Pascoe, Hemery, Jenkins
3:00.58 UK 30 Jun 91
Sanders, Akabusi, Whittle, Black
3:00.68 UK 11 Sep 82
Jenkins, Cook, Bennett, Brown
3:00.93 UK 19 Jun 92
Redmond, Akabusi, Ladejo, Black
3:01.03 UK - Under 23 19 Jul 92
McKenzie, Grindley, Richardson, Ladejo
3:01.12 UK 28 Jun 87
Harmsworth, Whittle, Bennett, Black
3:01.20 UK 7 Aug 92
Richardson, Akabusi, Black, Ladejo
3:01.21 A UK 20 Oct 68
Winbolt-Lewis, Campbell, Hemery,Sherwood
3:01.22 UK 12 Aug 95
McKenzie, Patrick, Hylton, Richardson
3:01.26 UK 9 Sep 72 20
Reynolds, Pascoe, Hemery, Jenkins
3:01.26 UK 5 Aug 86
Akabusi, Black, Bennett, Brown
3:01.34 UK 11 Sep 94
McKenzie, Ladejo, Baulch, Black
3:01.47 UK 5 Sep 87
Thomas, Akabusi, Bennett, Brown
3:01.6 a UK 21 Oct 64
Graham, Metcalfe, Cooper, Brightwell
3:01.65 UK 7 Jul 85
Redmond, Akabusi, Slack, Bennett
3:02.00 UK 1 Oct 88
Whittle, Akabusi, Bennett, Brown
3:02.14 England 28 Aug 94
McKenzie, Crampton, Patrick, Ladejo
3:02.15 UK 21 Aug 93
Ladejo, Bullock, McDonald, Mafe
3:02.20 UK 14 Sep 84
Dickens, Akabusi, Bennett, Brown

# UNDER 20

## 100 METRES

| | | | |
|---|---|---|---|
| 10.21 | Jamie Henderson | 6 Aug 87 | |
| 10.25 | Jason Livingston ¶ | 9 Aug 90 | |
| 10.25 | Jason Gardener | 21 Jul 94 | |
| 10.29 | Peter Radford (10.31?) | 13 Sep 58 | |
| 10.32 | Mike McFarlane | 6 Aug 78 | |
| 10.34 | Lincoln Asquith | 25 Aug 83 | |
| 10.37 | Darren Campbell | 26 Jul 91 | |
| 10.38 | Elliot Bunney | 22 Aug 85 | |
| 10.39 | Jason John | 28 Jul 90 | |
| 10.41 | Dwain Chambers | 28 Jul 95 | |
| 10.41 | Jamie Henthorn | 28 Jul 95 | |

**wind assisted**

| | | |
|---|---|---|
| 10.22 | Lincoln Asquith | 26 Jun 83 |
| 10.28 | Darren Campbell | 26 Jul 91 |
| 10.29 | Mike McFarlane | 7 Aug 78 |
| 10.29 | Elliot Bunney | 27 May 84 |
| 10.29 | Trevor Cameron | 11 Jun 94 |
| 10.34 | Darren Braithwaite | 25 Jun 88 |
| 10.34 | Julian Golding | 17 Sep 94 |
| 10.37 | Courtney Rumbolt | 25 Jun 88 |
| 10.37 | Allyn Condon | 3 Jul 93 |

**hand timing**

| | | |
|---|---|---|
| 10.3 | Martin Reynolds | 29 Jun 68 |

## 200 METRES

| | | |
|---|---|---|
| 20.54 | Ade Mafe | 25 Aug 85 |
| 20.67 | David Jenkins | 4 Sep 71 |
| 20.73 A | Ralph Banthorpe | 15 Oct 68 |
| 20.78 | John Regis | 29 Sep 85 |
| 20.80 | Mike McFarlane | 1 Jul 79 |
| 20.85 | Richard Ashby | 25 Aug 85 |
| 20.86 | Lincoln Asquith | 28 Aug 83 |
| 20.86 | Roger Hunter | 5 May 84 |
| 20.87 | Donovan Reid | 7 Oct 82 |
| 20.87 | Mark Smith | 28 Jul 90 |
| 20.87 | Darren Campbell | 19 Sep 92 |

**wind assisted**

| | | |
|---|---|---|
| 20.61 | Darren Campbell | 11 Aug 91 |
| 20.73 | Julian Golding | 17 Sep 94 |
| 20.85 | Mark Smith | 1 Jul 90 |

**hand timing**

| | | |
|---|---|---|
| 20.6 | David Jenkins | 19 Sep 71 |

**wind assisted**

| | | |
|---|---|---|
| 20.7 | Lincoln Asquith | 2 Jul 83 |

## 400 METRES

| | | |
|---|---|---|
| 45.36 | Roger Black | 24 Aug 85 |
| 45.41 | David Grindley | 10 Aug 91 |
| 45.45 | David Jenkins | 13 Aug 71 |
| 45.53 | Mark Richardson | 10 Aug 91 |
| 45.83 | Mark Hylton | 16 Jul 95 |
| 46.03 | Peter Crampton | 8 Aug 87 |
| 46.13 | Guy Bullock | 31 Jul 93 |
| 46.22 | Wayne McDonald | 17 Jun 89 |
| 46.32 | Derek Redmond | 9 Sep 84 |
| 46.48 | Roger Hunter | 20 May 84 |

**hand timing**

| | | |
|---|---|---|
| 45.7 | Adrian Metcalfe | 2 Sep 61 |

## 800 METRES (* 880 yards time less 0.70)

| | | |
|---|---|---|
| 1:45.64 | David Sharpe | 5 Sep 86 |
| 1:45.77 | Steve Ovett | 4 Sep 74 |
| 1:46.46 | John Gladwin | 7 Jul 82 |
| 1:46.63 | Curtis Robb | 6 Jul 91 |
| 1:46.70* | John Davies I | 3 Jun 68 |
| 1:47.0 | Ikem Billy | 12 Jun 83 |
| 1:47.02 | Chris McGeorge | 8 Aug 81 |
| 1:47.08 | Atle Douglas | 22 Aug 87 |
| 1:47.22 | Kevin McKay | 5 Jun 88 |
| 1:47.35 | Peter Elliott | 23 Aug 81 |

## 1000 METRES

| | | |
|---|---|---|
| 2:18.98 | David Sharpe | 19 Aug 86 |
| 2:19.92 | Graham Williamson | 8 Jul 79 |
| 2:20.0 | Steve Ovett | 17 Aug 73 |
| 2:20.02 | Darryl Taylor | 18 Aug 84 |
| 2:20.37 | Johan Boakes | 17 Jun 84 |
| 2:21.17 | Curtis Robb | 16 Sep 90 |
| 2:21.41 | Stuart Paton | 17 Sep 82 |
| 2:21.7 A | David Strang | 26 Jan 87 |
| 2:21.71 | Kevin Glastonbury | 18 Jun 77 |
| 2:22.3 | Chris McGeorge | 19 Jul 81 |

## 1500 METRES

| | | |
|---|---|---|
| 3:36.6 + | Graham Williamson | 17 Jul 79 |
| 3:40.09 | Steve Cram | 27 Aug 78 |
| 3:40.68 | Brian Treacy | 24 Jul 90 |
| 3:40.72 | Gary Taylor | 8 Jul 81 |
| 3:40.90 | David Robertson | 28 Jul 92 |
| 3:41.59 | Chris Sly | 22 Jul 77 |
| 3:42.2 | Paul Wynn | 9 Aug 83 |
| 3:42.5 | Colin Reitz | 8 Aug 79 |
| 3:42.67 | Matthew Hibberd | 28 Jul 92 |
| 3:42.7 | David Sharpe | 17 Oct 85 |

## ONE MILE

| | | |
|---|---|---|
| 3:53.15 | Graham Williamson | 17 Jul 79 |
| 3:57.03 | Steve Cram | 14 Sep 79 |
| 3:58.68 | Steve Flint | 26 May 80 |
| 3:59.4 | Steve Ovett | 17 Jul 74 |
| 4:00.31 | Johan Boakes | 5 Aug 86 |
| 4:00.6 | Simon Mugglestone | 16 Sep 87 |
| 4:00.67 | Brian Treacy | 22 Aug 90 |
| 4:01.0 | David Sharpe | 3 May 86 |
| 4:01.5 | Tony Leonard | 12 Sep 77 |
| 4:01.5 | Gary Staines | 19 Sep 82 |

## 3000 METRES

| | | |
|---|---|---|
| 7:48.28 | Jon Richards | 9 Jul 83 |
| 7:51.84 | Steve Binns | 8 Sep 79 |
| 7:56.28 | John Doherty | 13 Jul 80 |
| 7:59.55 | Paul Davies-Hale | 8 Aug 81 |
| 8:00.1 a | Micky Morton | 11 Jul 78 |
| 8:00.7 | Graham Williamson | 29 Jul 78 |
| 8:00.73 | David Black | 24 Jul 71 |
| 8:00.8 | Steve Anders | 1 Aug 78 |
| 8:00.88 | Paul Taylor | 12 Jun 85 |
| 8:01.2 | Ian Stewart I | 7 Sep 68 |

46

## 5000 METRES

| | | |
|---|---|---|
| 13:27.04 | Steve Binns | 14 Sep 79 |
| 13:35.95 | Paul Davies-Hale | 11 Sep 81 |
| 13:37.4 | David Black | 10 Sep 71 |
| 13:43.82 | Simon Mugglestone | 24 May 87 |
| 13:44.64 | Julian Goater | 14 Jul 72 |
| 13:48.74 | Jon Richards | 28 May 83 |
| 13:48.84 | John Doherty | 8 Aug 80 |
| 13:49.1 a | Nat Muir | 21 Aug 77 |
| 13:53.30 | Ian Stewart I | 3 Aug 68 |
| 13:53.3 a | Nick Lees | 21 Aug 77 |

## 2000 METRES STEEPLECHASE

| | | |
|---|---|---|
| 5:29.61 | Colin Reitz | 18 Aug 79 |
| 5:31.12 | Paul Davies-Hale | 22 Aug 81 |
| 5:32.84 | Tom Hanlon | 20 Jul 86 |
| 5:34.8 a | Micky Morris | 24 Aug 75 |
| 5:38.01 | Ken Baker | 1 Aug 82 |
| 5:38.2 | Spencer Duval | 8 Jul 89 |
| 5:39.3 a | Graeme Fell | 11 Jul 78 |
| 5:39.93 | Eddie Wedderburn | 9 Sep 79 |
| 5:40.2 | Paul Campbell | 31 Jul 77 |
| 5:40.2 | John Hartigan | 27 Jun 84 |

## 3000 METRES STEEPLECHASE

| | | |
|---|---|---|
| 8:29.85 | Paul Davies-Hale | 31 Aug 81 |
| 8:42.75 | Colin Reitz | 6 Jun 79 |
| 8:44.68 | Alastair O'Connor | 12 Aug 90 |
| 8:44.91 | Ken Baker | 30 May 82 |
| 8:45.65 | Spencer Duval | 17 Jun 89 |
| 8:47.1 | Tom Conlon | 6 Jul 80 |
| 8:47.49 | Tom Hanlon | 8 Jun 86 |
| 8:48.43 | Graeme Fell | 16 Jul 78 |
| 8:50.14 | Dave Long I | 13 Jul 73 |
| 8:51.02 | Tony Staynings | 14 Jul 72 |

## 110 METRES HURDLES (3'3")

| | | |
|---|---|---|
| 13.77 | Kevin Lumsdon | 8 Aug 92 |
| 13.8 | Jon Ridgeon | 13 Jul 84 |
| 13.8 | Paul Gray | 16 Jul 88 |
| 14.0 | Paul Brice | 25 Jun 83 |
| 14.0 | Colin Jackson | 27 Aug 84 |
| 14.0 | Neil Owen | 2 Aug 92 |
| | 14.06 | 4 Jul 92 |
| 14.0 | James Hughes | 11 May 93 |
| 14.0 | Damien Greaves | 8 Jul 95 |
| 14.01 | Jamie Quarry | 13 Jul 91 |
| 14.1 | Mark Holtom | 19 Jun 77 |
| 14.1 | Brett St Louis | 3 Aug 86 |

**wind assisted**

| | | |
|---|---|---|
| 13.6 | Mark Holtom | 9 Jul 77 |
| 13.8 | Paul Brice | 9 Jul 83 |
| 13.8 | Colin Jackson | 15 Jul 84 |
| 13.8 | Brett St Louis | 11 Jul 87 |

## 110 METRES HURDLES (3'6")

| | | |
|---|---|---|
| 13.44 | Colin Jackson | 19 Jul 86 |
| 13.46 | Jon Ridgeon | 23 Aug 85 |
| 13.72 | Tony Jarrett | 24 May 87 |
| 13.91 | David Nelson | 21 Jun 86 |
| 13.97 | Paul Gray | 30 Jul 88 |

| | | |
|---|---|---|
| 14.03 | Brett St Louis | 27 Jun 87 |
| 14.06 | Mark Holtom | 7 Aug 77 |
| 14.08 | Paul Brice | 26 Aug 83 |
| 14.14 | Neil Owen | 17 Sep 92 |
| 14.18 | James Archampong | 21 Jul 94 |

**wind assisted**

| | | |
|---|---|---|
| 13.42 | Colin Jackson | 27 Jul 86 |
| 13.82 | David Nelson | 5 Jul 86 |

## 400 METRES HURDLES

| | | |
|---|---|---|
| 50.22 | Martin Briggs | 28 Aug 83 |
| 50.70 | Noel Levy | 8 Jul 94 |
| 51.07 | Philip Beattie | 20 Aug 82 |
| 51.15 A | Andy Todd | 18 Oct 67 |
| 51.31 | Gary Oakes | 9 Sep 77 |
| 51.48 | Bob Brown | 19 Jun 88 |
| 51.51 | Max Robertson | 24 Jul 82 |
| 51.55 | Mark Whitby | 26 Aug 83 |
| 51.66 | Paul Goacher | 2 Aug 80 |
| 51.73 | Matt Douglas | 29 Jul 95 |

## HIGH JUMP

| | | |
|---|---|---|
| 2.37 | Steve Smith | 20 Sep 92 |
| 2.27 | Brendan Reilly | 27 May 90 |
| 2.25 | Geoff Parsons | 9 Jul 83 |
| 2.24 | John Hill | 23 Aug 85 |
| 2.23 | Mark Lakey | 29 Aug 82 |
| 2.22 | Dalton Grant | 3 Jul 85 |
| 2.20 | Byron Morrison | 14 Jul 84 |
| 2.18 | Ossie Cham | 14 Jun 80 |
| 2.18 | Alex Kruger | 26 Jun 82 |
| 2.18 | Steve Ritchie | 15 Jul 89 |
| 2.18 | Hopeton Lindo | 23 Jul 89 |
| 2.18 i | James Brierley | 5 Feb 95 |

## POLE VAULT

| | | |
|---|---|---|
| 5.50 | Neil Winter | 9 Aug 92 |
| 5.30 | Matthew Belsham | 15 Sep 90 |
| 5.21 | Andy Ashurst | 2 Sep 84 |
| 5.20 | Billy Davey | 5 Jun 83 |
| 5.20 | Warren Siley | 4 Aug 90 |
| 5.20 | Nick Buckfield | 31 May 92 |
| 5.10 | Brian Hooper | 1 Oct 72 |
| 5.10 | Michael Edwards | 20 Jun 87 |
| 5.05 | Ian Tullett | 22 Aug 87 |
| 5.05 | Dean Mellor | 7 Jul 90 |

## LONG JUMP

| | | |
|---|---|---|
| 7.98 | Stewart Faulkner | 6 Aug 88 |
| 7.91 | Steve Phillips | 10 Aug 91 |
| 7.84 | Wayne Griffith | 25 Aug 89 |
| 7.76 | Carl Howard | 31 Jul 93 |
| 7.73 | Jason Canning | 20 Apr 88 |
| 7.72 | Daley Thompson | 21 May 77 |
| 7.70 | Kevin Liddington | 27 Aug 88 |
| 7.66 | Barry Nevison | 7 Jul 85 |
| 7.62 | Colin Mitchell | 11 Jul 78 |
| 7.61 | Darren Gomersall | 19 Jul 87 |

**wind assisted**

| | | |
|---|---|---|
| 8.04 | Stewart Faulkner | 20 Aug 88 |
| 7.96 | Colin Jackson | 17 May 86 |
| 7.82 | Kevin Liddington | 25 Jun 89 |
| 7.72 | John Herbert | 15 Jun 80 |

## TRIPLE JUMP

| 16.58 | Tosi Fasinro | 15 Jun 91 |
|---|---|---|
| 16.53 | Larry Achike | 24 Jul 94 |
| 16.24 | Aston Moore | 11 Jun 75 |
| 16.22 | Mike Makin | 17 May 81 |
| 16.13 | Steven Anderson | 11 Jun 83 |
| 16.03 | John Herbert | 23 Jun 81 |
| 15.95 | Keith Connor | 30 Aug 76 |
| 15.94 | Vernon Samuels | 27 Jun 82 |
| 15.93 | Tayo Erogbogbo | 17 Sep 94 |
| 15.92 | Lawrence Lynch | 13 Jul 85 |

**wind assisted**

| 16.81 | Tosi Fasinro | 15 Jun 91 |
|---|---|---|
| 16.67 | Larry Achike | 24 Jul 94 |
| 16.43 | Mike Makin | 14 Jun 81 |
| 16.31 | Aston Moore | 9 Aug 75 |
| 16.07 | Vernon Samuels | 14 Aug 82 |
| 16.01 | Julian Golley | 22 Jul 90 |

## SHOT (7.26kg)

| 18.21 i | Matt Simson | 3 Feb 89 |
|---|---|---|
| 18.11 | | 27 Aug 89 |
| 17.78 i | Billy Cole | 10 Mar 84 |
| 17.72 | | 2 Jun 84 |
| 17.36 i | Chris Ellis | 8 Dec 84 |
| 17.10 | | 7 Jul 85 |
| 17.26 i | Geoff Capes | 16 Nov 68 |
| 16.80 | | 30 Jul 68 |
| 17.22 | Anthony Zaidman | 4 Jul 81 |
| 16.61 | Simon Williams | 10 Aug 86 |
| 16.60 | Alan Carter | 11 May 63 |
| 16.48 | Martyn Lucking | 24 Aug 57 |
| 16.47 | Paul Buxton | 25 May 75 |
| 16.21 | Mike Lindsay | 29 Jul 57 |

## SHOT (6.25kg)

| 19.47 | Matt Simson | 20 May 89 |
|---|---|---|
| 19.15 | Billy Cole | 19 May 84 |
| 18.66 i | Simon Williams | 15 Nov 86 |
| 18.52 | | 11 Jul 86 |
| 18.20 i | Chris Ellis | 16 Feb 85 |
| 18.13 | | 14 Jul 84 |
| 17.81 | Anthony Zaidman | 16 May 81 |
| 17.58 | Nigel Spratley | 28 May 89 |
| 17.32 | Andy Vince | 15 May 77 |
| 17.31 | Mitchell Smith | 11 Jun 85 |
| 17.30 | Jamie Cockburn | 20 Sep 92 |
| 17.26 | Neil Gray | 19 May 84 |
| 17.26 i | Neal Brunning ¶ | 9 Dec 89 |

## DISCUS (2kg)

| 55.10 | Glen Smith | 31 Aug 91 |
|---|---|---|
| 53.42 | Paul Mardle | 25 Jul 81 |
| 53.40 | Bob Weir | 10 Aug 80 |
| 53.32 | Paul Buxton | 9 Aug 75 |
| 53.02 | Simon Williams | 16 Aug 86 |
| 52.94 | Lee Newman | 29 Aug 92 |
| 52.84 | Jamie Murphy | 14 Jun 92 |
| 52.14 | Robert Russell | 4 Jul 93 |
| 51.70 | Richard Slaney | 27 Jul 75 |
| 51.66 | Neal Brunning ¶ | 30 Jul 89 |

## DISCUS (1.75kg)

| 60.76 | Glen Smith | 26 May 91 |
|---|---|---|
| 56.64 | Jamie Murphy | 19 May 90 |
| 56.10 | Lee Newman | 4 Jul 92 |
| 56.00 | Simon Williams | 17 May 86 |
| 55.94 | Mark Davies | 19 Aug 90 |
| 55.44 | Neal Brunning ¶ | 8 Jul 89 |
| 55.00 | Robert Russell | 16 May 93 |
| 54.70 | Emeka Udechuku | 18 Jun 95 |
| 54.50 | Paul Mardle | 27 Jun 81 |
| 53.84 | Bob Weir | 14 Sep 80 |

## HAMMER (7.26kg)

| 67.48 | Paul Head | 16 Sep 84 |
|---|---|---|
| 67.10 | Jason Byrne | 6 Aug 89 |
| 66.14 | Martin Girvan | 21 Jul 79 |
| 65.86 | Bob Weir | 6 Sep 80 |
| 65.30 | Karl Andrews | 2 Jul 94 |
| 64.14 | Ian Chipchase | 25 Sep 71 |
| 63.84 | Andrew Tolputt | 7 Sep 86 |
| 63.72 | Gareth Cook | 10 Jul 88 |
| 62.82 | Mike Jones | 29 Aug 82 |
| 62.02 | Peter Vivian | 1 Jul 89 |

## HAMMER (6.25kg)

| 74.92 | Jason Byrne | 17 Dec 89 |
|---|---|---|
| 73.28 | Bob Weir | 14 Sep 80 |
| 72.66 | Paul Head | 2 Sep 84 |
| 71.84 | Gareth Cook | 28 May 88 |
| 70.36 | Andrew Tolputt | 21 Sep 86 |
| 69.10 | Karl Andrews | 1 Aug 94 |
| 68.84 | Eric Berry | Jul 73 |
| 67.80 | Martin Girvan | 7 Jul 79 |
| 67.52 | Vaughan Cooper | 19 May 84 |
| 67.48 | Mike Jones | 2 Jun 82 |

## JAVELIN

| 79.50 | Steve Backley | 5 Jun 88 |
|---|---|---|
| 74.54 | Gary Jenson | 19 Sep 86 |
| 74.24 | Mark Roberson | 18 Jul 86 |
| 73.76 | Nigel Bevan | 29 Aug 87 |
| 71.74 | Myles Cottrell | 29 Jul 89 |
| 70.16 r | James Hurrion | 19 Jul 91 |
| 69.62 | Stefan Baldwin | 8 Jul 89 |
| 68.74 | Jon Clarke | 14 Jun 86 |
| 68.38 | James Drennen | 12 Jul 91 |
| 68.30 | Mark Lawrence | 31 Jul 88 |

## DECATHLON (1985 Tables)

| 8082 | Daley Thompson | 31 Jul 77 |
|---|---|---|
| 7488 | David Bigham | 9 Aug 90 |
| 7299 | Eugene Gilkes | 24 May 81 |
| 7274 | James Stevenson | 24 Jun 90 |
| 7247 h | Brian Taylor | 7 May 89 |
| 7169 | Barry Thomas | 5 Aug 90 |
| 7126 | Fidelis Obikwu | 16 Sep 79 |
| 7112 | Gavin Sunshine | 30 Jul 93 |
| 7018 | Jamie Quarry | 30 Jun 91 |
| 6958 h | Roy Mitchell | 29 Sep 74 |

**Junior implements**

| 7134 | Dean Macey | 17 Sep 95 |
|---|---|---|

## 3000 METRES TRACK WALK

| | | |
|---|---|---|
| 11:54.23 | Tim Berrett | 23 Jun 84 |
| 12:01.89 i | Philip King | 21 Feb 93 |
| 12:02.0 | | 12 May 92 |
| 12:02.04 | Phil Vesty | 24 Jul 82 |
| 12:16.5 | David Hucks | 5 Aug 84 |
| 12:19.8 | Gordon Vale | 11 Mar 81 |
| 12:23.2 | Martin Rush | 18 Sep 83 |
| 12:23.53 | Darrell Stone | 19 Sep 87 |
| 12:24.45 | Richard Dorman | 5 Sep 80 |
| 12:25.8 | Gareth Holloway | 17 Jun 89 |
| 12:29.3 | Ian Ashforth | 19 May 85 |

## 10000 METRES TRACK WALK

| | | |
|---|---|---|
| 41:52.13 | Darrell Stone | 7 Aug 87 |
| 42:06.35 | Gordon Vale | 2 Aug 81 |
| 42:46.3 | Phil Vesty | 20 Mar 82 |
| 42:47.7 | Philip King | 2 May 92 |
| 43:04.09 | Tim Berrett | 25 Aug 83 |
| 43:42.75 | Martin Rush | 29 May 83 |
| 43:54.25 | Gareth Brown | 7 Aug 87 |
| 44:22.12 | Gareth Holloway | 5 Jun 88 |
| 44:22.38 | Jon Vincent | 1 Apr 89 |
| 44:30.0 | Andy Penn | 15 Mar 86 |

## UNDER 17

### 100 METRES

| | | |
|---|---|---|
| 10.51 o | Lincoln Asquith | 4 Oct 80 |
| 10.67 | Michael Nartey | 28 Sep 91 |
| 10.69 | Mike McFarlane | 13 Aug 76 |
| 10.70 | Steve Green | 15 Jul 72 |
| 10.72 | Peter Little | 6 Aug 77 |
| 10.72 | Trevor Cameron | 7 Aug 93 |
| 10.73 | Danny Joyce | 17 Aug 91 |
| 10.75 | Elliot Bunney | 28 May 83 |
| 10.75 | Dwain Chambers | 28 May 94 |
| 10.76 | Paul Ashen | 1 Aug 81 |
| 10.76 | Kevin Mark | 15 Aug 92 |

**wind assisted**

| | | |
|---|---|---|
| 10.38 | Kevin Mark | 3 Jul 93 |
| 10.56 | Dwain Chambers | 9 Jul 94 |
| 10.57 | Trevor Cameron | 3 Jul 93 |
| 10.62 | Elliot Bunney | 25 Jun 83 |
| 10.62 | Jamie Nixon | 7 Jul 85 |
| 10.65 | Michael Williams | 20 Jun 87 |
| 10.66 | David Jackson | 1 Jul 89 |

**hand timing**

| | | |
|---|---|---|
| 10.5 | Mike Powell | 17 Sep 78 |

### 200 METRES

| | | |
|---|---|---|
| 20.92 | Ade Mafe | 27 Aug 83 |
| 21.24 | Peter Little | 21 Aug 77 |
| 21.25 | Mark Richardson | 24 Jul 88 |
| 21.44 | Roger Hunter | 2 Aug 81 |
| 21.51 | Darren Campbell | 15 Sep 90 |
| 21.53 | Steven Eden | 2 Aug 81 |
| 21.56 | Trevor Cameron | 8 Aug 93 |
| 21.58 | Christian Malcolm | 9 Jul 95 |
| 21.63 | Richard Ashby | 7 Aug 83 |
| 21.64 | Elliot Bunney | 7 Aug 83 |

**wind assisted**

| | | |
|---|---|---|
| 21.17 | Mark Richardson | 20 Aug 88 |
| 21.25 | Trevor Cameron | 25 Sep 93 |
| 21.32 | Graham Beasley | 9 Jul 94 |
| 21.38 | Elliot Bunney | 13 Aug 83 |

**hand timing**

| | | |
|---|---|---|
| 21.5 | Steve Green | 6 Aug 72 |
| 21.5 | Phil Brown | 20 May 78 |
| 21.5 | Lincoln Asquith | 23 Aug 80 |
| 21.5 | Jamie Nixon | 12 May 85 |
| 21.5 | Philip Perigo | 12 Aug 95 |

**wind assisted**

| | | |
|---|---|---|
| 21.0 | Peter Little | 30 Jul 77 |

### 400 METRES

| | | |
|---|---|---|
| 46.43 | Mark Richardson | 28 Jul 88 |
| 46.74 | Guy Bullock | 17 Sep 92 |
| 47.81 | Mark Hylton | 17 Jul 93 |
| 48.11 | Gary Thomas | 18 Sep 82 |
| 48.25 | Adrian Patrick | 2 Sep 89 |
| 48.34 | Richard McNabb | 27 Aug 95 |
| 48.35 | James Hilston | 6 Aug 95 |
| 48.36 | David Simpson | 29 May 89 |
| 48.41 | Mark Tyler | 11 Aug 84 |
| 48.46 | Philip Harvey | 24 Jun 79 |

**hand timing**

| | | |
|---|---|---|
| 48.2 | David Simpson | 8 Jul 89 |
| 48.3 | David McKenzie | 21 Sep 86 |
| 48.4 | Steve Ovett | 20 Aug 72 |
| 48.4 | Chris Thompson | 1 Aug 81 |

### 800 METRES

| | | |
|---|---|---|
| 1:49.9 | Mark Sesay | 18 Jul 89 |
| 1:50.7 | Peter Elliott | 16 Sep 79 |
| 1:50.90 | Craig Winrow | 21 Aug 88 |
| 1:51.0 | Chris McGeorge | 1 Jul 78 |
| 1:51.05 | Malcolm Edwards | 20 Sep 74 |
| 1:51.3 | Julian Spooner | 3 Aug 77 |
| 1:51.4 | Kevin McKay | 19 Aug 85 |
| 1:51.6 | Neil Horsfield | 31 Aug 83 |
| 1:51.6 | David Gerard | 21 Jul 84 |
| 1:51.8 | Paul Burgess | 14 Jul 87 |

### 1500 METRES

| | | |
|---|---|---|
| 3:47.7 | Steve Cram | 14 May 77 |
| 3:48.49 | Johan Boakes | 28 Jun 84 |
| 3:49.9 | Kelvin Newton | 20 Jun 79 |
| 3:51.1 | Jason Lobo | 30 Aug 86 |
| 3:51.4 | Darren Mead | 26 Jul 85 |
| 3:51.7 | Martin Forder | 19 Sep 86 |
| 3:51.8 | Mark Sesay | 22 Aug 89 |
| 3:52.0 | Stuart Poore | 6 Sep 89 |
| 3:52.47 | Simon Young | 4 Aug 90 |
| 3:52.6 | Glen Stewart | 19 Sep 87 |

### ONE MILE

| | | |
|---|---|---|
| 4:06.7 | Barrie Williams | 22 Apr 72 |
| 4:09.5 | Colin Clarkson | 29 Aug 77 |
| 4:09.6 | Alistair Currie | 9 Jun 81 |

## 3000 METRES

| | | |
|---|---|---|
| 8:13.42 | Barrie Moss | 15 Jul 72 |
| 8:15.34 | Kevin Steere | 30 Aug 71 |
| 8:19.08 | Darren Mead | 26 Aug 85 |
| 8:19.38 | Johan Boakes | 24 Jun 84 |
| 8:23.6 o | Ian Stewart II | 14 Dec 77 |
| 8:24.2 | Simon Goodwin | 16 Jul 80 |
| 8:24.2 | Jason Lobo | 13 Aug 86 |
| 8:25.2 | Colin Clarkson | 3 Aug 77 |
| 8:26.3 | Paul Williams | 10 Aug 83 |
| 8:26.6 | Jon Dennis | 23 Apr 86 |

## 1500 METRES STEEPLECHASE

| | | |
|---|---|---|
| 4:11.2 | Steve Evans | 15 Jul 74 |
| 4:12.3 | Chris Sly | 15 Jul 74 |
| 4:13.1 | John Crowley | 15 Jul 74 |
| 4:13.2 | David Lewis | 1 Jul 78 |
| 4:13.2 o | Darren Mead | 16 Oct 85 |
| 4:13.7 | Danny Fleming | 31 Jul 77 |
| 4:13.9 | Eddie Wedderburn | 31 Jul 77 |
| 4:14.0 | David Robertson | 8 Jul 89 |
| 4:14.4 | Steven Arnold | 7 Sep 85 |
| 4:15.0 | David Caton | 9 Jun 84 |
| 4:15.0 | Spencer Duval | 12 Jul 86 |

## 100 METRES HURDLES

| | | |
|---|---|---|
| 12.68 | Matthew Clements | 8 Aug 93 |
| 12.90 | Stephen Markham | 17 Aug 91 |
| 12.97 | Jon Snade | 8 Aug 93 |
| 13.01 | Hugh Teape | 3 Aug 80 |
| 13.05 | Brett St Louis | 4 Aug 85 |
| 13.07 | Jon Ridgeon | 7 Aug 83 |
| 13.09 | Damien Greaves | 8 Jul 94 |
| 13.10 | Ricky Glover | 17 Aug 91 |
| 13.12 | Ross Baillie | 13 Aug 94 |
| 13.15 | Perry Batchelor | 4 Jul 92 |
| **wind assisted** | | |
| 12.47 | Matthew Clements | 9 Jul 94 |
| 12.70 | Damien Greaves | 9 Jul 94 |
| 12.88 | Nick Csemiczky | 13 Jul 91 |
| 12.90 | Ricky Glover | 13 Jul 91 |
| 12.90 | Ben Warmington | 8 Jul 95 |
| 12.99 | Neil Owen | 1 Jul 90 |
| 13.01 | Berian Davies | 30 Jul 89 |
| **hand timing** | | |
| 12.8 | Brett St Louis | 28 Jul 85 |
| 12.8 | Richard Dunn | 29 Jun 91 |
| 12.9 | Hugh Teape | 31 Aug 80 |
| **wind assisted** | | |
| 12.6 | Brett St Louis | 20 Jul 85 |
| 12.9 | Jon Ridgeon | 9 Jul 83 |

## 400 METRES HURDLES (2'9")

| | | |
|---|---|---|
| 53.06 | Philip Beattie (3'0") | 2 Aug 80 |
| 53.14 | Martin Briggs | 2 Aug 80 |
| 53.30 | Mark Rowlands | 31 Jul 94 |
| 53.55 | Charles Robertson-Adams | 31 Jul 94 |
| 53.58 | Noel Levy | 13 Jul 91 |
| 53.64 | Dean Park | 17 May 94 |
| 53.69 | Max Robertson | 2 Aug 80 |
| 53.69 | Bob Brown | 9 Aug 86 |
| 53.71 | Andrew Bargh | 11 Jul 92 |
| 53.82 | Robert Taylor | 9 Aug 86 |
| **hand timing** | | |
| 53.2 | Philip Beattie | 24 May 80 |

## HIGH JUMP

| | | |
|---|---|---|
| 2.23 | Mark Lakey | 29 Aug 82 |
| 2.15 | Ossie Cham | 14 Jul 79 |
| 2.15 | Brendan Reilly | 7 May 89 |
| 2.15 | Stanley Osuide | 1 Sep 91 |
| 2.12 | Femi Abejide | 11 Jul 81 |
| 2.11 | Leroy Lucas | 6 Aug 83 |
| 2.10 | Dalton Grant | 18 Sep 82 |
| 2.10 | Tim Blakeway | 29 Aug 87 |
| 2.10 | James Brierley | 16 May 93 |
| 2.09 | Steve Smith | 10 Sep 89 |

## POLE VAULT

| | | |
|---|---|---|
| 5.20 | Neil Winter | 2 Sep 90 |
| 4.90 | Warren Siley | 8 Sep 89 |
| 4.81 | Christian Linskey | 30 Jul 95 |
| 4.80 | Billy Davey | 14 Sep 80 |
| 4.76 | Nick Buckfield | 11 Jun 89 |
| 4.72 | Ian Lewis | 24 Aug 85 |
| 4.66 | Michael Edwards | 24 Aug 85 |
| 4.60 | Ben Flint | 10 Jun 95 |
| 4.53 | Keith Stock | 5 Sep 73 |
| 4.50 | Christian North | 26 Aug 90 |
| 4.50 | Michael Barber | 15 Sep 90 |
| 4.50 | Neil Young | 5 Jun 93 |

## LONG JUMP

| | | |
|---|---|---|
| 7.32 | Kevin Liddington | 16 May 87 |
| 7.25 | Alan Slack | 12 Jun 76 |
| 7.21 | Hugh Teape | 17 May 80 |
| 7.20 | Hugh Davidson | 21 Jun 80 |
| 7.19 | Onochie Onuorah | 8 Jul 89 |
| 7.18 | Barry Nevison | 1 May 83 |
| 7.17 | Hugh Whyte | 15 Jul 79 |
| 7.15 | Matthew John | 29 Jun 86 |
| 7.14 | Stewart Faulkner | 17 Aug 85 |
| 7.13 | Mark Findlay | 24 Sep 94 |
| **wind assisted** | | |
| 7.40 | Matthew John | 10 May 86 |
| 7.25 | Nathan Morgan | 27 Aug 94 |
| 7.23 | Onochie Onuorah | 26 May 90 |
| 7.22 | Paul Hanson | 7 Jul 78 |

## TRIPLE JUMP

| | | |
|---|---|---|
| 15.65 | Vernon Samuels | 18 Jul 81 |
| 15.50 | Junior Campbell | 18 May 86 |
| 15.45 | Steven Anderson | 2 Aug 81 |
| 15.28 | Larry Achike | 22 Jun 91 |
| 15.14 | Marvin Bramble | 8 Aug 93 |
| 14.94 | Hugh Teape | 17 May 80 |
| 14.93 | Mark Whitehead | 26 Aug 85 |
| 14.90 | Lawrence Lynch | 21 Jul 84 |
| 14.88 o | Ian Timbers | 5 Oct 80 |
| 14.84 | Peter Vaughan | 2 May 83 |

**wind assisted**

| | | | |
|---|---|---|---|
| 15.25 | Marvin Bramble | 3 Jul 93 | |
| 15.08 | Lawrence Lynch | 29 Apr 84 | |
| 15.06 | Craig Duncan | 7 Aug 82 | |
| 14.88 | Carl Howard | 13 Jul 90 | |

**SHOT** (5kg)

| | | | |
|---|---|---|---|
| 19.22 | Chris Ellis | 4 Jun 82 | |
| 18.90 dh | Matt Simson | 23 Aug 86 | |
| 18.90 | Neal Brunning | 6 Sep 87 | |
| 18.43 | Emeka Udechuku | 28 May 95 | |
| 18.25 | Billy Cole | 1 Aug 81 | |
| 17.91 | Anthony Zaidman | 28 May 78 | |
| 17.76 | George Brocklebank | 22 Jul 79 | |
| 17.68 | Carl Myerscough | 24 Sep 95 | |
| 17.37 io | Guy Litherland | 15 Dec 85 | |
| 17.36 | Piers Selby | 10 Jul 92 | |
| 17.30 io | Simon Williams | 1 Dec 84 | |
| 17.30 | Jason Mulcahy | 7 Jul 89 | |
| 17.24 | Mark Edwards | 20 Aug 91 | |

**DISCUS** (1.5kg)

| | | | |
|---|---|---|---|
| 62.22 | Emeka Udechuku | 10 Jul 95 | |
| 56.14 | Chris Symonds | 6 Sep 87 | |
| 55.94 | Simon Williams | 9 Sep 84 | |
| 55.90 | Guy Litherland | 14 Sep 85 | |
| 55.72 | Keith Homer | 27 Jun 82 | |
| 55.52 | Glen Smith | 14 May 88 | |
| 55.36 | Neal Brunning ¶ | 7 Jun 87 | |
| 54.18 | Matthew Symonds | 21 Jul 84 | |
| 53.80 | Paul Mardle | 19 May 79 | |
| 52.76 | Julian Willett | 17 Jun 89 | |
| 52.76 | James South | 1 Sep 91 | |
| 52.76 | Carl Myerscough | 24 Sep 95 | |

**HAMMER** (5kg)

| | | | |
|---|---|---|---|
| 76.28 | Andrew Tolputt | 11 Aug 84 | |
| 73.90 | Paul Head | 29 Aug 81 | |
| 73.00 | Nick Steinmetz | 17 Jul 93 | |
| 71.34 | Tony Kenneally | 7 Sep 80 | |
| 70.82 | Jason Byrne | 20 Jun 87 | |
| 68.62 | Peter Vivian | 16 May 87 | |
| 67.64 | Gareth Cook | 22 Sep 85 | |
| 67.48 | Christopher Howe | 24 Jun 84 | |
| 66.92 | Paul Murden | 8 May 85 | |
| 66.30 | Malcolm Croad | 21 Jul 90 | |

## UNDER 15

### 100 METRES

| | | | |
|---|---|---|---|
| 11.0 | Norman Ellis | 23 Jul 89 | |
| 11.05 | Jamie Nixon | 21 Jul 84 | |
| 11.10 | Courage Edo | 15 Aug 92 | |
| 11.1 | Michael Hitchen | 24 Apr 77 | |
| 11.1 | Malcolm James | 77 | |
| 11.1 | Ray Burke | 25 Aug 84 | |
| 11.1 | Duncan Game | 11 May 86 | |
| 11.1 | Michael Williams | 31 Aug 86 | |
| 11.1 | Jeffrey Anderson | 3 Jul 89 | |
| 11.1 | Matthew Clements | 23 Aug 92 | |

**JAVELIN** (700g)

| | | | |
|---|---|---|---|
| 72.78 | Gary Jenson (800g) | 10 Sep 83 | |
| 72.48 | | 3 Jul 83 | |
| 70.30 | Colin Mackenzie | 6 Jul 79 | |
| 68.32 | David Parker | 15 Jul 95 | |
| 68.26 | Ian Marsh | 30 Jul 77 | |
| 68.18 | James Hurrion | 3 Jun 90 | |
| 66.88 | David Messom | 4 Jul 81 | |
| 66.86 | Michael Williams | 16 Jul 79 | |
| 66.52 | Marcus Humphries | 17 Sep 78 | |
| 65.68 | Tim Eldridge | 18 Aug 91 | |
| 65.16 | Mark Wells | 31 May 77 | |

**OCTATHLON** (1985 Tables) (* with 100m)

| | | | |
|---|---|---|---|
| 5531 * | Jim Stevenson | 18 Sep 88 | |
| 5423 | Leo Barker | 17 Sep 95 | |
| 5378 | Matthew Lewis | 20 Sep 92 | |
| 5311 | Dean Macey | 18 Sep 94 | |
| 5304 * | Tom Leeson | 28 Sep 80 | |
| 5208 | Fyn Corcoran | 18 Sep 94 | |
| 5194 * | Bryan Long | 26 Sep 76 | |
| 5149 | Paul Hourihan | 19 Sep 93 | |
| 5144 | Marc Newton | 17 Sep 95 | |
| 5121 | Chris Hindley | 20 Sep 92 | |
| 5106 * | Jeremy Lay | 29 Sep 85 | |

**3000 METRES TRACK WALK**

| | | | |
|---|---|---|---|
| 12:04.9 | Philip King | 18 May 91 | |
| 12:35.94 | David Hucks | 30 Aug 82 | |
| 12:44.8 o | Gordon Vale | 11 Oct 78 | |
| 12:50.9 | Jon Vincent | 8 Jul 87 | |
| 12:50.67 i | Stuart Monk | 18 Feb 95 | |
| | 12:52.9 | 12 Jul 95 | |
| 13:03.5 | Ian Ashforth | 16 Sep 84 | |
| 13:05.8 | Sean Maxwell | 8 Aug 76 | |
| 13:08.4 | Ian McCombie | 8 Aug 76 | |

**5000 METRES TRACK WALK**

| | | | |
|---|---|---|---|
| 20:46.5 | Philip King | 29 Sep 91 | |
| 21:52.7 | Stuart Monk | 22 Jul 95 | |
| 22:17.5 | Russell Hutchings | 27 Sep 86 | |
| 22:32.5 | Gareth Holloway | 27 Sep 86 | |
| 22:35.0 | Ian Ashforth | 6 Jun 84 | |
| 22:37.0 | Jonathan Bott | 27 Sep 86 | |
| 22:42.0 | Martin Young | 20 Aug 88 | |
| 22:42.19 | Jon Vincent | 6 Jun 86 | |
| 22:53.7 | Tim Berrett | 28 Jun 81 | |
| 22:53.8 | David Hucks | 10 Mar 82 | |

**wind assisted**

| | | | |
|---|---|---|---|
| 10.9 dt | Ronald Don | 20 Jun 81 | |
| 11.00 | Steve Wiggans | 9 Jul 94 | |
| 11.0 | Malcolm James | 24 Jun 77 | |
| 11.0 | Ian Strange | 24 Jun 77 | |
| 11.0 | John Burt | 6 Sep 80 | |
| 11.0 | Milton Thompson | 6 Aug 89 | |
| 11.0 | Jeffrey Anderson | 6 Aug 89 | |
| 11.0 | Matthew Clements | 15 Sep 91 | |
| 11.05 | Ray Burke | 11 Aug 84 | |

## 200 METRES

| | | |
|---|---|---|
| 22.2 | Michael Williams | 12 Jul 86 |
| 22.30 | Jamie Nixon | 29 Sep 84 |
| 22.3 | Anthony Cairns | 12 Jul 86 |
| 22.40 | Ben Lewis | 8 Jul 95 |
| 22.4 o | Ade Mafe | 11 Nov 81 |
| 22.4 | Duncan Game | 29 Jun 86 |
| 22.54 | Matthew Clements | 16 Aug 92 |
| 22.6 | Stuart Lawrenson | 27 Jun 76 |
| 22.69 | Chris Blake | 8 Aug 93 |

**wind assisted**

| | | |
|---|---|---|
| 21.9 | Anthony Cairns | 21 Jun 86 |
| 22.26 | Stephen Daly | 9 Jul 94 |
| 22.39 | André Duffus | 9 Jul 94 |
| 22.46 | Robert Allenby | 9 Jul 94 |

## 400 METRES

| | | |
|---|---|---|
| 49.8 | Mark Tyler | 25 Aug 82 |
| 49.9 | David McKenzie | 11 Aug 85 |
| 50.0 | Simon Heaton | 7 Jul 79 |
| 50.1 | Ade Mafe | 6 Sep 81 |
| 50.3 | Malcolm James | 29 Aug 77 |
| 50.5 io | Cephas Howard | 14 Dec 91 |
| | 50.7 | 19 May 91 |
| 50.65 | Ian Lowthian | 29 Jul 95 |
| 50.9 | Alan Leonard | 30 Aug 78 |
| 50.9 | Noel Goode | 7 Jul 79 |
| 51.00 | Paul Roberts | 22 Jul 84 |

## 800 METRES

| | | |
|---|---|---|
| 1:53.6 o | David Gerrard | 9 Nov 83 |
| 1:56.1 | Craig Winrow | 12 Jul 86 |
| 1:56.6 | Paul Burgess | 13 Jul 85 |
| 1:57.1 | Delroy Smith | 12 Jul 86 |
| 1:57.12 | Michael Combe | 14 Aug 93 |
| 1:57.2 a | Tony Jarman | 15 Sep 78 |
| 1:57.5 | Noel Goode | 11 Jul 79 |
| 1:57.7 o | Stephen Gilbey | 17 Oct 73 |
| 1:57.7 | Eric Kimani | 15 Sep 81 |
| 1:57.7 | Mark Sesay | 12 Aug 87 |

## 1500 METRES

| | | |
|---|---|---|
| 4:03.0 | Glen Stewart | 28 Aug 85 |
| 4:03.0 | Scott West | 28 Aug 90 |
| 4:03.52 | Mike Isherwood | 17 Sep 82 |
| 4:03.56 | Richard Youngs | 17 Sep 82 |
| 4:03.6 | Douglas Stones | 7 Jul 79 |
| 4:03.7 | David Gerard | 31 Jul 83 |
| 4:05.7 | Ben Mabon | 1 Sep 85 |
| 4:05.8 | Graham Green | 19 Jun 79 |
| 4:06.0 | Eric Kimani | 29 Jul 81 |
| 4:06.5 | Paul Hemmings | 18 Jul 82 |

## ONE MILE

| | | |
|---|---|---|
| 4:21.9 | Glen Stewart | 11 Sep 85 |

## 3000 METRES

| | | |
|---|---|---|
| 8:47.0 | Ben Mabon | 16 Jul 85 |
| 8:48.8 | Dale Smith | 14 Aug 85 |
| 8:51.1 | Mark Slowikowski | 4 Jun 80 |
| 8:54.6 | Gary Taylor | 14 Sep 77 |
| 8:54.6 | David Bean | 22 Jul 79 |
| 8:56.0 | Paul Ryder | 29 Aug 79 |
| 8:56.4 | Stuart Bond | 10 Sep 91 |
| 8:56.9 o | David Gerard | 12 Oct 83 |
| 8:57.0 | Philip Hennessy | 28 Jul 82 |
| 8:57.6 | Chris Taylor | 16 Jul 69 |

## 80 METRES HURDLES

| | | |
|---|---|---|
| 10.71 | Matthew Clements | 15 Aug 92 |
| 11.0 | Austin Drysdale | 22 Jun 75 |
| 11.04 | Leon McRae | 8 Jul 95 |
| 11.07 | Robert Hollinger | 8 Jul 95 |
| 11.1 | Ricky Glover | 8 Jul 89 |
| 11.1 | Tom Bradwell | 13 Jul 90 |
| 11.20 | Tony Lashley | 13 Jul 91 |
| 11.2 | David Colford | 13 May 84 |
| 11.2 | Dominic Lewis | 26 Sep 87 |
| 11.2 | Nick Dowsett | 18 Sep 93 |

**wind assisted**

| | | |
|---|---|---|
| 11.00 | Tom Benn | 9 Jul 94 |
| 11.02 | Nick Dowsett | 10 Jul 93 |
| 11.12 | Sam Allen | 10 Jul 93 |
| 11.17 | Tony Lashley | 18 Aug 91 |

## HIGH JUMP

| | | |
|---|---|---|
| 2.04 | Ross Hepburn | 22 Aug 76 |
| 1.97 | Andrew Lynch | 29 Aug 88 |
| 1.97 | Wayne Gray | 3 Sep 95 |
| 1.95 | Mark Lakey | 14 Sep 80 |
| 1.94 io | Paul Byrne | 10 Dec 77 |
| 1.93 | Ewan Gittins | 21 Jul 84 |
| 1.91 | Mark Smith | 15 Jul 89 |
| 1.91 io | Lee Broomfield | 19 Dec 92 |
| 1.91 | Edward Willers | 9 Jul 94 |
| 1.91 | Matthew Brereton | 9 Jul 94 |

## POLE VAULT

| | | |
|---|---|---|
| 4.40 o | Neil Winter | 1 Oct 88 |
| 4.31 | Richard Smith | 28 Aug 95 |
| 4.30 | Christian Linskey | 18 Jun 94 |
| 4.18 | Ian Lewis | 24 May 83 |
| 4.00 | Jimmy Lewis | 9 Sep 79 |
| 3.90 | Peter Eyre | 2 Jul 89 |
| 3.90 | Martin Parley | 6 Jun 92 |
| 3.90 | Steve Francis | 11 Sep 93 |
| 3.80 | 3 athletes | |

## LONG JUMP

| | | |
|---|---|---|
| 6.79 | Onochie Onuorah | 17 Sep 88 |
| 6.77 | Barry Nevison | 30 Aug 81 |
| 6.74 | Kevin Hibbins | 17 Jun 95 |
| 6.62 | Martin Giraud | 25 May 92 |
| 6.60 | Courage Edo | 8 Aug 92 |
| 6.59 | Danny Smith | 29 Aug 87 |
| 6.59 io | David Gilkes | 19 Dec 92 |
| 6.59 io | Marcellas Peters | 11 Dec 93 |
| 6.58 | Tony Allen | 8 Aug 82 |
| 6.52 | Julian Danquah | 7 Jul 67 |
| 6.52 | Ian Strange | 24 Jun 77 |

**wind assisted**
| | | |
|---|---|---|
| 7.12 | Onochie Onuorah | 17 Sep 88 |
| 6.72 | David Gilkes | 6 Apr 92 |
| 6.61 | Kirk King | 7 Jul 95 |

**downhill**
| | | |
|---|---|---|
| 6.77 | Eric Wood | 25 Aug 58 |

**TRIPLE JUMP**
| | | |
|---|---|---|
| 13.86 | Jamie Quarry | 10 Jul 87 |
| 13.79 | Paul Dundas | 11 Jun 88 |
| 13.77 | Eugene Hechevarria | 16 Sep 78 |
| 13.71 | Larry Achike | 10 Jun 89 |
| 13.69 | Vernon Samuels | 25 Aug 79 |
| 13.60 | Steven Anderson | 9 Jun 79 |
| 13.60 | Steve Folkard | 11 Jul 80 |
| 13.58 | Daniel Puddick | 26 May 93 |
| 13.57 | Errol Burrows | 11 Jul 80 |
| 13.56 | Delroy Ricketts | 18 Jun 88 |

**wind assisted**
| | | |
|---|---|---|
| 13.92 | Eugene Hechevarria | 8 Jul 78 |
| 13.87 | Vernon Samuels | 20 Sep 79 |
| 13.73 | Donovan Fraser | 7 Jul 79 |

**SHOT** (4kg)
| | | |
|---|---|---|
| 18.71 | Chris Ellis | 14 Jun 80 |
| 16.54 | Geoff Hodgson | 8 Jul 72 |
| 16.39 | Peter Waterman | 2 Jul 94 |
| 16.36 io | Billy Cole | 1 Nov 79 |
| 16.11 | | 7 Jul 79 |
| 16.29 | Neal Brunning ¶ | 11 Sep 85 |
| 16.14 | Andrew Monaghan | 19 Sep 70 |
| 16.05 | John Nicholls | 29 Jun 80 |
| 16.01 | Ian McLaughlin | 18 Sep 91 |
| 15.96 | James Muirhead | 14 Sep 85 |
| 15.95 | Spencer English | 3 Aug 86 |

**DISCUS** (1.25kg)
| | | |
|---|---|---|
| 53.08 | Emeka Udechuku | 5 Sep 93 |
| 50.80 | Paul Mardle | 3 Sep 77 |
| 50.32 | Chris Symonds | 23 Jul 85 |
| 50.04 | Keith Homer | 12 Jul 80 |
| 49.36 | James Muirhead | 12 May 85 |
| 49.32 | Julian Douglas | 16 Sep 79 |
| 49.22 | Spencer English | 1 Jun 86 |
| 48.84 | Witold Leonowicz | 23 Aug 80 |
| 48.78 | Neville Lynch | 7 Sep 80 |
| 48.76 | Ben Walker | 15 Aug 92 |

**HAMMER** (4kg)
| | | |
|---|---|---|
| 70.78 | Andrew Tolputt | 9 Jul 82 |
| 67.24 | Peter Vivian | 22 Sep 85 |
| 64.28 | Jason Byrne | 22 Sep 85 |
| 63.68 | Paul Binley | 29 Sep 85 |
| 63.30 | Richard Fedder | 26 Aug 79 |
| 63.16 | Tony Kenneally | 29 May 78 |
| 62.06 | Nick Steinmetz | 4 Aug 91 |
| 61.08 | Neil Curtis | 11 Sep 88 |
| 60.52 | Ian McLaughlin | 21 Aug 91 |
| 59.94 | Mike Rowlatt | 2 Sep 90 |

**JAVELIN** (600g)
| | | |
|---|---|---|
| 62.70 | Paul Godwin | 21 May 89 |
| 60.56 | David Messom | 6 Jul 79 |
| 60.56 | Clifton Green | 3 Jul 94 |
| 59.88 | James Hurrion | 17 Sep 88 |
| 59.52 | Paul Price | 19 Aug 79 |
| 58.94 | Dan Carter | 7 Aug 94 |
| 58.74 | Philips Olwenu | 6 Aug 95 |
| 58.58 | Justin Rubio | 11 Jun 83 |
| 58.48 | Andrew Ravenscroft | 9 Aug 80 |
| 58.22 | Michael Williams | 21 Jul 77 |

**PENTATHLON** (1985 Tables)
(* with 100 metres - rescored)
| | | |
|---|---|---|
| 3199 * | Onochie Onuorah | 17 Sep 88 |
| 3187 | Mark Newton | 27 Aug 94 |
| 3163 | Kevin Drury | 27 Aug 94 |
| 3085 *w | Cephas Howard | 21 Sep 91 |
| 3035 * | Ricky Glover | 17 Sep 89 |
| 3024 | Tom Benn | 17 Sep 94 |
| 2995 | Marcellas Peters | 19 Sep 93 |
| 2993 | Sam Allen | 19 Sep 93 |
| 2989 | Ian Leaman | 19 Sep 93 |
| 2925 | Scott Walker | 20 Sep 92 |

**3000 METRES TRACK WALK**
| | | |
|---|---|---|
| 12:59.7 o | Philip King | 10 Oct 89 |
| 13:35.0 | Russell Hutchings | 7 Sep 85 |
| 13:45.0 | John Murphy | 14 May 95 |
| 13:51.0 | Robert Mecham | 12 May 92 |
| 13:58.0 | Jon Vincent | 7 Sep 85 |
| 14:03.0 | Neil Simpson | 1 Apr 89 |
| 14:03.5 | Nathan Kavanagh | 20 Sep 81 |
| 14:13.0 | Karl Atton | 15 Mar 86 |
| 14:15.1 o | Matthew Hales | 9 Oct 94 |
| 14:15.3 | | 14 May 94 |

**Road** - *where superior to track time*
| | | |
|---|---|---|
| 13:20 | Jonathan Deakin | 18 Sep 88 |
| 13:29 | Robert Mecham | 20 Apr 92 |
| 13:32 | Russell Hutchings | 10 Nov 84 |
| 13:39 | Neil Simpson | 6 May 89 |
| 13:43 | Nathan Kavanagh | 21 Feb 81 |
| 13:44 o | Matthew Hales | 3 Dec 94 |
| 13:52 | Ben Allkins | 2 Dec 89 |
| 13:54 | John Jones | 18 Sep 88 |
| 13:56 | Martin Young | 23 Aug 86 |

**5000 METRES TRACK WALK**
| | | |
|---|---|---|
| 23:17.0 o | Philip King | 17 Dec 89 |
| 23:53.9 | | 27 Jun 89 |
| 24:03.6 o | John Murphy | 15 Oct 95 |
| 24:22.0 | Robert Mecham | 14 Jul 92 |
| 25:32.4 | Gareth Brown | 4 Apr 82 |

**Road** - *where superior to track time*
| | | |
|---|---|---|
| 23:15 o | Philip King | 9 Dec 89 |
| 23:31 | Martin Young | 14 Sep 85 |
| 24:34 o | Karl Atton | 6 Dec 86 |
| 23:25 o | John Murphy | 18 Nov 95 |

53

# UK ALL TIME LISTS - WOMEN

## 100 METRES

|  |  |  |
|---|---|---|
| 11.10 | Kathy Cook | 5 Sep 81 |
| 11.15 | Paula Thomas | 23 Aug 94 |
| 11.16 | Andrea Lynch | 11 Jun 75 |
| 11.20 | Sonia Lannaman | 25 Jul 80 |
| 11.20 | Heather Oakes | 26 Sep 80 |
| 11.22 A | Beverley Callender | 8 Sep 79 |
| 11.35 | | 22 Jul 81 |
| 11.27 | Stephanie Douglas | 26 Jul 91 |
| 11.29 | Beverly Kinch | 6 Jul 90 |
| 11.31 | Wendy Hoyte | 4 Oct 82 |
| 11.31 | Shirley Thomas | 3 Jul 83 |
| 11.31 | Simmone Jacobs | 24 Sep 88 |
| 11.32 | Joan Baptiste | 24 Aug 83 |
| 11.34 | Katharine Merry | 25 Jun 94 |
| 11.35 | Sharon Danville | 20 Aug 77 |
| 11.36 A | Della Pascoe | 14 Oct 68 |
| 11.39 A | Val Peat | 14 Oct 68 |
| 11.39 | Sallyanne Short | 12 Jul 92 |
| 11.40 | Helen Golden | 20 Jul 74 |
| 11.41 | Jayne Christian | 27 May 84 |
| 11.45 | Helen Burkart | 26 Aug 83 |
| 11.45 | Marcia Richardson | 14 Jul 93 |

### wind assisted

|  |  |  |
|---|---|---|
| 10.93 | Sonia Lannaman | 17 Jul 77 |
| 11.01 | Heather Oakes | 21 May 80 |
| 11.08 | Kathy Cook | 24 Aug 83 |
| 11.13 | Beverly Kinch | 6 Jul 83 |
| 11.13 | Shirley Thomas | 27 May 84 |
| 11.13 | Paula Thomas | 20 Aug 88 |
| 11.18 | Wendy Hoyte | 4 Oct 82 |
| 11.19 | Beverley Callender | 21 May 80 |
| 11.23 | Joan Baptiste | 24 Aug 83 |
| 11.23 | Jayne Christian | 17 Jul 84 |
| 11.26 | Simmone Jacobs | 27 May 84 |
| 11.27 | Katharine Merry | 11 Jun 94 |
| 11.34 | Sandra Whittaker | 22 May 83 |
| 11.36 | Sallyanne Short | 26 Aug 89 |
| 11.37 | Val Peat | 17 Jul 70 |
| 11.37 | Kaye Jeffrey | 22 May 83 |
| 11.37 | Helen Burkart | 11 Sep 83 |
| 11.39 | Pippa Windle | 24 Jul 87 |
| 11.39 | Marcia Richardson | 11 Jun 94 |
| 11.40 | Phylis Smith | 3 Jun 90 |

### hand timing

|  |  |  |
|---|---|---|
| 10.9 | Andrea Lynch | 28 May 77 |
| 11.1 | Sonia Lannaman | 29 Jun 80 |
| 11.1 | Heather Oakes | 29 Jun 80 |
| 11.2 | Helen Golden | 29 Jun 74 |
| 11.2 | Sharon Danville | 25 Jun 77 |
| 11.2 | Beverly Kinch | 14 Jul 84 |
| 11.2 | Geraldine McLeod | 21 May 94 |

### wind assisted

|  |  |  |
|---|---|---|
| 10.8 | Sonia Lannaman | 22 May 76 |
| 11.1 | Sharon Danville | 22 May 76 |
| 11.1 | Joan Baptiste | 16 Jul 85 |
| 11.1 | Beverly Kinch | 9 May 87 |

## 200 METRES

|  |  |  |
|---|---|---|
| 22.10 | Kathy Cook | 9 Aug 84 |
| 22.58 | Sonia Lannaman | 18 May 80 |
| 22.69 | Paula Thomas | 26 Aug 94 |
| 22.72 | Beverley Callender | 30 Jul 80 |
| 22.73 | Jennifer Stoute | 3 Aug 92 |
| 22.75 | Donna Hartley | 17 Jun 78 |
| 22.80 | Michelle Scutt | 12 Jun 82 |
| 22.85 | Katharine Merry | 12 Jun 94 |
| 22.86 | Joan Baptiste | 9 Aug 84 |
| 22.92 | Heather Oakes | 28 Aug 86 |
| 22.98 | Sandra Whittaker | 8 Aug 84 |
| 23.10 | Diane Smith | 11 Aug 90 |
| 23.12 | Simmone Jacobs | 15 Jun 91 |
| 23.14 | Helen Golden | 7 Sep 73 |
| 23.14 | Helen Burkart | 17 Jul 82 |
| 23.15 | Andrea Lynch | 25 Aug 75 |
| 23.17 | Stephanie Douglas | 12 Jun 94 |
| 23.18 | Joslyn Hoyte-Smith | 9 Jun 82 |
| 23.24 | Sallyanne Short | 28 Jun 92 |
| 23.29 | Verona Elder | 17 Jun 78 |
| 23.29 | Aileen McGillivary | 25 Jul 93 |

### wind assisted

|  |  |  |
|---|---|---|
| 22.48 | Michelle Scutt | 4 Jul 82 |
| 22.69 | Beverley Callender | 24 Jun 81 |
| 22.90 | Andrea Lynch | 11 Jun 75 |
| 22.97 | Helen Golden | 26 Jul 74 |
| 23.00 | Joslyn Hoyte-Smith | 13 Jun 82 |
| 23.01 | Simmone Jacobs | 28 May 84 |
| 23.11 | Linsey Macdonald | 5 Jul 80 |
| 23.14 | Shirley Thomas | 28 May 84 |
| 23.15 | Margaret Critchley | 22 Jul 70 |

### hand timing

|  |  |  |
|---|---|---|
| 22.9 | Heather Oakes | 3 May 80 |
| 22.9 | Helen Burkart | 6 Aug 83 |
| 23.0 | Helen Golden | 30 Jun 74 |
| 23.1 | Andrea Lynch | 21 May 77 |
| 23.1 | Linda Keough | 5 Jul 89 |
| 23.2 | Dorothy Hyman | 3 Oct 63 |
| 23.2 | Margaret Critchley | 2 Aug 70 |

### wind assisted

|  |  |  |
|---|---|---|
| 23.1 | Margaret Critchley | 14 Jul 74 |
| 23.1 | Sharon Danville | 17 Sep 77 |
| 23.1 | Linda McCurry | 2 Jul 78 |

## 300 METRES

|  |  |  |
|---|---|---|
| 35.46 | Kathy Cook | 18 Aug 84 |
| 36.01 | Michelle Scutt | 13 Jul 80 |
| 36.44 | Sally Gunnell | 30 Jul 93 |
| 36.45 | Joslyn Hoyte-Smith | 5 Jul 80 |
| 36.46 | Linsey Macdonald | 13 Jul 80 |
| 36.65 | Joan Baptiste | 18 Aug 84 |
| 36.69 | Helen Burkart | 9 Sep 83 |
| 36.95 | Jennifer Stoute | 21 Jul 91 |
| 36.97 | Donna Hartley | 4 Jul 75 |
| 37.30 | Verona Elder | 26 May 76 |

### hand timing

|  |  |  |
|---|---|---|
| 36.2 | Donna Hartley | 7 Aug 74 |
| 37.0 | Linda Keough | 22 Jul 89 |

54

## 400 METRES

| | | |
|---|---|---|
| 49.43 | Kathy Cook | 6 Aug 84 |
| 50.40 | Phylis Smith | 3 Aug 92 |
| 50.63 | Michelle Scutt | 31 May 82 |
| 50.75 | Joslyn Hoyte-Smith | 18 Jun 82 |
| 50.93 | Lorraine Hanson | 26 Aug 91 |
| 50.98 | Linda Keough | 26 Aug 91 |
| 51.04 | Sally Gunnell | 20 Jul 94 |
| 51.16 | Linsey Macdonald | 15 Jun 80 |
| 51.18 | Melanie Neef | 6 Aug 95 |
| 51.28 | Donna Hartley | 12 Jul 75 |
| 51.41 | Sandra Douglas | 2 Aug 92 |
| 51.53 | Jennifer Stoute | 12 Aug 89 |
| 51.70 | Verona Elder | 10 Jun 78 |
| 51.93 | Janine MacGregor | 28 Aug 81 |
| 51.97 | Linda Forsyth | 31 May 82 |
| 52.04 | Donna Fraser | 13 Sep 95 |
| 52.12 A | Lillian Board | 16 Oct 68 |
| 52.13 | Helen Burkart | 28 Jun 84 |
| 52.20 | Ann Packer | 17 Oct 64 |
| 52.26 | Pat Beckford | 14 Aug 88 |
| **hand timing** | | |
| 51.2 | Donna Hartley | 28 Jul 78 |
| 51.4 | Verona Elder | 22 May 76 |
| 52.2 | Liz Barnes | 22 May 76 |

## 800 METRES

| | | |
|---|---|---|
| 1:56.21 | Kelly Holmes | 9 Sep 95 |
| 1:57.42 | Kirsty Wade | 24 Jun 85 |
| 1:58.65 | Diane Modahl | 14 Jul 90 |
| 1:58.97 | Shireen Bailey | 15 Sep 87 |
| 1:59.05 | Christina Cahill | 4 Aug 79 |
| 1:59.67 | Lorraine Baker | 15 Aug 86 |
| 1:59.76 | Paula Fryer | 17 Jul 91 |
| 1:59.81 | Ann Griffiths | 10 Aug 94 |
| 2:00.15 | Rosemary Wright | 3 Sep 72 |
| 2:00.20 | Anne Purvis | 7 Jul 82 |
| 2:00.30 | Cherry Hanson | 25 Jul 81 |
| 2:00.39 | Bev Nicholson | 28 Aug 88 |
| 2:00.6 a | Jane Finch | 9 Jul 77 |
| 2:00.80 | Yvonne Murray | 10 Jul 87 |
| 2:01.1 a | Ann Packer | 20 Oct 64 |
| 2:01.11 | Lynne MacIntyre | 18 Aug 84 |
| 2:01.2 | Joan Allison | 1 Jul 73 |
| 2:01.2 | Christine Whittingham | 26 Aug 78 |
| 2:01.24 | Christine Benning | 28 Jul 79 |
| 2:01.35 | Liz Barnes | 10 Jul 76 |

## 1000 METRES

| | | |
|---|---|---|
| 2:32.83 | Kelly Holmes | 23 Jul 95 |
| 2:33.70 | Kirsty Wade | 9 Aug 85 |
| 2:34.92 | Christina Cahill | 9 Aug 85 |
| 2:35.32 | Shireen Bailey | 19 Jul 86 |
| 2:35.51 | Lorraine Baker | 19 Jul 86 |
| 2:35.86 | Diane Modahl | 29 Aug 93 |
| 2:37.05 | Christine Whittingham | 27 Jun 86 |
| 2:37.29 | Yvonne Murray | 14 Jul 89 |
| 2:37.61 | Bev Nicholson | 14 Jul 89 |
| 2:37.82 | Gillian Dainty | 11 Sep 81 |
| 2:38.44 | Evelyn McMeekin | 23 Aug 78 |
| 2:38.58 | Jo White | 9 Sep 77 |

## 1500 METRES

| | | |
|---|---|---|
| 3:59.96 | Zola Budd | 30 Aug 85 |
| 4:00.57 | Christina Cahill | 6 Jul 84 |
| 4:00.73 | Kirsty Wade | 26 Jul 87 |
| 4:01.20 | Yvonne Murray | 4 Jul 87 |
| 4:01.38 | Liz McColgan | 4 Jul 87 |
| 4:01.41 | Kelly Holmes | 12 Jun 94 |
| 4:01.53 | Christine Benning | 15 Aug 79 |
| 4:02.32 | Shireen Bailey | 1 Oct 88 |
| 4:03.17 | Alison Wyeth | 7 Aug 93 |
| 4:04.14 | Wendy Sly | 14 Aug 83 |
| 4:04.81 | Sheila Carey | 9 Sep 72 |
| 4:05.66 | Bev Nicholson | 20 Jul 90 |
| 4:05.75 | Lynn Gibson | 20 Jul 94 |
| 4:05.96 | Lynne MacIntyre | 20 Aug 84 |
| 4:06.0 | Mary Cotton | 24 Jun 78 |
| 4:06.24 | Christine Whittingham | 5 Jul 86 |
| 4:06.84 | Paula Radcliffe | 2 Jul 95 |
| 4:07.11 | Janet Marlow | 18 Aug 82 |
| 4:07.59 | Ann Williams | 9 Jun 92 |
| 4:07.69 | Teena Colebrook | 19 Aug 90 |

## ONE MILE

| | | |
|---|---|---|
| 4:17.57 | Zola Budd | 21 Aug 85 |
| 4:19.41 | Kirsty Wade | 27 Jul 85 |
| 4:22.64 | Christina Cahill | 7 Sep 84 |
| 4:22.64 | Yvonne Murray | 22 Jul 94 |
| 4:24.57 | Christine Benning | 7 Sep 84 |
| 4:24.87 | Alison Wyeth | 6 Jul 91 |
| 4:26.11 | Liz McColgan | 10 Jul 87 |
| 4:26.16 | Teena Colebrook | 14 Jul 90 |
| 4:26.52 | Bev Hartigan | 14 Aug 92 |
| 4:27.80 | Lisa York | 14 Aug 92 |
| 4:28.07 | Wendy Sly | 18 Aug 84 |
| 4:28.8 | Karen Hutcheson | 20 Aug 89 |
| 4:28.93 | Paula Radcliffe | 18 Aug 95 |
| 4:29.15 | Suzanne Morley | 18 Aug 84 |
| 4:30.08 | Lynne MacIntyre | 7 Sep 84 |
| 4:30.29 | Jane Shields | 9 Sep 83 |
| 4:30.89 | Ruth Partridge | 18 Aug 84 |
| 4:31.17 | Lynn Gibson | 1 Jul 94 |
| 4:31.24 i | Jo White | 5 Feb 83 |
| 4:31.45 | Shireen Bailey | 17 Sep 89 |
| 4:31.65 | Gillian Dainty | 26 Jun 82 |

## 2000 METRES

| | | |
|---|---|---|
| 5:26.93 | Yvonne Murray | 8 Jul 94 |
| 5:30.19 | Zola Budd | 11 Jul 86 |
| 5:33.85 | Christina Cahill | 13 Jul 84 |
| 5:37.00 | Christine Benning | 13 Jul 84 |
| 5:38.50 | Alison Wyeth | 29 Aug 93 |
| 5:39.20 | Paula Radcliffe | 29 Aug 93 |
| 5:40.24 | Liz McColgan | 22 Aug 87 |
| 5:42.15 | Wendy Sly | 17 Sep 82 |
| 5:43.24 | Suzanne Morley | 13 Jul 84 |
| 5:45.0 i | Bev Hartigan | 20 Feb 93 |
| 5:45.15 | Debbie Gunning | 29 Aug 93 |
| 5:45.34 | Lisa York | 10 Jul 92 |
| 5:45.45 | Ruth Partridge | 13 Jul 84 |
| 5:45.81 i | Kirsty Wade | 13 Mar 87 |
| 5:46.40 | Sonia McGeorge | 29 Aug 93 |

55

## 3000 METRES

| | | |
|---|---|---|
| 8:28.83 | Zola Budd | 7 Sep 85 |
| 8:29.02 | Yvonne Murray | 25 Sep 88 |
| 8:34.80 i | Liz McColgan | 4 Mar 89 |
| 8:38.23 | | 15 Jul 91 |
| 8:37.06 | Wendy Sly | 10 Aug 83 |
| 8:38.42 | Alison Wyeth | 16 Aug 93 |
| 8:40.40 | Paula Radcliffe | 16 Aug 93 |
| 8:44.46 | Christine Benning | 22 Aug 84 |
| 8:45.69 | Jane Shields | 10 Aug 83 |
| 8:47.36 | Jill Hunter | 17 Aug 88 |
| 8:47.59 | Angela Tooby | 5 Jul 88 |
| 8:47.7 | Kirsty Wade | 5 Aug 87 |
| 8:47.71 | Lisa York | 31 Jul 92 |
| 8:48.72 | Karen Hutcheson | 28 Jan 90 |
| 8:48.74 | Paula Fudge | 29 Aug 78 |
| 8:49.89 | Christina Cahill | 20 Jul 85 |
| 8:50.52 | Debbie Peel | 7 Aug 82 |
| 8:51.33 | Sonia McGeorge | 29 Aug 90 |
| 8:51.40 | Ruth Partridge | 7 Aug 82 |
| 8:52.79 | Ann Ford | 28 Aug 77 |
| 8:53.52 i | Nicola Morris | 4 Mar 89 |

## 5000 METRES

| | | |
|---|---|---|
| 14:48.07 | Zola Budd | 26 Aug 85 |
| 14:49.27 | Paula Radcliffe | 7 Jul 95 |
| 14:56.94 | Yvonne Murray | 7 Jul 95 |
| 14:59.56 | Liz McColgan | 22 Jul 95 |
| 15:00.37 | Alison Wyeth | 7 Jul 95 |
| 15:09.98 | Jill Hunter | 18 Jul 92 |
| 15:13.22 | Angela Tooby | 5 Aug 87 |
| 15:14.51 | Paula Fudge | 13 Sep 81 |
| 15:21.45 | Wendy Sly | 5 Aug 87 |
| 15:28.63 | Andrea Wallace | 2 Jul 92 |
| 15:31.78 | Julie Holland | 18 Jul 90 |
| 15:32.19 | Susan Tooby | 26 May 85 |
| 15:32.34 | Jane Shields | 5 Jun 88 |
| 15:34.16 | Jill Clarke | 26 May 85 |
| 15:38.84 | Ann Ford | 5 Jun 82 |
| 15:40.14 | Helen Titterington | 17 Jul 89 |
| 15:41.11 | Angela Hulley | 18 Jul 90 |

## 10,000 METRES

| | | |
|---|---|---|
| 30:57.07 | Liz McColgan | 25 Jun 91 |
| 31:07.88 | Jill Hunter | 30 Jun 91 |
| 31:53.36 | Wendy Sly | 8 Oct 88 |
| 31:55.30 | Angela Tooby | 4 Sep 87 |
| 31:56.97 | Yvonne Murray | 24 Aug 94 |
| 32:20.95 | Susan Tooby | 2 Jul 88 |
| 32:21.61 | Andrea Wallace | 6 Jun 92 |
| 32:24.63 | Sue Crehan | 4 Jul 87 |
| 32:32.42 | Vikki McPherson | 15 Jul 93 |
| 32:36.09 | Helen Titterington | 29 Aug 89 |
| 32:41.29 | Jenny Clague | 20 Jun 93 |
| 32:42.0 | Jane Shields | 24 Aug 88 |
| 32:42.84 | Angela Hulley | 6 Aug 89 |
| 32:44.06 | Suzanne Rigg | 27 Jun 93 |
| 32:47.78 | Julie Holland | 31 Aug 90 |
| 32:57.17 | Kathy Binns | 15 Aug 80 |
| 32:58.2 | Claire Lavers | 20 Apr 91 |
| 33:05.43 | Elspeth Turner | 1 Jun 88 |
| 33:10.25 | Shireen Samy | 5 Jul 86 |
| 33:10.94 | Marina Samy | 28 Jul 86 |

## MARATHON

| | | |
|---|---|---|
| 2:25:56 | Véronique Marot | 23 Apr 89 |
| 2:26:51 | Priscilla Welch | 10 May 87 |
| 2:27:32 | Liz McColgan | 3 Nov 91 |
| 2:28:06 | Sarah Rowell | 21 Apr 85 |
| 2:28:38 | Sally-Ann Hales | 21 Apr 85 |
| 2:29:29 | Sally Eastall | 8 Dec 91 |
| 2:29:43 | Joyce Smith | 9 May 82 |
| 2:29:47 | Paula Fudge | 30 Oct 88 |
| 2:30:38 | Ann Ford | 17 Apr 88 |
| 2:30:51 | Angela Hulley | 23 Sep 88 |
| 2:30:53 | Yvonne Danson | 17 Apr 95 |
| 2:31:33 | Susan Tooby | 23 Sep 88 |
| 2:31:33 | Andrea Wallace | 12 Apr 92 |
| 2:31:45 | Lynn Harding | 23 Apr 89 |
| 2:32:36 | Marian Sutton | 15 Oct 95 |
| 2:32:53 | Gillian Burley | 2 Dec 84 |
| 2:33:04 | Sheila Catford | 23 Apr 89 |
| 2:33:07 | Nicola McCracken | 22 Apr 90 |
| 2:33:16 | Karen Macleod | 27 Aug 94 |
| 2:33:22 | Carolyn Naisby | 6 Dec 87 |

## 100 METRES HURDLES

| | | |
|---|---|---|
| 12.82 | Sally Gunnell | 17 Aug 88 |
| 12.87 | Shirley Strong | 24 Aug 83 |
| 12.90 | Jacqui Agyepong | 25 Jun 95 |
| 12.91 | Kay Morley-Brown | 2 Feb 90 |
| 13.03 | Lesley-Ann Skeete | 3 Aug 90 |
| 13.04 | Clova Court | 9 Aug 94 |
| 13.05 | Judy Simpson | 29 Aug 86 |
| 13.07 | Lorna Boothe | 7 Oct 82 |
| 13.08 | Samantha Farquharson | 4 Jul 94 |
| 13.11 | Sharon Danville | 22 Jun 76 |
| 13.16 | Wendy Jeal | 27 Aug 86 |
| 13.24 | Kim Hagger | 31 Aug 87 |
| 13.24 | Keri Maddox | 12 Jun 93 |
| 13.25 | Diane Allahgreen | 21 Jul 94 |
| 13.26 | Michelle Edwards | 3 Aug 90 |
| 13.28 | Angela Thorp | 29 Aug 93 |
| 13.29 | Mary Peters | 2 Sep 72 |
| 13.32 | Sam Baker | 29 Aug 93 |
| 13.34 | Judy Vernon | 7 Sep 73 |
| 13.34 | Melanie Wilkins | 15 Jul 95 |

**wind assisted**

| | | |
|---|---|---|
| 12.78 | Shirley Strong | 8 Oct 82 |
| 12.80 | Sally Gunnell | 29 Jul 88 |
| 12.84 A | Kay Morley-Brown | 8 Aug 90 |
| 12.90 | Lorna Boothe | 8 Oct 82 |
| 13.01 | Lesley-Ann Skeete | 1 Feb 90 |
| 13.06 | Sharon Danville | 14 Jul 84 |
| 13.08 | Michelle Campbell | 26 May 95 |
| 13.12 | Pat Rollo | 27 May 84 |
| 13.20 | Keri Maddox | 2 Jul 93 |

**hand timing**

| | | |
|---|---|---|
| 13.0 | Judy Vernon | 29 Jun 74 |
| 13.0 | Blondelle Caines | 29 Jun 74 |

**wind assisted**

| | | |
|---|---|---|
| 12.7 | Kay Morley-Brown | 10 Jan 90 |
| 12.9 | Judy Vernon | 18 May 74 |

## 400 METRES HURDLES

| | | |
|---|---|---|
| 52.74 | Sally Gunnell | 19 Aug 93 |
| 54.63 | Gowry Retchakan | 3 Aug 92 |
| 55.91 | Elaine McLaughlin | 26 Sep 88 |
| 56.04 | Sue Morley | 10 Aug 83 |
| 56.05 | Wendy Cearns | 13 Aug 89 |
| 56.06 | Christine Warden | 28 Jul 79 |
| 56.15 | Jacqui Parker | 27 Jul 91 |
| 56.26 | Louise Fraser | 7 Jun 92 |
| 56.46 | Yvette Wray | 11 Jul 81 |
| 56.70 | Lorraine Hanson | 13 Aug 89 |
| 56.72 | Gladys Taylor | 6 Aug 84 |
| 57.00 | Simone Laidlow | 6 Aug 88 |
| 57.07 | Verona Elder | 15 Jul 83 |
| 57.30 | Louise Brunning | 27 Jun 95 |
| 57.38 | Sarah Dean | 27 Jul 91 |
| 57.41 | Jennifer Pearson | 6 Aug 88 |
| 57.43 | Liz Sutherland | 6 Jul 78 |
| 57.49 | Maureen Prendergast | 16 Jun 84 |
| 57.52 | Clare Sugden | 3 Jun 90 |
| 57.55 | Sharon Danville | 8 May 81 |

**hand timing**

| | | |
|---|---|---|
| 57.5 | Vicky Lee | 28 Jun 86 |

## HIGH JUMP

| | | |
|---|---|---|
| 1.95 | Diana Davies | 26 Jun 82 |
| 1.94 | Louise Gittens | 25 May 80 |
| 1.94 i | Debbie Marti | 3 Feb 91 |
| | 1.93 | 5 Sep 92 |
| 1.94 i | Jo Jennings | 13 Mar 93 |
| | 1.90 | 29 Sep 88 |
| 1.92 | Barbara Simmonds | 31 Jul 82 |
| 1.92 | Judy Simpson | 8 Aug 83 |
| 1.92 | Janet Boyle | 29 Sep 88 |
| 1.92 i | Julia Bennett | 10 Mar 90 |
| | 1.89 | 11 Jun 94 |
| 1.91 | Ann-Marie Cording | 19 Sep 81 |
| 1.91 | Gillian Evans | 30 Apr 83 |
| 1.91 | Jayne Barnetson | 7 Jul 89 |
| 1.91 | Lea Haggett | 2 Jun 91 |
| 1.90 | Kim Hagger | 17 May 86 |
| 1.90 | Sharon Hutchings | 1 Aug 86 |
| 1.88 i | Debbie McDowell | 17 Jan 88 |
| 1.88 i | Kerry Roberts | 16 Feb 92 |
| 1.88 i | Kelly Mason | 16 Feb 92 |
| 1.87 | Barbara Lawton | 22 Sep 73 |
| 1.87 | Moira Maguire | 11 May 80 |
| 1.87 | Louise Manning | 6 May 84 |
| 1.87 | Michelle Dunkley | 7 Jul 95 |
| 1.87 | Rachael Forrest | 7 Jul 95 |

## POLE VAULT

| | | |
|---|---|---|
| 3.90 ns | Kate Staples | 14 Jun 95 |
| | 3.80 i | 4 Feb 95 |
| | 3.80 | 2 Jul 95 |
| 3.72 | Linda Stanton | 11 Jun 95 |
| 3.60 i | Janine Whitlock | 30 Dec 95 |
| | 3.41 | 17 Sep 95 |
| 3.50 i | Paula Wilson | 28 Jan 95 |
| | 3.45 | 29 Aug 94 |
| 3.50 | Rhian Clarke | 20 Jul 95 |
| 3.45 | Clare Ridgley | 28 Aug 95 |

| | | |
|---|---|---|
| 3.40 i | Claire Morrison | 26 Feb 95 |
| | 3.30 | 18 Jun 95 |
| 3.30 | Louise Schramm | 9 Jul 95 |

## LONG JUMP

| | | |
|---|---|---|
| 6.90 | Beverly Kinch | 14 Aug 83 |
| 6.88 | Fiona May | 18 Jul 90 |
| 6.83 | Sue Telfer | 6 May 84 |
| 6.76 | Mary Rand | 14 Oct 64 |
| 6.75 | Joyce Oladapo | 14 Sep 85 |
| 6.73 | Sheila Sherwood | 23 Jul 70 |
| 6.73 | Yinka Idowu | 7 Aug 93 |
| 6.70 | Kim Hagger | 30 Aug 86 |
| 6.69 | Sue Reeve | 10 Jun 79 |
| 6.67 | Denise Lewis | 28 May 95 |
| 6.63 | Mary Berkeley | 17 Jun 89 |
| 6.57 | Joanne Wise | 25 May 92 |
| 6.55 | Ann Simmonds | 22 Jul 70 |
| 6.52 | Gillian Regan | 29 Aug 82 |
| 6.52 | Georgina Oladapo | 16 Jun 84 |
| 6.51 i | Ruth Howell | 23 Feb 74 |
| | 6.49 | 16 Jun 72 |
| 6.45 | Carol Zeniou | 12 May 82 |
| 6.45 | Margaret Cheetham | 18 Aug 84 |
| 6.44 | Sharon Danville | 15 Jun 77 |
| 6.44 | Barbara Clarke | 13 Sep 81 |

**wind assisted**

| | | |
|---|---|---|
| 7.00 | Sue Telfer | 27 May 84 |
| 6.98 | Fiona May | 4 Jun 89 |
| 6.93 | Beverly Kinch | 14 Aug 83 |
| 6.84 | Sue Reeve | 25 Jun 77 |
| 6.80 | Joyce Oladapo | 22 Jun 85 |
| 6.69 | Joanne Wise | 30 Jul 88 |
| 6.65 | Mary Berkeley | 4 Jun 89 |
| 6.57 | Ann Simmonds | 22 Aug 70 |
| 6.56 | Judy Simpson | 30 Aug 86 |
| 6.54 | Ruth Howell | 16 Jun 72 |
| 6.54 | Myra Nimmo | 19 Jun 76 |

## TRIPLE JUMP

| | | |
|---|---|---|
| 14.66 | Ashia Hansen | 21 Aug 95 |
| 14.08 | Michelle Griffith | 11 Jun 94 |
| 13.64 | Rachel Kirby | 7 Aug 94 |
| 13.56 | Mary Agyepong | 5 Jun 92 |
| 13.46 | Evette Finikin | 26 Jul 91 |
| 13.31 | Connie Henry | 9 Jul 94 |
| 12.94 | Lorna Turner | 9 Jul 94 |
| 12.89 | Karen Skeggs | 17 May 92 |
| 12.64 | Liz Ghojefa | 4 Sep 93 |
| 12.44 | Debbie Rowe | 9 Sep 95 |
| 12.43 | Shani Anderson | 26 Jun 93 |
| 12.42 | Elizabeth Gibbens | 2 Jul 95 |

**wind assisted**

| | | |
|---|---|---|
| 12.93 | Karen Hambrook | 13 Jun 92 |
| 12.55 | Lauraine Cameron | 29 Aug 93 |
| 12.44 | Shani Anderson | 9 Jul 94 |
| 12.37 | Jane Falconer | 29 Aug 93 |
| 12.34 | Nicola Barr | 10 Jun 92 |
| 12.31 | Caroline Miller | 23 Jul 94 |

## SHOT

| | | |
|---|---|---|
| 19.36 | Judy Oakes | 14 Aug 88 |
| 19.06 i | Venissa Head | 7 Apr 84 |
| 18.93 | | 13 May 84 |
| 19.03 | Myrtle Augee | 2 Jun 90 |
| 18.99 | Meg Ritchie | 7 May 83 |
| 17.53 | Angela Littlewood | 24 Jul 80 |
| 17.45 | Yvonne Hanson-Nortey | 28 Jul 89 |
| 16.57 | Maggie Lynes | 20 Jul 94 |
| 16.40 i | Mary Peters | 28 Feb 70 |
| 16.31 | | 1 Jun 66 |
| 16.29 | Brenda Bedford | 26 May 76 |
| 16.05 | Janis Kerr | 15 May 76 |
| 15.85 i | Alison Grey | 12 Feb 94 |
| 15.69 | | 11 Jun 94 |
| 15.80 | Sharon Andrews | 30 Jul 93 |
| 15.75 i | Caroline Savory | 23 Feb 83 |
| 15.50 | | 19 Jun 83 |
| 15.60 i | Justine Buttle | 27 Feb 88 |
| 15.45 | | 25 Aug 88 |
| 15.48 | Mary Anderson | 8 Sep 85 |
| 15.46 | Vanessa Redford | 14 Jun 80 |
| 15.45 | Susan King | 27 Mar 83 |
| 15.41 | Fatima Whitbread | 29 Apr 84 |
| 15.32 i | Helen Hounsell | 13 Feb 82 |
| 15.23 | Judy Simpson | 18 Jun 88 |

## DISCUS

| | | |
|---|---|---|
| 67.48 | Meg Ritchie | 26 Apr 81 |
| 64.68 | Venissa Head | 18 Jul 83 |
| 60.72 | Jacqui McKernan | 18 Jul 93 |
| 58.02 | Rosemary Payne | 3 Jun 72 |
| 57.32 | Lynda Whiteley | 16 Jun 84 |
| 57.00 | Debbie Callaway | 24 Jun 95 |
| 56.24 | Sharon Andrews | 12 Jun 94 |
| 56.06 | Kathryn Farr | 27 Jun 87 |
| 55.70 | Shelley Drew | 25 Jun 95 |
| 55.52 | Jane Aucott | 17 Jan 90 |
| 55.42 | Lesley Bryant | 12 Sep 80 |
| 55.06 | Janet Kane | 17 Jun 78 |
| 55.04 | Lorraine Shaw | 14 May 94 |
| 54.72 | Karen Pugh | 27 Jul 86 |
| 54.68 | Emma Beales | 10 Jun 95 |
| 54.46 | Ellen Mulvihill | 14 May 86 |
| 54.46 | Janette Picton | 17 Aug 90 |
| 54.40 | Tracy Axten | 17 Jul 93 |
| 54.24 | Nicola Talbot | 15 May 93 |
| 53.96 | Julia Avis | 27 Apr 86 |

## HAMMER

| | | |
|---|---|---|
| 64.90 | Lorraine Shaw | 10 Jun 95 |
| 56.76 | Esther Augee | 15 May 93 |
| 55.44 | Lyn Sprules | 19 Jul 94 |
| 54.42 | Diana Holden | 2 Sep 95 |
| 54.02 | Ann Gardner | 19 May 93 |
| 53.00 | Sarah Moore | 13 May 95 |
| 52.84 | Fiona Whitehead | 29 Jun 93 |
| 51.62 | Julie Lavender | 15 May 94 |
| 50.12 | Jean Clark | 28 Aug 95 |
| 49.48 | Samantha Burns-Salmond | 13 Aug 95 |
| 48.56 | Julie Kirkpatrick | 20 Jun 95 |
| 47.74 | Irene Duffin | 10 Jun 95 |
| 47.10 | Karen Brown | 11 Sep 93 |
| 47.06 | Caroline Manning | 22 Jul 95 |
| 46.98 | Helen Arnold | 29 Jul 95 |
| 46.88 | Janet Smith | 25 Jun 94 |
| 46.64 | Myrtle Augee | 5 Jul 95 |
| 46.64 | Angela Bonner | 30 Jul 95 |
| 46.48 | Helen McCreadie | 6 May 95 |
| 45.06 | Kim Thompson | 18 Jun 94 |
| 45.04 | Suzanne Last | 3 Sep 94 |
| 44.70 | Rachael Beverley | 15 Jul 95 |

## JAVELIN

| | | |
|---|---|---|
| 77.44 | Fatima Whitbread | 28 Aug 86 |
| 73.58 | Tessa Sanderson | 26 Jun 83 |
| 62.32 | Sharon Gibson | 16 May 87 |
| 62.22 | Diane Royle | 18 May 85 |
| 60.10 | Shelley Holroyd | 17 Jul 93 |
| 60.00 | Julie Abel | 24 May 87 |
| 59.40 | Karen Hough | 28 Aug 86 |
| 59.36 | Kirsty Morrison | 4 Sep 93 |
| 58.60 | Jeanette Rose | 30 May 82 |
| 57.90 | Anna Lockton | 1 Jul 87 |
| 57.84 | Amanda Liverton | 3 Jun 90 |
| 56.96 | Nicola Emblem | 1 Feb 90 |
| 56.50 | Caroline White | 8 Jun 91 |
| 55.72 | Karen Martin | 25 Jul 92 |
| 55.70 | Lynn Hayhoe | 31 May 92 |
| 55.60 | Susan Platt | 15 Jun 68 |
| 55.48 | Lorna Jackson | 16 Jul 95 |
| 55.38 | Catherine Garside | 19 May 84 |
| 55.36 | Jackie Zaslona | 30 Aug 80 |
| 55.30 | Clova Court | 27 Aug 91 |

## HEPTATHLON (1985 Tables)

| | | |
|---|---|---|
| 6623 | Judy Simpson | 30 Aug 86 |
| 6325 | Denise Lewis | 23 Aug 94 |
| 6259 | Kim Hagger | 18 May 86 |
| 6125 | Tessa Sanderson | 12 Jul 81 |
| 6094 h | Joanne Mulliner | 7 Jun 87 |
| 6022 | Clova Court | 27 Aug 91 |
| 5826 | Jenny Kelly | 3 Jul 94 |
| 5803 | Jayne Barnetson | 20 Aug 89 |
| 5776 | Kathy Warren | 12 Jul 81 |
| 5702 | Yinka Idowu | 21 May 95 |
| 5671 | Vikki Schofield | 3 Jul 94 |
| 5642 | Sarah Rowe | 23 Aug 81 |
| 5633 | Marcia Marriott | 18 May 86 |
| 5632 | Emma Beales | 1 Aug 93 |
| 5594 h | Gillian Evans | 22 May 83 |
| 5548 | Val Walsh | 18 May 86 |
| 5517 | Shona Urquhart | 21 Aug 88 |
| 5496 | Julia Bennett | 21 May 95 |
| 5495 | Charmaine Johnson | 24 May 92 |
| 5493 | Sally Gunnell | 28 May 84 |
| 5455 | Claire Phythian | 19 May 95 |
| 5446 | Manndy Laing | 7 Aug 83 |
| 5434 w | Debbie Woolgar | 8 Jul 90 |
| 5424 | Lisa Gibbs | 1 Aug 93 |
| 5420 | Pauline Richards | 19 Jun 94 |

## 3000 METRES TRACK WALK

| | | |
|---|---|---|
| 12:49.16 | Betty Sworowski | 28 Jul 90 |
| 12:59.3 | Vicky Lupton | 14 May 95 |
| 13:11.0 | Lisa Langford | 6 Jul 90 |
| 13:12.01 i | Julie Drake | 12 Mar 93 |
| 13:16.0 | | 11 Dec 90 |
| 13:13.3 | Carolyn Partington | 12 Jul 95 |
| 13:25.2 | Carol Tyson | 6 Jul 79 |
| 13:27.9 | Verity Snook | 14 May 94 |
| 13:28.0 | Helen Elleker | 22 Jul 90 |
| 13:37.1 | Beverley Allen | 16 May 87 |
| 13:42.10 | Sylvia Black | 23 May 90 |
| 13:43.0 | Melanie Wright | 5 Jul 94 |
| 13:44.0 | Virginia Birch | 19 Jun 84 |
| 13:46.3 + | Marion Fawkes | 30 Jun 79 |
| 13:48.0 | Sarah Brown | 16 May 87 |
| 13:52.0 | Lillian Millen | 7 May 83 |
| 13:56.0 | Irene Bateman | 20 Sep 80 |

## 5000 METRES TRACK WALK

| | | |
|---|---|---|
| 21:52.38 | Vicky Lupton | 9 Aug 95 |
| 21:57.68 | Lisa Langford | 25 Jun 90 |
| 22:02.06 | Betty Sworowski | 28 Aug 89 |
| 22:37.47 | Julie Drake | 17 Jul 93 |
| 22:40.19 | Carolyn Partington | 16 Jul 95 |
| 22:51.23 | Helen Elleker | 25 Jun 90 |
| 23:11.2 | Carol Tyson | 30 Jun 79 |
| 23:15.04 | Beverley Allen | 25 May 87 |
| 23:19.2 | Marion Fawkes | 30 Jun 79 |
| 23:20.00 | Virginia Birch | 25 May 85 |
| 23:22.52 | Verity Snook | 19 Jun 94 |
| 23:34.43 | Sylvia Black | 5 Jul 92 |
| 23:35.54 | Nicola Jackson | 25 May 87 |
| 23:38.3 | Irene Bateman | 28 Jun 81 |
| 23:46.7 | Lillian Millen | 28 Jun 81 |
| 23:47.0 | Melanie Wright | 29 May 94 |

## 5k Road - *where superior to track time*

| | | |
|---|---|---|
| 21:36 | Vicky Lupton | 18 Jul 92 |
| 21:50 | Betty Sworowski | 6 May 90 |
| 22:45 + | Verity Snook | 25 Aug 94 |
| 22:51 | Marion Fawkes | 29 Sep 79 |
| 22:59 | Carol Tyson | 29 Sep 79 |
| 23:00 + | Beverley Allen | 1 Sep 87 |
| 23:13 | Sylvia Black | 13 Feb 93 |
| 23:24 | Melanie Wright | 9 Apr 95 |

## 10,000 METRES TRACK WALK

| | | |
|---|---|---|
| 45:18.8 | Vicky Lupton | 2 Sep 95 |
| 45:53.9 | Julie Drake | 26 May 90 |
| 46:23.08 | Betty Sworowski | 4 Aug 91 |
| 46:25.2 | Helen Elleker | 26 May 90 |
| 47:10.07 | Verity Snook | 19 Jun 93 |
| 47:56.3 | Virginia Birch | 15 Jun 85 |
| 47:58.3 | Beverley Allen | 21 Jun 86 |
| 48:11.4 | Marion Fawkes | 8 Jul 79 |
| 48:20.0 | Carolyn Partington | 7 May 94 |
| 48:34.0 | Lisa Langford | 15 Mar 86 |
| 48:34.5 | Carol Tyson | 22 Aug 81 |
| 48:35.8 | Melanie Wright | 2 Sep 95 |
| 48:52.5sh | Irene Bateman | 19 Mar 83 |
| 48:56.5 | Sarah Brown | 18 Apr 91 |
| 49:27.0 | Sylvia Black | 22 Apr 95 |
| 49:39.0 | Karen Smith | 22 May 91 |
| 49:41.0 | Elaine Callanin | 22 Apr 95 |
| 50:10.2 | Brenda Lupton | 17 Mar 84 |
| 50:11.2sh | Jill Barrett | 19 Mar 83 |
| 50:25.0mx | Lisa Simpson | 1 Apr 87 |
| 50:28.0 | Andrea Crofts | 21 Jul 92 |

## Road - *where superior to track time*

| | | |
|---|---|---|
| 45:42 | Lisa Langford | 3 May 87 |
| 45:59 | Betty Sworowski | 24 Aug 91 |
| 46:06 | Verity Snook | 25 Aug 94 |
| 46:26 | Carolyn Partington | 1 Jul 95 |
| 47:19 | Melanie Wright | 23 Sep 95 |
| 47:58 | Nicola Jackson | 27 Jun 87 |
| 47:59 | Sylvia Black | 29 Mar 92 |
| 48:30 | Karen Smith | 16 Apr 94 |

## 4 x 100 METRES RELAY

| | | |
|---|---|---|
| 42.43 | UK | 1 Aug 80 |
| | Oakes, Cook, Callender, Lannaman | |
| 42.66 | UK | 11 Sep 82 |
| | Hoyte, Cook, Callender, S.Thomas | |
| 42.71 | UK | 10 Aug 83 |
| | Baptiste, Cook, Callender, S.Thomas | |
| 42.72 | UK | 3 Sep 78 |
| | Callender, Cook, Danville, Lannaman | |
| 43.02 | UK | 26 Sep 80 |
| | Oakes, Cook, Callender, Scutt | |
| 43.03 | UK | 15 Aug 81 |
| | Hoyte, Cook, Callender, S.Thomas | |
| 43.06 | UK | 10 Aug 83 |
| | Baptiste, Cook, Callender, S.Thomas | |
| 43.11 | UK | 11 Aug 84 |
| | Jacobs, Cook, Callender, Oakes | |
| 43.15 | England | 9 Oct 82 |
| | Hoyte, Cook, Callender, Lannaman | |
| 43.18 | UK | 4 Aug 79 |
| | Barnett, Hoyte, Cook, Oakes | |
| 43.18 | UK | 20 Aug 83 |
| | Baptiste, Cook, Callender, S.Thomas | |
| 43.19 | UK | 20 Sep 80 |
| | Oakes, Cook, Callender, Scutt | |
| 43.21 | UK | 18 Aug 82 |
| | Hoyte, Cook, Callender, S.Thomas | |
| 43.26 A | UK Students | 13 Sep 79 |
| | Luker, Cook, Patten, Callender | |
| 43.30 | UK | 30 Aug 86 |
| | P. Thomas, Cook, Baptiste, Hoyte | |
| 43.32 | UK | 5 Jun 80 |
| | Oakes, Cook, Callender, Lannaman | |
| 43.32 | UK | 1 Sep 90 |
| | Douglas, Kinch, Jacobs, P.Thomas | |
| 43.35 | UK | 17 Aug 85 |
| | Christian, Baptiste, Joseph, Oakes | |
| 43.36 | UK | 13 Jul 80 |
| | Oakes, Cook, Callender, Lannaman | |
| 43.36 | UK | 23 Jun 81 |
| | Hoyte, Cook, Callender, S.Thomas | |

## 4 x 400 METRES RELAY

| | | | | | |
|---|---|---|---|---|---|
| 3:22.01 | UK | 1 Sep 91 | 3:25.51 | UK | 11 Aug 84 |
| Hanson, Smith, Gunnell, Keough | | | Scutt, Barnett, Taylor, Hoyte-Smith | | |
| 3:23.41 | UK | 22 Aug 93 | 3:25.82 | UK | 11 Sep 82 |
| Keough, Smith, Goddard, Gunnell | | | Cook, Macdonald, Taylor, Hoyte-Smith | | |
| 3:23.89 | UK | 31 Aug 91 | 3:25.87 | UK | 19 Jun 82 |
| Hanson, Smith, Gunnell, Keough | | | Forsyth, Hoyte-Smith, Elder, Scutt | | |
| 3:24.14 | UK | 14 Aug 94 | 3:26.54 | UK | 6 Aug 89 |
| Neef, Keough, Smith, Gunnell | | | Keough, Stoute, Piggford, Gunnell | | |
| 3:24.23 | UK | 8 Aug 92 | 3:26.6 a | UK | 17 Aug 75 |
| Smith, Douglas, Stoute, Gunnell | | | Roscoe, Taylor, Elder, Hartley | | |
| 3:24.25 | UK | 30 Jun 91 | 3:26.89 | UK | 1 Oct 88 |
| Gunnell, Hanson, Stoute, Keough | | | Keough, Stoute, Piggford, Gunnell | | |
| 3:24.36 | UK | 5 Jun 93 | 3:26.89 | UK | 13 Aug 95 |
| Smith, Goddard, Stoute, Gunnell | | | Neef, Llewellyn, Hanson, Oladapo | | |
| 3:24.78 | UK | 1 Sep 90 | 3:27.04 | UK | 21 Aug 93 |
| Gunnell, Stoute, Beckford, Keough | | | Keough, Smith, Goddard, Gunnell | | |
| 3:25.20 | UK | 7 Aug 92 | 3:27.06 | England | 28 Aug 94 |
| Douglas, Smith, Stoute, Gunnell | | | Smith, Goddard, Keough, Gunnell | | |
| 3:25.50 | UK | 12 Aug 95 | 3:27.09 | UK | 30 Jul 76 |
| Neef, Llewellyn, Hanson, Oladapo | | | Barnes, Taylor, Elder, Hartley | | |

## UNDER 20

### 100 METRES

| | | |
|---|---|---|
| 11.27 A | Kathy Smallwood | 9 Sep 79 |
| 11.30 | Bev Kinch | 5 Jul 83 |
| 11.36 A | Della James | 14 Oct 68 |
| 11.43 | Shirley Thomas | 7 Aug 82 |
| 11.45 | Sonia Lannaman | 1 Sep 72 |
| 11.45 | Simmone Jacobs | 6 Jul 84 |
| 11.52 | Katharine Merry | 16 Sep 92 |
| 11.53 | Marcia Richardson | 21 Jul 91 |
| 11.54 | Wendy Clarke | 8 Jun 75 |
| 11.59 | Heather Hunte | 9 Sep 77 |
| 11.59 | Stephanie Douglas | 23 Jul 88 |
| 11.59 | Rebecca Drummond | 8 Jul 95 |

**wind assisted**

| | | |
|---|---|---|
| 11.13 | Bev Kinch | 6 Jul 83 |
| 11.25 | Shirley Thomas | 20 Aug 81 |
| 11.26 | Simmone Jacobs | 27 May 84 |
| 11.40 | Katharine Merry | 3 Jul 93 |
| 11.43 | Dorothy Hyman | 2 Sep 60 |
| 11.45 | Stephanie Douglas | 25 Jun 88 |
| 11.47 | Helen Golden | 17 Jul 70 |
| 11.50 | Rebecca Drummond | 9 Jul 94 |

**hand timing**

| | | |
|---|---|---|
| 11.3 | Sonia Lannaman | 9 Jun 74 |
| 11.3 | Heather Hunte | 15 Jul 78 |
| 11.5 | Jennifer Smart | 1 Sep 61 |
| 11.5 | Anita Neil | 19 Jul 68 |

**wind assisted**

| | | |
|---|---|---|
| 11.2 | Wendy Clarke | 22 May 76 |
| 11.3 | Helen Golden | 30 May 70 |
| 11.3 | Linsey Macdonald | 3 May 80 |
| 11.4 | Anita Neil | 30 Jun 68 |
| 11.4 | Helen Barnett | 16 May 76 |
| 11.4 | Jane Parry | 5 Jul 80 |

### 200 METRES

| | | |
|---|---|---|
| 22.70 A | Kathy Smallwood | 12 Sep 79 |
| 23.10 | Diane Smith | 11 Aug 90 |
| 23.20 | Katharine Merry | 13 Jun 93 |
| 23.23 | Sonia Lannaman | 25 Aug 75 |
| 23.24 | Sandra Whittaker | 12 Jun 82 |
| 23.28 | Simmone Jacobs | 28 Aug 83 |
| 23.33 | Linsey Macdonald | 9 Jun 82 |
| 23.35 | Donna Murray | 26 May 74 |
| 23.42 | Deborah Bunn | 17 Jun 78 |
| 23.46 | Shirley Thomas | 31 May 82 |

**wind assisted**

| | | |
|---|---|---|
| 23.01 | Simmone Jacobs | 28 May 84 |
| 23.11 | Linsey Macdonald | 5 Jul 80 |
| 23.16 | Donna Murray | 27 Jul 74 |
| 23.42 | Helen Golden | 22 Jul 70 |

**hand timing**

| | | |
|---|---|---|
| 23.1 | Sonia Lannaman | 7 Jun 75 |
| 23.3 | Donna Murray | 9 Jun 74 |
| 23.3 | Sharon Colyear | 30 Jun 74 |
| 23.3 | Linsey Macdonald | 8 May 82 |
| 23.4 | Helen Barnett | 17 Jul 76 |

**wind assisted**

| | | |
|---|---|---|
| 22.9 | Donna Murray | 14 Jul 74 |
| 23.2 | Deborah Bunn | 2 Jul 78 |
| 23.3 | Angela Bridgeman | 15 Aug 82 |

### 400 METRES

| | | |
|---|---|---|
| 51.16 | Linsey Macdonald | 15 Jun 80 |
| 51.77 | Donna Murray | 30 Jul 74 |
| 52.54 | Donna Fraser | 10 Aug 91 |
| 52.65 | Jane Parry | 11 Jun 83 |
| 52.80 | Sian Morris | 18 Jun 83 |
| 52.98 | Karen Williams | 6 Aug 78 |
| 52.99 | Angela Bridgeman | 24 Jul 82 |
| 53.01 i | Marilyn Neufville | 14 Mar 70 |
| 53.08 | Loreen Hall | 29 Jul 84 |
| 53.14 | Michelle Probert | 28 Jul 79 |

**hand timing**

| | | |
|---|---|---|
| 52.6 | Marilyn Neufville | 20 Jun 70 |
| 52.8 | Lillian Board | 9 Jul 67 |
| 52.9 | Verona Bernard | 15 Sep 72 |

## 800 METRES

| | | |
|---|---|---|
| 2:01.11 | Lynne MacDougall | 18 Aug 84 |
| 2:01.66 | Lorraine Baker | 26 Jun 82 |
| 2:02.00 | Diane Edwards | 14 Sep 85 |
| 2:02.0 | Jo White | 13 Aug 77 |
| 2:02.18 | Lynne Robinson | 18 Jul 86 |
| 2:02.8 a | Lesley Kiernan | 2 Sep 74 |
| 2:02.88 i | Kirsty McDermott | 22 Feb 81 |
| 2:04.01 | | 29 Jul 81 |
| 2:03.11 | Janet Prictoe | 19 Aug 78 |
| 2:03.18 | Paula Newnham | 17 Jun 78 |
| 2:03.53 | Christine McMeekin | 25 Aug 75 |

## 1500 METRES

| | | |
|---|---|---|
| 3:59.96 | Zola Budd | 30 Aug 85 |
| 4:05.96 | Lynne MacDougall | 20 Aug 84 |
| 4:11.12 | Bridget Smyth | 26 May 85 |
| 4:13.40 | Wendy Smith | 19 Aug 78 |
| 4:14.40 | Janet Lawrence | 20 Aug 77 |
| 4:14.50 | Wendy Wright | 20 Jun 87 |
| 4:14.56 | Andrea Whitcombe | 22 Aug 90 |
| 4:14.58 | Ruth Smeeth | 16 Jul 78 |
| 4:14.73 | Mary Stewart | 2 Feb 74 |
| 4:15.1 | Yvonne Murray | 18 Jul 82 |

## 3000 METRES

| | | |
|---|---|---|
| 8:28.83 | Zola Budd | 7 Sep 85 |
| 8:51.78 | Paula Radcliffe | 20 Sep 92 |
| 9:03.35 | Philippa Mason | 19 Jul 86 |
| 9:04.14 | Yvonne Murray | 28 May 83 |
| 9:06.16 | Helen Titterington | 19 Jun 88 |
| 9:07.02 | Carol Haigh | 24 Jun 85 |
| 9:09.14 | Lisa York | 19 Jul 89 |
| 9:10.9 | Julie Holland | 7 Apr 84 |
| 9:12.28 | Hayley Haining | 20 Jul 91 |
| 9:12.97 | Bernadette Madigan | 30 Jun 79 |

## 100 METRES HURDLES

| | | |
|---|---|---|
| 13.25 | Diane Allahgreen | 21 Jul 94 |
| 13.30 | Sally Gunnell | 16 Jun 84 |
| 13.32 | Keri Maddox | 21 Jul 91 |
| 13.45 | Natasha Danvers | 6 Aug 95 |
| 13.46 | Nathalie Byer | 26 Aug 83 |
| 13.47 | Samantha Baker | 30 Jun 91 |
| 13.49 | Angela Thorp | 30 Jun 91 |
| 13.50 | Lesley-Ann Skeete | 6 Jun 86 |
| 13.56 | Wendy McDonnell | 3 Jun 79 |
| 13.57 | Bethan Edwards | 29 Aug 92 |

**wind assisted**

| | | |
|---|---|---|
| 13.24 | Lesley-Ann Skeete | 7 Jun 86 |
| 13.39 | Lauraine Cameron | 1 Jul 90 |
| 13.45 | Louise Fraser | 30 Jul 89 |
| 13.45 | Samantha Baker | 30 Jun 91 |
| 13.46 | Wendy McDonnell | 30 Jun 79 |

**hand timing**

| | | |
|---|---|---|
| 13.5 | Christine Perera | 19 Jul 68 |

**wind assisted**

| | | |
|---|---|---|
| 13.1 | Sally Gunnell | 7 Jul 84 |
| 13.3 | Keri Maddox | 14 Jul 90 |

## 400 METRES HURDLES

| | | |
|---|---|---|
| 58.02 | Vyvyan Rhodes | 28 Jun 92 |
| 58.37 | Alyson Evans | 1 Sep 85 |
| 58.68 | Kay Simpson | 15 Jul 83 |
| 58.76 | Simone Gandy | 28 May 84 |
| 59.00 | Diane Heath | 19 Jul 75 |
| 59.01 | Sara Elson | 24 Aug 89 |
| 59.04 | Allison Curbishley | 31 Jul 93 |
| 59.12 | Tracy Allen | 29 Jul 89 |
| 59.13 | Sue Morley | 12 Aug 79 |
| 59.52 | Deborah Church | 25 Jul 81 |

**hand timing**

| | | |
|---|---|---|
| 58.3 | Simone Gandy | 14 Jul 84 |
| 58.7 | Sara Elson | 18 Jun 89 |
| 59.0 | Tracy Allen | 9 Jul 88 |
| 59.3 | Michelle Cooney | 13 Jul 85 |
| 59.4 | Diane Wade | 21 Jul 79 |

## HIGH JUMP

| | | |
|---|---|---|
| 1.91 | Lea Haggett | 2 Jun 91 |
| 1.90 | Jo Jennings | 29 Sep 88 |
| 1.89 | Debbie Marti | 2 Jun 84 |
| 1.88 | Jayne Barnetson | 3 Aug 85 |
| 1.87 | Louise Manning | 6 May 84 |
| 1.87 | Michelle Dunkley | 7 Jul 95 |
| 1.87 | Rachael Forrest | 7 Jul 95 |
| 1.86 | Barbara Simmonds | 9 Sep 79 |
| 1.86 | Claire Summerfield | 7 Aug 82 |
| 1.86 | Michele Wheeler | 31 May 87 |

## POLE VAULT

| | | |
|---|---|---|
| 3.50 | Rhian Clarke | 20 Jul 95 |
| 3.45 | Clare Ridgley | 28 Aug 95 |
| 3.10 | Dawn-Alice Wright | 10 Jul 94 |
| 3.10 | Leanne Mellor | 21 Aug 94 |
| 3.05 | Fiona Harrison | 19 Jul 95 |
| 3.00 | Katherine Horner | 25 Mar 95 |
| 2.90 i | Elizabeth Hughes | 24 Feb 95 |
| 2.90 | Becky Ridgley | 29 Jul 95 |
| 2.90 | Rebacca Roles | 9 Sep 95 |

## LONG JUMP

| | | |
|---|---|---|
| 6.90 | Beverly Kinch | 14 Aug 83 |
| 6.82 | Fiona May | 30 Jul 88 |
| 6.68 | Sue Hearnshaw | 22 Sep 79 |
| 6.63 | Yinka Idowu | 21 May 89 |
| 6.55 | Joyce Oladapo | 30 Jul 83 |
| 6.52 | Georgina Oladapo | 16 Jun 84 |
| 6.47 | Joanne Wise | 30 Jul 88 |
| 6.45 | Margaret Cheetham | 18 Aug 84 |
| 6.43 | Moira Walls | 18 Sep 70 |
| 6.43 | Myra Nimmo | 27 May 73 |

**wind assisted**

| | | |
|---|---|---|
| 6.93 | Beverly Kinch | 14 Aug 83 |
| 6.88 | Fiona May | 30 Jul 88 |
| 6.71 | Yinka Idowu | 15 Jun 91 |
| 6.69 | Joanne Wise | 30 Jul 88 |
| 6.49 | Margaret Cheetham | 4 Sep 83 |

## TRIPLE JUMP

| | | |
|---|---|---|
| 13.05 | Michelle Griffith | 16 Jun 90 |
| 12.43 | Shani Anderson | 26 Jun 93 |
| 12.42 | Elizabeth Gibbens | 2 Jul 95 |
| 12.27 | Lorna Turner | 25 May 91 |
| 12.22 | Mary Bignal | 18 Jun 59 |
| 12.14 | Jayne Ludlow | 21 May 94 |
| 12.10 | Jane Falconer | 29 Aug 93 |
| 12.10 | Pamela Anderson | 2 Jul 95 |
| 11.91 | Lisa Brown | 30 Jul 95 |
| 11.84 | Jayne McCoy | 7 Sep 91 |

**wind assisted**

| | | |
|---|---|---|
| 12.48 | Lorna Turner | 30 Jun 91 |
| 12.44 | Shani Anderson | 9 Jul 94 |
| 12.37 | Jane Falconer | 29 Aug 93 |
| 11.96 | Lisa Brown | 24 Jun 95 |
| 11.93 | Jessie Aru | 15 May 93 |
| 11.90 | Katie Evans | 25 May 91 |

## SHOT

| | | |
|---|---|---|
| 17.10 | Myrtle Augee | 16 Jun 84 |
| 16.24 i | Judith Oakes | 26 Feb 77 |
| 16.05 | | 26 Aug 77 |
| 15.72 i | Alison Grey | 29 Feb 92 |
| 15.26 | | 13 Jul 91 |
| 15.60 i | Justine Buttle | 27 Feb 88 |
| 15.45 | | 25 Aug 88 |
| 15.48 | Mary Anderson | 8 Sep 85 |
| 15.45 | Susan King | 27 Mar 83 |
| 14.75 i | Cynthia Gregory | 12 Dec 81 |
| 14.70 | | 29 Aug 81 |
| 14.66 i | Terri Salt | 7 Jan 84 |
| 14.59 | Dawn Grazette | 19 May 91 |
| 14.54 | Carol Cooksley | 9 Jul 88 |
| 14.54 i | Jayne Berry | 18 Mar 89 |

## DISCUS

| | | |
|---|---|---|
| 54.78 | Lynda Whiteley | 4 Oct 82 |
| 53.10 | Kathryn Farr | 19 Jul 86 |
| 52.58 | Emma Merry | 22 Aug 93 |
| 51.82 | Catherine Bradley | 20 Jul 85 |
| 51.24 | Jane Aucott | 11 Jun 86 |
| 51.12 | Janette Picton | 6 Jun 82 |
| 51.04dh | Fiona Condon | 7 Jul 79 |
| 50.44 | Karen Pugh | 8 Jul 83 |
| 50.34 | Angela Sellers | 27 Jul 86 |
| 50.30 | Julia Avis | 19 Sep 82 |
| 49.74 | Shelley Drew | 10 May 92 |

## HAMMER

| | | |
|---|---|---|
| 55.44 | Lyn Sprules | 19 Jul 94 |
| 53.34 | Diana Holden | 13 Aug 94 |
| 51.62 | Julia Lavender | 15 May 94 |
| 49.48 | Sam Burns-Salmond | 13 Aug 95 |
| 46.98 | Helen Arnold | 29 Jul 95 |

## JAVELIN

| | | |
|---|---|---|
| 60.14 | Fatima Whitbread | 7 May 80 |
| 59.40 | Karen Hough | 28 Aug 86 |
| 59.36 | Kirsty Morrison | 4 Sep 93 |
| 57.84 | Amanda Liverton | 3 Jun 90 |
| 57.82 | Shelley Holroyd | 9 Aug 92 |
| 57.80 | Julie Abel | 5 Jun 83 |
| 56.96 | Nicola Emblem | 1 Feb 90 |
| 55.72 | Karen Martin | 25 Jul 92 |
| 55.38 | Catherine Garside | 19 May 84 |
| 55.04 | Tessa Sanderson | 26 Sep 74 |

## HEPTATHLON (1985 Tables)

| | | |
|---|---|---|
| 5833 | Joanne Mulliner | 11 Aug 85 |
| 5642 | Sarah Rowe | 23 Aug 81 |
| 5496 | Yinka Idowu | 3 Sep 89 |
| 5493 | Sally Gunnell | 28 May 84 |
| 5484 | Denise Lewis | 30 Jun 91 |
| 5459 | Jennifer Kelly | 30 Jul 88 |
| 5391 w | Jackie Kinsella | 22 Jun 86 |
| 5331 | | 19 Jul 86 |
| 5377 | Uju Efobi | 18 Jul 93 |
| 5299 | Emma Beales | 26 Aug 90 |
| 5273 w | Debbie Marti | 11 Aug 85 |
| 5246 | Val Walsh | 7 Aug 83 |

## 3000 METRES TRACK WALK

| | | |
|---|---|---|
| 13:03.4 | Vicky Lupton | 18 May 91 |
| 13:47.0 | Julie Drake | 5 Jul 88 |
| 13:53.0 e+ | Lisa Langford | 23 Aug 85 |
| 14:04.1 | Susan Ashforth | 19 May 85 |
| 14:10.2 | Carol Tyson | 5 Sep 76 |
| 14:11.8 | Carolyn Brown | 18 Sep 92 |
| 14:12.0 | Jill Barrett | 11 Jun 83 |
| 14:12.8 | Nicola Jackson | 5 May 84 |
| 14:18.0 | Gill Edgar | 28 May 81 |

## 5000 METRES TRACK WALK

| | | |
|---|---|---|
| 22:36.81 | Vicky Lupton | 15 Jun 91 |
| 23:31.67 | Lisa Langford | 23 Aug 85 |
| 23:55.27 | Susan Ashforth | 25 May 85 |
| 23:56.9 | Julie Drake | 24 May 88 |
| 24:02.15 | Nicola Jackson | 27 May 84 |
| 24:08.4 | Jill Barrett | 28 May 83 |
| 24:19.0 | Victoria Lawrence | 13 Jun 87 |
| 24:24.31 | Andrea Crofts | 4 Jun 89 |
| 24:27.73 | Carolyn Brown | 29 Aug 92 |

**Road** - *where superior to track time*

| | | |
|---|---|---|
| 23:05 | Lisa Langford | 2 Nov 85 |
| 23:18 | Julie Drake | 27 Feb 88 |
| 23:35 | Lisa Simpson | 31 Oct 87 |

## 10,000 METRES TRACK WALK

| | | |
|---|---|---|
| 47:04.0 | Vicky Lupton | 30 Mar 91 |
| 48:34.0 | Lisa Langford | 15 Mar 86 |
| 49:48.7 | Julie Drake | 7 Feb 88 |
| 50:11.2 sh | Jill Barrett | 19 Mar 83 |
| 50:25.0mx | Lisa Simpson | 1 Apr 87 |
| 51:00.0 | Karen Nipper | 21 Feb 81 |
| 51:31.2 | Helen Ringshaw | 17 Mar 84 |
| 52:09.0 | Elaine Cox | 8 Apr 78 |
| 52:10.4 | Sarah Brown | 20 Mar 82 |

**Road** - *where superior to track time*

| | | |
|---|---|---|
| 49:10 | Victoria Lawrence | 14 Mar 87 |
| 49:14 | Carolyn Brown | 29 Mar 92 |
| 49:26 | Julie Drake | 21 May 88 |

Note: LJ, Hep. Although Idowu competed for UK
Juniors, she was a Nigerian citizen at the time.

## UNDER 17

### 100 METRES

| | | |
|---|---|---|
| 11.45 | Sonia Lannaman | 1 Sep 72 |
| 11.59 | Simmone Jacobs | 25 Aug 83 |
| 11.60 | Katharine Merry | 28 Jul 90 |
| 11.61 | Diane Smith | 9 Aug 90 |
| 11.65 | Linsey Macdonald | 22 May 79 |
| 11.69 | Jane Parry | 6 Jun 81 |
| 11.73 | Etta Kessebeh | 20 Aug 81 |
| 11.77 | Hayley Clements | 26 Jul 85 |
| 11.78 | Tatum Nelson | 16 May 94 |
| 11.79 | Janet Smith | 26 Jul 85 |

**wind assisted**

| | | |
|---|---|---|
| 11.50 | Rebecca Drummond | 9 Jul 94 |
| 11.61 | Linsey Macdonald | 16 Jun 79 |
| 11.62 | Kathleen Lithgow | 25 Jun 88 |
| 11.63 | Sharon Dolby | 10 Aug 85 |

**hand timing**

| | | |
|---|---|---|
| 11.6 | Denise Ramsden | 19 Jul 68 |
| 11.6 | Linsey Macdonald | 25 May 80 |
| 11.6 | Jane Parry | 2 Aug 80 |

**wind assisted**

| | | |
|---|---|---|
| 11.3 | Linsey Macdonald | 3 May 80 |
| 11.4 | Sonia Lannaman | 3 Jun 72 |
| 11.4 | Jane Parry | 5 Jul 80 |
| 11.5 | Sharon Dolby | 20 Jul 85 |

### 200 METRES

| | | |
|---|---|---|
| 23.10 | Diane Smith | 11 Aug 90 |
| 23.28 | Simmone Jacobs | 28 Aug 83 |
| 23.42 | Deborah Bunn | 17 Jun 78 |
| 23.43 | Linsey Macdonald | 20 Aug 80 |
| 23.50 | Katharine Merry | 20 Jul 91 |
| 23.60 | Michelle Probert | 12 Sep 76 |
| 23.66 | Jane Parry | 15 Jun 80 |
| 23.69 | Donna Fraser | 1 Jul 89 |
| 23.79 | Sharon Colyear | 5 Sep 71 |
| 23.90 | Angela Bridgeman | 20 Aug 80 |

**wind assisted**

| | | |
|---|---|---|
| 23.11 | Linsey Macdonald | 5 Jul 80 |
| 23.41 | Katharine Merry | 15 Jun 91 |
| 23.64 | Jane Parry | 5 Jul 80 |
| 23.70 | Sonia Lannaman | 16 Jun 72 |

**hand timing** (* 220 yards less 0.1)

| | | |
|---|---|---|
| 23.8 * | Marilyn Neufville | 27 Jul 78 |
| 23.8 | Janet Smith | 1 Jun 85 |

**wind assisted**

| | | |
|---|---|---|
| 23.2 | Deborah Bunn | 2 Jul 78 |
| 23.4 | Hayley Clements | 10 Aug 85 |

### 300 METRES

| | | |
|---|---|---|
| 36.46 | Linsey Macdonald | 13 Jul 80 |
| 38.2 | Marilyn Neufville | 6 Sep 69 |
| 38.21 | Lesley Owusu | 27 Aug 95 |
| 38.6 | Fay Nixon | 10 Sep 77 |
| 38.7 | Katharine Merry | 1 Sep 91 |
| 38.95 | Maria Bolsover | 8 Jul 95 |
| 39.2 | Allison Curbishley | 30 Aug 92 |
| 39.3 | Sinead Dudgeon | 13 Sep 92 |
| 39.40 | Sophie Cocker | 15 Aug 92 |
| 39.42 | Alison Shingler | 26 May 91 |

### 400 METRES

| | | |
|---|---|---|
| 51.16 | Linsey Macdonald | 15 Jun 80 |
| 53.08 | Loreen Hall | 29 Jul 84 |
| 53.75 | Linda Keough | 8 Aug 80 |
| 54.01 | Angela Bridgeman | 16 Aug 80 |
| 54.25 | Emma Langston | 19 Jun 88 |
| 54.57 | Lesley Owusu | 9 Sep 95 |
| 54.84 | Carol Candlish | 25 Jul 81 |
| 54.86 | Ruth Kennedy | 20 Jul 73 |

**hand timing**

| | | |
|---|---|---|
| 53.7 | Linda Keough | 2 Aug 80 |
| 54.2 o | Marilyn Neufville | 9 Oct 69 |
| 54.4 | | 23 Aug 69 |
| 54.6 | Evelyn McMeekin | 15 Sep 73 |
| 54.6 | Ruth Kennedy | 19 Sep 73 |

### 800 METRES

| | | |
|---|---|---|
| 2:02.0 | Jo White | 13 Aug 77 |
| 2:03.66 | Lesley Kiernan | 26 Aug 73 |
| 2:03.72 | Lorraine Baker | 15 Jun 80 |
| 2:04.85 | Louise Parker | 28 Jul 79 |
| 2:06.5 | Emma Langston | 10 Aug 88 |
| 2:06.53 | Lynne Robinson | 6 Jul 85 |
| 2:06.8 | Jayne Heathcote | 31 May 87 |
| 2:07.0 | Bridget Smyth | 27 Jun 84 |
| 2:07.3 | Amanda Alford | 7 May 80 |
| 2:07.53 | Sandra Arthurton | 17 Sep 78 |

### 1500 METRES

| | | |
|---|---|---|
| 4:15.20 | Bridget Smyth | 29 Jul 84 |
| 4:15.55 | Sandra Arthurton | 29 Jul 78 |
| 4:16.8 | Jo White | 30 Jul 77 |
| 4:21.88 | Jeina Mitchell | 20 Jul 91 |
| 4:22.25 | Karen Hughes | 24 May 81 |
| 4:22.25 | Clare Keller | 7 Jul 85 |
| 4:22.51 | Elise Lyon | 31 Jul 82 |
| 4:23.11 | Gillian Stacey | 2 Sep 89 |
| 4:23.25 | Denise Kiernan | 20 Aug 77 |
| 4:23.37 | Dawn Hargan | 14 Jun 87 |

### 3000 METRES

| | | |
|---|---|---|
| 9:26.4 o | Jo White | 7 Dec 77 |
| 9:28.9 | Bridget Smyth | 21 Apr 84 |
| 9:30.0 | Yvonne Murray | 4 Jul 81 |
| 9:32.20 | Nicola Slater | 28 Aug 93 |
| 9:33.1 | Alison Hollington | 6 Jun 81 |
| 9:34.5 | Louise Watson | 28 Aug 88 |
| 9:34.79 | Helen Titterington | 28 Jun 86 |
| 9:36.8 | Karen Hughes | 4 Jun 80 |
| 9:38.1 | Elise Lyon | 12 Sep 81 |
| 9:38.2 | Amanda Alford | 7 Mar 79 |

### 80 METRES HURDLES

| | | |
|---|---|---|
| 11.07 | Amanda Parker | 7 Jun 86 |
| 11.10 Ao | Sue Scott | 15 Oct 68 |
| 11.12 | Samantha Farquharson | 7 Jun 86 |
| 11.13 | Claire St John | 2 Jun 79 |
| 11.16 | Ann Girvan | 4 Jul 81 |
| 11.16 | Stephanie Douglas | 27 Jul 85 |
| 11.20 | Ann Wilson | 11 Aug 66 |
| 11.20 | Louise Brunning | 25 Jul 87 |
| 11.23 | Rachel Rigby | 25 Jul 87 |
| 11.25 | Louise Fraser | 25 Jul 87 |

**wind assisted**

| | | |
|---|---|---|
| 11.03 | Wendy McDonnell | 20 Aug 77 |
| 11.11 | Liz Fairs | 9 Jul 94 |

**hand timing**

| | | |
|---|---|---|
| 11.0 | Wendy McDonnell | 2 Jul 77 |
| 11.1 | Ann Wilson | 18 Sep 66 |
| 11.1 | Angela Thorp | 7 Jul 89 |
| 11.1 | Liz Fairs | 29 May 93 |

**wind assisted**

| | | |
|---|---|---|
| 10.9 | Ann Wilson | 16 Jul 66 |
| 10.9 | Wendy McDonnell | 9 Jul 77 |
| 10.9 | Samantha Farquharson | 20 Jul 85 |
| 11.0 | Stephanie Douglas | 20 Jul 85 |

## 100 METRES HURDLES (2'9")

| | | |
|---|---|---|
| 13.73 | Ann Girvan | 7 Aug 82 |
| 13.88 | Natasha Danvers | 28 Aug 93 |
| 13.98 | Claire St John | 11 Aug 79 |
| 14.04 | Lauraine Cameron | 7 Aug 88 |
| 14.24 | Pamela St Ange | 2 Oct 82 |
| 14.24 | Angela Thorp | 9 Jul 89 |
| 14.39 | Michelle Stone | 18 Aug 84 |
| 14.40 | Vicki Jamison | 22 Jun 93 |
| 14.51 | Susan Jones | 29 May 94 |
| 14.52 | Louise Brunning | 26 Jun 88 |

**wind assisted**

| | | |
|---|---|---|
| 13.67 | Ann Girvan | 4 Jul 82 |
| 13.76 | Natasha Danvers | 27 Aug 94 |
| 14.10 | Sue Mapstone | 25 Aug 73 |

**hand timing**

| | | |
|---|---|---|
| 13.7 | Ann Girvan | 29 Aug 81 |
| 14.1 | Pamela St Ange | 7 Aug 83 |

**wind assisted**

| | | |
|---|---|---|
| 13.7 | Nathalie Byer | 4 Sep 82 |
| 13.9 | Angela Thorp | 9 Sep 89 |
| 14.1 | Heather Ross | 2 Jul 78 |

## 300 METRES HURDLES

| | | |
|---|---|---|
| 41.99 | Natasha Danvers | 10 Jul 93 |
| 42.67 | Vicki Jamison | 17 Jul 93 |
| 42.91 | Allison Curbishley | 18 Aug 91 |
| 43.03 | Valerie Theobalds | 13 Aug 89 |
| 43.06 | Claire Griffiths | 18 Aug 91 |
| 43.12 | Keri Maddox | 6 Aug 88 |
| 43.28 | Denise Bolton | 5 Sep 93 |
| 43.38 | Dextene McIntosh | 31 Jul 94 |
| 43.44 | Joanne Mersh | 13 Jul 91 |
| 43.53 | Catherine Murphy | 21 Jul 90 |

**hand timing**

| | | |
|---|---|---|
| 42.4 | Keri Maddox | 8 May 88 |
| 42.5 | Louise Brunning | 8 May 88 |
| 42.8 | Rachel Stafford | 8 Jul 89 |
| 42.8 | Vyvyan Rhodes | 8 Jul 89 |
| 42.9 | Valerie Theobalds | 17 Jun 89 |
| 43.1 | Patricia Byford | 17 Jun 89 |
| 43.1 | Charlotte Knowles | 8 Jul 89 |

## 400 METRES HURDLES

| | | |
|---|---|---|
| 60.87 | Karin Hendrickse | 31 Jul 82 |
| 61.02 | Claire Edwards | 8 Sep 91 |
| 61.04 | Allison Curbishley | 26 Jul 92 |
| 61.10 | Vicki Jamison | 26 Jun 93 |
| 61.27 | Kay Simpson | 25 Jul 81 |
| 61.32 | Debra Duncan | 27 Jul 85 |
| 61.33 | Denise Kiernan | 17 Jul 77 |
| 61.59 | Donna Pert | 31 Jul 82 |

**hand timing**

| | | |
|---|---|---|
| 59.7 | Keri Maddox | 9 Jul 88 |
| 60.8 | Jayne Puckeridge | 9 Jul 88 |

## HIGH JUMP

| | | |
|---|---|---|
| 1.89 | Debbie Marti | 2 Jun 84 |
| 1.85 | Louise Manning | 11 Sep 82 |
| 1.85 | Jayne Barnetson | 21 Jul 84 |
| 1.84 | Ursula Fay | 6 Aug 83 |
| 1.83 | Jo Jennings | 26 Jul 85 |
| 1.83 | Tracey Clarke | 2 Aug 87 |
| 1.82 | Elaine Hickey | 9 Aug 80 |
| 1.82 | Kerry Roberts | 16 Jul 83 |
| 1.82 | Susan Jones | 20 May 94 |
| 1.81 | Barbara Simmonds | 22 Jul 78 |

## POLE VAULT

| | | |
|---|---|---|
| 3.44 | Clare Ridgley | 10 Sep 94 |
| 3.30 mx | Rhian Clarke | 4 Jul 93 |
| 3.25 | | 11 Sep 93 |
| 2.95 | Dawn-Alice Wright | 5 Jul 92 |
| 2.90 | Becky Ridgley | 29 Jul 95 |
| 2.90 | Rebecca Roles | 9 Sep 95 |
| 2.85 | Tracey Bloomfield | 15 Jul 95 |
| 2.80 | Kirsty Armstrong | 12 Jul 95 |

## LONG JUMP

| | | |
|---|---|---|
| 6.45 | Margaret Cheetham | 18 Aug 84 |
| 6.32 | Georgina Oladapo | 23 Jul 83 |
| 6.27 | Fiona May | 14 Jun 86 |
| 6.26 | Joanne Wise | 31 May 87 |
| 6.25 | Sue Hearnshaw | 9 Jul 77 |
| 6.23 | Sue Scott | 27 Jul 68 |
| 6.22 | Ann Wilson | 18 Sep 66 |
| 6.22 | Michelle Stone | 28 Apr 84 |
| 6.18 | Sheila Parkin | 4 Aug 62 |
| 6.14 | Bev Kinch | 26 Jul 80 |

**wind assisted**

| | | |
|---|---|---|
| 6.49 | Margaret Cheetham | 23 Sep 84 |
| 6.47 | Fiona May | 28 Jun 86 |
| 6.41 | Sue Hearnshaw | 9 Jul 77 |
| 6.33 | Sue Scott | 27 Aug 68 |
| 6.28 | Bev Kinch | 6 Sep 80 |

## TRIPLE JUMP

| | | |
|---|---|---|
| 12.14 | Jayne Ludlow | 21 May 94 |
| 11.81db | Fiona Hunter | 24 Jun 95 |
| 11.44 | Donna Quirie | 8 Aug 93 |
| 11.41 | Shani Anderson | 8 Sep 91 |
| 11.36 | Rebecca White | 10 May 95 |
| 11.35 | Kathryn MacKenzie | 24 Jul 93 |
| 11.28 | Julia Johnson | 30 Jul 95 |
| 11.25 i | Jessica Aru | 24 Mar 91 |
| 11.24 | Pamela Anderson | 25 Aug 93 |

**wind assisted**

| | | |
|---|---|---|
| 11.50 | Pamela Anderson | 8 Aug 93 |
| 11.45 | Nicky Ladrowski | 13 Aug 95 |

## SHOT

| | | |
|---|---|---|
| 15.08 | Justine Buttle | 16 Aug 86 |
| 14.40 | Susan King | 17 May 81 |
| 14.20 io | Terri Salt | 10 Dec 83 |
| 13.77 | | 17 Sep 83 |
| 14.04 | Mary Anderson | 6 May 84 |
| 13.94 | Jennifer Bloss | 13 May 67 |
| 13.89 i | Alison Grey | 11 Feb 89 |
| 13.83 | | 20 May 89 |
| 13.68 i | Philippa Roles | 26 Feb 94 |
| 13.65 | | 6 Aug 94 |
| 13.64 | Cynthia Gregory | 20 Aug 80 |
| 13.58 i | Natalie Hart | 19 Mar 88 |
| 13.49 | Lana Newton | 11 Jul 75 |

## DISCUS

| | | |
|---|---|---|
| 51.60 | Emma Merry | 27 Jun 90 |
| 49.56 | Jane Aucott | 3 Aug 85 |
| 48.88 | Philippa Roles | 13 Aug 94 |
| 48.84 | Karen Pugh | 7 Aug 82 |
| 47.58 | Catherine Bradley | 14 Jul 84 |
| 47.54 | Lauren Keightley | 12 Jul 95 |
| 47.50 | Sarah Symonds | 16 May 90 |
| 47.24 | Amanda Barnes | 3 Aug 85 |
| 46.76 | Fiona Condon | 6 Aug 77 |
| 46.34 | Janette Picton | 26 Mar 79 |

## HAMMER

| | | |
|---|---|---|
| 47.68 | Diana Holden | 31 Jul 91 |
| 46.98 | Helen Arnold | 29 Jul 95 |
| 45.58 | Julie Lavender | 13 Sep 92 |
| 44.70 | Rachel Beverley | 15 Jul 95 |
| 43.64 | Catherine Garden | 30 Apr 95 |

## UNDER 15

## 100 METRES

| | | |
|---|---|---|
| 11.67 | Katharine Merry | 13 May 89 |
| 11.86 | Hayley Clements | 2 Jul 83 |
| 11.89 | Joanne Gardner | 20 Aug 77 |
| 11.92 | Jane Parry | 20 Aug 77 |
| 11.95 | Tatum Nelson | 7 Aug 93 |
| 12.00 | Diane Smith | 15 Sep 89 |
| 12.02 | Renate Chinyou | 28 Aug 88 |
| 12.02 | Sarah Wilhelmy | 28 May 94 |
| 12.07 | Margaret Cheetham | 29 Jul 83 |
| 12.09 | Libby Alder | 8 Jul 95 |

**wind assisted**

| | | |
|---|---|---|
| 11.47 | Katharine Merry | 17 Jun 89 |
| 11.67 | Tatum Nelson | 10 Jul 93 |
| 11.78 | Jane Parry | 8 Aug 78 |
| 11.84 | Janis Walsh | 26 May 74 |
| 11.88 | Sarah Claxton | 9 Jul 94 |
| 11.97 | Yvonne Anderson | 16 Jun 79 |
| 11.97 | Renate Chinyou | 20 Aug 88 |
| 12.07 | Leanne Eastwood | 26 May 91 |

**hand timing**

| | | |
|---|---|---|
| 11.7 dt | Sonia Lannaman | 14 May 70 |
| 11.7 dt | Helen Barnett | 20 Sep 72 |
| 11.8 | Janis Walsh | 7 Jul 74 |
| 11.8 | Joanne Gardner | 2 Jul 77 |

## JAVELIN

| | | |
|---|---|---|
| 56.02 | Mandy Liverton | 11 Jun 89 |
| 53.42 | Karen Hough | 15 Jul 84 |
| 53.22 | Kirsty Morrison | 15 Aug 92 |
| 51.50 | Shelley Holroyd | 22 Jul 89 |
| 50.82 | Nicola Emblem | 19 Jun 87 |
| 50.04 | Kim Lisbon | 19 Feb 84 |
| 50.02 | Angelique Pullen | 31 Aug 85 |
| 49.24 | Jacqui Barclay | 7 Aug 82 |
| 48.34 | Fatima Whitbread | 29 Aug 77 |
| 48.00 | Claire Taylor | 17 Jun 92 |

## HEPTATHLON (1985 Tables) with 80mH

| | | |
|---|---|---|
| 5037 | Michelle Stone | 1 Jul 84 |
| 5031 | Yinka Idowu | 18 Sep 88 |
| 4915 | Denise Lewis | 24 Jul 88 |
| 4861 | Clover Wynter-Pink | 26 Jun 94 |
| 4841 | Rebecca Lewis | 18 Sep 94 |
| 4839 | Jackie Kinsella | 21 Jul 85 |
| 4794 | Claire Phythian | 22 May 88 |
| 4742 | Julie Hollman | 26 Sep 93 |
| 4673 | Denise Bolton | 19 Sep 93 |
| 4653 | Anne Hollman | 6 May 90 |

## 5000 METRES TRACK WALK

| | | |
|---|---|---|
| 23:55.27 | Susan Ashforth | 25 May 85 |
| 24:22.3 | Victoria Lawrence | 21 Jun 86 |
| 24:34.6 | Tracey Devlin | 17 Sep 89 |
| 24:45.4 | Karen Eden | 9 Jul 78 |
| 24:57.5 | Angela Hodd | 24 Jun 86 |
| 25:08.0 o | Julie Drake | 22 Dec 85 |
| 25:13.8 | Carla Jarvis | 2 Jun 91 |
| 25:15.3 | Vicky Lupton | 3 Sep 88 |
| 25:18.5 | Jill Barrett | 16 Aug 80 |

**wind assisted**

| | | |
|---|---|---|
| 11.7 | Diane Smith | 30 Jul 89 |
| 11.8 | Sonia Lannaman | 30 May 70 |
| 11.8 | Deborah Bunn | 28 Jun 75 |
| 11.8 | Delmena Doyley | 6 Jul 79 |

## 200 METRES

| | | |
|---|---|---|
| 23.72 | Katharine Merry | 17 Jun 89 |
| 23.90 | Diane Smith | 3 Sep 89 |
| 24.05 | Jane Parry | 16 Jul 78 |
| 24.39 | Hayley Clements | 3 Jul 83 |
| 24.44 | Rachel Kay | 8 Jul 95 |
| 24.51 | Tatum Nelson | 8 Aug 93 |
| 24.54 | Sarah Wilhelmy | 31 Jul 94 |
| 24.58 | Simmone Jacobs | 25 Jul 81 |
| 24.58 | Donna Fraser | 22 Aug 87 |
| 24.59 | Janet Smith | 30 Jul 83 |

**wind assisted**

| | | |
|---|---|---|
| 23.54 | Katharine Merry | 30 Jul 89 |
| 23.99 | Sarah Wilhelmy | 9 Jul 94 |
| 24.35 | Tatum Nelson | 27 Jun 93 |

**hand timing**

| | | |
|---|---|---|
| 23.8 | Janis Walsh | 23 Jun 74 |

**wind assisted**

| | | |
|---|---|---|
| 23.6 | Jane Parry | 9 Jul 77 |
| 23.8 | Diane Smith | 9 Sep 89 |

## 800 METRES

| | | | |
|---|---|---|---|
| 2:06.5 | Rachel Hughes | 19 Jul | 82 |
| 2:08.7 | Emma Langston | 12 Jul | 86 |
| 2:09.58 | Sally Ludlam | 8 Jun | 75 |
| 2:09.6 | Isabel Linaker | 1 Aug | 90 |
| 2:09.77 | Lorraine Baker | 19 Aug | 78 |
| 2:09.80 | Hannah Curnock | 15 Aug | 92 |
| 2:10.1 | Lesley Kiernan | 9 Jul | 71 |
| 2:10.3 | Carol Pannell | 9 Jul | 71 |
| 2:10.6 | Christina Boxer | 10 Jul | 71 |
| 2:10.6 | Natalie Tait | 12 Jul | 86 |
| 2:10.66 | Amanda Pritchard | 15 Jul | 94 |

## 1500 METRES

| | | | |
|---|---|---|---|
| 4:23.45 | Isabel Linaker | 7 Jul | 90 |
| 4:27.9 | Joanne Davis | 9 Jul | 88 |
| 4:29.0 | Claire Allen | 8 Jul | 89 |
| 4:29.1 | Valerie Bothams | 16 Jul | 89 |
| 4:29.6 | Lynne MacDougall | 16 Jul | 79 |
| 4:29.9 | Heidi Hosking | 9 Jul | 88 |
| 4:30.4 | Claire Nicholson | 18 Jun | 87 |
| 4:31.12 | Karen Hughes | 31 Aug | 79 |
| 4:31.45 | Amanda Alford | 22 Jul | 78 |
| 4:31.6 | Michelle Lavercombe | 13 Jun | 81 |

## 75 METRES HURDLES

| | | | |
|---|---|---|---|
| 10.93 | Rachel Halstead-Peel | 27 Jul | 85 |
| 11.00 | Louise Fraser | 27 Jul | 85 |
| 11.01 | Nathalie Byer | 16 Aug | 80 |
| 11.08 | Nicola Hall | 29 May | 94 |
| 11.09 | Catherine Murphy | 6 Aug | 88 |
| 11.09 | Orla Bermingham | 25 Aug | 90 |
| 11.13 | Lydia Chadwick | 7 Jun | 86 |
| 11.13 | Naomi Hodge-Dallaway | 30 Jul | 95 |
| 11.14 | Serena Bailey | 30 Jul | 95 |
| 11.15 | Rachel Rigby | 27 Jul | 85 |

**wind assisted**

| | | | |
|---|---|---|---|
| 11.01 | Naomi Hodge-Dallaway | 8 Jul | 95 |
| 11.06 | Kate Forsyth | 10 Jul | 93 |

**hand timing**

| | | | |
|---|---|---|---|
| 11.0 | Wendy McDonnell | 31 Aug | 75 |
| 11.0 | Lydia Chadwick | 12 Jul | 86 |
| 11.0 | Nina Thompson | 4 Jul | 87 |

**wind assisted**

| | | | |
|---|---|---|---|
| 10.7 | Orla Bermingham | 14 Jul | 90 |
| 10.8 | Nathalie Byer | 12 Jul | 80 |
| 10.8 | Ann Girvan | 12 Jul | 80 |
| 10.9 | Lauraine Cameron | 16 Aug | 86 |
| 10.9 | Nina Thompson | 7 Jun | 87 |

## HIGH JUMP

| | | | |
|---|---|---|---|
| 1.83 | Ursula Fay | 5 Jun | 82 |
| 1.81 | Debbie Marti | 18 Sep | 82 |
| 1.81 | Lea Haggett | 6 Jun | 86 |
| 1.80 | Jo Jennings | 19 Aug | 84 |
| 1.79 i | Julia Charlton | 24 Feb | 80 |
| 1.78 | | 13 Jul | 80 |
| 1.78 | Claire Summerfield | 28 Jul | 79 |

| | | | |
|---|---|---|---|
| 1.75 | Anne Gilson | 2 Jun | 73 |
| 1.75 | Claire Smith (Nun) | 8 Aug | 82 |
| 1.75 io | Alison Purton | 12 Dec | 87 |
| 1.75 | Jane Falconer | 10 Jun | 89 |

## LONG JUMP

| | | | |
|---|---|---|---|
| 6.34 | Margaret Cheetham | 14 Aug | 83 |
| 6.30 | Fiona May | 7 Jul | 84 |
| 6.07 | Georgina Oladapo | 21 Jun | 81 |
| 5.98 | Sandy French | 22 Jul | 78 |
| 5.93 io | Sue Scott | 19 Nov | 66 |
| 5.88 | | 11 Aug | 66 |
| 5.93 | Jackie Harris | 10 Jul | 87 |
| 5.86 | Tammy McCammon | 18 Aug | 91 |
| 5.85 | Kim Hagger | 20 Aug | 76 |
| 5.81 | Yvonne Hallett | 24 Aug | 86 |
| 5.78 | Pamela St Ange | 15 Aug | 81 |

**wind assisted**

| | | | |
|---|---|---|---|
| 6.49 | Margaret Cheetham | 4 Sep | 83 |
| 6.05 | Katharine Merry | 18 Sep | 88 |
| 6.02 | Michelle Stone | 10 Jul | 82 |
| 5.99 | Sandy French | 8 Jul | 78 |
| 5.85 | Karen Glen | 8 Jul | 78 |

## SHOT (3.25kg)

| | | | |
|---|---|---|---|
| 14.27 | Susan King | 19 May | 79 |
| 13.69 | Gloria Achille | 21 Jun | 80 |
| 13.61 | Justine Buttle | 6 Aug | 84 |
| 13.50 io | Philippa Roles | 19 Dec | 92 |
| 13.45 io | Susan Coyne | 28 Oct | 82 |
| 13.43 io | Navdeep Dhaliwal | 19 Dec | 92 |
| 13.04 | | 16 May | 92 |
| 13.22 | Emily Steele | 23 Jul | 89 |
| 13.11 | Amy Wilson | 2 Sep | 95 |
| 13.08 | Ashley Morris | 11 Aug | 84 |
| 13.05 | Tracy Page | 21 Jun | 86 |

## DISCUS

| | | | |
|---|---|---|---|
| 44.12 | Philippa Roles | 30 Aug | 92 |
| 41.92 | Catherine Garden | 12 Sep | 93 |
| 40.92 | Sandra McDonald | 24 Jun | 78 |
| 40.84 | Natalie Kerr | 24 Jul | 94 |
| 40.44 | Catherine MacIntyre | 12 Sep | 82 |
| 40.34 | Natalie Hart | 23 Mar | 86 |
| 40.22 | Emma Merry | 27 Aug | 88 |
| 40.18 | Kelly Mellis | 17 Sep | 94 |
| 40.14 | Clare Tank | 29 Aug | 88 |
| 39.76 | Alix Gallagher | 6 Jun | 87 |

## JAVELIN

| | | | |
|---|---|---|---|
| 48.40 | Mandy Liverton | 31 Aug | 87 |
| 46.98 | Kirsty Morrison | 30 Jun | 90 |
| 43.16 | Shelley Holroyd | 27 Jun | 87 |
| 43.08 | Karen Hough | 4 Sep | 82 |
| 42.70 | Emily Steele | 23 Sep | 89 |
| 41.50 | Kelly Morgan | 9 Jul | 94 |
| 41.22 | Maxine Worsfold | 12 Jul | 80 |
| 41.06 | Heather Derbyshire | 15 Aug | 93 |
| 40.86 | Julie Hawkins | 28 Aug | 77 |
| 40.80 | Jenny Foster | 16 Aug | 92 |

## PENTATHLON (with 800m & 75m hdls)

| | | |
|---|---|---|
| 3518 | Katharine Merry | 18 Sep 88 |
| 3333 | Jackie Harris | 27 Jun 87 |
| 3296 | Claire Everett | 19 Sep 93 |
| 3225 | Amy Nuttall | 26 Jun 94 |
| 3216 | Sally Gunnell | 23 Aug 80 |
| 3213 | Julie Hollman | 22 Sep 91 |
| 3195 | Julia Charlton | 10 May 80 |
| 3193 | Samantha Foster | 26 Jun 94 |
| 3186 | Lauraine Cameron | 16 Aug 86 |
| 3175 | Linda Wong | 14 Sep 80 |

## UNDER 13

### 80 METRES

| | | |
|---|---|---|
| 10.2 | Jane Riley | 1 Jun 85 |
| 10.2 | Helen Seery | 20 May 89 |
| 10.3 | Katharine Merry | 6 Jun 87 |
| 10.3 | Emma Ania | 7 Sep 91 |
| 10.4 | Susan Briggs | 9 Sep 79 |
| 10.4 | Tatum Nelson | 1 Sep 91 |
| 10.5 | Claire Ransome | 1 Jun 85 |
| 10.5 | Lynsey Scammens | 18 Jun 89 |
| 10.5 | Sarah Wilhelmy | 12 Sep 92 |
| 10.5 | Ayeesha Charles | 12 Sep 92 |

### 100 METRES (y = 100 yards)

| | | |
|---|---|---|
| 11.92 | Jane Parry | 20 Aug 77 |
| 12.1 | Katharine Merry | 26 Sep 87 |
| 11.1y | Sonia Lannaman | 10 Aug 68 |
| 12.3 | Joanne Gardner | 24 Jun 75 |
| 12.3 | Deborah Bunn | 30 Aug 75 |
| 12.4 | Lorraine Broxup | 13 Jun 76 |
| 12.4 | Sarah Claxton | 31 Aug 92 |
| **wind assisted** | | |
| 11.8 | Deborah Bunn | 28 Jun 75 |
| 12.3 | Barbara Parham | 7 Jul 73 |
| 12.3 | Susan Croker | 17 Jun 78 |
| 12.3 | Gail Hayes | 7 Jul 78 |

### 150 METRES

| | | |
|---|---|---|
| 19.1 | Emma Ania | 7 Sep 91 |
| 19.2 | Helen Seery | 19 Feb 89 |
| 19.2 | Kelly Rea | 30 Apr 95 |
| 19.2 | Rebecca Smith | 30 Apr 95 |
| 19.5 | Karlene Palmer | 1 Aug 93 |
| 19.6 | Sarah Wilhelmy | 13 Sep 92 |
| 19.6 | Laverne Slater | 24 Jul 94 |
| 19.6 | Stacy Hilling | 27 Jul 94 |
| 19.6 | Sarah Zawada | 11 Sep 94 |

### 200 METRES

| | | |
|---|---|---|
| 24.2 | Jane Parry | 28 May 77 |
| 25.4 | Katharine Merry | 21 Jun 87 |
| 25.4 | Myra McShannon | 8 May 88 |
| 25.6 | Debbie Bunn | 5 Jul 75 |
| 25.6 | Joanne Gardner | 24 Aug 75 |
| 25.6 | Jane Riley | 30 Jun 85 |
| 25.7 | Jane Bradbeer | 1 Aug 81 |
| 25.7 | Donna Fraser | 28 Sep 85 |
| **wind assisted** | | |
| 23.6 | Jane Parry | 9 Jul 77 |

## 3000 METRES TRACK WALK

| | | |
|---|---|---|
| 14:56.4 | Sarah Bennett | 26 Sep 93 |
| 15:00.0 | Susan Ashforth | 19 Jun 84 |
| 15:00.6 | Sally Wish | 16 Jul 72 |
| 15:16.0 o | Helen Ringshaw | 11 Nov 80 |
| 15:18.3 | Victoria Lawrence | 17 Jul 83 |
| 15:18.7sh | Sharon Tonks | 19 Mar 83 |
| 15:19.0 | Tracey Devlin | 28 Mar 87 |
| 15:28.0 | Kim Macadam | 3 Sep 83 |
| 15:30.0 | Nikola Ellis | 1 Sep 84 |
| 15:36.0 | Joanne Ashforth | 11 Jun 86 |

### 600 METRES

| | | |
|---|---|---|
| 1:37.5 | Hannah Wood | 17 Jul 94 |
| 1:38.5 | Jennifer Meadows | 4 Apr 93 |
| 1:38.9 | Emma Ward | 17 Jul 94 |
| 1:40.9 | Amanda O'Shea | 25 Jul 92 |
| 1:42.1 | Alison Kerboas | 26 Sep 93 |
| 1:42.2 | Holly O'Connor | 25 Jun 95 |
| 1:42.26 | Ellie Childs | 14 May95 |
| 1:42.5 | Francesca Green | 26 Jul 92 |
| 1:42.5 | Catherine Roberts | 16 Jul 95 |

### 800 METRES

| | | |
|---|---|---|
| 2:14.8 | Janet Lawrence | 10 Jul 71 |
| 2:15.05 | Rachel Hughes | 11 Sep 81 |
| 2:16.8 | Angela Davies | 25 Jul 83 |
| 2:17.20 | Emma Langston | 7 Sep 84 |
| 2:17.6 | Michelle Wilkinson | 22 Jun 85 |
| 2:17.9 | Melissa Rooney | 20 Jun 81 |
| 2:18.1 | Lileath Rose | 19 Jun 76 |
| 2:18.50 | Jennifer Meadows | 3 Jul 93 |
| 2:18.6 | Jayne Heathcote | 11 Jun 83 |
| 2:19.0 | Michelle Cherry | 6 Aug 83 |
| 2:19.0 | Dawn Simpson | 21 Jun 86 |

### 1500 METRES

| | | |
|---|---|---|
| 4:35.5 o | Rachel Hughes | 2 Dec 81 |
| | 4:36.9 | 20 Jul 81 |
| 4:42.1 | Stacy Washington | 18 Jul 84 |
| 4:43.0 | Julie Adkin | 18 Jul 84 |
| 4:44.0 | Paula Matheson | 20 Jul 76 |
| 4:44.2 | Clare Keller | 13 Jun 81 |
| 4:44.7 | Deborah Russell | 18 Jul 76 |
| 4:44.9 | Susan Jordan | 20 Sep 81 |
| 4:46.8 | Amanda Alford | 11 Sep 76 |
| 4:47.1 | Susan Byrom | 29 Jun 85 |

### 70 METRES HURDLES

| | | |
|---|---|---|
| 11.0 | Katharine Merry | 20 Sep 87 |
| 11.1 | Sarah Claxton | 14 Jun 92 |
| 11.17 | Ann-Marie Massey | 3 Sep 95 |
| 11.2 | Claire Stuart | 19 Jun 88 |
| 11.3 db | Sarah Culkin | 18 Jun 89 |
| 11.3 | Katie Challinor | 22 Sep 91 |
| 11.3 | Nicola Hall | 23 Aug 92 |
| 11.3 | Caroline Pearce | 1 Aug 93 |
| 11.3 | Naomi Hodge-Dallaway | 30 Aug 93 |
| **wind assisted** | | |
| 11.21 | Sandra Gunn | 4 Sep 88 |

## 75 METRES HURDLES

| | | |
|---|---|---|
| 11.3 | Katharine Merry | 26 Sep 87 |
| 11.6 | Jenny Vanes | 26 Sep 87 |
| 11.78 | Caroline Pearce | 7 Aug 93 |
| 11.9 | Cheryl Cox | 4 Sep 71 |
| 11.9 | Sharon McKinley | 8 Aug 81 |
| 11.9 | Adele Mesney | 30 Jul 88 |
| 12.0 | Julie Goldthorpe | 13 Jun 70 |
| 12.0 | Sandra White | 11 Sep 77 |
| 12.1 o | Carole Petitjean | 15 Nov 70 |
| 12.1 | Beverley Cox | 24 Sep 72 |
| 12.1 | Elizabeth Fairs | 1 Sep 90 |
| 12.1 | Kelly Williamson | 21 Jun 92 |
| 12.1 | Sarah Claxton | 1 Aug 92 |

**wind assisted**

| | | |
|---|---|---|
| 11.6 | Sarah Claxton | 5 Jul 92 |

## HIGH JUMP

| | | |
|---|---|---|
| 1.69 | Katharine Merry | 26 Sep 87 |
| 1.68 | Julia Charlton | 6 Aug 78 |
| 1.65 | Debbie Marti | 20 Sep 80 |
| 1.65 | Jane Falconer | 20 Sep 87 |
| 1.63 | Lindsey Marriott | 11 Aug 79 |
| 1.63 | Paula Davidge | 13 Sep 81 |
| 1.62 io | Claire Summerfield | 20 Nov 77 |
| 1.60 | Denise Wilkinson | 17 Jul 76 |
| 1.59 | Julie O'Dell | 28 Jul 74 |
| 1.59 | Julia Cockram | 18 May 80 |
| 1.59 | Beverley Green | 30 Aug 86 |

## LONG JUMP

| | | |
|---|---|---|
| 5.71 | Sandy French | 20 Aug 76 |
| 5.45 | Sarah Wilhelmy | 31 Aug 92 |
| 5.43 | Margaret Cheetham | 19 Sep 81 |
| 5.42 | Katharine Merry | 7 Jun 87 |
| 5.40 | Kerrie Gray | 1 Sep 84 |
| 5.38 | Toyin Campbell | 6 Aug 77 |
| 5.35 | Deborah Bunn | 7 Sep 75 |
| 5.34 | Fiona May | 12 Jun 82 |
| 5.33 | Kathryn Dowsett | 7 Sep 91 |
| 5.32 | Ann Flannery | 18 Sep 82 |

**wind assisted**

| | | |
|---|---|---|
| 5.55 | Katharine Merry | 10 Jul 87 |

## SHOT (2.72kg)

| | | |
|---|---|---|
| 11.57 io | Navdeep Dhaliwal | 12 Dec 90 |
| 11.04 | Amy Wilson | 12 Sep 93 |
| 10.91 | Catherine Garden | 8 Sep 91 |
| 10.60 | Lucy Rann | 29 Aug 93 |
| 10.48 | Julie Robin | 1 Jul 89 |
| 10.48 | Natalie Kerr | 9 Aug 92 |
| 10.46 | Sandra Biddlecombe | 4 Jul 90 |
| 10.41 | Eleanor Garden | 3 Sep 89 |

## SHOT (3.25kg)

| | | |
|---|---|---|
| 12.20 | Susan King | 3 Sep 77 |
| 10.77 | Michele Morgan | 19 Jun 82 |
| 10.68 io | Rebecca Hyams | 21 Dec 85 |
| 10.64 io | Roxanne Blackwood | 10 Nov 86 |
| 10.54 | Claire Burnett | 1 Sep 85 |
| 10.49 | Alison Grey | 3 Aug 85 |

## DISCUS (0.75kg)

| | | |
|---|---|---|
| 39.44 | Catherine Garden | 8 Sep 91 |
| 37.64 | Sandra Biddlecombe | 4 Jul 90 |
| 32.70 | Claire Smithson | 26 Aug 95 |
| 30.54 | Eleanor Garden | 10 Sep 89 |
| 29.76 | Navdeep Dhaliwal | 19 Aug 90 |
| 29.62 | Helen Gates | 3 Jul 93 |
| 29.48 | Rebecca Roles | 16 May 92 |
| 29.18 | Lucille Shaw | 10 Jul 94 |
| 29.00 | Elizabeth Hay | 12 Sep 92 |
| 28.86 | Celyn Samuels | 15 Sep 91 |

## DISCUS (1kg)

| | | |
|---|---|---|
| 34.22 | Catherine Garden | 25 Aug 91 |
| 33.86 o | Fiona Condon | 13 Oct 73 |
| 31.34 | Sandra Biddlecombe | 9 Sep 90 |
| 30.02 | Alison Moffitt | 6 Jul 82 |
| 29.88 | Iona Doyley | 2 Sep 78 |
| 29.42 | Eleanor Garden | 27 Aug 89 |
| 29.12 | Natalie Kerr | 26 Jul 92 |
| 28.88 | Jane Chapman | 13 Sep 81 |
| 28.56 | Amanda Franks | 25 Aug 74 |
| 28.38 | Sarah Hughes | 9 Sep 84 |

## JAVELIN (400gm)

| | | |
|---|---|---|
| 33.46 | Emma Claydon | 26 Jul 92 |
| 33.32 | Melanie Vaggers | 27 Sep 94 |
| 32.38 | Eve Russell | 30 Jul 95 |
| 31.58 | Louise Telford | 20 Aug 94 |
| 30.16 | Tanya Hunt | 27 Aug 95 |
| 30.82 | Gillian Stewart | 13 Sep 92 |
| 30.54 | Lesley Richardson | 16 Aug 92 |
| 30.46 | Lucy Rann | 8 Aug 93 |
| 29.94 | Stacey McLelland | 12 Sep 93 |
| 29.70 | Kelly Sloan | 15 Sep 91 |

## JAVELIN (600gm)

| | | |
|---|---|---|
| 32.02 | Claire Lacey | 20 Sep 87 |
| 31.60 | Emma Langston | 2 Sep 84 |
| 31.44 | Alison Moffitt | 6 Jul 82 |
| 31.28 | Eve Russell | 2 Sep 95 |
| 31.04 | Shelley Holroyd | Jun 85 |
| 30.82 | Diane Williams | 10 Jun 72 |
| 30.44 | Heather Derbyshire | 12 Sep 91 |
| 30.32 | Debra Smith | 83 |
| 30.28 | Emily Steele | 1 Aug 87 |
| 29.84 | Lucy Rann | 12 Jun 93 |

## 2500 METRES TRACK WALK

| | | |
|---|---|---|
| 12:48.9 | Claire Walker | 20 Jul 85 |
| 12:49.0 o | Karen Eden | 11 Oct 75 |
| 12:50.5 | Victoria Lawrence | 4 Jul 82 |
| 12:57.66 | Kelly Mann | 28 May 95 |
| 12:59.0 | Jo Pickett | 22 Jun 92 |
| 13:08.2 | Joanne Ashforth | 20 Jul 85 |
| 13:10.2 | Stephanie Cooper | 9 May 82 |
| 13:18.0 | Alison Warren | 4 Jun 78 |
| 13:18.0 | Karen Bowers | 14 Apr 79 |
| 13:18.8 | Janette McKenzie | 20 May 79 |
| 13:00.0 | Sarah Bennett | 22 Jun 92 |

# UK CLUB RELAY RECORDS

## MEN

**Seniors**

| | | | |
|---|---|---|---|
| 4 x 100m | 39.49 | Haringey | 1 Jun 91 |
| 4 x 200m | 1:23.5 | Team Solent | 19 Jul 87 |
| 4 x 400m | 3:04.48 | Team Solent | 29 Jun 90 |
| 1600m Medley | 3:20.8 | Wolverhampton & Bilston | 1 Jun 75 |
| 4 x 800m | 7:24.4* | North Staffs and Stone | 27 Jun 65 |
| 4 x 1500m | 15:12.6 | Bristol | 5 Aug 75 |

* = 4 x 880y time less 2.8sec

**Under 20**

| | | | |
|---|---|---|---|
| 4 x 100m | 41.30 | Victoria Park | 14 Aug 76 |
| 4 x 200m | 1:27.6 | Enfield | 13 Jun 82 |
| 4 x 400m | 3:15.3 | Enfield | 5 Sep 82 |
| 1600m Medley | 3:31.6 | Cardiff | 14 Aug 71 |
| 4 x 800m | 7:35.3 | Liverpool H | 14 Aug 90 |
| 4 x 1500m | 16:04.3 | Blackburn | 15 Sep 79 |
| 4 x 110H | 1:04.8 | Oundle Sch | 19 May 79 |

**Under 17**

| | | | |
|---|---|---|---|
| 4 x 100m | 42.22 | Thames V H | 24 Jun 89 |
| 4 x 200m | 1:31.2 | Hercules-W. | 12 Jul 78 |
| 4 x 400m | 3:23.1 | Enfield | 1 Oct 80 |
| 1600m Medley | 3:36.1 | Thurrock | 13 Jun 84 |
| 4 x 800m | 7:52.1 | Clydebank | 29 Aug 87 |
| 4 x 1500m | 16:27.0 | Liverpool H | 14 Sep 88 |

**Under 15**

| | | | |
|---|---|---|---|
| 4 x 100m | 44.62 | Sale | 29 Aug 93 |
| 4 x 200m | 1:36.9 | Belgrave | 19 Sep 93 |
| 4 x 400m | 3:31.5 | Ayr Seaforth | 5 Sep 82 |
| 1600m Medley | 3:48.4 | Blackheath | 29 Sep 86 |
| 4 x 800m | 8:13.28 | Clydebank | 2 Sep 89 |
| 4 x 1500m | 17:52.4 | Stretford | 22 Oct 85 |

**Under 13**

| | | | |
|---|---|---|---|
| 4 x 100m | 50.5 | Blackheath | 12 Sep 93 |
| 4 x 200m | 1:49.7 | Braintree | 29 Aug 94 |
| 4 x 400m | 4:04.5 | Blackheath | 12 Sep 93 |
| 1600m Medley | 4:13.7 | Blackheath | 28 Sep 86 |
| 4 x 800m | 9:29.8 | Sale | 28 Jun 88 |

## WOMEN

**Seniors**

| | | | |
|---|---|---|---|
| 4 x 100m | 43.79 | Hounslow | 18 Sep 82 |
| 4 x 200m | 1:35.15 | Stretford | 14 Jul 91 |
| 4 x 400m | 3:31.62 | Essex Ladies | 31 May 92 |
| 1600m Medley | 3:50.6 | Coventry Godiva | 5 May 84 |
| 3 x 800m | 6:32.4 | Cambridge H | 29 Jun 74 |
| 4 x 800m | 8:41.0 | Cambridge H | 26 May 75 |

**Under 20**

| | | | |
|---|---|---|---|
| 4 x 100m | 48.07 | Sale | 14 Sep 91 |
| 4 x 200m | 1:47.7 | Edinburgh WM | 12 Aug 90 |
| 4 x 400m | 3:51.67 | Sale | 23 Sep 89 |
| 3 x 800m | 7:33.2 | Essex Ladies | 12 Jun 94 |

**Under 17**

| | | | |
|---|---|---|---|
| 4 x 100m | 47.52 | Hounslow | 2 Oct 82 |
| 4 x 200m | 1:42.2 | London Oly. | 19 Aug 72 |
| 4 x 400m | 3:52.1 | City of Hull | 3 Jul 82 |
| 1600m Medley | 4:07.8 | Warrington | 14 Aug 75 |
| 3 x 800m | 6:46.5 | Haslemere | 15 Sep 79 |
| | 6:46.5 | Bromley L | 1 Jul 84 |
| 4 x 800m | 8:53.1 | Havering | 24 May 80 |

**Under 15**

| | | | |
|---|---|---|---|
| 4 x 100m | 48.5 | Haringey | 15 Sep 79 |
| 4 x 200m | 1:44.0 | Bristol | 15 Sep 79 |
| 3 x 800m | 6:39.8 | Havering | 13 Sep 78 |
| 4 x 800m | 9:21.4 | Sale | 5 Aug 78 |

**Under 13**

| | | | |
|---|---|---|---|
| 4 x 100m | 51.2 | Aberdeen | 20 Aug 89 |
| 4 x 200m | 1:52.5 | Mitcham | 24 Jul 82 |
| 3 x 800m | 7:18.0 | Mid Hants | 14 Sep 83 |
| 4 x 800m | 10:02.4 | Warrington | 16 Sep 75 |

# MEN

## 60 Metres
1. COLIN JACKSON — 6.58
2. MICHAEL ROSSWESS — 6.63
3. Alek Porkhomovskiy RUS — 6.71
4. Andrei Grigorev RUS — 6.72
5. JOHN REGIS gst — 6.73

## 200 Metres
1. JOHN REGIS — 20.65
2. SOLOMON WARISO gst — 20.84
3. DARREN BRAITHWAITE — 21.02
4. Konstantin Dyomin RUS — 21.43
5. Aleksandr Sokolov RUS — 21.47

## 400 Metres
1. Dmitriy Golovastov RUS — 47.09
2. Mikhail Vdovin RUS — 47.24
3. BRIAN WHITTLE — 47.50
4. GUY BULLOCK — 47.64
5. Dmitriy Kosov gst/RUS — 48.07
6. MARK HYLTON gst — 48.19

## 800 Metres
1. TOM MCKEAN — 1:50.04
2. MARTIN STEELE — 1:50.31
3. Pavel Dolgushev RUS — 1:50.58
   CRAIG WINROW — DNF

## 1500 Metres
1. IAN GRIME — 3:52.02
2. Andrey Zadorozhny RUS — 3:52.06
3. BRIAN TREACY — 3:52.12
4. TONY MORRELL gst — 3:52.45
5. Sergey Melnikov RUS — 3:55.19

## 3000 Metres
1. Vyach Shabunin RUS — 8:14.49
2. ANTHONY WHITEMAN — 8:14.71
3. DARRIUS BURROWS gst — 8:19.83
4. STEFFAN WHITE — 8:23.61
5. Vladimir Pronin RUS — 8:27.91

## 60 Metres Hurdles
1. COLIN JACKSON — 7.43
2. TONY JARRETT — 7.58
3. Aleks Gorshenin RUS — 7.71
4. Yevgeniy Pechonkin RUS — 7.75
5. PAUL GRAY gst — 7.88
6. Sergey Vetrov gst/RUS — 8.01

## High Jump
1. BRENDAN REILLY — 2.26
2. Grigoriy Fedorkov RUS — 2.26
3. Sergei Klyugin RUS — 2.23
4. Stuart Ohrland — 2.05

## Pole Vault
1. Vadim Strogalyov RUS — 5.20
2. ANDY ASHURST — 5.00
3. KEVIN HUGHES — 5.00
   Valeriy Ishutin RUS — NHC

## Long Jump
1. BARRINGTON WILLIAMS — 7.54
2. Kiril Sosunov RUS — 7.49
3. Yuri Sotnikov RUS — 7.27
4. STEVE PHILLIPS — 7.17

## Triple Jump
1. Genadi Markov RUS — 17.00
2. Yuriy Sotnikov RUS — 16.24
3. FRANCIS AGYEPONG — 16.15
4. JULIAN GOLLEY — 15.38

## Shot
1. Sergey Smirnov RUS — 18.71
2. Viktor Kapustin RUS — 18.66
3. MARK PROCTOR — 18.02
4. LEE NEWMAN — 17.03

## 4 x 400 Metres Relay
1. GREAT BRITAIN — 3:09.22
   (BULLOCK, HYLTON, CONDON, WHITTLE)
2. Russia — 3:09.27
   (Vdovin, Kosov, Machenko, Golovastov)

# WOMEN

## 60 Metres
1. PAULA THOMAS — 7.29
2. Natalya Merzlyakova RUS — 7.35
3. STEPHANIE DOUGLAS — 7.35
4. Natalya Anisimova RUS — 7.44

## 200 Metres
1. PAULA THOMAS — 23.61
2. Yulia Sotnikova RUS — 23.95
3. Yelena Ruzina gst — 23.98
4. Yelena Mizera gst/RUS — 24.36
5. SHARON WILLIAMS — 24.54

## 400 Metres
1. Elena Andreeva RUS — 52.57
2. Tatiana Alekseeva RUS — 52.81
3. Olga Nazarova gst/RUS — 52.99
4. SUSAN RAWLINSON — 53.82
5. MICHELLE THOMAS gst — 54.31
6. TRACY JOSEPH — 54.81

## 800 Metres
1. Yelena Afansyeva RUS — 2:05.14
2. Irina Samrokova RUS — 2:05.26
3. SONYA BOWYER — 2:06.44
4. CATHY DAWSON — 2:09.12
5. JILLIAN JONES gst — 2:09.69

## 1500 Metres
1. ANN GRIFFITHS — 4:14.74
2. Yek Podkopayeva RUS — 4:17.32
3. Lyudmila Mikhailova RUS — 4:20.17
4. MICHELLE FAHERTY — 4:33.66

## 3000 Metres
1. Klara Kashapova RUS — 9:15.45
2. Olga Kovpotina RUS — 9:16.43
3. ZAHARA HYDE — 9:17.97
4. DEBBIE GUNNING — 9:23.68
5. SARAH BENTLEY gst — 9:39.01

## 60 Metres Hurdles
1. JACQUI AGYEPONG — 8.05
2. Svetlana Laukhova RUS — 8.14
3. Natalya Yudakova RUS — 8.27
4. SAM FARQUHARSON — 8.35
5. CLOVA COURT gst — 8.35

## Pole Vault
1. KATE STAPLES — 3.75
2. PAULA WILSON — 3.50
3= Nat Mekhanoshina RUS — 3.35
3= Galina Yenvarenko RUS — 3.35

## Long Jump
1. Lyudmila Galkina RUS — 6.58
2. OLUYINKA IDOWU — 6.46
3. Vera Olenchenko RUS — 6.42
4. DENISE LEWIS — 6.12

## Triple Jump
1. ASHIA HANSEN — 14.17
2. Lyudmila Dubkova RUS — 13.71
3. MICHELLE GRIFFITH — 13.57
4. Natalya Kayukova RUS — 13.40

## Shot
1. Larisa Peleshenko RUS — 19.57
2. Irina Khudorzhkina RUS — 18.32
3. JUDY OAKES — 17.78
4. MAGGIE LYNES — 15.88

## 4 x 400 Metres Relay
1. Russia — 3:32.26
   (Ruzina, Andreeva, Alekseeva, Nazarova)
2. GREAT BRITAIN — 3:37.90
   (NEEF, RAWLINSON, JOSEPH, THOMAS)

## Match Result Men
1. GREAT BRITAIN & NI — 72
2. Russia — 64

## Match Result Women
1. Russia — 70
2. GREAT BRITAIN & NI — 58

## Combined Match Result
1. Russia — 134
2. GREAT BRITAIN & NI — 130

# AAA INDOOR CHAMPIONSHIPS  Birmingham  3 - 4 February 1995

## MEN

### 60 Metres  (4 Feb)
1. MICHAEL ROSSWESS — 6.63
2. DARREN BRAITHWAITE — 6.69
3. JASON FERGUS — 6.70
4. JOHN REGIS — 6.72
5. KEVIN WILLIAMS — 6.77
6. JASON GARDENER — 6.81
7. TREMAYNE RUTHERFORD — 6.83
8. DOUGLAS TURNER — 6.93

### 200 Metres  (4 Feb)
1. SOLOMON WARISO — 20.87
2. DARREN BRAITHWAITE — 20.95
3. ALLYN CONDON — 21.32
4. PETER MAITLAND — 21.68
5. SUNNY ADEPEGBA — 22.14
6. AYO FALOLA — 22.19

### 400 Metres  (4 Feb)
1. MARK HYLTON — 46.56
2. BRIAN WHITTLE — 47.26
3. Jaques Farraudiere  FRA — 47.28
4. KENT ULYATT — 47.97
5. LEE FAIRCLOUGH — 48.63

### 800 Metres  (4 Feb)
1. MARTIN STEELE — 1:49.17
2. CRAIG WINROW — 1:49.25
3. EWAN CALVERT — 1:50.15
4. PAUL WALKER — 1:50.81
5. John O'Reilly  IRE — 1:51.97
6. CLIVE GILBY — 1:54.30

### 1500 Metres  (4 Feb)
1. GRANT GRAHAM — 3:55.68
2. IAN CAMPBELL — 3:55.75
3. MARTIN YELLING — 3:57.09
4. LEE CADWALLADER — 3:58.16
5. STEVE MOSLEY — 3:58.84
6. GARTH WATSON — 3:59.92
7. DAVID PAMAH — 4:00.99

### 3000 Metres  (4 Feb)
1. STEPHEN GREEN — 8:08.71
2. DARRIUS BURROWS — 8:09.08
3. NICK COMERFORD — 8:09.64
4. BASHIR HUSSAIN — 8:13.14
5. DAVID LEE — 8:13.44
6. PATRICK DAVOREN — 8:15.94
7. Nigel Brunton  IRE — 8:16.07
8. NICK HAWKINS — 8:16.62

### 60 Metres Hurdles  (4 Feb)
1. PAUL GRAY — 7.83
2. BRIAN TAYLOR — 7.90
3. NEIL OWEN — 7.93
4. Sean Cahill  IRE — 8.02
5. MARK LAMBETH — 8.05
6. JAMES HUGHES — 8.14
7. KEVIN LUMSDON — 8.16
8. JAMES ARCHAMPONG — 8.20

### High Jump  (4 Feb)
1. GEOFF PARSONS — 2.24
2. ROB BROCKLEBANK — 2.07

### Pole Vault  (3 Feb)
1. PAUL WILLIAMSON — 5.20
2= MICHAEL BARBER — 5.20
2= KEVIN HUGHES — 5.20
4. IAN TULLETT — 5.10
5. MARK GRANT — 5.00
6. DUNCAN PEARCE — 4.80

### Long Jump  (3 Feb)
1. BARRINGTON WILLIAMS — 7.55
2. JOHN MUNROE — 7.54
3. STEVE PHILLIPS — 7.35
4. NIGEL BOURNE — 7.17
5. ANTHONY WOOD — 7.08
6. Jonathon Kron  IRE — 7.01

### Triple Jump  (4 Feb)
1. JOHN HERBERT — 16.48
2. JOHN MACKENZIE — 16.07
3. FEMI AKINSANYA — 15.43
4. REZ CAMERON — 15.40
5. JOSEPH SWEENEY — 15.25
6. MICHAEL MCDONALD — 15.06
7. JON HILTON — 14.45

### Shot  (3 Feb)
1. LEE NEWMAN — 17.30
2. STEPHEN WHYTE — 16.95
3. NIGEL SPRATLEY — 16.59
4. JAMES MASON — 16.54
5. PAUL REED — 16.03
6. SIMON MATTHEWS — 14.87

## WOMEN

### 60 Metres  (4 Feb)
1. STEPHANIE DOUGLAS — 7.28
2. AILEEN MCGILLIVARY — 7.36
3. DANAA CALLOW — 7.47
4. JACKIE AGYPEPONG — 7.47
5. DIANE ALLAHGREEN — 7.55
6. EVADNE MCKENZIE — 7.58

### 200 Metres  (4 Feb)
1. JACKIE AGYEPONG — 24.22
2. MARCIA RICHARDSON — 24.41
3. SARAH OXLEY — 24.59
4. SUSAN BRIGGS — 24.95
5. REBECCA KILGOUR — 25.85

### 400 Metres  (4 Feb)
1. MELANIE NEEF — 52.82
2. MICHELLE THOMAS — 54.50
3. STEPHANIE McCANN — 54.64
4. STEPHANIE LLEWELLYN — 54.84
5. ALLISON CURBISHLEY — 54.96

### 800 Metres  (4 Feb)
1. ABIGAIL HUNTE — 2:08.06
2. Aisling Molloy  IRE — 2:08.54
3. JEINA MITCHELL — 2:09.63
4. HELEN DANIEL — 2:09.81
5. NATALIE TAIT — 2:11.98
6. PAULA FRYER — 2:12.04

### 1500 Metres  (4 Feb)
1. LYNN GIBSON — 4:18.41
2. MICHELLE FAHERTY — 4:19.19
3. SHIRLEY GRIFFITHS — 4:20.84
4. SARAH BENTLEY — 4:25.40
5. ALYSON LAYZELL — 4:25.80
6. LISA CARTHEW — 4:33.76
7. ANGELA JOINER — 4:41.74

### 60 Metres Hurdles  (4 Feb)
1. CLOVA COURT — 8.22
2. SAM FARQUHARSON — 8.29
3. DENISE LEWIS — 8.49
4. DIANE ALLAHGREEN — 8.49
5. MELANIE WILKINS — 8.66
6. UJU EFOBI — 8.66
7. ORLA BERMINGHAM — 8.72
8. BETHAN EDWARDS — 8.87

### High Jump  (3 Feb)
1. LEA HAGGETT — 1.86
2. DEBBI MARTI — 1.80
3. JULIA BENNETT — 1.80
4. KELLY THIRKLE — 1.75
5= AILSA WALLACE — 1.70
5= LINDSAY EVANS — 1.70
5= Sharon Foley  IRE — 1.70
8. MICHELLE DUNKLEY — 1.70

### Pole Vault  (4 Feb)
1. KATE STAPLES — 3.80
2. LINDA STANTON — 3.50
3. RHIAN CLARKE — 3.30
4. CLAIRE MORRISON — 3.20
5. SUSAN DRUMMIE — 3.10

### Long Jump  (3 Feb)
1. DENISE LEWIS — 6.28
2. OLUYINKA IDOWU — 6.26
3. ANN BROOKS — 5.87
4. JACQUELINE WHITE — 5.67
5. JULIE HOLLMAN — 5.60

### Triple Jump  (4 Feb)
1. ASHIA HANSEN — 13.61
2. RACHEL KIRBY — 13.11
3. EVETTE FINIKIN — 12.63
4. KAREN SKEGGS — 12.13
5. KERENSA DENHAM — 11.22

### Shot  (3 Feb)
1. JUDITH OAKES — 17.81
2. MAGGIE LYNES — 15.71
3. ALISON GREY — 15.30
4. PHILIPPA ROLES — 13.96
5. DENISE LEWIS — 13.29
6. ANNA-LISA HOWARD — 11.69

# GB & NI v FRA (indoors)   Glasgow   11 February 1995

## MEN

### 60 Metres
1. LINFORD CHRISTIE          6.56
2. DARREN BRAITHWAITE  gst   6.65
3. Needy Guims          FRA  6.70
4. MICHAEL ROSSWESS          6.72
5. JOHN REGIS          gst   6.73
6. Sebastien Carrat     FRA  6.73

### 200 Metres
1. JOHN REGIS                20.67
2. SOLOMON WARISO            21.19
3. Christophe Cheval   FRA   21.47
4. Jerome Pani         FRA   21.69

### 400 Metres
1. MARK HYLTON              47.06
2. Jacques Farraudiere FRA  47.34
3. BRIAN WHITTLE            47.60
4. David Divad             47.67

### 800 Metres
1. TOM MCKEAN              1:48.72
2. MARTIN STEELE           1:48.95
3. Thierry Caquelard  FRA  1:49.05
4. CRAIG WINROW       gst  1:50.49
5. Frederic Taillard  FRA  1:50.57

### 1500 Metres
1. Eric Dubus         FRA  3:41.66
2. IAN GRIME               3:43.30
3. IAN CAMPBELL       gst  3:43.54
4. GRANT GRAHAM            3:46.97
5. Vincent Terrier    FRA  3:51.18

### 3000 Metres
1. Jacky Carlier      FRA  7:58.03
2. STEPHEN GREEN           8:03.82
3. Nadir Bosch        FRA  8:05.95
4. DARRIUS BURROWS         8:09.43
5. GLEN STEWART       gst  8:16.80

### 60 Metres Hurdles
1. COLIN JACKSON           7.39
2. TONY JARRETT            7.44
3. Vincent Clarico    FRA  7.78
4. PAUL GRAY          gst  7.93
5. Emmanuel Romary    FRA  7.96

### High Jump
1. Didier Detchenique FRA  2.23
2. BRENDAN REILLY          2.20
3. J-Charles Gicquel  FRA  2.20
4. JAMES BRIERLEY          2.15

### Pole Vault
1. Alain Andji        FRA  5.30
2. Philippe D'Encausse FRA 5.30
3. MICHAEL BARBER          5.20
4. PAUL WILLIAMSON         5.00

### Long Jump
1. Kader Klouchi      FRA  7.65
2. JOHN MUNROE             7.65
3. Olivier Borderan   FRA  7.61
4. BARRINGTON WILLIAMS     7.48

### Triple Jump
1. JOHN HERBERT            16.50
2. Garfield Anselm    FRA  16.22
3. JULIAN GOLLEY           16.18
4. Kenny Boudine      FRA  15.87

### Shot
1. MARK PROCTOR            18.39
2. Jean-Louis Lebon   FRA  17.69
3. LEE NEWMAN              16.85
4. J-Pierre Totele         16.72

### 4 x 400 Metres Relay
1. GREAT BRITAIN                3:09.28
(CRAMPTON, HYLTON, WARISO, WHITTLE)
2. France                       3:09.81
(Farraudiere, Divad, Seradin, Lauret)

### Match Result
1. GREAT BRITAIN & NI  77
2. France              62

## WOMEN

### 60 Metres
1. STEPHANIE DOUGLAS         7.21
2. Patricia Girard     FRA   7.24
3. PAULA THOMAS             7.28
4. Fabienne Ficher     FRA   7.35
5. AILEEN MCGILLIVARY  gst   7.39

### 200 Metres
1. PAULA THOMAS             23.42
2. Fabienne Ficher     FRA  23.64
3. Natacha Cilirie     FRA  24.02
4. SARAH OXLEY             24.79

### 400 Metres
1. MELANIE NEEF            53.67
2. Marie-Louis Bevis   FRA  53.71
3. SUSAN RAWLINSON         54.16
4. Valerie Jaunatre    FRA  55.32

### 800 Metres
1. Patricia Djaté      FRA  2:02.99
2. SONYA BOWYER            2:04.83
3. ABIGAIL HUNTE           2:08.49
4. M Christine Dampa   FRA  2:09.51

### 1500 Metres
1. Frederique Quentin  FRA  4:18.04
2. MICHELLE FAHERTY         4:18.65
3. LYNN GIBSON             4:22.02
4. SHIRLEY GRIFFITHS  gst  4:24.10
5. Severine Foulon     FRA  4:36.85

### 3000 Metres
1. Laurence Duquenoy  FRA  9:20.49
2. ZAHARA HYDE             9:22.07
3. DEBBIE GUNNING          9:29.92
4. Sylvie Drapp       FRA  10:00.60

### 60 Metres Hurdles
1. JACQUI AGYEPONG          8.08
2. Monique Tourret    FRA   8.13
3. SAM FARQUHARSON gst     8.18
4. CLOVA COURT            8.21
5. Annette Simon      FRA  8.43

### High Jump
1. Katell Courgeon    FRA  1.86
2. DEBBIE MARTI            1.86
3. LEA HAGGETT            1.83
4. Maryse Maury       FRA  1.83

### Pole Vault
1. KATE STAPLES            3.60
2. Catherine Oberson  FRA  3.50
3. Caroline Ammel     FRA  3.40
   LINDA STANTON           NH

### Long Jump
1. DENISE LEWIS            6.35
2. Anastasia Mahob    FRA  6.21
3. Sarah Gautreau     FRA  6.18
4. VIKKI SCHOFIELD         6.11

### Triple Jump
1. MICHELLE GRIFFITH       13.76
2. Caroline Honore    FRA  13.26
3. RACHEL KIRBY            13.15
4. Sandrine Domain    FRA  12.38

### Shot
1. JUDITH OAKES            17.15
2. MAGGIE LYNES            16.08
3. Annick Lefebvre    FRA  15.71
4. Nathalie Bellotti  FRA  14.83

### 4 x 400 Metres Relay
1. GREAT BRITAIN               3:37.60
(LLEWELLYN, RAWLINSON, STOUTE,
MCCANN)
2. France                      3:38.58
(Bevis, Domenech, Pierre, Jaunatre)

### Match Result
1. GREAT BRITAIN & NI  78
2. France              60

# England v AUT/HUN v CZE (indoors)  Vienna, Austria  18 February 1995

## MEN

### 60 Metres
1. JASON GARDENER 6.73
2. Jiri Valik CZE 6.77
3. AYO FALOLA 6.82
4. Gabor Dobos HUN 6.87

### 200 Metres Race 1
1. ALLYN CONDON 21.24
2. Thomas Griesser AUT 21.63
3. Martin Morkes CZE 21.99

### 200 Metres Race 2
1. Istvan Sami HUN 21.86
2. Wolfgang Sinzinger gst/AUT 22.21
3. Jiri Ondracek CZE 22.32
4. SUNNY ADEPEGPA 22.39

### 400 Metres Race 1
1. GUY BULLOCK 47.30
2. Lukas Soucek CZE 47.61
3. Dusan Kovacs HUN 47.63

### 400 Metres Race 2
1 Andreas Rechbauer AUT 48.22
2. Jiri Benda CZE 48.34
3. KENT ULYATT 48.66

### 800 Metres
1. Thomas Ebner gst/AUT 1:50.74
2. David Somfay HUN 1:50.80
3. Oliver Münzer AUT 1:51.02
4. CRAIG WINROW 1:51.32
6. PAUL WALKER 1:51.78

### 1500 Metres
1. ANTHONY WHITEMAN 3:48.74
2. Lukas Vydra CZE 3:49.04
3. Jaromir Skalicky CZE 3:49.45
4. Bekim Bahtiri gst/SLO 3:49.48
5. ADAM DUKE 3:52.61

### 3000 Metres
1. Tamas Kliszek HUN 8:13.23
2. Radomir Soukup CZE 8:14.69
3. BASHIR HUSSAIN 8:15.05
4. STEFFAN WHITE 8:17.28

### 60 Metres Hurdles
1. Christian Miaslinger AUT 7.76
2. Jiri Hudec CZE 7.79
3. BRIAN TAYLOR 7.81
4. ANDY TULLOCH 7.83

### High Jump
1. BRENDAN REILLY 2.18
2= Tomas Janku CZE 2.14
2= Janos Somogyi HUN 2.14
11. ANDREW LYNCH 2.05

### Pole Vault
1. Jan Netscher CZE 5.40
2. PAUL WILLIAMSON 5.40
3. Zdenek Safar CZE 5.30
4. Gabor Molnar HUN 5.10
7. KEVIN HUGHES 4.80

### Long Jump
1. Ivan Pedroso gst/CUB 8.18
2. FRED SALLE 7.90
3. Teddy Steinmayr AUT 7.71
4. Cherick Toure gst/SEN 7.69
5. JOHN MUNROE 7.65

### Triple Jump
1. FRANCIS AGYEPONG 16.46
2. Zsolt Czingler HUN 15.85
3. Jaroslav Mrstik CZE 15.74
4. FEMI AKINSANYA 15.65

### Shot
1. Jenö Koczian HUN 18.32
2. MARK PROCTOR 17.57
3. Jan Bartl CZE 16.49
4. Gerd Matuschek AUT 15.91
5. NIGEL SPRATLEY 15.88

### 4 x 200 Metres Relay
1. ENGLAND 1:26.71
(GARDENER, TAYLOR, FAYOLA, CONDON )
2. Czech Republic 1:27.06
(Valik, Svenek, Ondracek, Morkes)
3. Austria/Hungary 1:27.41
(Bartl, Klocker, Dobos, Sami)

### Match Result
1. ENGLAND 106
2. Austria/Hungary 90
3. Czech Republic 80

## WOMEN

### 60 Metres
1. Sabine Tröger AUT 7.35
2. Eva Barati HUN 7.37
3. DIANE ALLAGREEN 7.38
4. Hana Benesova CZE 7.44
5. DANAA CALLOW 7.50

### 200 Metres Race 1
1. Hana Benesova CZE 23.60
2. SHARON WILLIAMS 24.22
3. Alinka Bikar gst/SLO 24.80
4. Evlyn Fiala AUT 25.92

### 200 Metres Race 2
1. SARAH OXLEY 24.42
2. Denisa Obdrzalkova CZE 24.51
3. Monika Madai HUN 24.59

### 400 Metres Race 1
1. Nada Kostolova CZE 52.70
2. SUSAN EARNSHAW 53.70
3. Orsolya Doczi HUN 55.95

### 400 Metres Race 2
1. Ludmila Formanova CZE 53.45
2. ELAINE SUTCLIFFE 55.18
3. Fiona Ritchie AUT 55.59

### 800 Metres
1. ABIGAIL HUNTE 2:04.97
2. Andrea Suldesova CZE 2:05.97
3. Stefanie Graf AUT 2:07.82
4. Radka Lukavska CZE 2:08.00
5. JEINA MITCHELL 2:08.59

### 1500 Metres
1. MICHELLE FAHERTY 4:24.49
2. Viktoria Barta HUN 4:25.84
3. SHIRLEY GRIFFITHS 4:26.11
4. Jana Biolkova CZE 4:26.25

### 60 Metres Hurdles
1. Iveta Rudova CZE 8.33
2. DIANE ALLAHGREEN 8.38
3. Elke Wölfling AUT 8.39
4. Zita Balint HUN 8.51
5. Nikola Spinova CZE 8.51
6. JULIA BENNETT 9.25

### High Jump
1. Sigrid Kirchmann AUT 1.95
2. Monika Gollner gst/AUT 1.86
3. Sarka Makowkova CZE 1.86
4. Dora Györffy HUN 1.82
5. LEA HAGGETT 1.82
6. JULIA BENNETT 1.82

### Long Jump
1. Tunde Vaszi HUN 6.45
2. DENIS LEWIS 6.37
3. Dagmar Urbankova CZE 5.98
6. ANN BROOKS 5.82

### Triple Jump
1. Yolanda Chen gst/RUS 14.27
2. Sarka Kasparkova CZE 13.46
3. RACHEL KIRBY 13.27
4. EVETTE FINIKIN 12.62

### Shot
1. Alice Matejkowa CZE 15.77
2. MAGGIE LYNES 15.72
3. Sonja Spendelhofer AUT 15.26
5. SHARON ANDREWS 14.44

### 4 x 200 Metres Relay
1. Czech Republic 1:35.94
(Klapacova, Dziurova, Obdrzalkova, Benesova)
2. ENGLAND 1:37.00
(SUTCLIFFE, EARNSHAW, CALLOW, OXLEY)
3. Austria 1:37.87

### Match Result
1. Czech Republic 85
2. ENGLAND 79
3. Austria/Hungary 69

## AAA INDOOR JUNIOR CHAMPIONSHIPS  Birmingham  18 February 1995

### MEN    Under 20

| | | |
|---|---|---|
| 60 | Martin Giraud | 6.76 |
| 200 | Mark Hylton | 21.52 |
| 400 | Hugh Kerr | 48.39 |
| 800 | James Nolan (IRE) | 1:52.88 |
| 1500 | Des Roache | 3:57.06 |
| 3000 | | |
| 60H | James Archampong | 8.08 |
| HJ | Michael Robbins | 2.15 |
| PV | Neil Young | 4.70 |
| LJ | Ciaran McDonagh (IRE) | 7.37 |
| TJ | Kori Stennett | 14.59 |
| SP | Bruce Robb | 14.38 |
| 3kW | Stuart Monk | 12:50.67 |

### Under 17

| | | |
|---|---|---|
| | Christian Malcolm | 6.96 |
| | Christian Malcolm | 22.25 |
| | Nizamul Hoque | 50.88 |
| | Matthew Dixon | 1:58.43 |
| | Matthew Dixon | 4:04.62 |
| | Gareth Turnbull | 8:54.1 |
| | Liam Collins | 8.30 |
| | Edward Willers | 1.96 |
| | Christian Linskey | 4.60 |
| | David Butler | 6.45 |
| | Michael McKernan | 14.17 |
| | Emeka Udechuku | 18.14 |

### Under 15

| | | |
|---|---|---|
| | Wayne Gray | 7.34 |
| | Wayne Gray | 23.68 |
| | | |
| | Barry Woodward | 2:05.26 |
| | | |
| | | |
| | Brian Pearce | 8.80 |
| | Wayne Gray | 1.88 |
| | Richard Smith | 3.91 |
| | Kevin Hibbins | 6.24 |
| | | |
| | Adrian Cluskey | 14.74 |

### WOMEN Under 20

| | | |
|---|---|---|
| 60 | Ellana Ruddock | 7.75 |
| 200 | Victoria Shipman | 25.16 |
| 400 | Allison Curbishley | 54.43 |
| 800 | Rhonda MacPhee | 2:11.96 |
| 1500 | Anne Connolly | 4:40.98 |
| 3000 | Ann Welsh | 10:24.47 |
| 60H | Natasha Danvers | 8.60 |
| HJ | Michelle Dunkley | 1.79 |
| PV | Clare Ridgley | 3.00 |
| LJ | Tammy McCammon | 5.76 |
| TJ | Catherine Burrows | 11.72 |
| SP | Philippa Roles | 13.72 |
| 3kW | Sarah Bennett | 15:22.58 |

### Under 17

| | | |
|---|---|---|
| | Sarah Wilhelmy | 7.54 |
| | Sarah Wilhelmy | 24.52 |
| 300 | Gael Davies | 40.58 |
| | Emma Davies | 2:16.36 |
| | Maria Lynch (IRE) | 4:46.79 |
| | | |
| | Julie Pratt | 8.82 |
| | Lee McConnell | 1.74 |
| | Becky Ridgley | 2.60 |
| | Jade Johnson | 5.61 |
| | Rebecca White | 11.34 |
| | Helen Arnold | 11.72 |

### Under 15

| | | |
|---|---|---|
| | Dianne Howell | 7.81 |
| | Karlene Palmer | 25.38 |
| | | |
| | Aoife Byrne (IRE) | 2:16.30 |
| | | |
| | | |
| | Rachel Kay | 8.99 |
| | Lynsey Rankine | 1.60 |
| | | |
| | Emma Hughes | 5.26 |
| | | |
| | Amy Wilson | 11.32 |

## GB & NI v GER v RUS (U20) (indoors)  Erfurt, Germany  25 February 1995

### MEN

**60 Metres**
1. MARTIN GIRAUD — 6.76
2. DWAIN CHAMBERS — 6.90

**200 Metres**
1. MARLON DEVONISH — 21.51
2. TREVOR CAMERON — 21.68

**400 Metres**
1. HUGH KERR — 47.69
2. STEVEN MCHARDY — 48.65

**800 Metres**
1. A Mastrow RUS 1:50.57
4. ANDREW BLACKMORE — 1:53.65
6. ANDREW YOUNG — 1:55.01

### WOMEN

**60 Metres**
1. S Abel GER 7.47
4. DAWN ROSE — 7.67

**200 Metres**
1. C Bertmaring GER 24.25
2. SINEAD DUDGEON — 24.38

**400 Metres**
1. P Kotlyarova RUS 53.26
2. ALLISON CURBISHLEY — 54.53

**800 Metres**
1. O Rbruschek RUS 2:06.64
5. RHONDA MACPHEE — 2:11.30

**1500 Metres**
1. S Rordysheva RUS 4:26.73
5. CAROLYN SMITH — 4:40.03

**1500 Metres**
1. G Generalow RUS 3:50.00
2. DES ROACHE — 3:55.83

**60 Metres Hurdles**
1. A Kisllykh RUS 7.89
3. JAMES ARCHAMPONG — 8.03

**High Jump**
1. JAMES BRIERLEY — 2.14
2. MICHAEL ROBBINS — 2.11

**Pole Vault**
1. J Smiryagin RUS 5.45
5. MARK DAVIS — 4.40

**Long Jump**
1. C Walter GER 7.45
3. NATHAN MORGAN — 7.28

**60 Metres Hurdles**
1. NATASHA DANVERS — 8.42
6. RACHEL KING — 9.00

**High Jump**
1. O Kaliturina RUS 1.92
3. SUSAN JONES — 1.77

**Pole Vault**
1. K Recht GER 3.50
3. CLARE RIDGLEY — 3.40

**Long Jump**
1. S Stube GER 5.96
4. TAMMY MCCAMMON — 5.89

**Triple Jump**
1. V Tokovaja RUS 12.94
5. CATHERINE BURROWS — 11.71

**Triple Jump**
1. V Gushshinakij RUS 15.86
5. MARVIN BRAMBLE — 14.36

**Shot**
1. R Sack GER 16.92
5. BRUCE ROBB — 14.24

**5kWalk**
1. J Shmaliuk RUS 19:57.73
5. STUART MONK — 22:23.53

**Medley Relay**
1. GREAT BRITAIN — 4:25.34

**Match Result**
1. Russia — 213.5
2. Germany — 184.5
3. GREAT BRITAIN &NI — 145

**Shot**
1. O Ryabinkina RUS 15.97
5. PHILIPPA ROLES — 13.44
6. ELEANOR GATRELL — 12.97

**3kWalk**
1. T Gudkova RUS 12:52.69
5. SARAH BENNETT — 15:35.65
6. HELEN FORD-DUNN — 16:29.41

**Medley Relay**
1. GREAT BRITAIN — 2:44.54

**Match Result**
1. Russia — 104.5
2. Germany — 103.5
3. GREAT BRITAIN & NI — 56

## BAF CROSS COUNTRY CHAMPIONSHIPS Druridge Bay 5 March 1995

### MEN
1. SPENCER DUVAL — 39:29
2. DAVE CLARKE — 39:42
3. KEITH CULLEN — 40:00
4. TOMMY MURRAY — 40:16
5. ROBERT QUINN — 40:27
6. CHRISTIAN STEPHENSON — 40:30
7. MARTIN JONES — 40:35
8. RICHARD FINDLOW — 40:38
9. DAVE PAYNE — 40:41
10. ADRIAN PASSEY — 40:42
11. BRIAN RUSHWORTH — 40:47
12. MARK HUDSPITH — 40:51

### WOMEN
1. PAULA RADCLIFFE — 21:46
2. ANGIE HULLEY — 22:17
3. ALISON WYETH — 22:27
4. BEV HARTIGAN — 22:37
5. LUCY ELLIOTT — 22:43
6. HELEN TITTERINGTON — 22:52
7. ANDREA DUKE — 22:59
8. VIKKI McPHERSON — 23:01
9. JAYNE SPARK — 23:02
10. JANE SHIELDS — 23:10
11. HEATHER HEASMAN — 23:15
12. HAYLEY YELLING — 23:20

### JUNIOR MEN
1. BEN REESE — 28:09
2. ALLEN GRAFFIN — 28:14
3. ROBERT BROWN — 28:23
4. TONY FORREST — 28:34
5. NATHANIEL LANE — 28:37

### JUNIOR WOMEN
1. HEIDI MOULDER — 15:37
2. ALISON OUTRAM — 15:56
3. BEV GRAY — 15:56
4. ALICE BRAHAM — 16:01
5. NICOLA SLATER — 16:16

## ENGLISH CROSS COUNTRY CHAMPIONSHIPS Luton 11 March 1995

### MEN
1. SPENCER DUVAL — 43:43
2. ANDREW PEARSON — 44:28
3. CHRIS ROBISON — 44:40
4. GLYN TROMANS — 44:50
5. DAVE PAYNE — 44:57
6. DAVE TAYLOR — 45:13
7. KEITH ANDERSON — 45:17
8. DOMINIC BANNISTER — 45:23
9. TIM DICKINSON — 45:26
10. JOHN NUTTALL — 45:33
11. SPENCER NEWPORT — 45:34
12. DARREN COONEY — 45:46

### MEN Under 20
1. DANNY McCORMACK — 30:18
2. WILL LEVETT — 30:23
3. BRUNO WITCHALLS — 30:30
4. JOE FORESHEW — 30:36
5. NEIL CADDY — 30:47
6. MARK STEINLE — 30:48

### MEN Under 17
1. ANDREW GRAFFIN — 18:54
2. ALISTAIR MOSES — 18:57
3. JAMES HUNTER — 19:02
4. MIKE EAST — 19:11
5. DALE CANNING — 19:19
6. DANIEL GETLIFFE — 19:24

### WOMEN
1. Kate McCandless USA — 19:55
2. ALISON WYETH — 20:13
3. SUSAN McGEORGE — 20:27
4. ANDREA WALLACE — 20:33
5. HELEN TITTERINGTON — 20:37
6. LOUISE WATSON — 20:43
7. JILL HARRISON — 20:49
8. ANDREA DUKE — 20:52
9. ANDREA WHITCOMBE — 20:57
10. LYNNE ROBINSON — 21:02
11. LUCY ELLIOTT — 21:13
12. SUE PARKER — 21:16

### WOMEN Under 20
1. ALICE BRAHAM — 16:59
2. BEV GRAY — 17:11
3. ALISON OUTRAM — 17:29
4. JESSICA TURNBULL — 17:38

### WOMEN Under 17
1. VICKY ROBINSON — 18:14
2. CLARE DUNCAN — 18:24
3. JENNIFER GIBSON — 18:25
4. ANDREA KERSHAW — 18:40

### WOMEN Under 15
1. JACKIE HOGAN — 12:34
2. JODIE SWALLOW — 12:34
3. CLARE CAMPBELL — 12:39
4. SARAH DUGDALE — 12:40

### WOMEN Under 13
1. CARLEY WILSON — 10:47
2. EMMA WARD — 10:55
3. C DICKINSON — 11:07
4. ELIZABETH WHEELER — 11:11

## WORLD CROSS COUNTRY CHAMPIONSHIPS Durham 25 March 1995

### SENIOR MEN (12,020m)
1. Paul Tergat KEN — 34:05
2. Ismael Kirui KEN — 34:13
3. Salah Hissou MAR — 34:14
4. Haile Gebrselassie ETH — 34:26
5. Brahim Lahlafi MAR — 34:34
6. Paulo Guerra MAR — 34:38
7. James Songok KEN — 34:41
8. Simon Chemoiywo KEN — 34:46
9. Todd Williams USA — 34:47
10. Martín Fiz ESP — 34:50
20. ANDREW PEARSON — 35:07
55. KEITH CULLEN — 36:00
59. MARTIN JONES — 36:02
71. ADRIAN PASSEY — 36:14
72. CHRISTIAN STEPHENSON — 36:14
77. DAVE CLARKE — 36:17
81. TOMMY MURRAY — 36:20
100. ROBERT QUINN — 36:36
121. SPENCER DUVAL — 37:03

### Men's Teams
1. Kenya — 62
2. Morocco — 111
3. Spain — 120
9. GREAT BRITAIN & NI — 354

### SENIOR WOMEN (6,470m)
1. Derartu Tulu ETH — 20:21
2. Catherina McKiernan IRL — 20:29
3. Sally Barsosio KEN — 20:39
4. Margaret Ngotho KEN — 20:40
5. Gete Wami ETH — 20:49
6. Joan Nesbit USA — 20:50
7. Merima Denboba ETH — 20:53
8. Rose Cheruiyot KEN — 20:54
9. Albertina Dias POR — 20:56
10. Gabriela Szabo ROM — 20:57
11. Catherine Kirui KEN — 20:58
12. Zahra Ouaziz MAR — 21:06
18. PAULA RADCLIFFE — 21:14
24. BEV HARTIGAN — 21:21
44. ALISON WYETH — 21:38
78. ANGIE HULLEY — 22:07
83. LUCY ELLIOTT — 22:09
102. ANDREA DUKE — 22:31

### Women's Teams
1. Kenya — 26
2. Ethiopia — 38
3. Romania — 84
4. Japan — 102
9. GREAT BRITAIN & NI — 164

### JUNIOR MEN (8,470m)
1. Assefa Mezgebu ETH — 24:12
2. Dejene Lidetu ETH — 24:14
67. ALLEN GRAFFIN — 26:46
76. TONY FORREST — 26:54
85. MATTHEW O'DOWD — 27:04
92. BEN REESE — 27:10
107. ROBERT BROWN — 27:36
128. NATHANIAL LANE — 28:46

### Junior Men's Teams
1. Kenya — 23
15. GREAT BRITAIN & NI — 320

### JUNIOR WOMEN (4,470m)
1. Annemari Sandell FIN — 14:04
2. Jebiwot Keitany KEN — 14:09
20. ALICE BRAHAM — 14:58
27. NICOLA SLATER — 15:08
30. BEVERLEY GRAY — 15:15
56. HEIDI MOULDER — 15:41
58. ALISON OUTRAM — 15:44
78. MICHELLE MANN — 16:10

### Junior Women's Teams
1. Kenya — 18
6. GREAT BRITAIN & NI — 133

# WORLD INDOOR CHAMPIONSHIPS Barcelona, Spain 10-12 March 1995

## MEN

### 60 Metres (10 Mar)

| 1. | Bruny Surin | CAN | 6.46 |
|----|----|----|----|
| 2. | DARREN BRAITHWAITE | | 6.51 |
| 3. | Robert Esmie | CAN | 6.55 |
| 4. | Marc Blume | GER | 6.59 |
| 6. | Gus Nketia | NZL | 6.63 |
| 7. | Patrick Strenius | SWE | 6.64 |
| 8. | Vitaliy Savin | KZK | 6.65 |

3s1 MICHAEL ROSSWESS  6.62

### 200 Metres (11 Mar)

| 1. | Geir Moen | NOR | 20.58 |
|----|----|----|----|
| 2. | Troy Douglas | BER | 20.94 |
| 3. | Sebastian Keitel | CHI | 20.98 |
| 4. | Donovan Bailey | CAN | 21.08 |

2s1 JOHN REGIS  dns f  20.94
1h2 SOLOMON WARISO  dns s/f  21.39

### 400 Metres (12 Mar)

| 1. | Darnell Hall | USA | 46.17 |
|----|----|----|----|
| 2. | Sunday Bada | NGR | 46.38 |
| 3. | Mikhail Vdovin | RUS | 46.65 |
| 4. | Carlos Silva | POR | 46.87 |
| 5. | Son Ju-Il | KOR | 47.90 |
| 6. | Calvin Davis | USA | 47.19 |

5h2 PAUL SLYTHE  47.66
5h3 MARK HYLTON  50.26

### 800 Metres (12 Mar)

| 1. | Clive Terrelonge | JAM | 1:47.30 |
|----|----|----|----|
| 2. | Benson Koech | KEN | 1:47.51 |
| 3. | Pavel Soukup | CZE | 1:47.74 |
| 4. | Tor Oyvind Odegård | NOR | 1:48.34 |
| 5. | Mahjoub Haïda | MAR | 1:48.63 |
| 6. | Joseph Tengelei | KEN | 1:49.22 |

### 1500 Metres (11 Mar)

| 1. | Hicham El Guerrouj | MAR | 3:44.54 |
|----|----|----|----|
| 2. | Mateo Cañellas | ESP | 3:44.85 |
| 3. | Eric Nedeau | USA | 3:44.91 |
| 4. | Niall Bruton | IRL | 3:45.05 |
| 5. | Vyacheslav Shabunin | RUS | 3:45.40 |
| 6. | Fermin Cacho | ESP | 3:45.46 |
| 7. | Rudiger Stenzel | GER | 3:45.64 |
| 8. | Dominique Loser | GER | 3:46.09 |

11. ANTHONY WHITEMAN  3:47.50
6h2 BRIAN TREACY  3:47.18

### 3000 Metres (12 Mar)

| 1. | Gennaro Di Napoli | ITA | 7:50.89 |
|----|----|----|----|
| 2. | Anacleto Jiménez | SPA | 7:50.98 |
| 3. | Brahim Jabbour | MAR | 7:51.42 |
| 4. | Mohamed Suleiman | QAT | 7:51.73 |
| 5. | JOHN MAYOCK | | 7:51.86 |
| 6. | Reuben Reina | USA | 7:53.86 |
| 7. | Shaun Creighton | AUS | 7:54.46 |
| 8. | Isaac Viciosa | ESP | 8:01.00 |

### 60 Metres Hurdles (12 Mar)

| 1. | Allen Johnson | USA | 7.39 |
|----|----|----|----|
| 2. | Courtney Hawkins | USA | 7.41 |
| 3. | TONY JARRETT | • | 7.42 |
| 4. | Mark McKoy | AUT | 7.46 |
| 5. | Emilio Valle | CUB | 7.67 |
| 6. | Antti Haapakoski | FIN | 7.70 |
| 7. | Frank Busemann | GER | 7.70 |
| 8. | Kyle Vander-Kuyp | AUS | 7.73 |

6h4 BRIAN TAYLOR  8.00

### High Jump (12 Mar)

| 1. | Javier Sotomayor | CUB | 2.38 |
|----|----|----|----|
| 2. | Lambros Papakostas | GRE | 2.35 |
| 3. | Tony Barton | USA | 2.32 |
| 4. | Steinar Hoen | NOR | 2.32 |
| 5. | Ralf Sonn | GER | 2.38 |
| 6. | Stevan Zoric | YUG | 2.28 |
| 7. | Steve Smith | USA | 2.28 |
| 8= | DALTON GRANT | | 2.28 |
| 8= | Ettore Ceresoli | ITA | 2.28 |

15QBRENDAN REILLY  2.20

### Pole Vault (11 Mar)

| 1. | Sergey Bubka | UKR | 5.90 |
|----|----|----|----|
| 2. | Igor Potapovich | KZK | 5.80 |
| 3= | Okkert Brits | RSA | 5.75 |
| 3= | ANdrej Tiwontschik | GER | 5.75 |
| 5= | Nick Hysong | USA | 5.70 |
| 5= | José Manuel Arcos | ESP | 5.70 |
| 7= | Javier García | ESP | 5.60 |
| 7= | Maksim Tarasov | RUS | 5.60 |

### Long Jump (11 Mar)

| 1. | Iván Pedroso | CUB | 8.51 |
|----|----|----|----|
| 2. | Mattias Sunneborn | SWE | 8.20 |
| 3. | Erick Walder | USA | 8.14 |
| 4. | Joe Greene | USA | 8.12 |
| 5. | Bogdan Tudor | ROM | 8.11 |
| 6. | Milan Gombala | CZE | 7.95 |
| 7. | Erik Nijs | BEL | 7.88 |
| 8. | Huang Geng | CHN | 7.83 |

17QFRED SALLE  7.69

### Triple Jump (12 Mar)

| 1. | Brian Wellman | BER | 17.72 |
|----|----|----|----|
| 2. | Yoelvis Quesada | CUB | 17.62 |
| 3. | Serge Hélan | FRA | 17.06 |
| 4. | Lars Hedman | SWE | 16.86 |
| 5. | Arne Holm | SWE | 16.81 |
| 6. | LaMArk Carter | USA | 16.80 |
| 7. | FRANCIS AGYEPONG | | 16.74 |
| 8. | Garfield Anselm | FRA | 16.51 |

### Shot (10 Mar)

| 1. | Mika Halvari | FIN | 20.74 |
|----|----|----|----|
| 2. | C. J. Hunter | USA | 20.58 |
| 3. | Dragan Peric | YUG | 20.36 |
| 4. | Manuel Martínez | ESP | 19.97 |
| 5. | Yuriy Belonog | UKR | 19.74 |
| 6. | Petur Gudmundsson | ISL | 19.67 |
| 7. | Paolo Dal Soglio | ITA | 19.44 |
| 8. | Oliver Dück | GER | 19.24 |

### Heptathlon (11-12 Mar)

| 1. | Christian Plaziat | FRA | 6246 |
|----|----|----|----|
| 2. | Tomás Dvorák | CZE | 6169 |
| 3. | Henrik Dagård | SWE | 6142 |
| 4. | Ricky Barker | USA | 6120 |
| 5. | ALEX KRUGER | | 5978 |
| 6. | Antonio Peñalver | ESP | 5939 |
| 7. | Erki Nool | EST | 5887 |
| 8. | Sébastian Levicq | FRA | 5870 |

### 4 x 400 Metres Relay (12 Mar)

| 1. | United States | 3:07.37 |
|----|----|----|
| 2. | Italy | 3:09.12 |
| 3. | Japan | 3:09.73 |
| 4. | GREAT BRITAIN & NI | 3:10.89 |

## WOMEN

### 60 Metres (10 Mar)

| 1. | Merlene Ottey | JAM | 6.97 |
|----|----|----|----|
| 2. | Melanie Paschke | GER | 7.10 |
| 3. | Carlette Guidry | USA | 7.11 |
| 4. | Liliana Allen | CUB | 7.13 |
| 5. | Beverly McDonald | JAM | 7.16 |
| 6. | Nelli Fiere-Cooman | HOL | 7.17 |
| 7. | Chryste Gaines | USA | 7.22 |
| 8. | Lalao Ravaonirina | MAD | 7.28 |

7s2 STEPHANIE DOUGLAS  7.30
6h3 AILEEN MCGILLIVARY  7.44

### 200 Metres (10 Mar)

| 1. | Melinda Gainsford | AUS | 22.64 |
|----|----|----|----|
| 2. | Pauline Davis | BAH | 22.68 |
| 3. | Natalya Voronova | RUS | 23.01 |
| 4. | Silke Lichtenhagen | GER | 23.23 |
| 5. | Zlatka Georgieva | BUL | 23.36 |
| 6. | Juliet Cuthbert | JAM | 23.43 |

5h4 SHARON WILLIAMS  24.28

### 400 Metres (12 Mar)

| 1. | Irina Privalova | RUS | 50.23 |
|----|----|----|----|
| 2. | Sandie Richards | JAM | 51.38 |
| 3. | Daniela Georgieva | BUL | 51.78 |
| 4. | Deon Hemmings | JAM. | 52.01 |
| 5. | Jearl Miles | USA | 52.01 |
| 6. | Marie-Louise Bévis | FRA | 53.27 |

4h2 MELANIE NEEF  53.34
5h3 SUSAN EARNSHAW  53.85

**800 Metres** (12 Mar)
1. Maria Mutola MOZ 1:57.62
2. Yelena Afanasyeva RUS 1:59.79
3. Letitia Vriesde SUR 2:00.36
4. Irina Samorokova RUS 2:00.43
5. Stella Jongmans HOL 2:01.14
6. Inez Turner JAM 2:02.00

4h3 ABIGAIL HUNTE 2:07.82

**1500 Metres** (12 Mar)
1. Regina Jacobs USA 4:12.61
2. Carla Sacramento POR 4:13.02
3. Maite Zúñiga ESP 4:16.63
4. Kristen Seabury USA 4:16.77
5. Yvonne van der Kolk HOL 4:17.00
6. Paula Schnurr CAN 4:19.26
7. LYNN GIBSON 4:20.85
8. C Mabel Arrura ARG 4:31.15

**3000 Metres** (11 Mar)
1. Gabriela Szabo ROM 8:54.50
2. Lynn Jennings USA 8:55.23
3. Joan Nesbit USA 8:56.08
4. Elisa Rea ITA 8:56.21
5. Lidiya Vasilevskaya RUS 8:58.28
6. Marta Domínguez ESP 9:01.79
7. Zahra Ouaziz MAR 9:03.84
8. Annette Sergent-Palluy FRA 9:04.03

**60 Metres Hurdles** (12 Mar)
1. Aliuska López CUB 7.92
2. Olga Shishiginia KZK 7.92
3. Brigita Bukovec SLO 7.93

4. Monique Tourret FRA 7.98
5. JACKIE AGYEPONG 8.01
6. Cheryl Dickey USA 8.19
7. Michelle Freeman JAM 8.21

5h4 SAM FARQUHARSON 8.21

**High Jump** (11 Mar)
1. Alina Astafei GER 2.01
2. Britta Bilac SLO 1.99
3. Heike Henkel GER 1.99
4. Tatyana Motkova RUS 1.96
5. Yelena Gulyayeva RUS 1.96
6. Tatyana Shevchik BLR 1.96
7. Tisha Waller USA 1.93
8. Sigrid Kirchmann AUT 1.93

**Long Jump** (12 Mar)
1. Lyudmila Galkina RUS 6.95
2. Irina Mushayilova RUS 6.90
3. Susen Tiedke-Greene GER 6.90
4. Nicole Boegman AUS 6.81
5. Renata Nielsen DEN 6.77
6. Claudia Gerhardt GER 6.65
7. Yao Weili CHN 6.57
8. Marieta Ilcu ROM 6.52

**Triple Jump** (11 Mar)
1. Yolanda Chen RUS 15.03
2. Iva Prandzheva BUL 14.71
3. Ren Ruiping CHN 14.37
4. Sarka Kaspárková CZE 14.25

5. Mariya Sokova RUS 14.22
6. Niurka Montalvo CUB 14.04
7. Yelena Govorova UKR 14.04
8. Sheila H-Strudwick USA 13.88

**Shot** (11 Mar)
1. Larisa Peleshenko RUS 19.93
2. Kathrin Neimke GER 19.40
3. Connie Price-Smith USA 19.12
4. Grit Hammer GER 19.02
5. Zhang Liuhong CHN 18.84
6. Sui Xinmei CHN 18.81
7. Valentina Fedyushina UKR 18.48
8. Mihaela Oana ROM 18.07
9. JUDY OAKES 17.77

**Pentathlon** (10 Mar)
1. Svetlana Moskalets RUS 4834
2. Kym Carter USA 4632
3. Irina Tyukhay RUS 4622
4. Svetlana Buraga BLR 4466
5. Liliana Nastase ROM 4447
6. Mona Steigauf GER 4445
7. Anzhela Atroshchenko BLR 4441
8. Sharon Jaklofsky HOL 4434

**4 x 400 Metres Relay** (12 Mar)
1. Russia 3:29.29
2. Czech Republic 3:30.27
3. United States 3:31.43
4. GREAT BRITAIN & NI 3:35.39
5. China 3:39.76

## LONDON MARATHON
2 April 1995

**MEN**
1. Dionicio Ceron MEX 2:08:30
2. Steve Moneghetti AUS 2:08:33
3. Antonio Pinto POR 2:08:48
4. Xolile Yawa RSA 2:10:22
5. PAUL EVANS 2:10:31
6. Joaquim Pinheiro POR 2:10:35
7. Willie Mtolo RSA 2:11:35
8. Luigi Di Lello ITA 2:11:36
11. MARK HUDSPITH 2:11:58
12. PETER WHITEHEAD 2:12:23
13. EAMONN MARTIN 2:12:44
16. COLIN MOORE 2:15:02
23. CHRIS BUCKLEY 2:19:05

**WOMEN**
1. Malgorzata Sobanska POL 2:27:43
2. Manuela Machado POR 2:27:53
3. Ritva Lemettinen FIN 2:28:00
4. Renata Kokowska POL 2:30:35
5. LIZ MCCOLGAN 2:31:14
6. Kim Jones USA 2:31:35
7. Katrin Dorre GER 2:32:16
8. Nyla Carroll NZL 2:33:19
14. HAYLEY NASH 2:39:59
16. LYNN HARDING 2:41:20
17. JULIE COLEBY 2:41:37
19. ERYL DAVIES 2:44:43
20. CHRISTINA SCOBEY 2:46:24

## IAAF WORLD MARATHON CUP
Athens, Greece   9 April 1995

**MEN**
1. Douglas Wakiihuri KEN 2:12:01
2. Takahiro Sunada JAP 2:13:16
3. Davide Milesi ITA 2:13:23
4. Juan Torres ESP 2:14:48
5. Moges Taye ETH 2:14:53
6. Marco Gozzano ITA 2:14:58
7. Roberto Crosio ITA 2:15:21
8. Jean Marie Gehin FRA 2:15:27
9. Bartolomé Serrano ESP 2:15:43
10. Joseph Skosana RSA 2:15:47
11. Dominique Chauvelier FRA 2:15:58
12. Pascal Fetizon FRA 2:17:22
13. Aleksandr Vychyuzhanin RUS 2:17:41
14. Shingo Nakamura JAP 2:17:54
15. Vladimir Plykin RUS 2:18:14
16. Anatoliy Archakov RUS 2:18:19
17. Giovanni Ruggiero ITA 2:18:26
18. BILL FOSTER 2:18:45
34. DANIEL RATHBONE 2:22:48
40. TREVOR CLARK 2:24:10
44. IAN BLOOMFIELD 2:24:51
50. ROBIN NASH 2:26:31

**Teams**
1. Italy 6:43:32
2. France 6:48:47
3. Spain 6:51:05
9. GREAT BRITAIN & NI 7:05:43

**WOMEN**
1. Anuta Catuna ROM 2:31:10
2. Lidia Simon ROM 2:31:46
3. Cristina Pomacu ROM 2:32:09
4. Ornella Ferrara ITA 2:32:56
5. María Luisa Munoz ESP 2:34:35
6. Larisa Zyusko RUS 2:34:43
7. Cristina Burca ROM 2:34:55
8. Nadezhda Ilyina RUS 2:35:16
9. Maria Rebelo FRA 2:35:17
10. Josette C-Janin FRA 2:36:33
11. Marina Belyayeva RUS 2:37:40
12. Adriana Barbu ROM 2:37:46
13. Olga Yudenkova BLR 2:37:47
14. Emebet Abosa ETH 2:38:19
15. Maura Viceconte ITA 2:38:22
16. Antonella Bizioli ITA 2:39:28
17. Maryse Le Gallo FRA 2:39:50
24. ALISON ROSE 2:42:42
25. TRUDI THOMSON 2:42:44
27. CAROLINE HORNE 2:43:19
33. LESLEY TURNER 2:46:46
dnf ZINA MARCHANT

**Teams**
1. Romania 7:35:05
2. Russia 7:47:39
3. Italy 7:50:46
7. GREAT BRITAIN & NI 8:08:45

# IAAF WORLD RACE WALKING CUP
## Beijing, China   29 - 30 April 1995

**Men**

**20 Kilometres** (29 Apr)

| | | |
|---|---|---|
| 1. Li Zewen | CHN | 1:19:44 |
| 2. Mikhail Shchennikov | RUS | 1:19:58 |
| 3. Bernardo Segura | MEX | 1:20:32 |
| 4. Yevgeniy Misyulya | BLR | 1:20:39 |
| 5. Michele Didoni | ITA | 1:20:50 |
| 6. Chen Shaogua | CHN | 1:20:57 |
| 7. Thierry Toutain | FRA | 1:21:06 |
| 8. Bu Lingtang | CHN | 1:21:11 |
| 9. Robert Korzeniowski | POL | 1:21:28 |
| 10. Li Mingcai | CHN | 1:21:41 |
| 29. DARRELL STONE | | 1:24:49 |
| 58. STEVE PARTINGTON | | 1:30:02 |
| 70. ANDREW PENN | | 1:31:45 |
| 80. CHRIS CHEESEMAN | | 1:34:23 |

**Team**

| | |
|---|---|
| 1. China | 436 |
| 2. Italy | 422 |
| 3. Mexico | 420 |
| 4. France | 409 |
| 5. Poland | 392 |
| 6. Byelorus | 384 |
| 7. Japan | 357 |
| 8. Slovak Republic | 340 |
| 13. GREAT BRITAIN & NI | 314 |

**50 Kilometres** (30 Apr)

| | | |
|---|---|---|
| 1. Zhao Yongshen | CHN | 3:41:20 |
| 2. Jesús Garcia | ESP | 3:41:54 |
| 3. Valentin Kononen | FIN | 3:42:50 |
| 4. Valeriy Spitsyn | RUS | 3:43:36 |
| 5. Miguel Rodríguez | MEX | 3:44:07 |
| 6. Viktor Ginko | BLR | 3:45:48 |
| 7. René Piller | FRA | 3:45:56 |
| 8. Carlos Mercenario | MEX | 3:46:46 |
| 9. Sergey Korepanov | KZK | 3:48:06 |
| 10. Alexey Voyevodin | RUS | 3:48:55 |
| 42. MARK EASTON | | 4:06:01 |
| 44. LES MORTON | | 4:08:52 |
| 72. GRAHAM WHITE | | 4:29:41 |

**Team**

| | |
|---|---|
| 1. Mexico | 426 |
| 2. Russia | 419 |
| 3. Spain | 413 |
| 4. Slovak Republic | 395 |
| 5. France | 394 |
| 6. Italy | 393 |
| 7. Byelorus | 386 |
| 8. Finland | 376 |
| 16. GREAT BRITAIN & NI | 311 |

**The Lugano Trophy -** sum of points above GREAT BRITAIN & NI 14th

**Women**

**10 Kilometres** (29 Apr)

| | | |
|---|---|---|
| 1. Gao Hongmiao | CHN | 42:19 |
| 2. Yelena Nikolayeva | RUS | 42:32 |
| 3. Liu Hongyu | CHN | 42:49 |
| 4. Gu Yan | CHN | 42:55 |
| 5. Kerry Saxby-Junna | AUS | 42:58 |
| 6. Elisabetta Perrone | ITA | 43:13 |
| 7. Olga Leonenko | UKR | 43:34 |
| 8. Rosella Giordano | ITA | 43:44 |
| 9. Annarita Sidoti | ITA | 43:55 |
| 10. Tamara Kovalenko | RUS | 43:56 |
| 36. LISA LANGFORD | | 46:00 |
| 51. VICKY LUPTON | | 47:04 |
| 60. CAROLYN PARTINGTON | | 48:17 |
| 69. VERITY SNOOK | | 48:42 |
| 82. MELANIE WRIGHT | | 50:50 |

**Team - The Eschborn Cup**

| | |
|---|---|
| 1. China | 443 |
| 2. Italy | 427 |
| 3. Russia | 422 |
| 4. Byelorus | 400 |
| 5. Australia | 386 |
| 6. Mexico | 378 |
| 7. Spain | 376 |
| 8. Ukraine | 374 |
| 16. GREAT BRITAIN & NI | 323 |

## U23 International Men   Zorfingen, Switzerland   5 June 1995

**100 Metres Race 1**  wind -1.5

| | |
|---|---|
| 1. IAN MACKIE | 10.65 |

**100 Metres Race 2**  wind -0.5

| | |
|---|---|
| 1. OWUSU DAKO | 10.42 |
| 2. PETER MAITLAND | 10.43 |

**200 Metres Race 1** wind -0.9

| | |
|---|---|
| 1. PETER MAITLAND | 21.02 |

**200 Metres Race 2**  wind -1.4

| | | |
|---|---|---|
| 1. K Wildmer | SUI | 20.97 |
| 4. IAN MACKIE | | 21.53 |

**400 Metres Race 1**

| | | |
|---|---|---|
| 1. GUY BULLOCK | | 46.64 |
| 2. D Zichenberger | SUI | 47.90 |

**400 Metres Race 2**

| | | |
|---|---|---|
| 1. M Rusterholz | SUI | 46.02 |
| 2. ADRIAN PATRICK | | 46.33 |

**800 Metres Race 1**

| | |
|---|---|
| 1. EWAN CALVERT | 1:50.09 |

**800 Metres Race 2**

| | | |
|---|---|---|
| 1. F Amrein | SUI | 1:48.99 |
| 5. JUSTIN SWIFT-SMITH | | 1:50.14 |

**1500 Metres**

| | | |
|---|---|---|
| 1. A Bucher | SUI | 3:45.80 |
| 3. NEIL CADDY | | 3:46.43 |

**5000 Metres**

| | | |
|---|---|---|
| 1. G Tanui | KEN | 14:09.89 |
| 2. SPENCER BARDEN | | 14:10.88 |

**3000 Metres Steeplechase**

| | | |
|---|---|---|
| 1. CHRIS ELLIOTT | | 9:08.81 |
| 2. J Schwarz | SUI | 9:08.83 |
| 3. NORMAN OLIVER | | 9:11.13 |

**110 Metres Hurdles 1**  wind -0.9

| | | |
|---|---|---|
| 1. NEIL OWEN | | 14.18 |
| 2. O Shmueli | ISR | 14.72 |

**110 Metres Hurdles 2**  wind -1.2

| | | |
|---|---|---|
| 1. NEIL OWEN | | 13.87 |
| 2. G Schnorr | SUI | 14.05 |

**400 Metres Hurdles Race 1**

| | |
|---|---|
| 1. TONY BURSUMATO | 51.99 |

**400 Metres Hurdles Race 2**

| | | |
|---|---|---|
| 1. S Pluckiger | SUI | 51.50 |
| 3. BARRY MIDDLETON | | 52.96 |

**High Jump**

| | |
|---|---|
| 1. ANDREW LYNCH | 2.17 |
| 2. STUART OHRLAND | 2.11 |

**Pole Vault**

| | | |
|---|---|---|
| 1. NEIL WINTER | | 5.40 |
| 2. S Klien | AUT | 4.80 |
| MICHAEL BARBER | | no ht |

**Long Jump**

| | |
|---|---|
| 1. CARL HOWARD | 7.41 |
| 2. ONOCHIE ONUORAH | 7.36 |

**Triple Jump**

| | | |
|---|---|---|
| 1. A Tayari | ISR | 15.87 |
| 2. R Nachum | ISR | 15.79 |
| 3. TAYO EREGBOGBU | | 15.50 |

**Shot**

| | | |
|---|---|---|
| 1. M Sandmeiser | SUI | 17.35 |
| 4. LEE NEWMAN | | 15.90 |
| 7. MARK EDWARDS | | 14.83 |

**Discus**

| | | |
|---|---|---|
| 1. LEE NEWMAN | | 52.76 |
| 2. P Buchs | GER | 52.48 |
| 3. JAMIE MURPHY | | 52.44 |
| 4. ROBERT RUSSELL | | 48.34 |

**Javelin**

| | | |
|---|---|---|
| 1. A Grossenbacher | SUI | 70.38 |
| 2. STUART FABEN | | 69.34 |

**MEN**    # EUROPEAN CUP   Villeneuve d'Ascq, France   24 - 25 June 1995

### 100 Metres wind 2.0 (24 Jun)
1. LINFORD CHRISTIE   10.05
2. Andrei Grigorjev   RUS   10.27
3= Ezio Madonia   ITA   10.32
3= Matias Ghansah   SWE   10.32
5. Marc Blume   GER   10.37
6. Jordi Mayoral   ESP   10.46
7. Dmitriy Vanyaikin   UKR   10.48
8. Marek Zalewski   POL   10.64

### 200 Metres wind 1.9 (25 Jun)
1. LINFORD CHRISTIE   20.11
2. Vladislav Dologodin   UKR   20.35
3. Aleksander Sokolov   RUS   20.64
4. Christian Konieczny   GER   20.65
5. Torbjörn Eriksson   SWE   20.81
6. Krzysztof Sienko   POL   20.95
7. Francisco Navarro   ESP   21.00
8. Andrea Colombo   ITA   21.00

### 400 Metres (24 Jun)
1. MARK RICHARDSON   45.43
2. Andrea Nuti   ITA   46.40
3. Karsten Just   GER   46.42
4. Valentin Kulbatskiy   UKR   46.47
5. Dmitriy Kosov   RUS   46.84
6. Marko Granat   SWE   47.18
7. Pawel Januszewski   POL   47.44
8. Cayetano Cornet   ESP   47.56

### 800 Metres (25 Jun)
1. Nico Motchebon   GER   1:46.75
2. Andrzej Jakubiec   POL   1:47.15
3. Andrea Giocondi   ITA   1:47.33
4. Andrey Loginov   RUS   1:47.33
5. José Cerezo   ESP   1:47.54
6. Torbjörn Johansson   SWE   1:48.01
7. Anatoly Yakimovitch   UKR   1:48.76
8. CRAIG WINROW   1:48.84

### 1500 Metres (24 Jun)
1. Rudiger Stenzel   GER   3:42.58
2. Vyacheslav Shabunin   RUS   3:42.59
3. Fermin Cacho   ESP   3:44.20
4. GARY LOUGH   3:45.11
5. Andrey Bulkovski   UKR   3:45.87
6. Piotr Rostowski   POL   3:46.08
7. Giuseppe D'Urso   ITA   3:49.46
8. Jörgen Zaki   SWE   3:50.96

### 5000 Metres (25 Jun)
1. Gennaro Di Napoli   ITA   13:45.57
2. JOHN NUTTALL   13:46.82
3. Manuel Pancorbo   ESP   13:48.93
4. Vener Kashayev   RUS   13:49.69
5. Michal Bartoszak   POL   13:53.57
6. Thorsten Naumann   GER   13:55.91
7. Claes Nyberg   SWE   14:00.68
8. Victor Rogovoy   RUS   14:36.67

### 10000 Metres (24 Jun)
1. Stefano Baldini   ITA   28:45.77
2. Stephan Freigang   GER   28:46.34
3. Alejandro Gomez   ESP   28:46.76
4. Oleg Strizhakov   RUS   29:00.78
5. Valery Chesak   UKR   29:22.07
6. JUSTIN HOBBS   29:25.92
7. Bjarne Thysell   SWE   29:48.42
8. Piotr Gladki   POL   30:52.47

### 3000 Metres Steeplechase (25 Jun)
1. Aless. Lambruschini   ITA   8:21.94
2. Steffen Brand   GER   8:24.00
3. Javier Rodriguez   ESP   8:25.03
4. Vladimir Pronin   RUS   8:25.93
5. JUSTIN CHASTON   8:26.82
6. Rafal Wojcik   POL   8:38.98
7. Alexey Patserin   UKR   8:42.32
8. Magnus Bengtsson   SWE   8:58.87

### 110 Metres Hurdles 1.0 (25 Jun)
1. Florian Schwarthoff   GER   13.28
2. ANDREW TULLOCH   13.64
3. Dimitry Kolenichenko   UKR   13.67
4. Niklas Eriksson   SWE   13.69
5. Gennadiy Dakshevich   RUS   13.76
6. Ronald Mehlich   POL   13.79
7. M De Los Santos   ESP   13.92
8. Dario Volturara   ITA   14.12

### 400 Metres Hurdles (24 Jun)
1. Laurent Ottoz   ITA   49.30
2. Ruslan Mashchenko   RUS   49.49
3. Sven Nylander   SWE   49.64
4. GARY JENNINGS   50.43
5. Gennadiy Gorbenko   UKR   50.54
6. Michael Kaul   GER   50.63
7. Piotr Kotlarski   POL   50.84
8. Iñigo Monreal   ESP   51.86

### High Jump (24 Jun)
1. STEVE SMITH   2.31
2. Patrik Sjöberg   SWE   2.31
3. Artur Partyka   POL   2.25
4. Hendrik Beyer   GER   2.25
5. Vyacheslav Tyrtyshnik   UKR   2.25
6. Arturo Ortiz   ESP   2.21
7. Grigoriy Fyodorkov   RUS   2.15
8. Ettore Ceresoli   ITA   2.15

### Pole Vault (25 Jun)
1. Igor Trandenkov   RUS   5.80
2. Patrik Stenlund   SWE   5.60
3. Javier Garcia   ESP   5.50
4. Andrea Pegoraro   ITA   5.50
5. Vyacheslav Shuteyev   UKR   5.50
6. NICK BUCKFIELD   5.20
7. Adam Kolasa   POL   5.20
   Tim Lobinger   GER   nh

### Long Jump (24 Jun)
1. Stanislav Tarasenko   RUS   8.32w
2. Konstantin Krause   GER   8.11
3. Vitaliy Kirilenko   UKR   8.11w
4. Roberto Coltri   ITA   8.11
5. Krzystof Luczak   POL   7,96w
6. Jesús Olivan   ESP   7.86w
7. Peter Oldin   SWE   7.69w
8. JOHN MUNROE   7.64

### Triple Jump (25 Jun)
1. JONATHAN EDWARDS   18.43w
2. Jacek Butkiewicz   POL   17.14w
3. Arne Holm   SWE   16.70w
4. Julio Lopez   ESP   16.67w
5. Volker Mai   GER   16.57
6. Andrea Matarazzo   ITA   16.44
7. Viktor Sotnikov   RUS   16.28w
8. Gennadiy Glushenko   UKR   16.20w

### Shot (24 Jun)
1. Aleksandr Bagach   UKR   20.65
2. Sven-Oliver Buder   GER   20.28
3. Paolo Dal Soglio   ITA   19.80
4. Manuel Martinez   ESP   18.97
5. Thomas Hammarsten   SWE   18.54
6. Sergey Nikolayev   RUS   18.49
7. Piotr Perzylo   POL   18.11
8. MATT SIMSON   17.72

### Discus (25 Jun)
1. Lars Riedel   GER   68.76
2. Sergey Lyakhov   RUS   63.82
3. ROBERT WEIR   62.94
4. Kristian Pettersson   SWE   62.52
5. Vladimir Zinchenko   UKR   59.74
6. Diego Fortuna   ITA   58.52
7. David Martinez   ESP   57.48
8. Andrey Krawczyk   POL   55.62

### Hammer (25 Jun)
1. Ilya Konovalov   RUS   79.66
2. Vadim Kolesnik   UKR   76.66
3. Karsten Kobs   GER   76.32
4. Per Karlsson   SWE   75.22
5. Enrico Sgrulletti   ITA   75.14
6. Szymon Ziolkowski   POL   72.66
7. PETER VIVIAN   71.28
8. Jose Perez   ESP   66.76

### Javelin (24 Jun)
1. Raymond Hecht   GER   87.24
2. Andrey Moruyev   RUS   82.80
3. STEVE BACKLEY   81.96
4. Miroslaw Witek   POL   78.00
5. Andrey Uglov   UKR   75.82
6. Peter Borglund   SWE   73.76
7. Carlo Sonego   ITA   68.92
8. Julián Sotelo   ESP   64.58

### 4 x 100 Metres Relay (24 Jun)
1. GREAT BRITAIN & NI   38.73
   (GARDENER, JARRETT,
   BRAITHWAITE, CHRISTIE)
2. Germany   39.12
3. Italy   39.19
4. Sweden   39.31
5. Ukraine   39.31
6. Spain   39.77
7. Poland   39.86
8. Russia   40.93

### 4 x 400 Metres Relay (25 Jun)
1. GREAT BRITAIN & NI   3:00.34
   (THOMAS, PATRICK,
   RICHARDSON, BLACK)
2. Italy   3:04.27
3. Germany   3:04.28
4. Poland   3:04.42
5. Russia   3:04.46
6. Ukraine   3:05.54
7. Sweden   3:06.96
8. Spain   3:07.67

## WOMEN

### 100 Metres  wind 2.0  (24 Jun)
1. Melanie Paschke      GER   11.08
2. Yekaterina Leshchova RUS   11.16
3. Delphine Combe       FRA   11.30
4. STEPHANIE DOUGLAS          11.30
5. Irina Pukha          UKR   11.35
6. Natalya Vinogradova  BLR   11.49
7. Laura Ardissone      ITA   11.55
8. Izabela Czajko       POL   11.64

### 200 Metres  wind 0.8  (25 Jun)
1. Silke Knoll          GER   22.45
2. Marina Trandenkova   RUS   22.67
3. Viktoriya Fomenko    UKR   22.75
4. PAULA THOMAS               22.89
5. Delphine Combe       FRA   23.11
6. Natalya Vinogradova  BLR   23.15
7. Giada Gallina        ITA   23.53
8. Izabela Czajko       POL   23.93

### 400 Metres  (24 Jun)
1. MELANIE NEEF               51.35
2. Yulia Sotnikova      RUS   51.81
3. Yelena Rurak         UKR   52.92
4. Evelyne Elien        FRA   52.92
5. Linda Kisabaka       GER   53.06
6. Danielle Perpoli     ITA   53.12
7. Anna Kozak           BLR   53.59
8. Barbara Grzywocz     POL   54.90

### 800 Metres  (24 Jun)
1. Yelena Afanasyeva    RUS  1:59.26
2. Patricia Djate       FRA  1:59.73
3. Natalya Dukhnova     BLR  2:00.07
4. SONYA BOWYER              2:01.67
5. Lidia Chojecka       POL  2:02.42
6. Kati Kovacs          GER  2:02.95
7. Eleonara Berlanda    ITA  2:04.63
8. Svetlana Tverdokhleb UKR  2:04.87

### 1500 Metres  (25 Jun)
1. KELLY HOLMES              4:07.02
2. Yekat. Podkopajeva   RUS  4:07.88
3. Svetlana Miroshnik   UKR  4:07.94
4. Carmen Wuestenhagen  GER  4:09.77
5. Yel. Bychkovskaya    BLR  4:10.79
6. Frédérique Quentin   FRA  4:11.95
7. Malgorzata Rydz      POL  4:14.78
8. Serenella Sbrissa    ITA  4:16.52

### 5000 Metres  (24 Jun)
1. Viktoriya Nenasheva  RUS 15:16.06
2. ALISON WYETH             15:19.44
3. TAMARA KOBA         UKR 15:20.97
4. Silvia Sommaggio     ITA 15:32.20
5. Rosario Murcia       FRA 15:32.80
6. Yelena Mazovka       BLR 15:36.09
7. Claudia Dreher       GER 15:54.93
8. Renata Sobiesiak     POL 16:56.87

### Match Results

### 10000 Metres  (25 Jun)
1. Maria Guida          ITA  32:01.75
2. Uta Pippig           GER  32:14.66
3. Alla Zhilyaeva       RUS  32:17.62
4. LIZ MCCOLGAN              32:22.09
5. Natalya Galushko     BLR  32:50.12
6. Nicole Leveque       FRA  33:57.31
7. Yulia Kovalyova      UKR  34:29.74
8. Dorota Gruca         POL  35:50.11

### 100 Metres Hurdles  1.5 (25 Jun)
1. Yuliya Graudyn       RUS   12.86
2. Yelena Ovtcharova    UKR   12.88
3. JACQUI AGYEPONG            12.90
4. Monique Tourret      FRA   12.92
5. Lidiya Yurkova       BLR   13.01
6. Caren Jung           GER   13.13
7. Carla Tuzzi          ITA   13.16
8. Urszula Wlodarczyk   POL   13.56

### 400 Metres Hurdles  (24 Jun)
1. Marie-Jose Perec     FRA   54.51
2. Tatyana Kurochkina   BLR   55.59
3. Tatyana Tereshchuk   UKR   56.05
4. Heike Meissner       GER   56.25
5. Monika Warnicka      POL   57.35
6. Olga Nazarova        RUS   57.61
7. LOUISE FRASER              57.91
8. Virna De Angeli      ITA   58.16

### High Jump  (25 Jun)
1. Alina Astafei        GER   2.00
2. Tatyana Motkova      RUS   1.98
3. Tatyana Shevchik     BLR   1.96
4. Katarzyna Majchrzak  POL   1.92
5. Larisa Serebryanskaya UKR  1.89
6. LEA HAGGETT               1.86
7. Isabelle Jeanne      FRA   1.86
8. Stefania Lovison     ITA   1.80

### Long Jump  (25 Jun)
1. Heike Drechsler      GER   7.04w
2. Fiona May            ITA   6.98w
3. Nadine Caster        FRA   6.94
4. Olga Rubleva         RUS   6.93w
5. Agata Karczmarek     POL   6.72
6. Yelena Khlopotnova   UKR   6.69
7. Anzhela Atroshchenko BLR   6.51w
8. DENISE LEWIS              6.51

### Triple Jump  (24 Jun)
1. ASHIA HANSEN              14.37
2. Yelena Sinchukova    RUS  14.30w
3. Zhanna Gureyeva      BLR  14.25
4. Yelena Khlusovich    UKR  14.08
5. Barbara Lah          ITA  14.06w
6. Caroline Honore      FRA  13.73w
7. Ramona Molzan        GER  13.39w
8. Ilona Pazola         POL  13.31

### MEN
1. Germany                   117
2. GREAT BRITAIN & NI        107
3. Russia                    105
4. Italy                     96.5
5. Ukraine                   82
6. Sweden                    78.5
7. Spain                     67
8. Poland                    66

### Shot  (24 Jun)
1. Astrid Kumbernuss    GER   20.00
2. Irina Korzhanenko    RUS   18.32
3. JUDY OAKES                18.17
4. Nadezhda Lukyniv     UKR   17.40
5. Natalya Gurskaya     BLR   16.77
6. Mara Rosolen         ITA   16.57
7. Laurence Manfredi    FRA   15.67
8. Katarzyna Zakowicz   POL   15.59

### Discus  (24 Jun)
1. Natalya Sadova       RUS   66.86
2. Ilke Wyludda         GER   66.04
3. Irina Yatchenko      BLR   64.46
4. Renata Katewicz      POL   61.70
5. JACKIE MCKERNAN           59.06
6. Isabelle Devaluez    FRA   57.68
7. Agnese Maffeis       ITA   57.26
8. Viktoriya Boyko      UKR   55.24

### Javelin  (25 Jun)
1. Steffi Nerius        GER   68.42
2. Natalya Shikolenko   BLR   50.83
3. Yekaterina Ivakina   RUS   61.36
4. Martine Begue        FRA   55.86
5. Olga Ivankova        UKR   55.82
6. Ewa Rybak            POL   54.84
7. SHARON GIBSON             54.38
8. Claudia Coslovich    ITA   53.48

### 4 x 100 Metres Relay  (24 Jun)
1. Russia                    42.74
2. Germany                   43.15
3. France                    43.63
4. GREAT BRITAIN & NI        44.10
   (DOUGLAS, MURPHY,
    JACOBS, THOMAS)
5. Italy                     44.27
6. Ukraine                   44.35
7. Belarus                   44.85
8. Poland                    45.47

### 4 x 400 Metres Relay  (25 Jun)
1. Russia                   3:24.69
2. Germany                  3:26.23
3. Ukraine                  3:27.33
4. GREAT BRITAIN & NI       3:28.34
   (NEEF, HANSON,
    TUNALEY, OLADAPO)
5. Italy                    3:29.39
6. France                   3:29.64
7. Belarus                  3:29.65
8. Poland                   3:34.72

### WOMEN
1. Russia                    117
2. Germany                   100
3. GREAT BRITAIN & NI        85
4. France                    75
5. Ukraine                   75
6. Belarus                   71
7. Italy                     52
8. Poland                    37

## U23 International Women   Basle, Switzerland   5 June 1995

**100 Metres Race 1**  wind -0.3
1.  SOPHIE SMITH             11.83
2.  M Donders         GER    11.87
3.  CATHERINE MURPHY         11.95

**100 Metres Race 2**  wind -0.5
1.  CATHERINE MURPHY         11.79
2.  M Donders         GER    11.79
3.  SOPHIE SMITH             11.97

**200 Metres**  wind -1.7
1.  CATHERINE MURPHY         23.57
2.  JOICE MADUAKA            23.98
3.  M Donders         GER    23.91

**400 Metres Race 1**
1.  JULIE MOORE              55.44

**400 Metres Race 2**
1.  R Zurcher         GER    53.28
3.  MICHELLE PIERRE          54.05

**800 Metres**
1.  U Friedmann       GER    2:05.74
3.  VICKY LAWRENCE           2:07.14

**1500 Metres**
1.  ELIZABETH TALBOT         4:19.85

**100 Metres Hurdles  1**  wind -0.2
1.  L Solli           SUI    13.49
2.  H Blassneck       GER    13.51
3.  DIANE ALLAHGREEN         13.66
6.  MELANIE WILKINS          14.11

**100 Metres Hurdles  2**  wind 0.5
1.  P Nadlac          GER    13.90
2.  UJU EFOBI                14.15

**Shot**
1.  N Ganguillec      FRA    16.07
3.  UJU EFOBI                13.71

**Discus**
1.  SHELLEY DREW             53.66
5.  SARAH HENTON             44.92

**Javelin**
1.  C Sogli           GER    55.06
2.  KAREN MARTIN             53.20
6.  LORNA JACKSON            43.62

**4 x 100 Metres Relay**
1.  GREAT BRITAIN            46.17
    (ALLAHGREEN, MADUAKA,
    SOPHIE SMITH, WILKINS)

## European Cup Combined Events Women   Helmond, Holland  1 - 2 July 1995

**Heptathlon**
1.  DENISE LEWIS             6299
    (13.66, 1.78, 13.19, 25.13, 6.52, 49.34, 2:18.54)
2.  Sharon Jaklofsky    HOL   6197
    (13.60, 1.78, 13.38, 25.17, 6.59, 41.06, 2:17.37)
3.  Anzhela Atroshchenko  BLR  6186
    (13.87, 1.84, 13.36, 24.58, 6.45, 40.26, 2:20.26)
4.  Irina Vostrikova    RUS   6122
    (13.99, 1.81, 14.61, 26.23, 6.12, 47.88, 2:19.32)
5.  Peggy Beer          GER   6080
    (13.82, 1.72, 13.61, 24.95, 5.99, 47.94, 2:16.47)
6.  Natalie Teppe       FRA   6072
    (14.22, 1.78, 13.00, 26.26, 6.12, 53.68, 2:13.98)
17. YINKA IDOWU               5655
    (14.05, 1.69, 12.74, 25.74, 6.54, 37.30, 2:31.33)
22. EMMA BEALES               5524
    (14.42, 1.69, 12.94, 25.30, 5.61, 40.40, 2:23.76)
24. JULIA BENNETT             5422
    (14.74, 1.87, 10.93, 25.81, 5.87, 29.78, 2:22.34)

**Team Result**
1.  Belarus               18,150
2.  Germany               17,755
3.  Russia                17,705
4.  Holland/Netherlands   17,552
5.  GREAT BRITAIN         17,479
6.  France                17,473
7.  Ukraine               16,939
8.  Poland                15,582

## U23 Wal v HOL v BEL   Utrecht, Holland   9 July 1995

**MEN**

**100 Metres**  wind 0.6
1.  JAMIE HENTHORN           10.48
5.  NEIL POWELL              11.02

**200 Metres**  wind 0.7
1.  JAMIE HENTHORN           21.12
3.  CHRISTIAN MALCOLM        21.58

**400 Metres**
1.  MARK PUNTING             48.02
4.  STEVEN EVANS             51.29

**800 Metres**
1.  Jeroen van Dijke   HOL   1:52.59
3.  RUSSELL CARTWRIGHT       1:54.36
5.  MATTHEW MCHUGH           1:56.55

**1500 Metres**
1.  Gunther Methot     BEL   3:54.60
2.  DAVID DAVEY              3:55.36
5.  CHRIS GRIFFITHS          4:04.48

**3000 Metres**
1.  Jeroen Broekzitter  HOL   8:32.76
2.  ANDRES JONES             8:33.96
6.  NATHANIEL LANE           8:47.25

**3000 Metres Steeplechase**
1.  Ramses Bekkenk     HOL   9:24.48
5.  LEIGH KINROY             10:24.36
6.  SIMON TYPE               10:24.36

**110 Metres Hurdles**  wind 1.5
1.  Sven Pieters       BEL   14.13
5.  STEVEN EDWARDS           15.83
6.  MATTHEW EVELEIGH         15.96

**400 Metres Hurdles**
1.  Freek Wilkens      HOL   54.38
2.  JAMES HILLIER            54.45
3.  JAMIE SHEFFIELD          54.91

**High Jump**
1.  Patrick de Paepe   BEL   2.05
2.  ANDREW PENK              2.05
4=  MATTHEW PERRY            1.95

**Pole Vault**
1.  Rudy Senecaut      BEL   4.60
2.  STEVEN FRANCIS           4.40
4.  PAUL JONES               3.80

**Long Jump**
1.  ANTHONY MALCOLM          6.88
2.  Jermaine Sedoc     HOL   6.74
5.  ANDREW WOODING           6.45

**Triple Jump**
1.  Patrick Huteba     BEL   14.35
2.  CHARLES COLE             14.06
6.  DARREN MORGAN            12.01

**Shot**

1. Mike van der Bilt  HOL  15.63
5. GARETH MARKS  12.09
6. STEVEN BRADLEY  11.30

**Discus**

1. Mike van der Bilt  HOL  55.38
2. GARETH MARKS  44.68
6. STEVEN BRADLEY  32.14

**Hammer**

1. Wim Guldentops  BEL  61.90
3. ROSS BLIGHT  46.12
6. JAMES ELTON  34.60

**Javelin**

1. Rene Smit  HOL  59.10
2. Roel Emans  HOL  58.88
4. MATTHEW DAVIES  52.86
6. DEREK HERRMAN  48.38

**4 x 100 Metres Relay**

1. Belgium  41.12
2. WALES  41.60
   (POWELL, MALCOLM,
   HENTHRON, O'HARE)
3. Holland  42.48

**4 x 400 Metres Relay**

1. Belgium  3:22.42
2. WALES  3:24.92
   (S EVANS, SHEFFIELD,
   HILLIER, BANNISTER)
3. Holland  3:26.87

**Match Result**

1. Belgium  142
2. Holland  130.5
3. WALES  118.5

## WOMEN

**100 Metres**  wind 0.5

1. Myrlam Tschomba  BEL  12.25
3. STACEY RODD  12.44
6. LEANNE ROWLANDS  12.98

**200 Metres**  wind 0.6

1. Elke Boegmans  BEL  24.46
5. KATHRYN WILLIAMS  25.62
6. HANNAH PAINES  25.70

**400 Metres**

1. KATE WILLIAMS  56.71
4. MICHELLE JON  59.04

**800 Metres**

1. AMANDA PRITCHARD  2:13.91
6. KATHRYN BRIGHT  2:20.55

**1500 Metres**

1. Anjoile Wisse  HOL  4:32.81
4. CLAIRE MARTIN  4:38.09
5. CLAIRE THOMAS  4:46.65

**3000 Metres**

1. Fueline Coussement  BEL  9:55.39
5. HELEDD GRUFFUDD  10:45.64
6. CORI WENSLEY  10:59.17

**100 Metres Hurdles**  wind -1.5

1. Myriam Tschomba  BEL  13.91
2. RACHEL KING  14.60
6. RACHEL STANNARD  15.67

**400 Metres Hurdles**

1. KATHRYN WILLIAMS  1:02.34
5. LUCY ROBERTS  1:10.81

**High Jump**

1. Karlijn van Beurden  HOL  1.79
3. TERESA ANDREWS  1.73
5. KELLY MORETON  1.60

**Long Jump**

1. Danielle Varsseveld  HOL  5.93
5. TERESA ANDREWS  5.33
6. CERI MCDERMOTT  5.26

**Triple Jump**

1. JAYNE LUDLOW  11.93
5. JOANNE TOMLINSON  10.56

**Shot**

1. Corrie de Bruin  HOL  17.58
5. TERESA ANDREWS  10.42
6. BETHAN DEVERALL  10.38

**Discus**

1. Corrie de Bruin  HOL  59.34
4. SARAH JOHNSON  36.12
5. BETHAN DEVERALL  32.62

**Javelin**

1. Kitty van Haperen  HOL  46.10
5. RHIAN HUGHES  35.72
6. CLARE LOCKWOOD  32.00

**4 x 100 Metres Relay**

1. Belgium  46.56
2. Holland  47.08
3. WALES  48.23
   (RUDD, ROWLANDS, KING,
   KATHRYN WILLIAMS)

**4 x 400 Metres Relay**

1. WALES  3:57.41
   (KATE WILLIAMS, JOHN,
   PRITCHARD, MEAD)
2. Holland  4:00.06
3. Belgium  4:01.61

**Match Result**

1. Holland  127
2. Belgium  114
3. WALES  85

## Welsh Games Wales v England v Select  Cwmbran  9 July 1995

### MEN

**100 Metres**  wind 1.6

1. DARREN CAMPBELL  10.34
2. JASON GARDENER  10.36
3. JOHN REGIS  gst  10.41
4. KEVIN WILLIAMS  WAL  10.58
5. Ricky Nalatu  AUS  10.69
6. PETER MAITLAND  WAL  10.74
7. Ryan Whitnish  AUS  10.86

**200 Metres**  wind 4.0

1. DOUG TURNER  WAL  20.68w
2. JASON JOHN  20.74w
3. Darryl Wohlson  AUS  20.76w
4. JAMIE BAULCH  WAL  20.86w
5. PHILIP GOEDLUCK  21.13w

**400 Metres**

1. DAVID NOLAN  46.61
2. Mark Ladbrook  AUS  47.19
3. PETER MAITLAND  WAL  47.29
4. NIGEL WILL  47.81
5. Callan Taylor  NZ  48.04
6. JAMES WESTON  WAL  48.21
7. JOE LLOYD  gst/WAL  48.84

**800 Metres**

1. Paul Byrne  AUS  1:48.73
2. CRAIG WINROW  gst  1:48.84
3. MATTHEW YATES  gst  1:49.24
4. LEE CADWALLADER  1:49.42
5. MARK SESAY  1:50.42
6. DARRELL MAYNARD  WAL  1:50.47
7. PAUL ROBERTS  WAL  1:50.80
8. Prince Amara  SLE  1:51.23

**1500 Metres**

1. JON WILD  3:42.43
2. CIARAN MURPHY  3:43.42
3. Nigel Adkin  AUS  3:43.55
4. NICK COMMERFORD  WAL  3:46.66
5. ROBERT SIMON  WAL  3:53.78

**3000 Metres**

1. KEITH CULLEN  7:58.25
2. GLYN TROMANS  8:07.17
3. MARK MORGAN  WAL  8:20.56
4. COLIN JONES  WAL  8:28.38

**3000 Metres Steeplechase**

1. CARL WARREN  8:53.61
2. SIMON BELL  9:00.54
3. PHIL COOK  WAL  9:24.60

82

## 110 Metres Hurdles  wind 4.4
1.  COLIN JACKSON  WAL  13.17w
2.  NEIL OWEN  13.65w
3.  HUGHIE TEAPE  14.18w
4.  Paul Edmiston  AUS  14.36w
5.  JAMES HUGHES  gst/WAL 14.49w
6.  COLIN BOVELL  gst/WAL 14.76w

## 400 Metres Hurdles
1.  LLOYD COWAN  50.99
2.  Chris Carroll  AUS  52.00
3.  DAVID GRIFFIN  WAL  52.50
4.  MARVIN GRAY  gst/WAL  54.47
5.  CHRIS CASHELL  WAL  54.66
6.  Amimbola Ilo  NIG  58.09

## High Jump
1.  ANDREW LYNCH  2.18
2.  COLIN BENT  2.05
3.  STUART BROWN  WAL  2.00
4.  ROWAN GRIFFITHS  WAL  1.95

## Pole Vault
1.  Nick Hyson  USA  5.70
2.  NEIL WINTER  WAL  5.40
3.  MATTHEW BELSHAM  5.30
4.  Simon Arkell  AUS  5.30
7=  KEVIN HUGHES  5.00
9.  TIM THOMAS  WAL  4.80

## Long Jump
1.  STEVE PHILLIPS  7.77
2.  JON MUNROE  7.46
3.  Shane Casey  AUS  7.40
4.  GARRY SLADE  WAL  7.16
5.  GARETH DAVIES  WAL  7.07

## Shot
1.  MARK PROCTOR  18.09
2.  SHAUN PICKERING  gst  17.69
3.  NIGEL SPRATLEY  16.65
4.  DAVE CALLAWAY  gst  16.42
5.  ANDY TURNER  WAL  14.24
6.  ALAN THOMAS  WAL  13.00

## Hammer
1.  Sean Carlin  AUS  73.52
2.  PETER VIVIAN  70.92
3.  DAVID SMITH  69.42
4.  ADRIAN PALMER  WAL  59.26
5.  GARETH JONES  WAL  55.42

## Javelin
1.  NIGEL BEVAN  WAL  77.14
2.  NICK NIELAND  72.66
3.  STUART FABEN  63.38
4.  STUART LOUGHRAN  WAL  55.24

## 4 x 100 Metres Relay
1.  WALES  40.04
   (K WILLIAMS, JACKSON, BAULCH, RUTHERFORD)
2.  ENGLAND  40.44
   (GARDENER, CAMPBELL, GOEDLUCK, JOHN)
3.  Select  41.08

## 4 x 400 Metres Relay
1.  WALES  3:12.73
   (GRIFFIN, BAULCH, LLOYD, WESTON)
2.  ENGLAND  3:15.05
   (WILL, FAYOLA, WINROW, SESAY)

## Match Result
1.  ENGLAND  156
2.  WALES  106
3.  Select  59

# WOMEN
## 100 Metres  wind 3.3
1.  SALLY ANNE SHORT  WAL  11.57w
2.  CATHERINE MURPHY  WAL  11.65w
3.  DONNA HOGGARTH  11.74w
4.  SOPHIE SMITH  11.81w
5.  Elly Hutton  AUS  11.90w

## 200 Metres  wind 2.0
1.  DONNA FRASER  23.47
2.  SALLY ANNE SHORT  WAL  23.79
3.  JOICE MADUAKA  24.00
4.  JOANNE GRONOW  WAL  25.09

## 400 Metres
1.  STEPH. LLEWELLYN  gst  52.54
2.  Lee Naylor  AUS  52.67
3.  LINDA KEOUGH  53.72
4.  SUSAN RAWLINSON  53.85
5.  ELAINE SUTCLIFFE  gst  55.80
6.  RACHEL NEWCOMBE  WAL  56.17
7.  DAWN HIGGINS  WAL  60.79

## 800 Metres
1.  ABIGAIL HUNTE  2:06.22
2.  LYNNE GIBSON  gst  2:06.66
3.  HELEN DANIEL  2:06.77
4.  ALYSON LAYZELL  WAL  2:07.06
5.  ALISON PARRY  WAL  2:11.29
6.  LISA THOMPSON  gst/ENG 2:12.18

## 1500 Metres
1.  MICHELLE FAHERTY  4:19.56
2.  DEBBIE GUNNING  4:20.36
3.  SARAH BENTLEY  4:22.51
4.  AMANDA THORPE  4:25.92
5.  HAYLEY PARRY  WAL  4:28.22
6.  ESTHER EVANS  WAL  4:42.85

## 100 Metres Hurdles  wind -0.9
1.  KERI MADDOX  13.50
2.  CLOVA COURT  13.51
3.  Sally Heagney  AUS  14.14
4.  NON EVANS  WAL  14.44
5.  BETHAN EDWARDS  WAL  14.52

## High Jump
1.  LEA HAGGETT  1.88
2.  DEBBI MARTI  1.82
3.  JULIE CRANE  WAL  1.79
4.  AILSA WALLACE  WAL  1.70

## Shot
1.  TRACY AXTEN  14.51
2.  PHILIPPA ROLES  WAL  13.24
3.  JO DUNCAN  12.67
4.  LESLEY BRANNEN  WAL  11.64

## Discus
1.  Lisa Vizaniari  AUS  59.84
2.  DEBBIE CALLOWAY  54.34
3.  TRACY AXTEN  53.62
4.  PHILIPPA ROLES  WAL  49.12
5.  JAYNE FISHER  WAL  43.94

## Hammer
1.  LORRAINE SHAW  60.24
2.  LYN SPRULES  52.16
3.  SARAH MOORE  WAL  50.42
4.  ANGELA BONNER  WAL  42.98

## Javelin
1.  Kate Farrow  AUS  54.64
2.  KAREN MARTIN  50.38
3.  AMANDA LIVERTON  48.68
4.  MICHELLE FIELDS  44.18
5.  ONYEMI AMADI  WAL  43.48
6.  SIAN LAX  WAL  41.58

## 4 x 100 Metres Relay
1.  ENGLAND  45.41
   (S SMITH, HOGGARTH, MADUAKA, COURT)
2.  WALES  46.68
   (MILES, C MURPHY, B EDWARDS, SHORT)

## 4 x 400 Metres Relay
1.  ENGLAND  3:45.25
   (PIERRE, KEOUGH, FRASER, RAWLINSON)
2.  WALES  3:54.18
   (NEWCOMBE, PARRY, GRONOW, LAYZELL)

## Match Result
1.  ENGLAND  139
2.  WALES  85
3.  Select  32

## AAA CHAMPIONSHIPS  Birmingham  15 - 16 July 1995

### MEN

**100 Metres**  wind -1.2 (15 Jul)
1. LINFORD CHRISTIE  gst    10.18
2. DARREN BRAITHWAITE       10.33
3. JASON JOHN               10.34
4. DARREN CAMPBELL          10.37
5. TOBY BOX                 10.41
6. JAMIE HENDERSON          10.44
7. Josephus Thomas  SLE     10.60
8. JASON GARDENER           10.71
MICHAEL ROSSWESS         withdrew

**200 Metres**  wind 0.5  (16 Jul)
1. JOHN REGIS               20.37
2. SOLOMON WARISO           20.53
3. DAREEN BRAITHWAITE       20.64
4. TONY JARRETT             20.67
5. JULIAN GOLDING           20.77
6. Dean Capobianco  AUS     20.79
7. TOBY BOX                 20.86
8. OWUSU DAKO               21.01

**400 Metres**  (16 Jul)
1. MARK RICHARDSON          44.94
2. MARK HYLTON              45.83
3. ADRIAN PATRICK           46.11
4. TIM O'DELL               46.42
5. Bobang Phiri  RSA        46.65
6. Michael Joubert  AUS     46.76
7. DAVID MCKENZIE           46.99
   BRIAN WHITTLE               dnf

**800 Metres**  (16 Jul)
1. CURTIS ROBB            1:46.78
2. DAVID STRANG           1:47.06
3. GARY LOUGH             1:48.03
4. LEE CADWALLADER        1:48.28
5. Paul Byrne  AUS        1:48.30
6. CRAIG WINROW           1:48.90
7. TOM MCKEAN             1:50.70
8. MARTIN STEELE          1:53.49

**1500 Metres**  (16 Jul)
1. JOHN MAYOCK            3:40.55
2. KEVIN MCKAY            3:40.83
3. BRUNO WITCHALLS        3:41.51
4. BRIAN TREACY           3:41.73
5. ANDY KEITH             3:41.96
6. ANDY HART              3:42.03
7. NEIL CADDY             3:42.15
8. JOHN NUTTALL           3:42.66
9. Sammy Mutai  KEN       3:43.07
10. GLEN STEWART          3:44.77

**5000 Metres**  (15 Jul)
1. ROB DENMARK           13:37.54
2. JONATHON BROWN        13:37.83
3. Peter Ndrangu  KEN    13:39.57
4. Simeon Rono  KEN      13:43.41
5. Paul Koech  KEN       13:45.27
6. JOHN SHERBAN          13:46.76
7. JUSTIN CHASTON        13:51.86
8. JON SOLLY             13:58.43
9. SPENCER NEWPORT       14:00.24

**10000 Metres**  (11 Jun Loughbro)
1. GARY STAINES          28:49.29
2. JON SOLLY             28:59.29
3. CHRIS ROBISON         29:03.69
4. ANDY LYONS            29:04.87
5. MARK STEINLE          29:07.33
6. ROBERT QUINN          29:14.23
7. BILL FOSTER           29:17.11
8. SPENCER NEWPORT       29:23.49
9. RICHARD FINDLOW       29:32.67
10. Jamie Harrison  AUS  29:36.58

**3000 Metres Steeplechase** (16 Jul)
1. SPENCER DUVAL           8:24.64
2. Godgrey Siamusiye  ZIM  8:25.49
3. KEITH CULLEN            8:29.64
4. ROB HOUGH               8:36.29
5. MICK HAWKINS            8:36.55
6. CARL WARREN             8:40.74
7. DAVID LEE               8:51.41
8. PADDY BRICE             8:55.05

**110 Metres Hurdles**  -0.3 (16 Jul)
1. NEIL OWEN                 13.63
2. ANDY TULLOCH              13.76
3. LLOYD COWAN               13.96
4. KENNETH CAMPBELL          13.98
5. David Cooper  AUS         14.02
6. HUGHIE TEAPE              14.10
7. DAMIEN GREAVES            14.47
8. JAMES HUGHES              14.53

**400 Metres Hurdles**  (16 Jul)
1. Rohan Robinson  AUS       49.21
2. GARY CADOGAN              49.70
3. GARY JENNINGS             50.34
4. LAWRENCE LYNCH            50.64
5. CHRIS RAWLINSON           50.90
6. PAUL HIBBERT              51.33
7. DAVID SAVAGE              51.39
8. RICHARD HOLT              53.10

**High Jump**  (15 Jul)
1. STEVE SMITH               2.35
2. Chris Anderson  AUS       2.22
3. DALTON GRANT              2.17
4. BRENDAN REILLY            2.17
5= DAVID BARNETSON           2.12
5= JAMES BRIERLEY            2.12
7. ANDREW LYNCH              2.12
8= STUART OHRLAND            2.07
8= COLIN BENT                2.07
10. RICHARD ASPDEN           2.07
11. ROB BROCKLEBANK          2.07

**Pole Vault**  (16 Jul)
1. NICK BUCKFIELD            5.50
2. ANDY ASHURST              5.10
3. MIKE EDWARDS              5.10
4. MIKE BARBER               5.10
5. IAN TULLETT               5.10
6. DEAN MELLOR               4.80

**Long Jump**  (15 Jul)
1. FRED SALLE                7.66
2. Jai Taurima  AUS          7.63
3. BARRINGTON WILLIAMS       7.50
4. ONOCHIE ONUORAH           7.50
5. STEWART FAULKNER          7.46
6. JOHN MUNROE               7.38
7. CHRIS DAVIDSON            7.33
8. NATHAN MORGAN             7.27

**Triple Jump**  (16 Jul)
1. FRANCIS AGYEPONG         17.13
2. TAYO EROGBOGBO           15.83
3. TOSI FASINRO             15.65
4. PAUL RALPH               15.27
5. JULIAN GOLLEY            15.26
6. JOSEPH SWEENEY           14.90
7. MATTHEW RANDALL          14.70
8. Mathias Ogbeta  NIG      14.70

**Shot**  (16 Jul)
1. MARK PROCTOR             18.81
2. MATTHEW SIMSON           18.27
3. SHAUN PICKERING          17.71
4. LEE NEWMAN               17.62
6. DAVID CALLAWAY           16.45
7. GARY SOLLITT             16.33
8. NIGEL SPRATLEY           16.09
9. STEPHAN HAYWARD          16.05

**Discus**  (15 Jul)
1. Nick Sweeney  IRL        60.34
2. ROBERT WEIR              60.18
3. SIMON WILLIAMS           58.20
4. KEVIN BROWN              57.24
5. GARY HERRINGTON          52.98
6. GLEN SMITH               52.70
7. LEITH MARAR              52.54
8. Kyle Taylor  USA         51.44
9. MATTHEW SYMONDS          51.30

**Hammer**  (16 Jul)
1. Sean Carlin  AUS         73.40
2. MICHAEL JONES            69.44
3. JASON BYRNE              69.44
4. PETER VIVIAN             69.34
5. DAVID SMITH              68.32
6. SHANE PEACOCK            64.08
7. CHRIS HOWE               62.86
8. WILLIAM BEAUCHAMP        60.52
9. PAUL BARNARD             59.98

**Javelin**  (15 Jul)
1. MICHAEL HILL             80.54
2. COLIN MACKENZIE          77.50
3. NIGEL BEVAN              76.58
4. NICK NIELAND             73.54
5. MARK ROBERSON            72.66
6. STEPHEN HARRISON         70.18
7. STUART FABEN             69.94
8. DUNCAN MACDONALD         65.96

**10000 Metres Walk** (16 Jul)
1. DARRELL STONE 41:10.11
2. STEVE PARTINGTON 41:14.61
3. MARTIN BELL 41:16.13
4. PHILIP KING 42:33.30
5. MARK EASTON 42:49.59
6. CHRIS MADDOCKS 42:51.50
7. LES MORTON 43:35.98
8. CHRIS CHEESEMAN 43:50.44

# WOMEN
**100 Metres** wind 1.5 (15 Jul)
1. PAULA THOMAS 11.48
2. SIMMONE JACOBS 11.50
3. STEPHANIE DOUGLAS 11.53
4. MARCIA RICHARDSON 11.66
5. SOPHIA SMITH 11.71
6. DONNA HOGGARTH 11.93
7. JOICE MADUAKA 11.96
8. AILEEN MCGILLIVARY 12.00

**200 Metres** wind 0.1 (16 Jul)
1. CATHERINE MURPHY 23.40
2. SIMMONE JACOBS 23.48
3. JOICE MADUAKA 23.95
4. ALISON DAVIES 24.06
5. MARCIA RICHARDSON 24.11
6. SOPHIA SMITH 24.16
7. Anne Deller AUS 24.31
8. SHARON WILLIAMS 24.38

**400 Metres** (16 Jul)
1. MELANIE NEEF 51.63
2. LORRAINE HANSON 52.68
3. GEORGINA OLADAPO 52.71
4. STEPHANIE LLEWELLYN 53.13
5. SUSAN RAWLINSON 53.69
6. LINDA KEOUGH 54.05
7. ELAINE SUTCLIFFE 55.15
   DONNA FRASER dnf

**800 Metres** (16 Jul)
1. KELLY HOLMES 1:57.56
2. Jill Stamison USA 2:02.27
3. ABIGAIL HUNTE 2:02.47
4. NATALIE TAIT 2:02.69
5. PAULA RADCLIFFE 2:05.22
6. VICKIE LAWRENCE 2:05.93
7. MARY KITSON 2:07.78
   SONYA BOWYER dnf

**1500 Metres** (16 Jul)
1. YVONNE MURRAY 4:11.47
2. DEBBIE GUNNING 4:14.42
3. UNA ENGLISH 4:16.37
4. SUE PARKER 4:17.11
5. MICHELLE FAHERTY 4:18.44
6. ELIZABETH TALBOT 4:19.66
7. LYNN GIBSON 4:21.73
8. SHARON KING 4:24.99

**5000 Metres** (15 Jul)
1. ALISON WYETH 15:39.14
2. Nnenna Lynch USA 16:10.69
3. LOUISE WATSON 16:11.23
4. ANDREA WHITCOMBE 16:12.96
5. SARAH BENTLEY 16:22.80

6. JILL HARRISON 16:30.85
7. ZARA HYDE 16:38.52
8. GABRIELLE COLLISON 16:45.43

**100 Metres Hurdles** 1.6 (15 Jul)
1. MELANIE WILKINS 13.34
2. MICHELLE CAMPBELL 13.36
3. KERI MADDOX 13.40
4. DIANE ALLAHGREEN 13.53
5. DENISE LEWIS 13.58
6. NATASHA DANVERS 13.63
7. Jane Fleming AUS 13.93
8. CLOVA COURT 14.11

**400 Metres Hurdles** (16 Jul)
1. GOWRY RETCHAKAN 57.18
2. STEPHANIE MCCANN 58.21
3. LOUISE BRUNNING 58.58
4. VYVYAN RHODES 58.86
5. Asa Carlsson SWE 58.90
6. LOUISE FRASER 58.90
7. CLARE BLEASDALE 63.40
   VICKY DAY dnf

**High Jump** (16 Jul)
1. LEA HAGGETT 1.85
2. DIANA DAVIES 1.85
3. DEBBI MARTI 1.85
4= JULIE MAJOR 1.75
4= JULIE CRANE 1.75
6= JULIA BENNETT 1.75
6= RACHAEL FORREST 1.75
8= VIKKI SCHOFIELD 1.70
8= MICHELLE DUNKLEY 1.70

**PoleVault** (15 Jul)
1. Melissa Price USA 3.70
2. KATE STAPLES 3.50
3. CLAIRE MORRISON 3.30
4. LOUISE SCHRAMM 3.20
5. CLAIRE RIDGLEY 3.20
6. LINDA STANTON 3.00

**Long Jump** (16 Jul)
1. Nicole Boegman AUS 6.50
2. DENISE LEWIS 6.42
3. YINKA IDOWU 6.35
4. VIKKI SCHOFIELD 6.28
5. LIZ GHOJEFA 6.01
6. ANN BROOKS 5.98
7. ADELE FORRESTER 5.82
8. JACQUELINE WHITE 5.78

**Stoke 3 - 4 June**
# MEN

**Decathlon**
1. STEPHEN ROGERS 7295
2. STEPHEN ROWBOTHAM 6637
3. MATTHEW GILLARD 5466

**Triple Jump** (15 Jul)
1. MICHELLE GRIFFITH 13.43
2. RACHEL KIRBY 12.96
3. KAREN SKEGGS 12.11
4. CAROLINE STEAD 11.97
5. DEBORAH ROWE 11.67
6. KERENSA DENHAM 11.63
7. KATIE EVANS 11.50
8. FIONA WATT 11.20

**Shot** (15 Jul)
1. JUDY OAKES 17.75
2. MAGGIE LYNES 15.67
3. CAROL COOKSLEY 14.07
4. TRACY AXTEN 13.89
5. HELEN WILDING 13.64
6. CHARMAINE JOHNSON 13.35
7. UJU EFOBI 13.18

**Discus** (16 Jul)
1. Lisa-Marie Vizaniari AUS 61.98
2. JACQUI MCKERNAN 58.88
3. SHELLEY DREW 53.74
4. DEBORAH CALLAWAY 53.50
5. EMMA BEALES 51.60
6. MYRTLE AUGEE 47.92
7. TRACY AXTEN 47.76

**Hammer** (15 Jul)
1. Debbie Sosimenko AUS 65.24
2. Brenda MacNaughton AUS 56.62
3. LORRAINE SHAW 56.26
4. LYN SPRULES 52.36
5. DIANA HOLDEN 52.14
6. SARAH MOORE 50.40
7. JEAN CLARK 48.06

**Javelin** (16 Jul)
1. LORNA JACKSON 55.48
2. SHARON GIBSON 55.14
3. KAREN MARTIN 54.96
4. SHELLEY HOLROYD 54.92
5. Kate Farrow AUS 52.26
6. KIRSTY MORRISON 49.84
7. ONYEMA AMADI 48.34

**5000 Metres Walk** (16 Jul)
1. LISA LANGFORD 22:20.03
2. VICKY LUPTON 22:23.80
3. CAROLYN PARTINGTON 22:40.19
4. PERRI WILLIAMS 23:58.84
5. VERITY SNOOK 24:04.57
6. MELANIE WRIGHT 24:09.66

# WOMEN

**Heptathlon**
1. EMMA BEALES 5524
2. JENNY KELLY 5298
3. KERRY JURY 5037
4. CHARMAINE JOHNSON 4832
5. TRACY JOSEPH 4720
6. LEAH LACKERBY 4710
7. JENNY BROWN 4303

# WAL v SCO v NI v TUR   Cardiff   22 - 23 July 1995

## MEN

**100 Metres**  wind -1.7  (22 Jul)
1. KEVIN WILLIAMS   WAL   10.9
2. Resat Oguz   TUR   10.9
3. IAN CRAIG   NI   11.0
4. JAMIE HENDERSON   SCO   11.0

**200 Metres**  wind -0.8  (23 Jul)
1. MARK ALLEN   NI   21.62
2. Resat Oguz   TUR   21.95
3. BARRY MIDDLETON   SCO   22.74
4. JOE LLOYD   WAL   23.02

**400 Metres**  (22 Jul)
1. PAUL MCBURNEY   NI   47.25
2. PETER MAITLAND   WAL   47.31
3. Bulent Eren   TUR   48.18
4. IAN HORSBURGH   SCO   49.59

**800 Metres**  (23 Jul)
1. DARRELL MAYNARD   WAL   1:51.62
2. KHEREDINE IDESSANE   SCO   1:52.54
3. Salih Cakir   TUR   1:53.63
4. CHRIS BLOUNT   gst/WAL   1:54.16
5. JOHN ROGAN   NI   1:54.78

**1500 Metres**  (22 Jul)
1. GRANT GRAHAM   SCO   3:45.02
2. Zeki Ozturk   TUR   3:45.72
3. NICK COMMERFORD   WAL   3:48.02
4. Salih Gakir   gst/TUR   3:58.86
5. DAVID WRIGHT   NI   4:02.71

**5000 Metres**  (23 Jul)
1. Zeki Ozturk   TUR   13:53.94
2. Fatih Cintimar   gst/TUR   14:17.91
3. RICHARD BLAKELEY   NI   14:38.62
4. ANDRES JONES   WAL   14:45.21
5. JAMES AUSTON   SCO   15:47.68
6. Abdulkadir Oz   gst/TUR   16:03.09

**3000 Metres Steeplechase**  (22 Jul)
1. Nihat Bagci   TUR   8:59.41
2. STEVEN CAIRNS   NI   9:03.45
3. PHIL COOK   WAL   9:07.25
4. WILLIAM JENKINS   SCO   9:28.77

## WOMEN

**100 Metres**  wind -1.1  (22 Jul)
1. Askel Gurcan   TUR   11.96
2. SALLY ANNE SHORT   WAL   11.98
3. AILEEN MCGILLIVARY   SCO   12.17
4. DAWN FLOCKHART   gst/SCO   12.46
5. CLARE O'CONNOR   NI   12.62
6. Asli Ergenc   gst/TUR   12.83
7. DONNA LENNON   gst/NI   13.07

**200 Metres**  wind -0.5  (23 Jul)
1. Aksel Gurcan   TUR   24.47
2. STEPHANIE MCCANN   NI   24.54
3. DAWN FLOCKHART   SCO   25.56
4. CLARE O'CONNOR   gst/NI   25.56
5. LOUISE SHARPS   WAL   26.18

**110 Metres Hurdles**  (23 Jul)  0.5
1. KEN CAMPBELL   SCO   14.29
2. JAMES HUGHES   WAL   14.43
3. Alper Kosapoglu   TUR   14.76
4. GARY GALLAGHER   NI   15.99

**400 Metres Hurdles**  (22 Jul)
1. BARRY MIDDLETON   SCO   52.55
2. DAVE GRIFFIN   WAL   52.85
3. MARK ROWLANDS   gst/WAL   53.14
4. MATTHEW DOUGLAS   NI   53.89
5. DAVID GOODGER   gst/WAL   54.16
6. Fethi Bildirici   TUR   54.18

**High Jump**  (22 Jul)
1. Isik Bayraktar   TUR   2.10
2. ADAM SMITH   NI   2.00
3. STUART BROWN   WAL   1.95
4. TONY GILHOOLY   SCO   1.90
5. ROWAN GRIFFITHS   gst/WAL   1.85

**Pole Vault**  (22 Jul)
1. Ruhan Isim   TUR   5.00
2. NEIL YOUNG   NI   4.70
3. IAN BLACK   SCO   4.20

**Long Jump**  (22 Jul)
1. DARREN RITCHIE   SCO   7.23
2. Erim May   TUR   7.18
3. Alper Kasapoglu   gst/TUR   7.17
4. GARY SLADE   WAL   7.16
5. GARETH DAVIES   gst/WAL   6.70
6. GARETH DEVLIN   NI   6.68

**Triple Jump**  (23 Jul)
1. Murat Ayaydin   TUR   15.42
2. ADAM SMITH   NI   14.71
3. NEIL MCMENEMY   SCO   14.47
4. GARETH DAVIES   WAL   14.29

**Shot**  (22 Jul)
1. STEVE WHYTE   SCO   15.72
2. JAMES MUIRHEAD   gst/SCO   15.63
3. Huseyin Yilmaz   TUR   14.27
4. ANDY TURNER   WAL   14.22
5. DAVID SWEENEY   NI   13.80

**400 Metres**  (22 Jul)
1. Oznur Dursun   TUR   55.02
2. LISA VANNET   SCO   56.29
3. RACHEL NEWCOMBE   WAL   57.31
4. CLARE HILL   NI   57.59
5. MICHELLE JOHN   gst/WAL   59.66

**800 Metres**  (23 Jul)
1. ALYSON LAYZELL   WAL   2:07.38
2. VICKY LAWRENCE   SCO   2:08.76
3. Lale Debreli   TUR   2:14.37
4. CLAIRE BROOK   NI   2:15.89

**1500 Metres**  (22 Jul)
1. ANN TEREK   NI   4:23.1
2. Sepap Aktas   TUR   4:25.0
3. HAYLEY PARRY   WAL   4:25.9
4. VAL BOTHAMS *   SCO   4:41.7

**Discus**  (22 Jul)
1. GARY HERRINGTON   gst/ENG   54.22
2. H Yilmaz   TUR   53.54
3. JOHN MORELAND   NI   49.84
4. JAMES MUIRHEAD   SCO   47.34
5. ANDY TURNER   WAL   44.92
6.˙ DAVID SWEENEY   gst/NI   44.20

**Hammer**  (22 Jul)
1. STEVE WHYTE   SCO   60.44
2. ADRIAN PALMER   WAL   60.02
3. GARETH JONES   gst/WAL   55.78
4. Omer Ozcicek   TUR   55.44
5. DAVID NICHOLL   NI   47.34

**Javelin**  (22 Jul)
1. Fikret Ozsoy   TUR   69.62
2. JON CLARKE   WAL   61.72
3. DEAN SMAHON   NI   58.98
4. CHRIS SMITH   SCO   58.42

**10000 Metres Walk**  (22 Jul)
1. MARTIN BELL   SCO   41:13.65
2. Abdulkadir Oz   TUR   46:11.96
3. GARETH HOLLOWAY   WAL   46:44.96
4. MARTIN FLOOD   NI   50:20.85
5. KIRK TAYLOR   gst/WAL   50:35.97

**4 x 100 Metres Relay**  (22 Jul)
1. WALES   40.1
(K WILLIAMS, TURNER, BAULCH, MAITLAND)
2. SCOTLAND   40.7
(BUNNEY, CAMPBELL, HENDERSON, WALKER)
3. Turkey   41.2
4. NORTHERN IRELAND   41.7
(SLOAN, CRAIG, BRIZZELL, ALLEN)
5. WALES B TEAM   42.1

**4 x 400 Metres Relay**  (23 Jul)
1. WALES   3:11.85
(MAITLAND, BAULCH, GRIFFIN, WESTON)
2. NORTHERN IRELAND   3:15.30
(MCCOY, THORN, FORBES, MCBURNEY)
3. Turkey   3:15.82
4. SCOTLAND   3:17.77
(HORSBURGH, MIDDLETON, IDESSANE, GRAHAM)

**5000 Metres**  (23 Jul)
1. Serap Aktas   TUR   16:06.82
2. ANN TEREK   NI   16:54.47
3. DINAH CHEVERTON   WAL   17:23.72
4. VAL BOTHAMS   SCO   18:00.87

**100 Metres Hurdles**  (23 Jul)  0.8
1. RACHEL KING   WAL   14.03
2. BETHAN EDWARDS   gst/WAL   14.21
3. NON EVANS   gst/WAL   14.28
4. Filiz Turker   TUR   14.35
5. CLAIRE MACKINTOSH   SCO   14.74
6. ELAINE FAULKNER   NI   15.85

86

**400 Metres Hurdles** (22 Jul)
1. STEPHANIE MCCANN NI 59.44
2. JANE LOW SCO 60.31
3. ALISON MAHINDU gst/SCO 60.95
4. CLARE EDWARDS WAL 62.82
5. VICKY JAMISON gst/NI 62.93
6. Hazer Cetin TUR 66.34

**High Jump** (23 Jul)
1. JULIE CRANE WAL 1.78
2. Gulsun Durak TUR 1.75
3. LISA BROWN SCO 1.65
4. JACKIE VYFSCHAFT NI 1.65
5. AILSA WALLACE gst/WAL 1.65

**Long Jump** (22 Jul)
1. Fatma Yuksel TUR 6.08
2. RUTH IRVING SCO 5.68
3. SALLY ANNE SHORT WAL 5.67
4. ELIZABETH ORR NI 5.05

**Triple Jump** (23 Jul)
1. KAREN SKEGGS SCO 12.31
2. JAYNE LUDLOW WAL 11.65
3. Billur Dulkadir TUR 11.03
4. ELIZABETH ORR NI 10.19w

**Shot** (23 Jul)
1. PHILIPPA ROLES WAL 13.95
2. Aysel Tas TUR 13.24
3. TRACEY SHORTS SCO 12.03
4. JULIE MCCORRY NI 11.50

**Discus** (22 Jul)
1. Husniye Keskin TUR 50.56
2. PHILIPPA ROLES WAL 47.24
3. SUSAN FREEBAIRN SCO 41.90
4. TRACEY SHORTS gst/SCO 38.40
5. JULIE KIRKPATRICK NI 36.08

**Hammer** (23 Jul)
1. SARAH MOORE WAL 52.88
2. JEAN CLARKE SCO 47.62
3. JULIE KIRKPATRICK NI 44.96
4. Nesrin Kaya TUR 43.88

**Javelin** (23 Jul)
1. Aysel Tas TUR 54.38
2. LORNA JACKSON SCO 52.52
3. ONEYEMI AMADI WAL 44.38
4. ALISON MOFFITT NI 43.68

**5000 Metres Walk** (23 Jul)
1. VERITY SNOOK SCO 23:38.85
2. KIRRIE J WALLACE WAL 30:37.09

**4 x 100 Metres Relay** (22 Jul)
1. SCOTLAND 46.96
(BROWN, HYND, HEGNEY, MCGILLIVARY)
2. WALES 47.77
(MILES, SHARPS, EDWARDS, KING)
3. Turkey 47.80

**4 x 400 Metres Relay** (23 Jul)
1. N IRELAND 3:42.20
(HILL, O'CONNOR, MCCANN, JAMISON)
2. SCOTLAND 3:44.24
(LOW, MAHINDRU, FLOCKHART, VANNET)
3. WALES 3:51.37
(NEWCOMBE, PARRY, JOHN, SHARPS)
4. Turkey 3:54.30

**Men Match Result**
1. Turkey 79
2. SCOTLAND 69
3. WALES 67
4. N IRELAND 63

**Women Match Result**
1. WALES 68
2. Turkey 66
3. SCOTLAND 65
4. N IRELAND 46

**Overall Match Result**
1. Turkey 145
2. WALES 135
3. SCOTLAND 134
4. N IRELAND 109

# European Junior Championships Nyiregyhaza, Hungary 27 - 30 July 1995

**MEN**

**100 Metres** wind -0.9 (28 Jul)
1. DWAIN CHAMBERS 10.41
2. JAMIE HENTHORN 10.41
3. Angelos Pavlakakis GRE 10.47

**200 Metres** wind -0.6 (29 Jul)
1. MARLON DEVONISH 21.04
2. Alessio Comparini ITA 21.21
3. DANIEL MONEY 21.29

**400 Metres** (28 Jul)
1. MARK HYLTON 45.97
2. Jacek Bocian POL 46.59
3. Tsvetomir Marinov BUL 46.66
4. GEOFF DEARMAN 47.13

**800 Metres** (29 Jul)
1. Roberto Parra ESP 1:45.90
2. André Bucher SWZ 1:46.73
3. Wojciech Kaldowski POL 1:47.67
7s2 ALASDAIR DONALDSON 1:51.16
8s1 ANDREW BLACKMORE 1:55.53

**1500 Metres** (30 Jul)
1. Reyes Estevez ESP 3:45.74
2. José Redolat ESP 3:46.70
3. Gert-Jan Liefers HOL 3:47.17
dnf DESMOND ROACHE fell
6h2 MARK MILES 3:54.99

**5000 Metres** (30 Jul)
1. Benoit Zwierzchiewski FRA 13:55.75
2. Juan José Gomez ESP 14:15.65
3. Iván Perez ESP 14:17.83

**10000 Metres** (27 Jul)
1. Benoit Zwierzchiewski FRA 29:46.42
2. Iván Perez ESP 30:06.69
3. Damiano Polti ITA 30:06.91

**3000 Metres Steeplechase** (30 Jul)
1. Antonio Alvarez ESP 8:50.75
2. Christian Knoblich GER 8:50.85
3. Jerome Cochet FRA 8:52.92
8s2 STUART STOKES 9:12.46
9s1 KEVIN NASH 9:18.57

**110 Metres Hurdles** (29 Jul) -2.0
1. Sven Pieters BEL 14.06
2. Robert Kronberg SWE 14.16
3. Tomasz Scigaczewski POL 14.18
8. DAMIEN GREAVES 15.06

**400 Metres Hurdles** (29 Jul)
1. Daniel Hechler GER 50.42
2. Marcel Schelbert SUI 50.44
3. MATTHEW DOUGLAS 51.73
3s1 CHARLES ROBERTSON-ADAMS 52.84

**High Jump** (28 Jul)
1. Oskari Frösen FIN 2.19
2. Martin Buss GER 2.19
3. JAMES BRIERLEY 2.17
Q MICHAEL ROBBINS 2.07

**Pole Vault** (29 Jul)
1. Yevgeniy Smiryagin RUS 5.50
2. Timo Makkonen FIN 5.45
3. Nicolas Jolivet FRA 5.40

**Long Jump** (28 Jul)
1. Roman Shchurenko UKR 7.78w
2. Andrey Kislykh RUS 7.76
3. Dmitriy Myshka UKR 7.74w

**Triple Jump** (30 Jul)
1. Ronald Servius FRA 16.71
2. Dmitriy Vasilyev BLR 16.14
3. Pawel Zdrajkowski POL 15.96

**Shot** (27 Jul)
1. Tepa Reinikainen FIN 17.20
2. Rene Sack GER 16.89
3. Iker Sukia ESP 16.74

**Discus** (29 Jul)
1. Andrzej Krawczyk POL 58.22
2. Mike Van Der Bilt HOL 55.40
3. Tolga Köseoglu GER 52.06

**Hammer** (30 Jul)
1. Szymon Ziolkowski POL 75.42
2. Nikolay Avlasevich BLR 68.80
3. Vasiliy Shevchenko UKR 68.64

**Javelin** (29 Jul)
1. Christian Nicolay GER 76.88
2. Harri Haatainen FIN 74.28
3. Daniel Gustafsson SWE 72.38

**Decathlon** (29/30 Jul)
1. Glenn Lindqvist FIN 7363
2. Rick Wassenaar HOL 7299
3. Jiri Ryba CZE 7271
19. MARK BUSHELL 6630
dnf ROGER HUNTER

**10000 Metres Walk** (29 Jul)
1. Andreas Erm GER 40:51.38
2. Francisco Fernandez ESP 41:02.34
3. David Abellan ESP 41:57.84

**4 x 100 Metres Relay** (30 Jul)
1. GREAT BRITAIN 39.43
   (CHAMBERS, DEVONISH,
   HENTHORN, MONEY)
2. Italy 39.61
   (Alaimo, Ibba, Paggi, Comparini)
3. Germany 40.29
   (Kosenkow, Martin, Viel, Schulz)

**4 x 400 Metres Relay** (30 Jul)
1. GREAT BRITAIN 3:07.09
   (DEARMAN, MCHARDY,
   LERWILL, HYLTON)
2. France 3:07.72
   (Bouche, Zami, Letzelter, Loubli)
3. Poland 3:09.65
   (Boucian, Haczek, Lewandowski, Trelka)

## WOMEN

**100 Metres** wind -2.2 (28 Jul)
1. Frederique Bangue FRA 11.48
2. Nora Ivanova BUL 11.58
3. Viara Georgieva BUL 11.59
7. REBECCA DRUMMOND 12.06
6s2 ELLANA RUDDOCK 11.93

**200 Metres** wind -2.1 (29 Jul)
1. Nora Ivanova BUL 23.44
2. Fabé Dia FRA 23.68
3. Sylviane Felix FRA 23.81
5h2 SUSAN WILLIAMS 25.02
6h1 VICTORIA SHIPMAN 24.98

**400 Metres** (28 Jul)
1. Olga Kotlyarova RUS 52.03
2. Andrea Burlacu ROM 53.53
3. Jitka Burianova CZE 53.69
6. ALLISON CURBISHLEY 54.59

**800 Metres** (29 Jul)
1. Mioara Cosulianu ROM 2:04.15
2. Plamena Aleksandrova BUL 2:04.50
3. Anca Safta ROM 2:04.55

**1500 Metres** (30 Jul)
1. Lidia Chojecka POL 4:17.29
2. Lavinia Miroiu ROM 4:19.11
3. Jolanda Steblovnik SLO 4:20.22
7. JULIETTE OLDFIELD 4:25.96

**3000 Metres** (29 Jul)
1. Danisa Costescu ROM 9:13.44
2. Anita Weyermann SUI 9:15.45
3. Olivera Jevtic YUG 9:15.61
7. ALICE BRAHAM 9:35.16

**10000 Metres** (30 Jul)
1. Nadia Singeorzan ROM 33:24.94
2. Olivera Jevtic YUG 33:48.61
3. Sandica Mihalache ROM 34:10.22

**100 Metres Hurdles** (28 Jul) -1.2
1. Yelena Ovcharova UKR 13.09
2. NATASHA DANVERS 13.46
3. Linda Ferga FRA 13.61

**400 Metres Hurdles** (29 Jul)
1. Ionela Tirlea ROM 56.04
2. Ulrike Urbansky GER 57.21
3. Rikke Rönholt DEN 57.71
7s2 VICKI JAMISON 62.81

**High Jump** (30 Jul)
1. Viktoriya Styopina UKR 1.91
2. Yulya Lyakhova RUS 1.89
3. Kajsa Bergqvist SWE 1.89
8. MICHELLE DUNKLEY 1.80
Q RACHAEL FORREST 1.73

**Long Jump** (30 Jul)
1. Linda Ferga FRA 6.56
2. Cristina Nicolau ROM 6.35w
3. Iliana Ilieva BUL 6.25w

**Triple Jump** (28 Jul)
1. Tereza Marinova BUL 13.90
2. Tatyana Lebedeva RUS 13.88
3. Melinda Marton ROM 13.71

**Shot** (28 Jul)
1. Corrie De Bruin HOL 17.76
2. Yanina Korolchik BLR 16.95
3. Olga Ryabinkina RUS 16.55

**Discus** (30 Jul)
1. Corrie De Bruin HOL 57.46
2. Olga Tsander BLR 54.66
3. Lieja Koeman HOL 53.24
19Q RACHEL HOPGOOD 41.58

**Javelin** (29 Jul)
1. Tania Uppa FIN 60.72
2. Mirlea Manjani ALB 59.36
3. Angeliki Tsolakoudi GRE 54.76

**Heptathlon** (27/28 Jul)
1. Annu Montell FIN 5546
2. Yelena Shalygina RUS 5476
3. Katja Ripatti FIN 5394

**5000 Metres Walk** (27 Jul)
1. Sofia Avoila POR 22:13.23
2. Olga Panferova RUS 22:24.95
3. Jana Weidemann GER 22:30.90

**4 x 100 Metres Relay** (30 Jul)
1. Germany 44.77
   (Elmers, Möller, Bertmaring, Wagner)
2. Italy 45.37
   (Sordelli, Grillo, Cosolo, Levorato)
3. Poland 45.56
   (Kaminska, Dybowska, Glowacka, Trywianska)
4. GREAT BRITAIN 45.57
   (RUDDOCK, SHIPMAN,
   WILLIAMS, DRUMMOND)

**4 x 400 Metres Relay** (30 Jul)
1. France 3:32.79
   (Thiebaud, Ega, Marival, Felix)
2. Russia 3:36.10
   (Kozlova, Mistyukevich, Misyakova, Kotlyarova)
3. GREAT BRITAIN 3:38.23
   (WILLIAMS, SLOANE, CURBISHLEY, THORNE)

## International Multi-Events Vladimir, Russia 4 - 5 August 1995

### WOMEN
**Heptathlon**
1. Elizaveta Shalygina RUS 5260
2. Hatalya Roschupkina RUS 5226
3. Anna Panfilova RUS 4991
4. CLOVER WYNTER-PINK 4973
5. Debora Feltrin ITA 4946
6. Alexandra Barle FRA 4888
7. REBECCA LEWIS 4818
8. KELLY SOTHERTON 4812
9. Sonya Shoy SUI 4809
10. JULIE HOLLMAN 4772

**Match Result**
1. Russia 15477
2. GREAT BRITAIN 14603
3. France 14335
4. Italy 13885
5. Belarus 13307

## MEN

### 100 Metres  wind 1.0  (6 Aug)

| | | |
|---|---|---|
| 1. | Donovan Bailey | CAN --- 9.97 |
| 2. | Bruny Surin | CAN 10.03 |
| 3. | Ato Boldon | TRI 10.03 |
| 4. | Frank Fredericks | NAM 10.07 |
| 5. | Michael Marsh | USA 10.10 |
| 6. | LINFORD CHRISTIE | 10.12 |
| 7. | Olapade Adeniken | NGR 10.20 |
| 8. | Ray Stewart | JAM 10.29 |
| 7s2 | DARREN BRAITHWAITE | 10.28 |
| 5q3 | JASON JOHN | 10.39 |

### 200 Metres  wind 0.5  (11 Aug)

| | | |
|---|---|---|
| 1. | Micahel Johnson | USA 19.79 |
| 2. | Frank Fredericks | NAM 20.12 |
| 3. | Jeff Williams | USA 20.18 |
| 4. | Robson da Silva | BRA 20.21 |
| 5. | Claudenel da Silva | BRA 20.40 |
| 6. | Geir Moen | NOR 20.51 |
| 7. | JOHN REGIS | 20.67 |
| 8. | Iván Garcia | CUB 20.77 |
| 5s2 | SOLOMON WARISO | 20.58 |
| 4h2 | DARREN BRAITHWAITE | 20.87 |

### 400 Metres  (8 Aug)

| | | |
|---|---|---|
| 1. | Michael Johnson | USA 43.39 |
| 2. | Butch Reynolds | USA 44.22 |
| 3. | Greg Haughton | JAM 44.56 |
| 4. | Samson Kitur | KEN 44.71 |
| 5. | MARK RICHARDSON | 44.81 |
| 6. | Darnell Hall | USA 44.83 |
| 7. | ROGER BLACK | 45.28 |
| 8. | Sunday Bada | NGR 45.50 |
| 7q2 | ADRIAN PATRICK | 46.27 |

### 800 Metres  (8 Aug)

| | | |
|---|---|---|
| 1. | Wilson Kipketer | DEN 1:45.08 |
| 2. | Arthémon Hatungimana | BUR 1:45.64 |
| 3. | Vebjørn Rodal | NOR 1:45.68 |
| 4. | Nico Motchebon | GER 1:45.97 |
| 5. | Brandon Rock | USA 1:46.42 |
| 6. | Jose Parilla | USA 1:46.44 |
| 7. | Andrea Giocondi | ITA 1:47.78 |
| 8. | Mark Everett | USA 1:53.12 |
| 8s1 | CURTIS ROBB | 1:50.12 |
| 4h3 | CURTIS STRANG | 1:48.76 |

### 1500 Metres  (13 Aug)

| | | |
|---|---|---|
| 1. | Noureddine Morceli | ALG 3:33.73 |
| 2. | Hicham El Guerrouj | MAR 3:35.28 |
| 3. | Vénuste Niyongabo | BUR 3:35.56 |
| 4. | Rachid El Basir | BUR 3:35.96 |
| 5. | Kevin Sulivan | CAN 3:36.73 |
| 6. | Abdelkader Chekhémani | FRA 3:36.90 |
| 7. | Mohamed Suleiman | QAT 3:36.96 |
| 8. | Fermin Cacho | ESP 3:37.02 |
| 9. | GARY LOUGH | 3:37.59 |
| 9s1 | JOHN MAYOCK | 3:40.20 |
| 6h2 | KEVIN MCKAY | 3:43.87 |

### 5000 Metres  (13 Aug)

| | | |
|---|---|---|
| 1. | Ismael Kirui | KEN 13:16.77 |
| 2. | Khalid Boulami | MAR 13:17.15 |
| 3. | Shem Kororia | KEN 13:17.59 |
| 4. | Smail Sghir | MAR 13:17.86 |
| 5. | Brahim Lahlafi | MAR 13:18.89 |

| | | |
|---|---|---|
| 6. | Worku Bikila | ETH 13:20.12 |
| 7. | Bob Kennedy | USA 13:32.10 |
| 8. | Fita Bayissa | ETH 13:34.52 |
| 14. | JOHN NUTTALL | 13:49.25 |
| 6h1 | ROB DENMARK | 13:37.14 |
| 12h3 | ADRIAN PASSEY | 14:08.06 |

### 10000 Metres  (8 Aug)

| | | |
|---|---|---|
| 1. | Haile Gebrselassie | ETH 27:12.95 |
| 2. | Khalid Skah | MAR 27:14.53 |
| 3. | Paul Tergat | KEN 27:14.70 |
| 4. | Salah Hissou | MAR 27:19.30 |
| 5. | Josephat Machuka | ETH 27:23.72 |
| 6. | Joseph Kimani | ETH 27:30.02 |
| 7. | Stephane Franke | GER 27:48.88 |
| 8. | Paulo Guerra | POR 27:52.55 |
| 9h1 | PAUL EVANS | 28:14.76 |

### Marathon  (12 Aug)

| | | |
|---|---|---|
| 1. | Martin Fiz | ESP 2:11:41 |
| 2. | Dionisio Cerón | MEX 2:12:13 |
| 3. | Luiz dos Santos | BRA 2:12:49 |
| 4. | PETER WHITEHEAD | 2:14:08 |
| 5. | Alberto Juzdado | ESP 2:15:29 |
| 6. | Diego Garcia | ESP 2:15:34 |
| 7. | RICHARD NERURKAR | 2:15:47 |
| 8. | Steve Moneghetti | AUS 2:16:13 |
| dnf | MARK HUDSPITH | |

### 3000 Metres Steeplechase  (11 Aug)

| | | |
|---|---|---|
| 1. | Moses Kiptanui | KEN 8:04.16 |
| 2. | Christopher Koskei | KEN 8:09.30 |
| 3. | Sa'ad Shad. Al-Asmari | SAU 8:12.95 |
| 4. | Angelo Carosi | ITA 8:19.73 |
| 5. | Steffen Brand | GER 8:14.37 |
| 6. | Florian Ionescu | ROM 8:15.44 |
| 7. | Vladimir Pronin | RUS 8:16.59 |
| 8. | Martin Strege | GER 8:18.57 |
| 8s2 | JUSTIN CHASTON | 8:38.90 |
| 11h1 | SPENCER DUVAL | 8:38.01 |
| 8h2 | KEITH CULLEN | 8:32.07 |

### 110 Metres Hurdles  -0.1  (12 Aug)

| | | |
|---|---|---|
| 1. | Allen Johnson | USA 13.00 |
| 2. | TONY JARRETT | 13.04 |
| 3. | Roger Kingdom | USA 13.19 |
| 4. | Jack Pierce | USA 13.27 |
| 5. | Kyle Vander-Kuyp | AUS 13.30 |
| 6. | Dan Philibert | FRA 13.34 |
| 7. | Erik Batle | CUB 13.38 |
| 8. | Emilio Valle | CUB 13.43 |
| 7s1 | ANDY TULLOCH | 13.62 |
| 7s2 | NEIL OWEN | 13.92 |

### 400 Metres Hurdles  (10 Aug)

| | | |
|---|---|---|
| 1. | Derrick Adkins | USA 47.98 |
| 2. | Samuel Matete | ZAM 48.03 |
| 3. | Stéphane Diagana | FRA 48.14 |
| 4. | Ruslan Mashchenko | RUS 48.83 |
| 5. | Sven Nylander | SWE 48.84 |
| 6. | Ken Harnden | ZIM 48.89 |
| 7. | Kazuhiko Yamazaki | JAP 49.22 |
| 8. | Eronilde Araujo | BRA 49.86 |
| dqh | GARY JENNINGS | |
| dqh | GARY CADOGAN | |

### High Jump  (8 Aug)

| | | |
|---|---|---|
| 1. | Troy Kemp | BAH 2.37 |
| 2. | Javier Sotomayor | CUB 2.37 |
| 3. | Artur Partyka | POL 2.35 |
| 4= | Steinar Hoen | NOR 2.35 |
| 4= | STEVE SMITH | 2.35 |
| 6. | Patrik Sjöberg | SWE 2.32 |
| 7. | Tony Barton | USA 2.29 |
| 15Q | DALTON GRANT | 2.27 |
| 17=Q | BRENDAN REILLY | 2.24 |

### Pole Vault  (11 Aug)

| | | |
|---|---|---|
| 1. | Sergey Bubka | UKR 5.92 |
| 2. | Maksim Tarasov | RUS 5.86 |
| 3. | Jean Galfione | FRA 5.86 |
| 4. | Okkert Brits | RSA 5.80 |
| 5. | Rodion Gataullin | RUS 5.70 |
| 5. | Scott Huffman | USA 5.70 |
| 7. | Igor Trandenkov | RUS 5.70 |
| 8. | Dean Starkey | USA 5.60 |
| 17Q | NICK BUCKFIELD | 5.55 |

### Long Jump  (12 Aug)

| | | |
|---|---|---|
| 1. | Iván Pedroso | CUB 8.70 |
| 2. | James Beckford | JAM 8.30 |
| 3. | Mike Powell | USA 8.29 |
| 4. | Georg Ackermann | GER 8.14 |
| 5. | Bogdan Tudor | ROM 8.01 |
| 6. | Kostas Koukodimos | GRE 8.00 |
| 7. | Huang Geng | CHN 7.94 |
| 8. | Ivaylo Mladenov | BUL 7.93 |
| Q | FRED SALLE | 3nj |

### Triple Jump  (7 Aug)

| | | |
|---|---|---|
| 1. | JONATHAN EDWARDS | 18.29 |
| 2. | Brian Wellman | BER 17.62w |
| 3. | Jerome Romain | DMN 17.59w |
| 4. | Yoelvis Quesada | CUB 17.59w |
| 5. | Joel Garcia | CUB 17.16 |
| 6. | James Beckford | JAM 17.13w |
| 7. | Mike Conley | USA 16.96w |
| 8. | Galin Georgiev | BUL 16.93 |
| 14Q | FRANCIS AGYEPONG | 16.58 |

### Shot  (9 Aug)

| | | |
|---|---|---|
| 1. | John Godina | USA 21.47 |
| 2. | Mika Halvari | FIN 20.93 |
| 3. | Randy Barnes | USA 20.41 |
| 4. | Aleksandr Bagach | UKR 20.38 |
| 5. | Brent Noon | USA 20.13 |
| 6. | Oliver-Sven Buder | GER 20.11 |
| 7. | Roman Virastyuk | UKR 19.66 |
| 8. | Dmitriy Goncharuk | BLR 19.38 |
| 25Q | MARK PROCTOR | 18.08 |

### Discus  (11 Aug)

| | | |
|---|---|---|
| 1. | Lars Riedel | GER 68.76 |
| 2. | Vladimir Dubrovshchik | BLR 65.98 |
| 3. | Vasiliy Kaptyukh | BLR 65.88 |
| 4. | Attila Horváth | HUN 65.72 |
| 5. | Jürgen Schult | GER 64.44 |
| 6. | Adewale Olukoju | NGR 63.66 |
| 7. | Alexis Elizalde | CUB 63.28 |
| 8. | Dmitriy Shevchenko | RUS 63.18 |
| 9. | ROBERT WEIR | 63.14 |

**Hammer** (6 Aug)
1. Andrey Abduvaliyev TJK 81.56
2. Igor Astapkovich BLR 81.10
3. Tibor Gécsek HUN 80.98
4. Balázs Kiss HUN 79.02
5. Lance Deal USA 78.66
6. Sergey Alay BLR 76.66
7. Ilya Konovalov RUS 76.50
8. Aleksandr Seleznyov RUS 76.18
34Q PETER VIVIAN 67.28

**Javelin** (13 Aug)
1. Jan Zelezny CZE 89.58
2. STEVE BACKLEY 86.30
3. Boris Henry GER 86.08
4. Raymond Hecht GER 83.30
5. Dag Wennlund SWE 82.04
6. MICK HILL 81.06
7. Yuriy Rybin RUS 81.00
8. Andreas Linden GER 80.76

**Decathlon** (6/7 Aug)
1. Dan O'Brien USA 8695
2. Eduard Hämäläinen BLR 8489
3. Mike Smith CAN 8419
4. Erki Nool EST 8268
5. Tomás Dvorák CZE 8236
6. Christian Plaziat FRA 8206
7. Lev Lobodin UKR 8196
8. Chris Huffins USA 8193
12. ALEX KRUGER 7993

**WOMEN**
**100 Metres** wind 0.9 (6 Aug)
1. Gwen Torrence USA 10.85
2. Merlene Ottey JAM 10.94
3. Irina Privalova RUS 10.96
4. Carlette Guidry USA 11.07
5. Zhanna Pintusevich UKR 11.07
6. Melanie Paschke GER 11.10
7. Mary Onyali NGR 11.15
8. Juliet Cuthbert JAM 11.44
5q4 PAULA THOMAS 11.33
6h1 STEPHANIE DOUGLAS 11.67
5h3 SIMMONE JACOBS 11.60

**200 Metres** wind -2.2 (10 Aug)
1. Merlene Ottey JAM 22.12
2. Irina Privalova RUS 22.12
3. Galina Malchugina RUS 22.37
4. Melanie Paschke GER 22.60
5. Silke Knoll GER 22.66
6. Mary Onyali NGR 22.71
7. Marina Trandenkova RUS 22.84
dq Gwen Torrence (21.77)
8s1 PAULA THOMAS 23.03w

**400 Metres** (8 Aug)
1. Marie-José Pérec FRA 49.28
2. Pauline Davis BAH 49.96
3. Jearl Miles USA 50.00
4. Cathy Freeman AUS 50.60
5. Fatima Yusuf NGR 50.70
6. Falilat Ogunkoya NGR 50.77
7. Maicel Malone USA 50.99
8. Sandie Richards JAM 51.13
4s1 MELANIE NEEF 51.18

**20 Kilometres Walk** (6 Aug)
1. Michele Didoni ITA 1:19:59
2. Valentin Massana ESP 1:20:23
3. Yevgeniy Misyulya BLR 1:20:48
4. Ilya Markov RUS 1:21:28
5. Li Zewen CHN 1:21:39
6. Mikhail Shchennikov RUS 1:22:16
7. Denis Langlois FRA 1:22:21
8. Igor Kollár SVK 1:22:30
25. DARRELL STONE 1:28:48

**50 Kilometres Walk** (10 Aug)
1. Valentin Kononen FIN 3:43:42
2. Giovanni Perricelli ITA 3:45:11
3. Robert Korzeniowski POL 3:45:57
4. Miguel Rodriguez MEX 3:46:34
5. Jesus Angel Garcia ESP 3:48:05
6. Aleksandar Rakovic YUG 3:49:35
7. Arturo Di Mezza ITA 3:49:46
8. René Piller FRA 3:49:47
dq LES MORTON

**4 x 100 Metres Relay** (13 Aug)
1. Canada 38.31
(Esmie, Gilbert, Surin, Bailey)
2. Australia 38.50
(Henderson, Jackson, Brimacombe, Marsh)
3. Italy 39.07
(Puggioni, Madonia, Cipollini, Floris)

**800 Metres** (13 Aug)
1. Ana Quirot CUB 1:56.11
2. Letitia Vriesde SUR 1:56.68
3. KELLY HOLMES 1:56.95
4 Patricia Djaté FRA 1:57.04
5. Meredith Rainey USA 1:58.20
6. Ellen van Langen HOL 1:58.98
7. Lyubov Gurina RUS 1:59.16
8. Tatyana Grigoryeva RUS 2:05.55

**1500 Metres** (9 Aug)
1. Hassiba Boulmerka ALG 4:02.42
2. KELLY HOMES 4:03.04
3. Carla Sacramento POR 4:03.79
4. Angela Chalmers CAN 4:04.74
5. Lyudmila Borisova RUS 4:04.78
6. Anna Brzezinska POL 4:05.65
7. Ruth Wysocki USA 4:07.08
8. Mayte Zuñiga ESP 4:07.27

**5000 Metres** (12 Aug)
1. Sonia O'Sullivan IRL 14:46.47
2. Fernanda Ribeiro POR 14:48.54
3. Zohra Ouaziz MAR 14:53.77
4. Gabriela Szabo ROM 14:56.57
5. PAULA RADCLIFFE 14:57.02
6. Maria Pantyukhova RUS 15:01.23
7. Rose Cheruiyot KEN 15:02.45
8. Gwen Griffiths RSA 15:08.05
h ALISON WYETH dnf

**10000 Metres** (9 Aug)
1. Fernanda Ribeiro POR 31:04.99
2. Derartu Tulu ETH 31:08.10
3. Tecia Lorupe KEN 31:17.66

4. Jamaica 39.10
(Beckford, Green, Gordon, Stewart)
5. Japan 39.33
(Suzuki, K Ito, Inoue, Y Ito)
6. Brazil 39.35
(A da Silva, S T de Souza, Ribeiro, R da Silva)
7. Ukraine 39.39
(Chikhachov, Vanyaikin, Kramarenko, Osovich)
5s2 GREAT BRITAIN 38.75
(GARDENER, BRAITHWAITE, REGIS, WARISO)

**4 x 400 Metres Relay** (13 Aug)
1. USA 2:57.32
(Ramsey, Mills, Reynolds, Johnson)
2. Jamaica 2:59.88
(McDonald, D Clarke, McFarlane, Haughton)
3. Nigeria 3:03.18
(Ekyepong, Adejuyigbe, Monye, Bada)
4. GREAT BRITAIN 3:03.75
(MCKENZIE, HYLTON, PATRICK, BLACK)
5. Poland 3:03.84
(Rysiukiewicz, Januszewski, Mackowiak, Jedrusik)
6. Cuba 3:07.65
(Garcia, Crusellas, Mena, Tellez)
dq Germany

4. Maria Guida ITA 31:27.82
5. Elana Meyer RSA 31:31.96
6. LIZ MCCOLGAN 31:40.14
7. Alla Zhilyayeva RUS 31:52.15
8. Hiromi Suzuki JAP 31:54.01
15. JILL HUNTER 32:24.93
YVONNE MURRAY dnf

**Marathon** (5 Aug) 400m short
1. Manuela Machado POR 2:25:39
2. Anuta Catuna ROM 2:26:25
3. Ornella Ferrara ITA 2:30:11
4. Malgorzata Sobanska POL 2:31:10
5. Ritva Lemettinen FIN 2:31:19
6. Monica Pont ESP 2:31:53
7. Linda Somers USA 2:32:12
8. Sonj Krolik GER 2:32:17
22. TRUDI THOMSON 2:41:42
28. ALISON ROSE 2:45:52

**100 Metres Hurdles** 0.2 (6 Aug)
1. Gail Devers USA 12.68
2. Olga Shishigina KZK 12.80
3. Yuliya Graudyn RUS 12.85
4. Tatyana Reshetnikova RUS 12.87
5. Julie Baumann SUI 12.95
6. Gillian Russell JAM 12.96
7. Dionne Rose JAM 12.98
8. Brigita Bukovec SLO 13.02
7s1 JACQUI AGYEPONG 13.14

## 400 Metres Hurdles (10 Aug)
1. Kim Batten USA 52.61
2. Tonja Buford USA 52.62
3. Deon Hemmings JAM 53.48
4. Heike Meissner GER 54.86
5. Tatyana Tereshchuk UKR 54.94
6. Silvia Rieger GER 55.01
7. Ionela Tirlea ROM 55.46
8. Natalya Torshina KZK 56.75
6h1 LOUISE FRASER 57.99

## High Jump (13 Aug)
1. Stefka Kostadinova BUL 2.01
2. Alina Astafei GER 1.99
3. Inga Babakova UKR 1.99
4. Tatyana Motkova RUS 1.96
5. Tatyana Shevchik BLR 1.96
6. Hanne Haugland NOR 1.96
7. Svetlana Leseva BUL 1.93
8= Amy Acuff USA 1.93
8= Nelé Zilinskiené LIT 1.93
35Q LEA HAGGETT 1.75

## Long Jump (6 Aug)
1. Fiona May ITA 6.98w
2. Niurka Montalvo CUB 6.86
3. Irina Mushayilova RUS 6.83w
4. Olga Rublyova RUS 6.78
5. Valentina Uccheddu ITA 6.76
6. Jackie Joyner-Kersee USA 6.74w
7. Agata Karzmarek POL 6.71
8. Viktoriya Vershinina UKR 6.66

## Triple Jump (10 Aug)
1. Inessa Kravets UKR 15.50
2. Iva Prandzheva BUL 15.18
3. Anna Biryukova RUS 15.08
4. Inna Lasovskaya RUS 14.90
5. Rodica Petrescu ROM 14.82w
6. Ren Ruipeng CHN 14.25
7. Zhanna Gureyeva BLR 14.22
8. Barbara Lah ITA 14.18w
12. MICHELLE GRIFFITH 13.59
21Q ASHIA HANSEN 13.61

## Shot (5 Aug)
1. Astrid Kumbernuss GER 21.22
2. Huang Zhihong CHN 20.04
3. Svetla Mitkova BUL 19.56
4. Kathrin Neimke GER 19.30
5. Sui Xinmei CHN 19.09
6. Zhang Liuhong CHN 19.07
7. Ramona Pagel USA 18.81
8. Stephanie Storp GER 18.81
13Q JUDITH OAKES 17.87

## Discus (12 Aug)
1. Ellina Zveryova BLR 68.64
2. Ilke Wyludda GER 67.20
3. Olga Chernyavskaya RUS 68.64
4. Maritsa Martén CUB 64.36
5. Natalya Sadova RUS 62.60
6. Metta Bergmann NOR 62.48
7. Franka Dietzsch GER 61.28
8. Lyudmila Filimonova BLR 61.16
26Q JACKIE MCKERNAN 54.78

## Javelin (8 Aug)
1. Natalya Shikolenko BLR 67.56
2. Felicia Tilea ROM 65.22
3. Mikaela Ingberg FIN 65.16
4. Heli Rantanen FIN 65.04
5. Joanna Stone AUS 63.74
6. Tanja Damaske GER 62.32
7. Isel López CUB 60.80
8. Yekaterina Ivakina RUS 59.82

## Heptathlon (9/10 Aug)
1. Ghada Shouaa SYR 6651
2. Svetlana Moskalets RUS 6575
3. Rita Ináncsi HUN 6522
4. Eunice Barber SLE 6340
5. Kym Carter USA 6329
6. Regia Cardeñas CUB 6306
7. DENISE LEWIS 6299
8. DeDe Nathan USA 6258

## 10 Kilometres Walk (7 Aug)
1. Irina Stankina RUS 42:13
2. Elisabetta Perrone ITA 42:16
3. Yelena Nikolayeva RUS 42:20
4. Sari Essayah FIN 42:20
5. Larisa Ramazanova RUS 42:25
6. Rossella Giordano ITA 42:26
7. Maria Urbanik HUN 42:34
8. Liu Hongyu CHN 42:46
35. LISA LANGFORD 46:06

## 4 x 100 Metres Relay (13 Aug)
1. USA 42.12
(Mondie-Miller, Guidry, Gaines, Torrence)
2. Jamaica 42.25
(Duhaney, Cuthbert, McDonald, Ottey)
3. Germany 43.01
(Paschke, Lichtenhagen, Knoll, Becker)
4. Bahamas 43.14
(Clarke, Ferguson, Fynes, Davis)
5. France 43.35
(Singa, Bangue, Girard, Combe)
6. Finland 44.46
(Kemila, Hemesniemi, Suomi, Koivula)
7. Colombia 44.61
(Mera, Palacios, Rodriguez, Brock)
dnf Russia
5h2 GREAT BRITAIN 43.90
(RICHARDSON, MURPHY, JACOBS, THOMAS)

## 4 x 400 Metres Relay (13 Aug)
1. USA 3:22.39
(Graham, Stevens, Jones, Miles)
2. Russia 3:23.98
(Chebykina, Goncharenko, Sotnikova, Andreyeva)
3. Australia 3:25.88
(Naylor, Poetschka, Gainsford, Freeman)
4. Germany 3:26.10
(Janke, Knoll, Kisabaka, Rohländer)
5. GREAT BRITAIN 3:26.89
(NEEF, LLEWELLYN, HANSON, OLADAPO)
6. Nigeria 3:27.85
(Ogunkoya, Afolabi, L Akinremi, Yusuf)
7. Cuba 3:29.27
(Bonne, Quirot, McLeon, Duporty)
dq Jamaica (3:23.76)

# GB & NI v FRA v ESP v ITA (U23) Narbonne, France 29 July 1995

## MEN

### 100 Metres wind 1.3
1. JULIAN GOLDING 10.34
2. Guillaume Piherry FRA 10.49
3. Needy Guims FRA 10.50
4. ALLYN CONDON 10.55

### 200 Metres wind 0.4
1. OWUSU DAKO 20.80
2. DOUG WALKER 20.95
3. William Hourcade FRA 21.16

### 400 Metres
1. JAMIE BAULCH 45.40
2. Ashraf Saber ITA 46.72
3. JARED DEACON 46.98

### 800 Metres
1. Boris Le Helloco FRA 1:51.42
2. EWAN CALVERT 1:51.64
3. Jaime Rodriguez ESP 1:51.92
7. EDDIE KING 1:54.28

### 1500 Metres
1. BRUNO WITCHALLS 3:43.88
2. NEIL CADDY 3:44.23
3. Carlos Garcia ESP 3:44.78

### 5000 Metres
1. Maurizio Leone ITA 13:55.8
2. Francesco Ingargiola ITA 14:03.6
3. Hallel Taguelmint FRA 14:10.6
4. PHIL MOWBRAY 14:13.2
6. JON WILD 14:19.8

### 3000 Metres Steeplechase
1. Guiseppe Maffei ITA 8:36.68
2. Eliseo Marten ESP 8:37.06
3. Nadir Bosch FRA 8:42.34
7. DARREN PRESTON 9:02.72
8. SIMON O'CONNOR 9:03.60

### 110 Metres Hurdles wind 0.6
1. Balcot S Bianay FRA 13.88
6. KEVIN LUMSDON 14.35
7. JAMES HUGHES 14.47

## 400 Metres Hurdles
| | | | |
|---|---|---|---|
| 1. | Inigo Monreal | ESP | 51.06 |
| 2. | David Lopez | ESP | 51.66 |
| 3. | Jean Laurent Heusse | FRA | 51.77 |
| 4. | NOEL LEVY | | 51.78 |
| 8. | BARRY MIDDLETON | | 52.99 |

## High Jump
| | | | |
|---|---|---|---|
| 1. | Mustafa Raifak | FRA | 2.23 |
| 2. | Luca Zampieri | ITA | 2.21 |
| 3. | Javier Villalobos | ESP | 2.18 |
| 6. | ANDREW LYNCH | | 2.12 |
| 7. | STUART OHRLAND | | 2.09 |

## Pole Vault
| | | | |
|---|---|---|---|
| 1. | M. Mariani | ITA | 5.40 |
| 2. | Alain Andji | FRA | 5.40 |
| 3. | NEIL WINTER | | 5.40 |
| 6= | MICHAEL BARBER | | 5.00 |

## Long Jump
| | | | |
|---|---|---|---|
| 1. | Nicola Trentin | ITA | 7.61 |
| 2. | Simone Bianchi | ITA | 7.59 |
| 3. | ONOCHIE ONUORAH | | 7.58 |
| 7. | CARL HOWARD | | 6.97 |

## Triple Jump
| | | | |
|---|---|---|---|
| 1. | TAYO EROGBOGBO | | 16.31 |
| 2. | Kenny Boudine | FRA | 16.17 |
| 3. | Daniel Roman | ESP | 16.13 |
| 7. | LARRY ACHIKE | | 15.40 |

## Shot
| | | | |
|---|---|---|---|
| 1. | Rocky Vaitanaki | FRA | 17.18 |
| 2. | STEPHAN HAYWARD | | 16.88 |
| 3. | Erik Boes | FRA | 16.40 |
| 7. | MARK EDWARDS | | 15.41 |

## Discus
| | | | |
|---|---|---|---|
| 1. | JAMIE MURPHY | | 55.52 |
| 2. | Jose L. Valencia | ESP | 54.86 |
| 3. | Simone Serogio | ITA | 53.12 |
| 7. | SCOTT HAYES | | 48.74 |

## Hammer
| | | | |
|---|---|---|---|
| 1. | David Chaussinand | FRA | 72.58 |
| 2. | Nicola Vizzoni | ITA | 72.44 |
| 3. | Jose M. Perez | ESP | 70.76 |
| 5. | DAVID SMITH | | 65.70 |
| 7. | MALCOLM CROAD | | 57.66 |

## Javelin
| | | | |
|---|---|---|---|
| 1. | STUART FABEN | | 74.24 |
| 2. | Gaet Siakinuu Schmidt | FRA | 71.26 |
| 3. | Philippe Gandrey | FRA | 70.90 |
| 7. | DUNCAN MACDONALD | | 63.54 |

## 5000 Metres Walk
| | | | |
|---|---|---|---|
| 1. | Eddy Riva | FRA | 19:51.2 |
| 2. | Alessandra Gandellini | ITA | 19:55.3 |
| 3. | Giovanni Mancino | ITA | 20:05.4 |
| 4. | PHILLIP KING | | 20:05.7 |
| 8. | GARRY WITTON | | 22:14.0 |

## 4 x 100 Metres Relay
| | | |
|---|---|---|
| 1. | GREAT BRITAIN | 39.51 |
| | (WHITE, GOLDING, WALTER, DAKO) | |
| 2. | France | 40.17 |
| 3. | Italy | 40.33 |

## 4 x 400 Metres Relay
| | | |
|---|---|---|
| 1. | GREAT BRITAIN | 3:04.90 |
| | (BUDDEN, SLYTHE, MAITLAND, BAULCH) | |
| 2. | France | 3:06.73 |
| 3. | Italy | 3:07.56 |

## Match Result
| | | |
|---|---|---|
| 1. | France | 210 |
| 2. | GREAT BRITAIN | 185 |
| 3. | Italy | 177 |
| 4. | Spain | 133 |

# WOMEN

## 100 Metres  wind 0.0
| | | | |
|---|---|---|---|
| 1. | Marie Joelle Dogbo | FRA | 11.64 |
| 2. | Isabelle Correa | FRA | 11.66 |
| 3. | SOPHIA SMITH | | 11.69 |
| 5. | DONNA HOGGARTH | | 11.89 |

## 200 Metres  wind 0.0
| | | | |
|---|---|---|---|
| 1. | CATHERINE MURPHY | | 23.41 |
| 2. | Aline Andre | FRA | 23.87 |
| 3. | JOICE MADUAKA | | 24.04 |

## 400 Metres
| | | | |
|---|---|---|---|
| 1. | Christine Arron | FRA | 53.76 |
| 2. | Lucie Rangassamy | FRA | 54.33 |
| 3. | MICHELLE PIERRE | | 54.57 |
| 7. | JOANNA CLARK | | 56.13 |

## 800 Metres
| | | | |
|---|---|---|---|
| 1. | VICKY LAWRENCE | | 2:06.75 |
| 2. | Dolores Rodriguez | ESP | 2:07.58 |
| 3. | Elisabeth Grousselle | FRA | 2:07.97 |
| 7. | MICHELLE WILKINSON | | 2:14.14 |

## 1500 Metres
| | | | |
|---|---|---|---|
| 1. | Elisa Vagnini | ITA | 4:22.32 |
| 2. | Jaqueline Martin | ESP | 4:23.70 |
| 3. | Stephanie Berthevas | FRA | 4:24.04 |
| 5. | HAYLEY PARRY | | 4:25.51 |
| 7. | CATHERINE BERRY | | 4:28.72 |

## 3000 Metres
| | | | |
|---|---|---|---|
| 1. | Marina Mainelli | ITA | 9:29.59 |
| 2. | LIZ TALBOT | | 9:34.17 |
| 3. | ANDREA DUKE | | 9:44.50 |

## 100 Metres Hurdles  wind 0.0
| | | | |
|---|---|---|---|
| 1. | Nadege Joseph | FRA | 12.98 |
| 2. | Hay Aron | FRA | 13.51 |
| 3. | MELANIE WILKINS | | 13.55 |
| 4. | DIANE ALLAHGREEN | | 13.62 |

## 400 Metres Hurdles
| | | | |
|---|---|---|---|
| 1. | Isabelle Dhersecourt | FRA | 58.13 |
| 2. | Eva Paniavgua | ESP | 58.45 |
| 3. | VYVYAN RHODES | | 59.29 |
| 7. | LORNA SILVER | | 61.54 |

## High Jump
| | | | |
|---|---|---|---|
| 1. | Marta Mendia | ESP | 1.83 |
| 2. | C Castrejana | ESP | 1.80 |
| 3. | Marie Collonville | FRA | 1.77 |
| 5. | JULIE CRANE | | 1.77 |
| 7. | NICOLA BAKER | | 1.74 |

## Long Jump
| | | | |
|---|---|---|---|
| 1. | Marie Collonville | FRA | 6.11 |
| 2. | M Mazarin | FRA | 6.09 |
| 3. | Etchenique | ESP | 6.08 |
| 6. | RUTH IRVING | | 5.90 |
| 8. | DIANA BENNETT | | 5.52 |

## Triple Jump
| | | | |
|---|---|---|---|
| 1. | Nadia Morandini | ITA | 13.13 |
| 2. | Veronique Pierode | FRA | 12.67 |
| 3. | Noemi Calvigioni | ITA | 12.81 |
| 6. | LIZ GIBBENS | | 12.20 |
| 8. | JANE FALCONER | | 11.10 |

## Shot
| | | | |
|---|---|---|---|
| 1. | Martina D L Fuente | ESP | 16.71 |
| 2. | Laurence Manfredi | FRA | 15.90 |
| 3. | Esperanza Orts | ESP | 14.81 |
| 6. | HELEN WILDING | | 13.24 |
| 8. | EMMA MERRY | | 12.25 |

## Discus
| | | | |
|---|---|---|---|
| 1. | SHELLEY DREW | | 53.40 |
| 2. | Rita Lora | ESP | 52.72 |
| 3. | Scilla Castellini | ITA | 50.04 |
| 6. | SARAH WINCKLESS | | 46.94 |

## Javelin
| | | | |
|---|---|---|---|
| 1. | Marta Miguez | ESP | 54.16 |
| 2. | LORNA JACKSON | | 51.34 |
| 3. | Stephanie Hautavoine | FRA | 49.20 |
| 4. | KAREN MARTIN | | 49.20 |

## 3000 Metres Walk
| | | | |
|---|---|---|---|
| 1. | Micaela Hafner | ITA | 12:43.9 |
| 2. | Nora Leksir | FRA | 13:19.8 |
| 3. | Eva Perez Trujillo | ESP | 13:24.9 |
| 7. | CATH CHARNOCK | | 14:49.3 |
| 8. | KATHERINE HORWILL | | 15:05.2 |

## 4 x 100 Metres Relay
| | | |
|---|---|---|
| 1. | France | 44.43 |
| 2. | GREAT BRITAIN | 45.02 |
| | (MADUAKA, MURPHY, S SMITH, HOGGARTH) | |
| 3. | Spain | 46.26 |

## 4 x 400 Metres Relay
| | | |
|---|---|---|
| 1. | France | 3:37.23 |
| 2. | Italy | 3:39.65 |
| 3. | GREAT BRITAIN | 3:43.92 |

## Match Result
| | | |
|---|---|---|
| 1. | France | 194 |
| 2. | GREAT BRITAIN | 137 |
| 3. | Spain | 137 |
| 4. | Italy | 130 |

## GB & NI v FRA v BEN  Belfort, France  6 August 1995

### WOMEN

**100 Metres** wind -5.0
1. REBECCA DRUMMOND          12.17
2. Isabelle Beaumont  FRA    12.25
3. Sandra Citte  FRA         12.32
4. ELLANA RUDDOCK            12.33

**200 Metres** wind 0.5
1. Fabe Dia  FRA             24.04
2. Nadine Mahobah  FRA       24,47
3. Elke Bogemans  BEN        24.66
4. VICKY SHIPMAN             24.73
5. SUSAN WILLIAMS            24.83

**400 Metres**
1. ALISON CURBISHLEY         54.28
2. JO SLOANE                 54.59
3. Katiana Rene  FRA         54.79

**800 Metres**
1. Karen Goetze  FRA       2:09.33
2. RACHEL OGDEN            2:09.76
3. Betty Dubois  FRA       2:10.48
5. JANE GROVES             2:13.28

**1500 Metres**
1. AMANDA TREMBLE          4:22.70
.2. Hanan Najih  FRA       4:26.67
3. SHEILA FAIRWEATHER      4:28.67

**3000 Metres**
1. Charlotte Audier  FRA   9:22.13
2. MICHELLE MANN           9:46.92
3. Meriem Mered  FRA       9:59.25
5. LISA MOODY             10:26.22

**100 Metres Hurdles**
1. NATASHA DANVERS           13.45
2. RACHEL KING               14.13
3. Lydie Potin  FRA          14.30

**400 Metres Hurdles**
1. Sonia Bernard  FRA        59.16
2. KATRINA NORMAN            61.03
3. Emmanuelle Roggemans  FRA 61.22
4. VICKI JAMIESON            61.67

**High Jump**
1. MICHELLE DUNKLEY           1.81
2. Caroline V Beurden  BEN    1.79
3. RACHAEL FORREST            1.77

**Pole Vault**
1. Marie Poissonnier  FRA     3.80
2. RHIAN CLARKE               3.40
3. CLAIRE RIDGLEY             3.30

**Long Jump**
1. Marie-V Mazarin  FRA       6.09
2. JADE JOHNSON               5.99
3. Eugénie Boncoeur  FRA      5.79
5. ADELE FORRESTER            5.59

**Triple Jump**
1. Eugénie Elisabeth  FRA    12.23
2. PAMELA ANDERSON           11.71
3. JAYNE LUDLOW              11.49

**Shot**
1. Noria Nesnas  FRA         14.79
2. PHILIPPA ROLES            13.75
3. NATASHA SMITH             13.46

**Discus**
1. PHILIPPA ROLES            47.62
2. Helene Gipoulou  FRA      45.52
3. RACHEL HOPGOOD            44.06

**Hammer**
1. Florence Ezeh  FRA        56.04
2. Stéphanie Vaillant  FRA   52.41
3. SAM BURNS-SALMOND         48.42
6. HELEN ARNOLD              43.98

**Javelin**
1. Evelyne Blumet  FRA       48.58
2. Nadia Vigliano  FRA       46.66
3. JOANNE WALKER             45.24
5. KELLY MORGAN              44.32

**3000 Metres Walk**
1. Estelle Delamere  FRA    14:43.7
2. Christine Guinaudeau  FRA 14:54.3
3. NINA HOWLEY              15:10.0
4. NICOLA HUCKERBY          15:15.0

**4 x 100 Metres Relay**
1. France                    45.60
(CITTE, MAHOBAH, BEAUMONT, DIA)
2. GREAT BRITAIN             47.15
(DUDGEON, SHIPMAN, WILLIAMS, DRUMMOND)
3. Benelux                   47.33
(L. Mortier, Bogemans, J Mortier, Som)

**4 x 400 Metres Relay**
1. GREAT BRITAIN           3:43.42
(WILLIAMS, SLOANE, CURBISHLEY, THORNE)
2. France                 3:45.67
(Mendy, Roggermans, Camara, Rene)
3. Benelux                4:00.16
(Som, Van Gorp, Oortgiese, Elsoucht)

**Match Result**
1. France                    174
2. GREAT BRITAIN             157
3. Benelux                    67

## GB & NI v USA  Gateshead  21 August 1995

### MEN

**100 Metres** wind -0.4
1. Tony McCall  USA          10.26
2. Vince Henderson  USA      10.30
3. JASON JOHN                10.38
4. DARREN BRAITHWAITE        10.41
5. Slip Watkins  USA         10.48
6. JASON GARDENER            10.51

**200 Metres** wind 0.2
1. JOHN REGIS                20.63
2. SOLOMON WARISO            20.74
3. JULIAN GOLDING            21.06
4. Aki Bradley  USA          21.07
5. Rohsaan Griffin  USA      21.42
dq Anthur Maybank  USA

**400 Metres**
1. Marlon Ramsey  USA        44.96
2. MARK RICHARDSON           45.00
3. JAMIE BAULCH              45.15
4. ROGER BLACK               45.20
5. Kevin Lyles  USA          45.36
6. Tony Miller  USA          47.25

**800 Metres**
1. Terrance Herrington  USA 1:46.52
2. DAVID STRANG            1:46.68
3. CRAIG WINROW            1:46.68
4. Rich Kenah  USA         1:46.70
5. MATTHEW YATES           1:47.98
6. Brad Sumner  USA        1:49.44

**1500 Metres**
1. Paul McMullen  USA      3:46.87
2. JOHN MAYOCK             3:47.19
3. GARY LOUGH              3:47.30
4. KEVIN MCKAY             3:47.78
5. Bryan Hyde  USA         3:48.51
6. Ronnie Harris  USA      3:57.89

**3000 Metres**
1. ROB DENMARK             8:02.16
2. JOHN NUTTALL            8:02.51
3. Bob Henes  USA          8:03.34
4. Brian Baker  USA        8:04.19
5. IAN GILLESPIE           8:10.42
6. Ronnie Harris  USA      8:14.53

**3000 Metres Steeplechase**
1. TOM HANLON              8:24.37
2. KEITH CULLEN            8:26.05
3. SPENCER DUVAL           8:35.47
4. Karl VanCalcar  USA     8:40.17
5. Gavin Gaynor  USA       8:41.41
6. Sam Wilbur  USA         8:46.31

**110 Metres Hurdles** wind 0.2
1. COLIN JACKSON             13.18
2. TONY JARRETT              13.26
3. Terry Reese  USA          13.44
4. Derek Knight  USA         13.47
5. NEIL OWEN                 13.87
dnf Tony Dees  USA

**400 Metres Hurdles**
1. Danny Harris  USA         48.70
2. Bryan Bronson  USA        49.60
3. Eric Thomas  USA          50.91
4. LAWRENCE LYNCH            51.03
5. LLOYD COWAN               52.33
6. CHRIS RAWLINSON           52.76

## High Jump
1. Charles Austin　USA　2.31
2. Tony Barton　USA　2.28
3. STEVE SMITH　2.15
4. JAMES BRIERLEY　2.15
5. RICHARD ASPDEN　2.10

## Pole Vault
1. Scott Huffman　USA　5.70
2. NICK BUCKFIELD　5.50
3. Pat Manson　USA　5.50
4. DEAN MELLOR　5.20
5. MICHAEL BARBER　5.00
nh Bill Payne　USA

## Long Jump
1. Percy Knox　USA　7.90w
2. ONOCHIE ONUORAH　7.81w
3. Marcus Bailey　USA　7.56w
4. Tony Walton　USA　7.56
5. STEVE PHILLIPS　7.47w
6. FRED SALLE　7.02

## Triple Jump
1. JONATHAN EDWARDS　17.49
2. FRANCIS AGYEPONG　17.05
3. Tyrone Scott　USA　16.55

# WOMEN
## 100 Metres　wind -0.5
1. PAULA THOMAS　11.62
2. D'Andre Hill　USA　11.67
3. Wenda Vereen　USA　11.79
4. SOPHIA SMITH　11.88
5. Treshell Mayo　USA　12.12
6. SALLY ANNE SHORT　12.28

## 200 Metres　wind 0.2
1. Celena Mondie-Milner　USA　22.99
2. PAULA THOMAS　23.00
3. Aspen Burkett　USA　23.39
4. MELANIE NEEF　23.42
5. Richelle Webb　USA　24.11
6. DONNA FRASER　24.31

## 400 Metres
1. Kim Graham　USA　51.15
2. Rochelle Stevens　USA　51.26
3. LORRAINE HANSON　52.47
4. STEPHANIE LLEWELLYN　52.79
5. Nicole Green　USA　52.93
6. GEORGINA OLAPADO　52.97

## 800 Metres
1. Amy Wickus　USA　2:00.58
2. Alisa Hill　USA　2:01.63
3. ANNE GRIFFITHS　2:01.94
4. Jill Stamison　USA　2:03.55
5. ABIGAIL HUNTE　2:04.25
6. VICKIE LAWRENCE　2:04.77

## 1500 Metres
1. Ruth Wysocki　USA　4:05.03
2. Sarah Thorsett　USA　4:08.84
3. SUE PARKER　4:13.36
4. DEBBIE GUNNING　4:14.55
5. Kathy Franey　USA　4:16.89
6. LIZ TALBOT　4:26.58

4. TAYO EROGBOGBO　16.32
5. Charles Rogers　USA　16.20
6. Ivory Angello　USA　15.81

## Shot
1. Kevin Toth　USA　20.57
2. C J Hunter　USA　19.55
3. Scott Petersen　USA　18.13
4. MARK PROCTOR　17.99
5. SHAUN PICKERING　17.85
6. NIGEL SPRATLEY　16.15

## Discus
1. ROBERT WEIR　62.54
2. Randy Heisler　USA　60.10
3. Mike Buncic　USA　59.10
4. KEVIN BROWN　56.90
5. GARY HERRINGTON　54.50
nt Adam Stiff　USA

## Hammer
1. DAVE SMITH　69.20
2. Jim Driscoll　USA　69.14
3. John Walker　USA　67.88
4. PETER VIVIAN　66.80
5. MICHAEL JONES　66.32
6. Brian Murer　USA　65.84

## 3000 Metres
1. YVONNE MURRAY　8:59.80
2. Lynn Jennings　USA　9:04.34
3. Darcy Arreola　USA　9:04.78
4. Cheri Goddard　USA　9:07.37
5. ANDREA WHITCOMBE　9:10.29
6. SARAH BENTLEY　9:12.72

## 100 Metres Hurdles　wind 0.5
1. JACKIE AGYEPONG　13.09
2. Marsha Guialdo　USA　13.09
3. Dawn Bowles　USA　13.10
4. Doris Williams　USA　13.25
5. MICHELLE CAMPBELL　13.47
6. MELANIE WILKINS　13.63

## 400 Metres Hurdles
1. Trevaia Williams　USA　56.48
2. Tonya Willaims　USA　57.36
3. Tonya Lee　USA　57.58
4. JACKIE PARKER　57.90
5. LOUISE FRASER　58.18
6. VYVYAN RHODES　58.85

## High Jump
1. LEA HAGGETT　1.88
2. DIANA DAVIES　1.85
3. Yolanda Henry　USA　1.85
4. Connie Teaberry　USA　1.85
5= DEBBI MARTI　1.80
5= Tanya Hughes　USA　1.80

## Pole Vault
1. Melissa Price　USA　3.80
2. Stacey Dragila　USA　3.70
3. LINDA STANTON　3.60
4= Phil Raschker　USA　3.30
4= RHIAN CLARKE　3.30
6. CLAIRE MORRISON　3.20

## Javelin
1. STEVE BACKLEY　83.00
2. Tom Pukstys　USA　81.52
3. MICK HILL　81.40
4. COLIN MACKENZIE　74.04
5. Jim Connolly　USA　71.06
6. Erik Smith　USA　69.74

## 4 x 100 Metres Relay
1. USA　38.55
　(Watkins, Clark, McCall, Henderson)
2. GREAT BRITAIN　39.44
(JOHN, GOLDING, BRAITHWAITE, WARISO)

## 4 x 400 Metres Relay
1. GREAT BRITAIN　3:03.16
(MCKENZIE, BAULCH, O'DELL, HYLTON)
2. USA　3:12.01
　(Minor, Thomas, Bronson, Lyles)

## Match Result
1. GREAT BRITAIN　203
2. USA　182

## Long Jump
1. DENISE LEWIS　6.56
2. Shana Williams　USA　6.46
3. Sharon Couch　USA　6.29
4. VIKKIE SCHOFIELD　6.16
5. LIZ GHOJEFA　5.93

## Triple Jump
1. ASHIA HANSEN　14.66
2. MICHELLE GRIFFITH　13.98
3. Cynthea Rhodes　USA　13.98
4. Diana Orrange　USA　13.67
5. Amanda Banks　USA　13.16
6. RACHEL KIRBY　12.98

## Shot
1. Connie Price-Smith　USA　19.52
2. Ramona Pagel　USA　19.00
3. JUDY OAKES　18.13
4. Eileen Vanisi　USA　17.43
5. MAGGIE LYNES　15.57
6. TRACY AXTEN　14.08

## Discus
1. Pam Dukes　USA　56.50
2. Edie Boyer　USA　56.20
3. JACKIE MCKERNAN　56.16
4. DEBBIE CALLAWAY　52.32
5. Erica Ahmann　USA　52.20
6. SHELLEY DREW　51.20

## Hammer
1. LORRAINE SHAW　59.68
2. Sonia Fitts　USA　56.24
3. Alexandria Givan　USA　56.00
4. DIANA HOLDEN　52.32
5. Dawn Ellerbe　USA　51.96
6. LYN SPRULES　50.10

**Javelin**
1. SHARON GIBSON   58.10
2. Christine Stancliff   USA   55.84
3. Erica Wheeler   USA   53.86
4. Donna Mayhew   USA   53.70
5. LORNA JACKSON   52.86
6. KAREN MARTIN   49.90

**4 x 100 Metres Relay**
1. USA   43.10
   (Burkett, M-Milner, Gaines, Hill)
2. GREAT BRITAIN   45.46
(S SMITH, FRASER, SHORT, MCLEOD)

**4 x 400 Metres Relay**
1. USA   3:28.22
   (Hill, Green, Wickus, Miles)
2. GREAT BRITAIN   3:29.65
(NEEF, OLAPADO, HANSON, RAWLINSON)

**Match Result**
1. USA   210.5
2. GREAT BRITAIN   156.5

# WORLD UNIVERSITY CHAMPIONSHIPS   Fukuoka, Japan   28 Aug - 3 Sep 1995

## MEN

**100 Metres** wind 1.3 (1 Sep)
1. David Oaks   USA   10.28
2. Obadele Thompson   BAR   10.34
3. Terrence Bowen   USA   10.36
5. TOBY BOX   10.39
6. PAUL WHITE   10.45

**200 Metres** wind 0.6 (30 Aug)
1. Anthuan Maybank   USA   20.46
2. David Dopek   USA   20.47
3. Thomas Sbokos   GRE   20.75
7s2 OWUSU DAKO   21.32
4q5 DOUGLAS WALKER   21.38

**400 Metres** (1 Sep)
1. Eswort Coombs   STV   45.38
2. Udeme Ekpenyong   NGR   45.57
3. Dmitri Kossov   RUS   45.70
5s2 DAVID GRINDLEY   46.15
5s1 JARED DEACON   46.45

**800 Metres** (30 Aug)
1. Hezekiel Sepeng   RSA   1:47.87
2. Andres Diaz   ESP   1:48.06
3. Pavel Soukup   CZE   1:48.15

**1500 Metres** (3 Sep)
1. Abdelkader Chekhemani   FRA   3:46.53
2. Andrea Giocondi   ITA   3:47.11
3. Abdohamid Slimani   ALG   3:47.43
4. BRUNO WITCHALLS   3:47.79
9. BRIAN TREACY   3:48.88

**5000 Metres** (31 Aug)
1. Katsuhiro Kawauchi   JPN   13:53.86
2. Brahim Boulami   MAR   13:54.05
3. Maurizio Leone   ITA   13:54.13

**10000 Metres** (2 Sep)
1. Yasuyuki Watanabe   JPN   28:47.78
2. Stephen Mayaka   KEN   28:55.02
3. Gabino Apolonio   MEX   29:07.95

**Marathon** (3 Sep)
1. Takaki Morikawa   JPN   2:21:32
2. Patrick Muturi   KEN   2:24:29
3. Yi young Kim   KOR   2:24:43

**3000 Metres Steeplechase** (2 Sep)
1. Daniel Muturi   KEN   8:27.03
2. Joel Bourgeois   CAN   8:28.44
3. Brahim Boulami   MAR   8:35.53
5. JUSTIN CHASTON   8:39.28
   ROBERT HOUGH   dnf

**110 Metres Hurdles** 0.4 (30 Aug)
1. Jon Nsenga   BEL   13.51
2. Brian Amos   USA   13.59
3. Krzysztof Mehlich   POL   13.66
5. NEIL OWEN   13.72

**400 Metres Hurdles** (31 Aug)
1. Kazuhiko Yamazaki   JPN   48.58
2. Octavius Terry   USA   48.95
3. Yoshihiko Saito   JPN   49.18
8s2 GARY JENNINGS   51.22
5h3 TONY WILLIAMS   50.73

**High Jump** (1 Sep)
1. Dragutin Topic   YUG   2.29
2. Wolfgang Kreissig   GER   2.29
3. BRENDAN REILLY   2.27

**Pole Vault** (31 Aug)
1. Istvan Bagyula   HUN   5.70
2. Lawrence Johnson   USA   5.60
3. Nuno Fernandes   POR   5.55
Q PAUL WILLIAMSON   4.60

**Long Jump** (3 Sep)
1. Kiril Sosunov   RUS   8.21
2. Georg Ackermann   GER   8.21
3. Gregor Cankar   SLO   8.18

**Triple Jump** (30 Aug)
1. Andrey Kourennoy   RUS   17.30
2. Armen Martirosyan   ARM   16.82
3. LaMark Carter   USA   16.62
5. TOSI FASINRO   16.56
11. JULIAN GOLLEY   15.89

**Shot** (31 Aug)
1. Yury Belonog   UKR   19.70
2. Viktor Bulat   BLR   19.69
3. Thorsten Herbrand   GER   18.88

**Discus** (1 Sep)
1. Vitaliy Sidorov   UKR   62.16
2. Frits Potgieter   RSA   61.38
3. Diego Fortuna   ITA   61.16

**Hammer** (29 Aug)
1. Balazs Kiss   HUN   79.74
2. Alexandr Krykun   UKR   77.06
3. Sergey Gavrilov   RUS   75.50

**Javelin** (1 Sep)
1. Zhang Lianbiao   CHN   79.30
2. Gregor Hoegler   AUT   77.52
3. Andrey Uglov   UKR   76.16

**Decathlon** (31 Aug / 1 Sep)
1. Dezso Szabo   HUN   8051
2. Sebastian Chmara   POL   8014
3. Dmitriy Sukhomazov   BLR   7971
9. BARRY THOMAS   7766
15. JAMIE QUARRY   7401

**20 Kilometres Walk** (2 Sep)
1. Daniel Garcia   MEX   1:24:11
2. Giovanni Perricelli   ITA   1:24:19
3. Arturo Di Mezza   ITA   1:24:33

**4 x 100 Metres Relay** (3 Sep)
1. USA   38.96
   (Bowen, Oaks, Hargraves, Dopek)
2. GREAT BRITAIN   39.39
   (WHITE, BOX, WALKER, AFILAKA)
3. Italy   39.64
   (Cipolloni, Orlandi, Occhiena, Colombo)

**4 x 400 Metres Relay** (3 Sep)
1. USA   3:00.40
   (Hayden, Byrd, Morris, Maybank)
2. Russia   3:01.95
   (Zharov, Bei, Voronine, Kossov)
3. GREAT BRITAIN   3:02.42
(WILLIAMS, DEACON, JENNINGS, GRINDLEY)

## WOMEN

**100 Metres** wind 0.7 (1 Sep)
1. Melanie Paschke   GER   11.16
2. Ekaterina Thanou   GRE   11.30
3. Mary Tombiri   NGR   11.43
6. MARCIA RICHARDSON   11.60
8. SHARON WILLIAMS   11.89

**200 Metres** wind 1.7 (30 Aug)
1. Du Xiujie   CHN   22.53
2. Oksana Dyachenko   RUS   22.89
3. Zlatka Georguieva   BUL   23.04
5s2 CATHERINE MURPHY   23.74
8s1 JOICE MADUAKA   25.08

**400 Metres** (1 Sep)
1. Olabisi Afolabi   NGR   50.50
2. Tatyana Chebykina   RUS   51.01
3. Yelena Rurak   UKR   51.76
4h5 LOUISE WHITEHEAD   54.92

**800 Metres**  (31 Aug)
1.  Stella Jongmans   HOL   2:02.13
2.  Svetlana Tverdokhleb  UKR   2:02.92
3.  NATALIE TAIT   2:03.32

**1500 Metres**  (3 Sep)
1.  Gabriela Szabo   ROM   4:11.73
2.  Julianne Henner   USA   4:12.70
3.  Ursula Friedmann   GER   4:13.32
7.  ANGELA DAVIES   4:16.75

**5000 Metres**  (29 Aug)
1.  Gabriela Szabo   ROM   15:29.86
2.  Silvia Sommaggio   ITA   15:34.32
3.  Yumi Sato   JPN   15:35.28
9.  LOUISE WATSON   16:07.09

**10000 Metres**  (1 Sep)
1.  Iulia Negura   ROM   32:28.25
2.  Camelia Tecuta   ROM   32:43.38
3.  Yasuko Kimura   JPN   33:03.01
6.  LOUISE WATSON   33:33.71

**Marathon**  (3 Sep)
1.  Masako Kusakaya   JPN   2:53:03
2.  Nao Otani   JPN   2:57:09
3.  Kristi Klinnert   USA   2:57:29

**100 Metres Hurdles**  0.6 (2 Sep)
1.  Nicole Ramalalanirina   MAD   13.02
2.  Yelena Ovcharova   UKR   13.07
3.  Svetlana Laukhova   RUS   13.08

**400 Metres Hurdles**  (31 Aug)
1.  Heike Meissner   GER   55.57
2.  Ionela Tirlea   ROM   55.99
3.  Tonya Williams   USA   56.04

**High Jump**  (2 Sep)
1.  Viktoriya Fedorova   RUS   1.92
2.  Svetlana Zalevskaya   KAZ   1.92
3.  Nataliya Jonckheere   BEL   1.88

**Long Jump**  (31 Aug)
1.  Viktoria Vershinina   UKR   6.76
2.  Sharon Jaklofsky   HOL   6.74
3.  Lyudmila Galkina   RUS   6.55

**Triple Jump**  (1 Sep)
1.  Sarka Kasparkova   CZE   14.20
2.  Lyudmila Dubkova   RUS   13.87
3.  Barbara Lah   ITA   13.85

**Shot**  (2 Sep)
1.  Wu Xianchun   CHN   18.31
2.  Cheng Xiaoyan   CHN   17.95
3.  Corrie De Bruin   HOL   17.82

**Discus**  (31 Aug)
1.  Nataliya Sadova   RUS   62.92
2.  Anja Gundler   GER   60.78
3.  Bao Dongying   CHN   59.30

**Javelin**  (3 Sep)
1.  Felicea Tilea   ROM   62.16
2.  Claudia Isaila   ROM   61.74
3.  Young-Sun Lee   KOR   61.62

**Heptathlon**  (28/29 Aug)
1.  Jane Jamieson   AUS   6123
2.  Mona Steigauf   GER   6102
3.  Irina Tyukhay   RUS   5989

**10 Kilometres Walk**  (2 Sep)
1.  Anna rita Sidoti   ITA   43:22
2.  Rossella Giordano   ITA   43:30
3.  Larisa Ramazanova   RUS   43:56

**4 x 100 Metres Relay**  (3 Sep)
1.  USA   43.58
    (Taplin, Miller, Ball, Walton)
2.  Russia   44.06
    (Anisimova, Dyatchenko, Voronova, Levacheva)
3.  Nigeria   44.08
    (Akpan, Aladefa, Itanyi, Tombiri)
6.  GREAT BRITAIN   44.93
    (MADUAKA, MURPHY, RICHARDSON, WILLIAMS)

**4 x 400 Metres Relay**  (3 Sep)
1.  Russia   3:28.32
    (Sotnikova, Khrushchelyova, Andreyeva, Chebykina)
2.  USA   3:30.25
    (Green, C. Jones, J. Jones, Warren)
3.  Ukraine   3:30.57
    (Fomenko, Tverdokhleb, Movchan, Rurak)

## GB & NI v HUN V RUS V UKR (Jumps) Salgotargan, Hungary 11 September 1995

**MEN**
**High Jump**
1.  Javier Sotomayor   gst/CUB   2.37
2.  BRENDAN REILLY   2.25
3.  Aleksey Makurin   RUS   2.22
4.  Péter Deutsch   HUN   2.22
10. STUART OHRLAND   2.10

**Pole Vault**
1.  Maksim Tarasov   gst/RUS   5.91
2.  Viktor Chistyakov   RUS   5.71
3.  Istvan Bagyula   HUN   5.51
4.  Yevgeniy Smiryagin   RUS   5.41
6.  MIKE BARBER   5.31
7.  DEAN MELLOR   5.21

**WOMEN**
**High Jump**
1.  Natalya Golodnova   RUS   1.90
2.  Erzébet Fazekas   HUN   1.87
3.  Dora Gyorffy   HUN   1.87
4.  Rita Inancsi   HUN   1.84
9=  MICHELLE DUNKLEY   1.80
9=  RACHAEL FORREST   1.80

**Pole Vault**
1.  Daniela Bartová   gst/CZE   4.22
2.  Zsuzaria Szabo   HUN   3.46
3.  LINDA STANTON   3.46
4.  Fanni Juhasz   HUN   3.16

**Match Result**
1.  Russia   37.5
2.  Hungary   32
3.  GREAT BRITAIN   23
4.  Ukraine   11.5

## BAF HALF MARATHON CHAMPIONSHIPS South Shields 17 September 1995

**MEN**
1.  Moses Tanui   KEN   60:39
2.  Benson Masya   KEN   61:59
3.  James Kariuki   KEN   62:29
4.  PAUL EVANS   62:30
5.  GARY STAINES   62:38
6.  Fekadu Degethu   ETH   62:38
7.  Oleg Strizhakov   RUS   64:13
8.  EAMONN MARTIN   64:35
9.  DAVE BUZZA   64:38
10. DALE RIXON   64:38
11. BARRY ROYDEN   64:39

12. PAUL RODEN   64:39
13. BRAIN RUSHWORTH   64:48
14. DALE LAUGHLIN   65:05
15. ROBIN NASH   66:09

**WOMEN**
1.  LIZ McCOLGAN   71:42
2.  Fatuma Roba   ETH   72:05
3.  Manuela Machado   POR   73:22
4.  MARIAN SUTTON   74:19
5.  AMANDA WRIGHT   76:06

6.  HEATHER HEASMAN   77:36
7.  ELAINE FOSTER   77:59
8.  DEBBIE KILNER   78:17
9.  TRACY SWINDELL   78:18
10. LINDA RUSHMERE   78:50
11. JANICE MOOREKITE   80:47
12. JAN RASHLEIGH   80:49
13. ALISON DAVIDSON   81:34
14. K SHAW   82:51
15. LOUISE COOPER   83:19

# IAAF WORLD HALF MARATHON CHAMPIONSHIPS
## Belfort, France 1 October 1995

**MEN**

| | | | |
|---|---|---|---|
| 1. | Moses Tanui | KEN | 61:45 |
| 2. | Paul Yego | KEN | 61:46 |
| 3. | Charles Tangus | KEN | 61:50 |
| 4. | Antono Serrano | ESP | 61:56 |
| 5. | Josiah Thugwane | RSA | 62:28 |
| 6. | Delmir-A D Santos | BRA | 62:32 |
| 7. | Herder Vasquez | COL | 62:32 |
| 8. | Nobuyuki Sato | JPN | 62:36 |
| 9. | Yoshifumi Miyamoto | JPN | 62:38 |
| 10. | Joaquim Pinheiro | POR | 62:40 |
| 11. | Bartolome Serrano | ESP | 62:41 |
| 12. | Vicenzo Modica | ITA | 62:48 |
| 13. | D Goffi | ITA | 62:49 |
| 14. | Oleg Strizhakov | RUS | 62:54 |
| 15. | G Leone | ITA | 62:54 |
| 44. | MARTIN McCLOUGHLIN | | 64:26 |
| 51. | DAVE TAYLOR | | 64:47 |
| 66. | MARK FLINT | | 66:48 |
| 104. | BASHIR HUSSAIN | | 67:48 |

**Team Result**

| | | |
|---|---|---|
| 1. | Kenya | 3:05:21 |
| 2. | Spain | 3:07:51 |
| 3. | Italy | 3:08:31 |
| 4. | Japan | 3:08:44 |
| 5. | Brazil | 3:09:34 |
| 6. | Russia | 3:10:17 |
| 7. | France | 3:11:39 |
| 8. | Portugal | 3:11:51 |
| 16. | GREAT BRITAIN & NI | 3:16:01 |

**WOMEN**

| | | | |
|---|---|---|---|
| 1. | Valentina Yegorova | RUS | 69:58 |
| 2. | Cristina Pomacu | ROM | 70:22 |
| 3. | Anuta Catuna | ROM | 70:28 |
| 4. | Colleen de Reuck | RSA | 70:34 |
| 5. | Alla Zhilyayeva | RUS | 70:39 |
| 6. | Elena Fidatov | ROM | 70:39 |
| 7. | Ava-Isabel Alonso | ESP | 70:43 |
| 8. | Zaiha Dahmani | FRA | 71:28 |
| 9. | Maura Viceconte | ITA | 71:32 |
| 10. | Rocio Rios | ESP | 71:42 |
| 11. | Aurica Buai | ROM | 71:44 |
| 12. | Kamila Gradus | POL | 71:45 |
| 13. | Marleen Renders | BEL | 71:52 |
| 14. | L Doering | USA | 71:54 |
| 15. | Carmen Fuentas | ESP | 72:01 |
| 34 | CATH MIJOVIC | | 74:13 |
| 35 | ANGIE HULLEY | | 74:19 |
| 38 | VIKKI McPHERSON | | 74:27 |
| 48 | TRUDI THOMSON | | 75:48 |
| 78 | KATH BAILEY | | 80:16 |

**Team Result**

| | | |
|---|---|---|
| 1. | Romania | 3:31:29 |
| 2. | Russia | 3:33:12 |
| 3. | Spain | 3:34:26 |
| 4. | France | 3:38:00 |
| 5. | Italy | 3:39:40 |
| 6. | Japan | 3:41:51 |
| 7. | Netherlands | 3:42:04 |
| 8. | GREAT BRITAIN & NI | 3:42:59 |

# EUROPEAN CROSS COUNTRY CHAMPIONSHIPS
## Alnwick 2 December 1995

**MEN**

| | | | |
|---|---|---|---|
| 1. | Paulo Guerra | POR | 26:40 |
| 2. | Alejandra Gomez | ESP | 26:46 |
| 3. | ANDREW PEARSON | | 26:47 |
| 4. | KEITH CULLEN | | 26:48 |
| 5. | Mustapha Essaid | FRA | 26:52 |
| 6. | JON BROWN | | 26:56 |
| 7. | Alfredo Bras | POR | 27:01 |
| 8. | José Manuel Garcia | ESP | 27:03 |
| 9. | Giuliano Batocletti | ITA | 27:05 |
| 10. | Manuel Pancorbo | ESP | 27:05 |
| 42. | DAVID TAYLOR | | 28:04 |
| 55. | COLIN JONES | | 28:26 |
| 99. | CARL UDALL | | 30:19 |

**Team Result**

| | | |
|---|---|---|
| 1. | Spain | 32 |
| 2. | Portugal | 37 |
| 3. | GREAT BRITAIN | 55 |
| 4. | France | 60 |
| 5. | Italy | 111 |
| 6. | Russia | 131 |
| 7. | Ireland | 133 |
| 8. | Denmark | 160 |

**WOMEN**

| | | | |
|---|---|---|---|
| 1. | Annemari Sandell | FIN | 13:52 |
| 2. | Sara Wedlund | SWE | 14:07 |
| 3. | Nina Belikova | RUS | 14:09 |
| 4. | Elena Fidatov | ROM | 14:10 |
| 5. | Alla Zhilyayeva | RUS | 14:17 |
| 6. | Annette Palluy-Sergent | FRA | 14:18 |
| 7. | Sinead Delahunty | IRL | 14:18 |
| 8. | Stela Olteanu | ROM | 14:20 |
| 9. | Ana Dias | POR | 14:22 |
| 10. | LIZ TALBOT | | 14:23 |
| 31. | JANE SHIELDS | | 14:47 |
| 44. | SARAH BENTLEY | | 14:58 |
| 48. | SARAH YOUNG | | 14:59 |

**Team Result**

| | | |
|---|---|---|
| 1. | Russia | 20 |
| 2. | Romania | 23 |
| 3. | France | 41 |
| 4. | Spain | 55 |
| 5. | Portugal | 55 |
| 6. | Belgium | 59 |
| 7. | GREAT BRITAIN | 65 |
| 8. | Italy | 83 |

# REGIONAL CHAMPIONSHIPS

| | SCOTLAND<br>Edinburgh, 23-24 June | | WALES<br>Newport , 17 June | | NORTHERN IRELAND<br>Antrim, 1 July | |
|---|---|---|---|---|---|---|
| **MEN** | | | | | | |
| 100 | Ian Mackie | 10.72 | Kevin Williams | 10.6 | Ian Craig | 10.9 |
| 200 | Cypren Edmunds | 21.38 | Doug Turner | 21.58 | Mark Allen | 21.56 |
| 400 | Paul McBurney | 47.16 | Iwan Thomas | 46.40 | Paul McBurney | 47.14 |
| 800 | Paul Walker | 1:49.71 | Darrell Maynard | 1:55.6 | Phillip Healy | 1:54.98 |
| 1500 | Phil Mowbray | 3:43.81 | Nick Comerford | 4:09.74 | Phillip Healy | 3:50.01 |
| 5000 | Dermot Donnolly | 14:16:40 | Justin Hobbs | 14:30.08 | Dermot Donnolly | 14:05.45 |
| 10000 | Graeme Croll | 29:50.69 | Bruce Chinnick | 30:49.5 | Dermot Donnolly | 29:33.3 |
| 3kSt | Graeme Croll | 9:00.98 | Phil Cook | 9:27.14 | Steven Cairns | 9:24.6 |
| 110H | Ken Campbell | 14.5 | Colin Bovell | 14.5 | Trevor McGlynn | 15.60 |
| 400H | Mark Davidson | 52.22 | David Griffin | 52.7 | Douglas Thom | 53.80 |
| HJ | David Barnetson | 2.13 | Stuart Brown | 2.05 | Derek Gillespie (IRL) | 2.00 |
| | | | | | 2. Trevor McGlynn | 1.90 |
| PV | Des Fitzgerald | 4.40 | Tim Thomas | 5.00 | Richard Ramsey | 4.25 |
| LJ | Duncan Mathieson | 7.49 | Gary Slade | 7.24 | Michael McDonald | 6.33 |
| TJ | Neil McMenemy | 14.74 | Gareth Davies | 14.39 | Padraig Martin | 11.90 |
| SP | Steve Whyte | 16.52 | Lee Wiltshire | 14.93 | Mike Atkinson | 13.48 |
| DT | Paul Reed | 51.52 | Andy Turner | 43.44 | John Moreland | 51.76 |
| HT | Paul Barnard | 60.84 | Adrian Palmer | 60.50 | David Nicholl | 51.24 |
| JT | Phil Parry | 67.28 | Stuart Loughran | 58.98 | Dean Smahon | 64.14 |
| Dec | Duncan Mathieson | 7272 | Robert Treu | 6051 | Ian Condron (IRL) | 5957 |
| | | | | | | |
| **WOMEN** | | | | | | |
| 100 | Michelle Carroll (IRL) | 12.38 | Catherine Murphy | 11.80 | Stephanie McCann | 12.2 |
| | 2. Gillian Hegney | 12.46 | | | | |
| 200 | Sinead Dudgeon | 24.63 | Catherine Murphy | 24.3 | Stephanie McCann | 24.28 |
| 400 | Stephanie McCann | 55.39 | Kate Williams | 57.7 | Stephanie McCann | 56.28 |
| 800 | Vickie Lawrence | 2:07.20 | Alyson Layzell | 2:07.5 | Claire Brook | 2:13.44 |
| 1500 | Ann Terek | 4:25.27 | Liz Thomas | 4:36.80 | Ann Terek | 4:32.59 |
| 5000 | Hayley Haining | 16:36.6 | Dinah Cheverton | 17:33.4 | 3000 Jill Bruce (IRL) | 9:22.6 |
| 100H | Jocelyn Harwood | 14.55 | Rachel King | 14.2 | | |
| 400H | Stephanie McCann (NI) | 58.8 | Claire Edwards | 63.6 | Stephanie McCann | 63.2 |
| | 2. Jane Low | 59.9 | | | | |
| HJ | Lisa Brown | 1.81 | Julie Crane | 1.78 | Jackie Vyschaft | 1.70 |
| PV | Janine Whitlock | 2.85 | Rebecca Roles | 2.50 | | |
| LJ | Linda Davidson | 5.83 | Nicola Short | 5.66 | Liz Orr | 4.91 |
| TJ | Karen Skeggs | 12.47 | Jayne Ludlow | 11.29 | Liz Orr | 10.82 |
| SP | Alison Grey | 13.61 | Philippa Roles | 13.21 | Alison Moffitt | 11.06 |
| DT | Helen Cowe | 45.34 | Philippa Roles | 44.16 | Jackie McKernan | 56.58 |
| HT | Jean Lavender | 49.46 | Sarah Moore | 51.82 | Julie Kirkpatrick | 48.12 |
| JT | Lorna Jackson | 51.04 | Onyema Amadi | 41.82 | Alison Moffitt | 44.38 |
| Hep | Emma Lindsay | 50.56 | Amanda Wate | 4076 | | |

# AREA CHAMPIONSHIPS

| | SOUTH London (CP), 17 June | | MIDLANDS Birmingham, 17-18 June | | NORTH Gateshead, 17 June | |
|---|---|---|---|---|---|---|
| **MEN** | | | | | | |
| 100 | Josephus Thomas (SLE) | 10.67 | Marlon Devonish | 10.63 | Darren Campbell | 10.37 |
| 200 | Mark Smith | 21.32 | Dalton Powell | 21.71w | Allyn Condon | 21.05 |
| 400 | Nigel Will | 47.04 | Steve McHardy | 48.218 | David Nolan | 46.75 |
| 800 | Andy Knight | 1:51.24 | John Gercs | 1:53.2 | Martin Steele | 1:51.47 |
| 1500 | Philip Hogston | 3:46.17 | Stuart Margiotta | 3:56.22 | Tony Mate | 3:59.24 |
| 5000 | Nick Hopkins | 14:05.08 | Stephen Platts | 14:46.95 | Neil Rimmer | 14:32.88 |
| 3kSt | Simon Bell | 8:57.87 | Mark Dalkins | 9:29.91 | Martin Roscoe | 9:02.72 |
| 110H | Lloyd Cowan | 13.83 | Adrian Caines | 14.93 | Kevin Lumsdon | 14.55 |
| 400H | Eddie Betts | 51.24 | Paul Thompson | 53.56 | Tony Williams | 51.03 |
| HJ | Richard Aspden | 2.10 | Andrew Lynch | 2.10 | Rob Brocklebank | 2.14 |
| PV | Kevin Hughes | 5.10 | Michael Barber | 5.10 | Dean Mellor | 5.20 |
| LJ | Jonathon Kron (IRL) | 7.68 | Steve Phillips | 7.74w | Mathias Ogbeta | 7.26 |
| TJ | Femi Akinsanya | 16.03 | Paul Weston | 14.88w | Mathias Ogbeta | 15.66 |
| SP | Felix Hyde (GHA) | 16.38 | Kevin Brown | 13.84 | Paul Reed | 14.78 |
| DT | Neville Thompson | 54.42 | Glen Smith | 57.60 | Paul Reed | 52.04 |
| HT | Peter Vivian | 66.94 | John Pearson | 62.46 | David Smith | 64.30 |
| JT | Colin Mackenzie | 78.20 | David Wilson | 59.50 | | |
| 3kW | Mark Easton | 12:15.45 | | | 10kW Les Morton | 45:27.35 |
| | | | | | | |
| Dec | Terry Fidler | 6669 | Par Esegbona | 6258 | Tony Brannen | 7861 |

| | SOUTH | | MIDLANDS | | NORTH | |
|---|---|---|---|---|---|---|
| **WOMEN** | | | | | | |
| 100 | Joice Maduaka | 11.95 | Katharine Merry | 11.50 | Louise Fraser | 11.61 |
| 200 | Joice Maduaka | 24.23 | Geraldine McLeod | 24.46w | Susan Briggs | 24.83 |
| 400 | Georgina Oladapo | 54.13 | Lorraine Hanson | 54.19 | Elaine Sutcliffe | 54.35 |
| 800 | Natalie Tait | 2:05.33 | Victoria Sterne | 2:11.79 | Michelle Faherty | 2:07.53 |
| 1500 | Liz Talbot | 4:25.09 | Sonia Bowyer | 4:24.79 | Amanda Thorpe | 4:27.50 |
| 3000 | Zahara Hyde | 9:25.41 | | | Jill Hunter | 9:29.77 |
| 100H | Melanie Wilkins | 13.60 | Kerri Maddox | 13.5 | Louise Fraser | 13.51 |
| 400H | Clare Bleasdale | 59.29 | Sarah Veysey | 63.26 | Katy Bartlett | 61.88 |
| HJ | Debbie Marti | 1.85 | Michelle Dunkley | 1.80 | Gillian Howard | 1.76 |
| PV | Louise Schramm | 3.20 | Claire Adams | 3.30 | Linda Stanton | 3.60 |
| LJ | Liz Ghojefa | 6.07w | Denise Lewis | 6.66w | Adele Forester | 5.78 |
| TJ | Evette Finikin | 12.39 | Debbie Rowe | 12.01 | Margaret Still | 11.07 |
| SP | Judy Oakes | 18.25 | Lorraine Shaw | 14.03 | Helen Wilding | 12.99 |
| DT | Debbie Callaway | 54.52 | Lorraine Shaw | 51.38 | Rachel Hopgood | 44.72 |
| HT | Lyn Sprules | 52.30 | Lorraine Shaw | 59.78 | Julie Lavender | 49.86 |
| JT | Amanda Liverton | 49.94 | Sharon Gibson | 57.26 | | |
| 3kW | Perry Williams (IRL) | 13:27.87 | | | 5kW Vicky Lupton | 22:38.93 |
| Hept | Tracy Joseph | 4790 | Pauline Richards | 5417 | Michaela Gee | 4449 |

# AGE CHAMPIONSHIPS

## Under 20 MEN — Bedford, 1-2 July

| | | |
|---|---|---|
| 100 | Jamie Henthorn | 10.64 |
| 200 | Mark Hylton | 21.4 |
| 400 | Geoff Dearman | 47.55 |
| 800 | Andrew Blackmore | 1:50.8 |
| 1500 | Des Roache | 3:45.6 |
| 5000 | Alan Dunleavy (IRL) | 14:26.54 |
| | 2. Allen Graffin | 14:30.42 |
| 3kSt | Kevin Nash | 9:07.22 |
| 110H | Damien Greaves | 14.4w |
| 400H | Matthew Douglas | 52.21 |
| HJ | James Brierley | 2.16 |
| PV | Matt Filsell (AUS) | 4.80 |
| | 2. Christian Linskey | 4.70 |
| LJ | Dean Stevens (AUS) | 7.35 |
| | Nathan Morgan | 7.23 |
| TJ | Marvin Bramble | 15.23 |
| SP | Felix Hyde (GHA) | 17.38 |
| | 3. Bill Fuller | 15.64 |
| DT | Bruce Robb | 46.34 |
| HT | Jeff Ayres (AUS) | 56.06 |
| | 3. Matthew Bell | 54.00 |
| JT | Paul Cooper | 61.68 |

Bimingham, 29 July

| | | |
|---|---|---|
| 3000 | Matthew O'Dowd | 8:25.0 |

## Under 17 — Birmingham, 29-30 July

| | | |
|---|---|---|
| 100 | Christian Malcolm | 10.85 |
| 200 | Phillip Perigo | 21.77 |
| 400 | Richard McNabb | 48.93 |
| 800 | Neil Kirk | 1:55.65 |
| 1500 | Gareth Turnbull | 3:58.15 |
| 1500St | David Mitchinson | 4:23.17 |
| 100H | Christopher Hargrave | 13.34 |
| | Ruben Tabares | 54.52 |
| | Danny Graham | 2.03 |
| | Christian Linskey | 4.81 |
| | Geoffrey Ojok | 6.83w |
| | Jonathan Wallace | 14.48w |
| | Emeka Udechucku | 17.41 |
| | Emeka Udechucku | 58.00 |
| | James Hawkins | 56.44 |
| | David Parker | 65.16 |
| 5kW | Stuart Monk | 24:39.7 |

Bedford, 2 July

| | | |
|---|---|---|
| | Steven Lawrence | 8:52.59 |

## Under 15 — Birmingham, 29-30 July

| | | |
|---|---|---|
| | Wayne Gray | 11.29 |
| | Ben Lewis | 23.08 |
| | Ian Lowthian | 50.65 |
| | Austin Ferns | 2:01.26 |
| | Stephen Holmes | 4:16.68 |
| 80H | Robert Hollinger | 11.11 |
| | Neil Dixon | 1.87 |
| | Richard Smith | 4.11 |
| | Richard Gawthorpe | 5.86 |
| | Michael Ferraro | 12.39 |
| | Adrian Cluskey | 15.18 |
| | Simon Williams | 44.88 |
| | Ross Kidner | 54.14 |
| | Philip Olwenu | 55.54 |
| 3kW | John Murphy | 14:48.4 |

Bedford, 1 July

| | | |
|---|---|---|
| | Gareth Melvin | 9:19.47 |

## Under 20 WOMEN — Bedford, 3-4 July

| | | |
|---|---|---|
| 100 | Rebecca Drummond | 11.88 |
| 200 | Victoria Shipman | 24.08 |
| 400 | Jo Sloane | 55.17 |
| 800 | Alison Chiu (AUS) | 2:10.35 |
| | 2. Jane Groves | 2:11.37 |
| 1500 | Juliette Oldfield | 4:27.16 |
| 3000 | Alice Braham | 9:35.77 |
| 100H | Natasha Danvers | 13.51w |
| 400H | Josephine Fowley (AUS) | 59.00 |
| | 2. Vicki Jamison | 59.81 |
| HJ | Rachael Forrest | 1.85 |
| PV | Rhian Clarke | 3.40 |
| LJ | Adele Forrester | 5.87 |
| TJ | Gillian Ting (AUS) | 12.62 |
| | 2. Elizabeth Gibbens | 12.42 |
| SP | Philippa Roles | 14.11 |
| DT | Monique Nelson (AUS) | 48.28 |
| | 2. Phillipa Roles | 48.16 |
| HT | Brenda MacNaughton (AUS) | 53.3 |
| | 2. Sam Burns-Salmond | 47.56 |
| JT | Kelly Morgan | 46.94 |

## Under 17 — Birmingham, 30-31 July

| | | |
|---|---|---|
| | Tatum Nelson | 11.92 |
| | Lesley Owusu | 24.43 |
| 300 | Lesley Owusu | 38.54 |
| | Rachel Ogden | 2:12.70 |
| | Maria Lynch (IRL) | 4:36.51 |
| | 2. Karen Montador | 4:38.54 |
| | *Nicola Lilley | 10:16.38 |

* Bedford 3 July

| | | |
|---|---|---|
| 80H | Claire Pearson | 11.44 |
| 300H | Tracey Duncan | 44.44 |
| | Rachel Martin | 1.74 |
| | Becky Ridgley | 2.90 |
| | Jade Johnson | 5.69 |
| | Jayne Ludlow | 11.76w |
| | Catherine Garden | 11.94 |
| | Lauren Keightley | 44.10 |
| | Helen Arnold | 46.98 |
| | Sian Lax | 44.78 |
| 5kW | Sarah Bennett | 27:01.1 |

## Under 15 — Birmingham, 30-31 July

| | | |
|---|---|---|
| | Chantell Manning | 12.4 |
| | Karlene Palmer | 25.03 |
| | Jennifer Meadows | 2:15.13 |
| | Emma Ward | 4:41.58 |
| 75H | Naomi Hodge-Dalloway | 11.13 |
| | Alison Kerboas | 1.65 |
| | Caroline Pearce | 5.47 |
| | Amy Wilson | 11.93 |
| | Joan MacPherson | 35.90 |
| | Lucy Rann | 37:36 |
| 3kW | Kelly Mann | 15:41.0 |

# UK MERIT RANKINGS 1995 Compiled by Peter Matthews

This is the 28th successive year that I have compiled annual merit rankings of British athletes. As usual they are based on an assessment of form during the outdoor season. The major factors by which the rankings are determined are win-loss record, performances in the major meetings, and sequence of marks.

I endeavour to be as objective as possible, but form can often provide conflicting evidence, or perhaps an athlete may not have shown good enough results against leading rivals, or in very important competition, to justify a ranking which his or her ability might otherwise warrant.

I can only rank athletes on what they have actually achieved. Much depends on having appropriate opportunities. It is obviously harder for an athlete living in a remote part of the UK than one who is close to the major centres of competition, and it may be hard to break into the élite who get the invitations for the prestige meetings. Difficulties also arise when athletes reach peak form at different parts of the season or through injury miss significant competition. Once again it should be pointed out that the rankings are by no means necessarily the order in which I think the athletes would have finished in an idealised contest, but simply my attempt to assess what has actually happened in 1995.

I hope that I have not missed many performances, but I would be very pleased to receive any missing results at 10 Madgeways Close, Great Amwell, Herts SG12 9RU.

For each event the top 12 are ranked. On the first line is shown the athletes name, then their date of birth followed, in brackets, by the number of years ranked in the top 12 (including 1995) and their ranking last year (1994), and finally, their best mark prior to 1995. The following lines include their best six performances of the year (followed, for completeness, by significant indoor marks indicated by 'i', although indoor form, the subject of a separate assessment, is not considered in the rankings). Then follow placings at major meetings, providing a summary of the athlete's year at the event.

**Abbreviations include**

| | |
|---|---|
| AAA v LC | AAA v Loughborough Students |
| BL | British League |
| BUPA | BUPA International at Sheffield |
| CAU | Inter-Counties at Bedford |
| Cork | Cork City Sports |
| Cup | Guardian Cup Final at Stoke-on-Trent |
| E.Clubs | European Clubs Cup |
| ECup | European Cup |
| EJ | European Junior Championships |
| E.Sch | English Schools |
| GhG | BUPA Gateshead Games |
| GPF | Grand Prix Final at Monaco |
| HCI | Home Countries International |
| IR | Inter-regional at Birmingham |
| IS | Inter-Services |
| KP | KP Games at Crystal Palace |
| McD | McDonald Games at Crystal Palace |
| NvST | North v South of Thames v West at Enfield |
| TSB-CP | TSB Grand Prix at Crystal Palace |
| TSB-Ed | TSB Challenge at Edinburgh |
| U23 Int | Under 23 international at Narbonne |
| v Fra J | Junior International v France at Belfort |
| v USA | At Gateshead |
| S.Nat | Small Nations Int. - Wales v Scot, Israel, Turkey at Istanbul |
| WCh | World Championships |
| WG | Welsh Games at Cwmbrân |
| WSG | World Student Games |

# BRITISH MERIT RANKINGS 1995 - MEN

## 100 METRES
1. **Linford Christie** 2.4.60 (13y, 1) 9.87 '93    9.97A, 10.00, 10.02w, 10.03, 10.03w, 10.05, 10.06, 10.08, 10.08, 10.09, 10.10, 10.11;    1 BL1 (2), 2 Rome, 1 ECp, 4 Lausanne, 4h1 + 1g AAA, 6 WCh, 1 Zürich, 1 Brussels, 1= McD, 2 Berlin, 5 Monaco, 1 Tokyo, 1 Jo'burg
2. **Darren Braithwaite** 20.1.69 (7y, 7) 10.26 '94, 10.25w '90    10.12, 10.16w, 10.18A, 10.19, 10.22, 10.22; 2 Helsinki, 4 GhG, 5 KP, 2 (1) AAA, 7s2 WCh, 6 Zürich, 4 v USA, 6 Brussels, 5 McD
3. **Jason John** 17.10.71 (6y, 2) 10.23/10.08w '94    10.25, 10.26A, 10.28, 10.29w, 10.31A, 10.34; 10.3; 1 BL1 (3), 3 AAA, 2 Cup sf Derby, 5q3 WCh, 3 v USA, 4 McD, 1 Cannock
4. **Darren Campbell** 12.9.73 (4y, -) 10.37/10.28w '91    10.34, 10.37, 10.37w, 10.38, 10.39, 10.46w; 1 North, 1 WG, 4 AAA, BL2: -,1B,1B,-
5. **Julian Golding** 17.2.75 (2y, 11) 10.43/10.34w '94    10.30, 10.34, 10.34, 10.38, 10.70; 10.4, 10.4w; 3 Helsinki, 1B AAA v LC, 2 Geneva, 1 U23 Int, 3 Kilkenny, 2 Cannock; BL1: 2,-,-,2
6. **Toby Box** 9.9.72 (3y, 4) 10.34 '93, 10.07w '94    10.31w, 10.32, 10.34w, 10.39, 10.41, 10.41; 5 Helsinki, 1 BL2 (3), 5 AAA, 1 Cup sf Derby, 5 WSG, 3 Cannock
7. **Michael Rosswess** 11.6.65 (7y, 5) 10.15 '91, 10.07w '94    10.29A, 10.32w, 10.34, 10.34w, 10.36A, 10.37; 6 Helsinki, dnr AAA, BL1: 1,-,4,-
8. **Jason Gardener** 18.9.75 (2y, 8) 10.25 '94    10.33, 10.36, 10.37, 10.38, 10.47, 10.48; 10.4; 7 AAA v LC, 2 Zofingen, 1 Geneva, 2 WG, 8 AAA, 6 v USA
9. **John Regis** 13.10.66 (10y, 9) 10.15 '93, 10.07w '90    10.32, 10.41, 10.45, 10.48, 10.50, 10.52w; 7 Rome, 2 BL1 (3), 3 WG
10. **Owusu Dako** 23.5.73 (1y, -) 10.60/10.5w '93, 10.59w '92    10.42, 10.50w, 10.54, 10.61, 10.74; 10.5; 1 BL2 (1), 1 IR, 1 CAU, 1 AAA v LC
11. **Solomon Wariso** 11.11.66 (2y, -) 10.33 '94    10.40w, 10.43, 10.57, 10.61A, 10.62, 10.72A; 10.3; 2 Bedford, 1 Cup sf Liverpool, BL1: -,2, -,1
12. **Danny Joyce** 9.9.74 (2y, -) 10.47/10.40w '93    10.33w, 10.44w, 10.52, 10.56, 10.56, 10.59w; 10.5, 10.5w; 3 IR, 3 CAU, 3 Zofingen, 1 Bedford, 4 AAA v LC, 6sf South, 4 KP Dev, 4s1 AAA, 1 BUPA, 3 Cup sf Liverpool

Not ranked

   **Dwain Chambers** 5.4.78 (0y, ) 10.75/10.56w '94    10.41, 10.56w, 10.57, 10.62, 10.65, 10.70; 10.5w; 1 South-J, 3 BL1 (1), 5 AAA v LC, 2 AAA-J, 7s2 AAA, 1 Yth Oly, 1 EJ

   **Jamie Henthorn** 20.2.77 (0y, ) 10.78/10.6w '94    10.41, 10.48, 10.64, 10.67, 10.70, 10.71w; 10.6w; 4 CAU, 4 Welsh, 1 AAA-J, 1 W v B,Hol-J, 2 EJ, 2 v Fra-J

Christie completed ten successive years as the British number one, matching Geoff Capes's record at the shot 1971-80. Christie won 13 of his 18 finals, including his tie with Jon Drummond. There was again excellent depth in British sprinting, with Braithwaite having his best ever season to rank second. John was a clear third, with Campbell, in a limited season, doing enough for 4th. Those ranked 5th to 8th were very evenly matched; Golding beat Box 2-0 and Box beat Gardener at the AAAs, yet Gardener beat Golding in their one clash. Just missing out on the top 12 were Chambers and Henthorn, European Junior 1-2, and still juniors in 1996, and Andrew Mensah.

## 200 METRES
1. **Linford Christie** 2.4.60 (11y, 1) 20.09 '88    20.11, 20.12w, 20.53, 20.80, 20.87; 20.25i; 3 Rome, 2 BL1 (2), 1 ECp, 3 Lausanne
2. **John Regis** 13.10.66 (11y, 1) 19.87A '94, 19.94 '93    20.26, 20.28w, 20.32, 20.37, 20.39, 20.51; 6 Rome, 1 BL1 (3), 4 Lausanne, 1 Nice, 1 v USA, 3 Monaco, 7 WCh, 1 v USA, 8 GPF, 4 Rieti
3. **Solomon Wariso** 11.11.66 (4y, 4) 20.51 '94    20.50, 20.50, 20.51, 20.54w, 20.55, 20.55w; 1 Ljubljana, 1 Bedford, 3 Soria, 3 KP, 2 AAA, 5s2 WCh, 2 v USA, 2 Copenhagen, 5 Rieti, 1 Cup, BL1: -,1,-,1
4. **Darren Braithwaite** 20.1.69 (4y, 11) 20.72 '92    20.47, 20.54A, 20.63, 20.64, 20.87; 21.04; 20.87i; 1 Soria, 3 AAA, 4h2 WCh
5. **Tony Jarrett** 13.8.68 (4y, -) 20.67 '90    20.50, 20.67, 21.13; 4 AAA
6. **Julian Golding** 17.2.75 (2y, 10) 21.02/20.73w '94    20.69w, 20.75, 20.77, 20.82, 20.83, 20.92; 20.9w; 1 Middx, 2 AAA v LC, 2 GhG, 4 KP, 5 AAA, 3 v USA, 4 Copenhagen, 1 Kilkenny, BL1: 1,3,-,-
7. **Owusu Dako** 23.5.73 (2y, -) 21.10 '94, 20.80w '93    20.57, 20.79, 20.80, 20.84, 20.95, 21.01; 8 AAA, 1 U23 Int, 7sf WSG, BL2: 1B,-
8= **Doug Walker** 28.7.73 (2y, 7) 20.71 '94    20.53w, 20.88, 20.95, 20.96, 21.02, 21.07; 1 B.Univs, 1 AAA v LC, 5s1 AAA, 2 U23 Int, 4q5 WSG, 1 BL4 (3)
8= **Doug Turner** 2.12.66 (1y, -) 21.50 '94    20.68w, 20.75, 20.85, 20.90, 21.02, 21.12; 21.0; 1 IR, 1 Welsh, 1 WG, 6s2 AAA, 2 Cup sf Enfield, 1 v USA Dev, 2 Cup, BL2: 2,2B,1,1
10. **Toby Box** 9.9.72 (3y, 6) 20.72 '94    20.78, 20.86, 21.27, 21.36; 21.0; 21.65i; 2 Ljubljana, 7 AAA, 1 Cup sf Derby
11. **Jason John** 17.10.71 (4y, 8) 20.86 '94, 20.51w '93    20.74w, 20.86, 20.90, 21.08A; 5 Soria, 2 BL1 (3), 2 WG, dnf h7 AAA
12. **Marlon Devonish** 1.6.76 (1y, -) 21.25/21.20w '94    20.88w, 20.94, 20.99, 21.04, 21.11, 21.14; 1 Mid J, 1B AAA v LC, 3 AAA J, 1 v Fra J, 1 EJ

Not ranked
   **Adrian Patrick** 15.6.73 (0y, -) 21.4/21.49w '94    20.62w, 21.17, 21.33; 21.0, 21.4w, 21.5;
   1 CAU, 2 Bedford, BL3: -,1,1,-
   **Phil Goedluck** 10.9.67 (1y, 5) 20.79 '94    20.73w, 20.88w, 20.98, 21.13w, 21.20, 21.30;
   3 Bedford, 2 South, 8 GhG, 5 WG, 1 Cup sf Enfield, 6 Cup, BL1: 3,-,1B,2
Christie again won at the European Cup and takes over at No.1 from Regis, having beaten him 2-0, although Regis
had much better depth of marks. The AAA race settled the next four placings, with Wariso running a series of good
times during the year. The AAAs was Jarrett's only meeting but he beat Golding clearly there.
The 10th best standard of 20.86 is the best ever and Goedluck, 5th in 1994 just misses the top 12, despite a best of
20.73w, while Patrick, who ran mainly 400s ran even faster at 20.62w.

## 400 METRES
1.  **Mark Richardson** 26.7.72 (6y, -) 45.09 '92    44.81, 44.92, 44.94, 45.00, 45.06, 45.30;
    1 Dijon, 1 ECp, 2 GhG, 3 Oslo, 1 AAA, 5 WCh, 2 v USA, 6 Brussels, 3 McD
2.  **Roger Black** 31.3.66 (10y, 2) 44.59 '86    44.59, 45.01, 45.07, 45.15, 45.16, 45.18;
    3 Lausanne, 2 KP, 2 BUPA, 7 WCh, 4 v USA, 4 Berlin, 2 McD, 2 Rieti
3.  **Jamie Baulch** 3.5.73 (2y, 7) 46.45 '94    45.14, 45.15. 45.40, 45.57, 45.93;
    1 U23 Int, 2 Copenhagen, 3 v USA, 5 McD, 1 Cup
4.  **Mark Hylton** 24.9.76 (2y, 8) 46.37 '94    45.83, 45.97, 46.04, 46.26, 46.57, 46.67; 46.56i, 46.56i;
    5 Dijon, 1 AAA v LC, 1 ESch, 2 AAA, 1 EJ, 6 McD
5.  **Adrian Patrick** 28.6.73 (3y, 9) 46.11 '94    45.63, 46.02, 46.10, 46.11, 46.11, 46.27;
    2 Helsinki, 7 Lausanne, 3 AAA, 5 BUPA, 7q2 WCh, 8 McD
6.  **Iwan Thomas** 5.1.74 (2y, 5) 45.98 '94    45.58, 45.73, 46.03, 46.40, 46.53, 47.06;
    4 Fort-de-France, 1 Ljubljana, 1 Welsh, 3 Helsinki, 7 BUPA
7.  **Du'aine Ladejo** 14.2.71 (5y, 1) 44.94 '94    45.74, 45.97, 46.18, 46.85, 47.03, 47.4;
    2 Ljubljana, 1 Ostrava, 5 Helsinki, dnf GhG
8.  **David McKenzie** 3.9.70 (4y, 3) 45.47 '95    45.96, 46.20, 46.27, 46.32, 46.37, 46.48;
    1 Fort-de-France, 2 Ostrava, 1 BL1 (3), 7 AAA, 2 Cup
9.  **Tim O'Dell** 29.5.70 (1y, -) 47.37 '90    46.34, 46.42, 46.44, 46.71, 46.81, 47.16;
    3 CAU, 2 South, 4 AAA, 8 BUPA, 1 Kilkenny, 4 Cup, BL1: -,3,2,1
10. **David Grindley** 29.10.72 (5y, -) 44.50 '93    46.15, 46.86,.47.04, 47.3, 47.67, 47.68;
    5 GhG, 8 KP, 5s2 WSG
11. **Jared Deacon** 15.10.75 (1y, -) 47.53/47.5 '94    46.45, 46.58, 46.70, 46.8, 46.98, 47.03;
    3 Cork, 3 KP Dev, 5s2 AAA, 3 U23 Int, 5s1 WSG
12. **David Nolan** 25.7.69 (1y, -) 47.5/47.66 '94    46.61, 46.75, 46.82, 46.82, 47.03, 47.1;
    1 CAU, 1 North, 1 IS, 1 WG, 5s1 AAA, 3 Cup, BL1: 1,-,-,2
Not ranked
    **Kent Ulyatt** 10.4.72 (0y, -) 46.82 '95    46.31, 46.7, 47.0, 47.5; 47.97i, 48.26i;
    1 East, 1 Plate, unbeaten outdoors
    **Guy Bullock** 15.10.75 (1y, -) 46.13 '93    46.41, 46.64, 46.7, 47.31, 47.45, 48.23; 47.30i;
    2 IR, 1B Zofingen, 1B AAA v LC, 7h2 AAA
    **Mark Smith** 18.11.71 (0y, 12) 46.7/46.75 '94    46.44A, 46.60, 46.99, 47.05, 47.10, 47.71;
    1 IR, 2 AAA v LC, 1 KP Dev, 6s1 AAA
Richardson came back to such effect that he ranked no.1 for the first time, beating Black 2-1, including, crucially in
the World Championships. Black equalled his 9-year-old pb in Lausanne, but thereafter was consistent, when fit, at
just over 45 secs. Baulch excelled in late season with three Welsh records from 45.40 in his first 400m of the year on
July 29, while Hylton continued his progress, winning the European Junior title as clear favourite, and both these two
and Patrick moved up four places from 1994. Britain has great strength in this event, but once again injuries knocked
back too many of our top men - Ladejo and Thomas (three Welsh records before Baulch) had their seasons cut short,
while Grindley made his way back slowly. McKenzie broke 46 in his first race of the year, but not thereafter.
The 10th best of 46.31 (Kent Ulyatt) is the best ever, just ahead of 46.35 (1993) and 46.39 (1986 and 1994).

## 800 METRES
1.  **Curtis Robb** 7.6.72 (5y, 9) 1:44.92 '93    1:46.34, 1.46.35, 1:46.78, 1:47.14, 1:47.7, 1:48.72;
    1 BL2 (1), 6 KP, 1 AAA, 1 BUPA, 8s1 WCh
2.  **David Strang** 13.12.68 (3y, 7) 1:45.85 '92    1:46.02, 1:46.68, 1:47.0, 1:47.06, 1:48.11, 1:48.76;
    2 AAA. 2B Oslo, 3 BUPA, 4h3 WCh, 1 BL1 (4), 2 v USA, 8 McD
3.  **Craig Winrow** 22.12.71 (4y, 1) 1:46.54 '94    1:46.68, 1:47.6, 1:47.67, 1:48.11, 1:48.14, 1:48.25;
    6 Rome, 8 ECp, 2 WG, 6 AAA, 4 BUPA, 2 Stretford 1/8, 3 v USA, 9 McD, 3 BLQ
4.  **Lee Cadwallader** 17.1.69 (1y, -) 1:47.53 '93    1:47.8, 1:48.28, 1:48.45, 1:48.62, 1:49.0, 1:49.01;
    1r2 Wyth, 2 IR, 1 BMC Lough, 1 Stretford 27/6, 2 KP Dev, 4 WG, 4 AAA, 6 BUPA, 1 Stretford 22/8, BL2: -,1B,-,2
5.  **Gary Lough** 6.7.70 (1y, -) 1:49.01 '93    1:48.03, 1:48.88, 1:49.03, 1:49.30, 1:49.5; 3 La Celle, 9 GhG, 3 AAA
6.  **Tom McKean** 27.10.63 (11y, 3) 1:43.88 '89    1:47.46, 1:48.07, 1:49.9, 1:50.17, 1:50.38, 1:50.70; 1:48.72i,
    1:49.85i, 1:50.04i; dnf Scot, 1 BL1 (3), 7 GhG, 10 KP, 7 AAA

7.  **Clive Gilby** 24.2.66 (2y, -) 1:47.90 '92    1:47.33, 1:48.15, 1:49.07, 1:49.7, 1:49.79, 1:50.67;
    3 Wyth, 1 AAA v LC, 1 BL2 (2), 5 GhG, 11 KP, 4h5 AAA, 10 BUPA
8.  **Matthew Yates** 4.2.69 (6y, -) 1:45.05 '92    1:47.98, 1:48.11, 1:49.24, 1:49.9, 1:51.10; 1:49.82+i;
    8 GhG, 3 WG, 5 v USA, 1 Cup
9.  **Jason Lobo** 18.9.69 (1y, -) 1:47.7 '89    1:48.14, 1:48.5, 1:48.66, 1:48.73, 1:49.02, 1:49.36;
    5 Wyth, 2 North, 3 Cork, 2h1 AAA, 2 Stretford 22/8, 13 Berlin
10. **Andy Hart** 13.9.69 (1y, -) 1:48.06 '92    1:48.2, 1:49.2, 1:49.3, 1:49.5, 1:50.0; 1:50.9; 1:51.80i;
    1 IR, 2 Stretford 27/6, 1 Cup sf Derby, 2 BLQ
11. **Martin Steele** 30.9.62 (9y, 2) 1:43.84 '93    1:49.15, 1:49.4, 1:49.7, 1:50.28, 1:51.47; 1:48.95i, 1:49.17i;
    1 Wyth, 1 North, 3 Stretford 27/6, 8 AAA
12= **Kevin McKay** 9.2.69 (6y, -) 1:45.35 92    1:48.0, 1:49.59, 1:50.5, 1:52.1, 1:52.14;
    2 Cup sf Derby, 3 Stretford 1/8, BL4: -,1,-,1
12= **Tony Morrell** 3.5.62 (8y, -) 1:44.59 '88    1:48.7, 1:49.01, 1:49.41, 1:49.8, 1:50.32, 1:50.4;
    3 Scot, 3h5 AAA, 8 BUPA, 3 Stretford 22/8, BL5: -,-,1,1
Not ranked
    **Andy Keith** 25.12.71 (0y, -) 1:47.56 '92    1:47.59; 5B Stockholm
Robb was back as AAA champion and at the top of the rankings, and Strang joined him in Gothenburg, but Winrow was not as good as in 1994 and it was, as in 1994, a very poor year by the usually excellent British 800m standards. Lobo made a fine comeback, but did not run as fast as in 1989 when with 1:47.7 he was 20th fastest in Britain. Morrell just makes the top 12, for the first time since 1991. In 1988 he was ranked 5th with a best of 1:44.59 - anyone who had run such a time in 1995 would be way ahead of the list. In 1988 the 10th best was 1:46.13, this year's standard of 1:48.14 is a little better than in 1994.

## 1500 METRES - 1 MILE
1.  **John Mayock** 26.10.70 (5y, 2) 3:36.45 '93, 3:56.90M '91
    3:34.05, 3:34.58, 3:34.63, 3:51.89M/3:36.54, 3:37.32, 3:55.36M, 3:55.42M;
    6 Moscow, 1 GhG, 4 KP, 1 AAA, 9s1 WCh, 7 Zürich, 5 Köln, 2 v USA, 6 Brussels, 1 E.Carr, 6 Berlin, 6 GPF
2.  **Gary Lough** 6.7.70 (3y, 4) 3:35.83/3:59.48M '94
    3:34.76, 3:34.82, 3:36.01, 3:36.39, 3:37.59, 3:37.73, 3:37.78, 3:55.91M;
    1 AAA v LC, 4 ECp, 5= KP, 9 Oslo, 9 WCh,11 Köln, 3 v USA, 7 Brussels, 5 E.Carr, 7 Berlin, 7 GPF
3.  **Kevin McKay** 9.2.69 (7y, 3) 3:35.94 '92, 3:53.64M '94    3:37.27, 3:38.13, 3:40.83; 3:41.81, 3:42.13, 3:43.87;
    1 BL2 (2), 2 AAA v LC, 1 Lucerne, 8 GhG, 14 KP, 2 AAA, 6 Oslo, 6h2 WCh, 4 v USA
4.  **Bruno Witchalls** 22.3.75 (1y, -) 3:45.11 '94, 4:10.5M '93    3:41.51, 3:42.37, 3:42.81, 3:43.26, 3:43.88,
    3:47.79; 2 B.Univs, 3 Wyth 4 AAA v LC, 2 GhG Dev, 3 AAA, 1 U23 Int, 4 WSG
5.  **Brian Treacy** 29.7.71 (2y, 6) 3:38.93 '94, 4:00.67M '90
    3:39.87, 3:40.91, 3:41.69, 3:41.73, 3:42.15, 3:43.23; 4 Granada, 4 AAA, 3 Maia, 9 WSG
6.  **Andrew Keith** 25.12.71 (2y, 7) 3:39.06/3:57.7iM '93, 3:58.97M '94
    3:39.17, 3:57.96M, 3:41.32, 3:41.96, 3:42.82, 3:43.33; 3:59.52iM, 4:00.15iM; 2 Cork, 5 St Petersburg, 5 AAA
7.  **David Strang** 13.12.68 (3y, 5) 3:36.53/3:54.30M '94
    3:56.05M, 3:39.94, 3:41.39, 4:02.6M; 8 Eugene, 5 GhG, 11 KP
8.  **Neil Caddy** 18.3.75 (1y, -) 3:46.16 '94, 4:04.9M '94 3:39.67, 3:59.6M, 3:42.1, 3:42.15, 3:42.2, 3:43.12;
    1 Wyth, 1 Bath, 7 AAA, 1 Ch'ham, 2 U23 Int, 5 Copenhagen, 1 McD Dev, 1 So'ton
9.  **Rob Denmark** 23.11.68 (5y, -) 3:38.34 '92, 3:55.38M '90 3:37.99, 3:40.82; 4 Hengelo, 13 KP
10. **Simon Fairbrother** 28.3.68 (5y, -) 3:38.64 '92, 3:59.5M '89    3:41.92, 3:42.54, 3:43.37, 3:44.72, 4:04.13M,
    3:47.25; 3 AAA v LC, 4 Geneva, 11 AAA, 13 Copenhagen, 11 E.Carr, 3 Kilkenny, 1 Cup, BL1: -,1,1,1
11. **Steve Green** 18.2.71 (1y, nr) 3:39.19/3:59.6iM '94, 4:06.5M '90    3:42.4, 3:42.49, 3:42.95, 3:43.02, 3:43.54,
    3:43.85; 2 Wyth, 1 AAA v LC, 12 GhG, 3h3 AAA, 3 McD Dev
12. **Andy Hart** 13.9.69 (1y, -) 3:44.9 '94, 4:02.7M '91    3:42.03, 3:42.41, 3:42.7, 3:43.42, 3:43.47, 4:01.8M;
    3 B.Univs, 3 Wyth, 2 Bath, 2 Nurmijärvi, 8 AAA v LC, 1 Salisbury, 6 AAA, 2B Oslo, 3 Ch'ham, 12 McD Dev
Not ranked
    **Jon Wild** 30.8.73 (0y, -) 3:42.50 '94
    3:41.40, 3:59.79M, 3:42.12, 3:42.43, 3:42.7, 3:42.73; 8 NCAA, 1 GhG Dev, 1 WG, 4h3 AAA
    **Matthew Yates** 4.2.69 (5y, 1) 3:34.00 '9, 3:52.75M '93
    3:40.69, 4:01.66M, 3:46.05, 4:08.1M, 4:09.53M; dnf Nice, 6B Oslo, 12 Brussels, 10 E Carr, 15 Berlin
    **Tony Whiteman** 13.11.71 (1y, -) 3:41.92/4:03.87M '94    3:59.44M, 3:43.4, 3:45.50, 3:45.9, 3:47.54;
    3:41.28i, 3:44.21i; 2 Salisbury, 3h2 AAA, 1 Birmingham, 11 McD Dev, 1 Hong Kong

M = 1 mile time. Equivalents: 3:35.0m = 3:52.0M, 3:38.0m = 3:55.3M, 3:41.0m = 3:58.6M, 3:44.0m = 4:01.8M
    (Times in brackets are 1500m times en route to 1 mile)
Sadly Yates, top in 1994, dropped out of the rankings, and again missed most important British races. Mayock and Lough made progress and ran consistently well in Grand Prix races. Mayock made his first no.1 ranking and won the Emsley Carr Mile. McKay is a clear 3rd and Witchalls, although yet to run very fast times, is the highest newcomer; his 4th place ensured by his AAA 3rd and WSG 4th. The next best newcomer was Caddy, who had a splendid series of wins in BMC races. After him there was little to choose between a large group.

## 3000 METRES  (Not ranked this year)

**John Mayock** 26.10.70  7:48.47i '92, 8:03.75/8:32.54M '91
7:47.28, 7:52.99; 7:46.80i, 7:49.85i, 7:51.57i, 7:51.86i; 1 Cork, 1 Sheffield
**Rob Denmark** 23.11.68  7:39.55 '93, 8:26.05M '92
7:47.80, 7:56.22, 7:59.8+, 8:02.16; 2 BUPA, 1 v USA, 8 McD
**John Nuttall** 11.1.67  7:51.58 '93     7:48.59, 7:53.59, 7:59+, 8:02.51; 4 BUPA, 2 v USA, 5 McD
**Gary Lough** 6.7.70  0     7:49.45, 7:59.9; 1 Lough, 3 Bratislava
**Andrew Keith** 25.12.71  8:02.81/7:49.83i '94     7:54.37, 7:57.38; 7:59.19i, 8:10.75i; 6 New York, 10 BUPA
**Jon Wild** 30.8.73     7:55.16; 8:03.87i, 8:07.07i, 8:08.62i; 5 Cork

## 5000 METRES

1.  **Rob Denmark** 23.11.68 (5y, 1) 13:10.24 '92
    13:13.77, 13:15.83, 13:37.14, 13:37.57, 13:37.88; 1 Nuremburg, 3 GhG, 1 AAA, 13 Oslo, 6h1 WCh
2.  **John Nuttall** 11.1.67 (7y, 2) 13:23.54 '94
    13:16.70, 13:20.91, 13:25.18, 13:46.82, 13:49.25; 5 Rome, 2 ECp, 12 Stockholm, 14 WCh
3.  **Adrian Passey** 2.9.64 (1y, -) 13:30.99 '89     13:22.73, 13:28.83, 13:32.88, 13:35.69, 14:08.06, 14:15;
    8 Nuremburg, 8 Helsinki, 8 GhG, dnf AAA, 9 Hechtel, 12h3 WCh
4.  **Jon Brown** 27.2.71 (5y, 3) 13:19.78 '93     13:37.83, 13:39.68, 13:49.77, 14:03.4; 13 Lausanne, 2 AAA. 1 Nivelles
5.  **Paul Evans** 13.4.61 (5y, 11) 13:30.83 '92     13:25.38; 4 Helsinki
6.  **John Sherban** 30.7.64 (2y, -)  13:39.43 '91     13:46.76, 14:01.24, 14:08.21, 14:20.9; 6 AAA; BL1: -,2,1,1
7.  **Gary Staines** 3.7.63 (8y, 7) 13:14.28 '90     13:38.42, 14:03.74; 9 Helsinki, 10 AAA
8.  **Ian Robinson** 21.4.69 (1y, -) 14:03.93 '92     13:42.85, 14:07.88; 13:59.38i, 13:59.96i, 14:09.56i; 4 Madison
9.  **Justin Chaston** 4.11.68 (1y, -) 13:59.59 '94     13:51.86; 7 AAA
10. **Jon Solly** 28.6.63 (4y, -) 13:22.39 '86     13:56.96, 13:58.43, 14:17.5; 18 GhG, 8 AAA
11. **Glyn Tromans** 17.3.69 (1y, -) 0     13:55.23, 14:00.27, 14:06.29; 1 CAU, 16 Helsinki, 11 AAA
12. **Andrew Keith** 25.12.71 (1y, -) 0     13:48.13; 12 Philadelphia
    **Jon Wild** 30.8.73 (0y, -) 0     13:49.15, 14:19.8; 10 Walnut, 6 U23 Int

Denmark made it five years at the top of the UK 5000m rankings, but he got stuck at 13:37s after two fast times. Nuttall, 2nd again, improved his best time and made the world final, and Passey ranks for the first time at 5000m, six years after his last ranking at 1500m - a triumph for perseverance, but unfortunately he got injured in Gothenburg. Only the top four showed consistent form, and the overall standard was far below what it used to be in Britain, so that some athletes who just had one or two moderate runs made the rankings. The 10th best of 13:49.15 is the worst since 1970 (record 13:28.44 in 1984).

## 10,000 METRES

1.  **Paul Evans** 13.4.61 (4y, -) 27:47.79 '93     27:49.54, 28:07.15, 28:14.76; 5 KP, 9h1 WCh, 14 Brussels
2.  **John Nuttall** 11.1.67 (2y, -) 28:42.6 '92     28:07.43; 15 Brussels
3.  **Jon Brown** 27.2.71 (3y, -) 28:19.6 '92     28:08.31; 16 Brussels
4.  **Gary Staines** 3.7.63 (7y, 3) 27:48.73 '91     28:33.49, 28:49.29; 1 AAA, 17 KP
5.  **Ian Robinson** 21.4.69 (1y, -) 29:32.92 '92     28:34.84, 29:31.51; 9 Walnut, 4 NCAA
6.  **Jon Solly** 28.6.63 (6y, -) 27:51.76 '86     28:58.29; 2 AAA
7.  **Chris Robison** 16.3.61 (2y, 8) 28:39.35 '86     29:03.69; 3 AAA
8.  **Steve Brooks** 8.6.70 (1y, -) 29:37.75 '94     29:04.63, 29:48.40; 18 Walnut, 7 NCAA
9.  **Andrew Lyons** 24.12.69 (1y, -) 29:04.05 '91     29:04.87; 4 AAA
10. **Mark Steinle** 27.11.74 (1y, -) 0     29:07.33; 5 AAA
11. **Robert Quinn** 10.12.65 (1y, -) 29:37.4 '93     29:14.23, 29:55.20; 6 AAA, 3 Scot
12. **Bill Foster** 9.8.58 (1y, -) 29:37.11 '94     29:17.11, 30:01.88; 1 CAU, 7 AAA

Evans returned to the top ranking he also had in 1992 and 1993. He ran bravely in Gothenburg but missed the final by one place, and led Brown and Nuttall at Brussels, where they were 14th -16th. Last year's 1 and 2, Rob Denmark and Martin Jones did not run a 10,000m in 1995. We have few runners left who attempt 10,000m on the track, but 6 of the top 12 are newcomers to the rankings. Only Evans ran even three track races at this distance. The 10th best of 29:07.33 is the worst since 1965 (allowing for 6 miles conversions in the 1960s). The only other year above 29 minutes was 1985.

## MARATHON

1.  **Paul Evans** 13.4.61 (4y, -) 2:10:36 '92     2:10:31 (5) London, 2:11:05 (2) New York
2.  **Peter Whitehead** 3.12.64 (2y, 7) 2:13:40 '95     2:12:23 (12) London, 2:14:08 (4) WCh
3.  **Richard Nerurkar** 6.1.64 (3y, 1) 2:10:03 '93     2:11:03 (2) Kyongju, 2:15:47 (7) WCh
4.  **Eamonn Martin** 9.10.58 (3y, 2) 2:10:50 '93     2:11:18 (1) Chicago, 2:12:44 (13) London
5.  **Mark Hudspith** 19.1.69 (2y, 3) 2:12:52 '94     2:11:58 (11) London, dnf WCh
6.  **Peter Fleming** 5.1.61 (4y, 9) 2:13:33 '93     2:13:35 (5) Houston, 2:15:25 (12) Chicago, 2:16:00 (5) Pittsburgh
7.  **Bill Foster** 8.8.58 (2y, 12) 2:17:12 '95     2:15:19 (11) Berlin, 2:18:45 (18) WCp
8.  **Colin Moore** 25.11.60 (2y, 5) 2:13:35 '94     2:15:02 (16) London
9.  **Gary Staines** 3.7.63 (1y, -) 0     2:16:04 (4) Vienna
10. **John Ferrin** 20.2.67 (1y, -) 2:21:07 '94     2:18:40 (1) Belfast, 2:24:44 (5) Crete

11. **Chris Buckley** 26.7.61 (1y, -) 2:15:48 '91    2:19:05 (23) London
12. **Hugh Jones** 1.11.55 (12y, -) 2:09:24 '82
      2:19:58 (29) New York, 2:22:27 (2) Big Sur, 2:22:33 (2) Hanoi, 2:29:26 (1) Iceland?
Evans ran the fastest time of the year, and was the best at London, and then ran marvellously for 2nd in New York to take the top ranking over the two men who excelled in the heat of Gothenburg. Whitehead's great run there means that he is no.2, with Nerurkar moving down two places after two years at the top. Hugh Jones, now a vet, ranks for the 12th time over a 14-year span, both records for the event.

## 3000 METRES STEEPLECHASE
1. **Spencer Duval** 5.1.70 (5y, 6) 8:28.33 '94    8:24.64, 8:26.20, 8:28.99, 8:35.47, 8:38.01, 8:56.24;
   12 KP, 1 AAA, 7 Oslo, 11h1 WCh, 3 v USA
2. **Justin Chaston** 4.11.68 (6y, 3) 8:23.90 '94    8:24.97, 8:26.35, 8:26.82, 8:32.07, 8:32.3, 8:33.22;
   3 Eugene, 5 ECp, 13 KP, 8 Oslo, 8s2 WCh, 5 WSG
3. **Keith Cullen** 13.6.72 (4y, 7) 8:31.72 '92    8:26.05, 8:29.64, 8:32.07, 8:41.38, 8:46.92. 8:49.34;
   8 Granada, 2 AAA v LC, 1 Innsbruck, 3 AAA, 8h2 WCh, 2 v USA
4. **Tom Hanlon** 20.5.67 (9y, 4) 8:12.58 '91    8:24.37, 8:34.81; 7 Hechtel, 1 v USA
5. **Robert Hough** 3.6.72 (3y, 9) 8:38.80 '94    8:36.18, 8:36.29, 8:55.43; 4 AAA, 1 BUPA, dnf WSG
6. **Carl Warren** 28.9.69 (1y, -) 8:47.00 '94    8:40.74, 8:44.93, 8:50.01, 8:53.61, 8:55.02, 9:01.18;
   1 CAU, 3 AAA v LC, 1 WG, 6 AAA, 10 Linz
7. **Graeme Croll** 1.2.66 (3y, 12) 8:41.94 '93    8:40.49, 8:51.30, 9:00.98; 4 AAA v LC, 1 Scot, 2 BUPA
8. **Michael Hawkins** 24.10.61 (9y, 8) 8:37.15 '89    8:36.55, 8:51.96, 8:52.17, 8:53.26, 8:53.81, 8:59.5;
   5 AAA v LC, 5 AAA, 4 BUPA, 14 Linz
9. **David Lee** 16.9.65 (5y, 11) 8:31.22 '92    8:47.63, 8:47.97, 8:48.84, 8:51.41, 8:51.55, 8:59.55;
   1  AAA v LC, 7 AAA, 1 BL1 (3), 8 BUPA
10. **Spencer Newport** 5.10.66 (4y, -) 8:40.87 '92    8:45.3, 8:52.49; 1 Cup sf WL, 2 BL1 (4)
11. **Patrick Brice** 8.2.69 (0y, -) 8:54.03 '92    8:55.05, 8:57.42, 8:57.44, 9:01.07, 9:12.7;
   1 BL1 (1), 2 South, 8 AAA, 7 BUPA
12. **Simon O'Connor** 3.9.73 (0y, -) 9:04.09 '93    8:57.55, 8:58.13, 9:01.4, 9:03.60; 9 AAA, 8 U23 Int
Although he was the slowest of our trio in Gothenburg, Duval just makes it to top ranking. He beat Chaston 2-0, and his AAA win was the decider. Cullen began to fulfil the promise shown in 1992 and Hanlon came back to win the USA match, but as he ran only twice is ranked 4th. There was quite a gap after the top four and the 10th best of 8:47.63 is the worst since 1984.

## 110 METRES HURDLES
1. **Colin Jackson** 18.2.67 (12y, 1) 12.91 '93, 12.8 '90    13.17, 13.17w, 13.18, 13.18, 13.19, 13.20; 1 AUS Ch,
   1 Rome, 3 Nuremburg, 1 Madrid, 2 Nice, 3 Duisburg, 3 Paris, 1 WG, 2 Zürich, 1 v USA, 3 McD, 2 Berlin, 2 Tokyo
2. **Anthony Jarrett** 13.8.68 (10y, 2) 13.00 '93    13.04, 13.11, 13.13, 13.14, 13.19, 13.20;
   1 Helsinki, 2 GhG, 1 KP, 1 Oslo, 2 BUPA, 2 WCh, 5 Zürich, 2 Köln, 2 v USA, 2 McD, 3 Berlin, fs GPF
3. **Andrew Tulloch** 1.4.67 (9y, 4) 13.52 '94    13.62, 13.62, 13.64, 13.66, 13.69, 13.70;
   3 Moscow, 2 ECp, 6 GhG, 2 Tallinn, 2B Oslo, 7 BUPA, 7s1 WCh, 6 McD
4. **Neil Owen** 18.10.73 (4y, 6) 13.80 '94    13.60, 13.63, 13.65w, 13.71w, 13.72, 13.74;
   1 AAA v LC, 2 South, 8 KP, 2 WG, 1 AAA, 3B Oslo, 6 BUPA, 7s2 WCh, 5 v USA, 5 WSG, 1 Cup, BL1: -,1,-,1
5. **Paul Gray** 25.5.69 (6y, 3) 13.53 '94    13.86, 13.87, 13.90, 13.90, 13.98, 14.00
   3 AUS Ch, 6 Rome, 8 Nuremburg, 5 Madrid, 2B Duisburg, 1 BL2 (1), dnf WG
6. **Lloyd Cowan** 8.7.62 (8y, 5) 13.75 '94    13.79w, 13.83, 13.96, 13.97, 14.15, 14.20; 13.7w;
   1 IR, 2 AAA v LC, 1 South, 3 AAA, 8 BUPA, 8 McD, 3 Cup, BL1: 1,2, -,-
7. **Kenneth Campbell** 8.4.64 (3y, 7) 13.86 '94    13.98, 14.00, 14.02, 14.06, 14.11, 14.12;
   1 CAU, 1 Scot, 4 AAA, 1 S.Nat, 7 McD, BL2: -,2,1,-
8. **Hugh Teape** 26.12.63 (13y, 8) 13.44 '92    14.10, 14.10, 14.13, 14.18w; 14.9; 3 South, 1 BL3 (3), 3 WG, 6 AAA
9. **Mark Lambeth** 3.9.72 (3y, 11=) 14.24/14.20w '93, 14.2 '94    14.02, 14.28, 14.30, 14.36, 14.53, 14.54; 14.2;
   2 IR, 2 CAU, 4 South, 5 Tallinn, BL1: 3,3,1,-
10. **Damien Greaves** 19.9.77 (1y, -) 0    14.34, 14.37, 14.47, 14.50, 14.69, 15.06; 14.4w;
   1 AAA-J, 7 AAA, 8 EJ, 3 BL1 (4), 3 v Fra J
11. **Kevin Lumsdon** 3.3.74 (2y, 10) 14.20 '94    14.33w, 14.35, 14.44, 14.48, 14.55, 14.55;
   1B AAA v LC, 1 North, 2 Scot, 4h1 AAA, 6 U23 Int, 1 Nth IC, BL5: -,-,1,1
12. **Martin Nicholson** 9.12.70 (3y, 9) 14.14/13.8 '94    14.29, 14.41, 14.56, 14.60, 14.66, 14.67; 14.3;
   3 IR, 4 CAU, 4 AAA v LC, 2 North, 2 Cork, 2h2 AAA, BL1: 2,4,2,-
Not ranked
      **James Hughes** 8.11.74 (0y, -) 14.39/14.2 '94
   14.37, 14.43, 14.47, 14.49w, 14.53, 14.69w; 4 Cork, 5 WG, 8 AAA, 7 U23 Int, 2 S.Nat, BL2: -,1B,2,6
Jackson is UK No. 1 for the 7th time, a record for the event and Jarrett is ranked in the UK top two for the 8th successive year. Jarrett was 2nd in the Worlds and ran four times faster than Jackson's best, but crucially lost 3-1 to Jackson. Owen beat Tulloch 2-1 including at the AAAs, but Tulloch ran much faster in the Worlds and excelled with European Cup 2nd. Although in slightly different order, the top 11 are the same as in 1994.

## 400 METRES HURDLES

1. **Gary Jennings** 21.2.72 (3y, 6) 50.60 '94    49.82, 49.82, 50.03, 50.30, 50.30, 50.34;
   1 CAU, 1 BL1 (2), 1 AAA v LC, 6 Madrid, 4 ECp, 1 Barcelona, 3 AAA, 5 BUPA, dq h3 WCh, 8s2 WSG, 1 Cup
2. **Peter Crampton** 4.6.69 (3y, 2) 49.26 '94    49.58, 50.06, 50.35, 50.36A, 50.5, 50.76;
   4 Nairobi, 4 Malmö, 5 GhG, 6 KP, 7 BUPA
3. **Gary Cadogan** 8.10.66 (3y, 1) 49.25 '93    49.70, 50.82, 50.98; 2 AAA, dnf BUPA, dq h7 WCh
4. **Tony Williams** 1.5.72 (3y, 7) 50.98 '94    50.31, 50.40, 50.73, 50.96, 51.03, 51.2;
   1 B.Univs, 2B AAA v LC, 1 North, 3 Barcelona, 2h4 AAA, 1 BUPA Dev, 5h3 WSG
5. **Lawrence Lynch** 1.11.67 (7y, 3) 50.19 '91    50.62, 50.64, 50.70, 50.88, 50.89, 51.03;
   2 AAA v LC, 4 AAA, 6 BUPA, 4 v USA, 7 McD, 2 Cup, BL1: -,3,1,1
6. **Chris Rawlinson** 19.5.72 (1y, -) 52.0/52.32 '94    50.90, 51.08, 51.15, 51.20, 51.2, 51.31;
   1 IR, 2 CAU, 1B AAA v LC, 5 AAA, 3 Cup sf WL, 6 v USA
7. **Lloyd Cowan** 8.7.62 (3y, -) 51.22 '84    50.79, 50.99, 51.87, 52.33, 52.62, 52.70;
   2 BL1 (2), 1 WG, 3h4 AAA, 5 BUPA Dev, 5 v USA, 8 McD, 3 Kilkenny
8. **Gary Telfer** 10.1.65 (2y, 9=) 51.51 '94    51.29, 51.4, 51.75, 51.80, 51.9, 52.0;
   1 Middlesex, 2 IR, 3 E.Clubs, 1 Cup sf WL, BL1: 1,4,-,2
9. **Eddie Betts** 18.2.71 (2y, 8) 51.15 '94    51.24, 51.48, 51.57, 51.95, 52.16, 52.6;
   2 Middlesex, 3 CAU, 1 South, 1 KP Dev, 3h2 AAA, 3 BUPA Dev
10. **David Savage** 13.11.72 (1y, -) 51.87 '94    51.39, 51.44, 51.6, 51.70, 51.99, 52.13;
    4 CAU, 4 AAA v LC, 2 KP Dev, 7 AAA, 6 BUPA Dev, BL2: -,1,1,1
11. **Paul Hibbert** 31.3.65 (3y, -) 51.58 '93    51.33, 51.36, 52.79, 53.86; 6 AAA, BL1: -,-,1B,5
12. **Matthew Douglas** 26.11.76 (1y, -) 53.34 '94    51.73, 51.97, 52.03, 52.03, 52.21, 52.38;
    1 South J, 3 AAA v LC, 4 South, 1 AAA J, 2 E.Sch, 3h3 AAA, 4 S.Nat, 3 EJ, 1 v Fra J, 1 Jnr IA

Not ranked
   **Noel Levy** 22.6.75 (3y, 5) 50.70 '95    51.78, 52.17, 52.34, 52.62, 52.76, 52.81;
   4 KP Dev, 3h AAA, 4 BUPA Dev, 4 U23 Int, 6 Copenhagen, 3 Cup, BL1: -,dnf,-,3

Injury hit last year's top two, Cadogan and Crampton, and Jennings not only broke though the 50-second barrier, but leapt from 6th to 1st. Williams moved up three places after two years at no. 7 and at 6th Rawlinson is the top newcomer to the rankings.

## HIGH JUMP

1. **Steve Smith** 29.3.73 (6y, 1) 2.37 '92, 2.38i '94    2.35, 2.35, 2.31, 2.31, 2.30, 2.29; 1 BL2 (2), 2 V d'Ascq,
   1 ECp, 6 GhG, 3 KP, 2 Stockholm, 1 AAA, 1 Oslo, 3 BUPA, 4= WCh, 5 Zürich, 3 v USA, 5 Brussels, 7 McD, 3= Berlin
2. **Dalton Grant** 8.4.66 (12y, 2) 2.36 '91    2.35, 2.30, 2.30, 2.28, 2.27, 2.25; 2.32i;
   3 Eberstadt, 7 KP, 3 AAA, dnq 15 WCh, 12 Zürich, 4 Brussels, 1 McD, 10 Berlin, 1 Cup, BL1: -,1,1,-
3. **Brendan Reilly** 23.12.72 (7y, 3) 2.31 '92, 2.32i '94    2.27, 2.25, 2.25, 2.25, 2.24, 2.24; 2.26i;
   1 AAA v LC, 3 GhG, 9= KP, 4 AAA, 2 BUPA, dnq 17= WCh, 3 WSG, 2 Cup, 2 HUN Int
4. **James Brierley** 31.7.77 (2y, 8) 2.16 '94    2.17, 2.16, 2.16, 2.15, 2.15, 2.15; 2.18i; 1 Mid J, 1 CAU,
   2 AAA v LC, 1 AAA-J, 2= E.Sch, 5= AAA, 3 EJ, 1 v Fra J, 4 v USA, 8 McD, 2 Plate, 3 Jnr IA, 2 BLQ
5. **Geoff Parsons** 14.8.64 (14y, 4) 2.31 '94    2.20, 2.15, 2.13, 2.10, 2.08, 2.02; 2.24i;
   5 Budapest, nh AAA, 12 Oslo, 7= BUPA
6. **David Barnetson** 1.7.71 (6y, 11) 2.19 '92    2.17, 2.16, 2.13, 2.13, 2.12, 2.10; 1 Scot, 5= AAA, BL2: -,2,1,-
7. **Andrew Lynch** 28.6.74 (3y, 12=) 2.16 '93    2.18, 2.17, 2.13, 2.13, 2.12, 2.12; 2.14i;
   2 B.Univs, 4 CAU, 3 AAA v LC, 1 Mid, 1 WG, 7 AAA, 6 U23 Int, 5 Cup, BL1: -,3/4,7,2
8. **Richard Aspden** 15.10.76 (1y, -) 2.05 '93    2.16, 2.15, 2.11, 2.10, 2.10, 2.10;
   1 South J, 2 IR, 1 South, 6 AAA J, 1 E.Sch, 10 AAA, 2 v Fra J, 5 v USA, 2 Kilkenny, 1= Jnr IA, BL1: 2,6,-,3/4
9. **Stuart Ohrland** 6.9.75 (2y, 7) 2.17 '94    2.15, 2.13, 2.11, 2.10, 2.10, 2.10;
   1 NvST, 1 B.Univs, 4 AAA v LC, 2 AAA, 7 U23 Int, 3 Kilkenny, 2 Plate, 10 HUN Int
10. **Robert Brocklebank** 12.10.76 (2y, 9) 2.13 '94    2.16, 2.14, 2.12, 2.10, 2.10, 2.10;
    1 North-J, 3 IR, 6= AAA v LC, 1 North, 3 Cork, 3 AAA-J, 2= E.Sch, 11 AAA, 2 Nth IC, 1= Jnr IA
11. **Michael Robbins** 14.3.76 (2y, 10) 2.14 '94    2.17, 2.14, 2.11, 2.10, 2.10, 2.10; 2.15i, 2.11i, 2.11i;
    2 North-J, 4 IR, 2 North, 7 Cork, 2 AAA-J, dnq EJ, 1 Nth IC
12. **Alex Kruger** 18.11.63 (11y, 12=) 2.20 '88
    2.17, 2.15, 2.13, 2.10, 2.10, 2.10; 2.16i, 2.13i; 12 AAA, BL5: 1,1,-,1

Not ranked
   **Mark Mandy** (Ireland) 19.11.72 2.24 '93    2.25, 2.23, 2.21, 2.21, 2.20, 2.20; 2.24i;
   1 IR, 3 CAU, 1 ECp C1, 1 Cork, 1 GhG, 1 KP, 1 BLE, 7= BUPA, dnq 32 WCh, 5 McD, 1 Kilkenny, 1 BLQ

It was 1. Smith, 2. Grant, 3. Reilly for the third successive year. Brierley, still a junior in 1996, moves up to 4th. Parsons ranks in the top five, just, for the 14th successive year and Grant has been in the top three for ten successive years. Very close amongst the youngsters 7-11, followed by Kruger, who might have been higher if he had contested more high jump competitions as opposed to decathlons. The 10th best standard of 2.16 ties the record set in 1984 and 1989.

## POLE VAULT

1. **Nick Buckfield** 5.6.73 (5y, 3) 5.41 '93    5.70, 5.60, 5.55, 5.50, 5.50, 5.50;
   1 NvST, 6 ECp, 2 GhG, 8 KP, 1 AAA, 3 BUPA, dnq 17 WCh, 2 v USA, BL2: 1,1,1,-
2. **Neil Winter** 21.3.74 (5y, 1) 5.50 '92    5.60, 5.40, 5.40, 5.40, 5.40, 5.40;
   1 CAU, 1 GhG, 10 KP, 2 WG, 3 U23 Int, BL1: -,1=,1,1
3. **Paul Williamson** 16.6.74 (2y, 9) 5.22 '94    5.40, 5.35, 5.25, 5.20, 5.00, 5.00; 5.40i, 5.30i;
   2 B.Univs, 3 IR, 2 CAU, 1 AAA v LC, dnq WSG, 4 Cup, BL1: -,1=,-,8
4. **Michael Barber** 19.10.73 (4y, 6) 5.20 '94    5.42, 5.35, 5.31, 5.30, 5.20, 5.10; 5.20i;  1 B.Univs, 5 IR,
   3= CAU, 3 AAA v LC, 1 Mid, 5 WG, 4 AAA, 6= U23 Int, 1 Blackburn, 5 v USA, 2 UKPVA, 6 HUN Int, BL1: -,nh,3,6
5. **Ian Tullett** 15.8.69 (9y, 8) 5.30 '92    5.30, 5.30, 5.20, 5.20, 5.20, 5.15;
   4 IR, 6 WG, 5 AAA, 6= BUPA, 3 McD, 2 P'bor, BL1: 1,7,2,2
6. **Andrew Ashurst** 2.1.65 (12y, 4) 5.40 '88, 5.45i '92    5.20, 5.20, 5.20, 5.10, 5.00, 5.00;
   nh CAU, 2 AAA, 6= BUPA, 2 Cup sf Derby, 2 Blackburn, 4 McD, 3 P'bor, BL2: 4,2,-,1
7. **Dean Mellor** 25.11.71 (6y, 11) 5.22 '91    5.30, 5.21, 5.20, 5.20, 5.20, 5.15;
   1 IR, 3= CAU, 2 AAA v LC, 1 North, 1 Cork, 6 AAA, 9 BUPA, 1 Nth IC, 4 v USA, 7 HUN Int
8. **Michael Edwards** 19.10.68 (10y, 2) 5.52 '92    5.20, 5.11, 5.10, 5.10, 5.00, 5.00;
   4 AAA v LC, 4 GhG, 7= WG, 3 AAA, 8 BUPA, 1 Cup, BL1: 4,5=,4=,3
9. **Kevin Hughes** 30.4.73 (3y, 5) 5.25 '94    5.30, 5.20, 5.20, 5.10, 5.10, 5.10; 5.30i;
   nh CAU, 1 South, 7= WG, nh AAA, 1 P'bor, 1 UKPVA, 2 Cup, BL1: -,4,nh,4
10. **Matt Belsham** 11.10.71 (6y, 7) 5.35 '93    5.30, 5.20, 4.90, 4.80, 4.80;
    2 North, 2 Cork, 3 WG, nh AAA, BL2: 2,-,-,nh
11= **Mark Grant** 17.5.71 (3y, -) 5.06 '94    5.10, 5.00, 5.00, 4.80, 4.80; 5.09i, 5.00i, 5.00i;
    2 IR, 2 South, nh AAA, 6 P'bor, BL1: 3=,5=?,-,-
11= **Mark Hogkinson** 20.7.72 (2y, -) 5.00 '94    5.10, 5.00, 5.00, 5.00, 4.80, 4.80;
    7= IR, nh CAU, nh AAA, nh Blackburn, 3 UKPVA, BL1: 2,3,4=,5

Buckfield excelled to take Keith Stock's 14 year-old British record and well deserve his first top ranking. Winter was consistent at 5.40, before improving his Welsh record to 5.60, but injuring himself in the process to end his season prematurely. Williamson and Barber made good progress, the former, though missing a couple of months, just doing enough for 3rd. As last year there was remarkably little change in the men ranked, with no newcomers.
The progress in Britain at this event is shown by the fact that the tenth best standard of 5.20 improves upon the previous best of 5.11 in 1994 and 5.00 each year 1991-3.

## LONG JUMP

1. **Fred Salle** 10.9.64 (9y, 1) 7.97 '86    7.95w, 7.80Aw (7.57), 7.66, 7.62, 7.44w, 7.02; 7.90i, 7.69i;
   5 Seville, 1 AAA, 5 Sestriere, dnq WCh, 6 v USA, 3 Cup, BL1: 1,-,-,7
2. **Onochie Onuorah** 16.10.73 (2y, 12) 7.39 '94, 7.43w '92    7.81w, 7.58, 7.58, 7.50, 7.41, 7.40w;
   3 CAU, 3 AAA v LC, 9 South, 4 AAA, 3 U23 Int, 2 v USA, 1 Kilkenny, 1 Cup, BL1: 3,5,-,-
3. **Steve Phillips** 17.3.72 (5y, 4) 7.91 '91    7.77, 7.76w, 7.74w, 7.61, 7.59, 7.54; 7.59i;
   3 IR, 5 CAU, 1 Mid, 1 WG, 11 AAA, 5 v USA, 3 London, 2 Watford, BL1: -,-,1,2
4. **Stewart Faulkner** 19.2.69 (8y, -) 8.15 '90    7.69, 7.68, 7.48, 7.46, 7.43, 7.38;
   5 AAA, 3 Kilkenny, 1 London, 3 Watford, BL1: -,2,3,1
5. **John Munroe** 6.1.69 (3y, 5) 7.57/7.62w '93    7.64, 7.53?w, 7.53w, 7.51w, 7.46, 7.41; 7.65i, 7.65i, 7.54i;
   1 Middlesex, 1 IR, 6 E.Clubs, 1 AAA v LC, 2 WG, 6 AAA, 3 Cup sf WL, BL1: -,1,4,3
6. **Barrington Williams** 11.9.55 (9y, 2) 8.05i/8.01 '89    7.50, 7.48w (7.31), 7.41w (7.12), 7.33, 7.25, 7.06;
   7.65i, 7.55i, 7.54i, 7.48i; 2 IR, 2 CAU, 3 AAA, 1 Watford, BL3: 1,2,-,-
7. **Carl Howard** 27.1.74 (4y, 7) 7.76 '93    7.51, 7.51w?, 7.50, 7.48w, 7.41, 7.34; 7.41i;
   1 NvST, 2 AAA v LC, 2 South, 12 AAA, 7 U23 Int, 2 Cup, BL1: 2,nj,7,-
8. **Duncan Mathieson** 8.3.69 (4y, 10) 7.60 '94    7.62, 7.49w (7.43), 7.46, 7.37, 7.21, 7.19;
   1 Scot, 1 Cup sf WL, BL3: -,-,3,2
9. **Nathan Morgan** 30.6.78 (1y, -) 6.81/7.25w '94    7.43w, 7.39, 7.28, 7.28, 7.27, 7.25; 7.28i;
   6 CAU, 4 AAA v LC, 2 AAA-J, 5 Yth Oly, 8 AAA, 2 v Fra J, 1 Jnr IA
10= **Courtney Charles** 13.11.68 (3y, 6) 7.54 '94    7.44w, 7.40?w, 7.33, 7.31, 7.25, 7.22;
    2 Middlesex, 5 South, 13 AAA, BL1: 4,3,2,-
10= **John Shepherd** 23.12.61 (8y, -) 7.66 '88, 7.89w '86    7.48w, 7.46w, 7.38, 7.30w, 7.29, 7.26;
    4 CAU, 3 South, 18 AAA, BL3: -,1,2,3
12. **Darren Ritchie** 14.2.75 (1y, -) 7.00 '93, 7.15w '94    7.46w?, 7.33w, 7.30w (7.28), 7.26w, 7.23, 7.22;
    2 Scot, 10 AAA, 1 S.Nat, BL4: -,1,1,1
    **Ennyina Chukukere** 31.7.73 (1y, 11) 7.43 '90, 7.81w '94    7.57, 7.39, 7.30; 7.47i; 2 IC4A, 1 Cup sf Derby

Salle's AAA win is just enough to ensure that he retains his top ranking, and his 12-year span of rankings is the record for the event, but he was far from his 1994 form. There was little to choose between the top five or so. Williams, now 40, remains well in the top ten, and possibly deserves to rank higher on his fine competitive record, but he did not compete very often and his marks were much inferior to those ranked immediately above him. Leaping up from 12th to 2nd is Onuorah, who ended the year in fine form. Faulkner also ended the year well and showed promise of returnng to something like the athlete who was British no. 1 each year 1987-90.

108

# TRIPLE JUMP

1.  **Jonathan Edwards** 10.5.66 (10y, 1) 17.44/17.70w '93     18.43w (17.72), 18.29, 18.08w (17.45), 18.03w
    (17.74), 18.00, 17.98, 17.69, 17.60, 17.58, 17.58Aw, 17.49, 17.46, 17.46, 17.35, 17.29; 1 AAA v LC, 1 ECp,
    1 GhG, 1 KP, 1 BUPA, 1 Sestriere, 1 WCh, 1 v USA, 1 Brussels, 1 McD, 1 Berlin; won 14/14.
2.  **Francis Agyepong** 16.6.65 (13y, 3) 16.95 '94, 17.00w '92     17.29Aw, 17.24w, 17.18, 17.13, 17.05, 16.75;
    2 AAA v LC, 2 GhG, 3 KP, 1 AAA, 3 Sestriere, dnq 14 WCh, 7 Berlin, 2 v USA, 5 McD, 6 Rieti, BL1: -,1,-,1
3.  **Tayo Erogbogbo** 8.3.75 (2y, 7) 15.93 '94     16.32, 16.31, 16.22, 15.83, 15.73, 15.70;
    1 B.Univs, 6 AAA v LC, 2 AAA, 4 BUPA, 1 U23 Int, 4 v USA, 8 McD,  BL1: 2,-,1,3
4.  **Tosi Fasinro** 28.3.72 (6y, 4) 17.21/17.30w '93     16.56, 16.31, 16.20w (15.82), 16.08, 16.08w, 15.82;
    2 B.Univs, 1 IR, 1 Middx, 3 AAA v LC, 8 GhG, 9 KP, 3 AAA, 5 BUPA, 5 WSG, BL1: -,2,-,4
5.  **Julian Golley** 12.9.71 (6y, 5) 17.06 '94     16.06, 15.89w (15.75), 15.85, 15.26; 16.18i, 15.99i, 15.47i;
    5 AAA, 11 WSG
6.  **Femi Akinsanya** 29.11.69 (3y, 10) 15.98 '94     16.03, 16.00, 15.97w (15.90), 15.72, 15.64, 15.63w; 15.65i;
    2 NvST, 1 CAU, 4 AAA v LC, 1 South, 12 AAA, BL4: 1,1,-,-
7.  **Joe Sweeney** 17.7.65 (8y, -) 16.26 '91     15.95w (15.60), 15.75w, 15.45, 15.34, 15.26, 14.92; 15.25i;
    2 CAU, 2 South, 6 AAA, 1 Cup sf WL, BL3: 1,1,2,-
8.  **Onochie Achike** 31.1.75 (4y, 5) 16.53/16.67w '94     15.94w (15.91), 15.40, 14.93; 1 BL2 (2),
    5 AAA v LC, 7 U23 Int
9.  **John Herbert** 20.4.62 (15y, -) 17.41 '85     16.00w; 16.50, 16.28i; 2 BL1 (4)
10. **Paul Ralph** 16.12.67 (1y, -) 15.54 '93     15.72w, 15.67, 15.54, 15.49, 15.29, 15.27;
    4 NvST, 3 CAU, 3 South, 4 AAA, 2 Cup sf Derby, BL4: 2,2,1,1
11. **Rez Cameron** 18.5.60 (9y, 12) 16.20 '88, 16.32w '89     15.68w (15.55), 15.39, 15.31, 15.23, 15.05, 14.86;
    15.40i; 1 NvST, 2 Middx, 6 E.Clubs, 2 Cup sf WL, 3 Cup, BL1: 1,12,4,5
12. **Carl Howard** 27.1.74 (2y, 11) 15.84 '94     15.97, 15.44w?, 15.33; 3 NvST, 3 B.Univs, 10 BL1 (3)
    **John Mackenzie** (Australia) 23.8.65 (2y, 8) 16.17 '94
    15.77; 16.07i, 15.97i

Edwards produced one of the greatest series of performances in the history of sport; his season was perfect. After
some frustration with wind readings on his huge jumps at the European Cup, he duly took the world record in
Salamanca, and those two further records on successive jumps in Gothenburg were wondrous. His breaching of the
18m and 60ft barriers place him firmly amongst the all-time greats; he is UK no.1 for the 6th time.
Agyepong quietly improved to the edge of the world top ten, but injury hit our other talented leaders in this event.
Erogbogdo, now eligible for Britain, excelled to rank 3rd, having a 4-1 advantage over Fasinro, who ended the year
well, but Golley was a shadow of his 1994 self. Herbert, after a highly promising return indoors, only competed once
outdoors, but is one of only three men ranked this year who first appeared in the top 12 back in the 1970s (the others:
Neville Thompson and Chris Maddocks). Achike only competed three times outdoors, and Mackenzie not at all after
two indoor appearances until November in Australia. Cameron ranked for the ninth time; remarkably, for such a long
run, he has never been higher than 8th. Including indoor marks, the 10th best of 15.91 equals the record set in 1991.

# SHOT

1.  **Mark Proctor** 15.1.63 (5y, 4) 18.15 '94     19.37, 18.81, 18.55, 18.53, 18.10, 18.09; 18.39i;
    1 CAU, 1 AAA v LC, 1 IS, 1 WG, 1 AAA, dnq 25 WCh, 4 v USA, 1 McD, 1 Cup, BL1: nt,1,-,9
2.  **Matthew Simson** 28.5.70 (9y, 1) 19.49 '94     18.68, 18.27, 17.72, 17.40; 18.50i; 8 ECp, 2 AAA
3.  **Shaun Pickering** 14.11.61 (13y, 8) 18.31 '92     18.94, 17.85, 17.71, 17.69, 17.48, 17.00;
    2 WG, 3 AAA, 5 v USA, BL1: -,2,1,1
4.  **Lee Newman** 1.5.73 (3y, 3) 17.94 '95     18.46, 17.75, 17.64, 17.64, 17.62, 17.47; 17.80i;
    4 AAA, 1 Braintree, 2 McD, BL1: 3,3,-,2
5.  **Nigel Spratley** 1.4.70 (6y, 2) 17.96 '94     16.97, 16.86, 16.81, 16.80, 16.68, 16.65; 16.87i;
    nt NvST, 1 IR, 3 CAU, 2 AAA v LC, 3 S'ton 13/6, 2 South, 3 WG, 8 AAA, 6 v USA, 4 McD
6.  **David Callaway** 4.9.63 (8y, 5) 17.55 '93     16.60, 16.59, 16.58, 16.57, 16.56, 16.53;
    2 NvST, 2 Hants, 4 Bedford, 1 So'ton 13/6, 3 South, 4 WG, 6 AAA, 2 Braintree, 3 McD, 2 Cup, BL1: 1,7,2,3
7.  **Gary Sollitt** 13.1.72 (2y, 9) 16.68 '94     16.94, 16.89, 16.64, 16.60, 16.43, 16.33;
    1 NvST, 1 Hants, 2 IR, 4 CAU, 3 AAA v LC, 2 Soton 13/6, 7 AAA, 5 McD
8.  **Steve Whyte** 14.3.64 (8y, 7) 17.78 '89     16.66, 16.55, 16.52, 16.27, 16.18, 16.02; 16.95i, 16.87i, 16.69i;
    7 E.Clubs, 2 Bedford, 5 South, 1 Scot, 10 AAA, 1 S.Nat; 3 Cup; BL1: 3,6,3,5
9.  **Paul Reed** 2.6.62 (6y, 10) 17.04 '88     16.68, 16.45, 16.29, 16.23, 16.18, 16.00; 16.13i;
    5 CAU, 1 North, 2 Scot, 1 Nth IC, BL5: -,1,1,1
10. **Jim Mason** 22.3.72 (1y, -) 16.12i/15.94 '94     16.74, 16.41, 16.38, 16.25, 16.25, 15.96; 16.54i;
    3 Bedford, 4 South, 3 Scot, 12 AAA, 7 McD, BL1: 4,4,5,-
11= **James Muirhead** 26.1.71 (1y, -) 16.14 '93     16.60, 16.14, 16.12, 15.99, 15.83, 15.72; 2 S.Nat, BL2: 1,1,1,1
11= **Stefan Hayward** 30.7.74 (1y, -) 15.74 '94     16.88, 16.13, 16.05, 15.62, 15.08, 15.05; 15.23i;
    4 Scot, 2 U23 Int, BL4: 1,1,1,1
    **Simon Williams** 17.10.67 (7y, -) 19.44i '89, 19.14 '91     16.93, 15.55; 1 BL3 (3), 13 AAA
    **Felix Hyde** (Ghana) 7.8.76 16.70 '94     17.38, 17.06, 16.94, 16.84, 16.67, 16.41;
    2 CAU, 1 Bedford, 1 South, 1 AAA-J, 11 AAA, 6 McD

Proctor made a big improvement to reach the top for the first time from Simson, who only had four meetings. The standard in depth was down on 1994. Pickering, at the age of 33, set a new pb and Newman also passed the 18m line. Callaway was 4-3 v Spratley, but the latter had much better marks.

## DISCUS

1. **Robert Weir** 4.2.61 (8y, 1) 62.50 '84    63.56, 63.14, 62.94, 62.54, 62.50, 62.38;
   3 ECp, 2 AAA, 9 WCh, 10 Zürich, 1 v USA, 1 BL1 (4)
2. **Kevin Brown** 10.9.64 (11y, 2) 59.20 '91    59.50, 58.46, 58.32, 57.26, 57.24, 56.90;
   12 Halle, 1 IR, 1 CAU, 1 AAA v LC, 3 Mid, 1 Lough 21/6, 5 Budapest, 4 AAA, 4 v USA, BL1: 1,1,1,2
3. **Simon Williams** 17.10.67 (9y, 7) 61.14 '92    58.20, 56.54, 55.78, 54,74; 1 BL3 (3), 3 AAA
4. **Glen Smith** 21.5.72 (5y, 3) 59.78 '94    58.70, 57.60, 57.38, 57.06, 56.64, 56.58;
   15 Halle, 3 IR, 2 AAA v LC, 1 Mid, 2 Lough 21/6, 6 Budapest, 6 AAA, ML2: 1,-,1,-
5. **Gary Herrington** 31.3.61 (7y, 10) 56.02 '87    56.32, 56.28, 55.44, 55.08, 55.06, 54.50;
   2 Mid, 5 AAA, 1g S.Nat, 5 v USA, ML2: 2,1,2,1
6. **Leith Marar** 7.11.68 (3y, 9) 54.58 '93    55.38, 55.36, 55.32, 55.06, 54.12, 53.78;
   1 N v ST, 2 South, 7 AAA, BL1: 3,3,-,3
7. **Jamie Murphy** 20.3.73 (3y, 8) 55.24 '94    55.52, 55.50, 54.72, 53.32, 52.92, 52.44;
   2 CAU, 3 Zofingen, 12 AAA, 1 U23 Int, ML2: 3,2,3,2
8. **Neville Thompson** 28.3.55 (16y, 6) 55.68 '93    54.76, 54.42, 53.42, 52.84, 52.08, 50.88;
   3 CAU, 1 South, nt AAA, 5 Kilkenny, 3 Cup, BL1: 5,4,3,4
9. **Lee Newman** 1.5.73 (3y, 4) 58.34 '94    53.52, 53.46, 53.38, 53.06, 53.04, 52.92; 1 Zofingen, BL1: 2,2,-,5
10. **Paul Reed** 2.6.62 (6y, 11=) 54.50 '94    52.46, 52.46, 52.04, 51.52, 51.52, 51.36;
    4 CAU, 1 North, 1 Scot, BL5: -,1,1,1
11. **Denzil McDonald** 11.10.65 (1y, -) 51.62 '91    55.04, 53.24, 50.36, 50.10, 49.92, 49.52;
    6 BL1 (1), 3 IR, 6 CAU, 1 Croydon, 2 Cup
12. **Matt Symonds** 31.7.68 (1y, -) 52.16 '94    54.36, 51.30, 50.68, 50.66, 50.66, 50.44;
    4 IR, 5 E.Clubs, 3 South, 9 AAA, 7 Kilkenny, 5 Cup, BL1: 7,6,-,10
    **Mark Proctor** 15.1.63 (1y, -) 54.28 '93    52.86, 50.82, 50.74, 50.14, 48,76, 47.80; 1 IS, BL1: 4,5,-,12
    **John Moreland** 13.9.58 (0y, -) 50.80 '94    51.76, 51.26, 49.84, 49.70, 49.38, 49.22;
    9 CAU, 4 Mid, 1 NI, 11 AAA, 3 S.Nat, ML2: 4,-,4,3

Weir is clearly top, in that position for the third sucessive year to add to his 1st place in 1981 and 1984; he improved his 11 year-old pb and with 10th place in the world rankings had his best ever year. Brown is again second and Williams, although he competed only four times, gets third over Smith due to his fine AAA performance.

## HAMMER

1. **Peter Vivian** 5.11.70 (5y, 2) 70.80 '94    71.28, 70.92, 70.70, 70.26, 69.88, 69.84;
   3 IR, 5 EClubs, 1 AAA v LC, 1 South, 7 ECp, 2 WG, 4 AAA, dnq 34 WCh, 4 v USA, BL1: 2,2,1,2
2. **David Smith** 2.11.74 (2y, 4) 67.74 '94    71.52, 71.18, 70.12, 69.62, 69.46, 69.42;
   1 Colindale, 1 IR, 1 CAU, 2 AAA v LC,
   1 North, 3 WG, 5 AAA, 5 U23 Int, 1 v USA, 5 Königs W, 2 Kilkenny
3. **Michael Jones** 23.7.63 (14y, 3) 72.10 '88    70.48, 70.28, 70.08, 69.44, 69.00, 68.30;
   2 Colindale, 2 IR, 2 CAU, 2 AAA, 1 Cup sf Derby, 5 v USA, 3 Kilkenny, 1 Cup, BL1: 1,1,2,3
4. **Jason Byrne** 9.9.70 (7y, -) 73.80 '92    69.44, 67.72, 66.86, 63.52, 62.70, 62.40; 4 IR, 3 AAA, ML1: 1,1,1,-
5. **Paul Head** 1.7.65 (13y, 1) 74.02 '90    68.88, 67.80, 67.02, 66.28, 65.62, 64.34;
   2 Cup sf Derby, 6 Königs W, 4 Kilkenny, 2 Cup
6. **Shane Peacock** 5.3.63 (10y, 5) 71.60 '90    64.08, 64.00, 62.96, 61.70; 2 North, 3 BL1 (3), 6 AAA
7. **John Pearson** 30.4.66 (7y, 7) 66.54 '94    63.50, 63.26, 62.68, 62.48, 61.96, 61.54;
   2 B.Univs, 3 AAA v LC, 1 Mid, ML1: 2,2,2,1
8. **Chris Howe** 17.11.67 (8y, 11) 63.74 '90    62.86, 61.50, 60.94, 60.84, 59.86, 59.00;
   3 CAU, 2 South, 7 AAA, BL1: 6,5,4,-
9. **Bill Beauchamp** 9.9.70 (1y, -) 60.98 '93    62.92, 62.38, 62.04, 62.02, 61.74, 61.50;
   2 N vST, 4 CAU, 4 South, 8 AAA, 5 Kilkenny
10. **Gareth Cook** 20.2.69 (8y, 12) 67.32 '91    63.00, 62.96, 62.80, 62.54, 62.14, 61.72; 1 Surrey
11. **Paul Barnard** 27.7.72 (1y, -) 60.34 '94    62.70, 61.12, 60.84, 60.84, 60.50, 60.40;
    6 IR, 5 CAU, 3 North, 1 Scot, 9 AAA
12. **Robert Earle** 15.9.60 (1y, -) 61.68 '94    62.60, 60.66, 60.62, 60.56, 60.48, 59.94;
    3 South, 1 East, 10 AAA, 4 Cup, BL1: 7,4,6,6
    **David Smith** 21.6.62 (11y, -) 77.30 '85    65.02, 57.74
    **Phil Spivey** (Australia) 15.5.61 70.94 '86    63.46, 61.90, 60.88, 60.66, 60.02, 59.76;
    2 Surrey, 3 Cup, BL1: 3,3,5,5

The top three are extremely close. Vivian's early season form just enabled him to rank top for the first time. He had a 3-2 advantage over Smith, who maintained his rapid improvement to pass the 70m barrier and end as our best at the end of the year. Jones was 4-3 v Vivian, but 1-5 v Smith. After the top five the standard was down a few metres from the previous year. Howe, for instance, did not throw as far but rose three ranking places.

## JAVELIN

1. **Steve Backley** 12.2.69 (9y, 1) 91.46 '92    88.54, 87.62A, 86.46, 86.30, 86.30, 85.90, 85.26, 84.78,
   3 V d'Ascq, 3 ECp, 2 GhG, 3 Oslo, 1 BUPA, 2 WCh, 3 Zürich, 1 v USA, 3 Brussels, 6 McD, 3 GPF
2. **Michael Hill** 22.10.64 (12y, 2) 86.94 '93    84.14, 83.60, 83.54, 83.48, 83.40, 82.94;
   2 V d'Ascq, 3 GhG, 6 KP, 1 AAA, 4 Oslo, 2 BUPA, 6 WCh, 8 Zürich, 3 v USA, 8 Brussels, 3 McD, 6 Berlin
3. **Colin Mackenzie** 30.6.63 (14y, 3) 82.60 roughened tail '91, 82.38 '93    79.90, 79.80, 79.54, 79.30, 78.20,
   77.92; 1 South, 6 GhG, 11 KP, 2 AAA, 4 BUPA, 1 Cup sf Derby, 4 v USA, 8 McD, 1 Cup, BL1: -,1,1,1
4. **Nigel Bevan** 3.1.68 (9y, 4) 81.70 '92    77.14, 76.86, 76.58, 76.52, 74.78, 74.50;
   1 CAU, 1 WG, 3 AAA, 5 BUPA, 7 McD, 2 Cup, BL1: 3,3,-,2
5. **Mark Roberson** 13.3.67 (10y, 5) 80.92 '88    78.44, 78.44, 76.78, 76.44, 76.06, 75.66;
   1 NvST, 1 IR, 2 AAA v LC, 5 AAA, 1 Kilkenny, 3 Cup, BL1: 1,4,2,-
6. **Nick Nieland** 31.1.72 (4y, 7) 76.28 '94    76.30, 75.12, 74.58, 73.60, 73.54, 72.76;
   1 AAA v LC, 7 GhG, 4 AAA, 2 South, 3 WG, 3 Kilkenny, 4 Cup
7. **Steve Harrison** 19.12.72 (2y, 10) 71.94 '94    75.32, 71.72, 70.88, 70.86, 70.66, 70.18;
   1 B.Univs, 2 CAU, 3 AAA v LC, 3 South, 6 AAA, BL1: -,5,-,4
8. **Stuart Faben** 28.2.75 (1y, -) 66.74 '94    74.24, 73.56, 69.94, 69.52, 69.34, 69.00;
   2 NvST, 2 IR, 3 CAU, 4 AAA v LC, 2 South, 3 WG, 7 AAA, 1 U23 Int, BL1: 4,6,-,8
9. **Roald Bradstock** 24.4.62 (16y, 6) 83.84 '87
   75.64, 73.30, 71.42, 70.16; is becoming US citizen
10. **Phil Parry** 4.10.65 (2y, 12) 70.00 '94    67.28, 66.80, 66.32, 64.80, 63.88, 63.36;
    1 Scot, BL3: 2,1,1,-
11. **Duncan MacDonald** 30.3.74 (1y, -) 65.70 '93    65.96, 64.92, 64.16, 63.58, 63.54, 63.22;
    2 B.Univs, 4 CAU, 5 South, 8 AAA, 7 U23 Int, 5 Cup, BL1: -,9,5,7
12. **Dean Smahon** 8.12.61 (1y, -) 67.60 '94    66.00, 64.76, 64.72, 64.50, 64.14;
    5 CAU, 3 Scot, 1 NI

Backley is number one for the 6th time and was over 81m in all 18 competitions and Hill was over 80m in 14 of his
15. Mackenzie was a clear third, unlucky not quite to reach 80m. The top five retain their 1994 rankings.
The 10th best standard of 68.34 (Tony Smith) is the worst since the introduction of the new javelin in 1986, but this
is misleading as the 9th man threw 74.24, and this is the second best in this time span.

## DECATHLON

1. **Alex Kruger** 18.11.63 (10y, 1) 8078 '94    8131, 8098, 7993; 7008 (1Hr);    9 Götzis, 2 ECp, 12 WCh, dnf Talence
2. **Barry Thomas** 28.4.72 (6y, 5) 7616 '92    7766, 7737w, 7602, 7482; 2 North, 4 Alhama, 14 ECp, 9 WSG
3. **Anthony Brannen** 16.9.68 (6y, -) 7656 '91    7861; 1 North, dnf Alhama
4. **Simon Shirley** 3.8.66 (3y, 2) 8036 '88    7822; 20 Götzis, dnf ECp
5. **Paul Field** 24.6.67 (3y, 9) 7157 '95    7425w, 7295, 7196;    3g North, 8 Alhama, 20 ECp, dnf HCl
6. **Stephen Rogers** 1.9.71 (3y, 8) 7203 '94    7295, 7293, 7021; 4 North, 1 AAA, dnf Bebington, 1 HCl
7. **Jamie Quarry** 15.11.72 (4y, 4) 7610 '94    7401, 7082; 1 B.Univs, dnf AAA, 15 WSG
8. **Duncan Mathieson** 8.3.69 (6y, -) 7535 '90    7272, 7051; 1 Scot, 3 HCl
9. **Anthony Southward** 31.1.71 (1y, -) 6883 '94    7075, 6808w; 1 Bebington, 2 HCl
10. **Roger Hunter** 10.3.76 (1y, -) 6565w/6563 '94
    6925, 6871, 6825w; 10 B.Univs, 1 North J, 1 AAA J, dnf EJ, 4 HCl
11. **Mark Bushell** 22.10.76 (1y, -) 6622 '94    6839, 6782w, 6630, 6544; 2 North J, 2 AAA J, 19 EJ, 5 HCl
12. **Gavin Sunshine** 19.2.74 (2y, -) 7112 '93    6805, 6531; 6 North, 14 U23 v Rus

Kruger, top for the 5th time, improved his best at both Götzis and with a splendid European Cup 2nd place. After
winning the AAA indoor heptathlon and a splendid pb in April, Brannen had the misfortune to be sidelined by injury,
and Shirley also only completed one decathlon, but Thomas made excellent progress to rank second.

## 20 KILOMETRES WALK

1. **Darrell Stone** 2.2.68 (7y, 1) 1:25:05 '92, 1:23:27 sh? '93
   1:24:49, 1:25:22, 1:26:18, 1:26:51.6t, 1:27:44, 1:28:48; 1 Manx, 1 UK, 29 WCp, 4 Fana, 25 WCh, 1 v Ire
2. **Chris Maddocks** 28.3.57 (13y, 6) 1:22:12 '92
   1:26:35, 1:28:11, 1:28:33, 1:30:12, 1:33:00, 1:34:00+; 1 Plymouth, 4 Manx, 4 UK, 19 7N, 2 v Ire
3. **Steve Partington** 17.9.65 (10y, 3) 1:24:09 '94
   1:26:32, 1:27:25, 1:28:35, 1:28:50, 1:30:02; 2 Manx, 58 WCp, 20 7N, 1 Stockport, 4 v Ire
4. **Martin Bell** 9.4.61 (6y, 2) 1:25:42 '92    1:27:05, 1:27:24, 1:34:15, 1:35:40;
   6 UK, 5 Stockport, 1 Yverdon, 3 v Ire
5. **Andy Penn** 31.3.67 (6y, -) 1:23:34 '92    1:28:29, 1:30:30, 1:31:45, 1:32:28;
   3 UK, 70 WCp, 22 7N, 3 Yverdon
6. **Chris Cheeseman** 11.12.58 (2y, 4) 1:29:11 '94
   1:29:55, 1:30:21, 1:30:29, 1:31:30.0t, 1:34:23; 5 Manx, 2 UK, 80 WCp, 3 Stockport, 2 Lough
7. **Philip King** 25.11.74 (2y, 7) 1:29:49 '94    1:29:07, 1:29:14, 1:36:25, 1:36:40;
   dnf UK, 12 Ozd, 2 Stockport, 4 Yverdon, 8 v Ire

111

8.   **Martin Young** 11.7.72 (1y, -) 1:32:53 '92   1:30:28.6t, 1:31:17, 1:33:51; 1 Sutton Park, 4 Stockport, 1 Lough
9.   **Les Morton** 1.7.58 (10y, -) 1:27:16 '89,   1:26:31sh '93 1:33:37; 5 UK
10.  **Jamie O'Rawe** 3.2.73 (1y, -) 1:39:44 '93   1:34:52, 1:35:02, 1:36:32, 1:37:37;
     8 UK, 13 Ozd, 6 Stockport, 7 Dublin
Stone retains top ranking, with Maddocks just pipping Partington for 2nd. The 10th best performer level is 1:34:52, the worst since 1968.

## 50 KILOMETRES WALK
1.   **Chris Maddocks** 28.3.57 (9y, -) 3:51:37 '90
     1 Constanza 3:53:14, 2 Rotterdam 4:02:47, 2 Burrator 4:31:24, dnf Fana
2.   **Les Morton** 1.7.58 (12y, 1) 3:57:48 '89
     1 RWA 4:01:36, 2 Fana 4:06:46.0t, 44 WCp 4:08:52, dnf Rotterdam
3.   **Mark Easton** 24.5.63 (2y, -) 4:09:33 '92   42 WCp 4:06:01, 14 Palma 4:08:51
4.   **Tim Watt** 19.9.66 (2y, 2) 4:36:35 '94   6 Rotterdam 4:20:43, 2 RWA 4:28:14, 19 Palma 4:29:16
5.   **Graham White** 28.3.59 (2y, 4) 4:46:15 '94   1 Burrator 4:14:59, 72 WCp 4:29:41
6.   **Gareth Brown** 10.5.68 (1y, -) 4:51:10 '90   3 RWA 4:28:44, dnf Rotterdam
7.   **Jonathan Cocker** (1y, -)   4:33:01 (4) RWA, dnf Rotterdam
8=   **Chris Berwick** 1.5.46 (12y, 3) 4:23:22'86   5 RWA 4:39:27
8=   **Carl Thomson** 8.4.65 (2y, -) 4:39:17 '90   21 Palma 4:38:10
It was very difficult to determine who should rank first, should it be RWA champion Morton, who has ranked top in nine of the previous ten years, just ahead of Easton, who was a place ahead of him at the World Cup, or should it be Maddocks? In the end I decided that the latter's feat of producing by far the fastest time, and another better than Morton or Easton, should get the verdict despite his poor early season form. Maddocks has a 17-year span in the rankings at this event. I was able to rank nine men this year in contrast to just four in 1994.

# BRITISH MERIT RANKINGS 1995 - WOMEN
## 100 METRES
1.   **Paula Thomas** 3.12.64 (10y, 1) 11.15 '94, 11.13w '88   11.33, 11.34, 11.36w, 11.37, 11.43, 11.46w; 11.4,
     11.4; 2 Bedford, 5 GhG, 1 AAA, 5 q4 WCh, 1 v USA, BL1: 1,-,1
2.   **Simmone Jacobs** 5.9.66 (13y, 4) 11.31 '88, 11.26w '84   11.34, 11.48, 11.50, 11.54, 11.60, 11.68;
     1 Ljubljana, 1 AAA v LC, 1 Celje, 1 KP, 2 AAA, 5h3 WCh
3.   **Stephanie Douglas** 22.1.69 (7y, 3) 11.27 '91   11.30, 11.39w, 11.39Aw, 11.53, 11.54, 11.59;
     1 IR, 1 Bedford, 4 ECp, 3 AAA, 1 Cup sf WL, 6h1 WCh
4.   **Marcia Richardson** 10.2.72 (5y, 5) 11.45 '93, 11.39w '94   11.51w, 11.52, 11.53, 11.59, 11.59, 11.60
     4 Granada, 2 Ljubljana, 2 Celje, 2 KP, 4 AAA, 2 Cup sf WL, 6 WSG, 1 Cup, BL3: 1,1,1
5.   **Katharine Merry** 21.9.74 (7y, 2) 11.34/11.27w '94   11.47, 11.50, 11.74; 3 Granada, 1 Mid
6.   **Clova Court** 10.2.60 (1y, -) 11.77 '94, 11.6 '87, 11.5w '90   11.55w, 11.69, 11.80, 11.81w, 11.91; 11.7;
     1 CAU, 2 Mid, 2 Cup
7.   **Catherine Murphy** 21.9.75 (1y, -) 12.00/11.63w '94   11.65w, 11.74w, 11.78, 11.79, 11.80, 11.90;
     2 BL1 (1), 3 CAU, 1 Basel, 3 AAA v LC, 1 Welsh, 4 KP, 2 WG, 4 Cup
8.   **Sophia Smith** 8.12.74 (3y, 10) 11.70/11.56w '93   11.50w, 11.69, 11.69, 11.71, 11.80, 11.81w;
     6 CAU, 3 Basel, 4 WG, 5 AAA, 1 BUPA, 3 U23 Int, 4 v USA, BL2: 1,1,-
9.   **Donna Hoggarth** 14.10.73 (4y, 11) 11.61/11.55w '92   11.61w, 11.74w, 11.81w, 11.83, 11.88w, 11.89;
     2 IR, 2 North, 3 WG, 6 AAA, 2 BUPA, 5 U23 Int
10.  **Sallyanne Short** 6.3.68 (9y, -) 11.39 '92, 11.36w '89   11.57, 11.57w, 11.86, 11.98, 12.05; 11.8
     2 Welsh, 3 KP, 1 WG, dnr sf AAA, 2 S.Nat, 6 v USA
11.  **Sharon Williams** 20.5.70 (1y, -) 12.01 '92, 11.90w '93, 11.9 '90   11.53, 11.62, 11.83, 11.83, 11.89, 12.03;
     11.6w; 2 AAA v LC, 8s2 AAA, 3 WSG, 1 Plate
12.  **Rebecca Drummond** 18.4.78 (2y, 12) 11.92 '93, 11.50w '94   11.59, 11.71, 11.73, 11.87, 11.88, 11.88;
     1 BL4 (1), 4 IR, 6 AAA v LC, 1 Mid-J, 1 AAA-J, 1 ESch, 2 Yth Oly, 7 EJ, 1 v Fra J
Not ranked
     **Aileen McGillivary** 13.8.70 (4y, 8) 11.54 '92, 11.43w '93   11.62, 11.67w, 11.74w, 11.80, 11.80, 12.00;
     4 Bedford, 8 AAA, 3 S.Nat
     **Melanie Neef** 26.5.70 (0y, -) 11.88 '91, 11.69w '88   11.70, 11.80w; 11.6w, 11.7; 2 CAU, 2 BL1 (3)
     **Louse Fraser** 10.10.70 (0y, -) 11.88 '89, 11.6/11.68w '90)   11.61w, 11.74w; 11.8, 11.8; 1 North
Thomas is a clear choice for no.1; her six years there is a record for the event. Jacobs, Douglas and Richardson followed Thomas at the AAAs and in this ranking. The injury-struck Merry is 5th, followed by Court, who at age 35 makes her first ever ranking at this event.

## 200 METRES

1. **Paula Thomas** 3.12.64 (8y, 1=) 22.69 '94    22.89, 22.95, 23.00, 23.03w, 23.20w. 23.24; 23.31i;
   1 BL1 (4), 1 Bedford, 4 ECp, 5 GhG, 8 KP, 8s1 WCh, 2 v USA, 6 McD
2. **Melanie Neef** 26.5.70 (2y, 8) 23.64 '94    23.35, 23.42, 24.14, 24.50; 23.9, 24.0w; 23.73i, 24.03i, 24.16i;
   1 CAU, 2 GhG, 1 BL1 (3), 4 v USA
3. **Catherine Murphy** 21.9.75 (2y, 10) 23.85/23.83w '94    23.40, 23.41, 23.57, 23.58, 23.63, 23.66;
   2 BL1 (1), 7 CAU, 1B AAA v LC, 1 Welsh, 6 GhG, 1 AAA, 6 Oslo, 1 U23 Int, 5s2 WSG, 2 Cup
4. **Simmone Jacobs** 5.9.66 (12y, 4) 23.12 '91, 23.01w '84    23.44, 23.48, 23.48w, 23.58, 24.21, 24.58; 23.8;
   2 CAU, 3 Bedford, 4 Helsinki, 2 AAA
5. **Marcia Richardson** 10.2.72 (4y, 6) 23.55 '94, 23.4 '93    23.53, 23.94, 24.10, 24.11; 23.6w, 23.7, 23.8w,
   23.8w; 1 IR, 5 AAA, 2 Cup sf WL,1 Cup, BL3: 1,1,1
6. **Donna Fraser** 7.11.72 (4y, -) 23.69 '89    23.44w, 23.47, 23.94, 24.28, 24.28, 24.31; 23.7w, 24.0w;
   1 NvST, 3 CAU, 2 South, 1 WG, 6 v USA, 1 Kilkenny, BL2: 1,-,1
7. **Stephanie Douglas** 22.1.69 (8y, 3) 23.17 '94    23.33w, 23.50A, 23.91; 23.85i; 2 Bedford, 7 Helsinki
8. **Joice Maduaka** 30.9.73 (1y, -) 23.96 '94    23.81, 23.84, 23.88, 23.95, 24.00, 24.04;
   2 IR, 8 CAU, 1 South, 3 WG, 3 AAA, 3 U23 Int, 8s1 WSG
9. **Sharon Williams** 20.5.70 (1y, 0) 24.16/23.86w '93
   23.80w, 23.91, 23.95, 23.96, 24.32, 24.34; 23.9; 24.20i, 24.22i; 1 B.Univs, 1 AAA v LC, 8 AAA, 1 Plate
10. **Clova Court** 10.2.60 (2y, -) 23.57 '90    23.64; 24.0, 24.0; 2 BL1 (3), 3 Cup
11. **Louise Fraser** 10.10.70 (2y, -) 23.98i/24.1 '92, 24.13/23.41w '91    24.68; 23.4, 23.5w, 24.2;
    5 CAU, 1 Cup sf WL; BL1: -,1,3
12. **Alison Davies** 6.4.61 (1y, -) 23.87 '93
    24.06, 24.21, 24.51, 24.58; 24.0, 24.0, 24.1w?, 24.2w; 2 NvST, 3 South, 4 AAA, 1 Cup sf Derby

Not ranked
   **Sallyanne Short** 6.3.68 (6y, -) 23.24 '92, 23.19w '90)    23.79; 2 WG
   **Sharon Tunaley** 2.9.68 (0y, -) 24.26/24.2/23.8w '87, 23.94w '88    23.6, 24.0w, 24.2, 24.4, 24.6; 1 BL2 (3)
Thomas was no.1 for the 4th time at 200m. In second place is Neef, who found time amidst her splendid 400m campaign to run some good 200m races, beating those following her in the rankings. The depth of fast times was thin this year.

## 400 METRES

1. **Melanie Neef** 26.5.70 (2y, 3) 52.09 '94    51.18, 51.35, 51.39, 51.45, 51.63, 51.70;
   1 ECp, 1 BL1 (2), 1 AAA, 2 BUPA, 2 Rhede, 4s1 WCh, 1 Copenhagen, 7 McD, 4 Berlin
2. **Lorraine Hanson** 22.4.65 (6y, -) 50.93 '91    52.47, 52.6, 52.68, 53.05, 53.1, 53.22;
   1 Mid, 2 AAA, 6 BUPA, 1 Cup sf Liverpool, 3 v USA, 2 Cup, BL1: 1,3,2
3. **Stephanie Llewellyn** 31.12.68 (1y, -) 54.77 '94    52.4, 52.5, 52.54, 52.79, 53.13, 53.55;
   1B AAA v LC, 2 BL (2), 1 WG, 4 AAA, 1 Cup sf Derby, 4 v USA
4. **Georgina Oladapo** 15.5.67 (1y, -) 53.9 '94    52.71, 52.94, 53.05, 53.5, 53.51, 54.12;
   1 South, 3 AAA, 6 v USA
5. **Phylis Smith** 29.9.65 (6y, 2) 50.40 '92    52.5, 53.03, 53.19, 54.08. 54.22A;
   1 Soria, 1 BL1 (3), 1 Cup
6. **Donna Fraser** 7.11.72 (3y, 7=) 52.54 '91    52.04, 53.27, 53.32, 53.8, 53.9, 54.21;
   3 AAA v LC, 1 BL2 (2), 1B WG, dnf AAA, 1 McD Dev, 2 Pune
7. **Linda Keough** 26.12.63 (12y, 4) 50.98 '91    53.72, 53.86, 54.01, 54.05, 54.4, 54.42;
   1 CAU, 2B AAA v LC, 3 WG, 6 AAA
8. **Susan Rawlinson** 13.10.70 (1y, -) 53.89 '94    53.4, 53.69, 53.85, 54.24, 54.39, 54.9; 53.70i, 53.82i, 53.85i;
   2 IR, 3 CAU, 1 AAA v LC, 4 WG, 5 AAA, 2 Cup sf Derby
9. **Sally Gunnell** 29.7.66 (7y, 1) 51.04 '94    53.27, 53.34; 3 Lindau, 6 Rhede
10. **Sharon Tunaley** 2.9.68 (1y, -) 57.14 '94    53.58, 53.66, 53.8, 54.8, 54.96A, 55.1;
    1 BL4 (1), 2 Soria, 2 McD Dev
11. **Stephanie McCann** 26.10.65 (3y, 10) 53.91 '94    53.5, 54.31, 54.83, 55.39, 56.28; 54.39i, 54.62i, 54.64i,
    54.71i; 2 E.Clubs, 3B AAA v LC, 1 NI, 1 Scot, 2 Cup sf Liverpool
12. **Michelle Pierre** 30.9.73 (1y, -) 54.9/55.39 '92    54.05, 54.14, 54.57, 54.6, 54.63, 54.71;
    1 BL2 (1), 2 CAU, 2 AAA v LC, 1 U23 Int, 3 McD Dev

Not ranked
   **Louise Fraser** 10.10.70 (1y, -) 53.55 '92    53.9, 54.5; 4 BL1 (2)
After a fine début season at 400m in 1994, when she ranked third, Neef improved a further second and was splendidly consistent at a new level, running nine times under her 1994 best of 52.09. Comebacks were a feature of the rankings, with Hanson 2nd after a year out, and Oladapo, whose last top ten place had been 3rd equal at 200m in 1986, was 4th. A place ahead of her was Llewellyn, also ranked for the first time at this event. Keough's 15-year span of ranking, 1980-95, is a record for the event. The 10th best of 53.58 is the best since 1985 (record 53.0 in 1982).

113

## 800 METRES
1. **Kelly Holmes** 19.4.70 (4y, 1) 1:58.64 '93    1:56.21, 1:56.95, 1:57.56, 1:58.27, 1:58.77, 2:00.23;
   1 Helsinki, 1 IS, 1 KP, 1 AAA, 3 WCh, 1 McD, 3 Berlin, 2 GPF
2= **Ann Griffiths** 20.8.65 (5y, 2) 1:59.81 '94    2:01.94, 2:02.12, 2:03.3mx, 2:04.03, 2:04.9mx, 2:06.4mx;
   3 v USA, 6 Copenhagen, 6 McD
2= **Sonya Bowyer** 18.9.72 (2y, 3) 2:02.30 '94    2:01.67, 2:02.60, 2:04.43, 2:04.53, 2:05.9, 2:07.66; 2:04.83i;
   8 Moscow, 1 AAA v LC, 4 ECp, 10 KP, dnf AAA,
4. **Natalie Tait** 24.8.72 (1y, -) 2:05.1 '89    2:02.69, 2:03.2, 2:03.32, 2:03.79, 2:04.31, 2:04.50;
   3 AAA v LC, 1 South, 6 Helsinki, 1 Tallinn, 4 AAA, 3 WSG, 1 Cup
5. **Abigail Hunte** 12.5.71 (1y, -) 2:04.50 '94    2:02.47, 2:04.25, 2:04.26, 2:06.22, 2:07.29, 2:09.72; 2:04.97i,
   2:06.31i; 1 WG, 3 AAA, 5 v USA, 9 McD
6. **Vicki Lawrence** 9.6.73 (2y, 11) 2:04.69 '94    2:04.42, 2:04.77, 2:04.8mx, 2:05.93, 2:06.57, 2:06.67;
   3 Basel, 1 Scot, 6 AAA, 2 S.Nat, 1 U23 Int, 6 v USA,1 McD Dev, 4 Rieti
7. **Paula Radcliffe** 17.12.73 (1y, -) 2:05.97 '93    2:05.22, 2:06.55; 5 AAA
8. **Helen Daniel** 24.10.63 (9y, 9) 2:01.86 '87    2:05.96, 2:06.77, 2:06.80, 2:07.87, 2:08.18, 2:08.28;
   1 NvST, 1 CAU, 5 Crawley, 2 AAA v LC, 3 WG, 2h3 AAA, 6 McD Dev
9. **Mary Kitson** 2.4.63 (3y, -) 2:02.83 '91    2:03.8mx, 2:06.36, 2:06.8mx, 2:07.25, 2:07.78, 2:08.93;
   2 South, 5 GhG Dev, 7 AAA, 8 Stockholm
10. **Alison Layzell** 16.12.66 (1y, -) 2:04.84 '94    2:07.06, 2:07.17, 2:07.38, 2:07.38, 2:07.5, 2:08.3;
   1 Wyth, 1 IR, 3 Crawley, 1 Welsh, 4 WG, 2h2 AAA, 1 S.Nat
11. **Michelle Faherty** 10.8.68 (1y, -) 2:05.38 '94    2:05.3, 2:07.06, 2:07.53, 2:09.0, 2:10.11, 2:10.13;
   2 IR, 7 Crawley, 1 North, 1 Nth IC, 2 McD Dev, 1 Stretford 5/9
12. **Vicky Sterne** 12.10.68 (1y, -) 2:18.72 '82    2:06.1, 2:07.09, 2:08.0, 2:08.60;
   1 Mid, 5h4 AAA, 3 McD Dev, 2 Stretford 5/9
Not ranked
   **Jacqui Parker** 15.10.66 (0y, -) 2:03.78i '93, 2:08.9 '94    2:04.8 mx, 2:06.44
   **Angela Davies** 21.10.70 (1y, 7) 2:03.67 '94    2:05.41, 2:06.1mx, 2:07.3, 2:08.7; 2:09.51i; 3 Lough 20/5
Holmes's marvellous season included the English record for 800m to win the AAA title and then new British marks for
World 3rd and Grand Prix 2nd. The first three are the same as in 1994; injuries meant that Griffiths did not start
competitive running until July, while Bowyer's season ended then. There are six newcomers to the rankings at this
event. They are headed in 4th and 5th places by Tait, who began to fulfil her youthful promise, especially with her
World Student Games bronze, and Abigail Hunte, who returned from the US to run for Britain internationally.
The 10th best of 2:05.3 is the worst since 1976 (record 2:02.75 in 1984).

## 1500 METRES
1. **Kelly Holmes** 19.4.70 (2y, 1) 4:01.41 '94    4:03.04, 4:04.20, 4:07.02, 4:09.15, 4:10.98, 4:11.87;
   1 V d'Ascq, 1 ECp, 1 GhG, 2 WCh
2. **Yvonne Murray** 4.10.64 (13y, 2) 4:01.20 '87, 4:22.64M '94    4:05.61, 4:11.47, 4:17.92; 3 GhG, 1 AAA
3. **Paula Radcliffe** 17.12.73 (2y, -) 4:11.6/4:36.4eM 93    4:06.84, 4:28.93M, 4:11.91; 1 Dijon, 4 GhG, 9 Köln
4. **Alison Wyeth** 26.5.64 (9y, 3) 4:03.17 '93, 4:24.87M '91    4:06.58, 4:08.56, 4:12.67, 4:16.1, 4:27.07;
   1 IR, 3 V d'Ascq, 5 GhG, 6 Monaco
5. **Debbie Gunning** 31.8.65 (5y, 10) 4:12.69 '90, 4:32.32M '91    4:14.42, 4:14.55, 4:16.89, 4:18.16, 4:20.36,
   4:20.61; 1 KP Dev, 2 WG, 2 AAA, 3 Kvarrnsveden, 4 v USA, 2 Pune
6. **Bev Hartigan** 10.6.67 (7y, 5) 4:05.66 '90, 4:26.52M '92    4:11.96, 4:17.05; 3 Waldschut, 5 Nuremburg
7. **Una English** 14.8.70 (2y, -) 4:11.82/4:33.01M '92    4:13.26, 4:16.37, 4:17.31, 4:17.34, 4:19.10, 4:19.37;
   4 Waldschut, 7 Nuremburg, 3 AAA. 8 Linz
8. **Susan Parker** 24.3.70 (3y, 11) 4:12.3 '93, 4:37.82M '94    4:13.36, 4:37.52M, 4:17.11, 4:18.3, 4:19.12,
   4:19.8; 5 AAA v LC, 1 BL1 (2), 5 Cork, 4 AAA, 2 Cup sf WL, 3 v USA, 1 Cup
9. . **Angela Davies** 21.10.70 (3y, 6) 4:09.29/4:31.83M '94    4:12.8mx, 4:15.05, 4:35.89M, 4:16.75, 4:17.99,
   4:21.80; 2 AAA v LC, 2 Cork, 9 AAA, 7 WSG
10. **Karen Hargrave** 23.9.65 (6y, -) 4:09.46/4:28.8M '89    4:15.83, 4:18.36, 4:21.03, 4:22.78, 4:24.43; 6 French
11. **Sonia McGeorge** 2.11.64 (6y, 9) 4:10.75 '90, 4:33.12M '94    4:17.22, 4:18.1; 1 Lough 20/5, 1 AAA v LC
12. **Michelle Faherty** 10.8.68 (3y, 12) 4:15.37/4:41.69M '93    4:38.64M, 4:18.30, 4:18.44, 4:19.56, 4:20.5;
   4:18.65i, 4:19.19i; 3 AAA v LC, 6 Cork, 1 WG, 5 AAA
Not ranked
   **Lynn Gibson** 6.7.69 (2y, 6) 4:05.75/4:31.17M '94    4:16.2, 4:19.29, 4:19.94, 4:21.73, 4:22.64, 4:25.41;
   4:18.41i, 4:20.85i; 2 Nurmijärvi, 10 GhG, 7 AAA
   **Ann Griffiths** 20.8.65 (3y, 7) 4:07.59/4:33.12M '92    4:14.74i
M = 1 mile time. Equivalents: 4:05.0m = 4:24.6M, 4:10.0m = 4:30.1M, 4:15.0m = 4:35.5M, 4:20.0m = 4:41.0M
Holmes was clearly Britain's top woman athlete of 1995, and she again ranks first at both 800m and 1500m. There
were no newcomers to the rankings at this event, and the depth was weak. 2nd to 4th places went to the 5000m
specialists, all of course, world-class athletes. Hartigan made 5th ranking despite racing only twice, but she beat the
AAA 3rd placer English on both occasions.

114

# 3000 METRES
1.  **Paula Radcliffe** 17.12.73 (3y, -) 8:40.40 93    8:40.82, 8:42.55, 8:49.31, 8:56.6+, 8:58.19+, 8:58.3+;
    4 Zürich, 4 McD, 4 GPF
2.  **Yvonne Murray** 4.10.64 (14y, 1) 8:29.02 '88    8:42.82, 8:50.2+, 8:51.57, 8:58.1+, 8:59.80, 9:00.2+;
    13 Zürich, 1 v USA, 2 McD
3.  **Alison Wyeth** 26.5.64 (7y, 3) 8:38.42 '93    8:48.94, 8:58.6+; 6 Rome
4.  **Liz McColgan** 24.5.64 (9y, -) 8:38.23 '91, 8:34.80i '89    8:50.52, 8:57.2+, 9:01.?+; 2 Linz,
5.  **Jill Hunter** 14.10.66 (6y, -) 8:47.36 '88  9:02.30, 9:29.77, 9:29.95, 9:31.4+; 3 BMC Lough, 1 North, 6 Lappeenranta
6.  **Andrea Whitcombe** 8.6.71 (2y, -) 8:58.59 '91    9:10.29, 9:16.9mx, 9:18.6, 9:18.9; 5 v USA
7.  **Sarah Bentley** 21.5.67 (2y, 9) 9:18.09 '94
    9:10.9mx, 9:12.72, 9:24.8, 9:27.12; 9:28.94i, 9:39.01i; 1 Yorks, 1 AAA, 6 v USA
8.  **Kelly Holmes** 19.4.70 (1y, -) 0    9:08.7; 1 IS
9.  **Una English** 14.8.70 (1y, -) 9:10.0 '92    9:12.7, 9:23.24; 9:10.6i; 1 St Gallen, dnf McD, 2 Swiss Clubs
10. **Bev Hartigan** 10.6.67 (2y, -) 9:03.88i '90, 9:10.4 '92    9:17.19; 1 BMC Lough
11. **Debbie Gunning** 31.8.65 (2y, 5) 9:12.12 '94    9:22.43, 9:31.7; 9:23.68i, 9:29.92i;1 Cheltenham, 2 Kilkenny
12. **Susan Parker** 24.3.70 (2y, 7) 9:06.2 '92    9:18.92, 9:24.94; 12 McD, 3 Kilkenny
Not ranked
    **Kate McCandless** (USA) 22.6.70  8:56.00 '93    9:07.29; 8 Lappeenranta
    **Louise Watson** 13.12.71 (0y, -) 9:16.45 '92    9:18.1mx, 9:25.90; 2 AAA v LC
Radcliffe, who was 3rd in 1993, returned to head the list at this event, which although replaced by 5000m as a championships event contines to be run enough to justify a ranking. Also returning, in their cases, for the first time since 1992, are McColgan and Hunter. Whitcombe previously ranked in 1991 and Hartigan in 1987. Murray's 14 years in the rankings is a record for 3000m, and she has completed ten successive years in the top two.

## 5000 METRES (Previously ranked 1982-90 and 1992)
1.  **Paula Radcliffe** 17.12.73 (1y, -) 16:16.77i '92    14:49.27, 14:57.02, 15:00.83, 15:02.87, 15:14.32, 15:14.77;
    1 Hengelo, 2 KP, 5 WCh, 4 Brussels, 8 Berlin
2.  **Yvonne Murray** 4.10.64 (3y, -) 15:50.54 '84    14:56.94, 14:57.98, 16:06.1+, 16:18.0+;
    4 KP, dnf Brussels, 4 Berlin
3.  **Liz McColgan** 24.5.64 (6y, -) 15:01.08 '87    14:59.56, 15:04.88, 15:14.67, 15:54.7+, 15:59.6+, c.16:21.4+;
    3 Hechtel, 6 Köln, 6 Brussels
4 . **Alison Wyeth** 26.5.64 (3y, -) 15:10.38 '94    15:00.37, 15:19.44, 15:39.14; 2 ECp, 5 KP, 1 AAA, dnf ht WCh
5.  **Jill Hunter** 14.10.66 (4y, -) 15:09.98 '92    15:28.46, 15:39.85, 15:48.16, 15:59.8+, 16:0??+, 16:17.9+;
    3 Cork, 11 KP, 7 Oslo
6.  **Louise Watson** 13.12.71 (1y, -) 16:23.85i '94, 16:25.4 '92    15:57.06, 16:07.09, 16:11.23, 16:16.23 16:07.32i;
    7 Cork, 3 AAA, 9 WSG
7.  **Sarah Bentley** 21.5.67 (1y, -) 16:16.82 '94    15:53.86, 16:22.80, 16:22.93, 16:27;
    3 Hexham, 5 AAA, 15 Hechtel, 1 Königs W
8.  **Jane Shields** 23.8.60 (3y, -)  15:32.34 '88    15:54.80; 6 Cork, dnf AAA
9.  **Andrea Whitcombe** 8.6.71 (1y, -) 0    16:12.96; 4 AAA
10  **Sonia McGeorge** 2.11.64 (1y, -) 16:23.52 '91    16:17.32; 1 CAU, dnf AAA
11  **Heather Heasman** 27.9.63 (1y, -) 16:19.4 '93    16:14; 1 Hexham
12= **Shirley Griffiths** 23.6.72 (1y, -) 0    16:23.0; 1 N.East
12= **Liz Talbot** 5.12.74 (1y, -) 0    16:24.86, 16:42.8; 2 Tessenderlo
Not ranked
    **Katy McCandless** (USA) 22.6.70  15:34.93 '93    15:34.11, 15:45.87; 5 Moscow, 7 US Ch
    **Nnenna Lynch** (USA) 3.7.71  0    16:10.69, 16:11.81, 16:28.0mx, 16:36.93; 16 Hengelo, 26 US Ch, 2 AAA
Radcliffe excelled on her return from injury to take her first UK no.1 ranking; she had been 3rd at 3000m in 1993. McColgan and Hunter also returned in good style. Three women inside 15 minutes and one, Wyeth, just outside represented world-class strength at the top, but after Hunter there was then a very big gap to the rest, with a lack of quality races.

## 10000 METRES
1.  **Liz McColgan** 24.5.64 (8y, -) 30:57.07 '91    31:40.14, 32:22.09, 32:33.89; 4 ECp, 6 WCh
2.  **Jill Hunter** 14.10.66 (5y, 2) 31:07.88 '91    32:22.93, 32:24.93, 32:26.12; 1 AAA, 15 WCh
3.  **Yvonne Murray** 4.10.64 (3y, 1) 31:56.97 '94    32:16.76; dnf WCh
4.  **Louise Watson** 13.12.71 (1y, -) 34:36.83    33:33.71, 33:38.52; 2 AAA, 6 WSG
5.  **Jane Shields** 23.8.60 (3y, -) 32:42.0 '88    33:46.07; 3 AAA
6.  **Angela Hulley** 8.2.62 (5y, 7) 32:42.84 '89    34:05.42; 4 AAA
7.  **Heather Heasman** 27.9.63 (3y, -) 33:19.48 '92    34:18.68; 5 AAA
8.  **Zahara Hyde** 12.1.63 (2y, 4) 33:23.25 '94    34:24.33; 25 Walnut, dnf AAA
McColgan returned for her 7th year at no.1 at 10,000m and Hunter for her 5th year at no.2; both last appeared in 1992. Shields was last ranked in 1990. There was insufficient competition at this event to rank more than eight.

## MARATHON

1.  **Liz McColgan** 24.5.64 (4y, -) 2:27:32 '91    2:30:32 (7) Tokyo, 2:31:14 (5) London
2.  **Yvonne Danson** 22.5.59 (3y, 1) 2:32:24 '94    2:30:53 (5) Boston, 2:34:41 (2) S.E.Asian
    (now competing for Singapore)
3.  **Marion Sutton** 7.10.63 (5y, 2=) 2:34:38 '92    2:32:26 (4) Chicago
4=  **Suzanne Rigg** 29.11.63 (1y, -) 2:41:03 '94    2:34:21 (8) Berlin
4=  **Karen Macleod** 24.4.58 (5y, 2) 2:33:16 '94    2:34:23 (2) Sacramento
6.  **Trudi Thomson** 18.1.59 (1y, -) 2:43:18 '94    2:38:23 (1) Dublin, 2:42:44 (25) WCp, 2:41:42Sh (22) WCh
7.  **Alison Rose** 27.9.67 (2y, 12) 2:45:55 '94    2:42:42 (24) WCp, 2:45:52Sh (28) WCh
8.  **Catherine Mijovic** 11.4.61 (1y, -) 2:48:31 '94    2:37:14 (1) Reims, 2:44:30 (7) Rotterdam
9.  **Julie Coleby** 5.11.55 (5y, 10) 2:35:53 '84    2:38:25 (4) Sacramento, 2:41:37 (17) London
10. **Sally Goldsmith** 18.1.61 (1y, -) 2:38:39 '94    2:39:08 (3) Venice
11. **Hayley Nash** 30.5.63 (2y, 4) 2:35:39 '94    2:39:59 (14) London
12. **Lynn Harding** 10.8.61 (5y, 11) 2:31:45 '89    2:41:20 (16) London
Not ranked
    **Caroline Horne** 7.11.56 (0y, -) 2:37:26 '85    2:43:19 (27) WCp, 2:48:53 (5) Dublin
    **Lesley Turner** 1.8.66 (1y, 12) 2:41:09 '93    2:46:23 (33) WCp, 2:59:22 (1) Harrow
Danson and McColgan were both 5th in major spring marathons, with McColgan securing her fourth top ranking with her 7th in Tokyo. Rigg and Macleod produced similar times to share 4th ahead of Thomson and Rose.

## 100 METRES HURDLES

1.  **Jackie Agyepong** 5.1.69 (8y, 1) 12.93 '94    12.90, 13.03w, 13.06, 13.06, 13.09, 13.14;
    1 Hengelo, 1 Bedford, 3 ECp, 7s1 WCh, 7 Linz, 1 v USA, 5 McD, 1 Cup
2.  **Michelle Campbell** 24.2.69 (6y, -) 13.26 '90    13.08w, 13.24w, 13.26Aw, 13.28w, 13.32, 13.35;
    1 NAIA, 6 GhG, dq KP, 2 AAA, 3 BUPA, 6 Sestriere, 2 BL1 (3), 5 v USA
3=  **Clova Court** 10.2.60 (5y, 3) 13.04 '94    13.19w, 13.36, 13.42, 13.44, 13.48, 13.51; 13.4;
    1 IR, 2 WG, 8 AAA, 1 Nike Gh, 1 BL1 (3), 6 McD, 2 Cup
3=  **Keri Maddox** 4.7.72 (6y, 8) 13.24/13.20w '93    13.36, 13.40, 13.48, 13.48, 13.50, 13.56; 13.5;
    1 Staffs, 3 Ljubljana, 3 CAU, 2 AAA v LC, 1 Mid, 1 WG, 3 AAA, 4 BUPA, 3 Nike Gh, BL4: 1,-,1
5.  **Melanie Wilkins** 18.1.73 (2y, 10) 13.67 '93, 13.65w '94    13.34, 13.41, 13.55, 13.57, 13.60, 13.60; 13.1;
    1 NvST, 1 BL2 (1), 3 IR, 4 CAU, 3 AAA v LC, 1 South, 6 Basel, 1 AAA, 2 Tessenderlo, 5 BUPA,
    3 U23 Int, 2 Nike Gh, 6 v USA
6.  **Diane Allahgreen** 21.2.75 (3y, 7) 13.25 '94    13.47w, 13.53, 13.62, 13.65, 13.66, 13.69;
    2 BL2 (1), 4 IR, 2 CAU, 1 AAA v LC, 7 Basel, 8 GhG, 4 AAA, 8 BUPA, 4 U23 Int, 4 Nike Gh
7.  **Denise Lewis** 27.8.72 (4y, 9) 13.47 '94    13.51, 13.52, 13.58, 13.66, 13.70, 13.86; 13.6, 13.6;
    2 Staffs, 2 Mid, 5 AAA, BL1: 2,-,1B
8.  **Natasha Danvers** 19.9.77 (2y, 12) 13.88 '93, 13.76w '94    13.45, 13.46, 13.49w, 13.51w, 13.54, 13.63;
    13.6w; 2 BL2 (1), 1 Sth-J, 1 AAA-J, 1 E.Sch, 6 AAA, 2 EJ, 1 v Fra J, 7 McD
9.  **Louise Fraser** 10.10.70 (4y, -) 13.36 '91    13.51w, 13.71; 13.6, 13.6w, 13.9; 2 IR, 1 North, BL1: 1,-,3
10. **Angela Thorp** 7.12.72 (5y, 5) 13.28 '93    13.62, 13.70; 13.7; 1 Yorks, 1 CAU
11. **Orla Bermingham** 7.10.75 (1y, -) 14.01/13.87w '94    13.93, 13.97, 14.07, 14.22, 14.38, 14.42; 13.8w,
    13.8w, 14.1; 5 CAU, 4 AAA v LC, 2 South, 3h2 AAA, 5 Nike Gh, 2 Kilkenny, 3 Cup, BL1: 3,1,2B
12. **Samantha Farquharson** 15.12.69 (6y, 2) 13.08 '94    13.53; 4 Jena
Agyepong retains her top ranking, and improved her pb, but injury meant that she did not have the depth of fast times
of 1994. Campbell returned from the USA to take 2nd place, beating Maddox 2-0, while Court and Maddox were 1-
1 and ahead of Wilkins, the surprise AAA champion on win-loss, 2-1 and 3-2 respectively.

## 400 METRES HURDLES

1.  **Jacqui Parker** 15.10.66 (9y, 1) 56.15 '91    56.50, 56.64, 57.18, 57.32, 57.45, 57.52;
    1 Australian, 4 GhG, 8 KP, 4 Hechtel, 4 v USA
2.  **Gowry Retchakan** 21.6.60 (7y, 2) 54.63 '92    57.18, 57.52, 57.78, 57.85, 57.86, 58,3;
    1 CAU, 6 GhG, 1 AAA, BL3: -,1,1
3.  **Louise Fraser** 10.10.70 (3y, 3) 56.26 '92    57.07, 57.76, 57.91, 57.99, 58.18, 58.76;
    2 CAU, 1 AAA v LC, 7 ECp, 6 AAA, 3 Hechtel, 6h1 WCh, 5 v USA
4.  **Louise Brunning** 6.3.72 (2y, 6=) 58.07 '94    57.30, 58.18, 58.58, 59.15, 59.3, 59.6;
    1 Surrey, 2 AAA v LC, 3 AAA, 6h1 WSG
5.  **Stephanie McCann** 26.10.65 (2y, 4) 58.09 '94    58.21, 58.8, 59.00, 59.1, 59.44, 59.53;
    1 Scot, 1 NI, 1 S.Nat, 2 AAA, 1 Cup sf Liverpool
6.  **Vyvyan Rhodes** 5.5.73 (5y, 8) 58.02 '92    58.85, 58.86, 59.29, 59.89; 4 AAA, 3 U23 Int, 6 v USA
7.  **Clare Bleasdale** 6.7.71 (4y, 5) 58.04 '94    59.29, 59.65, 59.8, 59.9, 60.1, 60.11;
    2 NvST, 2 Surrey, 1 IR, 5 CAU, 1 South, 7 AAA
8.  **Heather Myers** 5.12.64 (2y, 11) 59.46 '94    59.9, 60.12, 60.24, 60.29, 60.36;
    1 NvST, 2 IR, 3 CAU, 1B AAA v LC, 7h3 AAA, 2 Cup, BL2: 1,1,1
9   **Jane Low** 26.8.60 (3y, 6=) 58.43 '94    59.9, 60.0, 60.31, 60.39, 60.4, 60.58; 4 CAU, 2 Scot, 3h2 AAA, 2 S.Nat

116

10. **Vicky Day** 19.6.72 (1y, -) 59.72 '94    60.15, 60.15, 60.55, 60.6; 2 BL1 (2), 2 South, 4h3 AAA
11. **Jennifer Pearson** 3.7.62 (9y, 10) 57.41 '88    60.0, 60.4, 61.11, 61.3, 61.3, 61.39;
    dns CAU, 2 Cup sf Liverpool. 1 Plate
12. **Katrina Norman** 1.1.76 (1y, -) 62.8/63.20 '94    60.15, 60.57, 60.9, 61.03, 61.38, 61.44;
    1 Sth J, 3B AAA v LC, 3 AAA-J, 1 E.Sch, 6h2 AAA, 2 v Fra J
    **Vikki Jamieson** 19.5.77 (1y, -) 60.07 '94    59.81, 61.3, 61.67, 61.7, 62.93;
    5 Scot, 2 AAA-J, 5 S.Nat, 4 v Fra J
After seven successive years at no.1 Sally Gunnell was sorely missed. Parker, although not running quite as fast as in 1994 and with a previous high of 3rd (four times), ranks top ahead of Retchakan, who won her 5th AAA title but declined Gothenburg selection through persistent injury and is second for the 6th successive year, and Fraser, who made a promising comeback. Brunning moved up two places, followed by McCann, but the overall standard declined this year and the 10th best of 59.9 is the worst since 1979. Pearson made it a 400mh record of 11 years in the rankings.

## HIGH JUMP
1. **Lea Haggett** 9.5.72 (5y, 3) 1.91 '91    1.90, 1.88, 1.88, 1.86, 1.85, 1.85; 1.88i, 1.86i;
   1 Bedford, 1 BL2 (2), 4 Geneva, 6 ECp, 1 WG, 1 AAA, dnq WCh, 1 v USA
2. **Diana Davies** 7.5.61 (18y, 6) 1.95 '82    1.85, 1.85, 1.83, 1.80, 1.80, 1.80;
   1 IR, 1 CAU, 1 AAA v LC, 2 AAA, 2= v USA
3. **Debbie Marti** 14.5.68 (11y, 1) 1.93 '92, 1.94i '91    1.85, 1.85, 1.85, 1.84, 1.82, 1.82; 1.86i, 1.85i;
   3 AAA v LC, 1 South, 2 WG, 3 AAA, 5= v USA, 2 Croydon, 4 Kilkenny, 1 Plate
4. **Michelle Dunkley** 26.1.78 (1y, -) 1.77 '94    1.87, 1.85, 1.84, 1.83, 1.83, 1.83;   2/3 IR, 1 Mid J, 2 CAU,
   2 AAA v LC, 1 Mid, 2 AAA-J, 1 ESch, 3= Yth Oly, 8 AAA, 8 EJ, 1 v Fra J, 1 Telford, 9= HUN Int, 1 Jnr IA
5. **Julia Bennett** 26.3.70 (8y, 2) 1.89 '94, 1.92i '90    1.87, 1.87, 1.85, 1.85, 1.83, 1.82, 1.80; 1.83i;
   3= CAU, 4= AAA v LC, 6= AAA, 1 Croydon, 2 Kilkenny, 2 Plate
6. **Rachael Forrest** 25.12.77 (1y, -) 1.78 '94    1.87, 1.85, 1.80, 1.80, 1.78, 1.77;
   2 Mid J, 5= CAU, 6 AAA v LC, 1 AAA-J, 2 ESch, 6= AAA, dnq EJ, 3 v Fra J, 5 Telford, 9= HUN Int, 2 Cup
7= **Denise Lewis** 27.8.72 (3y, 12) 1.81 '94    1.80, 1.80, 1.80, 1.78, 1.78, 1.75; 2 Mid, BL1: 1,-,1
7= **Julie Crane** 26.9.76 (2y, 7) 1.81 '94    1.81, 1.80, 1.79, 1.78, 1.78, 1.78; 2/3 IR, 2 Welsh J, 5= CAU,
   4= AAA v LC, 1 Welsh, 3 AAA-J, 3 ESch, 3 WG, 4= AAA, 1 S.Nat, 5 U23 Int, 3 Jnr IA
9. **Julie Major** 19.8.70 (4y, 4) 1.85 '94    1.81, 1.80, 1.75, 1.75, 1.75, 1.75;
   2 Bedford, 2 South, 4= AAA, 1 Cup, BL1: -,1,2
10. **Lisa Brown** 16.3.76 (2y, -) 1.76 '93    1.81, 1.76, 1.75, 1.75, 1.75, 1.73;
    3 BL1 (1), 3= CAU, 1 Scot, 4 AAA-J, 1 Scot J, 3 S.Nat, 3 Cup
11. **Susan Jones** 8.6.78 (2y, 11) 1.82 '94    1.81, 1.75, 1.75, 1.75, 1.73, 1.71; 1.77i, 1.76i;
    1 North J, 6 AAA-J, 4 ESch, 10 AAA, 5 Nth IC, 2 Jnr IA
12= **Kelly Thirkle** (née Mason) 29.3.71 (5y, 10) 1.88i '92, 1.85 '91    1.76, 1.75. 1.75, 1.70, 1.70, 1.70; 1.80i,
    1.75i, 1.75i; 2 North, 11= AAA, 3 Nth IC, BL1: 2,2,3
12= **Gillian Howard** 14.4.69 (3y, -) 1.81i '92, 1.80 '90    1.76, 1.76, 1.75; 1 BL2 (1), 1 North, 2 Cork, nh AAA
Not ranked
    **Dalia Mikneviciute** (Lit) 5.9.70 1.87?    1.80, 1.80, 1.78, 1.75, 1.75, 1.70; 1.83i; 3 South
Overall it was not a particularly good year for British women's high jumping, although 11 women over 1.80 was the same as in 1994. Haggett regained the top ranking she had enjoyed in 1990 and Davies, in her record 18th year in the rankings, was never worse than 2nd in any competition outdoors and achieved her highest position since 1988. There was encouragement to be gained from the big improvements made by the juniors Dunkley and Forrest, both newcomers to the rankings, with three more under 20s in the top ten.

## POLE VAULT
1. **Kate Staples** 2.11.65 (3y, 1) 3.65 '94    3.80, 3.70, 3.60, 3.52, 3.50; 3.90 ex, 3.75 ex; 3.80i, 3.75i, 3.70i;
   1 Bedford, 2 GhG, 1 WG, 2 AAA
2. **Linda Stanton** 22.6.73 (3y, 4) 3.40 '93    3.72, 3.70, 3.70, 3.70, 3.70, 3.60; 3 Ljubljana, 1 CAU,
   1 AAA v LC, 1 North, 3 GhG, 2 WG, 6 AAA, 3 BUPA, 3 v USA, 1 U23 Int, 1 Copenhagen, 3 HUN int, 1 Stoke
3= **Clare Ridgley** 11.9.77 (3y, 3) 3.44 '94    3.45, 3.40, 3.40, 3.40, 3.30, 3.30; 3.40i;
   1 NvST, 1 Sth J, 2 CAU, 2 AAA v LC, 5 GhG, 2 AAA-J, 5 AAA, 3 v Fra J, 2 Stoke
3= **Rhian Clarke** 19.4.77 (3y, 5) 3.30 '93    3.50, 3.40, 3.40, 3.40, 3.35, 3.30;
   3 N vST, 1 IR, 7 CAU, 2 Bedford, 3 AAA v LC, 1 AAA-J, 2 v Fra J, 4= v USA
5. **Claire Morrison** 30.5.69 (3y, 6) 3.24 '94    3.30, 3.30, 3.20, 3.20, 3.20, 3.20; 3.40i, 3.30i, 3.30i;
   3 IR, 3 CAU, 4 AAA v LC, 1 Mid, 3 AAA, 6 BUPA, 6 v USA
6. **Louise Schramm** 18.12.71 (2y, -) 2.90 '93    3.30, 3.20, 3.20, 3.10, 3.10, 3.00;
   2 NvST, 2 B.Univs, 2 IR, 4 CAU, 4 Bedford, 5 AAA v LC, 1 South, 3 WG, 4 AAA,1 Grimsby
7= **Janine Whitlock** 11.8.73 (1y, -) 3.10i '94    3.41, 3.31, 3.15, 3.11, 3.10, 3.00; 3.60i, 3.20i;
   6 IR, 2 North, 1 Scot, 8 AAA, 3 U23 Int, 1 Nth IC, 1 UKPVA, 2 Grimsby
8. **Katie Alexander** 28.4.74 (2y, 10) 3.00 '94    3.10, 3.00, 3.00, 3.00;
   4 NvST, 1 B.Univs, 5 CAU, 6 AAA v LC
9. **Paula Wilson** 20.11.69 (2y, 2) 3.45 '94    3.20; 3.50i; 4 Ljubljana

10.　**Dawn-Alice Wright** 20.1.76 (3y, 7) 3.10 '94　　3.00, 3.00, 2.90, 2.90, 2.90, 2.80; 3.00i;
　　　5 IR, 6 CAU, 5 Bedford, 2 Mid, 3 AAA-J, 3 Stoke
11.　**Katharine Horner** 6.1.78 (1y, -) 2.70 '94　　3.00, 3.00, 3.00, 2.90, 2.80, 2.80;
　　　2 Sth J, 7 Bedford, 2 South, 12= AAA, 3 Stoke
12.　**Susie Drummie** 19.6.71 (1y, -) 2.95 '93　3.00, 2.90, 2.80, 2.80, 2.80; 3.10i, 3.00i, 3.00i; 6 Bedford, 12= AAA
Ranked for the third year, there was again a good improvement in standards with eight women clearing 3.20 or higher.
Staples added five indoor and two outdoor British records to her collection, although her sequence was interrupted
by Stanton, who joined her in international class. Ridgley and Clarke, third equal, remain juniors for 1996.

## LONG JUMP
1.　**Denise Lewis** 27.8.72 (4y, 2) 6.56 '94　　6.67, 6.66w, 6.57, 6.56, 6.52, 6.51;
　　　1 Mid, 8 ECp, 3H Helmond, 2 AAA, 1 v USA, 1 Cup
2.　**Yinka Idowu** 25.2.72 (7y, 1) 6.73 '93　　6.54w, 6.38, 6.35, 6.34, 6.20; 6.46i, 6.35i;
　　　1 E Clubs, 2H Helmond, 3 AAA, 4 Hechtel
3.　**Vikki Schofield** 29.12.72 (2y, 8=) 6.07 '94　6.28, 6.16, 6.03, 6.00, 5.97; 6.13i, 6.11i, 5.98i;　4 AAA, 4 v USA
4.　**Liz Ghojefa** 24.2.69 (3y, 6) 6.25 '94　　6.27, 6.18, 6.07w (6.03), 6.06, 6.03, 6.01;
　　　1 NvST, 3 Surrey, 4 CAU, 2 AAA v LC, 1 South, 5 AAA, 5 v USA, 2 Kilkenny, 2 Plate
5.　**Ann Brooks** 4.5.71 (2y, 4) 6.14/6.38w '94　6.16, 6.12, 6.12w (6.07), 6.02, 5.98, 5.98; 6.00i;
　　　2 Lough 26/4, 1 IR, 1 CAU, 3 AAA v LC, 2 WG, 6 AAA, BL3: 1,-,1
6.　**Jade Johnson** 7.6.80 (1y, -) 5.68 '94　　6.24w (6.13), 6.22w, 5.99, 5.95w, 5.90w, 5.84;
　　　1 Sth U17, 2 AAA-J, 1 E.Sch-I, 1 Sch.Int, 1 AAA U17, 2 v Fra J, 1 Jnr IA
7.　**Jacqui White** 12.1.71 (3y, 11) 5.98 '94, 6.06w '93　　6.11w, 6.01w, 5.98w (5.85), 5.97, 5.95w (5.87), 5.88;
　　　2 IR, 3 CAU, 2 Mid, 1 WG
8.　**Diana Davies** 8.6.75 (2y, -) 6.17/6.32w '88　　6.05, 6.01, 5.88w (5.82), 5.85, 5.76; 3 IR, 2 CAU
9.　**Ruth Irving** 20.7.74 (3y, 3) 6.28 '94　　6.13, 6.00, 5.95, 5.90, 5.87, 5.82;
　　　1 Lough 26/4, 1 B.Univs, 1 CU v OU, 4 AAA v LC, 2 North, 9 AAA, 2 S.Nat, 6 U23 Int
10.　**Debbie Marti** 14.5.68 (2y, -) 6.19 '92, 6.22w '85　　6.21w, 5.98, 5.81; 1 Surrey, 1 Cup sf WL, 1 Plate
11.　**Paula Thomas** 3.12.64 (1y, -) 6.01 '86, 6.07w '88　　6.04, 6.03, 5.83; BL1: 1,1,1
12.　**Julia Bennett** 26.3.70 (1y, -) 6.12 '94　　6.02w, 6.00w, 5.99w, 5.93, 5.87, 5.79; 2 Surrey, 5 AAA v LC, 1 Kilkenny
not ranked
　　　**Ashia Hansen** 5.12.71 (2y, 5) 6.27 '94　　6.12w; 1 Middlesex
Lewis and Idowu swap places at the top, while Fiona May, our no.1 1987-93, became world champion for Italy. Coming
in at no.6 is Jade Johnson, at 16 the youngest to be ranked that high since Joanne Wise in 1987. Davies has only once
before been ranked, 6th equal in1988. The tenth best level on the UK lists (legal jumps) was 5.98, the lowest since
1973. Back in 1970 the 10th best was 6.09 and the record 10th best is 6.30 in 1984.

## TRIPLE JUMP
1.　**Ashia Hansen** 5.12.71 (5y, 2) 14.22 '94　　14.66, 14.45, 14.45, 14.38, 14.37, 14.16; 14.29i;
　　　2 Ljubljana, 3 Bratislava, 3 Moscow, 1 ECp, 3 GhG, 6 KP, dnq 21 WCh, 6 Zürich, 1 v USA, 3 Brussels, 5 GPF
2.　**Michelle Griffith** 6.10.71 (6y, 1) 14.08 '94　　14.03, 13.98, 13.80, 13.78w, 13.73, 13.68; 13.80i, 13.76i;
　　-6 Seville, 8 Rome, 2 B'zona, 7 GhG, 8 KP, 1 AAA, 7 Oslo, 3 BUPA, 12 WCh, 11 Zürich, 2 v USA, 3 McD, 1 Cup
3.　**Rachel Kirby** 18.5.69 (5y, 3) 13.64 '94　　13.23, 13.18w, 13.15, 13.13, 12.98, 12.96; 13.38i, 13.27i, 13.15i;
　　　5 Ljubljana, 3 B'zona, 8 GhG, 13 KP, 2 AAA, 6 BUPA, 6 v USA
4.　**Karen Skeggs** 26.10.69 (6y, 7=) 12.89/12.93w '92　　12.50, 12.47w, 12.37, 12.31, 12.21w, 12.12; 12.24i;
　　　2 CAU, 2 South, 1 Scot, 3 AAA, 1 S.Nat, 2 Cup sf Liverpool, 1 Plate
5.　**Liz Ghojefa** 24.2.69 (5y, 9) 12.64 '93　　12.49w, 12.37, 12.25, 12.22, 12.09; 1 Croydon, 2 Plate
6.　**Evette Finikin** 25.9.63 (6y, 5) 13.46 '91　　12.39, 12.11, 12.11, 11.99, 11.66; 12.68i, 12.63i, 12.62i, 12.56i,
　　　12.34i; 1 CAU, 1 South, 1 Cup sf Derby, 5 Cup, BL1: -,4,4
7.　**Elizabeth Gibbens** 5.4.77 (1y, -) 11.35/11.65w '94　　12.42, 12.28, 12.20, 11.95w, 11.94w;
　　　2 AAA-J, 1 E.Sch, 6 U23 Int, 2 Croydon, 1 Jnr IA
8.　**Debbie Rowe** 8.9.72 (2y, 12) 12.00 '94　　12.44, 12.19w, 12.16, 12.10, 12.10, 12.01;
　　　3 B.Univs, 1 IR, 3 CAU, 1 Mid, 5 AAA, 2 Cup, BL1: -,2,1
9.　**Lorna Turner** 11.5.72 (4y, 6) 12.94 '94　 ̄12.40w, 12.34w, 12.32, 12.16, 11.93, 11.92;
　　　3 South, 1 Cup sf Liverpool, 3 Cup, BL1: 1,1,3
10.　**Katie Evans** 4.2.74 (1y, -) 12.01 '94　　12.20, 12.17w (12.12), 12.14, 11.99w; 2 Mid, 2 BL1 (3), 4 Cup
11　**Caroline Stead** 14.9.71 (2y, 11) 12.17 '94　　12.15w (11.94), 12.14, 12.02, 11.99, 11.97, 11.89;
　　　2 IR, 4 CAU, 4 South, 4 AAA, 3 Cup sf Derby, 3 Plate
12　**Pamela Anderson** 16.10.76 (1y, -) 11.43 '94. 11.50w '93　　12.10, 11.91, 11.77, 11.71, 11.56;
　　　3 Scot, 4 AAA-J, 1 Scot-J, 2 v Fra J, 5 BL1 (3)
not ranked
　　　**Connie Henry** 15.4.72 (3y, 4) 13.31 '94　　13.01i
Hansen set two British records indoors and five outdoors to rank in the world top ten and become UK no.1 for the first
time. Griffith again showed great competitive ability, making her second World Championships final, and Kirby

118

remains 3rd. There was then, however, a big gap to the rest.

## SHOT
1. **Judy Oakes** 14.2.58 (19y, 1) 19.36 '88    18.44, 18.26, 18.25, 18.20, 18.17, 18.13; 1 South, 3 ECp, 6 KP,
   4 GhG, 1 AAA, 1 Braintree, 1 Cup sf Enfield, dnq 17 WCh, 3 v USA, 6 McD, 1 Kilkenny, 1 London
2. **Margaret Lynes** 19.2.63 (11y, 3) 16.57 '94    16.24, 16.15, 16.12, 16.05, 16.02, 16.02; 16.15i, 16.08i;
   1 Kent, 2 E.Clubs, 1 AAA v LC, 2 South, 7 GhG, 2 AAA, 2 Braintree, 1 Cup sf Liverpool, 5 v USA, 8 McD, 1 Cup
3. **Myrtle Augee** 4.2.65 (14y, 2) 19.03 '90    15.70, 13.68, 13.56; 1 Cup sf WL, 1 Plate
4. **Tracy Axten** 20.7.63 (1y, -) 14.15 '94    14.90, 14.51, 14.51, 14.50, 14.50, 14.47;
   2 CAU, 4 South, 4 AAA, 3 Braintree, 1 WG, 2 Cup sf Liverpool, 6 v USA, 2 London, BL3: 1,-,1
5. **Debbie Callaway** 15.7.64 (4y, 7) 14.88 '93    14.80, 14.53, 14.44, 14.39, 14.37, 14.34;
   1 NvST, 2 Essex, 2 IR, 1 CAU, 2 AAA v LC, 4 Braintree, 2 Cup sf Enfield, 2 Kilkenny, 2 Cup, 3 London, BL2: 1,1,1
6. **Alison Grey** 12.5.73 (6y, 6) 15.85i/15.69 '94    14.43, 14.39, 13.61, 13.44; 15.36i, 15.30i, 15.20i;
   1 Scot, BL1: 1,-,1
7. **Sharon Andrews** 4.7.67 (11y, 5) 15.80 '93    14.60, 14.35, 14.04, 13.85; 14.95i, 14.88i, 14.44i;
   1 Essex, BL1: -,1,2
8. **Carol Cooksley** 22.9.69 (9y, 11) 14.71 '90, 14.76i '91    14.23, 14.15, 14.09, 14.07, 14.05, 13.90;
   1 IR, 4 CAU, 2 Mid, 3 AAA, 3 Cup sf Enfield, 3 Cup, BL1: 2,2,3
9. **Uju Efobi** 10.10.74 (3y, 8) 15.21 '94    14.42, 14.25, 14.21, 13.84, 13.83, 13.71; 13.85i;
   2 Kent, 3 CAU, 5 South, 7 AAA
10. **Philippa Roles** 1.3.78 (1y, -) 13.68i/13.65 '94    14.11, 13.95, 13.84, 13.77, 13.75, 13.66; 13.96i;
    1 BL4 (1), 1 Welsh J, 4 IR, 3 AAA v LC, 1 AAA J, 3 Yth Oly, 1 S.Nat, 2 WG, 2 v Fra J, 1 Jnr IA
11. **Helen Wilding** 25.10.76 (1y, -) 13.17 '94    13.88, 13.73, 13.72, 13.70, 13.65, 13.64;
    1 North J, 4 AAA v LC, 1 North, 1 E.Sch, 2 AAA J, 5 AAA, 6 U23 Int, BL3: 2,-,3
12. **Joanne Duncan** 27.12.66 (2y, -) 14.17 '93    14.29, 13.98, 13.36, 13.22, 12.74, 12.67;
    3 Essex, 3 South, 3 WG, 9 AAA, BL1: -,3,5
not ranked
    **Clova Court** 10.2.60 (2y, -) 14.23 '93    14.08, 13.45, 13.40; 2 IR, 3 Cup sf Liverpool
Judy Oakes achieves a record 13th number one ranking and was a long way ahead of Lynes in the absence for most
of the year of Augee. Axten had not ranked before at this event, but was most consistent and jumped in at no.4.The
other newcomer to the top ten was 16 year-old Roles.

## DISCUS
1. **Jacqueline McKernan** 1.7.65 (11y, 1) 60.72 '93    59.06, 58.90, 58.88, 58.62, 58.38, 56.58;
   1 B.Univs, 8 Halle, 1 E.Clubs, 2 AAA v LC, 5 ECp, 1 NI, 2 AAA, 1 Cup sf Liverpool, dnq 26 WCh, 3 v USA, 1 Plate
2. **Debbie Callaway** 15.7.64 (12y, 3) 55.66 '94    57.00, 55.72, 54.56, 54.52, 54.34, 54.10;
   1 NvST, 1 Essex, 1 IR, 1 AAA v LC, 1 South, 2 WG, 4 AAA, 1 Braintree, 1 Cup sf Enfield, 4 v USA,
   1 Croydon, 2 Kilkenny, 1 Cup, 2 London, BL2: 1,1,1
3. **Shelley Drew** 8.8.73 (4y, 6) 54.60 '94    55.70, 55.18, 54.06, 54.00, 53.76, 53.74;
   2 NvST, 2 B.Univs, 10 Halle, 2 IR, 1 CAU, 3 AAA v LC, 2 South, 3 AAA, 1 U23 Int, 6 v USA, 2 Croydon
4. **Emma Beales** 7.12.71 (5y, 4) 53.78 '93    54.68, 53.34, 51.60, 51.52, 51.46, 50.84;
   3 CAU, 1 Bedford, 5 AAA, 2 Cup sf Enfield, 4 Plate
5. **Tracy Axten** 20.7.63 (7y, 7) 54.40 '93    53.62, 53.62, 52.06, 51.96, 51.06, 51.04;
   2 CAU, 2 Bedford, 4 AAA v LC, 3 South, 3 WG, 7 AAA, 2 Braintree, 2 Cup sf Liverpool, 1 London, BL3: 1,-,1
6. **Sharon Andrews** 4.7.67 (9y, 2) 56.24 '94    53.18, 51.34, 51.18, 50.28, 49.52, 48.82;
   2 Essex, 4 E Clubs, 3 Cup sf Liverpool, 2 Cup, BL1: -,1,2
7. **Sarah Winckless** 18.10.73 (4y, 16) 53.16 '94    52.58, 51.10, 48.76, 48.42, 48.10, 47.20;
   3 NvST, 6 AAA v LC, 6 U23 Int, 4 Croydon, 2 Plate
8. **Lorraine Shaw** 2.4.68 (3y, 5) 55.04 '94    51.38, 50.72, 50.42, 49.58, 49.48, 49.06; 3 IR, 1 Mid
9. **Emma Merry** 2.7.74 (6y, 11=) 52.58 '93    50.58, 49.32, 49.14, 48.52, 47.68, 47.56;
   3 B.Univs, 6 CAU, 7 AAA v LC, 1 BL1 (3)
10. **Judy Oakes** 14.2.58 (8y, -) 53.44 '88    50.56, 49.90, 48.22, 46.00, 43.66; 1 Surrey, 4 Kilkenny, 2 London
11. **Myrtle Augee** 4.2.65 (1y, -) 46.64 '92    49.44, 47.92, 47.84, 47.76, 47.70, 47.58;
    7 CAU, 5 South, 6 AAA, 3 Braintree, 3 Plate
12. **Philippa Roles** 1.3.78 (1y, -) 48.88 '94    49.12, 48.16, 48.00, 47.62, 47.24, 46.60;
    1 Welsh J, 1 BL4 (1), 1 IR, 1 Welsh, 3 AAA-J, 4 WG, 10 AAA, 2 S.Nat, 1 v Fra J, 12 EJ, 1 Jnr IA
not ranked
    **Rosanne Lister** (5y, 9) 53.66 '91    48.64, 47.90, 47.48, 47.02, 46.80, 46.56
3 Essex, 6 South, 8 AAA, 3 Croydon
    **Nicola Talbot** 17.2.72 (3y, 11=) 54.24 '93    48.32, 47.78, 47.64, 46.84, 46.70, 46.26; 4 IR, 2 Mid, 11 AAA
McKernan was number one for the 7th time. Callaway beat Drew 6-1 for a clear second place. Drew in turn was 3-0
up on Beales, who beat Axten 2-1. There were no newcomers to the rankings.

# HAMMER

1. **Lorraine Shaw** 2.4.68 (3y, 1) 59.92 '94    64.90, 63.80, 62.30, 61.56, 60.96, 60.76, 60.56, 60.24;
   1 Colindale, 1 Wimb. Pk, 1 Rehlingen, 3 Halle, 1 IR, 1 Bedford, 1 Mid, 1 WG, 3 AAA, 1 v USA
2. **Lyn Sprules** 11.9.75 (3y, 2) 55.44 '94    55.32, 54.44, 53.52, 53.50, 53.04, 52.86;
   1 CAU, 4 Bedford, 1 South, 2 WG, 4 AAA, 2 U23 Int, 6 v USA, BL3: 1,1,-
3. **Diana Holden** 12.2.75 (5y, 3) 53.34 '94    54.42, 53.24, 52.32, 52.14, 50.88, 50.64;
   2 B.Univs, 1 N v ST, 5 IR, 6 Bedford, 9 South, 5 AAA, 3 U23 Int, 4 v USA, 1 Kilkenny
4. **Sarah Moore** 15.3.73 (4y, 4) 50.52 '94    53.00, 52.88, 51.82, 51.56, 51.40, 51.24;
   1 B.Univs, 4 Colindale, 4 IR, 2 CAU, 5 Bedford, 1 Welsh, 3 WG, 6 AAA, 1 S.Nat, 1 BL4 (2)
5. **Ann Gardner** 11.10.68 (4y, 4) 54.02 '93    51.72, 51.32, 50.88, 50.46, 50.10, 50.04;
   3/3 Colindale, 3 Wimb. Pk, 3 IR, 5 CAU, 7 Bedford, 2 Mid, 9 AAA
6. **Jean Clark** 5.10.68 (5y, 7=) 49.78 '92    50.12, 48.78, 48.06, 47.86, 47.82, 47.78;
   6 Colindale, 4 Wimb. Pk, 4 CAU, 2 South, 2 Scot, 7 AAA, 2 S.Nat, 1 Cup sf Enfield, 2 Kilkenny, 1 Plate
7. **Samantha Burns-Salmond** 13.4.76 (2y, 12=) 45.48 '94    49.48, 49.46, 48.68, 48.42, 48.42, 47.86;
   3 B.Univs, 1 Nth J, 6 IR, 3 CAU, 8 Bedford, 2 North, 4 Scot, 3 AAA-J, 8 AAA, 3 v Fra J, 1 Jnr IA, 1 BL3 (3)
8. **Julie Lavender** 9.11.75 (4y, 6) 51.62 '94    49.86, 49.46, 48.10, 47.16, 45.84, 45.44;
   7/5 Colindale, 7 IR, 1 North, 1 Scot, 13 AAA, 1 Nth IC
9. **Julie Kirkpatrick** 14.7.72 (2y, -) 46.68 '93    48.56, 48.12, 46.64, 46.02, 45.76, 45.56;
   3 Scot, 1 NI, 11 AAA, 3 S.Nat, 2 Cup sf Liverpool
10. **Irene Duffin** 10.8.60 (2y, 9=) 46.14 '94    47.74, 47.36, 47.22, 46.84, 46.58, 46.56;
    5 Colindale, 2 N v ST, 6 CAU, 9 Bedford, 3 South, 10 AAA, 1 Cup sf Derby, 3 Cup, BL1: 1,1,1
11. **Caroline Manning** 5.3.73 (2y, -) 46.82 '93    47.06, 46.86, 46.60, 46.54, 46.10, 45.54;
    4 B.Univs, 5 Wimb. Pk, 9 CAU, 4 South, 12 AAA, 3 Cup sf Derby
12. **Helen Arnold** 5.10.78 (1y, -) 42.12 '94    46.98, 45.30, 45.12, 44.50, 44.18, 44.14;
    1 Sth J, 4 AAA J, 1 AAA U17, 6 v Fra J, 2 Jnr IA

not ranked

**Angela Bonner** 22.11.73 (3y, 12=) 45.44 '94    46.64, 46.64, 44.48, 43.84, 42.98, 40.86;
4 WG, 2 Cup sf Enfield, BL3: 3,3,2

**Esther Augee** 1.1.64 (3y, 7=) 56.76 '93    46.52, 44.32, 43.82; 3 Cup sf Liverpool, 4 BL1 (3), 1 Cup

Shaw was top for the third successive year and improved the British record seven times in all to add a further five metres to her 1994 best and to rank 5th in the world. She later won against the USA on the first occasion that the women's hammer has been included in a UK international match. Sprules and Holden retain their 2nd and 3rd place rankings, while Moore and Gardner swap places. The 10th best of 47.74 is the best yet.

# JAVELIN

1. **Sharon Gibson** 31.12.61 (16y, 1) 62.32 '87    58.10, 57.46, 57.24, 56.98, 55.14, 548;
   1 Mid, 7 ECp, 2 AAA, 1 v USA, 5 Copenhagen
2. **Shelley Holroyd** 17.5.73 (7y, 2) 60.10 '93    55.16, 54.92, 52.76, 52.08; 1 BL1 (2), 4 AAA, 1 Cup
3. **Lorna Jackson** 9.1.74 (3y, 10) 54.62 '94    55.48, 52.86, 52.52, 52.08, 51.88, 51.34;
   1 CAU, 1 Scot, 1 AAA, 2 S.Nat, 2 U23 Int, 5 v USA, 2 Cup, BL1: 2,2,1
4. **Karen Martin** 24.11.74 (4y, 7) 55.72 '92    54.96, 53.52, 53.20, 52.24, 50.44, 50.38;
   3 IR, 2 Bedford 25/6, 1 IS, 2 WG, 3 AAA, 4 U23 Int, 6 v USA, 1 Nth IC, BL2: 1,-,1
5. **Kirsty Morrison** 28.10.75 (5y, 6) 59.36 '93    53.80, 50.34, 49.84, 49.42, 48.22, 47.50;
   1 NvST, 4 CAU, 1 Bedford 25/6, 6 AAA, 1 Kilkenny, BL3: 2,2,1
6. **Denise Lewis** 27.8.72 (1y, -) 53.68 '94    49.76, 49.70, 49.34, 48.98, 45.76, 45.60;
   3 Mid, 3 BL1 (2), 2 Cup sf Liverpool, 3 Cup
7. **Amanda Liverton** 1.9.72 (8y, 8) 57.84 '90    49.94, 49.08, 48.68; 1 South, 3 WG
8. **Noelle Bradshaw** 18.12.63 (4y, 9) 52.40 '93    49.66, 49.34, 48.24, 47.76, 47.36, 47.10;
   1 NvST, 2 IR, 2 CAU, 2 South, 8 AAA
9. **Janine King** 18.2.73 (1y, -) 49.50 '94    49.24, 48.54, 48.42, 47.90, 47.76, 46.78;
   1 IR, 10 AAA, BL1: 1,4,3
10. **Karen Costello** 21.10.68 (2y, 4) 54.50 '94    48.82, 48.50; 3 BL1 (2), 2 Scot
11. **Michelle Fields** 15.5.73 (2y, -) 50.48 '93    48.30, 47.46, 46.56, 46.46, 46.30, 46.28;
    4 IR, 5 CAU, 2 Mid, 4 WG, 11 AAA, 1 Cup sf Liverpool, BL2: 2,1,2
12. **Onyema Amadi** 28.6.73 (1y, -) 49.04 '94    48.34, 47.64, 47.32, 46.28, 44.38, 43.48;
    7 IR, 1 Welsh, 5 WG, 7 AAA, 3 S.Nat, BL3: 1,1,2

Gibson is 1st for the third successive year. Holroyd only had four competitions, but beat Jackson, who made the most progress, 2-1 to take second ranking. Disappointingly only five women beat 50 metres, and the 10th best of 48.82 is the worst since 1981.

# HEPTATHLON

1. **Denise Lewis** 27.8.72 (7y, 1) 6325 '94    6299, 6299, 6255; 6 Götzis, 1 ECp, 7 WCh
2. **Yinka Idowu** 25.2.72 (4y, -) 5496 '89    5702, 5655; 6 Alhama, 17 ECp
3. **Emma Beales** 7.12.71 (5y, -) 5632 '93    5609, 5524, 5524w; 1 AAA, 22 ECp, 1 HCI
4. **Vikki Schofield** 29.12.72 (5y, 3) 5671 '94    5551, 5506; 1g Mid, 3 HCI
5. **Julia Bennett** 26.3.70 (4y, 11) 5239 '94    5496, 5422, 5244; 2g North, 8 Alhama, 24 ECp
6. **Claire Phythian** 7.2.73 (4y, 8) 5372 '94    5455, 5451, 5173; 8 Azusa, 8 NCAA, dnf U23 v Rus
7. **Pauline Richards** 30.6.68 (2y, 5) 5420 '94    5417, 5160; 2 (1) Mid, 3 HCI
8. **Sarah Damm** 12.9.70 (1y, -) 5112 '94    5392, 5364; 1g North, 9 Alhama, dnf AAA
9. **Jennifer Kelly** 20.6.70 (8y, 2) 5826 '94    5338, 5298; 11 Alhama, 2 AAA
10. **Kerry Jury** 19.11.68 (6y, 9) 5335 '93    5368, 5037, 5018; 4g North, 3 AAA, 3g Mid
11. **Diana Bennett** 14.6.74 (2y, 10) 5212 '94    5220, 5052; 3g North, dnf AAA, 6 U23 v Rus
12. **Emma Lindsay** 11.4.71 (4y, 7) 5353 '94    5108, 5056, 4895; 1 B.Univs, 1 Scot, 5 HCI
not ranked
    **Clova Wynter-Pink** 29.11.77 (0y, -) 4861 '94    5143, 4973, 4890; 2 AAA-J, 1 Portsmouth, 4 v Rus-J
With three scores over 6250 Lewis consolidated her position as a world-class multi-eventer. Some way back in second place, Idowu returned successfully to the event, for the first time since 1991. The 10th best of 5338 is the highest ever. HCI = Home Countries International

# WALKS
At 3000m to 10,000m performances are on the track, unless indicated by R for road marks. All longer distances are on the road. Previous bests are shown for track 5000m and road or track 10km.
Priority is given in these rankings to form at the standard international distance of 10 kilometres, although performances at 3000m, 5000m and 20km are also taken into account.
1. **Lisa Langford** 15.3.67 (11y, 2)  21:57.68 '90, 45:42R '87, 48:34.0t '86    3km: 13:12.6, 13:29.4+; 1 B.Univs
    5km: 22:20.03; 22:22R, 23:00R, 23:24R, 23:25+R; 1 AAA; 1 Mid, 1 NAT
    10km: 46:00R, 46:06R, 46:34R, 47:13R, 47:30R, 48:04R; 2 UK, 36 WCp, 16 7N, 35 WCh, 1 Leicester (Mid)
2. **Victoria Lupton** 17.4.72 (7y, 1)  22:12.21 '92, 46:30.0t/45:46R '94, 45:28 sh '94
    3km: 12:59.3, 13:17.68, 13:29.5+, 13:51.0; 13:22R; 1 CAU
    5km: 21:52.38, 22:15.4, 22:23.80, 22:38.93, 23:21.0; 23:12R, 23:20R; 1 North, 2 AAA; 1 C'field, 2 NAT
    10km: 45:18.8, 46:40R, 47:02R, 47:02R, 47:04R, 47:13+R, 47:26.2; 3 Manx, 1 UK, 51 WCp, 4 Fana, 15 7N,
    1 AAA, 2 Leicester, 2 v IRE    10M: 1:21:23; 1 RWA    20km: 1:42:47; 1 RWA
3. **Carolyn Partington** 27.6.66 (3y, 4) 24:38.68 '93, 47:21R '94, 50:43.87 '93
    3km: 13:13.3, 13:19.29, 13:33.6+; 2 CAU    5km: 22:41.19; 23:50R; 3 AAA
    10km: 46:26R, 47:14R, 47:21R, 48:17R; 2 Manx, 60 WCp, 17 7N, 1 Stockport
4. **Verity Snook** (née Larby) 13.11.70 (7y, 3)  23:22.52 '94, 46:06R '94
    3km: 13:32.90, 13:38.19, 13:55.0; 13:41.53i; 1 IR, 4 CAU
    5km: 23:38.85, 23:58.84; 22:58R, 23:35R, 24:07R; 5 AAA, 1 S.Nat
    10km: 48:47R, 48:50R; 13 Palma, 16 WCp
5. **Melanie Wright** (née Brookes) 5.4.64 (6y, 6)  23:57.0 '94, 48:18R/49:15.2t '92, 47:40Rsh '93
    3km: 13:59.58, 14:10.0; 2 IR    5km: 24:04.57; 23:24R, 24:30R; 6 AAA; 2 C'field
    10km: 48:35.8, 48:44R, 48:48R, 49:19R, 49:23R, 49:28R; 3 UK, 16 Palma, 82 WCp, 21 7N, 7 Fana, 1
    Yverdon, 2 AAA, 3 Leicester (2 Mid), 3 v IRE
6. **Kim Baird** 28.2.56 (3y, 10) 26:35.0 '91, 51:46R '93    3km: 14:17.74; 3 IR;  5km: 24:16.4
    10km: 49:39R, 49:43R , 51:00R, 51:06R; 1 Welsh, 10 Ozd, 3 Stockport, 4g v IRE
7. **Elaine Callanin** 13.9.60 (11y, 6)  24:13.4 '81, 49:17R '94, 51:51.0t '80
    5km: 24:09.66; 23:45R, 24:05R, 24:06R, 24:35R; 7 AAA; 4 C'field
    10km: 49:41.0, 50:05R, 50:53R, 51:12R; 4 UK, 3 IA, 3 Welsh, 11 Ozd    20km: 1:46:31R; 2 RWA
8. **Sylvia Black** 16.4.58 (12y, 7)  23:34.43 '92, 47:59R '92    3km: 13:54.2i, 14:14.05i; 13:38R
    5km: 24:52.95; 23:32R, 24:10R, 24:28R, 24:32R; 8 AAA; 2 Mid, 3 C'field, 4 NAT
    10km: 49:27.0, 50:10R, 50:18R, 50:34R, 51:31R, 52:40.9; 6 UK, 2 IA, 2 Welsh, 24 Ozd, 3 AAA, 5 v Ire
    10M: 1:26:23; 2 RWA
9. **Karen Kneale** 23.4.69 (2y, 9) 51:22t '94    3km: 14:05.1, 14:18.1; 1 Manx
    5km: 24:21R    10km: 51:03.0, 51:09R, 51:23R, 51:51R, 52:56R; 5 UK, 5 IA, 17 Ozd, 4 Stockport, 6 v IRE
10. **Liz Corran** 23.9.55 (1y, -) 51:24.0t '94    3km: 14:11.1; 2 Manx    5km: 25:13.03; 2 North
    10km: 51:03.0, 51:34R, 51:38R, 52:50R; 4 Manx, 7 UK, 4 IA, 1 North    20km: 1:55:10R; 4 RWA
WCp = World Cup, 7N = international at Forgères
Langford beat Lupton in both World Cup and Champs and 3-2 overall at 10k, so these two exchange places and Langford is top for the first time since 1990. Her four years at the top equals the record for women's walks. Partington and Snook also swap places. Black's 21-year span in the rankings is a record for any woman's event, beating the previous best set, 1972-92, by Chris Cahill.

*With thanks to Tony Miller, Alan Lindop, Ian Hodge, Tony O'Neill, Martin Rix, Matthew Fraser-Moat, John Powell and Colin Young for their comments.*

# 28 Years of UK Merit Rankings

Summary of achievements at standard events (not including occasional rankings for such events as men's 3000m, women's 200mh, 5000m)    + indicates would have added rankings pre 1968

## Leading points scorers    all events - 12 points for a first place to 1 point for 12th

### Men
| | | |
|---|---|---|
| 1. | Daley Thompson | 417.5 |
| 2. | Steve Ovett | 288 |
| 3. | Mike Winch | 281.5 |
| 4. | David Jenkins | 276 |
| 5. | Sebastian Coe | 262 |
| 6. | Linford Christie | 254 |
| 7. | Steve Cram | 252.5 |
| 8. | Brendan Foster | 244.5 |
| 9. | Alan Pascoe | 225 |
| 10. | Peter Tancred | 218 |
| 11. | John Regis | 213.5 |
| 12. | Bob Dobson | 213 |

### Women
| | | |
|---|---|---|
| 1. | Judy Simpson | 379 |
| 2. | Yvonne Murray | 311.5 |
| 3. | Sally Gunnell | 306.5 |
| 4. | Christina Cahill | 300.5 |
| 5. | Tessa Sanderson | 287 |
| 6. | Ann Simmonds + | 281 |
| 7. | Judy Oakes | 273.5 |
| 8. | Kathy Cook | 272.5 |
| 9. | Liz McColgan | 271.5 |
| 10. | Venissa Head | 243.5 |
| 11. | Sonia Lannaman | 234.5 |
| 12. | Margaret Ritchie | 234 |
| 13. | Sharon Colyear | 232 |

## Ranked at most events

### Men
9 Daley Thompson
   100m, 200m, 400m, 110mh, 400mh, HJ, PV, LJ, Dec
5 Paul Davies-Hale
   1500m, 5000m, 10,000m, Mar, 3000mSt
5 Peter Gabbet
   100m, 400m, PV, LJ, Dec
5 David Lewis
   1500m, 5000m, 10,000m, Mar, 3000mSt
5 Gus McKenzie
   200m, 110mh, HJ, LJ, Dec

## Range of distances
100m to 800m: Verona Elder
200m to 1500m: Lillian Board
800m to 10,000m: Yvonne Murray
1500m to Mar: Paul Davies-Hale
             David Lewis
             Liz McColgan
400m, 800m and Mar: Rosemary Wright

### Women
7 Sharon Colyear
   100m, 200m, 400m, 100mh, 400mh, LJ, Pen
6 Judy Vernon
   100m, 200m, 100mh, HJ, LJ, Hep
6 Mary Peters
   200m, 100mh, HJ, LJ, SP, Pen
6 Gladys Taylor
   100m, 200m, 400m, 400mh, LJ, Hep
6 Clova Court
   100m, 200m, 100mh, SP, JT, Hep
5 Verona Elder
   100m, 200m, 400m, 800m, 400mh
5 Sally Gunnell
   200m, 400m, 100mh, 400mh, Hep
5 Sue Reeve
   100mh, HJ, LJ, SP, Pen
5 Judy Simpson
   100mh, HJ, LJ, SP, Hep
5 Liz Sutherland

## Ranked at No.1 at three events
| | |
|---|---|
| David Bedford | 5000m, 10,000m, 3000mSt |
| Brendan Foster | 1500m, 5000m, 10,000m |
| Alan Lerwill | HJ, LJ, TJ |

| | |
|---|---|
| Lillian Board | 200m, 400m, 800m (all in '68) |
| Kathy Cook | 100m, 200m, 400m |
| Liz McColgan | 3000m, 10,000m, Mar |
| Joyce Smith | 1500m, 3000m, Mar |
| Yvonne Murray | 1500m, 3000m, 10,000m |

## Most successive years at No.1
| | | |
|---|---|---|
| 10 | Geoff Capes | SP 1971-80 |
| 10 | Margaret Ritchie | DT 1975-84 |
| 10 | Linford Christie | 100m 1968-95 |
| 8 | Mike Bull + | PV 1968-75 (1 tie) |
| 8 | David Travis | JT 1968-75 |
| 8 | Tessa Sanderson | JT 1974-81 |
| | (also 84, 89-92) | |

## Most perfect record
| | |
|---|---|
| Daley Thompson | No.1 all 12 years in Decathlon |
| Kriss Akabusi | No.1 all  7 years in 400mh |
| Sally Gunnell | No.1 all 7 years in 400mh |

## Most consecutive years ranked at an event
| | | |
|---|---|---|
| 25 | Bob Dobson | 50km W 1969-93 |
| 21 | Tessa Sanderson | JT 1972-92 |
| 19 | Keith Stock | PV 1973-91 |
| 19 | Peter Yates | JT 1976-94 |

# 1995 LISTS - MEN

## 60 METRES - Indoors

| | | | | | | | | |
|---|---|---|---|---|---|---|---|---|
| 6.47 | Linford Christie | | 2.04.60 | 1 | Lievin, FRA | | 19 | Feb |
| | 6.49 | | | 1 | Sindelfingen, GER | | 4 | Mar |
| | 6.55 | | | 2 | Birmingham | | 25 | Feb |
| | 6.56 | | | 1r1 | Glasgow | | 11 | Feb |
| | 6.56 | | | 1h1 | Lievin, FRA | | 19 | Feb |
| | 6.58 | | | 2 | Stockholm, SWE | | 27 | Feb |
| | 6.60 | | | 1 | Maebashi, JAP | | 5 | Feb |
| | 6.62 | | | 1 | Vienna, AUT | | 18 | Feb |
| | 6.64 | | | 1h1 | Birmingham | | 25 | Feb |
| | 6.65 | | | 1h2 | Vienna, AUT | | 18 | Feb |
| | 6.65 | | | 1h2 | Stockholm, SWE | | 27 | Feb |
| | 6.68 | | | 1h1 | Maebashi, JAP | | 5 | Feb |
| | 6.70 | | | 2h1 | Sindelfingen, GER | | 4 | Mar |
| 6.51 | Darren Braithwaite | | 20.01.69 | 2 | Barcelona, SPA | | 10 | Mar |
| | 6.54 | | | 1 | Birmingham | | 25 | Feb |
| | 6.54 | | | 1h3 | Barcelona, SPA | | 10 | Mar |
| | 6.57 | | | 1s3 | Barcelona, SPA | | 10 | Mar |
| | 6.58 | | | 5 | Lievin, FRA | | 19 | Feb |
| | 6.60 | | | 2h1 | Lievin, FRA | | 19 | Feb |
| | 6.61 | | | 2h2 | Birmingham | | 25 | Feb |
| | 6.63 | | | 1h1 | Stockholm, SWE | | 27 | Feb |
| | 6.65 | | | 1 | Glasgow | | 22 | Jan |
| | 6.65 | | | 2r1 | Glasgow | | 11 | Feb |
| | 6.65 | | | 3 | Stockholm, SWE | | 27 | Feb |
| | 6.67 | | | 1s1 | Glasgow | | 22 | Jan |
| | 6.69 | | | 2 | Birmingham | | 4 | Feb |
| | 6.70 | | | 1r2 | Glasgow | | 11 | Feb |
| 6.58 | Colin Jackson | | 18.02.67 | 1r1 | Birmingham | | 28 | Jan |
| | 6.62 | | | 3 | Stuttgart, GER | | 5 | Feb |
| 6.62 | Michael Rosswess | | 11.06.65 | 3s1 | Barcelona, SPA | | 10 | Mar |
| | 6.63 | | | 2r1 | Birmingham | | 28 | Jan |
| | 6.63 | | | 1 | Birmingham | | 4 | Feb |
| | 6.66 | | | 1s1 | Birmingham | | 4 | Feb |
| | 6.66 | | | 1 | Moscow, RUS | | 14 | Feb |
| | 6.68 | | | 2h7 | Barcelona, SPA | | 10 | Mar |
| 6.68 | Jason Fergus | U23 | 11.10.73 | 1r2 | Birmingham | | 28 | Jan |
| | 6.70 | | | 3 | Birmingham | | 4 | Feb |
| 6.70 | Dwain Chambers | U20 | 5.04.78 | 1r2 | Birmingham | | 29 | Jan |
| 38 performances to 6.70 by 6 athletes | | | | | | | | |
| 6.71 | Kevin Williams | | 15.12.71 | 7 | Birmingham | | 25 | Feb |
| 6.72 | John Regis | | 13.10.66 | 4 | Birmingham | | 4 | Feb |
| 6.73 | Jason Gardener | U23 | 18.09.75 | 1h1 | Vienna, AUT | | 18 | Feb |
| 6.74 | Tremayne Rutherford | | 19.06.72 | 5h2 | Birmingham | | 25 | Feb |
| | (10) | | | | | | | |
| 6.75 | Peter Maitland | U23 | 21.01.73 | 1r2 | Birmingham | | 25 | Feb |
| 6.76 | Martin Giraud | U20 | 16.11.77 | 1 | Birmingham | | 18 | Feb |
| 6.79 | Brian Taylor | | 13.08.70 | 3 | Vienna, AUT | | 18 | Feb |
| 6.79 | Andrew Mensah | | 30.11.71 | 2r1 | Birmingham | | 26 | Feb |
| 6.80 | Michael Afilaka | | 16.11.71 | 3 | St. Petersburg, RUS | 28 | Jan |
| 6.81 | Jamie Henderson | | 28.03.69 | 3 | Glasgow | | 22 | Jan |
| 6.82 | Doug Turner | | 2.12.66 | 2s2 | Birmingham | | 4 | Feb |
| 6.82 | Ayo Falola | | 29.07.68 | 3h1 | Vienna, AUT | | 18 | Feb |
| 6.84 | Terence Stamp | | 18.02.70 | 2h3 | Birmingham | | 4 | Feb |
| 6.84 | Allyn Condon | U23 | 24.08.74 | 1r2 | Birmingham | | 26 | Feb |
| | (20) | | | | | | | |
| *6.84* | *Josephus Thomas* | | *11.07.68* | *2* | *Nenagh, IRE* | | *5* | *Mar* |
| 6.85 | Trevor Cameron | U20 | 25.11.76 | 4r2 | Birmingham | | 28 | Jan |

| | | | | | | | | |
|---|---|---|---|---|---|---|---|---|
| 6.86 | Owusu Dako | U23 | 23.05.73 | 5s1 | Birmingham | 4 | Feb |
| 6.86 | Tony Ene | | 2.03.68 | 2h1 | Birmingham | 4 | Feb |
| 6.87 | Steve Gookey | | 21.04.71 | 1 | Sheffield | 22 | Jan |
| 6.87 | Toby Box | | 9.09.72 | 5r2 | Birmingham | 28 | Jan |
| 6.87 | Ejike Wodu | U23 | 15.12.74 | 3h2 | Birmingham | 4 | Feb |
| *6.87* | *Haroun Korjie* | | *17.02.72* | *6h5* | *Barcelona, SPA* | *10* | *Mar* |
| 6.89 | Ross Baillie | U20 | 26.09.77 | 1 | Glasgow | 14 | Jan |
| 6.89 | Fred Salle | | 10.09.64 | 5s3 | Birmingham | 4 | Feb |
| 6.89 | Marlon Devonish | U20 | 1.06.76 | 3h1 | Birmingham | 4 | Feb |
| 6.90 | Ewan Clark | | 4.04.69 | 2 | Glasgow | 15 | Jan |
| | (30) | | | | | | |
| 6.90 | Richard Rubenis | U23 | 10.11.73 | 4s2 | Glasgow | 22 | Jan |
| 6.90 | Mark Walcott | U23 | 24.11.73 | 3s2 | Glasgow | 22 | Jan |
| 6.91 | Steve Shanks | | 3.11.69 | 5s2 | Glasgow | 22 | Jan |
| 6.91 | Cypren Edmunds | | 20.06.70 | 4r1 | Birmingham | 29 | Jan |
| 6.91 | Daniel Money | U20 | 7.10.76 | 2s2 | Birmingham | 19 | Feb |
| 6.93 | Tunde Afilaka | | | 1h1 | Glasgow | 22 | Jan |
| 6.93 | Ray Burke | | 11.11.69 | 2h8 | Birmingham | 4 | Feb |
| 6.94 | Mclean Okotie | | 31.07.69 | 4h3 | Birmingham | 4 | Feb |
| 6.95 | Christian Malcolm | U17 | 3.06.79 | 1 | Birmingham | 28 | Jan |
| 6.95 | Paul Field | | 24.06.67 | 1H | Birmingham | 4 | Feb |
| | (40) | | | | | | |
| 6.96 | Maxwell Asare | | 14.09.68 | 3 | Sheffield | 22 | Jan |
| 6.96 | Bryn Middleton | U20 | 16.02.76 | 5 | Birmingham | 19 | Feb |
| 6.97 | Sam Omonua | U20 | 16.06.76 | 2s1 | Birmingham | 19 | Feb |
| 6.98 | Paul White | U23 | 1.09.74 | 4r2 | Birmingham | 29 | Jan |
| 6.98 | Jamie Baulch | U23 | 3.05.73 | 2h5 | Birmingham | 4 | Feb |
| 6.98 | Uvie Ugono | U20 | 8.03.78 | 3h5 | Birmingham | 19 | Feb |
| 6.99 | Neil Powell | U20 | 5.03.77 | 6 | Birmingham | 19 | Feb |

**Hand Timing**

| | | | | | | | |
|---|---|---|---|---|---|---|---|
| 6.8 | Danny Joyce | U23 | 9.09.74 | 1s | London (CP) | 21 | Jan |
| 6.9 | Mclean Okotie | | (6.94) | 1r10 | London (CP) | 11 | Jan |
| 6.9 | Ray Burke | | (6.93) | 1r12 | London (CP) | 11 | Jan |
| 6.9 | Tunde Afilaka | | (6.93) | 1 | London (CP) | 11 | Jan |
| 6.9 | Mark Lambeth | | 3.09.72 | 1h | London (Ha) | 14 | Jan |
| 6.9 | Terry Williams | | 15.11.68 | 1r1 | London (CP) | 15 | Feb |

**Additional Under 17** (1 above)

| | | | | | | | |
|---|---|---|---|---|---|---|---|
| 7.0 | Daniel Bonich | | 22.11.78 | 1 | London (CP) | 26 | Feb |
| 7.08 | | | | 3 | Birmingham | 28 | Jan |
| 7.01 | John Skeete | | 8.09.78 | 2 | Birmingham | 18 | Feb |
| 7.07 | Marlon Dickson | | 17.11.78 | 3 | Birmingham | 18 | Feb |

# 100 METRES

| | | | | | | | | |
|---|---|---|---|---|---|---|---|---|
| 9.97 A | 0.1 | Linford Christie | | 2.04.60 | 1 | Johannesburg, RSA | 23 | Sep |
| 10.00 | 0.6 | | | | 1 | Tokyo, JAP | 15 | Sep |
| 10.03 | -1.0 | | | | 1r1 | Zurich, SWZ | 16 | Aug |
| 10.05 | 2.0 | | | | 1 | Villeneuve d'Ascq, FRA | 24 | Jun |
| 10.06 | 0.8 | | | | 1 | Paris, FRA | 3 | Jul |
| 10.08 | 0.9 | | | | 1h2 | Oslo, NOR | 21 | Jul |
| 10.08 | -0.4 | | | | 1 | Brussels, BEL | 25 | Aug |
| 10.09 | 0.2 | | | | 1h3 | Zurich, SWZ | 16 | Aug |
| 10.10 | 0.0 | | | | 2r1 | Berlin, GER | 1 | Sep |
| 10.11 | 1.6 | | | | 1h1 | Perth, AUS | 29 | Jan |
| 10.12 | -0.8 | | | | 1 | Oslo, NOR | 21 | Jul |
| 10.12 | -0.2 | | | | 4s1 | Gothenburg, SWE | 6 | Aug |
| 10.12 | 1.0 | | | | 6 | Gothenburg, SWE | 6 | Aug |
| 10.15 | 0.8 | | | | 2r1 | Rome, ITA | 8 | Jun |
| 10.15 | 0.0 | | | | 1q2 | Gothenburg, SWE | 5 | Aug |

| | | | | | | | |
|---|---|---|---|---|---|---|---|
| (Christie) | 10.18 | -1.2 | | | 1 | Birmingham | 15 Jul |
| | 10.20 | 0.8 | | | 1 | Rieti, ITA | 5 Sep |
| | 10.20 | 0.1 | | | 5 | Monaco, MON | 9 Sep |
| | 10.26 | -0.1 | | | 1h8 | Gothenburg, SWE | 5 Aug |
| | 10.29 | 0.7 | | | 3h2 | Tokyo, JAP | 15 Sep |
| | 10.35 | -4.0 | | | 1 | Madrid, SPA | 20 Jun |
| | 10.45 | -1.4 | | | 1 | London (CP) | 3 Jun |
| | 10.48 | -2.0 | | | 1 | Adelaide, AUS | 26 Jan |
| 10.12 | 1.6 | Darren Braithwaite | | 20.01.69 | 1s1 | Birmingham | 15 Jul |
| | 10.18 A | 0.9 | | | 1h1 | Soria, SPA | 16 Jun |
| | 10.19 | 0.8 | | | 3h2 | Zurich, SWZ | 16 Aug |
| | 10.22 | 1.4 | | | 2r1 | Helsinki, FIN | 28 Jun |
| | 10.22 | -1.0 | | | 6 | Zurich, SWZ | 16 Aug |
| | 10.23 | -0.5 | | | 4q5 | Gothenburg, SWE | 5 Aug |
| | 10.24 | 1.0 | | | 3h1 | Oslo, NOR | 21 Jul |
| | 10.25 | 0.6 | | | 2h1 | Gothenburg, SWE | 5 Aug |
| | 10.26 | 0.8 | | | 2 | Bratislava, SVK | 30 May |
| | 10.28 | 1.8 | | | 7s2 | Gothenburg, SWE | 6 Aug |
| | 10.30 | -0.3 | | | 5 | London (CP) | 7 Jul |
| | 10.31 | -0.4 | | | 6 | Brussels, BEL | 25 Aug |
| | 10.33 | -1.5 | | | 1h3 | Birmingham | 15 Jul |
| | 10.33 | -1.2 | | | 2 | Birmingham | 15 Jul |

*Note AAA Champion, Christie ran as a guest*

| | | | | | | | |
|---|---|---|---|---|---|---|---|
| | 10.41 | -0.4 | | | 4 | Gateshead | 21 Aug |
| | 10.44 | 1.2 | | | 4 | Gateshead | 2 Jul |
| | 10.44 | 0.8 | | | 4 | Rieti, ITA | 5 Sep |
| | 10.45 | -0.9 | | | 3r2 | Berlin, GER | 1 Sep |
| 10.25 | 0.0 | Jason John | | 17.10.71 | 3h4 | Gothenburg, SWE | 5 Aug |
| | 10.26 A | 0.9 | | | 2h1 | Soria, SPA | 16 Jun |
| | 10.28 | 0.6 | | | 1s2 | Birmingham | 15 Jul |
| | 10.31 A | 1.5 | | | 1 | Soria, SPA | 16 Jun |
| | 10.34 | -1.2 | | | 3 | Birmingham | 15 Jul |
| | 10.38 | -0.4 | | | 3 | Gateshead | 21 Aug |
| | 10.39 | -0.8 | | | 5q3 | Gothenburg, SWE | 5 Aug |
| | 10.40 | -0.6 | | | 1r1 | Birmingham | 1 Jul |
| | 10.49 | -0.2 | | | 1h7 | Birmingham | 15 Jul |
| 10.29 A | 0.8 | Michael Rosswess | | 11.06.65 | 1 | Krugersdorp, RSA | 10 Apr |
| | 10.32 | 0.0 | | | 1 | Granada, SPA | 27 May |
| | 10.34 | 1.4 | | | 6r1 | Helsinki, FIN | 28 Jun |
| | 10.36 A | -0.7 | | | 1 | Pietersburg, RSA | 3 Apr |
| | 10.37 | -0.2 | | | 1 | Stellenbosch, RSA | 17 Apr |
| | 10.37 | 0.0 | | | 1 | Ljubljana, SLO | 21 May |
| | 10.40 | 1.6 | | | 2s1 | Birmingham | 15 Jul |
| | 10.49 | -2.0 | | | 1h1 | Granada, SPA | 27 May |
| 10.30 | 1.4 | Julian Golding | U23 | 17.02.75 | 3r1 | Helsinki, FIN | 28 Jun |
| | 10.34 | 1.3 | | | 1 | Narbonne, FRA | 29 Jul |
| | 10.38 | 0.8 | | | 1h1 | Geneva, SWZ | 17 Jun |
| | 10.38 | -0.5 | | | 2 | Geneva, SWZ | 17 Jun |
| 10.32 | 1.4 | Toby Box | | 9.09.72 | 5r1 | Helsinki, FIN | 28 Jun |
| | 10.39 | 1.3 | | | 5 | Fukuoka, JAP | 1 Sep |
| | 10.41 | 1.6 | | | 3s1 | Birmingham | 15 Jul |
| | 10.41 | -1.2 | | | 5 | Birmingham | 15 Jul |
| | 10.43 | -0.5 | | | 2q3 | Fukuoka, JAP | 31 Aug |
| | 10.49 | -0.5 | | | 1h2 | Birmingham | 15 Jul |
| 10.32 | 0.7 | John Regis | | 13.10.66 | 6r2 | Lausanne, SWZ | 5 Jul |
| | 10.41 | 1.6 | | | 3r1 | Cwmbran | 9 Jul |
| | 10.45 | 0.6 | | | 5 | Nuremberg, GER | 15 Jun |
| | 10.48 | 0.8 | | | 7r1 | Rome, ITA | 8 Jun |
| | 10.50 | -0.6 | | | 2r1 | Birmingham | 1 Jul |

| 10.33 | -0.5 | Jason Gardener | U23 | 18.09.75 | 1 | Geneva, SWZ | 17 | Jun |
| 10.36 | 1.6 | | | | 2r1 | Cwmbran | 9 | Jul |
| 10.37 | 1.1 | | | | 1h2 | Geneva, SWZ | 17 | Jun |
| 10.38 | 0.2 | | | | 1s3 | Birmingham | 15 | Jul |
| 10.47 | -0.9 | | | | 2r3 | Zofingen, SWZ | 5 | Jun |
| 10.48 | 0.1 | | | | 1h6 | Birmingham | 15 | Jul |
| 10.34 | 1.6 | Darren Campbell | U23 | 12.09.73 | 1r1 | Cwmbran | 9 | Jul |
| 10.37 | -1.2 | | | | 4 | Birmingham | 15 | Jul |
| 10.38 | -3.1 | | | | 1h1 | Birmingham | 15 | Jul |
| 10.39 | 0.2 | | | | 2s3 | Birmingham | 15 | Jul |
| 10.48 | 1.0 | | | | 1h1 | Gateshead | 17 | Jun |
| 10.40 | -0.3 | Paul White | U23 | 1.09.74 | 1q4 | Fukuoka, JAP | 31 | Aug |
| 10.45 | 1.3 | | | | 6 | Fukuoka, JAP | 1 | Sep |
| 10.49 | 2.0 | | | | 4s2 | Fukuoka, JAP | 1 | Sep |
| (10) | | | | | | | | |
| 10.41 | -0.9 | Dwain Chambers | U20 | 5.04.78 | 1 | Nyiregyhaza, HUN | 28 | Jul |
| 10.41 | -0.9 | Jamie Henthorn | U20 | 20.02.77 | 2 | Nyiregyhaza, HUN | 28 | Jul |
| 10.48 | 0.5 | | | | 1 | Utrecht, HOL | 9 | Jul |
| 10.42 | 0.6 | Peter Maitland | U23 | 21.01.73 | 1r1 | Edinburgh | 3 | Jun |
| 10.43 | -0.5 | | | | 2r2 | Zofingen, SWZ | 5 | Jun |
| 10.42 | -0.5 | Owusu Dako | U23 | 23.05.73 | 1r2 | Zofingen, SWZ | 5 | Jun |
| 10.43 | 1.2 | Solomon Wariso | | 11.11.66 | 3 | Cagliari, ITA | 20 | Sep |
| *10.45* | *0.6* | *Josephus Thomas* | | *11.07.68* | *3s2* | *Birmingham* | *15* | *Jul* |
| 10.46 | 1.9 | Jason Fergus | U23 | 11.10.73 | 1h1 | Barking | 13 | May |
| 10.47 | | Terence Stamp | | 18.02.70 | 1r1 | Aldershot | 23 | Jul |
| 10.48 | 0.2 | Allyn Condon | U23 | 24.08.74 | 3s3 | Birmingham | 15 | Jul |
| 10.49 | | Roger Black | | 31.03.66 | 1 | Irvine, USA | 1 | Apr |
| *10.50* | | *Thomas Ganda* | | *9.10.72* | *1* | *Tucson, USA* | *19* | *May* |
| 10.50 | 0.6 | Kevin Williams | | 15.12.71 | 2r1 | Edinburgh | 3 | Jun |
| (20) | | | | | | | | |
| 10.50 | 0.6 | Ayo Falola | | 29.07.68 | 4s2 | Birmingham | 15 | Jul |

120 performances to 10.50 by 21 athletes

| 10.51 | -1.0 | Andrew Mensah | | 30.11.71 | 1r2 | London (CP) | 7 | Jul |
| 10.51 | -1.1 | Jamie Baulch | U23 | 3.05.73 | 1r2 | Cardiff | 22 | Jul |
| 10.52 | 1.6 | Danny Joyce | U23 | 9.09.74 | 4s1 | Birmingham | 15 | Jul |
| 10.55 | | Mark Smith | | 18.11.71 | 2 | Irvine, USA | 1 | Apr |
| 10.55 | 0.1 | Marlon Devonish | U20 | 1.06.76 | 2h6 | Birmingham | 15 | Jul |
| 10.55 | 2.0 | Onochie Onuorah | U23 | 16.10.73 | 2 | Stoke | 9 | Sep |
| 10.58 | -1.1 | Doug Turner | | 2.12.66 | 2r2 | Cardiff | 22 | Jul |
| 10.60 | 1.0 | Daniel Money | U20 | 7.10.76 | 2r1 | Cardiff | 19 | Aug |
| 10.61 | -0.5 | Phil Goedluck | | 10.09.67 | 2 | Geneva, SWZ | 17 | Jun |
| (30) | | | | | | | | |
| 10.61 | 1.6 | Tremayne Rutherford | | 19.06.72 | 2r2 | Cwmbran | 9 | Jul |
| 10.61 | 1.1 | Ed White | U23 | 16.11.73 | 1r2 | Cardiff | 19 | Aug |
| 10.63 | -0.5 | Colin Jackson | | 18.02.67 | 3h2 | Birmingham | 15 | Jul |
| 10.63 | 0.2 | Michael Afilaka | | 16.11.71 | 6s3 | Birmingham | 15 | Jul |
| *10.63* | *-0.5* | *Haroun Korjie* | | *17.02.72* | *2r2* | *Enfield* | *19* | *Aug* |
| 10.64 | 0.0 | Andrew Walcott | U23 | 11.01.75 | 6 | Granada, SPA | 27 | May |
| 10.65 | -1.5 | Ian Mackie | U23 | 27.02.75 | 1r3 | Zofingen, SWZ | 5 | Jun |
| 10.67 | | Ian Craig | | 20.08.69 | 1 | Dublin (M), IRE | 16 | Jul |
| 10.68 | -1.1 | Mark Woodhouse | U23 | 1.11.75 | 2 | Birmingham | 17 | Jun |
| 10.71 | 0.0 | Trevor Cameron | U20 | 25.11.76 | 4 | Ljubljana, SLO | 21 | May |
| 10.72 | 0.7 | Andi Knight | U23 | 11.11.73 | 1 | Alfaz Del Pi, SPA | 13 | Apr |
| (40) | | | | | | | | |
| 10.73 | -0.5 | Mark Findlay | U20 | 20.03.78 | 3r2 | Enfield | 19 | Aug |
| 10.74 | 0.7 | Darren Scott | | 7.03.69 | 1 | Bebington | 23 | Jul |
| 10.74 | | Ian Lonsdale | | 8.09.71 | 2 | Peterborough | 28 | Aug |
| 10.74 | | Cypren Edmunds | | 20.06.70 | 2 | London (CP) | 10 | Sep |
| 10.76 | | Paul Brizzell | U20 | 3.10.76 | 1 | Tullamore, IRE | 25 | Jun |
| 10.77 | 0.4 | Mark McIntyre | | 14.10.70 | 2h4 | Bedford | 28 | May |
| 10.78 | 1.8 | James Egan | U23 | 12.11.75 | 1 | Hull | 5 | Aug |
| 10.79 | 1.0 | Paul Sampson | U20 | 12.07.77 | 2 | Sheffield | 27 | May |

| | | | | | | | | |
|---|---|---|---|---|---|---|---|---|
| 10.79 | 0.6 | Jamie Henderson | | 28.03.69 | 4r1 | Edinburgh | 3 | Jun |
| 10.79 | | Tim O'Dell | | 29.05.70 | 2 | Aldershot | 26 | Jun |
| | (50) | | | | | | | |
| 10.79 | -1.5 | Doug Walker | U23 | 28.07.73 | 1r1 | Edinburgh | 1 | Jul |
| 10.79 | | Mclean Okotie | | 31.07.69 | 3 | London (CP) | 10 | Sep |
| 10.80 | 1.8 | Phillip Perigo | U17 | 25.09.78 | 1 | Sheffield | 28 | May |
| 10.80 | | Clarence Callender | | 16.11.61 | 3 | Aldershot | 26 | Jun |
| 10.81 | -2.3 | Clayton Archer | U20 | 29.05.76 | 4 | London (CP) | 17 | Jun |
| 10.81 | -0.2 | Ray Burke | | 11.11.69 | 4h4 | Birmingham | 15 | Jul |
| 10.82 | -0.6 | Terry Williams | | 15.11.68 | 6r1 | Birmingham | 1 | Jul |
| 10.82 | 2.0 | Ejike Wodu | U23 | 15.12.74 | 4h5 | Birmingham | 15 | Jul |
| 10.82 | 1.8 | Michael Tietz | U20 | 14.09.77 | 2 | Hull | 5 | Aug |
| 10.82 | | Dave Deacon | | 19.03.65 | 3 | Peterborough | 28 | Aug |
| | (60) | | | | | | | |
| 10.82 | 1.9 | Jamie Quarry | | 15.11.72 | 1D | Fukuoka, JAP | 1 | Sep |
| 10.83 | | Akinola Lashore | U23 | 28.03.73 | 4 | London (CP) | 10 | Sep |
| 10.85 | 1.2 | Christian Malcolm | U17 | 3.06.79 | 1 | Birmingham | 29 | Jul |
| 10.86 | 1.8 | Andrew Row | U17 | 17.10.78 | 2 | Sheffield | 28 | May |
| 10.87 | 0.4 | Mark Allen | | 23.09.66 | 3h4 | Bedford | 28 | May |
| *10.87* | *-3.1* | *Carl Afilaka* | | *13.07.68* | *2h1* | *Birmingham* | *15* | *Jul* |
| 10.87 | -0.6 | Sam Omonua | U20 | 16.06.76 | 6h8 | Birmingham | 15 | Jul |
| 10.87 | -1.1 | John Bowen | | 20.05.63 | 4r2 | Cardiff | 22 | Jul |
| 10.87 | | Nigel Vidal | | 18.11.72 | 5 | London (CP) | 10 | Sep |
| 10.88 | 1.8 | Wayne Mitchell | U23 | 25.12.74 | 3 | Hull | 5 | Aug |
| 10.89 | | Lee Fairclough | | 23.06.70 | 4 | Aldershot | 26 | Jun |
| | (70) | | | | | | | |
| 10.90 | | Richard Rubenis | U23 | 10.11.73 | 1 | Wrexham | 5 | Aug |
| 10.92 | -1.0 | Kevin Mark | U20 | 15.09.76 | 1h8 | London (CP) | 17 | Jun |
| 10.92 | 2.0 | Richard Johnson | | 13.10.71 | 7h5 | Birmingham | 15 | Jul |
| 10.94 | -2.5 | Uvie Ugono | U20 | 8.03.78 | 4 | London (CP) | 28 | May |
| 10.94 | 0.7 | Andrew Bull | | 26.06.69 | 1h4 | Gateshead | 17 | Jun |
| 10.94 | -2.2 | Lenny Paul | | 25.05.58 | 4s3 | London (CP) | 17 | Jun |
| 10.96 | -0.7 | Andy Lewis | | 9.03.68 | 4 | Edinburgh | 6 | May |
| 10.96 | 0.5 | Kevin Farrell | U20 | 31.10.77 | 2 | Barking | 13 | May |
| 10.96 | 0.4 | Scott Dorset | | 10.04.69 | 4h4 | Bedford | 28 | May |
| 10.96 | 0.6 | Onochie Achike | U23 | 31.01.75 | 6r1 | Edinburgh | 3 | Jun |
| | (80) | | | | | | | |
| 10.96 | -2.3 | Ross Baillie | U20 | 26.09.77 | 3 | Edinburgh | 24 | Jun |
| 10.96 | 2.0 | Barry Thomas | | 28.04.72 | 1D | Fukuoka, JAP | 1 | Sep |
| 10.97 | -1.2 | Dalton Powell | | 20.08.63 | 2h2 | Birmingham | 17 | Jun |
| 10.98 | 1.9 | Paul Slythe | U23 | 5.09.74 | 4 | Tonsberg, NOR | 17 | Jun |
| 10.99 | 0.2 | Steve Shanks | | 3.11.69 | 1 | Wishaw | 13 | May |
| 10.99 | 2.0 | Angus MacDonald | | 21.12.64 | 2 | Grangemouth | 13 | May |
| 10.99 | -0.5 | Graeme Welsh | U23 | 8.10.75 | 4h2 | Birmingham | 15 | Jul |
| 10.99 | | Graham Beasley | U20 | 24.10.77 | 1 | Peterborough | 28 | Aug |

**doubtful**

| | | | | | | | |
|---|---|---|---|---|---|---|---|
| 10.59 | | Andy Hughes | | | 1r1 | Ranstein, GER | 27 | Jun |
| 10.71 | | Byrne Currie | | | 1h1 | Ranstein, GER | 27 | Jun |

**Wind Assisted**

| | | | | | | | |
|---|---|---|---|---|---|---|---|
| 10.02 | 3.5 | Christie | | (9.97A) | 1 | Perth, AUS | 29 | Jan |
| | | 10.03 | 2.3 | | 4r1 | Lausanne, SWZ | 5 | Jul |
| | | 10.11 | 2.2 | | 1= | London (CP) | 27 | Aug |
| 10.16 | 2.6 | Braithwaite | | (10.12) | 1 | Eagle Rock, USA | 13 | May |
| | | 10.33 | 2.2 | | 5 | London (CP) | 27 | Aug |
| 10.29 | 2.2 | John | | (10.25) | 4 | London (CP) | 27 | Aug |
| 10.31 | 2.2 | Toby Box | | (10.32) | 3h2 | Moscow, RUS | 5 | Jun |
| | | 10.34 | 3.0 | | 3s1 | Fukuoka, JAP | 1 | Sep |
| 10.33 | 3.6 | Danny Joyce | U23 | (10.52) | 1r1 | Bedford | 10 | Jun |
| | | 10.44 | 2.5 | | 1 | Sheffield | 23 | Jul |

| 10.34 | 2.7 | Rosswess | | (10.29A) | 1 | La Laguna, SPA | 30 May |
|---|---|---|---|---|---|---|---|
| 10.37 | 2.7 | Campbell | U23 | (10.34) | 1 | Gateshead | 17 Jun |
| 10.46 | 2.1 | | | | 1r1 | Edinburgh | 3 Jun |
| 10.40 | 3.6 | Solomon Wariso | | (10.43) | 2r1 | Bedford | 3 Jun |
| 10.43 | 3.6 | Phil Goedluck | | (10.61) | 3r1 | Bedford | 10 Jun |
| 10.48 | | | | | 3r2 | Irvine, USA | 23 Apr |
| 10.44 | 3.4 | Marlon Devonish | U20 | (10.55) | 1 | Nottingham | 8 Jul |
| 10.49 | 3.7 | | | | 1 | Telford | 26 Aug |
| | | | | | | | |
| 10.46 | 2.5 | Michael Afilaka | | (10.63) | 2 | Sheffield | 23 Jul |
| 10.47 | 2.6 | Tony Jarrett | | 13.08.68 | 3 | Eagle Rock, USA | 13 May |
| 10.47 | 2.7 | Allyn Condon | U23 | (10.48) | 2 | Gateshead | 17 Jun |
| 10.48 | 3.6 | Andrew Mensah | | (10.51) | 4r1 | Bedford | 10 Jun |
| 10.48 | 2.5 | | | | 3 | Sheffield | 23 Jul |
| 10.48 | 3.4 | Daniel Money | U20 | (10.60) | 2 | Nottingham | 8 Jul |
| 10.50 | 3.0 | Dako | U23 | (10.42) | 1r1 | Birmingham | 20 May |

25 performances to 10.50 by 16 athletes

| 10.55 | 3.4 | Mark Findlay | U20 | (10.73) | 3 | Nottingham | 8 Jul |
|---|---|---|---|---|---|---|---|
| 10.59 | 3.6 | Cypren Edmunds | | (10.74) | 6r1 | Bedford | 10 Jun |
| 10.60 | 3.6 | Andrew Walcott | U23 | (10.64) | 7r1 | Bedford | 10 Jun |
| 10.61 | 3.6 | Mark McIntyre | | (10.77) | 8r1 | Bedford | 10 Jun |
| | | | | | | | |
| 10.61 | 3.1 | Sam Omonua | U20 | (10.87) | 1 | London (He) | 6 Aug |
| 10.63 | 3.1 | Paul Field | | 24.06.67 | 1D | Alhama, SPA | 20 May |
| 10.64 | 3.4 | Uvie Ugono | U20 | (10.94) | 4 | Nottingham | 8 Jul |
| 10.64 | 2.5 | James Egan | U23 | (10.78) | 6 | Sheffield | 23 Jul |
| 10.70 | 3.3 | Darren Scott | | (10.74) | 2=s1 | Gateshead | 17 Jun |
| 10.71 | | Ray Burke | | (10.81) | 1r1 | Irvine, USA | 23 Apr |
| 10.72 | 3.3 | David Jackson | U23 | 12.05.73 | 4s1 | Gateshead | 17 Jun |
| 10.74 | 2.2 | John Skeete | U17 | 8.09.78 | 1 | Nottingham | 8 Jul |
| 11.06 | -1.3 | | | | 1s1 | Nottingham | 7 Jul |
| 10.77 | 3.7 | Richard Rubenis | U23 | (10.90) | 4 | Telford | 26 Aug |
| 10.78 | 3.2 | Lee Fairclough | | (10.89) | 1 | Portsmouth | 14 May |
| | | | | | | | |
| 10.78 | 3.4 | Martin Giraud | U20 | 16.11.77 | 5 | Nottingham | 8 Jul |
| 10.78 | 3.0 | Ross Baillie | U20 | (10.96) | 1 | Pitreavie | 8 Jul |
| 10.79 | 2.1 | John Bowen | | (10.87) | 2r1 | Edinburgh | 3 Jun |
| 10.80 | 2.1 | Rohan Samuel | | 30.01.66 | 3r3 | Bedford | 10 Jun |
| 10.81 | | Michael Nartey | U23 | 12.06.75 | 1r2 | Irvine, USA | 23 Apr |
| 10.81 | 3.0 | Andrew Bull | | (10.94) | 8r1 | Birmingham | 20 May |
| 10.87 | 3.3 | Alistair Audsley | | 17.08.65 | 5s1 | Gateshead | 17 Jun |
| 10.88 | 3.2 | Barry Thomas | | (10.96) | 1D | Alhama, SPA | 20 May |
| 10.88 | 2.4 | Thomas Begen | U17 | 14.04.79 | 1 | Pitreavie | 8 Jul |
| 11.03 | 0.7 | | | | 2s1 | Birmingham | 30 Jul |
| 10.88 | 2.1 | Graham Thomas | U20 | 23.09.77 | 6 | London (He) | 9 Sep |
| | | | | | | | |
| 10.89 | 3.7 | Andy Lewis | | (10.96) | 1D | Alhama, SPA | 20 May |
| 10.90 | 3.2 | Matthew Dangerfield | | | 2 | Portsmouth | 14 May |
| 10.90 | 3.7 | Dalton Powell | | (10.97) | 4r2 | Birmingham | 20 May |
| 10.92 | 3.7 | James Weston | | 9.01.70 | 5r2 | Birmingham | 20 May |
| 10.92 | 2.1 | Ancell Maxwell | | 17.01.69 | 3r2 | Edinburgh | 3 Jun |
| 10.93 | 2.8 | Daniel Bonich | U17 | 22.11.78 | 1 | London (CP) | 13 May |
| 10.94 | 3.1 | Richard Davis | U20 | 3.05.78 | 2 | London (He) | 6 Aug |
| 10.96 | 2.2 | Luke Grinnell | U17 | 21.03.79 | 2 | Nottingham | 8 Jul |
| 11.07 | 1.2 | | | | 4 | Birmingham | 30 Jul |
| 10.97 | 2.1 | Brendon Ghent | U20 | 7.09.76 | 8 | London (He) | 9 Sep |
| 10.99 | 2.4 | Chris Carson | U17 | 26.10.79 | 2 | Pitreavie | 8 Jul |
| 11.15 | 1.9 | | | | 2h2 | Grangemouth | 13 May |

**Hand Timing**

| 10.3 | 1.7 | Solomon Wariso | | (10.43) | 1 | Liverpool | 30 Jul |
|---|---|---|---|---|---|---|---|

| Time | Wind | Name | Cat | Mark | Pos | Venue | Date | |
|---|---|---|---|---|---|---|---|---|
| 10.3 | | John | | (10.25) | 1 | Cannock | 9 | Sep |
| 10.5 | | | | | 2 | Derby | 30 | Jul |
| 10.3 w | | Phil Goedluck | | (10.48w) | 1 | Fullerton, USA | 27 | Apr |
| 10.3 w | | Ayo Falola | | (10.50) | 2 | Fullerton, USA | 27 | Apr |
| 10.3 w | | Mark McIntyre | | (10.77) | 3 | Fullerton, USA | 27 | Apr |
| 10.4 | | White | U23 | (10.40) | 1 | Loughborough | 24 | May |
| 10.4 | | Gardener | U23 | (10.33) | 1r1 | Bath | 31 | May |
| 10.4 | | Golding | U23 | (10.30) | 2 | Cannock | 9 | Sep |
| 10.4 w 2.8 | | | | | 2r1 | London (He) | 7 | May |
| 10.4 w | | Ray Burke | | (10.81) | 6 | Fullerton, USA | 27 | Apr |
| 10.4 w | 2.8 | Michael Rosswess | | (10.29A) | 1r1 | London (He) | 7 | May |
| 10.4 w | | Mark Woodhouse | U23 | (10.68) | 1r1 | Loughborough | 20 | May |
| 10.4 w | 3.5 | Box | | (10.32) | 1r1 | Crawley | 1 | Jul |
| 10.5 | | Tremayne Rutherford | | (10.61) | 1 | Norwich | 13 | May |
| 10.5 | | Marlon Devonish | U20 | (10.55) | 2r1 | Bath | 31 | May |
| 10.5 | 1.7 | Danny Joyce | U23 | (10.52) | 3 | Liverpool | 30 | Jul |
| 10.5 | 1.7 | Ian Mackie | U23 | (10.65) | 4 | Liverpool | 30 | Jul |
| 10.5 | | Jamie Henthorn | U20 | (10.41) | 1 | Swansea | 28 | Aug |
| 10.5 w | | Mark Phills | | 26.07.64 | 1 | Harrow | 9 | Jul |
| 10.7 | | | | | 3 | Enfield | 30 | Jul |

20 performances to 10.5 by 18 athletes including 9 wind assisted

| Time | Wind | Name | Cat | Mark | Pos | Venue | Date | |
|---|---|---|---|---|---|---|---|---|
| 10.6 | | John Bowen | | (10.87) | | Cardiff | 7 | Jun |
| 10.6 | | John Kenny | | 17.12.70 | 1 | London (Nh) | 15 | Jun |
| 10.6 | | Jamie Paul | | 17.07.70 | 1 | London (PH) | 2 | Aug |
| 10.6 w | 2.3 | Uvie Ugono | U20 | (10.94) | 1 | Croydon | 13 | May |
| 10.8 | | | | | 2 | London (TB) | 29 | Jul |
| 10.6 w | | Andi Knight | U23 | (10.72) | 2r1 | Loughborough | 20 | May |
| 10.6 w | | Martin Giraud | U20 | (10.78w) | 1 | London (CP) | 31 | May |
| 10.6 w | | Evans Danso | | 29.11.72 | 1 | London (PH) | 2 | Aug |
| 10.8 | | | | | 1 | London (WL) | 5 | Aug |
| 10.6 w | | Richard Rubenis | U23 | (10.90) | 1r1 | Mansfield | 19 | Aug |
| 10.8 | | | | | 1 | Telford | 3 | Jun |
| 10.7 | | Maxwell Asare | | 14.09.68 | 1 | Valetta, MAL | 8 | Apr |
| 10.7 | | Bryn Middleton | U20 | 16.02.76 | | Cardiff | 17 | Apr |
| 10.7 | | Wayne Mitchell | U23 | (10.88) | 1r1 | Stretford | 25 | Apr |
| 10.7 | | Chike Emeagi | U23 | 25.09.74 | 1 | Oxford | 26 | Apr |
| 10.7 | | Jonathan Edwards | | 10.05.66 | 1r1 | Jarrow | 6 | May |
| 10.7 | | Andrew Bull | | (10.94) | 1r2 | Bournemouth | 6 | May |
| 10.7 | 1.8 | Steve McCourt | | 6.05.71 | 3r2 | London (He) | 7 | May |
| 10.7 | 1.8 | Mark Lambeth | | 3.09.72 | 4r2 | London (He) | 7 | May |
| *10.7* | | *Jonathon Kron* ¶ | *U23* | *16.02.73* | *1r2* | *Loughborough* | *20* | *May* |
| 10.7 | | Dave Deacon | | (10.82) | 2 | Loughborough | 24 | May |
| 10.7 | | Steve Coupland | | 15.06.65 | 1r1 | Barking | 3 | Jun |
| 10.7 | | Graeme Welsh | U23 | (10.99) | 2r2 | Barking | 3 | Jun |
| *10.7* | | *Carl Afilaka* | | *(10.87)* | *1* | *Oxford* | *1* | *Jul* |
| 10.7 | | Bode Oluwa | U20 | 15.11.76 | 1 | London (TB) | 29 | Jul |
| 10.7 | | Tim O'Dell | | (10.79) | 1 | Basingstoke | 6 | Aug |
| 10.7 | | Terry Williams | | (10.82) | 1 | London (WL) | 13 | Aug |
| 10.7 | | Tim Barton | | 3.10.70 | 2r1 | Mansfield | 19 | Aug |
| 10.7 | | Mark Findlay | U20 | (10.73) | 1 | Birmingham | 28 | Aug |
| *10.7 A* | | *Joslyn Thomas* | | *11.07.71* | *2h6* | *Harare, ZIM* | *14* | *Sep* |
| 10.7 w | 3.2 | Ejike Wodu | U23 | (10.82) | 2h2 | Hayes | 13 | May |
| 10.7 w | 2.5 | Rohan Samuel | | (10.80w) | 1h1 | Hayes | 14 | May |
| 10.8 0.6 | | | | | 2 | Hayes | 14 | May |
| 10.7 w | | Nigel Bourne | | 18.04.72 | 1r2 | Harrow | 9 | Jul |
| 10.7 w | | Scott Herbert | U23 | 12.02.74 | 3 | Harrow | 9 | Jul |
| 10.8 | | Kevin Mark | U20 | (10.92) | 1r1 | Perivale | 24 | Apr |

| Time | Wind | Name | Cat | DOB | Pos | Venue | Date |
|------|------|------|-----|-----|-----|-------|------|
| 10.8 | | Ronan Kearney | | | 3r1 | Stretford | 25 Apr |
| 10.8 | | N. Sharp | | | 4r1 | Stretford | 25 Apr |
| 10.8 | | Andy Gibson | U23 | 20.09.73 | 1 | York | 30 Apr |
| 10.8 | | Derek Morgan | | 4.04.69 | 2r1 | Bournemouth | 6 May |
| 10.8 | | Nigel Vidal | | (10.87) | 1r1 | Brighton | 6 May |
| 10.8 | | Graham Beasley | U20 | (10.99) | 1 | Bedford | 13 May |
| 10.8 | | Scott Dorset | | (10.96) | 1 | Bracknell | 13 May |
| 10.8 | | Darren Ward | U23 | 5.03.73 | 1 | Grantham | 13 May |
| 10.8 | | Alan Leaming | U20 | 2.11.76 | 1r1 | Lancaster | 3 Jun |
| 10.8 | -0.9 | Sam Kabiswa | | 28.10.66 | 1r1 | Bracknell | 3 Jun |
| 10.8 | 0.6 | Mark Hylton | U20 | 24.09.76 | 1r2 | Bracknell | 3 Jun |
| 10.8 | | Rupert Williams | | 17.03.64 | 1 | Portsmouth (RN) | 14 Jun |
| 10.8 | | Michael Tietz | U20 | (10.82) | 1 | Rugby | 28 Jun |
| 10.8 | | Jared Deacon | U23 | 15.10.75 | 1r1 | Jarrow · | 19 Jul |
| 10.8 | 0.7 | Steve Shanks | | (10.99) | 2 | Birmingham | 19 Jul |
| 10.8 | | Curtis Browne | U23 | 11.09.75 | 1r1 | Cannock | 22 Jul |
| 10.8 | | Chris Davidson | U23 | 4.12.75 | 1 | London (TB) | 29 Jul |
| 10.8 | | Nigel Will | | 18.10.67 | 4 | Enfield | 30 Jul |
| 10.8 | | Nick Swaby | U20 | 28.10.77 | 1 | Rugby | 2 Aug |
| 10.8 | | Oladipo Scott-Boyle | U23 | 17.06.74 | 1r1 | London (Elt) | 5 Aug |
| 10.8 | | Dan Donovan | | 8.10.70 | 4 | Basingstoke | 6 Aug |
| 10.8 | | Paul Edwards | | 13.06.68 | 1 | Cheltenham | 16 Aug |
| 10.8 | | Guy Bullock | U23 | 15.10.75 | 1r1 | Blackpool | 19 Aug |
| 10.8 w | 3.1 | Richard Johnson | | (10.92) | 1h3 | Hayes | 14 May |
| 10.8 w | | D. Jameson | | | 4r1 | Loughborough | 20 May |
| 10.8 w | 3.9 | Scott Fraser | U20 | 31.12.77 | 1 | Grangemouth | 17 Jun |
| 10.8 w | 4.7 | Mark Davidson | | 15.11.68 | 1 | Aberdeen | 23 Jul |

**Additional Under 20** (1 - 35 above)

| Time | Wind | Name | Cat | DOB | Pos | Venue | Date |
|------|------|------|-----|-----|-----|-------|------|
| 10.9 | | Andrew Lees | U17 | 11.05.79 | 1 | Edinburgh | 16 Apr |
| 11.05 | 1.9 | | | | 1h2 | Grangemouth | 13 May |
| 10.9 | | James Shipp | | 10.11.77 | 3 | Norwich | 13 May |
| 10.9 | | Jason Cox | | 1.04.77 | 1 | Cheltenham | 17 Jun |
| 10.9 | | Antonio Matarazzo | U17 | 27.03.80 | 1 | Portsmouth | 25 Jun |
| 10.9 | 1.9 | Mark Bushell | | 22.10.76 | 1D | Kilkenny, IRE | 26 Aug |
| 10.9 w | 5.5 | Marlon Dickson | U17 | 17.11.78 | 1h1 | Croydon | 13 May |
| 11.0 | | | | | 1 | London (BP) | 17 May |
| 11.06 w | 2.2 | | | | 3= | Nottingham | 8 Jul |
| 11.11 | 0.2 | | | | 2s2 | Birmingham | 30 Jul |
| 10.9 w | | Daniel Bonich | U17 | (10.93w) | 1 | Dartford | 21 May |
| 10.9 w | 3.9 | Adam Lowles | | 29.01.77 | 2 | Grangemouth | 17 Jun |
| 10.9 w | 2.6 | Chris Carson | U17 | (10.99w) | 2 | Grangemouth | 17 Jun |
| 11.0 | 1.7 | | | | 1 | Grangemouth | 21 Jun |

**Additional Under 17** (1 - 13 above)

| Time | Wind | Name | Cat | DOB | Pos | Venue | Date |
|------|------|------|-----|-----|-----|-------|------|
| 11.00 | 1.7 | Nick Long | | 1.02.79 | 1r1 | Stoke | 17 Jun |
| 11.0 | | Darren Carter | | 29.10.78 | 1 | Bournemouth | 13 May |
| 11.0 | 1.7 | Begen | | (10.88w) | 2 | Grangemouth | 21 Jun |
| 11.0 | | Chris Blake | | 8.11.78 | 1 | Hull | 25 Jun |
| 11.0 | | James Hilston | | 25.02.79 | 1r2 | Sutton | 19 Jul |
| 11.06 | 0.9 | | | | 2h3 | Birmingham | 30 Jul |
| 11.0 | | Papa Domi | | | 1 | Feltham | 27 Aug |
| 11.0 | | Luke Davis | | 1.01.80 | 1 | Worcester | 17 Sep |
| 11.14 | 1.4 | | | | 1h1 | Birmingham | 30 Jul |
| 11.07 | | Ian Leaman | | 14.10.78 | 1 | Braunton | 13 May |
| | (20) | | | | | | |
| 11.1 | | Soloman Povey | | 8.02.80 | 2 | Bournemouth | 13 May |
| 11.1 | | Nana Wilson | | 14.01.79 | 2 | Croydon | 10 Jun |
| 11.19 w | 2.2 | | | | 6 | Nottingham | 8 Jul |

130

| | | | | | | |
|---|---|---|---|---|---|---|
| 11.1 | | Andy Edmonds | 17.09.78 | 1 | Southampton | 8 Aug |
| 11.13 w 4.3 | | | | 1 | Portsmouth | 14 May |
| 11.1 | | Stuart Smith | 20.12.79 | 1 | Grimsby | 24 Sep |
| 11.1 w | 2.6 | Allan McBride | 31.12.79 | 3 | Grangemouth | 17 Jun |
| 11.12 w 3.2 | | Steven Daly | 29.12.79 | 1r2 | Stoke | 17 Jun |
| 11.19 | 0.2 | | | 4s2 | Birmingham | 30 Jul |
| 11.19 | 1.4 | Andre Duffus | 30.10.79 | 2h1 | Birmingham | 30 Jul |

**Under 15**

| | | | | | | |
|---|---|---|---|---|---|---|
| 11.20 w 2.2 | | Dominic Gordon | 7.01.81 | 1 | Nottingham | 8 Jul |
| 11.4 | | | | 1 | Newport | 25 Jun |
| 11.53 -1.3 | | | | 1s1 | Nottingham | 7 Jul |
| 11.2 w | | Andre Silva | 18.11.80 | 1 | Swansea | 28 Aug |
| 11.29 | | | | 1 | Cardiff | 22 Jul |
| 11.29 w 2.2 | | Wayne Gray | 7.11.80 | 1 | Birmingham | 30 Jul |
| 11.3 | | | | 1 | London (TB) | 25 Jun |
| 11.45 -1.2 | | | | 1s2 | Nottingham | 7 Jul |
| 11.30 | 0.6 | Ben Lewis | 6.03.81 | 1 | Birmingham | 3 Sep |
| 11.3 | | Russell Johnson | 14.09.80 | 1 | Basildon | 10 Jun |
| 11.44 w 2.2 | | | | 5 | Nottingham | 8 Jul |
| 11.33 | 1.2 | Daniel Plummer | 4.01.81 | 1r2 | Birmingham | 3 Sep |
| 11.37 w 2.2 | | Adam Newton | 4.12.80 | 3 | Nottingham | 8 Jul |
| 11.5 | | | | 1 | Bracknell | 10 Jun |
| 11.51 -1.2 | | | | 2s2 | Nottingham | 7 Jul |
| 11.4 | | Lewis Short | 26.10.80 | 1s1 | Grangemouth | 17 Jun |
| 11.43 w 2.2 | | Myrone Levy | 12.02.81 | 4 | Nottingham | 8 Jul |
| 11.5 | | | | 1 | Yeovil | 4 Jun |
| 11.49 w 2.2 | | Simon Collins | 23.11.80 | 7 | Nottingham | 8 Jul |
| (10) | | | | | | |
| 11.5 | | Alex Chaffe | 5.12.80 | 2 | Newport | 25 Jun |
| 11.51 | | Mike Ferraro | 21.11.80 | 2 | Cardiff | 22 Jul |
| 11.53 | 1.2 | Steven Jackson | | 2r2 | Birmingham | 3 Sep |
| 11.56 | | Henry Richards | 15.05.81 | 1 | Peterborough | 28 Aug |
| 11.59 w 4.1 | | Jamie Moore | 4.11.80 | 1 | Pitreavie | 9 Jul |
| 11.59 w 2.1 | | Gregory D'Almeida | 16.11.80 | 3 | London (He) | 6 Aug |

**Under 13**

| | | | | | | |
|---|---|---|---|---|---|---|
| 11.6 | | T. Anthony | | 1 | Welwyn | 28 Aug |
| 12.14 | 0.3 | Mark Francis | 4.09.82 | 1 | Birmingham | 3 Sep |
| 12.2 | | Lance Salmon | | 1 | Manchester (BV) | 13 Aug |
| 12.4 | | Ian Blake | 9.05.83 | 1 | Blackpool | 30 Apr |
| 12.50 w 4.8 | | David Love | 17.12.82 | 1 | Pitreavie | 9 Jul |

# 150 METRES

| | | | | | | |
|---|---|---|---|---|---|---|
| 14.74 w 3.9 | Linford Christie | | 2.04.60 | 1 | Sheffield | 23 Jul |
| 15.09 w 3.9 | Darren Braithwaite | | 20.01.69 | 3 | Sheffield | 23 Jul |
| 15.25 w 3.9 | John Regis | | 13.10.66 | 4 | Sheffield | 23 Jul |
| 15.25 w 3.9 | Solomon Wariso | | 11.11.66 | 6 | Sheffield | 23 Jul |
| 15.38 w 3.9 | Julian Golding | U23 | 17.02.75 | 7 | Sheffield | 23 Jul |

# 200 METRES

| | | | | | | |
|---|---|---|---|---|---|---|
| 20.11 | 1.9 | Linford Christie | 2.04.60 | 1 | Villeneuve d'Ascq, FRA | 25 Jun |
| 20.25 i | | | | 1r1 | Lievin, FRA | 19 Feb |
| 20.53 | 0.0 | | | 3 | Rome, ITA | 8 Jun |
| 20.80 | 0.9 | | | 5 | St. Denis, FRA | 1 Jun |
| 20.87 | -1.0 | | | 2r1 | London (CP) | 3 Jun |

| | | | | | | |
|---|---|---|---|---|---|---|
| 20.26 | -0.7 | John Regis | 13.10.66 | 1 | Nice, FRA | 12 Jul |
| 20.32 | 0.2 | | | 3 | Monaco, MON | 25 Jul |
| 20.37 | 0.5 | | | 1 | Birmingham | 16 Jul |
| 20.39 | 0.3 | | | 4s1 | Gothenburg, SWE | 11 Aug |
| 20.48 i | | | | 1r1 | Stuttgart, GER | 5 Feb |
| 20.51 | 0.8 | | | 3q3 | Gothenburg, SWE | 10 Aug |
| 20.52 | -0.6 | | | 1r1 | Birmingham | 1 Jul |
| 20.62 | 1.2 | | | 3r1 | Eagle Rock, USA | 13 May |
| 20.63 | 0.2 | | | 1 | Gateshead | 21 Aug |
| 20.65 i | | | | 1r1 | Birmingham | 28 Jan |
| 20.67 i | | | | 1 | Glasgow | 11 Feb |
| 20.67 | 0.5 | | | 7 | Gothenburg, SWE | 11 Aug |
| 20.74 | 1.9 | | | 3 | Duisburg, GER | 18 Jun |
| 20.75 | -0.3 | | | 8 | Monaco, MON | 9 Sep |
| 20.77 | 0.9 | | | 6 | Rome, ITA | 8 Jun |
| 20.77 | 0.3 | | | 2s2 | Birmingham | 16 Jul |
| 20.78 | 1.0 | | | 2h6 | Gothenburg, SWE | 10 Aug |
| 20.83 | -1.1 | | | 4 | Rieti, ITA | 5 Sep |
| 20.94 i | | | | 2s1 | Barcelona, SPA | 10 Mar |
| 20.47 | 1.5 | Darren Braithwaite | 20.01.69 | 1r2 | Eagle Rock, USA | 13 May |
| 20.54 A | 1.5 | | | 1 | Soria, SPA | 16 Jun |
| 20.63 | 0.3 | | | 1s2 | Birmingham | 16 Jul |
| 20.64 | 0.5 | | | 3 | Birmingham | 16 Jul |
| 20.87 i | | | | 1 | Birmingham | 1 Jan |
| 20.87 | 0.2 | | | 4h2 | Gothenburg, SWE | 10 Aug |
| 20.90 i | | | | 4 | Birmingham | 25 Feb |
| 20.95 i | | | | 2 | Birmingham | 4 Feb |
| 20.50 | 0.6 | Tony Jarrett | 13.08.68 | 1s1 | Birmingham | 16 Jul. |
| 20.67 | 0.5 | | | 4 | Birmingham | 16 Jul |
| 20.50 | 0.6 | Solomon Wariso | 11.11.66 | 2s1 | Birmingham | 16 Jul |
| 20.50 | 1.7 | | | 1 | Stoke | 9 Sep |
| 20.51 | 2.0 | | | 2h7 | Gothenburg, SWE | 10 Aug |
| 20.53 | 0.5 | | | 2 | Birmingham | 16 Jul |
| 20.55 | -0.1 | | | 4q4 | Gothenburg, SWE | 10 Aug |
| 20.58 | -0.9 | | | 5s2 | Gothenburg, SWE | 11 Aug |
| 20.67 | 0.0 | | | 3 | Lucerne, SWZ | 27 Jun |
| 20.68 | -0.5 | | | 3 | London (CP) | 7 Jul |
| 20.74 | 0.2 | | | 2 | Gateshead | 21 Aug |
| 20.77 | 0.9 | | | 2 | Bratislava, SVK | 30 May |
| 20.77 | -1.0 | | | 1r1 | London (CP) | 3 Jun |
| 20.84 i | | | | 2r1 | Birmingham | 28 Jan |
| 20.87 i | | | | 1 | Birmingham | 4 Feb |
| 20.87 | 0.8 | | | 1 | Cagliari, ITA | 20 Sep |
| 20.93 | 0.5 | | | 1h2 | Birmingham | 16 Jul |
| 20.96 | -2.2 | | | 1 | Ljubljana, SLO | 21 May |
| 20.99 i | | | | 2 | Birmingham | 1 Jan |
| 21.00 A | 1.5 | | | 3 | Soria, SPA | 16 Jun |
| 20.57 | 0.6 | Owusu Dako | U23 23.05.73 | 3s1 | Birmingham | 16 Jul |
| 20.79 | -1.1 | | | 1q2 | Fukuoka, JAP | 29 Aug |
| 20.80 | 0.4 | | | 1 | Narbonne, FRA | 29 Jul |
| 20.84 | -1.1 | | | 1h5 | Birmingham | 16 Jul |
| 20.95 | -0.4 | | | 1h3 | Fukuoka, JAP | 29 Aug |
| 20.75 | -0.5 | Julian Golding | U23 17.02.75 | 5 | London (CP) | 7 Jul |
| 20.77 | 0.5 | | | 5 | Birmingham | 16 Jul |
| 20.82 | -0.5 | | | 1r2 | Geneva, SWZ | 17 Jun |
| 20.83 | 0.3 | | | 3s2 | Birmingham | 16 Jul |
| 20.92 | -0.1 | | | 1 | Kilkenny, IRE | 2 Sep |
| 20.75 | 1.7 | Doug Turner | 2.12.66 | 2 | Stoke | 9 Sep |
| 20.85 | 1.1 | | | 1r1 | Cardiff | 19 Aug |
| 20.90 | -1.7 | | | 1 | London (CP) | 27 Aug |

| 20.78 | 0.6 | Toby Box | | 9.09.72 | 4s1 | Birmingham | 16 Jul |
| 20.86 | 0.5 | | | | 7 | Birmingham | 16 Jul |
| 20.86 | -0.6 | Jason John | | 17.10.71 | 2r1 | Birmingham | 1 Jul |
| 20.90 | | | | | 1 | Andujar, SPA | 7 Sep |
| | (10) | | | | | | |
| 20.88 | -0.6 | Michael Rosswess | | 11.06.65 | 2 | Stellenbosch, RSA | 17 Apr |
| 20.88 | 0.6 | Doug Walker | U23 | 28.07.73 | 5s1 | Birmingham | 16 Jul |
| 20.95 | 0.4 | | | | 3 | Narbonne, FRA | 29 Jul |
| 20.96 | | | | | 1s1 | Edinburgh | 8 May |
| *20.93 A* | *0.0* | *Josephus Thomas* | | *11.07.68* | *6* | *Harare, ZIM* | *18 Sep* |
| *21.28* | *-0.1* | | | | *2* | *Kilkenny, IRE* | *2 Sep* |
| 20.94 | 0.8 | Marlon Devonish | U20 | 1.06.76 | 1 | Belfort, FRA | 6 Aug |
| 20.99 | 0.9 | | | | 1s2 | Bedford | 2 Jul |
| 21.00 | 1.6 | Mark Smith | | 18.11.71 | 1 | Barking | 14 May |
| 21.00 | 1.8 | | | | 3 | Tallinn, EST | 9 Jul |
| 21.00 | 0.3 | Allyn Condon | U23 | 24.08.74 | 5s2 | Birmingham | 16 Jul |

78 performances to 21.00 by 15 athletes including 11 indoors

| 21.02 | -0.9 | Peter Maitland | U23 | 21.01.73 | 1r1 | Zofingen, SWZ | 5 Jun |
| 21.09 | 1.9 | Mark Hylton | U20 | 24.09.76 | 1h4 | Bedford | 2 Jul |
| 21.10 | 1.7 | Mark Allen | | 23.09.66 | 3 | Stoke | 9 Sep |
| 21.12 | 0.7 | Jamie Henthorn | U20 | 20.02.77 | 1 | Utrecht, HOL | 9 Jul |
| 21.12 | 1.1 | Ed White | U23 | 16.11.73 | 2r1 | Cardiff | 19 Aug |
| | (20) | | | | | | |
| 21.16 | | David Nolan | | 25.07.69 | 1 | Aldershot | 26 Jun |
| 21.17 | 0.5 | Adrian Patrick | U23 | 15.06.73 | 1 | Bedford | 29 May |
| 21.19 | -1.1 | Andrew Mensah | | 30.11.71 | 2h5 | Birmingham | 16 Jul |
| 21.20 | 1.6 | Ayo Falola | | 29.07.68 | 2 | Barking | 14 May |
| 21.20 | | Phil Goedluck | | 10.09.67 | 5r1 | Geneva, SWZ | 17 Jun |
| 21.21 | 1.9 | Daniel Money | U20 | 7.10.76 | 2h4 | Bedford | 2 Jul |
| 21.22 | 1.7 | Michael Afilaka | | 16.11.71 | 4 | Stoke | 9 Sep |
| 21.25 A | 1.4 | Guy Bullock | U23 | 15.10.75 | 1 | Albuquerque, USA | 22 Apr |
| *21.27* | | *Thomas Ganda* | | *9.10.72* | *1* | *Los Gatos, USA* | *8 Jul* |
| 21.28 | -1.1 | Steve McCourt | | 6.05.71 | 3h5 | Birmingham | 16 Jul |
| 21.29 | -1.3 | Paul White | U23 | 1.09.74 | 3r1 | Loughborough | 1 Jun |
| | (30) | | | | | | |
| 21.31 | | Cypren Edmunds | | 20.06.70 | 2 | Aldershot | 26 Jun |
| 21.31 | | Tim O'Dell | | 29.05.70 | 3 | Aldershot | 26 Jun |
| 21.32 | -0.4 | Jamie Baulch | U23 | 3.05.73 | 4h4 | Birmingham | 16 Jul |
| 21.34 | 0.9 | Graham Beasley | U20 | 24.10.77 | 3s2 | Bedford | 2 Jul |
| 21.35 | 1.1 | Darren Scott | | 7.03.69 | 3r1 | Cardiff | 19 Aug |
| 21.36 | -0.4 | Andrew Walcott | U23 | 11.01.75 | 3r2 | Loughborough | 11 Jun |
| 21.36 | 0.9 | Mark Findlay | U20 | 20.03.78 | 4s2 | Bedford | 2 Jul |
| 21.37 | 1.9 | Dwain Chambers | U20 | 5.04.78 | 3h4 | Bedford | 2 Jul |
| 21.38 | 0.9 | Uvie Ugono | U20 | 8.03.78 | 5s2 | Bedford | 2 Jul |
| 21.38 | 0.0 | Nick Budden | U23 | 17.11.75 | 2 | Stoke | 10 Sep |
| | (40) | | | | | | |
| 21.46 | 0.6 | Paul McBurney | | 14.03.72 | 1r2 | Antrim | 20 Jun |
| 21.46 | 0.4 | Kent Ulyatt | | 10.04.72 | 4 | Tessenderlo, BEL | 2 Jul |
| 21.50 | 0.8 | Paul Brizzell | U20 | 3.10.76 | 1r1 | Antrim | 20 Jun |
| 21.50 | | Andy Gibson | U23 | 20.09.73 | 1 | Wrexham | 5 Aug |
| 21.53 | -1.4 | Ian Mackie | U23 | 27.02.75 | 4r2 | Zofingen, SWZ | 5 Jun |
| 21.54 | 1.9 | Clayton Archer | U20 | 29.05.76 | 4h4 | Bedford | 2 Jul |
| 21.58 | 0.7 | Christian Malcolm | U17 | 3.06.79 | 3 | Utrecht, HOL | 9 Jul |
| 21.60 | 0.4 | Trevor Cameron | U20 | 25.11.76 | 4s1 | Bedford | 2 Jul |
| 21.66 | 0.5 | Jared Deacon | U23 | 15.10.75 | 5 | Bedford | 29 May |
| 21.69 | -2.4 | Michael Champion | U23 | 3.01.75 | 1 | Enfield | 29 Apr |
| | (50) | | | | | | |
| 21.69 | 1.9 | Phillip Perigo | U17 | 25.09.78 | 1 | Nottingham | 8 Jul |
| 21.70 | 0.3 | Kevin Williams | | 15.12.71 | 8s2 | Birmingham | 16 Jul |
| 21.71 | -1.3 | Steve Simmons | U23 | 10.11.74 | 3h7 | Birmingham | 16 Jul |
| 21.72 | 0.5 | Steve Coupland | | 15.06.65 | 6 | Bedford | 29 May |

| Time | Wind | Name | Cat | DOB | Pos | Venue | Date |
|---|---|---|---|---|---|---|---|
| 21.72 | -1.8 | Steve Shanks | | 3.11.69 | 2 | Edinburgh | 23 Jun |
| 21.75 | -1.2 | Ross Baillie | U20 | 26.09.77 | 1 | Wishaw | 14 May |
| 21.78 | -2.2 | Paul Slythe | U23 | 5.09.74 | 2r1 | Edinburgh | 1 Jul |
| 21.78 | -0.8 | John Skeete | U17 | 8.09.78 | 2 | Birmingham | 29 Jul |
| 21.79 | 1.1 | Sunny Adepegba | | 6.06.71 | 3r2 | Enfield | 19 Aug |
| 21.82 | -0.3 | Quincy Douglas | U23 | 7.09.75 | 1 | Fana, NOR | 19 Jul |
| (60) | | | | | | | |
| 21.84 A | 1.4 | Peter Crampton | | 4.06.69 | 5 | Albuquerque, USA | 22 Apr |
| 21.84 | -3.0 | Donley Jack | | 7.11.66 | 5 | London (CP) | 18 Jun |
| 21.84 | 1.9 | Chris Blake | U17 | 8.11.78 | 2 | Nottingham | 8 Jul |
| 21.85 | 0.6 | Lloyd Cowan | | 8.07.62 | 7 | Birmingham | 20 May |
| 21.86 | 0.5 | Graeme Welsh | U23 | 8.10.75 | 7 | Bedford | 29 May |
| 21.86 | -1.9 | Mark Lambeth | | 3.09.72 | 5r2 | Birmingham | 1 Jul |
| 21.86 | | Ian Craig | | 20.08.69 | 1r1 | Antrim | 8 Jul |
| 21.86 | | Dave Deacon | | 19.03.65 | 1 | Peterborough | 28 Aug |
| 21.88 | 0.5 | Sam Kabiswa | | 28.10.66 | 8 | Bedford | 29 May |
| 21.88 | 1.9 | Corri Henry | U20 | 9.12.76 | 5h4 | Bedford | 2 Jul |
| (70) | | | | | | | |
| 21.89 i | | Mark Walcott | U23 | 24.11.73 | 2s2 | Glasgow | 22 Jan |
| *21.89* | *1.1* | *Haroun Korjie* | | *17.02.72* | *4r2* | *Enfield* | *19 Aug* |
| 21.90 | -0.4 | Andi Knight | U23 | 11.11.73 | 5r2 | Loughborough | 11 Jun |
| 21.90 | 1.9 | Antonio Matarazzo | U17 | 27.03.80 | 3 | Nottingham | 8 Jul |
| 21.90 | -1.3 | James Egan | U23 | 12.11.75 | 5h7 | Birmingham | 16 Jul |
| *21.92* | | *Joslyn Thomas* | | *11.07.71* | *4h6* | *Harare, ZIM* | *17 Sep* |
| 21.94 | -1.1 | Dan Donovan | | 8.10.70 | 5h5 | Birmingham | 16 Jul |
| 21.95 i | | Alex Fugallo | | 28.01.70 | 3s3 | Birmingham | 1 Jan |
| 21.96 | | Lee Fairclough | | 23.06.70 | 2r1 | Aldershot | 23 Jul |
| 21.98 | 1.4 | Wayne Mitchell | U23 | 25.12.74 | h | Hull | 5 Aug |
| 21.99 | | Kevin Farrell | U20 | 31.10.77 | 2 | Barking | 14 May |
| 21.99 | 0.4 | Marcus Lindall | U23 | 23.01.75 | 5s2 | London (CP) | 18 Jun |
| (80) | | | | | | | |
| *21.99* | *0.8* | *Trevor Davis* | | *26.03.63* | *8h5* | *Gothenburg, SWE* | *10 Aug* |
| 22.01 | | Jason Smith | | 20.05.68 | 2 | Peterborough | 28 Aug |
| 22.03 | -0.6 | Mike Rey | | 19.07.68 | 2h2 | London (CP) | 18 Jun |
| 22.06 | | W. St.Hiller | | | 1 | Ranstein, GER | 27 Jun |
| 22.06 | 0.9 | Philip Ellershaw | U20 | 9.02.76 | 8s2 | Bedford | 2 Jul |
| 22.07 | | Bryan McCoy | U23 | 31.12.75 | 1 | Antrim | 8 Jul |
| 22.07 | 0.7 | Mark McIntyre | | 14.10.70 | 3h1 | Birmingham | 16 Jul |
| 22.07 | -1.9 | Onochie Onuorah | U23 | 16.10.73 | 5h6 | Birmingham | 16 Jul |
| 22.08 i | | Mark Hopkinson | U23 | 16.04.75 | 3s2 | Birmingham | 1 Jan |
| 22.09 | 1.6 | Clive Farrow | | 24.04.70 | 3 | Barking | 14 May |
| 22.10 | 0.4 | Alan Leaming | U20 | 2.11.76 | 6s1 | Bedford | 2 Jul |
| (90) | | | | | | | |
| 22.10 | 0.7 | Mark Phills | | 26.07.64 | 4h1 | Birmingham | 16 Jul |
| 22.13 | -0.6 | Martin Bennett | | 14.10.67 | 3h2 | London (CP) | 18 Jun |
| 22.13 | 2.0 | Philip Robson | U20 | 7.02.77 | 2 | London (He) | 6 Aug |
| 22.14 | | Terry McAdams | | | 1 | Wrexham | 25 Jun |
| 22.15 | | Phil Lewis | | 12.01.70 | 1 | London (CP) | 14 May |
| 22.15 | -0.4 | Onochie Achike | U23 | 31.01.75 | 5h4 | Birmingham | 16 Jul |
| 22.17 | 1.6 | Keith Palmer | | 19.11.64 | 4 | Barking | 14 May |
| 22.18 i | | Tremayne Rutherford | | 19.06.72 | 3r1 | Birmingham | 29 Jan |
| 22.19 i | | Bryn Middleton | U20 | 16.02.76 | 3h2 | Birmingham | 18 Feb |
| 22.20 | | Peter Brend | U20 | 2.02.77 | 1 | Braunton | 13 May |
| (100) | | | | | | | |
| 22.20 | | Paul Jamieson | U23 | 21.06.73 | 2 | Bebington | 23 Jul |
| 22.20 | 2.0 | Bode Oluwa | U20 | 15.11.76 | 3 | London (He) | 6 Aug |

**doubtful**

| Time | Wind | Name | Cat | DOB | Pos | Venue | Date |
|---|---|---|---|---|---|---|---|
| 22.10 | 1.1 | Dave Clark | | 16.02.64 | 4r1 | Cardiff | 19 Aug |

## Wind Assisted

| | | | | | | | | |
|---|---|---|---|---|---|---|---|---|
| 20.12 | 2.3 | Christie | | (20.11) | 3r1 | Lausanne, SWZ | 5 | Jul |
| 20.28 | 2.3 | Regis | | (20.26) | 4r1 | Lausanne, SWZ | 5 | Jul |
| | 20.76 | 3.7 | | | 7 | Paris, FRA | 3 | Jul |
| 20.53 | 3.4 | Doug Walker | U23 | (20.88) | 1 | Edinburgh | 8 | May |
| 20.55 | 4.3 | Wariso | | (20.50) | 1r1 | Bedford | 10 | Jun |
| | 20.58 | 2.2 | | | 2 | Oslo, NOR | 21 | Jul |
| 20.62 | 4.3 | Adrian Patrick | U23 | (21.17) | 2r1 | Bedford | 10 | Jun |
| 20.68 | 4.0 | Doug Turner | | (20.75) | 1r1 | Cwmbran | 9 | Jul |
| 20.69 | 2.2 | Julian Golding | U23 | (20.75) | 2 | Gateshead | 2 | Jul |
| 20.73 | | Phil Goedluck | | (21.20) | 1r3 | Irvine, USA | 23 | Apr |
| | 20.88 | 4.3 | | | 3 | Bedford | 10 | Jun |
| | 20.98 | 3.1 | | | 1 | Pomona, USA | 15 | Apr |
| 20.74 | 4.0 | Jason John | | (20.86) | 2r1 | Cwmbran | 9 | Jul |
| 20.86 | 4.0 | Jamie Baulch | U23 | (21.32) | 4r1 | Cwmbran | 9 | Jul |
| 20.88 | 4.0 | Marlon Devonish | U20 | (20.94) | 1 | Telford | 26 | Aug |
| 20.92 | | Mark Smith | | (21.00) | 3r3 | Irvine, USA | 23 | Apr |
| 20.93 | | Ayo Falola | | (21.20) | 4r3 | Irvine, USA | 23 | Apr |
| 20.96 | 3.4 | Peter Maitland | U23 | (21.02) | 2 | Edinburgh | 8 | May |

18 performances to 21.00 by 14 athletes

| | | | | | | | | |
|---|---|---|---|---|---|---|---|---|
| *21.18* | | *Thomas Ganda* | | *(21.27)* | *3* | *Los Angeles, USA* | *12* | *May* |
| 21.28 | 4.3 | Andrew Walcott | U23 | (21.36) | 6r1 | Bedford | 10 | Jun |
| 21.41 | 2.9 | Jared Deacon | U23 | (21.66) | 2 | Gateshead | 17 | Jun |
| 21.41 | 4.1 | Christian Malcolm | U17 | (21.58) | 1 | Cardiff | 1 | Jul |
| 21.50 | | Mark McIntyre | | (22.07) | 7r3 | Irvine, USA | 23 | Apr |
| 21.54 | 4.0 | Richard Rubenis | U23 | 10.11.73 | 3 | Telford | 26 | Aug |
| 21.62 | 3.1 | James Egan | U23 | (21.90) | 2 | Hull | 5 | Aug |
| 21.70 | 2.6 | Phil Lewis | | (22.15) | 1h6 | Edinburgh | 7 | May |
| 21.71 | 2.3 | Dalton Powell | | 20.08.63 | 1 | Birmingham | 18 | Jun |
| 21.78 | 2.9 | Lewis Samuel | | 12.02.66 | 5 | Gateshead | 17 | Jun |
| 21.78 | 2.5 | Corri Henry | U20 | (21.88) | 2 | Nottingham | 8 | Jul |
| 21.85 | 3.1 | Alan Leaming | U20 | (22.10) | 3 | Hull | 5 | Aug |
| 21.88 | | Ray Burke | | 11.11.69 | 2r2 | Irvine, USA | 23 | Apr |
| 21.91 | 2.3 | Jason Smith | | (22.01) | 2 | Birmingham | 18 | Jun |
| 21.92 | 2.3 | Nigel Hamer | U20 | 1.01.76 | 2 | Sheffield | 28 | May |
| 21.94 | 2.1 | Andrew Lees | U17 | 11.05.79 | 1 | Grangemouth | 14 | May |
| | 22.47 i | | | | 1 | Glasgow | 4 | Feb |
| 21.95 | 4.3 | Richard Johnson | | 13.10.71 | 8r1 | Bedford | 10 | Jun |
| 22.01 | 3.4 | Darren Walker | U23 | 21.03.75 | 7 | Edinburgh | 8 | May |
| 22.05 | 2.6 | Alex Francis | U23 | 15.07.74 | 3s3 | Edinburgh | 8 | May |
| 22.08 | 5.7 | Craig Hurst | | 30.12.70 | 2 | Stoke | 13 | May |
| 22.08 | 2.9 | Alistair Audsley | | 17.08.65 | 6 | Gateshead | 17 | Jun |
| 22.13 | 2.5 | Daniel Bruce | U20 | 29.09.76 | 4 | Nottingham | 8 | Jul |
| 22.15 | 3.7 | Greg Jones | | | 1h1 | Edinburgh | 7 | May |
| 22.17 | 2.3 | Matt Bartsch | | 12.12.64 | 4r1 | Edinburgh | 3 | Jun |
| 22.18 | 2.8 | Barry Middleton | U23 | 10.03.75 | 1 | Grangemouth | 14 | May |

## Hand Timing

| | | | | | | | | |
|---|---|---|---|---|---|---|---|---|
| 20.6 w | 2.9 | Dako | U23 | 23.05.73 | 1r2 | Crawley | 1 | Jul |
| 20.7 | 1.4 | Julian Golding | U23 | (20.75) | 1 | Hayes | 13 | May |
| | 20.9 w | 2.9 | | | 1h1 | Hayes | 13 | May |
| 21.0 | | Adrian Patrick | U23 | (21.17) | 1 | Bracknell | 14 | May |
| 21.0 | 1.2 | Turner | | 2.12.66 | 1r1 | Crawley | 1 | Jul |
| 21.0 | | Box | | 9.09.72 | 1 | Derby | 30 | Jul |
| 21.0 w | 2.9 | Baulch | U23 | 3.05.73 | 2r2 | Crawley | 1 | Jul |
| 21.0 w | 3.0 | Mark Allen | | (21.10) | 1 | London (WL) | 30 | Jul |
| 21.1 | | Paul White | U23 | (21.29) | 1 | Loughborough | 24 | May |
| 21.1 w | | John Kenny | | 17.12.70 | 1 | London (Nh) | 22 | Jun |

10 performances to 21.1 by 9 athletes incuding 5 wind assisted

| Time | Wind | Name | Cat | Mark/DOB | Pos | Venue | Date |
|---|---|---|---|---|---|---|---|
| 21.2 | | Michael Afilaka | | (21.22) | 2 | Derby | 30 Jul |
| | | | | | | | |
| 21.2 w | 3.0 | Cypren Edmunds | | (21.31) | 2 | London (WL) | 30 Jul |
| 21.3 | 1.0 | Steve Coupland | | (21.72) | 2 | Sheffield | 13 May |
| 21.3 | 1.1 | Andrew Bull | | 26.06.69 | 1 | Sheffield | 14 May |
| 21.3 | | Darren Scott | | (21.35) | 1 | Wakefield | 12 Aug |
| 21.3 w | 2.4 | David McKenzie | | 3.09.70 | 1r1 | Croydon | 28 Aug |
| 21.6 | -0.5 | | | | 4r1 | London (He) | 7 May |
| 21.4 | | Ian Mackie | U23 | (21.53) | 1 | Carlisle | 30 Apr |
| 21.4 | | Donley Jack | | (21.84) | 1 | London (PH) | 2 Aug |
| 21.4 w | 2.9 | Sunny Adepegba | | (21.79) | 2h1 | Hayes | 13 May |
| 21.4 w | 3.1 | Mark Lambeth | | (21.86) | 2h3 | Hayes | 13 May |
| 21.5 | 1.4 | | | | 2 | Hayes | 13 May |
| 21.4 w | 4.7 | Mark Davidson | | 15.11.68 | 1 | Aberdeen | 23 Jul |
| | | | | | | | |
| 21.5 | | Jared Deacon | U23 | (21.66) | 1r1 | Barking | 3 Jun |
| 21.5 | | Jason Fergus | U23 | 11.10.73 | 1r1 | Basildon | 1 Jul |
| 21.5 | | Richard Ralph | | 14.07.71 | 1r1 | London (WL) | 5 Aug |
| 21.5 | | Phillip Perigo | U17 | (21.69) | 2 | Wakefield | 12 Aug |
| 21.5 | -1.8 | Nigel Will | | 18.10.67 | 1r1 | Watford | 19 Aug |
| 21.5 w | 4.0 | Mark Woodhouse | U23 | 1.11.75 | 1r2 | Bedford | 26 Aug |
| 21.6 | | | | | 1 | Loughborough | 20 May |
| 21.6 w | 3.9 | Ross Baillie | U20 | (21.75) | 1 | Grangemouth | 17 Jun |
| 21.7 | -1.2 | | | | 1 | Ayr | 18 Jul |
| 21.6 w | 3.0 | Stefan Rose | U23 | 7.04.75 | 3 | London (WL) | 30 Jul |
| 21.6 w | 2.3 | Dave Deacon | | (21.86) | 3 | Grimsby | 3 Sep |
| 21.7 | | | | | 3 | Loughborough | 24 May |
| 21.7 | -0.9 | Lee Fairclough | | (21.96) | 1 | Portsmouth | 13 May |
| | | | | | | | |
| 21.7 | 1.4 | Alex Fugallo | | (21.95i) | 5 | Hayes | 13 May |
| 21.7 | | Andi Knight | U23 | (21.90) | 2r1 | Loughborough | 20 May |
| 21.7 | | Paul Jamieson | U23 | (22.20) | 3r1 | Loughborough | 20 May |
| 21.7 | 1.3 | Paul Slythe | U23 | (21.78) | 1r1 | Wakefield | 3 Jun |
| 21.7 | 0.7 | Scott Dorset | | 10.04.69 | 1 | Croydon | 25 Jun |
| 21.7 | 0.7 | Scott Herbert | U23 | 12.02.74 | 2 | Croydon | 25 Jun |
| 21.7 | | Guy Bullock | U23 | (21.25A) | 1 | Stretford | 1 Jul |
| 21.7 | | Mike Rey | | (22.03) | 2r1 | Harrow | 9 Jul |
| 21.7 | | Justin Sleath | | 9.02.67 | 3r1 | Harrow | 9 Jul |
| 21.7 | -0.8 | Steve Shanks | | (21.72) | 2 | Birmingham | 19 Jul |
| | | | | | | | |
| 21.7 | | David Grindley | | 29.10.72 | 3 | Wakefield | 12 Aug |
| 21.7 | -0.6 | Steve Simmons | U23 | (21.71) | 2r1 | Sheffield | 19 Aug |
| 21.8 | 1.3 | Andy Tulloch | | 1.04.67 | 1r1 | Stoke | 6 May |
| 21.8 | | Kevin Mark | U20 | 15.09.76 | 1r1 | Croydon | 6 May |
| 21.8 | | Nigel Hamer | U20 | (21.92w) | 1r1 | Derby | 3 Jun |
| 21.8 | | Ian Craig | | (21.86) | 2r2 | Barking | 3 Jun |
| 21.8 | | Graeme Welsh | U23 | (21.86) | 3r1 | Barking | 3 Jun |
| 21.8 | | Tony Waddington | U23 | 30.06.75 | 2 | London (Nh) | 22 Jun |
| 21.8 | | Trevor Painter | | 10.08.71 | 1 | Stretford | 27 Jun |
| 21.8 | | James Egan | U23 | (21.90) | 1r1 | Leeds | 1 Jul |
| | | | | | | | |
| 21.8 | | Mark Phills | | (22.10) | 4r1 | Harrow | 9 Jul |
| 21.9 | 1.3 | Rohan Samuel | | 30.01.66 | 3r1 | Stoke | 6 May |
| 21.9 | | Kahindi Sanusi | U20 | 17.01.77 | 1 | Reading | 1 Jul |
| 21.9 | | Chris Davidson | U23 | 4.12.75 | 3 | London (TB) | 29 Jul |
| 21.9 | | Oladipo Scott-Boyle | U23 | 17.06.74 | 1r1 | London (Elt) | 5 Aug |
| 21.9 | | Ray Salami | U23 | 11.04.74 | 1r2 | Ilford | 19 Aug |
| 21.9 | | Dan Donovan | | (21.94) | 1 | Carshalton | 17 Sep |
| 21.9 w | 2.3 | Andrew Lees | U17 | (21.94w) | 1 | Grangemouth | 17 Jun |
| 22.2 | 1.3 | | | | 3 | Wakefield | 3 Jun |
| 22.0 | | Richard Workman | | 31.05.71 | 1 | Wakefield | 30 Apr |

| Time | Wind | Name | Cat | DOB | Pos | Venue | Date |
|---|---|---|---|---|---|---|---|
| 22.0 | 1.3 | Kevin Stephens | | 17.08.72 | 1r2 | Bournemouth | 6 May |
| 22.0 | 1.3 | Tony Leigh | | 27.12.65 | 4r1 | Stoke | 6 May |
| 22.0 | | Paul Field | | 24.06.67 | 2 | Thurrock | 6 May |
| 22.0 | | Daniel Bruce | U20 | (22.13w) | 1r1 | Telford | 6 May |
| 22.0 | 1.0 | Matthew Gillard | U23 | 11.07.75 | 3 | Sheffield | 13 May |
| 22.0 | 1.0 | Mark Huggins | | 20.12.68 | 4 | Sheffield | 13 May |
| 22.0 | | Chris Millard | | 19.07.66 | 1 | Yate | 14 May |
| 22.0 | | Martin Bennett | | (22.13) | 2 | Watford | 14 May |
| 22.0 | | Gary Ghent | U23 | 2.11.73 | 1r1 | Telford | 3 Jun |
| 22.0 | | Matthew Douglas | U20 | 26.11.76 | 2r1 | Milton Keynes | 3 Jun |
| 22.0 | | Tim Barton | | 3.10.70 | 1r1 | Cannock | 22 Jul |
| 22.0 | | Steve McHardy | U20 | 8.01.76 | 2r1 | Cannock | 22 Jul |
| 22.0 | | Jamie Paul | | 17.07.70 | 2 | London (PH) | 2 Aug |
| 22.0 | | Onochie Onuorah | U23 | (22.07) | 1 | London (He) | 5 Aug |
| 22.0 | | Kieran Gajjar | U20 | 25.09.76 | 1r1 | Hull | 19 Aug |
| 22.0 | | Michael Tietz | U20 | 14.09.77 | 2r1 | Hull | 19 Aug |
| 22.0 | | Dalton Powell | | (21.71w) | 1 | Sutton Coldfield | 26 Aug |
| 22.0 w | 2.1 | Matt Bartsch | | (22.17w) | 5r1 | Liverpool | 6 May |
| 22.0 w | 2.9 | Eddie Betts | | 18.02.71 | 4h1 | Hayes | 13 May |
| 22.0 w | 3.1 | Eric John | | 28.06.61 | 2 | Crawley | 25 Jun |

**Additional Under 17** (1 - 6 above)

| Time | Wind | Name | Cat | DOB | Pos | Venue | Date |
|---|---|---|---|---|---|---|---|
| 22.2 | | James Hilston | | 25.02.79 | 1 | Sutton | 19 Jul |
| 22.2 w | 2.3 | Chris Carson | | 26.10.79 | 2 | Grangemouth | 17 Jun |
| 22.4 | | | | | 1 | Wishaw | 17 Sep |
| 22.63 w 2.1 | | | | | 1 | Grangemouth | 14 May |
| 22.21 | 1.9 | Ian Leaman | | 14.10.78 | 4 | Nottingham | 8 Jul |
| 22.22 | 1.9 | Jonathan Moss | | 24.09.78 | 5 | Nottingham | 8 Jul |
| (10) | | | | | | | |
| 22.27 w | 3.1 | Nick Long | | 1.02.79 | 5 | Hull | 5 Aug |
| 22.6 | | | | | 1 | Middlesbrough | 25 Jun |
| 22.31 | 1.9 | Andy Edmonds | | 17.09.78 | 2s1 | Nottingham | 8 Jul |
| 22.38 | 0.0 | Andrew Row | | 17.10.78 | 2 | Sheffield | 27 May |
| 22.40 | 1.6 | Ben Lewis | U15 | 6.03.81 | 1 | Nottingham | 8 Jul |
| 22.40 | -0.7 | Luke Davis | | 1.01.80 | 1h4 | Birmingham | 29 Jul |
| 22.4 | | Daniel Bonich | | 22.11.78 | 1 | Dartford | 21 May |
| 22.4 | | Thomas Begen | | 14.04.79 | 1 | Coatbridge | 18 Jun |
| 22.5 | | Remi Edu | | 14.12.78 | 1 | Welwyn | 10 Jun |
| 22.5 | | K. Augustus | | | 1 | Perivale | 16 Jul |
| 22.5 | | David Lawson | | 12.05.79 | 1 | Manchester | 16 Jul |
| 22.65 | 0.6 | | | | 2h1 | Birmingham | 29 Jul |
| (20) | | | | | | | |
| 22.51 w | 3.2 | Steven Daly | | 29.12.79 | 2 | Hull | 5 Aug |
| 22.58 w | 2.7 | Andrew Crossley | | 22.05.79 | 5s2 | Nottingham | 8 Jul |
| 22.6 | | Daniel Cannes | | | 1 | Birmingham | 10 Jun |
| 22.6 | | Matthew Still | | 1.12.79 | 2 | Portsmouth | 10 Jun |
| 22.6 | | Barry Halpin | | 20.07.79 | 1 | Cleckheaton | 14 Jun |
| 22.6 w | 3.5 | Marlon Dickson | | 17.11.78 | 1 | Croydon | 13 May |
| 22.6 w | 3.8 | Michael Bruce | | 8.10.78 | 1h2 | Grangemouth | 21 Jun |
| 22.62 | -1.4 | | | | 1 | Pitreavie | 8 Jul |
| 22.61 | | Kris Stewart | | 11.04.80 | 1 | Antrim | 12 Aug |
| 22.62 | -0.8 | Robert Allan | | 4.11.78 | 3h1 | Birmingham | 29 Jul |
| 22.65 w | 2.7 | Christian Creaby | | 11.10.78 | 6s2 | Nottingham | 8 Jul |
| (30) | | | | | | | |
| 22.69 | 1.9 | James Shawcross | | 12.02.79 | 5s1 | Nottingham | 8 Jul |

**Additional Under 15** (1 above)

| | | | | | | | | |
|---|---|---|---|---|---|---|---|---|
| 23.0 w | | Andre Silva | | 18.11.80 | 1 | Swansea | 28 | Aug |
| | | 23.41 1.3 | | | 1 | Cardiff | 1 | Jul |
| 23.09 | 1.6 | Alex Chaffe | | 5.12.80 | 2 | Nottingham | 8 | Jul |
| 23.12 | 1.6 | Daniel Plummer | | 4.01.81 | 3 | Nottingham | 8 | Jul |
| 23.16 | 0.7 | Dominic Gordon | | 7.01.81 | 1r1 | Stoke | 17 | Jun |
| 23.2 | | Kevin Hibbins | | 7.11.80 | 1 | Grantham | 11 | Jun |
| 23.23 | 1.6 | Alex Wilkinson | | 10.10.80 | 4 | Nottingham | 8 | Jul |
| 23.24 w | 2.2 | Matthew Butler | | 27.02.81 | 1 | London (He) | 6 | Aug |
| 23.3 | | Adam Newton | | 4.12.80 | 1 | Windsor | 25 | Jun |
| 23.39 | 1.6 | Tom Oswald | | 17.12.80 | 5 | Nottingham | 8 | Jul |
| | (10) | | | | | | | |
| 23.4 | | Russell Johnson | | 14.09.80 | 1 | London (TB) | 25 | Jun |
| 23.41 | -2.4 | Myrone Levy | | 12.02.81 | 2r1 | Birmingham | 29 | Jul |
| 23.46 w | 3.2 | Simon Collins | | 23.11.80 | 1 | Hull | 5 | Aug |
| 23.48 w | 3.2 | Ian Lowthian | | 10.10.80 | 2 | Hull | 5 | Aug |
| 23.5 | | Christopher Bennett | | 18.10.80 | 1 | Bournemouth | 23 | Jul |
| 23.51 | 2.0 | John Blackman | | 12.11.80 | 2s1 | Nottingham | 8 | Jul |
| 23.54 | -1.6 | Leon Connikie | | 6.01.81 | 2 | London (CP) | 28 | May |
| 23.6 | | Matthew Jones | | 5.12.80 | 1 | Cheltenham | 17 | Jun |
| 23.67 | 2.0 | Paul Crick | | 9.10.80 | 3s1 | Nottingham | 8 | Jul |
| 23.68 i | | Wayne Gray | | 7.11.80 | 1 | Birmingham | 18 | Feb |

**Under 13**

| | | | | | | | |
|---|---|---|---|---|---|---|---|
| 24.1 | T. Anthony | | | 1 | London (TB) | 30 | Jul |
| 25.2 | Mark Francis | | 4.09.82 | 1 | Birmingham | 25 | Jun |
| 25.5 | J. Davies | | | 1 | Watford | 9 | Jul |
| 25.7 | Tim Suswain | | 22.02.83 | 1 | Harrow | 4 | Jun |
| 25.7 | Chris Palmer | | | 1 | Southend | 25 | Jun |
| 25.7 | B. Heasley | | | 1 | Londonderry | 8 | Aug |

## 300 METRES

| | | | | | | | |
|---|---|---|---|---|---|---|---|
| 33.0 | David McKenzie | | 3.09.70 | 1 | Southampton | 3 | Sep |
| 33.0 | Mark Hylton | U20 | 24.09.76 | 1 | Cannock | 9 | Sep |
| | 33.70 | | | 1 | Tonsberg, NOR | 17 | Jun |
| 33.12 | Jared Deacon | U23 | 15.10.75 | 1 | Gateshead | 12 | Aug |
| 33.2 | Kent Ulyatt | | 10.04.72 | 2 | Cannock | 9 | Sep |
| 33.5 | Tim O'Dell | | 29.05.70 | 1 | Basingstoke | 6 | Aug |
| 33.6 | Adrian Patrick | U23 | 15.06.73 | 3 | Cannock | 9 | Sep |
| 33.8 | Paul McBurney | | 14.03.72 | 1 | Belfast | 22 | Apr |
| 33.8 | Lee Fairclough | | 23.06.70 | 2 | Southampton | 3 | Sep |
| 33.88 | Dave Deacon | | 19.03.65 | 2 | Gateshead | 12 | Aug |
| 33.9 | Dan Donovan | | 8.10.70 | 2 | Basingstoke | 6 | Aug |
| | (10) | | | | | | |

## 400 METRES

| | | | | | | | |
|---|---|---|---|---|---|---|---|
| 44.59 | Roger Black | | 31.03.66 | 3 | Lausanne, SWZ | 5 | Jul |
| | 45.01 | | | 3q1 | Gothenburg, SWE | 6 | Aug |
| | 45.07 | | | 1 | Madrid, SPA | 20 | Jun |
| | 45.15 | | | 1 | Granada, SPA | 27 | May |
| | 45.16 | | | 2r1 | London (CP) | 7 | Jul |
| | 45.18 | | | 2 | London (CP) | 27 | Aug |
| | 45.20 | | | 4 | Gateshead | 21 | Aug |
| | 45.23 | | | 4 | Berlin, GER | 1 | Sep |
| | 45.28 | | | 7 | Gothenburg, SWE | 8 | Aug |
| | 45.32 | | | 4s1 | Gothenburg, SWE | 7 | Aug |
| | 45.42 | | | 2 | Rieti, ITA | 5 | Sep |
| | 45.54 | | | 2 | Sheffield | 23 | Jul |
| | 45.81 | | | 1h1 | Gothenburg, SWE | 5 | Aug |

| 44.81 | Mark Richardson | | 26.07.72 | 5 | Gothenburg, SWE | 9 | Aug |
|---|---|---|---|---|---|---|---|
| | 44.92 | | | 1r1 | Dijon, FRA | 28 | May |
| | 44.94 | | | 1 | Birmingham | 16 | Jul |
| | 45.00 | | | 2 | Gateshead | 21 | Aug |
| | 45.06 | | | 3 | Oslo, NOR | 21 | Jul |
| | 45.30 | | | 2q3 | Gothenburg, SWE | 6 | Aug |
| | 45.35 | | | 1 | Khania, GRE | 4 | Jun |
| | 45.39 | | | 3 | London (CP) | 27 | Aug |
| | 45.42 | | | 4s2 | Gothenburg, SWE | 7 | Aug |
| | 45.43 | | | 1 | Villeneuve d'Ascq, FRA | 24 | Jun |
| | 45.53 | | | 6 | Brussels, BEL | 25 | Aug |
| | 45.61 | | | 1h3 | Gothenburg, SWE | 5 | Aug |
| | 45.82 | | | 2 | Gateshead | 2 | Jul |
| | 45.95 | | | 1s2 | Birmingham | 15 | Jul |
| | 46.36 | | | 1h2 | Birmingham | 15 | Jul |
| 45.14 | Jamie Baulch | U23 | 3.05.73 | 2 | Copenhagen, DEN | 23 | Aug |
| | 45.15 | | | 3 | Gateshead | 21 | Aug |
| | 45.40 | | | 1 | Narbonne, FRA | 29 | Jul |
| | 45.57 | | | 5 | London (CP) | 27 | Aug |
| | 45.93 | | | 1 | Stoke | 9 | Sep |
| 45.58 | Iwan Thomas | U23 | 5.01.74 | 2 | Bellinzona, SWZ | 20 | Jun |
| | 45.73 | | | 1 | Ljubljana, SLO | 21 | May |
| | 46.03 | | | 3 | Helsinki, FIN | 28 | Jun |
| | 46.40 | | | 1 | Newport | 17 | Jun |
| 45.63 | Ad.ian Patrick | U23 | 15.06.73 | 7 | Lausanne, SWZ | 5 | Jul |
| | 46.02 | | | 2 | Helsinki, FIN | 28 | Jun |
| | 46.10 | | | 1 | Oslo (Lam), NOR | 14 | Jun |
| | 46.11 | | | 3 | Birmingham | 16 | Jul |
| | 46.11 | | | 4h4 | Gothenburg, SWE | 5 | Aug |
| | 46.27 | | | 7q2 | Gothenburg, SWE | 6 | Aug |
| | 46.32 | | | 2r1 | Zofingen, SWZ | 5 | Jun |
| | 46.34 | | | 1 | Caslav, CS | 20 | Jun |
| | 46.43 | | | 5 | Sheffield | 23 | Jul |
| 45.74 | Du'aine Ladejo | | 14.02.71 | 2 | Ljubljana, SLO | 21 | May |
| | 45.97 | | | 1 | Azusa, USA | 22 | Apr |
| | 46.18 | | | 1 | Ostrava, CS | 1 | Jun |
| 45.83 | Mark Hylton | U20 | 24.09.76 | 2 | Birmingham | 16 | Jul |
| | 45.97 | | | 1 | Nyiregyhaza, HUN | 28 | Jul |
| | 46.04 | | | 6 | London (CP) | 27 | Aug |
| | 46.26 | | | 1 | Nottingham | 8 | Jul |
| | 46.44 | | | 5 | Dijon, FRA | 28 | May |
| 45.96 | David McKenzie | | 3.09.70 | 1 | Fort-de-France, MRT | 1 | May |
| | 46.20 | | | 4 | Bellinzona, SWZ | 20 | Jun |
| | 46.27 | | | 2 | Ostrava, CS | 1 | Jun |
| | 46.32 | | | 2s2 | Birmingham | 15 | Jul |
| | 46.37 | | | 1 | Birmingham | 1 | Jul |
| | 46.48 | | | 2 | Stoke | 9 | Sep |
| 46.15 | David Grindley | | 29.10.72 | 5s2 | Fukuoka, JAP | 1 | Sep |
| 46.31 | Kent Ulyatt | | 10.04.72 | 1 | Stoke | 10 | Sep |
| | (10) | | | | | | |
| 46.34 | Tim O'Dell | | 29.05.70 | 1r1 | Enfield | 19 | Aug |
| | 46.42 | | | 4 | Birmingham | 16 | Jul |
| | 46.44 | | | 3 | Pune, IND | 13 | Sep |
| 46.41 | Guy Bullock | U23 | 15.10.75 | 2 | Malmo, SWE | 29 | Jun |
| 46.44 A | Mark Smith | | 18.11.71 | 5 | Nairobi, KEN | 27 | May |
| | 46.60 | | | 1r2 | London (CP) | 7 | Jul |
| 46.45 | Jared Deacon | U23 | 15.10.75 | 5s1 | Fukuoka, JAP | 1 | Sep |
| | 69 performances to 46.5 by 14 athletes | | | | | | |
| 46.61 | David Nolan | | 25.07.69 | 1 | Cwmbran | 9 | Jul |
| 46.68 | Paul McBurney | | 14.03.72 | 2r2 | London (CP) | 7 | Ju! |

| 46.95 | Gary Jennings | | 21.02.72 | 1 | Edinburgh | 8 May |
|---|---|---|---|---|---|---|
| 47.01 | Brian Whittle | | 26.04.64 | 4s1 | Birmingham | 15 Jul |
| 47.02 | Geoff Dearman | U20 | 4.08.77 | 1 | Belfort, FRA | 6 Aug |
| 47.03 | Paul Slythe | U23 | 5.09.74 | 3r2 | London (CP) | 7 Jul |
| (20) | | | | | | |
| 47.04 | Nigel Will | | 18.10.67 | 1 | London (CP) | 18 Jun |
| 47.2 | Peter Maitland | U23 | 21.01.73 | 1r1 | Crawley | 1 Jul |
| 47.29 | | | | 3 | Cwmbran | 9 Jul |
| 47.23 | Eddie Williams | | 1.10.70 | 4r1 | Birmingham | 1 Jul |
| 47.30 | Chas McCaw | | 21.01.72 | 2 | Edinburgh | 8 May |
| 47.33 i | Doug Walker | U23 | 28.07.73 | 1 | Glasgow | 15 Jan |
| 47.42 | Alex Francis | U23 | 15.07.74 | 1r2 | Enfield | 19 Aug |
| 47.42 | Quincy Douglas | U23 | 7.09.75 | 2 | Lillehammer, NOR | 19 Aug |
| *47.49* | *Callum Taylor* | | *25.10.72* | *2r2* | *Enfield* | *19 Aug* |
| 47.5 | Nick Budden | U23 | 17.11.75 | 1 | Bedford | 26 Aug |
| 47.76 | | | | 2r2 | Loughborough | 11 Jun |
| 47.53 | Steve McHardy | U20 | 8.01.76 | 4h3 | Birmingham | 15 Jul |
| 47.57 | Justin Sleath | | 9.02.67 | 4h5 | Birmingham | 15 Jul |
| (30) | | | | | | |
| 47.57 | Tom Lerwill | U20 | 17.05.77 | 3 | Belfort, FRA | 6 Aug |
| 47.6 | Peter Crampton | | 4.06.69 | 2 | Sheffield | 13 May |
| 48.40 i | | | | 1 | Birmingham | 1 Jan |
| 47.6 | Lee Fairclough | | 23.06.70 | 1r1 | Hoo | 19 Aug |
| 47.80 | | | | 1 | Aldershot | 26 Jun |
| 47.69 i | Hugh Kerr | U20 | 4.01.76 | 1 | Erfurt, GER | 25 Feb |
| 47.75 | | | | 3 | Edinburgh | 8 May |
| 47.69 | Simon Ciaravella | U23 | 24.11.73 | 1 | Barking | 14 May |
| 47.7 | Mark Sesay | | 13.12.72 | 1 | Stretford | 1 Aug |
| 47.73 | Jim Beattie | U23 | 22.07.73 | 1h1 | Edinburgh | 23 Jun |
| 47.76 i | Andy Gibson | U23 | 20.09.73 | 2r1 | Birmingham | 26 Feb |
| 48.1 | | | | 1 | Wrexham | 5 Aug |
| 48.26 | | | | 4r2 | Loughborough | 11 Jun |
| 47.79 A | Trevor Painter | | 10.08.71 | 2 | Albuquerque, USA | 22 Apr |
| 48.07 | | | | 2 | Gateshead | 17 Jun |
| 47.8 | Steve Coupland | | 15.06.65 | 1r1 | Bournemouth | 6 May |
| 48.10 | | | | 3 | Birmingham | 20 May |
| (40) | | | | | | |
| 47.8 | Phil Lewis | | 12.01.70 | 2r1 | Norwich | 3 Jun |
| 47.83 | Vince Rose | | 21.08.71 | 5 | Vila Real, POR | 27 May |
| 47.88 | Alex Fugallo | | 28.01.70 | 4 | Ljubljana, SLO | 21 May |
| 47.9 | James Weston | | 9.01.70 | 7 | Cork, IRE | 24 Jun |
| 48.21 | | | | 6 | Cwmbran | 9 Jul |
| 47.9 | Sam Kabiswa | | 28.10.66 | 3 | London (WL) | 30 Jul |
| 48.05 | | | | 4 | London (CP) | 18 Jun |
| 47.99 | Dave Savage | | 13.11.72 | 1r1 | Edinburgh | 3 Jun |
| 48.02 | Mark Ponting | U20 | 28.04.77 | 1 | Utrecht, HOL | 9 Jul |
| 48.10 | Dan Donovan | | 8.10.70 | 5 | London (CP) | 18 Jun |
| 48.13 | Lawrence Lynch | | 1.11.67 | 3r2 | Enfield | 19 Aug |
| 48.19 | Lloyd Cowan | | 8.07.62 | 2r2 | Irvine, USA | 23 Apr |
| (50) | | | | | | |
| 48.2 | Matthew Douglas | U20 | 26.11.76 | 1 | Croydon | 25 Jun |
| 48.61 | | | | 1 | London (CP) | 28 May |
| 48.2 | Brian Darby | | 14.10.72 | 2 | Derby | 30 Jul |
| 48.84 | | | | 6h3 | Birmingham | 15 Jul |
| 48.2 | Richard Rubenis | U23 | 10.11.73 | 1r1 | Mansfield | 19 Aug |
| 48.22 | | | | 2 | Stoke | 10 Sep. |
| 48.23 | Kermitt Bentham | | 16.04.60 | 4r2 | Enfield | 19 Aug |
| 48.28 | Simon Haynes | U23 | 12.08.74 | 1r3 | Oslo (Lam), NOR | 14 Jun |
| 48.28 | Richard Knowles | U23 | 12.11.75 | 1 | Haguenau, FRA | 17 Jun |
| 48.3 | Tony Williams | | 1.05.72 | 1r1 | Loughborough | 20 May |
| 48.3 | Bruce Craven | | 18.03.72 | 3 | Derby | 30 Jul |

| | | | | | | | |
|---|---|---|---|---|---|---|---|
| 48.3 | Dave Deacon | | 19.03.65 | 1 | Gateshead | 2 | Aug |
| 48.34 | Richard McNabb | U17 | 22.02.80 | 1 | London (CP) | 27 | Aug |
| (60) | | | | | | | |
| 48.35 | James Hilston | U17 | 25.02.79 | 1 | London (He) | 6 | Aug |
| 48.4 | Dave Griffin | | 5.12.63 | 8 | Cork, IRE | 24 | Jun |
| 48.4 | Neil Jennings | U20 | 18.09.77 | 1r1 | Bolton | 16 | Sep |
| 48.58 | | | | 2 | London (He) | 9 | Sep |
| 48.41 | Carl Southam | U23 | 11.01.74 | 3r2 | Oslo (Lam), NOR | 14 | Jun |
| 48.44 | James Shipp | U20 | 10.11.77 | 3 | Nottingham | 8 | Jul |
| 48.45 | Clive Farrow | | 24.04.70 | 2 | Barking | 14 | May |
| 48.46 | Paul Field | | 24.06.67 | 1D | Alhama, SPA | 20 | May |
| 48.5 | Simon James | U23 | 31.08.73 | 1 | Perivale | 30 | Apr |
| 48.5 | Marlon Devonish | U20 | 1.06.76 | 1r2 | Coventry | 6 | May |
| 48.5 | Eddie Betts | | 18.02.71 | 1 | Plymouth | 6 | May |
| (70) | | | | | | | |
| 48.5 | Alan Murray | | 2.05.67 | 1r1 | Coatbridge | 6 | Aug |
| 48.57 | | | | 2h2 | Edinburgh | 23 | Jun |
| 48.5 | Pete Clarke | | 9.07.65 | 2r1 | Mansfield | 19 | Aug |
| 48.5 | Paul Bergqvist | | 17.08.72 | 2r1 | Bolton | 16 | Sep |
| 48.51 | Michael Bell | U20 | 23.11.77 | 3 | Stoke | 10 | Sep |
| 48.52 | Greg Dunson | | 2.12.63 | 1r1 | Ranstein, GER | 27 | Jun |
| 48.55 | Terry Gould | | 12.06.65 | 1r2 | Ranstein, GER | 27 | Jun |
| 48.55 | Simon Heggie | U20 | 12.01.76 | 5s2 | Bedford | 1 | Jul |
| 48.56 i | Malcolm McPhail | | 8.06.67 | 2 | Glasgow | 22 | Jan |
| 48.57 | Matthew Aldwinkle | U23 | 23.08.74 | 4 | Stoke | 10 | Sep |
| 48.59 | Justin Bird | | 3.05.71 | 4 | Gateshead | 17 | Jun |
| (80) | | | | | | | |
| 48.6 | Darrell Maynard | | 21.08.61 | 1 | Birmingham | 9 | Aug |
| 48.64 i | Adam Mole | U23 | 31.08.75 | 1r3 | Birmingham | 26 | Feb |
| 48.66 | Grant Purves | U23 | 6.04.73 | 4r1 | Edinburgh | 3 | Jun |
| 48.66 | Mark Bishop | | 12.02.67 | 4r1 | Zofingen, SWZ | 5 | Jun |
| 48.66 | Simon Shirley | | 3.08.66 | 4D | Valladolid, SPA | 1 | Jul |
| 48.66 | Nizamul Hoque | U17 | 19.09.78 | 6r2 | Enfield | 19 | Aug |
| 48.67 | Peter Brend | U20 | 2.02.77 | 2 | London (CP) | 28 | May |
| 48.70 | Steve Kneller | | 9.11.71 | 6h1 | Birmingham | 15 | Jul |
| 48.7 | Alasdair Donaldson | U20 | 21.06.77 | 1 | Pitreavie | 25 | Jun |
| 48.7 | Paul Walker | U23 | 2.12.73 | 2r1 | Crawley | 1 | Jul |
| (90) | | | | | | | |
| 48.7 | Robert Scantlebury | U20 | 9.11.76 | 1h3 | Nottingham | 7 | Jul |
| 48.78 | | | | 5 | Nottingham | 8 | Jul |
| 48.7 | Shane Patel | U23 | 4.03.74 | 1 | London (Elt) | 29 | Jul |
| 48.74 | Graham Healy | | 27.04.70 | 3h1 | London (CP) | 17 | Jun |
| 48.79 | Chris Carson | U17 | 26.10.79 | 1 | Pitreavie | 8 | Jul |
| 48.79 | Sean Baldock | U20 | 3.12.76 | 2 | London (He) | 6 | Aug |
| 48.80 i | Gregor McMillan | | 4.04.70 | 4s1 | Birmingham | 3 | Feb |
| 48.80 | Bryan McCoy | U23 | 31.12.75 | 4 | Dublin (M), IRE | 16 | Jul |
| 48.8 | | | | 1r1 | Antrim | 29 | Jul |
| 48.80 | Ryan Patis | U20 | 4.11.77 | 3 | London (He) | 6 | Aug |
| 48.80 | Michael Gallagher | | 25.04.66 | 7 | Stoke | 9 | Sep |
| 48.8 | Martin Steele | | 30.09.62 | 1 | Stretford | 22 | Jul |
| (100) | | | | | | | |
| 48.8 | Scott Herbert | U23 | 12.02.74 | 1r1 | Milton Keynes | 19 | Aug |
| 48.84 i | Barry Middleton | U23 | 10.03.75 | 2 | Glasgow | 15 | Jan |
| 48.84 | Joe Lloyd | U23 | 9.04.73 | 7 | Cwmbran | 9 | Jul |
| 48.86 | Tim Slocombe | U20 | 15.11.77 | 6 | Nottingham | 8 | Jul |
| 48.9 | Richard Dawson | | 7.12.70 | 2 | Perivale | 30 | Apr |
| 48.9 | Barry O'Brien | U20 | 3.07.76 | 1r1 | Jarrow | 6 | May |
| 49.28 | | | | 1 | Sheffield | 27 | May |
| 48.9 | Steve McCourt | | 6.05.71 | 1 | London (TB) | 24 | Jun |
| 48.9 | Noel Levy | U23 | 22.06.75 | 2 | Harrow | 5 | Jul |
| 48.9 | Chris Rawlinson | | 19.05.72 | 1D | Cudworth | 26 | Aug |

| | | | | | | | |
|---|---|---|---|---|---|---|---|
| 48.91 i | Gary Telfer | | 10.01.65 | 3 | Glasgow | 22 | Jan |
| (110) | Tim Gwynne | | 20.01.71 | 2h1 | Birmingham | 3 | Feb |
| 48.91 i | | | | | | | |
| 48.92 | Brian Forbes | U23 | 6.09.74 | 3 | Antrim | 1 | Jul |
| 48.96 | Wayne Martin | U20 | 12.08.76 | 3r2 | Bedford | 2 | Jul |
| 48.96 | Andrew Mitchell | U20 | 30.07.76 | 1 | Pitreavie | 8 | Jul |
| 48.97 | Alan Harrison | | 20.11.57 | 5h1 | London (CP) | 17 | Jun |
| 48.99 | Keith Palmer | | 19.11.64 | 4 | Barking | 14 | May |
| 49.0 | Glenn Gray | | 21.04.68 | 2 | Harrow | 28 | May |
| 49.0 | Martyn Bucknall | | 2.11.70 | 2 | Wrexham | 25 | Jun |
| 49.0 | Darren Bernard | | 15.06.69 | 1 | Croydon | 3 | Sep |

**Additional Under 20** (1 - 21 above)

| | | | | | | | |
|---|---|---|---|---|---|---|---|
| 49.1 | Gavin Mason | | 6.04.77 | 1 | London (TB) | 14 | Jun |
| 49.21 | Ahmed Al-Kowarri | U17 | 30.11.78 | 2 | Pitreavie | 8 | Jul |
| 49.25 i | Laurence Baird | | 14.12.77 | 3 | Birmingham | 19 | Feb |
| 49.25 | | | | 7r2 | London (CP) | 27 | Aug |
| 49.39 | Ian Horsburgh | | 10.01.78 | 2 | Pitreavie | 8 | Jul |
| 49.47 | Lee Black | U17 | 26.11.78 | 3 | Nottingham | 8 | Jul |
| 49.48 | Ben Harper | U17 | 9.11.78 | 1 | Barking | 14 | May |
| 49.49 | Philip Sadler | | 22.04.77 | 4 | London (CP) | 27 | May |
| 49.49 | Simon Mathieson | U17 | 20.01.79 | 2s1 | Nottingham | 8 | Jul |
| 49.5 | Dean Park | | 23.09.77 | 3 | Croydon | 25 | Jun |
| (30) | | | | | | | |

**Additional Under 17** (1 - 8 above)

| | | | | | | | |
|---|---|---|---|---|---|---|---|
| 49.7 | John Skeete | | 8.09.78 | 1 | London (TB) | 25 | Jun |
| 49.8 | Richard McDonald | | 11.01.80 | 1 | Glasgow | 11 | Jun |
| 50.18 | | | | 2 | Grangemouth | 13 | May |
| (10) | | | | | | | |
| 49.8 | Kris Stewart | | 11.04.80 | 2 | Grangemouth | 17 | Jun |
| 50.16 | | | | 1 | Grangemouth | 13 | May |
| 49.86 | Robert Fanning | | 31.10.78 | 3h2 | Nottingham | 7 | Jul |
| 49.95 | Nick Hamilton | | 13.03.79 | 4h2 | Nottingham | 7 | Jul |
| 49.97 | Simon Plaskett | | 9.04.79 | 4s2 | Nottingham | 8 | Jul |
| 50.0 | Graham Hedman | | 6.02.79 | 2 | Basildon | 10 | Jun |
| 50.26 | | | | 5s1 | Nottingham | 8 | Jul |
| 50.01 | David Naismith | | 15.12.79 | 5s2 | Nottingham | 8 | Jul |
| 50.09 | Noel Morgan | | 20.11.78 | 4s1 | Nottingham | 8 | Jul |
| 50.47 | Neil Akester | | 6.09.79 | 5h2 | Nottingham | 7 | Jul |
| 50.50 | Richard Singer | | 7.02.79 | 6h1 | Edinburgh | 23 | Jun |
| 50.53 | Martin Elks | | 26.01.80 | 1 | Stoke | 27 | May |
| (20) | | | | | | | |
| 50.59 | James Colclough | | 29.06.79 | 4h1 | Nottingham | 7 | Jul |
| 50.6 | Andrew Thomas | | 15.05.79 | 1 | Gateshead | 21 | May |
| 50.6 | Alex Guthrie | | 6.07.79 | 1 | Linwood | 24 | Aug |
| 50.65 | Ian Lowthian | U15 | 10.10.80 | 1 | Birmingham | 29 | Jul |
| 50.7 | Glen Howe | | 20.10.78 | 1 | Newcastle | 17 | Jun |
| 50.75 | Gareth Noble | | 1.05.79 | 4h4 | Nottingham | 7 | Jul |
| 50.8 | Ruben Tabares | | 22.10.78 | 1r2 | London (TB) | 25 | Jun |
| 50.86 | David Powell | | 11.09.78 | 6h1 | Nottingham | 7 | Jul |
| 51.0 | C. Richardson | | | 6 | Bath | 31 | May |

**Additional Under 15** (1 above)

| | | | | | | | |
|---|---|---|---|---|---|---|---|
| 51.11 | Leon Connikie | | 6.01.81 | 2 | Birmingham | 29 | Jul |
| 51.84 | Christopher Bennett | | 18.10.80 | 1h2 | Nottingham | 7 | Jul |
| 52.36 | Simon Bullock | | 22.11.80 | 2r2 | Stoke | 17 | Jun |
| 52.64 | Sam Murray | | 7.09.80 | 3h2 | Nottingham | 7 | Jul |
| 52.65 | Jonathan Beharie | | 21.09.80 | 3s2 | Nottingham | 8 | Jul |
| 52.79 | Neil Hewson | | 4.09.80 | 5 | Nottingham | 8 | Jul |
| 52.79 | John Shenava | | 5.02.81 | 1 | Pitreavie | 9 | Jul |

| | | | | | | |
|---|---|---|---|---|---|---|
| 52.89 | Ian Smith | | 7.01.81 | 3s1 | Nottingham | 8 Jul |
| 53.1 | Stuart Mathieson | | 5.02.81 | 1 | Grangemouth | 17 Jun |
| | (10) | | | | | |
| 53.2 | D. Spindley | | | 2 | Stretford | 10 Jun |
| 53.21 | Suone Lebari | | 25.10.80 | 4s2 | Nottingham | 8 Jul |
| 53.5 | Daniel Everett | | 30.01.81 | 3h3 | Birmingham | 29 Jul |
| | 53.60 | | | 3h3 | Nottingham | 7 Jul |
| 53.62 | Jonathan Pritchard | | 21.12.80 | 5s2 | Nottingham | 8 Jul |
| 53.69 | Oliver Rogan | | 22.04.81 | 6s2 | Nottingham | 8 Jul |
| 53.7 | David Moulton | | 7.09.81 | 2h1 | Birmingham | 29 Jul |
| 53.81 | Jonathan Groenen | | 12.09.80 | 1 | Horsham | 13 May |
| 53.9 | Gregg Dale | | 2.10.80 | 3h3 | Birmingham | 29 Jul |
| 53.95 | Nick Daniel | | 18.01.81 | 4h3 | Nottingham | 7 Jul |

**Under 13**

| | | | | | |
|---|---|---|---|---|---|
| 57.4 | Mark Alexander | 17.09.82 | 1 | Aberdeen | 7 May |
| 58.5 | Tim Suswain | 22.02.83 | 1 | Andover | 2 Jul |
| 58.7 | Glen Coppin | 16.01.83 | 2 | Watford | 9 Jul |
| 58.87 | Rick Howson | 9.02.83 | 1 | Crewe | 29 Jun |
| 59.7 | T. Anthony | | 1 | Welwyn | 23 Aug |
| 59.8 | J. Stephenson | | 1 | Ayr | 20 Aug |

## 600 METRES

| | | | | | | |
|---|---|---|---|---|---|---|
| 1:19.4 i | Adam Mole | U23 | 31.08.75 | 1r1 | Birmingham | 1 Mar |
| 1:19.6 | Peter Crampton | | 4.06.69 | 1 | Manchester | 17 May |

## 800 METRES

| | | | | | | |
|---|---|---|---|---|---|---|
| 1:46.02 | David Strang | 13.12.68 | 2r2 | Oslo, NOR | 21 Jul |
| | 1:46.68 | | 2 | Gateshead | 21 Aug |
| | 1:47.0 | | 1 | Dedham, USA | 27 May |
| | 1:47.06 | | 2 | Birmingham | 16 Jul |
| | 1:48.11 | | 3 . | Sheffield | 23 Jul |
| 1:46.34 | Curtis Robb | 7.06.72 | 2h1 | Gothenburg, SWE | 5 Aug |
| | 1:46.35 | | 6r1 | London (CP) | 7 Jul |
| | 1:46.78 | | 1 | Birmingham | 16 Jul |
| | 1:47.14 | | 1 | Sheffield | 23 Jul |
| | 1:47.7 | | 1r1 | Liverpool | 6 May |
| 1:46.68 | Craig Winrow | 22.12.71 | 3 | Gateshead | 21 Aug |
| | 1:47.6 | | 2r1 | Stretford | 1 Aug |
| | 1:47.67 | | 10 | Duisburg, GER | 18 Jun |
| | 1:48.11 | | 6 | Nuremberg, GER | 15 Jun |
| | 1:48.14 | | 4 | Sheffield | 23 Jul |
| | 1:48.25 | | 6r2 | Rome, ITA | 8 Jun |
| 1:47.33 | Clive Gilby | 24.02.66 | 5 | Gateshead | 2 Jul |
| | 1:48.15 | | 1r1 | Loughborough | 11 Jun |
| 1:47.46 | Tom McKean | 27.10.63 | 7 | Gateshead | 2 Jul |
| | 1:48.07 | | 10r1 | London (CP) | 7 Jul |
| 1:47.59 | Andy Keith | 25.12.71 | 5r2 | Stockholm, SWE | 10 Jul |
| 1:47.8 | Lee Cadwallader | 17.01.69 | 1r1 | Stretford | 22 Aug |
| | 1:48.28 | | 4 | Birmingham | 16 Jul |
| | 1:48.45 | | 6 | Sheffield | 23 Jul |
| 1:47.98 | Matthew Yates | 4.02.69 | 5 | Gateshead | 21 Aug |
| | 1:48.11 | | 8 | Gateshead | 2 Jul |
| 1:48.0 | Kevin McKay | 9.02.69 | 3r1 | Stretford | 1 Aug |
| 1:48.03 | Gary Lough | 6.07.70 | 3 | Birmingham | 16 Jul |
| | (10) | | | | |
| 1:48.14 | Jason Lobo | 18.09.69 | 13 | Berlin, GER | 1 Sep |
| | 1:48.5 | | 2r1 | Stretford | 22 Aug |
| 1:48.2 | Andy Hart | 13.09.69 | 1r1 | Birmingham (Un) | 20 Aug |

31 performances to 1:48.5 by 12 athletes

| Time | Name | | DOB | Pos | Venue | Date | |
|---|---|---|---|---|---|---|---|
| 1:48.7 | Tony Morrell | | 3.05.62 | 3r1 | Stretford | 22 | Aug |
| 1:48.9 | Steve Green | | 18.02.71 | 4r1 | Stretford | 22 | Aug |
| 1:48.95 i | Martin Steele | | 30.09.62 | 2 | Glasgow | 11 | Feb |
| 1:49.15 | | | | 4h2 | Birmingham | 15 | Jul |
| 1:49.02 | Mark Sesay | | 13.12.72 | 2r1 | Loughborough | 11 | Jun |
| 1:49.06 | Ewan Calvert | U23 | 28.11.73 | 3r1 | Loughborough | 11 | Jun |
| 1:49.14 | Robin Hooton | U23 | 5.05.73 | 7 | Tucson, USA | 20 | May |
| 1:49.18 | Des Roache | U20 | 5.01.76 | 3r2 | London (CP) | 7 | Jul |
| 1:49.36 | Andi Knight | | 26.10.68 | 4r2 | London (CP) | 7 | Jul |
| | (20) | | | | | | |
| 1:49.39 | Jon Wild | U23 | 30.08.73 | 1 | Arlington, USA | 6 | May |
| 1:49.48 | Bruno Witchalls | U23 | 22.03.75 | 5r2 | London (CP) | 7 | Jul |
| 1:49.55 | Grant Graham | | 27.12.72 | 1 | Edinburgh | 30 | May |
| 1:49.55 | Gary Brown | | 21.07.67 | 3 | Kilkenny, IRE | 2 | Sep |
| 1:49.56 | John Gercs | | 7.06.69 | 2r2 | Loughborough | 11 | Jun |
| 1:49.60 | Tony Whiteman | | 13.11.71 | 4 | Kilkenny, IRE | 2 | Sep |
| 1:49.6 | Matt Hibberd | U23 | 23.06.73 | 1 | Loughborough | 21 | Jun |
| 1:49.66 | Simon Fairbrother | | 28.03.68 | 2 | Celle Ligure, ITA | 22 | Jun |
| 1:49.69 | Simon Brown | | 22.03.69 | 4r1 | Loughborough | 11 | Jun |
| 1:49.7 | John Mayock | | 26.10.70 | 1 | Cannock | 16 | Sep |
| | (30) | | | | | | |
| 1:49.71 | Paul Walker | U23 | 2.12.73 | 1 | Edinburgh | 24 | Jun |
| 1:49.75 | Grant Purves | U23 | 6.04.73 | 2r1 | Edinburgh | 6 | Aug |
| 1:49.89 | Brian Treacy | | 29.07.71 | 1 | Avila, SPA | 24 | May |
| 1:49.9 | Sean Kelly | | 8.11.72 | 1h2 | Loughborough | 10 | Jun |
| 1:49.93 | Jason Boothroyd | | 26.11.69 | 2r2 | Tallahassee, USA | 18 | Mar |
| 1:49.95 | Richard Girvan | U20 | 26.07.76 | 5r1 | Loughborough | 11 | Jun |
| 1:49.95 | Keri Idessane | | 1.12.69 | 3r2 | Loughborough | 11 | Jun |
| 1:49.95 | Paul Roberts | | 24.12.69 | 6 | Cork, IRE | 24 | Jun |
| 1:49.96 | Eddie King | U23 | 26.11.75 | 6 | Kevelaar, HOL | 3 | Jun |
| 1:50.10 | Peter Hackley | | 19.02.71 | 2h4 | Birmingham | 15 | Jul |
| | (40) | | | | | | |
| 1:50.1 | Adam Duke | U23 | 5.10.73 | 7r1 | Manchester | 17 | May |
| 1:50.1 | Ian Grime | | 29.09.70 | 3 | Loughborough | 21 | Jun |
| 1:50.1 | Nick Bentham | | 7.12.70 | 3r1 | Solihull | 26 | Jul |
| 1:50.14 | Justin Swift-Smith | U23 | 28.08.74 | 5r2 | Zofingen, SWZ | 5 | Jun |
| 1:50.20 | Alasdair Donaldson | U20 | 21.06.77 | 2h2 | Nyiregyhaza, HUN | 27 | Jul |
| 1:50.2 | Neil Caddy | U23 | 18.03.75 | 1 | Carn Brea | 4 | Jul |
| 1:50.2 | Garth Watson | U23 | 20.04.73 | 5r1 | Stretford | 22 | Aug |
| 1:50.3 | Rupert Waters | | 3.01.72 | 3r1 | Stretford | 5 | Sep |
| 1:50.47 | Darrell Maynard | | 21.08.61 | 6 | Cwmbran | 9 | Jul |
| 1:50.49 | Tom Lerwill | U20 | 17.05.77 | 1 | Nottingham | 8 | Jul |
| | (50) | | | | | | |
| 1:50.51 i | Ian Campbell | | 6.09.71 | 2 | Glasgow | 22 | Jan |
| 1:50.73 | | | | 3 | Edinburgh | 30 | May |
| 1:50.53 | Neil Emberton | | 11.09.72 | | Fayetteville, USA | 6 | May |
| 1:50.53 | Martin Airey | | 28.10.70 | 6r2 | Loughborough | 11 | Jun |
| 1:50.6 | Andrew Walling | U23 | 3.04.73 | 7r1 | Stretford | 22 | Aug |
| 1:50.7 | Andrew Blackmore | U20 | 12.07.76 | 3r1 | Loughborough | 20 | May |
| 1:50.7 | Bruce Craven | | 18.03.72 | 8r1 | Stretford | 22 | Aug |
| 1:50.7 | John Rigg | | 3.06.67 | 9r1 | Stretford | 22 | Aug |
| 1:50.73 | Phillip Tulba-Morrison | U23 | 20.09.73 | 5h2 | Birmingham | 15 | Jul |
| 1:50.8 | Tony Balogun | | 7.02.66 | 1 | Watford | 19 | Jul |
| 1:50.8 | Matt Kloiber | | 22.11.71 | 5r1 | Stretford | 5 | Sep |
| | (60) | | | | | | |
| 1:50.83 | Ciaran Murphy | | 2.09.71 | 2r2 | Edinburgh | 3 | Jun |
| 1:50.9 | Tony Mate | U23 | 15.12.74 | 10r1 | Stretford | 22 | Aug |
| 1:51.00 | David Sharpe | | 8.07.67 | 4 | Fort-de-France, MRT | 1 | May |
| 1:51.0 | David Thornton | U23 | 27.07.73 | 6r1 | Stretford | 5 | Sep |
| *1:51.2* | *Des English* | | *6.06.67* | *2r1* | *Bournemouth* | *6* | *May* |
| 1:51.2 | Terry West | | 19.11.68 | 1r1 | Bournemouth | 6 | May |

| | | | | | | | |
|---|---|---|---|---|---|---|---|
| 1:51.23 | *Prince Amara* | *U23* | *15.03.73* | *8* | *Cwmbran* | *9* | *Jul* |
| 1:51.3 | Sean Price | | 4.01.63 | 3r1 | Liverpool | 6 | May |
| 1:51.3 | David Locker | U23 | 28.03.75 | 2h6 | Loughborough | 10 | Jun |
| 1:51.3 | Jason Dupuy | | 31.01.71 | 3r1 | Watford | 9 | Aug |
| 1:51.4 | Ian Mansfield | U23 | 27.11.74 | 1 | Grimsby | 27 | May |
| 1:51.4 | Ben Reese | U20 | 29.03.76 | 7r1 | Stretford | 27 | Jun |
| | (70) | | | | | | |
| 1:51.4 | Glen Stewart | | 7.12.70 | 3r1 | Edinburgh | 6 | Aug |
| 1:51.5 | John MacFadyen | | 1.08.72 | 3r2 | Manchester | 17 | May |
| 1:51.5 | Jason Thompson | | 16.11.71 | 2 | Watford | 19 | Jul |
| 1:51.5 | Luke Veness | U23 | 5.12.73 | 1 | London (TB) | 2 | Aug |
| 1:51.6 | Stuart Margiotta | | 19.11.69 | 4r1 | Solihull | 26 | Jul |
| 1:51.69 | Dominic Hall | | 21.02.71 | 3r1 | London (CP) | 18 | Jun |
| 1:51.70 | Martin Forder | | 7.08.70 | 4r1 | London (CP) | 18 | Jun |
| 1:51.7 | Simon Stebbings | | 23.04.71 | 5r1 | Watford | 9 | Aug |
| 1:51.80 | Stuart Taylor | | 6.06.75 | 7h2 | Birmingham | 15 | Jul |
| 1:51.8 | Rod Finch | | 5.08.67 | 6r2 | Manchester | 17 | May |
| | (80) | | | | | | |
| 1:51.8 | Andy Stuckey | | 24.04.72 | 4 | Loughborough | 21 | Jun |
| 1:51.8 | Philip Healy | | 1.10.70 | 1 | Londonderry | 25 | Jul |
| 1:51.8 | Paul Bennett | | 9.08.71 | 8r1 | Stretford | 5 | Sep |
| 1:51.9 | Stewart Allen | | 1.02.70 | 1r1 | Southampton | 3 | Jun |
| *1:51.9* | *Bobby Farren* | | *15.05.70* | *1* | *Antrim* | *29* | *Jul* |
| 1:51.9 | Matthew Davies | | 23.07.71 | 1r3 | Birmingham (Un) | 20 | Aug |
| 1:51.9 | Andy Young | U20 | 20.06.77 | 5r2 | Birmingham (Un) | 20 | Aug |
| 1:51.93 | Bradley Donkin | | 6.12.71 | 1 | Hull | 5 | Aug |
| 1:52.0 | Dale Canning | U20 | 12.06.78 | 5r1 | Bedford | 2 | Jul |
| 1:52.0 | Glyn Tromans | | 17.03.69 | 5r1 | Solihull | 26 | Jul |
| 1:52.04 | Gareth Manning | | 3.10.69 | 3r2 | London (CP) | 18 | Jun |
| | (90) | | | | | | |
| 1:52.04 | Mike Guegan | | 19.09.66 | 1r1 | Edinburgh | 1 | Jul |
| 1:52.06 | Mark Barrow | | 30.06.68 | 8h2 | Birmingham | 15 | Jul |
| 1:52.10 | Eddie Williams | | 1.10.70 | 2r1 | Birmingham | 1 | Jul |
| *1:52.19 i* | *Shane Daly* | *U23* | *21.03.73* | *2h1* | *Birmingham* | *3* | *Feb* |
| 1:52.2 | Jeremy Smith | U23 | 16.08.74 | 2 | Rotherham | 6 | May |
| 1:52.21 | Terry Salt | | 6.11.65 | 3 | Uster, SWZ | 17 | Jun |
| 1:52.3 | Noel Edwards | | 16.12.72 | 3h6 | Loughborough | 10 | Jun |
| 1:52.3 | Mark Griffin | U23 | 16.02.75 | 1r1 | Milton Keynes | 19 | Aug |
| 1:52.3 | Richard Ashe | U23 | 5.10.74 | 2r1 | Sutton | 17 | Sep |
| 1:52.4 | Larry Mangleshot | | 28.05.63 | 4r1 | Bedford | 19 | Jul |
| 1:52.41 | Richard Dawson | | 7.12.70 | 4r2 | London (CP) | 18 | Jun |
| | (100) | | | | | | |
| 1:52.44 | Paul Gardner | | 5.08.69 | 2 | Aldershot | 23 | Jul |
| 1:52.5 | Andrew Parker | U23 | 20.11.74 | 8r2 | Manchester | 17 | May |
| 1:52.5 | Steven Turville | U23 | 17.02.75 | 2 | Salisbury | 9 | Jul |
| 1:52.5 | Michael Combe | U17 | 24.12.78 | 1r2 | Stretford | 1 | Aug |
| *1:52.53* | *Patrick O'Reilly* | | *5.01.68* | *6r1* | *London (CP)* | *18* | *Jun* |
| 1:52.58 | Alan Wray | | 6.01.71 | 5r2 | London (CP) | 18 | Jun |
| 1:52.59 | Roger Morley | U20 | 20.09.77 | 2 | Nottingham | 8 | Jul |
| 1:52.6 | Toby Gosnall | | 21.04.71 | 2h2 | Loughborough | 10 | Jun |
| 1:52.6 | Peter Broadley | | 10.10.71 | 3 | Nottingham | 25 | Jun |
| 1:52.6 | Peter McDevitt | | 1.03.68 | 2 | Pitreavie | 25 | Jun |
| 1:52.6 | David Heath | | 22.05.65 | 5r1 | Bedford | 19 | Jul |
| | (110) | | | | | | |
| 1:52.6 | Alan Tatham | U20 | 29.04.77 | 2r2 | Birmingham (Un) | 20 | Aug |
| 1:52.6 | Andrew Prophett | U23 | 10.06.74 | 2r2 | Stretford | 22 | Aug |
| 1:52.64 | Ryan Davoile | U17 | 29.09.78 | 1 | Nottingham | 8 | Jul |
| 1:52.7 | Mark Benson | | 21.12.63 | 2r1 | Wakefield | 3 | Jun |
| 1:52.7 | Chris Beswick | U23 | 9.10.75 | 1h1 | Loughborough | 10 | Jun |
| 1:52.7 | Mark Miles (relay leg?) | U20 | 24.03.77 | 1 | Oxford | 16 | Jun |
| 1:52.7 | David Pamah | | 27.11.64 | 1r2 | London (TB) | 5 | Jul |

145

## Additional Under 20 (1 - 11 above)

| | | | | | | | |
|---|---|---|---|---|---|---|---|
| 1:52.85 | Gavin Mason | | 6.04.77 | 3 | Nottingham | 8 | Jul |
| 1:52.9 | Matthew Clarke | | 15.11.76 | 1 | Watford | 19 | Jul |
| 1:53.42 | Neil Kirk | U17 | 14.09.78 | 2 | Nottingham | 8 | Jul |
| 1:53.50 | Jon Quint | | 22.11.76 | 5 | Nottingham | 8 | Jul |
| 1:53.7 | David Stanley | U17 | 16.01.79 | 1r4 | Birmingham (Un) | 20 | Aug |
| 1:53.9 | Ian Mitchell | | 10.03.76 | 5r2 | Stretford | 22 | Aug |
| 1:53.91 | Andrew Graffin | | 20.12.77 | 3 | London (CP) | 28 | May |
| 1:54.09 | James Clack | | 14.08.76 | 1r2 | Bedford | 2 | Jul |
| 1:54.2 | Sam Illidge | | 4.02.77 | 7r1 | Bedford | 2 | Jul |
| (20) | | | | | | | |
| 1:54.36 | Russell Cartwright | | 13.10.77 | 3 | Utrecht, HOL | 9 | Jul |
| 1:54.4 | Andrew Hennessy | | 24.08.77 | 1 | Yeovil | 14 | May |
| 1:54.49 | Chris Moss | U17 | 17.06.79 | 4r2 | Birmingham | 1 | Jul |
| 1:54.62 | Andrew Brown | | 17.06.77 | 3r2 | Bedford | 1 | Jun |
| 1:54.70 | P. Jackson | | | 4r1 | Cheltenham | 6 | Aug |
| 1:54.8 | Alistair Moses | | 5.07.78 | 3r1 | London (CP) | 31 | May |
| 1:54.8 | Richard Mann | | 11.04.77 | 5r1 | Cardiff | 24 | Jun |
| 1:54.9 | Stuart Bailey | | 6.08.78 | 6 | Stretford | 18 | Jul |
| 1:54.9 | Matthew Dixon | U17 | 26.12.78 | 2r3 | Stretford | 22 | Aug |
| 1:55.0 | Huw Jenkins | | | 5r1 | Barry | 25 | Jul |
| (30) | | | | | | | |
| 1:55.0 | David Davey | | 8.09.77 | 6r1 | Barry | 25 | Jul |

## Additional Under 17 (1 - 6 above)

| | | | | | | | |
|---|---|---|---|---|---|---|---|
| 1:55.04 | Stephen Briffett | | 22.10.78 | 3 | Nottingham | 8 | Jul |
| 1:55.04 | Matthew De'Ath | | 27.10.78 | 4 | Nottingham | 8 | Jul |
| 1:55.06 | Andrew Thomas | | 15.05.79 | 5 | Nottingham | 8 | Jul |
| 1:55.27 | Sion Owen | | 6.03.79 | 6 | Nottingham | 8 | Jul |
| (10) | | | | | | | |
| 1:56.1 | Scott Hughes | | 20.11.78 | 2r3 | Stretford | 18 | Jul |
| 1:56.4 | Kevin Corr | | 17.04.79 | 1 | Carlisle | 9 | Jul |
| 1:56.6 | Paul Morby | | 15.01.79 | 5r7 | Manchester | 17 | May |
| 1:57.0 | Ben Harper | | 9.11.78 | 2 | London (Elt) | 18 | Jun |
| 1:57.38 | Stuart Austin | | 21.03.79 | 3 | London (CP) | 28 | May |
| 1:57.5 | Andrew Philips | | 9.04.79 | 4r4 | Stretford | 5 | Sep |
| 1:57.6 | Charles Boddam-Whetham | | 25.09.78 | 1 | Welwyn | 10 | Jun |
| 1:57.65 | Craig Blackman | | 3.04.79 | 2 | Sheffield | 27 | May |
| 1:57.7 | Martyn Gordon | | 29.09.79 | 1 | Middlesbrough | 10 | Jun |
| 1:57.7 | Lee Garrett | | 2.09.78 | 3r4 | Stretford | 27 | Jun |
| (20) | | | | | | | |
| 1:57.7 | Gareth Beard | | 28.02.79 | 2h3 | Birmingham | 29 | Jul |
| 1:57.9 | Lee Salter | | 12.12.78 | 1 | Exeter | 29 | Aug |

## Under 15

| | | | | | | | |
|---|---|---|---|---|---|---|---|
| 2:00.1 | Austin Ferns | | 12.01.81 | 1 | Walton | 1 | Jul |
| 2:00.5 | Jonathon Keith | | 5.11.80 | 1 | Cleckheaton | 10 | Sep |
| 2:00.6 | Michael Church | | 7.09.80 | 1 | London (Nh) | 16 | Jul |
| 2:00.61 | Barry Woodward | | 20.11.80 | 1 | Nottingham | 8 | Jul |
| 2:00.64 | John Heanley | | 25.09.80 | 2 | Nottingham | 8 | Jul |
| 2:01.29 | Jonathan Hockey | | 18.09.80 | 3 | Nottingham | 8 | Jul |
| 2:01.73 | Matthew Bailey | | 16.02.81 | 4 | Nottingham | 8 | Jul |
| 2:02.54 | Gregg Dale | | 2.10.80 | 2 | Birmingham | 30 | Jul |
| 2:02.6 | Ian Smith | | 7.01.81 | 1h5 | Birmingham | 30 | Jul |
| 2:02.6 | Danny Hermann | | 3.03.81 | 2h5 | Birmingham | 30 | Jul |
| (10) | | | | | | | |
| 2:02.7 | Russell Pittam | | 12.10.80 | | Horsham | 14 | Aug |
| 2:03.1 | William Goudie | | 16.12.80 | 1 | Stockport | 16 | Jul |
| 2:03.46 | David Luard | | 6.09.80 | 1h3 | Nottingham | 7 | Jul |
| 2:03.70 | Craig Michie | | 2.12.80 | 1 | Boblingen, GER | 30 | Jul |
| 2:03.91 | Paul Oliver | | 19.09.80 | 6 | Nottingham | 8 | Jul |
| 2:04.01 | Eric Tollett | | 29.04.81 | 3h1 | Nottingham | 7 | Jul |

| | | | | | | |
|---|---|---|---|---|---|---|
| 2:04.36 | Dominic Young | | 2.06.81 | 2h3 | Nottingham | 7 Jul |
| 2:04.€2 | Christopher Marshall | | 4.10.80 | 1r1 | Stoke | 17 Jun |
| 2:04.75 | Richard Jones | | 14.05.81 | 4h1 | Nottingham | 7 Jul |
| 2:04.8 | Stephen Holmes | | 17.10.80 | 1 | Bromley | 3 May |
| | (20) | | | | | |
| 2:04.9 | Gary Macey | | 25.10.80 | 1 | Portsmouth | 10 Jun |
| 2:04.94 | Paul Gilbert | | 21.06.81 | 4h3 | Nottingham | 7 Jul |
| 2:04.95 | Chris Batty | | 6.09.80 | 2 | London (CP) | 28 May |
| 2:04.96 | Matthew Peleszok | | 17.10.81 | 5h3 | Nottingham | 7 Jul |

**Under 15**

| | | | | | | |
|---|---|---|---|---|---|---|
| 2:12.7 | Glen Coppin | | 16.01.83 | 1 | Watford | 19 Jul |
| 2:13.0 | Tim Suswain | | 22.02.83 | 1 | Harrow | 16 Jul |
| 2:16.27 | Brian McIlroy | | | 1 | Birmingham | 3 Sep |
| 2:18.1 | M. Lewis | | | 1 | Swansea | 26 Aug |
| 2:18.2 | Richard Woods | | 4.09.82 | 1 | Sutton | 17 Sep |
| 2:18.49 | Matthew Hill | | | 2 | Birmingham | 3 Sep |

# 1000 METRES

| | | | | | | |
|---|---|---|---|---|---|---|
| 2:18.26 i | Matthew Yates | | 4.02.69 | 2 | Stockholm, SWE | 27 Feb |
| 2:18.61 | Lee Cadwallader | | 17.01.69 | 5 | Rhede, GER | 30 Jul |
| 2:22.0 | Steve Green | | 18.02.71 | 1 | Stretford | 18 Jul |
| 2:22.7 | Matt Hibberd | U23 | 23.06.73 | 2 | Stretford | 18 Jul |
| 2:23.0 i | Tony Whiteman | | 13.11.71 | 1r1 | Birmingham | 1 Mar |
| 2:23.2 | Stuart Margiotta | | 19.11.69 | 3 | Stretford | 18 Jul |
| 2:24.0 i | Nick Bentham | | 7.12.70 | 2r1 | Birmingham | 1 Mar |
| 2:24.6 | Ian Gillespie | | 18.05.70 | 1 | Street | 8 May |
| 2:24.6 | Ciaran Murphy | | 2.09.71 | 4 | Stretford | 18 Jul |
| 2:24.93 | Terry Salt | | 6.11.65 | 5 | Langenthal, SWZ | 25 May |

# 1500 METRES

| | | | | | | |
|---|---|---|---|---|---|---|
| 3:34.05 | John Mayock | | 26.10.70 | 5r1 | Cologne, GER | 18 Aug |
| | 3:34.58 | | | 4 | London (CP) | 7 Jul |
| | 3:34.63 | | | 6 | Monaco, MON | 9 Sep |
| | 3:36.54 + | | | 7m | Zurich, SWZ | 16 Aug |
| | 3:37.32 | | | 6 | Brussels, BEL | 25 Aug |
| | 3:40.09 | | | 1r1 | Gateshead | 2 Jul |
| | 3:40.20 | | | 9s1 | Gothenburg, SWE | 11 Aug |
| | 3:40.55 | | | 1 | Birmingham | 16 Jul |
| | 3:40.69 | | | 6 | Moscow, RUS | 5 Jun |
| | 3:40.70 | | | 2 | Nuremberg, GER | 15 Jun |
| | 3:42.27 | | | 1h1 | Birmingham | 15 Jul |
| 3:34.76 | Gary Lough | | 6.07.70 | 7 | Monaco, MON | 9 Sep |
| | 3:34.82 | | | 5= | London (CP) | 7 Jul |
| | 3:36.01 | | | 11r1 | Cologne, GER | 18 Aug |
| | 3:36.39 | | | 2 | Duisburg, GER | 18 Jun |
| | 3:37.59 | | | 9 | Gothenburg, SWE | 13 Aug |
| | 3:37.73 | | | 7 | Brussels, BEL | 25 Aug |
| | 3:37.78 | | | 4s2 | Gothenburg, SWE | 11 Aug |
| | 3:38.62 | | | 2h3 | Gothenburg, SWE | 10 Aug |
| | 3:39.36 | | | 9r1 | Oslo, NOR | 21 Jul |
| | 3:41.08 | | | 1r1 | Loughborough | 11 Jun |
| 3:37.27 | Kevin McKay | | 9.02.69 | 6r1 | Oslo, NOR | 21 Jul |
| | 3:38.13 | | | 1 | Lucerne, SWZ | 27 Jun |
| | 3:40.83 | | | 2 | Birmingham | 16 Jul |
| | 3:41.81 | | | 2r1 | Loughborough | 11 Jun |
| | 3:42.13 | | | 8r1 | Gateshead | 2 Jul |
| 3:37.99 | Rob Denmark | | 23.11.68 | 4 | Hengelo, HOL | 5 Jun |
| | 3:40.82 | | | 13 | London (CP) | 7 Jul |

| | | | | | | | |
|---|---|---|---|---|---|---|---|
| 3:39.17 | Andy Keith | | 25.12.71 | 5 | St. Petersburg, RUS | 30 | Jun |
| | 3:41.32 | | | 2 | Dedham, USA | 3 | Jun |
| | 3:41.96 | | | 5 | Birmingham | 16 | Jul |
| | 3:42.82 | | | 1 | Dedham, USA | 27 | May |
| 3:39.67 | Neil Caddy | U23 | 18.03.75 | 5 | Copenhagen, DEN | 23 | Aug |
| | 3:42.1 | | | 1 | Southampton | 3 | Sep |
| | 3:42.15 | | | 7 | Birmingham | 16 | Jul |
| | 3:42.2 | | | 1r1 | Manchester | 17 | May |
| 3:39.87 | Brian Treacy | | 29.07.71 | 3 | Maia, POR | 19 | Jul |
| | 3:40.91 | | | 4 | Alcala de Henares, SPA | 1 | Jul |
| | 3:41.69 | | | 4 | Granada, SPA | 27 | May |
| | 3:41.73 | | | 4 | Birmingham | 16 | Jul |
| | 3:42.15 | | | 2 | La Laguna, SPA | 30 | May |
| 3:39.94 | David Strang | | 13.12.68 | 11 | London (CP) | 7 | Jul |
| | 3:41.39 | | | 5r1 | Gateshead | 2 | Jul |
| 3:40.69 | Matthew Yates | | 4.02.69 | 12 | Brussels, BEL | 25 | Aug |
| 3:41.28 i | Tony Whiteman | | 13.11.71 | 2 | Birmingham | 25 | Feb |
| | 3:43.4 | | | 1r1 | Birmingham (Un) | 20 | Aug |
| (10) | | | | | | | |
| 3:41.40 | Jon Wild | U23 | 30.08.73 | 8 | Knoxville, USA | 3 | Jun |
| | 3:42.12 | | | 1r2 | Gateshead | 2 | Jul |
| | 3:42.43 | | | 1 | Cwmbran | 9 | Jul |
| | 3:42.7 | | | 2 | Ames, USA | 16 | May |
| | 3:42.73 | | | 6h2 | Knoxville, USA | 1 | Jun |
| 3:41.51 | Bruno Witchalls | U23 | 22.03.75 | 3 | Birmingham | 16 | Jul |
| | 3:42.37 | | | 2r2 | Gateshead | 2 | Jul |
| | 3:42.81 | | | 3h1 | Birmingham | 15 | Jul |
| 3:41.92 | Simon Fairbrother | | 28.03.68 | 4 | Geneva, SWZ | 17 | Jun |
| | 3:42.54 | | | 3r1 | Loughborough | 11 | Jun |
| 3:42.03 | Andy Hart | | 13.09.69 | 6 | Birmingham | 16 | Jul |
| | 3:42.41 | | | 2r2 | Oslo, NOR | 21 | Jul |
| | 3:42.7 | | | 3r1 | Manchester | 17 | May |
| 3:42.32 | Matt Hibberd | U23 | 23.06.73 | 5 | Budapest, HUN | 9 | Jul |
| 3:42.4 | Steve Green | | 18.02.71 | 2r1 | Manchester | 17 | May |
| | 3:42.49 | | | 1 | Nurmijarvi, FIN | 4 | Jun |
| | 3:42.95 | | | 12r1 | Gateshead | 2 | Jul |
| 3:42.66 | John Nuttall | | 11.01.67 | 8 | Birmingham | 16 | Jul |
| | 3:42.71 | | | 2h1 | Birmingham | 15 | Jul |
| *3:42.67* | *Des English* | | *6.06.67* | *13* | *Lucerne, SWZ* | *27* | *Jun* |
| 3:42.73 | Ian Grime | | 29.09.70 | 11r1 | Gateshead | 2 | Jul |
| 3:42.75 | Glen Stewart | | 7.12.70 | 3r2 | Gateshead | 2 | Jul |
| 3:42.9 | Richard Ashe | U23 | 5.10.74 | 1r1 | Watford | 9 | Aug |
| (20) | | | | | | | |
| 3:42.92 | Rod Finch | | 5.08.67 | 10 | Hengelo, HOL | 5 | Jun |
| 3:42.96 | Matt Barnes | | 12.01.68 | 4 | Ljubljana, SLO | 21 | May |
| 3:42.99 | Gary Brown | | 21.07.67 | 4r2 | Gateshead | 2 | Jul |
| | 3:43.0 | | | 4r1 | Manchester | 17 | May |

72 performances to 3:43.0 by 23 athletes including 1 indoors

| | | | | | | | |
|---|---|---|---|---|---|---|---|
| 3:43.2 | Grant Graham | | 27.12.72 | 5r1 | Manchester | 17 | May |
| 3:43.39 | Lee Cadwallader | | 17.01.69 | 5r2 | Gateshead | 2 | Jul |
| 3:43.42 | Ciaran Murphy | | 2.09.71 | 2 | Cwmbran | 9 | Jul |
| 3:43.54 i | Ian Campbell | | 6.09.71 | 3 | Glasgow | 11 | Feb |
| | 3:47.31 | | | 12r2 | Gateshead | 2 | Jul |
| 3:43.58 | Karl Keska | | 7.05.72 | 6 | Eugene, USA | 13 | May |
| 3:43.81 | Phil Mowbray | U23 | 19.03.73 | 1 | Edinburgh | 24 | Jun |
| 3:44.03 | Ian Gillespie | | 18.05.70 | 4h4 | Birmingham | 15 | Jul |
| (30) | | | | | | | |
| 3:44.26 | Stuart Margiotta | | 19.11.69 | 5 | London (CP) | 27 | Aug |
| 3:44.3 | Spencer Barden | U23 | 31.03.73 | 7r1 | Manchester | 17 | May |
| 3:44.3 | Nick Comerford | | 23.04.66 | 4r1 | Birmingham (Un) | 20 | Aug |
| 3:44.63 | Jason Boothroyd | | 26.11.69 | 2 | South Bend, USA | 6 | May |

148

| 3:44.63 | Tony Mate | U23 | 15.12.74 | 2r2 | Loughborough | 11 | Jun |
|---|---|---|---|---|---|---|---|
| 3:44.75 | Tony Morrell | | 3.05.62 | 11 | Geneva, SWZ | 17 | Jun |
| 3:44.8 | Glyn Tromans | | 17.03.69 | 4r1 | Stretford | 1 | Aug |
| 3:44.98 | Des Roache | U20 | 5.01.76 | 6r1 | Loughborough | 11 | Jun |
| 3:45.07 | Carl Leonard | U23 | 19.01.73 | | Indianapolis, USA | | |
| *3:45.1* | *Bobby Farren* | | *15.05.70* | *1* | *Antrim* | *20* | *Jun* |
| 3:45.39 i | Adam Duke | U23 | 5.10.73 | 1r1 | Birmingham | 29 | Jan |
| | 3:52.41 | | | 2h2 | London (CP) | 17 | Jun |

(40)

| 3:45.6 | Philip Healy | | 1.10.70 | 2 | Antrim | 20 | Jun |
|---|---|---|---|---|---|---|---|
| 3:45.6 | John Sherban | | 30.07.64 | 3 | Derby | 30 | Jul |
| 3:45.64 | Paul Gardner | | 5.08.69 | 6h4 | Birmingham | 15 | Jul |
| 3:45.78 | Jason Lobo | | 18.09.69 | 9r2 | Gateshead | 2 | Jul |
| 3:46.17 | Philip Hogston | U23 | 25.04.73 | 1r1 | London (CP) | 18 | Jun |
| 3:46.2 | Paul Freary | | 3.04.68 | 2r1 | Stretford | 6 | Jun |
| 3:46.45 i | Rob Scanlon | U23 | 13.04.74 | 5 | Birmingham | 25 | Feb |
| 3:46.58 | Justin Chaston | | 4.11.68 | 16r1 | Gateshead | 2 | Jul |
| 3:46.7 | Kim Critchley | U23 | 15.07.73 | 3r1 | Stretford | 6 | Jun |
| 3:46.7 | Stuart Poore | | 30.12.72 | 4r1 | Salisbury | 9 | Jul |

(50)

| 3:46.83 | Ewan Calvert | U23 | 28.11.73 | 11r2 | Gateshead | 2 | Jul |
|---|---|---|---|---|---|---|---|
| 3:46.9 | Clive Gilby | | 24.02.66 | 1r1 | Peterborough | 6 | May |
| 3:46.92 | Martin Yelling | | 7.02.72 | 2r2 | London (CP) | 18 | Jun |
| 3:47.02 | Martin Forder | | 7.08.70 | 6h3 | Birmingham | 15 | Jul |
| 3:47.3 | Ian Mitchell | U20 | 10.03.76 | 6r1 | Stretford | 1 | Aug |
| 3:47.31 | Terry West | | 19.11.68 | 10 | London (CP) | 27 | Aug |
| 3:47.5 | Andrew Pearson | | 14.09.71 | 1 | Stretford | 5 | Sep |
| 3:47.72 | Carl Warren | | 28.09.69 | 1 | Wrexham | 25 | Jun |
| 3:47.89 | David Heath | | 22.05.65 | 4r1 | London (CP) | 18 | Jun |
| 3:47.9 | Paul Bennett | | 9.08.71 | 7r1 | Stretford | 1 | Aug |

(60)

| 3:48.1 | Mark Miles | U20 | 24.03.77 | 2 | Bedford | 2 | Jul |
|---|---|---|---|---|---|---|---|
| 3:48.1 | Matthew Davies | | 23.07.71 | 5 | Southampton | 3 | Sep |
| 3:48.2 | Darren Spawforth | | 1.08.69 | 1 | Sheffield | 13 | May |
| 3:48.2 | Dave Lee | | 16.09.65 | 3 | Loughborough | 21 | Jun |
| 3:48.4 | Keith Cullen | | 13.06.72 | 1 | Oxford | 1 | Jul |
| 3:48.4 | Alan Tatham | U20 | 29.04.77 | 3 | Bedford | 2 | Jul |
| 3:48.46 | Dave Robertson | U23 | 4.08.73 | 1r1 | Crawley | 27 | May |
| 3:48.5 | Ben Reese | U20 | 29.03.76 | 2r2 | Manchester | 17 | May |
| 3:48.5 | Ben Rieper | U23 | 20.12.73 | 5r1 | Stretford | 6 | Jun |
| 3:48.7 | Peter Hackley | | 19.02.71 | 6r1 | Stretford | 6 | Jun |

(70)

| *3:48.7* | *John Downes* | | *21.07.67* | *1* | *London (WL)* | *19* | *Jul* |
|---|---|---|---|---|---|---|---|
| 3:48.8 | Brendan Smith | U20 | 20.07.77 | 8r1 | Stretford | 1 | Aug |
| 3:48.8 | Matthew Smith | U23 | 26.12.74 | 7r1 | Watford | 9 | Aug |
| 3:48.9 | Andrew Graffin | U20 | 20.12.77 | 4 | Bedford | 2 | Jul |
| 3:49.1 | Nick Bentham | | 7.12.70 | 1 | London (PH) | 5 | Jul |
| 3:49.1 | Steve Moseley | | 10.01.66 | 9r1 | Watford | 9 | Aug |
| 3:49.2 | Matt Skelton | | 8.11.72 | 2 | Crawley | 19 | Jul |
| 3:49.21 | Patrick Davoren | | 13.03.72 | 2r1 | Crawley | 27 | May |
| 3:49.4 | Chris Elliott | U23 | 29.05.75 | 6r2 | Manchester | 17 | May |
| 3:49.4 | Ivan Hollingsworth | U23 | 20.05.75 | 10r1 | Watford | 9 | Aug |
| 3:49.5 | Patrick O'Keefe | | | 2 | London (PH) | 5 | Jul |

(80)

| 3:49.57 | Larry Mangleshot | | 28.05.63 | 6h2 | Birmingham | 15 | Jul |
|---|---|---|---|---|---|---|---|
| 3:49.63 | Steve Edmonds | | 15.05.69 | 7h2 | Birmingham | 15 | Jul |
| 3:49.66 | David Locker | U23 | 28.03.75 | 2 | Wrexham | 25 | Jun |
| 3:49.7 | Chris Nicolson | U23 | 19.09.73 | 6 | Southampton | 3 | Sep |
| 3:49.79 | Andy Renfree | U23 | 18.05.75 | 4r1 | Crawley | 27 | May |
| 3:50.0 | Darrell Smith | | 10.04.67 | 4 | Crawley | 19 | Jul |
| 3:50.2 | Darius Burrows | U23 | 8.08.75 | 5r1 | Salisbury | 9 | Jul |

| | | | | | | | |
|---|---|---|---|---|---|---|---|
| 3:50.3 | Peter McColgan | | 20.02.63 | 2 | Edinburgh | 6 | Aug |
| 3:50.3 | Peter Jones | | 2.12.70 | 3 | Stretford | 5 | Sep |
| 3:50.4 | Keri Idessane | | 1.12.69 | 5 | Derby | 30 | Jul |
| (90) | | | | | | | |
| 3:50.7 | David Castle | | 30.07.71 | 5 | Crawley | 19 | Jul |
| 3:50.8 | Frank McGowan | | 23.08.70 | 7r1 | Stretford | 6 | Jun |
| 3:50.9 | Eric Crowther | U23 | 23.01.75 | 8r1 | Stretford | 6 | Jun |
| 3:51.2 | Vince Wilson | U23 | 1.04.73 | 1 | Gateshead | 24 | May |
| 3:51.2 | Luke Veness | U23 | 5.12.73 | 2h2 | ʼhborough | 10 | Jun |
| 3:51.2 | Russell Cartwright | U20 | 13.10.77 | 7 | ɔdiord | 2 | Jul |
| 3:51.2 | Richard Taylor | U23 | 5.12.73 | 11r1 | Watford | 9 | Aug |
| 3:51.3 | Tom Mayo | U20 | 2.05.77 | 3h2 | Loughborough | 10 | Jun |
| 3:51.3 | Spencer Newport | | 5.10.66 | 9r1 | Stretford | 1 | Aug |
| 3:51.32 | Peter Atkinson | | 13.12.65 | 4 | Edinburgh | 1 | Jul |
| (100) | | | | | | | |
| 3:51.5 | Mark Howard | | 7.02.66 | 6 | Crawley | 19 | Jul |
| 3:51.6 | Peter Baker | U23 | 6.02.73 | 2r1 | Solihull | 31 | May |
| 3:51.7 | Mike Simpson | | 6.01.70 | 3r2 | Watford | 9 | Aug |
| 3:51.7 | Ken Harker | | 25.02.71 | 5 | Stretford | 5 | Sep |
| 3:51.74 | Chris Stephenson | U23 | 22.07.74 | 3 | Edinburgh | 3 | Jun |
| 3:51.8 | Barry Royden | | 15.12.66 | 1 | Kingston | 22 | Jul |
| 3:51.8 | James Tonner | U23 | 3.06.75 | 2 | Glasgow | 16 | Aug |
| 3:51.90 | Donal O'Riordan | | 2.04.70 | 6r2 | Loughborough | 11 | Jun |
| 3:51.9 | Mark Barrow | | 30.06.68 | 9r1 | Stretford | 6 | Jun |
| *3:51.9* | *John Burke* | | *18.05.70* | *7r1* | *Salisbury* | *9* | *Jul* |
| 3:51.9 | Jon McCallum | U23 | 19.11.75 | 7 | Crawley | 19 | Jul |
| (110) | | | | | | | |
| 3:51.95 | Phillip Tulba-Morrison | U23 | 20.0ˌ/3 | 5r1 | Crawley | 27 | May |
| 3:52.0 | Steve Wright | | 12.02.71 | 2 | Gateshead | 24 | May |
| 3:52.0 | ï-rank Boyne | | 28.02.66 | 3r2 | Birmingham (Un) | 20 | Aug |

**Additional Under 20** (1 - 9 above)

| | | | | | | |
|---|---|---|---|---|---|---|
| 3:53.0 | Yacin Yusuf | 20.12.77 | 2 | Woking | 22 | Jul |
| (10) | | | | | | |
| 3:54.16 | Alistair Moses | 5.07.78 | 3 | Nottingham | 8 | Jul |
| 3:54.6 | Allen Graffin | 20.12.77 | 1 | Tonbridge | 3 | Sep |
| 3:54.8 | Craig Wheeler | 14.06.76 | 3r1 | Stretford | 27 | Jun |
| 3:54.9 | Grant Cuddy | 6.01.77 | 2 | Stretford | 10 | Jun |

**Under 17**

| | | | | | | |
|---|---|---|---|---|---|---|
| 3:56.67 | Gareth Turnbull | | 1 | Colwyn Bay | 15 | Jul |
| 3:58.76 | Matthew Dixon | 26.12.78 | 2 | Birmingham | 30 | Jul |
| 3:59.5 | Lee Garrett | 2.09.78 | 1 | Mansfield | 19 | Aug |
| 4:00.7 | Andrew Beckwith | 22.04.79 | 1 | Tonbridge | 10 | Sep |
| 4:01.19 | Aaron Hargreaves | 5.12.78 | 3 | Birmingham | 30 | Jul |
| 4:01.54 | Simon Burton | 23.04.79 | 1 | Nottingham | 8 | Jul |
| 4:02.01 | Chris Moss | 17.06.79 | 1h2 | Nottingham | 7 | Jul |
| 4:02.25 | Ross Fittall | 4.09.79 | 5 | Birmingham | 30 | Jul |
| 4:02.38 | Tom Salmon | 12.04.79 | 6 | Birmingham | 30 | Jul |
| 4:02.5 | Paul Fisher | 17.05.79 | 1 | Watford | 14 | Jun |
| (10) | | | | | | |
| 4:02.6 | Paul Morby | 15.01.79 | 2h1 | Birmingham | 30 | Jul |
| 4:03.33 | Simon Lees | 19.11.79 | 5h2 | Nottingham | 7 | Jul |
| 4:03.5 | Tom Hall | 8.07.79 | 3h1 | Birmingham | 30 | Jul |
| 4:04.1 | Tom Cartwright | 22.06.79 | 1 | Coventry | 30 | Jul |
| 4:05.5 | Stuart Austin | 21.03.79 | 4h3 | Birmingham | 30 | Jul |
| 4:05.7 | David Stanley | 16.01.79 | 1 | Kingston | 13 | Aug |
| 4:05.8 | Stephen Briffett | 22.10.78 | 1 | Watford | 12 | Jul |
| 4:06.1 | Chris Owen | 9.07.79 | 2h2 | Birmingham | 30 | Jul |
| 4:06.5 | James Bowskill | 19.05.79 | 2 | Mansfield | 14 | May |
| 4:07.0 | Bradley Yewer | 10.02.79 | 6h3 | Birmingham | 30 | Jul |

## Under 15

| | | | | | | | |
|---|---|---|---|---|---|---|---|
| 4:08.18 | Jonathon Keith | | 5.11.80 | 1 | Nottingham | 8 | Jul |
| 4:12.31 | Gareth Melvin | | 11.12.80 | 2 | Nottingham | 8 | Jul |
| 4:12.58 | Russell Pittam | | 12.10.80 | 1 | London (He) | 6 | Aug |
| 4:12.71 | Kieron Farrelly | | 14.10.80 | 3 | Nottingham | 8 | Jul |
| 4:13.52 | Stephen Holmes | | 17.10.80 | 2 | London (He) | 6 | Aug |
| 4:13.79 | Daniel Carthy | | 3.12.80 | 3 | London (He) | 6 | Aug |
| 4:14.63 | Andrew Brabin | | 19.10.80 | 4 | Nottingham | 8 | Jul |
| 4:15.7 | John Baker | | 28.01.81 | 1 | Horsham | 1 | Jul |
| 4:17.31 | Brian O'Reilly | | 3.10.80 | 1 | Tullamore, IRE | 3 | Jun |
| 4:17.76 | Andrew Rosson | | 2.12.80 | 6 | Nottingham | 8 | Jul |
| | (10) | | | | | | |
| 4:19.20 | Philip Harper | | 18.11.80 | 3 | Birmingham | 29 | Jul |
| 4:19.5 | David Brennan | | 26.06.81 | 2r5 | Stretford | 18 | Jul |
| 4:19.9 | Gary Blackman | | 24.09.80 | 1 | Solihull | 10 | Sep |
| 4:20.3 | Gary Macey | | 25.10.80 | 1 | Southampton | 18 | Jun |
| 4:20.9 | Michael Church | | 7.09.80 | 1 | London (Nh) | 16 | Jul |
| 4:21.3 | Daniel Gray | | 23.10.80 | 1 | Bolton | 16 | Jul |
| 4:21.63 | James Wardman | | 26.10.80 | 9 | Nottingham | 8 | Jul |
| 4:21.73 | Craig Hamilton | | 10.05.81 | 10 | Nottingham | 8 | Jul |

## Under 13

| | | | | | | | |
|---|---|---|---|---|---|---|---|
| 4:32.5 | Glen Coppin | | 16.01.83 | 2 | Watford | 19 | Jul |
| 4:42.0 | Malcolm Hassan | | | 1 | Barnsley | 16 | Jul |
| 4:42.2 | Terry Lyszyk | | | 1 | London (TB) | 30 | Jul |
| 4:42.8 | Ben Foreman | | 18.03.83 | 2 | London (TB) | 30 | Jul |
| 4:43.9 | Mohammed Farah | | | 1 | Perivale | 16 | Jul |
| 4:44.0 | Richard Waters | | 30.11.82 | 1 | Oldham | 23 | Aug |
| 4:44.1 | Chris Iddon | | 8.10.82 | 1 | Bolton | 16 | Jul |

## 1 MILE

| | | | | | | | | |
|---|---|---|---|---|---|---|---|---|
| 3:51.89 | John Mayock | | | 26.10.70 | 7 | Zurich, SWZ | 16 | Aug |
| | 3:55.36 | | | | 3 | London (CP) | 27 | Aug |
| | 3:55.42 | | | | 6 | Berlin, GER | 1 | Sep |
| 3:55.91 | Gary Lough | | | 6.07.70 | 5 | London (CP) | 27 | Aug |
| | 3:57.02 | | | | 7 | Berlin, GER | 1 | Sep |
| 3:56.05 | David Strang | | | 13.12.68 | 8 | Eugene, USA | 4 | Jun |
| 3:57.96 | Andy Keith | | | 25.12.71 | 2 | Cork, IRE | 24 | Jun |
| | 3:59.52 i | | | | 1 | Boston, USA | 19 | Feb |
| | 4:00.15 i | | | | 2 | Boston, USA | 21 | Jan |
| 3:58.68 | Ciaran Murphy | | | 2.09.71 | 4 | Cork, IRE | 24 | Jun |
| 3:59.44 | Tony Whiteman | | | 13.11.71 | 1 | Hong Kong, HK | 15 | Oct |
| 3:59.6 | Neil Caddy | U23 | | 18.03.75 | 1 | Cheltenham | 6 | Aug |
| | 4:01.1 | | | | 1 | Bath | 31 | May |
| 3:59.79 | Jon Wild | U23 | | 30.08.73 | 4 | Hot Springs, USA | 1 | Apr |
| | 4:01.19 i | | | | 1 | Kansas City, USA | 24 | Feb |
| 4:00.15 | Kim Critchley | U23 | | 15.07.73 | 7 | Cork, IRE | 24 | Jun |
| 4:01.4 | Robert Hough | | | 3.06.72 | 2 | Cheltenham | 6 | Aug |
| | (10) | | | | | | | |
| 4:01.66 | Matthew Yates | | | 4.02.69 | 10 | London (CP) | 27 | Aug |
| 4:01.8 | Andy Hart | | | 13.09.69 | 2 | Bath | 31 | May |

19 performances to 4:02.00 by 12 athletes including 3 indoors

| | | | | | | | |
|---|---|---|---|---|---|---|---|
| *4:02.5* | *Bobby Farren* | | *15.05.70* | *1* | *Londonderry* | *19* | *Aug* |
| 4:02.72 i | James Ellis-Smith | | 72 | 1 | Ames, USA | 10 | Feb |
| 4:02.8 | Grant Graham | | 27.12.72 | 2 | Londonderry | 19 | Aug |
| 4:02. ? | Ian Gillespie | | 18.05.70 | 2 | Gothenburg, SWE | | Aug |
| | 4:03.7 | | | 3 | Bath | 31 | May |
| 4:03.4 | Rob Simon | | | 10 | Cork, IRE | 24 | Jun |
| 4:04.0 | Philip Healy | | 1.10.70 | 3 | Londonderry | 19 | Aug |
| 4:04.13 | Simon Fairbrother | | 28.03.68 | 11 | London (CP) | 27 | Aug |

| | | | | | | | |
|---|---|---|---|---|---|---|---|
| 4:04.3 | Steffan White | | 21.12.72 | 4 | Bath | 31 | May |
| 4:04.3 | Stuart Margiotta | | 19.11.69 | 1 | Kings Lynn | 14 | Aug |
| | (20) | | | | | | |
| 4:04.6 | Patrick Davoren | | 13.03.72 | 5 | Bath | 31 | May |
| 4:05.6 | Peter McColgan | | 20.02.63 | 4 | Londonderry | 19 | Aug |
| 4:06.2 | Paul Gardner | | 5.08.69 | 4 | Cheltenham | 6 | Aug |
| 4:06.72 | Kevin McKay | | 9.02.69 | 12 | London (CP) | 27 | Aug |
| 4:06.73 i | Jason Boothroyd | | 26.11.69 | 1 | Ann Arbor, USA | 4 | Mar |
| 4:07.0 | Ian Grime | | 29.09.70 | 1 | Stretford | 18 | Jul |
| 4:08.0 | Peter Davies | | 24.02.63 | 6 | Bath | 31 | May |
| 4:08.2 | Des Roache | U20 | 5.01.76 | 5 | Londonderry | 19 | Aug |
| 4:08.91 | Terry West | | 19.11.68 | 1 | Gateshead | 12 | Aug |
| 4:09.4 | Steve Moseley | | 10.01.66 | 13 | Cork, IRE | 24 | Jun |
| | (30) | | | | | | |
| 4:09.6 | Matthew Davies | | 23.07.71 | 2 | Kings Lynn | 14 | Aug |
| 4:09.9 | David Heath | | 22.05.65 | 3 | Kings Lynn | 14 | Aug |
| 4:10.0 | Martin Yelling | | 7.02.72 | 1 | Bedford | 10 | May |

**Under 13**

| | | | | | | | |
|---|---|---|---|---|---|---|---|
| 5:19.6 | M. Slesser | | | 1 | Jarrow | 9 | Aug |

## 3000 METRES

| | | | | | | | |
|---|---|---|---|---|---|---|---|
| 7:46.80 i | John Mayock | | 26.10.70 | 3 | Birmingham | 25 | Feb |
| 7:47.28 | | | | 1 | Sheffield | 23 | Jul |
| 7:49.85 i | | | | 3 | Ghent, BEL | 12 | Feb |
| 7:51.57 i | | | | 2 | Seville, SPA | 17 | Feb |
| 7:51.86 i | | | | 5 | Barcelona, SPA | 12 | Mar |
| 7:52.99 | | | | 1 | Cork, IRE | 24 | Jun |
| 7:57.91 i | | | | 2h2 | Barcelona, SPA | 10 | Mar |
| 7:47.80 | Rob Denmark | | 23.11.68 | 2 | Sheffield | 23 | Jul |
| 7:56.22 | | | | 8 | London (CP) | 27 | Aug |
| 7:59.8 + | | | | 4m | Gateshead | 2 | Jul |
| 7:48.59 | John Nuttall | | 11.01.67 | 4 | Sheffield | 23 | Jul |
| 7:53.59 | | | | 5 | London (CP) | 27 | Aug |
| 7:59. | | | | m | Rome, ITA | 8 | Jun |
| 7:49.45 | Gary Lough | | 6.07.70 | 3 | Bratislava, SVK | 30 | May |
| 7:59.9 | | | | 1 | Loughborough | 20 | May |
| 7:54.37 | Andy Keith | | 25.12.71 | 10 | Sheffield | 23 | Jul |
| 7:57.38 | | | | 6 | New York, USA | 21 | May |
| 7:59.19 i | | | | 3 | New York, USA | 3 | Feb |
| 7:54.81 | Jon Brown | | 27.02.71 | 4 | Cork, IRE | 24 | Jun |
| 7:55.16 | Jon Wild | U23 | 30.08.73 | 5 | Cork, IRE | 24 | Jun |
| 7:56.17 | Paul Evans | | 13.04.61 | 6 | Cork, IRE | 24 | Jun |
| 7:56.71 | Tom Hanlon | | 20.05.67 | 10 | London (CP) | 27 | Aug |
| 7:58.25 | Keith Cullen | | 13.06.72 | 1 | Cwmbran | 9 | Jul |
| 7:58.59 | | | | 12 | London (CP) | 27 | Aug |
| | (10) | | | | | | |
| 7:59.27 | Glyn Tromans | | 17.03.69 | 1 | Nurmijarvi, FIN | 4 | Jun |

25 performances to 8:00.00 by 11 athletes including 6 indoors

| | | | | | | | |
|---|---|---|---|---|---|---|---|
| 8:00.1 | Davey Wilson | | 7.09.68 | 1 | Belfast | 22 | Apr |
| *8:00.24* | *John Downes* | | *21.07.67* | *11* | *Sheffield* | *23* | *Jul* |
| 8:00.4 + | Adrian Passey | | 2.09.64 | 6m | Gateshead | 2 | Jul |
| 8:16.7 | | | | 1 | Corby | 3 | Jun |
| 8:00.46 | Spencer Barden | U23 | 31.03.73 | 14 | London (CP) | 27 | Aug |
| 8:00.54 | Nick Comerford | | 23.04.66 | 8 | Cork, IRE | 24 | Jun |
| 8:00.9 | Ian Gillespie | | 18.05.70 | 1 | Watford | 9 | Aug |
| 8:01.0 | Darren Mead | | 4.10.68 | 2 | Loughborough | 20 | May |
| *8:02.84* | *John Burke* | | *18.05.70* | *11* | *Cork, IRE* | *24* | *Jun* |
| 8:03.82 i | Steve Green | | 18.02.71 | 2 | Glasgow | 11 | Feb |
| 8:05.45 | | | | 12 | Sheffield | 23 | Jul |

| Time | Name | Cat | DOB | Pos | Venue | Date |
|---|---|---|---|---|---|---|
| 8:03.86 | Neil Caddy | U23 | 18.03.75 | 1 | Birmingham | 20 May |
| 8:03.9 | Ian Hudspith | | 23.09.70 | 2 | Watford | 9 Aug |
| (20) | | | | | | |
| 8:04.5 | Darrell Smith | | 10.04.67 | 3 | Watford | 9 Aug |
| 8:04.66 | Kris Bowditch | U23 | 14.01.75 | 2 | Birmingham | 20 May |
| *8:04.69* | *Bobby Farren* | | *15.05.70* | *1* | *Antrim* | *8 Jul* |
| 8:04.9 | Julian Moorhouse | | 13.11.71 | 4 | Watford | 9 Aug |
| 8:05.0 | Chris Nicolson | U23 | 19.09.73 | 5 | Watford | 9 Aug |
| 8:05.02 | Dave Taylor | | 9.01.64 | 4 | Birmingham | 20 May |
| 8:05.67 | Spencer Duval | | 5.01.70 | 15 | London (CP) | 27 Aug |
| 8:05.74 | Mark Morgan | | 19.08.72 | 5 | Birmingham | 20 May |
| 8:06.29 | Steve Hope | | 8.02.72 | 6 | Birmingham | 20 May |
| 8:07.02 | Colin Jones | U23 | 8.04.74 | 14 | Cork, IRE | 24 Jun |
| 8:07.86 | Ged Davey | | 21.08.68 | 7 | Birmingham | 20 May |
| (30) | | | | | | |
| 8:08.26 | Toby Tanser | | 21.07.68 | 3 | Stockholm, SWE | 26 Jul |
| 8:08.7 | Andrew Pearson | | 14.09.71 | 1 | Stretford | 22 Aug |
| 8:09.08 i | Darius Burrows | U23 | 8.08.75 | 2 | Birmingham | 4 Feb |
| 8:09.19 | Paul Freary | | 3.04.68 | 16 | Cork, IRE | 24 Jun |
| 8:09.4 i | Glen Stewart | | 7.12.70 | 1 | Glasgow | 14 Jan |
| 8:09.75 | Dermot Donnelly | | 23.09.70 | 3r1 | Loughborough | 11 Jun |
| 8:09.79 i | Steffan White | | 21.12.72 | 1 | Birmingham | 1 Jan |
| | 8:13.31 | | | 7r1 | Loughborough | 11 Jun |
| 8:10.1 | Mark Steinle | U23 | 22.11.74 | 6 | Watford | 9 Aug |
| 8:10.2 i | Rod Finch | | 5.08.67 | 1r1 | Birmingham | 1 Mar |
| 8:10.43 | Phil Mowbray | U23 | 19.03.73 | 4r1 | Loughborough | 11 Jun |
| (40) | | | | | | |
| 8:10.8 | Paul Taylor | | 9.01.66 | 1r1 | Stretford | 18 Jul |
| 8:11.0 i | Rob Scanlon | U23 | 13.04.74 | 2r1 | Birmingham | 1 Mar |
| 8:11.86 | Nick Hopkins | | 28.08.66 | 1r1 | Birmingham | 30 Jul |
| 8:12.0 i | Alan Puckrin | | 2.04.64 | 3 | Glasgow | 14 Jan |
| 8:12.02 i | Ian Robinson | | 21.04.69 | 2 | Manhattan Ka, USA | 25 Feb |
| 8:12.78 i | Bashir Hussain | | 20.12.64 | 1 | Birmingham | 26 Feb |
| 8:13.4 | Bruno Witchalls | U23 | 22.03.75 | 1 | Loughborough | 21 Jun |
| 8:13.44 i | Dave Lee | | 16.09.65 | 5 | Birmingham | 4 Feb |
| | 8:19.9 | | | 1 | Loughborough | 24 May |
| *8:13.72* | *David Burke* | | *68* | *3r1* | *Birmingham* | *30 Jul* |
| 8:14.43 i | Robert Whalley | | 11.02.68 | 3 | Birmingham | 1 Jan |
| 8:14.71 i | Tony Whiteman | | 13.11.71 | 2 | Birmingham | 28 Jan |
| (50) | | | | | | |
| 8:15.94 i | Patrick Davoren | | 13.03.72 | 6 | Birmingham | 4 Feb |
| 8:16.1 | Robert Quinn | | 10.12.65 | 1 | Grangemouth | 3 May |
| 8:16.1 | Neil Rimmer | | 22.04.62 | 1 | Stretford | 1 Aug |
| 8:16.5 | Ian Grime | | 29.09.70 | 2 | Loughborough | 21 Jun |
| 8:16.62 i | Mick Hawkins | | 24.10.61 | 8 | Birmingham | 4 Feb |
| 8:17.3 i | Matt Skelton | | 8.11.72 | 3r1 | Birmingham | 1 Mar |
| | 8:21.8 | | | 1 | Watford | 26 Apr |
| 8:17.8 | John Kendall | | 23.09.69 | 8 | Watford | 9 Aug |
| 8:18.0 | Mark Benson | | 21.12.63 | 1r1 | Stretford | 27 Jun |
| 8:19.5 | Stephen Green | | 28.07.70 | 2r1 | Stretford | 27 Jun |
| 8:19.7 | Dave Tune | | 29.10.70 | 2 | Stretford | 1 Aug |
| (60) | | | | | | |
| 8:19.9 | Adrian Callan | | 28.11.62 | 1 | Glasgow | 16 Aug |
| 8:20.1 | Dave Robertson | U23 | 4.08.73 | 1 | Woking | 16 Aug |
| 8:20.6 | Brendan Smith | U20 | 20.07.77 | 2r1 | Stretford | 18 Jul |
| 8:20.7 | Colin Moore | | 25.11.60 | 3r1 | Stretford | 27 Jun |
| 8:20.9 | Carl Warren | | 28.09.69 | 1 | Telford | 3 Jun |
| 8:21.12 | Martin Jones | | 21.04.67 | 10r1 | Loughborough | 11 Jun |
| 8:21.2 | Jeff Hornby | | 17.01.66 | 3 | Stretford | 1 Aug |
| 8:21.5 | Richard Blakely | | 19.05.72 | 3 | Antrim | 20 May |
| 8:22.1 | Tim Hyde | | 22.02.72 | 2 | Woking | 16 Aug |

153

| 8:22.8 | Lee Hurst | | 29.07.72 | 2r1 | Stretford | 6 | Jun |
| (70) | | | | | | | |
| 8:23.4 | Graeme Croll | | 1.02.66 | 1 | Wishaw | 18 | Jun |
| 8:23.5 | Billy Dee | | 18.12.61 | 9 | Watford | 9 | Aug |
| 8:23.6 | Richard Taylor | U23 | 5.12.73 | 1 | Telford | 23 | Aug |
| 8:23.6 | Alan Guilder | | 10.12.61 | 2 | Telford | 23 | Aug |
| 8:23.7 | Paul Green | | 7.04.72 | 2 | Stretford | 22 | Aug |
| 8:23.9 | Matt Hibberd | U23 | 23.06.73 | 1 | Loughborough | 26 | Apr |
| 8:23.9 | Matt Kinnane | | | 3 | Woking | 16 | Aug |
| 8:24.0 | John O'Shea | | 13.04.67 | 1 | Woking | 12 | Jul |
| *8:24.1* | *Ian Harpur* | | *24.04.67* | *1* | *Aldershot* | *26* | *Jun* |
| 8:24.23 | Paddy Brice | | 8.02.69 | 6r1 | Birmingham | 30 | Jul |
| 8:24.25 | Mike Shevyn | | 12.12.71 | 1r2 | Loughborough | 11 | Jun |
| (80) | | | | | | | |
| 8:24.4 | Terry Booth | | 19.10.66 | 4 | Woking | 16 | Aug |
| 8:24.5 | Jason Lobo | | 18.09.69 | 4r1 | Stretford | 6 | Jun |
| 8:25.0 | Gareth Deacon | | 8.08.66 | 1 | Loughborough | 14 | May |
| 8:25.0 | Matt O'Dowd | U20 | 13.04.76 | 1r2 | Birmingham | 29 | Jul |

**Additional Under 20** (1 - 2 above)

| 8:28.3 | Andres Jones | | 3.02.77 | 1 | Street | 8 | May |
| 8:29.1 | Des Roache | | 5.01.76 | 2 | Glasgow | 16 | Aug |
| 8:29.23 | Andrew Hennessy | | 24.08.77 | 2 | Nottingham | 8 | Jul |
| 8:29.3 | Daniel Hyde | | 5.10.77 | 2 | Street | 8 | May |
| 8:30.3 | Julian Wilkie | | 18.03.76 | 4 | Telford | 23 | Aug |
| 8:30.34 | Allen Graffin | | 20.12.77 | 2 | Belfort, FRA | 6 | Aug |
| 8:30.5 | Russell Cartwright | | 13.10.77 | 3r2 | Birmingham | 29 | Jul |
| 8:31.2 | Chris Davies | | 19.10.76 | 9r1 | Stretford | 6 | Jun |
| (10) | | | | | | | |
| 8:33.7 | Kevin Nash | | 6.02.77 | 1 | Woking | 12 | Jul |
| 8:34.7 | Theo Boyce | | 11.12.76 | 4r2 | Birmingham | 29 | Jul |
| 8:35.0 | Matthew Vaux-Harvey | | 30.03.76 | 5 | Birmingham | 29 | Jul |

**Under 17**

| 8:42.8 | Paul Fisher | | 17.05.79 | 1 | Watford | 31 | May |
| 8:45.1 | Aaron Hargreaves | | 5.12.78 | 5 | Stretford | 22 | Aug |
| 8:48.8 | Simon Burton | | 23.04.79 | 1 | Coventry | 30 | Apr |
| 8:50.40 | Andrew Beckwith | | 22.04.79 | 2 | Colwyn Bay | 15 | Jul |
| 8:50.5 | Colin McLean | | 7.06.80 | 3 | Colwyn Bay | 15 | Jul |
| 8:52.59 | Steven Lawrence | | | 1 | Bedford | 2 | Jul |
| 8:52.7 | Oliver Laws | | 18.03.80 | 1 | Telford | 10 | Jun |
| 8:53.4 | Christopher Lindesay | | 11.02.79 | 11r1 | Stretford | 18 | Jul |
| 8:54.1 i | Gareth Turnbull | | | 1 | Birmingham | 19 | Feb |
| 8:54.61 | Simon Holley | | 2.09.78 | 2 | Bedford | 2 | Jul |
| (10) | | | | | | | |
| 8:55.3 | Matthew Dixon | | 26.12.78 | 12r1 | Stretford | 18 | Jul |
| 8:55.6 | Daniel Hicks | | 17.12.78 | | Brighton | 23 | Aug |
| 8:55.9 | Martyn Potter | | 16.02.80 | 2 | St. Albans | 21 | May |
| 8:56.1 | Simon Curwen | | 26.10.78 | 13r1 | Stretford | 18 | Jul |
| 8:57.3 | James Bowskill | | 19.05.79 | 1 | Telford | 21 | May |
| 8:57.82 | Joel Ellis | | 2.09.79 | 3 | Bedford | 2 | Jul |
| 8:57.97 | Sam Haughian | | 9.07.79 | 3 | Nottingham | 8 | Jul |
| 8:58.3 | Tommy Yule | | 13.09.78 | 1 | Linwood | 24 | Aug |
| 8:59.4 | Matthew Watson | | 23.02.80 | 1 | Sheffield | 13 | May |
| 8:59.4 | Adam Crosland | | 27.08.79 | 2 | Sheffield | 13 | May |

**Under 15**

| 9:19.47 | Gareth Melvin | | 11.12.80 | 1 | Bedford | 1 | Jul |
| 9:20.8 | Russell Pittam | | 12.10.80 | | Brighton | 23 | Aug |
| 9:26.3 | Andrew Franklin | | 13.09.80 | 1 | Walton | 1 | Jul |
| 9:29.1 | Stephen Holmes | | 17.10.80 | 1 | London (He) | 4 | Jun |

| 9:32.7 | Keith Chapman | 15.02.81 | 1 | Stockport | 16 | Jul |
|---|---|---|---|---|---|---|
| 9:32.9 | Chris Bolt | 21.09.80 | 1 | Bracknell | 10 | Sep |
| 9:34.10 | Lee Wolstencroft | 19.07.81 | 2 | Bedford | 1 | Jul |
| 9:34.6 | Robert Whittle | 14.06.81 | 2 | Bracknell | 10 | Sep |
| 9:34.9 | Idris Ahmed | 30.10.80 | 1 | Sheffield | 25 | Jun |
| 9:35.4 | W. Langley | | 1 | Brighton | 23 | Aug |
| 9:35.6 | Jamie McCullagh | 9.11.80 | 2 | Walton | 1 | Jul |
| 9:37.15 | Daniel Samuels | 21.12.80 | 3 | Sheffield | 28 | May |
| 9:37.0 | Richard Ward | 5.05.82 | | London (TB) | 2 | Aug |
| 9:37.4 | Gary Blackman | 24.09.80 | 1 | Harrow | 16 | Jul |
| 9:37.43 | Tsegay Berhre | 15.01.81 | 1 | Enfield | 13 | Aug |
| 9:37.79 | Paul Hunt | 26.03.81 | 3 | Bedford | 1 | Jul |
| 9:38.1 | Darren Middleton | 14.11.80 | 1 | Barnsley | 16 | Jul |
| 9:38.9 | Abdi Madar | 25.11.81 | 1 | Croydon | 16 | Jul |
| 9:39.2 | Adam Conway | 2.10.80 | 1 | London (Nh) | 6 | Jul |
| 9:40.82 | Stephen Vernon | 17.10.80 | 4 | Sheffield | 28 | May |
| 9:41.93 | Chris Thompson | 17.04.81 | 4 | Bedford | 2 | Jul |

**Under 13**

| 10:23.0 | Chris Gay | 10.02.83 | 1 | Watford | 13 | Sep |
|---|---|---|---|---|---|---|
| 10:29.7 | Richard Skornia | | 1 | Exeter | 26 | Sep |
| 10:30.7 | Richard Waters | 30.11.82 | 1 | Stoke | 6 | Sep |
| 10:31.5 | O. Josephson | | 1 | Watford | 28 | Jun |
| 10:32.7 | Richard Hardwick | 1.09.82 | 1 | Sheffield | 16 | Apr |

## 5000 METRES

| 13:13.77 | Rob Denmark | | 23.11.68 | 1 | Nuremberg, GER | 15 | Jun |
|---|---|---|---|---|---|---|---|
| | 13:15.83 | | | 3 | Gateshead | 2 | Jul |
| | 13:37.14 | | | 6h1 | Gothenburg, SWE | 11 | Aug |
| | 13:37.57 | | | 1 | Birmingham | 15 | Jul |
| | 13:37.88 | | | 13 | Oslo, NOR | 21 | Jul |
| 13:16.70 | John Nuttall | | 11.01.67 | 5 | Rome, ITA | 8 | Jun |
| | 13:20.91 | | | 12 | Stockholm, SWE | 10 | Jul |
| | 13:25.18 | | | 6h2 | Gothenburg, SWE | 11 | Aug |
| | 13:46.82 | | | 2 | Villeneuve d'Ascq, FRA | 25 | Jun |
| | 13:49.25 | | | 14 | Gothenburg, SWE | 13 | Aug |
| 13:22.73 | Adrian Passey | | 2.09.64 | 8 | Gateshead | 2 | Jul |
| | 13:28.83 | | | 9 | Hechtel, BEL | 22 | Jul |
| | 13:32.88 | | | 8 | Nuremberg, GER | 15 | Jun |
| | 13:35.69 | | | 8r1 | Helsinki, FIN | 28 | Jun |
| 13:25.38 | Paul Evans | | 13.04.61 | 4r1 | Helsinki, FIN | 28 | Jun |
| 13:37.83 | Jon Brown | | 27.02.71 | 2 | Birmingham | 15 | Jul |
| | 13:39.68 | | | 13 | Lausanne, SWZ | 5 | Jul |
| | 13:49.77 | | | 1 | Nivelles, BEL | 19 | Aug |
| 13:38.42 | Gary Staines | | 3.07.63 | 9r1 | Helsinki, FIN | 28 | Jun |
| 13:42.85 | Ian Robinson | | 21.04.69 | 4 | Madison, USA | 6 | May |
| | 13:59.38 i | | | 1 | Ames, USA | 3 | Mar |
| | 13:59.96 i | | | 4 | Indianapolis, USA | 11 | Mar |
| 13:46.76 | John Sherban | | 30.07.64 | 6 | Birmingham | 15 | Jul |
| 13:48.13 | Andy Keith | | 25.12.71 | 6 | Philadelphia, USA | 27 | Apr |
| 13:49.15 | Jon Wild | U23 | 30.08.73 | 10 | Walnut, USA | 14 | Apr |
| (10) | | | | | | | |
| 13:51.86 | Justin Chaston | | 4.11.68 | 7 | Birmingham | 15 | Jul |
| 13:54.02 | Dermot Donnelly | | 23.09.70 | 4 | Kevelaar, HOL | 3 | Jun |
| 13:55.23 | Glyn Tromans | | 17.03.69 | 16r1 | Helsinki, FIN | 28 | Jun |
| 13:56.96 | Jon Solly | | 28.06.63 | 18 | Gateshead | 2 | Jul |
| | 13:58.43 | | | 8 | Birmingham | 15 | Jul |
| 13:57.63 | Spencer Barden | U23 | 31.03.73 | 1 | London (CP) | 14 | May |
| 13:59.45 | Chris Robison | | 16.03.61 | 1 | Wishaw | 13 | May |

32 performances to 14:00.00 by 16 athletes including 2 indoors

| | | | | | | | |
|---|---|---|---|---|---|---|---|
| *14:00.2* | *Bobby Farren* | | *15.05.70* | *6* | *Kevelaar, HOL* | *3* | *Jun* |
| 14:00.24 | Spencer Newport | | 5.10.66 | 9 | Birmingham | 15 | Jul |
| 14:00.91 | Robert Quinn | | 10.12.65 | 2 | Wishaw | 13 | May |
| 14:01.45 | Richard Findlow | | 4.12.66 | 2 | Bedford | 29 | May |
| 14:04.2 | Dave Taylor | | 9.01.64 | 1 | London (He) | 7 | May |
| (20) | | | | | | | |
| 14:04.4 | Paul Taylor | | 9.01.66 | 2 | Barking | 3 | Jun |
| 14:05.08 | Nick Hopkins | | 28.08.66 | 1 | London (CP) | 17 | Jun |
| 14:05.58 | Adrian Callan | | 28.11.62 | 3 | Wishaw | 13 | May |
| 14:05.66 | Philip Hogston | U23 | 25.04.73 | 1 | London (CP) | 3 | Jun |
| 14:06.3 | Eamonn Martin | | 9.10.58 | 1 | Walton | 22 | Jul |
| 14:07.86 | Kris Bowditch | U23 | 14.01.75 | 3 | Bedford | 29 | May |
| 14:08.08 | Phil Mowbray | U23 | 19.03.73 | 12 | Birmingham | 15 | Jul |
| 14:08.22 | Dominic Middleton | | 22.10.69 | 3 | South Bend, USA | 6 | May |
| 14:08.85 | Dominic Bannister | | 1.04.68 | 3 | London (CP) | 3 | Jun |
| 14:09.12 | Carl Leonard | U23 | 19.01.73 | 15 | Philadelphia, USA | 27 | Apr |
| (30) | | | | | | | |
| 14:11.17 | Barry Royden | | 15.12.66 | 1 | Aldershot | 23 | Jul |
| *14:11.42* | *John Burke* | | *18.05.70* | *4* | *Bedford* | *29* | *May* |
| 14:12.04 | Bashir Hussain | | 20.12.64 | 5 | Bedford | 29 | May |
| 14:12.35 | Darius Burrows | U23 | 8.08.75 | 14 | Birmingham | 15 | Jul |
| *14:12.59* | *John Downes* | | *21.07.67* | *6* | *Bedford* | *29* | *May* |
| 14:14.89 | Darren Mead | | 4.10.68 | 2 | Birmingham | 1 | Jul |
| 14:15.2 | Rod Finch | | 5.08.67 | 1 | Brighton | 23 | Aug |
| 14:15.43 | Ian Hudspith | | 23.09.70 | 15 | Birmingham | 15 | Jul |
| 14:16.0 | Keith Anderson | | 10.08.57 | 3 | Hexham | 4 | May |
| 14:16.0 | Patrick Davoren | | 13.03.72 | 2 | Brighton | 23 | Aug |
| 14:16.6 | Tony O'Brien | | 14.11.70 | 1 | Grimsby | 3 | Sep |
| 14:16.8 | Darrell Smith | | 10.04.67 | 3 | Brighton | 23 | Aug |
| (40) | | | | | | | |
| 14:16.8 | Allen Graffin | U20 | 20.12.77 | 4 | Brighton | 23 | Aug |
| 14:16.88 | Mark Steinle | U23 | 22.11.74 | 4 | London (CP) | 3 | Jun |
| 14:17.3 | Graeme Croll | | 1.02.66 | 3 | Pitreavie | 28 | May |
| 14:18.3 | Colin Moore | | 25.11.60 | 1 | Bebington | 3 | Jun |
| 14:18.84 | Andrew Pearson | | 14.09.71 | 20 | Seville, SPA | 3 | Jun |
| 14:19.0 | Martin Jones | | 21.04.67 | 6 | Hexham | 4 | May |
| 14:19.5 | Andrew Morgan-Lee | | 1.03.69 | 5 | Brighton | 23 | Aug |
| 14:19.64 | Toby Tanser | | 21.07.68 | 16r1 | Gavle, SWE | 6 | Jul |
| 14:19.9 | Mark Morgan | | 19.08.72 | 1 | Swansea | 19 | Jul |
| 14:20.2 | Matt O'Dowd | U20 | 13.04.76 | 6 | Brighton | 23 | Aug |
| (50) | | | | | | | |
| 14:20.96 | Bill Foster | | 9.08.58 | 17 | Birmingham | 15 | Jul |
| 14:21.97 i | Steve Brooks | | 8.06.70 | 4 | Ames, USA | 10 | Feb |
| 14:22.0 | Mick Hawkins | | 24.10.61 | 7 | Hexham | 4 | May |
| 14:22.5 | Gary Nagel | | 4.06.62 | 1 | Gateshead | 14 | May |
| 14:22.7 | Stephen Green | | 28.07.70 | 1 | Stretford | 22 | Jul |
| 14:22.79 | Mike Simpson | | 6.01.70 | 4r1 | London (CP) | 17 | Jun |
| *14:23.0* | *Kassa Tadesse* | U23 | *21.08.74* | *8* | *Hexham* | *4* | *May* |
| 14:23.01 | Justin Pugsley | | 15.04.71 | 5 | London (CP) | 3 | Jun |
| 14:23.1 | Stuart Bell | | 29.07.67 | 2 | Gateshead | 14 | May |
| 14:24.2 | Jeff Hornby | | 17.01.66 | 2 | Stretford | 22 | Jul |
| 14:24.54 | Julian Moorhouse | | 13.11.71 | 7 | Bedford | 29 | May |
| (60) | | | | | | | |
| 14:24.7 | Darren Daniels | | 2.09.70 | 2 | Enfield | 19 | Aug |
| 14:24.83 | Ian Hamilton | | 8.03.65 | 5r1 | London (CP) | 17 | Jun |
| 14:25.27 | Dale Laughlin | | 28.12.66 | 1 | Barking | 13 | May |
| 14:26.7 | Alaister Russell | | 17.06.68 | 3 | Barking | 3 | Jun |
| 14:26.97 | Peter Haynes | | 18.09.64 | 2 | Aldershot | 23 | Jul |
| 14:27.21 | John Kendall | | 23.09.69 | 6r1 | London (CP) | 17 | Jun |
| 14:27.6 | Wayne Oxborough | | 10.11.66 | 7 | Brighton | 23 | Aug |
| 14:28.0 | Carl Thackery | | 14.10.62 | 9 | Hexham | 4 | May |

| 14:28.0 | Tommy Murray | | 18.05.61 | 10 | Hexham | 4 May |
| 14:28.62 | Nigel Gates | V40 | 18.05.53 | 7r1 | London (CP) | 17 Jun |
| (70) | | | | | | |
| 14:28.83 | Rob Birchall | | 14.06.70 | 2 | Edinburgh | 1 Jul |
| 14:29.1 | Kevin Blake | | 29.05.67 | 2 | Swansea | 19 Jul |
| 14:29.59 | Graeme Wight | | 3.06.65 | 4 | Edinburgh | 24 Jun |
| 14:29.60 | Richard Blakely | | 19.05.72 | 2 | Antrim | 1 Jul |
| 14:29.9 | Dave Tune | | 29.10.70 | 1r1 | Stretford | 1 Jul |
| 14:30.08 | Justin Hobbs | | 12.03.69 | 1 | Newport | 17 Jun |
| 14:31.1 | Terry Wall | | 12.06.70 | 2 | Grimsby | 3 Sep |
| 14:31.24 | Martin Roscoe | | 19.09.64 | 8 | Bedford | 29 May |
| 14:31.34 | Andrew Wedlake | | 30.11.71 | 32 | Philadelphia, USA | 27 Apr |
| 14:32.41 | Terry Booth | | 19.10.66 | 4 | Aldershot | 23 Jul |
| (80) | | | | | | |
| 14:32.54 | Steve Hope | | 8.02.72 | 9 | Bedford | 29 May |
| 14:32.88 | Neil Rimmer | | 22.04.62 | 1 | Gateshead | 17 Jun |
| 14:33.34 | Stephen Platts | | 12.03.66 | 10 | Bedford | 29 May |
| *14:33.51* | *John Lisiewicz* | | *18.07.62* | *2* | *Gateshead* | *17 Jun* |
| 14:33.54 | Peter Wilson | | 28.06.62 | 8r1 | London (CP) | 17 Jun |
| 14:33.6 | Andrew Graffin | U20 | 20.12.77 | 9 | Brighton | 23 Aug |
| 14:33.83 | Andy Eynon | | 1.09.62 | 1 | Cardiff | 19 Aug |
| 14:33.9 | Martin McLoughlin | | 23.12.58 | 1 | Wakefield | 3 Jun |
| 14:33.9 | Chris Slowley | | 16.02.63 | 3r1 | Wakefield | 3 Jun |
| 14:34.0 | Ian Johnston | | 4.06.64 | 1r1 | Coatbridge | 23 Apr |
| 14:34.03 | Ken Conley | | 24.12.61 | 11 | Bedford | 29 May |
| (90) | | | | | | |
| 14:34.1 | Carl Warren | | 28.09.69 | 1 | Liverpool | 30 Jul |
| 14:34.14 | Kevin Jacques | | 17.09.58 | 1r2 | London (CP) | 17 Jun |
| 14:34.18 | Nick Francis | | 29.08.71 | 3 | Edinburgh | 1 Jul |
| 14:34.2 | Michael Bulstridge | U23 | 23.01.73 | 6 | Enfield | 19 Aug |
| 14:35.52 | Steve Wright | | 12.02.71 | 3 | Gateshead | 17 Jun |
| 14:35.58 | Ian Grime | | 29.09.70 | 1 | Edinburgh | 7 May |
| 14:35.58 | Robert Malseed | | 16.09.71 | 3 | Crawley | 27 May |
| 14:35.6 | David Ross | | 2.11.65 | 3r1 | Coatbridge | 23 Apr |
| 14:35.8 | Simon Kinson | | 3.12.70 | 1 | Leamington | 14 May |
| 14:35.9 | Ian Harkness | | 23.08.68 | 2r1 | Stoke | 7 May |
| (100) | | | | | | |
| 14:36.0 | Mark Benson | | 21.12.63 | 1 | Stretford | 18 Jul |

**Illegally paced** - athletes dropping out and rejoining

| 14:05.3 | Graeme Croll | | 1.02.66 | 1 | Glasgow | 1 Aug |

**Additional Under 20** (1 - 3 above)

| 14:36.35 | Andres Jones | | 3.02.77 | 3 | Bedford | 2 Jul |
| 14:38.10 | Matthew Vaux-Harvey | | 30.03.76 | 4 | Bedford | 2 Jul |
| 14:44.7 | Tony Forrest | | 22.12.76 | 2 | Milton Keynes | 3 Jun |
| 14:57.36 | Nathaniel Lane | | 10.04.76 | 5 | Bedford | 2 Jul |
| 14:59.8 | Adrian White | | 10.09.76 | | Cannock | 16 Sep |
| 15:01.03 | Chris Davies | | 19.10.76 | 6 | Bedford | 2 Jul |
| 15:04.72 | Martin Palmer | | 5.04.77 | 7 | Bedford | 2 Jul |
| (10) | | | | | | |
| 15:05.74 | Mark Beerling | | 16.03.76 | 8 | Bedford | 2 Jul |

# 10000 METRES

| 27:49.54 | Paul Evans | | 13.04.61 | 5 | London (CP) | 7 Jul |
| 28:07.15 | | | | 14 | Brussels, BEL | 25 Aug |
| 28:14.76 | | | | 9h1 | Gothenburg, SWE | 5 Aug |
| 28:07.43 | John Nuttall | | 11.01.67 | 15 | Brussels, BEL | 25 Aug |
| 28:08.31 | Jon Brown | | 27.02.71 | 16 | Brussels, BEL | 25 Aug |
| 28:33.49 | Gary Staines | | 3.07.63 | 17 | London (CP) | 7 Jul |
| 28:49.29 | | | | 1 | Loughborough | 11 Jun |
| 28:34.84 | Ian Robinson | | 21.04.69 | 9 | Walnut, USA | 14 Apr |

| 28:58.29 | Jon Solly | | 28.06.63 | 2 | Loughborough | 11 | Jun |
|---|---|---|---|---|---|---|---|
| | 9 performances to 29:00.0 by 6 athletes | | | | | | |
| 29:03.69 | Chris Robison | | 16.03.61 | 3 | Loughborough | 11 | Jun |
| 29:04.63 | Steve Brooks | | 8.06.70 | 18 | Walnut, USA | 14 | Apr |
| 29:04.87 | Andy Lyons | | 24.12.69 | 4 | Loughborough | 11 | Jun |
| 29:07.33 | Mark Steinle | U23 | 22.11.74 | 5 | Loughborough | 11 | Jun |
| (10) | | | | | | | |
| 29:14.23 | Robert Quinn | | 10.12.65 | 6 | Loughborough | 11 | Jun |
| 29:17.11 | Bill Foster | | 9.08.58 | 7 | Loughborough | 11 | Jun |
| 29:23.49 | Spencer Newport | | 5.10.66 | 8 | Loughborough | 11 | Jun |
| 29:25.92 | Justin Hobbs | | 12.03.69 | 6 | Villeneuve d'Ascq, FRA | 24 | Jun |
| 29:28.0 | Colin Moore | | 25.11.60 | 1 | Stretford | 22 | Jul |
| 29:32.67 | Richard Findlow | | 4.12.66 | 9 | Loughborough | 11 | Jun |
| 29:33.8 | Dermot Donnelly | | 23.09.70 | 1 | Antrim | 12 | Aug |
| *29:36.58* | *Jamie Harrison* | | *21.12.63* | *10* | *Loughborough* | *11* | *Jun* |
| 29:36.80 | Justin Pugsley | | 15.04.71 | 11 | Loughborough | 11 | Jun |
| 29:44.03 | Stephen Green | | 28.07.70 | 12 | Loughborough | 11 | Jun |
| 29:45.6 | Stuart Bell | | 29.07.67 | 1 | Grimsby | 3 | Sep |
| (20) | | | | | | | |
| 29:50.69 | Graeme Croll | | 1.02.66 | 1 | Edinburgh | 23 | Jun |
| 29:52.16 | Alaister Russell | | 17.06.68 | 2 | Edinburgh | 23 | Jun |
| 29:58.09 | Ian Hudspith | | 23.09.70 | 13 | Loughborough | 11 | Jun |
| 29:59.5 | Jeff Hornby | | 17.01.66 | 2 | Grimsby | 3 | Sep |
| 30:01.20 | Andrew Wedlake | | 30.11.71 | 1 | Williamsburg, USA | 31 | Mar |
| 30:03.52 | Toby Tanser | | 21.07.68 | 6 | Sollentuna, SWE | 21 | Jul |
| *30:08.36* | *John Downes* | | *21.07.67* | *3* | *Tallinn, EST* | *10* | *Jun* |
| 30:08.41 | Martin Hula | | 2.01.66 | 14 | Loughborough | 11 | Jun |
| 30:16.20 | Rob Birchall | | 14.06.70 | 15 | Loughborough | 11 | Jun |
| 30:19.0 | Geoff Hill | | 8.02.63 | 1 | Crawley | 10 | Sep |
| 30:19.1 | Steve Murdoch | | 16.04.61 | 3 | Grimsby | 3 | Sep |
| (30) | | | | | | | |
| 30:27.19 | Karl Keska | | 7.05.72 | 1 | Tucson, USA | 19 | May |
| 30:29.1 | Kevin Smith | | 28.01.67 | 4 | Grimsby | 3 | Sep |
| 30:30.1 | Dave Gratton | | 25.10.55 | 5 | Grimsby | 3 | Sep |
| 30:32.2 | Tony O'Brien | | 14.11.70 | 1 | Liverpool | 30 | Jul |
| 30:35.45 | Dave Tune | | 29.10.70 | 4 | Edinburgh | 23 | Jun |
| 30:36.1 | Darren Daniels | | 2.09.70 | 2 | Liverpool | 30 | Jul |
| 30:37.0 | Alan Reid | | 19.04.66 | 1 | Inverness | 12 | Sep |
| 30:37.7 | Terry Wall | | 12.06.70 | 2 | Jarrow | 9 | Aug |
| 30:39.38 | Wayne Oxborough | | 10.11.66 | 3 | Bedford | 28 | May |
| 30:41.7 | Tony Graham | | 15.10.63 | 1 | Nottingham | 25 | Jun |
| (40) | | | | | | | |
| 30:43.0 | Eddie Stewart | | 15.12.56 | 9 | Ostrava, CS | 6 | Jul |
| 30:44.90 | Peter Wilson | | 28.06.62 | 4 | Bedford | 28 | May |
| 30:48.58 | Martin Ferguson | | 17.09.64 | 5 | Edinburgh | 23 | Jun |
| 30:49.5 | Bruce Chinnick | | 25.04.60 | 1 | Newport | 17 | Jun |
| 30:49.66 | Alan Puckrin | | 2.04.64 | 6 | Edinburgh | 23 | Jun |
| 30:49.84 | James Jackson | | 12.09.63 | 5 | Bedford | 28 | May |
| 30:54.9 | Jimmy Newnes | | 9.09.67 | 1 | Stretford | 22 | Jul |
| 30:57.0 | Charlie Thomson | | 17.06.65 | 1r1 | Edinburgh | 6 | Aug |
| 30:59.6 | Greg Hull | | 16.08.65 | 1 | Leeds | 20 | Jun |
| 31:01.15 | Ian Grime | | 29.09.70 | 1 | Stoke | 9 | Sep |
| (50) | | | | | | | |
| 31:04.69 | Robert Malseed | | 16.09.71 | 16 | Loughborough | 11 | Jun |
| 31:06.87 | Andrew Little | | 1.01.64 | 7 | Edinburgh | 23 | Jun |
| 31:19.0 | Neil Ovington | | 26.01.63 | 1 | Leicester | 13 | Sep |
| 31:19.38 | M. Griffiths | | | 2 | Edinburgh | 8 | May |
| 31:19.65 | Nigel Adams | | 17.07.62 | 3 | Edinburgh | 8 | May |

# 10 KILOMETRES Road

| | | | | | | |
|---|---|---|---|---|---|---|
| 28:13 | Paul Evans | 13.04.61 | 1 | Dusseldorf, GER | 8 | Jan |
| | 29:01 | | 1 | Perivale | 10 | Sep |
| 28:21 | Andrew Pearson | 14.09.71 | 1 | Barnsley | 5 | Nov |
| | 28:35 | | 2 | Coventry | 15 | Oct |
| | 28:50 | | 2 | Edinburgh | 1 | Oct |
| | 29:00 | | 2 | Swansea | 10 | Sep |
| 28:23 | Peter Whitehead | 3.12.64 | | Ensenada, MEX | 12 | Feb |
| | 28:39 | | 7 | Atlanta, USA | 4 | Jul |
| | 29:02 | | 1 | , BER | 15 | Jan |
| 28:34 | Gary Staines | 3.07.63 | 1 | Cardiff | 4 | Jun |
| | 28:40 | | 1 | Ewell | 5 | Feb |
| | 28:44 | | 3 | Coventry | 15 | Oct |
| | 28:48 | | 1 | Edinburgh | 1 | Oct |
| 28:35 | Justin Hobbs | 12.03.69 | 2 | Cardiff | 4 | Jun |
| 28:42 | Keith Cullen | 13.06.72 | 1 | Mondeville, FRA | 14 | Oct |
| 28:48 | Jon Brown | 27.02.71 | 4 | Mobile, USA | 25 | Mar |
| | 28:59 | | 6 | Bolzano, ITA | 31 | Dec |
| 28:57 | Paul Taylor | 9.01.66 | 4 | Coventry | 15 | Oct |
| | 29:03 | | 1 | Cardiff | 3 | Sep |
| 29:05 | Jon Solly | 28.06.63 | 3 | Cardiff | 4 | Jun |
| *29:05* | *David Burke* | *68* | *5* | *Coventry* | *15* | *Oct* |
| 29:09 | Martin Jones | 21.04.67 | 6 | Coventry | 15 | Oct |
| (10) | | | | | | |
| 29:10 | Spencer Duval | 5.01.70 | 3 | Belfast | 8 | Apr |
| 29:11 | Dave Taylor | 9.01.64 | 4 | Cardiff | 4 | Jun |
| 29:12 | Mark Peters | 66 | 7 | Coventry | 15 | Oct |
| 29:13 | Brian Rushworth | 14.12.62 | 1 | Sunderland | 7 | May |
| 29:15 | Dale Laughlin | 28.12.66 | 3 | Cardiff | 3 | Sep |
| 29:17 | Steve Brace | 7.07.61 | 4 | Belfast | 8 | Apr |
| 29:17 | Paul Davies-Hale | 21.06.62 | 4 | Cardiff | 3 | Sep |
| 29:19 | Paul Rowan | 20.03.66 | 6 | Belfast | 8 | Apr |
| 29:21 | Tony O'Brien | 14.11.70 | 7 | Swansea | 10 | Sep |
| *29:23* | *John Burke* | *18.05.70* | *7* | *Belfast* | *8* | *Apr* |
| 29:23 | Keith Anderson | 10.08.57 | 6 | Cardiff | 4 | Jun |
| (20) | | | | | | |
| 29:24 | Dermot Donnelly | 23.09.70 | 1 | | 2 | Aug |
| 29:24 | Tommie Swart | | 9 | Swansea | 10 | Sep |
| *29:25* | *Eddie Hyland* | *23.07.60* | *1* | *Blackpool* | *7* | *May* |
| 29:31 | Eamonn Martin | 9.10.58 | 1 | Eastleigh | 19 | Mar |
| 29:31 | Mark Flint | 19.02.63 | 1 | Milton | 6 | Aug |
| 29:32 | Martin McLoughlin | 23.12.58 | 14 | Dusseldorf, GER | 8 | Jan |
| 29:34 | Alan Puckrin | 2.04.64 | 1 | Helensburgh | 25 | May |
| 29:34 | Tommy Murray | 18.05.61 | 5 | Bangor | 10 | Sep |
| 29:35 | Darren Mead | 4.10.68 | 1 | Thetford | 30 | Apr |
| 29:35 | Chris Robison | 16.03.61 | 5 | Edinburgh | 1 | Oct |
| 29:36 | Wayne Oxborough | 10.11.66 | 7 | Cardiff | 3 | Sep |
| (30) | | | | | | |
| *29:36* | *John Lisiewicz* | *18.07.62* | | *Chester* | *29* | *Oct* |
| 29:36 | Davey Wilson | 7.09.68 | 1 | Northern Ireland | 18 | Nov |
| 29:37 | Stephen Harris | 27.04.71 | 1 | Chichester | 5 | Feb |
| 29:37 | Ian Robinson | 21.04.69 | 6 | Los Angeles, USA | 19 | Nov |
| 29:39 | Mark Howard | 7.02.66 | 2 | Chichester | 5 | Feb |
| 29:41 | Andrew Morgan-Lee | 1.03.69 | 3 | Chichester | 5 | Feb |
| 29:41 | Paul Roden | 18.04.65 | 9 | Cardiff | 3 | Sep |
| 29:42 | Adrian Callan | 28.11.62 | 2 | Cumbernauld | 14 | May |
| 29:42 | Chris Sweeney | 3.03.66 | 1 | Teddington | 4 | Jun |
| 29:42 | Colin Moore | 25.11.60 | 4 | Milton | 6 | Aug |
| 29:42 | Richard Findlow | 4.12.66 | 10 | Coventry | 15 | Oct |
| (40) | | | | | | |

| Time | Name | Cat | Birth | Pos | Venue | Date | |
|---|---|---|---|---|---|---|---|
| 29:43 | Richard Nerurkar | | 6.01.64 | 1 | Barnsley | 16 | Jul |
| 29:43 | Steve Knight | | 17.10.63 | 10 | Cardiff | 3 | Sep |
| 29:44 | Steve Jones | V40 | 4.08.55 | 1 | Harrow | 2 | Apr |
| 29:44 | Mark Croasdale | | 10.01.60 | 12 | Coventry | 15 | Oct |
| *29:45* | *Jamie Lewis* | | *8.03.69* | *7* | *Cardiff* | *4* | *Jun* |

**downhill**

| Time | Name | Cat | Birth | Pos | Venue | Date | |
|---|---|---|---|---|---|---|---|
| 27:20 | Jon Brown | | 27.02.71 | | Pittsburgh, USA | 23 | Sep |

**relay leg**

| Time | Name | Cat | Birth | Pos | Venue | Date | |
|---|---|---|---|---|---|---|---|
| 28:41 | Paul Taylor | | 9.01.66 | | Chiba, JAP | 20 | Nov |

# 10 MILES Road

| Time | Name | Cat | Birth | Pos | Venue | Date | |
|---|---|---|---|---|---|---|---|
| 46:19 | Richard Nerurkar | | 6.01.64 | 1 | Leyland | 23 | Jul |
| 46:35 | | | | 1 | Woking | 5 | Mar |
| 47:00 | Gary Staines | | 3.07.63 | 1 | Ballycotton, IRE | 12 | Mar |
| 47:47 | | | | 2 | Portsmouth | 8 | Oct |
| 47:38 | Peter Fleming | | 5.01.61 | 9 | Washington, USA | 9 | Apr |
| 47:51 | Martin McLoughlin | | 23.12.58 | 8 | New York, USA | 8 | Apr |
| 47:56 | Mark Flint | | 19.02.63 | 1 | Stockport | 3 | Dec |
| 48:07 | Stephen Green | | 28.07.70 | 1 | The Hague, HOL | 17 | Dec |
| 48:20 | Colin Jones | U23 | 8.04.74 | 2 | Llandudno | 12 | Nov |
| 48:22 | Steve Jones | | 4.08.55 | 13 | Washington, USA | 9 | Apr |
| 48:24 | Steve Brace | | 7.07.61 | 1 | Newport | 15 | Apr |
| 48:30 | Darren Mead | | 4.10.68 | 1 | Colchester | 4 | Jun |
| (10) | | | | | | | |
| 48:44 | Bashir Hussain | | 20.12.64 | 1 | Sale | 6 | Aug |
| 48:45 | Eamonn Martin | | 9.10.58 | 6 | Erewash | 3 | Sep |
| *48:53* | *Jamie Harrison* | | *21.12.63* | *2* | *Woking* | *5* | *Mar* |
| 48:54 | Bill Foster | | 9.08.58 | 7 | Erewash | 3 | Sep |

**downhill**

| Time | Name | Cat | Birth | Pos | Venue | Date | |
|---|---|---|---|---|---|---|---|
| 47:35 | Adrian Callan | | 28.11.62 | 1 | Motherwell | 9 | Apr |
| 47:54 | Graeme Wight | | 3.06.65 | 2 | Motherwell | 9 | Apr |
| 48:08 | Brian Kirkwood | V40 | 20.09.52 | 3 | Motherwell | 9 | Apr |
| 48:10 | Charlie Thomson | | 17.06.65 | 4 | Motherwell | 9 | Apr |

**short course**

| Time | Name | Cat | Birth | Pos | Venue | Date | |
|---|---|---|---|---|---|---|---|
| 47:46 | Brian Currie | | 7.10.62 | 1 | Llandudno | 12 | Nov |

# HALF MARATHON

| Time | Name | Cat | Birth | Pos | Venue | Date | |
|---|---|---|---|---|---|---|---|
| 1:00:09 | Paul Evans | | 13.04.61 | 1 | Marrakech, MOR | 15 | Jan |
| *some statisticians feel this course is short* | | | | | | | |
| 1:02:30 | | | | 4 | South Shields | 17 | Sep |
| 1:02:33 | Peter Whitehead | | 3.12.64 | 3 | Indianapolis, USA | 5 | May |
| 1:02:38 | Gary Staines | | 3.07.63 | 5 | South Shields | 17 | Sep |
| 1:02:39 | Richard Nerurkar | | 6.01.64 | 1 | Gothenburg, SWE | 13 | May |
| 1:02:50 | Mark Hudspith | | 19.01.69 | 1 | Malta | 19 | Feb |
| *this course may be downhill* | | | | | | | |
| 1:02:58 | Ian Hudspith | | 23.09.70 | 2 | Malta | 19 | Feb |
| 1:03:23 | Colin Walker | | 29.10.62 | 1 | Doncaster | 9 | Apr |
| 1:03:28 | Carl Thackery | | 14.10.62 | 6 | Glasgow | 20 | Aug |
| 1:03:30 | Steve Brace | | 7.07.61 | | Peterborough | 14 | May |
| 1:03:31 | Dave Taylor | | 9.01.64 | 7 | Glasgow | 20 | Aug |
| (10) | | | | | | | |
| 1:03:32 | Jon Solly | | 28.06.63 | 8 | Glasgow | 20 | Aug |
| 1:03:50 | Barry Royden | | 15.12.66 | | Marrakech, MOR | 15 | Jan |
| 1:03:55 | Mark Flint | | 19.02.63 | 9 | Glasgow | 20 | Aug |
| *1:04:06* | *Kassa Tadesse* | *U23* | *21.08.74* | *6* | *Paris, FRA* | *5* | *Mar* |
| 1:04:08 | Stephen Harris | | 27.04.71 | 9 | Portsmouth | 12 | Mar |

| 1:04:13 | Peter Fleming | | 5.01.61 | 15 | Philadelphia, USA | 17 | Apr |
|---|---|---|---|---|---|---|---|
| 1:04:32 | | | | 13 | Glasgow | 20 | Aug |
| 1:04:13 | Bashir Hussain | | 20.12.64 | 10 | Glasgow | 20 | Aug |
| 1:04:16 | Eamonn Martin | | 9.10.58 | 3 | Hastings | 12 | Jun |
| 1:04:35 | | | | 8 | South Shields | 17 | Sep |
| 1:04:25 | Martin McLoughlin | | 23.12.58 | 7 | Gothenburg, SWE | 13 | Jan |
| 1:04:26 | | | | 44 | Belfort, FRA | 1 | Oct |
| 1:04:26 | Brian Rushworth | | 14.12.62 | 11 | Glasgow | 20 | Aug |
| 1:04:38 | Keith Anderson | | 10.08.57 | 14 | Glasgow | 20 | Aug |
| | (20) | | | | | | |
| 1:04:38 | Dave Buzza | | 6.12.62 | 9 | South Shields | 17 | Sep |
| 1:04:38 | Dale Rixon | | 8.07.66 | 10 | South Shields | 17 | Sep |
| 1:04:39 | Andy Green | | 14.12.62 | 1 | Wilmslow | 19 | Mar |
| 1:04:39 | Paul Roden | | 18.04.65 | 12 | South Shields | 17 | Sep |
| 1:04:40 | Dale Laughlin | | 28.12.66 | 9 | Hastings | 12 | Jun |
| 1:04:45 | Stephen Green | | 28.07.70 | 15 | Glasgow | 20 | Aug |
| 1:04:46 | Bill Foster | | 9.08.58 | 2 | Wilmslow | 19 | Mar |
| 1:04:46 | Colin Moore | | 25.11.60 | 16 | Glasgow | 20 | Aug |

**downhill** (217m)

| 1:03:06 | Justin Chaston | | 4.11.68 | 7 | Las Vegas, USA | 4 | Feb |
|---|---|---|---|---|---|---|---|

# MARATHON

| 2:10:31 | Paul Evans | | 13.04.61 | 5 | London | 2 | Apr |
|---|---|---|---|---|---|---|---|
| 2:11:05 | | | | 2 | New York, USA | 12 | Nov |
| 2:11:03 | Richard Nerurkar | | 6.01.64 | 2 | Seoul, SKO | 18 | Mar |
| 2:15:47 | | | | 7 | Gothenburg, SWE | 12 | Aug |
| 2:11:18 | Eamonn Martin | | 9.10.58 | 13 | Chicago, USA | 15 | Oct |
| 2:12:44 | | | | 13 | London | 2 | Apr |
| 2:11:58 | Mark Hudspith | | 19.01.69 | 11 | London | 2 | Apr |
| 2:12:23 | Peter Whitehead | | 3.12.64 | 12 | London | 2 | Apr |
| 2:14:08 | | | | 4 | Gothenburg, SWE | 12 | Aug |
| 2:13:35 | Peter Fleming | | 5.01.61 | 5 | Houston, USA | 15 | Jan |
| 2:15:25 | | | | 12 | Chicago, USA | 15 | Oct |
| 2:16:00 | | | | 5 | Pittsburgh, USA | 7 | May |
| 2:15:02 | Colin Moore | | 25.11.60 | 16 | London | 2 | Apr |
| 2:15:49 | Bill Foster | | 9.08.58 | 11 | Berlin, GER | 24 | Sep |
| 2:18:45 | | | | 18 | Athens, GRE | 9 | Apr |
| 2:16:04 | Gary Staines | | 3.07.63 | 4 | Vienna, AUT | 23 | Apr |
| 2:18:40 | John Ferrin | | 20.02.67 | 1 | Belfast | 8 | May |
| | (10) | | | | | | |
| *2:18:48* | *Eddie Hyland* | | *23.07.60* | *2* | *Karlsruhe, GER* | *17* | *Sep* |
| 2:19:05 | Chris Buckley | | 26.07.61 | 23 | London | 2 | Apr |
| 2:19:58 | Hugh Jones | V40 | 1.11.55 | 29 | New York, USA | 12 | Nov |
| | 19 performances to 2:20:0 by 12 athletes | | | | | | |
| 2:20:17 | Scott Cohen | | 6.12.64 | 27 | London | 2 | Apr |
| 2:20:39 | Chris Penney | | 10.05.57 | 1 | Utrecht, HOL | 21 | May |
| 2:21:05 | Tony Graham | | 15.10.63 | 31 | London | 2 | Apr |
| 2:21:16 | Barry Royden | | 15.12.66 | 3 | Dublin, IRE | 30 | Oct |
| 2:21:19 | Mark Croasdale | | 10.01.60 | 2 | Belfast | 8 | May |
| 2:21:19 | Dennis Walmsley | | | 2 | Calvia, SPA | 3 | Dec |
| *2:21:30* | *Jamie Harrison* | | *21.12.63* | *33* | *London* | *2* | *Apr* |
| 2:21:40 | Tom Buckner | | 16.04.63 | 28 | Boston, USA | 17 | Apr |
| 2:21:50 | Terry Mitchell | | 23.08.59 | 3 | Belfast | 8 | May |
| | (20) | | | | | | |
| 2:21:59 | Peter Haynes | | 18.09.64 | 34 | London | 2 | Apr |
| 2:22:16 | I. McMahon | | | 4 | Belfast | 8 | May |
| 2:22:23 | Toby Tanser | | 21.07.68 | 15 | Lisbon, POR | 26 | Nov |
| 2:22:32 | Nick Rose | V40 | 30.12.51 | 35 | London | 2 | Apr |
| 2:22:41 | Brian Rushworth | | 14.12.62 | 4 | Dublin, IRE | 30 | Oct |

| | | | | | | | |
|---|---|---|---|---|---|---|---|
| 2:22:48 | Dan Rathbone | | 9.04.69 | 34 | Athens, GRE | 9 | Apr |
| 2:23:25 | Dave Mansbridge | | 4.06.64 | 4 | Calvia, SPA | 3 | Dec |
| 2:23:32 | David Cavers | | 9.04.63 | 40 | London | 2 | Apr |
| 2:23:40 | Eddie Stewart | | 15.12.5 | 6 | Prague, CZE | | Aug |
| 2:23:47 | Peter Banks | | 9.12.60 | 6 | Dublin, IRE | 30 | Oct |
| | (30) | | | | | | |
| 2:23:48 | Ian Bloomfield | V40 | 23.11.52 | 18 | Minneapolis/St Paul, USA | 8 | Oct |
| 2:23:57 | Shaun Tobin | | 13.10.62 | 42 | London | 2 | Apr |
| 2:24:04 | Gary Bishop | | 3.08.63 | 44 | London | 2 | Apr |
| 2:24:07 | Peter Pleasants | | 29.07.62 | 46 | London | 2 | Apr |
| 2:24:10 | Trevor Clark | | 29.04.56 | 40 | Athens, GRE | 9 | Apr |
| 2:24:21 | Tony Barden | | 15.10.60 | 48 | London | 2 | Apr |
| 2:24:26 | Alan Chilton | | 16.04.71 | 48 | New York, USA | 12 | Nov |
| 2:24:27 | Jon Hooper | | 22.07.64 | 1 | Leeds | 15 | Jul |
| 2:24:28 | Trevor Wilson | | 20.03.62 | 49 | London | 2 | Apr |
| 2:24:41 | Alan Guilder | | 10.12.61 | 50 | London | 2 | Apr |
| | (40) | | | | | | |
| 2:24:53 | Mike O'Reilly | | 23.04.58 | 53 | Otsu, JAP | 19 | Mar |
| 2:24:56 | Anthony Pooley | | 14.01.64 | 51 | London | 2 | Apr |
| 2:24:57 | Peter Dymoke | | 30.10.61 | 25 | Stockholm, SWE | 10 | Jun |
| 2:25:09 | Ieuan Ellis | | 11.05.60 | 2 | Leeds | 16 | Jul |
| 2:25:11 | Robin Nash | | 9.02.59 | 19 | Beijing, CHN | 15 | Oct |
| 2:25:14 | Paul Smith | V40 | 12.08.54 | 52 | London | 2 | Apr |
| 2:25:17 | Simon Kinson | | 3.12.70 | 3 | Chiswick | 24 | Sep |
| 2:25:31 | John Wieczorek | | 22.11.66 | 53 | London | 2 | Apr |
| 2:25:36 | Mark Hargreaves | | 26.08.60 | 1 | Poole | 4 | Jul |
| 2:25:47 | Phillip Smith | | 26.05.64 | 54 | London | 2 | Apr |
| | (50) | | | | | | |
| 2:25:47 | Mark Cooper | | 3.09.62 | 4 | Chiswick | 24 | Sep |
| 2:26:01 | Andy Holt | | 23.02.64 | 55 | London | 2 | Apr |
| 2:26:02 | A. Annand | | | 5 | Chiswick | 24 | Sep |
| 2:26:07 | Joe Loader | U23 | 21.07.73 | 56 | London | 2 | Apr |
| 2:26:29 | Alan Shepherd | | 28.04.69 | 6 | Chiswick | 24 | Sep |
| 2:26:34 | Greg Hull | | 16.08.65 | 7 | Chiswick | 24 | Sep |
| 2:26:35 | Ronnie James | | 14.12.64 | 8 | Chiswick | 24 | Sep |
| 2:26:38 | Mark Roberts | | 12.02.59 | 1 | Stoke | 18 | Jun |
| 2:26:39 | Dave Buzza | | 6.12.62 | 30 | Belgrade, YUG | 22 | Apr |
| 2:26:45 | Martin Ferguson | | 17.09.64 | 59 | London | 2 | Apr |
| | (60) | | | | | | |
| 2:26:56 | Bashir Hussain | | 20.12.64 | 23 | Sacramento, USA | 3 | Dec |
| 2:27:00 | Steve Davies | | 4.02.58 | 21 | Reims, FRA | | |
| 2:27:09 | Ginge Gough | | 10.02.56 | 60 | London | 2 | Apr |
| 2:27:12 | John Parker | V40 | 31.10.54 | 61 | London | 2 | Apr |
| 2:27:15 | Tim Jones | | 15.09.57 | 62 | London | 2 | Apr |
| 2:27:27 | Chris Starbuck | | | 9 | Chiswick | 24 | Sep |
| 2:27:32 | Dennis Smith | V45 | 26.01.49 | 10 | Dublin, IRE | 30 | Oct |
| 2:27:39 | Wayne Buxton | | 16.04.62 | 22 | Caen, FRA | | |
| 2:27:47 | Martyn Lee | | 13.07.55 | 65 | London | 2 | Apr |
| 2:27:47 | Ray Dzikowski | | 6.03.63 | 10 | Chiswick | 24 | Sep |
| | (70) | | | | | | |
| 2:27:54 | Eric Williams | | 6.05.56 | 2 | Stoke | 18 | Jun |
| 2:28:13 | Mike Greally | | 18.06.60 | 2 | New Forest | 13 | Sep |
| 2:28:22 | Mark King | | 16.09.62 | 70 | London | 2 | Apr |
| 2:28:28 | Mike Bowering | | 19.05.63 | 73 | London | 2 | Apr |
| 2:28:31 | A. Jones | | | 8 | Washington, USA | 22 | Oct |
| 2:28:36 | Andy Wetherill | | 6.12.57 | 4 | Nottingham | 24 | Sep |
| 2:28:38 | Evan Cook | | | 14 | Toronto, CAN | 7 | May |
| 2:28:42 | Ian Hamer | | 15.04.61 | 75 | London | 2 | Apr |
| 2:28:46 | Dave Lacy | V50 | 9.09.44 | 77 | London | 2 | Apr |
| 2:28:54 | Mike McGeoch | | 15.08.55 | 79 | London | 2 | Apr |
| | (80) | | | | | | |

| 2:28:57 | Paul Kilgallon | | | 10 | Benidorm, SPA | 26 Nov |
|---|---|---|---|---|---|---|
| 2:28:58 | Kelvin Turner | | | 80 | London | 2 Apr |
| 2:29:00 | Richard Beaumont | | 2.05.71 | 81 | London | 2 Apr |
| 2:29:02 | F. McWilliams | | | 5 | Belfast | 8 May |
| 2:29:05 | K. Bowers | | | 82 | London | 2 Apr |
| 2:29:19 | Neil Moore | | 1.04.61 | 84 | London | 2 Apr |
| 2:29:20 | Paul Harris | U23 | 16.09.73 | 1 | Abingdon | 22 Oct |
| 2:29:22 | Davie Shaw | | | 85 | London | 2 Apr |
| 2:29:34 | S. Mills | | | 86 | London | 2 Apr |
| 2:29:36 | Gary Eagle | | 28.12.60 | 88 | London | 2 Apr |
| (90) | | | | | | |
| 2:29:44 | Bill Speake | | 24.01.71 | 89 | London | 2 Apr |
| 2:29:49 | Colin Walker | | 29.10.62 | 36 | Stockholm, SWE | 10 Jun |
| 2:29:50 | Lionel Gowland | V40 | 5.02.55 | 91 | London | 2 Apr |
| 2:29:57 | Geoffrey Rawlinson | | 2.08.57 | 92 | London | 2 Apr |
| 2:30:03 | N. Brookes | | | 2 | Poole | 4 Jun |
| 2:30:11 | Dave Ellis | | 4.09.59 | 94 | London | 2 Apr |
| 2:30:11 | Allister Bristow | | 27.04.72 | 95 | London | 2 Apr |
| 2:30:16 | Paul Bettridge | | 27.02.57 | 96 | London | 2 Apr |
| 2:30:21 | Gary McIlroy | | 6.04.67 | 14 | Dublin, IRE | 30 Oct |
| 2:30:30 | W. O'Donnell | | | 97 | London | 2 Apr |
| (100) | | | | | | |
| 2:30:40 | Robert Elstone | | | 99 | London | 2 Apr |
| 2:30:46 | Simon Watts | | 30.03.61 | 100 | London | 2 Apr |

## 100 KILOMETRES (Track)

| 7:07:29 | Don Ritchie | V50 | 6.07.44 | | London (TB) | 14 Oct |
|---|---|---|---|---|---|---|

## 100 KILOMETRES (Road)

| 6:55:12 | Shane Downes | | | Torhout, BEL | 16 Jun |
|---|---|---|---|---|---|
| 6:56:02 | Simon Lund | | 22.12.65 | Nottingham | 20 May |
| 6:58:29 | Patrick Macke | V40 | 18.06.55 | Saroma, JAP | 25 Jun |
| 7:03:05 | Greg Dell | | 20.11.64 | Winschoten, HOL | 16 Sep |
| 7:09:49 | Don Ritchie | V50 | 6.07.44 | Winschoten, HOL | 16 Sep |
| 7:12:15 | Steve Moore | V45 | 17.12.47 | Chavagnes-en-P, FRA | 27 May |
| 7:13:25 | Mike Hartley | | | Winschoten, HOL | 16 Sep |
| 7:22:48 | Martin Eccles | | 16.01.57 | Nottingham | 20 May |
| 7:26:56 | Robin Gardner | | | Chavagnes-en-P, FRA | 27 May |
| 7:28:18 | Willie Sichel | | | Edinburgh | 30 Jun |
| (10) | | | | | |
| 7:31:19 | Dave Lacy | V50 | 9.09.44 | Chavagnes-en-P, FRA | 27 May |
| 7:45:15 | Paul Bream | | | Nottingham | 20 May |
| 7:48:52 | James Zarei | V50 | 12.01.44 | Nottingham | 20 May |
| 7:56:03 | Malcolm Griffiths | | | Chavagnes-en-P, FRA | 27 May |

## 24 HOURS (Track)

| 221.920 | Alden Barlow | Doncaster | 28 May |
|---|---|---|---|
| 215.954 | Stephen Till | Doncaster | 28 May |
| 213.133 | Mike Aris | London (TB) | 15 Oct |
| 210.151 | Jim Carruth | Brechin | 11 Jun |
| 205.131 | Brian Bosher | Humberside | 16 Jul |
| 204.833 | Derek Ricketts | Doncaster | 28 May |

## 1500 METRES STEEPLECHASE - Under 17

| 4:22.5 | Mark Warmby | 12.12.78 | 1 | Cleckheaton | 10 Jun |
|---|---|---|---|---|---|
| 4:22.97 | David Mitchinson | 4.09.78 | 1 | Nottingham | 8 Jul |
| 4:24.80 | Simon Lees | 19.11.79 | 2 | Birmingham | 30 Jul |
| 4:25.29 | Simon Curwen | 26.10.78 | 2 | Nottingham | 8 Jul |
| 4:25.72 | Matthew Amos | 20.11.78 | 3 | Birmingham | 30 Jul |
| 4:26.53 | Richard Brady | 20.09.78 | 3 | Nottingham | 8 Jul |

| 4:27.7 | Scott Hughes | | 20.11.78 | 1 | Stretford | 10 | Jun |
| 4:29.38 | Keith Grant | | 17.03.80 | 5 | Birmingham | 30 | Jul |
| 4:29.5 | Paul Morby | | 15.01.79 | 1 | Yeovil | 4 | Jun |
| 4:29.51 | Richard Matthews | | 23.10.78 | 6 | Birmingham | 30 | Jul |
| | (10) | | | | | | |
| 4:30.0 | Richard Vint | | 16.02.79 | 1 | Harrow | 4 | Jun |
| 4:30.0 | Jason Ward | | 15.09.78 | 1 | Sheffield | 25 | Jun |
| 4:30.91 | Conor Basquil | | 2.04.79 | 1 | Birmingham | 2 | Sep |
| 4:31.83 | Gordon Irvine | | 29.11.78 | 7 | Birmingham | 30 | Jul |
| 4:32.2 | Simon Walker | | 5.06.79 | 1 | Aberdeen | 24 | Jun |
| 4:32.7 | Delroy Simon | | 27.11.78 | 1 | Harrow | 16 | Jul |
| 4:33.1 | Chris Parkin | | 6.07.79 | 6h1 | Nottingham | 7 | Jul |
| 4:34.3 | Carl Jackson | | 31.07.79 | 2 | Stretford | 10 | Jun |
| 4:34.34 | Ian Ratcliffe | | 28.05.79 | 3h2 | Birmingham | 29 | Jul |
| 4:34.4 | Shane Coney | | | 3 | Colwyn Bay | 15 | Jul |
| | (20) | | | | | | |
| 4:35.10 | Tobens Tymmons | | | 4 | Colwyn Bay | 15 | Jul |
| 4:35.2 | Ian Puntan | | 6.04.79 | 1 | Hoo | 10 | Jun |
| 4:37.2 | Mark Rogers | | 14.03.79 | 2 | Kingston | 13 | Aug |
| 4:37.8 | Kirk Watts | | | 1 | London (He) | 4 | Jun |
| 4:38.4 | Daniel Rowen | | 30.12.79 | 1 | Solihull | 16 | Jul |
| 4:38.7 | Nigel Maull | | 14.11.79 | 1 | Leamington | 14 | May |
| 4:38.75 | Keith Round | | 23.11.78 | 5h2 | Birmingham | 29 | Jul |
| 4:39.1 | John Peake | | 14.02.79 | 1 | Stoke | 17 | Jun |
| 4:39.89 | David Moore | | 25.04.79 | 1 | Pitreavie | 8 | Jul |

**no water jump**

| 4:34.4 | Bobby Madden | | 25.10.78 | 1 | Greenock | 25 | Jun |

## 2000 METRES STEEPLECHASE

| 5:37.9 | Carl Warren | | | 28.09.69 | 1 | Cannock | 9 | Sep |
| 5:38.0 | Dave Lee | | | 16.09.65 | 2 | Cannock | 9 | Sep |
| 5:39.0 | Spencer Duval | | | 5.01.70 | 1 | Solihull | 31 | May |
| 5:42.3 | Mick Hawkins | | | 24.10.61 | 3 | Cannock | 9 | Sep |
| 5:46.5 | Matt Barnes | | | 12.01.68 | 1 | Woodford | 22 | Apr |
| 5:46.9 | Andrew Morgan-Lee | | | 1.03.69 | 1 | Watford | 30 | Aug |
| 5:50.4 | Karl Palmer | | | 5.02.66 | 1 | Aldershot | 26 | Jun |
| 5:51.97 | Ray Plant | | | 13.05.68 | 1 | Stoke | 13 | May |
| 5:52.6 | Chris Symonds | U23 | 21.11.73 | 2 | Watford | 30 | Aug |
| 5:52.7 | Sean Fenwick | | | | 1 | Watford | 19 | Jul |
| | (10) | | | | | | | |
| 5:53.02 | Stuart Stokes | U20 | 15.12.76 | 1 | Sheffield | 28 | May |
| 5:53.62 | Craig Wheeler | U20 | 14.06.76 | 2 | Sheffield | 28 | May |
| 5:55.38 | Andy Coleman | U23 | 29.09.74 | 1 | Enfield | 29 | Apr |
| 5:55.42 | Chris Elliott | U23 | 29.05.75 | 2 | Enfield | 29 | Apr |
| 5:57.60 | Robert Brown | U20 | 3.03.78 | 3 | Sheffield | 28 | May |
| 5:58.58 | Darren Reilly | | | 19.09.65 | 1 | Hull | 5 | Aug |
| 5:58.80 | Jon Pavis | | | 4.10.66 | 2 | Hull | 5 | Aug |

**Additional Under 20** (1 - 3 above)

| 5:59.26 | Mark McGarry | | 16.02.77 | 1 | Nottingham | 8 | Jul |
| 5:59.63 | Matthew Plano | | 8.10.76 | 3 | Nottingham | 8 | Jul |
| 5:59.67 | Ben Whitby | | 6.01.77 | 1 | London (CP) | 27 | May |
| 5:59.67 | Kevin Nash | | 6.02.77 | 3 | Belfort, FRA | 6 | Aug |
| 6:00.20 | Damian Roland | | 15.01.77 | 2 | London (CP) | 27 | May |
| 6:02.78 | Tim Davis | | 25.01.78 | 1 | London (He) | 6 | Aug |
| 6:03.86 | Simon Wurr | | 7.01.77 | 1 | Birmingham | 26 | Apr |
| | (10) | | | | | | |
| 6:05.0 | James Calvert | | 5.11.77 | 1 | Hoo | 10 | Jun |
| 6:06.3 | Martin Dobson | | 20.12.76 | 1 | London (He) | 10 | Jun |
| 6:06.38 | David Freeman | | 5.08.77 | 1 | Stoke | 28 | May |

# 3000 METRES STEEPLECHASE

| | | | | | | |
|---|---|---|---|---|---|---|
| 8:24.37 | Tom Hanlon | | 20.05.67 | 1 | Gateshead | 21 Aug |
| 8:34.81 | | | | 7 | Hechtel, BEL | 22 Jul |
| 8:24.64 | Spencer Duval | | 5.01.70 | 1 | Birmingham | 16 Jul |
| 8:26.20 | | | | 7 | Oslo, NOR | 21 Jul |
| 8:28.99 | | | | 12 | London (CP) | 7 Jul |
| 8:35.47 | | | | 3 | Gateshead | 21 Aug |
| 8:38.01 | | | | 11h1 | Gothenburg, SWE | 7 Aug |
| 8:24.97 | Justin Chaston | | 4.11.68 | 8h3 | Gothenburg, SWE | 7 Aug |
| 8:26.35 | | | | 8 | Oslo, NOR | 21 Jul |
| 8:26.82 | | | | 5 | Villeneuve d'Ascq, FRA | 25 Jun |
| 8:32.07 | | | | 3 | Eugene, USA | 4 Jun |
| 8:32.3 | | | | 1 | Walnut, USA | 14 Apr |
| 8:33.22 | | | | 13 | London (CP) | 7 Jul |
| 8:38.90 | | | | 8s2 | Gothenburg, SWE | 9 Aug |
| 8:39.28 | | | | 5 | Fukuoka, JAP | 2 Sep |
| 8:43.18 | | | | 1 | Enfield | 19 Aug |
| 8:26.05 | Keith Cullen | | 13.06.72 | 2 | Gateshead | 21 Aug |
| 8:29.64 | | | | 3 | Birmingham | 16 Jul |
| 8:32.07 | | | | 8h2 | Gothenburg, SWE | 7 Aug |
| 8:41.38 | | | | 1 | Innsbruck, AUT | 28 Jun |
| 8:46.92 | | | | 8 | Granada, SPA | 29 May |
| 8:49.34 | | | | 2 | Loughborough | 11 Jun |
| 8:36.18 | Robert Hough | | 3.06.72 | 1 | Sheffield | 23 Jul |
| 8:36.29 | | | | 4 | Birmingham | 16 Jul |
| 8:36.55 | Mick Hawkins | | 24.10.61 | 5 | Birmingham | 16 Jul |
| 8:40.49 | Graeme Croll | | 1.02.66 | 2 | Sheffield | 23 Jul |
| 8:40.74 | Carl Warren | | 28.09.69 | 6 | Birmingham | 16 Jul |
| 8:44.93 | | | | 10 | Linz, AUT | 22 Aug |
| 8:45.3 | Spencer Newport | | 5.10.66 | 1 | London (WL) | 30 Jul |
| 8:47.63 | Dave Lee | | 16.09.65 | 1 | Loughborough | 11 Jun |
| 8:47.97 | | | | 2 | K. Wusterhausen, GER | 2 Sep |
| 8:48.84 | | | | 1 | Birmingham | 1 Jul |

32 performances to 8:50.0 by 10 athletes

| | | | | | | |
|---|---|---|---|---|---|---|
| 8:52.4 | Andrew Morgan-Lee | | 1.03.69 | 1 | Aldershot | 23 Jul |
| 8:53.9 | Matt Barnes | | 12.01.68 | 1 | Stoke | 6 May |
| 8:54.01 | Lee Hurst | | 29.07.72 | 5 | Sheffield | 23 Jul |
| 8:54.3 | Simon Bell | | 26.12.66 | 1 | Wakefield | 3 Jun |
| 8:54.59 | Hugh Brasher | | 28.09.64 | 6 | Sheffield | 23 Jul |
| 8:55.05 | Paddy Brice | | 8.02.69 | 8 | Birmingham | 16 Jul |
| 8:56.02 | Mike Jubb | | 20.06.70 | 4h1 | Birmingham | 15 Jul |
| 8:56.3 | Martin Roscoe | | 19.09.64 | 2 | Wakefield | 3 Jun |
| 8:56.46 | Adrian Green | | 30.05.68 | 12 | Barcelona, SPA | 27 Jun |
| 8:56.83 | Andy Fooks | U23 | 26.04.75 | 1 | Tessenderlo, BEL | 2 Jul |
| | (20) | | | | | |
| 8:57.55 | Simon O'Connor | U23 | 3.09.73 | 5h2 | Birmingham | 15 Jul |
| 8:58.72 | Darren Preston | U23 | 19.12.74 | 6h1 | Birmingham | 15 Jul |
| 9:00.16 | Ben Rieper | U23 | 20.12.73 | 6 | Loughborough | 11 Jun |
| 9:00.74 | Oliver Norman | U23 | 6.09.73 | 11 | Sheffield | 23 Jul |
| 9:03.45 | Steve Cairns | | 3.11.67 | 2 | Cardiff | 22 Jul |
| 9:04.3 | Mark Dalkins | | 9.09.71 | 2 | Walnut, USA | 13 Apr |
| 9:04.43 | Chris Elliott | U23 | 29.05.75 | 1 | Edinburgh | 8 May |
| 9:04.64 | Jon Sear | | 3.04.64 | 1 | Stoke | 9 Sep |
| 9:05.84 | Stuart Stokes | U20 | 15.12.76 | 7 | Loughborough | 11 Jun |
| 9:06.03 | Billy Jenkins | | 13.07.71 | 1 | Wishaw | 13 May |
| | (30) | | | | | |
| 9:06.20 | Steve Wright | | 12.02.71 | 2 | Edinburgh | 24 Jun |
| 9:06.34 | Phil Cook | | 7.05.69 | 2 | Edinburgh | 8 May |
| 9:06.6 | Mike Hoey | | 29.04.69 | 1 | Portsmouth | 25 Jun |
| 9:07.0 | Tim Hyde | | 22.02.72 | 2 | Enfield | 1 Jul |

| 9:07.22 | Kevin Nash | U20 | 6.02.77 | 1 | Bedford | 1 | Jul |
|---|---|---|---|---|---|---|---|
| 9:08.10 | Joe Loader | U23 | 21.07.73 | 8 | Loughborough | 11 | Jun |
| 9:08.9 | Andy Eynon | | 1.09.62 | 1 | Crawley | 1 | Jul |
| 9:08.92 | Jason Humm | | 11.01.71 | 6 | London (CP) | 18 | Jun |
| 9:10.2 | Sean Fenwick | | | 2 | Loughborough | 21 | Jun |
| 9:10.41 | Ian Hobdell | | 30.07.68 | 7 | London (CP) | 18 | Jun |
| (40) | | | | | | | |
| 9:11.0 | Karl Palmer | | 5.02.66 | 2 | Aldershot | 23 | Jul |
| 9:11.5 | Frank Boyne | | 28.02.66 | 2 | Grangemouth | 13 | May |
| 9:11.6 | Dean Coventon | | 3.11.70 | 4 | Bracknell | 3 | Jun |
| 9:11.95 | Craig Wheeler | U20 | 14.06.76 | 3 | Bedford | 1 | Jul |
| 9:12.05 | David Ross | | 2.11.65 | 4 | Edinburgh | 24 | Jun |
| 9:12.2 | James Austin | | 9.08.65 | 1 | Pitreavie | 25 | Jun |
| 9:12.34 | Dave Farrell | | 29.06.64 | 2 | Stoke | 9 | Sep |
| 9:14.9 | Eddie Broome | | 3.09.72 | 1 | Cambridge | 20 | May |
| 9:15.5 | Ken Stirrat | | 1.03.70 | 1 | Coatbridge | 23 | Apr |
| 9:15.70 | Kerry Hayes | | 22.01.63 | 4h2 | London (CP) | 17 | Jun |
| (50) | | | | | | | |
| 9:15.95 | Colin Palmer | | 27.07.67 | 3h1 | London (CP) | 17 | Jun |
| 9:16.40 | Matt O'Dowd | U20 | 13.04.76 | 4 | Bedford | 1 | Jul |
| 9:16.6 | Darren Reilly | | 19.09.65 | 1 | Wakefield | 12 | Aug |
| 9:16.8 | Roger Hackney | | 2.09.57 | 1 | Cosford | 5 | Jul |
| 9:16.9 | Stuart Bell | | 29.07.67 | 1 | Jarrow | 3 | Jun |
| 9:17.0 | Martin Ferguson | | 17.09.64 | 2 | Peterborough | 6 | May |
| 9:17.0 | James Fitzsimmons | U23 | 20.04.74 | 2 | Cambridge | 20 | May |
| 9:17.2 | Harvey Cossell | U23 | 1.12.74 | 4 | Aldershot | 23 | Jul |
| 9:17.34 | Justin Reid | | 26.09.69 | 3 | New York, USA | 16 | May |
| 9:17.50 | Steve Goss | | 15.12.68 | 3 | Stoke | 9 | Sep |
| (60) | | | | | | | |
| 9:17.84 | Andy Coleman | U23 | 29.09.74 | 4 | Birmingham | 20 | May |
| 9:18.0 | Sam Stevenson | | 20.12.63 | 2 | Cannock | 16 | Sep |
| 9:18.3 | Charlie Low | U23 | 9.10.74 | 1 | Loughborough | 20 | May |
| 9:19.1 | Donald Lennon-Jones | | 9.05.68 | 3 | Croydon | 28 | Aug |
| 9:19.2 | Mike Nolan | | 15.07.67 | 3 | Cambridge | 20 | May |
| 9:19.9 | Kevin Usher | | 3.11.65 | 5 | Bracknell | 3 | Jun |
| 9:20.3 | John Steel | | 27.02.63 | 2 | Liverpool | 6 | May |
| 9:20.8 | Brian Rushworth | | 14.12.62 | 1 | Middlesbrough | 3 | Jun |
| 9:21.35 | Ciaran McGuire | U23 | 1.07.74 | 1 | Stoke | 10 | Sep |
| 9:22.2 | Jeff Gill | | 15.09.71 | 1 | Yeovil | 10 | Sep |
| (70) | | | | | | | |
| 9:22.4 | A. Beavers | | | 3h1 | Edinburgh | 6 | May |
| 9:22.9 | Mark Keeley | | 4.01.72 | 1 | Blackburn | 25 | Jun |
| 9:23.10 | Jon Pavis | | 4.10.66 | 1 | Cardiff | 19 | Aug |
| 9:23.2 | Kevin Downie | | 7.07.69 | 4 | Coatbridge | 23 | May |
| 9:23.3 | Matthew Bateson | | 14.05.72 | 3 | Watford | 19 | Aug |
| 9:23.8 | Peter Banks | | 9.12.60 | 2 | Blackburn | 25 | Jun |
| 9:24.3 | Stephen Parr | | 18.03.59 | 1 | Bolton | 16 | Sep |
| 9:24.43 | Bruce Barton | | 2.02.64 | 6 | Enfield | 19 | Aug |
| 9:24.5 | Craig Siddons | U23 | 4.06.73 | 3 | Jarrow | 2 | Jul |
| 9:25.0 | Matthew Plano | U20 | 8.10.76 | 2 | Bath | 31 | May |

**1 barrier short**

| 9:14.3 | Grant Graham | | 27.12.72 | 1 | Antrim | 30 | Apr |
|---|---|---|---|---|---|---|---|

**Additional Under 20** (1 - 5 above)

| 9:28.4 | Robert Brown | | 3.03.78 | 2 | Jarrow | 3 | Jun |
|---|---|---|---|---|---|---|---|
| 9:29.8 | Simon Marwood | | 6.04.78 | 1 | Hull | 27 | Aug |
| 9:32.26 | Ben Whitby | | 6.01.77 | 6 | Bedford | 1 | Jul |
| 9:33.3 | David Connelly | | 6.02.76 | 1 | Carlisle | 30 | Apr |
| 9:35.2 | Matthew Whitfield | | 23.01.76 | 1 | Bebington | 3 | Jun |
| (10) | | | | | | | |

| | | | | | | |
|---|---|---|---|---|---|---|
| 9:38.8 | Mark McGarry | 16.02.77 | 1r1 | Gateshead | 19 | Aug |
| 9:39.0 | Stuart Bailey | 6.08.78 | 2r2 | Blackpool | 19 | Aug |
| 9:44.1 | Joe Foreshew | 2.05.77 | 1 | Horsham | 14 | May |
| 9:47.21 | Matthew Hillier | 10.08.77 | 4r2 | London (CP) | 3 | Jun |
| 9:48.58 | Damian Roland | 15.01.77 | 7 | Bedford | 1 | Jul |

## 60 METRES HURDLES - Indoor

| | | | | | | |
|---|---|---|---|---|---|---|
| 7.39 | Colin Jackson | 18.02.67 | 1 | Glasgow | 11 | Feb |
| | 7.39 | | 1h2 | Karlsruhe, GER | 12 | May |
| | 7.42 | | 2 | Madrid, SPA | 9 | Feb |
| | 7.43 | | 1 | Birmingham | 28 | Jan |
| | 7.44 | | 1 | Stuttgart, GER | 5 | Feb |
| | 7.54 | | 1h2 | Madrid, SPA | 9 | Feb |
| 7.42 | Tony Jarrett | 13.08.68 | 2 | Lievin, FRA | 19 | Feb |
| | 7.42 | | 3 | Barcelona, SPA | 12 | Mar |
| | 7.44 | | 2= | Stuttgart, GER | 5 | Feb |
| | 7.44 | | 2 | Glasgow | 11 | Feb |
| | 7.44 | | 1 | Birmingham | 25 | Feb |
| | 7.46 | | 1h2 | Lievin, FRA | 19 | Feb |
| | 7.46 | | 2s1 | Barcelona, SPA | 11 | Mar |
| | 7.57 | | 1 | Stockholm, SWE | 27 | Feb |
| | 7.58 | | 2 | Birmingham | 28 | Jan |
| | 7.58 | | 1h6 | Barcelona, SPA | 11 | Mar |
| 7.78 | Paul Gray | 25.05.69 | 6 | Madrid, SPA | 9 | Feb |
| | 7.79 | | 3h1 | Madrid, SPA | 9 | Feb |
| | 7.83 | | 1 | Birmingham | 4 | Feb |
| | 7.87 | | 5h2 | Karlsruhe, GER | 12 | Feb |
| | 7.88 | | 5 | Birmingham | 28 | Jan |
| 7.81 | Brian Taylor | 13.08.70 | 3h1 | Vienna, AUT | 18 | Feb |
| | 7.89 | | 6 | Vienna, AUT | 18 | Feb |
| | 7.90 | | 2 | Birmingham | 4 | Feb |
| | 7.90 | | 8 | Birmingham | 25 | Feb |
| 7.83 | Mark Lambeth | 3.09.72 | 1r2 | Birmingham | 28 | Jan |
| | 7.88 | | 2 | Stange, NOR | 12 | Feb |
| 7.83 | Andy Tulloch | 1.04.67 | 4h1 | Vienna, AUT | 18 | Feb |
| 28 performances to 7.90 by 6 athletes | | | | | | |
| 7.93 | Neil Owen | U23 | 18.10.73 | 3 | Birmingham | 4 | Feb |
| 8.00 | Ken Campbell | | 30.09.72 | 2 | Glasgow | 22 | Jan |
| 8.03 | James Archampong | U20 | 14.03.76 | 3r1 | Erfurt,GER | 25 | Feb |
| 8.04 | Ross Baillie | U20 | 26.09.77 | 2h2 | Glasgow | 22 | Jan |
| | (10) | | | | | | |
| 8.05 | Anthony Brannen | | 16.09.68 | 1 | Birmingham | 26 | Feb |
| 8.09 | Kevin Lumsdon | U23 | 3.03.74 | 2h3 | Birmingham | 4 | Feb |
| 8.13 | Martin Nicholson | | 9.12.70 | 4 | Glasgow | 22 | Jan |
| 8.14 | James Hughes | U23 | 8.11.74 | 6 | Birmingham | 4 | Feb |
| 8.26 | Ererton Harrison | | 8.04.66 | 3 | Birmingham | 26 | Feb |
| 8.29 | Andrew David | | 9.09.69 | 4 | Birmingham | 26 | Feb |
| 8.30 | Paul Field | | 24.06.67 | H | Birmingham | 5 | Feb |
| 8.33 | Adrian Caines | U23 | 13.11.74 | 4h1 | Birmingham | 4 | Feb |
| 8.35 | Keith Bunce | | 5.04.66 | 3h1 | Glasgow | 22 | Jan |
| 8.36 | Barry Thomas | | 28.04.72 | H | Birmingham | 5 | Feb |
| | (20) | | | | | | |
| 8.36 | Alex Kruger | | 18.11.63 | 5H | Barcelona, SPA | 12 | Mar |
| 8.37 | Simon McAree | U23 | 28.12.75 | 5h1 | Birmingham | 4 | Feb |

### Hand Timing

| | | | | | | |
|---|---|---|---|---|---|---|
| 8.1 | Jamie Quarry | | 15.11.72 | 1 | Birmingham | 1 | Mar |
| 8.3 | Kirk Harries | U23 | 7.08.74 | 4 | London (CP) | 21 | Jan |
| *8.3* | *Pascal Renaud* | | *20.04.70* | *2r3* | *London (CP)* | *11* | *Feb* |
| 8.3 | Andy Lewis | | 9.03.68 | 1 | London (Ha) | 25 | Feb |

## 60 METRES HURDLES - Indoor - Under 20 (3'3")

| | | | | | | | |
|---|---|---|---|---|---|---|---|
| 8.09 | James Archampong | 14.03.76 | 1 | Birmingham | 29 | Jan |
| 8.16 | James Allard | 11.05.77 | 1 | Birmingham | 5 | Feb |
| 8.28 | Paul Gripton | 9.11.76 | h | Birmingham | 5 | Feb |
| 8.41 | Dominic Bradley | 22.12.76 | 2 | Birmingham | 29 | Jan |
| 8.41 | Jon Snade | 31.03.77 | 3 | Birmingham | 5 | Feb |

## 60 METRES HURDLES - Indoor - Under 17 (3'0")

| | | | | | | | |
|---|---|---|---|---|---|---|---|
| 8.28 | Liam Collins | 23.10.78 | 1 | Glasgow | 4 | Feb |
| 8.34 | Ian Cawley | 21.11.78 | 2 | Birmingham | 18 | Feb |
| 8.4 | Chris Hargrave | 27.02.79 | 1 | London (CP) | 21 | Jan |
| | 8.45 | | 4 | Birmingham | 18 | Feb |
| 8.41 | Nick Dowsett | 24.11.78 | 3 | Birmingham | 18 | Feb |
| 8.41 | Garry Turner | 21.12.78 | 1h2 | Birmingham | 18 | Feb |
| 8.43 | Tom Benn | 20.04.80 | 1 | Birmingham | 26 | Feb |
| 8.46 | Ben Warmington | 20.03.79 | 5 | Birmingham | 18 | Feb |
| 8.50 | Richard Singer | 7.02.79 | 2 | Glasgow | 4 | Feb |

## 60 METRES HURDLES - Indoor - Under 15 (2'9")

| | | | | | | | |
|---|---|---|---|---|---|---|---|
| 8.80 | Brian Pearce | 9.12.80 | 1 | Birmingham | 19 | Feb |
| 8.93 | Andrew Turner | 19.09.80 | 1 | Birmingham | 5 | Feb |
| 9.01 | Graeme Allan | 24.09.80 | 1 | Glasgow | 5 | Feb |

## 70 METRES HURDLES - Under 13 (2'3")

| | | | | | | | |
|---|---|---|---|---|---|---|---|
| 12.1 | | B. Copeland | 1 | London (WL) | 21 | Jun |
| 12.2 | -1.4 | A. Clements | 1 | Portsmouth | 1 | Jul |

## 75 METRES HURDLES - Under 13 (2'3")

| | | | | | | | |
|---|---|---|---|---|---|---|---|
| 12.41 w 3.8 | William Beattie | 22.10.82 | 1 | Pitreavie | 9 | Jul |
| 12.5 | Craig Fleming | 29.01.83 | 1 | Coatbridge | 13 | Aug |
| 12.6 | David Watsman | 20.10.82 | 1 | Inverness | 24 | Sep |

## 80 METRES HURDLES - Under 13 (2'3")

| | | | | | | | |
|---|---|---|---|---|---|---|---|
| 12.1 | D. Borrett | | 1 | Great Yarmouth | 17 | Aug |
| 12.5 | T. Anthony | | | | | |
| 12.7 | Tim Greenwood | 22.11.82 | 1 | Bournemouth | 23 | Jul |

## 80 METRES HURDLES - Under 15 (2'9")

| | | | | | | | |
|---|---|---|---|---|---|---|---|
| 11.04 | 1.0 | Leon McRae | 3.11.80 | 1 | Nottingham | 8 | Jul |
| 11.07 | 1.0 | Robert Hollinger | 11.10.80 | 2 | Nottingham | 8 | Jul |
| 11.21 | 1.0 | Joseph Maxwell | 23.12.80 | 3 | Nottingham | 8 | Jul |
| 11.4 w | 3.6 | Robert Newton | 10.05.81 | 1h1 | Nottingham | 7 | Jul |
| | | 11.79 -3.0 | | 2 | Stoke | 27 | May |
| 11.41 | -0.3 | Finlay Wright | 23.12.80 | 2 | Birmingham | 29 | Jul |
| 11.44 w | 4.7 | Chris Baillie | 21.04.81 | 1 | Pitreavie | 9 | Jul |
| | | 11.7 1.7 | | 1 | Grangemouth | 17 | Jun |
| | | 11.87 -0.3 | | 4 | Birmingham | 29 | Jul |
| 11.46 | 1.9 | Wayne Gray | 7.11.80 | 2P | Stoke | 16 | Sep |
| 11.5 | | Andrew Turner | 19.09.80 | 1 | Nottingham | 10 | Jun |
| | | 11.63 1.0 | | 5 | Nottingham | 8 | Jul |
| 11.67 | -1.9 | Tony Seston | 21.12.80 | 2 | London (CP) | 28 | May |
| 11.7 | | Daniel Johnstone | 10.01.81 | 1 | Basildon | 10 | Jun |
| | | 11.85 -4.1 | | 2s1 | Nottingham | 7 | Jul |
| | (10) | | | | | | |
| 11.7 | 1.9 | Nicky Rawling | 28.12.80 | 2h3 | Nottingham | 7 | Jul |
| 11.7 w | 3.0 | Ken McKeown | 6.03.82 | 1 | Grangemouth | 17 | Jun |
| 11.76 w | 4.7 | Graeme Allan | 24.09.80 | 2 | Pitreavie | 9 | Jul |
| 11.8 | | G. Cowie | | 1 | Glasgow | 6 | Jun |
| 11.8 | 1.6 | James Milburn | 17.07.81 | 3h2 | Nottingham | 7 | Jul |
| | | 11.85 -2.0 | | 6s2 | Nottingham | 7 | Jul |

| 11.8 w | 3.5 | Darren Chapman | | 2.10.80 | 1h4 | Nottingham | 7 | Jul |
|---|---|---|---|---|---|---|---|---|
| 11.89 | -4.1 | | | | 3s1 | Nottingham | 7 | Jul |
| 11.8 w | 3.5 | Pak Wai Wan | | 1.09.80 | 2h4 | Nottingham | 7 | Jul |
| 11.85 | -3.5 | Andrew Umpleby | | 31.10.80 | 1h1 | Stoke | 27 | May |
| 11.86 | | Brian Pearce | | 9.12.80 | 1 | London (CP) | 14 | May |
| 11.88 | -0.3 | A. Henry | | | 5 | Birmingham | 29 | Jul |

**overage** (NI)

| 11.72 | -2.2 | Joe Rafferty | U17 | 5.02.80 | 1 | Antrim | 12 | Aug |
|---|---|---|---|---|---|---|---|---|

# 100 METRES HURDLES - Under 17 (3'0")

| 12.90 w | 2.2 | Ben Warmington | 20.03.79 | 1 | Nottingham | 8 | Jul |
|---|---|---|---|---|---|---|---|
| 13.2 | -2.0 | | | 1s1 | Nottingham | 7 | Jul |
| 13.27 | 1.8 | | | 1 | Sheffield | 28 | May |
| 13.27 w | 2.2 | Chris Hargrave | 27.02.79 | 2 | Nottingham | 8 | Jul |
| 13.34 | -0.8 | | | 1 | Birmingham | 29 | Jul |
| 13.3 | | Nick Dowsett | 24.11.78 | 1 | Basildon | 10 | Jun |
| 13.56 | -2.0 | | | 1h5 | Nottingham | 7 | Jul |
| 13.34 w | 2.2 | Tom Benn | 20.04.80 | 3 | Nottingham | 8 | Jul |
| 13.4 | | | | 2 | Basildon | 10 | Jun |
| 13.66 | -3.2 | | | 1 | Colwyn Bay | 15 | Jul |
| 13.44 | 1.8 | Liam Collins | 23.10.78 | 2 | Sheffield | 28 | May |
| 13.44 | -0.8 | David O'Leary | 3.08.80 | 2 | Birmingham | 29 | Jul |
| 13.45 w | 2.2 | Andrew Charles | 14.01.79 | 4 | Nottingham | 8 | Jul |
| 13.5 | | | | 1h | London (He) | 10 | Jun |
| 13.91 | -1.1 | | | 2h4 | Nottingham | 7 | Jul |
| 13.53 | 1.6 | Leo Barker | 26.12.78 | 1O | Stoke | 16 | Sep |
| 13.60 | 1.5 | Gordon Menzies | 13.03.79 | 1 | Pitreavie | 8 | Jul |
| 13.70 | -0.8 | Courtney Joseph | 25.12.78 | 4 | Birmingham | 29 | Jul |
| | (10) | | | | | | |
| 13.7 | | Greig Goodey | 14.09.78 | 1 | London (Elt) | 30 | Apr |
| 13.7 | | Christian Bird | 19.09.78 | 1 | Bracknell | 10 | Jun |
| 13.92 | -0.8 | | | 7 | Birmingham | 29 | Jul |
| 13.7 | | Andrew Boon | 7.10.78 | 1 | Birmingham | 10 | Jun |
| 13.78 | 1.5 | | | 3h3 | Birmingham | 29 | Jul |
| 13.7 | | Remi Edu | 14.12.78 | 1 | Welwyn | 10 | Jun |
| 13.98 | -2.7 | | | 2h3 | Nottingham | 7 | Jul |
| 13.7 | | Ian Cawley | 21.11.78 | 1 | Hayes | 16 | Jul |
| 13.84 | -0.8 | | | 5 | Birmingham | 29 | Jul |
| 13.7 | | Adam Tibbets | 14.12.78 | 1 | Yate | 16 | Jul |
| 13.80 w | 2.4 | Garry Turner | 21.12.78 | 2 | Birmingham | 2 | Sep |
| 14.1 | | | | 1 | Coventry | 30 | Apr |
| 13.8 | | Tim Dalton | 18.01.79 | 2h2 | London (He) | 10 | Jun |
| 14.10 | -2.0 | | | 3h5 | Nottingham | 7 | Jul |
| 13.8 | | Steven Scott | 5.06.79 | 1 | Croydon | 10 | Jun |
| 13.86 | -0.9 | | | 2h2 | Nottingham | 7 | Jul |
| 13.90 w | 3.0 | Gareth Lewis | 5.10.78 | 1 | Cardiff | 1 | Jul |
| 14.0 | | | | 1 | Cwmbran | 11 | Jun |
| | (20) | | | | | | |
| 13.9 | 1.9 | Richard Singer | 7.02.79 | 2 | Grangemouth | 17 | Jun |
| 14.10 | -3.2 | | | 3 | Colwyn Bay | 15 | Jul |
| 13.9 | 1.9 | Kevin MacLennan | 5.12.78 | 3 | Grangemouth | 17 | Jun |
| 13.94 | -0.3 | Mark Ridler | 20.07.79 | 3h1 | Birmingham | 29 | Jul |
| 14.0 | | Austen Smith | 26.09.79 | 1h1 | Cheltenham | 17 | Jun |
| 14.0 | -0.2 | Chris Low | 24.04.80 | 2 | Grangemouth | 21 | Jun |
| 14.01 | 1.2 | | | 1O | Aberdeen | 16 | Jul |
| 14.0 | | Kevin Drury | 30.09.79 | 1O | Blackpool | 24 | Jun |
| 14.10 | -0.9 | | | 4h2 | Nottingham | 7 | Jul |
| 14.0 | | Alex Kelly | 1.04.79 | 1 | Newport | 25 | Jun |
| 14.0 | -0.7 | Roland Eva | 6.09.78 | 5s2 | Nottingham | 7 | Jul |
| 14.08 | -0.9 | | | 3h2 | Nottingham | 7 | Jul |

| 14.0 w | 5.9 | Steve Francis | | 31.01.79 | 1 | Cardiff | 27 | May |
|--------|-----|---------------|---|----------|---|---------|----|-----|
| 14.04 | 1.6 | Sam Bonsall | | 15.03.79 | 3O | Stoke | 16 | Sep |
| (30) | | | | | | | | |
| 14.05 w | 2.4 | Ruben Tabares | | 22.10.78 | 4 | Birmingham | 3 | Sep |
| 14.10 | -0.9 | Darren Kabengele | | 11.02.79 | 5h2 | Nottingham | 7 | Jul |

## 110 METRES HURDLES - Under 17 (3'0")

| 14.16 | -1.1 | Ben Warmington | | 20.03.79 | 3 | Bath | 12 | Jul |
|-------|------|----------------|---|----------|---|------|----|-----|

## 110 METRES HURDLES - Under 20 (3'3")

| 14.36 w | 2.7 | Dominic Bradley | | 22.12.76 | 1 | Stoke | 17 | Jun |
|---------|-----|-----------------|---|----------|---|-------|----|-----|
| 14.54 | 2.0 | | | | 1 | Sheffield | 27 | May |
| 14.40 | -0.8 | Damien Greaves | | 19.09.77 | 1 | London (He) | 9 | Sep |
| 14.41 w | 2.7 | Paul Gripton | | 9.11.76 | 2 | Stoke | 17 | Jun |
| 14.94 | -3.1 | | | | 1 | Stoke | 27 | May |
| 14.44 | | James Archampong | | 14.03.76 | 1 | Brecon | 6 | Aug |
| 15.08 | -1.8 | Dean Macey | | 12.12.77 | 1D | Stoke | 17 | Sep |
| 15.15 | 1.7 | Mensah Elliott | | 29.08.76 | 1D | Stoke | 17 | Sep |
| 15.16 w | 2.7 | Mark Anderson | | 5.11.77 | 3 | Stoke | 17 | Jun |
| 15.21 | -3.1 | | | | 2 | Stoke | 27 | May |
| 15.22 w | 3.5 | Adam Carswell | | 8.01.76 | 1h1 | London (He) | 6 | Aug |
| 15.38 | -0.6 | | | | 1 | London (He) | 6 | Aug |
| 15.23 w | | Stuart Cope | | | 2 | Stoke | 13 | May |
| 15.36 w | 3.2 | Michael Serra | | 1.07.77 | 1h2 | London (He) | 6 | Aug |
| (10) | | | | | | | | |
| 15.40 | 2.0 | Anthony Gill | | 19.09.77 | 2 | Sheffield | 27 | May |
| 15.42 w | 3.5 | Ian Cawley | U17 | 21.11.78 | 2h1 | London (He) | 6 | Aug |
| 15.44 | -0.6 | | | | 2 | London (He) | 6 | Aug |
| 15.45 w | 2.4 | Mark Bushell | | 22.10.76 | 1D | Derby | 30 | Apr |
| 15.49 | -0.8 | James Allard | | 11.05.77 | 4 | London (He) | 9 | Sep |

**Hand Timing**

| 14.0 | 1.6 | Damien Greaves | | (14.40) | 1 | Nottingham | 8 | Jul |
|------|-----|----------------|---|---------|---|------------|---|-----|
| 14.3 w | 5.7 | James Archampong | | (14.44) | 1 | Cardiff | 27 | May |
| 14.6 | 1.6 | James Storey | | 26.11.76 | 2 | Nottingham | 8 | Jul |
| 14.6 w | | Ross Baillie | | 26.09.77 | 1 | Grangemouth | 17 | Jun |
| 14.8 | -1.7 | | | | 1 | Ayr | 18 | Jul |
| 14.7 | | Adam Carswell | | (15.38) | 1h1 | Cheltenham | 17 | Jun |
| 14.8 | 1.6 | Richard Churchill | | 29.09.77 | 3 | Nottingham | 8 | Jul |
| 15.38 | -0.8 | | | | 3 | London (He) | 9 | Sep |
| 14.8 | | Steven Scott | U17 | 5.06.79 | 1 | Southend | 30 | Jul |
| 14.8 | | Anthony Gill | | (15.40) | 1 | Ashton-U-Lyne | 27 | Aug |
| 14.9 | | Trevor McGlynn | | 6.06.78 | 1 | Antrim | 15 | May |
| 15.0 | -1.7 | Stephen Edwards | | 13.06.77 | 2 | Ayr | 18 | Jul |
| 15.2 | | Rupert Fleming | | 15.11.76 | 1 | Bournemouth | 10 | Jun |
| 15.2 | | Ben Gritz | | 21.11.77 | 2 | Welwyn | 10 | Jun |
| 15.2 | | Charles Robertson-Adams | | 5.12.77 | 1 | Telford | 18 | Jun |
| 15.2 | | Mark Bushell | | (15.45w) | 1D | Portsmouth | 25 | Jun |
| 15.2 | 1.6 | James Allard | | (15.49) | 5 | Nottingham | 8 | Jul |
| 15.2 | | Liam Collins | U17 | 23.10.78 | 1 | Middlesbrough | 30 | Jul |
| 15.3 | | James Wood | | 9.07.77 | 2 | Cheltenham | 17 | Jun |
| 15.3 | | Jon Snade | | 31.03.77 | 3 | Middlesbrough | 30 | Jul |
| 15.3 | | Matthew Douglas | | 26.11.76 | 1 | Kingston | 13 | Aug |
| 15.3 | | Ruben Tabares | U17 | 22.10.78 | 1r2 | Birmingham | 27 | Aug |
| 15.4 | | Scott Exley | | 9.02.78 | 1 | Yeovil | 10 | Jun |
| 15.4 | | James Smith | | 2.08.77 | 1 | Leicester | 10 | Jun |
| 15.4 | | James Hillier | | 3.04.78 | 1 | Newport | 18 | Jun |
| 15.4 | | Brad Knowles | | 17.11.76 | 2r2 | Birmingham | 27 | Aug |

**doubtful**

| 14.6 | | Mark Butland | | | 1 | Swansea | 8 | Jul |
|------|---|--------------|---|---|---|---------|---|-----|

# 110 METRES HURDLES

| Time | Wind | Name | | DOB | Pos | Location | Date |
|---|---|---|---|---|---|---|---|
| 13.04 | -0.1 | Tony Jarrett | | 13.08.68 | 2 | Gothenburg, SWE | 12 Aug |
| 13.11 | 0.2 | | | | 2 | Cologne, GER | 18 Aug |
| 13.13 | 0.6 | | | | 1 | Helsinki, FIN | 28 Jun |
| 13.14 | -0.6 | | | | 2 | London (CP) | 27 Aug |
| 13.19 | 1.1 | | | | 1s2 | Gothenburg, SWE | 12 Aug |
| 13.20 | -0.3 | | | | 1 | London (CP) | 7 Jul |
| 13.23 | 0.2 | | | | 1q3 | Gothenburg, SWE | 11 Aug |
| 13.25 | -1.5 | | | | 1 | Nurmijarvi, FIN | 4 Jun |
| 13.26 | 0.2 | | | | 2 | Gateshead | 21 Aug |
| 13.31 | -0.6 | | | | 1 | Oslo, NOR | 21 Jul |
| 13.33 | -0.3 | | | | 3 | Berlin, GER | 1 Sep |
| 13.57 | -0.3 | | | | 1h6 | Gothenburg, SWE | 11 Aug |
| 13.58 | 1.5 | | | | 5 | Zurich, SWZ | 16 Aug |
| 13.17 | -0.3 | Colin Jackson | | 18.02.67 | 1 | Baden, SWZ | 12 Aug |
| 13.18 | 0.7 | | | | 1 | Rome, ITA | 8 Jun |
| 13.18 | 0.2 | | | | 1 | Gateshead | 21 Aug |
| 13.19 | 0.0 | | | | 3 | Tokyo, JAP | 15 Sep |
| 13.20 | -0.6 | | | | 3 | London (CP) | 27 Aug |
| 13.21 | 1.5 | | | | 2 | Zurich, SWZ | 16 Aug |
| 13.29 | -0.7 | | | | 3 | Duisburg, GER | 18 Jun |
| 13.29 | -0.3 | | | | 2 | Berlin, GER | 1 Sep |
| 13.32 | -0.9 | | | | 1 | Sydney, AUS | 5 Mar |
| 13.32 | -1.9 | | | | 1 | Padua, ITA | 16 Jul |
| 13.35 | -1.0 | | | | 2 | Nice, FRA | 12 Jul |
| 13.37 | -1.0 | | | | 1 | Melbourne, AUS | 23 Feb |
| 13.38 | 0.9 | | | | 1h2 | Tokyo, JAP | 15 Sep |
| 13.43 | -0.5 | | | | 3 | Nuremberg, GER | 15 Jun |
| 13.51 | -2.7 | | | | 1h2 | Sydney, AUS | 5 Mar |
| 13.60 | 1.5 | Neil Owen | U23 | 18.10.73 | 2r2 | Helsinki, FIN | 28 Jun |
| 13.63 | -0.3 | | | | 1 | Birmingham | 16 Jul |
| 13.71 | 2.5 | | | | 6 | Sheffield | 23 Jul |
| 13.72 | 0.4 | | | | 5 | Fukuoka, JAP | 30 Aug |
| 13.74 | 1.7 | | | | 4h3 | Gothenburg, SWE | 11 Aug |
| 13.75 | 0.6 | | | | 1 | Tessenderlo, BEL | 2 Jul |
| 13.84 | -0.3 | | | | 8 | London (CP) | 7 Jul |
| 13.85 | 0.4 | | | | 4s2 | Fukuoka, JAP | 30 Aug |
| 13.87 | -1.2 | | | | 1r2 | Zofingen, SWZ | 5 Jun |
| 13.87 | 0.8 | | | | 1h3 | Birmingham | 16 Jul |
| 13.87 | 0.2 | | | | 5 | Gateshead | 21 Aug |
| 13.88 | -1.1 | | | | 1 | Loughborough | 11 Jun |
| 13.89 | -0.6 | | | | 3q2 | Fukuoka, JAP | 29 Aug |
| 13.92 | 0.1 | | | | 1h2 | Tessenderlo, BEL | 2 Jul |
| 13.92 | 1.1 | | | | 7s2 | Gothenburg, SWE | 12 Aug |
| 13.95 | -2.1 | | | | 2 | London (CP) | 18 Jun |
| 13.96 | -1.3 | | | | 3r2 | Oslo, NOR | 21 Jul |
| 13.62 | 0.6 | Andy Tulloch | | 1.04.67 | 4q1 | Gothenburg, SWE | 11 Aug |
| 13.62 | -0.1 | | | | 7s1 | Gothenburg, SWE | 12 Aug |
| 13.64 | 1.0 | | | | 2 | Villeneuve d'Ascq, FRA | 25 Jun |
| 13.66 | 1.3 | | | | 2 | Tallinn, EST | 9 Jul |
| 13.69 | 0.8 | | | | 3h1 | Gothenburg, SWE | 11 Aug |
| 13.70 | 0.9 | | | | 3r2 | Tallinn, EST | 9 Jul |
| 13.76 | 0.6 | | | | 3 | Moscow, RUS | 5 Jun |
| 13.76 | -0.3 | | | | 2 | Birmingham | 16 Jul |
| 13.79 | -0.4 | | | | 1h2 | Birmingham | 16 Jul |
| 13.81 | -0.6 | | | | 6 | London (CP) | 27 Aug |
| 13.82 | 0.3 | | | | 3 | Bellinzona, SWZ | 20 Jun |
| 13.82 | -1.3 | | | | 2r2 | Oslo, NOR | 21 Jul |
| 13.86 | 0.6 | | | | 8 | Helsinki, FIN | 28 Jun |
| 13.87 | -0.4 | | | | 2 | Oslo (Lam), NOR | 14 Jun |
| 13.94 | 0.0 | | | | 2 | Ljubljana, SLO | 21 May |

| | | | | | | | | |
|---|---|---|---|---|---|---|---|---|
| 13.83 | -2.1 | Lloyd Cowan | | 8.07.62 | 1 | London (CP) | 18 | Jun |
| 13.96 | -1.1 | | | | 2 | Loughborough | 11 | Jun |
| 13.97 | -0.3 | | | | 3 | Birmingham | 16 | Jul |
| 13.86 | -1.2 | Paul Gray | | 25.05.69 | 2r2 | Duisburg, GER | 18 | Jun |
| 13.87 | 0.7 | | | | 6 | Rome, ITA | 8 | Jun |
| 13.90 | 1.1 | | | | 1 | Edinburgh | 3 | Jun |
| 13.90 | -0.5 | | | | 8 | Nuremberg, GER | 15 | Jun |
| 13.98 | | | | | 2h1 | Sydney, AUS | 5 | Mar |
| 13.98 | -0.3 | Ken Campbell | | 30.09.72 | 4 | Birmingham | 16 | Jul |
| | | 69 performances to 13.99 by 7 athletes | | | | | | |
| 14.02 | 1.3 | Mark Lambeth | | 3.09.72 | 5 | Tallinn, EST | 9 | Jul |
| *14.02* | *-0.3* | *Darren Cooper* | | *1.02.66* | *5* | *Birmingham* | *16* | *Jul* |
| 14.10 | 1.0 | Hugh Teape | | 26.12.63 | 1h1 | Birmingham | 16 | Jul |
| *14.14* | *-1.0* | *Paul Edmiston* | | *16.02.72* | *4* | *Melbourne, AUS* | *23* | *Feb* |
| 14.29 | | Martin Nicholson | | 9.12.70 | 2 | Cork, IRE | 24 | Jun |
| | (10) | | | | | | | |
| 14.34 | 1.0 | Damien Greaves | U20 | 19.09.77 | 2h1 | Birmingham | 16 | Jul |
| 14.35 | 0.6 | Kevin Lumsdon | U23 | 3.03.74 | 6 | Narbonne, FRA | 29 | Jul |
| 14.37 | 1.0 | James Hughes | U23 | 8.11.74 | 3h1 | Birmingham | 16 | Jul |
| 14.45 | 0.6 | Greg Dunson | | 2.12.63 | 2 | Enfield | 19 | Aug |
| 14.46 | -3.3 | Simon McAree | U23 | 28.12.75 | 2 | Gateshead | 12 | Aug |
| 14.47 | 1.0 | Mark Stern | | 22.05.72 | 3h2 | Birmingham | 16 | Jul |
| 14.48 | | Colin Bovell | | 9.03.72 | 3 | Cork, IRE | 24 | Jun |
| 14.53 | 1.8 | James Archampong | U20 | 14.03.76 | 1 | Cardiff | 19 | Aug |
| 14.54 | -0.9 | Ross Baillie | U20 | 26.09.77 | 5h2 | Birmingham | 16 | Jul |
| 14.59 | 0.7 | Chris Rawlinson | | 19.05.72 | 3h2 | Bedford | 28 | May |
| | (20) | | | | | | | |
| 14.61 | -1.1 | Jamie Quarry | | 15.11.72 | 3 | Loughborough | 11 | Jun |
| 14.67 | -0.1 | Ererton Harrison | | 8.04.66 | 3h4 | Birmingham | 16 | Jul |
| 14.76 | -0.4 | Alex Kruger | | 18.11.63 | 2D | Gotzis, AUT | 28 | May |
| 14.76 | -3.0 | Kirk Harries | U23 | 7.08.74 | 3h1 | London (CP) | 18 | Jun |
| 14.81 | -0.1 | Chris Dorgu | | 11.12.69 | 4h4 | Birmingham | 16 | Jul |
| 14.81 | | Adrian Carter | | 7.02.68 | 1r2 | Gateshead | 12 | Aug |
| 14.83 | | Andrew David | | 9.09.69 | 1 | London (CP) | 10 | Sep |
| 14.88 | 1.0 | Adrian Caines | U23 | 13.11.74 | 5h1 | Birmingham | 16 | Jul |
| 14.88 | 0.8 | Barry Thomas | | 28.04.72 | 4h3 | Birmingham | 16 | Jul |
| 14.89 | | Ayo Falola | | 29.07.68 | 2 | London (CP) | 10 | Sep |
| | (30) | | | | | | | |
| 14.92 | 0.6 | Clarence Allen | | 1.04.64 | 4 | Bedford | 10 | Jun |
| *14.95* | *1.8* | *Pascal Renaud* | | *20.04.70* | *2* | *Cardiff* | *19* | *Aug* |
| 14.97 | 1.4 | Sebastian Rosato | | 19.11.72 | 2= | Oxford | 28 | Jun |
| 14.97 | 1.4 | Stephen Booth | | 21.10.71 | 2= | Oxford | 28 | Jun |
| 14.99 | 1.0 | Richard Hunter | | 12.01.71 | 6h1 | Birmingham | 16 | Jul |
| 15.02 | | Tim Tomkinson | | 31.10.68 | 1 | Aldershot | 7 | Jun |
| 15.05 | -0.4 | Simon Shirley | | 3.08.66 | 4D | Gotzis, AUT | 28 | May |
| 15.06 | -3.6 | Paul Field | | 24.06.67 | 4D | Valladolid,SPA | 2 | Jul |
| 15.10 | 0.1 | Nick Dakin | | 13.11.63 | 3r2 | Barcelona, SPA | 27 | Jun |
| 15.10 | 0.4 | Tony Southward | | 31.01.71 | 1D | Bebington | 23 | Jul |
| 15.13 | 1.5 | Paul Gripton | U20 | 9.11.76 | 3r2 | Loughborough | 11 | Jun |
| | (40) | | | | | | | |
| 15.15 | 1.4 | Marvin Gray | | 18.12.71 | 1r2 | Cardiff | 19 | Aug |
| 15.20 | 2.0 | Charles Edsall | U23 | 2.05.74 | 1 | Portsmouth | 14 | May |
| 15.23 | 1.7 | David Barnetson | | 1.07.71 | 2r2 | Edinburgh | 3 | Jun |
| 15.25 | 2.0 | Jeremy Thompson | U23 | 11.06.73 | 2 | Portsmouth | 14 | May |
| 15.26 | 1.8 | Trevor McGlynn | U20 | 6.06.78 | 1 | Antrim | 20 | Jun |
| 15.26 | | Andrew Smailes | | 22.04.68 | 2 | Frankenthal, GER | 27 | Jun |
| 15.26 | 1.8 | Kevin Furlong | | 19.05.70 | 2 | Hull | 5 | Aug |
| 15.26 | | Dean Macey | U20 | 12.12.77 | 1D | Vladimir, RUS | 5 | Aug |
| 15.27 | 1.8 | Dominic Bradley | U20 | 22.12.76 | 3 | Hull | 6 | Aug |
| 15.27 | -0.5 | Max Robertson | | 27.12.63 | 4r2 | Enfield | 19 | Aug |
| | (50) | | | | | | | |

| | | | | | | | |
|---|---|---|---|---|---|---|---|
| 15.28 | 2.0 | Paul Warrillow | | 8.07.70 | 3 | Portsmouth | 14 May |
| 15.28 | 1.7 | Nick Buckfield | U23 | 5.06.73 | 3r2 | Edinburgh | 3 Jun |
| 15.28 | | Gary Myles | | 3.02.63 | 1 | Wrexham | 25 Jun |
| 15.30 | 1.2 | Richard Leggate | U23 | 20.07.74 | 3h2 | Gateshead | 17 Jun |
| 15.31 | | David Vidgen | U23 | 27.09.74 | D | Enfield | 13 Aug |
| 15.34 | | David Brooking | | 22.10.68 | 1 | Braunton | 13 May |
| 15.34 | 1.8 | Gareth Hughes | U23 | 22.10.73 | 4 | Cardiff | 19 Aug |
| 15.34 | 1.8 | Dave Savage | | 13.11.72 | 3 | Cardiff | 19 Aug |
| 15.35 | 0.6 | David Humphreys | | 10.10.69 | 5 | Enfield | 19 Aug |
| 15.36 | | Terry Fidler | | 13.10.71 | 1D | Enfield | 13 Aug |
| | (60) | | | | | | |
| 15.38 | -1.5 | Perry Batchelor | U23 | 11.12.75 | 4r2 | Loughborough | 11 Jun |
| 15.40 | -1.4 | Adam Carswell | U20 | 8.01.76 | 3h1 | Bedford | 2 Jul |
| 15.42 | 0.9 | Stephen Rogers | | 1.09.71 | 1D | Derby | 30 Apr |
| 15.43 | 1.9 | Les Antoine | | 16.12.65 | 2r2 | Birmingham | 20 May |
| 15.44 | 1.4 | Rob Laing | | 30.07.66 | 2r2 | Cardiff | 19 Aug |
| 15.46 | 0.7 | Andy Gill | | 19.02.70 | 5h2 | Bedford | 28 May |
| 15.47 | -0.3 | William Gilles | U23 | 15.02.73 | 2D | Stoke | 25 Jun |
| 15.54 | | Robert Mason | U23 | 13.09.75 | 2 | Wrexham | 25 Jun |
| 15.56 | -1.5 | Martyn Hendry | U23 | 10.04.75 | 2 | Edinburgh | 1 Jul |
| 15.56 | 0.6 | Andy Hodge | | 18.12.68 | 6 | Enfield | 19 Aug |
| | (70) | | | | | | |
| 15.57 | 1.8 | Richard Churchill | U20 | 29.09.77 | 5 | Hull | 5 Aug |
| 15.63 | 1.0 | Gary Smith | | 20.02.71 | 7h1 | Birmingham | 16 Jul |
| 15.66 | 1.8 | Anthony Gill | U20 | 19.09.77 | 6 | Hull | 5 Aug |

**Wind Assisted**

| | | | | | | | |
|---|---|---|---|---|---|---|---|
| 13.17 | 4.4 | Jackson | | (13.17) | 1 | Cwmbran | 9 Jul |
| 13.28 | 3.0 | | | | 3 | Paris, FRA | 3 Jul |
| 13.32 | 2.5 | Jarrett | | (13.04) | 2 | Sheffield | 23 Jul |
| 13.35 | 3.0 | | | | 2 | Gateshead | 2 Jul |
| 13.65 | 4.4 | Owen | U23 | (13.60) | 2 | Cwmbran | 9 Jul |
| 13.82 | 2.8 | | | | 4q2 | Gothenburg, SWE | 11 Aug |
| 13.75 | 2.5 | Andy Tulloch | | (13.62) | 7 | Sheffield | 23 Jul |
| 13.76 | 3.0 | | | | 6 | Gateshead | 2 Jul |
| 13.79 | 2.5 | Lloyd Cowan | | (13.83) | 8 | Sheffield | 23 Jul |
| *13.98* | *4.3* | *Paul Edmiston* | | *(14.14)* | *1* | *Perth, AUS* | *15 Oct* |
| 14.23 | 4.1 | Jamie Quarry | | (14.61) | 1 | Edinburgh | 8 May |
| 14.25 | 2.2 | Anthony Brannen | | 16.09.68 | 1D | Derby | 30 Apr |
| 14.33 | 2.2 | Kevin Lumsdon | U23 | (14.35) | 1h | Hull | 5 Aug |
| 14.62 | 4.1 | Barry Thomas | | (14.88) | 4D | Alhama, SPA | 21 May |
| 14.68 | 4.1 | Paul Field | | (15.06) | 6D | Alhama, SPA | 21 May |
| 14.68 | 3.5 | Adrian Caines | U23 | (14.88) | 3 | Telford | 26 Aug |
| 14.72 | 3.5 | Mark Bushell | U20 | 22.10.76 | 1D | Stoke | 4 Jun |
| 14.79 | 4.1 | Sebastian Rosato | | (14.97) | 2 | Edinburgh | 8 May |
| 14.87 | 4.1 | Andy Lewis | | 9.03.68 | 3 | Edinburgh | 8 May |
| 14.91 | 4.1 | Richard Leggate | U23 | (15.30) | 4 | Edinburgh | 8 May |
| 15.05 | 2.2 | Gavin Sunshine | U23 | 19.02.74 | 4D | Derby | 30 Apr |
| 15.05 | 3.5 | Stephen Rogers | | (15.42) | 2D | Stoke | 4 Jun |
| 15.07 | 6.0 | Andrew Smailes | | (15.26) | 1 | Stoke | 13 May |
| 15.33 | 3.5 | Roger Hunter | U20 | 10.03.76 | 3D | Stoke | 4 Jun |
| 15.37 | 4.1 | Andrew Bargh | U20 | 21.08.76 | 7 | Edinburgh | 8 May |
| 15.42 | 2.2 | Duncan Mathieson | | 8.03.69 | 1D | Aberdeen | 16 Jul |
| 15.48 | 2.6 | Gavin Streather | | 14.04.71 | 6 | Stoke | 9 Sep |
| 15.52 | 2.2 | Adrian Ferrand | | 5.02.68 | 5D | Derby | 30 Apr |
| 15.57 | 3.7 | William Wyllie | U23 | 12.07.73 | 4h1 | Edinburgh | 7 May |
| 15.65 | 3.5 | Par Esegbona | | 16.04.68 | 4D | Stoke | 4 Jun |
| 15.67 | 2.6 | Danny Heywood | | 27.05.71 | 7 | Stoke | 9 Sep |

**Hand Timing**

| | | | | | | | | |
|---|---|---|---|---|---|---|---|---|
| 13.7 w | | Lloyd Cowan | | (13.83) | 4 | Fullerton, USA | 27 | Apr |

1 performances to 14.0 wind assisted

| | | | | | | | | |
|---|---|---|---|---|---|---|---|---|
| 14.2 | 0.0 | Anthony Brannen | | (14.25w) | 1 | Stoke | 6 | May |
| 14.4 | | Greg Dunson | | (14.45) | 1 | Cosford | 5 | Jul |
| 14.4 w | 2.8 | Ross Baillie | U20 | (14.54) | 2 | Bedford | 2 | Jul |
| 14.6 | 0.0 | Chris Dorgu | | (14.81) | 2 | Stoke | 6 | May |
| 14.7 w | 4.2 | Mark Bushell | U20 | (14.72w) | 1D | Kilkenny, IRE | 27 | Aug |
| 14.8 | | Tim Tomkinson | | (15.02) | 1 | Loughborough | 24 | May |
| 14.8 | | Paul Field | | (15.06) | 2 | Loughborough | 24 | May |
| 14.8 | | Richard Hunter | | (14.99) | 1 | Harrow | 9 | Jul |
| 14.8 w | 3.1 | Tony Southward | | (15.10) | 1D | Kilkenny, IRE | 27 | Aug |
| | | | | | | | | |
| 14.9 | | Gary Smith | | (15.63) | 2 | Harrow | 9 | Jul |
| 14.9 | | Clarence Allen | | (14.92) | 2 | Tonbridge | 5 | Aug |
| 14.9 w | 3.1 | Duncan Mathieson | | (15.42w) | 2D | Kilkenny, IRE | 27 | Aug |
| 15.0 | | Stephen Rogers | | (15.42) | 1 | Loughborough | 20 | May |
| 15.0 | 1.6 | Andy Gill | | (15.46) | 1 | Wakefield | 3 | Jun |
| 15.0 | | Andrew Smailes | | (15.26) | | Ranstein, GER | 27 | Jun |
| 15.0 | | Eric Hollingsworth | | 6.12.62 | 2 | Melbourne, AUS | 21 | Oct |
| 15.1 | | Paul Gripton | U20 | (15.13) | 1 | Telford | 6 | May |
| 15.1 | 2.0 | David Bigham | | 4.07.71 | 5 | London (He) | 7 | May |
| 15.1 | | Dominic Bradley | U20 | (15.27) | 1 | Crewe | 13 | May |
| | | | | | | | | |
| 15.1 | | Kevin Furlong | | (15.26) | 1 | Blackpool | 13 | May |
| 15.1 | | Trevor McGlynn | U20 | (15.26) | 1 | Tullamore, IRE | 25 | Jun |
| 15.1 | | David Vidgen | U23 | (15.31) | 1 | London (PH) | 5 | Aug |
| 15.1 w | 4.9 | Paul Warrillow | | (15.28) | 2 | Croydon | 28 | Aug |
| | | 15.2 | -1.7 | | 3 | London (WL) | 30 | Jul |
| 15.2 | | Perry Batchelor | U23 | (15.38) | 1 | Coventry | 6 | May |
| 15.2 | | Richard Leggate | U23 | (15.30) | 1 | York | 1 | Jul |
| 15.2 | | John Franklin | | 1.03.66 | 3 | Harrow | 9 | Jul |
| 15.2 | | Dean Macey | U20 | (15.26) | 1 | Ipswich | 22 | Jul |
| 15.2 | -1.7 | Gary Telfer | | 10.01.65 | 2 | London (WL) | 30 | Jul |
| 15.2 w | 2.8 | Adam Carswell | U20 | (15.40) | 3 | Bedford | 2 | Jul |
| | | | | | | | | |
| 15.2 w | 4.9 | Andy Hodge | | (15.56) | 3r2 | Croydon | 28 | Aug |
| 15.2 w | 2.4 | Gary Myles | | (15.28) | 2 | Cannock | 16 | Sep |
| 15.3 | | David Humphreys | | (15.35) | 2 | Coventry | 6 | May |
| 15.3 | 1.5 | William Wyllie | U23 | (15.57w) | 3 | Leamington | 14 | May |
| 15.3 | 1.5 | Les Antoine | | (15.43) | 4 | Leamington | 14 | May |
| 15.3 | | Mark Perman | | 6.01.68 | 3 | Barking | 3 | Jun |
| 15.3 w | 4.9 | Terry Fidler | | (15.36) | 3 | Croydon | 28 | Aug |
| 15.4 | | Mark Purser | | 18.04.72 | 2 | Loughborough | 20 | May |
| 15.4 | | D. Sweetman | | | 2r2 | Loughborough | 24 | May |
| 15.4 | 1.6 | Martyn Hendry | U23 | (15.56) | 3 | Wakefield | 3 | Jun |
| | | | | | | | | |
| 15.4 | 0.3 | Rob Laing | | (15.44) | 5 | Crawley | 1 | Jul |
| 15.4 w | 4.0 | Ian Wells | | 18.02.62 | 2 | Bedford | 26 | Aug |
| | | 15.5 | 1.6 | | 4r2 | London (Ha) | 7 | May |
| 15.5 | 0.0 | Steve Leader | | 24.11.66 | 3 | Stoke | 6 | May |
| 15.5 | 0.9 | Trevor Sloman | | 21.03.68 | 2r2 | Stoke | 6 | May |
| 15.5 | -1.6 | Gavin Streather | | (15.48w) | 3r2 | London (He) | 7 | May |
| 15.5 | | Marcus Hole | | 18.06.71 | 2 | Exeter | 28 | May |
| 15.5 | 1.6 | Bill McDonagh | | 11.07.72 | 4 | Wakefield | 3 | Jun |
| 15.5 | | Phil Brilus | | 29.12.68 | 1 | Harlow | 22 | Jul |
| 15.5 | | Andrew Haines | | 15.10.72 | 2 | Southampton | 22 | Jul |
| 15.5 | | William Morris | U23 | 18.08.73 | 1 | Colchester | 22 | Jul |
| | | | | | | | | |
| 15.5 | | Andrew Bargh | U20 | (15.37w) | 1 | Southampton | 22 | Jul |
| 15.5 w | 4.9 | John Hadler | | 18.08.69 | 5 | Croydon | 28 | Aug |

| | | | | | | | |
|---|---|---|---|---|---|---|---|
| 15.5 w | 2.4 | Sean Saxon | | 11.12.71 | 3 | Cannock | 16 Sep |
| 15.6 | | Des Wilkinson | | 7.01.63 | 2 | Thurrock | 6 May |
| 15.6 | | Gavin Sunshine | U23 | (15.05w) | 7 | London (He) | 7 May |
| 15.6 | | Jon Gregory | | 3.10.72 | 4 | Loughborough | 20 May |
| 15.6 | | Peter Crampton | | 4.06.69 | 1r2 | Derby | 3 Jun |
| 15.6 | | Billy Jewers | | 27.09.62 | 2 | Croydon | 25 Jun |
| 15.6 | | Gary Gallagher | | 7.06.71 | 4 | Derby | 30 Jul |
| 15.6 | | Nathan Hart | U23 | 1.07.73 | 2 | Watford | 19 Aug |
| 15.6 | | John McIlwham | | 29.02.72 | 2 | Blackpool | 19 Aug |

# 400 METRES HURDLES

| | | | | | |
|---|---|---|---|---|---|
| 49.58 | Peter Crampton | 4.06.69 | 4 | Malmo, SWE | 29 Jun |
| 50.06 | | | 6 | London (CP) | 7 Jul |
| 50.35 | | | 5 | Gateshead | 2 Jul |
| 50.36 A | | | 4 | Nairobi, KEN | 27 May |
| 50.5 | | | 1 | Derby | 14 May |
| 50.76 | | | 8 | St. Denis, FRA | 1 Jun |
| 49.70 | Gary Cadogan | 8.10.66 | 2 | Birmingham | 16 Jul |
| 50.82 | | | 5 | Bellinzona, SWZ | 20 Jun |
| 50.98 | | | 1h2 | Birmingham | 15 Jul |
| 49.82 | Gary Jennings | 21.02.72 | 1 | Barcelona, SPA | 27 Jun |
| 49.82 | | | 3h5 | Fukuoka, JAP | 30 Aug |
| 50.03 | | | 1 | Bedford | 29 May |
| 50.30 | | | 1 | London (CP) | 3 Jun |
| 50.30 | | | 2 | Nivelles, BEL | 19 Aug |
| 50.34 | | | 3 | Birmingham | 16 Jul |
| 50.38 | | | 1 | Loughborough | 11 Jun |
| 50.43 | | | 4 | Villeneuve d'Ascq, FRA | 24 Jun |
| 50.47 | | | 6 | Madrid, SPA | 20 Jun |
| 50.48 | | | 6 | Gateshead | 2 Jul |
| 50.84 | | | 1h4 | Birmingham | 15 Jul |
| 50.95 | | | 5 | Sheffield | 23 Jul |
| 50.96 | | | 1 | Stoke | 9 Sep |
| 51.22 | | | 8s2 | Fukuoka, JAP | 31 Aug |
| 50.31 | Tony Williams | 1.05.72 | 3 | Barcelona, SPA | 27 Jun |
| 50.40 | | | 2 | Lahti, FIN | 27 Jul |
| 50.73 | | | 5h3 | Fukuoka, JAP | 30 Aug |
| 50.96 | | | 1r2 | Sheffield | 23 Jul |
| 51.03 | | | 1 | Gateshead | 17 Jun |
| 51.2 | | | 1 | Sheffield | 19 Jul |
| 50.62 | Lawrence Lynch | 1.11.67 | 3 | Ljubljana, SLO | 21 May |
| 50.64 | | | 4 | Birmingham | 16 Jul |
| 50.70 | | | 2h3 | Birmingham | 15 Jul |
| 50.88 | | | 1 | Enfield | 19 Aug |
| 50.89 | | | 1 | Birmingham | 1 Jul |
| 51.03 | | | 4 | Gateshead | 21 Aug |
| 51.05 | | | 2 | Stoke | 9 Sep |
| 51.08 | | | 6 | Sheffield | 23 Jul |
| 51.22 | | | 2 | Celje, SLO | 16 Jun |
| 51.3 | | | 1 | Liverpool | 30 Jul |
| 51.31 | | | 2 | Loughborough | 11 Jun |
| 51.38 | | | 3 | London (CP) | 3 Jun |
| 50.79 | Lloyd Cowan | 8.07.62 | 2 | London (CP) | 3 Jun |
| 50.99 | | | 1 | Cwmbran | 9 Jul |
| 50.90 | Chris Rawlinson | 19.05.72 | 5 | Birmingham | 16 Jul |
| 51.08 | | | 1 | Birmingham | 20 May |
| 51.15 | | | 2 | Geneva, SWZ | 17 Jun |
| 51.20 | | | 1r2 | Loughborough | 11 Jun |
| 51.2 | | | 1 | Rotherham | 6 May |
| 51.31 | | | 2h2 | Birmingham | 15 Jul |

| | | | | | | | |
|---|---|---|---|---|---|---|---|
| 51.24 | Eddie Betts | | 18.02.71 | 1 | London (CP) | 18 | Jun |
| 51.48 | | | | 1r2 | London (CP) | 7 | Jul |
| 51.29 | Gary Telfer | | 10.01.65 | 3 | Vila Real, POR | 27 | May |
| 51.4 | | | | 1 | Hayes | 14 | May |
| 51.33 | Paul Hibbert | | 31.03.65 | 6 | Birmingham | 16 | Jul |
| 51.36 | | | | 1h5 | Birmingham | 15 | Jul |
| (10) | | | | | | | |
| 51.39 | Dave Savage | | 13.11.72 | 7 | Birmingham | 16 | Jul |
| 51.44 | | | | 2h5 | Birmingham | 15 | Jul |

57 performances to 51.50 by 11 athletes

| | | | | | | | |
|---|---|---|---|---|---|---|---|
| 51.73 | Matthew Douglas | U20 | 26.11.76 | 3 | Nyiregyhaza, HUN | 29 | Jul |
| 51.78 | Noel Levy | U23 | 22.06.75 | 4 | Narbonne, FRA | 29 | Jul |
| 51.8 | Greg Dunson | | 2.12.63 | 1 | Cosford | 5 | Jul |
| 52.03 | | | | 3 | London (CP) | 18 | Jun |
| 51.94 | Mark Davidson | | 15.11.68 | 2 | Birmingham | 1 | Jul |
| 51.96 | Mark Bishop | | 12.02.67 | 2 | London (CP) | 18 | Jun |
| 51.99 | Anthony Borsumato | U23 | 13.12.73 | 1r3 | Zofingen, SWZ | 5 | Jun |
| 52.07 | Dave Griffin | | 5.12.63 | 2 | Edinburgh | 3 | Jun |
| 52.11 | Richard Holt | | 28.11.71 | 5 | London (CP) | 18 | Jun |
| 52.46 | Barry Middleton | U23 | 10.03.75 | 2 | Edinburgh | 7 | May |
| (20) | | | | | | | |
| 52.84 | Charles Robertson-Adams | U20 | 5.12.77 | 3h1 | Nyiregyhaza, HUN | 28 | Jul |
| 53.0 | Chris Cashell | | 11.05.66 | 1 | Peterborough | 6 | May |
| 53.16 | | | | 2 | Enfield | 29 | Apr |
| 53.0 | Mark Rowlands | U20 | 18.04.78 | 2 | Newport | 17 | Jun |
| 53.14 | | | | 3 | Cardiff | 22 | Jul |
| 53.1 | Mark Green | | 28.06.71 | 2 | Enfield | 1 | Jul |
| 53.1 | Andrew Kennard | | 2.01.66 | 1 | Aldershot | 8 | Jul |
| 53.59 | | | | 2h3 | London (CP) | 17 | Jun |
| 53.34 | Ian Wells | | 18.02.62 | 5h2 | Birmingham | 15 | Jul |
| 53.41 | Colin Anderson | | 18.02.59 | 3h4 | London (CP) | 17 | Jun |
| 53.43 | Douglas Thom | | 13.04.68 | 3 | Edinburgh | 24 | Jun |
| 53.47 | George Sandy | | 22.04.71 | 6 | London (CP) | 18 | Jun |
| 53.5 | Andy Gill | | 19.02.70 | 1 | Salisbury | 9 | Jul |
| 54.01 | | | | 1 | Edinburgh | 1 | Jul |
| (30) | | | | | | | |
| 53.51 | Adam Hartley | | 27.02.69 | 5 | Birmingham | 1 | Jul |
| 53.56 | Paul Thompson | | 22.03.72 | 1 | Birmingham | 17 | Jun |
| 53.6 | Andrew Bargh | U20 | 21.08.76 | 2 | Salisbury | 9 | Jul |
| 54.16 | | | | 5r1 | Bedford | 2 | Jul |
| 53.7 | Marvin Gray | | 18.12.71 | 3 | Newport | 17 | Jun |
| 54.06 | | | | 1r2 | Edinburgh | 3 | Jun |
| 53.7 | Richard Scott | U23 | 14.09.73 | 1 | Salisbury | 16 | Jul |
| 53.98 | | | | 2h2 | London (CP) | 17 | Jun |
| 53.73 | Andy Edwards | | 15.09.69 | 7 | Birmingham | 1 | Jul |
| 53.80 | Jon Parker | U20 | 1.05.76 | 6 | Birmingham | 20 | May |
| 53.80 | David Gifford | U23 | 9.03.73 | 1 | Wrexham | 25 | Jun |
| 53.8 | David Goodger | U23 | 19.09.75 | 4 | Newport | 17 | Jun |
| 54.09 | | | | 7h2 | Birmingham | 15 | Jul |
| 53.8 | Derek Paisley | U23 | 1.12.73 | 2 | Liverpool | 30 | Jul |
| 53.82 | | | | 1 | Antrim | 20 | Jun |
| (40) | | | | | | | |
| 53.88 | John Bell | U23 | 10.09.73 | 3h1 | Birmingham | 15 | Jul |
| 53.9 | Danny Heywood | | 27.05.71 | 5 | Newport | 17 | Jun |
| 54.53 | | | | 2 | Cardiff | 19 | Aug |
| 53.9 | Howard Moscrop | | 16.12.57 | 2 | Southampton | 22 | Jul |
| 54.0 | John McIlwham | | 29.02.72 | 2 | Rotherham | 6 | May |
| 54.0 | Mark Purser | | 18.04.72 | 1 | Loughborough | 20 | May |
| 54.51 | | | | 1 | Stoke | 10 | Sep |
| 54.0 | Paul Beaumont | | 27.03.63 | 2 | Cosford | 5 | Jul |
| 54.02 | Matthew Birchall | | 1.11.71 | 1h2 | London (CP) | 17 | Jun |

176

| | | | | | | | |
|---|---|---|---|---|---|---|---|
| 54.10 | Glenn Gray | | 21.04.68 | 2r2 | Birmingham | 1 | Jul |
| 54.17 | Ian Neely | U23 | 29.12.74 | 4 | Edinburgh | 24 | Jun |
| 54.2 | Carl Foster | U23 | 24.10.75 | 2 | Sheffield | 13 | May |
| | 54.58 | | | 3 | Nottingham | 8 | Jul |
| (50) | | | | | | | |
| 54.2 | Martin Holgate | | 2.11.65 | 1 | Birmingham | 9 | Aug |
| | 54.51 | | | 2r2 | Enfield | 19 | Aug |
| 54.22 | Jamie Sheffield | U20 | 26.06.78 | 2 | Wrexham | 25 | Jun |
| 54.3 | Simon Wassell | | 7.04.69 | 3 | Rotherham | 6 | May |
| 54.33 | Keith Newton | | 12.12.68 | 2 | Barking | 14 | May |
| 54.45 | Matt Lethbridge | U20 | 22.01.77 | 2 | London (CP) | 28 | May |
| 54.45 | James Hillier | U20 | 3.04.78 | 2 | Utrecht, HOL | 9 | Jul |
| 54.5 | John Garmston | | 3.03.65 | 3 | Watford | 19 | Aug |
| | 54.84 | | | 1h1 | Birmingham | 17 | Jun |
| 54.55 | Lee Thompson | U20 | 21.10.76 | 2h1 | Nottingham | 7 | Jul |
| 54.58 | Craig White | | 4.04.71 | 2r2 | Edinburgh | 3 | Jun |
| *54.59* | *Nigel Keogh* | | *18.07.67* | *3r2* | *London (CP)* | *3* | *Jun* |
| 54.60 | Gavin Streather | | 14.04.71 | 4r2 | London (CP) | 3 | Jun |
| (60) | | | | | | | |
| 54.60 | Mark Anderson | U20 | 5.11.77 | 3h1 | Nottingham | 7 | Jul |
| 54.6 | James Melville-Jackson | U23 | 24.01.74 | 3 | Basingstoke | 6 | Aug |
| 54.63 | Andrew Judge | U23 | 24.05.75 | 2 | Stoke | 10 | Sep |
| 54.74 | Martin Briggs | | 4.01.64 | 7 | Birmingham | 20 | May |
| 54.8 | Phil Harries | | 7.04.66 | 2 | Derby | 3 | Jun |
| 54.8 | Jeremy Bridger | U23 | 23.09.75 | 5 | Basingstoke | 6 | Aug |
| 54.87 | Andy Douglas | | 19.07.62 | 3 | Cardiff | 19 | Aug |
| 54.93 | Lee Murphy | U20 | 11.03.77 | 3 | London (CP) | 28 | May |
| 54.97 | Jon Goodwin | U20 | 22.09.76 | 3h1 | Bedford | 1 | Jul |
| 54.98 | Scott Chisholm | U20 | 20.10.77 | 3 | Stoke | 10 | Sep |
| (70) | | | | | | | |
| 55.10 | Simon Rush | U20 | 23.06.76 | 4 | London (CP) | 27 | May |
| 55.16 | Dean Park | U20 | 23.09.77 | 1r2 | Bedford | 2 | Jul |
| 55.2 | Gavin Sunshine | U23 | 19.02.74 | 1 | Croydon | 3 | Sep |
| 55.3 | Neil Tunstall | | 3.01.62 | 1 | Bedford | 25 | Jun |
| 55.41 | Trystan Bevan | U23 | 22.08.75 | 1r2 | Cardiff | 19 | Aug |
| 55.5 | Stephen Booth | | 21.10.71 | 2 | Oxford | 1 | Jul |
| 55.52 | Henrik Hartmann | | 7.09.72 | 5h1 | London (CP) | 17 | Jun |
| 55.69 | Stephen Pratt | U20 | 14.06.76 | 5 | London (CP) | 28 | May |
| 55.7 | Matthew Leslie | U20 | 17.06.76 | 1 | Ashton-U-Lyne | 6 | May |
| | 55.74 | | | 4h3 | Bedford | 1 | Jul |
| 55.9 | Paul Webb | U20 | 9.04.76 | 2 | Kettering | 19 | Aug |

**Additional Under 20** (1 - 18 above)

| | | | | | | | |
|---|---|---|---|---|---|---|---|
| 56.1 | Martin Troy | | 13.07.76 | 1 | London (Elt) | 18 | Jun |
| 56.16 | Steve Mitchell | | 1.09.77 | 6h2 | Nottingham | 7 | Jul |
| (20) | | | | | | | |
| 56.2 | Ruben Tabares | U17 | 22.10.78 | 2 | Telford | 18 | Jun |
| 56.3 | Andrew Mitchell | | 30.07.76 | 1 | Linwood | 24 | Aug |
| 56.38 | David Clifton | | 15.04.76 | 5r2 | Enfield | 19 | Aug |
| 56.46 | Fyn Corcoran | | 17.03.78 | 5h1 | Nottingham | 7 | Jul |
| 56.5 | Michael Serra | | 1.07.77 | 3 | Kingston | 13 | Aug |
| 56.6 | Alasdhair Love | | 29.07.77 | 3 | Ayr | 18 | Jul |
| 56.8 | Mark Chapman | | 28.12.76 | 2 | Basildon | 10 | Jun |
| | 56.95 | | | 6h3 | Bedford | 1 | Jul |
| 56.8 | Stefan Laffley | | 10.09.77 | 1 | Stretford | 10 | Jun |
| 56.8 | Keith Mason | | 10.02.76 | 4 | Ayr | 18 | Jul |

**Additional Under 17** (1 above)

| | | | | | | | |
|---|---|---|---|---|---|---|---|
| 57.9 | Carl McMullen | | 9.11.79 | 1 | Stretford | 19 | Aug |
| 57.9 | Kerrin Young | | 2.09.79 | 1 | Antrim | 26 | Aug |

# 400 METRES HURDLES - Under 17

| | | | | | | | |
|---|---|---|---|---|---|---|---|
| 54.10 | Russell Quelch | | 9.09.78 | 1 | Nottingham | 8 | Jul |
| 54.52 | Ruben Tabares | | 22.10.78 | 1 | Birmingham | 30 | Jul |
| 55.34 | Paul Morris | | 10.11.78 | 3 | Nottingham | 8 | Jul |
| 55.37 | Richard Singer | | 7.02.79 | 3 | Colwyn Bay | 15 | Jul |
| 55.53 | Robert Lewis | | 2.09.78 | 4 | Nottingham | 8 | Jul |
| 55.57 | Gareth Lewis | | 5.10.78 | 1 | Cardiff | 27 | May |
| 55.58 | Alastair Newmarch | | 28.11.78 | 5 | Nottingham | 8 | Jul |
| 55.96 | Greig Goodey | | 14.09.78 | 2 | London (CP) | 27 | May |
| 56.13 | Duncan Howarth | | 20.02.79 | 5 | Birmingham | 30 | Jul |
| 56.36 | Matthew Elias | | 25.04.79 | 2 | Cardiff | 27 | May |
| | (10) | | | | | | |
| 56.41 | Carl McMullen | | 9.11.79 | 1 | Hull | 5 | Aug |
| 56.50 | Colin Philip | | 8.06.79 | 4 | Colwyn Bay | 15 | Jul |
| 56.5 | Glen Howe | | 20.10.78 | 1 | Newcastle | 17 | Jun |
| 57.97 | | | | 7 | Birmingham | 30 | Jul |
| 56.62 | Kerrin Young | | 2.09.79 | 3 | Antrim | 12 | Aug |
| 56.8 | David Murphy | | 16.09.78 | 1 | Dublin (M), IRE | 24 | Jun |
| 56.8 | David Keoghan | | 9.10.78 | 1 | Bolton | 16 | Jul |
| 57.38 | | | | 3h2 | Nottingham | 7 | Jul |
| 56.9 | Sam Allen | | 26.10.78 | 1 | Sheffield | 13 | May |
| 57.14 | | | | 1 | Sheffield | 27 | May |
| 56.9 | Garry Turner | | 21.12.78 | 1 | Cannock | 21 | May |
| 56.9 | T. Aggard | | | 1 | Perivale | 16 | Jul |
| 57.0 | Michael Nesbeth | | 1.03.79 | 1 | London (TB) | 25 | Jun |
| | (20) | | | | | | |
| 57.14 | Andrew Hicks | | 30.07.79 | 2h1 | Nottingham | 7 | Jul |
| 57.2 | Paul Crossley | | 30.03.79 | 2 | Peterborough | 21 | May |
| 57.91 | | | | 4h1 | Nottingham | 7 | Jul |
| 57.2 | David Walker | | 24.11.78 | 2 | Newcastle | 17 | Jun |
| 57.2 | Mark Ridler | | 20.07.79 | 3h2 | Birmingham | 30 | Jul |
| 57.2 | Mark Tullett | | | 1 | Brecon | 5 | Aug |
| 57.2 | Gordon Menzies | | 13.03.79 | 2 | Linwood | 24 | Aug |
| 57.40 | | | | 3 | Pitreavie | 8 | Jul |
| 57.3 | Gary Stevenson | | 12.09.79 | 2 | Linwood | 24 | Aug |
| 57.35 | Martin Thomas | | 21.09.78 | 3h1 | Nottingham | 7 | Jul |
| 57.9 | Jon Heggie | | 8.12.79 | 4h3 | Birmingham | 30 | Jul |

**overage**

| | | | | | | | |
|---|---|---|---|---|---|---|---|
| 52.63 | Mark Rowlands | U20 | 18.04.78 | 2 | Bath | 13 | Jul |

# HIGH JUMP

| | | | | | | | |
|---|---|---|---|---|---|---|---|
| 2.35 | Dalton Grant | | 8.04.66 | 3 | Eberstadt, GER | 9 | Jul |
| | 2.32 i | | | 6 | Wuppertal, GER | 3 | Feb |
| | 2.30 | | | 4 | Brussels, BEL | 25 | Aug |
| | 2.30 | | | 1 | London (CP) | 27 | Aug |
| | 2.28 i | | | 8= | Barcelona, SPA | 12 | Mar |
| | 2.28 | | | 1 | Stoke | 9 | Sep |
| | 2.27 | | | 15Q | Gothenburg, SWE | 6 | Aug |
| | 2.25 i | | | 12 | Balingen, GER | 11 | Feb |
| | 2.25 | | | 1 | Granada, SPA | 27 | May |
| | 2.25 | | | 7 | London (CP) | 7 | Jul |
| | 2.25 | | | 3= | Nice, FRA | 12 | Jul |
| | 2.24 i | | | Q | Barcelona, SPA | 11 | Mar |
| | 2.20 i | | | 9= | Arnstadt, GER | 29 | Jan |
| | 2.20 i | | | 3 | Birmingham | 25 | Feb |
| | 2.20 | | | 1 | Jena, GER | 1 | Jun |
| | 2.20 | | | 1 | Birmingham | 1 | Jul |
| | 2.20 | | | 12 | Zurich, SWZ | 16 | Aug |
| | 2.20 | | | 10 | Berlin, GER | 1 | Sep |

| | | | | | | | | |
|---|---|---|---|---|---|---|---|---|
| 2.35 | Steve Smith | U23 | 29.03.73 | 1 | Birmingham | 15 | Jul |
| | 2.35 | | | 4= | Gothenburg, SWE | 8 | Aug |
| | 2.31 | | | 1 | Villeneuve d'Ascq, FRA | 24 | Jun |
| | 2.31 | | | 2 | Oslo, NOR | 21 | Jul |
| | 2.30 | | | 2 | St. Denis, FRA | 1 | Jun |
| | 2.29 | | | 2 | Stockholm, SWE | 10 | Jul |
| | 2.29 | | | Q | Gothenburg, SWE | 6 | Aug |
| | 2.28 | | | 3 | London (CP) | 7 | Jul |
| | 2.28 | | | 5 | Zurich, SWZ | 16 | Aug |
| | 2.27 | | | 2 | Villeneuve d'Ascq, FRA | 17 | Jun |
| | 2.27 | | | 5 | Brussels, BEL | 27 | Aug |
| | 2.25 | | | 3= | Berlin, GER | 1 | Sep |
| | 2.20 | | | 4= | Hamamatsu, JAP | 3 | May |
| | 2.20 | | | 6 | Gateshead | 2 | Jul |
| | 2.20 | | | 3 | Sheffield | 23 | Jul |
| 2.27 | Brendan Reilly | | 23.12.72 | 3 | Fukuoka, JAP | 1 | Sep |
| | 2.26 i | | | 1 | Birmingham | 28 | Jan |
| | 2.25 | | | 3 | Gateshead | 2 | Jul |
| | 2.25 | | | 2 | Sheffield | 23 | Jul |
| | 2.25 | | | 2 | Salgotarjan, HUN | 11 | Sep |
| | 2.24 | | | 17=Q | Gothenburg, SWE | 6 | Aug |
| | 2.24 | | | 2 | Stoke | 9 | Sep |
| | 2.22 | | | 1 | Pierre-Benite, FRA | 16 | Jun |
| | 2.21 i | | | 3 | Stafford | 29 | Jan |
| | 2.20 i | | | 2 | Glasgow | 11 | Feb |
| | 2.20 i | | | 4= | Birmingham | 25 | Feb |
| | 2.20 i | | | 14Q | Barcelona, SPA | 11 | Mar |
| | 2.20 | | | 1 | Loughborough | 11 | Jun |
| | 2.20 | | | 9= | London (CP) | 7 | Jul |
| | 2.20 | | | 1 | Enfield | 19 | Aug |
| *2.25* | *Mark Mandy* | | *19.11.72* | *1* | *Gateshead* | *2* | *Jul* |
| 2.24 i | Geoff Parsons | | 14.08.64 | 1 | Birmingham | 4 | Feb |
| | 2.20 | | | 12 | Oslo, NOR | 21 | Jul |
| 50 performances to 2.20 by 4 athletes including 12 indoors | | | | | | | |
| 2.18 i | James Brierley | U20 | 31.07.77 | 1 | Birmingham | 5 | Feb |
| | 2.17 | | | 3 | Nyiregyhaza, HUN | 28 | Jul |
| 2.18 | Andrew Lynch | U23 | 28.06.74 | 1 | Cwmbran | 9 | Jul |
| 2.17 | Alex Kruger | | 18.11.63 | 1D | Gotzis, AUT | 27 | May |
| 2.17 | David Barnetson | | 1.07.71 | 1 | Crawley | 1 | Jul |
| 2.17 | Mike Robbins | U20 | 14.03.76 | 1 | Hull | 5 | Aug |
| 2.16 | Richard Aspden | U20 | 15.10.76 | 1 | Nottingham | 7 | Jul |
| | (10) | | | | | | |
| 2.16 | Rob Brocklebank | U20 | 12.10.76 | 2= | Nottingham | 7 | Jul |
| 2.15 | Stuart Ohrland | U23 | 6.09.75 | 1 | Tessenderlo, BEL | 2 | Jul |
| 2.14 | Colin Bent | | 12.04.70 | 2 | Bedford | 29 | May |
| 2.13 | Damon Rutland | U23 | 10.07.75 | 1 | Bath | 31 | May |
| 2.13 | Ian Holliday | U23 | 9.12.73 | 1 | Gateshead | 22 | Jul |
| 2.13 | Dean Macey | U20 | 12.12.77 | 1D | Stoke | 16 | Sep |
| 2.11 | James Leaver | U23 | 15.09.75 | 1 | Bournemouth | 8 | Apr |
| 2.11 | Ben Challenger | U20 | 7.03.78 | 2 | Bath | 12 | Jul |
| 2.10 i | Gary Jones | | 15.07.72 | 2 | Birmingham | 26 | Feb |
| | 1.97 | | | 1 | Rotherham | 6 | May |
| 2.10 | Hopeton Lindo | | 25.08.70 | 1 | London (He) | 7 | May |
| | (20) | | | | | | |
| 2.10 | Adam Smith | U20 | 20.02.77 | 1 | Antrim | 20 | Jun |
| 2.10 | Richard Laws | U23 | 8.10.75 | 2 | Gateshead | 22 | Jul |
| 2.10 | Ian Massey | U20 | 9.09.76 | 1 | Kirkby | 10 | Sep |
| 2.08 | Paul Burraway | | 30.11.68 | 2 | Corby | 25 | Jun |
| 2.08 | Mark Roach | | 11.04.65 | 1 | Zurich, SWZ | 26 | Aug |
| 2.07 | Andrew Lowe | U20 | 6.03.76 | 1 | Stretford | 1 | Jul |
| 2.07 | David Franks | U20 | 21.04.78 | 7 | Nottingham | 7 | Jul |

179

| 2.07 | Mark Latham | U20 | 13.01.76 | 2 | London (WL) | 30 | Jul |
|------|-------------|-----|----------|---|-------------|----|-----|
| 2.06 | Chris Hindley | U20 | 21.01.76 | 1D | Worcester | 24 | Jun |
| 2.06 | Tom Vanhinsbergh | U17 | 28.12.78 | 1 | Crawley | 28 | Aug |
| (30) | | | | | | | |
| 2.06 | Phil Diamond | U23 | 15.10.74 | 1 | St Saviour, JER | 9 | Sep |
| 2.05 i | Darren Joseph | U20 | 4.04.78 | 2 | Birmingham | 5 | Feb |
| 2.05 | | | | 8 | Bedford | 2 | Jul |
| 2.05 i | Brad Knowles | U20 | 17.11.76 | 4 | Birmingham | 5 | Feb |
| 2.00 | | | | 1 | Dudley | 20 | Aug |
| 2.05 i | Dafydd Edwards | U23 | 19.09.74 | 5 | Birmingham | 26 | Feb |
| 2.05 | Paul Dovell | U20 | 5.05.77 | 2 | Bournemouth | 8 | Apr |
| 2.05 | Anthony Brannen | | 16.09.68 | 1 | Stoke | 6 | May |
| 2.05 | John Wallace | | 9.10.68 | 2 | Bournemouth | 6 | May |
| 2.05 | Fayyaz Ahmed | | 10.04.66 | 3 | London (He) | 7 | May |
| 2.05 | Stuart Smith | U20 | 2.08.76 | 1 | Leamington | 13 | May |
| 2.05 | Henderson Pierre | | 29.10.63 | | London (CP) | 3 | Jun |
| (40) | | | | | | | |
| 2.05 | Stuart Brown | | 27.11.72 | 1 | Newport | 17 | Jun |
| 2.05 | Stanley Osuide | U23 | 30.11.74 | 1 | Horsham | 5 | Jul |
| 2.05 | Andrew Penk | U17 | 19.09.78 | 2 | Utrecht, HOL | 9 | Jul |
| 2.05 | Andrew Weston | U23 | 4.12.73 | 2 | Bracknell | 22 | Jul |
| 2.05 | Ian Gidley | | 13.11.70 | 1 | Cardiff | 19 | Aug |
| 2.05 | Danny Graham | U17 | 3.08.79 | 2 | Cardiff | 19 | Aug |
| 2.04 | Robert Creese | U20 | 1.12.77 | 9 | Nottingham | 7 | Jul |
| 2.03 | Mike Toone | U20 | 25.09.76 | 1 | Crewe | 10 | Jun |
| 2.03 | Richard Dent | U17 | 2.11.78 | 1 | Colwyn Bay | 15 | Jul |
| 2.03 | Greg Dunson | | 2.12.63 | 1 | Bedford | 26 | Aug |
| (50) | | | | | | | |
| 2.02 | Tony Gilhooly | U20 | 26.03.76 | 10 | Bedford | 2 | Jul |
| 2.02 | Duncan Mathieson | | 8.03.69 | 1D | Aberdeen | 15 | Jul |
| 2.01 | Barry Thomas | | 28.04.72 | 2D | Derby | 29 | Apr |
| 2.01 | Jason Allan | | 17.09.72 | 1 | Antrim | 30 | Apr |
| 2.01 | Billy Jewers | | 27.09.62 | 2 | Aldershot | 26 | Jun |
| 2.01 | Trevor McSween | | 27.10.66 | 1 | Aldershot | 26 | Jun |
| 2.01 | Matt Perry | U20 | 15.02.78 | 1 | Cardiff | 1 | Jul |
| 2.01 | Simon Shirley | | 3.08.66 | 7D | Valladolid,SPA | 1 | Jul |
| 2.00 i | Dominic Norriss | | 29.12.71 | 3 | London (Ha) | 21 | Jan |
| 2.00 i | Martin Pate | U20 | 16.03.77 | 2= | Glasgow | 22 | Jan |
| (60) | | | | | | | |
| 2.00 | Elliot Dronfield | | 26.10.72 | 4 | Coventry | 6 | May |
| 2.00 | Marlon Huggins | | 11.02.71 | 4 | London (He) | 7 | May |
| 2.00 | Andrew Skelding | | 8.11.71 | 1 | Worcester | 13 | May |
| 2.00 | Aaron Robb | U20 | 1.11.76 | 1 | Wishaw | 14 | May |
| 2.00 | Edward Willers | U17 | 18.09.79 | 1 | Basildon | 10 | Jun |
| *2.00* | *Olu Robincocker* | *U23* | *27.11.75* | *6* | *Gateshead* | *17* | *Jun* |
| 2.00 | Daniel Slessor | U17 | 5.10.78 | 1 | Wigan | 25 | Jun |
| 2.00 | Clint Nicholls | U17 | 16.02.79 | 1 | Tonbridge | 25 | Jun |
| 2.00 | Darran Baker | | 30.03.67 | 1 | London (Col) | 28 | Jun |
| 2.00 | Andy Hodge | | 18.12.68 | 1 | Oxford | 28 | Jun |
| 2.00 | John Hopper | | 5.12.68 | 6 | Birmingham | 1 | Jul |
| (70) | | | | | | | |
| 2.00 | Martin Lloyd | U17 | 18.06.80 | 1 | Hoo | 1 | Jul |
| 2.00 | Ross McFarland | U17 | 13.10.78 | 4 | Birmingham | 30 | Jul |
| 2.00 | Andrew Palmer | U20 | 13.04.77 | 1 | | 30 | Jul |
| 2.00 | Richard Stevens | U20 | 17.07.76 | 1 | Southend | 30 | Jul |
| 2.00 | Alex Haworth | U20 | 12.04.78 | 4 | Hull | 5 | Aug |
| 2.00 | Andy Grant | | 26.01.72 | 1 | London (TB) | 27 | Aug |
| 2.00 | M. Roncia | | | 2 | Croydon | 3 | Sep |
| 1.98 | Robert Holton | U17 | 8.09.78 | 1 | Coventry | 30 | Apr |
| 1.98 | Matthew Webb | | 72 | 1 | Basingstoke | 6 | May |
| 1.98 | Dinkar Sabnis | U23 | 23.09.73 | 1 | Aberdeen | 4 | Jun |

| | | | | | | | |
|---|---|---|---|---|---|---|---|
| 1.98 | Mike Wright | U20 | 15.09.77 | 1 | York | 10 | Jun |
| 1.98 | Matthew Cordy | U23 | 29.09.75 | 2 | Portsmouth | 10 | Jun |
| 1.98 | Richard Bennett | U17 | 31.03.79 | 1 | Kingston | 26 | Jun |
| 1.98 | Mark Sweeney | U20 | 26.02.77 | 2D | Stoke | 16 | Sep |
| 1.97 | John Portway | U17 | 13.10.78 | 1 | Dartford | 21 | May |
| 1.97 | Gavin Neblett | U17 | 27.12.79 | 1 | London (He) | 10 | Jun |
| 1.97 | Daniel Turner | U17 | 27.11.78 | 1 | Portsmouth | 10 | Jun |
| 1.97 | Andrew Binns | U17 | 12.03.79 | 1 | Lancaster | 29 | Jul |
| 1.97 | Wayne Gray | U15 | 7.11.80 | 1 | Birmingham | 3 | Sep |

**Additional Under 17** (1 - 15 above)

| | | | | | | |
|---|---|---|---|---|---|---|
| 1.95 | James Howlett | 18.02.79 | 1 | Peterborough | 22 | Jul |
| 1.95 | Ian Wilson | 7.10.79 | 1 | Cheltenham | 6 | Aug |
| 1.95 | Neil Lucas | 2.10.78 | 1 | Antrim | 12 | Aug |
| 1.95 | Colin McMaster | 15.01.80 | 1 | Pitreavie | 19 | Aug |
| 1.94 | Alex Stergiou | 27.09.78 | 1 | Cheltenham | 17 | Jun |
| (20) | | | | | | |
| 1.94 | L. Fisher | | 1 | Colchester | 13 | Aug |
| 1.94 | Scott Kenny | 20.02.80 | 1 | Wishaw | 13 | Aug |
| 1.93 i | Peter Goodall | 7.05.79 | 1 | Glasgow | 14 | Jan |
| | 1.90 | | 1 | Ayr | 4 | Jun |
| 1.92 | Tony Kuiper | 25.10.79 | 1 | Kirkby | 10 | Sep |
| *1.91 i* | *Jon Orrelle* | *28.01.79* | *1P* | *London (CP)* | *22* | *Jan* |
| 1.91 | Paul Graham | 8.10.78 | 1 | Peterborough | 21 | May |
| 1.91 | William Phillips | 2.03.79 | 2 | Portsmouth | 10 | Jun |
| 1.91 | Marc Newton | 15.03.80 | 1O | Blackpool | 24 | Jun |
| 1.91 | Andrew Cresswell | 4.04.80 | Q | Birmingham | 30 | Jul |
| 1.90 | Laurent Peacock | 4.02.79 | 1 | Exeter | 21 | May |
| 1.90 | Richard Sear | 21.08.79 | 3 | London (CP) | 27 | May |
| (30) | | | | | | |
| 1.90 | Jason McDade | 3.04.80 | 1 | Great Yarmouth | 18 | Jun |
| 1.90 | R. Blanchard | | 1 | Northampton | 25 | Jun |
| 1.90 | Lee Black | 26.11.78 | 1O | Ipswich | 25 | Jun |
| 1.90 | Stuart Livingstone | 29.08.79 | 5 | Derby | 30 | Jul |
| 1.90 | Ian Murray-Tait | 80 | 1 | Antrim | 9 | Aug |
| 1.90 | James Hilston | 25.02.79 | 3= | Kingston | 13 | Aug |
| 1.90 | Andrew Smith | 10.01.80 | 3= | Kingston | 13 | Aug |
| 1.90 | Paul Martin | 7.09.79 | 1 | Wakefield | 17 | Sep |

**Additional Under 15** (1 above)

| | | | | | | |
|---|---|---|---|---|---|---|
| 1.87 | Neil Dixon | 16.09.80 | 1 | Birmingham | 29 | Jul |
| 1.86 | Gareth Dyball | 16.03.81 | 1 | Barking | 13 | May |
| 1.85 | Ken McKeown | 6.03.82 | 1 | Pitreavie | 9 | Jul |
| 1.82 | Chris Sweeney | 26.05.81 | 1 | Bebington | 21 | May |
| 1.81 | James Wood | 5.02.81 | 2 | Nottingham | 8 | Jul |
| 1.81 | Kevin McKinson | 6.09.80 | 3 | Nottingham | 8 | Jul |
| 1.81 | Ross Edgerton | 13.09.80 | 4 | Nottingham | 8 | Jul |
| 1.81 | Ben Davies | 24.08.81 | 6 | Birmingham | 29 | Jul |
| 1.80 | Andrew Umpleby | 31.10.80 | 1 | Telford | 21 | May |
| (10) | | | | | | |
| 1.80 | A. Brown | | 1 | Kirkby | 4 | Jun |
| 1.80 | Matthew Burden | 3.09.80 | 1 | Bournemouth | 10 | Jun |
| 1.80 | P. Edmonds | | 2 | Hull | 5 | Aug |
| 1.80 | Gareth Moir | 17.12.80 | 1 | St. Ives | 20 | Aug |
| 1.80 | Peter Watson | 30.06.81 | 2P | Stoke | 17 | Sep |
| 1.78 | Carl Wallace | 10.02.81 | 8 | Birmingham | 29 | Jul |
| 1.78 | Kevin Quigley | 28.12.80 | 1 | Wishaw | 13 | Aug |
| 1.76 i | Simon Bannister | 16.04.81 | 1 | Bedford | 4 | Mar |
| 1.76 | Leon McRae | 3.11.80 | 1 | Yate | 8 | May |
| 1.76 | Carl Wilkes | 7.11.80 | 1P | Worcester | 24 | Jun |

**Under 13**

| | | | | | | |
|---|---|---|---|---|---|---|
| 1.66 | Tim Greenwood | | 22.11.82 | | | |
| 1.60 | Richard Piper | | | 2 | Horsham | 9 Jul |
| 1.56 | Matt Paice | | | 1 | Windsor | 20 Aug |
| 1.55 | A. Bowland | | | 3 | London (TB) | 30 Jul |

## POLE VAULT

| | | | | | | |
|---|---|---|---|---|---|---|
| 5.70 | Nick Buckfield | U23 | 5.06.73 | 3 | Sheffield | 23 Jul |
| | 5.60 | | | 2 | La Valette, FRA | 19 Apr |
| | 5.55 | | | 17Q | Gothenburg, SWE | 9 Aug |
| | 5.50 | | | 1 | W -Tiengen, GER | 14 May |
| | 5.50 | | | 1 | Birmingham | 16 Jul |
| | 5.50 | | | 2 | Gateshead | 21 Aug |
| | 5.45 | | | 1 | Edinburgh | 3 Jun |
| | 5.40 | | | 1 | Horsham | 13 May |
| | 5.40 | | | 4 | Bratislava, SVK | 30 May |
| | 5.40 | | | 5 | Nuremberg, GER | 15 Jun |
| | 5.30 | | | 1 | Enfield | 29 Apr |
| | 5.30 | | | 8 | London (CP) | 7 Jul |
| | 5.20 | | | 6 | Villeneuve d'Ascq, FRA | 25 Jun |
| | 5.20 | | | 1 | Crawley | 1 Jul |
| | 5.20 | | | 2 | Gateshead | 2 Jul |
| 5.60 | Neil Winter | U23 | 21.03.74 | 1 | Enfield | 19 Aug |
| | 5.40 | | | 1 | Bedford | 28 May |
| | 5.40 | | | 1= | London (CP) | 3 Jun |
| | 5.40 | | | 1 | Zofingen, SWZ | 5 Jun |
| | 5.40 | | | 1 | Birmingham | 1 Jul |
| | 5.40 | | | 2 | Cwmbran | 9 Jul |
| | 5.40 | | | 3 | Narbonne, FRA | 29 Jul |
| | 5.40 | | | 1 | Cheltenham | 6 Aug |
| | 5.20 | | | 1 | Bath | 31 May |
| | 5.20 | | | 1 | Gateshead | 2 Jul |
| | 5.20 | | | 10 | London (CP) | 7 Jul |
| 5.42 | Mike Barber | U23 | 19.10.73 | 1 | Telford | 26 Aug |
| | 5.35 | | | 1 | Blackburn | 16 Aug |
| | 5.31 | | | 6 | Salgotarjan, HUN | 11 Sep |
| | 5.30 | | | 1 | Stoke | 25 Jun |
| | 5.20 i | | | 2= | Birmingham | 3 Feb |
| | 5.20 i | | | 3 | Glasgow | 11 Feb |
| | 5.20 | | | 5 | Cwmbran | 9 Jul |
| 5.40 i | Paul Williamson | U23 | 16.06.74 | 2 | Vienna, AUT | 18 Feb |
| | 5.40 | | | 1= | London (CP) | 3 Jun |
| | 5.35 | | | 2 | Bedford | 28 May |
| | 5.30 i | | | 6 | Birmingham | 25 Feb |
| | 5.25 | | | 1 | Grimsby | 14 May |
| | 5.20 i | | | 4 | St. Petersburg, RUS | 28 Jan |
| | 5.20 i | | | 1 | Birmingham | 3 Feb |
| | 5.20 | | | 1 | Loughborough | 11 Jun |
| 5.30 i | Kevin Hughes | U23 | 30.04.73 | 7 | Birmingham | 25 Feb |
| | 5.30 | | | 1 | Peterborough | 28 Aug |
| | 5.20 i | | | 2= | Birmingham | 3 Feb |
| | 5.20 | | | 1 | London (Ha) | 25 Jun |
| | 5.20 | | | 4 | Enfield | 19 Aug |
| 5.30 | Dean Mellor | | 25.11.71 | 1 | Gateshead | 17 Jun |
| | 5.21 | | | 7 | Salgotarjan, HUN | 11 Sep |
| | 5.20 | | | 1 | Sheffield | 19 Jul |
| | 5.20 | | | 1 | Wakefield | 12 Aug |
| | 5.20 | | | 4 | Gateshead | 21 Aug |
| 5.30 | Matt Belsham | | 11.10.71 | 3 | Cwmbran | 9 Jul |
| | 5.20 | | | 2 | Gateshead | 17 Jun |

| 5.30 | Ian Tullett | | 15.08.69 | 2 | Enfield | 19 Aug |
|------|-------------|--|----------|---|---------|--------|
| 5.30 | | | | 3 | London (CP) | 27 Aug |
| 5.20 | | | | 6 | Cwmbran | 9 Jul |
| 5.20 | | | | 6= | Sheffield | 23 Jul |
| 5.20 | | | | 2 | Peterborough | 28 Aug |
| 5.20 | Andy Ashurst | | 2.01.65 | 2 | Edinburgh | 3 Jun |
| 5.20 | | | | 6= | Sheffield | 23 Jul |
| 5.20 | | | | 1 | Cardiff | 19 Aug |
| 5.20 | Mike Edwards | | 19.10.68 | 3 | Enfield | 19 Aug |
| | 62 performances to 5.20 by 10 athletes including 8 indoors | | | | | |
| 5.10 | Mark Grant | | 17.05.71 | 2 | Birmingham | 20 May |
| 5.10 | Mark Hodgkinson | | 20.07.72 | 3 | London (CP) | 3 Jun |
| 5.00 | Mark Davis | U20 | 1.03.77 | 1 | Corby | 3 Jun |
| 5.00 | Tim Thomas | U23 | 18.11.73 | 3 | Edinburgh | 3 Jun |
| 5.00 | Bob Kingman | U23 | 21.02.73 | 1 | Cosford | 5 Jul |
| 4.90 i | Anthony Brannen | . | 16.09.68 | 2H | Birmingham | 5 Feb |
| 4.80 | | | | 1D | Derby | 30 Apr |
| 4.90 i | Barry Thomas | | 28.04.72 | 1H | Birmingham | 5 Feb |
| 4.83 | | | | 2 | Alfaz Del Pi, SPA | 13 Apr |
| 4.90 i | Alex Kruger | | 18.11.63 | 5H | Barcelona, SPA | 12 Mar |
| 4.90 | | | | 6=D | Gotzis, AUT | 28 May |
| 4.90 | Egryn Jones | | 1.11.71 | 1 | Cwmbran | 14 Jun |
| 4.85 | Matt Weaver | U23 | 14.11.73 | 2 | London (Ha) | 25 Jun |
| (20) | | | | | | |
| 4.85 | Neil Young | U20 | 20.02.77 | 1 | Antrim | 29 Jul |
| 4.81 | Christian Linskey | U17 | 14.06.80 | 1 | Birmingham | 30 Jul |
| 4.80 i | Duncan Pearce | | 21.10.70 | 6 | Birmingham | 3 Feb |
| 4.70 | | | | 1 | Sheffield | 6 May |
| 4.80 | Warren Siley | U23 | 16.01.73 | 2 | Liverpool | 3 Jun |
| 4.80 | Dominic Shepherd | U20 | 11.12.76 | 6 | Loughborough | 11 Jun |
| 4.80 | Ian Wilding | U23 | 3.03.75 | 2 | Cannock | 9 Sep |
| 4.75 i | Steve Leader | | 24.11.66 | 1 | London (Ha) | 25 Mar |
| 4.70 | | | | 2D | Derby | 30 Apr |
| 4.70 | Glyn Price | | 12.09.65 | 1 | Barry | 14 May |
| 4.70 | Simon Shirley | | 3.08.66 | 4 | London (CP) | 17 Jun |
| 4.70 | Robert Thickpenny | U20 | 17.07.76 | 3 | London (Ha) | 25 Jun |
| (30) | | | | | | |
| *4.70* | *Dylan McDermott* | | *1.12.70* | *1* | *Barn Elms* | *19 Jul* |
| 4.70 | Dave Gordon | | 20.03.68 | 3 | Wrexham | 5 Aug |
| 4.60 i | Gary Jackson | | 28.04.68 | 1 | Gateshead | 19 Jan |
| 4.60 | Warren Jousiffe | U20 | 27.05.77 | 3 | Stoke | 6 May |
| 4.60 | Wayne Weimann | | 2.05.66 | 1 | St. Ives | 14 May |
| 4.60 | Brett Armstrong | U20 | 9.09.76 | 2 | Corby | 3 Jun |
| 4.60 | Stephen Rogers | | 1.09.71 | 1D | Stoke | 4 Jun |
| 4.60 | Ben Flint | U17 | 16.09.78 | 2 | Sheffield (W) | 10 Jun |
| 4.60 | Adam Davis | | 19.11.72 | 1b | Corby | 22 Jun |
| 4.60 | Paul Beswick | | 5.12.68 | 7 | Peterborough | 28 Aug |
| 4.60 | Nick Pritchard | | 5.12.72 | 1 | Swansea | 28 Aug |
| (40) | | | | | | |
| 4.60 | Robin Hill | U20 | 23.02.77 | 2 | Grimsby | 24 Sep |
| 4.60 | Eric Hollingsworth | | 6.12.62 | 1 | Melbourne, AUS | 16 Nov |
| 4.55 | Matthew Evans | U23 | 19.11.75 | 4 | Stoke | 2 Sep |
| 4.50 | Dan Gilby | | 9.07.70 | 2 | Wakefield | 3 Jun |
| 4.50 | Jon Yapp | U23 | 1.02.75 | 5 | Stoke | 25 Jun |
| *4.50* | *Alan Burke* | | *23.05.65* | *3* | *Dublin (M), IRE* | *15 Jul* |
| 4.50 | Paul Hoad | | 29.10.63 | 1 | London (Elt) | 19 Aug |
| 4.45 | Steve Gutteridge | | 5.07.71 | 1 | Southend | 22 Jul |
| 4.45 | Iain Black | | 18.09.70 | 1 | Edinburgh | 6 Aug |
| 4.45 | David McLeod | | 26.03.63 | | Jarrow | 13 Aug |
| 4.45 | Rufus Cooper | U17 | 24.02.79 | 1 | Croydon | 3 Sep |
| (50) | | | | | | |

| | | | | | | | |
|---|---|---|---|---|---|---|---|
| 4.40 i | Gavin Sunshine | U23 | 19.02.74 | 2 | London (Ha) | 14 | Jan |
| 4.40 | | | | 8=D | Vladimir, RUS | 6 | Aug |
| 4.40 i | Neil Turner | U20 | 17.05.77 | 4 | Horsham | 22 | Jan |
| 4.40 | | | | 3= | Enfield | 9 | Apr |
| 4.40 i | Chris Wills | U20 | 18.05.76 | 2 | Birmingham | 5 | Feb |
| 4.30 | | | | 1 | Middlesbrough | 30 | Jul |
| 4.40 i | Jamie Quarry | | 15.11.72 | 3 | Birmingham | 1 | Mar |
| 4.30 | | | | 1D | Stoke | 25 | Jun |
| 4.40 | Matthew Buck | U23 | 5.04.74 | 3= | Enfield | 29 | Apr |
| *4.40* | *Brett Williams* | | | 2 | *Cambridge* | *20 May* | |
| 4.40 | Craig Guite | U20 | 19.08.77 | 1 | Sheffield | 27 | May |
| 4.40 | Kevin Treen | U20 | 1.02.76 | 2 | Telford | 3 | Jun |
| 4.40 | Des Fitzgerald | | 26.11.72 | 1 | Edinburgh | 24 | Jun |
| 4.40 | David O'Neill | U20 | 19.01.76 | 8 | Bedford | 2 | Jul |
| 4.40 | Steve McLennan | U17 | 17.11.78 | 2 | Nottingham | 7 | Jul |
| | (60) | | | | | | |
| 4.40 | Steve Francis | U17 | 31.01.79 | 2 | Utrecht, HOL | 9 | Jul |
| 4.40 | Glyn Slowly | | 19.05.71 | 1 | Exeter | 25 | Jul |
| 4.40 | Terry Fidler | | 13.10.71 | 1D | Enfield | 13 | Aug |
| 4.40 i | Edward Richards | U20 | 19.09.77 | 1 | Birmingham | 30 | Dec |
| 4.20 | | | | 4 | Bath | 31 | May |
| 4.31 | Richard Smith | U15 | 17.01.81 | 3 | Peterborough | 28 | Aug |
| 4.30 | Tim Anstiss | | 17.11.61 | 3 | Hayes | 13 | May |
| 4.30 | Martin Parley | U20 | 26.07.78 | 1 | Yate | 14 | May |
| 4.30 | D. Graham | | | 1 | Ipswich | 3 | Jun |
| 4.30 | Mark Bushell | U20 | 22.10.76 | 1 | Portsmouth | 10 | Jun |
| 4.30 | Andrew Penk | U17 | 19.09.78 | 1 | Bebington | 16 | Jul |
| | (70) | | | | | | |
| 4.30 | Tony Southward | | 31.01.71 | 3D | Kilkenny, IRE | 27 | Aug |
| 4.30 i | Klemmens Pollmeier | | 8.06.66 | 1 | Bath | 3 | Dec |
| 4.20 | | | | 5 | Bath | 31 | May |
| 4.55 unconfirmed | | | | | | | |
| 4.25 | Richard Ramsey | | 6.10.72 | 1 | Antrim | 1 | Jul |
| 4.25 | Jamie Webb | U23 | 18.12.75 | 1 | Sutton | 17 | Sep |
| 4.20 i | Rob Laing | | 30.07.66 | 8 | Wakefield | 21 | Jan |
| 4.20 | | | | 1 | Blackburn | 25 | Jun |
| 4.20 i | Simon Rush | U20 | 23.06.76 | 5 | Horsham | 22 | Jan |
| 4.10 | | | | 4 | London (CP) | 27 | May |
| *4.20 i* | *Nicholas Warchalowski* | | *10.11.71* | *2* | *Glasgow* | *22 Jan* | |
| 4.20 i | Owen Chaplin | U20 | 2.12.77 | 7 | Birmingham | 29 | Jan |
| 4.05 | | | | 4 | Stoke | 17 | Jun |
| 4.20 i | Gavin Showell | | 29.09.72 | 1=H | Birmingham | 4 | Feb |
| 4.20 | | | | 1D | Stoke | 5 | Aug |
| 4.20 i | James Robinson | U20 | 27.08.76 | 1=H | Birmingham | 4 | Feb |
| 4.20 i | Allan Leiper | | 23.07.60 | 3H | Birmingham | 4 | Feb |
| 4.20 | | | | 3 | Edinburgh | 24 | Jun |
| | (80) | | | | | | |
| 4.20 | Lee Walker | U20 | 17.08.77 | 1 | Portsmouth | 1 | Apr |
| 4.20 | Trevor Sloman | | 21.03.68 | 5D | Derby | 30 | Apr |
| 4.20 | Dean Robinson | | 25.06.70 | 1 | Hull | 30 | Apr |
| 4.20 | Geoff Gregory | U23 | 8.06.74 | 5 | Stoke | 6 | May |
| 4.20 | E. Mok | | | 4= | Edinburgh | 7 | May |
| 4.20 | Peter Holt | U20 | 12.02.77 | 2 | Cleckheaton | 10 | Jun |
| 4.20 | Ian Noble | U20 | 2.04.77 | 3 | Cleckheaton | 10 | Jun |
| 4.20 | James Palmer | U20 | 21.04.78 | 1 | Norwich | 10 | Jun |
| 4.20 | Mike Nicholl | | 29.07.61 | 5 | Birmingham | 17 | Jun |
| 4.20 | Gavin Card | U20 | 11.05.78 | 1 | Jarrow | 1 | Jul |
| | (90) | | | | | | |
| 4.20 | Steve Gascoigne | | 20.12.66 | 1 | Watford | 19 | Jul |
| 4.20 | Andy Buchanan | | 12.09.70 | 1 | Walton | 22 | Jul |
| 4.20 | Justin Richards | | 25.01.71 | 1 | Bracknell | 22 | Jul |

| 4.20 | Alan Hardy | | 4.09.58 | 3 | London (WL) | 30 Jul |
| 4.20 | Terry Gyorffy | | 28.01.65 | 1D | Cosford | 1 Aug |
| 4.20 | David Griffiths | U23 | 22.12.74 | 5 | Watford | 19 Aug |
| 4.15 i | Greg Conlon | U23 | 18.12.74 | 1 | London (CP) | 11 Feb |
| 4.10 | | | | 2 | Sheffield | 19 Aug |
| 4.15 i | Chris Bennett | U23 | | | Vancouver, CAN | 19 Jan |
| 4.15 | Neal Davis | U20 | 11.10.77 | 3 | Stoke | 2 Sep |
| 4.10 | Stephen Booth | | 21.10.71 | 2 | Kingston | 9 Apr |
| (100) | | | | | | |
| 4.10 | Tom Richards | U17 | 13.11.78 | 2 | Feltham | 30 Apr |
| 4.10 | John Taylor | | 13.05.57 | 1 | York | 30 Apr |
| 4.10 | Paul Field | | 24.06.67 | 12D | Alhama, SPA | 21 May |
| 4.10 | Paul Jones | U20 | 11.04.78 | | Swansea | 4 Jun |
| 4.10 | Garry Chiles | | 15.05.66 | 9 | London (CP) | 17 Jun |
| 4.10 | Scott Simpson | U17 | 21.07.79 | 4 | Nottingham | 7 Jul |
| 4.10 | Stuart Caudery | | 19.11.66 | 1 | Salisbury | 16 Jul |
| 4.10 | Paul Howard | | 19.10.66 | 1D | Bebington | 23 Jul |
| 4.10 | Ian Holdsworth | U20 | 12.01.78 | 2 | Yeovil | 19 Aug |
| 4.10 | Brett Heath | U23 | 6.01.75 | 1D | Thurrock | 24 Sep |

**Additional Under 17** (1 - 8 above)

| 4.00 i | Stephen Smith | | 13.02.80 | 5= | Birmingham | 19 Feb |
| 4.00 | | | | 3 | London (WF) | 6 May |
| 4.00 | Tom Benn | | 20.04.80 | 1 | London (CP) | 17 Apr |
| (10) | | | | | | |
| 4.00 | Ian Parkinson | | 12.02.79 | 1 | Harrow | 21 May |
| 4.00 | Richard Hulse | | 22.09.78 | 1 | Stockport | 16 Jul |
| 3.91 | Nick Waters | | 1.01.80 | 1 | Enfield | 30 Jun |
| 3.90 | Darren Neport | | 4.09.79 | 2 | Harrow | 9 Jul |
| 3.85 | Phil Prosser | | | 1 | Colwyn Bay | 2 Sep |
| 3.80 | David Ingram | | 19.01.80 | 1 | Woking | 3 Sep |
| 3.70 | Robert Gardner | | 23.12.78 | 3 | London (CP) | 27 May |
| 3.70 | Steven Atkinson | | 24.02.79 | 2 | Birmingham | 2 Sep |
| 3.60 | Ben Johnston | | 8.11.78 | 1 | Kirkby | 4 Jun |
| *3.60* | *Jon Orrelle* | | *28.01.79* | *4D* | *Stoke* | *4 Jun* |
| 3.60 | N. Manning | | | 1 | Oxford | 10 Jun |
| (20) | | | | | | |
| 3.60 | Alex Thomas | | 31.12.79 | 1 | Solihull | 16 Jul |
| 3.60 | Richard Carter | U15 | 3.02.81 | 1 | Yate | 16 Jul |
| 3.60 | Paul Harrison | | 17.11.79 | 1 | Southend | 30 Jul |
| 3.60 | Charles Rule | | 22.05.80 | 1 | Pitreavie | 19 Aug |

**Additional Under 15** (1 - 2 above)

| 3.50 | Martin Densley | | 1.05.81 | 2 | London (He) | 6 Aug |
| 3.50 | Ashley Swain | | 3.10.80 | 3 | London (He) | 6 Aug |
| 3.45 | Paul Miles | | 14.09.80 | 1 | Cannock | 16 Aug |
| 3.40 | Steven Fidler | | 18.10.80 | 1 | Horsham | 14 May |
| 3.40 | David Raw | | 1.02.81 | 1 | Northumberland | 17 Jun |
| 3.35 | Steven Brown | | 20.03.82 | 4 | Nottingham | 7 Jul |
| 3.30 | David Allister | | 22.09.80 | 1 | Bebington | 18 Jul |
| 3.30 | Mark Beharrell | | 10.01.81 | 6 | Birmingham | 29 Jul |
| (10) | | | | | | |
| 3.30 | Aaron Bullock | | 6.02.81 | 7 | Birmingham | 29 Jul |
| 3.20 | Craig Telford | | 6.05.81 | 1 | Carlisle | 10 Sep |
| 3.10 | Mark English | | 2.02.81 | 1 | Bolton | 16 Jul |
| 3.10 | Alex Stewart | | 30.09.80 | 8 | Birmingham | 29 Jul |
| 3.10 | Tom Abdy | | | 1 | Redditch | 28 Aug |
| 3.10 | Andrew Turner | | 19.09.80 | 4 | Barnsley | 3 Sep |

**Under 13**

| 2.25 | Iain Jackson | | 23.03.83 | 1 | Pitreavie | 19 Aug |

# LONG JUMP

| | | | | | | | | | |
|---|---|---|---|---|---|---|---|---|---|
| 7.95 w | 2.2 | Fred Salle | | | 10.09.64 | 3 | Seville, SPA | 3 | Jun |
| 7.90 i | | | | | | 2 | Vienna, AUT | 18 | Feb |
| 7.80 wA 4.1 | | | | | | 5 | Sestriere, ITA | 29 | Jul |
| 7.69 i | | | | | | 17Q | Barcelona, SPA | 10 | Mar |
| 7.66 | 1.1 | | | | | 1 | Birmingham | 15 | Jul |
| 7.62 | | | | | | 1 | London (He) | 7 | May |
| 7.56 | | | | | | 1 | Braunton | 13 | May |
| 7.81 w | 2.9 | Onochie Onuorah | U23 | 16.10.73 | | 2 | Gateshead | 21 | Aug |
| 7.58 | -1.1 | | | | | 3 | Narbonne, FRA | 29 | Jul |
| 7.58 | 1.8 | | | | | 1 | Stoke | 9 | Sep |
| 7.50 | 0.9 | | | | | 4 | Birmingham | 15 | Jul |
| *7.78* | *1.6* | *Jonathon Kron ¶* | *U23* | *16.02.73* | | *1* | *Cork, IRE* | *24* | *Jun* |
| *7.82* | *1.1 disqualified for drugs* | | | | | *5* | *Salamanca, SPA* | *18* | *Jul* |
| 7.77 | -0.8 | Steve Phillips | | | 17.03.72 | 1 | Cwmbran | 9 | Jul |
| 7.76 w | | | | | | 1 | Liverpool | 30 | Jul |
| 7.74 w | 3.0 | | | | | 1 | Birmingham | 17 | Jun |
| 7.61 | | | | | | 1 | Bath | 28 | Aug |
| 7.59 i | | | | | | 1 | Birmingham | 26 | Feb |
| 7.59 | | | | | | 1 | Rugby | 29 | Aug |
| 7.54 | | | | | | 2 | Enfield | 19 | Aug |
| 7.50 | 0.4 | | | | | 1 | Birmingham | 1 | Jul |
| 7.47 w | 3.4 | | | | | 5 | Gateshead | 21 | Aug |
| 7.46 | | | | | | 1 | Loughborough | 21 | Jun |
| 7.69 | | Stewart Faulkner | | | 19.02.69 | 1 | Enfield | 19 | Aug |
| 7.68 | | | | | | 1 | London (TB) | 29 | Jul |
| 7.48 | | | | | | 1 | Milton Keynes | 26 | Jul |
| 7.46 | -0.2 | | | | | 5 | Birmingham | 15 | Jul |
| 7.65 i | | John Munroe | | | 6.01.69 | 2 | Glasgow | 11 | Feb |
| 7.65 i | | | | | | 5 | Vienna, AUT | 18 | Feb |
| 7.64 | 0.5 | | | | | 8 | Villeneuve d'Ascq, FRA | 24 | Jun |
| 7.54 i | | | | | | 2 | Birmingham | 3 | Feb |
| 7.53 | | | | | | 1 | Hayes | 14 | May |
| 7.53 w | 2.6 | | | | | 1 | London (CP) | 3 | Jun |
| 7.51 w | 3.0 | | | | | 1 | Birmingham | 20 | May |
| 7.46 i | | | | | | 1 | London (Ha) | 21 | Jan |
| 7.46 | -0.8 | | | | | 2 | Cwmbran | 9 | Jul |
| *7.63* | | *Thomas Ganda* | | | *9.10.72* | *1* | *Los Angeles, USA* | *9* | *May* |
| 7.62 | 2.0 | Duncan Mathieson | | | 8.03.69 | 1 | London (WL) | 30 | Jul |
| 7.49 w | 2.8 | | | | | 1 | Edinburgh | 23 | Jun |
| 7.46 | 1.6 | | | | | 1D | Aberdeen | 15 | Jul |
| 7.57 | | Enyinna Chukukere | U23 | 31.07.73 | | 2 | Fairfax, USA | 20 | May |
| 7.47 i | | | | | | 3 | Princeton, USA | 3 | Mar |
| 7.55 i | | Barrington Williams | | | 11.09.55 | 1 | Birmingham | 3 | Feb |
| 7.54 i | | | | | | 1 | Birmingham | 28 | Jan |
| 7.50 | -0.8 | | | | | 3 | Birmingham | 15 | Jul |
| 7.48 i | | | | | | 4 | Glasgow | 11 | Feb |
| 7.48 w | 2.3 | | | | | 2 | Birmingham | 20 | May |
| 7.33 | | | V40 | | | 1 | Watford | 27 | Sep |
| 7.51 | | Carl Howard | U23 | 27.01.74 | | 1 | Loughborough | 20 | May |
| 7.51 | 1.7 | | | | | 2 | Stoke | 9 | Sep |
| 7.50 | -0.3 | | | | | 2 | London (CP) | 17 | Jun |
| 7.48 w | 2.6 | | | | | 1 | Enfield | 29 | Apr |
| 7.50 | | Julian Flynn | | | 3.07.72 | 1 | Rugby | 2 | Aug |
| | (10) | | | | | | | | |
| 7.48 w? | | John Shepherd | | | 23.12.61 | 2 | Enfield | 1 | Jul |
| 7.46 w | | | | | | 1 | Croydon | 28 | Aug |
| 7.38 | | | | | | 1 | Harrow | 25 | Jun |
| 7.46 | | Darren Ritchie | U23 | 14.02.75 | | 1 | Wakefield | 3 | Jun |

52 performances to 7.45 by 12 athletes including 11 indoors and 13 wind assisted

186

| Mark | Wind | Name | Cat | DOB | Pos | Venue | Date |
|---|---|---|---|---|---|---|---|
| 7.44 w | | Courtney Charles | | 13.11.68 | 2 | Birmingham | 1 Jul |
| 7.40 | | | | | 2 | Hayes | 14 May |
| 7.43 w | 3.6 | Nathan Morgan | U20 | 30.06.78 | 1 | Telford | 26 Aug |
| 7.28 i | | | | | 3 | Erfurt,GER | 25 Feb |
| 7.28 | 0.9 | | | | 2 | Belfort, FRA | 6 Aug |
| 7.42 | | Gary Jones | | 15.07.72 | 2 | Cork, IRE | 24 Jun |
| 7.41 w | | Garry Slade | | 10.10.68 | 1 | Sheffield | 14 May |
| 7.24 | | | | | 1 | Newport | 17 Jun |
| 7.40 w | 2.5 | Jamie Quarry | | 15.11.72 | 1 | Watford | 19 Aug |
| 6.88 | | | | | 2 | Edinburgh | 8 May |
| 7.35 w | 3.1 | Alex Kruger | | 18.11.63 | 4 | Stoke | 9 Sep |
| 7.30 | 1.0 | | | | 10D | Gotzis, AUT | 27 May |
| 7.34 | 1.0 | Onochie Achike | U23 | 31.01.75 | 1 | Alfaz Del Pi, SPA | 13 Apr |
| 7.34 | 2.0 | Anthony Brannen | | 16.09.68 | 1D | Derby | 29 Apr |
| | (20) | | | | | | |
| 7.33 | 0.5 | Chris Davidson | U23 | 4.12.75 | 7 | Birmingham | 15 Jul |
| 7.31 | 1.4 | Simon Shirley | | 3.08.66 | 6D | Valladolid,SPA | 1 Jul |
| 7.31 w | 3.5 | Paul Field | | 24.06.67 | 5D | Alhama, SPA | 20 May |
| 7.15 | | | | | 1 | Birmingham | 19 Jul |
| 7.30 w | | Nick Walne | U23 | 18.09.75 | 1 | Oxford | 28 Jun |
| 7.28 w | | Glyn Chidlow | | 21.10.71 | 2 | Oxford | 28 Jun |
| 6.90 | | | | | 1 | Oxford | 26 Apr |
| 7.26 i | | John Mackenzie | | 23.08.65 | 1 | London (Ha) | 14 Jan |
| 7.15 w | 3.0 | | | | 5 | Perth, AUS | 18 Nov |
| 7.26 | 1.5 | Mathias Ogbeta | | 19.06.68 | 1 | Gateshead | 17 Jun |
| 7.26 w | | Joe Sweeney | | 17.07.65 | 1 | Bracknell | 13 May |
| 7.08 | -0.1 | | | | 3 | Stoke | 6 May |
| *7.26 w* | | *Akin Oyediran* | | *27.11.59* | *1* | *Crawley* | *25 Jun* |
| *6.97* | | | | | *2* | *Cannock* | *16 Sep* |
| 7.25 | | Mark Bushell | U20 | 22.10.76 | 1 | Isle of Wight | 10 May |
| 7.24 i | | Andy Lewis | | 9.03.68 | 2 | London (Ha) | 14 Jan |
| 7.15 w | 3.8 | | | | 7 | London (CP) | 17 Jun |
| 7.09 | | | | | 17 | Birmingham | 15 Jul |
| | (30) | | | | | | |
| 7.23 w | 2.1 | John Herbert | | 20.04.62 | 4 | London (CP) | 3 Jun |
| 7.19 | 0.8 | | | | * | London (CP) | 3 Jun |
| 7.22 i | | Michael Morgan | | 30.07.66 | 3 | London (Ha) | 14 Jan |
| 7.21 | | Anthony Malcolm | U20 | 15.02.76 | 1 | London (He) | 6 Aug |
| 7.20 | | Gary Munroe | | 12.04.69 | 1 | Cosford | 5 Jul |
| 7.20 w | | Paul Ralph | | 16.12.67 | 2 | Croydon | 28 Aug |
| 7.19 | | | | | 2 | Hoo | 19 Aug |
| 7.17 i | | Nigel Bourne | | 18.04.72 | 4 | Birmingham | 3 Feb |
| 6.98 | | | | | 1 | Perivale | 30 Apr |
| 7.17 | 0.8 | Patrick Teape | | 14.01.70 | 6 | London (CP) | 17 Jun |
| 7.16 | | Alec Leonce | | 19.04.62 | 2 | Loughborough | 21 Jun |
| 7.16 w | 2.3 | Tendai Huntley | U20 | 12.09.76 | 2 | Nottingham | 8 Jul |
| 7.11 | 1.4 | | | | * | Nottingham | 8 Jul |
| 7.15 | 1.4 | Barry Thomas | | 28.04.72 | 12D | Fukuoka, JAP | 1 Sep |
| | (40) | | | | | | |
| 7.15 w | | Gary Smith | | 20.02.71 | 4 | Enfield | 19 Aug |
| 7.10 | | | | | 6 | Birmingham | 1 Jul |
| *7.14* | | *Olu Robincocker* | *U23* | *27.11.75* | *1* | *Cannock* | *16 Sep* |
| 7.13 i | | Paul Johnson | | 8.03.68 | 1 | Wakefield | 21 Jan |
| 7.13 | | | | | 1 | Sheffield | 14 Jun |
| 7.13 | | Dave Deacon | | 19.03.65 | 2 | Birmingham | 19 Jul |
| 7.13 | | Manny Nsudoh | | 8.04.72 | 1 | Sutton | 19 Aug |
| 7.13 w | 3.0 | Jan Irving | U20 | 4.03.77 | 1 | Bebington | 10 Jun |
| 6.99 | 0.7 | | | | 6 | Bedford | 2 Jul |
| 7.12 | | Ian Simpson | | 3.08.66 | 4 | Hoo | 19 Aug |
| 7.11 | | Kenny Thompson | | 28.02.71 | 5 | Birmingham | 1 Jul |

| Mark | Wind | Name | Cat | DOB | Pos | Venue | Date |
|---|---|---|---|---|---|---|---|
| 7.11 w | 3.1 | David Clerihew | U20 | 11.09.77 | 1 | Pitreavie | 8 Jul |
| 7.06 | 0.3 | | | | * | Pitreavie | 8 Jul |
| 7.11 w | | Tony Mason | U20 | 8.03.76 | 5 | Enfield | 19 Aug |
| 7.09 | | | | | 2 | Bedford | 26 Aug |
| 7.10 | | Ian Roberts | | 15.06.68 | | London (PH) | 5 Jul |
| (50) | | | | | | | |
| 7.08 i | | Anthony Wood | U23 | 30.03.74 | 5 | Birmingham | 3 Feb |
| 7.07 w | | | | | 4 | Enfield | 1 Jul |
| 6.82 | | | | | 4 | Bracknell | 3 Jun |
| 7.07 | -0.8 | Gareth Davies | | 11.05.71 | 5 | Cwmbran | 9 Jul |
| 7.07 | | Trevor Sinclair | | 6.08.61 | 3 | Bedford | 26 Aug |
| 7.07 w | | Femi Akinsanya | | 29.11.69 | 2 | Wakefield | 3 Jun |
| 7.00 | -0.2 | | | | 2 | Peterborough | 6 May |
| 7.07 w | 2.7 | Willie Stark | U20 | 11.03.77 | 2 | Pitreavie | 8 Jul |
| 7.06 | 1.0 | | | | 2 | Ayr | 18 Jul |
| 7.06 | 1.8 | Par Esegbona | | 16.04.68 | 4D | Derby | 29 Apr |
| 7.06 | | Steve Ingram | | 22.09.70 | 1 | Liverpool | 6 May |
| 7.06 w | | Matthew Randall | | 28.04.70 | 3 | Enfield | 29 Apr |
| 6.96 | -0.9 | | | | 4 | Tessenderlo, BEL | 2 Jul |
| 7.04 | | Dan Dugard | | 21.06.65 | 2 | Aldershot | 23 Jul |
| 7.04 w | | Gavin Sunshine | U23 | 19.02.74 | 6 | Enfield | 19 Aug |
| (60) | | | | | | | |
| 7.03 | | Steve Smith | U23 | 29.03.73 | 2 | Edinburgh | 3 Jun |
| 7.03 | | Andrew Roberts | U20 | 19.09.77 | 1 | Wakefield | 12 Aug |
| 7.02 w | 2.1 | Greg Richards | | 25.04.56 | 8 | London (CP) | 17 Jun |
| 6.96 | 1.5 | | | | * | London (CP) | 17 Jun |
| 7.01 | | Charles Madeira-Cole | U20 | 29.11.77 | 1 | Swansea | 28 Aug |
| 7.00 | | Stefan Rose | U23 | 7.04.75 | 1 | Salisbury | 9 Jul |
| 7.00 | | Leo Barker | U17 | 26.12.78 | 1 | Norwich | 30 Jul |
| 7.00 w | 4.7 | Nick Hubbard | U20 | 17.04.76 | 4 | Nottingham | 8 Jul |
| 6.93 | 1.5 | | | | * | Nottingham | 8 Jul |
| 6.99 i | | Chris Cotter | | 3.02.72 | 1 | London (CP) | 14 Jan |
| 6.93 | | | | | 1 | London (PH) | |
| 6.99 | | Lee Edwards | U23 | 14.09.75 | 1 | Barry | 13 May |
| 6.99 | | Kevin Rockhead | U20 | 23.04.77 | 2 | London (He) | 5 Aug |
| (70) | | | | | | | |
| 6.99 w | 5.1 | Stuart Finnie | U17 | 14.12.78 | 1 | Colwyn Bay | 15 Jul |
| 6.85 | | | | | 1 | Antrim | 26 Aug |
| 6.98 | | Jason Wing | | 12.10.65 | 1 | Corby | 25 Jun |
| 6.98 | | Gareth James | U20 | 16.08.77 | 4 | Ayr | 18 Jul |
| 6.98 w | 2.3 | Dinkar Sabnis | U23 | 23.09.73 | 5 | Edinburgh | 24 Jun |
| 6.95 | | | | | 2 | Aberdeen | 21 May |
| 6.97 | | Mark Lawrence | | 26.01.71 | 3 | Wakefield | 3 Jun |
| 6.97 | | Francis Adams | | 19.10.69 | 1 | London (WL) | 13 Aug |
| 6.96 | | Dave Sanderson | | 6.05.71 | 1 | Liverpool | 6 May |
| 6.96 w | | Jeremy Booth | | 26.05.71 | 3 | Croydon | 28 Aug |
| 6.95 | | | | | 2 | Sutton | 19 Aug |
| 6.95 | 0.4 | Tosi Fasinro | | 28.03.72 | 8 | Alicante, SPA | 13 Apr |
| 6.95 | | Stephen Rowbotham | | 6.03.68 | 3 | Cannock | 16 Sep |
| (80) | | | | | | | |
| 6.94 | 0.0 | Donald Campbell | U20 | 13.02.78 | 1 | Basildon | 10 Jun |
| 6.94 | | Alvin Walker | | 30.04.65 | 1 | Bolton | 16 Sep |
| 6.93 | | Dave Reeve | U23 | 25.05.73 | 1 | Loughborough | 26 Apr |
| 6.92 | 1.4 | Stuart Richmond | | 11.04.69 | 7 | Bedford | 29 May |
| 6.92 | | Essop Merrick | U23 | 24.05.74 | 5 | Wakefield | 3 Jun |
| 6.92 | | Gareth Brown | U23 | 2.09.73 | 1 | Cheltenham | 26 Jul |
| 6.92 | | Robin Hynes | U20 | 22.04.77 | 2 | Bebington | 30 Jul |
| 6.92 | | Ross McFarland | U17 | 13.10.78 | 1 | Antrim | 12 Aug |
| 6.91 i | | Gareth Devlin | U20 | 2.06.76 | 4 | Birmingham | 18 Feb |
| 6.85 | | | | | 1 | Antrim | 24 Jul |
| 6.90 i | | Jon Jones | U23 | 14.09.74 | 3 | Birmingham | 1 Mar |

| Mark | Wind | Name | Cat | DOB | Pos | Venue | Date |
|---|---|---|---|---|---|---|---|
| 6.90 | | Morris Philipson | U23 | 26.02.73 | 1 | Wakefield | 30 Apr |
| 6.90 | | Matthew Birchall | | 11.01.71 | 1 | Lancaster | 3 Jun |
| 6.90 | | Billy Jewers | | 27.09.62 | 2 | Basingstoke | 22 Jul |
| 6.90 | | Mark Findlay | U20 | 20.03.78 | 1 | Birmingham | 27 Aug |
| 6.90 w | 2.2 | Ererton Harrison | | 8.04.66 | 6 | Stoke | 9 Sep |
| 6.89 w | 2.1 | Steve Gordon | | 9.04.67 | 1 | Stoke | 10 Sep |
| 6.81 | 0.4 | | | | * | Stoke | 10 Sep |
| 6.88 | | Michael Collins | U17 | 12.11.78 | 2 | Lancaster | 3 Jun |
| 6.88 | | Paul White | U20 | 17.11.76 | 1 | London (He) | 10 Jun |
| 6.85 | | Eshref Hassan | U17 | 7.12.79 | 4 | Croydon | 13 May |
| 6.85 | -0.9 | Michael Bull | | 6.06.70 | 2 | Enfield | 30 Jul |
| (100) | | | | | | | |
| 6.85 | -0.1 | Mike Edwards | | 19.10.68 | 3 | Enfield | 30 Jul |

**Additional Under 20** (1 - 23 above)

| Mark | Wind | Name | Cat | DOB | Pos | Venue | Date |
|---|---|---|---|---|---|---|---|
| 6.85 | 1.5 | Dean Macey | | 12.12.77 | 1D | Stoke | 16 Sep |
| 6.83 w | | Alistair Gudgeon | U17 | 26.10.79 | 2 | Colwyn Bay | 15 Jul |
| 6.63 | -2.5 | | | | 2 | Nottingham | 8 Jul |
| 6.83 w | 2.4 | Geoffrey Ojok | U17 | 19.05.79 | 1 | Birmingham | 29 Jul |
| 6.75 w | | | | | 4 | Colwyn Bay | 15 Jul |
| 6.74 | | | | | 1 | Croydon | 10 Jun |
| 6.80 w | 3.3 | Neil Brown | | 6.04.78 | 1 | Birmingham | 17 Jun |
| 6.80 w | 3.3 | Andrew Thornton | | 29.11.77 | 6 | Nottingham | 8 Jul |
| 6.75 | 1.1 | | | | 8 | Bedford | 2 Jul |

**Additional Under 17** (1 - 7 above)

| Mark | Wind | Name | Cat | DOB | Pos | Venue | Date |
|---|---|---|---|---|---|---|---|
| 6.79 w | | Andrew Wooding | | 2.06.79 | 3 | Colwyn Bay | 15 Jul |
| 6.72 | | | | | 1 | Colwyn Bay | 10 Jun |
| 6.77 | | Nick Dowsett | | 24.11.78 | 1 | Barking | 14 May |
| 6.76 | 1.3 | Dave Butler | | 9.12.78 | 2 | Birmingham | 29 Jul |
| (10) | | | | | | | |
| 6.74 | | Kevin Hibbins | U15 | 7.11.80 | 1 | Derby | 17 Jun |
| 6.69 | | Stuart Wells | | 26.07.79 | 2 | Barking | 14 May |
| 6.67 | 1.2 | Darren Hatton | | 21.03.79 | 4 | Birmingham | 29 Jul |
| 6.63 | | Leroy Knowles | | 26.09.78 | 2 | Kings Lynn | 15 Jul |
| 6.62 w | 2.5 | Jonathan Wallace | | 1.01.79 | 1 | Birmingham | 3 Sep |
| 6.61 | | Johnathan Foley | | 24.10.78 | 1 | Cheltenham | 17 Jun |
| 6.61 | | Kevin Eaves | | 16.03.79 | 3 | Kingston | 4 Jul |
| 6.61 w | 4.3 | Kirk King | U15 | 18.09.80 | 1 | Nottingham | 7 Jul |
| 6.35 | | | | | 1 | Kingston | 17 Jun |
| 6.58 | | Nicholas Francis | | 26.11.78 | 4 | Kingston | 4 Jul |
| 6.57 | | Mark Tappenden | | | 1 | Harrow | 28 Aug |
| (20) | | | | | | | |
| 6.57 | | Kristian Mason | | 17.09.78 | 1 | Wakefield | 17 Sep |
| 6.56 | | Nicholas Myers | | 25.03.80 | 1 | Birmingham | 10 Jun |
| 6.56 | | Marc Newton | | 15.03.80 | 1 | Stoke | 17 Jun |
| 6.55 | | James Morris | | 2.12.79 | 2 | Cardiff | 27 May |
| 6.53 | | Ronnie Ingram | | 27.11.78 | 2 | Stoke | 17 Jun |
| 6.50 i | | Jon Orrelle | | 28.01.79 | 1P | London (CP) | 22 Jan |
| 6.50 | | Thomas Begen | | 14.04.79 | 1 | Glasgow | 13 Jun |
| 6.50 w | 5.0 | Wayne Hay | U15 | 25.09.80 | 2 | Nottingham | 7 Jul |
| 6.30 | | | | | 1 | Oxford | 4 Jun |
| 6.49 | | Rasheed Banda | | 18.03.80 | 1 | Horsham | 13 May |
| 6.48 | 1.5 | John-Paul Blake | | 2.08.79 | 3 | London (CP) | 28 May |
| 6.44 w | | Andrew Squire | | 30.09.79 | 2 | Stoke | 10 Jun |
| (30) | | | | | | | |
| 6.42 w | | Dean Rees | | | 2 | Cardiff | 1 Jul |

**Additional Under 15** (1 - 3 above)

| Mark | Wind | Name | Cat | DOB | Pos | Venue | Date |
|---|---|---|---|---|---|---|---|
| 6.34 w | 5.0 | Paul Wheatcroft | | 22.11.80 | 3 | Nottingham | 7 Jul |
| 6.10 | | | | | 1 | Stretford | 10 Jun |

| 6.33 | | Robert Worrall | 11.01.81 | 1 | Oldham | 9 | Jul |
|------|-----|----------------|----------|----|---------------|----|-----|
| 6.30 w | 4.5 | Benjamin Medder | 31.10.80 | 4 | Nottingham | 7 | Jul |
| 6.25 i | | Peter Watson | 30.06.81 | 1P | Glasgow | 10 | Dec |
| 6.00 | | | | 1 | High Wycombe | 13 | May |
| 6.24 w | 5.6 | Richard Gawthorpe | 28.01.81 | 5 | Nottingham | 7 | Jul |
| 6.03 | | | | 1 | Derby | 10 | Jun |
| 6.18 w | 4.0 | Peter McLean | 5.10.80 | 6 | Nottingham | 7 | Jul |
| 6.10 | | Brian Morrison | 3.09.80 | 1 | Birmingham | 3 | Sep |
| 5.97 w | | D. Simmons | | 1 | Stoke | 10 | Jun |
| | (10) | | | | | | |
| 5.95 | | Tony Seston | 21.12.80 | 1 | Ipswich | 14 | May |
| 5.90 | | Simon Lanyon | 8.01.81 | 1 | Cheltenham | 17 | Jun |
| 5.90 w | | Steven Smith | 4.12.80 | 1 | Pitreavie | 9 | Jul |
| 5.89 | | Adam Gilbert | 24.02.81 | 1 | Mansfield | 14 | May |
| 5.84 | 1.4 | Ezekiel May | 20.03.81 | Q | Nottingham | 7 | Jul |
| 5.81 w | 5.4 | S. Kenny | 21.12.80 | 10 | Nottingham | 7 | Jul |
| 5.80 | | Neil Dixon | 16.09.80 | 1 | Middlesbrough | 13 | May |
| 5.80 w | | Gareth Gittins | | 1 | Cardiff | 1 | Jul |

**Under 13**

| 5.55 | | D. Munn | | 1 | Horsham | 16 | Jul |
|------|-----|----------------|----------|----|---------------|----|-----|
| 5.37 | | Nathan Douglas | 19.06.83 | 1 | Daventry | 12 | Aug |
| 5.23 | | R. Tinker | | 1 | London (Elt) | 16 | Jul |
| 5.21 | | Chris Hackett | 1.03.83 | 2 | Daventry | 12 | Aug |
| 5.16 | | Matt Paice | | 1 | Watford | 4 | Jun |

# TRIPLE JUMP

| 18.43 w | 2.4 | Jonathan Edwards | 10.05.66 | 1 | Villeneuve d'Ascq, FRA | 25 | Jun |
|---------|-----|------------------|----------|----|------------------------|----|-----|

17.90w(2.5) - 18.43 - 17.72 - 18.39w(3.7) - p - p

| 18.29 | 1.3 | | | 1 | Gothenburg, SWE | 7 | Aug |

18.16(1.3)WR - 18.29WR - p - p - 17.49(0.8) - p

| 18.08 w | 2.5 | | | 1 | Sheffield | 23 | Jul |

17.81w(2.1) - x - p - 17.45(1.0) - p - 18.08w

| 18.03 w | 2.9 | | | 1 | Gateshead | 2 | Jul |

14.21 - 17.60(0.5) - 18.03w - 17.72(1.1)=NR - p - 17.74

| 18.00 | 1.3 | | | 1 | London (CP) | 27 | Aug |

17.42 - 17.42 - p - x - p - 18.00

| 17.98 | 1.8 | | | 1 | Salamanca, SPA | 18 | Jul |

17.39(1.9) - 17.98WR - p -13.43w(2.2) - p - p

| 17.74 | 1.7 | | | * | Gateshead | 2 | Jul |
| 17.72 | 0.5 | | | * | Villeneuve d'Ascq, FRA | 25 | Jun |
| 17.69 | 0.5 | | | 1 | London (CP) | 7 | Jul |

17.18 - 17.69 - 17.28 - p - p - p

| 17.60 | 0.3 | | | 1 | Brussels, BEL | 25 | Aug |

17.02 - 17.31 - 17.60 - p - p - p

| 17.58 | 1.2 | | | 1 | Loughborough | 11 | Jun |

17.01 - x - 17.58 - p - p

| 17.58wA | 3.3 | | | 1 | Sestriere, ITA | 29 | Jul |

15.97w - 13.45w - 17.41w - 15.12w - 17.58w - 14.67w

| 17.49 | 0.4 | | | 1 | Gateshead | 21 | Aug |

x - 17.49 - p - x - p - x

| 17.46 | -0.3 | | | 1 | Villeneuve d'Ascq, FRA | 17 | Jun |

16.90 - 17.46 - 17.22 - x - p - p

| 17.46 | 1.4 | | | Q | Gothenburg, SWE | 5 | Aug |

17.46 - p - p

| 17.45 | 1.0 | | | * | Sheffield | 23 | Jul |
| 17.35 | 0.8 | | | 1 | Berlin, GER | 1 | Sep |

16.89 - 17.34 - 17.35 - p - p - p

| 17.29 | 1.6 | | | 1 | Rieti, ITA | 5 | Sep |

16.86 - x - 17.29 - x - p - 17.12

| Mark | Wind | Name | Cat | DOB | Pos | Venue | Date | |
|---|---|---|---|---|---|---|---|---|
| 17.29 wA | 4.8 | Francis Agyepong | | 16.06.65 | 3 | Sestriere, ITA | 29 | Jul |
| 17.24 w | 4.1 | | | | 2 | Gateshead | 2 | Jul |
| 17.18 | 0.5 | | | | 3 | London (CP) | 7 | Jul |
| 17.13 | -1.0 | | | | 1 | Birmingham | 16 | Jul |
| 17.05 | -0.1 | | | | 2 | Gateshead | 21 | Aug |
| 16.75 | | | | | 1 | Enfield | 19 | Aug |
| 16.74 i | | | | | 7 | Barcelona, SPA | 12 | Mar |
| 16.67 | 1.1 | | | | 5 | London (CP) | 27 | Aug |
| 16.58 | 0.9 | | | | 14Q | Gothenburg, SWE | 5 | Aug |
| 16.51 | 1.4 | | | | 6 | Rieti, ITA | 5 | Sep |
| 16.49 i | | | | | Q | Barcelona, SPA | 10 | Mar |
| 16.46 i | | | | | 1 | Vienna, AUT | 18 | Feb |
| 16.44 | 0.0 | | | | 3 | Warsaw, POL | 16 | Jun |
| 16.37 | 1.7 | | | | * | Gateshead | 2 | Jul |
| 16.31 i | | | | | 8 | Birmingham | 25 | Feb |
| 16.29 i | | | | | 2 | Stuttgart, GER | 5 | Feb |
| 16.26 i | | | | | 4 | Berlin, GER | 10 | Feb |
| 16.25 | 1.0 | | | | 7 | Berlin, GER | 1 | Sep |
| 16.21 | 1.9 | | | | 1 | London (CP) | 3 | Jun |
| 16.18 | 0.8 | | | | 2 | Loughborough | 11 | Jun |
| 16.15 i | | | | | 3 | Birmingham | 28 | Jan |
| 16.13 i | | | | | 1 | Glasgow | 22 | Jan |
| 16.56 | 0.3 | Tosi Fasinro | | 28.03.72 | 5 | Fukuoka, JAP | 30 | Aug |
| 16.31 | 0.4 | | | | Q | Fukuoka, JAP | 29 | Aug |
| 16.20 w | 4.9 | | | | 8 | Gateshead | 2 | Jul |
| 16.08 | | | | | 2 | Edinburgh | 6 | May |
| 16.08 | 1.7 | | | | 3 | Birmingham | 11 | Jun |
| 16.50 i | | John Herbert | | 20.04.62 | 1 | Glasgow | 11 | Feb |
| 16.48 i | | | | | 1 | Birmingham | 4 | Feb |
| 16.28 i | | | | | 1 | London (Ha) | 21 | Jan |
| 16.00 w | | | | | 2 | Enfield | 19 | Aug |
| 16.32 | 0.3 | Tayo Erogbogbo | U23 | 8.03.75 | 4 | Gateshead | 21 | Aug |
| 16.31 | -0.9 | | | | 1 | Narbonne, FRA | 29 | Jul |
| 16.22 | | | | | 1 | Edinburgh | 6 | May |
| 16.18 i | | Julian Golley | | 12.09.71 | 3 | Glasgow | 11 | Feb |
| 16.06 | 1.4 | | | | Q | Fukuoka, JAP | 29 | Aug |
| 16.07 i | | John Mackenzie | | 23.08.65 | 2 | Birmingham | 4 | Feb |
| 16.05 w | | | | | 1 | Perth, AUS | 2 | Dec |
| 15.77 | | | | | 1 | Perth, AUS | 11 | Nov |
| 16.03 | 1.3 | Femi Akinsanya | | 29.11.69 | 1 | London (CP) | 18 | Jun |
| 16.00 | 1.5 | | | | 1 | Peterborough | 6 | May |

58 performances to 16.00 by 8 athletes including 13 indoors and 9 wind assisted

| Mark | Wind | Name | Cat | DOB | Pos | Venue | Date | |
|---|---|---|---|---|---|---|---|---|
| 15.97 | | Carl Howard | U23 | 27.01.74 | 2 | Edinburgh | 6 | May |
| 15.95 w | 2.7 | Joe Sweeney | | 17.07.65 | 2 | London (CP) | 18 | Jun |
| 15.60 | 0.6 | | | | * | London (CP) | 18 | Jun |
| | (10) | | | | | | | |
| 15.94 w | 2.3 | Onochie Achike | U23 | 31.01.75 | 5 | Loughborough | 11 | Jun |
| 15.91 | 0.7 | | | | * | Loughborough | 11 | Jun |
| 15.72 w | | Paul Ralph | | 16.12.67 | 1 | Croydon | 28 | Aug |
| 15.67 | | | | | 1 | Aldershot | 23 | Jul |
| 15.68 w | 2.2 | Rez Cameron | | 18.05.60 | 1 | Enfield | 29 | Apr |
| 15.55 | 1.0 | | | | * | Enfield | 29 | Apr |
| 15.66 | 1.1 | Mathias Ogbeta | | 19.06.68 | 1 | Gateshead | 17 | Jun |
| *15.57 w* | | *Akin Oyediran* | | *27.11.59* | *1* | *Crawley* | *25* | *Jun* |
| *14.80* | | | | | *2* | *Cannock* | *16* | *Sep* |
| 15.37 | 0.4 | Matthew Randall | | 28.04.70 | 1 | Tessenderlo, BEL | 2 | Jul |
| 15.36 i | | Ezra Clarke | U23 | 9.12.74 | 3 | Glasgow | 22 | Jan |
| 15.36 | | Keith Ible | | 9.11.68 | 1 | Derby | 30 | Jul |
| 15.29 | | Michael McDonald | | 24.08.65 | 1 | Bournemouth | 6 | May |
| 15.23 | 1.7 | Marvin Bramble | U20 | 10.06.77 | 1 | Bedford | 1 | Jul |

191

| Mark | Wind | Name | Cat | DOB | Pos | Venue | Date |
|---|---|---|---|---|---|---|---|
| 15.19 w | 2.1 | Dave Sanderson | | 6.05.71 | 2 | Birmingham | 20 May |
| 15.11 | | | | | 3 | Derby | 30 Jul |
| (20) | | | | | | | |
| 15.15 | | Delroy Hulme | | 14.09.72 | 1 | Enfield | 1 Jul |
| 15.11 | 1.3 | James Leaver | U23 | 15.09.75 | 1 | Nottingham | 8 Jul |
| 15.09 | | Paul Weston | | 6.10.67 | 2 | Bournemouth | 6 May |
| 15.06 w | 2.4 | Michael Brown | | 6.05.62 | 5 | London (CP) | 18 Jun |
| 14.83 | 1.8 | | | | * | London (CP) | 18 Jun |
| 15.05 | | Joe Allison | | 16.09.59 | 4 | Derby | 30 Jul |
| 15.04 | | Dave Reeve | U23 | 25.05.73 | 1 | Cambridge | 20 May |
| 15.04 | 1.6 | James Peacock | U20 | 29.09.77 | 1 | London (He) | 9 Sep |
| 15.03 | | Jon Hilton | U23 | 11.01.74 | 1 | Cardiff | 19 Aug |
| 15.01 | 1.8 | Denis Costello | | 3.12.61 | 2 | Stoke | 9 Sep |
| 14.99 w | | Dwayne Heard | | 2.02.64 | 1 | Oxford | 28 Jun |
| 14.28 | | | | | 4 | Aldershot | 23 Jul |
| (30) | | | | | | | |
| 14.96 | | Alvin Walker | | 30.04.65 | 2 | Aldershot | 23 Jul |
| 14.95 | | Ruddy Farquharson | | 26.03.61 | 1 | Cosford | 5 Jul |
| 14.95 | | Steve Phillips | | 17.03.72 | 1 | Liverpool | 30 Jul |
| *14.94* | | *Olu Robincocker* | *U23* | *27.11.75* | *1* | *Rotherham* | *6 May* |
| 14.87 | | Richard Edwards | | 4.06.67 | 1 | Birmingham | 19 Jul |
| 14.86 | 0.3 | Stuart Richmond | | 11.04.69 | 2 | Hoo | 19 Aug |
| 14.82 | 1.6 | Adam Smith | U20 | 20.02.77 | 2 | Bedford | 1 Jul |
| 14.76 | | Martin Rossiter | | 4.09.69 | 2 | Thurrock | 19 Aug |
| 14.76 | 1.8 | Jonathan Wallace | U17 | 1.01.79 | 1 | Birmingham | 3 Sep |
| 14.74 w | 2.6 | Neil McMenemy | | 6.04.67 | 1 | Edinburgh | 24 Jun |
| 14.58 | | | | | 4 | London (He) | 7 May |
| 14.68 | | Chris Cotter | | 3.02.72 | 1 | London (He) | 5 Aug |
| (40) | | | | | | | |
| 14.64 | | Kori Stennett | U20 | 2.09.76 | 2 | London (He) | 9 Sep |
| 14.60 | | Charles Madeira-Cole | U20 | 29.11.77 | 1 | Ayr | 18 Jul |
| 14.60 | | Paul Gilding | U23 | 2.01.75 | 2 | London (CP) | 10 Sep |
| 14.58 | | Junior Lewis | | 19.03.66 | 1 | Bedford | 26 Aug |
| 14.55 | | Delroy Ricketts | U23 | 17.07.74 | 3 | Stoke | 6 May |
| 14.55 | | Willie Stark | U20 | 11.03.77 | 1 | Glasgow | 11 Jun |
| 14.51 w | 4.4 | Mike McKernan | U17 | 28.11.78 | 2 | Nottingham | 7 Jul |
| 14.27 i | | | | | 1 | Birmingham | 7 Feb |
| 13.99 | | | | | 2 | Colwyn Bay | 15 Jul |
| 14.46 | | Sam Bobb | U23 | 29.08.75 | 3 | London (CP) | 10 Sep |
| 14.45 | | Wyn Morris | | 25.02.61 | 1 | Brighton | 19 Aug |
| 14.41 | | Gareth Davies | | 11.05.71 | 2 | Edinburgh | 3 Jun |
| (50) | | | | | | | |
| 14.40 | | Dave McCalla | | | 5 | Derby | 30 Jul |
| 14.32 | | Elphinston Hinds | | 15.07.60 | 1 | London (WF) | 22 Jul |
| 14.30 | | Mel Fowler | | 7.07.66 | 1 | Coatbridge | 23 Apr |
| 14.28 | | Henderson Pierre | | 29.10.63 | 2 | Liverpool | 30 Jul |
| 14.28 | | Julian Flynn | | 3.07.72 | 1 | Mansfield | 19 Aug |
| 14.27 | 1.4 | Ben Hodson | U20 | 25.01.76 | 7 | Loughborough | 11 Jun |
| 14.23 | | Eugene Hechevarria | | 30.12.63 | 1 | Northampton | 19 Aug |
| 14.21 w | 5.3 | Stuart McMillan | | 14.05.67 | 2 | Edinburgh | 24 Jun |
| 14.17 | | | | | 2 | Edinburgh | 6 Aug |
| 14.20 w | 3.3 | Colin McDonald | | 12.04.71 | 2 | Edinburgh | 1 Jul |
| 14.19 w | | Albert Earle | | 10.01.58 | 2 | Birmingham | 18 Jun |
| 14.15 | | | | | 2 | Nottingham | 25 Jun |
| (60) | | | | | | | |
| 14.18 i | | Mike Swift | | 27.08.72 | 1 | Sheffield | 22 Jan |
| 13.94 | | | | | 1 | Kirkby | 3 Jun |
| 14.18 | | Ray Smith | | 24.12.67 | 2 | Watford | 19 Aug |
| 14.16 i | | John Wiggins | | 1.07.71 | 4 | Birmingham | 26 Feb |
| 14.13 | | | | | 4 | Edinburgh | 24 Jun |
| 14.15 i | | Abu Garba | U20 | 6.05.76 | 1 | London (CP) | 11 Feb |

| | | | | | | | |
|---|---|---|---|---|---|---|---|
| 14.13 | | Simon Gee | U23 | 23.04.75 | 1 | Liverpool | 6 May |
| 14.13 | | Jeremy Booth | | 26.05.71 | 1 | Sutton | 19 Aug |
| 14.13 w | 2.1 | Rodger Harkins | | 7.06.60 | 3 | Edinburgh | 24 Jun |
| 14.10 | | Chris Wright | | | 1 | Bracknell | 30 Apr |
| 14.10 w | 3.8 | Leke Ilo | U20 | 25.06.78 | 4 | Nottingham | 8 Jul |
| 13.70 | 0.0 | | | | 1 | Kingston | 10 Jun |
| 14.05 | | Dinkar Sabnis | U23 | 23.09.73 | 2 | Aberdeen | 4 Jun |
| | (70) | | | | | | |
| 14.04 | | Daniel Davies | U20 | 2.02.76 | 1 | Cardiff | 27 May |
| 14.03 | 0.9 | Arif Shah | U17 | 29.11.78 | 3 | Nottingham | 7 Jul |
| 14.01 w | 2.5 | Ian Rowe | U17 | 28.09.78 | 2 | Birmingham | 29 Jul |
| 13.86 | | | | | 1 | Kingston | 13 Aug |
| 13.99 | | Mark Lawrence | | 26.01.71 | 3 | Hoo | 19 Aug |
| 13.96 | | Alan Ellis | | | 1 | Middlesbrough | 13 May |
| 13.95 w | 3.2 | Richard McDonald | U17 | 11.01.80 | 3 | Birmingham | 29 Jul |
| 13.60 | -1.3 | | | | 1 | Glasgow | 6 Aug |
| 13.94 w | 2.5 | Adrian Browne | U20 | 14.07.78 | 5 | Nottingham | 8 Jul |
| 13.58 | 1.1 | | | | * | Nottingham | 8 Jul |
| 13.91 | | Junior Campbell | | 13.02.70 | 12 | Enfield | 19 Aug |
| 13.90 | 1.3 | Phillips Idowu | U17 | 30.12.78 | 4 | Birmingham | 29 Jul |

**Additional Under 17** (1 - 6 above)

| | | | | | | | |
|---|---|---|---|---|---|---|---|
| 13.84 | | Nicholas Thomas | | 4.04.79 | 1 | London (TB) | 25 Jun |
| 13.84 | | Peter Francis | | 28.08.80 | 2 | London (TB) | 25 Jun |
| 13.76 | | Michael Nesbeth | | 1.03.79 | 1 | Birmingham | 2 Sep |
| 13.76 w | | Kevin MacLennan | | 5.12.78 | 3 | Colwyn Bay | 15 Jul |
| | (10) | | | | | | |
| 13.70 | | Adrian Jefferies | | 12.04.79 | 1 | Warley | 21 May |
| 13.69 | | Leo Barker | | 26.12.78 | 2 | London (Ha) | 19 Aug |
| 13.60 | | Leroy Knowles | | 26.09.78 | 1 | Kingston | 25 Jun |
| 13.53 | 1.0 | Christopher Platt | | 25.09.78 | 7 | Nottingham | 7 Jul |
| 13.44 | | Waqas Naqui | | 14.09.78 | 1 | Basildon | 10 Jun |

**Under 15**

| | | | | | | | |
|---|---|---|---|---|---|---|---|
| 13.18 w | 2.6 | Jonathon Miller | | 10.06.81 | 1 | Nottingham | 7 Jul |
| 12.97 | | | | | 1 | Stoke | 17 Jun |
| 12.80 | 0.8 | James Philip | | 11.12.80 | 2 | Nottingham | 7 Jul |
| 12.76 | 1.3 | John Heavyside | | 19.11.80 | 3 | Nottingham | 7 Jul |
| 12.73 w | 3.1 | C. Hanson | | | 4 | Nottingham | 7 Jul |
| 12.68 | 1.6 | | | | * | Nottingham | 7 Jul |
| 12.66 | 1.1 | George Allen | | 19.10.80 | 5 | Nottingham | 7 Jul |
| 12.59 | | Christian Kirkham | | 26.06.81 | 1 | Colchester | 28 Aug |
| 12.53 | 1.1 | Brian Robinson | | 3.09.80 | 6 | Nottingham | 7 Jul |
| 12.49 | | Kieron James | | 22.09.80 | 2 | Birmingham | 10 Jun |
| 12.49 | 1.1 | Chris Dunsdon | | 24.09.80 | 7 | Nottingham | 7 Jul |
| 12.47 | | Chris Mortimer | | 14.11.80 | 1 | Swindon | 10 Jun |
| | (10) | | | | | | |
| 12.39 | 0.4 | Mike Ferraro | | 21.11.80 | 1 | Birmingham | 30 Jul |
| 12.28 | | Nathan Rogers | | 11.11.80 | 1 | St. Ives | 17 Jun |
| 12.27 | | Nick Howe | | 15.02.81 | 1 | Stoke | 27 May |
| 12.15 | | Nathan Ford | | 17.09.80 | 1 | Derby | 17 Jun |
| 12.12 | | Tim Butterfield | | 2.01.81 | 1 | Cleckheaton | 10 Jun |
| 12.12 | | Henry Wismayer | | 26.11.80 | 1 | Croydon | 10 Jun |
| 12.01 | | Justin Gyphion | | 1.09.80 | 1 | Cheltenham | 10 Jun |
| 12.00 | | Andrew White | | 1.05.82 | 1 | Kingston | 10 Jun |
| 11.96 | | Alan Jones | | 11.09.80 | 3 | Stoke | 17 Jun |
| 11.95 | 0.9 | Neil Hewson | | 4.09.80 | 2 | Birmingham | 30 Jul |

**Under 13**

| | | | | | | | |
|---|---|---|---|---|---|---|---|
| 10.37 | | Craig Fleming | | 29.01.83 | 1 | Linwood | 10 Sep |

# SHOT

| | | | | | | | | |
|---|---|---|---|---|---|---|---|---|
| 19.37 | Mark Proctor | | 15.01.63 | 1 | Porta Westfalica, GER | 21 | Jul |
| | 18.81 | | | 1 | Birmingham | 16 | Jul |
| | 18.55 | | | 1 | Cosford | 5 | Jul |
| | 18.53 | | | 1 | Cosford | 14 | Jun |
| | 18.39 i | | | 1 | Glasgow | 11 | Feb |
| | 18.10 | | | 1 | London (CP) | 3 | Jun |
| | 18.09 | | | 1 | Cwmbran | 9 | Jul |
| | 18.08 | | | 25Q | Gothenburg, SWE | 8 | Aug |
| | 18.02 i | | | 3 | Birmingham | 28 | Jan |
| | 17.99 | | | 4 | Gateshead | 21 | Aug |
| | 17.97 | | | 1 | London (CP) | 27 | Aug |
| | 17.88 i | | | 1 | Braintree | 19 | Mar |
| | 17.86 | | | 1 | Cosford | 31 | May |
| | 17.57 i | | | 2 | Vienna, AUT | 18 | Feb |
| | 17.53 | | | 1 | London (WL) | 19 | Jul |
| | 17.42 | | | 1 | Croydon | 25 | Jun |
| | 17.40 | | | 1 | Bedford | 29 | May |
| | 17.31 | | | 1 | Loughborough | 11 | Jun |
| 18.94 | Shaun Pickering | | 14.11.61 | 1 | Enfield | 19 | Aug |
| | 17.85 | | | 5 | Gateshead | 21 | Aug |
| | 17.71 | | | 3 | Birmingham | 16 | Jul |
| | 17.69 | | | 2 | Cwmbran | 9 | Jul |
| | 17.48 | | | 1 | London (WL) | 13 | Aug |
| 18.68 | Matt Simson | | 28.05.70 | 1 | Gainesville, USA | 25 | Mar |
| | 18.50 i | | | 1 | Gainesville, USA | 2 | Mar |
| | 18.27 | | | 2 | Birmingham | 16 | Jul |
| | 17.72 | | | 8 | Villeneuve d'Ascq, FRA | 24 | Jun |
| | 17.40 | | | 1 | Perivale | 1 | Jul |
| 18.46 | Lee Newman | U23 | 1.05.73 | 1 | Horsham | 9 | Jul |
| | 17.80 i | | | 1 | London (CP) | 16 | Dec |
| | 17.75 | | | 1 | Braintree | 23 | Jul |
| | 17.64 | | | 1 | Tessenderlo, BEL | 2 | Jul |
| | 17.64 | | | 1 | Bromley | 5 | Jul |
| | 17.62 | | | 4 | Birmingham | 16 | Jul |
| | 17.47 | | | 1 | Feltham | 22 | Jul |
| | 17.43 | | | 1 | London (Elt) | 5 | Aug |
| | 17.31 | | | 1 | London (CP) | 10 | Sep |
| | 17.30 i | | | 1 | Birmingham | 3 | Feb |
| *18.06* | *John Gorddard* | | *21.09.71* | *Q* | *Fukuoka, JAP* | *30* | *Aug* |
| *17.38* | *Felix Hyde* | *U20* | *7.08.76* | *1* | *Bedford* | *1* | *Jul* |

38 performances to 17.30 by 4 athletes including 7 indoors

| | | | | | | | |
|---|---|---|---|---|---|---|---|
| 16.97 | Nigel Spratley | | 1.04.70 | 2 | Loughborough | 11 | Jun |
| 16.95 i | Steve Whyte | | 14.03.64 | 2 | Birmingham | 3 | Feb |
| | 16.66 | | | 2 | Bedford | 10 | Jun |
| 16.94 | Gary Sollitt | | 13.01.72 | 3 | Loughborough | 11 | Jun |
| 16.93 | Simon Williams | | 17.10.67 | 1 | Enfield | 1 | Jul |
| 16.88 | Stephan Hayward | U23 | 30.07.74 | 2 | Narbonne, FRA | 29 | Jul |
| 16.74 | Jim Mason | | 22.03.72 | 2 | Horsham | 9 | Jul |
| | (10) | | | | | | |
| 16.68 | Paul Reed | | 2.06.62 | 1 | Gateshead | 17 | Jun |
| 16.60 | Dave Callaway | | 4.09.63 | 1 | Southampton | 13 | Jun |
| 16.60 | James Muirhead | | 26.01.71 | 1 | Cardiff | 19 | Aug |
| 16.28 | Neil Gray | | 30.08.65 | 1 | Bracknell | 30 | Apr |
| 16.10 | Lee Wiltshire | | 26.07.62 | 2 | Portsmouth (RN) | 3 | Jun |
| 16.07 | Peter Weir | | 2.09.63 | 5 | London (CP) | 3 | Jun |
| 16.05 | Antony Zaidman | | 18.03.62 | 3 | London (WL) | 19 | Jul |
| 16.00 | Guy Marshall ¶ | | 24.09.71 | 1 | Grimsby | 13 | May |
| 15.98 i | Scott Hayes | U23 | 4.01.73 | 2 | Bedford | 4 | Mar |
| | 15.62 | | | 1 | Colchester | 26 | Mar |

| 15.90 | Denzil McDonald | | 11.10.65 | 2 | Croydon | 28 Aug |
|---|---|---|---|---|---|---|
| | (20) | | | | | |
| 15.72 | Emeka Udechuku | U17 | 10.07.79 | 3 | Belfort, FRA | 6 Aug |
| 15.66 | Simon Armstrong | | 29.05.62 | 1 | Bournemouth | 13 May |
| 15.65 | David Condon | | 11.04.72 | 7 | Bedford | 29 May |
| 15.64 | Bill Fuller | U20 | 19.10.76 | 3 | Bedford | 1 Jul |
| 15.60 | Mark Edwards | U23 | 2.12.74 | 1 | Exeter | 27 Aug |
| 15.59 | Matt Symonds | | 31.07.68 | 1 | High Wycombe | 13 May |
| 15.59 | Martyn Fletcher | | 21.01.69 | 2 | Cork, IRE | 24 Jun |
| 15.54 i | Jamie Murphy | U23 | 20.03.73 | 3 | Birmingham | 26 Feb |
| 14.40 | | | | 1 | Rugby | 22 Jul |
| 15.49 | Paul Corrigan | | 19.01.66 | 1 | Gateshead | 12 Aug |
| 15.48 | John Nicholls | | 1.09.65 | 1 | Stretford | 19 Aug |
| | (30) | | | | | |
| *15.44* | *B. Grays* | | | *8* | *Bedford* | *29 May* |
| *15.35 i* | *Terry McHugh* | | *22.08.63* | *2* | *Nenagh, IRE* | *5 Mar* |
| *14.43* | | | | *1* | *London (TB)* | *3 Jun* |
| 15.17 i | Simon Matthews | | 21.05.71 | 5 | Birmingham | 26 Feb |
| 14.54 | | | | 1 | Blackpool | 15 Apr |
| 15.12 | Steve Bergin | | 17.06.66 | 3 | Cork, IRE | 24 Jun |
| 15.09 | Jeff Clare | | 21.03.65 | 2 | Crawley | 1 Jul |
| 15.03 | Bruce Robb | U20 | 27.07.77 | 1 | Grangemouth | 11 May |
| 14.99 | Barry Nash | | 4.09.71 | 1 | Welwyn | 28 Aug |
| 14.95 | Morris Fox | | 30.04.63 | 3 | Watford | 19 Aug |
| 14.91 | Guy Perryman | | 2.11.58 | 2 | Tonbridge | 5 Aug |
| 14.90 | Chris Symonds | | 15.11.70 | 1 | Loughborough | 20 May |
| *14.90* | *John Farrelly* | | *4.12.67* | *1* | *Tullamore, IRE* | *20 Aug* |
| 14.79 i | Alex Kruger | | 18.11.63 | 8H | Barcelona, SPA | 10 Mar |
| 14.60 | | | | 4 | Stoke | 9 Sep |
| *14.76* | *John Menton* | | *2.05.70* | *1* | *Woodford* | *6 May* |
| 14.66 | Kevin Brown | | 10.09.64 | 6 | Birmingham | 1 Jul |
| | (40) | | | | | |
| 14.66 | Keith Ansell | | 30.03.62 | 3 | London (CP) | 10 Sep |
| 14.65 | Mark Wiseman | | | 1 | Aldershot | 7 Jun |
| 14.63 i | Andy Turner | | 29.08.63 | 1 | Horsham | 28 Jan |
| 14.57 | | | | 2 | Bournemouth | 13 May |
| 14.63 | Neville Thompson | V40 | 28.03.55 | 3 | Derby | 30 Jul |
| 14.62 | Simon Fricker | U23 | 14.07.75 | 1 | Horsham | 30 Jul |
| 14.59 | Simon Shirley | | 3.08.66 | 15D | Gotzis, AUT | 27 May |
| 14.59 | Eric Hollingsworth | | 6.12.62 | D | Perth, AUS | 16 Dec |
| 14.55 | Mike Oliver | V40 | 23.03.53 | 1 | Kingston | 19 Aug |
| 14.52 | Bryan Kelly | U23 | 29.12.73 | 4 | Edinburgh | 3 Jun |
| 14.52 | Andrew Wain | | 2.06.65 | 1 | Norwich | 3 Sep |
| | (50) | | | | | |
| *14.49* | *Philip Schussel* | | | *1* | *Guildford* | *30 Apr* |
| 14.47 | Mark Davies | | 10.01.71 | 1 | Bromley | 19 Aug |
| 14.43 | Graeme Stark | | 12.10.63 | 1 | Carlisle | 30 Apr |
| *14.43* | *Libor Krten* | *U23* | *26.02.73* | *1* | *Oxford* | *22 Jul* |
| 14.42 | Neil Elliott | | 10.04.71 | 2 | Grangemouth | 11 May |
| 14.40 | Simon Keller | U20 | 10.11.76 | 1 | Nottingham | 9 May |
| 14.37 i | David Burnett | U20 | 27.01.76 | 2 | Birmingham | 19 Feb |
| 13.26 | | | | 2 | Paris, FRA | 30 Sep |
| 14.31 | Andrew Kruszewski | | 7.04.59 | 2 | Wakefield | 3 Jun |
| 14.26 i | Dave Eastlake | | 2.07.63 | 5 | Glasgow | 22 Jun |
| 13.60 | | | | 3 | Middlesbrough | 13 May |
| 14.24 | Mark MacDonald | | 2.12.59 | 1 | Rothesay | 19 Aug |
| 14.23 i | Robert Russell | U23 | 5.08.74 | 1 | Sheffield | 8 Feb |
| 14.17 | | | | 2 | Cardiff | 19 Aug |
| 14.23 | Alun Thomas | | 16.03.57 | 2 | Horsham | 9 Apr |
| | (60) | | | | | |
| 14.16 | Liam McIntyre | U20 | 22.09.76 | 4 | Cardiff | 19 Aug |

| 14.14 | Steve Aitken | | 8.07.66 | 1 | Forres | 8 | Jul |
|---|---|---|---|---|---|---|---|
| 14.14 | Ian Lindley | | 3.12.55 | 1 | Stretford | 22 | Jul |
| 14.13 i | Malcolm Fenton | | 12.02.56 | 3 | Braintree | 19 | Mar |
| 14.09 | Guy Litherland | | 13.11.68 | 11 | Enfield | 19 | Aug |
| 14.06 | Anthony Brannen | | 16.09.68 | 1D | Derby | 29 | Apr |
| 14.06 | Neil Mason | | 10.02.71 | 2 | Forres | 8 | Jul |
| *14.05* | *Kengo Kubota* | | *26.06.68* | *3* | *Grangemouth* | *14* | *May* |
| 14.05 | Tony Soalla-Bell | U20 | 3.10.76 | 5 | London (CP) | 10 | Sep |
| 14.05 i | Leo Barker | U20 | 26.12.78 | 2P | Glasgow | 10 | Dec |
| 14.04 | Leith Marar | | 7.11.68 | 2 | Loughborough | 20 | May |
| (70) | | | | | | | |
| 14.02 | Nick Phipps | V40 | 8.04.52 | 3 | Portsmouth (RN) | 3 | Jun |
| 14.01 | Gareth Cook | | 20.02.69 | 1 | Sutton | 6 | May |
| 14.01 | Rob Smith | | 3.11.66 | 1 | Elgin | 15 | Jul |
| 14.00 | James South | U23 | 4.01.75 | 3 | Barking | 13 | May |
| 13.93 | Jamie Quarry | | 15.11.72 | 9D | Fukuoka, JAP | 1 | Sep |
| 13.89 | Clayton Turner | | 9.01.68 | 1 | Horsham | 3 | Jun |
| 13.86 | Brian Redman | | 25.10.68 | 7 | London (He) | 7 | May |
| 13.86 | George Baker | U20 | 14.08.76 | 1 | Woking | 12 | Jul |
| 13.86 | Craig Rogers | U20 | 14.02.76 | 2 | Telford | 16 | Sep |
| 13.85 | Matthew Twigg | | 18.07.69 | 2 | Peterborough | 6 | May |
| (80) | | | | | | | |
| 13.85 | Bill Fuller | V45 | 5.02.48 | 3 | Croydon | 13 | May |
| 13.84 | John Tyler | U23 | 6.03.74 | 1 | Stoke | 6 | May |
| 13.80 | Pete Lowe | | 4.07.65 | 1 | Happy Valley, CYP | 14 | Jun |
| 13.80 | Neal Hart | | 15.04.68 | 2 | Dumfries | 2 | Jul |
| 13.80 | David Sweeney | | 9.02.62 | 5 | Cardiff | 22 | Jul |
| 13.76 | Stewart McMillan | | 12.09.69 | 2 | Glasgow | 11 | Jun |
| 13.75 | Rob Earle | | 15.09.60 | 4 | Barking | 13 | May |
| 13.75 | Bruce Shepherd | | 20.03.67 | 1 | Nethybridge | 12 | Aug |
| 13.73 | John Painter ¶ | | 12.06.58 | 1 | Norwich | 13 | May |
| 13.68 | Rafer Joseph | | 21.07.68 | 1 | Watford | 1 | Jul |
| (90) | | | | | | | |
| 13.65 | Greg Richards | | 25.04.56 | 2 | St. Ives | 22 | Jul |
| 13.64 | Gareth Gilbert | | 24.08.72 | 7 | Stoke | 9 | Sep |
| 13.63 | Barry Thomas | | 28.04.72 | 18D | Valladolid,SPA | 1 | Jul |
| *13.55* | *P.D. Horne* | | | *2* | *Fort William* | *29* | *Jul* |
| 13.54 | Paul Howard | | 19.10.66 | 1D | Bebington | 22 | Jul |
| 13.53 | Glen Smith | | 21.05.72 | 7 | Birmingham | 20 | May |
| 13.52 | Ewart Hulse | | 21.01.62 | 6 | Cork, IRE | 24 | Jun |
| 13.49 | Jeremy Hames | | 17.11.70 | 2 | Loughborough | 13 | May |
| 13.48 | Neal Killen | | 10.04.59 | 2 | Aldershot | 7 | Jun |
| 13.48 | Mike Atkinson | | 6.03.58 | 1 | Antrim | 1 | Jul |
| 13.46 | Gary Herrington | | 31.03.61 | 3 | London (Ha) | 25 | Jun |
| (100) | | | | | | | |
| *13.41* | *Gareth Rees* | | *30.06.67* | *1* | *Oxford* | *28* | *Jun* |

**Additional Under 20** (1 - 10 above)

| 13.29 | Daniel Brunt | | 23.04.76 | 3 | Edinburgh | 7 | May |
|---|---|---|---|---|---|---|---|
| 13.20 | Carl Myerscough | U17 | 21.10.79 | 1 | Blackpool | 10 | Sep |

## SHOT - Under 20 - 6.25kg

| *18.67* | *Felix Hyde* | | *7.08.76* | *1* | *London (He)* | *9* | *Sep* |
|---|---|---|---|---|---|---|---|
| 16.96 | Bill Fuller | | 19.10.76 | 1 | London (CP) | 27 | May |
| 16.62 i | Emeka Udechuku | | 10.07.79 | 1 | London (CP) | 14 | Dec |
| 16.26 | | U17 | | 1 | Bromley | 23 | Apr |
| 16.18 | Bruce Robb | | 27.07.77 | 1 | Pitreavie | 8 | Jul |
| 16.17 | Dinos Alexopoulos | | 2.12.76 | 1 | Cheltenham | 17 | Jun |
| 16.02 | George Baker | | 14.08.76 | 2 | Nottingham | 8 | Jul |
| 15.72 | Liam McIntyre | | 22.09.76 | 2 | Ayr | 18 | Jul |
| 15.48 | Craig Rogers | | 14.02.76 | 4 | Nottingham | 8 | Jul |

| | | | | | |
|---|---|---|---|---|---|
| 15.39 | Simon Keller | 10.11.76 | 5 | Nottingham | 8 Jul |
| 15.38 | Tony Soalla-Bell | 3.10.76 | 2 | Kingston | 10 Jun |
| 14.92 | Simon James | 21.01.77 | 2 | Telford | 18 Jun |
| (10) | | | | | |
| 14.53 | Graham Lloyd-Bennett | 26.10.76 | 1 | Hoo | 10 Jun |
| 14.35 | Daniel Brunt | 23.04.76 | 1 | Derby | 13 May |
| | or 14th | | | | |
| 14.24 | Paul Williams | 21.09.77 | 4 | Stoke | 28 May |
| 14.18 | David Burnett | 27.01.76 | 1 | Watford | 27 Aug |
| 14.15 | Sudip Burman-Roy | 15.01.78 | 8 | Nottingham | 8 Jul |
| 14.07 | Ian McMullan | 15.06.78 | 1 | Antrim | 20 May |
| 13.91 | Iain Douglas | 4.01.77 | 3 | Pitreavie | 8 Jul |
| 13.89 i | Tim King | 10.12.77 | 1 | Bedford | 4 Mar |
| 13.74 | | | 2 | Grantham | 10 Jun |
| *13.89* | *Hayden Knowles* | *17.08.77* | *4* | *Pitreavie* | *8 Jul* |
| 13.81 | Matthew Cusack | 13.01.77 | 2 | Sheffield | 27 May |

**overage**

| | | | | | | |
|---|---|---|---|---|---|---|
| 14.61 | John Howard | U23 | 16.09.75 | 1 | Antrim | 27 May |
| 13.86 | Wayne Clarke | U23 | 24.12.75 | 1 | Grantham | 10 Jun |

# SHOT - Under 17 - 5kg

| | | | | | |
|---|---|---|---|---|---|
| 18.43 | Emeka Udechuku | 10.07.79 | 1 | London (CP) | 28 May |
| 17.68 | Carl Myerscough | 21.10.79 | 1 | Blackpool | 24 Sep |
| 16.64 | Alan Rudkin | 5.11.78 | 1 | Hull | 5 Aug |
| 16.29 | James Bull | 12.02.79 | 1 | Ipswich | 10 Jun |
| 15.89 | Pete Waterman | 12.09.79 | 1 | Crawley | 31 May |
| 15.76 | Nick Barber | 22.11.78 | 2 | Nottingham | 7 Jul |
| 15.72 | Dave Irwin | 18.12.78 | 1 | Antrim | 27 May |
| 15.15 | David Lovett | 13.09.78 | 1 | Perivale | 16 Jul |
| 15.02 | Jamie Hunt | 29.11.79 | 2 | St. Ives | 17 Jun |
| 14.92 | Quintan Caulfield | · | 3 | Tullamore, IRE | 3 Jun |
| (10) | | | | | |
| 14.70 | David Readle | 10.02.80 | 1 | Kirkby | 10 Sep |
| 14.69 i | Darren Hatton | 21.03.79 | 3 | London (CP) | 11 Feb |
| 14.64 i | Adrian Cluskey | 30.12.80 | 1 | London (CP) | 14 Dec |
| 14.62 | Simon Sephton | 27.09.78 | 1 | Hull | 9 Aug |
| 14.58 | Steven Scott | 29.05.79 | 2 | Hull | 5 Aug |
| 14.54 | John Thyer | 23.11.78 | 1 | Plymouth | 1 Jul |
| 14.51 | Andy Castle | 8.12.79 | 1 | Cheltenham | 17 Jun |
| 14.37 | Constantine Karayannis | 9.01.79 | 1 | Harrow | 16 Jul |
| 14.29 | Martin Mortley | 8.09.78 | 1 | Barking | 25 Jun |
| 14.15 | Stephen Reed | 7.09.78 | 1 | York | 10 Jun |
| (20) | | | | | |
| 14.15 | John Parkin | 23.02.79 | 1 | Brecon | 6 Aug |
| 14.08 | Warren Woad | 16.03.80 | 5 | Nottingham | 7 Jul |
| 14.07 | Ian Leaman | 14.10.78 | 1 | Exeter | 21 May |
| 14.03 i | Martin Hayes | 31.08.79 | 5 | Birmingham | 18 Feb |

**unconfirmed**

| | | | | | |
|---|---|---|---|---|---|
| *16.14 i* | *Jon Orrelle* | *28.01.79* | *1P* | *London (CP)* | *21 Jan* |

# SHOT - Under 15 - 4kg

| | | | | | |
|---|---|---|---|---|---|
| 15.78 | Adrian Cluskey | 30.12.80 | 1 | Nottingham | 7 Jul |
| 15.42 | Graeme Allan | 24.09.80 | 1 | Inverness | 16 Sep |
| 15.00 | Robin Wheldon | 7.12.80 | 2 | Nottingham | 7 Jul |
| 14.92 | Tony Quinn | 14.01.81 | 2 | Antrim | 12 Aug |
| 14.57 | Simon Williams | 5.10.80 | 1 | Windsor | 20 Aug |
| 14.49 | Ross Kidner | 12.09.80 | 1 | Milton Keynes | 10 Jun |
| 14.38 | Stuart Tynan | 3.10.80 | 3 | Antrim | 12 Aug |

| | | | | | | |
|---|---|---|---|---|---|---|
| 14.35 | Scot Thompson | 10.08.81 | 1 | Inverness | 13 | Aug |
| 14.10 | Adrian Rawling | 21.11.80 | 1 | Carn Brea | 17 | Sep |
| 13.90 | Lyndon Woodward | 22.11.80 | 1 | Cannock | 9 | Sep |
| | (10) | | | | | |
| 13.76 | Liam Walsh | 5.05.82 | 1 | Wrexham | 24 | Sep |
| 13.71 | Philip Sharpe | 6.03.81 | 1 | Blackpool | 10 | Sep |
| 13.67 | Carl Cheadle | 6.09.80 | 3 | Nottingham | 7 | Jul |
| 13.63 | William Spence | 29.12.80 | 1 | Manchester (BV) | 16 | Jul |
| 13.55 | Brian Pearce | 9.12.80 | 1P | Bromley | 18 | Jun |
| 13.51 | Geoffrey Reid-Hughes | 14.10.81 | 1 | Thurrock | 16 | Jul |
| 13.45 | Erik Sanders | 31.10.80 | 1 | Newcastle | 10 | Jun |
| 13.45 | Mark Hamilton | 18.11.80 | 1 | Derby | 17 | Jun |
| 13.38 | Craig Smith | 1.03.81 | 3 | Pitreavie | 9 | Jul |
| 13.22 | Steve Foster | | 1 | Grantham | 1 | Jul |
| | (20) | | | | | |
| 13.16 | Ben Marsden | 20.10.80 | 1 | Braintree | 24 | Jun |
| 13.11 | Andrew Frost | 17.04.81 | 1 | Crawley | 28 | Aug |
| 13.04 | Matthew Simpole | 6.07.81 | 1 | Enfield | 30 | Jun |
| 13.04 | Robert Hollinger | 11.10.80 | 1 | Barnsley | 9 | Jul |

## DISCUS

| | | | | | | |
|---|---|---|---|---|---|---|
| 63.56 | Robert Weir | 4.02.61 | 1 | Los Gatos, USA | 10 | Jun |
| | 63.14 | | 9 | Gothenburg, SWE | 11 | Aug |
| | 62.94 | | 3 | Villeneuve d'Ascq, FRA | 25 | Jun |
| | 62.54 | | 1 | Gateshead | 21 | Aug |
| | 62.50 | | Q | Gothenburg, SWE | 9 | Aug |
| | 62.38 | | 2 | Santa Cruz, USA | 1 | Jul |
| | 61.68 | | 1 | Liverpool | 30 | Jul |
| | 61.60 | | 10 | Zurich, SWZ | 16 | Aug |
| | 61.08 | | 1 | Enfield | 19 | Aug |
| | 60.92 | | 7 | Salinas, USA | 24 | May |
| | 60.44 | | 1 | Cannock | 22 | Jul |
| | 60.36 | | 9 | Monaco, MON | 25 | Jul |
| | 60.18 | | 2 | Birmingham | 15 | Jul |
| | 59.08 | | 7 | San Jose, USA | 27 | May |
| | 58.86 | | 1 | Stanford, USA | 12 | May |
| 59.50 | Kevin Brown | 10.09.64 | 1 | Stoke | 9 | Sep |
| | 58.46 | | 1 | Birmingham | 20 | May |
| | 58.32 | | 1 | Loughborough | 21 | Jun |
| | 57.26 | | 1 | Loughborough | 11 | Jun |
| | 57.24 | | 4 | Birmingham | 15 | Jul |
| | 56.90 | | 4 | Gateshead | 21 | Aug |
| | 56.88 | | 1 | London (CP) | 3 | Jun |
| | 56.84 | | 2 | Enfield | 19 | Aug |
| | 56.22 | | 5 | Budapest, HUN | 9 | Jul |
| | 56.18 | | 1 | London (He) | 7 | May |
| | 56.00 | | 12 | Halle, GER | 13 | May |
| | 55.88 | | 1 | Bedford | 28 | May |
| | 55.36 | | 3 | Birmingham | 17 | Jun |
| | 55.00 | | 1 | Birmingham | 1 | Jul |
| 58.70 | Glen Smith | 21.05.72 | 1 | Loughborough | 29 | Apr |
| | 57.60 | | 1 | Birmingham | 17 | Jun |
| | 57.38 | | 2 | Birmingham | 20 | May |
| | 57.06 | | 1 | Telford | 6 | May |
| | 56.64 | | 1 | Bath | 31 | May |
| | 56.58 | | 1 | Rugby | 22 | Jul |
| | 56.02 | | 2 | Loughborough | 21 | Jun |
| | 55.98 | | 2 | Loughborough | 11 | Jun |
| | 55.40 | | 6 | Budapest, HUN | 9 | Jul |
| | 55.18 | | 2 | Perth, AUS | 29 | Jan |

| | | | | | | | |
|---|---|---|---|---|---|---|---|
| 58.20 | Simon Williams | | 17.10.67 | 3 | Birmingham | 15 | Jul |
| | 56.54 | | | 1 | Harrow | 9 | Jul |
| | 55.78 | | | 1 | San Diego, USA | 4 | Mar |
| 56.32 | Gary Herrington | | 31.03.61 | 2 | Birmingham | 17 | Jun |
| | 56.28 | | | 2 | Rugby | 22 | Jul |
| | 55.44 | | | 1 | London (Ha) | 25 | Jun |
| | 55.08 | | | 1 | Redditch | 19 | Aug |
| | 55.06 | | | 1 | Rugby | 29 | Aug |
| 55.52 | Jamie Murphy | U23 | 20.03.73 | 1 | Narbonne, FRA | 29 | Jul |
| | 55.50 | | | 2 | Bedford | 28 | May |
| 55.38 | Leith Marar | | 7.11.68 | 1 | London (TB) | 24 | Jun |
| | 55.36 | | | 1 | Barn Elms | 5 | Aug |
| | 55.32 | | | 1 | Loughborough | 20 | May |
| | 55.06 | | | 3 | Enfield | 19 | Aug |
| 55.04 | Denzil McDonald | | 11.10.65 | 1 | Croydon | 28 | Aug |
| 54 performances to 55.00 by 8 athletes | | | | | | | |
| 54.76 | Neville Thompson | V40 | 28.03.55 | 5 | Kilkenny, IRE | 2 | Sep |
| 54.36 | Matt Symonds | | 31.07.68 | 1 | Braintree | 24 | Jun |
| (10) | | | | | | | |
| 53.62 | Perris Wilkins | | 12.11.68 | 1 | Loughborough | 22 | Jul |
| 53.52 | Lee Newman | U23 | 1.05.73 | 2 | London (TB) | 24 | Jun |
| 52.96 | Abi Ekoku | | 13.04.66 | 2 | Loughborough | 20 | May |
| 52.86 | Mark Proctor | | 15.01.63 | 1 | Cosford | 5 | Jul |
| 52.46 | Paul Reed | | 2.06.62 | 1 | Barnsley | 14 | Jun |
| *52.38* | *John Menton* | | *2.05.70* | *1* | *Cork, IRE* | *22* | *Apr* |
| 52.32 | Jeff Clare | | 21.03.65 | 1 | Bolton | 14 | May |
| 52.26 | Scott Hayes | U23 | 4.01.73 | 2 | Braintree | 24 | Jun |
| 51.76 | John Moreland | | 13.09.58 | 1 | Antrim | 1 | Jul |
| 51.64 | James Muirhead | | 26.01.71 | 3 | Loughborough | 20 | May |
| 51.20 | Steve Casey | | 26.02.66 | 6 | Enfield | 19 | Aug |
| (20) | | | | | | | |
| 51.08 | Robert Russell | U23 | 5.08.74 | 1 | Sheffield | 14 | May |
| 51.06 | Shaun Pickering | | 14.11.61 | 7 | Enfield | 19 | Aug |
| 50.92 | Nick Woolcott | | 7.04.61 | 4 | Stoke | 9 | Sep |
| 49.88 | Peter Gordon | V40 | 2.07.51 | 1 | Jarrow | 16 | Aug |
| 49.78 | Eric Hollingsworth | | 6.12.62 | 1 | Melbourne, AUS | 21 | Oct |
| 49.62 | Chris Symonds | | 15.11.70 | 4 | Crawley | 1 | Jul |
| 49.28 | Rafer Joseph | | 21.07.68 | 2 | London (WF) | 22 | Jul |
| 49.16 | Andrew Kruszewski | | 7.04.59 | 3 | Croydon | 28 | Aug |
| 48.96 | Emeka Udechuku | U17 | 10.07.79 | 9 | Enfield | 19 | Aug |
| 48.84 | Mark Wiseman | | | 3 | Loughborough | 24 | May |
| (30) | | | | | | | |
| 48.56 | Stephen Ayre | | 20.10.67 | 2 | Middlesbrough | 13 | May |
| 48.14 | Ian Taylor | | 2.07.67 | 1 | Telford | 3 | Jun |
| 48.10 | Steve Whyte | | 14.03.64 | 1 | Bedford | 13 | May |
| 47.70 | Gareth Cook | | 20.02.69 | 1 | Basildon | 5 | Aug |
| 47.48 | Ashley Knott | U23 | 30.08.75 | 1 | Exeter | 27 | Aug |
| 47.40 | Andy Turner | | 29.08.63 | 6 | Birmingham | 20 | May |
| 47.38 | Neil Sougrin | | 14.05.71 | 2 | Enfield | 1 | Jul |
| 47.08 | James South | U23 | 4.01.75 | 4 | Croydon | 28 | Aug |
| 46.94 | Mark Davies | | 10.01.71 | 5 | Croydon | 28 | Aug |
| 46.92 | Michael Jemi-Alade | | 13.10.64 | 5 | Crawley | 1 | Jul |
| (40) | | | | | | | |
| 46.90 | Stephan Hayward | U23 | 30.07.74 | 1 | Dumfries | 2 | Jul |
| 46.72 | David Sweeney | | 9.02.62 | 1 | Ilford | 19 | Aug |
| 46.64 | Bryan Kelly | U23 | 29.12.73 | 6 | Crawley | 2 | Jul |
| 46.58 | Matt Simson | | 28.05.70 | 2 | Perivale | 1 | Jul |
| 46.54 | Peter Weir | | 2.09.63 | 7 | Birmingham | 1 | Jul |
| 46.40 | Morris Fox | | 30.04.63 | 5 | Birmingham | 17 | Jun |
| 46.38 | Bruce Robb | U20 | 27.07.77 | 4 | Loughborough | 11 | Jun |
| 46.34 | Gareth Gilbert | | 24.08.72 | 1 | Stretford | 22 | Jun |

| 45.98 | Garry Power | | 1.09.62 | 1 | Woking | 19 | Aug |
|---|---|---|---|---|---|---|---|
| 45.92 | Libor Krten | U23 | 26.02.73 | 2 | Oxford | 22 | Jul |
| 45.74 | Simon Fricker | U23 | 14.07.75 | 1 | Horsham | 30 | Jul |
| 45.36 | Alex Kruger | | 18.11.63 | 3D | Valladolid,SPA | 2 | Jul |
| | (50) | | | | | | |
| 45.00 | Nigel Spratley | | 1.04.70 | 1 | Basingstoke | 6 | Aug |
| 44.86 | Simon Armstrong | | 29.05.62 | 2 | Portsmouth | 25 | Jun |
| 44.68 | Gareth Marks | U20 | 31.05.77 | 2 | Utrecht, HOL | 9 | Jul |
| 44.62 | Ivan Washington | | 18.11.56 | 2 | Wakefield | 12 | Aug |
| 44.52 | Hayden Knowles | U20 | 17.08.77 | 4 | Sydney, AUS | 2 | Mar |
| 44.44 | Greg Richards | | 25.04.56 | 1 | Barn Elms | 1 | Jul |
| 44.38 | Neil Griffin | V45 | 28.05.48 | 4 | Enfield | 1 | Jul |
| 44.26 | Matthew Twigg | | 18.07.69 | 3 | Peterborough | 6 | May |
| 44.20 | John Farrelly | | 4.12.67 | 4 | Tullamore, IRE | 20 | Jun |
| 44.10 | Neal Killen | | 10.04.59 | 1 | Aldershot | 26 | Jul |
| 44.08 | Paul Corrigan | | 19.01.66 | 3 | Middlesbrough | 13 | May |
| 44.06 | Rob Earle | | 15.09.60 | 3 | Barking | 13 | May |
| | (60) | | | | | | |
| 44.04 | Tegid Griffiths | | 19.04.60 | | Wrexham | 18 | Jun |
| 44.00 | Simon Shirley | | 3.08.66 | 7 | Irvine, USA | 23 | Apr |
| 43.86 | Ian McMullan | U23 | 3.05.74 | 1 | London (Col) | 12 | Jul |
| 43.86 | Jeremy Hames | | 17.11.70 | 4 | Cannock | 22 | Jul |
| 43.70 | John Little | V40 | 14.04.53 | 1 | Carlisle | 2 | Apr |
| 43.70 | Mike Conerney | | 30.10.72 | 1 | Cambridge | 20 | May |
| 43.68 | Ben Walker | U20 | 8.06.78 | 2 | Watford | 1 | Jul |
| 43.60 | Kengo Kubota | | 26.06.68 | 3 | Grangemouth | 14 | May |
| 43.48 | Liam McIntyre | U20 | 22.09.76 | 2 | Glasgow | 11 | Jun |
| 43.32 | Steven Lloyd | U23 | 20.03.74 | 1 | Carlisle | 25 | Jun |
| 43.32 | David Abernethy | V40 | 5.09.55 | 1 | Carlisle | 10 | Sep |
| | (70) | | | | | | |
| 43.20 | Stephen Rogers | | 1.09.71 | 5 | Loughborough | 20 | May |
| 43.18 | Jamie Quarry | | 15.11.72 | 2 | Watford | 19 | Aug |
| 42.96 | Peter Roberts | | 19.09.71 | | Cardiff | 2 | Aug |
| 42.74 | Hector Lawrence | U20 | 1.11.77 | 2 | London (Ha) | 25 | Jun |
| 42.72 | Peter Russell | | 7.05.60 | 4 | Birmingham | 19 | Jul |
| 42.46 | James Kindon | U20 | 18.06.76 | 2 | Cambridge | 20 | May |
| 42.38 | Maurice Hicks | | 1.01.70 | 1 | Haslemere | 17 | Aug |
| 42.24 | Andy Rutland | U20 | 13.01.76 | 1 | Jarrow | 6 | May |
| 42.24 | Glen Townsend | | 23.04.64 | 1 | Isle of Man | 11 | Jun |
| 42.20 | Mike Small | V40 | 31.03.54 | 3 | Ealing | 1 | Jul |
| | (80) | | | | | | |
| 42.12 | Simon Jones | | 23.02.65 | 1 | Horsham | 3 | Jun |
| 42.08 | Ewart Hulse | | 21.01.62 | | Wrexham | 29 | Jul |
| 42.00 | Alan Marriott | | 6.03.60 | 1 | Cudworth | 4 | Jul |
| 41.96 | Mark Edwards | U23 | 2.12.74 | 4 | Mansfield | 19 | Aug |
| 41.82 | Jan Drzewiecki | | 29.11.57 | 1 | London (WL) | 23 | Apr |
| 41.82 | Barry Thomas | | 28.04.72 | 5D | Alhama, SPA | 21 | May |
| 41.80 | Justin Bryan | | 16.08.69 | 1 | Brierley Hill | 30 | Apr |
| 41.72 | Neal Hart | | 15.04.68 | 4 | Edinburgh | 23 | Jun |
| 41.70 | Jason Byrne | | 9.09.70 | 2 | Coventry | 6 | May |
| 41.68 | Neil Elliott | | 10.04.71 | 1 | Coatbridge | 23 | Apr |
| | (90) | | | | | | |
| 41.60 | Danny Littlechild | U20 | 2.10.77 | 3 | Edinburgh | 6 | May |
| 41.60 | Geoff Tyler | V45 | 30.09.48 | 1 | Stretford | 19 | Aug |
| 41.50 | Andrew Brown | U23 | 22.09.73 | 2 | Southend | 22 | Jul |
| 41.40 | Iain Park | U23 | 16.07.74 | 4 | Edinburgh | 1 | Jul |
| 41.38 | Paul Head | | 1.07.65 | 3 | Derby | 30 | Jul |
| 41.34 | Paul Howard | | 19.10.66 | 10 | Birmingham | 2 | Jul |
| 41.34 | Euan Davidson | U23 | 8.12.73 | 2 | Haslemere | 5 | Aug |
| 41.34 | P. Curtis | | | 1 | Aldershot | | |
| 41.32 | Tony Satchwell | V40 | 3.02.53 | 1 | Portsmouth | 14 | May |

| Mark | Name | Cat | DOB | Pos | Venue | Date |
|---|---|---|---|---|---|---|
| 41.30 | Gary Parsons | | | 1 | Kings Lynn | 15 Jul |
| (100) | | | | | | |
| 41.28 | Guy Marshall ¶ | | 24.09.71 | 1 | Hull | 30 Apr |
| 41.28 | Matt Allison | U23 | 26.02.73 | 1D | Cudworth | 27 Aug |
| 41.24 | N. Dixon | U23 | 73 | 4 | Edinburgh | 6 May |
| 41.18 | Bill Fuller | U20 | 19.10.76 | 3 | Croydon | 14 May |
| 41.08 | Philip Davies | | 12.10.60 | 1 | Bolton | 16 Sep |
| *41.06* | *Terry McHugh* | | *22.08.63* | *2* | *Woking* | *22 Jul* |
| 41.00 | Peter Trayner | U23 | 27.09.73 | 2 | Loughborough | 13 May |

**Additional Under 20** (1 - 10 above)

| Mark | Name | Cat | DOB | Pos | Venue | Date |
|---|---|---|---|---|---|---|
| 40.98 | Andrew Rollins | | 20.03.78 | 3 | Wakefield | 12 Aug |
| 40.90 | Dean Daniels | | 1.02.76 | 5 | Bedford | 2 Jul |
| 40.42 | Craig Munden | | 24.12.76 | 4 | Derby | 30 Jul |

## DISCUS - Under 20 - 1.75kg

| Mark | Name | Cat | DOB | Pos | Venue | Date |
|---|---|---|---|---|---|---|
| 54.70 | Emeka Udechuku | U17 | 10.07.79 | 1 | Telford | 18 Jun |
| 51.38 | Gareth Marks | | 31.05.77 | 1 | Cardiff | 1 Jul |
| 48.86 | Bruce Robb | | 27.07.77 | 1 | Pitreavie | 8 Jul |
| *48.48* | *Hayden Knowles* | | *17.08.77* | *2* | *Pitreavie* | *8 Jul* |
| 46.50 | Liam McIntyre | | 22.09.76 | 2 | Ayr | 18 Jul |
| 45.82 | Andy Rutland | | 13.01.76 | 1 | Sheffield | 27 May |
| 45.76 | Michael Leonard | | 28.05.77 | 1 | Basildon | 10 Jun |
| 45.52 | Edward Griss | | 12.08.76 | 2 | Birmingham | 27 Aug |
| 45.50 | Bill Fuller | | 19.10.76 | 2 | London (CP) | 27 May |
| 44.84 | Ben Walker | | 8.06.78 | 1 | Welwyn | 10 Jun |
| 44.32 | Andrew Rollins | | 20.03.78 | 2 | Nottingham | 8 Jul |
| (10) | | | | | | |
| 44.10 | David Burnett | | 27.01.76 | 1 | Derby | 17 Sep |
| 43.72 | Hector Lawrence | | 1.11.77 | 1 | London (He) | 10 Jun |
| 43.70 | Alex Thompson | | 5.05.78 | 1 | Yeovil | 10 Jun |
| 43.20 | Scott Barker | | 22.07.77 | 1 | Corby | 10 Jun |
| 42.94 | Steven Hale | | 20.04.77 | 3 | Nottingham | 8 Jul |
| 42.86 | Louis Hodgson | | 29.12.76 | 2 | Hull | 5 Aug |
| 42.78 | Dean Daniels | | 1.02.76 | 2 | Telford | 18 Jun |
| 42.76 | Craig Munden | | 24.12.76 | 4 | London (CP) | 27 May |
| 41.92 | Tim King | | 10.12.77 | 3 | Hull | 5 Aug |
| 41.46 | Daniel Brunt | | 23.04.76 | 1 | Derby | 13 May |
| (20) | | | | | | |
| 41.10 | Simon Brisk | | 5.07.77 | 2 | Cheltenham | 17 Jun |

**overage**

| Mark | Name | Cat | DOB | Pos | Venue | Date |
|---|---|---|---|---|---|---|
| 42.36 | John Howard | U23 | 16.09.75 | 1 | Tullamore, IRE | 3 Jun |

## DISCUS - Under 17 - 1.5kg

| Mark | Name | DOB | Pos | Venue | Date |
|---|---|---|---|---|---|
| 62.22 | Emeka Udechuku | 10.07.79 | Q | Bath | 10 Jul |
| 52.76 | Carl Myerscough | 21.10.79 | 1 | Blackpool | 24 Jul |
| 49.12 | Alan Rudkin | 5.11.78 | 1 | Peterborough | 28 Aug |
| 47.42 | David Black | 9.10.78 | 1 | Cannock | 10 May |
| 47.10 | George Skevis | 12.10.79 | 1 | Croydon | 16 Jul |
| 45.96 | John Parkin | 23.02.79 | 1 | Colwyn Bay | 8 Jul |
| 43.70 dh | David Lovett | 13.09.78 | 4 | Nottingham | 7 Jul |
| 42.96 | Terry Attwood | 8.09.78 | 1 | Windsor | 25 Jun |
| 42.78 dh | Andrew Waters | 11.10.79 | 5 | Nottingham | 7 Jul |
| 42.32 | | | 2 | Braintree | 23 Jul |
| 42.00 | Pete Waterman | 12.09.79 | 2 | London (CP) | 28 May |
| (10) | | | | | |
| 42.00 | Martin Hayes | 31.08.79 | 1 | Rotherham | 20 Sep |
| 41.88 | Steven Stanford | 9.12.79 | 1 | Bebington | 10 Jun |
| 41.70 | Nick Barber | 22.11.78 | 1P | Cudworth | 26 Aug |
| 41.58 | John Thyer | 23.11.78 | 1 | Plymouth | 1 Jul |

| | | | | | | |
|---|---|---|---|---|---|---|
| 41.48 | Constantine Karayannis | 9.01.79 | 1 | London (He) | 4 | Jun |
| 41.42 | Simon Mathieson | 20.01.79 | 2 | Cwmbran | 16 | Jul |
| 41.16 | Darren Hatton | 21.03.79 | 2 | Hoo | 30 | Apr |
| 40.42 | Richard Greenhow | 13.02.80 | 1 | Carlisle | 10 | Jun |

## DISCUS - Under 15 - 1.25kg

| | | | | | | |
|---|---|---|---|---|---|---|
| 47.44 | Simon Williams | 5.10.80 | 1 | Nottingham | 7 | Jul |
| 46.18 | Scot Thompson | 10.08.81 | 1 | Aberdeen | 9 | Sep |
| 45.48 | Graeme Allan | 24.09.80 | 1 | Antrim | 12 | Aug |
| 44.96 | Tony Quinn | 14.01.81 | 1 | Antrim | 19 | Aug |
| 44.82 | Adrian Cluskey | 30.12.80 | 1 | Crawley | 19 | Jul |
| 42.66 | James Goforth | 7.12.80 | 2 | Nottingham | 7 | Jul |
| 42.04 | Daniel Lethbridge | 1.04.81 | 1 | Crawley | 28 | Aug |
| 41.04 | James Bryan | | 1 | Newport | 17 | Sep |
| 40.98 | Daniel Oliver | 11.10.80 | 1 | Cheltenham | 17 | Jun |
| 40.86 | Ben Marsden | 20.10.80 | 1 | Basildon | 10 | Jun |
| (10) | | | | | | |
| 40.08 | William Hardgrave | 17.09.80 | 4 | Nottingham | 7 | Jul |
| 39.96 | James Rumbold | 4.11.81 | 1 | Yeovil | 3 | Sep |
| 39.92 | Craig Smith | 1.03.81 | 1 | Pitreavie | 9 | Sep |
| 39.70 | Liam Walsh | 5.05.82 | 1 | Cardiff | 1 | Jul |
| 38.88 | Chris Marland | 9.11.80 | 1 | Cardiff | 22 | Jul |
| 38.80 | John Barnes | 6.05.82 | Q | Nottingham | 7 | Jul |
| 38.64 | Andrew Graham | 1.09.80 | Q | Nottingham | 7 | Jul |
| 38.64 | Liam McCaffrey | | 1 | Swansea | 26 | Aug |
| 38.60 | Daniel Waller | 1.10.80 | 1 | Welwyn | 10 | Jun |
| 38.60 | Philip Morley | 8.12.80 | 5 | Nottingham | 7 | Jul |
| (20) | | | | | | |
| 38.46 | James Provan | 23.09.80 | 5 | London (He) | 6 | Aug |
| 38.22 | Tom Hayman | 17.09.80 | 1 | Mansfield | 10 | Jun |
| 38.14 | Matthew Simpole | 6.07.81 | 1 | London (TB) | 25 | Jun |
| 37.86 | Craig Chatburn | 29.01.81 | 1 | Wigan | 25 | Jun |
| 37.68 | Mark Tinwell | 18.11.81 | 2 | Birmingham | 3 | Sep |
| 37.62 | Stuart Denny | 28.04.81 | Q | Nottingham | 7 | Jul |
| 37.52 | Guy Wnuk | 12.09.80 | 1 | Walton | 1 | Jul |

**overage**

| | | | | | | |
|---|---|---|---|---|---|---|
| 43.12 | William Kirkpatrick | U17 | 28.02.80 | 2 | Antrim | 12 | Aug |
| 42.28 | Eifion Robinson | U17 | | 3 | Antrim | 12 | Aug |

## DISCUS - Under 13 - 1kg

| | | | | | |
|---|---|---|---|---|---|
| 33.14 | C. Orr | 1 | Pitreavie | 9 | Jul |

## HAMMER

| | | | | | | | |
|---|---|---|---|---|---|---|---|
| 71.52 | David Smith | U23 | 2.11.74 | 1 | Hull | 22 | Jul |
| 71.18 | | | | 1 | Wakefield | 17 | Sep |
| 70.12 | | | | 1 | Birmingham | 20 | May |
| 69.62 | | | | 5 | K. Wusterhausen, GER | 30 | Aug |
| 69.46 | | | | 1 | Derby | 3 | Jun |
| 69.42 | | | | 1 | London (Col) | 22 | Apr |
| 69.42 | | | | 3 | Cwmbran | 9 | Jul |
| 69.20 | | | | 1 | Gateshead | 21 | Aug |
| 69.02 | | | | 2 | Kilkenny, IRE | 2 | Sep |
| 68.66 | | | | 1 | Hull | 2 | Apr |
| 68.32 | | | | 5 | Birmingham | 16 | Jul |
| 68.18 | | | | 1 | Bedford | 29 | May |
| 66.92 | | | | Q | Bedford | 29 | May |
| 66.64 | | | | 1 | Cleckheaton | 24 | Sep |
| 66.60 | | | | 1 | Manchester | 10 | Sep |
| 66.34 | | | | 1 | Wakefield | 6 | May |
| 66.02 | | | | 1 | Grimsby | 13 | May |

| | | | | | | |
|---|---|---|---|---|---|---|
| 71.28 | Peter Vivian | | 5.11.70 | 7 | Villeneuve d'Ascq, FRA | 25 Jun |
| | 70.92 | | | 2 | Cwmbran | 9 Jul |
| | 70.70 | | | 5 | Faro, POR | 27 May |
| | 70.26 | | | 3b | Rehlingen, GER | 5 Jun |
| | 69.88 | | | 1 | Loughborough | 11 Jun |
| | 69.84 | | | 2 | London (CP) | 3 Jun |
| | 69.78 | | | 1 | Birmingham | 1 Jul |
| | 69.34 | | | 4 | Birmingham | 16 Jul |
| | 68.92 | | | 2 | London (He) | 7 May |
| | 67.86 | | | 2 | Enfield | 19 Aug |
| | 67.60 | | | 3 | Birmingham | 20 May |
| | 67.42 | | | 1 | London (WL) | 30 Jul |
| | 67.38 | | | 1 | London (Col) | 28 Jun |
| | 67.28 | | | 34Q | Gothenburg, SWE | 5 Aug |
| | 66.94 | | | 1 | London (CP) | 18 Jun |
| | 66.80 | | | 4 | Gateshead | 21 Aug |
| 70.48 | Michael Jones | | 23.07.63 | 1 | London (CP) | 3 Jun |
| | 70.28 | | | 1 | London (He) | 7 May |
| | 70.08 | | | 2 | Birmingham | 20 May |
| | 69.44 | | | 2 | Birmingham | 16 Jul |
| | 69.00 | | | 1 | Derby | 30 Jul |
| | 68.30 | | | 1 | Stoke | 9 Sep |
| | 68.28 | | | 2 | Birmingham | 1 Jul |
| | 67.78 | | | 3 | Enfield | 19 Aug |
| | 67.06 | | | 3 | Kilkenny, IRE | 2 Sep |
| | 66.98 | | | 1 | Horsham | 13 May |
| | 66.74 | | | 2 | Bedford | 29 May |
| | 66.68 | | | 1 | Croydon | 28 Aug |
| | 66.32 | | | 5 | Gateshead | 21 Aug |
| | 66.24 | | | Q | Bedford | 29 May |
| 69.44 | Jason Byrne | | 9.09.70 | 3 | Birmingham | 16 Jul |
| | 67.72 | | | 1 | London (Col) | 21 Jun |
| | 66.86 | | | 1 | London (Col) | 5 Jul |
| 68.88 | Paul Head | | 1.07.65 | 1 | Enfield | 19 Aug |
| | 67.80 | | | 2 | Derby | 30 Jul |
| | 67.02 | | | 4 | Kilkenny, IRE | 2 Sep |
| | 66.28 | | | 2 | Stoke | 9 Sep |
| | 54 performances to 66.00 by 5 athletes | | | | | |
| 65.02 | David Smith | | 21.06.62 | 2 | Middlesbrough | 13 Aug |
| 64.08 | Shane Peacock | | 5.03.63 | 6 | Birmingham | 16 Jul |
| 63.50 | John Pearson | | 30.04.66 | 1 | Loughborough | 24 May |
| *63.46* | *Phil Spivey* | | *15.05.61* | *3* | *Stoke* | *9 Sep* |
| 63.00 | Gareth Cook | | 20.02.69 | 1 | Carshalton | 17 Sep |
| 62.96 | Stephen Pearson | | 13.09.59 | 2 | Manchester | 10 Sep |
| | (10) | | | | | |
| 62.92 | William Beauchamp | | 9.09.70 | 1 | Perivale | 23 Aug |
| 62.86 | Chris Howe | | 17.11.67 | 7 | Birmingham | 16 Jul |
| 62.70 | Paul Barnard | | 27.07.72 | 1 | Middlesbrough | 19 Jul |
| 62.60 | Rob Earle | | 15.09.60 | 1 | Ipswich | 1 Aug |
| 62.48 | Adrian Palmer | | 10.08.69 | 1 | Crawley | 1 Jul |
| 62.14 | Shaun Pickering | | 14.11.61 | 1 | London (WL) | 13 Aug |
| 61.90 | Robert Weir | | 4.02.61 | 4 | Enfield | 19 Aug |
| 61.62 | Malcolm Fenton | | 12.02.56 | 1 | London (BP) | 8 Apr |
| 61.02 | Steve Whyte | | 14.03.64 | 1 | Bedford | 13 May |
| 60.56 | Steve Minnikin | | 4.01.72 | 1 | Sheffield | 13 May |
| | (20) | | | | | |
| 60.12 | Dave Allan | | 17.10.70 | 1 | Edinburgh | 7 May |
| 60.04 | Malcolm Croad | U23 | 27.10.73 | 2 | London (Col) | 12 Jul |
| 59.18 | Chris Black | V45 | 1.01.50 | 1 | Grendon Hall | 15 Oct |
| 58.36 | Steve Angell | | 8.04.70 | 2 | Harrow | 5 Jul |

| | | | | | | | |
|---|---|---|---|---|---|---|---|
| 58.28 | Simon Bown | U23 | 21.11.74 | 3 | London (Col) | 12 | Jul |
| *57.98* | *Ed Healey* | *V40* | *54* | *1* | *Dublin (M), IRE* | *17* | *May* |
| 57.72 | Mike Floyd | U20 | 26.09.76 | 3 | Belfort, FRA | 6 | Aug |
| 57.50 | Gareth Jones | | 14.12.68 | 1 | Cwmbran | 10 | May |
| 57.46 | Craig Ellams | | 24.11.72 | 7 | Birmingham | 20 | May |
| 57.44 | Alan McNicholas | U23 | 10.12.74 | 1 | London (He) | 5 | Aug |
| 57.34 | Anthony Swain | U23 | 17.01.75 | 1 | Wakefield | 9 | Jul |
| (30) | | | | | | | |
| 57.20 | Steve Sammut | | 3.05.67 | 1 | Salisbury | 9 | Jul |
| 56.98 | Glen Kerr | U23 | 27.10.74 | 2 | London (He) | 5 | Aug |
| 56.92 | Graham Holder | | 16.01.72 | 1 | London (CP) | 14 | May |
| 56.84 | Mark Miller | | 10.11.71 | 3 | Enfield | 30 | Jul |
| 56.56 | Iain Park | U23 | 16.07.74 | 2 | London (Col) | 26 | Jul |
| 56.48 | Wayne Clarke | U23 | 24.12.75 | 2 | Wakefield | 24 | Jul |
| 55.70 | Dave Gisbey | | 2.05.60 | 4 | Edinburgh | 24 | Jun |
| 55.54 | Matt Spicer | | 18.05.71 | 1 | Bournemouth | 6 | May |
| 54.58 | Eric Kerr | | 9.12.64 | 2 | Sutton | 22 | Jul |
| 54.28 | Rob Careless | U23 | 7.09.74 | 1 | Corby | 25 | Jun |
| (40) | | | | | | | |
| 54.00 | Matthew Bell | U20 | 2.06.78 | 3 | Bedford | 1 | Jul |
| 54.00 | Steve McEvoy | | 23.05.63 | 1 | London (Col) | 12 | Jul |
| 53.90 | Neil Curtis | U23 | 30.07.74 | 2 | Corby | 25 | Jun |
| 53.66 | Bill Fuller | U20 | 19.10.76 | 4 | Bedford | 1 | Jul |
| 53.62 | Maurice Hicks | | 1.01.70 | 3 | Bracknell | 3 | Jun |
| 53.56 | Andrew Benn | U20 | 2.09.77 | 4 | Carshalton | 17 | Sep |
| 53.46 | Tony Irving | U23 | 30.04.75 | 5 | Edinburgh | 24 | Jun |
| 53.30 | Stuart Spratley | | 18.07.72 | 8 | London (CP) | 3 | Jun |
| 53.16 | John Nevis | | 24.12.69 | 7 | Gateshead | 17 | Jun |
| 53.04 | David Nicholl | | 16.09.69 | 5 | Dublin, IRE | 15 | Jul |
| (50) | | | | | | | |
| 52.96 | John Owen | | 28.10.64 | 4 | Crawley | 1 | Jul |
| 52.90 | Paul Dickenson | V45 | 4.12.49 | 2 | Loughborough | 20 | May |
| 52.68 | Russell Payne-Dwyer | | 11.09.60 | 4 | Birmingham | 18 | Jun |
| 52.56 | Stuart Thurgood | U20 | 17.05.76 | 7 | London (Col) | 5 | Jul |
| 52.56 | Barrie Dickinson | | 17.09.67 | 1 | Cannock | 16 | Sep |
| 52.54 | Calum Bruce | U23 | 28.02.75 | 1 | Antrim | 20 | Jun |
| *52.26* | *Hayden Knowles* | *U20* | *17.08.77* | *2* | *Cannock* | *16* | *Sep* |
| *52.22* | *Jiri Horak* | *U23* | *24.07.74* | *1* | *Oxford* | *22* | *Jul* |
| 52.02 | Nigel Winchcombe | | 10.12.59 | 2 | Hull | 19 | Aug |
| 51.80 | Mark Proctor | | 15.01.63 | 1 | Cosford | 5 | Jul |
| 51.48 | Ewart Hulse | | 21.01.62 | 1 | Newport | 12 | Aug |
| 51.24 | Mark Gulliver | | 11.02.72 | 1 | Leeds | 30 | May |
| (60) | | | | | | | |
| 51.24 | Graham Middleton | | 17.09.60 | 5 | Birmingham | 18 | Jun |
| 51.20 | Keith Robinson | V40 | 9.02.52 | 2 | Bournemouth | 6 | May |
| 51.20 | Andy Turner | | 29.08.63 | 1 | London (Nh) | 15 | Jun |
| 50.90 | Sean Jones | | 21.03.69 | 2 | Woodford | 29 | Apr |
| 50.76 | Damon Cripps | | 9.10.70 | 1 | Worcester | 3 | Jun |
| 50.58 | Geoffrey Whaley | | 9.06.58 | 1 | Braunton | 13 | May |
| 50.42 | Gary Curtis | | 21.11.61 | 9 | London (CP) | 3 | Jun |
| 50.40 | Michael Reiss | | 17.06.63 | 2 | Perivale | 30 | Apr |
| 50.34 | Michael Madden | | 13.09.65 | 1 | Plymouth | 6 | May |
| 50.34 | Simon Bowman | | 11.09.71 | 1 | Croydon | 1 | Jul |
| (70) | | | | | | | |
| 49.58 | Barry Williams | V45 | 5.03.47 | 2 | Stretford | 1 | Aug |
| 49.20 | Chris Mallon | | 4.08.72 | 1 | Bracknell | 30 | Apr |
| 49.16 | Bruce Shepherd | | 20.03.67 | 5 | Aberdeen | 20 | May |
| 49.10 | Peter Stark | V40 | 9.12.53 | 6 | Crawley | 1 | Jul |
| *49.06* | *Hugh Kennedy* | | | *4* | *Oxford* | *1* | *Jul* |
| 48.80 | Kenneth Smith | | 10.05.64 | 1 | Yate | 19 | Aug |
| 48.74 | John Urquhart | U20 | 14.11.77 | 1 | Glasgow | 16 | Aug |

| 48.64 | Jimmy Summers | | 7.10.65 | 1 | Ilford | 1 | Jul |
|---|---|---|---|---|---|---|---|
| 48.60 | Wesley Clarke | | 31.12.63 | 2 | Welwyn | 19 | Aug |
| 48.52 | Phil Tyley | | 11.10.66 | 2 | Portsmouth (RN) | 25 | Jun |
| 48.38 | Chris O'Connell | | 17.01.59 | 2 | Wakefield | 12 | Aug |
| | (80) | | | | | | |
| 48.24 | Jason Dibble | | 15.02.71 | 6 | Cannock | 16 | Sep |
| 48.16 | Bernard Reed | | 18.10.56 | 7 | Crawley | 1 | Jul |
| 47.74 | Eric Berry | V40 | 23.04.54 | 1 | High Wycombe | 6 | May |
| | 48.32 un | | | | | | |
| 47.74 | Len Steers | | 31.03.60 | 1 | Blackburn | 25 | Jun |
| 47.68 | Mark Broughton | | 23.10.63 | 2 | London (Col) | 12 | Jul |
| 47.64 | David Robinson | U20 | 12.01.78 | 2 | Jarrow | 6 | May |
| 47.64 | Chris Roberts | | | 1 | London (PH) | 5 | Aug |
| 47.54 | Gary Herrington | | 31.03.61 | 2 | Corby | 3 | Jun |
| 47.52 | Andy Charij | | | 6 | Aldershot | 23 | Jul |
| 47.44 | Terry Lalley | V45 | 12.11.49 | 8 | Crawley | 1 | Jul |
| | (90) | | | | | | |
| 47.34 | Neil Townsend | | 3.05.63 | 4 | Crawley | 25 | Jun |
| 47.30 | Andy Mitchell | | | 1 | Milton Keynes | 19 | Aug |
| 47.20 | Adam Devonshire | U17 | 2.03.79 | 1 | Watford | 22 | Jul |
| 47.18 | Greg Bastille | U23 | 25.04.73 | 5 | Enfield | 3 | Jun |
| 47.14 | Gary Parsons | | | 1 | Welwyn | 1 | Jul |
| 46.98 | Alan Woods | V40 | 27.03.51 | 1 | Bromley | 11 | Jun |
| 46.94 | Brian Lockley | V45 | 18.06.48 | 2 | Blackburn | 25 | Jun |
| 46.94 | David Shenton | U20 | 20.10.77 | 2 | Bolton | 16 | Sep |
| 46.60 | John Little | V40 | 14.04.53 | 2 | Carlisle | 2 | Apr |
| 46.52 | Chris Melluish | V50 | 15.07.44 | 1 | London (He) | 5 | Sep |
| | (100) | | | | | | |
| 46.42 | Matt Symonds | | 31.07.68 | 1 | Oxford | 13 | May |
| 46.38 | Simon Natham | | 28.11.66 | 1 | Bolton | 6 | May |
| 46.38 | Peter Aston | V50 | 21.02.45 | 2 | Reading | 1 | Jul |
| 46.16 | Michael McGinn | U23 | 13.12.75 | 3 | Portsmouth | 25 | Jun |
| 46.16 | Gavin Cook | | 30.03.70 | 1 | High Wycombe | 31 | Jul |
| 46.14 | Matt Hammond | | 26.09.68 | 1 | Hull | 16 | Apr |
| 46.14 | Stuart Devonshire | U20 | 19.09.76 | 4 | London (CP) | 10 | Sep |
| 46.12 | Ross Blight | U20 | 28.05.77 | 3 | Utrecht, HOL | 9 | Jul |
| 46.06 | Peter Gordon | V40 | 2.07.51 | 1 | Jarrow | | |
| 46.02 | Anthony Doran | | 22.10.72 | | Cardiff | 19 | Aug |

**Additional Under 20** (1 - 11 above)

| 45.72 | Carl Gregory | | 17.08.77 | 1 | London (WF) | 6 | May |
|---|---|---|---|---|---|---|---|
| 45.48 | Damien Slater | | 14.10.77 | 9 | Bedford | 1 | Jul |
| 45.44 | Neil Bulman | | 7.09.77 | 3 | Jarrow | 6 | May |
| 45.44 | Douglas Spikes | | 1.07.76 | 3 | Perivale | 1 | Jul |

## HAMMER - Under 20 - 6.25kg

| 63.94 | Mike Floyd | | 26.09.76 | 1 | Derby | 17 | Sep |
|---|---|---|---|---|---|---|---|
| 60.22 | Andrew Benn | | 2.09.77 | 1 | Birmingham | 28 | Aug |
| 57.14 | Matthew Bell | | 2.06.78 | 3 | Nottingham | 8 | Jul |
| 56.28 | Bill Fuller | | 19.10.76 | 1 | London (Col) | 19 | Jul |
| *55.74* | *Hayden Knowles* | | *17.08.77* | *1* | *Pitreavie* | *8* | *Jul* |
| 55.12 | John Urquhart | | 14.11.77 | 1 | Glasgow | 16 | Aug |
| 53.68 | Carl Gregory | | 17.08.77 | 1 | Haslemere | 16 | May |
| 53.24 | Paul Gorham | | 7.08.78 | 1 | Basildon | 10 | Jun |
| 52.62 | David Robinson | | 12.01.78 | 1 | Middlesbrough | 13 | May |
| 52.60 | Ross Blight | | 28.05.77 | 1 | Cardiff | 1 | Jul |
| 51.94 | Stuart Thurgood | | 17.05.76 | 3 | Kingston | 13 | Aug |
| | (10) | | | | | | |
| 51.92 | Kevin Davies | | 11.01.78 | 4 | Nottingham | 8 | Jul |
| 51.56 | David Shenton | | 20.10.77 | 2 | Cleckheaton | 24 | Sep |
| 51.18 | Damien Slater | | 14.10.77 | 1 | London (Col) | 12 | Jul |

| 51.10 | Stuart Devonshire | | 19.09.76 | 6 | Nottingham | 8 | Jul |
|---|---|---|---|---|---|---|---|
| 50.80 | Neil Bulman | | 7.09.77 | 1 | Middlesbrough | 18 | Jun |
| 50.28 | Robin Walker | | 8.02.78 | 1 | Hull | 10 | Jun |
| 49.40 | Brett Marsh | | 20.01.76 | 1 | Carn Brea | 17 | Sep |
| 48.76 | Chris Walsh | U17 | 1.10.78 | 1 | Cleckheaton | 24 | Sep |
| 48.68 | Lee Clift | | 12.10.76 | 1 | Croydon | 18 | Jun |
| 48.16 | Nicholas Fogg | | 24.03.78 | 2 | Derby | 17 | Sep |
| | (20) | | | | | | |
| 48.06 | Peter Fuller | | 30.04.78 | 2 | London (WP) | 29 | Apr |
| 47.40 | Douglas Spikes | | 1.07.76 | 4 | Kingston | 13 | Aug |
| 47.38 | Tim Wurr | U17 | 1.03.79 | 1 | Brierley Hill | 20 | Aug |
| 46.92 | Mark Elliott | | 3.04.78 | 1 | Birmingham | 17 | May |

**overage**

| 62.16 | Wayne Clarke | U23 | 24.12.75 | 1 | Grantham | 10 | Jun |
|---|---|---|---|---|---|---|---|

## HAMMER - Under 17 - 5kg

| 59.90 | Adam Devonshire | | 2.03.79 | 1 | London (CP) | 27 | May |
|---|---|---|---|---|---|---|---|
| 59.86 | Tim Wurr | | 1.03.79 | 1 | Nottingham | 7 | Jul |
| 59.80 | James Hawkins | | 14.12.79 | 1 | Kingston | 13 | Aug |
| 56.74 | Michael Sexton | | 26.05.79 | 1 | Haslemere | 18 | Jul |
| 55.92 | James Punch | | 19.12.79 | 2 | Corby | 7 | May |
| 55.72 | Chris Walsh | | 1.10.78 | 1 | Cleckheaton | 24 | Sep |
| 55.02 | Dean Hughes | | 22.09.78 | 1 | Haslemere | 16 | May |
| 54.10 | Martin Hayes | | 31.08.79 | 3 | Nottingham | 7 | Jul |
| 53.34 | Chris Aherne | | 21.12.79 | 1 | Cardiff | 27 | May |
| 52.86 | Tom Eden | | 16.05.79 | 5 | Birmingham | 29 | Jul |
| | (10) | | | | | | |
| 51.52 | Ross Kidner | U15 | 12.09.80 | 2 | Manchester | 10 | Sep |
| 51.40 | Paul McNamara | | 3.10.78 | 1 | Harrow | 4 | Jun |
| 51.20 | Andy Castle | | 8.12.79 | 1 | Solihull | 16 | Jul |
| 51.14 | Christian Vickery | | 10.11.78 | 3 | Kingston | 13 | Aug |
| 51.12 | Pete Waterman | | 12.09.79 | 1 | Peterborough | 21 | May |
| 50.74 | John Parkin | | 23.02.79 | 1 | Brecon | 6 | Aug |
| 50.36 | Mark Clinch | | 23.10.78 | 3 | Sheffield | 28 | May |
| 48.88 | Andrew Grierson | | 23.11.79 | 1 | Southampton | 21 | May |
| 48.18 | Emeka Udechuku | | 10.07.79 | 5 | Kingston | 13 | Aug |
| 47.42 | Anthony White | | 8.09.78 | 3 | Haslemere | 16 | May |

## HAMMER - Under 15 - 4kg

| 58.04 | Ross Kidner | | 12.09.80 | 1 | Manchester | 10 | Sep |
|---|---|---|---|---|---|---|---|
| | 58.72un | | | 1 | Carshalton | 17 | Sep |
| 53.46 | Matthew Sutton | | 8.09.81 | 2 | Manchester | 10 | Sep |
| 52.16 | Jason Stone | | 15.10.80 | 1 | Nottingham | 8 | Jul |
| 50.44 | Ross Thompson | | 7.12.81 | 1 | Birmingham | 3 | Sep |
| 49.80 | Graeme Allan | | 24.09.80 | 2 | Birmingham | 30 | Jul |
| 49.64 | David Jones | | 4.10.80 | 2 | Birmingham | 3 | Sep |
| 49.44 | John Barnes | | 6.05.82 | 1 | Grendon Hall | 15 | Oct |
| 49.04 | Andrew Frost | | 17.04.81 | 2 | London (He) | 6 | Aug |
| 49.00 | Alan Kelsall | | 3.09.80 | 1 | Basildon | 10 | Jun |
| 48.94 | Christopher Adams | | 18.07.81 | 1 | Colwyn Bay | 2 | Sep |
| | (10) | | | | | | |
| 48.48 | Marc Landon | | 9.11.81 | 3 | Birmingham | 30 | Jul |
| 48.22 | David Little | | 28.02.81 | 1 | Carlisle | 10 | Jun |
| 47.74 | Leslie McIntosh | | 25.02.81 | 2 | Stoke | 17 | Jun |
| 47.04 | Gavin Minns | | 5.12.80 | 1 | Kings Lynn | 2 | Jul |
| 47.02 | Michael Bennett | | 22.11.80 | 3 | Birmingham | 3 | Sep |
| 45.88 | Michael Brady | | 21.02.81 | 2 | Sheffield | 27 | May |
| 44.60 | Robin Wheldon | | 7.12.80 | 1 | Cheltenham | 4 | Jun |
| 43.68 | Erik Sanders | | 31.10.80 | 1 | | 17 | Jun |
| 43.22 | Gareth Driscoll | | 8.03.81 | 1 | Kings Lynn | 13 | Aug |

| 43.08 | Adam Miller | 4.11.80 | | Colchester | 13 Aug |
|---|---|---|---|---|---|
| (20) | | | | | |
| 43.04 | Gwynfor Lishman | 1.12.80 | 2 | Carlisle | 9 Jul |
| 41.62 | Damien Howard | 23.11.81 | 1 | Norwich | 3 Sep |

## JAVELIN

| 88.54 | Steve Backley | 12.02.69 | 1 | London (CP) | 7 Jul |
|---|---|---|---|---|---|
| 87.62 A | | | 1 | Pietersburg, RSA | 3 Apr |
| 86.46 | | | 3 | Oslo, NOR | 21 Jul |
| 86.30 | | | 1 | Sheffield | 23 Jul |
| 86.30 | | | 2 | Gothenburg, SWE | 13 Aug |
| 85.90 | | | 3 | Zurich, SWZ | 16 Aug |
| 85.26 | | | 1 | Lahti, FIN | 27 Jul |
| 84.78 | | | 3 | Brussels, BEL | 25 Aug |
| 83.84 | | | 3 | Monaco, MON | 9 Sep |
| 83.24 | | | 1 | Stellenbosch, RSA | 17 Apr |
| 83.20 | | | Q | Gothenburg, SWE | 11 Aug |
| 83.00 | | | 1 | Gateshead | 21 Aug |
| 82.92 A | | | 1 | Krugersdorp, RSA | 10 Apr |
| 82.82 | | | 2 | Gateshead | 2 Jul |
| 81.96 | | | 3 | Villeneuve d'Ascq, FRA | 24 Jun |
| 81.90 | | | 6 | London (CP) | 27 Aug |
| 81.52 | | | 3 | Villeneuve d'Ascq, FRA | 17 Jun |
| 81.00 | | | 1 | Ljubljana, SLO | 21 May |
| 84.14 | Mick Hill | 22.10.64 | 4 | Oslo, NOR | 21 Jul |
| 83.60 | | | 2 | Nurmijarvi, FIN | 4 Jun |
| 83.54 | | | Q | Gothenburg, SWE | 11 Aug |
| 83.48 | | | 3 | London (CP) | 27 Aug |
| 83.40 | | | 5 | Kuortane, FIN | 24 Jun |
| 82.94 | | | 2 | Villeneuve d'Ascq, FRA | 17 Jun |
| 82.38 | | | 2 | Sheffield | 23 Jul |
| 82.38 | | | 6 | Berlin, GER | 1 Sep |
| 82.18 | | | 8 | Zurich, SWZ | 16 Aug |
| 81.40 | | | 3 | Gateshead | 21 Aug |
| 81.34 | | | 6 | London (CP) | 7 Jul |
| 81.06 | | | 6 | Gothenburg, SWE | 13 Aug |
| 80.84 | | | 8 | Brussels, BEL | 25 Aug |
| 80.54 | | | 1 | Birmingham | 15 Jul |
| 79.38 | | | 3 | Gateshead | 2 Jul |
| 79.90 | Colin Mackenzie | 30.06.63 | 1 | London (CP) | 3 Jun |
| 79.80 | | | 1 | Stoke | 9 Sep |
| 79.54 | | | 1 | Birmingham | 1 Jul |
| 79.30 | | | 4 | Sheffield | 23 Jul |
| 78.20 | | | 1 | London (CP) | 18 Jun |
| 77.92 | | | 1 | Derby | 30 Jul |
| 77.50 | | | 2 | Birmingham | 15 Jul |
| 76.64 | | | 7 | Helsinki, FIN | 28 Jun |
| 76.56 | | | 1 | Enfield | 19 Aug |
| *79.06* | *Terry McHugh* | *22.08.63* | *1* | *Magglingen, SWZ* | *6 May* |
| 78.44 | Mark Roberson | 13.03.67 | 1 | Bedford | 26 Aug |
| 78.44 | | | 1 | Grimsby | 24 Sep |
| 76.78 | | | 1 | Andorra, AND | 17 Sep |
| 76.44 | | | 1 | Enfield | 29 Apr |
| 76.06 | | | 1 | Liverpool | 30 Jul |
| 77.14 | Nigel Bevan | 3.01.68 | 1 | Cwmbran | 9 Jul |
| 76.86 | | | 1 | Loughborough | 20 May |
| 76.58 | | | 3 | Birmingham | 15 Jul |
| 76.52 | | | 5 | Sheffield | 23 Jul |
| 76.30 | Nick Nieland | 31.01.72 | 2 | London (CP) | 3 Jun |

52 performances to 76.00 by 6 athletes

207

| | | | | | | |
|---|---|---|---|---|---|---|
| 75.64 | Roald Bradstock | | 24.04.62 | 2 | Walnut, USA | 15 Apr |
| 75.32 | Steve Harrison | | 19.12.72 | 6 | Tallinn, EST | 9 Jul |
| 74.24 | Stuart Faben | U23 | 28.02.75 | 1 | Narbonne, FRA | 29 Jul |
| 68.34 | Tony Smith | | 17.05.58 | 3 | Birmingham | 1 Jul |
| | (10) | | | | | |
| 67.78 | Stefan Baldwin | | 26.04.70 | 4 | Vila Real, POR | 27 May |
| 67.28 | Phil Parry | | 4.10.65 | 1 | Edinburgh | 24 Jun |
| 67.02 | Keith Beard | | 8.11.61 | 1 | Hoorn, HOL | 24 Sep |
| 66.00 | Dean Smahon | | 8.12.61 | 1 | Loughborough | 24 May |
| 65.96 | Duncan MacDonald | U23 | 30.03.74 | 8 | Birmingham | 15 Jul |
| 65.90 | Peter Yates | | 15.06.57 | 4 | London (CP) | 18 Jun |
| 65.34 | Paul Cooper | U20 | 4.12.76 | 5 | Loughborough | 11 Jun |
| 65.14 | Mark Pinner | | 12.05.64 | 1 | Cannock | 16 Aug |
| 65.02 | Dave Ottley | V40 | 5.08.55 | 1 | Telford | 24 Sep |
| 64.68 | Matt Atkins | U20 | 23.06.77 | 1 | Derby | 29 Apr |
| | (20) | | | | | |
| 64.66 | Demetrio Barros | | 29.06.71 | 1 | Bracknell | 3 Jun |
| 64.56 | Ken Hayford | | 10.03.63 | 1 | Peterborough | 6 May |
| 64.44 | Mark Francis | U20 | 23.09.77 | 1 | Carshalton | 17 Sep |
| 64.16 | Simon Bennett | | 16.10.72 | 1 | Braunton | 13 May |
| 63.90 | James Hurrion | U23 | 11.11.73 | 1 | Oxford | 28 Jun |
| 63.88 | Stuart Loughran | U20 | 19.02.76 | 1 | London (He) | 9 Sep |
| 63.64 | Damien Crawford | | 22.08.68 | 2 | Antrim | 1 Jul |
| 63.22 | David Hanna | U23 | 13.12.75 | 1 | Antrim | 20 Jun |
| 63.08 | David Wilson | | 5.09.70 | 1 | Hull | 30 Apr |
| 63.06 | Jon Clarke | | 20.11.67 | 1 | Cardiff | 19 Aug |
| | (30) | | | | | |
| 62.68 | Alan Holloway | | 22.06.60 | 2 | Corby | 25 Jun |
| 62.60 | David Parker | U17 | 28.02.80 | 1 | Jarrow | 19 Aug |
| 62.34 | Jon Wilkinson | | 17.02.62 | 2 | Sheffield | 14 May |
| 62.10 | Dave Bailey | U23 | 19.10.73 | 3 | Corby | 25 Jun |
| 62.06 | Simon Shirley | | 3.08.66 | 12D | Gotzis, AUT | 28 May |
| 62.02 | Robert Mullen | | 8.08.64 | 2 | Loughborough | 24 May |
| 61.98 | Matthew Bamford | | 19.09.58 | 2 | London (He) | 5 Aug |
| 61.96 | Steve Langdon | | 1.01.58 | 2 | London (Elt) | 5 Aug |
| 61.72 | Anthony Norman | | 5.07.63 | 1 | Bromley | 19 Aug |
| 61.56 | Chris Smith | U23 | 27.11.75 | 1 | Hoo | 19 Aug |
| | (40) | | | | | |
| 61.46 | James Drennen | | 16.08.72 | 1 | Bournemouth | 6 May |
| 61.38 | Simon Carter | U23 | 5.03.75 | 2 | Hoo | 19 Aug |
| 61.34 | Graham Lay | U23 | 13.11.75 | 1 | Loughborough | 26 Apr |
| 61.34 | A. Johnson | | | 1 | Thurrock | 19 Aug |
| 61.30 | Dean Macey | U20 | 12.12.77 | 1D | Stoke | 4 Jun |
| 61.26 | Paul Howard | | 19.10.66 | 1 | Croydon | 3 Sep |
| 61.22 | Kevin Hill | U23 | 17.06.73 | 1 | Stretford | 1 Jul |
| 61.20 | Rob Laing | | 30.07.66 | 4 | Birmingham | 20 May |
| 61.14 | Thomas Dobbing | U23 | 5.02.73 | 1 | Norwich | 13 May |
| 61.14 | Andy Clarke | | 10.08.70 | 1 | Stretford | 16 May |
| | (50) | | | | | |
| 60.98 | Alex Kruger | | 18.11.63 | 13D | Gotzis, AUT | 28 May |
| 60.92 | James Menhennitt | U23 | 14.12.74 | 1 | Jersey | 9 Sep |
| 60.80 | Andrew Benn | U20 | 2.09.77 | 1 | Kingston | 12 Mar |
| 60.70 | Stephen Rogers | | 1.09.71 | 2D | Stoke | 4 Jun |
| 60.38 | Andy Hayward | U23 | 26.10.74 | 1 | Hull | 16 Apr |
| 60.30 | Barry Thomas | | 28.04.72 | 6D | Fukuoka, JAP | 2 Sep |
| 60.26 | Jason Oakes | U20 | 29.09.77 | 1 | Middlesbrough | 30 Jul |
| 60.16 | Simon Achurch | U23 | 27.12.74 | 2 | London (Ha) | 25 Jun |
| 60.06 | Landley Darlington | U20 | 19.01.77 | 2 | Peterborough | 28 Aug |
| 59.96 | Alistair Gidley | | 5.09.72 | 2 | Hayes | 26 Mar |
| | (60) | | | | | |
| 59.90 | Trevor Ratcliffe | | 9.03.64 | 6 | London (CP) | 18 Jun |

208

| | | | | | | | |
|---|---|---|---|---|---|---|---|
| 59.84 | David Sketchley | U20 | 25.02.76 | 2 | Colchester | 26 | Mar |
| 59.76 | Seth Kirkham | U23 | 9.09.75 | 3 | London (Ha) | 25 | Jun |
| 59.64 | Sean Evans | U20 | 3.10.76 | 2 | Nottingham | 8 | Jul |
| 59.42 | Stewart McMillan | | 12.09.69 | 1 | Edinburgh | 6 | Aug |
| 59.28 | Michael Morgan | | 30.07.66 | 6 | London (He) | 7 | May |
| 59.22 | David Bigham | | 4.07.71 | 7 | London (He) | 7 | May |
| 58.78 | Kevin Murch | | 11.11.58 | 1 | Corby | 3 | Jun |
| 58.68 | Damian Huntingford | U20 | 11.06.77 | 5 | Nottingham | 8 | Jul |
| 58.62 | Wayne Powell | | 27.07.71 | 2 | Bath | 31 | May |
| | (70) | | | | | | |
| 58.60 | Fuat Fuat | | 20.09.71 | 4 | Watford | 19 | Aug |
| 58.44 | Stuart Bartlett | | 20.10.64 | 3 | Hayes | 13 | May |
| 58.38 | Shane Lewis | | 22.08.72 | 2 | Edinburgh | 3 | Jun |
| 58.20 | Sam Armstrong | U23 | 17.02.74 | 4 | Edinburgh | 24 | Jun |
| 58.20 | Kevin Sheppard | V45 | 9.06.48 | 1 | Crawley | 4 | Jul |
| 58.16 | David Brown | | 4.06.66 | 1 | Perivale | 1 | Jul |
| 58.10 | Wayne McLoughlin | | 27.03.66 | 1 | Wakefield | 30 | Apr |
| 58.08 | Roger Hunter | U20 | 10.03.76 | 3D | Stoke | 4 | Jun |
| 58.04 | Buster Watson | | 19.11.57 | 1 | Barn Elms | 5 | Aug |
| *58.00* | *Cyrus Doomasia* | *U23* | *31.03.73* | *2* | *Ilford* | *19* | *Aug* |
| 57.98 | Pawlo Ostapowycz | V40 | 1.07.52 | 2 | Blackpool | 19 | Aug |
| | (80) | | | | | | |
| 57.92 | Stephen Birse | U20 | 8.10.77 | 1 | Middlesbrough | 3 | Jun |
| 57.90 | Stewart Maxwell | | 29.06.58 | 2 | Derby | 29 | Apr |
| 57.86 | Sean O'Hanlon | U20 | 3.09.76 | 2 | Brighton | 3 | Jun |
| 57.14 | John Trower | | 6.02.56 | 1 | Telford | 6 | May |
| 57.10 | Anthony Brannen | | 16.09.68 | 1D | Derby | 30 | Apr |
| 57.04 | Terry Gyorffy | | 28.01.65 | 1 | Basingstoke | 6 | May |
| 57.00 | Peter Johnson | U23 | 25.09.75 | 2 | Liverpool | 23 | Apr |
| 56.94 | Matthew Phillips | U20 | 22.09.77 | 1 | Stoke | 27 | May |
| 56.94 | Damien McDaid | U20 | 17.07.78 | 6 | Bedford | 2 | Jul |
| 56.82 | Ben Jump | | 6.02.65 | 1 | Glasgow | 11 | Jun |
| | (90) | | | | | | |
| 56.80 | Greg Hayward | | 28.01.64 | 1 | Cosford | 14 | Jun |
| 56.72 | Paul Bale | U20 | 20.12.76 | 1 | Rugby | 22 | Jul |
| 56.72 | Josh Harrison | U23 | 14.08.75 | 5 | Liverpool | 30 | Jul |
| 56.64 | P. Berry | | | 1 | Andover | 5 | Aug |
| 56.62 | David Abernethy | V40 | 5.09.55 | 1 | Carlisle | 10 | Sep |
| 56.60 | Mark Welch | U23 | 9.11.74 | 2 | Aldershot | 7 | Jun |
| 56.48 | David Odwar | U20 | 23.12.76 | 7 | Nottingham | 8 | Jul |
| 56.44 | Andrew Whiting | U23 | 7.03.74 | 1 | Bedford | 25 | Jun |
| 56.34 | Peter Fraser | U20 | 28.01.78 | 2 | Edinburgh | 6 | Aug |
| 56.32 | Dean Johnson | U23 | 31.12.75 | 1 | Sheffield | 19 | Jul |
| | (100) | | | | | | |
| 56.32 | Ken Taylor | V45 | 24.10.48 | 1 | Blackburn | 19 | Aug |
| 56.24 | Roger Killick | U20 | 20.11.76 | 1 | Loughborough | 22 | Jul |
| 56.20 | David Hassall | | 11.10.70 | 4 | Derby | 29 | Apr |

**Additional Under 20** (1 - 21 above)

| | | | | | | | |
|---|---|---|---|---|---|---|---|
| 55.82 | David Evans | | 23.01.76 | 4 | Telford | 18 | Jun |
| 55.76 | Adam Carswell | | 8.01.76 | 2 | London (WP) | 1 | Jul |
| 55.62 | Tim Eldridge | | 15.03.76 | 4 | Barking | 13 | May |
| 55.58 | Andrew Yiannacou | | 18.08.78 | 1 | Enfield | 17 | Jul |
| 55.50 | Ben Cascoe | | 26.12.77 | 1 | Croydon | 10 | Jun |
| 55.48 | Tim Cattermole | | 17.08.77 | 1 | Yeovil | 10 | Jun |
| 55.44 | Stephen Cross | | 12.02.77 | 1 | Wrexham | 19 | Aug |
| 55.24 | Brent Starling | | 19.05.76 | 1 | Middlesbrough | 30 | Jul |
| 54.98 | Martin Troy | | 13.07.76 | 1 | Bedford | 14 | Jun |
| | (30) | | | | | | |
| 54.88 | Ian Burns | | 20.09.77 | 1 | Gateshead | | |
| 54.60 | Lee Hammond | | 13.11.77 | 2 | Stoke | 27 | May |

| | | | | | | |
|---|---|---|---|---|---|---|
| 53.74 | Keith Lavelle | | 13.05.77 | 1 | Liverpool | 13 May |
| 53.10 | Kevin Lajoie | | | 1 | Portsmouth | 13 May |
| 52.86 | Matthew Davies | U17 | 16.09.78 | 4 | Utrecht, HOL | 9 Jul |
| 52.62 | Harley Carter | | 28.06.78 | 11 | Nottingham | 8 Jul |
| 52.40 | David Ralson | | 22.02.77 | 1D | Stoke | 17 Sep |
| 52.18 | Simon Pavitt | | 12.07.76 | 2 | Braintree | 24 Jun |
| 52.16 | Jon Taylor | | 25.10.77 | 1 | Bournemouth | 10 Jun |
| 52.04 | Ben Cotton | | 10.03.78 | 1 | Peterborough | 10 Jun |

## JAVELIN - Under 17 - 700g

| | | | | | | |
|---|---|---|---|---|---|---|
| 68.32 | David Parker | | 28.02.80 | 1 | Colwyn Bay | 15 Jul |
| 64.18 | Clifton Green | | 10.10.79 | 1 | Hoo | 10 Jun |
| 63.74 | Steve Jamieson | | 4.02.79 | 2 | Colwyn Bay | 15 Jul |
| 59.62 | Stuart Walker | | 22.09.78 | 1 | Cannock | 21 May |
| 58.96 | Dan Carter | | 15.04.80 | 1 | Braintree | 21 Sep |
| 58.12 | Matthew Davies | | 16.09.78 | 2 | Cannock | 21 May |
| 57.74 | Robert Charlesworth | | 25.03.79 | 1 | Bedford | 26 Aug |
| 57.06 | Tim Phillips | | 13.01.79 | 1 | Welwyn | 10 Jun |
| 57.02 | Tim Kitney | | 26.04.80 | 1 | London (He) | 20 Jun |
| 56.56 | Stephen Melber | | 26.02.79 | 1 | Milton Keynes | 18 Jun |
| | (10) | | | | | |
| 56.42 | J. Pearson | | | 1 | Wrexham | 12 Mar |
| 56.24 | Matthew Pedrick | | 3.05.79 | 4 | Birmingham | 29 Jul |
| 55.78 | Patrick Boundy | | 19.02.79 | 1 | Kingston | 13 Aug |
| 55.32 | Greg Magee | | 27.09.78 | 1 | Pitreavie | 8 Jul |
| 55.18 | James Apps | | 29.04.80 | 1 | London (CP) | 13 May |
| 54.62 | Robert Southward | | 24.03.80 | 2 | Wrexham | 12 Mar |
| 54.46 | Martin Stringer | | 23.11.78 | 1 | Croydon | 10 Jun |
| 53.82 | Alan Rudkin | | 5.11.78 | 1 | Great Yarmouth | 13 Aug |
| 53.48 | Chris Gasson | | 28.02.79 | 1 | London (Elt) | 30 Apr |
| 53.40 | Neil McLellan | | 10.09.78 | 6 | Nottingham | 7 Jul |

**overage**

| | | | | | | |
|---|---|---|---|---|---|---|
| 60.42 o | Damien McDaid | U20 | 17.07.78 | 1 | Antrim | 13 May |

## JAVELIN - Under 15 - 600g

| | | | | | | |
|---|---|---|---|---|---|---|
| 58.74 | Philips Olwenu | | 14.02.81 | 1 | London (He) | 6 Aug |
| 54.06 | Shaun Groves | | 15.09.80 | 1 | Swansea | 28 Aug |
| 53.10 | Philip Sharpe | | 6.03.81 | 1 | Blackpool | 10 Sep |
| 52.10 | Tim Pamphlett | | 18.02.81 | 1 | Hoo | 10 Jun |
| 51.54 | Ian Creek | | 20.09.80 | 3 | Nottingham | 8 Jul |
| 50.82 | Ben Haughton | | | 1 | Dublin (M), IRE | 16 Jul |
| 50.42 | Liam Walsh | | 5.05.82 | 1 | Colwyn Bay | 10 Jun |
| 50.24 | Graeme Denholm | | 31.03.81 | 1 | Aalborg, DEN | 30 Jul |
| 49.98 | Jonathan Lundman | | 7.12.81 | 5 | Nottingham | 8 Jul |
| 49.30 | Stuart Denny | | 28.04.81 | 1 | Carlisle | 10 Sep |
| | (10) | | | | | |
| 49.26 | Steven Elliott | | 5.12.80 | 1 | Blackburn | 21 May |
| 49.06 | Tony Stanley-Clarke | | 10.10.80 | 1 | London (Elt) | 16 Jul |
| 48.86 | Ben Hansen | | 12.10.80 | 6 | Nottingham | 8 Jul |
| 48.82 | Chris Appleby | | | 3 | London (He) | 6 Aug |
| 48.74 | Scot Thompson | | 10.08.81 | 1 | Inverness | 17 Aug |
| 48.12 | Simon Williams | | 5.10.80 | 1 | Windsor | 20 Aug |
| 48.00 | Matthew Peleszok | | 17.10.81 | 1 | Grantham | 21 May |
| 47.78 | Mark Tinwell | | 18.11.81 | 1 | Stretford | 10 Jun |
| 47.48 | Matthew Patience | | 22.12.81 | 1 | Kingston | 17 Jun |
| 47.24 | James Dowsett | | 10.11.80 | 1 | Birmingham | 3 Sep |
| | (20) | | | | | |
| 46.50 | Rob Holmes | | 2.11.80 | 1 | Cwmbran | 16 Jul |
| 46.24 | Ben Poynter | | 23.09.80 | 1 | London (CP) | 27 May |
| 46.24 | J. Fowkes | | | 1 | Thurrock | 16 Jul |

46.14 Max Shale 20.01.81 1 Windsor 25 Jun

**Under 13**
39.78 C. Wade

## JAVELIN - Under 13 - 400g
38.70 M. Groves 1 Rhymney Valley 17 Sep
37.06 C. Taylor 11.11.82 1 Wakefield 17 Sep
36.52 M. Richardson 1 Woking 3 Sep
35.96 Tim Greenwood 22.11.82 1 Solihull 10 Sep
35.94 Tony Francis 6.07.83 1 Woking 16 Aug
35.32 Simon McKay 4 Paddington 3 Sep
34.80 C. Johnson 1 Whitehaven 20 May
34.24 B. Workman 1 London (TB) 30 Jul

## DECATHLON
8131 Alex Kruger 18.11.63 2 Valladolid,SPA 2 Jul
    11.23 7.30 14.20 2.13 49.27 14.77 45.36 4.80 57.90 4:34.83
    8098 9 Gotzis, AUT 28 May
    11.19 7.30 14.01 2.17 50.07 14.76 39.74 4.90 60.98 4:34.00
    7993 12 Gothenburg, SWE 7 Aug
    11.19 7.14 14.43 2.10 50.08 14.82 42.98 4.80 57.30 4:33.28
1 Hour 7008 3 Salzburg, AUT 23 Sep
    11.61 7.05 13.89 2.15 57.44 16.73 42.74 4.60 56.16 5:22.06
7861 Anthony Brannen 16.09.68 1 Derby 30 Apr
    11.2w 7.34 14.06 2.04 50.17 14.25w 39.92 4.80 57.10 4:41.22
7822 Simon Shirley 3.08.66 20 Gotzis, AUT 28 May
    11.12 7.24 14.59 1.93 49.80 15.05 40.84 4.40 62.06 4:27.14
7766 Barry Thomas 28.04.72 9 Fukuoka, JAP 2 Sep
    10.96 7.15 13.07 1.97 49.90 15.15 40.54 4.80 60.30 4:39.93
    7737 w 4 Alhama, SPA 21 May
    10.88w 7.03W 13.32 1.99 49.52 14.62W 41.82 4.40 54.24 4:32.42
    7602 14 Valladolid,SPA 2 Jul
    11.17 7.11 13.63 1.98 49.51 15.34 39.36 4.70 55.50 4:43.02
    7482 2 Derby 30 Apr
    11.2w 7.08w 13.07 2.01 50.17 14.97w 39.06 4.60 54.46 4:45.02
7425 w Paul Field 24.06.67 8 Alhama, SPA 21 May
    10.63w 7.31w 13.34 1.87 48.46 14.68W 35.44 4.10 44.08 4:33.66
    7295 20 Valladolid,SPA 2 Jul
    10.96 6.99 12.58 1.86 48.67 15.06 37.86 4.10 50.82 4:35.80
    7196 3 Derby 30 Apr
    10.9w 7.09w 12.54 1.92 49.45 15.00w 39.38 3.90 48.38 4:42.62
7401 Jamie Quarry 15.11.72 15 Fukuoka, JAP 2 Sep
    10.82 7.18 13.93 1.94 49.76 14.64 41.02 3.80 47.68 4:45.00
    7082 1 Stoke 25 Jun
    10.99 6.98 13.55 1.89 49.89 14.75 39.34 4.30 39.54 5:07.78
7295 Stephen Rogers 1.09.71 1 Stoke 4 Jun
    11.36 6.47 12.35 1.95 50.54 15.05w 39.92 4.60 60.70 4:52.72
    7293 1 Kilkenny, IRE 27 Aug
    11.2 6.65w 13.12 1.93 50.50 15.1w 39.76 4.60 58.14 4:49.74
    7021 4 Derby 30 Apr
    11.55w 6.51 11.98 1.89 50.69 15.42 35.38 4.40 56.66 4:37.32
7272 Duncan Mathieson 8.03.69 1 Aberdeen 16 Jul
    11.11w 7.46 13.10 2.02 49.49 15.42w 39.44 3.80 51.52 5:01.25
    7051 3 Kilkenny, IRE 27 Aug
    11.0 7.19 13.14 1.99 49.95 14.9w 37.08 3.70 51.82 5:09.22
7075 Tony Southward 31.01.71 2 Kilkenny, IRE 27 Aug
    11.2 6.83w 12.84 1.87 50.43 14.8w 40.32 4.30 50.20 4:55.37
    6808 w 1 Bebington 23 Jul
    11.4w 6.84W 12.82 1.89 50.98 15.10 38.06 4.00 41.30 4:46.76

| 6925 | Roger Hunter | | | U20 | 10.03.76 | 1 | | Stoke | | 4 Jun |
|---|---|---|---|---|---|---|---|---|---|---|
| 11.42 | 6.56 | 11.78 | 1.86 | 50.22 | 15.31w | | 36.92 | 4.00 | 58.08 | 4:48.22 |
| 6871 | | | | | | 1 | | Derby | | 30 Apr |
| 11.59 | 6.78 | 12.26 | 1.89 | 51.09 | 15.60w | | 34.14 | 4.00 | 54.76 | 4:39.62 |
| 6825 w | | | | | | 4 | | Kilkenny, IRE | | 27 Aug |
| 11.1 | 6.25 | 12.18 | 1.87 | 50.65 | 15.1W | | 37.22 | 3.70 | 54.32 | 4:36.34 |

(10)

| 6839 | Mark Bushell | | | U20 | 22.10.76 | 2 | | Derby | | 30 Apr |
|---|---|---|---|---|---|---|---|---|---|---|
| 11.38 | 6.95 | 12.17 | 1.92 | 50.55 | 15.45w | | 35.20 | 4.00 | 45.58 | 4:50.11 |
| 6782 w | | | | | | 5 | | Kilkenny, IRE | | 27 Aug |
| 10.9 | 7.11 | 10.44 | 1.90 | 51.34 | 14.7W | | 35.90 | 4.20 | 41.10 | 4:59.58 |
| 6630 | | | | | | 19 | | Nyiregyhaza, HUN | | 30 Jul |
| 11.28 | 6.96 | 11.36 | 1.93 | 50.67 | 15.75 | | 30.06 | 4.20 | 39.96 | 4:54.33 |
| 6544 | | | | | | 2 | | Stoke | | 4 Jun |
| 11.14 | 6.95 | 11.23 | 1.89 | 51.61 | 14.72w | | 31.96 | 4.20 | 32.24 | 5:08.04 |

| 6805 | Gavin Sunshine | | | U23 | 19.02.74 | 14 | | Vladimir, RUS | | 6 Aug |
|---|---|---|---|---|---|---|---|---|---|---|
| 11.42 | 6.73 | 11.29 | 1.91 | 50.60 | 15.13w | | 31.90 | 4.40 | 44.10 | 4:45.83 |
| 6531 | | | | | | 6 | | Derby | | 30 Apr |
| 11.3w | 6.77 | 10.73 | 1.86 | 51.61 | 15.05w | | 31.44 | 4.00 | 46.64 | 4:55.86 |

| 6745 | Steve Leader | | | | 24.11.66 | 5 | | Derby | | 30 Apr |
|---|---|---|---|---|---|---|---|---|---|---|
| 11.48w | 6.32 | 11.48 | 1.80 | 51.03 | 15.71 | | 35.48 | 4.70 | 45.06 | 4:38.93 |

| 6679 | Mike Edwards | | | | 19.10.68 | 7 | | San Angelo, USA | | 14 Apr |
|---|---|---|---|---|---|---|---|---|---|---|
| 11.01 | 6.74 | 11.50 | 1.85 | 49.92 | 15.93 | | 27.44 | 5.11 | 34.38 | 5:04.39 |

| 6669 | Terry Fidler | | | | 13.10.71 | 1 | | Enfield | | 13 Aug |
|---|---|---|---|---|---|---|---|---|---|---|
| 11.69 | 6.57 | 12.02 | 1.77 | 52.09 | 15.36 | | 34.54 | 4.40 | 48.12 | 4:43.4 |
| 6445 | | | | | | 4 | | Stoke | | 25 Jun |
| 11.75 | 6.59 | 11.16 | 1.74 | 52.32 | 15.68 | | 35.34 | 4.00 | 48.04 | 4:42.22 |

| 6662 | Dean Macey | | | U20 | 12.12.77 | 2 | | Vladimir, RUS | | 5 Aug |
|---|---|---|---|---|---|---|---|---|---|---|
| 11.88 | 6.64 | 12.63 | 1.97 | 51.95 | 15.26 | | 31.76 | 3.30 | 55.08 | 4:37.12 |
| 6489 w | | | | | | 3 | | Stoke | | 4 Jun |
| 11.55 | 6.48w | 11.43 | 1.98 | 52.40 | 15.66W | | 30.62 | 3.30 | 61.30 | 5:01.25 |

| 6648 | Terry Gyorffy | | | | 28.01.65 | 2 | | Bebington | | 23 Jul |
|---|---|---|---|---|---|---|---|---|---|---|
| 11.3w | 6.76 | 12.27 | 1.89 | 51.92 | 16.36 | | 30.04 | 3.60 | 55.22 | 4:56.78 |

| 6637 | Stephen Rowbotham | | | | 6.03.68 | 2 | | Stoke | | 4 Jun |
|---|---|---|---|---|---|---|---|---|---|---|
| 11.49 | 6.67 | 13.32 | 1.83 | 51.83 | 15.82w | | 38.58 | 3.80 | 52.32 | 5:10.56 |
| 6542 | | | | | | 1 | | Cudworth | | 27 Aug |
| 11.3 | 6.73 | 12.88 | 1.83 | 51.7 | 15.9 | | 38.44 | 3.60 | 53.02 | 5:08.7 |
| 6471 | | | | | | 8 | | Derby | | 30 Apr |
| 11.4w | 6.63 | 12.84 | 1.77 | 51.79 | 16.48 | | 39.24 | 3.80 | 53.42 | 5:11.01 |

| 6601 | William Gilles | | | U23 | 15.02.73 | 2 | | Stoke | | 25 Jun |
|---|---|---|---|---|---|---|---|---|---|---|
| 11.67 | 6.89 | 9.40 | 1.92 | 51.17 | 15.47 | | 30.64 | 3.70 | 50.26 | 4:28.30 |

| 6542 | Adrian Ferrand | | | | 5.02.68 | 7 | | Derby | | 30 Apr |
|---|---|---|---|---|---|---|---|---|---|---|
| 11.57w | 6.51 | 12.26 | 1.92 | 51.76 | 15.52w | | 36.74 | 4.00 | 37.18 | 4:51.29 |

(20)

| 6542 | David Vidgen | | | U23 | 27.09.74 | 2 | | Enfield | | 13 Aug |
|---|---|---|---|---|---|---|---|---|---|---|
| 11.10 | 6.73 | 12.19 | 1.83 | 52.85 | 15.31 | | 40.18 | 3.40 | 48.28 | 5:11.5 |

| 6481 | Paul Hourihan | | | U20 | 7.11.76 | 3 | | Stoke | | 25 Jun |
|---|---|---|---|---|---|---|---|---|---|---|
| 11.64 | 6.36 | 10.75 | 1.89 | 51.65 | 15.97 | | 33.10 | 4.00 | 45.96 | 4:35.63 |

| 6479 w | Paul Howard | | | | 19.10.66 | 3 | | Bebington | | 23 Jul |
|---|---|---|---|---|---|---|---|---|---|---|
| 11.9W | 6.53w | 13.54 | 1.95 | 55.48 | 16.84 | | 38.20 | 4.10 | 60.66 | 5:19.78 |

| 6443 | Par Esegbona | | | | 16.04.68 | 9 | | Derby | | 30 Apr |
|---|---|---|---|---|---|---|---|---|---|---|
| 11.39w | 7.06 | 11.22 | 1.95 | 53.03 | 15.95 | | 35.38 | 3.40 | 48.98 | 5:10.33 |

47 performances to 6400 by 24 athletes

| 6393 | Eric Hollingsworth | | | | 6.12.62 | 5 | | Perth, AUS | | 17 Dec |
|---|---|---|---|---|---|---|---|---|---|---|
| 11.35 | 3nj | 14.59 | 1.80 | 51.79 | 15.82 | | 47.12 | 4.50 | 54.80 | 5:10.82 |

| 6318 | Andrew Weston | | | U23 | 4.12.73 | 3 | | Enfield | | 13 Aug |
|---|---|---|---|---|---|---|---|---|---|---|
| 11.93 | 6.82 | 10.90 | 2.01 | 53.44 | 16.55 | | 32.80 | 4.00 | 44.20 | 5:01.0 |

| 6311 | Steve Garland | | | U23 | 12.01.73 | 5 | | Stoke | | 25 Jun |
|---|---|---|---|---|---|---|---|---|---|---|
| 11.63 | 6.00 | 10.81 | 1.83 | 51.12 | 16.28 | | 31.02 | 3.70 | 49.98 | 4:31.01 |

| 6306 | Matt Allison | | | U23 | 26.02.73 | 2 | | Cudworth | | 27 Aug |
|---|---|---|---|---|---|---|---|---|---|---|
| 11.6 | 6.48 | 11.37 | 1.69 | 50.9 | 16.0 | | 41.28 | 3.30 | 50.64 | 4:46.3 |

| 6299 | Simon Wassell | | | | 7.04.69 | 11 | Derby | | | 30 Apr |
| | 11.33w | 6.04 | 11.42 | 1.71 | 51.02 | 16.13 | 36.46 | 3.40 | 47.32 | 4:35.72 |
| 6291 | Chris Rawlinson | | | | 19.05.72 | 3 | Cudworth | | | 27 Aug |
| | 11.3 | 6.51 | 10.06 | 1.80 | 48.9 | 15.0 | 26.88 | 3.90 | 38.46 | 4:46.8 |

(30)

| 6258 | Trevor Sloman | | | | 21.03.68 | 10 | Derby | | | 30 Apr |
| | 11.7w | 6.41 | 9.84 | 1.83 | 52.65 | 15.89 | 33.92 | 4.20 | 46.70 | 4:54.48 |
| 6193 | Brett Heath | | U23 | 6.01.75 | 1 | | Thurrock | | | 24 Sep |
| | 11.8 | | | 6.50 | 12.87 | 1.86 | 53.7 | | | 16.5 |
| 36.60 | 4.10 | | | 41.62 | 5:08.8 | | | | | |
| 6127 w | Chris Hindley | | U20 | 21.01.76 | 5 | | Bebington | | | 23 Jul |
| | 11.9W | 6.63w | 12.77 | 2.01 | 54.80 | 17.80 | 33.44 | 3.60 | 42.02 | 4:45.28 |
| 5197 | | | | | | 17 | Vladimir, RUS | | | 5 Aug |
| | 12.31 | 6.25 | 11.79 | NHC | 53.78 | 18.22 | 36.26 | 3.60 | 43.02 | 4:47.24 |
| 6114 | Stephen Booth | | | | 21.10.71 | 7 | Stoke | | | 25 Jun |
| | 11.79 | 6.26 | 10.02 | 1.80 | 51.35 | 15.54 | 32.28 | 3.60 | 40.06 | 4:42.56 |
| *6096* | *Fintan McCabe* | | | | *27.03.72* | *5* | *Namur, BEL* | | | *1 Oct* |
| | *11.59* | *6.64* | *12.30* | *1.71* | *51.57* | *16.62* | *34.96* | *2.70* | *46.10* | *4:42.18* |
| 6077 | Jon Wilkinson | | | | 17.02.62 | 4 | Cudworth | | | 27 Aug |
| | 12.2 | 5.99 | 11.42 | 1.83 | 55.1 | 16.0 | 37.10 | 3.90 | 53.18 | 4:57.4 |
| 6075 | Robert Pope | | | | 24.01.69 | 4 | Enfield | | | 13 Aug |
| | 11.71 | 6.44 | 12.85 | 1.77 | 54.17 | 16.92 | 37.40 | 3.70 | 48.64 | 5:21.8 |
| 6051 | Robert Treu | | | | 1.12.69 | 1 | Cardiff | | | 23 Jul |
| | 11.6w | 5.87 | 11.68 | 1.72 | 51.82 | 16.16w | 36.50 | 3.80 | 44.08 | 5:00.73 |
| 5994 w | Richard Hunter | | | | 12.01.71 | 6 | Bebington | | | 23 Jul |
| | 11.2W | 6.55w | 9.71 | 1.71 | 51.28 | 15.26 | 30.56 | 3.20 | 35.44 | 4:41.96 |
| 5742 | | | | | | 10 | Stoke | | | 25 Jun |
| | 11.71 | 6.20 | 9.89 | 1.71 | 51.32 | 15.46 | 30.84 | 3.10 | 33.72 | 4:51.83 |
| 5981 | Iain Smith | | U23 | 12.05.73 | 2 | | Aberdeen | | | 16 Jul |
| | 11.41w | 6.26 | 10.49 | 1.84 | 54.33 | 16.67w | 34.28 | 3.20 | 51.48 | 5:03.62 |
| 5961 | Dan Gilby | | | | 9.07.70 | 1 | Hoo | | | 10 Sep |
| | 11.6 | 6.16 | 10.83 | 1.75 | 53.5 | 16.9 | 32.56 | 4.50 | 47.62 | 5:21.4 |

(40)

| *5957* | *Ian Condron* | | | | *7.10.59* | *1* | *Londonderry* | | | *6 Aug* |
| | *11.9* | *6.17* | *11.44* | *1.71* | *53.3* | *17.7* | *38.90* | *3.95* | *48.00* | *4:55.2* |
| 5926 w | David Ralson | | U20 | 22.02.77 | 4 | | Stoke | | | 4 Jun |
| | 11.51 | 6.22 | 10.95 | 1.77 | 52.63 | 16.23W | 30.32 | 3.60 | 47.14 | 5:17.00 |
| 5556 | | | | | | 16 | Vladimir, RUS | | | 5 Aug |
| | 11.57 | 6.56 | 10.87 | 1.88 | 51.46 | 17.81 | 28.12 | NHC | 49.18 | 4:57.07 |
| 5864 | Kenneth Pearson | | | | 9.07.72 | 3 | Aberdeen | | | 16 Jul |
| | 12.07w | 5.97 | 9.30 | 1.87 | 54.04 | 17.12w | 27.54 | 3.90 | 50.10 | 4:41.70 |
| 5817 | Matthew Gillard | | U23 | 11.07.75 | 12 | | Derby | | | 30 Apr |
| | 11.3w | 6.38 | 11.58 | 1.59 | 50.65 | 16.79 | 29.84 | 3.50 | 32.64 | 4:44.27 |
| 5805 | Michael Bull | | | | 6.06.70 | 2 | Stoke | | | 6 Aug |
| | 11.65 | | | 6.82w | 11.98 | 1.68 | 51.86 | | | 17.0 |
| 29.00 | 3.10 | | | 39.60 | 4:55.1 | | | | | |
| 5751 | Duncan Gauden | | | | 11.02.68 | 2 | Cardiff | | | 23 Jul |
| | 11.7w | 6.30 | 11.74 | 1.66 | 53.10 | 17.37w | 33.98 | 3.30 | 45.06 | 4:56.50 |
| 5746 | Allan Leiper | | | | 23.07.60 | 4 | Aberdeen | | | 16 Jul |
| | 11.90w | 6.06 | 11.78 | 1.66 | 54.80 | 16.52w | 30.74 | 4.00 | 48.66 | 5:25.22 |
| 5710 | Richard Czernik | | | | 12.07.72 | 3 | Stoke | | | 6 Aug |
| | 11.97 | 6.08w | 11.44 | 1.62 | 52.03 | 17.2 | 36.50 | 2.90 | 48.82 | 4:53.7 |
| 5705 | Mark Perman | | | | 6.01.68 | 2 | Thurrock | | | 24 Sep |
| | 11.8 | 6.46 | 10.67 | 1.77 | 53.9 | 16.0 | 38.00 | 3.60 | 40.04 | 5:45.5 |
| 5629 | Richard Stubbs | | | | 6.06.66 | 3 | Cardiff | | | 23 Jul |
| | 12.0 | 6.06 | 9.35 | 1.78 | 54.98 | 17.39w | 30.66 | 3.60 | 46.84 | 4:44.06 |
| 5611 | Alvin Walker | | | | 30.04.65 | 2 | Cosford | | | 1 Aug |
| | 11.5 | 6.58 | 9.85 | 1.85 | 51.4 | 17.5 | 32.60 | 2.20 | 39.58 | 4:49.8 |

(50)

| 5580 | Adam Davis | | | | 19.11.72 | 11 | Stoke | | | 25 Jun |
| | 11.74 | 6.16 | 12.79 | 1.68 | 56.99 | 18.03 | 34.36 | 4.50 | 37.30 | 5:47.33 |

```
5554      Geoff Ingram                   31.01.68   3   Cosford              1 Aug
          11.9      6.42    9.35   1.70  53.2    16.9    29.60   3.50  39.00  4:50.4
5544      Brett Shea                     17.04.71   1   Aldershot           16 Jun
          11.91     6.11    9.69   1.74  54.02   17.3    31.10   3.75  42.58  5:11.01
5491      Kevin Ricketts         U20     29.06.76  13   Kilkenny, IRE       27 Aug
          12.4      5.98    9.16   1.84  54.59   17.3w   27.20   3.30  46.64  4:34.03
5401 w    Jon Orrelle            U17     28.01.79   5   Stoke                4 Jun
          12.00     6.20   11.16   1.86  59.47   16.43W  21.86   3.60  47.58  5:29.85
5324      Chris Lawniczak                24.03.72   1   Peterborough        24 Sep
          12.3      6.11   10.26   1.84  55.2    17.1    25.80   4.00  31.32  5:08.7
5310      John Culshaw                   20.11.62   4   Stoke                6 Aug
          12.64     5.77   10.65   1.77  53.36   18.1    28.18   2.90  45.34  4:40.8
5296 w    Paul Curran            U20      5.04.77  15   Kilkenny, IRE       27 Aug
          12.2      5.74    8.11   1.87  53.51   16.8W   27.02   2.80  33.76  4:23.10
          5202                                     3   Cork, IRE            5 Jun
          12.1      5.85    9.34   1.82  54.2    17.7    25.18   2.73  39.18  4:33.4
5273 w    Gerry Murray           U20     13.02.78  16   Kilkenny, IRE       27 Aug
          11.4      5.95w  10.23   1.66  52.24   16.7W   21.62   2.40  39.64  4:43.59
5262      Jason Dickenson                11.11.69   4   Cosford              1 Aug
          12.3      5.91   10.89   1.76  54.3    17.5    31.08   2.70  39.58  4:47.3
5251      Gavin Showell                  29.09.72   5   Stoke                5 Aug
          12.24     6.05    9.77   1.71  55.16   17.4    25.30   4.20  34.54  5:17.3
     (60)
5249 w    Paul Jones             U20     11.04.78  17   Kilkenny, IRE       27 Aug
          11.8      6.24W   9.60   1.72  57.29   16.7W   24.70   3.80  42.54  5:29.47
5220      Glyn Chidlow                   21.10.71   6   Stoke                6 Aug
          12.03     6.54   10.19   1.74  55.22   19.2    22.62   3.20  43.96  4:56.3
5165 w    Mark Dobbie            U20      5.03.77  18   Kilkenny, IRE       27 Aug
          11.9      6.11w   9.85   1.69  56.98   16.6W   27.42   3.20  41.20  5:15.19
5161      Keith Mainstone        U23     15.03.74   6   Aberdeen            16 Jul
          12.31w    5.41    9.80   1.93  55.73   18.46w  25.36   2.30  44.62  4:27.64
5153      Damien Todd                    21.02.71   5   Cosford              1 Aug
          12.1      5.64    9.53   1.58  53.2    16.2    26.94   2.60  42.64  4:44.7
5104      Stephen Clark                  24.05.72   3   Thurrock            24 Sep
          12.0      5.55   10.99   1.71  55.1    19.2    30.98   3.40  43.32  5:11.5
5084      Russell Turner                  1.06.68   7   Enfield             13 Aug
          12.01     6.29   10.31   1.65  56.42   17.95   34.78   2.70  50.58  6:00.3
5054      Keith Bell             U23     31.12.74  15   Derby               30 Apr
          12.34w    5.62   11.03   1.74  58.82   19.65   33.52   3.50  44.80  5:14.64
5045      Nicholas Walker                24.02.64   3   Middlesbrough        1 Oct
          11.7      6.31   10.51   1.63  52.3    17.4    28.60   2.10  36.78  5:17.0
5027      Ian Tomkins                    23.03.68   2   Crawley             10 Sep
          12.5      6.08   10.84   1.82  54.1    18.5    26.62   2.50  34.38  4:45.8
     (70)
5000      Thomas Molloy          U23     25.03.73   2   Aldershot           16 Jun
          12.53     5.85    8.80   1.71  55.06   17.9    30.64   2.55  40.18  4:45.36

unconfirmed
5520      Andy Lewis                      9.03.68       Alhama, SPA         21 May
```

## DECATHLON - Under 20 with Under 20 Implements

```
7134      Dean Macey                     12.12.77   1   Stoke               17 Sep
          11.49     6.85   12.66   2.13  51.44   15.08   38.92   3.80  51.50  4:49.15
6672      Martin Troy                    13.07.76   2   Stoke               17 Sep
          11.67     6.39w  11.00   1.86  51.58   15.77   33.48   3.90  51.50  4:18.57
6570      David Ralson                   22.02.77   3   Stoke               17 Sep
          11.29     6.58   12.61   1.83  50.92   15.76   33.78   3.70  52.40  5:05.25
6457      Mark Bushell                   22.10.76   1   Portsmouth          25 Jun
          11.5      6.89   11.51   1.90  51.5    15.2    36.28   4.20  32.48  5:03.3
6417      Chris Hindley                  21.01.76   1   Worcester           25 Jun
          12.0      6.58   12.75   2.06  54.8    17.0    36.94   3.72  46.20  4:35.6
```

| 6180 | Fyn Corcoran | | | | 17.03.78 | 4 | Stoke | | 17 Sep |
| | 11.75 | 5.88 | 12.37 | 1.77 | 52.61 | 15.63 | 34.30 | 3.20 | 50.00 | 4:41.80 |
| 5981 | Mensah Elliott | | | | 29.08.76 | 5 | Stoke | | 17 Sep |
| | 11.43 | 6.52 | 12.02 | 1.77 | 52.01 | 15.15 | 31.16 | 2.70 | 43.20 | 5:13.44 |
| 5715 | Craig Holgate | | | | 21.09.76 | 6 | Stoke | | 17 Sep |
| | 11.93 | 6.19 | 10.04 | 1.71 | 52.34 | 17.12w | 30.48 | 3.40 | 34.80 | 4:27.36 |
| 5702 | Kevin Ricketts | | | | 29.06.76 | 1 | Cardiff | | 23 Jul |
| | 12.3w | 6.05 | 10.11 | 1.84 | 55.51 | 17.23w | 31.28 | 3.40 | 50.60 | 4:39.85 |
| 5639 | Scott Exley | | | | 9.02.78 | 2 | Yeovil | | 25 Jun |
| | 11.5 | 5.95 | 10.36 | 1.86 | 53.0 | 15.7 | 31.82 | 2.80 | 33.24 | 4:52.4 |
| | (10) | | | | | | | | | |
| 5632 | Mark Dobbie | | | | 5.03.77 | 1 | Aberdeen | | 16 Jul |
| | 12.19 | 6.41 | 11.31 | 1.75 | 56.43 | 16.36w | 35.54 | 3.50 | 39.16 | 5:16.50 |
| 5589 | Adam Pengilly | | | | 14.10.77 | 3 | Yeovil | | 25 Jun |
| | 11.6 | 6.08 | 10.20 | 1.62 | 54.5 | 16.6 | 29.84 | 3.60 | 44.50 | 4:54.5 |
| 5568 | Jon Goodwin | | | | 22.09.76 | 4 | Yeovil | | 25 Jun |
| | 11.7 | 5.66 | 9.91 | 1.74 | 51.5 | 15.4 | 24.12 | 2.70 | 39.50 | 4:29.5 |
| 5563 | Owen Chaplin | | | | 2.12.77 | 1 | Blackpool | | 25 Jul |
| | 11.4 | 6.10 | 10.92 | 1.59 | 54.3 | 16.8 | 26.70 | 4.00 | 43.64 | 5:14.3 |
| 5561 | Sam Oteng | | | | 12.04.78 | 7 | Stoke | | 17 Sep |
| | 11.73 | 5.30 | 10.67 | 1.74 | 52.92 | 16.24w | 36.26 | 2.70 | 42.68 | 4:59.16 |
| 5560 | Paul Carroll | | | | 25.01.78 | 8 | Stoke | | 17 Sep |
| | 12.55 | 6.00w | 12.11 | 1.71 | 54.82 | 17.63w | 35.82 | 3.50 | 40.34 | 4:55.55 |
| 5493 | Cliff Lowe | | | | 12.01.77 | 3 | Derby | | 30 Apr |
| | 11.88 | 6.39 | 10.26 | 1.71 | 54.34 | 17.63w | 30.90 | 3.00 | 38.42 | 4:45.18 |
| 5458 | Matthew Dowsett | | | | 18.09.76 | 9 | Stoke | | 17 Sep |
| | 11.76 | 6.27 | 10.11 | 1.65 | 53.60 | 15.65 | 33.36 | 2.20 | 39.46 | 5:02.80 |
| 5449 | Erik Toemen | | | | 1.07.78 | 10 | Stoke | | 17 Sep |
| | 12.28 | 5.86 | 9.44 | 1.80 | 54.55 | 16.63 | 27.88 | 3.50 | 38.82 | 4:51.96 |
| 5431 | David Bullock | | | | 1.12.76 | 11 | Stoke | | 17 Sep |
| | 11.91 | 6.18 | 9.30 | 1.71 | 52.06 | 17.75 | 29.48 | 2.90 | 35.84 | 4:36.81 |
| | (20) | | | | | | | | | |
| 5411 | Lee Parkes | | | | 23.12.76 | 1 | Cudworth | | 27 Aug |
| | 12.0 | 5.74 | 10.40 | 1.74 | 55.5 | 16.8 | 35.42 | 3.10 | 43.90 | 5:02.9 |
| 5368 | Clint Barrett | | | | 21.11.77 | 12 | Stoke | | 17 Sep |
| | 12.33 | 5.41 | 9.80 | 1.62 | 54.56 | 16.88 | 34.64 | 2.80 | 45.28 | 4:33.01 |
| 5305 | David Cuthill | | | | 18.01.78 | 2 | Aberdeen | | 16 Jul |
| | 12.08 | 6.03 | 11.14 | 1.72 | 54.21 | 18.03w | 24.30 | 2.80 | 39.80 | 4:35.41 |
| 5276 | Kevin Davies | | | | 11.01.78 | 5 | Yeovil | | 25 Jun |
| | 11.9 | 5.43 | 11.45 | 1.62 | 53.1 | 17.3 | 33.92 | 2.70 | 34.96 | 4:37.9 |
| 5268 | Paul Curran | | | | 5.04.77 | 1 | Londonderry | | 6 Aug |
| | 12.4 | 5.57 | 8.58 | 1.89 | 53.4 | 16.7 | 28.34 | 2.75 | 35.40 | 4:30.8 |
| 5267 | David Powell | | | U17 | 11.09.78 | 5 | Derby | | 30 Apr |
| | 11.70 | 5.77 | 11.37 | 1.59 | 52.79 | 17.21w | 32.40 | 2.20 | 32.30 | 4:40.56 |
| 5201 | Keith Oag | | | | 11.11.77 | 3 | Aberdeen | | 16 Jul |
| | 11.70 | 6.08w | 10.01 | 1.90 | 55.37 | 16.22w | 26.12 | 2.40 | 32.20 | 5:18.99 |
| 5175 | Michael Leonard | | | | 28.05.77 | 15 | Stoke | | 17 Sep |
| | 12.35 | 5.58 | 11.91 | 1.71 | 58.79 | 17.64w | 39.74 | 2.60 | 43.58 | 5:09.07 |
| 5162 | Robert Thickpenny | | | | 17.07.76 | 1 | Peterborough | | 24 Sep |
| | 12.0 | 5.96 | 9.38 | 1.51 | 55.5 | 17.0 | 20.80 | 4.20 | 44.46 | 5:12.8 |
| 5092 | Mark Sweeney | | | | 26.02.77 | 16 | Stoke | | 17 Sep |
| | 12.32 | 5.99 | 11.22 | 1.98 | 56.98 | 15.62 | 33.38 | 3.10 | 34.64 | DNF |
| | (30) | | | | | | | | | |
| 5090 | Lee Rudd | | | | 15.09.76 | 2 | Carlisle | | 5 May |
| | 11.4 | 5.53 | 8.13 | 1.69 | 53.4 | 16.9 | 22.26 | 2.70 | 44.98 | 4:55.6 |
| 5069 | Ian Duffy | | | | 1.12.77 | 4 | Blackpool | | 25 Jun |
| | 12.3 | 6.06 | 10.25 | 1.80 | 57.5 | 17.8 | 26.80 | 2.50 | 42.20 | 4:43.8 |

**overage**

| 5296 | Simon White | | | U23 | 2.10.75 | 13 | Stoke | | 17 Sep |
| | 12.09 | 5.71 | 11.00 | 1.71 | 55.11 | 16.34w | 30.78 | 2.80 | 36.18 | 4:57.29 |
| 5251 | Edward Galbraith | | | U23 | 3.10.75 | 4 | Portsmouth | | 25 Jun |
| | 12.0 | 6.50 | 10.21 | 1.84 | 56.9 | 16.8 | 32.52 | 3.10 | 34.62 | 5:31.6 |

## DECATHLON - Under 17 with Under 17 Implements

| 5618 | David Powell | | | | 11.09.78 | 1 | Middlesbrough | 1 Oct |
|---|---|---|---|---|---|---|---|---|
| | 11.7 | 31.64 | 2.40 | 37.86 52.6 | 14.4 | 5.90 13.23 1.64 | 4:43.0 | |
| 5252 | Daniel Carney | | | | 25.12.78 | 2 | Middlesbrough | 1 Oct |
| | 12.7 | 32.76 | 2.50 | 37.76 53.9 | 14.8 | 5.44 10.50 1.76 | 4:36.9 | |
| 5066 | Steven Atkinson | | | | 24.02.79 | 3 | Middlesbrough | 1 Oct |
| | 11.8 | 31.84 | 3.60 | 32.68 58.0 | 15.0 | 5.88 11.17 1.67 | 5:52.9 | |

## OCTATHLON - Under 17

| 5423 | Leo Barker | 26.12.78 | 1 | Stoke | 17 Sep |
|---|---|---|---|---|---|
| | 13.53 6.84 46.52 53.02 1.76 39.34 | 13.37 4:46.29 (a) | | | |
| 5144 | Marc Newton | 15.03.80 | 2 | Stoke | 17 Sep |
| | 14.15w 6.37 35.04 51.26 1.82 36.14 | 12.24 4:35.03 (a) | | | |
| 5039 | Alan Rudkin | 5.11.78 | 3 | Stoke | 17 Sep |
| | 14.68w 5.87 48.42 55.76 1.70 46.46 | 14.54 5:07.26 (a) | | | |
| 4993 | Darren Hatton | 21.03.79 | 4 | Stoke | 17 Sep |
| | 15.45w 6.39 50.58 54.03 1.85 35.86 | 12.45 5:00.62 (a) | | | |
| 4982 | Sam Allen | 26.10.78 | 1 | Bebington | 23 Jul |
| | 14.2w 6.40w 50.56 51.9 1.69 27.78 | 13.01 4:51.32 (a) | | | |
| 4932 | James Hodson | 28.09.78 | 2 | Blackpool | 25 Jun |
| | 15.1 5.88 43.82 54.4 1.73 39.48 | 12.64 4:32.0 (a) | | | |
| 4897 | David Powell | 11.09.78 | 6 | Stoke | 17 Sep |
| | 14.79w 5.87 38.24 51.69 1.64 39.66 | 12.69 4:41.92 (a) | | | |
| 4873 | Lee Black | 26.11.78 | 3 | Ipswich | 25 Jun |
| | 15.5 6.26 30.68 49.7 1.90 26.82 | 11.30 4:21.3 (a) | | | |
| 4827 | Gurmukh Sahans | 8.10.78 | 7 | Stoke | 17 Sep |
| | 14.53 6.31 45.32 53.88 1.73 35.44 | 11.41 5:01.33 (a) | | | |
| 4796 | Andrew Squire | 30.09.79 | 3 | Stoke | 6 Aug |
| | 15.18 5.99 47.82 54.22 1.88 34.24 | 12.04 5:10.66 (a) | | | |

(10)

| 4778 | Nick Dowsett | 24.11.78 | 9 | Stoke | 17 Sep |
|---|---|---|---|---|---|
| | 13.66 6.63w 41.70 53.68 1.73 34.88 | 11.13 5:28.22 (a) | | | |
| 4712 | Chris Low | 24.04.80 | 1 | Aberdeen | 16 Jul |
| | 11.71 6.17 1.69 53.53 14.01 26.24 | 41.14 5:04.35 (b) | | | |
| 4665 | Sion Owen | 6.03.79 | 10 | Stoke | 17 Sep |
| | 15.27w 5.88 37.44 51.19 1.73 29.78 | 9.82 4:26.02 (a) | | | |
| 4624 | Nick Barber | 22.11.78 | 3 | Bebington | 23 Jul |
| | 15.8w 6.13w 39.68 54.7 1.81 39.44 | 14.69 4:59.66 (a) | | | |
| 4612 | Sam Bonsall | 15.03.79 | 4 | Bebington | 23 Jul |
| | 14.1w 6.13 40.62 52.8 1.66 30.12 | 10.21 4:49.24 (a) | | | |
| 4545 | Edward Coats | 14.06.80 | 11 | Stoke | 17 Sep |
| | 14.87w 5.41 43.80 52.13 1.67 30.30 | 10.78 4:46.85 (a) | | | |
| 4495 | Johnathan Foley | 24.10.78 | 2 | Yeovil | 25 Jun |
| | 15.0 6.25 30.16 52.1 1.61 35.04 | 11.93 5:04.3 (a) | | | |
| 4462 | George Skevis | 12.10.79 | 1 | Crawley | 10 Sep |
| | 11.7 6.02 12.68 1.56 55.7 43.82 | 43.86 5:47.0 (c) | | | |
| 4415 | Daniel Carney | 25.12.78 | 12 | Stoke | 17 Sep |
| | 14.98 5.24 37.56 53.49 1.76 29.28 | 10.42 4:41.43 (a) | | | |
| 4350 | Paul Armstrong | 20.10.79 | 2 | Aberdeen | 16 Jul |
| | 11.97 5.16 1.69 52.02 14.69 22.96 | 25.74 4:32.47 (b) | | | |

(20)

| 4340 | Kevin Drury | 30.09.79 | 14 | Stoke | 17 Sep |
|---|---|---|---|---|---|
| | 14.35 5.50 42.50 55.77 1.76 29.42 | 11.06 5:18.62 (a) | | | |
| 4324 | Jonathan Holmes | 13.11.78 | 15 | Stoke | 17 Sep |
| | 14.66 5.87 40.50 54.63 1.58 27.16 | 10.34 4:51.31 (a) | | | |
| 4275 | Anthony Sawyer | 29.04.80 | 1 | Worcester | 25 Jun |
| | 15.1 5.76 28.42 53.1 1.65 30.82 | 10.13 4:43.5 (a) | | | |
| 4202 | Darren Wright | 7.09.79 | 17 | Stoke | 17 Sep |
| | 15.27w 5.77 36.34 57.95 1.85 28.08 | 10.37 5:06.71 (a) | | | |

Order of Events  a)  100mH, LJ, JT, 400m, HJ, DT, SP, 1500m
              b)  100m, LJ, HJ, 400m, 100mH, DT, JT, 1500m
              c)  100m, LJ, SP, HJ, 400m, DT, JT, 1500m

## PENTATHLON - Under 15

| 2898 | Peter Watson | | | | 30.06.81 | 1 | Stoke | 16 Sep |
|---|---|---|---|---|---|---|---|---|
| | 13.09 | 12.35 | 5.81 | 1.80 | 2:16.31 (a) | | | |
| 2878 | Daryl Russell | | | | 20.10.80 | 2 | Stoke | 16 Sep |
| | 12.00 | 10.83 | 5.89 | 1.74 | 2:16.97 (a) | | | |
| 2868 | Wayne Gray | | | | 7.11.80 | 3 | Stoke | 16 Sep |
| | 11.46 | 11.62 | 5.65 | 1.92 | 2:34.02 (a) | | | |
| 2822 | Leon McRae | | | | 3.11.80 | 4 | Stoke | 16 Sep |
| | 11.32 | 9.47 | 5.62 | 1.68 | 2:13.09 (a) | | | |
| 2816 | Richard Gawthorpe | | | | 28.01.81 | 1 | Stoke | 6 Aug |
| | 12.1 | 1.73 | 12.14 | 5.87 | 2:17.5 (b) | | | |
| 2739 | Richard Smith | | | | 17.01.81 | 5 | Stoke | 16 Sep |
| | 12.38 | 10.25 | 5.51 | 1.71 | 2:14.09 (a) | | | |
| 2692 | Jonathan Groenen | | | | 12.09.80 | 1 | Crawley | 10 Sep |
| | 5.56 | 13.5 | 1.69 | 12.11 | 2:15.3 (c) | | | |
| 2686 | Daniel Everett | | | | 30.01.81 | 1 | Enfield | 12 Aug |
| | 12.16 | 10.42 | 1.55 | 5.81 | 2:15.61 (d) | | | |
| 2661 | Martin Cowan | | | | 16.11.80 | 6 | Stoke | 16 Sep |
| | 12.92 | 11.18 | 5.38 | 1.71 | 2:17.60 (a) | | | |
| 2656 | Christopher Hopkins | | | | 11.11.80 | 7 | Stoke | 16 Sep |
| | 12.57 | 11.95 | 5.43 | 1.56 | 2:16.22 (a) | | | |
| (10) | | | | | | | | |
| 2626 | Brian Pearce | | | | 9.12.80 | 1 | Bromley | 18 Jun |
| | 12.8 | 13.55 | 4.91 | 1.65 | 2:19.5 (a) | | | |
| 2590 | Carl Wilkes | | | | 7.11.80 | 3 | Worcester | 24 Jun |
| | 12.7 | 9.33 | 5.18 | 1.76 | 2:14.8 (a) | | | |
| 2582 | Robert Hollinger | | | | 11.10.80 | 3 | Stoke | 6 Aug |
| | 12.2 | 1.61 | 11.88 | 5.35 | 2:17.1 (b) | | | |
| 2559 | Tony Seston | | | | 21.12.80 | 2 | Ipswich | 25 Jun |
| | 12.2 | 9.02 | 5.69 | 1.66 | 2:20.9 (a) | | | |
| 2546 | Andrew Turner | | | | 19.09.80 | 8 | Stoke | 16 Sep |
| | 11.77 | 9.07 | 5.62 | 1.59 | 2:22.24 (a) | | | |
| 2535 | Chris Pritchard | | | | 15.12.80 | 1 | Jarrow | 24 Jun |
| | 12.7 | 11.91 | 5.30 | 1.62 | 2:23.4 (a) | | | |
| 2535 | Neil Scrivener | | | | 18.09.80 | 9 | Stoke | 16 Sep |
| | 12.50 | 9.20 | 5.11 | 1.62 | 2:12.57 (a) | | | |
| 2533 | Kevin McKinson | | | | 6.09.80 | 2 | Bromley | 18 Jun |
| | 12.3 | 8.39 | 5.35 | 1.80 | 2:22.5 (a) | | | |

Order of Events
a)   80mH, SP, LJ, HJ, 800m        b)   80mH, HJ, SP, LJ, 800m
c)   LJ, 80H, HJ, SP, 800m         d)   80mH, SP, HJ, LJ, 800m

**Non Standard Events** - 80mH, LJ, 200m, SP, 1500m

| 2536 | Craig Loney | | | | 10.06.81 | 1 | Grangemouth | 10 Jun |
|---|---|---|---|---|---|---|---|---|
| | 13.2 | 5.03 | 25.8 | 11.18 | 5:08.6 (e) | | | |
| 2446 | Chris Baillie | | | | 21.04.81 | 2 | Grangemouth | 10 Jun |
| | 12.1 | 5.22 | 25.4 | 6.97 | 5:12.2 (e) | | | |

## OCTATHLON - Under 15 with Under 15 Implements

| 3933 | Aidan Turnbull | | | | | 1.09.81 | 1 | Middlesbrough | 1 Oct |
|---|---|---|---|---|---|---|---|---|---|
| | 12.6 | 1.53 | 26.48 | 58.1 | 41.70 | 5.47 | 10.20 | 4:54.3 | |

## PENTATHLON - Under 13

| 1866 | Craig Fleming | | | | 29.01.83 | 1 | Aberdeen | 15 Jul |
|---|---|---|---|---|---|---|---|---|
| | 4.79 | 12.71 | 9.08 | 1.53 | 2:47.16 | | | |
| 1815 | Paul Torry | | | | 17.10.82 | 2 | Aberdeen | 15 Jul |
| | 4.21 | 13.19 | 9.02 | 1.38 | 2:27.16 | | | |

## 2000 Metres Walk - Track - Under 13

| | | | | | | |
|---|---|---|---|---|---|---|
| 10:10.0 | Dominic King | | 30.05.83 | 3 | Colchester | 23 Mar |
| 10:12.0 | Daniel King | | 30.05.83 | 4 | Colchester | 23 Mar |
| 10:34.0 | Alan Hogg | | 3.06.83 | 2 | Leicester | 22 Apr |
| 11:20.0 | Andrew Ball | | 13.05.83 | 4 | Leicester | 22 Apr |
| 11:21.0 | Andrew Parker | | 10.12.83 | 5 | Leicester | 22 Apr |
| 11:24.0 | Simeon Adams | | 1.07.84 | 3 | Loughborough | 21 Oct |
| 11:26.0 | Liam Grange | | 18.08.83 | 6 | Leicester | 22 Apr |
| 11:32.0 | Paul Miles | | 28.04.84 | 7 | Leicester | 26 Sep |
| 11:59.0 | Tommy Green | | 6.05.83 | 8 | Leicester | 22 Apr |

## 3000 Metres Walk - Track

| | | | | | | |
|---|---|---|---|---|---|---|
| 11:33.4 | Steve Partington | | 17.09.65 | 1 | Douglas, IOM | 12 Jul |
| 12:04.19 | | | | 2 | Bedford | 29 May |
| 11:47.12 i | Philip King | U23 | 25.11.74 | 1 | Birmingham | 26 Feb |
| 11:49.64 | | | | 1 | Bedford | 29 May |
| 11:53.3 | Martin Bell | | 9.04.61 | 1 | Birmingham | 9 Aug |
| 11:56.62 i | | | | 2 | Birmingham | 26 Feb |
| 11:58.8 | | | | 1 | London (WL) | 19 Jul |
| 12:12.36 | Andy Penn | | 31.03.67 | 3 | Bedford | 29 May |
| 12:15.45 | Mark Easton | | 24.05.63 | 1 | London (CP) | 18 Jun |
| 12:20.38 | Martin Young | | 11.07.72 | 1 | Telford | 26 Aug |
| 12:21.8 | Jamie O'Rawe | U23 | 3.02.73 | 2 | Croydon | 28 Aug |
| 12:24.29 i | Gary Witton | U23 | 25.08.73 | 3 | Birmingham | 26 Feb |
| 12:30.6 | | | | 1 | Horsham | 13 May |
| 12:42.9 | Steve Taylor | | 19.03.66 | 2 | Douglas, IOM | 12 Jul |
| 12:43.57 | Les Morton | | 1.07.58 | 5 | Bedford | 29 May |
| (10) | | | | | | |
| 12:44.48 | Steve Hollier | U20 | 27.02.76 | 1 | London (He) | 9 Sep |
| 12:45.05 | Noel Carmody | | 24.12.56 | 1 | London (CP) | 14 May |
| 12:46.05 | David Keown | U23 | 18.07.74 | 4 | Telford | 26 Aug |
| 12:50.67 i | Stuart Monk | U17 | 23.03.79 | 1 | Birmingham | 18 Feb |
| 12:52.9 | | | | 1 | Woodford | 12 Jul |
| 12:55.70 | Richard Oldale | | 26.01.66 | 1 | Sheffield (W) | 9 Aug |
| 12:56.7 | Steve Brennan | | 4.11.65 | 3 | Douglas, IOM | 3 Sep |
| 12:58.56 i | Gareth Holloway | | 2.02.70 | 5 | Birmingham | 26 Feb |
| 13:00.0 | Gareth Brown | | 10.05.68 | 1 | Horsham | 13 Jun |
| 13:01.8 | Nick Barrable | U23 | 8.06.74 | 1 | Cosford | 29 Apr |
| 13:10.03 | Brian Adams | V45 | 13.03.49 | 2 | Loughborough | 14 May |
| (20) | | | | | | |
| 13:11.84 | Bob Care | V45 | 8.04.47 | 4 | Birmingham | 20 May |
| 13:14.65 | Derek Cross | V45 | 30.04.49 | 3 | Enfield | 29 Apr |
| 13:19.0 | Chris Smith | | 23.12.58 | 1 | Rugby | 14 Sep |
| 13:19.9 | Ray Craggs | | 9.07.63 | 2 | London (WL) | 19 Jul |
| 13:20.07 | Robert Mecham | U20 | 14.09.77 | 4 | Enfield | 29 Apr |
| 13:20.79 i | Colin Bradley | | 2.02.56 | 6 | Birmingham | 26 Feb |
| 13:22.64 | | | | 5 | Birmingham | 20 May |
| 13:27.4 | Martin Rush | | 25.12.64 | 1 | Salisbury | 16 Jul |
| 13:30.89 | Scott Davis | U23 | 3.04.75 | 2 | Barking | 14 May |
| 13:32.4 | Jimmy Ball | | 17.02.63 | 1 | Portsmouth | 13 May |
| 13:35.4 | Allan Callow | V50 | 4.09.45 | 4 | Douglas, IOM | 12 Jul |
| (30) | | | | | | |
| 13:42.8 | Allan King | | 3.12.56 | 3 | Rugby | 14 Sep |
| 13:45.0 | John Murphy | U15 | 6.03.81 | 4 | Loughborough | 14 May |
| 13:46.96 | Kirk Taylor | | 30.05.68 | 7 | Birmingham | 20 May |
| 13:47.3 | Steve Uttley | | 18.05.57 | 3 | London (WL) | 19 Jul |
| 13:48.4 | Darren Thorn | | 17.07.62 | 4 | Rugby | 14 Sep |

**Additional Juniors**

| 13:57.0 | Matthew Hales | U17 | 6.10.79 | 1 | Horsham | 11 | Apr |
|---|---|---|---|---|---|---|---|
| 14:53.6 | Scott Taylor | U20 | 28.07.78 | 5 | Rugby | 14 | Sep |
| 15:01.2 | Robert Warren | U15 | 17.07.81 | 1 | Horsham | 13 | May |
| 15:04.34 | Nigel Whorlow | U15 | 26.11.80 | 2 | Stoke | 17 | Sep |
| 15:43.0 | Dominic King | U13 | 30.05.83 | 2 | Colchester | 13 | Jul |
| 15:46.25 | Michael Deacon | U15 | 13.04.81 | 4 | Stoke | 17 | Sep |
| 15:48.0 | Paul Spilane | U17 | 27.09.79 | 6 | Loughborough | 14 | May |
| 15:58.49 | Nathan Adams | U15 | 14.04.82 | 5 | Stoke | 17 | Sep |
| 16:00.0 | Michael Kemp | U17 | 23.12.79 | 7 | Loughborough | 14 | May |
| 16:06.25 | R. Cummins | U15 | | 6 | Stoke | 17 | Sep |
| 16:10.0 | Alan Hogg | U13 | 3.06.83 | 5 | Horsham | 14 | Mar |
| 16:11.0 | Daniel King | U13 | 30.05.83 | 3 | Colchester | 13 | Jul |
| 16:18.0 | Stephen Garridge | U15 | 31.12.81 | 5 | Leicester | 22 | Apr |

## 3000 Metres Walk - Road - Juniors

| 13:20 | Robert Mecham | U20 | 14.09.77 | 1 | Steyning | 22 | Jan |
|---|---|---|---|---|---|---|---|
| 14:11 | John Murphy | U15 | 6.03.81 | 1 | Sutton Coldfield | 6 | May |
| 14:16 | Matthew Hales | U17 | 6.10.79 | 1 | Weymouth | 19 | Mar |
| 14:19 | Michael Kemp | U17 | 23.12.79 | 1 | Leicester | 7 | Oct |
| 14:53 | Paul Spilane | U17 | 27.09.79 | 3 | Dublin, IRE | 23 | Sep |
| 15:08 | Nigel Whorlow | U15 | 26.11.80 | 2 | Sutton Coldfield | 6 | May |
| 15:12 | Robert Warren | U15 | 17.07.81 | 3 | Sutton Coldfield | 6 | May |
| 15:20 | Alan Hogg | U13 | 3.06.83 | 1 | Holmewood | 9 | Apr |
| 15:20 | Dominic King | U13 | 30.05.83 | 2 | Holmewood | 9 | Apr |
| 15:30 | Nathan Adams | U15 | 14.04.82 | 1 | Solihull | 18 | Nov |
| 15:34 | Daniel King | U13 | 30.05.83 | 1 | Weymouth | 19 | Mar |

## 5000 Metres Walk - Track - Juniors

| 21:51.0 | Steve Hollier | U20 | 27.02.76 | 1 | Leicester | 22 | Apr |
|---|---|---|---|---|---|---|---|
| 21:52.7 | Stuart Monk | U17 | 23.03.79 | 2 | Dublin, IRE | 22 | Jul |
| 22:14.0 | Gary Witton | U23 | 25.08.73 | 8 | Narbonne, FRA | 29 | Jul |
| 23:52.4 | Matthew Hales | U20 | 6.10.79 | 4 | Brierley Hill | 15 | Oct |
| 24:21.0 | | U17 | | 2 | Horsham | 9 | May |
| 23:56.72 | Robert Mecham | U20 | 14.09.77 | 1 | Stoke | 17 | Sep |
| 24:03.6 o | John Murphy | U15 | 6.03.81 | 5 | Brierley Hill | 15 | Oct |
| 24:16.7 | Scott Taylor | U20 | 28.07.78 | 7 | Brierley Hill | 15 | Oct |
| 25:47.96 | Andrew Goudie | U17 | 4.10.78 | 3 | Stoke | 17 | Sep |
| 26:04.6 | Michael Kemp | U17 | 23.12.79 | 8 | Brierley Hill | 15 | Oct |
| 26:13.20 | Paul Spilane | U17 | 27.09.79 | 5 | Stoke | 17 | Sep |

**Road**

| 22:16 | Stuart Monk | U17 | 23.03.79 | 1 | Bexley | 11 | Feb |
|---|---|---|---|---|---|---|---|
| 22:48 + | Steve Hollier | U20 | 27.02.76 | | Fougeres, FRA | 11 | Jun |
| 23:24 | Matthew Hales | U17 | 6.10.79 | 1 | Bexley | 9 | Dec |
| 23:25 | John Murphy | U15 | 6.03.81 | 1 | Solihull | 18 | Nov |
| 24:04 | Michael Kemp | U17 | 23.12.79 | 2 | Solihull | 18 | Nov |

## 10000 Metres Walk - Track

| 41:10.11 | Darrell Stone | | 2.02.68 | 1 | Birmingham | 16 | Jul |
|---|---|---|---|---|---|---|---|
| 41:59.0 | | | | 1 | Brighton | 28 | Jan |
| 41:13.65 | Martin Bell | | 9.04.61 | 1 | Cardiff | 22 | Jul |
| 41:16.13 | | | | 3 | Birmingham | 16 | Jul |
| 41:14.61 | Steve Partington | | 17.09.65 | 2 | Birmingham | 16 | Jul |
| 41:37.0 | Mark Easton | | 24.05.63 | 1 | Hornchurch | 29 | Mar |
| 42:45.7 | | | | 1 | Brighton | 20 | Jul |
| 42:49.59 | | | | 5 | Birmingham | 16 | Jul |

| | | | | | | | |
|---|---|---|---|---|---|---|---|
| 42:28.0 | Philip King | U23 | 25.11.74 | 1 | Leamington | 17 | May |
| | 42:33.30 | | | 4 | Birmingham | 16 | Jul |
| | 42:45.7 | | | 2 | Brighton | 20 | Jul |
| | 43:15.0 | | | 1 | Leicester | 24 | Apr |
| 42:51.50 | Chris Maddocks | | 28.03.57 | 6 | Birmingham | 16 | Jul |
| 43:21.1 | Les Morton | | 1.07.58 | 1 | Sheffield | 19 | Sep |
| | 43:35.98 | | | 7 | Birmingham | 16 | Jul |
| 43:50.44 | Chris Cheeseman | | 11.12.58 | 8 | Birmingham | 16 | Jul |
| 43:53.97 | Martin Young | | 11.07.72 | 9 | Birmingham | 16 | Jul |
| 44:38.57 | Gary Witton | U23 | 25.08.73 | 10 | Birmingham | 16 | Jul |
| (10) | | | | | | | |
| 44:40.0 | Jamie O'Rawe | U23 | 3.02.73 | 2 | Leicester | 22 | Apr |
| 45:20.42 | Steve Hollier | U20 | 27.02.76 | 2 | Bedford | 2 | Jul |
| 46:02.0 | Andy Penn | | 31.03.67 | 3 | Leamington | 17 | May |
| 46:15.2 | Richard Oldale | | 26.01.66 | 2 | Sheffield | 19 | Sep |
| 46:20.6 | Gareth Brown | | 10.05.68 | 2 | Brighton | 28 | Jan |
| 46:30.0 | Steve Taylor | | 19.03.66 | 4 | Leicester | 22 | Apr |
| 46:41.8 | Derek Cross | V45 | 30.04.49 | 1 | London (BP) | 3 | May |
| 46:44.96 | Gareth Holloway | | 2.02.70 | 3 | Cardiff | 22 | Jul |
| 46:50.0 | Brian Adams | V45 | 13.03.49 | 5 | Leicester | 22 | Apr |
| 47:22.0 | Chris Smith | | 23.12.58 | 2 | Leicester | 26 | Sep |
| (20) | | | | | | | |
| 47:36.60 | Stuart Monk | U17 | 23.03.79 | 3 | Bedford | 2 | Jul |
| 47:49.7 | Noel Carmody | | 24.12.56 | 1 | Hoo | 10 | Sep |
| 48:04.0 | Allan Callow | V45 | 4.09.45 | 7 | Leicester | 22 | Apr |
| 48:26.0 | David Keown | U23 | 18.07.74 | 5 | Leamington | 17 | May |

## 10000 Metres Walk - Road - Juniors

| | | | | | | | |
|---|---|---|---|---|---|---|---|
| 42:29 | Steve Hollier | U20 | 27.02.76 | 1 | Birmingham | 10 | Dec |
| 46:11 | Stuart Monk | U17 | 23.03.79 | 3 | Weymouth | 19 | Mar |
| 49:14 | Michael Kemp | U17 | 23.12.79 | 2 | Leicester | 2 | Dec |
| 50:58 | Robert Mecham | U20 | 14.09.77 | 3 | Steyning | 4 | Nov |
| 51:00 | Matthew Hales | U17 | 6.10.79 | 3 | Brighton | 18 | Nov |
| 51:37 | Scott Taylor | U20 | 28.07.78 | 8 | Tamworth | 28 | Oct |
| 53:51 | Andrew Goudie | U17 | 4.10.78 | 6 | Bexley | 21 | Oct |

## 20 Kilometres Walk

| | | | | | | | |
|---|---|---|---|---|---|---|---|
| 1:24:49 | Darrell Stone | | 2.02.68 | 29 | Beijing, CHN | 29 | Apr |
| | 1:25:22 | | | 1 | Dublin, IRE | 23 | Sep |
| | 1:26:18 | | | 1 | Douglas, IOM | 25 | Feb |
| | 1:26:51.6 t | | | 4 | Fana, NOR | 25 | May |
| | 1:27:44 | | | 3 | Horsham | 25 | Mar |
| | 1:28:48 | | | 25 | Gothenburg, SWE | 6 | Aug |
| 1:26:32 | Steve Partington | | 17.09.65 | 2 | Douglas, IOM | 25 | Feb |
| | 1:27:25 | | | 4 | Dublin, IRE | 23 | Sep |
| | 1:28:35 | | | 20 | Fougeres, FRA | 11 | Jun |
| | 1:28:50 | | | 1 | Stockport | 1 | Jul |
| | 1:30:02 | | | 58 | Beijing, CHN | 29 | Apr |
| 1:26:35 | Chris Maddocks | | 28.03.57 | 2 | Dublin, IRE | 23 | Sep |
| | 1:28:11 | | | 19 | Fougeres, FRA | 11 | Jun |
| | 1:28:33.0 t | | | 1 | Plymouth | 8 | Jan |
| | 1:30:12 | | | 4 | Douglas, IOM | 25 | Feb |
| 1:27:05 | Martin Bell | | 9.04.61 | 3 | Dublin, IRE | 23 | Sep |
| | 1:27:24 | | | 1 | Yverdon, SWZ | 20 | Aug |
| 1:28:29 | Andy Penn | | 31.03.67 | 3 | Yverdon, SWZ | 20 | Aug |
| | 1:30:30 | | | 3 | Horsham | 25 | May |

| Time | Name | Cat | DOB | Pos | Location | Date |
|---|---|---|---|---|---|---|
| 1:29:07 | Philip King | U23 | 25.11.74 | 4 | Yverdon, SWZ | 20 Aug |
| 1:29:14 | | | | 2 | Stockport | 1 Jul |
| 1:29:55 | Chris Cheeseman | | 11.12.58 | 2 | Horsham | 25 Mar |
| 1:30:21 | | | | 3 | Stockport | 1 Jul |
| 1:30:29 | | | | 5 | Douglas, IOM | 25 Feb |
| 1:30:28.6 t | Martin Young | | 11.07.72 | 1 | Loughborough | 21 Oct |
| 1:33:37 | Les Morton | | 1.07.58 | 5 | Horsham | 25 Mar |
| 1:34:21.6 t | Richard Oldale | | 26.01.66 | 4 | Loughborough | 21 Oct |
| (10) | | | | | | |
| 1:34:52 | Jamie O'Rawe | U23 | 3.02.73 | 7 | Dublin, IRE | 23 Sep |
| 1:36:17 | Steve Taylor | | 19.03.66 | 7 | Horsham | 25 Mar |
| 1:37:43 | Steve Brennan | | 4.11.65 | 1 | Douglas, IOM | 14 May |
| 1:37:57 | Noel Carmody | | 24.12.56 | 1 | Colchester | 28 May |
| 1:38:21 | Jimmy Ball | | 17.02.63 | 9 | Horsham | 25 Mar |
| 1:38:21 | Gareth Brown | | 10.05.68 | 10 | Horsham | 25 Mar |
| 1:38:48.4 t | Brian Adams | V45 | 13.03.49 | 5 | Loughborough | 21 Oct |
| 1:39:29 | Allan Callow | V45 | 4.09.45 | 2 | Douglas, IOM | 14 May |
| 1:39:52 | Chris Smith | | 23.12.58 | 10 | Dublin, IRE | 23 Sep |

## 30 Kilometres Walk

| Time | Name | | DOB | Pos | Location | Date |
|---|---|---|---|---|---|---|
| 2:18:41 | Chris Maddocks | | 28.03.57 | 1 | Cardiff | 7 May |

## 35 Kilometres Walk

| Time | Name | | DOB | Pos | Location | Date |
|---|---|---|---|---|---|---|
| 2:40:49 | Darrell Stone | | 2.02.68 | 11 | Fougeres, FRA | 11 Jun |
| 2:43:18 + | Chris Maddocks | | 28.03.57 | 1m | Constanta, ROM | 25 Nov |
| 2:45:58 | Mark Easton | | 24.05.63 | 17 | Fougeres, FRA | 11 Jun |
| 2:49:15 | Les Morton | | 1.07.58 | 18 | Fougeres, FRA | 11 Jun |
| 2:53:59 | Graham White | | 28.03.59 | 19 | Fougeres, FRA | 11 Jun |

## 50 Kilometres Walk

| Time | Name | Cat | DOB | Pos | Location | Date |
|---|---|---|---|---|---|---|
| 3:53:14 | Chris Maddocks | | 28.03.57 | 1 | Constanta, ROM | 25 Nov |
| 4:02:47 | | | | 2 | Barendrecht, HOL | 8 Oct |
| 4:31:24 | | | | 2 | Burrator | 5 Mar |
| 4:01:36 | Les Morton | | 1.07.58 | 1 | Stockport | 1 Jul |
| 4:06:46.6 t | | | | 2 | Fana, NOR | 25 May |
| 4:08:52 | | | | 44 | Beijing, CHN | 30 Apr |
| 4:06:01 | Mark Easton | | 24.05.63 | 42 | Beijing, CHN | 30 Apr |
| 4:08:51 | | | | 14 | Palma, SPA | 4 Mar |
| 4:14:59 | Graham White | | 28.03.59 | 1 | Burrator | 5 Mar |
| 4:29:41 | | | | 72 | Beijing, CHN | 30 Apr |
| 4:20:43 | Tim Watt | | 19.09.66 | 6 | Rotterdam, HOL | 8 Oct |
| 4:28:14 | | | | 2 | Stockport | 1 Jul |
| 4:29:16 | | | | 19 | Palma, SPA | 4 Mar |
| 4:28:44 | Gareth Brown | | 10.05.68 | 3 | Stockport | 1 Jul |
| 4:33:01 | Jonathan Cocker | | 26.09.71 | 4 | Stockport | 1 Jul |
| 4:38:10 | Carl Thomson | | 8.04.65 | 21 | Palma, SPA | 4 Mar |
| 4:39:27 | Chris Berwick | V45 | 1.05.46 | 5 | Stockport | 1 Jul |
| 4:49:40 | Andy Trigg | | 23.06.62 | 3 | Burrator | 5 Mar |
| (10) | | | | | | |
| 4:51:57 | Colin Bradley | | 2.02.56 | 6 | Stockport | 1 Jul |
| 4:52:47 | Bob Dobson | V50 | 4.11.42 | 7 | Stockport | 1 Jul |

## 100 Miles Walk

| Time | Name | Cat | DOB | Pos | Location | Date |
|---|---|---|---|---|---|---|
| 19:23:16 | Richard Brown | V45 | 18.11.46 | 1 | London (BP) | 6 Aug |
| 21:24:32 | Chris Flint | V50 | 6.12.44 | 5 | London (BP) | 6 Aug |
| 21:41:37 | Kevin Perry | V45 | 7.12.48 | 7 | London (BP) | 6 Aug |

# 4 x 100 METRES

| | | | | | |
|---|---|---|---|---|---|
| 38.73 | National Team<br>(J Gardener, T Jarrett, D Braithwaite, L Christie) | 1 | Villeneuve d'Ascq, FRA | 24 | Jun |
| 38.75 | National Team<br>(J Gardener, D Braithwaite, J Regis, S Wariso) | 5s2 | Gothenburg, SWE | 12 | Aug |
| 39.07 | National Team<br>(J Gardener, D Braithwaite, J Regis, S Wariso) | 2h4 | Gothenburg, SWE | 12 | Aug |
| 39.39 | National Students Team<br>(P White, T Box, D Walker, M Afilaka) | 2 | Fukuoka, JAP | 3 | Sep |
| 39.43 | National Junior Team U20<br>(D Chambers, M Devonish, D Money, J Henthorn) | 1 | Nyiregyhaza, HUN | 30 | Jul |
| 39.44 | National Team<br>(J Gardener, J Golding, D Braithwaite, S Wariso) | 2 | Gateshead | 21 | Aug |
| 39.51 | National Under 23 Team<br>(P White, J Golding, D Walter, O Dako) | 1 | Narbonne, FRA | 29 | Jul |
| 39.57 | National Students Team<br>(P White, T Box, D Walker, M Afilaka) | 2h2 | Fukuoka, JAP | 2 | Sep |
| 39.8 | Sale Harriers<br>(A Condon, D Campbell, T Box, O Dako) | 1 | Crawley | 1 | Jul |
| 40.02 | National Junior Team U20 | 1 | Loughborough | 11 | Jun |
| 40.04 " | Wales<br>(K Williams, C Jackson, J Baulch, T Rutherford) | 1 | Cwmbran | 9 | Jul |
| 40.09 | National Students Team | 1 | Sheffield | 23 | Jul |
| 40.1 | Wales<br>(K Williams, D Turner, J Baulch, P Maitland) | 1 | Cardiff | 22 | Jul |
| 40.2 | Cardiff AAC<br>(K Williams, D Turner, J Baulch, J Bowen) | 1 | Enfield | 30 | Jul |
| 40.33 | National Students Team | 2 | Loughborough | 11 | Jun |
| 40.33 | Cardiff AAC<br>(K Williams, D Turner, J Baulch, T Rutherford) | 1 | Stoke | 9 | Sep |
| 40.39 | National Team<br>(O Dako, I Mackie, T Box, P Maitland) | 3 | London (CP) | 7 | Jul |
| 40.44 | England<br>(J Gardener, D Campbell, P Goedluck, J John) | 2 | Cwmbran | 9 | Jul |
| 40.47 | Woodford Green AC<br>(A Falola, Josephus Thomas, Joslyn Thomas, T O'Dell) | 2 | Stoke | 9 | Sep |
| 40.53 | Haringey AC<br>(D Chambers, A Mensah, M Lambeth, S Wariso) | 1 | London (CP) | 3 | Jun |

**Additional National Teams**

| | | | | | |
|---|---|---|---|---|---|
| 40.7 | Scotland<br>(E Bunney, K Campbell, J Henderson, D Walker) | 2 | Cardiff | 22 | Jul |
| 41.7 | Northern Ireland<br>(Sloan, I Craig, P Brizzell, M Allen) | 4 | Cardiff | 22 | Jul |

**Additonal Club Teams** (1 - 4 above)

| | | | | | |
|---|---|---|---|---|---|
| 40.72 | Newham & Essex Beagles | 3 | Stoke | 9 | Sep |
| 40.77 | Belgrave | 4 | Stoke | 9 | Sep |
| 40.97 | Thames Valley | 5 | Algarve, POR | 27 | May |
| 41.1 | Edinburgh Southern | 2 | Derby | 30 | Jul |
| 41.11 | Loughborough Students | 4 | Loughborough | 11 | Jun |
| 41.61 | Blackheath | 4 | Enfield | 19 | Aug |
| 41.7 | Shaftesbury Barnet | 4 | London (He) | 7 | May |
| 41.7 | Border | 1 | London (WL) | 30 | Jul |
| 42.06 | BT Pitreavie | 2 | Edinburgh | 6 | Aug |
| 42.1 | Peterborough | 1 | Peterborough | 6 | May |
| 42.1 | City of Stoke | 3 | London (WL) | 30 | Jul |
| 42.1 | Old Gaytonians | 1 | Watford | 19 | Aug |
| 42.1 | Coventry Godiva | 1 | Mansfield | 19 | Aug |
| 42.1 | Bedford & County | 1 | Sutton | 19 | Aug |
| 42.11 | Norfolk Olympiads | 1 | Stoke | 10 | Sep |

**Additional Under 20 Teams** (1 - 2 above)

| | | | | | |
|---|---|---|---|---|---|
| 40.55 | National Junior 'B' Team | | 3 | Loughborough | 11 Jun |
| 40.55 | National Junior Team | | 1h1 | Nyiregyhaza, HUN | 29 Jul |
| 40.65 | National Junior Team | | 1 | Belfort, FRA | 6 Aug |
| 40.68 | National Junior Team | U18 | 1 | Bath | 13 Jul |
| 41.60 | Wales | | 2 | Utrecht, HOL | 9 Jul |
| 41.79 | National Junior Team | U18 | h | Bath | 12 Jul |
| 41.9 | Scottish Schools | | 1 | Ayr | 18 Jul |
| 42.37 | Essex Schools | | 1 | Nottingham | 8 Jul |

**Under 20 Club Teams**

| | | | | | |
|---|---|---|---|---|---|
| 42.9 | Belgrave | | 1 | London (Elt) | 18 Jun |
| 43.14 | Blackheath | | 1 | Paris, FRA | 30 Sep |
| 43.3 | Belgrave | U17 | 1 | Kingston | 25 Jun |
| 43.32 | Ballyclare HS | | 1 | Tullamore, IRE | 3 Jun |
| 43.56 | Sale | U17 | 1 | Birmingham | 3 Sep |
| 43.69 | Norfolk Olympiads | U17 | 1h3 | Nottingham | 8 Jul |
| 43.76 | Blackheath | U17 | 2 | Birmingham | 3 Sep |
| 43.7 | King's School, Canterbury | | 1 | Oxford | 13 May |
| 43.79 | Shaftesbury Barnet | | 5 | Paris, FRA | 30 Sep |
| 44.0 | Gateshead | | 1 | Middlesbrough | 30 Jul |
| 44.0 | Derby & County | | 1 | Telford | 30 Jul |

**Additional Under 17 Teams**

| | | | | | |
|---|---|---|---|---|---|
| 42.83 | English Schools | | 1 | Colwyn Bay | 15 Jul |
| 43.01 | Scottish Schools | | 2 | Colwyn Bay | 15 Jul |
| 43.10 | Scotland | | 1 | Antrim | 12 Aug |
| 43.36 | Welsh Schools | | 3 | Colwyn Bay | 15 Jul |
| 43.42 | Merseyside Schools | | 1h1 | Nottingham | 8 Jul |
| 43.44 | Essex Schools | | 2h1 | Nottingham | 8 Jul |
| 43.45 | West Midlands Schools | | 2 | Nottingham | 8 Jul |

**Additional Under 17 Club Teams** (1 - 4 above)

| | | | | | |
|---|---|---|---|---|---|
| 44.5 | Liverpool Harriers | | 1 | Stockport | 16 Jul |
| 44.8 | Dundee Hawkhill | | 1 | Inverness | 28 May |
| 44.8 | Blackheath | U15 | 1 | London (TB) | 25 Jun |
| 44.9 | Dulwich College | | 1 | Oxford | 13 May |
| 45.0 | Newham & Essex Beagles | | 1 | London (WF) | 13 Jul |
| 45.08 | Methodist College Belfast | | 1 | Tullamore, IRE | 3 Jun |

**Additional Under 15 Teams** (1 above)

| | | | | | |
|---|---|---|---|---|---|
| 44.46 | West Midlands Schools | | 1h3 | Nottingham | 8 Jul |
| 45.19 | Scotland | | 1 | Antrim | 12 Aug |
| 45.34 | London Schools | | 1h1 | Nottingham | 8 Jul |
| 46.0 | Birchfield | | 1 | Solihull | 16 Jul |
| 46.18 | Staffordshire Schools | | 1h4 | Nottingham | 8 Jul |
| 46.28 | Wales | | 2 | Antrim | 12 Aug |

**Additional Under 15 Club Teams** (1 - 2 above)

| | | | | | |
|---|---|---|---|---|---|
| 47.36 | Airdrie | | 1 | Edinburgh | 24 Jun |
| 47.4 | Eastbourne Rovers | | 1 | Crawley | 11 Jun |
| 47.4 | Old Gaytonians | | 1 | Harrow | 16 Jul |
| 47.4 | Gateshead | | 1 | Bolton | 16 Jul |
| 47.5 | Windsor Slough & Eton | | 1 | Windsor | 25 Jun |
| 47.52 | Cannock & Stafford | | 1 | Birmingham | 2 Sep |
| 47.6 | Liverpool Harriers | | 1 | Liverpool | 30 Apr |
| 47.7 | Croydon | | 1 | London (TB) | 25 Jun |

## Under 13 Club Teams

| | | | | | |
|---|---|---|---|---|---|
| 52.25 | Birchfield | | 1 | Birmingham | 3 Sep |
| 52.7 | Havering Mayesbrook | | 1 | London (WF) | 13 Jul |
| 53.3 | Barnet | | 1 | Watford | 9 Jul |
| 53.4 | Blackheath | | 1 | Tonbridge | 17 Sep |
| 53.50 | L & L Track Club | | 1 | Edinburgh | 24 Jun |
| 53.89 | Enfield | | 1 | Birmingham | 2 Sep |
| 54.16 | Sale | | 2 | Birmingham | 3 Sep |
| 54.3 | Team Solent | | 1 | London (TB) | 25 Jun |
| 54.3 | Liverpool Harriers | | 1 | Stockport | 16 Jul |

# 4 x 200 METRES

| | | | | | |
|---|---|---|---|---|---|
| 1:26.65 i | AA of Wales | | 1 | Birmingham | 26 Feb |
| | (K Williams, D Turner, B Middleton, P Maitland) | | | | |
| 1:26.71 i | England | | 1 | Vienna, AUT | 18 Feb |
| | (J Gardener, B Taylor, A Falola, A Condon) | | | | |
| 1:26.95 i | North of England | | 2 | Birmingham | 26 Feb |
| | (D Money, A Clegg, S McCourt, A Condon) | | | | |
| 1:27.57 i | South of England | | 3 | Birmingham | 26 Feb |
| | (A Lewis, A Falola, L Fairclough, A Mensah) | | | | |
| 1:28.2 | Herne Hill | | 1 | London (TB) | 23 Aug |
| 1:29.20 i | Birmingham University | | 1 | Birmingham | 1 Mar |
| 1:30.1 | Hercules Wimbledon | | 1 | Sutton | 19 Jul |
| 1:30.2 | Belgrave | | 2 | London (TB) | 23 Aug |
| 1:30.3 i | Scottish Universities | | 2 | Glasgow | 11 Mar |
| 1:31.2 | Belgrave | U20 | 2 | Sutton | 19 Jul |

**Additional Club Teams** (1 - 4 above)

| | | | | | |
|---|---|---|---|---|---|
| 1:31.3 | Croydon | | 2 | Wimbledon | 30 Apr |
| 1:31.3 | Belgrave | U17 | 1 | London (TB) | 2 Aug |
| 1:31.5 | Coventry Godiva | | 1 | Cheltenham | 6 Aug |
| 1:32.32 i | Edinburgh University | | 1 | Glasgow | 28 Jan |
| 1:32.8 | South London | | 4 | London (TB) | 23 Aug |
| 1:33.0 | Ealing Southall & Middlesex | | 1 | Perivale | 26 Aug |
| 1:33.6 | Eton College | U20 | 1 | Oxford | 13 May |

**Additional Under 20 Teams** (1 - 3 above)

| | | | | | |
|---|---|---|---|---|---|
| 1:32.45 i | Scotland Schools | U17 | 1 | Birmingham | 26 Feb |
| 1:33.05 i | England Schools | U17 | 2 | Birmingham | 26 Feb |
| 1:34.6 | Dulwich College | U17 | 1 | Oxford | 13 May |
| 1:34.7 | Epsom College | | 2 | Oxford | 13 May |
| 1:34.85 i | Ayr Seaforth AAC | U17 | 1 | Glasgow | 29 Jan |
| 1:35.23 i | West Midlands Schools | U17 | 1 | Birmingham | 7 Feb |
| 1:35.66 i | Staffordshire Schools | U17 | 2 | Birmingham | 7 Feb |

**Additional Under 20 Club Teams** (1 - 5 above)

| | | | | | |
|---|---|---|---|---|---|
| 1:36.2 | St. Paul's School | | 1h1 | Oxford | 13 May |
| 1:36.2 | Highgate School | | 3h2 | Oxford | 13 May |
| 1:36.8 | Wellington College | U17 | 2 | Oxford | 13 May |
| 1:37.11 i | Falkirk Victoria | | 2 | Glasgow | 29 Jan |
| 1:37.5 | Pitreavie | | 1 | Pitreavie | 28 May |

**Additional Under 17 Teams** (1 - 8 above)

| | | | | | |
|---|---|---|---|---|---|
| 1:35.9 | Dundee Hawkhill | | 1 | Dundee | 30 Apr |
| 1:36.21 i | Nottinghamshire Schools | | 3 | Birmingham | 7 Feb |
| 1:36.26 i | Wales Schools | | 3 | Birmingham | 26 Feb |

**Additional Under 17 Club Teams** (1 - 5 above)

| | | | | |
|---|---|---|---|---|
| 1:37.7 | Sutton & District | 1 | London (TB) | 21 Jun |
| 1:37.7 | Lucozade Motherwell | 1 | Wishaw | 28 Jun |
| 1:37.7 | Minolta Black Isle | 1 | Inverness | 20 Aug |
| 1:37.73 i | IBM Spango Valley | 2 | Glasgow | 29 Jan |
| 1:37.8 | King's School, Canterbury | 3 | Oxford | 13 May |

**Under 15 Teams**

| | | | | |
|---|---|---|---|---|
| 1:38.6 | Eastbourne Rovers | 1 | Crawley | 11 Jun |
| 1:41.1 | Highgate School | 1 | Oxford | 13 May |
| 1:41.4 | Croydon | 1 | Croydon | 14 May |
| 1:41.7 | Notts | 1 | Nottingham | 20 Aug |
| 1:42.23 i | West Midlands Schools | 1 | Birmingham | 7 Feb |
| 1:42.3 X | Lagan Valley | 1 | Belfast | 1 Jun |
| 1:42.57 i | Nottinghamshire Schools | 2 | Birmingham | 7 Feb |
| 1:42.59 i | Staffordshire Schools | 3 | Birmingham | 7 Feb |
| 1:42.8 | Millfield School | 2 | Oxford | 13 May |
| 1:43.7 X | St. Columb's College | 1 | Templemore | 18 Jul |
| 1:43.9 | Epsom College | 3 | Oxford | 13 May |
| 1:44.7 | Lucozade Motherwell | 1 | Wishaw | 28 Jun |
| 1:44.9 | Wimbledon College | 1 | London (TB) | 21 Jun |

**Under 13 Teams**

| | | | | |
|---|---|---|---|---|
| 1:55.0 X | St. Columbs College | 1 | Templemore | 18 Jul |
| 1:55.7 | L & L Track Club | 1 | Wishaw | 28 Jun |
| 1:57.5 X | Lagan Valley | 2 | Londonderry | 8 Aug |
| 1:58.7 | Croydon | 1 | Croydon | 14 May |

# 4 x 400 METRES

| | | | | |
|---|---|---|---|---|
| 3:00.34 | National Team | 1 | Villenueve d'Ascq, FRA | 25 Jun |
| | (I Thomas, A Patrick, M Richardson, R Black) | | | |
| 3:01.22 | National Team | 2h3 | Gothenburg, SWE | 12 Aug |
| | (D McKenzie, A Patrick, M Hylton, M Richardson) | | | |
| 3:02.42 | Great Britain Students | 3 | Fukuoka, JAP | 3 Sep |
| | (A Williams, J Deacon, G Jennings, D Grindley) | | | |
| 3:03.16 | National Team | 1 | Gateshead | 21 Aug |
| | (D MacKenzie, J Baulch, T O'Dell, M Hylton) | | | |
| 3:03.75 | National Team | 4 | Gothenburg, SWE | 13 Aug |
| | (D MacKenzie, M Hylton, A Patrick, R Black) | | | |
| 3:04.90 | National U23 Team | 1 | Narbonne, FRA | 29 Jul |
| | (N Budden, P Slythe, P Maitland, J Baulch) | | | |
| 3:06.40 | Great Britain Students | 2h1 | Fukuoka, JAP | 2 Sep |
| | (A Williams, J Deacon, G Jennings, D Grindley) | | | |
| 3:07.09 | National Junior Team U20 | 1 | Nyiregyhaza, HUN | 30 Jul |
| | (G Dearman, S McHardy, T Lerwill, M Hylton) | | | |
| 3:07.33 | Newham & Essex Beagles | 1 | London (CP) | 3 Jun |
| | (A Francis, G Jennings, P McBurney, I Thomas) | | | |
| 3:08.6 | Windsor Slough & Eton AC | 1 | Stoke | 6 May |
| | (S Kabiswa, M Hylton, A Patrick, M Richardson) | | | |
| 3:09.20 | Thames Valley Harriers | 2 | London (CP) | 3 Jun |
| | (K Bentham, E Williams, G Telfer, V Rose) | | | |
| 3:09.22 i | National Team | 1 | Birmingham | 28 Jan |
| | (G Bullock, M Hylton, A Condon, B Whittle) | | | |
| 3:09.28 i | National Team | 1 | Glasgow | 11 Feb |
| | (P Crampton, M Hylton, S Wariso, B Whittle) | | | |
| 3:09.89 | National Junior Team U20 | 1 | Belfort, FRA | 6 Aug |
| | (S McHardy, M Douglas, T Lerwill, G Dearman) | | | |
| 3:10.89 i | National Team | 4 | Barcelona, SPA | 12 Mar |
| | (G Bullock, P Slythe, M Hylton, A Condon) | | | |
| 3:10.89 | Loughborough Students | 1 | Loughborough | 11 Jun |
| | ( , , ,G Jennings ) | | | |

| | | | | | |
|---|---|---|---|---|---|
| 3:10.94 | Newham & Essex Beagles | | 1 | Stoke | 9 Sep |
| | (A Francis, D Park, G Jennings, P McBurney) | | | | |
| 3:11.18 | England | | 2 | Loughborough | 11 Jun |
| | (G Bullock, C Rawlinson, D Nolan, M Smith) | | | | |
| 3:11.21 | Woodford Green | | 1 | Birmingham | 1 Jul |
| | (S Ciaravella, J Kenny, T O'Dell, M Smith) | | | | |
| 3:11.85 | Wales | | 1 | Cardiff | 23 Jul |
| | (P Maitland, J Baulch, D Griffin, J Weston) | | | | |
| 3:12.24 | Loughborough Students | | 1 | Edinburgh | 8 May |

**Additional National Teams**

| | | | | | |
|---|---|---|---|---|---|
| 3:15.30 | Northern Ireland | | 2 | Cardiff | 23 Jul |
| | (B McCoy, D Thom, B Forbes, P McBurney) | | | | |
| 3:17.77 | Scotland | | 4 | Cardiff | 23 Jul |
| | (I Horsburgh, B Middleton, K Idessane, G Graham) | | | | |

**Additional Club Teams** (1 - 5 above)

| | | | | | |
|---|---|---|---|---|---|
| 3:13.4 | Wigan | | 1 | Stretford | 1 Jul |
| 3:13.6 | Cardiff | | 1 | Crawley | 1 Jul |
| 3:13.62 | Belgrave | | 3 | Enfield | 19 Aug |
| 3:13.67 | Haringey | | 4 | Enfield | 19 Aug |
| 3:14.45 | Birchfield | | 3 | Birmingham | 1 Jul |
| 3:14.7 | Sale | | 2 | Derby | 30 Jul |
| ?3:14.75 | Haringey AC | | 5 | Stoke | 9 Sep |
| 3:15.32 | Staffordshire University | | 2 | Edinburgh | 8 May |
| 3:15.37 | Norfolk Olympiads | | 1 | Stoke | 10 Sep. |
| 3:16.24 | Team Solent | | 1 | Edinburgh | 1 Jul |
| 3:16.7 | Coventry Godiva | | 3 | Derby | 30 Jul |
| 3:16.8 | Morpeth | | 1 | Jarrow | 1 Jul |
| 3:17.22 | GEC Avionics | | 2 | Edinburgh | 1 Jul |
| 3:17.5 | Cambridge Harriers | | 2 | Wakefield | 3 Jun |
| 3:17.8 | Borough of Hounslow | | 2 | Bracknell | 3 Jun |
| 3:17.81 | Shaftesbury Barnet | | 6 | Stoke | 9 Sep |

**Additional Under 20 Teams** (1 - 2 above)

| | | | | | |
|---|---|---|---|---|---|
| 3:18.3 | Scotland Schools | | 1 | Ayr | 18 Jul |
| | (A Young, G Doyle, I Horsburgh, A Donaldson) | | | | |
| 3:18.8 | Scottish AA | | 2 | Ayr | 18 Jul |
| 3:19.07 | South | | 1 | London (He) | 9 Sep |
| 3:19.67 | Blackheath | | 2 | Paris, FRA | 30 Sep |
| 3:21.13 | England Schools | U17 | 1 | Colwyn Bay | 15 Jul |
| 3:21.70 | Midlands | | 2 | London (He) | 9 Sep |
| 3:22.12 | Scotland Schools | U17 | 2 | Colwyn Bay | 15 Jul |
| 3:22.52 | Humberside CAA | | 1 | | 5 Aug |
| 3:23.0 | Surrey CAA | | 1 | Kingston | 13 Aug |
| 3:23.1 | Welsh Schools | | 3 | Ayr | 18 Jul |
| 3:23.2 | AA of Wales | | 4 | Ayr | 18 Jul |

**Additional Under 20 Club Teams** (1 above)

| | | | | | |
|---|---|---|---|---|---|
| 3:23.74 | Blackheath | U17 | 1 | Birmingham | 3 Sep |
| 3:23.8 | Braintree & District | | 1 | Ipswich | 23 Apr |
| 3:26.8 | Kilbarchan | U17 | 1 | Edinburgh | 24 Jun |
| 3:26.9 | Hillingdon | | 1 | Dartford | 18 Jun |
| 3:27.2 | Telford | | 1 | Telford | 18 Jun |
| 3:28.0 | Birchfield | | 1 | Middlesbrough | 30 Jul |
| 3:28.1 | Belgrave | | 1 | Perivale | 23 Apr |
| 3:28.2 | Luton United | | 1 | Thurrock | 30 Jul |
| 3:29.1 | Medway | | 2 | Dartford | 18 Jun |
| 3:29.96 | Shaftesbury Barnet | | 4 | Paris, FRA | 30 Sep |

**Additional Under 17 Teams** (1 - 4 above)

| | | | | | |
|---|---|---|---|---|---|
| 3:26.14 | Wales Schools | 3 | Colwyn Bay | 15 | Jul |
| 3:27.7 | Hampshire CAA | 1 | Kingston | 13 | Aug |
| 3:27.8 | Kent CAA | 2 | Kingston | 13 | Aug |
| 3:30.1 | Essex CAA | 3 | Kingston | 13 | Aug |
| 3:30.5 | Crewe & Nantwich | 1 | Crewe | 27 | Jun |
| 3:31.1 | Basildon | 1 | London (WF) | 13 | Jul |

**Additional Under 17 Club Teams** (1 - 4 above)

| | | | | | |
|---|---|---|---|---|---|
| 3:31.3 | Berry Hill Mansfield | 1 | Solihull | 16 | Jul |
| 3:31.60 | Birchfield | 2 | Birmingham | 3 | Sep |
| 3:31.75 | Liverpool Harriers | 3 | Birmingham | 3 | Sep |
| 3:31.8 | Airdrie | 2 | Edinburgh | 24 | Jun |
| 3:32.1 | Leeds City | 1 | Leeds | 4 | Jun |
| 3:32.1 | Rowntrees | 1 | Jarrow | 16 | Jul |

**Under 15 Teams**

| | | | | | |
|---|---|---|---|---|---|
| 3:41.6 | Blackheath | 1 | Tonbridge | 17 | Sep |
| 3:42.29 | Shaftesbury Barnet | 1 | Birmingham | 3 | Sep |
| 3:42.4 | Wirral | 1 | Crewe | 27 | Jun |
| 3:42.7 | Croydon | 1 | Croydon | 16 | Jul |
| 3:43.5 | Rowntrees | 1 | York | 21 | May |
| 3:43.5 | Invicta East Kent | 2 | Tonbridge | 17 | Sep |
| 3:44.82 | Liverpool Harriers | 3 | Birmingham | 3 | Sep |
| 3:47.7 | Windsor Slough & Eton | 1 | Windsor | 25 | Jun |
| 3:47.9 | Cannock & Stafford | 2 | Birmingham | 2 | Sep |
| 3:48.85 | Sale | 4 | Birmingham | 3 | Sep |

**Under 13 Teams**

| | | | | | |
|---|---|---|---|---|---|
| 4:19.4 | Blackheath | 1 | Tonbridge | 17 | Sep |
| 4:23.0 | Team Solent | 1 | Bournemouth | 23 | Jul |
| 4:23.3 X | St Columb's College | 1 | Templemore | 13 | Jul |
| 4:28.1 | City of Porstmouth | 1 | Andover | 18 | Jun |
| 4:30.6 | GEC Avionics | 3 | Tonbridge | 17 | Sep |

## 1600 METRES MEDLEY

| | | | | | |
|---|---|---|---|---|---|
| 3:27.56 i | AA of Wales | 1 | Birmingham | 26 | Feb |
| 3:27.91 i | Midland Counties AA | 2 | Birmingham | 26 | Feb |
| 3:28.65 | Clydesdale | 1 | Greenock | 4 | Jun |
| 3:28.7 | Bexley Borough | 1 | Tonbridge | 17 | Sep |
| 3:29.58 | BT Pitreavie | 2 | Greenock | 4 | Jun |
| 3:29.66 i | North of England AA | 3 | Birmingham | 26 | Feb |
| 3:30.22 | Victoria Park | 3 | Greenock | 4 | Jun |
| 3:31.2 | Blackheath | 2 | Tonbridge | 17 | Sep |

**Under 20 Teams**

| | | | | | |
|---|---|---|---|---|---|
| 3:43.4 | City of Portsmouth | 1 | Portsmouth | 19 | Jul |

**Under 17 Teams**

| | | | | | |
|---|---|---|---|---|---|
| 3:45.2 | Lucozade Motherwell | 1 | Wishaw | 26 | Aug |
| 3:47.5 | Shettleston | 2 | Wishaw | 26 | Aug |
| 3:50.0 | Larkhall YMCA | 3 | Wishaw | 26 | Aug |
| 3:52.4 | City of Portsmouth | 1 | Portsmouth | 19 | Jul |
| 3:52.6 | Perth Strathtay | 1 | Dundee | 7 | Jun |

**Under 15 Teams**

| | | | | | |
|---|---|---|---|---|---|
| 4:12.6 | Winchester & District | 1 | Portsmouth | 19 | Jul |
| 4:14.8 | Lucozade Motherwell | 1 | Wishaw | 26 | Aug |
| 4:19.8 | City of Portsmouth | 2 | Portsmouth | 19 | Jul |
| 4:20.3 | Aberdeen | 1 | Peterhead | 18 | Jun |
| 4:20.6 | Minolta Black Isle | 1 | Inverness | 4 | Jun |

**Under 13 Teams**

| | | | | |
|---|---|---|---|---|
| 4:43.7 | L & L Track Club | 1 | Wishaw | 26 Aug |
| 4:52.4 | Lucozade Motherwell | 2 | Wishaw | 26 Aug |
| 4:56.4 | Law | 3 | Wishaw | 26 Aug |

# 4 x 800 METRES

| | | | | | |
|---|---|---|---|---|---|
| 7:26.2 | BMC Juniors | U20 | 1 | Oxford | 2 Sep |
| | (A Tatham, D Stanley, A Donaldson, A Blackmore) | | | | |
| 7:26.2 | Sale | | 2 | Oxford | 2 Sep |
| | (B Craven, R Waters, A Walling, S Green) | | | | |
| 7:32.0 | BMC Wales | | 3 | Oxford | 2 Sep |
| | (N Commerford, M Jones, D Povall, P Bristow) | | | | |
| 7:37.1 | BMC North | | 4 | Oxford | 2 Sep |
| | (G Watson, M Gooch, D Rankin, D Thornton) | | | | |
| 7:39.6 | BMC South West | | 5 | Oxford | 2 Sep |
| | (M Kloiber, M Wiscombe, D Cole, A Caple) | | | | |
| 7:46.9 | BMC Wales Juniors | U20 | 6 | Oxford | 2 Sep |
| | (R Cartwright, M McHugh, J Weybourne, D Davy) | | | | |
| 7:49.6 | BMC South | | 7 | Oxford | 2 Sep |
| | (J Mayo, D Clark, A McDougall, M Curzon) | | | | |
| 7:54.1 | BMC England | | 8 | Oxford | 2 Sep |
| | (M Griffin, J Thompson, J Dupuy, G Scott) | | | | |
| 8:04.5 | Gateshead | | 1 | Gateshead | 2 Aug |

**Additional Under 20 Teams** (1 - 2 above)

| | | | | |
|---|---|---|---|---|
| 8:04.8 | Millfield School | 1 | Oxford | 13 May |
| 8:09.6 | Trinity School | 2 | Oxford | 13 May |
| 8:14.0 | Oxford City | 1 | Oxford | 2 Sep |

**Under 17 Teams**

| | | | | |
|---|---|---|---|---|
| 8:17.4 | Crewe & Nantwich | 1 | Crewe | 11 Jul |
| 8:38.8 | Warrington | 2 | Crewe | 11 Jul |
| 8:40.0 | Berkhamstead School | 1 | Oxford | 13 May |

**Under 15 Teams**

| | | | | |
|---|---|---|---|---|
| 9:04.9 X | North Belfast | 1 | | 29 Jun |
| 9:11.6 | Eton College | 1 | Oxford | 13 May |
| 9:16.6 | Highgate School | 2 | Oxford | 13 May |

**Under 13 Teams**

| | | | | |
|---|---|---|---|---|
| 9:54.6 X | St Columbs College | 1 | | 29 Jun |
| 10:09.0 | Wakefield | 1 | Blackpool | 24 Sep |
| 10:15.8 | Warrington | 1 | Crewe | 27 Jun |
| 10:17.4 | Crewe & Nantwich | 2 | Crewe | 27 Jun |

# 4 x 1500 METRES

| | | | | |
|---|---|---|---|---|
| 17:05.3 | Cambridge University | 1 | Cambridge | 18 Feb |
| 18:11.3 | Oxford University | 2 | Cambridge | 18 Feb |

# 4 x 1 MILE

| | | | | |
|---|---|---|---|---|
| 16:28.9 | British Milers Club | 1 | Oxford | 2 Sep |
| | (L Cadwallader, A Hart, I Gillespie, N Caddy) | | | |
| 17:10.1 | Border | 3 | Oxford | 2 Sep |
| | (P Hackley, K Downie, D MacLachlan, D Farrell) | | | |
| 17:52.6 | BMC South | 4 | Oxford | 2 Sep |
| | (M O'Dowd, J Brooks, G Beard, T Grose) | | | |
| 18:06.4 | BMC East | 5 | Oxford | 2 Sep |
| | (I Hollingsworth, J Greenhough, I Chalk, D Hayes) | | | |

X as  Northern Ireland age groups and therefore possibly including older athletes.

# 1995 LISTS - WOMEN

## 60 METRES - Indoors

| | | | | | | | |
|---|---|---|---|---|---|---|---|
| 7.21 | Stephanie Douglas | | 22.01.69 | 1r1 | Glasgow | 11 | Feb |
| 7.28 | | | | 1 | Birmingham | 4 | Feb |
| 7.29 | | | | 3 | Birmingham | 25 | Feb |
| 7.30 | | | | 5 | Lievin, FRA | 19 | Feb |
| 7.30 | | | | 7s2 | Barcelona, SPA | 10 | Mar |
| 7.31 | | | | 4h2 | Lievin, FRA | 19 | Feb |
| 7.31 | | | | 3h2 | Barcelona, SPA | 10 | Mar |
| 7.33 | | | | 1s1 | Birmingham | 4 | Feb |
| 7.35 | | | | 3 | Birmingham | 28 | Jan |
| 7.35 | | | | 1r2 | Birmingham | 28 | Jan |
| 7.37 | | | | 1h1 | Birmingham | 4 | Feb |
| 7.48 | | | | 3h2 | Stockholm, SWE | 27 | Feb |
| 7.28 | Paula Thomas | | 3.12.64 | 3r1 | Glasgow | 11 | Feb |
| 7.29 | | | | 1 | Birmingham | 28 | Jan |
| 7.32 | | | | 3h1 | Lievin, FRA | 19 | Feb |
| 7.34 | | | | 6 | Birmingham | 25 | Feb |
| 7.36 | Melanie Neef | | 26.05.70 | 1 | Glasgow | 22 | Jan |
| 7.45 | | | | 2 | Glasgow | 15 | Jan |
| 7.49 | | | | 2h2 | Glasgow | 22 | Jan |
| 7.36 | Aileen McGillivary | | 13.08.70 | 2 | Birmingham | 4 | Feb |
| 7.37 | | | | 2 | Glasgow | 22 | Jan |
| 7.37 | | | | 5r1 | Glasgow | 11 | Feb |
| 7.39 | | | | 1 | Glasgow | 15 | Jan |
| 7.42 | | | | 1r2 | Glasgow | 11 | Feb |
| 7.44 | | | | 6h3 | Barcelona, SPA | 10 | Mar |
| 7.45 | | | | 2s1 | Birmingham | 4 | Feb |
| 7.38 | Diane Allahgreen | U23 | 21.02.75 | 3h1 | Vienna, AUT | 18 | Feb |
| 7.48 | | | | 2h4 | Birmingham | 4 | Feb |
| 7.43 | Jacqui Agyepong | | 5.01.69 | 1s2 | Birmingham | 4 | Feb |
| 7.44 | | | | 1h4 | Birmingham | 4 | Feb |
| 7.47 | | | | 4 | Birmingham | 4 | Feb |
| 7.45 | Marcia Richardson | | 10.02.72 | 2s2 | Birmingham | 4 | Feb |
| 7.46 | Danaa Myhill/Callow | | 16.10.70 | 1r2 | Vienna, AUT | 18 | Feb |
| 7.47 | | | | 1h2 | Birmingham | 4 | Feb |
| 7.47 | | | | 3 | Birmingham | 4 | Feb |
| 7.48 | | | | 3s2 | Birmingham | 4 | Feb |
| 7.50 | | | | 5h1 | Vienna, AUT | 18 | Feb |
| 7.49 | Sam Farquharson | | 15.12.69 | 1h2 | Glasgow | 22 | Jan |
| | 39 performances to 7.50 by 9 athletes | | | | | | |
| 7.54 | Sarah Wilhelmy | U17 | 2.02.80 | 1 | Birmingham | 18 | Feb |
| | (10) | | | | | | |
| *7.57* | *Evadne McKenzie* | *U23* | *19.05.75* | *4s2* | *Birmingham* | *4* | *Feb* |
| 7.58 | Rebecca Drummond | U20 | 18.04.78 | 1r1 | Birmingham | 29 | Jan |
| 7.61 | Sophia Smith | U23 | 8.12.74 | 2 | Birmingham | 26 | Feb |
| 7.63 | Dawn Rose | U17 | 25.01.79 | 2 | Birmingham | 18 | Feb |
| 7.63 | Clova Court | V35 | 10.02.60 | 3 | Birmingham | 30 | Dec |
| 7.66 | Sinead Dudgeon | U20 | 9.07.76 | 2h1 | Glasgow | 15 | Jan |
| 7.67 | Uju Efobi | U23 | 10.10.74 | 4s1 | Birmingham | 4 | Feb |
| 7.69 | Yinka Idowu | | 25.02.72 | 2 | Birmingham | 28 | Jan |
| 7.69 | Sarah Oxley | U23 | 3.07.73 | 1r1 | Birmingham | 29 | Jan |
| 7.69 | Ann Brooks | | 4.05.71 | 2h1 | Birmingham | 4 | Feb |
| 7.70 | Helen Miles | | 2.03.67 | 3 | Birmingham | 26 | Feb |
| | (20) | | | | | | |
| 7.71 | Rebecca Kilgour | U23 | 18.10.75 | 1 | Birmingham | 11 | Feb |
| 7.72 | Gillian Hegney | U20 | 4.11.77 | 1 | Glasgow | 9 | Feb |
| 7.73 | Ellena Ruddock | U20 | 23.02.76 | 2r1 | Birmingham | 29 | Jan |

| | | | | | | | |
|---|---|---|---|---|---|---|---|
| 7.73 | Lorraine Robins | | 13.05.70 | 2r1 | Birmingham | 29 | Jan |
| 7.74 | Elaine Sutcliffe | | 6.04.70 | 6 | Birmingham | 28 | Jan |
| 7.74 | Joan Booth | | 18.12.68 | 3h2 | Birmingham | 4 | Feb |
| 7.75 | Lesley Owusu | U17 | 21.12.78 | 1= | Birmingham | 28 | Jan |
| 7.75 | Vicky Shipman | U20 | 31.03.77 | 1r2 | Birmingham | 29 | Jan |
| 7.75 | Laura Seston | U17 | 9.02.79 | 1r1 | Birmingham | 29 | Jan |
| 7.75 | Elaine Pryce | U23 | 4.10.73 | 3h3 | Birmingham | 4 | Feb |
| | (30) | | | | | | |
| 7.75 | Zoe Wilson | U20 | 28.08.76 | 1s1 | Birmingham | 19 | Feb |
| 7.77 | Fiona Hutchison | U20 | 18.01.77 | 1h2 | Glasgow | 4 | Feb |
| 7.77 | Sarah Chesney | U23 | 3.03.73 | 5s2 | Birmingham | 4 | Feb |
| *7.77* | *Jean Oyeyemi* | *U15* | *24.08.81* | *1* | *Birmingham* | *26* | *Feb* |
| 7.78 | Dawn Flockhart | | 16.05.67 | 2h2 | Glasgow | 15 | Jan |
| 7.78 | Kirsty Payne | U20 | 22.10.77 | 3 | Birmingham | 5 | Feb |
| 7.78 | Mairi McEwen | U17 | 16.08.79 | 1 | Glasgow | 14 | Feb |
| 7.79 | Sue Briggs | | 26.03.67 | 3r1 | Birmingham | 29 | Jan |

**Additional Under 17** (1 - 5 above)

| | | | | | | | |
|---|---|---|---|---|---|---|---|
| 7.80 | Maria Bolsover | | 5.06.80 | 2 | Birmingham | 11 | Feb |
| 7.80 | Emma Ania | | 7.02.79 | 3 | Birmingham | 18 | Feb |
| 7.82 | Ayeesha Charles | | 4.09.79 | 3r1 | Birmingham | 29 | Jan |
| 7.82 | Elizabeth Hall | | 16.10.78 | 1h1 | Birmingham | 5 | Feb |
| 7.82 | Sarah Claxton | | 23.09.79 | 5 | Birmingham | 18 | Feb |
| | (10) | | | | | | |
| 7.83 | Claire Jelley | | 27.11.79 | 4r1 | Birmingham | 29 | Jan |
| 7.83 | Shelley-Anne Bowen | | 12.05.79 | 3s1 | Birmingham | 18 | Feb |
| 7.84 | Jade Johnson | | 7.06.80 | 1h4 | Birmingham | 18 | Feb |
| 7.87 | Lee McConnell | | 9.10.78 | 4 | Birmingham | 28 | Jan |
| 7.87 | Karen Scott | | 17.10.79 | 2 | Birmingham | 16 | Feb |
| 7.88 | Hannah Moody | | 26.07.79 | 4s1 | Birmingham | 18 | Feb |
| 7.89 | Sarah Miles | | 14.12.78 | 2h1 | Birmingham | 18 | Feb |
| 7.90 | Hannah Paines | | 6.04.79 | 5r1 | Birmingham | 29 | Jan |
| 7.90 | Helen Roscoe | | 4.12.79 | 3 | Birmingham | 11 | Feb |
| 7.92 | Amanda Forrester | | 29.09.78 | 2h2 | Birmingham | 18 | Feb |
| | (20) | | | | | | |
| 7.93 | Fiona MacNeill | | 8.09.79 | 2h5 | Birmingham | 18 | Feb |
| 7.94 | Kelly Lopez | | 29.11.78 | 4s3 | Birmingham | 18 | Feb |
| 7.96 | Sarah Beadle | | 16.05.79 | 3h2 | Birmingham | 18 | Feb |
| 7.97 | Samantha Davies | | 20.09.79 | 4h3 | Birmingham | 18 | Feb |
| 7.98 | Lucy Chaffe | | 25.03.79 | 5 | Birmingham | 28 | Jan |
| 7.98 | Susan Christie | | 7.03.79 | 2 | Glasgow | 4 | Feb |
| 7.99 | Penny Thomson | | 10.04.80 | 3 | Glasgow | 4 | Feb |
| 7.99 | Rebecca White | | 5.06.80 | 1 | Birmingham | 31 | Dec |

**Under 15**

| | | | | | | | |
|---|---|---|---|---|---|---|---|
| 7.81 | Dionne Howell | | 10.04.81 | 1 | Birmingham | 18 | Feb |
| 7.83 | Karlene Palmer | | 23.10.80 | 2 | Birmingham | 18 | Feb |
| 7.87 | Chantell Manning | | 4.09.80 | 3 | Birmingham | 18 | Feb |
| 7.97 | Sarah Zawada | | 9.04.82 | 3h2 | Birmingham | 18 | Feb |

**Hand Timing**

| | | | | | | | |
|---|---|---|---|---|---|---|---|
| 7.6 | Uju Efobi | U23 | (7.67i) | 1s1 | London (CP) | 21 | Jan |
| 7.7 | Natasha Danvers | U20 | 19.09.77 | 1r2 | London (CP) | 11 | Jan |
| 7.7 | Sarah Chesney | U23 | (7.77i) | 3 | London (CP) | 21 | Jan |

**Under 17**

| | | | | | | | |
|---|---|---|---|---|---|---|---|
| 7.8 | Shelley-Anne Bowen | | (7.83i) | 1 | London (CP) | 21 | Jan |
| 7.8 | Melanie Purkiss | | 11.03.79 | 3 | London (CP) | 21 | Jan |

**Under 15**

| | | | | | | | |
|---|---|---|---|---|---|---|---|
| 7.8 | Dionne Howell | | (7.81i) | 1r3 | London (CP) | 11 | Jan |

## 75 METRES - Under 13

| | | | | | | |
|---|---|---|---|---|---|---|
| 10.0 | Kelly Rea | 17.09.82 | 1r1 | Sheffield | 30 | Apr |
| *10.0* | *Nicole Froneberger* | *12.06.83* | *1r1* | *Hayes* | *30* | *Apr* |
| 10.1 | Rebecca Smith | 23.02.83 | 2r1 | Sheffield | 30 | Apr |
| 10.2 | Elaine Smith | 16.05.83 | 3r1 | Sheffield | 30 | Apr |
| 10.2 | Ruth Brooke | 2.09.83 | 1 | Bracknell | 25 | Jun |
| 10.2 | Kelly Gomeze | | 1 | Perivale | 25 | Jun |
| 10.2 | Nadya Nathan | 3.11.82 | 2 | Bromley | 16 | Jul |

## 80 METRES - Under 13

| | | | | | | |
|---|---|---|---|---|---|---|
| 10.69 | Andrea Maughan | | 1h1 | Gateshead | 12 | Aug |
| 10.7 | Michelle Nicholls | 26.09.82 | 1 | Woking | 17 | Sep |
| 10.77 | Lindsey Murphy | 26.06.83 | 1h3 | Gateshead | 12 | Aug |
| 10.85 | Elaine Smith | 16.05.83 | 1h4 | Gateshead | 12 | Aug |
| 10.9 | Nadya Nathan | 3.11.82 | 1 | Bromley | 23 | Jul |
| 10.9 | Ruth Brooke | 2.09.83 | 1 | Aldershot | 6 | Aug |
| 10.9 | Charlene Payne | 7.10.83 | 2 | Aldershot | 6 | Aug |
| 10.9 | Felicity Urbain | 11.11.82 | 3 | Aldershot | 6 | Aug |
| 10.97 | Amy Teale | 30.12.82 | 2h1 | Gateshead | 12 | Aug |
| 11.0 | Kelly Rea | 17.09.82 | 1 | Hull | 16 | Apr |
| (10) | | | | | | |
| 11.0 | Kelly Brady | 3.11.82 | 1 | Bolton | 14 | May |
| 11.0 | Helen Carberry | 16.12.82 | 1h3 | Liverpool | 14 | May |
| 11.0 | Anne Massey | 10.09.82 | 2h3 | Liverpool | 14 | May |
| 11.0 | Laura Meegan | 22.04.83 | 1 | Blackpool | 24 | Sep |

## 100 METRES

| | | | | | | | |
|---|---|---|---|---|---|---|---|
| 11.30 | 2.0 | Stephanie Douglas | | 22.01.69 | 4 | Villeneuve d'Ascq, FRA | 24 Jun |
| | | 11.53 | 1.5 | | 3 | Birmingham | 15 Jul |
| | | 11.54 | -1.2 | | 2s2 | Birmingham | 15 Jul |
| | | 11.59 | -1.0 | | 2h1 | Birmingham | 15 Jul |
| | | 11.63 | -2.0 | | 1 | Nurmijarvi, FIN | 4 Jun |
| 11.33 | 0.2 | Paula Thomas | | 3.12.64 | 5q4 | Gothenburg, SWE | 6 Aug |
| | | 11.34 | -0.3 | | 2h7 | Gothenburg, SWE | 6 Aug |
| | | 11.37 | 1.1 | | 1r2 | Rhede, GER | Jul |
| | | 11.43 | -0.7 | | 1s1 | Birmingham | 15 Jul |
| | | 11.48 | 1.5 | | 1 | Birmingham | 15 Jul |
| | | 11.54 | -1.0 | | 1h1 | Birmingham | 15 Jul |
| | | 11.55 | -1.1 | | 2 | Villeneuve d'Ascq, FRA | 17 Jun |
| | | 11.55 | 0.9 | | 4 | Gateshead | 2 Jul |
| | | 11.62 | -0.5 | | 1 | Gateshead | 21 Aug |
| 11.34 | 0.7 | Simmone Jacobs | | 5.09.66 | 1 | London (CP) | 7 Jul |
| | | 11.48 | -1.2 | | 1s2 | Birmingham | 15 Jul |
| | | 11.50 | 1.5 | | 2 | Birmingham | 15 Jul |
| | | 11.54 | 0.5 | | 1h2 | Birmingham | 15 Jul |
| | | 11.60 | 0.3 | | 5h3 | Gothenburg, SWE | 6 Aug |
| 11.47 | -0.3 | Katharine Merry | U23 | 21.09.74 | 3 | Granada, SPA | 27 May |
| | | 11.50 | -1.6 | | 1 | Birmingham | 17 Jun |
| 11.52 | 0.7 | Marcia Richardson | | 10.02.72 | 2 | London (CP) | 7 Jul |
| | | 11.53 | 1.1 | | 2 | Budapest, HUN | 9 Jul |
| | | 11.59 | -0.3 | | 4 | Granada, SPA | 27 May |
| | | 11.59 | -0.7 | | 2s1 | Birmingham | 15 Jul |
| | | 11.60 | -0.7 | | 6 | Fukuoka, JAP | 1 Sep |
| | | 11.61 | -0.1 | | 1h3 | Birmingham | 15 Jul |
| | | 11.63 | -1.1 | | 3q2 | Fukuoka, JAP | 31 Aug |
| | | 11.65 | 0.5 | | 4s1 | Fukuoka, JAP | 1 Sep |
| 11.53 | 0.6 | Sharon Williams | | 20.05.70 | 3h3 | Fukuoka, JAP | 31 Aug |
| | | 11.62 | 1.9 | | 4s2 | Fukuoka, JAP | 1 Sep |
| 11.57 | 0.7 | Sallyanne Short | | 6.03.68 | 3 | London (CP) | 7 Jul |
| 11.59 | 1.9 | Rebecca Drummond | U20 | 18.04.78 | 1 | Nottingham | 8 Jul |
| 11.62 | | Aileen McGillivary | | 13.08.70 | 1 | Greenock | 4 Jun |

34 performances to 11.65 by 9 athletes

| | | | | | | | |
|---|---|---|---|---|---|---|---|
| 11.69 | 1.6 | Clova Court | V35 | 10.02.60 | 1 | Bedford | 29 May |
| | (10) | | | | | | |
| 11.69 | -0.7 | Sophia Smith | U23 | 8.12.74 | 3s1 | Birmingham | 15 Jul |
| 11.70 | 1.6 | Melanie Neef | | 26.05.70 | 2 | Bedford | 29 May |
| 11.70 | 1.9 | Ellena Ruddock | U20 | 23.02.76 | 2 | Nottingham | 8 Jul |
| 11.78 | 0.7 | Catherine Murphy | U23 | 21.09.75 | 4 | London (CP) | 7 Jul |
| 11.81 | -0.7 | Joice Maduaka | U23 | 30.09.73 | 4s1 | Birmingham | 15 Jul |
| 11.83 | 1.8 | Sarah Wilhelmy | U17 | 2.02.80 | 1 | Barking | 13 May |
| 11.83 | -1.2 | Donna Hoggarth | U23 | 14.10.73 | 4s2 | Birmingham | 15 Jul |
| 11.90 | 1.6 | Elona Reinalda | U20 | 31.03.76 | 1 | Sydney, AUS | 28 Jan |
| 11.91 | 1.6 | Ann Brooks | | 4.05.71 | 2h1 | Bedford | 29 May |
| 11.91 | -1.6 | Michelle Thomas | | 16.10.71 | 3 | Birmingham | 17 Jun |
| | (20) | | | | | | |
| 11.91 | 0.7 | Geraldine McLeod | | 24.09.71 | 6 | London (CP) | 7 Jul |
| 11.92 | 0.2 | Tatum Nelson | U17 | 17.12.78 | 1 | Birmingham | 29 Jul |
| 11.93 | | Sinead Dudgeon | U20 | 9.07.76 | 1 | Greenock | 4 Jun |
| 11.97 | 0.7 | Alison Davies | | 6.04.61 | 7 | London (CP) | 7 Jul |
| 12.00 | | Natalie Hynd | U20 | 30.01.78 | 2 | Greenock | 4 Jun |
| 12.01 | | Ena Waldo | | 29.06.63 | 2r2 | Birmingham | 20 May |
| 12.03 | 1.9 | Helen Fee | U20 | 20.11.76 | 3 | Nottingham | 8 Jul |
| 12.04 | 1.6 | Tracy Goddard/Joseph | | 29.11.69 | 4h1 | Bedford | 29 May |
| 12.05 | 1.8 | Lucy Chaffe | U17 | 25.03.79 | 2 | Barking | 13 May |
| 12.05 | -0.7 | Annabel Soper | | 18.11.71 | 7s1 | Birmingham | 15 Jul |
| | (30) | | | | | | |
| 12.07 | -1.0 | Donna Fraser | | 7.11.72 | 1s2 | London (CP) | 17 Jun |
| 12.07 | | Jannette Niccolls | U20 | 7.09.76 | 1 | Aldershot | 26 Jun |
| 12.07 | 0.5 | Donna Bannister | | 27.12.72 | 5h2 | Birmingham | 15 Jul |
| 12.08 | | Morag Baxter/McGowan | | 22.08.69 | 2 | Greenock | 4 Jun |
| 12.08 | -0.5 | Laura Seston | U17 | 9.02.79 | 4r1 | Bedford | 1 Jul |
| 12.08 | 1.9 | Gillian Hegney | U20 | 4.11.77 | 1h2 | Pitreavie | 8 Jul |
| 12.09 | 1.1 | Libby Alder | U15 | 20.11.80 | 1 | Nottingham | 8 Jul |
| 12.10 | 1.6 | Diane Allahgreen | U23 | 21.02.75 | 7 | Bedford | 29 May |
| *12.10* | *-1.7* | *Evadne McKenzie* | *U23* | *19.05.75* | *5h4* | *Birmingham* | *15 Jul* |
| 12.12 | -1.7 | Sharon Tunaley | | 2.09.68 | 5 | Loughborough | 11 Jun |
| 12.13 | 1.6 | Dawn Cousins | | 16.03.68 | 5h1 | Bedford | 29 May |
| | (40) | | | | | | |
| 12.13 | 0.0 | Zoe Wilson | U20 | 28.08.76 | 6 | Birmingham | 17 Jun |
| 12.14 | | Fiona Calder | | 4.05.71 | 3 | Greenock | 4 Jun |
| 12.15 | -1.0 | Julie Howard | | 24.09.66 | 3s2 | London (CP) | 17 Jun |
| 12.16 | | Fiona Hutchison | U20 | 18.01.77 | 4 | Greenock | 4 Jun |
| 12.16 | 1.4 | Kirsty Payne | U20 | 22.10.77 | 2r1 | Stoke | 17 Jun |
| 12.16 | 1.9 | Adele Foster | U20 | 16.11.76 | 4 | Nottingham | 8 Jul |
| 12.17 | 0.2 | Emma Ania | U17 | 7.02.79 | 2 | Birmingham | 29 Jul |
| *12.18* | *1.1* | *Jean Oyeyemi* | *U15* | *24.08.81* | *2* | *Nottingham* | *8 Jul* |
| 12.19 | -1.5 | Uju Efobi | U23 | 10.10.74 | 3s1 | London (CP) | 17 Jun |
| 12.20 | -0.5 | Lesley Owusu | U17 | 21.12.78 | 5r1 | Bedford | 1 Jul |
| 12.22 | 0.9 | Leanne Eastwood | U20 | 23.11.76 | 1 | Sheffield | 28 May |
| | (50) | | | | | | |
| 12.22 | -1.5 | Jennifer Stoute | | 16.04.65 | 4s1 | London (CP) | 17 Jun |
| 12.22 | -1.3 | Sarah Claxton | U17 | 23.09.79 | 2s1 | Nottingham | 7 Jul |
| 12.24 | -1.5 | Christine Bloomfield | | 12.02.68 | 5s1 | London (CP) | 17 Jun |
| 12.25 | 1.8 | Amanda Waite | U20 | 1.02.78 | 1 | Barking | 13 May |
| 12.25 | 1.7 | Melanie Purkiss | U17 | 11.03.79 | 1 | Portsmouth | 13 May |
| 12.25 | 1.9 | Dawn Rose | U17 | 25.01.79 | 1 | Stoke | 28 May |
| 12.25 | | Sarah Zawada | U15 | 9.04.82 | 1 | London (He) | 6 Aug |
| 12.26 | -1.5 | Debbie Mant | U23 | 11.10.75 | 6s1 | London (CP) | 17 Jun |
| 12.26 | -1.0 | Shani Anderson | U23 | 7.08.75 | 6h1 | Birmingham | 15 Jul |
| 12.27 | | Dawn Flockhart | | 16.05.67 | 2 | Grangemouth | 13 May |
| | (60) | | | | | | |
| 12.29 | 1.6 | Lynne Draper | | 10.05.67 | 6h1 | Bedford | 29 May |
| 12.29 | -1.3 | Gahlie Davis | U17 | 3.05.79 | 3s1 | Nottingham | 7 Jul |

232

**Additional Under 17** (1 - 10 above)

| | | | | | | | |
|---|---|---|---|---|---|---|---|
| 12.34 | -0.1 | Helen Roscoe | 4.12.79 | 2 | Birmingham | 3 | Sep |
| 12.37 | 1.8 | Kelly Lopez | 29.11.78 | 4 | Barking | 13 | May |
| 12.37 | -2.4 | Kelli Bailey | 8.09.79 | 3s2 | Nottingham | 7 | Jul |
| 12.37 | 0.2 | Amanda Forrester | 29.09.78 | 3 | Birmingham | 29 | Jul |
| 12.37 | 0.2 | Shelley-Anne Bowen | 12.05.79 | 4 | Birmingham | 29 | Jul |
| 12.39 | | Mairi McEwen | 16.08.79 | 1 | Greenock | 4 | Jun |
| 12.39 | | Hannah Paines | 6.04.79 | 1 | Cardiff | 1 | Jul |
| 12.40 | -1.3 | Lisa Thomas | 22.06.80 | 5s1 | Nottingham | 7 | Jul |
| 12.41 | | Syreena Pinel | 13.01.79 | 1 | Peterborough | 28 | Aug |
| 12.42 | | Leanne Rowlands | 16.09.79 | 2 | Cardiff | 1 | Jul |
| (20) | | | | | | | |
| 12.44 | -2.4 | Ayeesha Charles | 4.09.79 | 4s2 | Nottingham | 7 | Jul |
| 12.44 | 2.0 | Susan Christie | 7.03.79 | 1h1 | Pitreavie | 8 | Jul |
| 12.44 | | Lee McConnell | 9.10.78 | 1 | Edinburgh | 10 | Sep |
| 12.47 | 1.7 | Kate Denham | 18.03.80 | 2 | Portsmouth | 13 | May |
| 12.48 | | Rebecca White | 5.06.80 | 1 | Wrexham | 5 | Aug |
| 12.49 | | Gail Evans | 23.07.80 | 3 | Cardiff | 1 | Jul |
| 12.50 | -1.3 | Jennifer Such | 5.10.79 | 6s1 | Nottingham | 7 | Jul |
| 12.51 | 0.6 | Sally Burnham | 25.08.79 | 1 | Sheffield | 27 | May |
| 12.52 | 2.0 | Karen Scott | 17.10.79 | 2h1 | Pitreavie | 8 | Jul |
| 12.53 | -2.4 | Emily Nicholls | 5.12.78 | 5s2 | Nottingham | 7 | Jul |
| (30) | | | | | | | |
| 12.54 | 0.6 | Hannah Eatough | 14.08.79 | 3 | Sheffield | 27 | May |
| 12.55 | -0.1 | Faithlyn Edwards | 26.11.78 | 3 | Birmingham | 3 | Sep |
| 12.56 | | Donna Lennon | 8.12.78 | 1 | Antrim | 10 | Jun |
| 12.56 | 0.2 | Claire Weston | 26.07.80 | 6 | Birmingham | 29 | Jul |
| 12.56 | -1.1 | Katherine Endacott | 29.01.80 | 1 | London (He) | 6 | Aug |
| 12.56 | 2.0 | Wendy Cox | 1.09.79 | 1 | Birmingham | 2 | Sep |
| 12.57 | 0.6 | Sonya Green | 6.03.80 | 4 | Sheffield | 27 | May |
| 12.57 | -2.4 | Madeleine Kilby | 16.01.80 | 6s2 | Nottingham | 7 | Jul |
| 12.57 | 0.2 | Tracy Bishop | 1.05.79 | 7 | Birmingham | 29 | Jul |

**Wind Assisted**

| | | | | | | | | |
|---|---|---|---|---|---|---|---|---|
| 11.36 | 2.9 | Thomas | | (11.33) | 2 | Bedford | 10 | Jun |
| | | 11.36 | 2.4 | | 2 | Hechtel, BEL | 22 | Jul |
| | | 11.46 | 2.9 | | 2 | Bedford | 10 | Jun |
| 11.39 | 2.9 | Douglas | | (11.30) | 1 | Bedford | 10 | Jun |
| | | 11.39 A | 3.3 | | 2 | Soria, SPA | 16 | Jun |
| | | 11.63 | | | 1 | Birmingham | 20 | May |
| 11.50 | 3.2 | Sophia Smith | U23 | (11.69) | 1 | Sheffield | 23 | Jul |
| 11.51 | 2.1 | Marcia Richardson | | (11.52) | 1 | Stoke | 9 | Sep |
| | | 11.60 A | 4.3 | | 2 | La Laguna, SPA | 30 | May |
| 11.55 | 2.1 | Clova Court | V35 | (11.69) | 2 | Stoke | 9 | Sep |
| 11.57 | 3.3 | Short | | (11.57) | 1 | Cwmbran | 9 | Jul |
| 11.61 | 2.3 | Louise Fraser | | 10.10.70 | 1 | Gateshead | 17 | Jun |
| 11.61 | 3.2 | Donna Hoggarth | U23 | (11.83) | 2 | Sheffield | 23 | Jul |
| 11.65 | 3.3 | Catherine Murphy | U23 | (11.78) | 2 | Cwmbran | 9 | Jul |

14 performances to 11.65 by 9 athletes

| | | | | | | | | |
|---|---|---|---|---|---|---|---|---|
| 11.71 | 2.1 | Phylis Smith | | 29.09.65 | 3 | Stoke | 9 | Sep |
| 11.72 | 2.9 | Jacqui Agyepong | | 5.01.69 | 3 | Bedford | 10 | Jun |
| 11.74 | 3.2 | Joice Maduaka | U23 | (11.81) | 3 | Sheffield | 23 | Jul |
| 11.77 | 3.2 | Alison Davies | | (11.97) | 4 | Sheffield | 23 | Jul |
| 11.86 | 2.3 | Danaa Myhill/Callow | | 16.10.70 | 3 | Gateshead | 17 | Jun |
| 11.87 | 5.0 | Julie Howard | | (12.15) | 1 | Braunton | 13 | May |
| 11.87 | 3.6 | Gillian Hegney | U20 | (12.08) | 1 | Pitreavie | 8 | Jul |
| 11.93 | 2.3 | Laura Seston | U17 | (12.08) | 2= | Nottingham | 8 | Jul |
| 11.93 | 2.3 | Sarah Claxton | U17 | (12.22) | 2= | Nottingham | 8 | Jul |
| 11.94 | 2.3 | Sue Briggs | | 26.03.67 | 4 | Gateshead | 17 | Jun |
| 11.95 | 3.8 | Natalie Hynd | U20 | (12.00) | 1 | Edinburgh | 17 | Jun |

| 11.96 | 2.8 | Diane Allahgreen | U23 | (12.10) | 4h2 | Bedford | 29 May |
|---|---|---|---|---|---|---|---|
| 11.98 | 2.1 | Christine Bloomfield | | (12.24) | 6 | Stoke | 9 Sep |
| 11.99 | | Donna Fraser | | (12.07) | 2 | Irvine, USA | 22 Apr |
| 12.00 | 2.9 | Ena Waldo | | (12.01) | 5 | Bedford | 10 Jun |
| 12.05 | 2.3 | Joan Booth | | 18.12.68 | 5 | Gateshead | 17 Jun |
| 12.08 | 2.9 | Amanda Forrester | U17 | (12.37) | 1r1 | Stoke | 17 Jun |
| 12.09 | 2.9 | Shani Anderson | U23 | (12.26) | 7 | Bedford | 10 Jun |
| 12.16 | 3.8 | Fiona Sinclair | U20 | 14.02.77 | 3 | Edinburgh | 17 Jun |
| 12.16 | 3.2 | Alison Thompson | U23 | 11.02.74 | 6 | Sheffield | 23 Jul |
| | | | | | | | |
| 12.19 | 4.3 | Karen Scott | U17 | (12.52) | 1 | Edinburgh | 17 Jun |
| 12.20 | 2.1 | Dawn Flockhart | | (12.27) | 7 | Stoke | 9 Sep |
| 12.21 | | Emma Symonds | U20 | 5.06.77 | 1 | Peterborough | 28 Aug |
| 12.24 | 3.7 | Evette Williams | U20 | 23.03.78 | 1 | London (CP) | 13 May |
| 12.24 | 7.0 | Katherine Endacott | U17 | (12.56) | 1 | Braunton | 14 May |
| 12.24 | 2.9 | Samantha Davies | U17 | 20.09.79 | 2r1 | Stoke | 17 Jun |
| 12.25 | 2.3 | Claire O'Connor | U23 | 24.09.74 | 1 | Antrim | 20 Jun |
| 12.26 | 2.1 | Christine Chambers | | 4.03.69 | 4s1 | Gateshead | 17 Jun |
| 12.26 | | Stacey Rodd | U20 | 19.05.78 | 1 | Cardiff | 1 Jul |
| 12.27 | 2.9 | Kelli Bailey | U17 | (12.37) | 3r1 | Stoke | 17 Jun |
| 12.29 | 4.3 | Susan Christie | U17 | (12.44) | 2 | Edinburgh | 17 Jun |
| 12.29 | | Jocelyn Kirby/Harwood | V35 | 21.11.57 | 1h | Buffalo, USA | 17 Jul |

**Additional Under 17**

| 12.30 | 4.3 | Mairi McEwen | | (12.39) | 3 | Edinburgh | 17 Jun |
|---|---|---|---|---|---|---|---|
| 12.39 | 2.3 | Rebecca White | | (12.48) | 1 | Blackpool | 20 Aug |
| 12.44 | 2.3 | Wendy Cox | | (12.56) | 2 | Blackpool | 20 Aug |
| 12.45 | 2.9 | Emily Nicholls | | (12.53) | 4r1 | Stoke | 17 Jun |
| 12.48 | 4.3 | Lorna Sinclair | | 15.06.79 | 4 | Edinburgh | 17 Jun |
| 12.49 | 2.7 | Amanda Freeman | | 16.10.79 | 1h1 | London (He) | 6 Aug |
| 12.51 | 2.4 | Ruth Watson | | 29.11.79 | 2h3 | London (He) | 6 Aug |
| 12.54 | 4.3 | Fiona Martin | | 17.09.79 | 5 | Edinburgh | 17 Jun |
| 12.57 | 7.0 | Karen Gear | | 30.09.79 | 2 | Braunton | 14 May |
| 12.59 | 4.3 | Nicola Hutchison | | 1.02.79 | 6 | Edinburgh | 17 Jun |

**Hand Timing**

| 11.4 | | Thomas | | (11.33) | 1 | Alfaz Del Pi, SPA | 13 Apr |
|---|---|---|---|---|---|---|---|
| | 11.4 | 1.1 | | | 1 | Birmingham | 19 Aug |
| | 11.6 | 0.9 | | | 1 | Glasgow | 6 May |
| 11.6 w | | Donna Hoggarth | U23 | (11.83) | 1 | Blackpool | 13 May |
| 11.6 w | 2.3 | Melanie Neef | | (11.70) | 1r2 | Coatbridge | 21 May |

5 performances to 11.6 by 3 athletes including 2 wind assisted

| 11.7 | | Ashia Hansen | | 5.12.71 | 2 | Alfaz Del Pi, SPA | 13 Apr |
|---|---|---|---|---|---|---|---|
| 11.7 w | | Danaa Myhill/Callow | | (11.86w) | 2 | Blackpool | 13 May |
| 11.8 | | Louise Fraser | | (11.61w) | 2r1 | Alfaz Del Pi, SPA | 13 Apr |
| 11.8 | 1.5 | Sharon Tunaley | | (12.12) | 1 | Mansfield | 13 May |
| 11.8 | | Sue Earnshaw/Rawlinson | | 13.10.70 | 2 | Rotherham | 6 Aug |
| 11.9 | | Geraldine McLeod | | (11.91) | .1 | London (He) | 1 Jul |
| 11.9 | 1.1 | Phylis Smith | | (11.71w) | 3 | Birmingham | 19 Aug |
| | | | | | | | |
| 11.9 w | 3.9 | Donna Fraser | | (12.07) | 1 | Croydon | 28 Aug |
| 12.0 | 1.8 | Gillian Hegney | U20 | (12.08) | 1r2 | Glasgow | 6 May |
| 12.0 | | Diane Allahgreen | U23 | (12.10) | 1 | Liverpool | 13 May |
| 12.0 | | Dawn Cousins | | (12.13) | 1 | Basildon | 20 May |
| 12.0 | | Julie Howard | | (12.15) | 1 | Bath | 31 May |
| 12.0 | | Shani Anderson | U23 | (12.26) | 2 | London (He) | 1 Jul |
| 12.0 | | Christine Bloomfield | | (12.24) | 1 | Harrow | 9 Jul |
| 12.0 | | Tracy Goddard/Joseph | | (12.04) | 1 | Basingstoke | 22 Jul |
| 12.0 | | Elaine Sutcliffe | | 6.04.70 | 1 | York | 23 Jul |
| *12.0* | | *Evadne McKenzie* | *U23* | *(12.10)* | *1* | *Basingstoke* | *12 Aug* |
| 12.0 | | Evette Williams | U20 | (12.24w) | 1 | Andover | 12 Aug |

234

| | | | | | | | |
|---|---|---|---|---|---|---|---|
| 12.0 | | Sarah Claxton | U17 | (12.22) | 1 | Colchester | 28 Aug |
| 12.0 w | | Leanne Eastwood | U20 | (12.22) | 1 | Telford | 18 Jun |
| 12.0 w | 4.2 | Morag Baxter/McGowan | | (12.08) | 1 | Aberdeen | 23 Jul |
| 12.1 | -1.8 | Helen Miles | | 2.03.67 | 2 | Cardiff | 23 Apr |
| 12.1 | 0.9 | Joan Booth | | (12.05w) | 3 | Glasgow | 6 May |
| 12.1 | 1.8 | Sue Briggs | | (11.94w) | 2r2 | Glasgow | 6 May |
| 12.1 | | Louise Whitehead | U23 | 26.03.75 | 2 | Liverpool | 13 May |
| 12.1 | 1.5 | Alison Mayfield | | 12.05.69 | 2 | Mansfield | 13 May |
| 12.1 | | Susan Williams | U20 | 2.06.77 | 1 | Walton | 20 May |
| 12.1 | | Susan Mary Douglas | U20 | 3.11.77 | 1 | Antrim | 27 May |
| | | | | | | | |
| 12.1 | | Gahlie Davis | U17 | (12.29) | 1r2 | Exeter | 28 May |
| 12.1 | | Zoe Wilson | U20 | (12.13) | 2 | Bath | 31 May |
| 12.1 | | Lesley Owusu | U17 | (12.20) | 1 | Bournemouth | 3 Jun |
| 12.1 | | Afi Amaku | | 6.05.70 | 2 | Bournemouth | 3 Jun |
| 12.1 | | Jacqui Agyepong | | (11.72w) | 1 | Brighton | 3 Jun |
| 12.1 | | Samantha Barr/Porter | | 14.08.70 | 1 | Welwyn | 21 Jun |
| 12.1 | | Rachael Kay | U15 | 8.09.80 | 1 | Derby | 25 Jun |
| 12.1 | | Lynne Draper | | (12.29) | 1 | Bedford | 2 Sep |
| 12.1 w | | Kim Goodwin | | 16.05.70 | 3 | Blackpool | 13 May |
| 12.1 w | 3.1 | Dawn Flockhart | | (12.27) | 3 | Inverness | 11 Jun |
| | | | | | | | |
| 12.1 w | | Lyndsey Fletcher | U20 | 18.09.76 | 2 | Telford | 18 Jun |

**Additional Under 17**

| | | | | | | | |
|---|---|---|---|---|---|---|---|
| 12.2 | | Amanda Forrester | | (12.37) | 1 | Sheffield | 30 Apr |
| 12.2 | | Dawn Rose | | (12.25) | 1 | Kettering | 21 May |
| 12.2 | | Lindsay Impett | | 4.01.80 | 2 | Cheltenham | 17 Jun |
| 12.2 | | Rebecca White | | (12.48) | 1 | Bebington | 22 Jul |
| 12.2 | | Kate Denham | | (12.47) | 1 | Walton | 22 Jul |
| 12.2 | | Tracy Bishop | | (12.57) | 2 | Bournemouth | 22 Jul |
| 12.2 | | Kelli Bailey | | (12.37) | 1 | Corby | 23 Jul |
| 12.2 | | Lee McConnell | | (12.44) | 1 | Glasgow | 23 Jul |
| 12.2 | -1.2 | Claudine Leger | | 17.05.80 | 2 | London (Nh) | 6 Aug |
| 12.2 | | Emily Nicholls | | (12.53) | 1 | Bath | 28 Aug |
| 12.2 w | 7.4 | Jade Johnson | | 7.06.80 | 1s1 | Croydon | 13 May |
| 12.3 | | Sonya Green | | (12.57) | 1 | Carlisle | 2 Apr |
| 12.3 | | Hannah Paines | | (12.39) | 1 | Barry | 11 May |
| 12.3 | | Helen Pryer | | 21.01.79 | 1 | Walton | 8 Jul |
| 12.3 | | Ayeesha Charles | | (12.44) | 2 | Bournemouth | 23 Jul |
| 12.3 | | Elizabeth Walker | | 30.05.79 | 1 | Lincoln | 23 Jul |
| 12.3 | | Faithlyn Edwards | | (12.55) | 1 | Middlesbrough | 30 Jul |
| 12.3 | | Ruth Watson | | (12.51w) | 1 | St. Ives | 30 Jul |
| 12.3 | | Gael Davies | | 5.02.79 | 1 | Reading | 28 Aug |
| 12.3 | | Shelley-Anne Bowen | | (12.37) | 1 | Reading | 3 Sep |
| 12.4 | | Julie Pratt | | 20.03.79 | 2 | Hornchurch | 2 Apr |
| 12.4 | | Leanne Palmer | | 22.03.80 | 2 | Carlisle | 2 Apr |
| 12.4 | | Wendy Cox | | (12.56) | 2 | Sheffield | 30 Apr |
| 12.4 | | Claire Weston | | (12.56) | 1 | Worcester | 13 May |
| 12.4 | | Madeleine Kilby | | (12.57) | 1 | Hayes | 14 May |
| 12.4 | 1.1 | Hannah Eatough | | (12.54) | 1 | Blackpool | 10 Jun |
| 12.4 | | Maria Bolsover | | 5.06.80 | 1 | Sheffield | 18 Jun |
| 12.4 | | Syreena Pinel | | (12.41) | 1 | Mansfield | 25 Jun |
| 12.4 | | Carly Moody | | 9.06.80 | 1 | Thurrock | 25 Jun |
| 12.4 | | Leanne Rowlands | | (12.42) | 1 | Cwmbran | 27 Jun |
| 12.4 | | Samantha Davies | | (12.24w) | 1 | Derby | 23 Aug |
| 12.4 | | Katherine Endacott | | (12.56) | 1 | Exeter | 27 Aug |
| 12.4 | | Sophie Williams | | 29.03.80 | 2 | Bath | 28 Aug |
| 12.4 w | | Katherine Livesey | | 15.12.79 | 2 | Blackpool | 13 May |

## Additional Under 15 (1 - 3 above)

| | | | | | | | | |
|---|---|---|---|---|---|---|---|---|
| 12.2 | | Karlene Palmer | 23.10.80 | 1 | Bournemouth | 4 | Jun |
| | | 12.43   -1.6 | | 1 | London (CP) | 27 | May |
| 12.2 w | 4.0 | Dionne Howell | 10.04.81 | 1 | Croydon | 13 | May |
| | | 12.53   -1.6 | | 2 | London (CP) | 27 | May |
| 12.3 | | Donna Naylor | 20.05.82 | 1r1 | Blackpool | 16 | Jul |
| 12.3 | | Chantell Manning | 4.09.80 | 1 | Basildon | 16 | Jul |
| | | 12.33   1.1 | | 3 | Nottingham | 8 | Jul |
| 12.3 w | | Petrina Alleyne | 10.07.81 | 1 | Isle of Wight | 25 | Sep |
| | | 12.5 | | 1 | Aldershot | 6 | Aug |
| 12.40 | 1.1 | Kate Hill | 13.12.80 | 4 | Nottingham | 8 | Jul |
| 12.4 | | Kelly Thomas | 9.01.81 | 1 | Ipswich | 4 | Jun |
| | | 12.59   -1.6 | | 3 | London (CP) | 27 | May |
| | (10) | | | | | | |
| 12.42 | 1.1 | Rachel Redmond | 7.12.81 | 5 | Nottingham | 8 | Jul |
| 12.47 w | 3.2 | Lisa Callan | 10.10.80 | 1 | Pitreavie | 9 | Jul |
| 12.49 w | 3.2 | Andrea Lang | 6.03.82 | 2 | Pitreavie | 9 | Jul |
| 12.5 | | Jennifer Meadows | 17.04.81 | 2r2 | Blackpool | 16 | Jul |
| 12.5 | | Jo Thorn | 19.02.81 | 1 | Yate | 26 | Jul |
| 12.5 | | Debbie Morgan | 9.10.80 | 1 | Cwmbran | 20 | Aug |
| | | 12.53 | | 1 | Cardiff | 22 | Jul |
| 12.53 w | 3.2 | Sinead Rattigan | 27.10.80 | 1r1 | Stoke | 17 | Jun |
| 12.55 w | 2.4 | Fiona Harrison | 30.11.81 | 1 | Sheffield | 28 | May |
| 12.59 w | 2.4 | Victoria Blair | 20.11.80 | 2 | Sheffield | 28 | May |

## Under 13

| | | | | | | | | |
|---|---|---|---|---|---|---|---|---|
| *12.6* | | *Nicole Froneberger* | *12.06.83* | *2* | *Ipswich* | *3* | *Jun* |
| | | *13.22   00.8* | | *6h3* | *Nottingham* | *7* | *Jul* |
| 12.89 | | Nicola Jarvie | 11.09.82 | 1 | Greenock | 4 | Jun |
| 12.9 | | Kelly Rea | 17.09.82 | 1 | Scunthorpe | 17 | Jun |
| 12.9 | | Sophie Allen | 7.09.82 | 1 | St. Ives | 20 | Aug |
| 13.0 | | Sarah Lane | 24.11.82 | 1 | Carmarthen | 11 | Jun |
| 13.0 | | Miranda Woodruff | 6.09.82 | 1 | Sutton | 15 | Jul |
| 13.0 | | Rosanna Maio | 28.03.83 | | | | |
| 13.10 w | 3.8 | Rebecca Smith | 23.02.83 | 1 | Stoke | 14 | May |
| | | 13.16   1.8 | | 1h | Stoke | 13 | May |
| 13.1 | | Susan Armstrong | 8.09.82 | 1 | Carlisle | 2 | Apr |
| 13.1 | | Nicola Lapczuk | 16.11.82 | 1 | Derby | 11 | Jul |
| 13.1 | | Nina Ezeogu | 11.10.82 | 1 | Southend | 20 | Aug |
| | (10) | | | | | | |
| 13.20 w | 4.6 | Fiona Godden | 17.12.82 | 2s1 | Pitreavie | 9 | Jul |
| 13.2 | | Stephanie Spinks | 6.09.82 | 1 | Norwich | 14 | May |
| 13.2 | | Sarah Hamilton | | 1 | Yate | 18 | Jun |
| 13.2 | | Lowri Jones | 22.07.83 | 1 | Newport | 17 | Sep |

## 150 METRES - Under 13

| | | | | | | | | |
|---|---|---|---|---|---|---|---|---|
| 19.2 | | Kelly Rea | 17.09.82 | 1r1 | Sheffield | 30 | Apr |
| 19.2 | | Rebecca Smith | 23.02.83 | 2r1 | Sheffield | 30 | Apr |
| *19.4* | | *Nicole Froneberger* | *12.06.83* | *1r1* | *Hayes* | *30* | *Apr* |
| 19.8 | | Nicola Lapczuk | 16.11.82 | 1r1 | Derby | 25 | Jun |
| 19.8 | | Elexi Walker | 28.10.82 | 1r1 | Blackpool | 16 | Jul |
| 19.8 | | Chevette Mais | 22.09.82 | 1 | Crawley | 28 | Aug |
| 19.9 | | Carolyn Maile | 5.04.83 | 3r1 | Sheffield | 30 | Apr |
| 19.9 | | Kimberly Haimes | 28.09.82 | 1r1 | Plymouth | 16 | Jul |
| 19.9 | | Bianca Simon | 28.12.82 | | | | |
| 20.1 | | Nicola Atkins | | 4r1 | Sheffield | 30 | Apr |
| 20.1 | | Helen Griffin | | 3r1 | Blackpool | 16 | Jul |
| | (10) | | | | | | |
| 20.1 | | Nadya Nathan | 3.11.82 | 1 | Bromley | 23 | Jul |
| 20.1 | | Rosanna Maio | 28.03.83 | 1 | Horsham | 3 | Aug |
| 20.2 | | Shelley Wilson | 17.01.83 | T | Bebington | 23 | Jul |

236

# 200 METRES

| Time | Wind | Name | Cat | DOB | Pos | Venue | Date | |
|---|---|---|---|---|---|---|---|---|
| 22.89 | 0.8 | Paula Thomas | | 3.12.64 | 4 | Villeneuve d'Ascq, FRA | 25 | Jun |
| 22.95 | -0.5 | | | | 3h3 | Gothenburg, SWE | 9 | Aug |
| 23.00 | 0.2 | | | | 2 | Gateshead | 21 | Aug |
| 23.24 | 1.6 | | | | 6 | London (CP) | 27 | Aug |
| 23.31 i | | | | | 2 | Birmingham | 25 | Feb |
| 23.34 | -0.5 | | | | 8 | London (CP) | 7 | Jul |
| 23.38 | -0.5 | | | | 2 | Villeneuve d'Ascq, FRA | 17 | Jun |
| 23.42 i | | | | | 1 | Glasgow | 11 | Feb |
| 23.51 | 0.9 | | | | 5 | Gateshead | 2 | Jul |
| 23.61 i | | | | | 1 | Birmingham | 28 | Jan |
| 23.35 | 0.9 | Melanie Neef | | 26.05.70 | 2 | Gateshead | 2 | Jul |
| 23.42 | 0.2 | | | | 4 | Gateshead | 21 | Aug |
| 23.73 i | | | | | 1 | Glasgow | 22 | Jan |
| 23.40 | 0.1 | Catherine Murphy | U23 | 21.09.75 | 1 | Birmingham | 16 | Jul |
| 23.41 | 0.0 | | | | 1 | Narbonne, FRA | 29 | Jul |
| 23.57 | 1.1 | | | | 1 | Bellinzona, SWZ | 20 | Jun |
| 23.58 | 1.3 | | | | 2 | Stoke | 9 | Sep |
| 23.63 | -0.5 | | | | 1r2 | Loughborough | 11 | Jun |
| 23.66 | -0.6 | | | | 1h4 | Birmingham | 16 | Jul |
| 23.66 | 0.8 | | | | 1h6 | Fukuoka, JAP | 29 | Aug |
| 23.67 | -1.7 | | | | 1 | Basel, SWZ | 5 | Jun |
| 23.73 | 0.9 | | | | 6 | Gateshead | 2 | Jul |
| 23.74 | 1.7 | | | | 5s2 | Fukuoka, JAP | 30 | Aug |
| 23.77 | -0.5 | | | | 4q2 | Fukuoka, JAP | 29 | Aug |
| 23.44 | 1.2 | Simmone Jacobs | | 5.09.66 | 4 | Helsinki, FIN | 28 | Jun |
| 23.48 | 0.1 | | | | 2 | Birmingham | 16 | Jul |
| 23.58 | -1.4 | | | | 1h2 | Birmingham | 16 | Jul |
| 23.47 | 2.0 | Donna Fraser | | 7.11.72 | 1 | Cwmbran | 9 | Jul |
| 23.50 A | 1.9 | Stephanie Douglas | | 22.01.69 | 1 | Soria, SPA | 16 | Jun |
| 23.85 i | | | | | 3 | Birmingham | 25 | Feb |
| 23.91 | 1.2 | | | | 7 | Helsinki, FIN | 28 | Jun |
| 23.53 | 1.3 | Marcia Richardson | | 10.02.72 | 1 | Stoke | 9 | Sep |
| 23.64 | 1.3 | Clova Court | V35 | 10.02.60 | 3 | Stoke | 9 | Sep |
| 23.79 | 2.0 | Sallyanne Short | | 6.03.68 | 2 | Cwmbran | 9 | Jul |

34 performances to 23.80 by 9 athletes including 5 indoors

| Time | Wind | Name | Cat | DOB | Pos | Venue | Date | |
|---|---|---|---|---|---|---|---|---|
| 23.81 | 2.0 (10) | Joice Maduaka | U23 | 30.09.73 | 2h3 | Fukuoka, JAP | 29 | Aug |
| 23.86 | 0.5 | Elona Reinalda | U20 | 31.03.76 | 1h | Sydney, AUS | 11 | Feb |
| 23.90 | -1.9 | Jennifer Stoute | | 16.04.65 | 1 | Cork, IRE | 24 | Jun |
| 23.91 | -1.2 | Sharon Williams | | 20.05.70 | 1r1 | Loughborough | 11 | Jun |
| 23.92 | -1.2 | Sophia Smith | U23 | 8.12.74 | 2r1 | Loughborough | 11 | Jun |
| 24.04 | 0.9 | Evette Williams | U20 | 23.03.78 | 1 | Nottingham | 8 | Jul |
| 24.06 | 0.1 | Alison Davies | | 6.04.61 | 4 | Birmingham | 16 | Jul |
| 24.08 | 1.2 | Vicky Shipman | U20 | 31.03.77 | 1r1 | Bedford | 2 | Jul |
| 24.19 | 1.8 | Aileen McGillivary | | 13.08.70 | 1 | Grangemouth | 14 | May |
| 24.19 | -1.2 | Sarah Wilhelmy | U17 | 2.02.80 | 4 | Loughborough | 11 | Jun |
| 24.22 i | (20) | Jacqui Agyepong | | 5.01.69 | 1 | Birmingham | 4 | Feb |
| 24.28 | | Sinead Dudgeon | U20 | 9.07.76 | 1 | Greenock | 4 | Jun |
| 24.28 | | Stephanie McCann | | 26.10.65 | 1 | Antrim | 1 | Jul |
| 24.30 | 1.2 | Susan Williams | U20 | 2.06.77 | 2r1 | Bedford | 2 | Jul |
| 24.32 | 1.8 | Emma Ania | U17 | 7.02.79 | 1s1 | Nottingham | 8 | Jul |
| 24.34 | -1.7 | Tracy Goddard/Joseph | | 29.11.69 | 2h2 | London (CP) | 18 | Jun |
| 24.38 i | | Sarah Oxley | U23 | 3.07.73 | 2 | Birmingham | 1 | Jan |
| 24.38 | -1.7 | Stephanie Llewellyn | | 31.12.68 | 3h2 | London (CP) | 18 | Jun |
| 24.41 | 0.3 | Lesley Owusu | U17 | 21.12.78 | 1 | Birmingham | 3 | Sep |
| 24.43 | -0.5 | Geraldine McLeod | | 24.09.71 | 2r2 | Loughborough | 11 | Jun |
| 24.44 | 1.6 (30) | Rachael Kay | U15 | 8.09.80 | 1 | Nottingham | 8 | Jul |

237

| | | | | | | | | |
|---|---|---|---|---|---|---|---|---|
| 24.48 | -0.9 | Michelle Thomas | | 16.10.71 | 4 | Bedford | 28 | May |
| 24.49 | 2.0 | Louretta Thorne | U20 | 6.05.77 | 2h1 | Bedford | 2 | Jul |
| 24.49 | 1.8 | Helen Roscoe | U17 | 4.12.79 | 1s2 | Nottingham | 8 | Jul |
| 24.52 | 0.9 | Rebecca Kilgour | U23 | 18.10.75 | 3 | Nottingham | 8 | Jul |
| 24.53 | 1.8 | Melanie Purkiss | U17 | 11.03.79 | 2s2 | Nottingham | 8 | Jul |
| 24.55 | 1.9 | Lucy Carter | U20 | 7.03.78 | 3s1 | Nottingham | 8 | Jul |
| 24.57 i | | Ashia Hansen | | 5.12.71 | 3h2 | Birmingham | 3 | Feb |
| 24.58 | 0.4 | Louise Whitehead | U23 | 26.03.75 | 3h3 | Birmingham | 16 | Jul |
| 24.59 i | | Christine Bloomfield | | 12.02.68 | 3 | Birmingham | 1 | Jan |
| 24.79 | | | | | 2 | London (CP) | 10 | Sep |
| 24.61 | 1.1 | Kerry Jury | | 19.11.68 | 1H | Stoke | 5 | Aug |
| (40) | | | | | | | | |
| 24.63 | | Fiona Calder | | 4.05.71 | 1 | Greenock | 4 | Jun |
| 24.64 | 1.8 | Lindsay Impett | U17 | 4.01.80 | 2s1 | Nottingham | 8 | Jul |
| 24.64 | 1.3 | Keeley Butler | U23 | 24.03.75 | 4 | Stoke | 9 | Sep |
| 24.65 i | | Elaine Sutcliffe | | 6.04.70 | 1 | Birmingham | 11 | Feb |
| 24.99 | 1.3 | | | | 5 | Birmingham | 20 | May |
| 24.66 | 1.8 | Wendy Cox | U17 | 1.09.79 | 3s2 | Nottingham | 8 | Jul |
| 24.68 | -0.9 | Louise Fraser | | 10.10.70 | 5 | Bedford | 28 | May |
| 24.69 | 1.8 | Samantha Davies | U17 | 20.09.79 | 3s1 | Nottingham | 8 | Jul |
| 24.69 | 1.8 | Kate Denham | U17 | 18.03.80 | 4s1 | Nottingham | 8 | Jul |
| 24.69 | 0.4 | Kim Goodwin | | 16.05.70 | 4h3 | Birmingham | 16 | Jul |
| *24.69* | *1.3* | *Dion Graham* | *U17* | *27.09.78* | *5* | *Stoke* | *9* | *Sep* |
| 24.72 | -1.7 | Julie Howard | | 24.09.66 | 4h2 | London (CP) | 18 | Jun |
| (50) | | | | | | | | |
| 24.72 | | Joanna Clark | U23 | 11.02.73 | 1 | Aldershot | 26 | Jun |
| 24.72 | 1.8 | Katherine Endacott | U17 | 29.01.80 | 5s1 | Nottingham | 8 | Jul |
| 24.74 | | Fiona Hutchison | U20 | 18.01.77 | 2 | Greenock | 4 | Jun |
| 24.74 | | Sue Briggs | | 26.03.67 | 1 | Wrexham | 5 | Aug |
| 24.75 | | Claire O'Connor | U23 | 24.09.74 | 1 | Antrim | 20 | Jun |
| 24.76 | -0.8 | Donna Bannister | | 27.12.72 | 2h3 | London (CP) | 18 | Jun |
| 24.76 | -0.5 | Shani Anderson | U23 | 7.08.75 | 4h1 | Birmingham | 16 | Jul |
| 24.78 | -1.3 | Lucy Chaffe | U17 | 25.03.79 | 2 | Birmingham | 30 | Jul |
| 24.80 | 0.7 | Maria Bolsover | U17 | 5.06.80 | 1r2 | Bedford | 2 | Jul |
| 24.81 | | Dawn Flockhart | | 16.05.67 | 1 | Edinburgh | 9 | Apr |
| (60) | | | | | | | | |
| 24.84 | 1.6 | Karlene Palmer | U15 | 23.10.80 | 2 | Nottingham | 8 | Jul |
| 24.85 | -1.7 | Debbie Mant | U23 | 11.10.75 | 4 | Enfield | 29 | Apr |
| 24.89 | -0.6 | Annabel Soper | | 18.11.71 | 3h4 | Birmingham | 16 | Jul |
| 24.92 | 1.5 | Emma Clapson | | 22.11.71 | 2h1 | London (CP) | 14 | May |
| 24.92 | 1.8 | Tracy Bishop | U17 | 1.05.79 | 4s2 | Nottingham | 8 | Jul |
| 24.92 | 1.1 | Pauline Richards | | 30.06.68 | 2H | Stoke | 5 | Aug |
| 24.93 | 1.8 | Lisa Vannet | U23 | 8.11.74 | 3 | Grangemouth | 14 | May |
| 24.94 | 0.2 | Denise Lewis | | 27.08.72 | 2H | Gotzis, AUT | 27 | May |
| 24.94 | 1.6 | Sarah Zawada | U15 | 9.04.82 | 3 | Nottingham | 8 | Jul |
| 24.95 | 1.1 | Vikki Schofield | | 29.12.72 | 3H | Stoke | 5 | Aug |
| (70) | | | | | | | | |
| 24.97 | 0.9 | Emma Symonds | U20 | 5.06.77 | 6 | Nottingham | 8 | Jul |
| 24.98 i | | Kelly Woods | U23 | 28.05.75 | 2r3 | Birmingham | 29 | Jan |
| 24.98 | 1.3 | Alison Thompson | U23 | 11.02.74 | 6 | Stoke | 9 | Sep |
| 24.99 | 1.9 | Emma Beales | | 7.12.71 | 1H | Kilkenny, IRE | 26 | Aug |
| 25.00 | 0.9 | Kirsty Payne | U20 | 22.10.77 | 7 | Nottingham | 8 | Jul |
| 25.00 | -1.5 | Natalie Hynd | U20 | 30.01.78 | 2 | Pitreavie | 8 | Jul |
| 25.01 | 0.2 | Helen Pryer | U17 | 21.01.79 | 2h1 | Birmingham | 30 | Jul |
| 25.01 | 0.0 | Emma Lindsay | | 11.04.71 | 1H | Kilkenny, IRE | 26 | Aug |
| 25.02 i | | Janet Levermore | | 7.06.69 | 4r1 | Birmingham | 29 | Jan |
| 25.02 | 0.4 | Leanne Eastwood | U20 | 23.11.76 | 1 | Sheffield | 27 | May |
| (80) | | | | | | | | |
| 25.02 | | Morag Baxter/McGowan | | 22.08.69 | 3 | Greenock | 4 | Jun |
| 25.03 | 1.8 | Syreena Pinel | U17 | 13.01.79 | 5s2 | Nottingham | 8 | Jul |
| 25.06 | 1.9 | Serena Wilkins | U20 | 7.08.78 | 4s1 | Nottingham | 8 | Jul |

| 25.07 | 2.0 | Helen Williams | U20 | 2.06.77 | 4h1 | Bedford | 2 | Jul |
|---|---|---|---|---|---|---|---|---|
| 25.09 | -1.7 | Dawn Cousins | | 16.03.68 | 5 | Enfield | 29 | Apr |
| 25.09 | 2.0 | Jo Gronow | | 29.11.72 | 4 | Cwmbran | 9 | Jul |
| 25.10 | 1.9 | Jenny Balogun | U20 | 23.02.77 | 5s1 | Nottingham | 8 | Jul |
| 25.11 | 0.8 | Ruth Watson | U17 | 29.11.79 | 2h2 | London (He) | 6 | Aug |
| 25.15 | -0.9 | Julie Hollman | U20 | 16.02.77 | H | Vladimir, RUS | 4 | Aug |
| 25.16 | 0.2 | Amanda Forrester | U17 | 29.09.78 | 3h2 | Birmingham | 30 | Jul |
| | (90) | | | | | | | |
| 25.18 | 1.9 | Sarah Damm | | 12.09.70 | 1H | Derby | 29 | Apr |
| 25.19 | -1.7 | Elaine Viney | | 20.12.71 | 6 | Enfield | 29 | Apr |
| 25.19 | 1.8 | Elizabeth Walker | U17 | 30.05.79 | 6s1 | Nottingham | 8 | Jul |
| 25.21 i | | Kate Bullen | | 12.02.71 | 5 | Birmingham | 1 | Jan |
| 25.24 | | Claire Cooper | | 4.01.72 | 2 | Braunton | 13 | May |
| 25.24 | | Gillian Hegney | U20 | 4.11.77 | 1r2 | Edinburgh | 10 | Sep |
| 25.26 | 1.9 | Sarah Godbeer | U20 | 10.06.77 | 6s1 | Nottingham | 8 | Jul |
| 25.26 | -0.3 | Lindsay Fleet | U15 | 1.06.81 | 2 | Birmingham | 30 | Jul |
| 25.29 | -1.0 | Claire Haslam | | 18.12.63 | 4h1 | London (CP) | 18 | Jun |
| 25.29 | 1.8 | Shelley-Anne Bowen | U17 | 12.05.79 | 6s2 | Nottingham | 8 | Jul |
| | (100) | | | | | | | |
| 25.29 | | Kelly Holmes | | 19.04.70 | 1 | Aldershot | 26 | Jul |

**Additional Under 17** (1 - 19 above)

| 25.34 | | Karen Gear | | 30.09.79 | 1 | Braunton | 13 | May |
|---|---|---|---|---|---|---|---|---|
| | (20) | | | | | | | |
| 25.42 | | Rebecca White | | 5.06.80 | 1 | Wrexham | 5 | Aug |
| 25.44 | -1.5 | Lee McConnell | | 9.10.78 | 1 | Wishaw | 14 | May |
| 25.51 i | | Dawn Rose | | 25.01.79 | 1 | Birmingham | 5 | Feb |
| 25.54 | 1.8 | Tracy Martin | | 4.04.80 | 7s2 | Nottingham | 8 | Jul |
| 25.55 i | | Gael Davies | | 5.02.79 | 1 | Birmingham | 29 | Jan |
| 25.58 i | | Ayeesha Charles | | 4.09.79 | 2h2 | Birmingham | 19 | Feb |
| 25.70 | 0.6 | Hannah Paines | | 6.04.79 | 6 | Utrecht, HOL | 9 | Jul |

**Wind Assisted**

| 23.03 | 2.3 | Thomas | | (22.89) | 8s1 | Gothenburg, SWE | 10 | Aug |
|---|---|---|---|---|---|---|---|---|
| | | 23.20 | 2.2 | | 1 | Bedford | 10 | Jun |
| 23.33 | 2.2 | Stephanie Douglas | | (23.91) | 2 | Bedford | 10 | Jun |
| 23.44 | | Donna Fraser | | (23.47) | 1 | Irvine, USA | 23 | Apr |
| 23.48 | 2.2 | Jacobs | | (23.44) | 3 | Bedford | 10 | Jun |
| 23.80 | 4.5 | Sharon Williams | | (23.91) | 1 | Edinburgh | 8 | May |
| | | 6 performances to 23.80 by 5 athletes | | | | | | |
| 23.95 | 2.8 | Evette Williams | U20 | (24.04) | 1s2 | Nottingham | 8 | Jul |
| 24.17 | 4.5 | Sinead Dudgeon | U20 | (24.28) | 2 | Edinburgh | 8 | May |
| 24.27 | 4.5 | Louise Whitehead | U23 | (24.58) | 3 | Edinburgh | 8 | May |
| 24.33 | 4.5 | Sarah Oxley | U23 | (24.38i) | 4 | Edinburgh | 8 | May |
| 24.34 | 2.9 | Lesley Owusu | U17 | (24.41) | 1h3 | Bedford | 2 | Jul |
| 24.37 | | Julie Howard | | (24.72) | 1 | Braunton | 13 | May |
| 24.40 | | Dawn Cousins | | (25.09) | 1 | Barking | 14 | May |
| 24.40 | 2.2 | Ena Waldo | | 29.06.63 | 4 | Bedford | 10 | Jun |
| 24.45 | | Vicky Day | | 19.06.72 | 2 | Barking | 14 | May |
| 24.45 | 2.8 | Rebecca Kilgour | U23 | (24.52) | 2s2 | Nottingham | 8 | Jul |
| 24.51 | 4.6 | Lucy Chaffe | U17 | (24.78) | 2 | London (He) | 6 | Aug |
| 24.54 | 4.5 | Keeley Butler | U23 | (24.64) | 5 | Edinburgh | 8 | May |
| 24.62 | 2.4 | Sue Briggs | | (24.74) | 1 | Blackpool | 20 | Aug |
| 24.69 | 3.8 | Lorraine Bell | U20 | 21.06.77 | 1 | Edinburgh | 17 | Jun |
| 24.72 | 2.3 | Linda Keough/Staines | | 26.12.63 | 1 | Portsmouth | 14 | May |
| 24.72 | 3.8 | Natalie Hynd | U20 | (25.00) | 2 | Edinburgh | 17 | Jun |
| 24.73 | 2.8 | Kirsty Payne | U20 | (25.00) | 3s2 | Nottingham | 8 | Jul |
| 24.74 | 2.8 | Emma Symonds | U20 | (24.97) | 4s2 | Nottingham | 8 | Jul |
| 24.79 | 3.8 | Suzanne McGowan | U20 | 13.04.78 | 3 | Edinburgh | 17 | Jun |

| Time | Wind | Name | Cat | | Pos | Venue | Date |
|---|---|---|---|---|---|---|---|
| 24.80 | 2.3 | Debbie Mant | U23 | (24.85) | 2 | Portsmouth | 14 May |
| 24.82 | 3.3 | Sarah Zawada | U15 | (24.94) | 1 | London (He) | 6 Aug |
| 24.84 | 2.8 | Amanda Waite | U20 | 1.02.78 | 5s2 | Nottingham | 8 Jul |
| 24.84 | 2.8 | Leanne Eastwood | U20 | (25.02) | 6s2 | Nottingham | 8 Jul |
| 24.86 | | Orla Bermingham | U23 | 7.10.75 | 3 | Barking | 13 May |
| 24.86 | 4.0 | Emma Lindsay | | (25.01) | 1H | Stoke | 24 Jun |
| | | | | | | | |
| 24.87 | | Elaine Viney | | (25.19) | 1 | Peterborough | 28 Aug |
| 24.88 | 4.7 | Emma Clapson | | (24.92) | 2 | London (CP) | 14 May |
| 24.96 | 4.6 | Jannette Niccolls | U20 | 7.09.76 | 4 | London (He) | 6 Aug |
| 24.98 | 4.4 | Sally Evans | U23 | 14.05.75 | 5 | Telford | 26 Aug |
| 24.99 | 4.6 | Ruth Watson | U17 | (25.11) | 5 | London (He) | 6 Aug |
| 25.00 | 4.5 | Kelly Woods | U23 | (24.98i) | 6 | Edinburgh | 8 May |
| 25.03 | 3.3 | Naomi Hodge-Dallaway | U15 | 1.06.81 | 2 | London (He) | 6 Aug |
| 25.05 | 3.3 | Lindsay Fleet | U15 | (25.26) | 3 | London (He) | 6 Aug |
| 25.10 | | Maureen Barnes | | 21.04.63 | 3 | Irvine, USA | 23 Apr |
| 25.15 | 2.5 | Denise Bolton | U20 | 1.02.77 | 2H | Aberdeen | 15 Jul |
| | | | | | | | |
| 25.20 | | Samantha Barr/Porter | | 14.08.70 | 4 | Barking | 13 May |
| 25.21 | 2.9 | Lyndsey Fletcher | U20 | 18.09.76 | 4h3 | Bedford | 2 Jul |
| 25.23 | 2.1 | Ellena Ruddock | U20 | 23.02.76 | 2 | Birmingham | 18 Jun |
| 25.24 | 3.7 | Zoe Wilson | U20 | 28.08.76 | 3s2 | Edinburgh | 8 May |
| 25.26 | 4.0 | Anne Hollman | U23 | 18.02.74 | 2H | Stoke | 24 Jun |
| 25.28 | 2.4 | Ruth Williams | | 18.03.70 | 3 | Blackpool | 20 Aug |

**Additional Under 17**

| Time | Wind | Name | | | Pos | Venue | Date |
|---|---|---|---|---|---|---|---|
| 25.35 | 3.7 | Gail Evans | | 23.07.80 | 1 | Cardiff | 1 Jul |
| 25.39 | 3.7 | Hannah Paines | | (25.70) | 2 | Cardiff | 1 Jul |
| 25.41 | 3.1 | Rebecca White | | (25.42) | 2 | Sheffield | 28 May |

**Hand Timing**

| Time | Wind | Name | Cat | | Pos | Venue | Date |
|---|---|---|---|---|---|---|---|
| 23.4 | 1.4 | Thomas | | (22.89) | 1 | Glasgow | 6 May |
| 23.4 | | Louise Fraser | | (24.68) | 1 | London (He) | 1 Jul |
| | | 23.5 w | 2.7 | | 1 | London (WL) | 30 Jul |
| 23.6 w | 2.7 | Richardson | | (23.53) | 2 | London (WL) | 30 Jul |
| | | 23.7 | 1.1 | | 1 | Bebington | 11 Jun |
| 23.6 w? | | Sharon Tunaley | | 2.09.68 | 1 | Rotherham | 6 Aug |
| | | 24.2 | | | 1 | Nottingham | 13 Aug |

6 performances to 23.7 by 4 athletes including 3 wind assisted

| Time | Wind | Name | Cat | | Pos | Venue | Date |
|---|---|---|---|---|---|---|---|
| 23.8 w? | | Sue Earnshaw/Rawlinson | | 13.10.70 | 2 | Rotherham | 6 Aug |
| | | 23.9 | | | 1 | Grimsby | 3 Sep |
| 23.9 | | Sharon Williams | | (23.91) | 1 | Portsmouth (RN) | 20 May |
| 24.0 | | Alison Davies | | (24.06) | 1 | Woking | 22 Jul |
| 24.1 | | Aileen McGillivary | | (24.19) | 2 | Derby | 30 Jul |
| 24.2 | | Stephanie Llewellyn | | (24.38) | 2 | Watford | 14 May |
| 24.2 | | Donna Hoggarth | U23 | 14.10.73 | 1 | Blackpool | 13 May |
| | | | | | | | |
| 24.2 | | Geraldine McLeod | | (24.43) | 2 | London (He) | 1 Jul |
| 24.2 | | Sue Briggs | | (24.74) | 1r2 | London (He) | 1 Jul |
| 24.2 | | Susan Williams | U20 | (24.30) | 1 | Watford | 20 Aug |
| 24.2 w | 2.7 | Phylis Smith | | 29.09.65 | 3 | London (WL) | 30 Jul |
| | | 24.6 | | | 2r2 | London (He) | 1 Jul |
| 24.2 w | 3.7 | Lesley Owusu | U17 | (24.41) | 2 | Croydon | 28 Aug |
| 24.3 | | Alanna Cooke/Rowbotham | | 11.01.70 | 1 | Sheffield | 14 May |
| 24.3 | | Elaine Sutcliffe | | (24.99) | 1 | York | 23 Jul |
| 24.3 | | Paula Cohen | | 5.02.71 | 1 | Derby | 23 Jul |
| 24.3 w | 2.7 | Donna Bannister | | (24.76) | 4 | London (WL) | 30 Jul |
| | | 24.4 | | | 1 | Bedford | 25 Jun |
| *24.4* | | *Dion Graham* | *U17* | *(24.69)* | *1* | *Telford* | *18 Jun* |
| 24.4 | | Lucy Carter | U20 | (24.55) | 2 | Bedford | 25 Jun |

| | | | | | | | |
|---|---|---|---|---|---|---|---|
| 24.4 | | Christine Bloomfield | | (24.79) | 1 | Harrow | 9 Jul |
| 24.5 | | Kim Goodwin | | (24.69) | 2 | Bebington | 11 Jun |
| 24.5 | | Dawn Flockhart | | (24.81) | 3 | London (He) | 1 Jul |
| 24.6 | | Dawn Cousins | | (25.09) | 1 | Basildon | 20 May |
| 24.6 | | Julie Howard | | (24.72) | 1 | Bath | 31 May |
| 24.6 | | Leanne Eastwood | U20 | (25.02) | 2 | Telford | 18 Jun |
| 24.6 | | Vicky Day | | (24.45w) | 4 | London (He) | 1 Jul |
| 24.6 | -0.9 | Emma Symonds | U20 | (24.97) | 2 | Kings Lynn | 15 Jul |
| 24.6 | | Joanna Clark | U23 | (24.72) | 1 | Bracknell | 22 Jul |
| 24.7 | | Fiona Hutchison | U20 | (24.74) | 1r2 | Glasgow | 7 May |
| 24.7 | | Claire Haslam | | (25.29) | 2 | Hayes | 13 May |
| 24.7 | | Louise Brunning | | 6.03.72 | 1 | Dartford | 20 May |
| 24.7 | | Lucy Chaffe | U17 | (24.78) | 1 | London (WF) | 25 Jun |
| 24.7 | | Shani Anderson | U23 | (24.76) | 3r2 | London (He) | 1 Jul |
| 24.7 | | Emma Clapson | | (24.92) | 2 | Bracknell | 22 Jul |
| 24.7 | | Janine Whitlock | U23 | 11.08.73 | 3 | Grimsby | 3 Sep |
| 24.7 w | 4.2 | Morag Baxter/McGowan | | (25.02) | 1 | Aberdeen | 23 Jul |
| | | 24.8 | | | 5 | London (He) | 1 Jul |
| 24.8 | 1.4 | Alison Thompson | U23 | (24.98) | 4 | Glasgow | 6 May |
| 24.8 | | Lynne Draper | | 10.05.67 | 1 | Horsham | 3 Jun |
| 24.8 | 1.3 | Michelle Pierre | U23 | 30.09.73 | 1 | Croydon | 25 Jun |
| 24.8 | | Orla Bermingham | U23 | (24.86w) | 4r2 | London (He) | 1 Jul |
| 24.8 | | Emma Lindsay | | (25.01) | 5r2 | London (He) | 1 Jul |
| 24.8 | | Jannette Niccolls | U20 | (24.96w) | 1 | London (WP) | 12 Aug |
| 24.8 w | 2.3 | Alison Mayfield | | 12.05.69 | 2 | Mansfield | 13 May |
| | | 24.9 | | | 1 | London (Ha) | 25 Jun |
| 24.8 w | | Keri Maddox | | 4.07.72 | 3 | Rotherham | 6 Aug |
| 24.9 | | Rebecca Drummond | U20 | 18.04.78 | 2r2 | Stafford | 7 May |
| 24.9 | | Marcia Walker | | 27.05.70 | 2h1 | Hayes | 13 May |
| 24.9 | | Dawn Rose | U17 | (25.51i) | 1 | Kettering | 21 May |
| 24.9 | | Sally Evans | U23 | (24.98w) | 2 | Kettering | 21 May |
| 24.9 | | Georgina Oladapo | | 15.05.67 | 3 | Bebington | 11 Jun |
| 24.9 | | Clare Bleasdale | | 6.07.71 | 3 | Crawley | 25 Jun |
| 24.9 | | Ruth Watson | U17 | (25.11) | 1 | St. Ives | 30 Jul |
| 25.0 i | | Jocelyn Kirby/Harwood | V35 | 21.11.57 | 1 | Birmingham | 12 Feb |
| 25.0 | | Amanda Forrester | U17 | (25.16) | 2 | Sheffield | 30 Apr |
| 25.0 | | Linda Keough/Staines | | (24.72w) | 1 | Basingstoke | 30 Apr |
| 25.0 | | Tania Findlay/Adlam | | 8.11.70 | 1 | Yate | 13 May |
| 25.0 | | Joan Booth | | 18.12.68 | 4 | Sheffield | 14 May |
| 25.0 | | Julie Moore | U23 | 5.12.73 | 1 | Loughborough | 20 May |
| 25.0 | | Leigh Ferrier | | 15.08.72 | 1 | Watford | 31 May |
| 25.0 | | Hayley Clements | | 17.09.68 | 1 | Ipswich | 3 Jun |
| 25.0 | -2.9 | Lorraine Bell | U20 | (24.69w) | 2 | Ayr | 18 Jul |
| 25.0 | | Rebecca White | U17 | (25.42) | 1 | Blackburn | 22 Jul |
| 25.0 | | Syreena Pinel | U17 | (25.03) | 1 | Corby | 23 Jul |
| 25.0 | | Tatum Nelson | U17 | 17.12.78 | 1 | Southampton | 12 Aug |
| 25.1 | | Lee McConnell | U17 | (25.44) | 3 | Sheffield | 30 Apr |
| 25.1 | | Shelley-Anne Bowen | U17 | (25.29) | 1 | Bracknell | 10 Jun |
| 25.1 | | Amanda Waite | U20 | (24.84w) | 1 | Basildon | 10 Jun |
| 25.1 | | Natalie Smethurst | U20 | 31.03.77 | 4 | Telford | 18 Jun |
| 25.1 | | Lyndsey Fletcher | U20 | (25.21w) | 3 | Telford | 18 Jun |
| 25.1 | | Zoe Wilson | U20 | (25.24w) | 1r2 | Derby | 23 Jul |
| 25.1 | | Helen Miles | | 2.03.67 | 1 | Yate | 23 Jul |
| 25.1 | | Abigail Hunte | | 12.05.71 | 1 | Windsor | 12 Aug |
| 25.1 w | 2.8 | Natasha Danvers | U20 | 19.09.77 | 1 | Croydon | 14 May |

### Additional Under 17

| | | | | | | |
|---|---|---|---|---|---|---|
| 25.2 | Amanda Gray | 22.03.79 | 1H | Worcester | 24 | Aug |
| 25.3 | Joanne McDougall | 23.08.79 | 1 | Bebington | 10 | Jun |
| 25.3 | Kelly Lopez | 29.11.78 | 2r2 | Telford | 18 | Jun |
| 25.3 | Laura Seston | 9.02.79 | 1 | Colchester | 28 | Aug |
| 25.3 | Gael Davies | (25.55i) | 1 | Reading | 28 | Aug |
| 25.5 | Carmel Triggs | 18.04.80 | 1 | Manchester | 2 | Jul |

### Additional Under 15 (1 - 4 above)

| | | | | | | | |
|---|---|---|---|---|---|---|---|
| 25.3 | | Jennifer Meadows | 17.04.81 | 1 | Blackpool | 16 | Jul |
| 25.34 | 0.5 | Natalie Law | 2.05.81 | 3s1 | Nottingham | 8 | Jul |
| 25.39 | 0.5 | Rhian Cains | 29.10.80 | 4s1 | Nottingham | 8 | Jul |
| 25.39 | -0.3 | Rachel Redmond | 7.12.81 | 3 | Birmingham | 30 | Jul |
| 25.4 | | Libby Alder | 20.11.80 | 1 | Cheltenham | 17 | Jun |
| 25.48 | 1.9 | Lois Cresswell | 12.01.81 | 3s2 | Nottingham | 8 | Jul |
| (10) | | | | | | | |
| 25.5 | | Dionne Howell | 10.04.81 | 1 | London (TB) | 22 | Apr |
| | 25.61 -3.5 | | | 2 | London (CP) | 28 | May |
| 25.5 | | Rachel Rogers | 20.11.80 | 2 | Kingston | 17 | Jun |
| | 25.60 1.9 | | | 4s2 | Nottingham | 8 | Jul |
| 25.6 | | Emily Freeman | 24.11.80 | 1 | Blackpool | 24 | Sep |
| 25.64 w 2.3 | | Lisa Callan | 10.10.80 | 1 | Edinburgh | 17 | Jun |

### Under 13

| | | | | | | |
|---|---|---|---|---|---|---|
| 26.8 | Sophie Allen | 7.09.82 | 1 | St. Ives | 20 | Aug |
| 26.96 w 2.5 | Nicola Jarvie | 11.09.82 | 1 | Pitreavie | 9 | Jul |
| 27.0 | Miranda Woodruff | 6.09.82 | 2 | Sutton | 22 | Jul |
| 27.07 | Nicola Lapczuk | 16.11.82 | 2 | Derby | 10 | Jun |
| 27.1 | Stephanie Spinks | 6.09.82 | 1 | Norwich | 30 | Jul |
| 27.17 | Sarah Lane | 24.11.82 | 1 | Cardiff | 23 | Jul |
| 27.3 | Lowri Jones | 22.07.83 | 1 | Newport | 17 | Sep |
| 27.36 w 4.4 | Sally Drew | 23.11.82 | 1 | Braunton | 14 | May |
| 27.4 | Nina Ezeogu | 11.10.82 | 1 | Southend | 20 | Aug |
| 27.4 w 3.7 | Rebecca Smith | 23.02.83 | 1 | Stoke | 13 | May |
| (10) | | | | | | |
| 27.53 | Susan Armstrong | 8.09.82 | 1 | Greenock | 4 | Jun |
| 27.6 | Kelly Rea | 17.09.82 | 1 | Cudworth | 6 | Aug |
| 27.6 | Lauren McLoughlin | 8.09.82 | 1 | Newport | 9 | Aug |

## 300 METRES

| | | | | | | | |
|---|---|---|---|---|---|---|---|
| 37.4 + | Georgina Oladapo | | 15.05.67 | | London (CP) | 18 | Jun |
| 38.21 | Lesley Owusu | U17 | 21.12.78 | 1 | London (CP) | 27 | Aug |
| *38.55* | *Dion Graham* | *U17* | *27.09.78* | *1* | *Nottingham* | *8* | *Jul* |
| 38.73 | Jacqui Parker | | 15.10.66 | 1 | Perth, AUS | 20 | Dec |
| 38.95 | Maria Bolsover | U17 | 5.06.80 | 2s2 | Nottingham | 8 | Jul |
| 39.00 i | Elaine Sutcliffe | | 6.04.70 | 1 | Birmingham | 11 | Feb |
| 39.1 | Sue Briggs | | 26.03.67 | 1 | Sheffield | 14 | Jun |
| 39.3 | Sharon Tunaley | | 2.09.68 | 1 | Burton | 11 | Apr |
| 39.47 | Lucy Chaffe | U17 | 25.03.79 | 1 | London (CP) | 28 | May |
| 39.49 | Lee McConnell | U17 | 9.10.78 | 1 | Edinburgh | 10 | Sep |
| 39.50 i | Louise Whitehead | U23 | 26.03.75 | 2 | Birmingham | 11 | Feb |
| (10) | | | | | | | |
| 39.6 | Elizabeth Williams | U20 | 2.06.77 | 1 | Bracknell | 21 | Jun |
| 39.68 | Ruth Watson | U17 | 29.11.79 | 2s1 | Nottingham | 8 | Jul |

### Additional Under 17 (1 - 5 above)

| | | | | | | |
|---|---|---|---|---|---|---|
| 40.01 | Rebecca White | 5.06.80 | 3s1 | Nottingham | 8 | Jul |
| 40.09 | Lindsay Impett | 4.01.80 | 2 | London (CP) | 27 | Aug |
| 40.09 | Helen Roscoe | 4.12.79 | 3 | London (CP) | 27 | Aug |
| 40.22 | Sarah Cootes | 3.11.78 | 4s1 | Nottingham | 8 | Jul |
| 40.3 | Karen Gear | 30.09.79 | 1 | Exeter | 10 | Jun |
| | 41.01 | | 5s1 | Nottingham | 8 | Jul |

| | | | | | |
|---|---|---|---|---|---|
| 40.33 | Claire Nichols | 14.05.79 | 2h1 | London (CP) | 27 May |
| 40.33 | Helen Lee | 27.08.80 | 3s2 | Nottingham | 8 Jul |
| 40.50 | Amanda Pritchard | 18.03.80 | 3 | Colwyn Bay | 15 Jul |
| 40.53 | Sharon Hollett | 26.12.78 | 1 | Pitreavie | 8 Jul |
| 40.57 | Emily De Nobrega | 23.10.78 | 4s2 | Nottingham | 8 Jul |
| 40.58 i | Gael Davies | 5.02.79 | 1h1 | Birmingham | 1 Jan |
| 40.6 | Kate Denham | 18.03.80 | 1 | Bournemouth | 23 Jul |
| 40.8 | Nina Rogers | 19.09.78 | 1 | Derby | 23 Jul |
| 40.9 | Melissa Okusanya | 2.01.80 | 1 | Derby | 17 Jun |
| 40.95 | | | 5s2 | Nottingham | 8 Jul |
| 40.9 | Abigail Naugher | 26.02.80 | 1 | Newcastle | 17 Jun |
| 40.99 | | | 3h3 | Nottingham | 7 Jul |
| | (20) | | | | |
| 40.9 | Joanne Vaughan-Jones | ⁻6.09.79 | 1 | Kings Lynn | 15 Jul |
| 40.92 | Susan Atavwigho | 19.10.78 | 2h2 | Nottingham | 7 Jul |
| 40.93 | Pamela Johnstone | 16.03.79 | 2 | Pitreavie | 8 Jul |
| 41.05 | Claire Smith | 6.01.79 | 1 | Derby | 10 Jun |
| 41.18 | Lyndsey Croton | 16.12.78 | 3h2 | Nottingham | 7 Jul |
| 41.22 | Lorna Rice | 10.01.79 | 4h3 | Nottingham | 7 Jul |
| 41.3 | Eve Miller | 1.12.79 | 1 | Hayes | 12 Mar |
| 41.3 | Emily Nicholls | 5.12.78 | 1 | Yate | 23 Jul |
| 41.3 | Ayeesha Charles | 4.09.79 | 3 | Bournemouth | 23 Jul |
| 41.38 | Claire Concannon | 2.03.79 | 4h2 | Nottingham | 7 Jul |
| | (30) | | | | |
| 41.40 | Melissa Forster | 30.03.80 | 5h3 | Nottingham | 7 Jul |
| 41.4 | Nicola Pankhurst | 27.09.79 | 1 | Kingston | 17 Jun |
| 41.4 | Laura Seston | 9.02.79 | 1 | St. Ives | 20 Aug |
| 41.45 | Rachel Wiseman | 25.09.79 | 6h3 | Nottingham | 7 Jul |
| 41.45 | Sarah Todd | 3.11.79 | 5h4 | Nottingham | 7 Jul |

## 400 METRES

| | | | | | |
|---|---|---|---|---|---|
| 51.18 | Melanie Neef | 26.05.70 | 4s1 | Gothenburg, SWE | 6 Aug |
| 51.35 | | | 1 | Villeneuve d'Ascq, FRA | 24 Jun |
| 51.39 | | | 2h1 | Gothenburg, SWE | 5 Aug |
| 51.45 | | | 2 | Rhede, GER | 30 Jul |
| 51.63 | | | 1 | Birmingham | 16 Jul |
| 51.70 | | | 1 | Nuremberg, GER | 15 Jun |
| 51.76 | | | 1 | Copenhagen, DEN | 23 Aug |
| 51.96 | | | 2 | Sheffield | 23 Jul |
| 52.0 | | | 1 | London (He) | 1 Jul |
| 52.15 | | | 4 | Berlin, GER | 1 Sep |
| 52.22 | | | 1 | Khania, GRE | 4 Jun |
| 52.49 | | | 7 | London (CP) | 27 Aug |
| 52.57 i | | | 3 | Birmingham | 25 Feb |
| 52.82 i | | | 1 | Birmingham | 4 Feb |
| 53.02 | | | 1h1 | Birmingham | 15 Jul |
| 53.34 i | | | 4h2 | Barcelona, SPA | 10 Mar |
| 53.67 i | | | 1s1 | Birmingham | 3 Feb |
| 53.67 i | | | 1r1 | Glasgow | 11 Feb |
| 52.04 | Donna Fraser | 7.11.72 | 2 | Pune, IND | 13 Sep |
| 53.27 | | | 1r2 | Cwmbran | 9 Jul |
| 53.32 | | | 1r2 | London (CP) | 27 Aug |
| 53.8 | | | 1 | Liverpool | 1 Jul |
| 53.9 | | | 1 | Croydon | 12 Aug |
| 52.4 | Stephanie Llewellyn | 31.12.68 | 2 | London (He) | 1 Jul |
| 52.5 | | | 1 | Derby | 30 Jul |
| 52.54 | | | 1r1 | Cwmbran | 9 Jul |
| 52.79 | | | 4 | Gateshead | 21 Aug |
| 53.13 | | | 4 | Birmingham | 16 Jul |
| 53.55 | | | 1h2 | Birmingham | 15 Jul |
| 53.6 | | | 1 | Brighton | 3 Jun |

| 52.47 | Lorraine Hanson | | 22.04.65 | 3 | Gateshead | 21 | Aug |
|---|---|---|---|---|---|---|---|
| | 52.6 | | | 2 | Birmingham | 19 | Aug |
| | 52.68 | | | 2 | Birmingham | 16 | Jul |
| | 53.05 | | | 1h3 | Birmingham | 15 | Jul |
| | 53.1 | | | 1 | Glasgow | 6 | May |
| | 53.22 | | | 1 | Tallinn, EST | 9 | Jul |
| | 53.25 | | | 6 | Sheffield | 23 | Jul |
| | 53.3 | | | 3 | London (He) | 1 | Jul |
| | 53.3 | | | 1 | Liverpool | 30 | Jul |
| | 53.57 | | | 2 | Stoke | 9 | Sep |
| 52.5 | Phylis Smith | | 29.09.65 | 1 | Birmingham | 19 | Aug |
| | 53.03 | | | 1 | Stoke | 9 | Sep |
| | 53.19 | | | 1 | Telford | 26 | Aug |
| 52.71 | Georgina Oladapo | | 15.05.67 | 3 | Birmingham | 16 | Jul |
| | 52.94 | | | 6 | Gateshead | 21 | Aug |
| | 53.05 | | | 1 | Jona, SWZ | 23 | Jul |
| | 53.5 | | | 1 | Welwyn | 3 | Jun |
| | 53.51 | | | 1h4 | Birmingham | 15 | Jul |
| 53.27 | Sally Gunnell | | 29.07.66 | 6 | Rhede, GER | 30 | Jul |
| | 53.34 | | | 3 | Lindau, GER | 28 | Jul |
| 53.4 | Sue Earnshaw/Rawlinson | | 13.10.70 | 2 | Derby | 30 | Jul |
| | 53.69 | | | 5 | Birmingham | 16 | Jul |
| | 53.70 i | | | 2r1 | Vienna, AUT | 18 | Feb |
| | 53.82 i | | | 4 | Birmingham | 28 | Jan |
| | 53.85 i | | | 5h3 | Barcelona, SPA | 10 | Mar |
| | 53.85 | | | 4r1 | Cwmbran | 9 | Jul |
| 53.5 | Stephanie McCann | | 26.10.65 | 2 | Liverpool | 30 | Jul |
| | 54.31 | | | 2 | Antrim | 28 | May |
| 53.58 | Sharon Tunaley | | 2.09.68 | 2r2 | London (CP) | 27 | Aug |
| | 53.66 | | | 2 | Granada, SPA | 27 | May |
| | 53.8 | | | 1 | Nottingham | 13 | Aug |
| | (10) | | | | | | |
| 53.72 | Linda Keough/Staines | | 26.12.63 | 3r1 | Cwmbran | 9 | Jul |
| | 53.86 | | | 1 | Aldershot | 23 | Jul |
| 53.9 | Louise Fraser | | 10.10.70 | 4 | London (He) | 1 | Jul |
| 64 performances to 54.0 by 12 athletes including 8 indoors | | | | | | | |
| 54.05 | Michelle Pierre | U23 | 30.09.73 | 3r2 | Basel, SWZ | 5 | Jun |
| 54.08 | Vicky Day | | 19.06.72 | 2 | Aldershot | 23 | Jul |
| 54.28 | Allison Curbishley | U20 | 3.06.76 | 1 | Belfort, FRA | 6 | Aug |
| 54.31 i | Michelle Thomas | | 16.10.71 | 5 | Birmingham | 28 | Jan |
| | 54.46 | | | 3 | Innsbruck, AUT | 28 | Jun |
| 54.35 | Elaine Sutcliffe | | 6.04.70 | 1 | Gateshead | 17 | Jun |
| 54.4 | Claire Raven | | 15.06.72 | 1 | Enfield | 30 | Jul |
| | 55.06 | | | 5r2 | London (CP) | 27 | Aug |
| 54.4 | Dawn Flockhart | | 16.05.67 | 1r2 | Birmingham | 19 | Aug |
| | 55.14 | | | 4 | Stoke | 9 | Sep |
| 54.5 | Jennifer Stoute | | 16.04.65 | 5 | London (He) | 1 | Jul |
| | 55.36 i | | | 5 | Birmingham | 25 | Jan |
| | (20) | | | | | | |
| 54.51 | Kelly Holmes | | 19.04.70 | 1 | Aldershot | 26 | Jul |
| 54.57 | Lesley Owusu | U17 | 21.12.78 | 3 | Stoke | 9 | Sep |
| 54.59 | Jo Sloane | U20 | 2.12.76 | 2 | Belfort, FRA | 6 | Aug |
| 54.64 | Kim Goodwin | | 16.05.70 | 2 | Gateshead | 17 | Jun |
| 54.7 | Alyson Layzell | | 16.12.66 | 1 | Portsmouth | 25 | Jun |
| 54.8 | Emma Clapson | | 22.11.71 | 2 | London (WL) | 30 | Jul |
| | 54.94 | | | 2 | London (CP) | 18 | Jun |
| 54.81 i | Tracy Goddard/Joseph | | 29.11.69 | 6 | Birmingham | 28 | Jan |
| 54.9 mx | Abigail Hunte | | 12.05.71 | | London (PH) | 2 | Aug |
| 54.92 | Louise Whitehead | U23 | 26.03.75 | 4h5 | Fukuoka, JAP | 31 | Aug |
| 54.99 | Joanna Clark | U23 | 11.02.73 | 3 | London (CP) | 18 | Jun |
| | (30) | | | | | | |

| | | | | | | | |
|---|---|---|---|---|---|---|---|
| 55.07 | Julie Moore | U23 | 5.12.73 | 3 | Gateshead | 17 | Jun |
| 55.08 | Sandra Leigh | | 26.02.66 | 4 | London (CP) | 18 | Jun |
| 55.25 | Louretta Thorne | U20 | 6.05.77 | 1h1 | Nottingham | 7 | Jul |
| 55.4 | Janet Levermore | | 7.06.69 | 2r2 | Birmingham | 19 | Aug |
| 56.99 | | | | 2h2 | Birmingham | 18 | Jun |
| 55.47 | Elizabeth Williams | U20 | 2.06.77 | 1h2 | Bedford | 2 | Jul |
| 55.50 | Clare Bleasdale | | 6.07.71 | 3 | Aldershot | 23 | Jul |
| 55.69 i | Nicola Crowther | | 15.05.70 | 1r1 | Birmingham | 29 | Jan |
| 55.7 | Alison Mayfield | | 12.05.69 | 2 | Peterborough | 7 | May |
| 55.7 | Alison Thorne | | 25.09.72 | 3 | London (WL) | 30 | Jul |
| 55.74 | Wendy Steele | | 7.01.66 | 2 | Edinburgh | 23 | Jun |
| | (40) | | | | | | |
| 55.8 | Sharon Williams | | 20.05.70 | 1 | Bromley | 22 | Apr |
| 55.85 | Stacey Jacques | U20 | 24.06.77 | 3 | Nottingham | 8 | Jul |
| 55.86 | Rosie Thorner | | 7.08.67 | 3 | Birmingham | 18 | Jun |
| 55.89 | Rachel Newcombe | | 25.02.67 | 4 | Gateshead | 17 | Jun |
| 55.9 | Sarah Stevenson | U23 | 31.12.73 | 2 | Mansfield | 14 | May |
| 56.26 | | | | 4 | Birmingham | 18 | Jun |
| 55.92 | Katharine Eustace | U23 | 16.04.75 | 2 | Edinburgh | 8 | May |
| 56.0 | Lisa Vannet | U23 | 8.11.74 | 2r2 | London (He) | 1 | Jul |
| 56.13 | | | | 3 | Edinburgh | 23 | Jun |
| 56.0 | Alanna Cooke/Rowbotham | | 11.01.70 | 1 | Wakefield | 12 | Aug |
| 56.01 | Denise Facey | | 8.02.69 | 5 | Gateshead | 17 | Jun |
| 56.02 | Maureen Barnes | | 21.04.63 | 1 | Irvine, USA | 23 | Apr |
| | (50) | | | | | | |
| 56.03 | Lorraine Bell | U20 | 21.06.77 | 1 | Wishaw | 13 | May |
| 56.1 | Ena Waldo | | 29.06.63 | 1 | Leamington | 14 | May |
| 56.1 | Alison Mahindru | | 15.07.68 | 3r2 | London (He) | 1 | Jul |
| 56.1 | Leigh Ferrier | | 15.08.72 | 4r2 | London (He) | 1 | Jul |
| 57.17 | | | | 6h1 | Birmingham | 15 | Jul |
| 56.14 | Kelly Woods | U23 | 28.05.75 | 3h1 | London (CP) | 17 | Jun |
| 56.17 | Clare Hill | U20 | 14.12.76 | 2h1 | Bedford | 2 | Jul |
| 56.2 | Paula Fryer | | 14.07.69 | 3r2 | Birmingham | 19 | Aug |
| 56.33 | | | | 7 | Gateshead | 17 | Jun |
| 56.24 i | Susan Hendry | U20 | 30.06.76 | 2 | Birmingham | 18 | Feb |
| 56.69 | | | | 7 | Bedford | 2 | Jul |
| 56.25 | Elaine Viney | | 20.12.71 | 1 | Enfield | 29 | Apr |
| 56.3 | Paula Cohen | | 5.02.71 | 1 | Alfaz Del Pi, SPA | 13 | Apr |
| | (60) | | | | | | |
| 56.4 | Lucy Chaffe | U17 | 25.03.79 | 1 | Bromley | 23 | Apr |
| 56.4 | Jayne Mallows | | 6.07.70 | 2 | Leamington | 14 | May |
| 57.49 i | | | | 4h3 | Birmingham | 3 | Feb |
| 56.4 | Christine Amede | | 7.08.63 | 1 | Hayes | 14 | May |
| 56.4 | Dawn Gandy | | 28.07.65 | 1 | Portsmouth | 20 | May |
| 56.4 | Sarah Damm | | 12.09.70 | 3 | Derby | 23 | Jul |
| 56.4 | Jacqui Parker | | 15.10.66 | 1 | Aldershot | 12 | Aug |
| 56.60 | | | | 1 | Stoke | 10 | Sep |
| 56.49 | Katharine Reeves | U23 | 2.03.73 | 3h2 | London (CP) | 17 | Jun |
| 56.50 | Coral Davis | | 15.05.61 | 1 | Pomona, USA | 15 | Apr |
| 56.5 | Vicki Jamison | U20 | 19.05.77 | 1 | Antrim | 9 | Aug |
| 56.5 | Natalie Tait | | 24.08.72 | 1 | Windsor | 12 | Aug |
| | (70) | | | | | | |
| 56.56 | Nicola Youden | U20 | 2.11.77 | 1 | Greenock | 4 | Jun |
| 56.6 | Suzanne Guise | | 3.02.62 | 1r2 | Birmingham | 23 | Apr |
| 56.63 | Claire Haslam | | 18.12.63 | 3 | Enfield | 29 | Apr |
| 56.7 | Maureen Williams | | 22.02.69 | 2 | Hayes | 14 | May |
| 57.13 | | | | 2h3 | London (CP) | 17 | Jun |
| 56.7 | Kate-Elin Williams | U20 | 18.04.77 | 8 | Cork, IRE | 24 | Jun |
| 56.71 | | | | 1 | Utrecht, HOL | 9 | Jul |
| 56.7 | Mary Kitson | | 2.04.63 | 1 | Corby | 25 | Jun |

| 56.7 | Jane Ridley | | 12.07.68 | 5r2 | London (He) | 1 | Jul |
| 57.29 | | | | 5h2 | London (CP) | 17 | Jun |
| 56.7 | Joanne Mersh | U23 | 19.10.74 | 1 | Harrow | 9 | Jul |
| 56.75 | Nicole Bowring | U23 | 27.01.74 | 6 | London (CP) | 18 | Jun |
| 56.80 | Simone Harrison | U20 | 2.09.77 | 8 | Bedford | 2 | Jul |
| | (80) | | | | | | |
| *56.8* | *Ronit Feigenbaum* | | *3.11.63* | *1* | *Horsham* | *20* | *Aug* |
| *57.11* | | | | *4h2* | *London (CP)* | *17* | *Jun* |
| 56.81 | Jenny Pearson | | 3.07.62 | 2h2 | London (CP) | 13 | May |
| 56.9 | Dyanna Clarke | V35 | 27.02.58 | 3 | Hayes | 14 | May |
| 57.45 | | | | 3h3 | London (CP) | 17 | Jun |
| 56.9 | Julie Asgill | V35 | 24.05.56 | 8r2 | London (He) | 1 | Jul |
| 56.9 | Emma Beales | | 7.12.71 | 1 | Harrow | 2 | Sep |
| 56.92 i | Pauline Richards | | 30.06.68 | 2h2 | Birmingham | 3 | Feb |
| 57.0 | Heather Myers | | 5.12.64 | 2 | Bracknell | 22 | Jul |
| 57.0 | Julia Moss | U20 | 2.07.77 | 1 | Wrexham | 5 | Aug |
| 57.06 | Caroline Swinbank | U23 | 16.06.75 | 2 | Birmingham | 23 | Apr |
| 57.09 i | Sally Evans | U23 | 14.05.75 | 3h1 | Birmingham | 3 | Feb |
| 57.5 | | | | 1 | Stoke | 23 | Jul |
| 57.2 | Lynn Gibson | | 6.07.69 | 1 | London (He) | 20 | May |
| | (90) | | | | | | |
| 57.2 | Helen Daniel | | 24.10.63 | 1 | Bromley | 23 | Jul |
| 57.22 | Lisa Thompson | | 12.07.62 | 2 | Aldershot | 26 | Jun |
| 57.28 | Emma Lindsay | | 11.04.71 | 2 | Greenock | 4 | Jun |
| 57.3 | Hayley Parry | U23 | 17.02.73 | 1 | Swansea | 19 | Jul |
| 57.3 | Sally Youden | U20 | 2.11.77 | 1 | Horsham | 30 | Jul |
| 57.3 | Emma Symonds | U20 | 5.06.77 | 3 | Norwich | 3 | Sep |
| 57.3 | Anita Pace | | 18.10.67 | 1 | Sheffield | 13 | Sep |
| 57.4 | Sue Briggs | | 26.03.67 | 2r2 | Glasgow | 6 | May |
| 57.4 | Melanie Brown | | 10.12.70 | 2 | Kingston | 22 | Jul |
| 57.4 | Lynn Taylor | | 5.08.67 | 2 | Woking | 22 | Jul |
| | (100) | | | | | | |
| 57.4 | Vicky Sterne | | 12.10.68 | 1 | Telford | 16 | Sep |
| 57.50 | Kathy Thurston | U20 | 2.01.76 | 2 | Wrexham | 5 | Aug |
| 57.5 | Claire-Marie Dillon | U23 | 1.03.73 | 1 | Nottingham | 27 | Apr |
| 57.5 | Jenny Holden | U23 | 21.09.73 | 3 | Gibraltar, GIB | 18 | Jul |

**Additional Under 17** (1 - 2 above)

| | | | | | | | |
|---|---|---|---|---|---|---|---|
| 57.8 | Amanda Pritchard | | 18.03.80 | 1 | Cardiff | 7 | Jun |
| 57.8 | Rachael Ogden | | 23.07.79 | 1 | Sheffield | 18 | Jun |
| 57.8 | Emily De Nobrega | | 23.10.78 | 1 | London (CP) | 12 | Jul |
| 58.2 | Emma Davies | | 9.10.78 | 2 | Horsham | 3 | Jun |
| 58.27 | Lindsay Impett | | 4.01.80 | 1h2 | London (He) | 6 | Aug |
| *58.4* | *Dion Graham* | | *27.09.78* | *1r2* | *Norwich* | *3* | *Jun* |
| 58.59 | Karen Gear | | 30.09.79 | 3 | London (He) | 6 | Aug |
| 58.6 | Sarah Cootes | | 3.11.78 | 1r2 | Basildon | 20 | May |
| 58.6 | Rebecca White | | 5.06.80 | 1 | Blackburn | 12 | Jul |
| | (10) | | | | | | |
| 58.8 | Sharon Hollett | | 26.12.78 | 3 | Ayr | 18 | Jul |
| 59.0 | Joanne Vaughan-Jones | | 6.09.79 | 2 | Bedford | 25 | Jun |
| 59.0 | Jade Himsworth | | 4.08.79 | 1 | Kings Lynn | 2 | Jul |
| 59.1 | Jennifer Learmouth | | 22.09.78 | 1 | Dundee | 13 | Jun |
| 59.1 | Nicola Pankhurst | | 27.09.79 | 1 | Horsham | 20 | Aug |

# 600 METRES

| | | | | | | |
|---|---|---|---|---|---|---|
| 1:26.0 + | Kelly Holmes | 19.04.70 | 2m | Gothenburg, SWE | 13 | Aug |
| 1:32.75 i | Abigail Hunte | 12.05.71 | 1 | Nenagh, IRE | 5 | Mar |
| 1:32.9 | Michelle Harries | 4.01.72 | 1 | Hayes | 12 | Jul |

## Under 13

| | | | | | | |
|---|---|---|---|---|---|---|
| 1:42.2 | Holly O'Connor | 9.12.83 | 1r1 | Kirkby | 25 | Jun |
| 1:42.26 | Ellie Childs | 26.05.83 | 1 | Barking | 14 | May |
| 1:42.5 | Catherine Roberts | 27.09.82 | 1r1 | Blackpool | 16 | Jul |
| 1:43.0 | Janet Madu | 3.02.83 | 1r1 | Derby | 25 | Jun |
| 1:43.11 | Louise Whittaker | 29.11.82 | 1r1 | Birmingham | 3 | Sep |
| 1:43.9 | Amanda Lucas | 23.05.83 | 1 | Walton | 1 | Jul |
| 1:44.2 | Francesca Doran | 5.02.83 | 1r1 | Enfield | 16 | Jul |
| 1:44.3 | Anastasia Hounslow | | 2 | Walton | 2 | Jul |
| 1:44.5 | Sarah Reeve | 16.12.82 | 1 | London (PH) | 3 | May |
| 1:44.9 | Kelly Deacon | 25.10.82 | 1 | Horsham | 14 | May |
| (10) | | | | | | |
| 1:45.0 | Minna Kane | 25.09.82 | 1 | Black Hole | 4 | Jun |
| 1:45.1 | Kerry Swyer | 2.12.82 | 1r1 | Cannock | 16 | Jul |
| 1:45.2 | Kim Wall | | 2r1 | Enfield | 16 | Jul |

# 800 METRES

| | | | | | | |
|---|---|---|---|---|---|---|
| 1:56.21 | Kelly Holmes | 19.04.70 | 2 | Monaco, MON | 9 | Sep |
| 1:56.95 | | | 3 | Gothenburg, SWE | 13 | Aug |
| 1:57.56 | | | 1 | Birmingham | 16 | Jul |
| 1:58.27 | | | 3 | Berlin, GER | 1 | Sep |
| 1:58.77 | | | 1 | London (CP) | 7 | Jul |
| 2:00.23 | | | 3h2 | Gothenburg, SWE | 10 | Aug |
| 2:00.43 | | | 1 | Helsinki, FIN | 28 | Jun |
| 2:00.78 | | | 1 | London (CP) | 27 | Aug |
| 2:01.52 | | | 2s1 | Gothenburg, SWE | 11 | Aug |
| 2:01.6 + | | | 2m | Brussels, BEL | 25 | Aug |
| 2:01.90 + | | | 1m | Sheffield | 23 | Jul |
| 2:02.36 | | | 1 | Nurmijarvi, FIN | 4 | Jun |
| 2:04.34 | | | 1 | Belle Vue, MAU | 30 | Sep |
| 2:04.5 | | | 1 | Cosford | 5 | Jul |
| 2:04.56 | | | 1h1 | Birmingham | 15 | Jul |
| 2:01.67 | Sonya Bowyer | 18.09.72 | 4 | Villeneuve d'Ascq, FRA | 24 | Jun |
| 2:02.60 | | | 10 | London (CP) | 7 | Jul |
| 2:04.43 | | | 2 | Aarhus, DEN | 29 | Jun |
| 2:04.53 | | | 8 | Moscow,RUS | 5 | Jun |
| 2:04.83 i | | | 2 | Glasgow | 11 | Feb |
| 2:01.94 | Ann Griffiths | 20.08.65 | 3 | Gateshead | 21 | Aug |
| 2:02.12 | | | 6 | Copenhagen, DEN | 23 | Aug |
| 2:03.3 mx | | | 2 | Stretford | 1 | Aug |
| 2:04.03 | | | 6 | London (CP) | 27 | Aug |
| 2:04.9 mx | | | | Stretford | 19 | Jul |
| 2:02.47 | Abigail Hunte | 12.05.71 | 3 | Birmingham | 16 | Jul |
| 2:04.25 | | | 5 | Gateshead | 21 | Aug |
| 2:04.26 | | | 1h4 | Birmingham | 15 | Jul |
| 2:04.97 i | | | 1 | Vienna, AUT | 18 | Feb |
| 2:02.69 | Natalie Tait | 24.08.72 | 4 | Birmingham | 16 | Jul |
| 2:03.2 | | | 1 | Woking | 16 | Aug |
| 2:03.32 | | | 3 | Fukuoka, JAP | 31 | Aug |
| 2:03.79 | | | 6 | Helsinki, FIN | 28 | Jun |
| 2:04.31 | | | 2h4 | Birmingham | 15 | Jul |
| 2:04.50 | | | 1 | Tallinn, EST | 9 | Jul |
| 2:03.8 mx | Mary Kitson | 2.04.63 | 1 | London (TB) | 5 | Jul |
| 2:06.36 | | | 2h1 | Birmingham | 15 | Jul |
| 2:04.42 | Vickie Lawrence U23 | 9.06.73 | 4 | Rieti, ITA | 5 | Sep |
| 2:04.77 | | | 6 | Gateshead | 21 | Aug |
| 2:04.8 mx | | | | Stretford | 1 | Aug |
| 2:04.8 mx | Jacqui Parker | 15.10.66 | 2 | Perth, AUS | 25 | Jan |
| 2:06.44 | | | 3 | Khania, GRE | 4 | Jun |

42 performances to 2:05.0 by 8 athletes including 2 indoors

| 2:05.22 | Paula Radcliffe | U23 | 17.12.73 | 5 | Birmingham | 16 Jul |
|---|---|---|---|---|---|---|
| 2:05.3 | Michelle Faherty | | 10.08.68 | 1 | Stretford | 5 Sep |
| (10) | | | | | | |
| 2:05.41 | Angela Davies | | 21.10.70 | 2 | Fukuoka, JAP | 26 Aug |
| 2:05.64 | Mary McClung | | 19.02.71 | 1 | Tuscaloosa, USA | 23 Apr |
| 2:05.96 | Helen Daniel | | 24.10.63 | 2 | Celje, SLO | 16 Jun |
| 2:06.1 | Vicky Sterne | | 12.10.68 | 2 | Stretford | 5 Sep |
| 2:06.16 | Bev Hartigan | | 10.06.67 | 2 | Crawley | 27 May |
| 2:06.29 | Dawn Gandy | | 28.07.65 | 3 | Sydney, AUS | 5 Mar |
| 2:06.66 | Lynn Gibson | | 6.07.69 | 2 | Cwmbran | 9 Jul |
| 2:07.06 | Alyson Layzell | | 16.12.66 | 4 | Cwmbran | 9 Jul |
| 2:07.1 | Linda Keough/Staines | | 26.12.63 | 1 | Watford | 9 Aug |
| 2:07.15 | Michelle Wilkinson | U23 | 1.01.73 | 4 | London (CP) | 27 Aug |
| (20) | | | | | | |
| 2:07.19 | Paula Fryer | | 14.07.69 | 4h4 | Birmingham | 15 Jul |
| 2:07.44 | Lisa Thompson | | 12.07.62 | 4h1 | Birmingham | 15 Jul |
| 2:07.46 | Christa Salt | | 17.06.64 | 3 | Neufeld, SWZ | 16 Sep |
| 2:07.79 | Una English | | 14.08.70 | 2 | Zurich, SWZ | 17 Sep |
| 2:07.80 | Michelle Harries | | 4.01.72 | 1 | Jona, SWZ | 23 Jul |
| 2:07.83 | Sue Parker | | 24.03.70 | 2 | Gateshead | 17 Jun |
| 2:07.9 | Lynn Taylor | | 5.08.67 | 1 | Horsham | 9 Jul |
| 2:08.0 | Debbie Gunning | | 31.08.65 | 1 | Andover | 12 Aug |
| 2:08.2 | Sarah Bentley | | 21.05.67 | 1 | London (WL) | 30 Jul |
| 2:08.27 | Sharon King | | 27.01.72 | 4 | Crawley | 27 May |
| (30) | | | | | | |
| 2:08.33 | Joanna Latimer | | 30.01.71 | 2 | Gateshead | 2 Jul |
| 2:08.37 | Claire Raven | | 15.06.72 | 3 | Gateshead | 2 Jul |
| 2:08.51 i | Catherine Allsopp | U23 | 30.11.73 | 6h2 | Indianapolis, USA | 10 Mar |
| 2:12.02 | | | | 7 | Loughborough | 11 Jun |
| 2:08.59 i | Jeina Mitchell | U23 | 21.01.75 | 5 | Vienna, AUT | 18 Feb |
| 2:09.62 | | | | 2 | Tessenderlo, BEL | 2 Jul |
| 2:08.65 | Shirley Griffiths | | 23.06.72 | 1 | Gateshead | 12 Aug |
| 2:08.73 | Maria Carville | U23 | 8.12.73 | 6h1 | Birmingham | 15 Jul |
| 2:08.78 | Rachael Ogden | U17 | 23.07.79 | 4 | Loughborough | 11 Jun |
| 2:08.8 | Dorothea Lee | U20 | 28.07.77 | 1 | Birmingham | 20 Aug |
| 2:09.05 | Jillian Jones | | 23.12.69 | 6 | Crawley | 27 May |
| 2:09.07 | Hayley Parry | U23 | 17.02.73 | 5 | Loughborough | 11 Jun |
| (40) | | | | | | |
| 2:09.12 i | Cathy Dawson | | 9.03.66 | 4 | Birmingham | 28 Jan |
| 2:09.35 | Ellen O'Hare | U20 | 4.02.78 | 2h3 | Bath | 11 Jul |
| 2:09.4 | Vicki Andrews | | 31.08.69 | 2 | Watford | 9 Aug |
| 2:09.5 | Maxine Newman | | 15.12.70 | 1 | Enfield | 30 Jul |
| 2:09.5 | Debbie France | | 16.10.65 | 3 | Blackpool | 20 Aug |
| 2:09.7 | Amanda Thorpe | | 21.07.71 | 3 | Stretford | 27 Jun |
| 2:10.0 | Rhonda MacPhee | U20 | 30.04.76 | 2 | Manchester | 17 May |
| 2:10.2 | Wendy Steele | | 7.01.66 | 1 | Inverness | 13 Aug |
| 2:10.25 | | | | 2 | Edinburgh | 6 Aug |
| 2:10.3 | Suzanne Guise | | 3.02.62 | 3 | Stoke | 9 Sep |
| 2:10.37 | Sue Bevan | V35 | 15.12.59 | 2 | Aldershot | 23 Jul |
| (50) | | | | | | |
| 2:10.5 | Julie Cruse | | 20.01.68 | 2 | Croydon | 14 May |
| 2:10.5 | Kerry Smithson | U20 | 13.09.76 | 2 | Stretford | 22 Aug |
| 2:10.80 | Jane Groves | U20 | 17.05.77 | 1 | Nottingham | 8 Jul |
| 2:10.8 | Jenny Harnett | U20 | 11.03.76 | 4 | Manchester | 17 May |
| 2:10.81 | Ann Terek | | 22.09.64 | 1 | Stoke | 10 Sep |
| 2:10.87 | Nicola Andrews | | 11.06.70 | 7h1 | Birmingham | 15 Jul |
| 2:10.9 | Janet Holt | V35 | 10.10.56 | 2 | Glasgow | 6 May |
| 2:10.96 | Emma Davies | U17 | 9.10.78 | 3 | Aldershot | 23 Jul |
| 2:11.0 | Amanda Tremble | U20 | 2.11.76 | 1 | Gateshead | 30 Jul |
| 2:11.0 | Helen Pattinson | U23 | 2.01.74 | 3 | Stretford | 22 Aug |
| (60) | | | | | | |

| | | | | | | | |
|---|---|---|---|---|---|---|---|
| 2:11.1 | Julie Swann | | 15.07.62 | 2 | Cheltenham | 6 | Aug |
| 2:11.1 | Sarah Bull | U23 | 4.06.75 | 3 | Birmingham (Un) | 20 | Aug |
| 2:11.2 | Claire Entwistle | U20 | 9.12.76 | 4 | Stretford | 22 | Aug |
| 2:11.29 | Alison Parry | | 19.06.66 | 5 | Cwmbran | 9 | Jul |
| 2:11.30 | Claire Brook | V35 | 13.03.60 | 4 | Antrim | 28 | May |
| 2:11.3 mx | Joanne Colleran | | 1.09.72 | 4 | Stretford | 18 | Jul |
| 2:11.38 | Zoe Peatfield | U20 | 8.12.77 | 2 | Nottingham | 8 | Jul |
| 2:11.4 | Michelle Mann | U20 | 6.02.77 | 5 | Stretford | 22 | Aug |
| 2:11.4 | Sarah Bouchard | U23 | 23.10.74 | 6 | Stretford | 22 | Aug |
| 2:11.60 | Hayley Parkinson | U23 | 5.12.75 | 3 | Edinburgh | 6 | Aug |
| (70) | | | | | | | |
| 2:11.8 | Pauline Quinn | | 2.08.70 | 2 | Belfast | 19 | Jul |
| 2:11.9 | Rachel Jordan | | 29.01.72 | 3 | Glasgow | 6 | May |
| 2:11.94 | Candy Perkins | | 26.02.71 | 3 | Stoke | 10 | Sep |
| 2:12.03 | Jayne Puckeridge | | 23.10.71 | 6 | London (CP) | 18 | Jun |
| 2:12.06 + | Yvonne Murray | | 4.10.64 | m | Birmingham | 16 | Jul |
| 2:12.08 i | Angela Coates | | 2.04.67 | 3h1 | Birmingham | 3 | Feb |
| 2:12.09 | Christina Bourne | | 24.09.69 | 4 | Stoke | 10 | Sep |
| 2:12.2 | Colette Kaufman | | 30.09.63 | 4 | Derby | 30 | Jul |
| 2:12.28 | Karen Johns | U17 | 18.08.80 | 3 | Nottingham | 8 | Jul |
| 2:12.3 | Sharon Orridge | | 7.03.66 | 3 | Enfield | 30 | Jul |
| (80) | | | | | | | |
| 2:12.5 | Liz Talbot | U23 | 5.12.74 | 1 | Bromley | 20 | May |
| 2:12.5 | Elinor Doubell | | 27.09.71 | 1 | Liverpool | 2 | Jul |
| 2:12.64 | Susan Hendry | U20 | 30.06.76 | 3 | Edinburgh | 24 | Jun |
| 2:12.7 | Laura McCabe | U17 | 24.01.80 | 1 | Stretford | 22 | Aug |
| 2:12.72 | Charlotte Goff | U20 | 6.07.77 | 4 | Nottingham | 8 | Jul |
| 2:12.77 | Diana Bennett | U23 | 14.06.74 | 5 | Stoke | 10 | Sep |
| 2:12.8 | Christine Amede | | 7.08.63 | 1 | Nottingham | 25 | Jun |
| 2:12.8 | Vyvyan Rhodes | U23 | 5.05.73 | 1r2 | Derby | 6 | Aug |
| 2:12.9 | Amanda Pritchard | U17 | 18.03.80 | 2 | Cardiff | 24 | Jun |

**Additional Under 17** (1 - 5 above)

| | | | | | | |
|---|---|---|---|---|---|---|
| 2:13.48 | Emily Hathaway | 22.12.79 | 4 | Nottingham | 8 | Jul |
| 2:14.07 | Jade Himsworth | 4.08.79 | 3h3 | Nottingham | 7 | Jul |
| 2:14.07 | Simone Hardy | 9.11.79 | 1 | Stoke | 5 | Aug |
| 2:14.1 | Jennifer Ward | 22.09.78 | 2 | Ayr | 18 | Jul |
| 2:15.2 | Francesca Green | 10.02.80 | 1 | Hoo | 10 | Jun |
| (10) | | | | | | |
| 2:15.36 | Kate Doherty | 23.07.79 | 6 | Nottingham | 8 | Jul |
| 2:15.47 | Karen Montador | 14.05.79 | 1 | Grangemouth | 14 | May |
| 2:15.8 | Hayley Griffin | 20.07.80 | 1 | Watford | 19 | Jul |
| 2:16.0 | Amber Gascoigne | 5.09.79 | 1 | Bath | 31 | May |
| 2:16.2 | Laura Hale | 21.01.80 | 1 | Cheltenham | 17 | Jun |
| 2:16.28 | Sarah Corlett | 28.05.79 | 3h2 | Nottingham | 7 | Jul |
| 2:16.5 | Sarah Fensome | 28.09.79 | 1 | Watford | 28 | Jun |
| 2:16.63 | Claire McCarthy | 6.11.79 | 2h3 | Birmingham | 30 | Jul |
| 2:16.8 | Georgie Salmon | 1.11.79 | 1 | Yate | 13 | May |
| 2:16.8 | Liz Canwell | 25.12.78 | 2 | Leeds | 30 | May |
| (20) | | | | | | |
| 2:16.94 | Suzanne Owen | 5.05.79 | 4h3 | Nottingham | 7 | Jul |

**Under 15**

| | | | | | | |
|---|---|---|---|---|---|---|
| 2:14.0 | Emma Ward | 2.01.82 | 1 | Cannock | 16 | Jul |
| 2:14.88 | Jennifer Meadows | 17.04.81 | 1 | Nottingham | 8 | Jul |
| 2:15.49 | Carley Wilson | 6.12.81 | 2 | Nottingham | 8 | Jul |
| 2:15.6 | Michelle Whalley | 1.10.80 | 1 | Blackpool | 16 | Jul |
| 2:15.8 | Jennifer Grogan | 7.09.80 | 1 | Hayes | 30 | Apr |
| 2:15.86 | Nikki Daniels | 25.08.82 | 3 | Nottingham | 8 | Jul |
| 2:16.30 | Suzanne Hasler | 7.04.82 | 2 | Birmingham | 29 | Jul |
| 2:17.4 | Anna Lomas | 28.09.80 | 2 | Birmingham | 30 | Apr |

| 2:17.5 | Sharon Whitby | | 29.09.80 | 1 | Barn Elms | 10 | Sep |
| 2:17.67 | Amanda Child | | 28.11.81 | 1 | London (CP) | 28 | May |
| (10) | | | | | | | |
| 2:17.69 | Louise Neville | | 18.09.80 | 5 | Nottingham | 8 | Jul |
| 2:17.75 | Tanya Brazier | | 14.11.80 | 3 | Birmingham | 29 | Jul |
| 2:17.96 | Bella Clayton | | 29.01.81 | 3 | London (CP) | 28 | May |
| 2:18.1 | Lyndsey Vernon | | 24.11.80 | 2 | Blackpool | 16 | Jul |
| 2:18.1 | Nichola Coates | | 24.03.82 | 1 | Scunthorpe | 28 | Aug |
| 2:18.23 | Ros Grant | | 18.06.81 | 6 | Nottingham | 8 | Jul |
| 2:18.9 | Kamila Braithwaite | | 26.01.81 | 2 | Hayes | 30 | Apr |
| 2:18.9 | Angela Dent | | 24.12.80 | 1 | Hull | 2 | Jul |
| 2:18.91 i | Donna Porazinski | | 29.01.81 | 1h3 | Birmingham | 18 | Feb |

**Under 13**

| 2:22.8 | Samantha Cochrane-Dyet | | 17.10.82 | 1 | Exeter | 2 | Sep |
| 2:23.7 | Joanne Bradford | | 22.03.83 | 1 | Blackpool | 10 | Sep |
| 2:24.2 | Louise Whittaker | | 29.11.82 | 3 | Wakefield | 6 | Aug |
| 2:24.39 | Iona McIntyre | | 14.03.83 | 1 | Edinburgh | 10 | Sep |
| 2:24.4 | Kelly Deacon | | 25.10.82 | | | | |
| 2:25.1 | Viktoria Boyle | | 1.05.83 | 1 | Oldham | 30 | Jul |
| 2:25.4 | Sarah Reeve | | 16.12.82 | 1 | Watford | 14 | May |
| 2:25.5 | Lorraine McAuley | | 9.06.83 | 1 | Wishaw | 3 | Sep |
| 2:26.2 | Minna Kane | | 25.09.82 | 2 | Oldham | 30 | Jul |
| 2:26.4 | Catherine Roberts | | 27.09.82 | 1 | Bebington | 10 | Jun |
| (10) | | | | | | | |
| 2:26.5 | Lorna King | | 22.01.83 | 1 | Solihull | 10 | Sep |
| 2:26.8 | Alice MacGregor | | 3.10.82 | 2 | Blackpool | 10 | Sep |
| 2:27.0 | Holly O'Connor | | 9.12.83 | 1 | Kirkby | 10 | Sep |
| 2:27.8 | Amanda Lucas | | 23.05.83 | 1 | Walton | 24 | Jun |
| 2:27.8 | Claire Rhodes | | 25.01.83 | 1 | Wakefield | 17 | Sep |
| 2:27.95 | Stephanie Cooper | | 16.09.82 | 2 | Peterborough | 28 | Aug |

# 1000 METRES

| 2:32.82 | Kelly Holmes | | 19.04.70 | 1 | Sheffield | 23 | Jul |
| | 2:33.18 | | | 3 | Brussels, BEL | 25 | Aug |
| 2:39.74 | Ann Griffiths | | 20.08.65 | 4 | Sheffield | 23 | Jul |
| 2:40.28 | Natalie Tait | | 24.08.72 | 5 | Sheffield | 23 | Jul |
| 2:40.81 | Sue Parker | | 24.03.70 | 6 | Sheffield | 23 | Jul |
| 2:43.57 | Michelle Faherty | | 10.08.68 | 7 | Sheffield | 23 | Jul |
| 2:44.81 | Vickie Lawrence | U23 | 9.06.73 | 6 | Zurich, SWZ | 16 | Aug |
| 2:45.34 | Michelle Wilkinson | U23 | 1.01.73 | 8 | Sheffield | 23 | Jul |
| 2:47.22 | Christa Salt | | 17.06.64 | 1 | Ettelbruck, SWZ | 9 | Sep |
| 2:48.11 | Karen Hargrave | | 23.09.65 | 1 | Beaupreau, FRA | 13 | May |

# 1500 METRES

| 4:03.04 | Kelly Holmes | | 19.04.70 | 2 | Gothenburg, SWE | 9 | Aug |
| | 4:04.20 | | | 1 | Gateshead | 2 | Jul |
| | 4:07.02 | | | 1 | Villeneuve d'Ascq, FRA | 25 | Jun |
| | 4:09.15 | | | 2s1 | Gothenburg, SWE | 7 | Aug |
| | 4:10.98 | | | 1 | Villeneuve d'Ascq, FRA | 17 | Jun |
| | 4:11.87 | | | 2h1 | Gothenburg, SWE | 6 | Aug |
| 4:05.61 | Yvonne Murray | | 4.10.64 | 3 | Gateshead | 2 | Jul |
| | 4:11.47 | | | 1 | Birmingham | 16 | Jul |
| 4:06.58 | Alison Wyeth | | 26.05.64 | 6 | Monaco, MON | 25 | Jul |
| | 4:08.56 | | | 5 | Gateshead | 2 | Jul |
| | 4:12.67 | | | 3 | Villeneuve d'Ascq, FRA | 17 | Jun |
| | 4:16.1 | | | 1 | Watford | 14 | Jun |
| 4:06.84 | Paula Radcliffe | U23 | 17.12.73 | 4 | Gateshead | 2 | Jul |
| | 4:11.91 | | | 1 | Dijon, FRA | 28 | May |
| 4:11.96 | Bev Hartigan | | 10.06.67 | 6 | Nuremberg, GER | 15 | Jun |

| | | | | | | |
|---|---|---|---|---|---|---|
| *4:12.44* | *Nnenna Lynch* | | *3.07.71* | *8* | *Rhede, GER* | *30 Jul* |
| 4:12.8 mx | Angela Davies | | 21.10.70 | 1 | Watford | 9 Aug |
| | 4:15.05 | | | 3h2 | Fukuoka, JAP | 2 Sep |
| | 4:16.75 | | | 7 | Fukuoka, JAP | 3 Sep |
| 4:12.9 mx | Amanda Thorpe | | 21.07.71 | 4 | Stretford | 5 Sep |
| | 4:25.92 | | | 4 | Cwmbran | 9 Jul |
| 4:13.26 | Una English | | 14.08.70 | 8 | Nuremberg, GER | 15 Jun |
| | 4:16.37 | | | 3 | Birmingham | 16 Jul |
| 4:13.36 | Sue Parker | | 24.03.70 | 3 | Gateshead | 21 Aug |
| 4:14.42 | Debbie Gunning | | 31.08.65 | 2 | Birmingham | 16 Jul |
| | 4:14.55 | | | 4 | Gateshead | 21 Aug |
| | 4:16.89 | | | 3 | Kvarnsveden, SWE | 28 Jul |
| (10) | | | | | | |
| 4:14.74 i | Ann Griffiths | | 20.08.65 | 1 | Birmingham | 28 Jan |
| 4:15.83 | Karen Hargrave | | 23.09.65 | 6 | Paris, FRA | 23 Jul |
| 4:16.2 | Lynn Gibson | | 6.07.69 | 1 | Southampton | 13 Jun |

29 performances to 4:17.0 by 13 athletes including 1 indoors

| | | | | | | |
|---|---|---|---|---|---|---|
| 4:17.22 | Sonia McGeorge | | 2.11.64 | 1 | Loughborough | 11 Jun |
| 4:17.9 | Natalie Tait | | 24.08.72 | 1 | London (WL) | 30 Jul |
| 4:18.30 | Michelle Faherty | | 10.08.68 | 3 | Loughborough | 11 Jun |
| 4:19.09 | Liz Talbot | U23 | 5.12.74 | 4 | Loughborough | 11 Jun |
| *4:20.18* | *Jill Bruce* | *U23* | *25.07.73* | *3* | *Kevelaar, HOL* | *3 Jun* |
| 4:20.84 i | Shirley Griffiths | | 23.06.72 | 3 | Birmingham | 4 Feb |
| | 4:33.01 | | | 3 | Gateshead | 17 Jun |
| 4:22.1 mx | Sonya Bowyer | | 18.09.72 | 3 | Stretford | 1 Aug |
| | 4:24.79 | | | 1 | Gateshead | 17 Jun |
| 4:22.49 | Sharon King | | 27.01.72 | 6 | Loughborough | 11 Jun |
| (20) | | | | | | |
| 4:22.51 | Sarah Bentley | | 21.05.67 | 3 | Cwmbran | 9 Jul |
| 4:22.70 | Amanda Tremble | U20 | 2.11.76 | 1 | Belfort, FRA | 6 Aug |
| 4:23.1 | Ann Terek | | 22.09.64 | 1 | Cardiff | 22 Ju |
| 4:24.1 | Andrea Whitcombe | | 8.06.71 | 1 | Harrow | 25 Jun |
| 4:24.55 | Jillian Jones | | 23.12.69 | 3 | London (CP) | 7 Jul |
| 4:24.7 mx | Michelle Mann | U20 | 6.02.77 | 6 | Stretford | 1 Aug |
| | 4:28.7 | | | 2 | Stretford | 6 Jun |
| 4:24.86 | Michelle Harries | | 4.01.72 | 6 | Treviso, ITA | 2 Sep |
| 4:25.37 i | Caroline Slimin | | 27.08.65 | 1 | Birmingham | 26 Feb |
| 4:25.51 | Hayley Parry | U23 | 17.02.73 | 5 | Narbonne, FRA | 29 Jul |
| 4:25.56 | Maxine Newman | | 15.12.70 | 1 | Birmingham | 23 Apr |
| (30) | | | | | | |
| 4:25.80 i | Alyson Layzell | | 16.12.66 | 5 | Birmingham | 4 Feb |
| 4:25.96 | Juliette Oldfield | U20 | 14.04.77 | 7 | Nyiregyhaza, HUN | 30 Jul |
| 4:26.18 | Christa Salt | | 17.06.64 | 1 | Dudelange, LUX | 5 Jul |
| 4:26.5 | Zahara Hyde | | 12.01.63 | 1 | Crawley | 25 Jun |
| 4:26.71 | Catherine Allsopp | U23 | 30.11.73 | 3 | Stanford, USA | 25 Mar |
| 4:27.1 mx | Helen Daniel | | 24.10.63 | 2 | Watford | 9 Aug |
| 4:27.2 | Lynne Robinson | | 21.06.69 | 1 | Solihull | 31 May |
| 4:27.4 mx | Gabby Collison | | 10.02.66 | 3 | Watford | 9 Aug |
| | 4:29.3 | | | 1 | Horsham | 9 Jul |
| *4:27.59* | *Edwige Pitel* | | *4.06.67* | *3* | *Paris, FRA* | *21 May* |
| 4:27.6 | Carolina Weatherill | | 13.05.68 | 4 | London (He) | 1 Jul |
| 4:27.7 | Helen Pattinson | U23 | 2.01.74 | 3 | Manchester | 17 May |
| (40) | | | | | | |
| 4:27.74 | Catherine Berry | U23 | 8.10.75 | 3 | Tessenderlo, BEL | 2 Jul |
| 4:27.92 | Vicky Sterne | | 12.10.68 | 5 | London (CP) | 7 Jul |
| 4:28.1 | Ellen O'Hare | U20 | 4.02.78 | 2 | Loughborough | 21 Jun |
| 4:28.2 | Valerie Bothams | U23 | 19.03.75 | 2 | Solihull | 31 May |
| 4:28.46 | Jo Davis | U23 | 20.09.73 | 6 | London (CP) | 7 Jul |
| 4:28.6 | Wendy Farrow | | 25.12.71 | 3 | Solihull | 31 May |
| 4:28.67 | Sheila Fairweather | U20 | 24.11.77 | 3 | Belfort, FRA | 6 Aug |
| 4:28.77 | Julie Swann | | 15.07.62 | 7 | London (CP) | 7 Jul |

| | | | | | | | |
|---|---|---|---|---|---|---|---|
| 4:28.9 | Louise Watson | | 13.12.71 | 3 | Loughborough | 21 | Jun |
| 4:29.09 | Teena Colebrook | V35 | 18.12.56 | 5 | Walnut, USA | 15 | Apr |
| | (50) | | | | | | |
| 4:29.3 | Penny Thackray | U23 | 18.08.74 | | Sheffield | 15 | Sep |
| 4:29.38 | Elinor Doubell | | 27.09.71 | 8 | London (CP) | 7 | Jul |
| 4:29.56 | Pauline Quinn | | 2.08.70 | 2 | Edinburgh | 24 | Jun |
| 4:29.92 | Adele Rankin | | 27.05.72 | 6 | Knoxville, USA | 7 | Apr |
| 4:30.08 | Ruth Carney | | 12.10.68 | | Dublin (M), IRE | 16 | Jul |
| 4:30.43 | Rachel Wallace | U23 | 7.11.74 | 2 | Blackpool | 20 | Aug |
| 4:31.1 | Alice Braham | U20 | 17.01.76 | 1 | Harrow | 9 | Jul |
| 4:31.6 | Janet Holt | V35 | 10.10.56 | 1 | Glasgow | 6 | May |
| 4:31.7 | Rhonda MacPhee | U20 | 30.04.76 | 1 | Dartford | 22 | Apr |
| 4:31.9 | Vickie Lawrence | U23 | 9.06.73 | 1 | Liverpool | 6 | Aug |
| | (60) | | | | | | |
| 4:31.99 | Jenny Harnett | U20 | 11.03.76 | 9 | London (CP) | 7 | Jul |
| 4:32.0 mx | Joanne Colleran | | 1.09.72 | 10 | Stretford | 1 | Aug |
| 4:32.37 | Tommy Kemp | U17 | 5.03.80 | 2 | Colwyn Bay | 15 | Jul |
| 4:32.4 | Julie Mitchell | U23 | 3.10.74 | 1 | Carshalton | 17 | Sep |
| 4:32.69 i | Lisa Carthew | | 6.04.71 | 4 | Birmingham | 26 | Feb |
| 4:33.0 | Liz Francis/Thomas | | 22.12.63 | 5 | Manchester | 17 | May |
| 4:33.0 | Alicia Hill | | 10.12.67 | 1 | Bebington | 11 | Jun |
| 4:33.01 | Sue Ridley | | 25.10.65 | 3 | Edinburgh | 24 | Jun |
| 4:33.07 | Andrea Duke | U23 | 6.07.73 | 4 | Gateshead | 17 | Jun |
| 4:33.7 | Angela Joiner | | 14.02.69 | 2 | Loughborough | 20 | May |
| | (70) | | | | | | |
| 4:33.8 | Karen Nicol | U20 | 1.11.77 | 3 | Stretford | 6 | Jun |

**Additional Under 17** (1 above)

| | | | | | | | |
|---|---|---|---|---|---|---|---|
| 4:34.6 | Clare Duncan | | 22.08.79 | 4 | Stretford | 6 | Jun |
| 4:35.4 mx | Karen Montador | | 14.05.79 | 6 | Grangemouth | 7 | Jun |
| | 4:35.61 | | | 3 | Colwyn Bay | 15 | Jul |
| 4:36.98 | Laura Hale | | 21.01.80 | 1 | Nottingham | 8 | Jul |
| 4:39.02 | Camilla Waite | | 24.05.80 | 3 | Nottingham | 8 | Jul |
| 4:39.1 | Rachel Felton | | 27.06.79 | 1 | Watford | 13 | Sep |
| 4:39.4 | Claire Demaine | | 6.09.78 | 1 | Stretford | 22 | Aug |
| 4:39.9 | Georgie Salmon | | 1.11.79 | 1 | Millfield | 8 | May |
| 4:40.0 | Rachael Ogden | | 23.07.79 | 1 | Hull | 7 | May |
| 4:40.09 | Katie Wallace | | 19.09.78 | 1 | Portsmouth | 13 | May |
| | (10) | | | | | | |
| 4:40.4 | Jackie Hogan | | 19.03.80 | 1 | Mandale | 9 | Apr |
| 4:40.48 | Emma Davies | | 9.10.78 | 2 | Portsmouth | 13 | May |
| 4:40.64 | Sonia Thomas | | 16.05.79 | 2 | Blackpool | 20 | Aug |
| 4:40.85 | Hayley Whitehead | | 14.05.79 | 4 | Nottingham | 8 | Jul |
| 4:40.9 | Heather Carson | | 18.07.79 | 1 | Blackpool | 16 | Jul |
| 4:41.2 | Amber Gascoigne | | 5.09.79 | 1 | Yeovil | 14 | May |
| 4:41.3 | Paula Whitney | | 21.03.79 | 3 | Bolton | 23 | Jul |
| 4:41.37 | Katie Dennison | | 8.06.80 | 4 | Birmingham | 29 | Jul |
| 4:41.77 | Louise Rowe | | 8.11.78 | 2 | London (CP) | 28 | May |
| 4:42.04 | Emma Alberts | | 22.11.79 | 1 | Sheffield | 27 | May |
| | (20) | | | | | | |
| 4:42.59 | Justina Heslop | | 3.03.79 | 2 | Sheffield | 27 | May |
| 4:42.8 | Kate Grimshaw | | 26.10.79 | 1 | Leeds | 16 | May |
| 4:43.46 i | Jennifer Ward | | 22.09.78 | 1 | Glasgow | 4 | Feb |
| | 4:43.6 | | | 1 | Pitreavie | 9 | Apr |
| 4:44.15 | Alexandra Carter | | 1.04.80 | 1h1 | Birmingham | 29 | Jul |
| 4:44.2 | Susannah Rutherford | | 26.02.79 | 1 | Middlesbrough | 27 | Jun |
| 4:44.32 | Clare Thomas | | 26.08.79 | 1 | Cardiff | 1 | Jul |
| 4:44.4 | Caroline Walsh | | 29.04.80 | 1 | London (He) | 10 | Jun |
| 4:44.43 | Kate Doherty | | 23.07.79 | 1 | Stoke | 28 | May |
| 4:44.64 | Michelle Harris | | 26.10.79 | 3h2 | Birmingham | 29 | Jul |
| 4:44.83 | Simone Hardy | | 9.11.79 | 2 | Stoke | 28 | May |
| 4:44.92 | Susan McNairney | | 22.02.79 | 2 | Pitreavie | 8 | Jul |

## Under 15

| | | | | | | | |
|---|---|---|---|---|---|---|---|
| 4:37.16 | Emma Ward | 2.01.82 | 1 | Nottingham | 8 | Jul |
| 4:37.7 | Nichola Coates | 24.03.82 | 1 | Newcastle | 10 | Jun |
| 4:39.95 | Michelle Whalley | 1.10.80 | 3 | Nottingham | 8 | Jul |
| 4:41.22 | Jodie Swallow | 23.06.81 | 4 | Nottingham | 8 | Jul |
| 4:41.67 | Tanya Brazier | 14.11.80 | 5 | Nottingham | 8 | Jul |
| 4:41.82 | Helen Pearson | 8.02.81 | 6 | Nottingham | 8 | Jul |
| 4:42.0 | Anna Lomas | 28.09.80 | 1 | Stretford | 1 | Aug |
| 4:42.74 | Emily Giles | 31.10.80 | 7 | Nottingham | 8 | Jul |
| 4:43.46 | Hannah Norman | 1.06.81 | 1 | Edinburgh | 10 | Sep |
| 4:43.99 | Jenny Mockler | 28.04.82 | 8 | Nottingham | 8 | Jul |
| (10) | | | | | | |
| 4:45.64 | Jeanette Shorthall | 9.09.80 | 3 | Blackpool | 20 | Aug |
| 4:47.0 | Jennifer Cliff | 9.05.81 | 1 | Basildon | 16 | Jul |
| 4:48.30 | Emma Rutland | 9.10.81 | 4 | Blackpool | 20 | Aug |
| 4:48.5 | Carley Wilson | 6.12.81 | 1 | Middlesbrough | 14 | May |
| 4:48.60 | Donna Brown | 1.05.81 | 1h2 | Birmingham | 30 | Jul |
| 4:49.9 | Ros Grant | 18.06.81 | 1 | Kingston | 24 | Jun |
| 4:50.1 | Charlotte Fearn | 26.11.80 | 1 | Basildon | 16 | Jul |

## Under 13

| | | | | | | | |
|---|---|---|---|---|---|---|---|
| 4:54.8 | Gemma Viney | 7.01.83 | 1 | Barn Elms | 20 | May |
| 4:57.5 | Samantha Cochrane-Dyet | 17.10.82 | 1 | Basingstoke | 22 | Jul |
| 4:57.8 | Louise Whittaker | 29.11.82 | 1 | Solihull | 10 | Sep |
| 4:58.3 | Sarah Raven | 22.11.82 | 1 | Grantham | 1 | Jul |
| 5:01.5 | Kelly Deacon | 25.10.82 | | | | |
| 5:01.9 | Layla Hall | 1.12.82 | | London (He) | 20 | May |
| 5:02.9 | Lorna King | 22.01.83 | 2 | London (TB) | 30 | Jul |
| 5:03.0 | Gemma Taylor | 18.09.82 | 1 | York | 2 | Jul |
| 5:03.3 | Helen Armitage | 13.12.82 | 1 | Middlesbrough | 27 | Jun |
| 5:04.0 | Kimberley Read | 31.12.82 | 2 | Newcastle | 7 | May |
| (10) | | | | | | |
| 5:04.5 | Lucie Michaelson | 18.04.83 | 5 | Bebington | 10 | Jun |
| 5:06.4 | Michelle Hudson | 11.11.82 | 2 | Jarrow | 5 | Aug |
| 5:07.0 | Catherine Terry | 17.11.82 | | Bebington | 10 | Jun |
| 5:07.1 | Stephanie Cooper | 16.09.82 | | Walton | 20 | May |
| 5:07.2 | Helen Lister | 6.08.83 | 1 | Middlesbrough | 7 | May |
| 5:07.2 | Kerry Thomas | 5.12.82 | 2 | Liverpool | 14 | May |
| 5:07.4 | Amanda Lucas | 23.05.83 | 1 | London (WL) | 22 | Jul |

## 1 MILE

| | | | | | | | |
|---|---|---|---|---|---|---|---|
| 4:28.93 | Paula Radcliffe | U23 | 17.12.73 | 9 | Cologne, GER | 18 | Aug |
| 4:35.89 | Angela Davies | | 21.10.70 | 2 | Cork, IRE | 24 | Jun |
| *4:37.34* | *Jill Bruce* | *U23* | *25.07.73* | *4* | *Cork, IRE* | *24* | *Jun* |
| 4:37.52 | Sue Parker | | 24.03.70 | 5 | Cork, IRE | 24 | Jun |
| 4:38.64 | Michelle Faherty | | 10.08.68 | 6 | Cork, IRE | 24 | Jun |
| 4:48.72 i | Catherine Allsopp | U23 | 30.11.73 | 2 | Ames, USA | 10 | Mar |
| 4:48.88 | Hayley Parry | U23 | 17.02.73 | 9 | Cork, IRE | 24 | Jun |
| 4:50.21 | Josie Gray | U20 | 6.03.76 | 10 | Cork, IRE | 24 | Jun |
| 4:52.58 | Liz Francis/Thomas | | 22.12.63 | 12 | Cork, IRE | 24 | Jun |

## 2000 METRES

| | | | | | | | |
|---|---|---|---|---|---|---|---|
| 5:46.1 + | Paula Radcliffe | U23 | 17.12.73 | 3m | Zurich, SWZ | 16 | Aug |
| | 5:50.6 + | | | 2m | London (CP) | 27 | Aug |
| | 5:50.6 + | | | 2m | Monaco, MON | 9 | Sep |
| 5:46.3 + | Yvonne Murray | | 4.10.64 | 2m | Zurich, SWZ | 16 | Aug |
| | 5:50.7 + | | | 3m | London (CP) | 27 | Aug |
| | 5:50.7 + | | | 3m | Monaco, MON | 9 | Sep |
| 5:53.4 + | Alison Wyeth | | 26.05.64 | 1m | Rome, ITA | 8 | Jun |
| 5:55.1 + | Liz McColgan | | 24.05.64 | 1m | Linz, AUT | 22 | Aug |
| *5:58.17* | *Nnenna Lynch* | | *3.07.71* | *4* | *Sheffield* | *23* | *Jul* |

# 3000 METRES

| | | | | | | | | |
|---|---|---|---|---|---|---|---|---|
| 8:40.82 | Paula Radcliffe | U23 | 17.12.73 | 4 | Zurich, SWZ | 16 | Aug |
| 8:42:55 | | | | 4 | Monaco, MON | 9 | Sep |
| 8:49.31 | | | | 4 | London (CP) | 27 | Aug |
| 8:56.6 + | | | | 5m | Berlin, GER | 1 | Sep |
| 8:58.20 + | | | | 1m | Gothenburg, SWE | 12 | Aug |
| 8:58.3 + | | | | 4m | London (CP) | 7 | Jul |
| 9:00.0 + | | | | 5m | Brussels, BEL | 25 | Aug |
| 9:06.04 + | | | | 2m | Hengelo, HOL | 5 | Jun |
| 8:42.82 | Yvonne Murray | | 4.10.64 | 2 | London (CP) | 27 | Aug |
| 8:50.2 +e | | | | 3m | Berlin, GER | 1 | Sep |
| 8:51.57 | | | | 13 | Zurich, SWZ | 16 | Aug |
| 8:58.1 + | | | | 3m | London (CP) | 7 | Jul |
| 8:59.80 | | | | 1 | Gateshead | 21 | Aug |
| 9:00.2 + | | | | 6m | Brussels, BEL | 25 | Aug |
| 8:48.94 | Alison Wyeth | | 26.05.64 | 6 | Rome, ITA | 8 | Jun |
| 8:58.6 + | | | | 6m | London (CP) | 7 | Jul |
| 8:50.52 | Liz McColgan | | 24.05.64 | 2 | Linz, AUT | 22 | Aug |
| 8:57.2 + | | | | 5m | Cologne, GER | 18 | Aug |
| 9:01.0 + | | | | | Brussels, BEL | 25 | Aug |
| 9:02.30 | Jill Hunter | | 14.10.66 | 6 | Lappeenranta, FIN | 16 | Jul |
| *9:07.29* | *Kate McCandless* | | *22.06.70* | *8* | *Lappeenranta, FIN* | *16* | *Jul* |
| 9:08.7 | Kelly Holmes | | 19.04.70 | 1 | Cosford | 5 | Jul |
| | 21 performances to 9:10.0 by 6 athletes | | | | | | |
| 9:10.29 | Andrea Whitcombe | | 8.06.71 | 5 | Gateshead | 21 | Aug |
| 9:10.6 i | Una English | | 14.08.70 | 1 | Glasgow | 22 | Jan |
| 9:12.47 | | | | 2 | Zurich, SWZ | 16 | Sep |
| 9:10.9 mx | Sarah Bentley | | 21.05.67 | 4r2 | Stretford | 27 | Jun |
| 9:12.72 | | | | 6 | Gateshead | 21 | Aug |
| 9:17.19 | Bev Hartigan | | 10.06.67 | 1 | Loughborough | 11 | Jun |
| | (10) | | | | | | |
| 9:17.97 i | Zahara Hyde | | 12.01.63 | 3 | Birmingham | 28 | Jan |
| 9:25.41 | | | | 1 | London (CP) | 18 | Jun |
| 9:18.1 mx | Louise Watson | | 13.12.71 | 2 | Watford | 9 | Aug |
| 9:25.90 | | | | 2 | Loughborough | 11 | Jun |
| *9:18.5* | *Nnenna Lynch* | | *3.07.71* | *1* | *Street* | *8* | *May* |
| 9:18.92 | Sue Parker | | 24.03.70 | 12 | London (CP) | 27 | Aug |
| *9:22.4* | *Berhane Dagne* | *U20* | *7.10.77* | *1* | *Watford* | *13* | *Sep* |
| 9:22.43 | Debbie Gunning | | 31.08.65 | 2 | Kilkenny, IRE | 2 | Sep |
| *9:22.6* | *Jill Bruce* | *U23* | *25.07.73* | *1* | *Antrim* | *1* | *Jul* |
| 9:23.1 | Carolina Weatherill | | 13.05.68 | 1 | Watford | 19 | Jul |
| 9:25.14 | Karen Hargrave | | 23.09.65 | 14 | London (CP) | 27 | Aug |
| 9:25.5 | Jane Shields | | 23.08.60 | 2 | Sheffield | 13 | May |
| 9:25.65 i | Angela Davies | | 21.10.70 | 1 | Birmingham | 19 | Feb |
| *9:26.8* | *Fransua Woldemarin* | | | *2* | *Watford* | *13* | *Sep* |
| 9:27.5 | Amanda Tremble | U20 | 2.11.76 | | Newcastle | 29 | Aug |
| 9:28.39 | Ann Terek | | 22.09.64 | 2 | Antrim | 28 | May |
| | (20) | | | | | | |
| 9:29.8 | Liz Talbot | U23 | 5.12.74 | 1 | Bracknell | 22 | Apr |
| 9:30.73 | Shirley Griffiths | | 23.06.72 | 1 | Blackpool | 20 | Aug |
| *9:31.05* | *Edwige Pitel* | | *4.06.67* | *4* | *Bugeat, FRA* | *5* | *Jun* |
| 9:31.31 i | Elaine Foster | | 21.07.63 | 1 | Birmingham | 26 | Feb |
| 9:32.5 mx | Jayne Spark | | 16.09.70 | 14 | Stretford | 6 | Jun |
| 9:33.49 | Alice Braham | U20 | 17.01.76 | 4 | Loughborough | 11 | Jun |
| 9:33.80 i | Joanne Symonds | | 19.02.68 | 3 | Birmingham | 19 | Feb |
| 9:34.11 | Andrea Duke | U23 | 6.07.73 | 5 | Loughborough | 11 | Jun |
| 9:36.1 mx | Penny Thackray | U23 | 18.08.74 | 15 | Stretford | 5 | Sep |
| 9:46.89 i | | | | 3 | Birmingham | 26 | Feb |
| 9:37.6 mx | Linden Wilde | | 11.05.61 | 23 | Stretford | 1 | Aug |

| | | | | | | | | |
|---|---|---|---|---|---|---|---|---|
| 9:38.0 mx | Michelle Mann | U20 | 6.02.77 | 20 | Stretford | | 18 | Jul |
| | 9:46.92 | | | 2 | Belfort, FRA | | 6 | Aug |
| (30) | | | | | | | | |
| 9:38.67 | Gabby Collison | | 10.02.66 | 2 | Birmingham | | 29 | Jul |
| 9:38.69 | Joanne Fairclough | | 24.12.71 | 3 | Ames, USA | | 15 | May |
| 9:39.3 i | Kirsten Scobie | | 13.11.67 | 2 | Glasgow | | 22 | Jan |
| *9:39.54* | *Teresa Duffy* | | *6.07.69* | *4* | *Kilkenny, IRE* | | *2* | *Sep* |
| 9:40.08 | Amanda Thorpe | | 21.07.71 | 3 | Birmingham | | 29 | Jul |
| 9:40.12 | Joanne Holden | | 20.02.65 | 2 | London (CP) | | 18 | Jun |
| *9:40.3* | *Getenesh Tamirat* | *U20* | *11.07.77* | *3* | *Watford* | | *13* | *Sep* |
| 9:40.58 | Jill Harrison | V35 | 20.06.58 | 6 | Loughborough | | 11 | Jun |
| 9:41.6 | Anna Kostilek | | 16.11.65 | 1 | Bracknell | | 21 | Jun |
| 9:41.84 | Sue Ridley | | 25.10.65 | 4 | Birmingham | | 29 | Jul |
| 9:45.0 i | Teresa Dyer | V35 | 29.09.59 | 1 | Birmingham | | 12 | Feb |
| 9:45.46 i | Michelle Ross | | 31.01.72 | 1 | Birmingham | | 20 | Jan |
| | 9:53.38 | | | 3 | Birmingham | | 20 | May |
| (40) | | | | | | | | |
| 9:46.25 i | Christa Salt | | 17.06.64 | 2 | Ghent, BEL | | 15 | Jan |
| 9:46.89 | Hayley Yelling | U23 | 3.01.74 | 3 | London (CP) | | 18 | Jun |
| 9:47.26 i | Sue Morley | V35 | 11.10.57 | 4 | Birmingham | | 26 | Feb |
| 9:48.42 | Antoinette Burleigh | V45 | 15.04.49 | | Venissieux, FRA | | 21 | May |
| 9:48.9 + | Sonia McGeorge | | 2.11.64 | m | Bedford | | 28 | May |
| 9:48.9 | Lisa Hollick | | 1.01.70 | 2 | Watford | | 30 | Aug |
| 9:49.78 | Sarah Bradbury | | 25.02.63 | 4 | London (CP) | | 18 | Jun |
| 9:50.1 | Rhona Makepeace | | 7.08.62 | 1 | Loughborough | | 13 | Aug |
| 9:50.4 | Sheila Fairweather | U20 | 24.11.77 | 1 | Livingston | | 26 | Jul |
| *9:51.03* | *Wendy Sutherland/Llewellyn* | | *30.05.63* | *2* | *Aldershot* | | *23* | *Jul* |
| 9:51.1 | Stephanie Forrester | | 30.04.69 | 2 | Watford | | 19 | Jul |
| (50) | | | | | | | | |
| 9:52.1 | Kath Bailey | | 25.03.68 | 1 | Aldershot | | 26 | Jun |
| 9:52.58 | Samantha Ashby/Bretherwick | | 16.04.69 | 3 | Blackpool | | 20 | Aug |
| 9:52.7 | Anne Ridley | | 7.05.65 | 1 | Kingston | | 22 | Jul |
| 9:53.55 | Clare Pauzers | | 2.08.62 | 3 | Aldershot | | 23 | Jul |
| 9:54.1 | Ann Taswell | | 31.05.71 | 3 | Street | | 8 | May |
| 9:54.4 | Caroline Horne | V35 | 7.11.56 | 1 | Crawley | | 4 | Jul |
| 9:54.7 mx | Sarah Young | | 2.01.70 | 23 | Stretford | | 18 | Jul |
| 9:55.3 | Claire Swift | U20 | 17.10.76 | | Stretford | | 22 | Aug |
| 9:55.70 | Jessica Turnbull | U23 | 4.07.75 | 4 | Gateshead | | 17 | Jun |
| 9:56.3 | Catherine Dugdale | U23 | 29.11.74 | 1 | Newport | | 13 | Sep |
| (60) | | | | | | | | |
| 9:56.9 | Julie Briggs | | 13.03.69 | 1 | Horsham | | 9 | Jul |
| *9:57.6* | *Fatmagul Bosnak* | | *23.01.69* | *1* | *London (WP)* | | *29* | *Apr* |
| 9:57.6 | Nicky Slater | U20 | 11.01.77 | 1 | Crawley | | 31 | May |
| 9:57.6 | Carol Holmes | | 13.12.63 | 1 | Nottingham | | 13 | Aug |
| 9:57.8 | Amanda Larby | | 13.11.70 | 2 | Aldershot | | 26 | Jun |
| 9:57.9 mx | Lynn Maddison | | 17.08.67 | 26 | Stretford | | 18 | Jul |
| 9:58.1 | Loretta Sollars | | 29.10.63 | 1 | Leeds | | 7 | May |
| 9:58.2 | Pamela Morgan | | 16.04.65 | 1 | Derby | | 6 | Aug |
| 9:58.21 | Nicola Brown | U23 | 17.03.74 | 5 | Gateshead | | 17 | Jun |
| 9:58.78 | Sarah Wallace | U23 | 31.05.73 | 4 | Blackpool | | 20 | Aug |
| 9:58.8 | Debbie Kilner | | 2.11.61 | 1 | Aberdeen | | 1 | Jun |
| (70) | | | | | | | | |
| 9:58.88 | Ann McPhail | | 3.05.70 | 2 | Antrim | | 20 | Jun |
| 9:59.2 | Alison Outram | U20 | 14.06.77 | 1 | London (He) | | 10 | Jun |
| 9:59.2 | Sheila Gollan | | 18.07.64 | 2 | Birmingham | | 19 | Aug |

**Under 17**

| | | | | | | | | |
|---|---|---|---|---|---|---|---|---|
| 10:01.6 | Kate Grimshaw | | 26.10.79 | 1 | Jarrow | | 13 | Aug |
| 10:09.7 mx | Heather Carson | | 18.07.79 | 31 | Stretford | | 1 | Aug |
| | 10:13.4 | | | 1 | Stretford | | 10 | Jun |
| 10:11.9 | Jackie Hogan | | 19.03.80 | 1 | Sheffield | | 16 | Apr |

| 10:12.45 | Clare Duncan | 22.08.79 | 2 | Nottingham | 7 | Jul |
|---|---|---|---|---|---|---|
| 10:14.0 | Clare Thomas | 26.08.79 | 1 | Newport | 13 | Sep |
| 10:15.2 | Katie Wallace | 19.09.78 | 1 | Portsmouth | 14 | May |
| 10:16.38 | Nicola Lilley | 17.02.80 | 1 | Bedford | 2 | Jul |
| 10:16.6 | Susannah Rutherford | 26.02.79 | 2 | Newcastle | 17 | Jun |
| 10:16.99 | Emma Brooker | 26.10.78 | 1 | London (He) | 12 | Aug |
| 10:18.0 | Gabby Hawson | 3.02.79 | 2 | Portsmouth | 14 | May |
| (10) | | | | | | |
| 10:18.50 | Jane Moss | 23.08.79 | 2 | Bedford | 2 | Jul |
| 10:18.9 | Suzanne McCormick | 10.02.79 | 1 | Antrim | 26 | Aug |
| 10:22.6 | Sarah Davey | 13.10.78 | 1 | Horsham | 9 | Jul |
| 10:23.2 | Wendy Bailey | 31.01.80 | 3 | Crewe | 27 | Jun |
| 10:24.25 | Claire Demaine | 6.09.78 | 5 | Nottingham | 7 | Jul |
| 10:24.9 | Sonia Thomas | 16.05.79 | 2 | Jarrow | 9 | Aug |
| 10:25.7 | Rebecca Wade | 11.06.80 | 1 | Yate | 10 | Jun |
| 10:26.9 | Rosanna Iannone | 15.06.79 | 1 | Watford | 12 | Aug |
| 10:28.0 | Camilla Waite | 24.05.80 | 3 | Portsmouth | 14 | May |
| 10:29.2 | Kathryn Hodkinson | 12.01.79 | 1 | Derby | 25 | Jun |
| (20) | | | | | | |
| 10:29.79 | Stacey Falk | 9.06.80 | 3 | Bedford | 2 | Jul |
| 10:31.4 | Rachel Felton | 27.06.79 | 1 | Welwyn | 10 | Jun |
| 10:31.8 | Christina Radon | 12.07.79 | 1 | Milton Keynes | 13 | May |
| 10:32.0 | Paula Whitney | 21.03.79 | 4 | Crewe | 27 | Jun |
| 10:32.51 | Ceri Davies | 19.08.80 | 3 | Stoke | 17 | Jun |
| 10:33.12 | Rebecca Everett | 10.03.80 | 4 | Bedford | 2 | Jul |
| 10:33.3 | Laura Hale | 21.01.80 | 5 | Bath | 31 | May |
| 10:33.7 | Samantha Northey | 18.04.80 | 1 | Bournemouth | 10 | Jun |
| 10:34.2 | Gayle Adams | 5.04.79 | 1 | Coventry | 16 | Jul |
| 10:34.4 | Sarah Corlett | 28.05.79 | 1 | Carlisle | 10 | Sep |
| (30) | | | | | | |
| 10:34.5 | Jody Eckersley | 23.02.80 | 1 | Basildon | 10 | Jun |

## 5000 METRES

| 14:49.27 | Paula Radcliffe | U23 | 17.12.73 | 2 | London (CP) | 7 | Jul |
|---|---|---|---|---|---|---|---|
| 14:57.02 | | | | 5 | Gothenburg, SWE | 12 | Aug |
| 15:00.83 | | | | 4 | Brussels, BEL | 25 | Aug |
| 15:02.87 | | | | 1 | Hengelo, HOL | 5 | Jun |
| 15:14.32 | | | | 8 | Berlin, GER | 1 | Sep |
| 15:14.77 | | | | 4h2 | Gothenburg, SWE | 10 | Aug |
| 14:56.94 | Yvonne Murray | | 4.10.64 | 4 | London (CP) | 7 | Jul |
| 14:57.98 | | | | 4 | Berlin, GER | 1 | Sep |
| 16:06.1 + | | | | | Gothenburg, SWE | 9 | Aug |
| 16:18.0 + | | | | 2h1m | Gothenburg, SWE | 6 | Aug |
| 14:59.56 | Liz McColgan | | 24.05.64 | 3 | Hechtel, BEL | 22 | Jul |
| 15:04.88 | | | | 6 | Cologne, GER | 18 | Aug |
| 15:14.67 | | | | 6 | Brussels, BEL | 25 | Aug |
| 15:54.7 + | | | | 6m | Gothenburg, SWE | 9 | Aug |
| 15:59.6 + | | | | 4m | Villeneuve d'Ascq, FRA | 25 | Jun |
| 16:21.4 + | | | | | Gothenburg, SWE | 6 | Aug |
| 15:00.37 | Alison Wyeth | | 26.05.64 | 5 | London (CP) | 7 | Jul |
| 15:19.44 | | | | 2 | Villeneuve d'Ascq, FRA | 24 | Jun |
| 15:39.14 | | | | 1 | Birmingham | 15 | Jul |
| 15:28.46 | Jill Hunter | | 14.10.66 | 7 | Oslo, NOR | 21 | Jul |
| 15:39.85 | | | | 3 | Cork, IRE | 24 | Jun |
| 15:48.16 | | | | 11 | London (CP) | 7 | Jul |
| 15:59.8 + | | | | 1m | Bedford | 1 | Jul |
| 16:17.9 + | | | | 1h1m | Gothenburg, SWE | 6 | Aug |
| *15:34.11* | *Kate McCandless* | | *22.06.70* | *5* | *Moscow, RUS* | *5* | *Jun* |

256

LINFORD CHRISTIE. Injury in the World Championships held him back to a number 2 world ranking.

JOHN REGIS. Again disappointment in the World Championships but highly ranked in the world.

ROGER BLACK. Equalled his personal best but hard pressed by Mark Richardson.

JOHN MAYOCK. Improved his best by over 2 seconds in the 1500m.

PETER WHITEHEAD. A magnificent 4th place in Gothenburg.

TONY JARRETT. 2nd in the World Championships.

COLIN JACKSON. Injured for part of the season but still ran impressively.

STEVE SMITH. Just missed a medal at the World Championships.

STEVE BACKLEY. A solid season with a silver medal at Gothenburg.

NICK BUCKFIELD. At last someone improves the British record.

DARREN BRAITHWAITE. Continues to improve but always overshadowed by Linford.

MELANIE NEEF. In the World Top 20.

KELLY HOLMES. A wonderful season with records and two World Championship medals.

PAULA RADCLIFFE. Twice under 15 minutes for a 5000m.

YVONNE MURRAY. Good performances for 3k - 10k.

LIZ McCOLGAN. Strong performances in 10k give an indication of a good marathon year in 1996.

KATE STAPLES. Continues to improve but the world standards are rapidly rising.

ASHIA HANSEN. A British record and placed in the World Top 10.

JUDY OAKES. Still at the top.

LORRAINE SHAW. Many British records and a number 5 World ranking.

| 15:53.86 | Sarah Bentley | | 21.05.67 | 15 | Hechtel, BEL | 22 | Jul |
|---|---|---|---|---|---|---|---|
| | 16:22.80 | | | 5 | Birmingham | 15 | Jul |
| | 16:22.93 | | | 1 | K Wusterhausen, GER | 30 | Aug |
| | 16:27 | | | 3 | Hexham | 4 | May |
| 15:54.80 | Jane Shields | | 23.08.60 | 6 | Cork, IRE | 24 | Jun |
| 15:57.06 | Louise Watson | | 13.12.71 | 7 | Cork, IRE | 24 | Jun |
| | 16:07.09 | | | 9 | Fukuoka, JAP | 29 | Aug |
| | 16:07.32 i | | | 7 | Boston, USA | 27 | Jan |
| | 16:11.23 | | | 3 | Birmingham | 15 | Jul |
| | 16:16.23 | | | 12 | Philadelphia, USA | 27 | Apr |
| *16:10.69* | *Nnenna Lynch* | | *3.07.71* | *2* | *Birmingham* | *15* | *Jul* |
| *16:12.65* | *Teresa Duffy* | | *6.07.69* | *8* | *Cork, IRE* | *24* | *Jun* |
| 16:12.96 | Andrea Whitcombe | | 8.06.71 | 4 | Birmingham | 15 | Jul |
| 16:14 | Heather Heasman | | 27.09.63 | 1 | Hexham | 4 | May |
| (10) | | | | | | | |
| 16:17.32 | Sonia McGeorge | | 2.11.64 | 1 | Bedford | 28 | May |
| *16:17.5 mx* | *Berhane Dagne* | *U20* | *7.10.77* | *1* | *London (CP)* | *26* | *Jul* |
| *16:22.25* | *Edwige Pitel* | | *4.06.67* | *7* | *Paris, FRA* | *22* | *Jul* |
| 16:23 | Shirley Griffiths | | 23.06.72 | 1 | Jarrow | 9 | Aug |
| 16:24.86 | Liz Talbot | U23 | 5.12.74 | 2 | Tessenderlo, BEL | 2 | Jul |
| 16:26.65 | Karen Hargrave | | 23.09.65 | >7 | Lisbon, POR | 17 | Jun |
| | 40 performances to 16:30.0 by 14 athletes including 1 indoors | | | | | | |
| 16:30.85 | Jill Harrison | V35 | 20.06.58 | 6 | Birmingham | 15 | Jul |
| 16:36.6 | Hayley Haining | | 6.03.72 | 1 | Edinburgh | 24 | Jun |
| 16:37.16 | Joanne Holden | | 20.02.65 | 1 | Stoke | 9 | Sep |
| 16:37.21 | Linden Wilde | | 11.05.61 | 2 | Stoke | 9 | Sep |
| 16:38.04 | Angie Hulley | | 8.02.62 | 2 | Bedford | 28 | May |
| 16:38.52 | Zahara Hyde | | 12.01.63 | 7 | Birmingham | 15 | Jul |
| (20) | | | | | | | |
| 16:41.0 | Andrea Duke | U23 | 6.07.73 | 2 | Edinburgh | 24 | Jun |
| 16:45.43 | Gabby Collison | | 10.02.66 | 8 | Birmingham | 15 | Jul |
| 16:46.94 | Joanne Fairclough | | 24.12.71 | 2 | Ames, USA | 16 | May |
| 16:47.18 | Catherine Mijovic | | 11.04.61 | 3 | Stoke | 9 | Sep |
| 16:49 | Caroline Horne | | 7.11.56 | 6 | Hexham | 4 | May |
| 16:50.4 | Amanda Tremble | U20 | 2.11.76 | 2 | Jarrow | 9 | Aug |
| 16:54.47 | Ann Terek | | 22.09.64 | 2 | Cardiff | 23 | Jul |
| 16:54.98 | Angela Joiner | | 14.02.69 | 12 | Birmingham | 15 | Jul |
| 16:55.9 | Hayley Yelling | U23 | 3.01.74 | 2 | Liverpool | 30 | Jul |
| *16:56.45* | *Wendy Sutherland/Llewellyn* | | *30.05.63* | *1* | *Enfield* | *13* | *Aug* |
| 16:56.98 | Hayley Nash | | 30.05.63 | 10 | Cork, IRE | 24 | Jun |
| (30) | | | | | | | |
| 16:57.5 | Jessica Turnbull | U23 | 4.07.75 | 11 | Cork, IRE | 24 | Jun |
| 16:57.5 | Sue Ridley | | 25.10.65 | 2 | London (He) | 1 | Jul |
| *16:58* | *Cathy Shum* | | *30.05.61* | *8* | *Hexham* | *4* | *May* |
| 17:03.04 | Michelle Ross | | 31.01.72 | 13 | Birmingham | 15 | Jul |
| 17:06 | Marian Sutton | | 7.10.63 | 9 | Hexham | 4 | May |
| 17:06.6 | Jane Harrop | V35 | 25.07.60 | 1 | Guildford | 30 | Apr |
| 17:07.24 | Sarah Bradbury | | 25.02.63 | 14 | Birmingham | 15 | Jul |
| *17:08.9 mx* | *Getenesh Tamirat* | *U20* | *11.07.77* | *13* | *London (CP)* | *6* | *Jul* |
| 17:09.62 | Lisa Hollick | | 1.01.70 | 2 | Enfield | 13 | Aug |
| 17:09.8 | Debbie Kilner | | 2.11.61 | 3 | Edinburgh | 24 | Jun |
| 17:09.9 | Elaine Foster | | 21.07.63 | 12 | Cork, IRE | 24 | Jun |
| 17:10 | Helen Titterington | | 24.10.69 | 10 | Hexham | 4 | May |
| (40) | | | | | | | |
| 17:10.1 | Lucy Wright | | 17.11.69 | 1 | Leeds | 20 | Jun |
| 17:14.3 | Anne Ridley | | 7.05.65 | 4 | London (He) | 1 | Jul |
| 17:15.9 | Paula Fudge | V40 | 30.03.52 | 2 | Bebington | 11 | Jun |
| 17:19.1 | Kath Bailey | | 25.03.68 | 1 | Crawley | 25 | Jun |
| 17:21.4 | Catriona Morrison | U20 | 11.01.77 | 2 | Edinburgh | 7 | May |
| 17:21.45 | Dawn Harris | | 22.06.69 | 4 | Lyss, SWZ | 14 | Jun |
| 17:22.5 | Anne-Marie Richards | | 15.01.61 | 3 | Bebington | 11 | Jun |

257

| | | | | | |
|---|---|---|---|---|---|
| 17:23.5 | Laura Woffenden | | 14.08.70 | 4 | Edinburgh | 7 May |
| 17:23.72 | Dinah Cheverton | | 24.03.65 | 3 | Cardiff | 23 Jul |
| 17:23.8 | Megan Smith | U23 | 19.04.74 | 5 | Edinburgh | 7 May |

(50)

| | | | | | |
|---|---|---|---|---|---|
| 17:24.00 | Angharad Mair | | 30.03.61 | 13 | Cork, IRE | 24 Jun |
| 17:27.4 | Teresa Dyer | V35 | 29.09.59 | 1 | Liverpool | 2 Jul |
| 17:28.6 | Ann McPhail | | 3.05.70 | 6 | Edinburgh | 7 May |
| 17:30.7 | Meryl Whitley | | 12.04.69 | 3 | Jarrow | 9 Aug |

## 10000 METRES

| | | | | | |
|---|---|---|---|---|---|
| 31:40.14 | Liz McColgan | | 24.05.64 | 6 | Gothenburg, SWE | 9 Aug |
| 32:22.09 | | | | 4 | Villeneuve d'Ascq, FRA | 25 Jun |
| 32:33.89 | | | | 2h2 | Gothenburg, SWE | 6 Aug |
| 32:16.76 | Yvonne Murray | | 4.10.64 | 2h1 | Gothenburg, SWE | 6 Aug |
| 32:22.93 | Jill Hunter | | 14.10.66 | 9h1 | Gothenburg, SWE | 6 Aug |
| 32:24.93 | | | | 15 | Gothenburg, SWE | 9 Aug |
| 32:26.12 | | | | 1 | Bedford | 1 Jul |
| 33:33.71 | Louise Watson | | 13.12.71 | 6 | Fukuoka, JAP | 1 Sep |
| 33:38.52 | | | | 2 | Bedford | 1 Jul |
| 33:46.07 | Jane Shields | | 23.08.60 | 3 | Bedford | 1 Jul |
| 34:05.42 | Angie Hulley | | 8.02.62 | 4 | Bedford | 1 Jul |
| 34:18.68 | Heather Heasman | | 27.09.63 | 5 | Bedford | 1 Jul |
| 34:24.33 | Zahara Hyde | | 12.01.63 | 25 | Walnut, USA | 19 Apr |
| *34:38.59* | *Cathy Shum* | | *30.05.61* | *6* | *Bedford* | *1 Jul* |
| *34:55.76* | *Teresa Duffy* | | *6.07.69* | *5* | *Tallinn, EST* | *10 Jun* |
| *35:12.14* | *Elizabeth Riley* | *U23* | *31.05.74* | *1* | *Edinburgh* | *8 May* |
| 35:29.67 | Jill Harrison | V35 | 20.06.58 | 7 | Bedford | 1 Jul |
| 35:29.77 | Joanne Holden | | 20.02.65 | 8 | Bedford | 1 Jul |

(10)

| | | | | | |
|---|---|---|---|---|---|
| 35:44.98 | Fiona Phillips | V35 | 8.03.60 | 9 | Bedford | 1 Jul |
| 36:16.29 | Catherine Mijovic | | 11.04.61 | 10 | Bedford | 1 Jul |
| 36:22.7 | Debbie Kilner | | 2.11.61 | 1 | Aberdeen | 2 May |
| 36:43.11 | Sharon Dixon | | 22.04.68 | 2 | Edinburgh | 8 May |

## 10 KILOMETRES ROAD

| | | | | | |
|---|---|---|---|---|---|
| 32:06 | Liz McColgan | | 24.05.64 | 1 | Coventry | 15 Oct |
| 32:27 | | | | 1 | Edinburgh | 1 Oct |
| 33:02 | Bev Hartigan | | 10.06.67 | 1 | Belfast | 8 Apr |
| 33:05 | Jill Hunter | | 14.10.66 | 1 | Cardiff | 4 Jun |
| 33:26 | | | | 3 | Bowling Green, USA | 30 Sep |
| 33:28 | | | | 6 | Boston, USA | 9 Oct |
| 33:43 | | | | 1 | Atlanta, USA | 4 Sep |
| 33:09 | Heather Heasman | | 27.09.63 | 1 | Eastleigh | 19 Mar |
| 33:44 | | | | 1 | Garstang | 14 Jan |
| 33:45 | | | | 3 | Cardiff | 4 Jun |
| 33:45 | | | | 3 | Barnsley | 5 Nov |
| 33:20 | Sarah Young | | 2.01.70 | 1 | Barnsley | 5 Nov |
| *33:21* | *Cathy Shum* | | *30.05.61* | *1* | *Dublin, IRE* | *18 Jun* |
| 33:22 | Jane Shields | | 23.08.60 | 2 | Cardiff | 4 Jun |
| 33:45 | | | | 4 | Coventry | 15 Oct |
| 33:25 | Lynne Robinson | | 21.06.69 | 2 | Belfast | 8 Apr |
| 33:58 | | | | 1 | Loughborough | 26 Feb |
| 33:25 | Marian Sutton | | 7.10.63 | 1 | London | 10 Sep |
| 33:31 | | | | 2 | Edinburgh | 1 Oct |
| 33:59 | | | | 1 | Milton Keynes | 6 Jun |
| 33:27 | Catherine Mijovic | | 11.04.61 | 1 | Bourton | 26 Feb |
| 33:30 | Yvonne Danson | V35 | 22.05.59 | 1 | Singapore, SIN | 2 Apr |

(10)

| | | | | | |
|---|---|---|---|---|---|
| *33:36* | *Kate McCandless* | | *22.06.70* | *3* | *Coventry* | *15 Oct* |
| 33:36 | Angie Hulley | | 8.02.62 | 2 | Barnsley | 5 Nov |
| 33:54 | | | | 1 | Leeds | 3 Dec |

258

| | | | | | | | |
|---|---|---|---|---|---|---|---|
| 33:42 | Lesley Morton | | 25.12.63 | 3 | Oslo, NOR | 1 | May |
| 33:45 | Lucy Elliott | | 9.03.66 | 1 | Paris, FRA | 12 | Nov |
| 33:46 | Zahara Hyde | | 12.01.63 | 2 | Eastleigh | 19 | Mar |
| 33:46 | Amanda Wright | | 14.07.68 | 1 | Telford | 17 | Dec |
| 33:49 | Karen Macleod | V35 | 24.04.58 | 2 | Schipol, HOL | 25 | Jun |
| 33:56 | Vikki McPherson | | 1.06.71 | 1 | Cardiff | 3 | Sep |
| 33:57 | | | | 1 | Troon | 10 | May |
| 33:59 | Jill Bruce | U23 | 25.07.73 | 1 | Enniskillen | 13 | May |
| 34:04 | Teresa Duffy | | 6.07.69 | 2 | Dublin, IRE | 18 | Jun |
| 34:07 | Kath Bailey | | 25.03.68 | 1 | Chichester | 5 | Feb |
| 34:08 | Carol Holmes | | 13.12.63 | 4 | Barnsley | 5 | Nov |
| 34:15 | Sarah Bradbury | | 25.02.63 | 1 | Seaford | 9 | Apr |
| 34:17 | Andrea Duke | U23 | 6.07.73 | 5 | Barnsley | 5 | Nov |
| 34:20 | Fiona Phillips | V35 | 8.03.60 | 1 | Totton | 9 | Apr |
| | (20) | | | | | | |
| 34:26 | Hayley Haining | | 6.03.72 | 6 | Barnsley | 5 | Nov |
| 34:29 | Jane Harrop | | 25.07.60 | 2 | Totton | 9 | Apr |
| 34:30 | Edwige Pitel | | 4.06.67 | 3 | Bordeaux, FRA | 24 | Sep |
| 34:30 | Clare Pauzers | | 2.08.62 | 1 | Brighton | 19 | Nov |
| 34:32 | Gabby Collison | | 10.02.66 | 4 | Eastleigh | 19 | Mar |
| 34:32 | Jill Harrison | V35 | 20.06.58 | 1 | Swansea | 10 | Sep |
| 34:35 | Jane Palmer | | 7.10.66 | 2 | Brighton | 19 | Nov |
| 34:37 | Caroline Slimin | | 27.08.65 | 3 | Totton | 9 | Apr |
| 34:37 | Wendy Sutherland/Llewellyn | | 30.05.63 | 2 | Redditch | 20 | Aug |
| 34:39 | Sarah Bentley | | 21.05.67 | 1 | London (CP) | 20 | May |
| 34:42 | Alice Braham | U20 | 17.01.76 | 4 | Belfast | 8 | Apr |
| 34:44 | Wendy Ore | | 23.05.66 | 2 | Swansea | 10 | Sep |
| | (30) | | | | | | |
| 34:44 | Debbie Percival | V35 | 22.04.58 | 3 | Brighton | 10 | Nov |
| 34:46 | Anna Kostilek | | 16.11.65 | 5 | Cardiff | 4 | Jun |
| 34:47 | S. Anderson | V35 | | 4 | Totton | 9 | Apr |
| 34:47 | Eileen McKenzie | U23 | 6.10.75 | 1 | Silverstone | 10 | May |
| 34:50 | Julie Coleby | V40 | 5.11.55 | 1 | Newcastle | 5 | Nov |
| 34:53 | Heather Jennings | | 10.07.60 | 2 | Burton | 26 | Feb |
| 34:54 | Nicola Brown | U23 | 17.03.74 | 4 | Brighton | 19 | Nov |
| 34:55 | Suzanne Rigg | | 29.11.63 | 3 | Liverpool | 21 | May |
| 34:55 | Laura Woffenden | | 14.08.70 | 2 | Leeds | 3 | Dec |
| 34:57 | Angela Joiner | | 14.02.69 | 3 | London | 10 | Sep |
| | (40) | | | | | | |
| 34:58 | Janet Holt | V35 | 10.10.56 | 1 | Barnsley | 5 | Nov |
| 34:59 | Trudi Thomson | V35 | 18.01.59 | 6 | Coventry | 15 | Oct |

**Short course** (110m)

| | | | | | | | |
|---|---|---|---|---|---|---|---|
| 34:24 | Alison Rose | | 27.09.67 | 2 | Grangemouth | 19 | Feb |

# 10 MILES ROAD

| | | | | | | | |
|---|---|---|---|---|---|---|---|
| 53:12 | Liz McColgan | | 24.05.64 | 1 | Portsmouth | 8 | Oct |
| 53:45 | Jill Hunter | | 14.10.66 | 2 | Flint, USA | 26 | Aug |
| 54:31 | Kate McCandless | | 22.06.70 | 2 | Portsmouth | 8 | Oct |
| 54:36 | Suzanne Rigg | | 29.11.63 | 1 | Erewash | 3 | Sep |
| 55:06 | Marian Sutton | | 7.10.63 | 2 | Erewash | 3 | Sep |
| 55:49 | Cathy Shum | | 30.05.61 | 1 | Leyland | 23 | Jul |
| 56:02 | Hayley Nash | | 30.05.63 | 1 | Woking | 5 | Mar |
| 56:02 | Amanda Wright | | 14.07.68 | 3 | Erewash | 3 | Sep |
| 56:27 | Angie Hulley | | 8.02.62 | 4 | Erewash | 3 | Sep |
| 56:29 | Karen Macleod | V35 | 24.04.58 | 1 | Bristol | 26 | Feb |
| 56:44 | Carol Holmes | | 13.12.63 | 5 | Erewash | 3 | Sep |
| 56:53 | Julie Coleby | V40 | 5.11.55 | 1 | Carlisle | 18 | Nov |
| | (10) | | | | | | |
| 56:55 | Angela Joiner | | 14.02.69 | 6 | Erewash | 3 | Sep |
| 57:35 | Janet Kenyon | V35 | 15.03.59 | 1 | Stockport | 3 | Dec |
| 58:02 | Fiona Phillips | | 8.03.60 | 2 | Woking | 5 | Mar |

| | | | | | | | |
|---|---|---|---|---|---|---|---|
| 58:09 | Caroline Horne | V35 | 7.11.56 | 1 | Barrow | 17 | Jun |
| 58:10 | Ruth Kingsborough | | 25.10.67 | 4 | Portsmouth | 8 | Oct |
| 58:16 | Elaine Foster | | 21.07.63 | 7 | Erewash | 3 | Sep |
| 58:18 | Paula Fudge | V40 | 30.03.52 | 3 | Woking | 5 | Mar |
| 58:24 | Sally Lynch | | 6.11.64 | 1 | Newport | 15 | Apr |
| 58:27 | Ann Ford | V40 | 30.03.52 | 8 | Erewash | 3 | Sep |
| 58:29 | Clare Pauzers | | 2.08.62 | 2 | Teddington | 1 | Oct |
| | (20) | | | | | | |
| 58:31 | Jackie Newton | | 28.08.64 | 1 | Erewash | 3 | Sep |
| 58:36 | Sally Eastall | | 5.01.63 | 1 | Hadleigh | 26 | Nov |
| 58:37 | Karen Cornwall | | 26.08.66 | 1 | Blyth | 23 | Apr |
| 58:40 | Janice Moorekite | V35 | 1.05.57 | 4 | Woking | 5 | Mar |
| 58:43 | Tracy Swindell | | 8.11.66 | 5 | Woking | 5 | Mar |
| 58:46 | Eileen McKenzie | U23 | 6.10.75 | 1 | Nuneaton | 10 | Sep |
| 58:46 | Sue Dilnot | | 14.01.62 | 1 | Hayling Island | 26 | Nov |

**downhill**

| | | | | | | | |
|---|---|---|---|---|---|---|---|
| 53:57 | Vikki McPherson | | 1.06.71 | 1 | Motherwell | 9 | Apr |
| 56:41 | Audrey Sym | | 2.08.66 | 2 | Motherwell | 9 | Apr |
| 57:33 | Elaine McBrinn | | 19.12.63 | 3 | Motherwell | 9 | Apr |

# HALF MARATHON

| | | | | | | | |
|---|---|---|---|---|---|---|---|
| 1:09:49 | Liz McColgan | | 24.05.64 | 3 | Lisbon, POR | 12 | Mar |
| 1:11:42 | | | | 1 | South Shields | 17 | Sep |
| 1:11:44 | Karen Macleod | V35 | 24.04.58 | 2 | Marrakech, MOR | 15 | Jan |
| 1:14:17 | | | | 1 | Bath | 19 | Mar |
| 1:14:55 | | | | 5 | Glasgow | 20 | Aug |
| 1:13:43 | Catherine Mijovic | | 11.04.61 | 1 | Portsmouth | 12 | Mar |
| 1:14:13 | | | | 34 | Belfort, FRA | 1 | Oct |
| 1:14:07 | Kath Bailey | | 25.03.68 | 2 | Portsmouth | 12 | Mar |
| 1:14:14 | Vikki McPherson | | 1.06.71 | 3 | Glasgow | 20 | Aug |
| 1:14:27 | | | | 38 | Belfort, FRA | 1 | Oct |
| 1:14:19 | Marian Sutton | | 7.10.63 | 4 | South Shields | 17 | Sep |
| 1:14:19 | Angie Hulley | | 8.02.62 | 35 | Belfort, FRA | 1 | Oct |
| *1:14:22* | *Cathy Shum* | | *30.05.61* | *1* | *Leyland* | *5* | *Mar* |
| 1:14:37 | Suzanne Rigg | | 29.11.63 | 4 | Glasgow | 20 | Aug |
| 1:15:16 | Carol Holmes | | 13.12.63 | 1 | Nottingham | 24 | Sep |
| 1:15:48 | Trudi Thomson | V35 | 18.01.59 | 48 | Belfort, FRA | 1 | Oct |
| | (10) | | | | | | |
| 1:15:51 | Heather Heasman | | 27.09.63 | 6 | Glasgow | 20 | Aug |
| *1:16:01* | *Edwige Pitel* | | *4.06.67* | *9* | *Villeneuve d'Ascq, FRA* | *2* | *Sep* |
| 1:16:06 | Amanda Wright | | 14.07.68 | 5 | South Shields | 17 | Sep |
| 1:16:38 | Karen Cornwall | | 26.08.66 | 1 | Helsby | 22 | Jan |
| 1:17:08 | Zina Marchant | V40 | 30.09.50 | 3 | Bath | 19 | Mar |
| 1:17:19 | Sally Eastall | | 5.01.63 | 2 | Norwich | 11 | Jun |
| 1:17:26 | Audrey Sym | | 2.08.66 | 2 | Helensburgh | 23 | Jul |
| 1:17:30 | Caroline Horne | V35 | 7.11.56 | 1 | Clowne | 26 | Nov |
| *1:17:36* | *Elizabeth Riley* | *U23* | *31.05.74* | *1* | *Alloa* | *26* | *Mar* |
| 1:17:37 | Marina Steadman | V35 | 4.09.60 | 2 | Reading | 30 | Apr |
| 1:17:37 | Sue Dilnot | | 14.01.62 | 1 | Angers, FRA | 24 | Sep |
| 1:17:38 | Nicola Swithenbank | | 10.12.63 | 2 | Nottingham | 24 | Sep |
| | (20) | | | | | | |
| 1:17:39 | Paula Fudge | V40 | 30.03.52 | 1 | Stroud | 22 | Oct |
| 1:17:44 | Jackie Leak | | 19.10.60 | 1 | Wokingham | 12 | Feb |
| 1:17:46 | Jackie Newton | | 28.08.64 | 8 | Glasgow | 20 | Aug |
| 1:17:56 | Antoinette Burleigh | V45 | 15.04.49 | | Lyons, FRA | 30 | Apr |
| 1:17:59 | Elaine Foster | | 21.07.63 | 7 | South Shields | 17 | Sep |
| 1:17:59 | Nicky Brookland | | 8.06.68 | 5 | Brest, FRA | 25 | Sep |
| 1:18:10 | Elaine Flather | | 2.02.66 | 3 | Portsmouth | 12 | Mar |
| 1:18:13 | Mandy Ayling | | 4.04.65 | 1 | Peterborough | 14 | May |
| 1:18:17 | Debbie Kilner | | 2.11.61 | 8 | South Shields | 17 | Sep |

| 1:18:18 | Tracy Swindell | | 8.11.66 | 9 | South Shields | 17 Sep |
|---|---|---|---|---|---|---|
| | (30) | | | | | |
| 1:18:20 | Lesley Turner | | 1.08.66 | 1 | Lake Vyrnwy | 24 Sep |
| 1:18:22 | Diane Underwood | V40 | 20.12.52 | 2 | Wilmslow | 19 Mar |
| 1:18:28 | Angela Allen | | | 2 | Stroud | 22 Oct |
| 1:18:39 | Elaine McBrinn | | 19.12.63 | 3 | Helensburgh | 23 Jul |
| 1:18:44 | Laura Woffenden | | 14.08.70 | 1 | York | 26 Mar |
| 1:18:45 | Ann Ford | V40 | 30.03.52 | 3 | Nottingham | 24 Sep |
| 1:18:50 | Linda Rushmere | V35 | 14.11.59 | 10 | South Shields | 17 Sep |

# MARATHON

| 2:30:32 | Liz McColgan | | 24.05.64 | 7 | Tokyo, JAP | 19 Nov |
|---|---|---|---|---|---|---|
| 2:31:14 | | | | 5 | London | 2 Apr |
| 2:30:53 | Yvonne Danson | V35 | 22.05.59 | 5 | Boston, USA | 17 Apr |
| 2:34:41 | (representing Singapore) | | | 2 | Chiangmai, THA | 13 Dec |
| 2:32:26 | Marian Sutton | | 7.10.63 | 5 | Chicago, USA | 15 Oct |
| 2:34:21 | Suzanne Rigg | | 29.11.63 | 8 | Berlin, GER | 24 Sep |
| 2:34:25 | Karen Macleod | V35 | 24.04.58 | 2 | Sacramento, USA | 3 Dec |
| 2:37:14 | Catherine Mijovic | | 11.04.61 | 9 | Reims, FRA | 22 Oct |
| 2:44:30 | | | | 7 | Rotterdam, HOL | 23 Apr |
| 2:38:23 | Trudi Thomson | V35 | 18.01.59 | 1 | Dublin, IRE | 30 Oct |
| 2:42:44 | | | | 25 | Athens, GRE | 9 Apr |
| 2:38:25 | Julie Coleby | V40 | 5.11.55 | 4 | Sacramento, USA | 3 Dec |
| 2:41:37 | | | | 17 | London | 2 Apr |
| 2:39:59 | Hayley Nash | | 30.05.63 | 14 | London | 2 Apr |
| *2:40:35* | *Wendy Sutherland/Llewellyn* | | *30.05.63* | *13* | *Reims, FRA* | *22 Oct* |
| 2:41:20 | Lynn Harding | | 10.08.61 | 16 | London | 2 Apr |
| | (10) | | | | | |
| 2:42:42 | Alison Rose | | 27.09.67 | 24 | Athens, GRE | 9 Apr |
| 2:43:19 | Caroline Horne | V35 | 7.11.56 | 27 | Athens, GRE | 9 Apr |
| 2:44:43 | Eryl Davies | | 30.11.60 | 19 | London | 2 Apr |
| 2:44:43 | Gillian Horovitz | V40 | 7.06.55 | 15 | Duluth, USA | 17 Jun |
| 2:45:26 | Linda Rushmere | V35 | 14.11.59 | 2 | Dublin, IRE | 30 Oct |
| 2:46:02 | Angharad Mair | | 30.03.61 | 19 | Berlin, GER | 24 Sep |
| *2:46:24* | *Christina Scobey* | | *1.06.66* | *20* | *London* | *2 Apr* |
| 2:46:46 | Lesley Turner | | 1.08.66 | 33 | Athens, GRE | 9 Apr |
| 2:47:11 | Elaine Flather · | | 2.02.66 | 22 | London | 2 Apr |
| 2:48:06 | Janice Moorekite | V35 | 1.05.57 | 23 | London | 2 Apr |
| 2:48:20 | Tracy Swindell | | 8.11.66 | 4 | Crete, GRE | 29 Oct |
| | (20) | | | | | |
| 2:49:28 | Zoe Lowe | | 7.07.65 | 24 | London | 2 Apr |
| 2:49:44 | Mandy Whittington | | 1.08.64 | 1 | Abingdon | 22 Oct |
| *2:51:06* | *Teresa Tuohy* | *V35* | *1.06.59* | *10* | *Rotterdam, HOL* | *23 Apr* |
| 2:51:36 | Eleanor Robinson | V45 | 20.11.47 | 25 | London | 2 Apr |
| 2:52:31 | Karen Cornwall | | 26.08.66 | 2 | Chiswick | 24 Sep |
| 2:52:49 | Debbie Percival | V35 | 22.04.58 | 26 | London | 2 Apr |
| 2:53:04 | Lucy Ramwell | | 16.08.67 | 1 | Hanoi, VIE | 15 Jan |
| 2:54:03 | Libby Jones | | 25.04.61 | 30 | London | 2 Apr |
| 2:54:20 | Carolyn Hunter-Rowe | | 25.01.64 | 6 | Dublin, IRE | 30 Oct |
| 2:54:50 | Gillian Kennedy | V35 | 16.01.56 | 31 | London | 2 Apr |
| 2:55:14 | Susan Abbiss | V35 | 20.10.59 | 2 | Belfast | 8 May |
| | (30) | | | | | |
| 2:55:25 | Ruth Kingsborough | | 25.10.67 | 7 | Dublin, IRE | 30 Oct |
| 2:55:59 | Marilyn Gradden | | 26.01.61 | 4 | Chiswick | 24 Sep |
| 2:56:42 | Lynne Quigley | | 19.02.69 | 32 | London | 2 Apr |
| 2:57:56 | Sandra Bower | V35 | | 9 | Dublin, IRE | 30 Oct |
| 2:58:00 | Janice Gjelseth | | 16.09.60 | 36 | London | 2 Apr |
| 2:58:11 | Heather Jennings | V35 | 10.07.60 | 28 | Berlin, GER | 24 Sep |
| 2:58:16 | Louise Cooper | U23 | 25.08.75 | 37 | London | 2 Apr |
| 2:58:30 | Lynne Duance | V45 | 28.12.46 | 10 | Dublin, IRE | 30 Oct |
| 2:58:50 | Bonny Appleby | V40 | 15.02.53 | 39 | London | 2 Apr |

| Time | Name | Cat | Date | Pos | Location | Date |
|------|------|-----|------|-----|----------|------|
| 2:58:56 | Kath Kaiser | V40 | 24.08.51 | 2 | Sheffield | 30 Apr |
| (40) | | | | | | |
| 2:59:30 | Jackie Coulson | | 10.08.61 | 40 | London | 2 Apr |
| 2:59:35 | Meredith Black | | | 2 | Harrow | 6 Nov |
| 2:59:41 | Barbara Stevens | V35 | 2.05.56 | 1 | Nottingham | 24 Sep |
| 3:00:09 | Avril Allen | V35 | 1.08.59 | 2 | Nottingham | 24 Sep |
| 3:00:09 | Kim Fisher | V35 | 6.04.57 | 11 | Dublin, IRE | 30 Oct |
| 3:00:30 | Sue Endersby | V35 | 12.10.57 | 42 | London | 2 Apr |
| 3:01:02 | Janette Picton | | 4.03.63 | 5 | Chiswick | 24 Sep |
| 3:01:18 | Lorraine Branch | V35 | 9.11.59 | 43 | London | 2 Apr |
| 3:02:03 | Rachel Wilson | V35 | 13.03.56 | 1 | Taunton | 2 Apr |
| 3:02:10 | Jane Boulton | V35 | 2.04.56 | 47 | London | 2 Apr |
| (50) | | | | | | |
| 3:02:15 | Julie Holdsworth | | 22.07.61 | 1 | Benidorm, SPA | 26 Nov |
| 3:02:16 | S. Kriel | | | 3 | Nottingham | 24 Sep |
| 3:02:19 | Barbara Parker | V35 | 29.04.58 | 48 | London | 2 Apr |
| 3:02:35 | Arlene Carswell | V35 | 14.12.55 | 49 | London | 2 Apr |
| 3:02:36 | Jane Bright | V45 | 24.03.50 | 50 | London | 2 Apr |
| 3:03:39 | Anne-Marie Hughes | | 8.05.62 | 51 | London | 2 Apr |
| 3:03:51 | Sylvia Kerambrum | V35 | 5.11.58 | 52 | London | 2 Apr |
| 3:03:53 | Margaret Healey | | | 12 | Dublin, IRE | 30 Oct |
| 3:03:57. | Wendy Jones | | 10.03.62 | 53 | London | 2 Apr |
| 3:03:58 | Sara Rhimes | V40 | 12.09.54 | 54 | London | 2 Apr |
| (60) | | | | | | |
| 3:04:15 | Karen Barlow | | 15.11.67 | 55 | London | 2 Apr |
| 3:04:37 | Deborah Southgate | V35 | 2.02.56 | 56 | London | 2 Apr |
| 3:04:38 | Margaret Mackenzie | V35 | 16.01.60 | 57 | London | 2 Apr |
| 3:04:41 | Liz Clarke | V35 | 14.02.57 | 58 | London | 2 Apr |
| 3:04:46 | Celia Findlay-Bada | | 19.06.62 | 1 | Lederle | 23 Apr |
| 3:05:08 | Alison Davidson | | 9.03.71 | 59 | London | 2 Apr |
| 3:05:34 | Patricia Sloan | | 22.03.66 | 61 | London | 2 Apr |
| 3:05:56 | Beverley Brown | | 9.05.65 | 2 | Lederle | 23 Apr |
| 3:05:56 | Julia McGowan | V35 | 12.05.59 | 10 | Lausanne, SWZ | 15 Oct |
| 3:06:12 | Hilary Walker | V40 | 9.11.53 | 63 | London | 2 Apr |
| (70) | | | | | | |
| 3:06:13 | Tracy Owen | | 29.04.64 | 64 | London | 2 Apr |
| 3:06:23 | Helen Slimon | | 18.02.71 | 1 | Glasgow | 10 Sep |
| 3:06:31 | Erica Christie | V35 | 10.03.56 | 65 | London | 2 Apr |
| 3:06:33 | Freida Brown | | 6.05.63 | 66 | London | 2 Apr |
| 3:06:36 | Andrea Dennison | | 22.04.63 | 67 | London | 2 Apr |
| 3:06:47 | Alison Carpenter | V35 | 3.01.58 | 68 | London | 2 Apr |
| 3:06:49 | Lynda Bain | V35 | 20.06.56 | 1 | Elgin | 3 Sep |
| 3:06:52 | Kathy Drake | V35 | 25.05.60 | 1 | Snowdonia | 29 Oct |
| 3:06:55 | Christine Naylor | V40 | 22.10.54 | 69 | London | 2 Apr |
| 3:06:59 | Penny Forse | V45 | 7.06.49 | 70 | London | 2 Apr |
| (80) | | | | | | |
| 3:07:00 | Catherine Nevin | V35 | 12.11.55 | 71 | London | 2 Apr |
| 3:07:14 | Wendy Leslie | V35 | 3.10.56 | 72 | London | 2 Apr |
| 3:07:17 | Margaret McLaren | V35 | 21.04.57 | 1 | Fort William | 23 Apr |
| 3:07:36 | Kathryn Lockhart | | 6.06.61 | 73 | London | 2 Apr |
| 3:08:22 | Gillian Johnson | | 25.08.63 | 76 | London | 2 Apr |
| 3:08:36 | Margaret Thompson | V40 | 8.07.54 | 2 | Stoke | 16 Jun |
| 3:08:43 | Margaret Levy | V40 | 8.09.52 | 78 | London | 2 Apr |
| 3:08:46 | P. Leach | | | 3 | Sheffield | 30 Apr |

**short** (Gothenburg 400m, Venice 80m?)

| Time | Name | Cat | Date | Pos | Location | Date |
|------|------|-----|------|-----|----------|------|
| 2:41:42 | Trudi Thomson | V35 | 18.01.59 | 22 | Gothenburg, SWE | 9 Aug |
| 2:39:06 | Sally Goldsmith | | 18.01.61 | 3 | Venice, ITA | 29 Oct |
| 2:45:52 | Alison Rose | | 27.09.67 | 28 | Gothenburg, SWE | 9 Aug |
| *2:43:10* | *Cathy Shum* | | *30.05.61* | *25* | *Gothenburg, SWE* | *9 Aug* |

## 100 KILOMETRES - Road

| | | | | | | | |
|---|---|---|---|---|---|---|---|
| 7:40:18 | Carolyn Hunter-Rowe | | 25.01.64 | 5 | Winschoten, HOL | 16 | Sep |
| 7:50:42 | Eleanor Robinson | V45 | 20.11.47 | 10 | Winschoten, HOL | 16 | Sep |
| 7:53:23 | Lynn Harding | | 10.08.61 | 2 | Chavagnes-en-P, FRA | 27 | May |
| 8:12:03 | Sharon Gayter | | | | Winschoten, HOL | 16 | Sep |
| 8:26:28 | Hilary Walker | V40 | 9.11.53 | 1 | Edinburgh | 30 | Jun |
| 8:39:41 | Marianne Savage | V45 | 26.01.49 | 1 | Nottingham | 20 | May |
| *8:47:03* | *Donna Nugent* | | *8.03.61* | *2* | *Nottingham* | *20* | *May* |

## 24 HOURS - Track

| | | | | | | |
|---|---|---|---|---|---|---|
| 213.504 | Eleanor Robinson | V45 | 20.11.47 | Humberside | 16 | Jul |
| 199.278 | Sandra Brown | V45 | 1.04.49 | London (TB) | 15 | Oct |
| 177.470 | Brenda Barnett | | | Doncaster | 28 | May |
| 170.599 | Mary Howarth | | | Doncaster | 28 | May |

## 24 HOURS - Road

| | | | | |
|---|---|---|---|---|
| 166.845 | Kay Dodson | | Brechin | 11 | Jun |

## 1500 METRES STEEPLECHASE

| | | | | | | | |
|---|---|---|---|---|---|---|---|
| 6:15.8 | Jane Davies | V45 | 7.09.48 | 1 | Crawley | 4 | Jul |
| 6:35.6 | Alison Jones | V35 | 11.08.59 | 2 | Crawley | 4 | Jul |

## 2000 METRES STEEPLECHASE (2' 6" Barriers)

| | | | | | | | |
|---|---|---|---|---|---|---|---|
| 7:37.20 | Sharon Dixon | | 22.04.68 | 1 | Edinburgh | 6 | May |
| 7:46.00 | J. Martin | | | 2 | Edinburgh | 6 | May |
| 7:51.32 | Esther Merchant | U20 | 9.01.76 | 3 | Edinburgh | 6 | May |

## 60 METRES HURDLES - Indoors

| | | | | | | | |
|---|---|---|---|---|---|---|---|
| 8.01 | Jacqui Agyepong | | 5.01.69 | 5 | Barcelona, SPA | 12 | Mar |
| | 8.02 | | | 2s2 | Barcelona, SPA | 11 | Mar |
| | 8.05 | | | 1 | Birmingham | 28 | Jan |
| | 8.06 | | | 4 | Birmingham | 25 | Feb |
| | 8.08 | | | 1 | Glasgow | 11 | Feb |
| | 8.09 | | | 2h2 | Barcelona, SPA | 11 | Mar |
| | 8.16 | | | 4 | Stockholm, SWE | 27 | Feb |
| 8.16 | Sam Farquharson | | 15.12.69 | 1h2 | Vienna, AUT | 18 | Feb |
| | 8.16 | | | 2 | Vienna, AUT | 18 | Feb |
| | 8.18 | | | 3 | Glasgow | 11 | Feb |
| | 8.19 | | | 8 | Birmingham | 25 | Feb |
| | 8.20 | | | 1 | Erfurt,GER | 15 | Feb |
| | 8.21 | | | 5h4 | Barcelona, SPA | 12 | Mar |
| | 8.27 | | | h | Budapest, HUN | 29 | Jan |
| | 8.29 | | | 2 | Birmingham | 4 | Feb |
| | 8.31 | | | 5 | Budapest, HUN | 29 | Jan |
| | 8.35 | | | 4 | Birmingham | 28 | Jan |
| | 8.38 | | | 1h2 | Birmingham | 4 | Feb |
| | 8.40 | | | 1 | Glasgow | 22 | Jan |
| | 8.42 | | | 1 | Birmingham | 1 | Jan |
| | 8.43 | | | 1h1 | Glasgow | 22 | Jan |
| 8.21 | Clova Court | V35 | 10.02.60 | 4 | Glasgow | 11 | Feb |
| | 8.22 | | | 1 | Birmingham | 4 | Feb |
| | 8.32 | | | 1h1 | Birmingham | 4 | Feb |
| | 8.35 | | | 5 | Birmingham | 28 | Jan |
| | 8.47 | | | 1 | Birmingham | 30 | Dec |
| 8.38 | Diane Allahgreen | U23 | 21.02.75 | 2h1 | Vienna, AUT | 18 | Feb |
| | 8.39 | | | 2h2 | Birmingham | 4 | Feb |
| | 8.49 | | | 4 | Birmingham | 4 | Feb |
| 8.42 | Natasha Danvers | U20 | 19.09.77 | 1 | Erfurt,GER | 25 | Feb |
| | 8.44 | | | 1r2 | Erfurt,GER | 25 | Feb |

| | | | | | | | | |
|---|---|---|---|---|---|---|---|---|
| 8.45 | Denise Lewis | | 27.08.72 | 3h2 | Birmingham | 4 | Feb |
| | 8.49 | | | 3 | Birmingham | 4 | Feb |
| 8.54 | Orla Bermingham | U23 | 7.10.75 | 2h1 | Birmingham | 4 | Feb |
| 8.60 | Vikki Schofield | | 29.12.72 | 1 | Sheffield | 22 | Jan |
| 8.61 | Uju Efobi | U23 | 10.10.74 | 3h1 | Birmingham | 4 | Feb |
| 8.65 | Kim Crowther-Price | | 19.01.66 | 3 | Sheffield | 22 | Jan |
| (10) | | | | | | | |
| 8.66 | Melanie Wilkins | U23 | 18.01.73 | 5 | Birmingham | 4 | Feb |
| 8.72 | Bethan Edwards | U23 | 2.05.73 | 4h1 | Birmingham | 4 | Feb |
| 8.81 | Keri Maddox | | 4.07.72 | 3 | Birmingham | 30 | Dec |
| 8.82 | Janine Whitlock | U23 | 11.08.73 | 2 | Glasgow | 22 | Jan |
| 8.82 | Julie Pratt | U17 | 20.03.79 | 1 | Birmingham | 18 | Feb |
| 8.83 | Katy Sketchley/Parsons | U23 | 9.07.73 | 3 | Glasgow | 22 | Jan |
| 8.84 | Sam Baker | | 14.04.72 | 4 | Glasgow | 22 | Jan |
| 8.84 | Claire Pearson | U17 | 23.09.78 | 2 | Birmingham | 18 | Feb |
| 8.84 | Nicola Hall | U17 | 14.12.79 | 1 | Birmingham | 26 | Feb |
| 8.88 | Lorna Silver | U23 | 10.01.74 | 1h2 | Glasgow | 22 | Jan |
| (20) | | | | | | | |
| 8.88 | Sarah Claxton | U17 | 23.09.79 | 3 | Birmingham | 18 | Feb |
| 8.89 | Sarah Damm | | 12.09.70 | 1P | Birmingham | 5 | Feb |
| 8.90 | Rachel King | U20 | 11.05.76 | 2 | Birmingham | 19 | Feb |
| 8.93 | Katherine Livesey | U17 | 15.12.79 | 1P | Glasgow | 9 | Dec |
| 8.94 | Kerry Jury | | 19.11.68 | 4P | Birmingham | 5 | Feb |
| 8.94 | Sharon Price | U23 | 10.12.75 | 1h3 | Birmingham | 19 | Feb |
| 8.96 | Joanne Suddes | U20 | 27.01.77 | 3 | Birmingham | 19 | Feb |
| 8.97 | Sarah Richmond | U23 | 6.01.73 | 2 | Glasgow | 28 | Jan |
| 8.98 | Jackie Tindal | U17 | 21.01.79 | 1 | Glasgow | 4 | Feb |
| 8.99 | Diana Bennett | U23 | 14.06.74 | 5h1 | Birmingham | 4 | Feb |

**Hand Timing**

| | | | | | | | |
|---|---|---|---|---|---|---|---|
| 8.5 | Yinka Idowu | | 25.02.72 | 1P | London (CP) | 22 | Jan |
| 8.6 | Uju Efobi | U23 | (8.61i) | 1 | London (CP) | 21 | Jan |
| 8.6 | Natasha Mighty | | 21.12.70 | 2h2 | London (CP) | 21 | Jan |
| 8.9 | Teresa Springate/Copeland | | 8.03.69 | 1r1 | London (CP) | 14 | Jan |

**Additional Under 17** (1 - 6 above)

| | | | | | | |
|---|---|---|---|---|---|---|
| 9.0 | Emma Brown | | 7.11.78 | 3 | London (CP) | 21 | Jan |
| 9.01 | Emma Anderson | | 19.06.79 | 2 | Birmingham | 5 | Feb |
| 9.09 | Katy Lestrange | | 17.09.79 | 6 | Birmingham | 18 | Feb |
| 9.10 | Gillian Stewart | | 21.01.80 | 2P | Glasgow | 9 | Dec |
| (10) | | | | | | | |
| 9.1 | Clare O'Sullivan | | 8.05.80 | 2 | London (CP) | 26 | Feb |
| 9.12 | Paula Woodland | | 21.12.78 | 3 | Birmingham | 11 | Feb |
| 9.14 | Anna Leyshon | | 19.01.80 | 7 | Birmingham | 18 | Feb |
| 9.15 | Chloe Cozens | | 9.04.80 | 1P | Glasgow | 9 | Dec |
| 9.18 | Julie Davis | | 16.11.79 | 3 | Birmingham | 26 | Feb |
| 9.21 | Deanne Kenney | | 8.09.78 | 3 | Birmingham | 5 | Feb |
| 9.23 | Karen Jousiffe | | 28.04.80 | 2h2 | Birmingham | 18 | Feb |
| 9.25 | Lesley McGoldrick | | 12.09.79 | 3h1 | Birmingham | 18 | Feb |
| 9.26 | Hayley Warrilow | | 10.04.80 | 1r2 | Birmingham | 29 | Jan |
| 9.26 | Niki Pocock | | 9.05.79 | 2h4 | Birmingham | 18 | Feb |

**Overage**

| | | | | | | |
|---|---|---|---|---|---|---|
| 9.17 | Clare Anning | | 26.05.79 | 3P | Glasgow | 9 | Dec |

**Under 15**

| | | | | | | |
|---|---|---|---|---|---|---|
| 8.99 | Rachael Kay | | 8.09.80 | 1h2 | Birmingham | 18 | Feb |
| 9.22 | Naomi Hodge-Dallaway | | 1.06.81 | 2 | Birmingham | 18 | Feb |

**Overage**

| | | | | | | |
|---|---|---|---|---|---|---|
| 9.17 | Caroline Pearce | | 1.09.80 | 1P | Glasgow | 9 | Dec |
| 9.2 | Sarah Akinbiyi | | 23.08.81 | 1 | London (CP) | 16 | Dec |

# 70 METRES HURDLES - Under 13

| | | | | | | | |
|---|---|---|---|---|---|---|---|
| 11.17 | 1.8 | Anne Massey | 10.09.82 | 1r1 | Birmingham | 3 | Sep |
| 11.4 | | Charlotte Haimes | 28.09.82 | 1r2 | London (TB) | 30 | Jul |
| 11.4 | | Rachel Webb | 1.12.82 | 1 | St. Ives | 20 | Aug |
| 11.5 | | Kelly Smith | | 1 | Carmarthen | 11 | Jun |
| 11.5 | | D. Mann | | 1 | Birmingham | 2 | Jul |
| 11.5 | | E. Cutts | | 2 | Birmingham | 2 | Jul |
| 11.5 | | Lauren McLoughlin | 8.09.82 | 1r1 | Plymouth | 16 | Jul |
| 11.5 | | Helen Barling | 5.10.82 | 1 | Bournemouth | 27 | Aug |
| 11.57 w 3.0 | | Laura Henderson | 10.09.82 | P | Aberdeen | 16 | Jul |
| 11.6 | | Jennifer Hoare | 15.10.82 | 3 | Birmingham | 2 | Jul |
| (10) | | | | | | | |
| 11.70 w 3.7 | | Gemma Archibald | 29.10.82 | 1 | Pitreavie | 9 | Jul |
| 11.70 w 3.0 | | Catriona Pennet | 10.10.83 | P | Aberdeen | 16 | Jul |
| 11.7 | | Nicola Atkins | | 1 | Cannock | 9 | Sep |
| 11.73 w 3.0 | | Jemma Scott | 14.03.83 | P | Aberdeen | 16 | Jul |
| 11.74 w 3.7 | | Clare McNeill | 10.10.82 | 2 | Pitreavie | 9 | Jul |

# 75 METRES HURDLES - Under 15

| | | | | | | | |
|---|---|---|---|---|---|---|---|
| 11.01 w 2.6 | | Naomi Hodge-Dallaway | 1.06.81 | 1 | Nottingham | 8 | Jul |
| 11.13 | -0.3 | | | 1r1 | Birmingham | 30 | Jul |
| 11.14 | -0.3 | Serena Bailey | 2.01.81 | 2r1 | Birmingham | 30 | Jul |
| 11.18 w 2.5 | | Sarah Akinbiyi | 23.08.81 | 1 | London (He) | 6 | Aug |
| 11.3 | | | | 1 | Croydon | 10 | Jun |
| 11.31 | -0.5 | | | 1h1 | Birmingham | 30 | Jul |
| 11.3 | | Sarah Lane | 4.06.81 | 1 | Cwmbran | 27 | Jun |
| 11.50 | -0.3 | Becki Marshall | 13.09.80 | 4r1 | Birmingham | 30 | Jul |
| 11.50 w 2.5 | | Caroline Pearce | 1.09.80 | 2 | London (He) | 6 | Aug |
| 11.52 | -0.3 | | | 5r1 | Birmingham | 30 | Jul |
| 11.5 | | Rachael Kay | 8.09.80 | 1 | Birmingham | 30 | Apr |
| 11.56 | 1.8 | | | 1 | Sheffield | 28 | May |
| 11.5 | | Jane Dutton | 6.09.80 | | | | |
| 11.6 | | | | 1 | Crewe | 10 | Jun |
| 11.64 | -0.7 | | | 3s2 | Nottingham | 7 | Jul |
| 11.58 | | Carolynne Sutherland | 4.09.80 | 1 | Greenock | 4 | Jun |
| 11.6 | | Clare Turner | 23.09.80 | 1 | Basildon | 16 | Jul |
| 11.61 | | | | 1 | Birmingham | 2 | Sep |
| (10) | | | | | | | |
| 11.6 | | Sarina Mantle | 19.01.81 | 2 | Colchester | 28 | Aug |
| 11.6 | | Emma Duck | 9.02.81 | 1 | Ryde | 24 | Sep |
| 11.61 | 1.8 | Laura Foster | 22.07.81 | 2 | Sheffield | 28 | May |
| 11.66 | 0.2 | Joanne Stringer | 17.03.81 | 2h2 | Birmingham | 30 | Jul |
| 11.7 | | Caroline Pugh | 13.10.80 | 1 | Walton | 1 | Jul |
| 11.7 | | Stephanie Little | 5.11.81 | 1 | Newport | 17 | Sep |
| 11.74 w 2.8 | | Ruth Dales | 29.10.80 | 1h1 | Pitreavie | 9 | Jul |
| 11.78 | 1.0 | Emma Reid | 5.01.81 | 1 | Grangemouth | 14 | May |
| 11.78 w 4.2 | | Gemma Whitton | 25.05.81 | 1h2 | Pitreavie | 9 | Jul |

**Under 13**

| | | | | | | | |
|---|---|---|---|---|---|---|---|
| 12.5 | | Helen Barling | 5.10.82 | 1 | Oxford | 11 | Jun |
| 12.6 | | Amy Teale | 30.12.82 | 2 | Carlisle | 10 | Sep |

# 80 METRES HURDLES - Under 17

| | | | | | | | |
|---|---|---|---|---|---|---|---|
| 11.32 | 1.5 | Julie Pratt | 20.03.79 | 1 | Nottingham | 8 | Jul |
| 11.40 | 1.5 | Nicola Hall | 14.12.79 | 2 | Nottingham | 8 | Jul |
| 11.44 | -0.2 | Claire Pearson | 23.09.78 | 1 | Birmingham | 29 | Jul |
| 11.49 | 1.5 | Emma Anderson | 19.06.79 | 3 | Nottingham | 8 | Jul |
| 11.5 | | Sarah Claxton | 23.09.79 | 1 | Colchester | 28 | Aug |
| 11.57 | | | | 2 | Barking | 13 | May |
| 11.56 w 2.6 | | Lynne Fairweather | 15.01.80 | 1 | Pitreavie | 8 | Jul |
| 11.89 | 2.0 | | | 1h1 | Edinburgh | 17 | Jun |

| 11.6 w | | Gael Davies | 5.02.79 | 1 | Cardiff | 27 May |
| | | 11.62 -0.2 | | 2 | Birmingham | 29 Jul |
| 11.65 | 1.5 | Victoria Henson | 9.01.79 | 5 | Nottingham | 8 Jul |
| 11.65 | | Kate Forsyth | 5.06.79 | 1 | Gateshead | 12 Aug |
| 11.69 w 2.6 | | Jackie Tindal | 21.01.79 | 2 | Pitreavie | 8 Jul |
| (10) | | | | | | |
| 11.7 | | Paula Woodland | 21.12.78 | 1 | Swansea | 30 Apr |
| 11.7 | | Deanne Kenney | 8.09.78 | 2 | Leicester | 10 Jun |
| | | 11.88 -0.2 | | 4 | Birmingham | 29 Jul |
| 11.7 | | Amanda Gray | 22.03.79 | 1 | Derby | 23 Jul |
| 11.71 | 1.5 | Lesley McGoldrick | 12.09.79 | 7 | Nottingham | 8 Jul |
| 11.8 | | Anna Leyshon | 19.01.80 | 2 | Swansea | 30 Apr |
| | | 11.94 w | | 1 | Cardiff | 1 Jul |
| 11.8 w | 4.0 | Michelle Winter | 18.06.79 | 1H | Bebington | 22 Jul |
| | | 12.0 | | 1H | Blackpool | 24 Jun |
| 11.86 | 1.3 | Nikita Thompson | 17.08.80 | 3 | Hagen, GER | 15 Jul |
| 11.88 | | Natalie Butler | 25.11.78 | 1H | Enfield | 12 Aug |
| 11.88 w 2.1 | | Debbie Harrison | 13.11.78 | 1H | Stoke | 16 Sep |
| 11.89 w 3.0 | | Gillian Stewart | 21.01.80 | 2 | Edinburgh | 17 Jun |
| | | 11.96 | | 1 | Greenock | 4 Jun |
| (20) | | | | | | |
| 11.9 | | Helen Martin | 19.08.80 | 1 | Glasgow | 28 Aug |
| 11.9 w | 5.2 | Emma Brown | 7.11.78 | 1 | Croydon | 13 May |
| 11.9 w | | Clare Anning | 26.05.79 | 2 | Cardiff | 27 May |
| | | 11.95 w | | 2 | Cardiff | 1 Jul |
| | | 12.0 | | 1 | Barry | 11 May |
| 11.9 w | | Danielle Sullivan | 11.12.78 | 4 | Cardiff | 27 May |
| 11.9 w | 4.0 | Katherine Livesey | 15.12.79 | 2H | Bebington | 22 Jul |
| | | 12.0 | | 1 | Blackpool | 13 May |
| 11.96 w 2.7 | | Katie Challoner | 18.09.78 | 2r1 | Stoke | 17 Jun |
| 12.0 | | Clare O'Sullivan | 8.05.80 | 1 | Dartford | 20 May |
| 12.0 | | Eve Miller | 1.12.79 | 2 | Enfield | 20 May |
| 12.0 | | Tasmin Stephens | 2.08.80 | 1h | Antrim | 27 May |
| 12.0 | | Amy Nuttell | 6.02.80 | 1 | Grantham | 10 Jun |
| (30) | | | | | | |
| 12.0 | | Laura Haylock | 20.02.80 | 2 | St. Ives | 17 Jun |
| 12.0 | | Karen Jousiffe | 28.04.80 | 1 | Kingston | 22 Jun |
| 12.0 | | Anna Biscoe | 13.09.79 | 1 | Grantham | 1 Jul |
| 12.0 w | | Amanda Humble | 15.08.79 | 2 | Middlesbrough | 13 May |
| 12.0 w | 3.6 | Pamela Johnstone | 16.03.79 | 1 | Inverness | 11 Jun |
| 12.0 w | 3.5 | Kate Bailey | 14.09.78 | 4h1 | Nottingham | 7 Jul |
| 12.0 w | 2.2 | Leanda Adams | 7.12.79 | 4h2 | Nottingham | 7 Jul |

## 100 METRES HURDLES

| 12.90 | 1.5 | Jacqui Agyepong | 5.01.69 | 3 | Villeneuve d'Ascq, FRA | 25 Jun |
| | | 13.06 1.3 | | 1 | Hengelo, HOL | 5 Jun |
| | | 13.06 -0.2 | | 3h4 | Gothenburg, SWE | 5 Aug |
| | | 13.09 0.5 | | 1 | Gateshead | 21 Aug |
| | | 13.14 0.1 | | 7s1 | Gothenburg, SWE | 5 Aug |
| | | 13.23 1.7 | | 1 | Stoke | 9 Sep |
| | | 13.28 0.2 | | 7 | Linz, AUT | 22 Aug |
| | | 13.35 -4.6 | | 2 | Madrid, SPA | 20 Jun |
| 13.32 | 0.7 | Michelle Campbell | 24.02.69 | 2 | Azusa, USA | 22 Apr |
| | | 13.35 1.2 | | 3 | Sheffield | 23 Jul |
| | | 13.36 1.6 | | 2 | Birmingham | 15 Jul |
| | | 13.37 1.7 | | 2 | Long Beach, USA | 10 Jun |
| | | 13.40 1.1 | | 1h1 | Azusa, USA | 25 May |
| | | 13.40 2.0 | | 6 | Gateshead | 2 Jul |
| | | 13.47 0.5 | | 5 | Gateshead | 21 Aug |
| | | 13.51 1.2 | | 1 | Budapest, HUN | 8 Jul |
| | | 13.55 0.4 | | 2 | Norwalk, USA | 4 Jun |

| Time | Wind | Name | Cat | Born | Pos | Venue | Date |
|---|---|---|---|---|---|---|---|
| 13.34 | 1.6 | Melanie Wilkins | U23 | 18.01.73 | 1 | Birmingham | 15 Jul |
| 13.41 | 1.2 | | | | 5 | Sheffield | 12 Jul |
| 13.55 | 0.0 | | | | 3 | Narbonne, FRA | 29 Jul |
| 13.36 | 1.2 | Keri Maddox | | 4.07.72 | 4 | Sheffield | 23 Jul |
| 13.40 | 1.6 | | | | 3 | Birmingham | 15 Jul |
| 13.48 | | | | | 1 | Wrexham | 25 Jun |
| 13.48 | -1.3 | | | | 1h3 | Birmingham | 15 Jul |
| 13.50 | -0.9 | | | | 1 | Cwmbran | 9 Jul |
| 13.36 | -2.4 | Clova Court | V35 | 10.02.60 | 1 | Gateshead | 12 Aug |
| 13.42 | 1.7 | | | | 2 | Stoke | 9 Sep |
| 13.44 | 0.4 | | | | 2 | K Wusterhausen, GER | 30 Aug |
| 13.48 | -1.1 | | | | 1h1 | Birmingham | 15 Jul |
| 13.51 | -0.9 | | | | 2 | Cwmbran | 9 Jul |
| 13.55 | 2.0 | | | | 1 | Birmingham | 20 May |
| 13.45 | 1.8 | Natasha Danvers | U20 | 19.09.77 | 1 | Belfort, FRA | 6 Aug |
| 13.46 | -1.2 | | | | 2 | Nyiregyhaza, HUN | 28 Jul |
| 13.54 | -0.7 | | | | 3r2 | Linz, AUT | 22 Aug |
| 13.51 | 1.0 | Denise Lewis | | 27.08.72 | 1h2 | Birmingham | 15 Jul |
| 13.52 | -0.6 | | | | 1H | Gothenburg, SWE | 9 Aug |
| 13.53 | 1.1 | Sam Farquharson | | 15.12.69 | 4 | Jena, GER | 1 Jun |
| 13.53 | 1.6 | Diane Allahgreen | U23 | 21.02.75 | 4 | Birmingham | 15 Jul |

38 performances to 13.55 by 9 athletes

| Time | Wind | Name | Cat | Born | Pos | Venue | Date |
|---|---|---|---|---|---|---|---|
| 13.62 | 0.8 | Angela Thorp | | 7.12.72 | 1 | Bedford | 28 May |
| (10) | | | | | | | |
| 13.71 | 2.0 | Louise Fraser | | 10.10.70 | 2 | Birmingham | 20 May |
| 13.87 | -1.2 | Yinka Idowu | | 25.02.72 | 1 | Edinburgh | 8 May |
| 13.93 | 1.0 | Orla Bermingham | U23 | 7.10.75 | 3h2 | Birmingham | 15 Jul |
| 14.03 | 0.8 | Rachel King | U20 | 11.05.76 | 1 | Cardiff | 22 Jul |
| 14.05 | 1.2 | Uju Efobi | U23 | 10.10.74 | 2h1 | Tessenderlo, BEL | 2 Jul |
| 14.09 | 1.8 | Jane Hale | U23 | 4.01.74 | 2h | Knoxville, USA | 7 May |
| 14.21 | 0.8 | Bethan Edwards | U23 | 2.05.73 | 2 | Cardiff | 22 Jul |
| 14.24 | | Clare Mackintosh | | 2.04.71 | 1 | Greenock | 4 Jun |
| 14.26 | -2.0 | Liz Fairs | U20 | 1.12.77 | 1s1 | Nottingham | 7 Jul |
| 14.28 | 0.8 | Non Evans | | 27.02.67 | 3 | Cardiff | 22 Jul |
| (20) | | | | | | | |
| 14.31 | 0.4 | Emma Beales | | 7.12.71 | 1H | Kilkenny, IRE | 26 Aug |
| 14.32 | 1.0 | Jacqui Parker | | 15.10.66 | 1 | Perth, AUS | 20 Dec |
| 14.35 | | Sarah Richmond | U23 | 6.01.73 | 2 | Greenock | 4 Jun |
| 14.38 | 1.0 | Teresa Springate/Copeland | | 8.03.69 | 4h2 | Birmingham | 15 Jul |
| 14.43 | | Claire Phythian | U23 | 7.02.73 | H | Tuscaloosa, USA | 18 May |
| 14.45 | 1.1 | Kerry Jury | | 19.11.68 | 1H | Stoke | 3 Jun |
| 14.46 | 1.9 | Denise Bolton | U20 | 1.02.77 | 1 | Blackpool | 20 Aug |
| 14.47 | 1.9 | Janine Whitlock | U23 | 11.08.73 | 2 | Blackpool | 20 Aug |
| 14.48 | 1.1 | Jenny Kelly | | 20.06.70 | 2H | Stoke | 3 Jun |
| 14.49 | 1.3 | Pauline Richards | | 30.06.68 | 2h2 | Birmingham | 18 Jun |
| (30) | | | | | | | |
| 14.50 | 1.1 | Kim Crowther-Price | | 19.01.66 | 1H | Stoke | 3 Jun |
| *14.50* | | *Olive Burke* | | *12.09.66* | *1* | *Aldershot* | *26 Jun* |
| 14.52 | -0.5 | Leah Lackenby | U23 | 18.09.74 | 1H | Vladimir, RUS | 5 Aug |
| 14.55 | -2.4 | Jocelyn Kirby/Harwood | V35 | 21.11.57 | 1 | Edinburgh | 24 Jun |
| 14.56 | | Katy Sketchley/Parsons | U23 | 9.07.73 | 1 | Barking | 13 May |
| 14.56 | 0.8 | Tracy Goddard/Joseph | | 29.11.69 | 7 | Bedford | 28 May |
| 14.56 | | Gail Walker | | 7.12.71 | 3 | Greenock | 4 Jun |
| 14.58 | 1.9 | Clare Bushby | U20 | 7.09.76 | 2 | Sheffield | 28 May |
| 14.58 | -0.3 | Katie Budd | U20 | 3.01.76 | 2h2 | Bedford | 2 Jul |
| 14.58 | 1.0 | Susan Jones | U20 | 8.06.78 | 1H | Stoke | 16 Sep |
| 14.61 | 1.5 | Sharon Price | U23 | 10.12.75 | 1 | Stoke | 17 Jun |
| (40) | | | | | | | |
| 14.73 | -1.2 | Josephine Peet | | 4.12.71 | 3 | Edinburgh | 8 May |
| 14.74 | -0.3 | Julia Bennett | | 26.03.70 | H | Helmond, HOL | 1 Jul |
| 14.74 | 0.5 | Kelly Sotherton | U20 | 13.11.76 | 3h3 | Bedford | 2 Jul |

| | | | | | | | | |
|---|---|---|---|---|---|---|---|---|
| 14.76 | | Sally Sagar | U20 | 28.03.77 | 2h2 | Sheffield | 28 | May |
| 14.77 | 1.1 | Charmaine Johnson | | 4.06.63 | 4H | Stoke | 3 | Jun |
| 14.78 | 1.3 | Sarah Damm | | 12.09.70 | 3H | Derby | 29 | Apr |
| 14.81 | 1.3 | Diana Bennett | U23 | 14.06.74 | 4H | Derby | 29 | Apr |
| 14.81 | -1.7 | Clover Wynter-Pink | U20 | 29.11.77 | 3s2 | Nottingham | 7 | Jul |
| 14.81 | 0.0 | Bianca Liston | U20 | 28.05.78 | 3 | Stoke | 10 | Sep |
| 14.84 | -0.1 | Julie Pratt | U17 | 20.03.79 | 4 | Alfaz Del Pi, SPA | 13 | Apr |
| (50) | | | | | | | | |
| 14.85 | | Kate Forsyth | U17 | 5.06.79 | 1r2 | Gateshead | 12 | Aug |
| 14.86 | 1.9 | Joanne Suddes | U20 | 27.01.77 | 3 | Sheffield | 28 | May |
| 14.87 | -0.2 | Anne Hollman | U23 | 18.02.74 | 2H | Vladimir, RUS | 5 | Aug |
| 14.96 | | Samantha Male | U20 | 11.04.76 | 2 | Aldershot | 26 | Jun |
| 14.98 | 1.9 | Wendy Laing | | 29.12.62 | 4 | Blackpool | 20 | Aug |
| 14.99 | 1.5 | Debbie Robson | U20 | 12.07.76 | 2 | Stoke | 17 | Jun |
| 15.00 | | Manndy Laing | V35 | 7.11.59 | 1 | Exeter | 6 | Aug |
| 15.06 | 1.4 | Louise Batho | U20 | 27.11.76 | 1H | Stoke | 16 | Sep |
| 15.08 | 0.5 | Julie Hollman | U20 | 16.02.77 | 4H | Stoke | 3 | Jun |
| 15.08 | 1.5 | Abigail Ashby | U20 | 23.11.77 | 2H | Stoke | 16 | Sep |
| (60) | | | | | | | | |
| 15.09 | 1.5 | Nicola Gautier | U20 | 21.03.78 | 3H | Stoke | 16 | Sep |
| 15.10 | 1.9 | Stephanie Nicholson | U20 | 28.06.76 | 5 | Sheffield | 28 | May |
| 15.10 | | Beverley Roker | | 22.06.62 | 3 | Aldershot | 26 | Jun |
| 15.11 | 1.7 | Rebecca Lewis | U20 | 31.12.77 | 5 | Stoke | 9 | Sep |
| 15.12 | -1.4 | Jackie Jenner | U20 | 25.10.76 | 2h3 | Nottingham | 7 | Jul |
| 15.12 | 1.4 | Michala Gee | U23 | 8.12.75 | 2H | Stoke | 16 | Sep |
| 15.15 | | Megan Jones | U20 | 10.07.76 | | Wrexham | 29 | Jul |
| 15.16 | | Claire Morrison/Adams | | 30.05.69 | 2 | Wrexham | 25 | Jun |
| 15.16 | -2.0 | Annette Stern | U20 | 9.09.76 | 5s1 | Nottingham | 7 | Jul |
| 15.17 | 1.5 | Jane O'Malley | U20 | 18.07.77 | 4H | Stoke | 16 | Sep |
| (70) | | | | | | | | |
| 15.19 | -0.5 | Rachel Hooker | U17 | 27.05.79 | 3 | London (He) | 6 | Aug |
| 15.20 | 1.9 | Katie Jones | U20 | 4.01.77 | 7 | Blackpool | 20 | Aug |
| 15.20 | 1.7 | Emma Lindsay | | 11.04.71 | 6 | Stoke | 9 | Sep |
| 15.23 | | Lorna Silver | U23 | 10.01.74 | 1 | Edinburgh | 10 | Sep |
| 15.28 | 1.0 | Clare Wise | | 22.08.69 | 2 | Portsmouth | 13 | May |
| 15.28 | 1.5 | Amanda Higgins | U20 | 13.09.76 | 3 | Stoke | 17 | Jun |
| 15.28 | -2.0 | Emma Nye | U20 | 17.07.77 | 6=s1 | Nottingham | 7 | Jul |
| 15.29 | 0.0 | Jenny Pearson | | 3.07.62 | 4 | Stoke | 10 | Sep |

**Wind Assisted**

| | | | | | | | | |
|---|---|---|---|---|---|---|---|---|
| 13.03 | 2.4 | Agyepong | | (12.90) | 5 | London (CP) | 27 | Aug |
| 13.08 | 4.0 | Michelle Campbell | | (13.32) | 1 | Azusa, USA | 26 | May |
| | | 13.17 | 2.7 | | 4 | Walnut, USA | 15 | Apr |
| | | 13.24 | 2.9 | | 2 | Oslo, NOR | 21 | Jul |
| | | 13.26 A | 3.8 | | 6 | Sestriere, ITA | 29 | Jul |
| | | 13.28 | 3.3 | | 1 | Los Angeles, USA | 6 | May |
| | | 13.54 | 2.3 | | 3 | Fresno, USA | 1 | Apr |
| 13.19 | 2.4 | Clova Court | V35 | (13.36) | 6 | London (CP) | 27 | Aug |
| 13.47 | 2.9 | Diane Allahgreen | U23 | (13.53) | 2 | Tallinn, EST | 9 | Jul |
| 13.49 | 2.4 | Danvers | U20 | (13.45) | 7 | London (CP) | 27 | Aug |
| | | 13.51 | 2.2 | | 1 | Bedford | 2 | Jul |
| 13.51 | 2.3 | Louise Fraser | | (13.71) | 1 | Gateshead | 17 | Jun |
| | | 12 performances to 13.55 by 6 athletes | | | | | | |
| 13.76 | 2.5 | Yinka Idowu | | (13.87) | 2H | Alhama, SPA | 20 | May |
| 13.94 | 2.4 | Jacqui Parker | | (14.32) | 2 | Perth, AUS | 17 | Dec |
| 13.99 | 2.2 | Rachel King | U20 | (14.03) | 2 | Bedford | 2 | Jul |
| 14.07 | 2.3 | Jocelyn Kirby/Harwood | V35 | (14.55) | 2 | Gateshead | 17 | Jun |
| | | | | | | | | |
| 14.17 | | Claire Phythian | U23 | (14.43) | H | Knoxville, USA | 2 | Jun |
| 14.24 | 2.2 | Liz Fairs | U20 | (14.26) | 4 | Bedford | 2 | Jul |
| 14.24 | 2.1 | Vikki Schofield | | 29.12.72 | 1H | Kilkenny, IRE | 26 | Aug |

| | | | | | | | | |
|---|---|---|---|---|---|---|---|---|
| 14.27 | 2.5 | Denise Bolton | U20 | (14.46) | 1H | Aberdeen | 15 | Jul |
| 14.37 | 2.3 | Clare Bushby | U20 | (14.58) | 4 | Gateshead | 17 | Jun |
| 14.43 | 2.3 | Paula Wilkin | U23 | 28.03.74 | 5 | Gateshead | 17 | Jun |
| 14.45 | 2.5 | Charmaine Johnson | | (14.77) | 5H | Alhama, SPA | 20 | May |
| 14.45 | | Susan Jones | U20 | (14.58) | 2h1 | Blackpool | 20 | Aug |
| 14.53 | 2.2 | Katie Budd | U20 | (14.58) | 6 | Bedford | 2 | Jul |
| 14.54 | 2.2 | Kelly Sotherton | U20 | (14.74) | 7 | Bedford | 2 | Jul |
| | | | | | | | | |
| 14.62 | 2.5 | Josephine Peet | | (14.73) | 2h1 | Birmingham | 18 | Jun |
| 14.64 | 2.3 | Joanne Suddes | U20 | (14.86) | 6 | Gateshead | 17 | Jun |
| 14.64 | 5.1 | Samantha Male | U20 | (14.96) | 1h1 | London (He) | 1 | Jul |
| 14.68 | 2.9 | Sarah Damm | | (14.78) | 5H | Alhama, SPA | 20 | May |
| 14.68 | 2.5 | Julia Bennett | | (14.74) | 6H | Alhama, SPA | 20 | May |
| 14.72 | | Wendy Laing | | (14.98) | 3h1 | Blackpool | 20 | Aug |
| 14.74 | 4.6 | Diana Bennett | U23 | (14.81) | 3h2 | Edinburgh | 7 | May |
| 14.79 | 4.6 | Julie Pratt | U17 | (14.84) | 1h2 | London (He) | 6 | Aug |
| 14.84 | | Jackie Jenner | U20 | (15.12) | 1 | London (CP) | 13 | May |
| 14.84 | | Marie Major | U23 | 4.05.74 | 2 | Barking | 13 | May |
| | | | | | | | | |
| 14.91 | 4.1 | Debbie Robson | U20 | (14.99) | 7 | Telford | 26 | Aug |
| 14.95 | 5.1 | Rachel Hooker | U17 | (15.19) | 2h1 | London (He) | 6 | Aug |
| 15.01 | 2.5 | Jane Saxelby | | 14.01.72 | 3h1 | Birmingham | 18 | Jun |
| 15.09 | 2.5 | Jackie Cooke | U20 | 20.06.76 | 4h1 | Birmingham | 18 | Jun |
| 15.11 | 2.5 | Claire White | U23 | 24.02.73 | 5h1 | Birmingham | 18 | Jun |
| 15.29 | 2.3 | Helen Blanchard | | 11.07.72 | 8 | Gateshead | 17 | Jun |

**Hand Timing**

| | | | | | | | | |
|---|---|---|---|---|---|---|---|---|
| 13.1 | 1.2 | Melanie Wilkins | U23 | (13.34) | 2 | Tessenderlo, BEL | 2 | Jul |
| 13.4 | -1.7 | Court | V35 | (13.36) | 1 | Birmingham | 19 | Aug |
| 13.4 w | 4.5 | Maddox | | (13.36) | 1 | Stoke | 13 | May |
| 13.5 | | Agyepong | | (12.90) | 1 | Derby | 30 | Jul |

4 performances to 13.5 by 4 athletes

| | | | | | | | | |
|---|---|---|---|---|---|---|---|---|
| 13.6 | -0.1 | Louise Fraser | | (13.71) | 1r2 | Alfaz Del Pi, SPA | 13 | Apr |
| 13.8 w | 2.7 | Orla Bermingham | U23 | (13.93) | 3 | Glasgow | 6 | May |
| 13.9 w | 4.9 | Jacqui Parker | | (14.32) | 3 | Perth, AUS | 9 | Dec |
| 14.0 w | 2.2 | Vikki Schofield | | (14.24w) | 1 | Grimsby | 3 | Sep |
| | | 14.2 | | | 1 | York | 23 | Jul |
| 14.1 | | Janine Whitlock | U23 | (14.47) | 2 | Sheffield | 14 | May |
| 14.1 | -0.5 | Lesley-Ann Skeete | | 20.02.67 | 1 | London (WL) | 30 | Jul |
| | | | | | | | | |
| 14.1 w | 3.1 | Clare Mackintosh | | (14.24) | 1 | Inverness | 11 | Jun |
| 14.1 w | 4.1 | Liz Fairs | U20 | (14.26) | 2 | Nottingham | 8 | Jul |
| 14.2 | | Non Evans | | (14.28) | 1 | Newport | 12 | Aug |
| 14.2 | | Katy Sketchley/Parsons | U23 | (14.56) | 1 | Bedford | 2 | Sep |
| 14.3 | | Paula Wilkin | U23 | (14.43w) | 1 | Grimsby | 13 | May |
| 14.3 | | Teresa Springate/Copeland | | (14.38) | 1 | Reading | 20 | May |
| 14.3 | | Jocelyn Kirby/Harwood | V35 | (14.55) | 1 | Bebington | 11 | Jun |
| 14.3 w | 3.1 | Lorna Silver | U23 | (15.23) | 2 | Inverness | 11 | Jun |
| 14.3 w | 4.1 | Clare Bushby | U20 | (14.58) | 3 | Nottingham | 8 | Jul |
| 14.3 w | 4.3 | Leah Lackenby | U23 | (14.52) | 1H | Bebington | 22 | Jul |
| | | | | | | | | |
| 14.4 | | Kerry Jury | | (14.45) | 1 | Worcester | 13 | May |
| 14.4 | | Denise Bolton | U20 | (14.46) | 1 | Middlesbrough | 30 | Jul |
| 14.4 | | Julie Pratt | U17 | (14.84) | 2 | Middlesbrough | 30 | Jul |
| 14.4 w | 4.1 | Sharon Price | U23 | (14.61) | 4 | Nottingham | 8 | Jul |
| 14.5 w | 2.7 | Katie Budd | U20 | (14.58) | 4 | Glasgow | 6 | May |
| 14.5 w | 4.1 | Clover Wynter-Pink | U20 | (14.81) | 5 | Nottingham | 8 | Jul |
| 14.6 | -0.1 | Dionne Ible | | 14.09.67 | 3 | Alfaz Del Pi, SPA | 13 | Apr |
| 14.6 | | Katy Bartlett | U23 | 6.05.73 | 2 | Grimsby | 13 | May |
| 14.6 | | Joanne Nicklin | | 12.07.67 | 1r2 | London (Elt) | 20 | May |
| 14.6 | | Claire White | U23 | (15.11w) | 1 | Kettering | 21 | May |

269

| | | | | | | | |
|---|---|---|---|---|---|---|---|
| 14.6 | | Anne Hollman | U23 | (14.87) | 1 | Peterborough | 22 Jul |
| 14.6 | -1.5 | Gowry Retchakan | V35 | 21.06.60 | 1 | Grimsby | 20 Aug |
| 14.7 | | Bianca Liston | U20 | (14.81) | 1 | Hoo | 10 Jun |
| 14.7 | -0.5 | Josephine Peet | | (14.73) | 5 | Birmingham | 18 Jun |
| 14.7 | | Debbie Nicklin | U23 | 9.12.75 | 1 | Ilford | 2 Sep |
| 14.7 w | 2.7 | Sam Baker | | 14.04.72 | 6 | Glasgow | 6 May |
| 14.7 w | 4.3 | Wendy Laing | | (14.98) | 3H | Bebington | 22 Jul |
| 14.8 | | Jane O'Malley | U20 | (15.17) | 1 | Grimsby | 13 May |
| 14.9 | | Jackie Cooke | U20 | (15.09w) | 1r2 | Stafford | 7 May |
| 14.9 | | Kay Reynolds | | 15.09.67 | 1 | Bromley | 20 May |
| | | | | | | | |
| 14.9 | | Joanne Bennett | U23 | 1.09.73 | 2 | Loughborough | 20 May |
| 14.9 | | Beverley Roker | | (15.10) | 1 | Basingstoke | 22 Jul |
| 14.9 | | Jane Fuller | U20 | 21.04.76 | 2 | Basingstoke | 22 Jul |
| 14.9 w | 2.9 | Alison Purton | | 25.11.72 | 2r2 | Glasgow | 6 May |
| 15.1 | -2.9 | | | | 3 | Leamington | 14 May |
| 15.0 | | Rachael Kennedy | U20 | 15.06.78 | 2 | Grimsby | 13 May |
| 15.0 | | Donna-Louise Hutt | | 6.06.72 | 1 | Milton Keynes | 13 May |
| 15.0 | | Abigail Ashby | U20 | (15.08) | 3 | Sheffield | 14 May |
| 15.0 | | Amanda Higgins | U20 | (15.28) | 1 | | 15 May |
| 15.0 | | Louise Batho | U20 | (15.06) | 1 | Portsmouth | 20 May |
| 15.0 | | Lian Miveld | U20 | 8.09.76 | 1r2 | Portsmouth | 20 May |
| | | | | | | | |
| 15.0 | | Jackie Jenner | U20 | (15.12) | 2 | Hoo | 10 Jun |
| 15.0 | | Jane Saxelby | | (15.01w) | 2 | Nottingham | 25 Jun |
| 15.0 | | Dextene McIntosh | U20 | 27.08.78 | 1r2 | London (He) | 1 Jul |
| 15.0 | | Rebecca Lewis | U20 | (15.11) | 3 | Middlesbrough | 30 Jul |
| 15.0 | | Megan Jones | U20 | (15.15) | | Newport | 12 Aug |
| 15.0 | | Vicki Jamison | U20 | 19.05.77 | 1 | Londonderry | 19 Aug |
| 15.0 | | Jenny Pearson | | (15.29) | 2 | Derby | 9 Sep |
| 15.0 w | 3.0 | Annette Stern | U20 | (15.16) | 1 | Bedford | 26 Aug |
| 15.0 w | 2.2 | Louise Eden | U20 | 11.12.77 | 4 | Grimsby | 3 Sep |
| 15.1 | | Helen Blanchard | | (15.29w) | 1 | Carlisle | 2 Apr |
| | | | | | | | |
| 15.1 | | Michala Gee | U23 | (15.12) | 3r1 | Stafford | 7 May |
| 15.1 | | Kirsty Mayhead | U20 | 17.02.78 | 2 | Basildon | 20 May |
| 15.1 | | Gael Davies | U17 | 5.02.79 | 1 | Sutton Coldfield | 26 Aug |
| 15.1 w | 4.0 | Emma Lindsay | | (15.20) | 1 | Coatbridge | 21 May |
| 15.1 w | 3.9 | Heather Myers | | 5.12.64 | 4 | Liverpool | 2 Jul |
| 15.1 w | 4.1 | Debbie Woolgar | | 10.03.65 | 5 | Croydon | 28 Aug |
| 15.1 w | 2.2 | Margaret Still | | 9.05.65 | 5 | Grimsby | 3 Sep |
| 15.2 | | Ruth Irving | U23 | 20.07.74 | 1 | Cambridge | 20 May |

**Additional Under 17**

| | | | | | | | |
|---|---|---|---|---|---|---|---|
| 15.4 | -0.4 | Yewande Ige | | 21.03.80 | 3 | London (WP) | 29 Apr |
| 15.6 | | Kelly Moreton | | 18.09.79 | 1 | Newport | 18 Jun |
| 15.7 | | Victoria Henson | | 9.01.79 | 1 | Bedford | 2 Sep |
| 15.8 w | 3.0 | Linda Crocker | | 2.04.79 | 1r2 | Bedford | 26 Aug |

## 300 METRES HURDLES - Under 17

| | | | | | | |
|---|---|---|---|---|---|---|
| 43.75 | Cicely Hall | | 12.10.78 | 1 | London (CP) | 28 May |
| 43.83 | Gael Davies | | 5.02.79 | 1 | Nottingham | 8 Jul |
| 43.88 | Tracey Duncan | | 16.05.79 | 2 | Nottingham | 8 Jul |
| 44.2 | Pamela Johnstone | | 16.03.79 | 1 | Glasgow | 25 Jun |
| | 44.47 | | | 1 | Edinburgh | 17 Jun |
| 44.23 | Eve Miller | | 1.12.79 | 2 | London (CP) | 28 May |
| 44.42 | Amanda Gray | | 22.03.79 | 3h3 | Nottingham | 7 Jul |
| 44.64 | Niki Pocock | | 9.05.79 | 3 | Nottingham | 8 Jul |
| 44.65 | Yewande Ige | | 21.03.80 | 1h1 | Nottingham | 7 Jul |
| 44.7 | Maria Bolsover | | 5.06.80 | 1 | Sheffield | 30 Apr |
| 44.75 | Jodi Hallett | | 8.11.78 | 1h2 | Nottingham | 7 Jul |

(10)

270

| 44.97 | Sarah Wilhelmy | 2.02.80 | 1 | Barking | 14 | May |
|---|---|---|---|---|---|---|
| 45.07 | Linda Crocker | 2.04.79 | 4 | London (CP) | 28 | May |
| 45.2 | Eleanor Chamberlain | 17.04.79 | 1 | Birmingham | 10 | Jun |
| | 45.83 | | 3h1 | Nottingham | 7 | Jul |
| 45.2 | Lesley Owusu | 21.12.78 | 1 | Woking | 17 | Sep |
| 45.34 | Katie Challoner | 18.09.78 | 2r1 | Stoke | 17 | Jun |
| 45.4 | Leanne Dennis | 30.12.79 | 1 | Cardiff | 25 | Jun |
| | 45.68 | | 1 | Cardiff | 1 | Jul |
| 45.69 | Alice Wright | 31.12.78 | 4h2 | Nottingham | 7 | Jul |
| 45.9 | Emma Brown | 7.11.78 | 3 | Kingston | 10 | Jun |
| | 46.45 | | 5h3 | Nottingham | 7 | Jul |
| 45.9 | Fiona Clasper | 16.10.79 | 2 | Pitreavie | 8 | Jul |
| | 46.17 | | 5 | Birmingham | 30 | Jul |
| 45.98 | Sarah Short | 27.11.79 | 1h2 | London (CP) | 27 | May |
| | (20) | | | | | |
| 46.0 | Sarah Cloke | 28.06.79 | 1 | Exeter | 10 | Jun |
| 46.04 | Kate Dyer | 12.07.79 | 4h3 | Nottingham | 7 | Jul |
| 46.10 | Lisa Bennington | 12.12.78 | 1 | Blackpool | 20 | Aug |
| 46.1 | Martha Jones | 31.07.80 | 2h1 | Birmingham | 30 | Jul |
| | 46.29 | | 6 | Birmingham | 30 | Jul |
| 46.2 | Kate Moody | 7.04.79 | 3 | Birmingham | 23 | Apr |
| 46.2 | Lizz Mitchell | 13.10.79 | 1 | Basildon | 10 | Jun |
| 46.2 | Emma Anderson | 19.06.79 | 1r2 | Cannock | 16 | Jul |
| 46.39 | Carrie Hancox | 8.08.80 | 5h2 | Nottingham | 7 | Jul |
| 46.4 | Paula Woodland | 21.12.78 | 2 | Swansea | 30 | Apr |
| | 46.74 | | 7 | London (CP) | 28 | May |
| 46.4 | Ruth McCallum | 1.03.79 | 3 | Pitreavie | 8 | Jul |
| | (30) | | | | | |
| 46.49 | Gemma Robinson | 30.12.78 | 6 | London (CP) | 28 | May |
| 46.6 | Tasmin Stephens | 2.08.80 | 1 | Dumfries | 2 | Jul |
| 46.77 | Sally Lindsay | 28.07.79 | 2 | Edinburgh | 17 | Jun |
| 46.8 | Fiona Hall | 19.04.79 | 1 | Grimsby | 14 | May |
| 46.8 | Lisa Whigham | 14.08.80 | 2 | Coatbridge | 27 | Aug |

## 400 METRES HURDLES

| 56.50 | Jacqui Parker | | 15.10.66 | 1 | Sydney, AUS | 5 | Mar |
|---|---|---|---|---|---|---|---|
| | 56.64 | | | 4 | Sao Paulo, BRZ | 14 | May |
| | 57.18 | | | 4 | Gateshead | 2 | Jul |
| | 57.32 | | | 8 | London (CP) | 7 | Jul |
| | 57.45 | | | 7 | New York, USA | 21 | May |
| | 57.52 | | | 1 | Perth, AUS | 29 | Jan |
| | 57.56 | | | 3 | Jena, GER | 1 | Jun |
| | 57.90 | | | 4 | Gateshead | 21 | Aug |
| | 58.30 | | | 2 | Perth, AUS | 24 | Jan |
| | 58.42 | | | 4 | Hechtel, BEL | 22 | Jul |
| | 58.8 | | | 1 | Bedford | 10 | Jun |
| 57.07 | Louise Fraser | | 10.10.70 | 3 | Hechtel, BEL | 22 | Jul |
| | 57.76 | | | 3 | Stockholm, SWE | 26 | Jul |
| | 57.91 | | | 7 | Villeneuve d'Ascq, FRA | 24 | Jun |
| | 57.99 | | | 6h1 | Gothenburg, SWE | 8 | Aug |
| | 58.18 | | | 5 | Gateshead | 21 | Aug |
| | 58.76 | | | 1 | Loughborough | 11 | Jun |
| 57.18 | Gowry Retchakan | V35 | 21.06.60 | 1 | Birmingham | 16 | Jul |
| | 57.52 | | | 5 | Lucerne, SWZ | 27 | Jun |
| | 57.65 | | | 4 | Hengelo, HOL | 5 | Jun |
| | 57.78 | | | 6 | St. Denis, FRA | 1 | Jun |
| | 57.86 | | | 6 | Gateshead | 2 | Jul |
| | 58.3 | | | 1 | Hayes | 14 | May |
| | 58.5 | | | 1 | Bebington | 11 | Jun |
| | 58.56 | | | 1 | Bedford | 29 | May |
| | 58.77 | | | 1h3 | Birmingham | 15 | Jul |
| | 58.8 | | | 1 | London (TB) | 29 | Jul |

| 57.30 | Louise Brunning | | 6.03.72 | 1 | Barcelona, SPA | 27 | Jun |
|---|---|---|---|---|---|---|---|
| 58.18 | | | | 1 | Jona, SWZ | 23 | Jul |
| 58.58 | | | | 3 | Birmingham | 16 | Jul |
| 58.21 | Stephanie McCann | | 26.10.65 | 2 | Birmingham | 16 | Jul |
| 58.8 | | | | 1 | Edinburgh | 24 | Jun |
| 58.85 | Vyvyan Rhodes | U23 | 5.05.73 | 6 | Gateshead | 21 | Aug |
| 33 performances to 59.0 by 6 athletes | | | | | | | |
| 59.29 | Clare Bleasdale | | 6.07.71 | 1 | London (CP) | 18 | Jun |
| 59.81 | Vicki Jamison | U20 | 19.05.77 | 2 | Bedford | 2 | Jul |
| 59.9 | Jane Low | | 26.08.60 | 2 | Edinburgh | 24 | Jun |
| 60.31 | | | | 2 | Cardiff | 22 | Jul |
| 59.9 | Heather Myers | | 5.12.64 | 1 | Enfield | 30 | Jul |
| 60.12 | | | | 1 | Enfield | 29 | Sep |
| (10) | | | | | | | |
| 59.91 | Allison Curbishley | U20 | 3.06.76 | 1 | Edinburgh | 7 | May |
| 60.0 | Alanna Cooke/Rowbotham | | 11.01.70 | 1 | Sheffield | 13 | May |
| 60.43 | | | | 2h1 | Bedford | 29 | May |
| 60.0 | Jenny Pearson | | 3.07.62 | 1 | Derby | 9 | Sep |
| 61.11 | | | | 1 | Stoke | 10 | Sep |
| 60.15 | Vicky Day | | 19.06.72 | 2 | London (CP) | 18 | Jun |
| 60.15 | Kate Norman | U20 | 1.01.76 | 3 | Bedford | 2 | Jul |
| 60.37 | Christine Amede | | 7.08.63 | 3 | London (CP) | 18 | Jun |
| 60.4 | Lorna Silver | U23 | 10.01.74 | 3 | Edinburgh | 24 | Jun |
| 60.63 | | | | 3h1 | Bedford | 29 | May |
| 60.6 | Keri Maddox | | 4.07.72 | 1 | Coventry | 13 | Aug |
| 60.7 | Alison Mahindru | | 15.07.68 | 4 | Edinburgh | 24 | Jun |
| 60.95 | | | | 3 | Cardiff | 22 | Jul |
| 60.73 | Jo Mahoney | U20 | 22.10.76 | 2 | Nottingham | 8 | Jul |
| (20) | | | | | | | |
| 60.8 | Margaret Still | | 9.05.65 | 2 | Derby | 9 | Sep |
| 62.12 | | | | 3 | Gateshead | 17 | Jun |
| 61.0 | Kathy Thurston | U20 | 2.01.76 | 1 | Stretford | 6 | Aug |
| 61.39 | | | | 5 | Bedford | 2 | Jul |
| 61.1 | Sarah Damm | | 12.09.70 | 1 | Rotherham | 6 | Aug |
| 61.2 | Katy Bartlett | U23 | 6.05.73 | 1 | Watford | 7 | May |
| 61.56 | | | | 5h3 | Birmingham | 15 | Jul |
| 61.31 | Anna Roze | U23 | 6.11.74 | 2r2 | Loughborough | 11 | Jun |
| 61.32 | Karen Spackman | | 20.08.69 | 4 | London (CP) | 18 | Jun |
| 61.34 | Sinead Dudgeon | U20 | 9.07.76 | 1 | Stoke | 9 | Sep |
| 61.61 | Janet Levermore | | 7.06.69 | 3 | Stoke | 9 | Sep |
| 62.2 | Louise Gregory | U23 | 11.05.74 | 1 | Birmingham | 19 | Aug |
| 62.22 | Anne Hollman | U23 | 18.02.74 | 5 | London (CP) | 18 | Jun |
| (30) | | | | | | | |
| 62.34 | Kate Williams | U20 | 10.11.77 | 1 | Utrecht, HOL | 9 | Jul |
| 62.36 | Jane Lapido | | 24.08.69 | 3h1 | London (CP) | 17 | Jun |
| 62.4 | Veronica Boden | V35 | 23.12.58 | 2 | Stretford | 6 | Aug |
| 62.5 | Clare Wise | | 22.08.69 | 2 | London (He) | 20 | May |
| 63.19 | | | | 4h2 | London (CP) | 17 | Jun |
| 62.5 | Claire Edwards | U23 | 20.10.74 | | Birmingham | 25 | Jun |
| 62.82 | | | | 4 | Cardiff | 22 | Jul |
| 62.5 | Pamela Johnstone | U17 | 16.03.79 | 1 | Ayr | 18 | Jul |
| 62.5 | Michele Gillham | U23 | 8.10.74 | 2 | Croydon | 28 | Aug |
| 65.09 | | | | 5h1 | London (CP) | 17 | Jun |
| 62.6 | Katie Jones | U20 | 4.01.77 | 1 | Stretford | 10 | Jun |
| 63.64 | | | | 2 | Sheffield | 27 | May |
| 62.7 | Denise Facey | | 8.02.69 | 1 | Corby | 25 | Jun |
| 62.7 | Jane Fuller | U20 | 21.04.76 | 1 | Derby | 30 | Jul |
| 63.20 | | | | 2h3 | Edinburgh | 6 | May |
| (40) | | | | | | | |
| 62.81 | Julia Bennett | | 26.03.70 | 4h1 | London (CP) | 17 | Jun |
| 62.90 | Julia Sykes | U23 | 27.05.75 | 1h3 | Edinburgh | 6 | May |

| 62.92 | Dextene McIntosh | U20 | 27.08.78 | 3 | Nottingham | 8 | Jul |
|---|---|---|---|---|---|---|---|
| 62.93 | Sara Elson | | 8.05.70 | 4 | Gateshead | 17 | Jun |
| 63.0 | Sarah Veysey | U23 | 4.03.75 | 1 | Loughborough | 26 | Apr |
| 63.34 | | | | 4 | Telford | 26 | Aug |
| 63.0 | Denise Bolton | U20 | 1.02.77 | 2 | Peterborough | 7 | May |
| 63.35 | | | | 3h1 | Bedford | 1 | Jul |
| 63.0 | Carolyn Smith | | 6.10.61 | 6 | Edinburgh | 24 | Jun |
| 64.13 | | | | 2 | Grangemouth | 14 | May |
| 63.0 | Cathy Yarwood | | 17.06.69 | 1 | Bolton | 2 | Jul |
| 63.74 | | | | 3 | Blackpool | 20 | Aug |
| 63.1 | Isobel Donaldson | | 24.01.64 | 1 | Aldershot | 12 | Aug |
| 64.19 | | | | 3 | Portsmouth | 14 | May |
| 63.2 | Sarah Baigent | | 22.12.71 | 2 | Aldershot | 12 | Aug |
| 65.50 | | | | 3h1 | Edinburgh | 6 | May |
| (50) | | | | | | | |
| 63.3 | Natasha Turner | U23 | 8.11.74 | 3 | London (He) | 20 | May |
| 65.39 | | | | 6h1 | London (CP) | 17 | Jun |
| 63.3 | Orla Bermingham | U23 | 7.10.75 | 4 | Birmingham | 19 | Aug |
| 63.80 | Jane O'Malley | U20 | 18.07.77 | 5 | Nottingham | 8 | Jul |
| 63.8 | Linda Gabriel | | 27.07.64 | 5 | Birmingham | 19 | Aug |
| 64.38 | | | | 2 | Birmingham | 17 | Jun |
| 63.9 | Sandra Leigh | | 26.02.66 | 1 | St. Ives | 30 | Apr |
| 64.04 | Elaine Donald | U23 | 30.04.74 | 2 | Wishaw | 14 | May |
| 64.05 | Cicely Hall | U17 | 12.10.78 | 1 | London (He) | 6 | Aug |
| 64.05 | Viginia Mitchell | | 29.01.63 | 3 | Stoke | 10 | Sep |
| 64.1 | Wendy Laing | | 29.12.62 | 1 | Liverpool | 13 | May |
| 64.1 | Julie Harkin | U23 | 8.08.74 | 3 | Carlisle | 25 | Jun |
| (60) | | | | | | | |
| 64.11 | Kate Bullen | | 12.02.71 | 7 | Birmingham | 20 | May |
| 64.19 | Debbie Duncan | | 13.02.69 | 4 | Antrim | 28 | May |
| 64.20 | Leanne Buxton | U20 | 27.05.78 | 2 | London (He) | 6 | Aug |
| 64.3 | Sarah Griffiths | U20 | 24.04.78 | 1 | Bracknell | 13 | May |
| 64.4 | Elizabeth Waters | U20 | 19.02.77 | 2 | Bedford | 26 | Aug |
| 65.87 | | | | 3 | Stoke | 28 | May |
| 64.6 | Juliana Palka | U20 | 9.05.77 | 3r2 | Birmingham | 19 | Aug |
| 64.7 | Jenny Holden | U23 | 21.09.73 | 2 | Woking | 12 | Aug |
| 65.0 | Gemma Smith | U23 | 16.01.75 | 2r2 | Peterborough | 7 | May |
| 65.0 | Alison McConnell | U17 | 9.10.78 | 1r2 | Walton | 20 | May |
| 65.0 | Teresa Springate/Copeland | | 8.03.69 | 1 | Southampton | 22 | May |
| (70) | | | | | | | |
| 65.03 | Celia Brown | U20 | 22.01.77 | 4 | London (CP) | 28 | May |
| 65.10 | Sara Johnson | | 10.07.70 | 1 | Wrexham | 29 | Jul |
| 65.1 | Alison Hesketh | | 29.04.63 | 3 | Stretford | 6 | Aug |
| 65.13 | Caroline Blackburn | | 6.08.71 | 4h3 | Edinburgh | 6 | May |
| 65.15 | Jackie Cooke | U20 | 20.06.76 | 2 | London (He) | 9 | Sep |
| 65.2 | Sally Sagar | U20 | 28.03.77 | 4 | Sheffield | 13 | May |
| 65.2 | Anya Hutchinson | U20 | 16.07.77 | 1 | Nottingham | 17 | Jun |
| 65.30 | | | | 1 | Stoke | 28 | May |
| 65.3 | Yvette Bennett | | 2.07.65 | 1r2 | Bebington | 11 | Jun |
| 65.4 | Laura Martin | U20 | 13.01.77 | 1 | Horsham | 14 | May |
| 65.4 | Joanna Cadman | | 1.06.68 | 3 | Derby | 30 | Jul |
| (80) | | | | | | | |
| 65.50 | Sally Youden | U20 | 2.11.77 | 1 | Greenock | 4 | Jun |
| 65.5 | Dyanna Clarke | V35 | 27.02.58 | 1 | Ilford | 30 | Apr |
| 65.6 | Susan Williams | U20 | 2.06.77 | 1 | Basingstoke | 30 | Apr |
| 65.6 | Carol Dawkins | V35 | 8.12.60 | 1 | Portsmouth | 20 | May |
| 65.6 | Fiona Andrews | U20 | 6.12.77 | 1 | Dumfries | 18 | Jun |
| 65.7 | Cathy Dawson | | 9.03.66 | 1 | Hastings | 20 | May |
| 65.7 | Carolyn May | U23 | 15.10.74 | 1 | Cambridge | 20 | May |
| 65.7 | Gayle Stanway | U20 | 29.10.77 | 3 | Ayr | 18 | Jul |
| 65.8 | Emma Lindsay | | 11.04.71 | 2 | Inverness | 11 | Jun |

| 65.8 | Michelle John | U20 | 13.04.78 | 4 | Ayr | 18 | Jul |
|---|---|---|---|---|---|---|---|

**Additional Under 17** (1 - 3 above)

| | | | | | | | |
|---|---|---|---|---|---|---|---|
| 66.1 | Linda Crocker | | 2.04.79 | 1 | St. Ives | 3 | May |
| 66.41 | Amanda Wilding | | 3.05.79 | 2 | Aldershot | 26 | Jun |
| 66.9 | Tracey Duncan | | 16.05.79 | 1r2 | Telford | 18 | Jun |
| 67.4 | Amina Ceesay | | 19.11.79 | 1 | London (WP) | 6 | Aug |
| 67.6 | Niki Pocock | | 9.05.79 | 1r2 | Aldershot | 12 | Aug |

# HIGH JUMP

| | | | | | | | |
|---|---|---|---|---|---|---|---|
| 1.90 | Lea Haggett | | 9.05.72 | 1 | Liverpool | 1 | Jul |
| | 1.88 i | | | 3 | Birmingham | 28 | Jan |
| | 1.88 | | | 1 | Cwmbran | 9 | Jul |
| | 1.88 | | | 1 | Gateshead | 21 | Aug |
| | 1.86 i | | | 1 | Birmingham | 3 | Feb |
| | 1.86 | | | 6 | Villeneuve d'Ascq, FRA | 25 | Jun |
| | 1.85 i | | | 1 | Birmingham | 1 | Jan |
| | 1.85 i | | | 1 | London (CP) | 25 | Feb |
| | 1.85 | | | 1 | Bedford | 10 | Jun |
| | 1.85 | | | 1 | Birmingham | 16 | Jul |
| | 1.85 | | | 2 | Perth, AUS | 17 | Dec |
| | 1.84 i | | | 1 | London (CP) | 14 | Jan |
| | 1.84 | | | 3 | Pierre-Benite, FRA | 16 | Jun |
| | 1.83 i | | | 3 | Glasgow | 11 | Feb |
| 1.87 | Julia Bennett | | 26.03.70 | 1H | Alhama, SPA | 20 | May |
| | 1.87 | | | 1H | Helmond, HOL | 1 | Jul |
| | 1.85 | | | 1 | Aldershot | 23 | Jul |
| | 1.83 i | | | 1P | Birmingham | 5 | Feb |
| | 1.83 | | | 1 | Croydon | 14 | May |
| 1.87 | Michelle Dunkley | U20 | 26.01.78 | 1 | Nottingham | 7 | Jul |
| | 1.85 | | | 2 | Bedford | 1 | Jul |
| | 1.84 | | | 1 | Loughborough | 21 | Jun |
| | 1.83 | | | 1 | Stoke | 27 | May |
| | 1.83 | | | 3= | Bath | 11 | Jul |
| | 1.83 | | | Q | Nyiregyhaza, HUN | 28 | Jul |
| 1.87 | Rachael Forrest | U20 | 25.12.77 | 2 | Nottingham | 7 | Jul |
| | 1.85 | | | 1 | Bedford | 1 | Jul |
| 1.86 i | Debbie Marti | | 14.05.68 | 2 | Glasgow | 11 | Feb |
| | 1.85 i | | | 4 | Birmingham | 28 | Jan |
| | 1.85 | | | 1 | London (CP) | 17 | Jun |
| | 1.85 | | | 3 | Birmingham | 16 | Jul |
| | 1.85 | | | 1 | London (WL) | 30 | Jul |
| | 1.84 | | | 1 | Bedford | 25 | Jun |
| 1.85 | Diana Davies | | 7.05.61 | 2 | Birmingham | 16 | Jul |
| | 1.85 | | | 2= | Gateshead | 21 | Aug |
| | 1.83 | | | 1 | Loughborough | 11 | Jun |
| *1.83 i* | *Dalia Mikneviciute* | | *5.09.70* | *1* | *London (CP)* | *16* | *Dec* |
| | *1.80* | | | *1* | *Bromley* | *2* | *Sep* |

36 performances to 1.83 by 6 athletes including 9 indoors

| | | | | | | | |
|---|---|---|---|---|---|---|---|
| 1.81 | Lisa Brown | U20 | 16.03.76 | 1 | Edinburgh | 24 | Jun |
| 1.81 | Julie Crane | U20 | 26.09.76 | 3 | Nottingham | 7 | Jul |
| 1.81 | Susan Jones | U20 | 8.06.78 | 4 | Nottingham | 7 | Jul |
| 1.81 | Julie Major | | 19.08.70 | 1 | Stoke | 9 | Sep |
| 1.80 i (10) | Kelly Thirkle | | 29.03.71 | 3 | Birmingham | 26 | Feb |
| | 1.76 | | | 2 | Gateshead | 17 | Jun |
| 1.80 | Denise Lewis | | 27.08.72 | 1 | Glasgow | 6 | May |
| 1.78 | Vikki Schofield | | 29.12.72 | 1 | Derby | 30 | Jul |
| 1.77 | Hayley Young | U17 | 26.09.79 | 1 | St. Ives | 17 | Jun |
| 1.77 | Nicola Baker | U23 | 8.10.74 | 1 | Blackpool | 20 | Aug |

| | | | | | | | |
|------|------|------|------|------|------|------|------|
| 1.76 | Claire Phythian | U23 | 7.02.73 | H | Tuscaloosa, USA | 18 | May |
| 1.76 | Gill Howard | | 14.04.69 | 1 | Gateshead | 17 | Jun |
| 1.76 | Lindsay Evans | U20 | 29.08.77 | | Lyons, FRA | 17 | Jul |
| 1.75 i | Alison Evans | U23 | 13.12.73 | 1 | Birmingham | 1 | Mar |
| 1.65 | | | | 4 | Birmingham | 17 | Jun |
| 1.75 | Nicole Smallwood | U20 | 9.10.77 | 3 | Stoke | 27 | May |
| (20) | | | | | | | |
| 1.75 | Teresa Andrews | U20 | 4.01.77 | 2 | Newport | 17 | Jun |
| 1.75 | Fiona McPhail | | 23.06.71 | 2 | Blackpool | 20 | Aug |
| 1.75 i | Chloe Cozens | U17 | 9.04.80 | 1P | Glasgow | 10 | Dec |
| 1.69 | | | | 1 | Kings Lynn | 15 | Jul |
| 1.74 i | Lee McConnell | U17 | 9.10.78 | 1 | Birmingham | 18 | Feb |
| 1.71 | | | | 1 | Antrim | 12 | Aug |
| 1.74 | Rachel Martin | U17 | 9.09.78 | 1 | Birmingham | 30 | Jul |
| 1.74 | Kerry Jury | | 19.11.68 | 2H | Stoke | 6 | Aug |
| 1.73 | Elizabeth Gibbens | U20 | 5.04.77 | 1 | Dartford | 22 | Apr |
| 1.73 | Diana Bennett | U23 | 14.06.74 | 1 | Barking | 22 | Apr |
| 1.73 | Yinka Idowu | | 25.02.72 | 2 | Edinburgh | 6 | May |
| 1.73 | Antonia Bemrose | U17 | 3.09.79 | 1 | Aldershot | 26 | Jun |
| (30) | | | | | | | |
| 1.72 | Emma Beales | | 7.12.71 | 1 | Enfield | 8 | Apr |
| 1.72 | Sam Foster | U17 | 9.09.79 | 1 | Basildon | 10 | Jun |
| 1.72 | Jenny Brown | V35 | 21.05.59 | 2 | Buffalo, USA | 18 | Jul |
| 1.72 | Laura White | U17 | 5.09.79 | 1H | Stoke | 16 | Sep |
| 1.71 | Kelly Moreton | U17 | 18.09.79 | 1H | Stoke | 5 | Aug |
| 1.70 i | Hazel Clarke | U17 | 17.03.79 | 1 | Wakefield | 21 | Jan |
| 1.65 | | | | 2 | Carlisle | 9 | Apr |
| 1.70 i | Cathy Boulton | U20 | 2.11.77 | 1 | London (Ha) | 28 | Jan |
| 1.70 i | Ailsa Wallace | U20 | 12.03.77 | 5= | Birmingham | 3 | Feb |
| 1.70 | | | | 1 | Watford | 7 | May |
| 1.70 i | Alison Purton | | 25.11.72 | 6= | Birmingham | 26 | Feb |
| 1.70 | | | | 4 | Glasgow | 6 | May |
| 1.70 i | Louise Gittens | V35 | 9.03.60 | 4 | Nenagh, IRE | 5 | Mar |
| 1.70 | | | | 1 | Basingstoke | 6 | Aug |
| (40) | | | | | | | |
| 1.70 | Anna Biscoe | U17 | 13.09.79 | 1 | Braintree | 30 | Apr |
| 1.70 | Fay Champion | | 27.09.66 | 1 | Cheltenham | 30 | Apr |
| 1.70 | Julie Hollman | U20 | 16.02.77 | 2 | Peterborough | 7 | May |
| 1.70 | Louise Gentle | U17 | 4.09.78 | 1 | London (CP) | 27 | May |
| 1.70 | Emma Lindsay | | 11.04.71 | 1 | Greenock | 4 | Jun |
| 1.70 | Emma Kerr | U20 | 15.10.77 | 2= | Greenock | 4 | Jun |
| 1.70 | Claire Farquharson | U17 | 28.12.78 | 1 | Brighton | 10 | Jun |
| 1.70 | Sharon Woolrich | U20 | 1.05.76 | 2 | Aldershot | 26 | Jun |
| 1.70 | Sarah Potter | U23 | 28.10.75 | 3 | Aldershot | 26 | Jun |
| 1.70 | Jackie Vyfschaft | | 15.12.64 | 1 | Antrim | 1 | Jul |
| (50) | | | | | | | |
| 1.70 | Julie Hynan | U17 | 23.05.80 | 1 | Budapest, HUN | 25 | Jul |
| 1.70 | Alison James | U17 | 9.03.79 | 1 | Cheltenham | 6 | Aug |
| 1.70 | Sara Veevers | U23 | 26.04.74 | 4 | Blackpool | 20 | Aug |
| 1.70 | Kerry Saunders | U20 | 28.03.77 | 1 | Mansfield | 15 | Sep |
| 1.70 i | Alison Kerboas | U17 | 21.05.81 | 1P | Glasgow | 9 | Dec |
| 1.66 | | U15 | | 1P | Bebington | 23 | Jul |
| 1.69 | Carolyn May | U23 | 15.10.74 | 1 | Oxford | 28 | Jun |
| 1.68 | Jane Lilford | | 28.11.70 | 1 | Leamington | 20 | May |
| 1.68 | Kate Franklin | U17 | 16.07.80 | 1 | Yate | 18 | Jun |
| 1.68 | Kelly Sotherton | U20 | 13.11.76 | 5H | Vladimir, RUS | 4 | Aug |
| 1.67 | Clover Wynter-Pink | U20 | 29.11.77 | 1 | London (WF) | 22 | Apr |
| (60) | | | | | | | |
| 1.67 | Justina Cruickshank | U20 | 27.09.77 | 1 | Bromley | 23 | Apr |
| 1.67 | Gayle O'Connor | U17 | 24.08.79 | 1 | Liverpool | 14 | May |
| 1.67 | Joanna Morris | U20 | 16.10.77 | 1 | Walton | 20 | May |

275

| | | | | | | | |
|---|---|---|---|---|---|---|---|
| 1.67 | Leone Dickinson | U23 | 5.11.75 | 1 | York | 2 | Jul |
| 1.67 | Joanne Hyslop | U17 | 13.03.80 | 6 | Nottingham | 8 | Jul |
| 1.67 | Maggie Ellis | | 4.01.64 | 1 | London (TB) | 22 | Jul |
| 1.67 | Keira Stout | U17 | 6.03.80 | 1 | Braintree | 27 | Aug |
| 1.67 | Rachel Harris | U15 | 15.02.82 | 1 | Birmingham | 3 | Sep |
| 1.66 | Jenny Reader | U20 | 23.12.77 | 1 | Hayes | 23 | Apr |
| 1.66 | Michala Gee | U23 | 8.12.75 | 3H | Derby | 29 | Apr |
| | (70) | | | | | | |
| 1.66 | Ione Fraser | U17 | 28.10.79 | 1 | Perivale | 3 | May |
| 1.66 | Basilie Moffat | U20 | 8.04.78 | 1 | Hull | 7 | May |
| 1.66 | Debbie McIlroy | U20 | 18.12.77 | 1 | Grimsby | 7 | May |
| 1.66 | Anne Hollman | U23 | 18.02.74 | 6H | Stoke | 24 | Jun |
| 1.66 | Eleanor Cave | U23 | 23.01.73 | 3 | Oxford | 28 | Jun |
| 1.66 | Beverley Howarth | U20 | 4.09.76 | 6= | Nottingham | 7 | Jul |
| 1.66 | Kellie Durham | U20 | 29.05.78 | 8= | Nottingham | 7 | Jul |
| 1.66 | Lisa Thompson | U15 | 25.04.81 | 1 | Brecon | 12 | Jul |
| 1.66 | Leah Lackenby | U23 | 18.09.74 | 1H | Bebington | 22 | Jul |
| 1.66 | Jackie Tindal | U17 | 21.01.79 | 1 | Boblingen, GER | 30 | Jul |
| | (80) | | | | | | |
| 1.66 | Rebecca Weale | U20 | 7.02.78 | 2H | Stoke | 16 | Sep |
| 1.65 i | Katherine Livesey | U17 | 15.12.79 | 1P | Glasgow | 18 | Feb |
| | 1.64 | | | 1 | Blackpool | 10 | Jun |
| 1.65 i | Kirsty Roger | U20 | 24.03.78 | 1P | Glasgow | 4 | Mar |
| 1.65 | Laura Freeman | U20 | 22.04.78 | 1 | Birmingham | 23 | Apr |
| 1.65 | Hannah Wise | U23 | 8.10.74 | 1 | Loughborough | 26 | Apr |
| 1.65 | Claudia Filce | | 11.11.72 | 1 | Telford | 30 | Apr |
| 1.65 | Jenny Kelly | | 20.06.70 | 5 | Peterborough | 7 | May |
| 1.65 | Jodie Hurst | U20 | 21.06.77 | 1 | Stafford | 8 | May |
| 1.65 | J. Wilkinson | U20 | | 2 | Bolton | 13 | May |
| 1.65 | Shelley Coffey | U20 | 22.10.76 | 3 | Sheffield | 27 | May |
| | (90) | | | | | | |
| 1.65 | Nicola McGovern | U17 | 26.11.79 | 4 | Sheffield | 28 | May |
| 1.65 | Helen Wanstall | U15 | 13.11.80 | 1 | London (CP) | 28 | May |
| 1.65 | Gillian Black | U17 | 27.10.79 | 1 | Greenock | 4 | Jun |
| 1.65 | Justine Gordon | U17 | 10.05.80 | 1 | Andover | 18 | Jun |
| 1.65 | Michelle Smith | U20 | 1.01.78 | 1 | Portsmouth | 25 | Jun |
| 1.65 | Jodi Hallett | U17 | 8.11.78 | 1 | Coventry | 16 | Jul |
| 1.65 | Sarah Claxton | U17 | 23.09.79 | 2 | London (TB) | 22 | Jul |
| 1.65 | Emily Tugwell | U20 | 26.05.78 | 1 | Walton | 22 | Jul |
| 1.65 | Nicola Richens | U17 | 26.10.79 | 1 | Bournemouth | 23 | Jul |
| 1.65 | Adele Jones | U20 | 23.09.77 | 2 | Derby | 23 | Jul |
| | (100) | | | | | | |
| 1.65 | Suzanne Ashton | U17 | 13.10.79 | 6 | Birmingham | 30 | Jul |
| 1.65 | Lorna Turner | | 11.05.72 | 2 | Liverpool | 30 | Jul |
| 1.65 | Roz Richer | U23 | 5.10.74 | 3 | London (WL) | 30 | Jul |
| 1.65 | Kim Hagger | | 2.12.61 | 2 | Windsor | 12 | Aug |
| 1.65 | Susan Noble | | 3.01.74 | 2 | Wakefield | 12 | Aug |
| 1.65 | Judith Payne | U17 | 7.07.80 | 1 | Blackpool | 20 | Aug |

**Additional Under 17** (1 - 30 above)

| | | | | | | |
|---|---|---|---|---|---|---|
| 1.64 | Donna McDonald | 28.11.79 | 1 | Coatbridge | 21 | May |
| 1.64 | Juliet Kennard | 26.01.79 | 1 | Swindon | 10 | Jun |
| 1.64 | Catherine Ledger | 6.02.79 | 1 | Great Yarmouth | 18 | Jun |
| 1.64 | Nadia Brewer | 14.04.80 | 1 | Perivale | 25 | Jun |
| 1.64 | Beth James | 12.02.79 | 1 | Barry | 8 | Jul |

**Additional Under 15** (1 - 4 above)

| | | | | | | |
|---|---|---|---|---|---|---|
| 1.64 | Beth Orford | 25.03.81 | 1 | Cannock | 16 | Jul |
| 1.64 | Rachel Snape | 21.12.80 | 1 | Derby | 23 | Jul |
| 1.63 | Jennifer Hills | 25.03.81 | 1 | Nottingham | 8 | Jul |
| 1.63 | Mary Onianwa | 20.01.81 | 1 | London (He) | 6 | Aug |
| 1.63 | Angela Martin | 26.11.80 | 1 | Carlisle | 10 | Sep |

| 1.63 | Sophie McQueen | 3.12.81 | 1 | Scunthorpe | 11 Sep |
|---|---|---|---|---|---|
| 1.62 | Irene Shokan | 7.03.81 | 1 | Colchester | 13 Aug |
| 1.61 | Lynsey Rankine | 26.01.81 | 1 | Edinburgh | 17 Jun |
| 1.60 | Tina Sayers | 19.07.81 | 1 | Rotherham | 30 Apr |
| 1.60 | Helen Colbourne | 28.08.81 | 1 | Kettering | 22 May |
| 1.60 | Emma Taylor | 29.11.80 | 1 | Kingston | 5 Jul |
| 1.60 | Emily Jackson | 16.10.80 | 5 | Nottingham | 8 Jul |
| 1.60 | Laura Smith | 16.11.80 | 1= | Barnsley | 9 Jul |
| 1.60 | Fiona Harrison | 30.11.81 | 1= | Barnsley | 9 Jul |
| 1.60 | Danielle Parkinson | 2.09.81 | 1 | Wakefield | 17 Sep |

**overage**

| 1.61 i | Laura Redmond | 19.04.81 | 2P | Glasgow | 9 Dec |
|---|---|---|---|---|---|

**Under 13**

| 1.50 | Kelly Smith | | 1 | Barry | 2 Jul |
|---|---|---|---|---|---|
| 1.46 | Natalie Clark | 4.09.82 | 1 | Cudworth | 9 Jul |
| 1.45 | Lara Richards | 7.03.83 | 1 | Brecon | 12 Jul |
| 1.45 | Victoria Kellaway | 21.10.82 | P | Hoo | 10 Sep |
| 1.45 | Gemma Fallon | 4.01.83 | 1 | East Kilbride | 17 Sep |
| 1.44 | I. Robertson | | 1 | Birmingham | 2 Jul |
| 1.44 | Kerry Swyer | 2.12.82 | 1 | Jarrow | 12 Aug |
| 1.43 | Barbara Parker | 8.11.82 | 1 | Colchester | 9 Jul |
| 1.43 | Ami Dornan | 13.10.82 | 1 | St. Albans | 9 Jul |
| 1.43 | Joanne Spencer | 1.11.82 | 3 | Southampton | 12 Aug |
| | (10) | | | | |
| 1.43 | Stephanie Higham | 26.12.83 | 1 | Carlisle | 3 Sep |
| 1.43 | Ruth Brooke | 2.09.83 | 1 | Ryde | 24 Sep |
| 1.42 | Bethan Gould | 23.02.83 | 1 | Bath | 3 Sep |
| 1.42 | Caroline Gore | 29.03.83 | 1 | Crewe | 24 Sep |

**overage**

| 1.51 | Odelle DeJonghe | 17.03.83 | 1 | Liverpool | 19 Nov |
|---|---|---|---|---|---|
| 1.48 | Caroline Gore | 29.03.83 | 2 | Liverpool | 19 Nov |
| 1.47 i | Kerry Swyer | 2.12.82 | 1 | Gateshead | 14 Dec |

# POLE VAULT

| 3.80 i | Kate Staples | | 2.11.65 | 1 | Birmingham | 4 Feb |
|---|---|---|---|---|---|---|
| | 3.80 | | | 2 | Gateshead | 2 Jul |
| | 3.90 City Square competition | | | 3 | Prague, CZE | 14 Jun |
| | 3.75 i | | | 1 | Birmingham | 28 Jan |
| | 3.75 ex | | | 1 | London (Ha) | 25 Jun |
| | 3.70 i | | | 1 | Horsham | 22 Jan |
| | 3.70 | | | 1 | Bedford | 10 Jun |
| | 3.60 i | | | 1 | Glasgow | 11 Feb |
| | 3.60 | | | 1 | Cwmbran | 9 Jul |
| | 3.55 i | | | 6 | Lindau, GER | 17 Feb |
| | 3.55 i | | | 2 | Atlanta, USA | 3 Mar |
| | 3.52 | | | 7 | Duisburg, GER | 18 Jun |
| | 3.50 | | | 2 | Birmingham | 15 Jul |
| 3.72 | Linda Stanton | U23 | 22.06.73 | 1 | Loughborough | 11 Jun |
| | 3.70 | | | 3 | Sheffield | 23 Jul |
| | 3.70 | | | 1 | Narbonne, FRA | 29 Jul |
| | 3.70 | | | 5 | Copenhagen, DEN | 23 Aug |
| | 3.70 | | | 1 | Stoke | 9 Sep |
| | 3.60 | | | 1 | Gateshead | 17 Jun |
| | 3.60 | | | 3 | Gateshead | 2 Jul |
| | 3.60 | | | 1 | Sheffield | 19 Jul |
| | 3.60 | | | 1 | Wakefield | 13 Aug |
| | 3.60 | | | 3 | Gateshead | 21 Aug |
| | 3.50 i | | | 2 | Birmingham | 4 Feb |

| Mark | Athlete | Class | DOB | Pos | Venue | Date |
|---|---|---|---|---|---|---|
| Stanton | 3.46 ex | | | 3 | Salgotarjan, HUN | 11 Sep |
| | 3.40 | | | 1 | Stoke | 7 May |
| | 3.40 | | | 3 | Ljubljana, SLO | 21 May |
| | 3.40 | | | 1 | Bedford | 29 May |
| | 3.40 | | | 2 | Cwmbran | 9 Jul |
| | 3.40 | | | 1 | Grimsby | 3 Sep |
| 3.60 i | Janine Whitlock | U23 | 11.08.73 | 1 | Birmingham | 30 Dec |
| | 3.41 | | | 1 | Sutton | 17 Sep |
| | 3.31 | | | 1 | Stoke | 2 Sep |
| 3.50 i | Paula Wilson | | 20.11.69 | 2 | Birmingham | 28 Jan |
| | 3.20 | | | 4 | Ljubljana, SLO | 21 May |
| 3.50 un | Rhian Clarke | U20 | 19.04.77 | 1 | Weston, USA | 20 Jul |
| | although unconfirmed this performance is thought genuine | | | | | |
| | 3.40 | | | 1 | Bedford | 1 Jul |
| | 3.40 | | | 2 | Belfort, FRA | 6 Aug |
| | 3.40 | | | 2 | Peterborough | 28 Aug |
| | 3.35 | | | 2 | Albany, USA | 15 Jul |
| | 3.30 i | | | 3 | Birmingham | 4 Feb |
| | 3.30 | | | 1 | Norwich | 4 Apr |
| | 3.30 | | | 4= | Gateshead | 21 Aug |
| 3.45 | Clare Ridgley | U20 | 11.09.77 | 1 | Croydon | 28 Aug |
| | 3.40 i | | | 3 | Erfurt,GER | 25 Feb |
| | 3.40 | | | 2 | Loughborough | 11 Jun |
| | 3.40 | | | 2 | Bedford | 1 Jul |
| | 3.40 | | | 5 | Gateshead | 2 Jul |
| | 3.30 | | | 1 | Cannes, FRA | 9 Apr |
| | 3.30 | | | 1 | Enfield | 29 Apr |
| | 3.30 | | | 1 | London (CP) | 28 May |
| | 3.30 | | | 3 | Belfort, FRA | 6 Aug |
| 3.40 i | Claire Morrison/Adams | | 30.05.69 | 1 | Birmingham | 26 Feb |
| | 3.30 i | | | 4 | Birmingham | 4 Feb |
| | 3.30 i | | | 1 | Birmingham | 11 Feb |
| | 3.30 | | | 1 | Birmingham | 18 Jun |
| | 3.30 | | | 3 | Birmingham | 15 Jul |
| 3.30 | Louise Schramm | | 18.12.71 | 3 | Cwmbran | 9 Jul |
| | 58 performances to 3.30 by 8 athletes including 14 indoors | | | | | |
| 3.10 i | Sue Drummie | | 19.06.71 | 5 | Birmingham | 4 Feb |
| | 3.00 | | | 1 | London (TB) | 14 Jun |
| 3.10 | Katie Alexander | U23 | 28.04.74 | 5 | Bedford | 29 May |
| (10) | | | | | | |
| 3.10 i | Emma Hornby | U23 | 12.12.73 | 2 | Birmingham | 30 Dec |
| | 2.90 | | | 1 | Telford | 16 Sep |
| 3.05 | Fiona Harrison | U15 | 30.11.81 | 2 | Sheffield | 19 Jul |
| 3.00 i | Maria Newton | | 22.07.66 | 2 | Horsham | 22 Jan |
| | 2.80 | | | 1 | Bromley | 9 Apr |
| 3.00 i | Dawn-Alice Wright | U20 | 20.01.76 | 2 | Birmingham | 29 Jan |
| | 3.00 | | | 3 | Enfield | 29 Apr |
| 3.00 | Katharine Horner | U20 | 6.01.78 | 1 | Crawley | 25 Mar |
| 3.00 | Claudia Filce | | 11.11.72 | 4 | Birmingham | 20 May |
| 2.90 i | Julia Cockram | | 1.01.68 | 2 | London (CP) | 11 Feb |
| | 2.80 | | | 2 | London (TB) | 14 Jun |
| 2.90 | Becky Ridgley | U17 | 26.02.80 | 1 | Birmingham | 29 Jul |
| 2.90 | Rebecca Roles | U17 | 14.12.79 | 2 | London (He) | 9 Sep |
| 2.90 | Larissa Lowe | | 19.08.69 | 1 | Reading | 1 Oct |
| (20) | | | | | | |
| 2.85 | Tracey Bloomfield | U17 | 13.09.79 | 7 | Birmingham | 15 Jul |
| 2.80 | Gail Marshall | | 1.04.71 | 1 | Grangemouth | 29 Apr |
| 2.80 | Fiona Peake | U20 | 31.05.77 | 3 | London (CP) | 28 May |
| 2.80 | Samantha Stapleton | U23 | 13.10.73 | 8 | Bedford | 29 May |
| 2.80 | Kirsty Armstrong | U17 | 14.05.80 | 1 | Woking | 12 Jul |
| 2.75 | Susan Crossland | U20 | 3.03.77 | 1 | Sheffield | 27 May |

| 2.75 | Elizabeth Beckingsale | U17 | 20.03.80 | | Albany, USA | 15 Jul |
|------|----------------------|-----|----------|---|-------------|--------|
| 2.75 | Alison Ronald | | 20.01.67 | 1 | Coatbridge | 3 Sep |
| 2.70 i | Joanna Whitfield | U20 | 5.01.78 | 2 | Birmingham | 19 Feb |
| 2.70 | | | | 1 | Stoke | 2 Aug |
| 2.70 | Rachel Foster | U20 | 1.09.76 | 1 | Hull | 7 May |
| (30) | | | | | | |
| 2.60 | Sarah Francis | U20 | 15.08.76 | 1 | Grimsby | 7 May |
| 2.60 | Liz Tapper | U20 | 2.06.78 | 1 | Loughborough | 13 May |
| 2.60 | Danielle Codd | U17 | 17.02.79 | 1 | Blackburn | 12 Jul |
| 2.60 | Barbara Bannon | | 25.04.70 | 1 | Salisbury | 16 Jul |
| 2.60 | Lynsay Perides | U17 | 24.05.79 | 5 | Birmingham | 29 Jul |
| 2.60 | Elizabeth Hughes | U20 | 9.06.77 | 7 | Croydon | 28 Aug |
| 2.50 | Bonny Elms | U17 | 30.10.79 | 2 | Newport | 17 Jun |
| 2.45 | Gillian Hevingham | V40 | 24.06.54 | 1 | Exeter | 6 Aug |
| 2.40 i | Julie Hynan | U17 | 23.05.80 | 3 | Birmingham | 18 Feb |
| 2.40 | Pamela Murray | | 13.01.67 | 5 | Edinburgh | 6 May |
| (40) | | | | | | |
| 2.40 | Helen Beddow | | 10.09.67 | 2 | Stoke | 7 May |
| 2.40 | Gisell Reddy | U17 | 25.09.79 | 1 | London (Ha) | 3 Sep |

**Additional Under 17** (1 - 10 above)

| 2.30 | Kathryn Hodgson | | 30.03.80 | 1= | Munster, GER | 22 Aug |
|------|----------------|---|----------|----|-------------|--------|
| 2.30 | Rachel Fox | | 25.02.80 | 1= | Munster, GER | 22 Aug |
| 2.20 | Clare Edis | | 26.11.79 | 1 | Hull | 14 Jun |

**Additional Under 15** (1 above)

| 2.20 i | Linda Dykes | | 1.09.80 | 1 | Liverpool | 5 Mar |
|--------|-------------|---|---------|---|-----------|--------|
| 2.20 | Sarah Hartley | | 4.05.81 | 1 | Stoke | 2 Sep |

**very doubtful and unconfirmed**

| 3.32 | Allie Murray-Jessee | | 13.01.67 | 1 | El Paso, USA | 28 Oct |
|------|---------------------|---|----------|---|-------------|--------|
| 3.00 | | | | 1 | Juarex, MEX | 2 Jul |

These and other marks in the El Paso region are thought most unlikely

## LONG JUMP

| 6.67 | 1.3 | Denise Lewis | 27.08.72 | 4H | Gotzis, AUT | 28 May |
|------|-----|-------------|----------|----|-------------|--------|
| | 6.66 w | 4.0 | | 1 | Birmingham | 18 Jun |
| | 6.57 | 0.4 | | 2H | Gothenburg, SWE | 10 Aug |
| | 6.56 | 0.2 | | 1 | Gateshead | 21 Aug |
| | 6.52 | -0.1 | | 3H | Helmond, HOL | 2 Jul |
| | 6.51 | 0.6 | | 8 | Villeneuve d'Ascq, FRA | 25 Jun |
| | 6.42 | 0.9 | | 2 | Birmingham | 16 Jul |
| | 6.37 i | | | 2 | Vienna, AUT | 18 Feb |
| | 6.35 i | | | 1 | Glasgow | 11 Feb |
| | 6.30 | -0.2 | | * | Birmingham | 18 Jun |
| | 6.28 i | | | 1 | Birmingham | 3 Feb |
| | 6.22 w | 2.1 | | 1 | Stoke | 9 Sep |
| | 6.15 w | | | 1 | Stoke | 13 May |
| | 6.12 i | | | 4 | Birmingham | 28 Jan |
| 6.54 w | 2.1 | Yinka Idowu | 25.02.72 | 3H | Helmond, HOL | 2 Jul |
| | 6.46 i | | | 2 | Birmingham | 28 Jan |
| | 6.38 | | | 1 | Antrim | 28 May |
| | 6.35 i | | | 1 | London (Ha) | 21 Jan |
| | 6.35 | -0.2 | | 3 | Birmingham | 16 Jul |
| | 6.34 | | | 4 | Hechtel, BEL | 22 Jul |
| | 6.26 i | | | 2 | Birmingham | 3 Feb |
| | 6.20 | 1.9 | | 4H | Alhama, SPA | 21 May |
| 6.28 | 0.2 | Vikki Schofield | 29.12.72 | 4 | Birmingham | 16 Jul |
| | 6.16 | 0.9 | | 4 | Gateshead | 21 Aug |
| | 6.11 i | | | 4 | Glasgow | 11 Feb |
| 6.27 | | Liz Ghojefa | 24.02.69 | 1 | Aldershot | 23 Jul |
| | 6.18 | | | 1 | Kingston | 22 Jul |

| Mark | Wind | Name | Cat | DOB | Pos | Venue | Date |
|---|---|---|---|---|---|---|---|
| 6.24 w | 2.7 | Jade Johnson | U17 | 7.06.80 | 1 | London (CP) | 28 May |
| 6.22 w | 3.0 | | | | 1 | Colwyn Bay | 15 Jul |
| 6.13 | 1.6 | | | | * | London (CP) | 28 May |
| 6.21 w | | Debbie Marti | | 14.05.68 | 1 | Croydon | 13 May |
| 5.98 | 1.4 | | | | 1 | Stoke | 10 Sep |
| 6.16 | 1.0 | Ann Brooks | | 4.05.71 | 1 | Birmingham | 20 May |
| 6.12 | | | | | 1 | Carlisle | 25 Jun |
| 6.12 w | 2.2 | | | | 1 | Bedford | 29 May |
| 6.13 | | Ruth Irving | U23 | 20.07.74 | 1 | Cambridge | 20 May |
| 6.12 w | 5.2 | Ashia Hansen | | 5.12.71 | 1 | Hayes | 13 May |
| 6.11 w | | Jackie White | | 12.01.71 | 1 | Leamington | 13 May |
| 5.97 | -0.5 | | | | 1 | Cwmbran | 9 Jul |

37 performances to 6.10 by 10 athletes including 8 indoors and 10 wind assisted

| Mark | Wind | Name | Cat | DOB | Pos | Venue | Date |
|---|---|---|---|---|---|---|---|
| 6.06 | 1.1 | Michelle Griffith | | 6.10.71 | 2 | Stoke | 9 Sep |
| 6.05 | | Diana Davies | | 7.05.61 | 1 | Corby | 23 Jul |
| 6.04 | | Paula Thomas | | 3.12.64 | 1 | London (He) | 1 Jul |
| 6.02 w | 3.4 | Julia Bennett | | 26.03.70 | H | Alhama, SPA | 21 May |
| 5.93 | | | | | 2 | Kingston | 23 Jul |
| 6.01 | | Sarah Claxton | U17 | 23.09.79 | 1 | Colchester | 2 Jul |
| 5.97 i | | Sarah Wilhelmy | U17 | 2.02.80 | 1 | London (Ha) | 21 Jan |
| 5.86 | | | | | 1 | Watford | 20 May |
| 5.97 w | 2.9 | Julie Hollman | U20 | 16.02.77 | 1 | Peterborough | 7 May |
| 5.84 | 0.0 | | | | 1H | Vladimir, RUS | 5 Aug |
| 5.97 w | 4.0 | Louise Eden | U20 | 11.12.77 | 1 | Nottingham | 8 Jul |
| 5.94 | 2.0 | | | | 1 | Sheffield | 28 May |
| 5.96 | | Joanne Dear | U23 | 8.06.75 | 1 | Bromley | 22 Apr |
| 5.95 w | 5.0 | Adele Forester | U20 | 27.03.76 | 2 | Nottingham | 8 Jul |
| 5.90 | | | | | 1 | Sheffield | 18 Jun |
| | (20) | | | | | | |
| 5.94 w | | Linda Davidson | | 29.05.70 | 1 | Greenock | 4 Jun |
| 5.86 | | | | | 2 | London (He) | 1 Jul |
| 5.93 | | Pauline Richards | | 30.06.68 | 1 | Coventry | 13 Aug |
| 5.92 | | Kim Hagger | | 2.12.61 | 1 | London (WF) | 2 Sep |
| 5.90 i | | Caroline Black | | 19.05.72 | 1 | Glasgow | 14 Jan |
| 5.73 | | | | | 1 | Coatbridge | 27 Aug |
| 5.90 | 1.2 | Jenny Kelly | | 20.06.70 | 2 | London (CP) | 18 Jun |
| 5.89 i | | Tammy McCammon | U20 | 17.10.76 | 4 | Erfurt, GER | 25 Feb |
| 5.64 | | | | | 2 | Braintree | May |
| 5.89 | | Sarah Damm | | 12.09.70 | 1 | Birmingham | 23 Apr |
| 5.89 w | 3.3 | Emma Beales | | 7.12.71 | 2H | Kilkenny, IRE | 27 Aug |
| 5.87 | -1.4 | | | | 1 | Enfield | 30 Jul |
| 5.88 | | Claire Phythian | U23 | 7.02.73 | 1 | Derby | 30 Jul |
| 5.87 | | Lynne Draper | | 10.05.67 | 1 | Horsham | 9 Jul |
| | (30) | | | | | | |
| 5.86 | | Diana Bennett | U23 | 14.06.74 | 2 | London (WF) | 2 Sep |
| 5.84 | | Kelly Sotherton | U20 | 13.11.76 | 1H | Portsmouth | 25 Jun |
| 5.82 | | Joyce Hepher | | 11.02.64 | 1 | Bromley | 20 May |
| 5.82 | | Karen Skeggs | | 26.10.69 | 1 | Derby | 9 Sep |
| 5.81 | | Lea Haggett | | 9.05.72 | 1 | Perth, AUS | 20 Dec |
| 5.81 w | 3.2 | Emma Lindsay | | 11.04.71 | 1H | Aberdeen | 16 Jul |
| 5.71 | -0.1 | | | | 1H | Stoke | 25 Jun |
| 5.79 | | Sarah Hanson | | 25.11.72 | 1 | Liverpool | 30 Jul |
| 5.77 | | Debbie Rowe | | 8.09.72 | 1 | Derby | 23 Jul |
| 5.74 w | 2.4 | Tracy Goddard/Joseph | | 29.11.69 | 5 | Bedford | 29 May |
| 5.62 | | | | | 1 | Portsmouth | 14 May |
| 5.74 w | 2.1 | Debbie Harrison | U17 | 13.11.78 | 2 | Nottingham | 7 Jul |
| 5.54 | 1.3 | | | | 3 | Birmingham | 29 Jul |
| | (40) | | | | | | |
| 5.71 | | Kerry Jury | | 19.11.68 | 1 | Worcester | 13 May |
| 5.71 | | Caroline Stead | | 14.09.71 | 1 | Harrow | 25 Jun |
| 5.70 | | Catriona Slater | U20 | 27.01.77 | 1 | Ipswich | 2 Apr |

| Mark | Wind | Name | Cat | DOB | Pos | Venue | Date | |
|---|---|---|---|---|---|---|---|---|
| 5.70 | 1.2 | Bianca Liston | U20 | 28.05.78 | 2 | London (CP) | 27 | May |
| 5.70 | | Katie Budd | U20 | 3.01.76 | 2 | Derby | 30 | Jul |
| 5.69 | 0.5 | Teresa Springate/Copeland | | 8.03.69 | 4 | London (CP) | 18 | Jun |
| 5.69 w | 4.4 | Davenia John | U20 | 29.12.77 | 4 | Nottingham | 8 | Jul |
| 5.51 | | | | | 4 | Watford | 7 | May |
| 5.68 | | Michelle Dunkley | U20 | 26.01.78 | 1 | Corby | 7 | May |
| 5.68 | 0.3 | Nicola Short | | 30.10.69 | 4 | Cwmbran | 9 | Jul |
| 5.67 | -0.3 | Sallyanne Short | | 6.03.68 | 3 | Cardiff | 22 | Jul |
| (50) | | | | | | | | |
| 5.67 | | Debbie Woolgar | | 10.03.65 | 1H | Crawley | 10 | Sep |
| 5.66 | | Carolyn May | U23 | 15.10.74 | 1 | Oxford | 28 | Jun |
| 5.66 | | Carol Zeniou | V35 | 30.11.56 | 1 | London (PH) | 5 | Jul |
| 5.64 w | | Fiona Hunter | U17 | 14.09.78 | 3 | Colwyn Bay | 15 | Jul |
| 5.63 | | Charmaine Johnson | | 4.06.63 | 3 | Watford | 7 | May |
| 5.63 | | Evette Finikin | | 25.09.63 | 5 | London (He) | 1 | Jul |
| 5.63 w | 2.3 | Sarah Ramminger | U23 | 1.10.75 | 2 | Edinburgh | 23 | Jun |
| 5.58 | 1.5 | | | | 2 | Edinburgh | 23 | Jun |
| 5.62 | | Josephine Peet | | 4.12.71 | 3 | Edinburgh | 7 | May |
| 5.62 | | Lisa Gibbs | | 9.01.69 | 1 | Barry | 14 | May |
| 5.62 | | Emma Hughes | U15 | 15.09.80 | 1 | Kings Lynn | 15 | Jul |
| (60) | | | | | | | | |
| 5.62 w | 3.3 | Pamela Anderson | U20 | 16.10.76 | 1 | Pitreavie | 8 | Jul |
| 5.57 i | | | | | 3 | Glasgow | 22 | Jan |
| 5.51 | | | | | * | Pitreavie | 8 | Jul |
| 5.62 w | 2.6 | Rebecca Lewis | U20 | 31.12.77 | 5 | Stoke | 9 | Sep |
| 5.61 | | Michala Gee | U23 | 8.12.75 | 2 | Stafford | 7 | May |
| 5.61 | | Caroline Miller/Warden | | 16.09.72 | 1 | Blackpool | 13 | May |
| 5.61 | | Teresa Andrews | U20 | 4.01.77 | 2 | Newport | 17 | Jun |
| 5.61 | | Kerensa Denham | U23 | 8.03.74 | 3 | Horsham | 9 | Jul |
| 5.61 | | Leigh Hubbard | U20 | 30.09.77 | 1 | Rugby | · 2 | Aug |
| 5.60 | | Nikita Thompson | U17 | 17.08.80 | 2 | Cologne, GER | 15 | Jul |
| 5.60 w | | Tina Malcolm | | 8.09.67 | 1 | London (CP) | 14 | May |
| 5.53 | 0.8 | | | | * | London (CP) | 18 | Jun |
| 5.60 w | 3.1 | Catherine Burrows | U20 | 11.02.76 | 3 | Sheffield | 28 | May |
| (70) | | | | | | | | |
| 5.59 | 1.2 | Hazel Melvin | U23 | 19.11.73 | 4 | Edinburgh | 23 | Jun |
| 5.59 | | Helen Silvey | U23 | 4.12.73 | 1 | Aldershot | 12 | Aug |
| 5.58 i | | Kelly Williamson | U17 | 4.12.79 | 1 | Birmingham | 26 | Feb |
| 5.49 w | 2.4 | | | | 4 | Nottingham | 7 | Jul |
| 5.46 | 1.3 | | | | 1 | Sheffield | 27 | May |
| 5.58 | | Joanne Glover | | 6.10.71 | 1 | Middlesbrough | 13 | May |
| 5.58 | | Paula Watson | | 5.09.70 | 2 | Windsor | 12 | Aug |
| 5.58 w | | Victoria Reynolds | U17 | 22.04.80 | 1 | Carlisle | 2 | Apr |
| 5.42 | 1.0 | | | | 6 | Nottingham | 7 | Jul |
| 5.57 | 1.6 | Lisa Brown | U20 | 16.03.76 | 2 | Pitreavie | 8 | Jul |
| 5.56 | | Nicola Hutchison | U17 | 1.02.79 | 1 | Greenock | 4 | Jun |
| 5.56 | | Fiona Paul | U17 | 5.09.78 | 2 | Greenock | 4 | Jun |
| 5.55 | | Nicola Gautier | U20 | 21.03.78 | 1 | Sheffield | 13 | May |
| (80) | | | | | | | | |
| 5.54 | 1.6 | Danielle Freeman | U17 | 11.02.80 | 3 | Nottingham | 7 | Jul |
| 5.54 | | Janine Whitlock | U23 | 11.08.73 | 2 | Derby | 9 | Sep |
| 5.53 | | Isobel Donaldson | | 24.01.64 | 1 | Cosford | 14 | Jun |
| 5.53 | | Becky Folds | U23 | 28.01.75 | 4 | Kingston | 22 | Jul |
| 5.52 | | Jackie Jenner | U20 | 25.10.76 | 1 | Bracknell | 30 | Apr |
| 5.52 w | 4.9 | Stephanie Nicholson | U20 | 28.06.76 | 4 | Sheffield | 28 | May |
| 5.51 | | Anna-Maria Thorpe | | 15.07.71 | 5 | Perivale | 30 | Apr |
| ·5.51 | | Angie Nyhan | U20 | 13.04.78 | 2 | Sheffield | 13 | May |
| 5.51 | | Ruth Williams | | 18.03.70 | 1 | Jarrow | 2 | Jul |
| 5.51 w | | Hayley Warrilow | U17 | 10.04.80 | 1 | Stoke | 13 | May |
| 5.49 | | | | | 1 | Stoke | 17 | Jun |
| (90) | | | | | | | | |

281

**Additional Under 17** (1 - 12 above)

| 5.48 i | | Belinda Samuels | 29.11.78 | 2 | Birmingham | 19 | Feb |
|--------|-----|-----------------|----------|----|----------------|----|-----|
| 5.48 w | 4.3 | | | 5 | Nottingham | 7 | Jul |
| 5.38 | 2.0 | | | 4 | Birmingham | 29 | Jul |
| 5.48 | | Jane Taylor | 18.02.80 | 1 | Stretford | 18 | Jun |
| 5.47 | | Gemma Jones | 25.02.79 | 1 | Cardiff | 27 | May |
| 5.47 | | Faithlyn Edwards | 26.11.78 | 1 | London (WF) | 25 | Jun |
| 5.45 | | Amy Nuttell | 6.02.80 | 1 | St. Ives | 17 | Jun |
| 5.45 | 0.5 | Katherine Livesey | 15.12.79 | 1H | Bebington | 23 | Jul |
| 5.42 | | Rebecca Lawford | 27.04.80 | 1 | Burton | 11 | Apr |
| 5.42 | | Kathryn Dowsett | 24.11.78 | 1 | Basildon | 10 | Jun |
| | (20) | | | | | | |
| 5.42 | | Victoria Henson | 9.01.79 | 2 | London (WF) | 25 | Jun |
| 5.41 i | | Syreena Pinel | 13.01.79 | 3 | Birmingham | 5 | Feb |
| 5.41 | | Jayne Ludlow | 7.01.79 | 2 | Cardiff | 27 | May |
| 5.40 | | Stephanie Phillips | 25.10.78 | 1 | Canvey Island | 3 | Jun |
| 5.39 | | Rebecca White | 5.06.80 | 2 | Blackpool | 14 | May |
| 5.39 | | Hannah Greenslade | 14.07.80 | 1 | Cheltenham | 17 | Jun |

**Additional Under 15** (1 above)

| 5.47 | 1.2 | Caroline Pearce | 1.09.80 | 1 | Birmingham | 30 | Jul |
|--------|------|-----------------|----------|----|----------------|----|-----|
| 5.45 | | Fiona Harrison | 30.11.81 | 1 | Barnsley | 9 | Jul |
| 5.43 | | Lucy Atunumuo | 4.11.80 | 1 | Harlow | 22 | Jul |
| 5.40 | 1.0 | Carli Bentley | 29.01.81 | 2 | Birmingham | 30 | Jul |
| 5.38 | | Jane Cuddy | 25.08.81 | 1 | Bebington | 10 | Jun |
| 5.36 | | Kim Clarke | 30.04.81 | 1 | Great Yarmouth | 28 | May |
| 5.33 | | Laura Yeardley | 21.12.80 | 1 | Wrexham | 18 | Jun |
| 5.33 | | Aimee Cutler | 7.10.81 | 1 | Swansea | 28 | Aug |
| 5.32 w | 4.8 | Helen Armishaw | 4.10.80 | 1 | Sheffield | 28 | May |
| | | 5.20 | | 1 | Stretford | 10 | Jun |
| | (10) | | | | | | |
| 5.31 w | | Sarah Lane | 4.06.81 | 1 | Cardiff | 27 | May |
| 5.27 | | Victoria Blair | 20.11.80 | 1 | Leeds | 7 | May |
| 5.26 | | Rachel Peacock | 18.05.82 | 1 | Cheltenham | 17 | Jun |
| 5.26 | | Tolu Jegede | 25.09.80 | 1 | Southend | 20 | Aug |
| 5.22 | | Rachel Houghton | 18.12.80 | 1 | Crewe | 13 | May |
| 5.22 | | Laura Smith | 16.11.80 | 1 | Barnsley | 9 | Jul |
| 5.21 | -1.5 | Donna Naylor | 20.05.82 | Q | Nottingham | 8 | Jul |
| 5.20 i | | Rachael Kay | 8.09.80 | 1 | Birmingham | 11 | Feb |
| 5.20 | | Kerry Powell | 28.02.82 | 2 | Cheltenham | 17 | Jun |

**Under 13**

| 4.92 | | Katrina Buccierri | 24.06.83 | 1 | Sheffield | 1 | Jul |
|--------|------|-------------------|----------|----|----------------|----|-----|
| 4.91 | | Nicola Lapczuk | 16.11.82 | 1 | Derby | 25 | Jun |
| 4.84 | | Vicky Weston | 14.03.83 | 4 | Aldershot | 12 | Aug |
| 4.83 | | Leanne Ogogo | | 1 | Great Yarmouth | 6 | Aug |
| 4.83 | | Nina Ezeogu | 11.10.82 | 1 | Southend | 20 | Aug |
| 4.79 | | Michelle Johansen | 1.02.84 | 1 | Portsmouth | 8 | May |
| 4.79 | | Elaine Smith | 16.05.83 | 1 | Glasgow | 25 | Jun |
| 4.78 | | Sarah Lane | 24.11.82 | 1 | Swansea | 26 | Aug |
| 4.75 | | Emma Wragg | 22.01.83 | 1 | Sheffield | 9 | Jun |
| 4.73 | | Sophie Allen | 7.09.82 | | Ipswich | 3 | Jun |
| | (10) | | | | | | |
| 4.72 | | Sally Drew | 23.11.82 | 1 | Millfield | 25 | Jun |
| 4.72 | | Ruth Brooke | 2.09.83 | 1 | London (WF) | 2 | Sep |
| 4.70 | | Rebecca Woodford | 26.02.83 | 1 | Cardiff | 23 | Apr |
| 4.70 | | Helen Carberry | 16.12.82 | 1 | Oldham | 20 | Aug |
| 4.67 | | Natalie Shaw | 2.01.83 | 1 | Watford | 19 | May |
| 4.66 | | Rebecca Essex | 16.11.82 | 1 | Bracknell | 25 | Jun |

# TRIPLE JUMP

| | | | | | | | |
|---|---|---|---|---|---|---|---|
| 14.66 | 0.8 | Ashia Hansen | | 5.12.71 | 1 | Gateshead | 21 Aug |
| 14.45 | 1.2 | | | | 3 | Brussels, BEL | 25 Aug |
| 14.45 | -0.6 | | | | 5 | Monaco, MON | 9 Sep |
| 14.38 | -0.3 | | | | 6 | Zurich, SWZ | 16 Aug |
| 14.37 | 1.0 | | | | 1 | Villeneuve d'Ascq, FRA | 24 Jun |
| 14.29 i | | | | | 2 | Birmingham | 25 Feb |
| 14.17 i | | | | | 1 | Birmingham | 28 Jan |
| 14.16 | 0.9 | | | | 3 | Moscow,RUS | 5 Jun |
| 13.98 | -0.4 | | | | 3 | Gateshead | 2 Jul |
| 13.98 | 0.7 | | | | 6 | London (CP) | 7 Jul |
| 13.96 | 1.4 | | | | 2 | Ljubljana, SLO | 21 May |
| 13.95 | 0.3 | | | | 3 | Bratislava, SVK | 30 May |
| 13.94 i | | | | | 1 | London (Ha) | 21 Jan |
| 13.84 i | | | | | 1 | London (CP) | 15 Jan |
| 13.61 i | | | | | 1 | Birmingham | 4 Feb |
| 13.61 | 1.5 | | | | 21Q | Gothenburg, SWE | 8 Aug |
| 14.03 | 1.1 | Michelle Griffith | | 6.10.71 | Q | Gothenburg, SWE | 8 Aug |
| 13.98 | 0.8 | | | | 2 | Gateshead | 21 Aug |
| 13.80 i | | | | | 4 | Birmingham | 25 Feb |
| 13.80 | -0.7 | | | | 8 | London (CP) | 7 Jul |
| 13.78 w | 3.9 | | | | 3 | Sheffield | 23 Jul |
| 13.76 i | | | | | 1 | Glasgow | 11 Feb |
| 13.73 | 1.5 | | | | 4 | Lucerne, SWZ | 27 Jun |
| 13.68 | 1.9 | | | | 3 | London (CP) | 27 Aug |
| 13.64 | 0.0 | | | | 2 | Bellinzona, SWZ | 20 Jun |
| 13.61 | | | | | * | Sheffield | 23 Jul |
| 13.59 | 1.5 | | | | 12 | Gothenburg, SWE | 10 Aug |
| 13.57 i | | | | | 3 | Birmingham | 28 Jan |
| 13.55 | 0.6 | | | | 7 | Gateshead | 2 Jul |
| 13.54 w | 3.0 | | | | 6 | Seville, SPA | 3 Jun |
| 13.53 | -0.8 | | | | 2 | Celje, SLO | 16 Jun |
| 13.51 | | | | | 1 | Bebington | 11 Jun |
| 13.50 | 0.5 | | | | 8 | Rome, ITA | 8 Jun |
| 13.48 | 1.2 | | | | 7 | Oslo, NOR | 21 Jul |
| 13.43 | 0.8 | | | | 1 | Birmingham | 15 Jul |
| 13.37 | 1.3 | | | | * | Seville, SPA | 3 Jun |
| 13.30 | | | | | 1 | Hayes | 13 May |
| 13.28 w | 3.7 | | | | 1 | Stoke | 9 Sep |
| 13.25 | 0.0 | | | | 11 | Zurich, SWZ | 16 Aug |
| 13.11 | | | | | 1 | Watford | 7 May |
| 13.05 | | | | | 1 | London (WL) | 30 Jul |
| 13.38 i | | Rachel Kirby | | 18.05.69 | 6 | Birmingham | 25 Feb |
| 13.27 i | | | | | 3 | Vienna, AUT | 18 Feb |
| 13.23 | 0.3 | | | | 3 | Bellinzona, SWZ | 20 Jun |
| 13.18 w | 2.1 | | | | 6 | Sheffield | 23 Jul |
| 13.15 i | | | | | 3 | Glasgow | 11 Feb |
| 13.15 | -0.4 | | | | 8 | Gateshead | 2 Jul |
| 13.13 | 0.0 | | | | 5 | Ljubljana, SLO | 21 May |
| 13.11 i | | | | | 2 | Birmingham | 4 Feb |
| 13.01 i | | Connie Henry | | 15.04.72 | 2 | London (Ha) | 21 Jan |

50 performances to 13.00 by 4 athletes including 13 indoors and 4 wind assisted

| | | | | | | | |
|---|---|---|---|---|---|---|---|
| 12.68 i | | Evette Finikin | | 25.09.63 | 2 | London (CP) | 14 Jan |
| 12.39 | 1.6 | | | | 1 | London (CP) | 17 Jun |
| 12.50 | 1.4 | Karen Skeggs | | 26.10.69 | 1 | Stoke | 10 Sep |
| 12.49 w | | Liz Ghojefa | | 24.02.69 | 1 | Croydon | 28 Aug |
| 12.37 | | | | | 1 | London (Ha) | 25 Jun |
| 12.44 | 1.3 | Debbie Rowe | | 8.09.72 | 2 | Stoke | 9 Sep |
| 12.42 | -0.4 | Elizabeth Gibbens | U20 | 5.04.77 | 2 | Bedford | 2 Jul |

| Mark | | Name | Cat | DOB | Pos | Venue | Date |
|---|---|---|---|---|---|---|---|
| 12.40 w 4.6 | | Lorna Turner | | | 11.05.72 | 3 | Stoke | 9 Sep |
| 12.32 | | | | | 1 | Glasgow | 6 May |
| | (10) | | | | | | |
| 12.20 | | Katie Evans | U23 | 4.02.74 | 1 | Bath | 28 Aug |
| 12.15 i | | Fiona Watt | U23 | 29.01.73 | 1 | Glasgow | 22 Jan |
| 11.67 | | | | | 1 | Wishaw | 14 May |
| 12.15 w 3.5 | | Caroline Stead | | 14.09.71 | 2 | Birmingham | 20 May |
| 12.14 | | | | | 1 | Harrow | 25 Jun |
| 12.11 | | Jayne Ludlow | U17 | 7.01.79 | 1 | Cardiff | 27 May |
| 12.10 0.4 | | Pamela Anderson | U20 | 16.10.76 | 4 | Bedford | 2 Jul |
| 11.98 | | Ruth Irving | U23 | 20.07.74 | 1 | Oxford | 25 Feb |
| 11.96 w 2.7 | | Lisa Brown | U20 | 16.03.76 | 2 | Edinburgh | 24 Jun |
| 11.91 | | | | | 2 | Derby | 30 Jul |
| 11.81 db1.5 | | Fiona Hunter | U17 | 14.09.78 | 4 | Edinburgh | 24 Jun |

*Both athlete and coach feel this mark is 10.81. However it has been ratified as a Scottish record. One explanation is that an official called 11 metres... before the measurement. Although officials and athletes sometimes disagree it is unusual for the officials to give the better performance. Who said statistics was exact - Ed*

| Mark | | Name | Cat | DOB | Pos | Venue | Date |
|---|---|---|---|---|---|---|---|
| 11.21 | | | | | 2 | Greenock | 4 Jun |
| 11.79 w 2.9 | | Catherine Burrows | U20 | 11.02.76 | 1 | Sheffield | 27 May |
| 11.72 i | | | | | 1 | Birmingham | 18 Feb |
| 11.69 | | | | | 1 | Bromley | 23 Apr |
| 11.77 | | Jane Falconer | U23 | 20.09.74 | 1 | Oxford | 28 Jun |
| | (20) | | | | | | |
| 11.74 i | | Caroline Miller/Warden | | 16.09.72 | 1 | Birmingham | 30 Dec |
| 11.40 | | | | | 1 | Stretford | 6 Aug |
| 11.65 0.4 | | Liz Patrick | U20 | 29.08.77 | 1 | London (He) | 6 Aug |
| 11.64 | | Stacy McGivern | U20 | 14.12.76 | | Kings Lynn | 15 Jul |
| 11.63 | | Kerensa Denham | U23 | 8.03.74 | 1 | Barn Elms | 20 May |
| 11.62 | | Margaret Still | | 9.05.65 | 1 | Blackpool | 20 Aug |
| 11.62 | | Louise Eden | U20 | 11.12.77 | 1 | Birmingham | 27 Aug |
| 11.60 | | Naomi Siddall | U23 | 2.04.75 | 1 | Barnsley | 3 Sep |
| 11.59 | | Joanna Morris | U20 | 16.10.77 | 1 | Andover | 12 Aug |
| 11.54 | | Marcia Walker | | 27.05.70 | 1 | London (He) | 20 May |
| 11.54 | | Kelly Sotherton | U20 | 13.11.76 | 1 | Portsmouth | 10 Jun |
| | (30) | | | | | | |
| 11.52 | | Annelies Stevens | U20 | 16.05.78 | 1 | St. Ives | 13 May |
| 11.51 w 3.6 | | Kerry Jury | | 19.11.68 | 1 | Peterborough | 7 May |
| 11.44 | | | | | 4 | Derby | 30 Jul |
| 11.49 | | Catherine Barnes | U20 | 28.09.77 | 2 | Portsmouth | 10 Jun |
| 11.49 | | Susan Harries | | 9.09.70 | 1 | Windsor | 12 Aug |
| 11.47 | | Stephanie Aneto | U20 | 23.08.77 | 4 | Antrim | 28 May |
| 11.45 w | | Nicky Ladrowski | U17 | 13.07.79 | 1 | Exeter | 13 Aug |
| 10.63 | | | | | 2 | Exeter | 27 Aug |
| 11.42 | | Danielle Rasbuary | U23 | 15.01.74 | 2 | Blackpool | 20 Aug |
| 11.40 i | | Joanne Scott | U20 | 31.12.76 | 2 | Birmingham | 18 Feb |
| 11.19 w 2.2 | | | | | 4 | Sheffield | 27 May |
| 11.09 | | | | | 1 | Middlesbrough | 13 May |
| 11.38 | | Jodie Hurst | U20 | 21.06.77 | 1 | Stoke | 10 Jun |
| 11.36 | | Rebecca White | U17 | 5.06.80 | 1 | Blackburn | 10 May |
| | (40) | | | | | | |
| 11.36 | | Jenny Brown | V35 | 21.05.59 | 1 | London (CP) | 13 May |
| 11.36 | | Miranda Fellows | U23 | 12.12.75 | 1 | Hereford | 10 Jun |
| 11.34 i | | Rachel Atkinson | U23 | 26.05.73 | 1 | Sheffield | 22 Jan |
| 11.33 | | | | | 6 | Birmingham | 19 Aug |
| 11.33 0.8 | | Debbie Marti | | 14.05.68 | 4 | Stoke | 10 Sep |
| 11.31 | | Lucy Clements | U20 | 20.07.78 | 1 | Corby | 25 Jun |
| 11.30 | | Debbie Woolgar | | 10.03.65 | 1 | Horsham | 13 May |
| 11.30 | | Kerry Saunders | U20 | 28.03.77 | 5 | Derby | 30 Jul |
| 11.30 | | Kathryn Blackwood | U20 | 31.03.76 | 1 | Southampton | 27 Aug |
| 11.30 | | Justina Cruickshank | U20 | 27.09.77 | 2 | Birmingham | 27 Aug |

| | | | | | | | |
|---|---|---|---|---|---|---|---|
| 11.28 | -0.7 | Julia Johnson | U17 | 21.09.79 | 2 | Birmingham | 30 Jul |
| (50) | | | | | | | |
| 11.25 | | Joanne Nicklin | | 12.07.67 | 1 | Barking | 13 May |
| 11.24 | | Clare Mackintosh | | 2.04.71 | 3 | Inverness | 11 Jun |
| 11.23 | | Lisa Vincent | U23 | 23.09.74 | 4 | Edinburgh | 8 May |
| 11.20 w | 3.0 | Emma Graves | U17 | 18.05.79 | 2 | London (CP) | 28 May |
| 11.02 | 1.0 | | | | * | London (CP) | 28 May |
| 11.18 i | | Nicola Clark | U20 | 14.04.77 | 2 | Sheffield | 22 Apr |
| 11.17 | | | | | 4 | Blackpool | 20 Aug |
| 11.16 | | Joanne Stanley | U20 | 30.03.77 | | Jarrow | 13 Aug |
| 11.15 | | Leigh Hubbard | U20 | 30.09.77 | 1 | Northampton | 10 May |
| 11.15 | 0.7 | Joanne Bennett | U23 | 1.09.73 | 3 | Birmingham | 17 Jun |
| 11.14 | | Andrea Hall | U20 | 28.01.77 | 1 | Bedford | 13 May |
| 11.12 i | | Hannah Moody | U17 | 26.07.79 | 2 | Birmingham | 19 Feb |
| 10.90 w | 4.4 | | | | 3 | Sheffield | 28 May |
| 10.83 | 1.6 | | | | * | Sheffield | 28 May |
| (60) | | | | | | | |
| 11.12 | | Kirsty Payne | U20 | 22.10.77 | 4 | Derby | 23 Jul |
| 11.11 | | Linda Davidson | | 29.05.70 | 1 | Aberdeen | 2 May |
| 11.10 | | Helen Silvey | U23 | 4.12.73 | 1 | Aldershot | 12 Aug |
| 11.09 i | | Sarah Ramminger | U23 | 1.10.75 | 1 | Glasgow | 15 Jan |
| 11.09 | | Gahlie Davis | U17 | 3.05.79 | 1 | London (CP) | 22 Apr |
| 11.07 w | | Meryl Woodger | | 3.11.66 | 1 | Aldershot | 12 Aug |
| 11.06 | | Hayley Young | U17 | 26.09.79 | 1 | Grantham | 13 May |
| 11.05 i | | Nicola Barr | | 26.04.70 | 2 | Glasgow | 15 Jan |
| 11.05 | 1.1 | Lindsay Jones | | 24.10.71 | 2 | Enfield | 30 Jul |
| 11.05 | | Dawn Jones | | 16.02.70 | 1 | Welwyn | 29 Aug |
| (70) | | | | | | | |
| 11.05 w | 2.9 | Victoria Reynolds | U17 | 22.04.80 | 2 | Sheffield | 28 May |
| 10.50 | 0.4 | | | · | * | Sheffield | 28 May |
| 11.03 | | Maurine Okwue | U20 | 13.05.78 | 1 | Canvey Island | 22 Apr |
| 11.03 | | Nikki Gilding | | 16.05.72 | 1 | Brighton | 3 Jun |
| 11.03 | | Janine Whitlock | U23 | 11.08.73 | 1 | Carshalton | 17 Sep |
| 11.00 | | Rachel Main | | 17.03.67 | 2 | Thurrock | 2 Sep |

**Additional Under 17** (1 - 10 above)

| | | | | | | |
|---|---|---|---|---|---|---|
| 10.94 | | Helen Baker | 5.02.79 | 1 | Woking | 12 Aug |
| 10.91 | | Hannah Lloyd | 14.11.78 | 2 | Crawley | 25 Jun |
| 10.89 | | Suzanne Sheppard | 24.09.78 | 1 | Belfast | 13 May |
| 10.88 | | Fiona Paul | 5.09.78 | 2 | Grangemouth | 14 May |
| 10.86 | -2.0 | Kelly Williamson | 4.12.79 | 5 | Birmingham | 30 Jul |
| 10.81 | | Natalie Butler | 25.11.78 | 3 | London (He) | 20 May |
| 10.81 | | Jacqueline Elliott | 13.09.78 | 1 | Jarrow | 13 Aug |
| 10.77 | -0.3 | Hayley Warrilow | 10.04.80 | 6 | Birmingham | 30 Jul |
| 10.76 | | Natalie Taylor | 2.01.80 | 3 | Greenock | 4 Jun |
| 10.74 | | Gemma Robinson | 30.12.78 | 2 | London (CP) | 14 May |
| (20) | | | | | | |
| 10.69 w | 4.2 | Kelly Brow | 24.09.78 | 4 | Sheffield | 28 May |
| 10.68 | | Danielle Collins | 8.12.79 | 1 | Sutton | 22 Jul |
| 10.66 | | Nicola Winship | 24.09.78 | 1 | Enfield | 18 Jun |
| 10.65 | | Claire Everett | 25.06.79 | 1 | Norwich | 14 May |
| 10.61 | | Caroline Doyle | 3.10.79 | 2 | Kingston | 12 Aug |
| 10.61 | | Carrie Hancox | 8.08.80 | 1 | Cheltenham | 27 Aug |
| 10.59 | | Annette Foster | 7.05.80 | 1 | Lincoln | 10 Sep |
| 10.58 | 0.8 | Jenny Todd | 23.10.78 | 4 | Montrevil, FRA | 30 Sep |
| 10.57 | | Alison Dodd | 8.09.78 | 2 | Derby | 14 May |
| 10.55 | | Sarah Wellstead | 22.10.79 | 1 | Sutton | 17 Sep |
| 10.54 i | | Kate Rogers | 14.02.79 | 8 | Birmingham | 19 Feb |
| 10.52 | | Nicola Bray | 14.10.79 | 2 | London (WL) | 22 Jul |
| 10.50 | | Sarah Fleetham | 9.01.79 | 2 | Colchester | 28 Aug |

**overage**

| | | | | | |
|---|---|---|---|---|---|
| 10.86 i | Natalie Butler | 25.11.78 | 4 | Birmingham | 30 Dec |

285

# SHOT

| | | | | | | | |
|---|---|---|---|---|---|---|---|
| 18.44 | Judy Oakes | V35 | 14.02.58 | 1 | Kilkenny, IRE | 2 | Sep |
| | 18.26 | | | 6 | London (CP) | 7 | Jul |
| | 18.25 | | | 1 | London (CP) | 18 | Jun |
| | 18.20 | | | 1 | Enfield | 30 | Jul |
| | 18.17 | | | 3 | Villeneuve d'Ascq, FRA | 24 | Jun |
| | 18.13 | | | 3 | Gateshead | 21 | Aug |
| | 18.11 | | | 6 | London (CP) | 27 | Aug |
| | 18.10 | | | 1 | Pl de Las Americas,SPA | | Apr |
| | 18.07 | | | 1 | Braintree | 23 | Jul |
| | 17.93 i | | | 1 | London (CP) | 16 | Dec |
| | 17.89 | | | 1 | Croydon | 13 | May |
| | 17.89 | | | 1 | Croydon | 3 | Jun |
| | 17.87 | | | 4 | Gateshead | 2 | Jul |
| | 17.87 | | | 13Q | Gothenburg, SWE | 5 | Aug |
| | 17.81 i | | | 1 | Birmingham | 3 | Feb |
| | 17.78 i | | | 3 | Birmingham | 28 | Jan |
| | 17.77 i | | | 8 | Barcelona, SPA | 11 | Mar |
| | 17.75 | | | 1 | Birmingham | 15 | Jul |
| | 17.72 | | | 1 | London (CP) | 10 | Sep |
| | 17.70 i | | | 1 | London (CP) | 14 | Jan |
| | 17.62 i | | | 1 | London (Ha) | 21 | Jan |
| | 17.58 i | | | 1 | London (CP) | 25 | Feb |
| | 17.15 i | | | 1 | Glasgow | 11 | Feb |
| 16.24 | Maggie Lynes | | 19.02.63 | 2 | Pl de Las Americas,SPA | | Apr |
| | 16.16 | | | 1 | London (CP) | 14 | May |
| | 16.15 i | | | 1 | Nenagh, IRE | 5 | Mar |
| | 16.12 | | | 2 | London (CP) | 18 | Jun |
| | 16.08 i | | | 2 | Glasgow | 11 | Feb |
| | 16.05 | | | 2 | Braintree | 23 | Jul |
| | 16.02 | | | 4 | Nurmijarvi, FIN | 4 | Jun |
| | 16.02 | | | 1 | Liverpool | 30 | Jul |
| | 16.01 i | | | 2 | London (CP) | 16 | Dec |
| | 15.97 | | | 2 | Antrim | 28 | May |
| | 15.91 | | | 1 | Braintree | 24 | Jun |
| | 15.90 | | | 1 | Loughborough | 11 | Jun |
| | 15.88 i | | | 4 | Birmingham | 28 | Jan |
| | 15.87 i | | | 2 | London (Ha) | 21 | Jan |
| | 15.76 i | | | 2 | London (CP) | 14 | Jan |
| | 15.74 | | | 1 | Windsor | 12 | Aug |
| | 15.72 i | | | 2 | Vienna, AUT | 18 | Feb |
| | 15.71 i | | | 2 | Birmingham | 3 | Feb |
| | 15.67 | | | 2 | Birmingham | 15 | Jul |
| | 15.67 | | | 1 | Stoke | 9 | Sep |
| | 15.62 | | | 1 | Croydon | 3 | Sep |
| | 15.57 | | | 5 | Gateshead | 21 | Aug |
| 15.70 | Myrtle Augee | | 4.02.65 | 1 | Stoke | 10 | Sep |
| | 46 performances to 15.50 by 3 athletes including 16 indoors | | | | | | |
| 15.36 i | Alison Grey | U23 | 12.05.73 | 1 | Glasgow | 22 | Jan |
| | 14.43 | | | 1 | Birmingham | 19 | Aug |
| 14.95 i | Sharon Andrews | | 4.07.67 | 3 | London (Ha) | 21 | Jan |
| | 14.60 | | | 1 | Norwich | 3 | Jun |
| 14.90 | Tracy Axten | | 20.07.63 | 2 | London (CP) | 10 | Sep |
| 14.80 | Debbie Callaway | | 15.07.64 | 1 | Derby | 6 | Aug |
| 14.42 | Uju Efobi | U23 | 10.10.74 | 2 | London (CP) | 14 | May |
| 14.35 i | Jayne Berry | | 18.07.70 | 1 | Birmingham | 26 | Feb |
| 14.29 | Jo Duncan | | 27.12.66 | 3 | London (CP) | 18 | Jun |
| | (10) | | | | | | |
| 14.23 | Carol Cooksley | | 22.09.69 | 1 | Loughborough | 21 | Jun |
| 14.19 i | Yinka Idowu | | 25.02.72 | 4 | London (Ha) | 21 | Jan |
| | 13.69 | | | H | Alhama, SPA | 20 | May |

| 14.11 | Philippa Roles | U20 | 1.03.78 | 1 | Bedford | 2 | Jul |
|---|---|---|---|---|---|---|---|
| 14.08 | Clova Court | V35 | 10.02.60 | 2 | Birmingham | 20 | May |
| 14.03 | Lorraine Shaw | | 2.04.68 | 1 | Birmingham | 18 | Jun |
| 13.88 | Helen Wilding | U20 | 25.10.76 | 1 | Nottingham | 8 | Jul |
| 13.78 | Helen Cowe | | 7.09.66 | 1 | Drumnadrochit | 26 | Aug |
| 13.71 | Emma Beales | | 7.12.71 | 1 | Southampton | 12 | Aug |
| 13.63 | Charmaine Johnson | | 4.06.63 | 4 | Stoke | 9 | Sep |
| 13.58 | Denise Lewis | | 27.08.72 | 3 | Glasgow | 6 | May |
| | (20) | | | | | | |
| 13.56 i | Natasha Smith | U20 | 6.06.77 | 3 | London (CP) | 16 | Dec |
| 13.46 | | | | 3 | Belfort, FRA | 6 | Aug |
| 13.53 | Debbie Woolgar | | 10.03.65 | 1 | Southend | 2 | Sep |
| 13.37 | Emma Merry | U23 | 2.07.74 | 1 | Loughborough | 26 | Apr |
| 13.37 | Eleanor Gatrell | U20 | 5.10.76 | 1 | Reading | 20 | May |
| 13.30 | Fay Champion | | 27.09.66 | 1 | Swindon | 14 | May |
| 13.24 | Christina Bennett | U20 | 27.02.78 | 1 | Kingston | 10 | Jun |
| 13.18 | Pauline Richards | | 30.06.68 | 5 | London (He) | 1 | Jul |
| 13.18 | Vickie Foster | | 1.04.71 | 1 | Southampton | 10 | Sep |
| 13.00 | Jenny Kelly | | 20.06.70 | 2 | Peterborough | 7 | May |
| 12.95 | Irene Duffin | V35 | 10.08.60 | 1 | London (He) | 20 | May |
| | (30) | | | | | | |
| 12.91 | Jacqui McKernan | | 1.07.65 | 3 | Stoke | 10 | Sep |
| 12.76 | Angela Lambourn | | 9.04.66 | 1 | Kings Lynn | 29 | Apr |
| 12.76 | Sharon Gibson | | 31.12.61 | 1 | Mansfield | 13 | May |
| 12.76 | Carol Bennett | U20 | 11.01.77 | 1 | Hull | 10 | Jun |
| 12.75 | Joanne Galligan/Mortimer | | 18.12.71 | 1 | Bolton | 13 | May |
| 12.65 | Sara Allen | | 7.12.70 | 2 | Bolton | 13 | May |
| 12.58 i | Sarah Damm | | 12.09.70 | 1P | Birmingham | 5 | Feb |
| 12.44 | | | | 4 | Birmingham | 23 | Apr |
| 12.56 | Nav Dhaliwal | U20 | 30.11.77 | 2 | Coatbridge | 27 | Aug |
| 12.55 | Tracy Shorts | | 4.11.72 | 8 | Bedford | 28 | May |
| 12.53 | Jacquie Burke | U20 | 12.09.76 | 1 | Hull | 16 | Apr |
| | (40) | | | | | | |
| 12.38 | Lorna Jackson | U23 | 9.01.74 | 6 | London (He) | 1 | Jul |
| 12.37 | Anna-Lisa Howard | U20 | 18.04.78 | 1 | St. Ives | 17 | Jun |
| 12.35 | Claire Burnett | | 17.10.72 | 1 | Braunton | 13 | May |
| 12.34 | Donna Williams | U17 | 7.10.78 | 1 | Bolton | 13 | May |
| 12.31 | Bronwin Carter | V40 | 25.04.51 | 1 | Portsmouth | 20 | May |
| 12.27 | Gaynor Haskell | U20 | 11.08.76 | 1 | Aldershot | 12 | Aug |
| 12.26 | Noelle Bradshaw | | 18.12.63 | 4 | Barking | 22 | Apr |
| 12.19 | Kim Crowther-Price | | 19.01.66 | 1H | Bebington | 22 | Jul |
| 12.13 | Lynne Barnett | U23 | 12.08.74 | 1 | Dundee | 4 | Jun |
| 12.11 | Nicola Gautier | U20 | 21.03.78 | 1H | Stoke | 16 | Sep |
| | (50) | | | | | | |
| 12.10 | Lesley Brannan | U20 | 13.09.76 | 1 | Colwyn Bay | 14 | May |
| 12.04 | Christine Mann | U20 | 24.10.76 | 1 | Greenock | 4 | Jun |
| 12.02 | Julie Dunkley | U17 | 11.09.79 | 1 | Dartford | 20 | Aug |
| 11.98 | Jan Marie Thompson | | 9.03.70 | 2 | Bolton | 2 | Jul |
| 11.96 | Rebecca Lewis | U20 | 31.12.77 | 1H | Blackpool | 24 | Jun |
| 11.94 | Catherine Garden | U17 | 4.09.78 | 1 | Birmingham | 30 | Jul |
| 11.93 | Rachel Hopgood | U20 | 2.06.78 | 1 | Jarrow | 27 | Aug |
| 11.92 i | Krissy Owen | U23 | 14.12.75 | 2 | Birmingham | 1 | Mar |
| 11.92 | Tracy Page | | 3.02.72 | 1 | Portsmouth | 14 | Jun |
| 11.92 i | Fiona Hunter | U20 | 14.09.78 | 1P | Glasgow | 9 | Dec |
| 11.11 | | U17 | | 5 | Colwyn Bay | 15 | Jul |
| | (60) | | | | | | |
| 11.86 | Helen Arnold | U17 | 5.10.78 | 1 | Portsmouth | 12 | Jul |
| 11.85 | Lisa Gibbs | | 9.01.69 | 1 | Brierley Hill | 30 | Apr |
| 11.84 | Cathy-Ann Hill | U20 | 4.05.77 | 1 | High Wycombe | 2 | Sep |
| 11.74 | Clover Wynter-Pink | U20 | 29.11.77 | 3 | Peterborough | 7 | May |
| 11.74 | Gillian Burns | | 12.07.64 | 3 | Bebington | 11 | Jun |

| | | | | | | | |
|---|---|---|---|---|---|---|---|
| 11.74 | Vikki Shepherd | U17 | 26.01.80 | 1 | Hemsworth | 25 | Jun |
| 11.73 * | Karen Martin | U23 | 24.11.74 | 1 | Cosford | 5 | Jul |
| 11.73 | Karen Skeggs | | 26.10.69 | 2 | Hoo | 12 | Aug |
| 11.69 | Eleanor Garden | U20 | 20.11.76 | 4 | Edinburgh | 24 | Jun |
| *11.67* | *Kelly Kane* | *U23* | *28.10.74* | *3* | *Blackpool* | *20* | *Aug* |
| 11.66 | Carole Hardy | | 31.12.66 | 1 | Cheltenham | 21 | May |
| (70) | | | | | | | |
| 11.66 | Julie McCorry | U17 | 7.11.79 | 2 | Birmingham | 30 | Jul |
| 11.63 | Alison George | | 11.12.62 | 2 | Rotherham | 6 | Aug |
| 11.62 | Jo Evans | | 3.10.68 | 2 | Cardiff | 23 | Apr |
| 11.61 | Michelle Harrison | U17 | 29.09.78 | 1 | Sheffield | 21 | Jun |
| 11.61 | Melanie Walker | U17 | 29.04.79 | 3 | Nottingham | 8 | Jul |
| 11.59 | Michelle Cornick | U20 | 21.09.76 | 8 | Nottingham | 8 | Jul |
| 11.59 i | Cheryl Done | | 25.09.70 | 2 | Birmingham | 30 | Dec |
| 11.58 | Louise Batho | U20 | 27.11.76 | 1 | Basildon | 10 | Jun |
| 11.51 | Jane Aucott | | 10.10.68 | 3 | Loughborough | 24 | May |
| 11.51 | Sharon Nash | U23 | 5.05.74 | 2 | Salisbury | 2 | Sep |
| (80) | | | | | | | |
| 11.50 i | Jackie Tindal | U20 | 21.01.79 | 2P | Glasgow | 9 | Dec |
| 11.04 | | U17 | | 1 | Coatbridge | 3 | Sep |
| 11.49 i | Pauline Shirt | U20 | 21.05.78 | 1 | Sheffield | 5 | Mar |
| 11.47 | Lisa Munden | U20 | 13.03.78 | 2 | Salisbury | 16 | Jul |
| 11.46 | Nicola Talbot | | 17.02.72 | 1 | Telford | 13 | May |
| 11.46 | Tracy Rea | U17 | 19.01.79 | 5 | Nottingham | 8 | Jul |
| 11.44 | Joanne Holloway | U20 | 10.05.76 | 4 | Kingston | 10 | Jun |
| 11.44 | Heather Seager | | 4.04.68 | 1 | Yeovil | 22 | Jul |
| 11.44 | Lyn Sprules | U23 | 11.09.75 | 1 | Exeter | 27 | Aug |
| 11.43 | Jackie Gordon | | 22.12.67 | 2 | Birmingham | 9 | Aug |
| 11.41 i | Vikki Schofield | | 29.12.72 | 5 | Wakefield | 21 | Jan |
| 11.25 | | | | 1 | York | 23 | Jul |
| (90) | | | | | | | |
| 11.37 | Karen Costello | | 21.10.68 | 9 | London (He) | 1 | Jul |
| 11.37 | Jennifer Elphick | | 24.11.66 | 3 | Birmingham | 9 | Aug |
| 11.36 | Irene Timmis | | 28.03.65 | 1 | Dartford | 20 | May |
| 11.35 | Anna Town | U23 | 22.04.75 | 1 | Watford | 14 | May |
| 11.31 | Jackie Barclay | | 17.01.66 | 2 | Glasgow | 23 | Apr |
| 11.30 | Julia Bennett | | 26.03.70 | 1 | London (CP) | 19 | Apr |
| 11.30 | Alison Moffitt | | 6.10.69 | 1 | Londonderry | 19 | Aug |
| 11.29 | Emma Lindsay | | 11.04.71 | 3 | Greenock | 4 | Jun |
| 11.29 | Alyson Hourihan | V35 | 17.10.60 | 3 | Newport | 17 | Jun |
| 11.26 | Frances Reid-Hughes | U17 | 18.03.80 | 2 | Horsham | 20 | May |
| (100) | | | | | | | |
| 11.25 | Michelle Woods | U17 | 2.08.80 | 4 | Norwich | 3 | Jun |
| 11.24 | Karen Ostersburg | | 23.09.65 | 4 | Derby | 23 | Jul |
| 11.23 | Angie Nyhan | U20 | 13.04.78 | 1 | York | 30 | Jul |
| 11.22 | Ann Gardner | | 11.10.68 | 1 | Lincoln | 30 | Apr |
| 11.20 | Sue Grant | | 10.05.69 | 1 | Wakefield | 9 | Jul |
| 11.20 | Rebecca Chamberlain | U17 | 7.09.79 | 7 | Birmingham | 30 | Jul |

**Additional Under 17** (1 - 14 above)

| | | | | | | | |
|---|---|---|---|---|---|---|---|
| 11.09 | Tuvola Akiwumi | | 15.10.79 | 1 | Kingston | 3 | Jun |
| 10.92 | Lauren Keightley | | 2.08.79 | 2 | Bracknell | 22 | Jul |
| 10.87 | Lynsey Herrington | | 31.05.79 | 1 | Bracknell | 25 | Mar |
| 10.83 | Emma Clarence | | 2.12.78 | 2 | Bolton | 13 | May |
| 10.80 | Joanne Smith | | 22.11.78 | 1b | Windsor | 12 | Aug |
| 10.74 i | Fran Wilkins | | 15.01.79 | 3 | Birmingham | 18 | Feb |
| (20) | | | | | | | |
| 10.65 i | Natalie Kerr | | 17.11.79 | 4 | Birmingham | 18 | Feb |
| 10.61 | | | | 1 | Birmingham | 10 | Jun |
| 10.50 | Michelle Ingham | | 1.09.78 | 1 | Ashton-U-Lyne | 27 | Aug |

## SHOT - Under 15 - 3.25kg

| | | | | | | |
|---|---|---|---|---|---|---|
| 13.11 | Amy Wilson | 31.12.80 | 1 | Welwyn | 2 | Sep |
| 12.86 | Lucy Rann | 5.09.80 | 1 | London (CP) | 28 | May |
| 12.16 | April Kalu | 31.03.82 | 1 | Blackpool | 20 | Aug |
| 12.10 | Maryann Naboya | 16.09.80 | 1 | Nottingham | 7 | Jul |
| 11.99 | Alex Hajipavlis | 3.10.80 | 2 | Sutton Coldfield | 30 | Apr |
| 11.91 | Joan MacPherson | 18.09.80 | 2 | Birmingham | 29 | Jul |
| 11.59 | Anna McHugh | 27.03.81 | 2 | Nottingham | 7 | Jul |
| 11.30 | Leigh Dargan | 31.03.81 | 1 | Brighton | 10 | Jun |
| 11.28 | Lesley Ann Roy | 3.01.82 | 1 | Greenock | 4 | Jun |
| 11.24 i | Sara Nesbitt | 9.10.80 | 2 | Birmingham | 18 | Feb |
| | 10.87 | | 5 | Nottingham | 7 | Jul |
| | (10) | | | | | |
| 10.82 | Eva Massey | 22.12.80 | 2 | Antrim | 12 | Aug |
| 10.81 | Emma Carpenter | 16.05.82 | 1 | Exeter | 27 | Aug |
| 10.79 | Linda Dykes | 1.09.80 | 1 | Liverpool | 13 | Aug |
| 10.74 | Elizabeth Bowyer | 8.09.81 | 6 | Nottingham | 7 | Jul |
| 10.62 | Natalie Buckland | 19.02.82 | 1 | Basildon | 10 | Jun |
| 10.54 | Alina Elliott | 4.08.81 | 1 | Cheltenham | 17 | Jun |

### Under 13

| | | | | | | |
|---|---|---|---|---|---|---|
| 9.64 | Onome Okwuosa | 2.08.83 | 1 | Salisbury | 2 | Sep |
| 8.97 | Lucy Newman | 2.03.83 | | | | |
| 8.53 | Eve Russell | 27.09.82 | 4 | Exeter | 2 | Sep |

## SHOT - Under 13 - 2.72kg

| | | | | | | |
|---|---|---|---|---|---|---|
| 10.40 | Lisa Thompson | 3.12.82 | 1 | Inverness | 17 | Aug |
| 10.02 | Shelley McLellan | 21.03.83 | 1 | London (TB) | 30 | Jul |
| 9.97 | Eve Russell | 27.09.82 | 1 | Reading | 3 | Sep |
| 9.81 | Kate Morris | 18.01.83 | 1 | Dartford | 19 | Aug |
| 9.72 | V. Chirneside | | 1 | Newcastle | 24 | Jun |
| 9.57 | Lucy Newman | 2.03.83 | 1 | Crawley | 3 | Sep |
| 9.49 | Petulia Thomas | | 1 | Carmarthen | 20 | Aug |
| 9.40 | Claire Smithson | 3.08.83 | 1 | Crawley | 28 | Aug |
| 9.17 | Laura Douglas | 4.01.83 | 1 | Wrexham | 24 | Sep |
| 9.16 | Joanna Thrift | 14.09.82 | | Windsor | 19 | Jul |
| | (10) | | | | | |
| 9.14 | Jemma Spellacy | 27.11.82 | 1 | Southend | 27 | Aug |
| 9.11 | Natalie Anderson | 7.10.82 | 1 | Colchester | 28 | Aug |

### Overage

| | | | | | | |
|---|---|---|---|---|---|---|
| 9.31 | Caroline Gore | 29.03.83 | 1 | Liverpool | 26 | Nov |

## DISCUS

| | | | | | | |
|---|---|---|---|---|---|---|
| 59.06 | Jacqui McKernan | 1.07.65 | 5 | Villeneuve d'Ascq, FRA | 24 | Jun |
| 58.90 | | | 1 | Oslo (Lam), NOR | 14 | Jun |
| 58.88 | | | 2 | Birmingham | 16 | Jul |
| 58.62 | | | 1 | Antrim | 8 | Jul |
| 58.38 | | | 1 | Edinburgh | 7 | May |
| 56.58 | | | 1 | Antrim | 1 | Jul |
| 56.38 | | | 1 | Liverpool | 30 | Jul |
| 56.16 | | | 3 | Gateshead | 21 | Aug |
| 55.50 | | | 2 | Kevelaar, HOL | 3 | Jun |
| 55.50 | | | 7 | Oslo, NOR | 21 | Jul |
| 55.38 | | | 8 | Halle, GER | 13 | May |
| 54.90 | | | 1 | Antrim | 28 | May |
| 54.78 | | | 26Q | Gothenburg, SWE | 10 | Aug |
| 53.32 | | | 5 | Byrkjelo, NOR | 23 | Jul |
| 53.12 | | | 2 | Loughborough | 11 | Jun |

| | | | | | | | |
|---|---|---|---|---|---|---|---|
| 57.00 | Debbie Callaway | | 15.07.64 | 1 | Braintree | 24 | Jun |
| 55.72 | | | | 1 | Enfield | 29 | Apr |
| 54.56 | | | | 1 | Croydon | 28 | Aug |
| 54.52 | | | | 1 | London (CP) | 18 | Jun |
| 54.34 | | | | 2 | Cwmbran | 9 | Jul |
| 54.10 | | | | 1 | Loughborough | 11 | Jun |
| 54.04 | | | | 1 | Barking | 13 | May |
| 54.00 | | | | 1 | Birmingham | 20 | May |
| 53.72 | | | | 1 | Southampton | 11 | Jul |
| 53.50 | | | | 4 | Birmingham | 16 | Jul |
| 52.84 | | | | 1 | Liverpool | 2 | Jul |
| 52.80 | | | | 1 | Derby | 6 | Aug |
| 52.70 | | | | 1 | Enfield | 30 | Jul |
| 52.32 | | | | 4 | Gateshead | 21 | Aug |
| 52.32 | | | | 2 | Kilkenny, IRE | 2 | Sep |
| 52.02 | | | | 1 | Braintree | 23 | Jul |
| 55.70 | Shelley Drew | U23 | 8.08.73 | 1 | Birmingham | 25 | Jun |
| 55.18 | | | | 2 | Edinburgh | 7 | May |
| 54.06 | | | | 1 | Bedford | 29 | May |
| 54.00 | | | | 10 | Halle, GER | 13 | May |
| 53.76 | | | | 1 | Horsham | 3 | Jun |
| 53.74 | | | | 3 | Birmingham | 16 | Jul |
| 53.66 | | | | 1 | Basel, SWZ | 5 | Jun |
| 53.52 | | | | 2 | Enfield | 29 | Apr |
| 53.40 | | | | 1 | Narbonne, FRA | 29 | Jul |
| 53.02 | | | | 2 | Croydon | 28 | Aug |
| 52.96 | | | | | | 28 | Jun |
| 52.58 | | | | 2 | Birmingham | 20 | May |
| 52.08 | | | | 2 | London (CP) | 18 | Jun |
| 54.68 | Emma Beales | | 7.12.71 | 1 | Bedford | 10 | Jun |
| 53.34 | | | | 1 | Braintree | 20 | May |
| 53.62 | Tracy Axten | | 20.07.63 | 2 | Bedford | 10 | Jun |
| 53.62 | | | | 3 | Cwmbran | 9 | Jul |
| 52.06 | | | | 1 | Melbourne, AUS | 3 | Mar |
| 53.18 | Sharon Andrews | | 4.07.67 | 2 | Barking | 13 | May |
| 52.58 | Sarah Winckless | U23 | 18.10.73 | 1 | London (Ha) | 25 | Jun |
| 51 performances to 52.00 by 7 athletes | | | | | | | |
| 51.38 | Lorraine Shaw | | 2.04.68 | 1 | Birmingham | 18 | Jun |
| 50.58 | Emma Merry | U23 | 2.07.74 | 1 | Loughborough | 20 | May |
| 50.56 | Judy Oakes | V35 | 14.02.58 | 1 | Pl de Las Americas,SPA | | Apr |
| (10) | | | | | | | |
| 49.44 | Myrtle Augee | | 4.02.65 | 1 | London (CP) | 14 | May |
| 49.12 | Philippa Roles | U20 | 1.03.78 | 4 | Cwmbran | 9 | Jul |
| 48.84 | Uju Efobi | U23 | 10.10.74 | 2 | London (CP) | 14 | May |
| 48.64 | Rosanne Lister | | 9.05.69 | 4 | Croydon | 28 | Aug |
| 48.32 | Nicola Talbot | | 17.02.72 | 2 | Corby | 25 | Jun |
| 48.18 | Sarah Henton | U23 | 4.05.73 | 4 | Edinburgh | 7 | May |
| 48.04 | Rachel Hopgood | U20 | 2.06.78 | 1 | York | 10 | Jun |
| 47.54 | Lauren Keightley | U17 | 2.08.79 | 1 | Woking | 12 | Jul |
| 47.56 dh | | | | 1 | Nottingham | 7 | Jul |
| 46.26 | Helen Cowe | | 7.09.66 | 1 | Aberdeen | 23 | Jul |
| 45.94 | Alison Grey | U23 | 12.05.73 | 1 | Edinburgh | 10 | Sep |
| (20) | | | | | | | |
| 44.82 | Sarah Symonds | U23 | 28.12.73 | 5 | Enfield | 29 | Apr |
| 44.74 | Susan Freebairn | | 22.08.65 | 3 | Birmingham | 19 | Aug |
| 44.64 | Fay Champion | | 27.09.66 | 1 | Basingstoke | 6 | Aug |
| 44.54 | Rebecca Hardy | | 11.11.68 | 2 | Hayes | 13 | May |
| 44.52 | Joanne Essex | | 16.04.63 | 1 | Harlow | 22 | Jul |
| 43.94 | Jayne Fisher | | 2.11.70 | 5 | Cwmbran | 9 | Jul |
| 43.72 | Michelle Wright | U23 | 26.04.74 | 3 | Derby | 23 | Jul |

| 43.60 | Vickie Foster | | 1.04.71 | 1 | Swindon | 14 May |
|---|---|---|---|---|---|---|
| 43.18 | Tasha Saint-Smith | U23 | 20.12.75 | 3 | Loughborough | 26 Apr |
| 42.92 | Jane Aucott | | 10.10.68 | 3 | Loughborough | 24 May |
| (30) | | | | | | |
| 42.90 | Sara Allen | | 7.12.70 | 1 | Bolton | 13 May |
| 42.90 | Helen Wilding | U20 | 25.10.76 | 1 | Pitreavie | 25 Jun |
| 42.68 | Lucy Capes | U23 | 1.12.75 | 2 | Sheffield | 14 May |
| 42.44 | Maggie Lynes | | 19.02.63 | 2 | Pl de Las Americas,SPA | Apr |
| 42.20 | Catherine Garden | U17 | 4.09.78 | 2 | Edinburgh | 10 Sep |
| 42.18 | Donna Williams | U17 | 7.10.78 | 1 | Bolton | 13 May |
| 42.02 | Jackie Wright | V40 | 8.10.53 | 1 | Exeter | 6 Aug |
| 41.96 | Kelly Mellis | U17 | 4.12.79 | 6 | Croydon | 28 Aug |
| 41.94 | Natalie Kerr | U17 | 17.11.79 | 1 | Sutton Coldfield | 26 Aug |
| 41.44 | Tracy Shorts | | 4.11.72 | 1 | Glasgow | 17 Sep |
| (40) | | | | | | |
| 41.36 | Karen Smith | U23 | 10.02.74 | 4 | London (He) | 1 Jul |
| 41.32 | Helen McCreadie | U23 | 10.05.75 | 5 | London (He) | 1 Jul |
| 41.30 | Alyson Hourihan | V35 | 17.10.60 | 1 | Newport | 12 Aug |
| 41.06 | Carol Cooksley | | 22.09.69 | 7 | London (He) | 1 Jul |
| 40.82 | Eleanor Garden | U20 | 20.11.76 | 6 | Edinburgh | 7 May |
| 40.70 | Donna McEwan | U20 | 17.01.78 | 1 | Redditch | 27 Aug |
| 40.64 | Jenny Hope | | 1.09.62 | 1 | Nottingham | 25 Jun |
| 40.12 | Charlotte Davies | U20 | 21.04.76 | 1 | Peterborough | 10 Jun |
| 39.72 | Joanna Wood | | 2.10.72 | 3 | Gateshead | 17 Jun |
| 39.72 | Susan Backhouse | U17 | 6.12.78 | 1 | York | 23 Jul |
| (50) | | | | | | |
| 39.66 | Lynsey Herrington | U17 | 31.05.79 | 2 | Woking | 12 Jul |
| | 41.86 dh | | | 3 | Nottingham | 7 Jul |
| 39.52 | Rachel Morris | | 20.09.70 | 1 | Watford | 14 May |
| 39.44 | Lyn Sprules | U23 | 11.09.75 | 3 | Feltham | 22 Jul |
| 39.42 | Claire Cameron | V35 | 3.10.58 | 2 | Wishaw | 13 May |
| 39.38 | Julie Robin | U20 | 16.01.77 | 5 | Edinburgh | 24 Jun |
| 39.38 | Alex Hajipavlis | U15 | 3.10.80 | 1 | Loughborough | 13 Aug |
| 39.34 | Nav Dhaliwal | U20 | 30.11.77 | 3 | Ayr | 18 Jul |
| 39.30 | Alison Faben | U20 | 7.02.77 | 2 | Nottingham | 7 Jul |
| 38.64 | Stephanie Buttle | | 27.03.72 | 1 | Dartford | 13 Aug |
| 38.62 | Michelle Wallace | | 1.11.72 | 3 | Stafford | 7 May |
| (60) | | | | | | |
| 38.62 | Sharon Nash | U23 | 5.05.74 | 1 | Dartford | 13 Aug |
| 38.60 | Catherine Lane | U20 | 18.11.76 | 2 | London (CP) | 27 May |
| 38.58 | Lynsey Braddock | U20 | 14.10.77 | 1 | Bracknell | 10 Jun |
| 38.46 | Julie Kirkpatrick | | 14.07.72 | 3 | Pitreavie | 25 Jun |
| 38.38 | Kate Semus | | 18.01.70 | 1 | Andover | 12 Aug |
| 38.26 | Alana Wallace | | | 1 | Antrim | 26 Aug |
| 38.12 | Christina Bennett | U20 | 27.02.78 | 1 | Crawley | 15 Apr |
| 38.10 | Sarah Ashbridge | U23 | 23.05.75 | 5 | Peterborough | 7 May |
| 38.04 | Irene Duffin | V35 | 10.08.60 | 8 | London (He) | 1 Jul |
| 37.82 | Imogen Martin | U23 | 13.02.74 | 1 | Bedford | 2 Sep |
| (70) | | | | | | |
| 37.76 | Noelle Bradshaw | | 18.12.63 | 4 | Barking | 22 Apr |
| 37.74 | Heather MacLeod | | 12.03.72 | 5 | Glasgow | 23 Apr |
| 37.74 | Nicola Derbyshire | U20 | 8.08.76 | 1 | Bolton | 13 May |
| 37.74 | Michelle Woods | U17 | 2.08.80 | 3 | London (CP) | 28 May |
| 37.72 | Leanne Grey | U20 | 6.02.78 | 1 | Stoke | 17 Jun |
| 37.68 | Amanda Sheppard | | 26.02.68 | 1 | Carlisle | 2 Jul |
| 37.50 | Rebecca West | U23 | 9.09.74 | 1 | Perivale | 22 Apr |
| 37.48 | Debbie Woolgar | | 10.03.65 | 5 | Croydon | 28 Aug |
| 37.48 | Suzanne Last | | 11.01.70 | 2 | Exeter | 2 Sep |
| 37.42 | Wendy Thomson | U23 | 24.06.75 | 5 | Barking | 13 May |
| (80) | | | | | | |
| 37.42 | Tammy Nicholls | U20 | 21.07.78 | 1 | Basildon | 10 Jun |

| 37.34 | Jo Evans | | 3.10.68 | 2 | Bebington | 11 | Jun |
| 37.22 | Debra Monds | U20 | 25.02.78 | 5 | Nottingham | 7 | Jul |
| 37.22 | Joan MacPherson | U15 | 18.09.80 | 1 | Ryde | 24 | Sep |
| 37.10 | Katie Hopkins | U20 | 6.11.77 | 2 | Bedford | 25 | Jun |
| 37.00 | Samantha Burns-Salmond | U20 | 13.04.76 | 1 | Grimsby | 13 | May |
| 37.00 | Heather Seager | | 4.04.68 | 1 | Yeovil | 22 | Jul |
| 36.90 | Elizabeth Whittle | U23 | 23.06.75 | 2 | Bolton | 13 | May |
| 36.72 | Laura Wood | U17 | 31.10.78 | 1 | Stockport | 30 | Apr |
| 36.68 | Joanne Coote | | 10.02.68 | 1 | York | 30 | Apr |
| | (90) | | | | | | |
| 36.64 | Rebecca Roles | U17 | 14.12.79 | 1 | Cardiff | 1 | Jul |
| 36.64 | Amie Hill | U15 | 9.09.80 | 1 | Braintree | 20 | Aug |
| 36.52 | Sandra Terry | | 28.04.69 | 1 | Aldershot | 7 | Jun |
| 36.46 | Claire Phillips | U23 | 13.03.75 | 7 | Edinburgh | 7 | May |
| 36.42 | V. Duffy | V35 | | 1 | London (BP) | 15 | May |
| 36.38 | Joanna Bradley | U17 | 23.08.79 | 1 | London (CP) | 14 | May |
| | 37.06 dh | | | 6 | Nottingham | 7 | Jul |
| 36.18 | Amy Burton | U20 | 24.06.77 | 2 | Aldershot | 7 | Jun |
| 36.14 | Sarah Moore | U23 | 15.03.73 | 2 | Wrexham | 25 | Jun |
| 36.12 | Bronwin Carter | V40 | 25.04.51 | 2 | Portsmouth | 20 | May |
| | 38.80 un | | | | | | |
| 36.12 | Sarah Johnson | U20 | 24.08.77 | 4 | Utrecht, HOL | 9 | Jul |
| | (100) | | | | | | |
| 36.08 | Ann-Marie Read | U23 | 24.05.75 | 3 | Milton Keynes | 22 | Apr |
| 36.06 | Tracey Quartey | | 16.12.71 | 1 | London (Elt) | 2 | Sep |
| 36.00 | Maria Hood | U17 | 20.12.79 | 1 | Welwyn | 28 | Aug |

**Additional Under 17** (1 - 12 above)

| 35.56 | Jennifer Hewitt | | 8.01.80 | 1b | Exeter | 2 | Sep |
| 35.46 | Sarah Strickleton | | 10.05.80 | 1 | Bolton | 14 | Jun |
| 35.34 | Charlene Sumnall | | 21.02.79 | 2 | Corby | 23 | Jul |
| 35.26 | Victoria Halliwell | | 6.11.78 | 1 | Wigan | 16 | May |
| 35.08 | Clare Wheatcroft | | 15.12.78 | 7 | Birmingham | 30 | Jul |
| 35.04 | Kelly Kirkham | | 2.03.79 | 1 | Redditch | 27 | Aug |
| 34.90 | Joanne Smith | | 22.11.78 | 2b | Norfolk | 3 | Jun |
| 34.82 | Llyn Perry | | 21.02.79 | 1 | Braintree | 24 | Jun |
| | (20) | | | | | | |
| 34.68 | Emma Clarence | | 2.12.78 | 1b | Telford | 18 | Jun |
| 34.52 | Frances Reid-Hughes | | 18.03.80 | 1 | Tonbridge | 3 | Sep |
| 34.32 | Michelle Higman | | 30.10.78 | 1 | Plymouth | 8 | May |
| 34.30 | Helen Arnold | | 5.10.78 | 1 | Oxford | 22 | Jul |
| 33.82 | Kelly Sloan | | 18.09.78 | 1 | Glasgow | 15 | Jun |
| 33.60 | Rachel Cox | | 27.06.80 | 1 | Coventry | 13 | Aug |
| 33.48 | Jacqui Loney | | 17.04.79 | 2 | Greenock | 4 | Jun |
| 33.24 dh | Julie Pinfold | | 18.07.79 | 10 | Nottingham | 7 | Jul |
| 33.16 | Janine Crosby | | 17.01.79 | 1 | Manchester (BV) | 30 | Jul |

**Additional Under 15** (1 - 3 above)

| 35.44 | Joanne John | | 12.11.80 | 1 | Hayes | 30 | Apr |
| 35.10 | Vicki Clark | | 23.09.80 | 1 | Hoo | 10 | Jun |
| 34.32 | Carly Burton | | 14.10.80 | 1 | Hoo | 2 | Jul |
| 32.64 | Lesley Ann Roy | | 3.01.82 | 1 | Pitreavie | 9 | Apr |
| 31.92 | Vicky Gibbons | | 19.12.80 | 1 | Cardiff | 1 | Jul |
| 31.84 | Tasha Nicholls | | 1.11.80 | | | | |
| 31.54 | Anwen James | | 17.02.81 | 1 | Swansea | 8 | Jul |
| | (10) | | | | | | |
| 31.04 | Zoe Derham | | 24.11.80 | | | | |
| 30.96 | Natalie Buckland | | 19.02.82 | 1 | Braintree | 20 | Aug |
| 30.86 | Laura Eastwood | | 7.04.81 | 1 | Colwyn Bay | 14 | May |
| 30.62 | Emma Carpenter | | 16.05.82 | 1 | Exeter | 27 | Aug |
| 30.52 | Katherine Langdon | | 24.10.80 | 1 | Walton | 24 | Jun |
| 30.20 | Josephine Andrews | | 3.05.81 | 1 | Nottingham | 10 | Jun |

292

**Under 13**

| 29.58 | Claire Smithson | | 3.08.83 | 1 | Crawley | 28 Aug |
|---|---|---|---|---|---|---|
| 24.90 | Kimberley Rawling | | 22.07.83 | 1b | Crawley | 3 Sep |

## DISCUS - Under 13 - 0.75kg

| 32.70 | Claire Smithson | | 3.08.83 | 1 | London (TB) | 26 Aug |
|---|---|---|---|---|---|---|
| 27.76 | Kate Morris | | 18.01.83 | 1 | Hoo | 2 Jul |
| 27.14 | Jemma Spellacy | | 27.11.82 | 1 | Southend | 28 Aug |
| 26.78 | Kimberley Rawling | | 22.07.83 | 1 | Carn Brea | 17 Sep |
| 26.04 | Rebecca Stowell | | 21.04.83 | 1 | Bath | 28 Aug |
| 25.94 | Barbara Kidimu | | 1.09.82 | 1 | Reading | 3 Sep |
| 25.30 | Rebecca Fox | | | 1 | Dartford | 13 Aug |
| 24.68 | Susan Stockdale | | | 1 | Loughborough | 14 May |
| 24.32 | Natalie Anderson | | 7.10.82 | 1 | London (WL) | 21 Jun |
| 24.32 | Joanne Clark | | 10.06.83 | 1 | Pitreavie | 9 Jul |
| (10) | | | | | | |
| 24.30 | Lauren Procter | | 9.09.82 | 1 | Bournemouth | 23 Jul |
| 24.04 | Petulia Thomas | | | 1 | Brecon | 5 Aug |
| 24.04 | Hayley Sargison | | 15.09.82 | 2 | Reading | 3 Sep |
| 24.02 | Sarah Nicholson | | 30.06.83 | 1b | London (TB) | 30 Jul |

## HAMMER

| 64.90 | Lorraine Shaw | | 2.04.68 | 1 | Bedford | 10 Jun |
|---|---|---|---|---|---|---|
| | 63.80 | | | 1 | Rehlingen, GER | 5 Jun |
| | 62.30 | | | 3 | Halle, GER | 13 May |
| | 61.56 | | | 1 | London (WP) | 29 Apr |
| | 60.96 | | | 1 | Birmingham | 20 May |
| | 60.76 | | | 2 | Stadtsteinach, GER | 14 May |
| | 60.56 | | | 1 | London (Col) | 22 Apr |
| | 60.24 | | | 1 | Cwmbran | 9 Jul |
| | 59.78 | | | 1 | Birmingham | 17 Jun |
| | 59.68 | | | 1 | Gateshead | 21 Aug |
| | 59.38 | | | 1 | Cheltenham | 19 Jul |
| | 59.06 | | | 1 | Peterborough | 28 Aug |
| | 58.08 | | | 1 | Barry | 30 Apr |
| | 56.66 | | | Q | Birmingham | 15 Jul |
| | 56.26 | | | 3 | Birmingham | 15 Jul |
| 55.32 | Lyn Sprules | U23 | 11.09.75 | 1 | Feltham | 22 Jul |
| | 54.44 | | | 2 | Narbonne, FRA | 29 Jul |
| | 53.52 | | | 2 | London (Col) | 22 Apr |
| | 53.50 | | | 4 | Bedford | 10 Jun |
| | 53.04 | | | 1 | Haslemere | 16 May |
| | 52.86 | | | 1 | Bedford | 28 May |
| | 52.78 | | | 8 | Halle, GER | 13 May |
| | 52.56 | | | 1 | Woking | 17 Apr |
| | 52.50 | | | 1 | Corby | 25 Jun |
| | 52.44 | | | 1 | Crawley | 15 Apr |
| | 52.36 | | | 4 | Birmingham | 15 Jul |
| | 52.32 | | | 1 | London (BP) | 8 Apr |
| | 52.30 | | | 1 | London (CP) | 17 Jun |
| | 52.30 | | | 1 | Southampton | 12 Aug |
| | 52.28 | | | 2 | Birmingham | 20 May |
| | 52.18 | | | 1 | Bebington | 11 Jun |
| | 52.16 | | | 2 | Cwmbran | 9 Jul |
| | 51.82 | | | 1 | Welwyn | 3 Jun |
| | 51.70 | | | 5 | Stadtsteinach, GER | 14 May |
| | 51.32 | | | 1 | Watford | 6 May |
| 54.42 | Diana Holden | U23 | 12.02.75 | 1 | Kilkenny, IRE | 2 Sep |
| | 53.24 | | | 3 | Narbonne, FRA | 29 Jul |
| | 52.32 | | | 4 | Gateshead | 21 Aug |
| | 52.14 | | | 5 | Birmingham | 15 Jul |

| | | | | | | | |
|---|---|---|---|---|---|---|---|
| 53.00 | Sarah Moore | U23 | 15.03.73 | 7 | Halle, GER | 13 | May |
| 52.88 | | | | 1 | Cardiff | 23 | Jul |
| 51.82 | | | | 1 | Newport | 17 | Jun |
| 51.56 | | | | 5 | Bedford | 10 | Jun |
| 51.40 | | | | 6 | Stadtsteinach, GER | 14 | May |
| 51.24 | | | | 1 | Rotherham | 6 | Aug |
| 51.02 | | | | 4 | Birmingham | 20 | May |
| 51.72 | Ann Gardner | | 11.10.68 | 3 | Birmingham | 20 | May |
| 51.32 | | | | 3 | London (Col) | 22 | Apr |

48 performances to 51.00 by 5 athletes

| | | | | | | | |
|---|---|---|---|---|---|---|---|
| 50.12 | Jean Clark | | 5.10.68 | 1 | Welwyn | 28 | Aug |
| 49.86 | Julie Lavender | U23 | 9.11.75 | 1 | Gateshead | 17 | Jun |
| 49.48 | Samantha Burns-Salmond | U20 | 13.04.76 | 1 | Middlesbrough | 13 | Aug |
| 48.56 | Julie Kirkpatrick | | 14.07.72 | 1 | Antrim | 20 | Jun |
| 47.74 | Irene Duffin | | 10.08.60 | 9 | Bedford | 10 | Jun |
| (10) | | | | | | | |
| 47.06 | Caroline Manning | U23 | 5.03.73 | 1 | Woking | 22 | Jul |
| 46.98 | Helen Arnold | U17 | 5.10.78 | 1 | Birmingham | 29 | Jul |
| *46.72* | *Marina Semenova* | | *12.07.64* | *1* | *Liverpool* | *30* | *Jul* |
| 46.64 | Myrtle Augee | | 4.02.65 | 2 | London (Col) | 5 | Jul |
| 46.64 | Angela Bonner | U23 | 22.11.73 | 2 | Enfield | 30 | Jul |
| 46.52 | Esther Augee | | 1.01.64 | 1 | Stoke | 9 | Sep |
| 46.48 | Helen McCreadie | U23 | 10.05.75 | 2 | Glasgow | 6 | May |
| 44.92 | Janet Smith | | 7.10.64 | 2 | Bebington | 11 | Jun |
| 44.72 | Suzanne Last | | 11.01.70 | 5 | London (CP) | 17 | Jun |
| 44.70 | Rachael Beverley | U17 | 23.07.79 | 15Q | Birmingham | 15 | Jul |
| 44.22 | Lesley Brannan | U20 | 13.09.76 | 1 | Colwyn Bay | 2 | Sep |
| (20) | | | | | | | |
| 43.64 | Catherine Garden | U17 | 4.09.78 | 1 | Carlisle | 30 | Apr |
| 43.58 | Debbie Callaway | | 15.07.64 | 7 | Bedford | 28 | May |
| 43.52 | Cheryl Cunnane | U20 | 8.02.77 | 1 | Leeds | 7 | May |
| 43.32 | Helen Cowe | | 7.09.66 | 4 | London (He) | 1 | Jul |
| 43.00 | Claire Burnett | | 17.10.72 | 1 | Exeter | 2 | Sep |
| 42.66 | Sheena Parry | U20 | 16.11.77 | 1 | Cardiff | 1 | Jul |
| 42.58 | Joanne Eley | U23 | 12.01.74 | 1 | Derby | 15 | Aug |
| 42.48 | Imogen Martin | U23 | 13.02.74 | 1 | Enfield | 20 | May |
| 42.12 | Emma Jones | U20 | 9.07.77 | 2 | Portsmouth | 25 | Jun |
| 41.96 | Karen Brown | | 31.08.68 | 6 | Stoke | 9 | Sep |
| (30) | | | | | | | |
| 41.94 | Leanne Jones | U23 | 13.05.74 | 1 | Colwyn Bay | 23 | Apr |
| 41.90 | Jenny Cunnane | V35 | 23.02.57 | | Middlesbrough | 9 | Apr |
| 41.42 | Louise Kay | U20 | 1.12.77 | 1 | Cleckheaton | 24 | Sep |
| 41.26 | Sarah Harrison | U17 | 1.03.79 | 4 | London (Col) | 5 | Jul |
| 41.14 | Diane Smith | V35 | 15.11.60 | 3 | Grendon Hall | 15 | Oct |
| 40.96 | Vickie Foster | | 1.04.71 | 3 | Enfield | 29 | Apr |
| 40.78 | Andrea Jenkins | U23 | 4.10.75 | 2 | Hoo | 12 | Aug |
| 40.62 | Fiona Whitehead | | 31.05.70 | 1 | Portsmouth | 14 | May |
| 40.58 | Sarah Symonds | U23 | 28.12.73 | 2 | Corby | 25 | Jun |
| 40.46 | Sally Giles | | 6.04.62 | 1 | Bournemouth | 22 | Apr |
| (40) | | | | | | | |
| 39.98 | Michelle Ingham | U17 | 1.09.78 | 2 | Middlesbrough | 13 | Aug |
| 39.98 | Marcelle Edwards | U20 | 9.01.78 | 7 | Birmingham | 19 | Aug |
| 39.84 | Gemma Rolfe | U17 | 18.12.78 | 7 | Bedford | 1 | Jul |
| 39.80 | Carice Allen | U20 | 25.09.77 | 1 | Telford | 30 | Apr |
| 39.40 | Marian Simpson | U20 | 2.11.77 | 1 | Aberdeen | 7 | May |
| 39.24 | Helen Wilding | U20 | 25.10.76 | 2 | Pitreavie | 25 | Jun |
| 39.18 | Christina Bennett | U20 | 27.02.78 | 4 | Liverpool | 30 | Jul |
| 39.10 | Lindsey Jones | U20 | 8.09.77 | 2 | Grendon Hall | 14 | Oct |
| 39.08 | Carol Cooksley | | 22.09.69 | 1 | Leamington | 13 | May |
| 38.92 | Philippa Roles | U20 | 1.03.78 | 5 | London (He) | 9 | Sep |
| (50) | | | | | | | |

| 38.30 | Kirsty Perrett | U20 | 17.03.76 | 2 | Middlesbrough | 16 May |
|---|---|---|---|---|---|---|
| 37.96 | Louise Campbell | U17 | 22.02.79 | 2 | Belfast | 22 Apr |
| 37.92 | Rachel Cox | U17 | 27.06.80 | 6 | London (He) | 9 Sep |
| 37.84 | Tracy Axten | | 20.07.63 | 1 | London (Col) | 12 Jul |
| 37.74 | Rosanne Lister | | 9.05.69 | 3 | Croydon | 28 Aug |
| 37.54 | Joanne Coote | | 10.02.68 | 3 | Sheffield | 14 May |
| 37.30 | Rachel Stott | U23 | 3.09.74 | | Woodford | 12 Aug |
| 37.30 | Susan Freebairn | | 22.08.65 | 1 | Glasgow | 16 Aug |
| 37.00 | Lindsey Oliver | U20 | 12.03.78 | 7 | Blackpool | 20 Aug |
| 36.72 | Sharon Nash | U23 | 5.05.74 | 2 | Salisbury | 2 Sep |
| | (60) | | | | | |
| 36.42 | Elizabeth Whittle | U23 | 23.06.75 | 5 | Derby | 30 Jul |
| 36.20 | Llyn Perry | U17 | 21.02.79 | 3 | Derby | 17 Sep |
| 36.10 | Natasha Smith | U20 | 6.06.77 | 4 | Southampton | 12 Aug |
| 35.62 | Nicola Roberts | | 22.01.70 | 3 | Derby | 6 Aug |
| 35.60 | Anna Town | U23 | 22.04.75 | 2 | Welwyn | 2 Sep |
| 35.38 | Angela Lambourn | | 9.04.66 | 1 | Kings Lynn | 29 Apr |
| 35.30 | Sarah Winckless | U23 | 18.10.73 | 1 | Cambridge | 20 May |
| 35.30 | Tracy Shorts | | 4.11.72 | 4 | Inverness | 11 Jun |
| 35.28 | Lisa Munden | U20 | 13.03.78 | 5 | Derby | 6 Aug |
| 35.18 | Alison Dutch | | 25.05.65 | 4 | Edinburgh | 10 Sep |
| | (70) | | | | | |
| 35.16 | Lindsay Ross | U20 | 27.12.77 | 2 | Wishaw | 13 May |
| 35.14 | Siobhan Hart | U23 | 15.06.75 | 3 | Haslemere | 18 Jul |
| 35.10 | Susie Keast | U20 | 28.03.77 | 4 | London (He) | 6 Aug |
| 35.06 | Bethan Deverell | U20 | 23.08.76 | | Brighton | 12 Apr |
| 35.04 | Rachael Dunn | U17 | 4.03.79 | 7 | Birmingham | 29 Jul |
| 34.96 | Rosemary Redmond | U17 | 3.10.78 | 2 | Walton | 22 May |
| 34.96 | Jenny Clarke | V40 | 19.10.52 | 1 | Wakefield | 17 Sep |
| 34.92 | Beatrice Simpson | V35 | | 1 | Crawley | 5 Jul |
| 34.72 | Suzanne Roberts | U17 | 19.12.78 | 1 | Cleckheaton | 24 Sep |
| 34.46 | Catherine Lane | U20 | 18.11.76 | 1 | London (Col) | 12 Aug |
| | (80) | | | | | |
| 34.38 | Alison George | | 11.12.62 | 1 | Colwyn Bay | 2 Sep |
| 34.38 | Jill Harnett | U20 | 26.02.76 | 1 | High Wycombe | 2 Sep |
| 34.34 | Emma Welbourn | U17 | 14.02.79 | 3 | Rotherham | 23 Apr |
| 34.24 | Gabrielle Brosch | | 8.07.65 | 1 | Peterborough | 2 Sep |
| 34.22 | Sarah Hughes | U23 | 14.03.75 | | Wrexham | 29 Jul |
| 34.18 | Carys Parry | U15 | 24.07.81 | 1 | Cardiff | 17 May |
| 34.00 | Dana Long | U20 | 1.10.76 | 2 | Bournemouth | 13 May |

**Additional Under 17** (1 - 13 above)

| 33.86 | Joanne Leeson | | 28.07.79 | 1 | Bedford | 14 Jun |
|---|---|---|---|---|---|---|
| 32.64 | Jacqui Findlayson | | 27.01.80 | 1 | Inverness | 22 Jul |
| 32.48 | Laura Wood | | 31.10.78 | 2 | Birmingham | 27 Aug |
| 32.46 | Kirsty Holland | | 23.10.78 | 3 | Pitreavie | 8 Jul |

# JAVELIN

| 58.10 | Sharon Gibson | | 31.12.61 | 1 | Gateshead | 21 Aug |
|---|---|---|---|---|---|---|
| 57.46 | | | | 1 | Birmingham | 17 Jun |
| 57.24 | | | | 1 | Rotherham | 6 Aug |
| 56.98 | | | | 1 | Yate | 23 Jul |
| 55.14 | | | | 2 | Birmingham | 16 Jul |
| 54.88 | | | | 1 | Enfield | 30 Jul |
| 54.64 | | | | 1 | Nottingham | 13 Aug |
| 54.38 | | | | 7 | Villeneuve d'Ascq, FRA | 25 Jun |
| 53.26 | | | | 5 | Copenhagen, DEN | 23 Aug |
| 51.94 | | | | 1 | Mansfield | 13 May |

| | | | | | | | | |
|---|---|---|---|---|---|---|---|---|
| 55.48 | Lorna Jackson | U23 | 9.01.74 | 1 | Birmingham | 16 | Jul |
| 52.86 | | | | 5 | Gateshead | 21 | Aug |
| 52.52 | | | | 2 | Cardiff | 23 | Jul |
| 52.08 | | | | 1 | Bedford | 28 | May |
| 51.88 | | | | 1 | Birmingham | 19 | Aug |
| 51.34 | | | | 2 | Narbonne, FRA | 29 | Jul |
| 51.28 | | | | 2 | Stoke | 9 | Sep |
| 51.04 | | | | 1 | Edinburgh | 23 | Jun |
| 50.94 | | | | 1 | Coatbridge | 27 | Aug |
| 50.56 | | | | 2 | London (He) | 1 | Jul |
| 50.00 | | | | 1 | Inverness | 11 | Jun |
| 55.16 | Shelley Holroyd | U23 | 17.05.73 | 1 | London (He) | 1 | Jul |
| 54.92 | | | | 4 | Birmingham | 16 | Jul |
| 52.76 | | | | 1 | Stoke | 9 | Sep |
| 52.08 | | | | 1 | Bolton | 13 | May |
| 54.96 | Karen Martin | U23 | 24.11.74 | 3 | Birmingham | 16 | Jul |
| 53.52 | | | | 1 | Birmingham | 23 | Apr |
| 53.20 | | | | 2 | Basel, SWZ | 5 | Jun |
| 52.24 | | | | 1 | Derby | 13 | May |
| 50.44 | | | | 1 | Derby | 6 | Aug |
| 50.38 | | | | 2 | Cwmbran | 9 | Jul |
| 53.80 | Kirsty Morrison | U23 | 28.10.75 | 1 | Kilkenny, IRE | 2 | Sep |
| 50.34 | | | | 1 | Bedford | 25 | Jun |

33 performances to 50.00 by 5 athletes

| | | | | | | | |
|---|---|---|---|---|---|---|---|
| 49.94 | Mandy Liverton | | 1.09.72 | 1 | London (CP) | 17 | Jun |
| 49.76 | Denise Lewis | | 27.08.72 | 3 | Stoke | 9 | Sep |
| 49.66 | Noelle Bradshaw | | 18.12.63 | 1 | Portsmouth | 14 | May |
| 49.24 | Janine King | U23 | 18.02.73 | 1 | Bolton | 23 | Jul |
| 48.82 | Karen Costello | | 21.10.68 | 3 | London (He) | 1 | Jul |
| (10) | | | | | | | |
| 48.34 | Onyema Amadi | U23 | 28.06.73 | 7 | Birmingham | 16 | Jul |
| 48.30 | Michelle Fields | U23 | 15.05.73 | 1 | London (Ha) | 25 | Jun |
| 47.28 | Jo Burton | U23 | 11.05.75 | 1 | Bournemouth | 13 | May |
| 47.14 | Joanne Walker | U20 | 2.03.78 | 3 | Bedford | 28 | May |
| 46.94 | Kelly Morgan | U17 | 17.06.80 | 1 | Bedford | 1 | Jul |
| 46.84 | Lucy Stevenson | U23 | 30.01.73 | 1 | Edinburgh | 7 | May |
| 46.80 | Clova Court | V35 | 10.02.60 | 1 | Derby | 23 | Jul |
| 46.62 | Tammie Francis | U17 | 14.11.78 | 1 | Bournemouth | 10 | Jun |
| 46.60 | Alison Moffitt | | 6.10.69 | 1 | Tullamore, IRE | 14 | May |
| 45.76 | Angelique McCormick | | 29.04.69 | 7 | Bedford | 28 | May |
| (20) | | | | | | | |
| 45.38 | Sian Lax | U17 | 4.08.79 | 1 | Telford | 13 | May |
| 45.02 | Katrina Campbell | | 8.03.72 | 1 | Pitreavie | 25 | Jun |
| 44.98 | Angharad Richards | U20 | 9.12.76 | 1 | Harrow | 22 | Apr |
| 44.96 | Wendy Newman | | 31.08.71 | 1 | Antrim | 28 | May |
| 44.80 | Helen Potter | U23 | 25.06.74 | 5 | London (He) | 1 | Jul |
| 44.62 | Jackie Barclay | | 17.01.66 | 1 | Coatbridge | 21 | May |
| 44.56 | Katie Amos | U17 | 13.11.78 | 1 | Basildon | 10 | Jun |
| 44.44 | Louise Smith | U20 | 11.07.77 | 1 | Norwich | 3 | Sep |
| 44.34 | Linda Gray | | 23.03.71 | 2 | Derby | 29 | Apr |
| 44.20 | Nicola Mackay | U20 | 26.08.78 | 1 | St. Ives | 3 | May |
| (30) | | | | | | | |
| 44.08 | Emma Lilley | U20 | 2.05.76 | 8 | Bedford | 28 | May |
| 44.00 | Katie Granger | U23 | 31.03.75 | 1 | Exeter | 2 | Sep |
| 43.88 | Paula Blank | U20 | 13.12.77 | 1 | Welwyn | 12 | Jul |
| 43.50 | Amanda Brown | U23 | 11.05.75 | 1 | Crawley | 2 | Apr |
| 43.16 | Katherine Evans | U20 | 19.11.77 | 3 | Bedford | 1 | Jul |
| 43.10 | Siona Kelly | U23 | 19.04.74 | 2 | Edinburgh | 7 | May |
| 43.06 | Hayley Martin | U20 | 25.05.76 | 1 | London (CP) | 14 | May |
| 43.06 | Mari-Anne Daykin | U23 | 16.02.73 | 2 | Hoo | 2 | Jul |
| 42.94 | Emma Rich | U20 | 14.05.77 | 1 | Yeovil | 13 | May |

| | | | | | | | |
|---|---|---|---|---|---|---|---|
| 42.82 | Nicky Rolfe | | 19.08.69 | 1 | Yeovil | 22 | Jul |
| (40) | | | | | | | |
| 42.80 | Julie Nightingale | U23 | 28.04.75 | 1 | Horsham | 9 | Jul |
| 42.72 | Clover Wynter-Pink | U20 | 29.11.77 | 1H | Portsmouth | 25 | Jun |
| 42.60 | Karen Moody | | 20.07.67 | 2 | Coventry | 13 | Aug |
| 42.56 | Uju Efobi | U23 | 10.10.74 | 3 | Bedford | 25 | Jun |
| 42.46 | Lucy Cook | U23 | 11.09.75 | 1 | Crawley | 15 | Apr |
| 42.40 | Pauline Richards | | 30.06.68 | 1H | Stoke | 6 | Aug |
| 42.34 | Claire Taylor | U20 | 6.08.76 | 1 | Telford | 13 | Aug |
| 42.18 | Tammy Carless | U20 | 10.01.77 | 1 | Colchester | 28 | Aug |
| 42.14 | Donna Loveland | U20 | 28.06.78 | 1 | Basildon | 10 | Jun |
| 42.06 | Jenny Kemp | U17 | 18.02.80 | 1 | Kirkby | 10 | Sep |
| (50) | | | | | | | |
| 42.04 | Emma Beales | | 7.12.71 | 1 | Croydon | 25 | Jun |
| 41.92 | Lynsay Munro | U20 | 1.02.77 | 5 | Edinburgh | 23 | Jun |
| 41.40 | Teri Oboh | U23 | 7.10.73 | 5 | Irvine, USA | 23 | Apr |
| 41.28 | Heather Derbyshire | U17 | 12.09.78 | 1 | Bromley | 23 | Apr |
| 41.22 | Joanne Bruce | U17 | 26.10.78 | 1 | Bedford | 2 | Sep |
| 41.00 | Katie Rowland | | 5.03.71 | 1 | Birmingham | 25 | Jun |
| 41.00 | Liz Pidgeon | U20 | 27.04.77 | 5 | Nottingham | 7 | Jul |
| 40.92 | Emily Steele | U23 | 10.09.74 | | Wrexham | 18 | Jul |
| 40.64 | Joanne Smith/Davis | U23 | 23.06.73 | 2 | Rotherham | 6 | Aug |
| 40.44 | Amanda Humble | U17 | 15.08.79 | 1 | Carlisle | 30 | Apr |
| (60) | | | | | | | |
| 40.42 | Lucy Rann | U15 | 5.09.80 | 1 | Portsmouth | 10 | Jun |
| 40.40 | Karen Miller/Shackel | | 4.02.64 | 2 | Horsham | 14 | May |
| 40.36 | Gemma Johnson | U20 | 21.07.78 | 2 | Mansfield | 13 | May |
| 40.30 | Isobel Donaldson | | 24.01.64 | 3 | Derby | 6 | Aug |
| 40.16 | Jenna Allen | U17 | 2.05.79 | 1 | Loughborough | 13 | May |
| 40.12 | Catherine Hawkins | U23 | 2.06.75 | 3 | Sheffield | 13 | May |
| 39.94 | Sarah Simmans | U17 | 29.11.78 | 1 | Oldham | 9 | Jul |
| 39.86 | Vicky Storey | U20 | 21.11.77 | 1 | Crewe | 10 | Jun |
| 39.82 | Llyn Perry | U17 | 21.02.79 | 2 | Thurrock | 25 | Jun |
| 39.80 | Leanne Morrall | U17 | 7.07.79 | 1 | Solihull | 6 | Aug |
| (70) | | | | | | | |
| 39.78 | Emma Claydon | U17 | 1.06.80 | 1 | Bromley | 9 | Apr |
| 39.50 | Esther Sneddon | U23 | 30.06.74 | 2 | Grangemouth | 14 | May |
| 39.48 | Hilary Davies | U23 | 9.02.75 | 1 | Barry | 30 | Apr |
| 39.40 | Laurie Morrison | U23 | 27.07.73 | 1 | Cosford | 5 | Jul |
| 39.36 | Sarah Damm | | 12.09.70 | 1 | Wrexham | 25 | Jun |
| 39.28 | Selby Croot | U23 | 18.06.75 | 1 | Leicester | 23 | Apr |
| 39.24 | Diane Nuttall | U20 | 10.06.77 | 2 | London (CP) | 28 | May |
| 39.22 | Nicky Cobb | | 2.11.71 | 5 | Stoke | 9 | Sep |
| 39.20 | Sylveen Monaghan | | 25.08.72 | 4 | Edinburgh | 7 | May |
| 39.18 | Tracy Page | | 3.02.72 | 1 | Portsmouth | 14 | Jun |
| (80) | | | | | | | |
| 39.06 | Tracy Shorts | | 4.11.72 | 2 | Edinburgh | 10 | Sep |
| 39.02 | Claire Archer | U20 | 30.09.76 | 1 | Yeovil | 10 | Jun |
| 38.96 | Anna-Lisa Howard | U20 | 18.04.78 | 1 | Norwich | 13 | May |
| 38.82 | Jenny Kelly | | 20.06.70 | H | Stoke | 4 | Jun |
| 38.82 | Debbie Woolgar | | 10.03.65 | 1H | Crawley | 10 | Sep |
| 38.76 | Rhian Hughes | U17 | 11.05.79 | 1 | Cardiff | 1 | Jul |
| 38.60 | Jenny Foster | U20 | 6.09.77 | 1 | Derby | 29 | Apr |
| 38.58 | Justine Curgenven | U23 | 5.11.73 | 1 | Cambridge | 20 | May |
| 38.56 | Christine Head | U17 | 18.12.79 | 5 | Nottingham | 7 | Jul |
| 38.54 | Nicola Connell | | 17.12.68 | | Scunthorpe | 5 | Mar |
| (90) | | | | | | | |
| 38.52 | Helen Skinsley | U23 | 19.03.74 | 7 | ,GER | 22 | Jun |
| 38.48 | Diana Bennett | U23 | 14.06.74 | 3 | Tessenderlo, BEL | 2 | Jul |
| 38.44 | Jean Lintern | V40 | 13.03.51 | 1 | Crawley | 19 | Jul |
| 38.42 | Evette Finikin | | 25.09.63 | 3 | Derby | 30 | Jul |

| 38.32 | Lesley Lavers | | 6.08.68 | 2 | Harrow | 22 | Apr |
|---|---|---|---|---|---|---|---|
| 38.32 | Debbie McIlroy | U20 | 18.12.77 | 1 | Jarrow | 13 | Jun |
| 38.30 | Jenny Grimstone | U17 | 30.04.79 | 1 | London (WP) | 10 | May |
| 38.30 | Michelle Woods | U17 | 2.08.80 | 2 | Barking | 14 | May |
| 38.06 | Sara Fry | | 19.01.62 | 1 | Birmingham | 19 | Jul |
| 38.04 | Natalie Duff | | 30.12.71 | 1 | Loughborough | 29 | May |
| 38.02 | Melanie Burrows | U20 | 7.08.76 | 1 | Exeter | 2 | Sep |

**Additional Under 17** (1 - 17 above)

| 37.22 | Louise Hepplethwaite | | 3.02.79 | 1 | Telford | 18 | Jun |
|---|---|---|---|---|---|---|---|
| 37.22 | Claire Allen | | 18.09.78 | 1 | Carlisle | 3 | Sep |
| 36.20 | Jemma Grant | | 17.09.78 | 1 | Inverness | 3 | Jun |
| | (20) | | | | | | |
| 36.14 | Nicola Lycett | | 10.03.80 | 1 | Stretford | 6 | Jun |
| 36.04 | Lynne Miles | | 14.06.79 | 1 | Sutton Coldfield | 10 | May |
| 35.86 | Melanie Walker | | 29.04.79 | 1b | Andover | 12 | Aug |
| 35.84 | Clare Lockwood | | 7.10.79 | 2 | Cardiff | 27 | May |
| 35.70 | Samantha Backshall | | 6.10.79 | 1 | Hull | 10 | Jun |
| 35.68 | Mary Townsley | | 20.10.78 | 1 | Glasgow | 23 | Apr |
| 35.60 | Rehanne Skinner | | 13.11.79 | 8 | Birmingham | 29 | Jul |
| 35.54 | Sarah Murray | | 24.04.79 | 1 | Brighton | 10 | Jun |
| 35.46 | Fiona Hunter | | 14.09.78 | 1 | Pitreavie | 8 | Jul |
| 35.08 | Kelly Sloan | | 18.09.78 | 1 | Grangemouth | 21 | Jun |
| 34.98 | Alison Neall | | 8.11.79 | 3 | Croydon | 13 | May |

**Additional Under 15** (1 above)

| 35.34 | Lydia Hanley | | 2.02.81 | 1 | Liverpool | 6 | Aug |
|---|---|---|---|---|---|---|---|
| 35.04 | Aileen Paxton | | 8.07.81 | 1 | Livingston | 16 | Aug |
| 34.60 | Karen Crouch | | | 1 | Walton | 1 | Jul |
| 34.02 | Tara Holman | | 13.10.80 | 1 | Watford | 4 | Jul |
| 34.00 | Jessica Brooker | | 6.01.81 | 1 | Exeter | 2 | Sep |
| 33.28 | Melanie Vaggers | | 16.06.82 | 1 | Plymouth | 29 | Jul |
| 32.52 | Katy Watts | | 25.03.81 | 1 | Salisbury | 2 | Sep |
| 32.40 | Emily Kitney | | 25.04.81 | 1 | London (WF) | 17 | Jun |
| 32.22 | J. Ayero | | | 1 | London (He) | 10 | Jun |
| | (10) | | | | | | |
| 32.00 | Amy Harvey | | | 1 | Norwich | 11 | Sep |
| 31.82 | Joanne John | | 12.11.80 | 1 | Perivale | 18 | Jun |
| 31.74 | Tracey Howard | | 11.02.81 | 2 | Croydon | 13 | Aug |
| 31.58 | Faye Moran | | 28.10.80 | 1 | Stretford | 10 | Jun |
| 31.20 | Victoria Bradshaw | | 10.12.80 | 1 | Ipswich | 13 | May |
| 31.04 | Kerrie Atkins | | 8.04.81 | 1 | Norwich | 10 | Jun |
| 30.86 | Natasha Campbell | | 6.08.82 | 1 | Hoo | 10 | Jun |

**Under 13**

| 31.28 | Eve Russell | | 27.09.82 | 2 | Exeter | 2 | Sep |
|---|---|---|---|---|---|---|---|
| 26.00 | Jemma Spellacy | | 27.11.82 | | Colchester | 2 | Jul |
| 25.40 | Susan Theobald | | 4.03.83 | 2 | Braintree | 20 | Aug |

## JAVELIN - Under 13 - 400 gram

| 32.38 | Eve Russell | | 27.09.82 | 1 | London (TB) | 30 | Jul |
|---|---|---|---|---|---|---|---|
| 30.16 | Tanya Hunt | | 14.09.83 | 1 | Bournemouth | 27 | Aug |
| 29.58 | Carol Wallbanks | | 9.12.82 | 1 | Barrow | 16 | Jul |
| 29.40 | Emma Higgins | | | 1 | Aldershot | 5 | Aug |
| 28.84 | Lisa Kenney | | 17.02.83 | T | Grimsby | 20 | May |
| 28.42 | Joanna McGilchrist | | 27.08.83 | 1 | Pitreavie | 19 | Aug |
| 27.76 | Susan Theobald | | 4.03.83 | 1 | Solihull | 10 | Sep |
| 27.52 | Loni Payne | | 17.12.82 | 2 | Reading | 3 | Sep |
| 27.38 | Becky Twort | | 26.07.83 | 1 | Reading | 3 | Sep |
| 27.26 | Samantha Redd | | | 1 | Brighton | 7 | Jun |
| | (10) | | | | | | |
| 27.24 | Adrienne Harvey | | 2.12.82 | 1 | Carmarthen | 20 | Aug |

| | | | | | | | |
|---|---|---|---|---|---|---|---|
| 26.72 | J. Sergeant | | | 1 | Birmingham | 2 | Jul |
| 26.00 | Jemma Spellacy | | 27.11.82 | 1 | Canvey Island | 6 | Jun |

## HEPTATHLON

| Score | Name | | Date/Pos | | Place | Date | |
|---|---|---|---|---|---|---|---|
| 6299 | Denise Lewis | | 27.08.72 | 1 | Helmond, HOL | 2 | Jul |
| 13.66 | 1.78 | 13.19 | 25.13 | 6.52 | 49.34 | 2:18.54 | |
| 6299 | | | | 7 | Gothenburg, SWE | 10 | Aug |
| 13.52 | 1.74 | 13.24 | 24.97 | 6.57 | 49.70 | 2:19.35 | |
| 6255 | | | | 6 | Gotzis, AUT | 28 | May |
| 13.70 | 1.78 | 12.81 | 24.94 | 6.67 | 45.76 | 2:19.21 | |
| 5702 | Yinka Idowu | | 25.02.72 | 6 | Alhama, SPA | 21 | May |
| 13.76w | 1.69 | 13.69 | 25.43 | 6.20 | 35.86 | 2:27.39 | |
| 5655 | | | | 17 | Helmond, HOL | 2 | Jul |
| 14.05 | 1.69 | 12.74 | 25.74 | 6.54w | 37.30 | 2:31.33 | |
| 5609 | Emma Beales | | 7.12.71 | 1 | Kilkenny, IRE | 27 | Aug |
| 14.31 | 1.68 | 13.01 | 24.99 | 5.89w | 39.14 | 2:24.68 | |
| 5524 | | | | 22 | Helmond, HOL | 2 | Jul |
| 14.42 | 1.69 | 12.94 | 25.30 | 5.61 | 40.40 | 2:23.76 | |
| 5524 w | | | | 1 | Stoke | 4 | Jun |
| 14.54 | 1.68 | 13.26 | 25.56 | -5.69W | 41.90 | 2:25.50 | |
| 5521 | | | | * | Stoke | 4 | Jun |
| | | | | 5.68w | | | |
| 5551 | Vikki Schofield | | 29.12.72 | 1 | Stoke | 6 | Aug |
| 14.97 | 1.74 | 11.05 | 24.95 | 6.03 | 37.76 | 2:19.5 | |
| 5506 | | | | 2 | Kilkenny, IRE | 27 | Aug |
| 14.24w | 1.74 | 10.83 | 24.22 | 5.97 | 33.88 | 2:20.50 | |
| 5496 | Julia Bennett | | 26.03.70 | 8 | Alhama, SPA | 21 | May |
| 14.68w | 1.87 | 10.68 | 25.95 | 6.02w | 29.70 | 2:18.68 | |
| 5422 | | | | 24 | Helmond, HOL | 2 | Jul |
| 14.74 | 1.87 | 10.93 | 25.81 | 5.87 | 29.78 | 2:22.34 | |
| 5244 | | | | 2 | Derby | 30 | Apr |
| 15.02 | 1.75 | 11.17 | 26.00 | 5.99w | 28.66 | 2:22.53 | |
| 5455 | Claire Phythian | U23 | 7.02.73 | 1 | Tuscaloosa, USA | 19 | May |
| 14.43 | 1.76 | 10.78 | 25.58 | 5.66 | 37.36 | 2:19.49 | |
| 5451 | | | | 8 | Knoxville, USA | 3 | Jun |
| 14.17w | 1.74 | 10.24 | 25.20 | 5.73w | 36.64 | 2:21.09 | |
| 5173 | | | | 8 | Azusa, USA | 14 | Apr |
| 14.94 | 1.70 | 9.65 | 25.97 | 5.56 | 39.28 | 2:22.41 | |
| 5417 | Pauline Richards | | 30.06.68 | 2 | Stoke | 6 | Aug |
| 14.94 | 1.56 | 12.78 | 24.92 | 5.70 | 42.40 | 2:21.8 | |
| 5160 | | | | 3 | Kilkenny, IRE | 27 | Aug |
| 14.53w | 1.53 | 11.62 | 25.38 | 5.53w | 38.48 | 2:24.40 | |
| 5392 | Sarah Damm | | 12.09.70 | 1 | Derby | 30 | Apr |
| 14.78 | 1.57 | 11.62 | 25.18 | 5.86w | 38.12 | 2:16.22 | |
| 5364 | | | | 9 | Alhama, SPA | 21 | May |
| 14.68w | 1.57 | 12.33 | 25.63 | 5.81w | 39.12 | 2:19.99 | |
| 5368 | Kerry Jury | | 19.11.68 | 3 | Stoke | 6 | Aug |
| 14.74 | 1.74 | 11.02 | 24.61 | 5.43 | 33.72 | 2:18.6 | |
| 5037 | | | | 3 | Stoke | 4 | Jun |
| 14.45 | 1.65 | 10.27 | 25.05 | 5.37w | 30.98 | 2:26.10 | |
| 5018 | | | | 4 | Derby | 30 | Apr |
| 14.47 | 1.66 | 8.95 | 25.47 | 5.47w | 33.40 | 2:24.62 | |
| 5338 | Jenny Kelly | | 20.06.70 | 11 | Alhama, SPA | 21 | May |
| 14.64w | 1.63 | 12.76 | 26.00 | 5.88w | 35.52 | 2:23.73 | |
| 5298 | | | | 2 | Stoke | 4 | Jun |
| 14.48 | 1.62 | 12.76 | 25.84 | 5.86w | 38.82 | 2:33.20 | |
| 5220 | Diana Bennett | U23 | 14.06.74 | 3 | Derby | 30 | Apr |
| 14.81 | 1.69 | 9.92 | 26.94 | 5.76 | 36.66 | 2:15.16 | |
| 5052 | | | | 6 | Vladimir, RUS | 6 | Aug |
| 15.28 | 1.64 | 10.88 | 27.43 | 5.72 | 37.38 | 2:20.35 | |

```
5143      Clover Wynter-Pink      U20    29.11.77  1    Portsmouth      25  Jun
          15.1       1.65   11.61   25.4        5.32    42.72    2:27.9
5108      Emma Lindsay                   11.04.71  1    Stoke           25  Jun
          15.49      1.66   10.46   24.86w      5.71    32.12    2:22.84
5056                                               1    Aberdeen        16  Jul
          15.32w     1.65   10.32   25.02w      5.81w   29.66    2:24.43
5107      Anne Hollman            U23    18.02.74  2    Stoke           25  Jun
          14.8       1.66   10.31   25.26w      5.43    36.66    2:25.73
5017 w    Kim Crowther-Price             19.01.66  1    Bebington       23  Jul
          14.5W      1.57   12.19   25.7w       5.39    32.06    2:32.24
          32 performances to 5000 by 15 athletes
4961      Kelly Sotherton         U20    13.11.76  2    Portsmouth      25  Jun
          15.0       1.65   10.63   25.9        5.84    29.10    2:26.4
4918 w    Leah Lackenby           U23    18.09.74  2    Bebington       23  Jul
          14.3W      1.66   10.49   25.5w       5.42    35.34    2:40.06
4846                                               8    Vladimir, RUS    6  Aug
          14.52      1.64   9.76    25.77       5.54    31.88    2:37.48
4907      Debbie Woolgar                 10.03.65  1    Crawley         10  Sep
          15.4       1.57   12.76   28.2        5.67    38.82    2:26.0
4832 w    Charmaine Johnson              4.06.63   4    Stoke            4  Jun
          14.77      1.59   13.52   26.50w      5.38W   33.74    2:45.89
4818      Rebecca Lewis           U20    31.12.77  7    Vladimir, RUS    5  Aug
          15.28      1.59   10.38   26.19       5.59    33.52    2:30.66
       (20)
4790      Tracy Goddard/Joseph           29.11.69  1    Enfield         13  Aug
          15.42      1.57   9.52    24.62       5.54    23.54    2:20.66
4788      Denise Bolton           U20    1.02.77   1    Aberdeen        16  Jul
          14.27w     1.53   8.80    25.15w      5.27w   28.60    2:22.92
4772      Julie Hollman           U20    16.02.77  10   Vladimir, RUS    5  Aug
          15.51      1.62   9.86    25.15       5.84    24.12    2:31.17
4768      Isobel Donaldson               24.01.64  1    Cosford          1  Aug
          15.5       1.57   9.13    26.5        5.37    37.82    2:19.9
4635 w    Louise Batho            U20    27.11.76  6    Kilkenny, IRE   27  Aug
          15.13W     1.56   11.00   26.91       5.07w   35.68    2:33.97
4626                                               4    Stoke            4  Jun
          15.27      1.56   11.16   26.88       4.77w   37.26    2:30.22
4632      Manndy Laing            V35    7.11.59   1    Sheffield       10  Sep
          15.0w      1.59   10.63   26.9w       5.08    35.84    2:32.8
4620      Katie Budd              U20    3.01.76   5    Derby           30  Apr
          14.59      1.54   10.31   27.29       5.33w   31.26    2:32.04
4543      Nicola Gautier          U20    21.03.78  3    Stoke           17  Sep
          15.09      1.51   12.11   26.47       4.61    35.20    2:35.54
4534      Teresa Springate/Copeland      8.03.69   1    Hoo             10  Sep
          14.7       1.46   10.87   26.8        5.25    35.12    2:36.8
4526      Anne Carr               U20    1.05.76   2    Aberdeen        16  Jul
          15.81      1.62   9.49    26.90w      5.03w   30.72    2:25.03
       (30)
4523      Angie Nyhan             U20    13.04.78  1    Jarrow          25  Jun
          15.7       1.53   10.73   26.6        5.40    31.12    2:31.4
4466      Abigail Ashby           U20    23.11.77  3    Jarrow          25  Jun
          15.0       1.59   9.71    26.7        5.14    29.74    2:34.7
4449      Michala Gee             U23    8.12.75   6    Derby           30  Apr
          15.21      1.66   8.77    26.90       5.42w   23.70    2:35.52
4349      Leanne Buxton           U20    27.05.78  8    Stoke           17  Sep
          15.41      1.45   8.98    26.03       5.09    28.54    2:29.13
4303 w    Jenny Brown             V35    21.05.59  7    Stoke            4  Jun
          16.73      1.65   9.19    27.99w      5.03W   32.16    2:30.50
4279                                               *    Stoke            4  Jun
                                               4.94w
```

300

| 4293 | Sarah Ramminger | U23 | 1.10.75 | 2 | Aberdeen | 16 Jul |
| | 15.74w | 1.56 | 9.40 | 26.40w | 5.41 | 26.74 | 2:45.08 |
| 4243 | Esther Sneddon | U23 | 30.06.74 | 9 | Kilkenny, IRE | 27 Aug |
| | 15.75w | 1.53 | 9.59 | 27.65 | 4.75w | 34.44 | 2:35.32 |
| 4220 | Jane O'Malley | U20 | 18.07.77 | 9 | Stoke | 17 Sep |
| | 15.17 | 1.54 | 9.38 | 26.68 | 4.72 | 21.60 | 2:29.21 |
| 4219 | Katy Sketchley/Parsons | U23 | 9.07.73 | 1 | Thurrock | 24 Sep |
| | 14.5 | 1.44 | 9.50 | 26.1 | 5.01 | 30.72 | 2:49.3 |
| 4209 | Joanna Morris | U20 | 16.10.77 | 3 | Portsmouth | 25 Jun |
| | 15.8 | 1.65 | 9.14 | 27.9 | 5.22 | 25.60 | 2:37.8 |
| (40) | | | | | | |
| 4161 | Janine Whitlock | U23 | 11.08.73 | 1 | Middlesbrough | 1 Oct |
| | 14.9 | 1.56 | 7.97 | 25.1 | 5.53 | 13.74 | 2:45.4 |
| 4157 | Sarah Still | U23 | 24.09.75 | 2 | Middlesbrough | 1 Oct |
| | 15.8 | 1.61 | 8.40 | 26.6 | 5.20 | 22.34 | 2:37.2 |
| 4154 | Rachel Smith | U20 | 3.03.76 | 3 | Stoke | 25 Jun |
| | 15.95 | 1.54 | 8.53 | 27.32w | 4.78 | 28.88 | 2:29.90 |
| 4142 | Susan Jones | U20 | 8.06.78 | 10 | Stoke | 17 Sep |
| | 14.58 | 1.75 | 8.15 | 26.62 | 4.91w | 17.34 | 2:56.29 |
| 4096 | Siona Kelly | U23 | 19.04.74 | 4 | Stoke | 25 Jun |
| | 18.89 | 1.51 | 9.04 | 27.47w | 5.29 | 39.58 | 2:35.64 |
| 4081 | Jackie Cooke | U20 | 20.06.76 | 11 | Stoke | 17 Sep |
| | 15.31 | 1.48 | 7.79 | 26.87 | 4.72w | 29.18 | 2:35.47 |
| 4076 | Amanda Wale | | 14.10.70 | 1 | Cardiff | 23 Jul |
| | 15.9w | 1.57 | 8.55 | 28.05 | 4.97 | 26.36 | 2:32.86 |
| 4067 | Claire Everett | U17 | 25.06.79 | 1 | Enfield | 13 Aug |
| | 16.55 | 1.54 | 9.98 | 27.51 | 4.87 | 28.20 | 2:38.67 |
| 4050 | Karen Martin | U23 | 24.11.74 | 2 | Cosford | 1 Aug |
| | 18.5 | 1.57 | 11.07 | 27.9 | 4.52 | 49.54 | 2:53.3 |
| 4001 | Samantha Male | U20 | 11.04.76 | 12 | Stoke | 17 Sep |
| | 15.18 | 1.48 | 8.45 | 27.39 | 5.12 | 26.84 | 2:49.67 |
| (50) | | | | | | |
| 3943 w | Kelly Moreton | U17 | 18.09.79 | 11 | Kilkenny, IRE | 27 Aug |
| | 15.76W | 1.65 | 7.10 | 26.74 | 4.82w | 14.92 | 2:35.72 |
| 3926 | Fiona Allan | U23 | 6.11.75 | 13 | Stoke | 17 Sep |
| | 15.26 | 1.51 | 9.29 | 27.45 | 5.15 | 25.08 | 2:49.65 |
| 3896 | Liz Churchley | | 17.07.66 | 3 | Cosford | 1 Aug |
| | 16.1 | 1.54 | 8.48 | 27.8 | 5.17 | 24.06 | 2:44.0 |
| 3883 | Sarah Godbeer | U20 | 10.06.77 | 1 | Yeovil | 25 Jun |
| | 16.6 | 1.51 | 8.47 | 25.6 | 4.80 | 23.58 | 2:43.5 |
| 3871 | Michelle Winter | U17 | 18.06.79 | 9 | Derby | 30 Apr |
| | 16.12w | 1.45 | 7.24 | 27.43 | 5.19 | 22.34 | 2:34.71 |
| 3866 | Jill Parker | U20 | 4.10.77 | 14 | Stoke | 17 Sep |
| | 16.14 | 1.45 | 7.04 | 27.15 | 4.61w | 24.06 | 2:25.95 |
| 3844 | Lucy Baden | U20 | 21.10.77 | 2 | Yeovil | 25 Jun |
| | 15.4 | 1.48 | 7.63 | 26.7 | 4.97 | 22.74 | 2:46.3 |
| 3825 | Amanda Horton | | 18.05.71 | 2 | Cardiff | 23 Jul |
| | 17.1w | 1.54 | 8.24 | 28.16 | 4.85 | 22.96 | 2:29.10 |
| 3819 | Anya Hutchinson | U20 | 16.07.77 | 15 | Stoke | 17 Sep |
| | 16.35 | 1.36 | 8.04 | 28.41 | 4.79 | 26.00 | 2:23.88 |

# HEPTATHLON - Under 17

| 4588 | Katherine Livesey | | 15.12.79 | 1 | Stoke | 17 Sep |
| | 12.29w | 1.63 | 8.80 | 25.85 | 5.30 | 25.96 | 2:25.37 |
| 4507 | Danielle Freeman | | 11.02.80 | 2 | Stoke | 17 Sep |
| | 12.52 | 1.63 | 8.73 | 26.15 | 5.17 | 26.28 | 2:24.72 |
| 4409 | Jackie Tindal | | 21.01.79 | 1 | Stoke | 6 Aug |
| | 12.15 | 1.59 | 10.71 | 26.60 | 5.11 | 29.82 | 2:44.4 |
| 4385 | Debbie Harrison | | 13.11.78 | 1 | Worcester | 25 Jun |
| | 12.2 | 1.53 | 8.87 | 25.8 | 5.51 | 27.36 | 2:39.6 |

| 4378 | Chloe Cozens | | | 9.04.80 | 3 | Stoke | | 17 Sep |
| | 12.46w | 1.69 | 8.60 | 26.61 | 4.77 | 32.54 | 2:38.46 | |
| 4366 | Claire Everett | | | 25.06.79 | 1 | Peterborough | | 24 Sep |
| | 12.5 | 1.57 | 9.89 | 26.9 | 5.12 | 28.60 | 2:32.1 | |
| 4333 | Amanda Gray | | | 22.03.79 | 1 | Derby | | 25 May |
| | 11.9 | 1.51 | 8.22 | 25.3 | 4.81 | 23.32 | 2:23.15 | |
| 4272 | Hayley Young | | | 26.09.79 | 1 | Lincoln | | 7 May |
| | 12.8 | 1.74 | 7.83 | 27.5 | 5.08 | 27.10 | 2:35.2 | |
| 4250 | Amanda Humble | | | 15.08.79 | 1 | Jarrow | | 21 May |
| | 12.1 | 1.58 | 9.25 | 27.6 | 4.82 | 36.92 | 2:45.6 | |
| 4237 | Sam Foster | | | 9.09.79 | 1 | Ipswich | | 25 Jun |
| | 12.9 | 1.70 | 9.32 | 28.0 | 5.17 | 26.88 | 2:39.8 | |
| (10) | | | | | | | | |
| 4200 | Christine Head | | | 18.12.79 | 5 | Stoke | | 17 Sep |
| | 12.73w | 1.60 | 9.49 | 28.08 | 4.81 | 36.46 | 2:43.89 | |
| 4177 | Jodi Hallett | | | 8.11.78 | 3 | Stoke | | 6 Aug |
| | 12.50 | 1.59 | 8.57 | 27.17 | 4.70 | 26.38 | 2:29.6 | |
| 4170 | Natalie Butler | | | 25.11.78 | 1 | London (He) | | 13 Aug |
| | 11.88 | 1.59 | 8.80 | 26.62 | 5.02 | 26.76 | 2:50.70 | |
| 4151 | Belinda Samuels | | | 29.11.78 | 3 | Worcester | | 25 Jun |
| | 12.2 | 1.50 | 9.51 | 26.3 | 5.08 | 31.34 | 2:53.7 | |
| 4104 | Hayley Warrilow | | | 10.04.80 | 4 | Stoke | | 6 Aug |
| | 12.37 | 1.56 | 9.04 | 27.19 | 5.11 | 20.80 | 2:37.0 | |
| 4099 | Amy Nuttell | | | 6.02.80 | 7 | Stoke | | 17 Sep |
| | 12.31 | 1.45 | 8.98 | 27.18 | 5.16 | 26.84 | 2:38.10 | |
| 4097 | Hazel Clarke | | | 17.03.79 | 1 | Carlisle | | 5 May |
| | 12.3 | 1.59 | 8.38 | 27.5 | 4.74 | 27.60 | 2:36.2 | |
| 4090 | Michelle Winter | | | 18.06.79 | 3 | Bebington | | 23 Jul |
| | 11.8w | 1.48 | 6.82 | 27.2 | 5.13 | 25.76 | 2:31.56 | |
| 4073 | Anna Biscoe | | | 13.09.79 | 5 | Ipswich | | 25 Jun |
| | 12.6 | 1.67 | 5.87 | 26.6 | 4.97 | 24.74 | 2:36.2 | |
| 4069 | Laura White | | | 5.09.79 | 8 | Stoke | | 17 Sep |
| | 12.54 | 1.72 | 8.15 | 27.32 | 5.02 | 17.78 | 2:41.63 | |
| (20) | | | | | | | | |
| 4068 | Catherine Ryan | | | 4.02.80 | 6 | Stoke | | 6 Aug |
| | 13.00 | 1.56 | 8.87 | 27.91 | 5.22 | 24.60 | 2:36.4 | |
| 4032 | Kathryn Dowsett | | | 24.11.78 | 9 | Stoke | | 17 Sep |
| | 12.72 | 1.54 | 7.64 | 26.88 | 5.32 | 23.90 | 2:42.01 | |
| 4014 | Kelly Moreton | | | 18.09.79 | 1 | Cardiff | | 23 Jul |
| | 12.2w | 1.63 | 7.41 | 27.71 | 4.85 | 17.38 | 2:29.77 | |
| 3993 | Leanne Milburn | | | 16.08.79 | 5 | Blackpool | | 25 Jun |
| | 12.6 | 1.45 | 6.47 | 25.8 | 5.08 | 29.26 | 2:40.6 | |
| 3989 | Cicely Hall | | | 12.10.78 | 6 | Ipswich | | 25 Jun |
| | 12.9 | 1.52 | 7.93 | 26.5 | 4.70 | 17.48 | 2:21.1 | |
| 3962 | Stephanie Phillips | | | 25.10.78 | 10 | Stoke | | 17 Sep |
| | 12.73 | 1.51 | 8.67 | 27.54 | 5.12 | 24.58 | 2:42.26 | |
| 3925 | Hannah Stares | | | 13.11.78 | 12 | Stoke | | 17 Sep |
| | 12.46 | 1.54 | 8.26 | 26.96 | 4.66 | 28.50 | 2:49.15 | |
| 3894 | Kate Rogers | | | 14.02.79 | 4 | Worcester | | 25 Jun |
| | 12.5 | 1.41 | 7.71 | 26.4 | 5.02 | 22.76 | 2:36.9 | |
| 3891 | Victoria Reynolds | | | 22.04.80 | 14 | Stoke | | 17 Sep |
| | 12.48 | 1.57 | 8.51 | 27.14 | 4.97 | 27.40 | 3:02.46 | |
| 3881 | Fran Wilkins | | | 15.01.79 | 8 | Stoke | | 6 Aug |
| | 13.89 | 1.53 | 9.35 | 28.01 | 4.74 | 30.80 | 2:42.2 | |
| (30) | | | | | | | | |
| 3867 | Eve Miller | | | 1.12.79 | 2 | Portsmouth | | 25 Jun |
| | 12.6 | 1.42 | 8.56 | 25.9 | 4.77 | 18.94 | 2:35.7 | |
| 3867 | Felicity White | | | 17.11.78 | 3 | Portsmouth | | 25 Jun |
| | 13.4 | 1.51 | 7.57 | 27.3 | 4.65 | 29.96 | 2:35.7 | |
| 3856 | Nikita Thompson | | | 17.08.80 | 9 | Stoke | | 6 Aug |
| | 12.20 | 1.44 | 7.09 | 26.24 | 4.89 | 22.76 | 2:42.8 | |

| 3832 | Helen Baker | | | 5.02.79 | 16 | Stoke | | 17 Sep |
| | 12.65 | 1.54 | 7.85 | 27.60 | 5.08 | 26.02 | 2:54.79 | |
| 3826 | Kate Dyer | | | 12.07.79 | 8 | Ipswich | | 25 Jun |
| | 13.7 | 1.40 | 8.08 | 26.4 | 5.04 | 17.80 | 2:25.5 | |
| 3816 | Joanne Stacey | | | 23.09.79 | 2 | London (He) | | 13 Aug |
| | 12.80 | 1.53 | 6.82 | 27.87 | 4.45 | 23.88 | 2:27.80 | |
| 3814 | Amy Baden | | | 30.05.79 | 17 | Stoke | | 17 Sep |
| | 12.05w | 1.45 | 8.32 | 27.15 | 4.86 | 20.34 | 2:44.75 | |

# PENTATHLON - Under 15

| 3062 | Alison Kerboas | | | 21.05.81 | 1 | Blackpool | 25 Jun |
| | 12.6 | 8.67 | 5.02 | 1.63 | 2:31.5 | | |
| 3017 | Caroline Pearce | | | 1.09.80 | 1 | Stoke | 17 Sep |
| | 11.68 | 8.19 | 5.18 | 1.51 | 2:33.30 | | |
| 2973 | Laura Curtis | | | 2.05.81 | 1 | Jarrow | 25 Jun |
| | 11.9 | 6.96 | 1.54 | 4.85 | 2:24.0 | | |
| 2927 | Lisa Thompson | | | 25.04.81 | 1 | Wrexham | 16 Sep |
| | 12.14 | 7.17 | 4.60 | 1.63 | 2:29.7 | | |
| 2869 | Gemma Swetman | | | 28.09.80 | 3 | Stoke | 17 Sep |
| | 12.20 | 7.31 | 1.45 | 5.18 | 2:30.50 | | |
| 2860 | Kay Goodman | | | 17.11.80 | 2 | Ipswich | 25 Jun |
| | 12.5 | 8.20 | 5.03 | 1.48 | 2:32.5 | | |
| 2774 | Syretta Williams | | | 3.05.81 | 5 | Stoke | 17 Sep |
| | 12.09w | 8.53 | 1.36 | 4.81 | 2:29.60 | | |
| 2772 | Rachel Houghton | | | 18.12.80 | 6 | Stoke | 17 Sep |
| | 12.67w | 7.07 | 1.57 | 5.09 | 2:42.50 | | |
| 2755 | Helen Thieme | | | 28.09.81 | 1 | Worcester | 25 Jun |
| | 13.0 | 8.70 | 4.48 | 1.50 | 2:29.6 | | |
| 2750 | Emma Reid | | | 5.01.81 | 1 | Grangemouth | 10 Jun |
| | 12.1 | 8.07 | 1.51 | 4.37 | 2:33.1 | | |
| (10) | | | | | | | |
| 2731 | Maria Pringle | | | 18.12.80 | 2 | Bebington | 23 Jul |
| | 4.60w | 12.3w | 9.96 | 1.54 | 2:52.0 | | |
| 2714 | Lucy Rann | | | 5.09.80 | 2 | Portsmouth | 25 Jun |
| | 12.6 | 12.36 | 1.42 | 4.46 | 2:49.6 | | |
| 2710 | Emily Buckwell | | | 25.09.80 | 1 | Bromley | 18 Jun |
| | 13.4 | 8.48 | 1.42 | 4.49 | 2:22.5 | | |
| 2705 | Tina Thirwell | | | 5.09.81 | 3 | Bebington | 23 Jul |
| | 4.79 | 12.6w | 7.88 | 1.51 | 2:40.3 | | |
| 2690 | Amy Fendley | | | 25.01.81 | 7 | Stoke | 17 Sep |
| | 12.01w | 8.52 | 1.42 | 5.07 | 2:49.30 | | |
| 2685 | Laura Redmond | | | 19.04.81 | 2 | Grangemouth | 10 Jun |
| | 13.5 | 8.77 | 1.51 | 4.68 | 2:36.9 | | |
| 2677 | Jennifer Grogan | | | 7.09.80 | 2 | Bromley | 18 Jun |
| | 4.29 | 14.0 | 7.89 | 1.45 | 2:17.1 | | |
| 2661 | Fiona Harrison | | | 30.11.81 | 1 | Cudworth | 27 Aug |
| | 5.28 | 13.4 | 7.80 | 1.53 | 2:51.0 | | |
| 2657 | Carys Vaughan | | | 15.09.81 | 3 | Ipswich | 25 Jun |
| | 13.3 | 7.31 | 5.11 | 1.42 | 2:34.3 | | |
| 2654 | Donna Porazinski | | | 29.01.81 | 2 | Wrexham | 16 Sep |
| | 12.38 | 6.65 | 4.58 | 1.39 | 2:24.8 | | |
| (20) | | | | | | | |
| 2641 | Rachael Kay | | | 8.09.80 | 1 | Stoke | 8 Apr |
| | 12.0 | 6.15 | 1.45 | 4.65 | 2:33.2 | | |
| 2625 | Vicky Gregory | | | 16.03.81 | 10 | Stoke | 17 Sep |
| | 12.35w | 9.45 | 1.45 | 4.71 | 2:51.60 | | |
| 2614 | Alexis Carter | | | 23.10.81 | 1 | Rugby | 25 May |
| | 12.9 | 4.85 | 7.22 | 1.54 | 2:46.4 | | |
| 2612 | Victoria Duffield | | | 23.07.81 | 1 | Jarrow | 21 May |
| | 13.5 | 8.14 | 1.49 | 4.93 | 2:43.5 | | |

2606 Stephanie Little 5.11.81 3 Wrexham 16 Sep
 12.08 6.60 4.62 1.36 2:29.3
2600 Nusrat Caesay 18.03.81 12 Stoke 17 Sep
 12.51 7.21 1.36 4.67 2:30.10
2598 Melanie Vaggers 16.06.82 2 Yeovil 25 Jun
 12.9 8.83 1.47 4.28 2:37.2
2579 Helen Walker 12.10.80 2 Jarrow 25 Jun
 12.0 7.67 1.33 4.62 2:35.3
2572 Seonaid Ferry 19.11.81 2 Aberdeen 16 Jul
 9.32 12.4w 1.35 4.73 2:45.64
2569 Cathy Young 14.03.82 4 Ipswich 25 Jun
 13.8 6.77 4.57 1.54 2:34.3
 (30)
2563 Rachel Peacock 18.05.82 3 Yeovil 25 Jun
 12.4 7.35 1.38 4.89 2:41.6
2562 Vickie Williams 11.04.81 3 Stoke 6 Aug
 12.0 1.38 7.37 4.78 2:43.2
2555 Davinia Hesp 24.03.81 3 Jarrow 25 Jun
 11.9 7.85 1.36 4.54 2:40.2
2553 Tracey Matuszkiewicz 30.07.82 13 Stoke 17 Sep
 12.18w 8.33 1.42 4.43 2:43.50

## PENTATHLON - Under 13

2299 Jemma Scott 14.03.83 1 Aberdeen 16 Jul
 4.34 11.73w 6.32 · 1.36 2:41.69
2226 Laura Henderson 10.09.82 2 Aberdeen 16 Jul
 4.25 11.57w 5.60 1.27 2:35.78
2127 Lauren McLoughlin 8.09.82 1 Cardiff 27 May
 4.27 12.38 6.87 1.31 2:48.58
2089 Lucy Newman 2.03.83 1 Crawley 10 Sep
 3.96 12.4 9.55 1.25 2:56.2
2022 Rebecca Essex 16.11.82 2 Crawley 10 Sep
 4.37 12.8 6.60 1.31 2:56.2
2016 Catriona Pennet 10.10.83 3 Aberdeen 16 Jul
 4.20 11.70w 6.02 1.24 2:52.43
2015 Claire Pleavin 25.04.83 1 Bebington 22 Jul
 3.96 12.6 5.86 1.29 2:42.58
2008 Kirsty Hodson 6.03.83 2 Bebington 22 Jul
 4.20w 12.9w 6.46 1.32 2:52.90
1993 Carly Austin 16.05.83 1 Woking 6 Aug
 3.94 12.1 5.48 1.21 2:39.2
1963 Fiona Godden 17.12.82 4 Aberdeen 16 Jul
 4.32 13.30w 7.15 1.27 2:56.25
 (10)
1932 Melissa Harris 20.10.83 3 Bebington 22 Jul
 4.23 12.2 5.02 1.38 3:04.90
1924 Melissa Tremarco 12.10.82 4 Bebington 22 Jul
 3.86 12.4 5.06 1.23 2:40.64
1913 Rosanna Maio U13 28.03.83 3 Crawley 10 Sep
 4.13 14.0 8.05 1.10 2:41.9

## 2000 METRES WALK - Track - Under 13

10:09.0 Kelly Mann 8.09.83 1 Solihull 10 Sep
10:56.0 Vanessa Caines 17.04.83 5 Leamington 12 Aug
11:22.9 Natalie Evans 15.11.83 2 Brierley Hill 15 Oct
11:34.0 Samantha Collins 19.08.83 3 Solihull 10 Sep
11:40.3 Hayley Hutchings 14.11.83 3 Brierley Hill 15 Oct
11:46.4 Hayley Coleman 24.05.83 2 Horsham 13 May

## 2500 METRES WALK - Road - Under 15

| | | | | | | |
|---|---|---|---|---|---|---|
| 12:57.66 | Kelly Mann | U13 | 8.09.83 | 1 | Stoke | 28 May |
| 13:01.9 | Amy Hales | | 16.03.82 | 1 | Horsham | 13 May |
| 13:22.12 | Katie Ford | | 21.10.81 | 2 | Stoke | 17 Sep |
| 13:29.04 | Louise Richmond | | 15.12.81 | 3 | Stoke | 17 Sep |
| 13:31.89 | Gemma Onions | | 6.03.81 | 2 | Stoke | 28 May |
| 13:51.9 | Natalie Watson | U13 | 29.01.83 | 2 | Leamington | 13 May |
| 13:58.02 | Lisa Airey | | 19.12.80 | 5 | Stoke | 17 Sep |
| 13:58.7 | Tracey Robinson | | 28.09.81 | 3 | Stoke | 28 May |
| 13:59.36 | Vanessa Caines | U13 | 17.04.83 | 6 | Stoke | 17 Sep |

## 3000 METRES WALK - Track

| | | | | | | |
|---|---|---|---|---|---|---|
| 12:59.3 | Vicky Lupton | | 17.04.72 | 1 | Sheffield | 13 May |
| | 13:17.68 | | | 1 | Bedford | 29 May |
| | 13:29.5 + | | | 2m | Birmingham | 16 Jul |
| | 13:51.0 | | | 1 | Leamington | 12 Aug |
| 13:12.6 mx | Lisa Langford | | 15.03.67 | 1 | Edinburgh | 8 May |
| | 13:29.4 + | | | 1m | Birmingham | 16 Jul |
| 13:13.3 | Carolyn Partington | | 27.06.66 | 1 | Douglas, IOM | 12 Jul |
| | 13:19.29 | | | 2 | Bedford | 29 May |
| | 13:33.6 + | | | | Birmingham | 16 Jul |
| *13:25.99* | *Perri Williams* | | *2.06.66* | *3* | *Bedford* | *29 May* |
| 13:32.90 | Verity Snook | | 13.11.70 | 1 | Birmingham | 20 May |
| | 13:38.19 | | | 4 | Bedford | 29 May |
| | 13:41.53 i | | | 1 | Birmingham | 26 Feb |
| | 13:55.0 | | | 1 | Portsmouth | 13 May |
| 13:54.2 i | Sylvia Black | V35 | 16.04.58 | 1 | Birmingham | 12 Feb |
| 13:59.58 | Melanie Wright | | 5.04.64 | 2 | Birmingham | 20 May |
| 14:05.1 | Karen Kneale | | 23.04.69 | 1 | Douglas, IOM | 11 Jun |
| 14:11.1 | Liz Corran | V40 | 23.09.55 | 2 | Douglas, IOM | 11 Jun |
| 14:17.74 | Kim Baird | V35 | 28.02.56 | 3 | Birmingham | 20 May |
| 14:28.25 | Catherine Charnock | U23 | 3.05.75 | 5 | Bedford | 29 May |
| (10) | | | | | | |
| 14:29.00 i | Lynsey Tozer | U23 | 6.12.75 | 4 | Birmingham | 26 Feb |
| 14:33.36 i | Gill Watson | | 26.05.64 | 5 | Birmingham | 26 Feb |
| | 14:46.0 | | | 3 | Leamington | 12 Aug |
| 14:38.5 | Sharon Tonks | | 18.04.70 | 1 | Worcester | 13 May |
| 14:42.0 | Sarah Brown | | 28.09.64 | 1 | Horsham | 11 Apr |
| 14:56.61 i | Brenda Lupton | V40 | 5.10.52 | 6 | Birmingham | 26 Feb |
| | 15:09.2 | | | 3 | Sheffield | 13 May |
| 14:59.0 | Sarah Bennett | U17 | 27.07.80 | 3 | Leamington | 12 Aug |
| 15:05.2 | Kath Horwill | U23 | 26.01.75 | 8 | Narbonne, FRA | 29 Jul |
| 15:10.0 | Nina Howley | U20 | 22.01.78 | 3 | Belfort, FRA | 6 Aug |
| 15:10.4 | Karen Smith/Ratcliffe | | 1.06.61 | 1 | Leamington | 13 May |
| 15:15.0 | Nikki Huckerby | U20 | 27.02.78 | 4 | Belfort, FRA | 6 Aug |
| (20) | | | | | | |
| 15:25.9 | Clare Ellis | U20 | 27.04.78 | 2 | Leamington | 13 May |
| 15:32.97 | Joanne Pope | | 17.01.71 | 2 | Enfield | 29 Apr |
| 15:35.9 | Claire Childs | | 8.10.72 | 3 | Leamington | 13 May |
| 15:38.0 | Suzanne Ford-Dunn | U23 | 25.04.73 | 2 | Horsham | 11 Apr |
| 15:40.6 | Sally Warren | U20 | 29.01.78 | 1 | Brighton | 20 Jul |
| 15:41.0 | Kelly Mann | U13 | 8.09.83 | 1 | Birmingham | 30 Jul |
| 15:41.36 | Cath Reader | V40 | 19.10.54 | 3 | Enfield | 29 Apr |
| 15:53.0 | Amy Hales | U15 | 16.03.82 | 1 | Horsham | 9 May |
| 15:58.9 | Ann Lewis | V45 | 29.12.47 | 1 | Crawley | 4 Jul |
| 15:59.0 | Helen Ford-Dunn | U20 | 20.10.77 | 2 | Horsham | 9 May |
| (30) | | | | | | |
| 16:10.0 | Liz Ford-Dunn | | 13.05.71 | 2 | Horsham | 13 Jun |
| 16:10.62 | Debbie Wallen | U17 | 28.05.79 | 1 | London (He) | 6 Aug |
| 16:20.1 | Lynne Bradley | | 21.05.67 | 2 | Sheffield | 13 May |

305

| | | | | | | | |
|---|---|---|---|---|---|---|---|
| 16:26.0 | Katie Ford | U15 | 21.10.81 | 2 | Leicester | 22 | Apr |
| 16:29.7 | Lynne Newton | V45 | 19.05.47 | 2 | Crawley | 4 | Jul |
| 16:33.0 | Lisa Airey | U15 | 19.12.80 | 3 | Leicester | 22 | Apr |
| 16:36.6 | Louise Richmond | U15 | 15.12.81 | 5 | Birmingham | 30 | Jul |

**Road - Junior**

| | | | | | | | |
|---|---|---|---|---|---|---|---|
| 15:08 | Sarah Bennett | U17 | 27.07.80 | 1 | Dublin, IRE | 23 | Sep |
| 15:22 | Nikki Huckerby | U20 | 27.02.78 | 4 | Coventry | 5 | Mar |
| 15:30 | Clare Ellis | U20 | 27.04.78 | 3 | Dublin, IRE | 23 | Sep |
| 15:39 | Louise Richmond | U15 | 15.12.81 | 1 | Solihull | 18 | Nov |
| 15:40 | Nina Howley | U20 | 22.01.78 | 6 | Coventry | 5 | Mar |
| 15:48 o | Natalie Watson | U13 | 29.01.83 | 2 | Solihull | 18 | Nov |
| 15:51 o | Rebecca Pridmore | U13 | 19.12.82 | 3 | Solihull | 18 | Nov |
| 15:52 | Amy Hales | U15 | 16.03.82 | 1 | Weymouth | 19 | Mar |

## 5000 METRES WALK - Track

| | | | | | | | |
|---|---|---|---|---|---|---|---|
| 21:52.4 | Vicky Lupton | | 17.04.72 | 1 | Sheffield (W) | 9 | Aug |
| 22:15.4 | | | | 1 | Cudworth | 3 | Sep |
| 22:23.80 | | | | 2 | Birmingham | 16 | Jul |
| 22:38.93 | | | | 1 | Gateshead | 17 | Jun |
| 23:21.0 | | | | 1 | Leamington | 12 | Aug |
| 22:20.03 | Lisa Langford | | 15.03.67 | 1 | Birmingham | 16 | Jul |
| 22:41.19 | Carolyn Partington | | 27.06.66 | 3 | Birmingham | 16 | Jul |
| *23:32.31* | *Perri Williams* | | *2.06.66* | *4* | *Birmingham* | *16* | *Jul* |
| 23:38.85 | Verity Snook | | 13.11.70 | 1 | Cardiff | 22 | Jul |
| 23:58.84 | | | | 5 | Birmingham | 16 | Jul |
| 24:04.57 | Melanie Wright | | 5.04.64 | 6 | Birmingham | 16 | Jul |
| 24:09.66 | Elaine Callanin | | 13.09.60 | 7 | Birmingham | 16 | Jul |
| 24:16.4 | Kim Baird | V35 | 28.02.56 | 1 | Solihull | 4 | Jun |
| 24:52.95 | Sylvia Black | V35 | 16.04.58 | 8 | Birmingham | 16 | Jul |
| 25:00.79 | Gill Watson | | 26.05.64 | 9 | Birmingham | 16 | Jul |
| 25:13.03 | Liz Corran | V35 | 23.09.55 | 2 | Gateshead | 17 | Jun |
| (10) | | | | | | | |
| 25:22.67 | Catherine Charnock | U23 | 3.05.75 | 10 | Birmingham | 16 | Jul |
| 25:27.72 | Kath Horwill | U23 | 26.01.75 | 11 | Birmingham | 16 | Jul |
| 25:33.0 | Sarah Brown | | 28.09.64 | 4 | Horsham | 9 | May |
| 25:41.4 | Nina Howley | U20 | 22.01.78 | 3 | Sheffield (W) | 9 | Aug |
| 25:50.7 | Brenda Lupton | V40 | 5.10.52 | 4 | Sheffield (W) | 9 | Aug |
| 26:03.46 | Nikki Huckerby | U20 | 27.02.78 | 1 | Bedford | 2 | Jul |
| 26:07.85 | Sharon Tonks | | 18.04.70 | 12 | Birmingham | 16 | Jul |
| 26:31.0 | Clare Ellis | U20 | 27.04.78 | 3 | Leicester | 22 | Apr |
| 26:49.87 | Sally Warren | U20 | 29.01.78 | 3 | Bedford | 2 | Jul |
| 27:01.1 | Sarah Bennett | U17 | 27.07.80 | 1 | Birmingham | 30 | Jul |
| (20) | | | | | | | |
| 27:04.40 | Suzanne Ford-Dunn | U23 | 25.04.73 | 16 | Birmingham | 16 | Jul |
| 27:16.04 | Cath Reader | V40 | 19.10.54 | 1 | Exeter | 6 | Aug |
| 27:21.7 | Lynne Bradley | | 21.05.67 | 5 | Sheffield (W) | 9 | Aug |
| 27:33.0 | Helen Ford-Dunn | U20 | 20.10.77 | 5 | Leicester | 22 | Apr |
| 27:41.50 | Ann Lewis | V45 | 29.12.47 | 2 | Exeter | 6 | Aug |

**Road**

| | | | | | | | |
|---|---|---|---|---|---|---|---|
| 22:22 | Lisa Langford | | 15.03.67 | 1 | Tamworth | 28 | Oct |
| 23:00 | | | | 1 | Enfield | 3 | Jun |
| 23:24 | | | | 1 | Sutton Coldfield | 11 | Feb |
| 23:25 + | | | | m | Horsham | 25 | Mar |
| 22:58 | Verity Snook | | 13.11.70 | 1 | Bexley | 11 | Mar |
| 23:35 | | | | 1 | Bexley | 11 | Feb |
| 23:12 | Vicky Lupton | | 17.04.72 | 2 | Enfield | 3 | Jun |
| 23:20 | | | | 1 | Holmewood | 9 | Apr |
| 23:50 + | | | | 1=m | Douglas, IOM | 25 | Feb |

| | | | | | | | |
|---|---|---|---|---|---|---|---|
| 23:19 | *Perri Williams* | | *2.06.66* | *1* | *Bexley* | *9* | *Dec* |
| 23:24 | Melanie Wright | | 5.04.64 | 2 | Holmewood | 9 | Apr |
| 23:32 | Sylvia Black | V35 | 16.04.58 | 3 | Holmewood | 9 | Apr |
| 23:45 | Elaine Callanin | | 13.09.60 | 1 | Coventry | 28 | Jan |
| 23:50 + | Carolyn Partington | | 27.06.66 | 1=m | Douglas, IOM | 25 | Feb |
| 24:21 | Karen Kneale | | 23.04.69 | 1 | Douglas, IOM | 14 | May |
| 24:46 | Catherine Charnock | U23 | 3.05.75 | 2 | Solihull | 18 | Nov |
| 24:51 | Liz Corran | V35 | 23.09.55 | 2 | Douglas, IOM | 14 | May |
| | (10) | | | | | | |
| 25:00 | Kath Horwill | U23 | 26.01.75 | 5 | Enfield | 3 | Jun |
| 25:04 | Sharon Tonks | | 18.04.70 | 2 | Coventry | 28 | Jan |
| 25:22 | Claire Childs | | 8.10.72 | 1 | Coventry | 25 | Jul |
| 25:31 | Sarah Brown | | 28.09.64 | 6 | Enfield | 3 | Jun |
| 25:38 | Clare Ellis | U20 | 27.04.78 | 4 | Solihull | 18 | Nov |
| 25:44 | Gill Watson | | 26.05.64 | 7 | Enfield | 3 | Jun |
| 25:50 | Brenda Lupton | V40 | 5.10.52 | 8 | Enfield | 3 | Jun |
| 25:51 | Sandra Brown | V45 | 1.04.49 | 3 | London (CP) | 4 | Feb |
| 26:01 | Nikki Huckerby | U20 | 27.02.78 | 1 | Holmewood | 9 | Apr |
| 26:01 | Lynsey Tozer | U23 | 6.12.75 | 5 | Solihull | 18 | Nov |
| | (20) | | | | | | |
| 26:02 | Karen Smith/Ratcliffe | | 1.06.61 | 9 | Enfield | 3 | Jun |
| 26:05 | Sarah Bennett | U17 | 27.07.80 | 6 | Solihull | 18 | Nov |
| 26:18 | Nina Howley | U20 | 22.01.78 | 2 | Holmewood | 9 | Apr |
| 26:34 | Sally Warren | U20 | 29.01.78 | 3 | Bexley | 9 | Dec |
| 26:36 | Cath Reader | V40 | 19.10.54 | 1 | Thundersley | 5 | Nov |
| 26:43 | Suzanne Ford-Dunn | U23 | 25.04.73 | 2 | Bexley | 11 | Mar |
| 26:48 | Joanne Pope | | 17.01.71 | 3 | Bexley | 11 | Feb |
| 27:19 + | Maureen Cox | V40 | 7.09.50 | 5m | Douglas, IOM | 25 | Feb |
| 27:19 | Debbie Wallen | U17 | 28.05.79 | 3 | Bexley | 21 | Oct |
| 27:27 | Ann Lewis | V45 | 29.12.47 | 4 | Bexley | 9 | Dec |
| | (30) | | | | | | |
| 27:40 | Sally Hall | | 14.02.71 | 7 | Solihull | 18 | Nov |
| 27:41 | Liz Ford-Dunn | | 13.05.71 | 5 | Bexley | 9 | Dec |
| 27:52 | Kelly Bartlett | U17 | 13.10.79 | 8 | Solihull | 18 | Nov |

## 10000 METRES WALK - Track

| | | | | | | | |
|---|---|---|---|---|---|---|---|
| 45:18.8 | Vicky Lupton | | 17.04.72 | 1 | Watford | 2 | Sep |
| | 47:26.2 | | | 4 | Fana, NOR | 25 | May |
| | 49:14.1 | | | 1 | Sheffield | 19 | Sep |
| 48:35.8 | Melanie Wright | | 5.04.64 | 2 | Watford | 2 | Sep |
| | 50:26.3 | | | 7 | Fana, NOR | 25 | May |
| *48:54.0* | *Perri Williams* | | *2.06.66* | *1* | *Leicester* | *22* | *Apr* |
| 49:27.0 | Sylvia Black | V35 | 16.04.58 | 2 | Leicester | 22 | Apr |
| 49:41.0 | Elaine Callanin | | 13.09.60 | 3 | Leicester | 22 | Apr |
| 51:03.0 | Liz Corran | V35 | 23.09.55 | 4 | Leicester | 22 | Apr |
| 51:03.0 | Karen Kneale | | 23.04.69 | 5 | Leicester | 22 | Apr |
| 52:25.0 | Sarah Brown | | 28.09.64 | 1 | Brighton | 28 | Jan |
| 53:05.6 | Brenda Lupton | V40 | 5.10.52 | 4 | Watford | 2 | Sep |
| 54:06.6 | Gill Watson | | 26.05.64 | 5 | Watford | 2 | Sep |
| 54:18.7 | Nina Howley | U20 | 22.01.78 | 6 | Watford | 2 | Sep |
| | (10) | | | | | | |
| 56:17.0 | Cath Reader | V40 | 19.10.54 | 1 | Hornchurch | 29 | May |
| 56:35.9 | Lynne Bradley | | 21.05.67 | 4 | Sheffield | 19 | Sep |

## 10000 METRES WALK - Road

| | | | | | | | |
|---|---|---|---|---|---|---|---|
| 46:00 | Lisa Langford | | 15.03.67 | 36 | Beijing, CHN | 29 | Apr |
| | 46:06 | | | 35 | Gothenburg, SWE | 7 | Aug |
| | 46:34 | | | 1 | Leicester | 10 | Sep |
| | 47:13 | | | 16 | Fougeres, FRA | 11 | Jun |
| | 47:30 | | | 1 | Dawlish | 19 | Nov |
| | 48:04 | | | 2 | Horsham | 25 | Mar |

| | | | | | | | |
|---|---|---|---|---|---|---|---|
| 46:26 | Carolyn Partington | | 27.06.66 | 1 | Stockport | 1 | Jul |
| 47:14 | | | | 2 | Douglas, IOM | 25 | Feb |
| 47:21 | | | | 17 | Fougeres, FRA | 11 | Jun |
| 48:17 | | | | 60 | Beijing, CHN | 29 | Apr |
| 46:40 | Vicky Lupton | | 17.04.72 | 15 | Fougeres, FRA | 11 | Jun |
| 47:02 | | | | 2 | Leicester | 10 | Sep |
| 47:02 | | | | 2 | Dublin, IRE | 23 | Sep |
| 47:04 | | | | 51 | Beijing, CHN | 29 | Apr |
| 47:13 + | | | | 2m | Stockport | 1 | Jul |
| 47:28 | | | | 3 | Douglas, IOM | 25 | Feb |
| 47:44 | | | | 1 | Horsham | 25 | Mar |
| 48:42 | Verity Snook | | 13.11.70 | 69 | Beijing, CHN | 29 | Apr |
| 48:50 | | | | 13 | Palma, SPA | 4 | Mar |
| 48:44 | Melanie Wright | | 5.04.64 | 3 | Horsham | 25 | Mar |
| 48:48 | | | | 21 | Fougeres, FRA | 10 | Jun |
| 49:39 | Kim Baird | V35 | 28.02.56 | 4 | Dublin, IRE | 23 | Sep |
| 50:05 | Elaine Callanin | | 13.09.60 | 4 | Horsham | 25 | Mar |
| 50:10 | Sylvia Black | V35 | 16.04.58 | 2 | Cardiff | 7 | May |
| 51:09 | Karen Kneale | | 23.04.69 | 6 | Dublin, IRE | 23 | Sep |
| 51:20 | Kath Horwill | U23 | 26.01.75 | 1 | Birmingham | 16 | Dec |
| (10) | | | | | | | |
| 51:34 | Liz Corran | V40 | 23.09.55 | 7 | Horsham | 25 | May |
| 52:46 | Sharon Tonks | | 18.04.70 | 4 | Cardiff | 7 | May |
| 53:17 | Gill Watson | | 26.05.64 | 2 | York | 20 | May |
| 53:19 | Brenda Lupton | V40 | 5.10.52 | 3 | York | 20 | May |
| 54:08 | Sarah Brown | | 28.09.64 | 8 | Horsham | 25 | Mar |
| 54:31 | Lynsey Tozer | U23 | 6.12.75 | 2 | Birmingham | 16 | Dec |
| 54:48 | Julie Drake | | 21.05.69 | 1 | Brighton | 18 | Nov |
| 54:56 | Nikki Huckerby | U20 | 27.02.78 | 3 | Birmingham | 16 | Dec |
| 55:24 | Nina Howley | U20 | 22.01.78 | 5 | Leicester | 10 | Sep |
| 55:31 | Suzanne Ford-Dunn | U23 | 25.04.73 | 11 | Horsham | 25 | Mar |
| (20) | | | | | | | |
| 55:40 | Cath Reader | V40 | 19.10.54 | 1 | Weymouth | 19 | Mar |
| 55:59 | Debbie Wallen | U17 | 28.05.79 | 1 | Steyning | 4 | Nov |
| 56:08 | Maureen Cox | V40 | 7.09.50 | 5 | Douglas, IOM | 25 | Feb |
| 56:15 | Sally Warren | U20 | 29.01.78 | 2 | Steyning | 4 | Nov |
| 56:22 | Andrea Crofts | | 7.09.70 | 6 | Leicester | 10 | Sep |
| 57:29 | Lynne Bradley | | 21.05.67 | 7 | Leicester | 10 | Sep |
| 57:42 | Ann Lewis | V45 | 29.12.47 | 16 | Horsham | 25 | Mar |
| 57:52 | Hazel Cross | | 29.04.66 | 1 | Macclesfield | 11 | Mar |
| 58:04 | Sally Hall | | 14.02.71 | 4 | Birmingham | 16 | Dec |

## 20 KILOMETRES WALK

| | | | | | | | |
|---|---|---|---|---|---|---|---|
| 1:42:47 | Vicky Lupton | | 17.04.72 | 1 | Stockport | 1 | Jul |
| 1:46:31 | Elaine Callanin | | 13.09.60 | 2 | Stockport | 1 | Jul |
| 1:53:14 | Brenda Lupton | V40 | 5.10.52 | 3 | Stockport | 1 | Jul |
| 1:53:28 | Cath Reader | V40 | 19.10.54 | 1 | Sutton Coldfield | 10 | Jun |
| 1:55:10 | Liz Corran | V35 | 23.09.55 | 4 | Stockport | 1 | Jul |
| 1:57:07 | Sarah Brown | | 28.09.64 | 5 | Stockport | 1 | Jul |
| 1:58:22 | Maureen Cox | V40 | 7.09.50 | 1 | Douglas, IOM | 14 | May |

## 50 KILOMETRES WALK

| | | | | | | | |
|---|---|---|---|---|---|---|---|
| 5:25:52 | Sandra Brown | V45 | 1.04.49 | 1 | Burrator | 5 | Mar |
| 5:54:43 | Jill Green | V50 | 10.10.41 | 2 | Burrator | 5 | Mar |
| 5:55:29 | Pam Ficken | V50 | 25.07.41 | 3 | Burrator | 5 | Mar |

## 100 MILES WALK

| | | | | | | | |
|---|---|---|---|---|---|---|---|
| 21:37:21 | Sandra Brown | V45 | 1.04.49 | 1 | London (BP) | 6 | Aug |
| 22:32:35 | Jill Green | V50 | 10.10.41 | 2 | London (BP) | 6 | Aug |
| 23:05:21 | Kath Crilley | V45 | 8.09.47 | 3 | London (BP) | 6 | Aug |

# 4 x 100 METRES

| 43.90 | National Team | | 5h2 | Gothenburg, SWE | 12 | Aug |
|---|---|---|---|---|---|---|
| | (M Richardson, C Murphy, S Jacobs, P Thomas) | | | | | |
| 44.10 | National Team | | 4 | Villeneuve d'Ascq, FRA | 24 | Jun |
| | (St Douglas, C Murphy, S Jacobs, P Thomas) | | | | | |
| 44.12 | National Team | | 1 | London (CP) | 7 | Jul |
| | (SA Short, P Thomas, S Jacobs, G McLeod) | | | | | |
| 44.93 | Great Britain Students | | 6 | Fukuoka, JAP | 3 | Sep |
| | (J Maduaka, C Murphy, M Richardson, S Williams) | | | | | |
| 45.02 | National U23 Team | | 2 | Narbonne, FRA | 29 | Jul |
| | (J Maduaka, C Murphy, S Smith, D Hoggarth) | | | | | |
| 45.14 | Great Britain Students | | 2 | London (CP) | 7 | Jul |
| | (J Maduaka, M Thomas, C Murphy, M Richardson) | | | | | |
| 45.37 | England | | 1 | Loughborough | 11 | Jun |
| | (S Smith, G McLeod, S Jacobs, S Rawlinson) | | | | | |
| 45.41 | England | | 1 | Cwmbran | 9 | Jul |
| | (S Smith, D Hoggarth, J Maduaka, C Court) | | | | | |
| 45.46 | National Team | | 2 | Gateshead | 21 | Aug |
| | (S Smith, D Fraser, SA Short, G McLeod) | | | | | |
| 45.57 | National Junior Team | U20 | 4 | Nyiregyhaza, HUN | 30 | Jul |
| | (E Ruddock, V Shipman, Susie Williams, R Drummond) | | | | | |
| 45.88 | National Junior Team | U20 | 2 | Loughborough | 11 | Jun |
| | (L Carter, S Wilhelmy, S Dudgeon, R Drummond) | | | | | |
| 45.91 | National U23 Team | | 1 | Sheffield | 23 | Jul |
| 45.98 | National Junior Team | U20 | 3h1 | Nyiregyhaza, HUN | 30 | Jul |
| | (E Ruddock, V Shipman, S Dudgeon, R Drummond) | | | | | |
| 46.04 | Great Britain Students | | 3 | Loughborough | 11 | Jun |
| 46.17 | National U23 Team | | 1 | Basle, SWZ | 5 | Jun |
| | (D Allahgreen, J Maduaka, S Smith, M Wilkins) | | | | | |
| 46.19 | Great Britain Students | | 2 | Sheffield | 23 | Jul |
| 46.22 | South | | 1 | Birmingham | 20 | May |
| | (J Maduaka, M Richardson, A Soper, St Douglas) | | | | | |
| 46.3 | Trafford | | 1 | Glasgow | 6 | May |

**Additional National Teams**

| 46.68 | Wales | | 2 | Cwmbran | 9 | Jul |
|---|---|---|---|---|---|---|
| | (H Miles, C Murphy, B Edwards, S-A Short) | | | | | |
| 46.96 | Scotland | | 1 | Cardiff | 22 | Jul |
| | (L Brown, N Hynd, G Hegney, A McGillivary) | | | | | |

**Additional Club Teams** (1 above)

| 46.6 | Edinburgh Woollen Mill | | 1 | Derby | 30 | Jul |
|---|---|---|---|---|---|---|
| 46.61 | Shaftesbury Barnet | | 1 | Stoke | 9 | Sep |
| 46.8 | Sale | | 1 | London (WL) | 30 | Jul |
| 46.8 | City of Glasgow | | 3 | Birmingham | 19 | Aug |
| 46.95 | Windsor Slough & Eton | | 2 | Stoke | 9 | Sep |
| 47.5 | Birchfield | | 1 | Liverpool | 30 | Jul |
| 47.6 | Essex Ladies | | 3 | London (He) | 1 | Jul |
| 47.67 | Team Solent | | 1 | Stoke | 10 | Sep |
| 47.7 | Croydon | | 1 | Peterborough | 7 | May |
| 47.9 | Coventry Godiva | | 1 | Coventry | 13 | Aug |
| 47.9 | Rotherham | | 1 | Grimsby | 3 | Sep |
| 48.1 | Bromley Ladies | | 2 | London (WL) | 30 | Jul |
| 48.3 | Essex Ladies | U17 | 1 | London (He) | 30 | Apr |
| 48.3 | Peterborough | | 2 | Peterborough | 7 | May |
| 48.3 | Basildon | | 1 | Basildon | 20 | May |
| 48.4 | Aldershot Farnham & District | | 3 | Peterborough | 7 | May |
| 48.4 | Borough of Hounslow | | 1 | Feltham | 22 | Jul |
| 48.6 | Essex Ladies | U20 | 1 | Bromley | 23 | Apr |
| 48.64 | Loughborough Students | | 1 | Edinburgh | 8 | May |

**Additional Under 20 Teams** (1 - 3 above)

| | | | | | |
|---|---|---|---|---|---|
| 46.66 | Surrey Schools | | 1 | Nottingham | 8 Jul |
| 46.75 | National Team | | 2h1 | Bath | 12 Jul |
| 47.09 | Kent Schools | | 2 | Nottingham | 8 Jul |
| 47.15 | National Team | | 2 | Belfort, FRA | 6 Aug |
| 47.18 | Suffolk Schools | U17 | 1h1 | Nottingham | 8 Jul |
| 47.19 | England Schools | U17 | 1 | Colwyn Bay | 15 Jul |
| 47.27 | Middlesex Schools | U17 | 1 | Nottingham | 8 Jul |
| 47.59 | West Midlands Schools | U17 | 2h1 | Nottingham | 8 Jul |
| 47.6 | Scotland Schools | | 1 | Ayr | 18 Jul |

**Additional National Teams**

| | | | | |
|---|---|---|---|---|
| 47.9 | Scotland | 2 | Ayr | 18 Jul |
| 48.23 | Wales | 3 | Utrecht, HOL | 9 Jul |

**Additional Under 20 Club Teams** (1 above)

| | | | | | |
|---|---|---|---|---|---|
| 48.7 | Wigan | | 2 | Telford | 18 Jun |
| 49.25 | Lucozade Motherwell | U17 | 1 | Edinburgh | 24 Jun |
| 49.44 | Sale | | | Montreuil, FRA | 30 Sep |
| 49.5 | Liverpool Harriers | U17 | 1 | Derby | 25 Jun |
| 49.6 | Hallamshire | | 1 | Sheffield | 18 Jun |
| 49.7 | City of Stoke | U17 | 1 | Derby | 23 Jul |
| 49.8 | Rugby & District | U17 | 1 | Sutton Coldfield | 30 Apr |
| 49.9 | Trafford | | 3 | Telford | 18 Jun |
| 49.9 | Derby Ladies | U17 | 2 | Derby | 23 Jul |

**Additional Under 17 Teams** (1 - 4 above)

| | | | | |
|---|---|---|---|---|
| 47.69 | Essex Schools | 2h3 | Nottingham | 8 Jul |
| 47.71 | Scotland Schools | 2 | Colwyn Bay | 15 Jul |
| 48.47 | Berkshire Schools | 3h3 | Nottingham | 8 Jul |
| 48.51 | Cambridgeshire Schools | 1h2 | Nottingham | 8 Jul |

**Additional Under 17 Club Teams** (1 - 6 above)

| | | | | | |
|---|---|---|---|---|---|
| 50.0 | Wigan | U15 | 1 | Derby | 25 Jun |
| 50.27 | Windsor Slough & Eton | | 3 | Birmingham | 3 Sep |
| 50.3 | Liverpool Harriers | U15 | 2 | Derby | 25 Jun |
| 50.3 | Telford | | 1 | Telford | 25 Jun |

**Under 15 Teams**

| | | | | |
|---|---|---|---|---|
| 48.66 | West Midlands Schools | 1 | Nottingham | 8 Jul |
| 48.98 | Greater Manchester Schools | 2 | Nottingham | 8 Jul |
| 49.49 | Hampshire Schools | 3 | Nottingham | 8 Jul |

**Under 15 National Teams**

| | | | | |
|---|---|---|---|---|
| 50.08 | Wales | 2 | Antrim | 12 Aug |
| 50.82 | Scotland | 3 | Antrim | 12 Aug |

**Additional Under 15 Club Teams** (1 - 2 above)

| | | | | |
|---|---|---|---|---|
| 50.6 | Derby Ladies | 3 | Derby | 25 Jun |
| 50.6 | Sale | 1 | Blackpool | 16 Jul |
| 50.8 | City of Glasgow | 1 | Glasgow | 25 Jun |
| 51.0 | City of Portsmouth | 1 | Oxford | 22 Jul |
| 51.0 | Birchfield | 1 | Derby | 23 Jul |
| 51.2 | Bromley Ladies | 1 | Tonbridge | 17 Sep |

**Under 13 Teams**

| | | | | |
|---|---|---|---|---|
| 53.7 | Liverpool Harriers | 1 | Kirkby | 10 Sep |
| 53.86 | Irvine | 1h1 | Edinburgh | 24 Jun |
| 54.11 | City of Stoke | 1 | Birmingham | 3 Sep |
| 54.3 | Dorset CAA | 1 | London (TB) | 30 Jul |
| 54.4 | Havering Mayesbrook | 1 | London (WF) | 13 Jul |
| 54.7 | Surrey CAA | 2 | London (TB) | 30 Jul |

# 4 x 200 METRES

| | | | | | |
|---|---|---|---|---|---|
| 1:37.00 i | England | | 2 | Vienna, AUT | 18 Feb |
| | (E Sutcliffe, S Earnshaw, D Callow, S Oxley) | | | | |
| 1:39.67 i | North of England AA | | 1 | Birmingham | 26 Feb |
| | (S Briggs, S Smith, L Whitehead, E Sutcliffe) | | | | |
| 1:41.36 i | Midland Counties AA | | 2 | Birmingham | 26 Feb |
| | (R Simpson, K Kury, Z Wilson, S Oxley) | | | | |
| 1:42.00 i | Birmingham University | | 1 | Birmingham | 1 Mar |
| 1:42.0 | Walton | | 1 | Walton | 31 May |
| 1:42.81 i | South of England AA | | 2 | Nenagh, IRE | 5 Mar |
| 1:43.2 i | Loughborough University | | 2 | Glasgow | 11 Mar |
| 1:43.41 i | Scotland Schools | U17 | 1 | Birmingham | 26 Feb |
| 1:43.8 | Dartford | | 1 | Tonbridge | 17 Sep |
| | (J Heap, S Simmons, M Jones, E Williams) | | | | |
| 1:43.91 i | AA of Wales | | 3 | Birmingham | 26 Feb |
| | (H Miles, B Edwards, K Williams) | | | | |

**Additional Club Teams** (1 - 4 above)

| | | | | | |
|---|---|---|---|---|---|
| 1:45.2 | Bromley Ladies | | 2 | Tonbridge | 17 Sep |
| 1:45.3 | Ashford | | 3 | Tonbridge | 17 Sep |
| 1:47.10 i | Brunel University | | 3 | Birmingham | 1 Mar |
| 1:47.3 | Southampton City | U17 | 1 | Portsmouth | 19 Jul |
| 1:47.4 | Medway | | 2 | Bromley | 23 Jul |
| 1:47.5 | Cambridge Harriers | U17 | 1 | Tonbridge | 17 Sep |

**Under 20 Team**

| | | | | | |
|---|---|---|---|---|---|
| 1:50.2 | Tonbridge | | 4 | Tonbridge | 17 Sep |

**Additional Under 17 Teams** (1 - 3 above)

| | | | | | |
|---|---|---|---|---|---|
| 1:45.33 i | England Schools | | 3 | Birmingham | 26 Feb |
| 1:46.01 i | Wales Schools | | 4 | Birmingham | 26 Feb |
| 1:47.7 | City of Glasgow | U15 | 1 | Edinburgh | 20 Aug |
| 1:48.0 | GEC Avionics | | 2 | Tonbridge | 17 Sep |
| 1:48.52 i | Victoria Park AAC | | 1 | Glasgow | 29 Jan |
| 1:48.8 | Bromley Ladies | U15 | 1 | Bromley | 23 Jul |
| 1:49.63 i | West Midlands Schools | U15 | 1 | Birmingham | 7 Feb |

**Additional Under 17 Club Teams** (1 - 6 above)

| | | | | | |
|---|---|---|---|---|---|
| 1:50.1 | Brighton & Hove | U15 | 1 | Crawley | 11 Jun |
| 1:50.4 | Wakefield | | 1 | Wakefield | 9 Jul |
| 1:50.9 | Dartford | U15 | 2 | Bromley | 23 Jul |
| 1:51.0 | Spenborough | U15 | 1 | Wakefield | 9 Jul |
| 1:51.0 | Bedford & County | | 1 | Bedford | 3 Sep |

**Additional Under 15 Club Teams** (1 - 5 above)

| | | | | | |
|---|---|---|---|---|---|
| 1:51.3 | Hercules Wimbledon | | 1 | Croydon | May |
| 1:51.9 | Sparta | | 1 | Templemore | 18 Jul |
| 1:52.5 | Ayr Seaforth | | 2 | Edinburgh | 20 Aug |
| 1:52.8 | Lucozade Motherwell | | 3 | Edinburgh | 20 Aug |
| 1:53.0 | Medway | | 3 | Bromley | 23 Jul |
| 1:53.0 | Dundee Hawkhill | | 4 | Edinburgh | 20 Aug |

**Under 13 Teams**

| | | | | | |
|---|---|---|---|---|---|
| 1:59.5 | Horsham Blue Star | | 1 | Crawley | 11 Jun |
| 1:59.5 | Aberdeen | | 1 | Peterhead | 18 Jun |
| 2:01.0 | Corstorphine | | 1 | Pitreavie | 20 May |
| 2:01.2 | Corby | | 1 | Corby | 22 Jun |
| 2:01.6 | Blackheath | | 1 | Bromley | 23 Jul |

# 4 x 400 METRES

| Time | Team | Place | Venue | Date |
|---|---|---|---|---|
| 3:25.50 | National Team | 5h2 | Gothenburg, SWE | 12 Aug |
| | (M Neef, S Llewellyn, L Hanson, G Oladapo) | | | |
| 3:26.89 | National Team | 5 | Gothenburg, SWE | 13 Aug |
| | (M Neef, S Llewellyn, L Hanson, G Oladapo) | | | |
| 3:28.34 | National Team | 4 | Villeneuve d'Ascq, FRA | 25 Jun |
| | (M Neef, L Hanson, S Tunaley, G Oladapo) | | | |
| 3:29.65 | National Team | 2 | Gateshead | 21 Aug |
| | (M Neef, G Oladapo, L Hanson, S Rawlinson) | | | |
| 3:35.39 i | National Team | 4 | Barcelona, SPA | 12 Mar |
| | (M Neef, S Earnshaw, A Curbishley, S McCann) | | | |
| 3:37.60 i | National Team | 1 | Glasgow | 11 Feb |
| | (S Llewellyn, S Earnshaw, J Stoute, S McCann) | | | |
| 3:37.90 i | National Team | 2 | Birmingham | 28 Jan |
| | (M Neef, S Earnshaw, T Joseph, M Thomas) | | | |
| 3:38.23 | National Junior Team | U20 3 | Nyiregyhaza, HUN | 30 Jul |
| | (E Williams, J Sloane, A Curbishley, L Thorne) | | | |
| 3:39.43 | National Junior Team | U20 2h2 | Nyiregyhaza, HUN | 29 Jul |
| | (E Williams, J Sloane, A Curbishley, L Thorne) | | | |
| 3:40.7 | Birchfield | 1 | Birmingham | 19 Aug |
| | (S Guise, J Levermore, L Hanson, C Court) | | | |
| 3:42.0 | Birchfield | 1 | London (He) | 1 Jul |
| 3:42.16 | England | 1 | Loughborough | 11 Jun |
| 3:42.20 | Northern Ireland | 1 | Cardiff | 23 Jul |
| | (C Hill, C O'Connor, S McCann, V Jamieson) | | | |
| 3:42.36 | Birchfield | 1 | Stoke | 9 Sep |
| | (S Guise, J Levermore, L Hansen, C Court) | | | |
| 3:42.85 | Great Britain Students | 2 | Loughborough | 11 Jun |
| 3:43.0 | Sale | 2 | Birmingham | 19 Aug |
| 3:43.42 | National Junior Team | U20 1 | Belfort, FRA | 6 Aug |
| | (E Williams, J Sloane, A Curbishley, L Thorne) | | | |
| 3:43.58 | Birchfield | 1 | Birmingham | 23 Apr |
| 3:43.63 | Windsor Slough & Eton | 2 | Stoke | 9 Sep |
| | (C Amede, M Richardson, N Tait, L Owusu) | | | |
| 3:43.92 | National U23 Team | 3 | Narbonne, FRA | 29 Jul |
| 3:44.0 | Sale | 1 | London (WL) | 30 Jul |
| 3:44.23 | National Junior Team | U20 3 | Loughborough | 11 Jun |
| | (E Williams, C Hill, L Bell, L Thorne) | | | |
| 3:44.24 | Scotland | 2 | Cardiff | 23 Jul |
| | (J Low, A Mahindru, D Flockhart, L Vannet) | | | |

**Additional National Team**

| Time | Team | Place | Venue | Date |
|---|---|---|---|---|
| 3:51.37 | Wales | 3 | Cardiff | 23 Jul |

**Additional Club Teams** (1 - 3 above)

| Time | Team | Place | Venue | Date |
|---|---|---|---|---|
| 3:44.86 | Shaftesbury Barnet | 3 | Stoke | 9 Sep |
| 3:44.99 | Loughborough Students | 4 | Loughborough | 11 Jun |
| 3:46.52 | Edinburgh Woollen Mill | 5 | Stoke | 9 Sep |
| 3:47.1 | Essex Ladies | 4 | London (He) | 1 Jul |
| 3:50.3 | Bromley Ladies | 3 | London (WL) | 30 Jul |
| 3:50.9 | Trafford | 1 | Glasgow | 7 May |
| 3:51.0 | Aldershot Farnham & District | 1 | Derby | 6 Aug |
| 3:51.01 | Birmingham University | 2 | Edinburgh | 8 May |
| 3:51.1 | Coventry Godiva | 1 | Coventry | 13 Aug |
| 3:51.3 | City of Glasgow | 6 | London (He) | 1 Jul |
| 3:52.1 | Croyden | 1 | Croydon | 6 Aug |
| 3:52.2 | Ashford | 1 | Tonbridge | 17 Sep |
| 3:52.9 | Hallamshire | 2 | Derby | 6 Aug |
| 3:53.4 | Peterborough | 1 | Peterborough | 7 May |
| 3:53.7 | Lisburn | 1 | | 20 May |
| 3:54.0 | Bristol | 2 | Birmingham | 23 Apr |

**Additional Under 20 Teams** (1 - 4 above)

| | | | | | |
|---|---|---|---|---|---|
| 3:54.2 | Scotland Schools | | 1 | Ayr | 18 Jul |
| 3:56.14 | South of England AA | | 1 | London (He) | 9 Sep |
| | (D McIntosh, L Buxton, Susie Williams, E Williams) | | | | |
| 3:56.8 | Scotland | | 2 | Ayr | 18 Jul |
| 3:57.41 | Wales | | 1 | Utrecht, HOL | 9 Jul |
| | (K Williams, M John, A Pritchard, S Mead) | | | | |
| 3:58.5 | Essex Ladies | | 1 | Telford | 18 Jun |
| 3:59.8 | Wales Schools | | 3 | Ayr | 18 Jul |

**Additional Under 20 Club Teams** (1 above)

| | | | | | |
|---|---|---|---|---|---|
| 4:01.4 | Wigan | | 2 | Telford | 18 Jun |
| 4:01.78 | Sale | | 2 | Montreuil, FRA | 30 Sep |
| 4:05.1 | Hallamshire | | 1 | Sheffield | 18 Jun |
| 4:06.7 | Trafford | | 3 | Telford | 18 Jun |
| 4:08.4 | North Shields Poly | | 1 | Gateshead | 30 Jul |

**Under 17 Teams**

| | | | | | |
|---|---|---|---|---|---|
| 4:13.5 | Hertford & Ware | | 3 | Welwyn GC | 2 Sep |
| 4:24.2 | Borough of Enfield | | 1 | Thurrock | 30 Jul |
| 4:27.5 | Newquay & Par | | 3 | Salisbury | 22 Jul |

## 1200 METRES MEDLEY

| | | | | | |
|---|---|---|---|---|---|
| 2:44.54 i | National Team | U20 | 1 | Erfurt, GER | 25 Feb |
| | (S Wilhelmy, S Dudgeon, S Hendry, N Danvers) | | | | |

## 1600 METRES MEDLEY

| | | | | | |
|---|---|---|---|---|---|
| 3:53.44 i | South of England | | 1 | Birmingham | 26 Feb |
| | (S Llewellyn, D Marti, A Hunte, A Davies) | | | | |
| 4:02.75 i | Midland Counties AA | | 2 | Birmingham | 26 Feb |
| | (J Sloane, S Evans, J Levermore, S Hardy) | | | | |
| 4:05.01 i | North of England AA | | 3 | Birmingham | 26 Feb |
| | (D Allahgreen, E Price, D Facey, P Fryer) | | | | |
| 4:17.07 i | AA of Wales | | 4 | Birmingham | 26 Feb |
| | (H Paines, D Higgins, K Bright, L Carthew) | | | | |
| 4:09.1 | Motherwell | | 1 | Edinburgh | 20 Aug |
| 4:10.2 | Dundee Hawkhill | | 2 | Edinburgh | 20 Aug |

## 3 x 800 METRES

| | | | | | |
|---|---|---|---|---|---|
| 6:57.5 | Vale Royal | U17 | 1 | Crewe | 11 Jul |
| 7:16.4 | Warrington AC | | 1 | Crewe | 11 Jul |
| 7:18.8 + | BMC East | | 3 | Oxford | 2 Sep |
| | First 3 legs of 4 x 800 Metres Relay | | | | |
| 7:20.5 | Warrington AC | U17 | 2 | Crewe | 11 Jul |
| 7:21.3 | Phoenix | U15 | 1 | Crawley | 11 Jun |
| 7:21.4 | Northampton Phoenix | | 1 | Corby | 22 Jun |
| 7:23.6 | Basildon | U17 | 1 | London (WF) | 13 Jul |
| 7:24.40 | Edinburgh AC | U17 | 1 | Edinburgh | 24 Jun |

**Additional Under 15 Teams** (1 above)

| | | | | | |
|---|---|---|---|---|---|
| 7:24.84 | Ayr Seaforth | | 1 | Edinburgh | 24 Jun |
| 7:25.15 | Pitreavie | | 2 | Edinburgh | 24 Jun |
| 7:28.0 | Blackpool North Schools | | 1 | Blackburn | 15 May |
| 7:31.1 | Tonbridge | | 1 | Tonbridge | 17 Sep |
| 7:31.3 | Essex Ladies | | 1 | London (WF) | 13 Jul |
| 7:31.9 | Dartford | | 2 | Tonbridge | 17 Sep |

**Under 13 Teams**

| | | | | | |
|---|---|---|---|---|---|
| 7:49.3 | Basildon | | 1 | London (WF) | 13 Jul |
| 7:52.5 | Invicta East Kent | | 1 | Tonbridge | 17 Sep |
| 7:53.7 | Stockport | | 1 | Crewe | 27 Jun |

# Leading Women Veterans

## 100 Metres

| | | | | | | |
|---|---|---|---|---|---|---|
| 11.69 | Clova Court | W35 | (Birchfield H) | Bedford | 29 | May |
| 12.5 | Lynn Talbert | W35 | (Thurrock H) | Bournemouth | 3 | Jun |
| 12.9 | Alison Brown | W35 | (Edin WM) | Carlisle | 2 | Apr |
| 12.8 | Irene Morrison | W40 | (Glasgow) | Glasgow | 7 | May |
| 12.9 | Helen Godsell | W40 | (Bromley V) | Thurrock | 4 | Jun |
| 13.2 | June Simpson | W40 | (Newq & Par) | Carn Brea | 20 | Aug |
| 12.9 | Vivien Bonner | W45 | (A F & D) | London (Col) | 3 | Sep |
| 13.25 | Maureen Lewington | W45 | (Birchfield H) | Buffalo, USA | 23 | Jul |
| 13.4 | Brenda Elliott | W45 | (Cramlington) | Jarrow | 29 | Jul |
| 14.1 | Judy Vernon | W50 | (Sutton AC) | Reading | 1 | Oct |
| 14.2 | Mary Axtell | W50 | (Team Sol) | Thurrock | 4 | Jun |
| 14.2 | Sylvia Wood | W50 | (Linlithgow) | Livingstone | 16 | Aug |
| 14.0 | Una Gore | W55 | (City of Bath) | Bath | 21 | Jun |
| 16.0 | Betty Steedman | W60 | (Mussel) | Inverness | 11 | Jun |
| 16.1 | Eileen Kear | W60 | (Radley L) | Windsor | 23 | Apr |
| 18.2 | Brenda Green | W65 | (Serpentine) | Exeter | 6 | Aug |
| 17.31 | Mary Wixey | W70 | (MVAC) | Buffalo, USA | 23 | Jul |
| 21.4 | Peggy Taylor | W75 | (Oxford City) | Exeter | 6 | Aug |
| 23.1 | Mavis Williams | W80 | (Worth & D) | Thurrock | 4 | Jun |

## 200 Metres

| | | | | | | |
|---|---|---|---|---|---|---|
| 23.64 | Clova Court | W35 | (Birchfield H) | Stoke | 9 | Sep |
| 25.4 | Jocelyn Harwood | W35 | (Midd & C) | Wirral | 11 | Jun |
| 25.5 | Gowry Retchakan | W35 | (Essex L) | Hoo | 12 | Aug |
| 26.39 | Amanda Day | W40 | (Bromley V) | Exeter | 6 | Aug |
| 26.5 | S Smith | W40 | (Lincoln Well) | Manchester (BV) | 6 | Aug |
| 26.80 | Helen Godsell | W40 | (Bromley V) | Exeter | 6 | Aug |
| 26.3 | Vivien Bonner | W45 | (A F & D) | London (Col) | 3 | Sep |
| 26.72 | Barbara Blurton | W45 | (Reigate Pr) | Detroit, USA | 9 | Jul |
| 27.4 | Brenda Elliott | W45 | (Cramlington) | Jarrow | 29 | Jul |
| 28.6 | Christine Scarles | W50 | (Kilbarchan) | Pitreavie | 23 | Apr |
| 29.6 | Majorie Hocknell | W50 | (Riddings) | Jarrow | 6 | Aug |
| 29.8 | Mary Axtell | W50 | (Team Sol) | Portsmouth. | 8 | May |
| 29.2 | Una Gore | W55 | (Trowbridge) | Bath | 21 | Jun |
| 29.8 i | Jean Hulls | W55 | (Bromley V) | Birmingham | 12 | Feb |
| 33.68 | Betty Steedman | W60 | (Mussel) | Exeter | 6 | Aug |
| 33.8 | Eileen Kear | W60 | (Radley L) | Reading | 25 | Jun |
| 37.69 | Brenda Green | W65 | (Serpentine) | Buffalo, USA | 23 | Jul |
| 38.14 | Mary Wixey | W70 | (MVAC) | Detroit, USA | 9 | Jul |
| 49.66 | Peggy Taylor | W75 | (Oxford City) | Exeter | 6 | Aug |

## 400 Metres

| | | | | | | |
|---|---|---|---|---|---|---|
| 56.9 | Julie Asgill | W35 | (Trafford AC) | London (He) | 1 | Jul |
| 56.9 | Dyanna Clarke | W35 | (Thames VH) | Hayes | 14 | May |
| 58.47 | Lynn Talbert | W35 | (Thurrock H) | Mayesbrook Pk | 14 | May |
| 59.2 | S Smith | W40 | (Lincoln Well) | Manchester (BV) | 6 | Aug |
| 61.3 | Amanda Day | W40 | (Bromley V) | Exeter | 6 | Aug |
| 62.5 | Marianne Layden | W40 | (North'ton Ph) | Corby | 14 | May |
| 57.91 | Barbara Blurton | W45 | (Reigate Pr) | Buffalo, USA | 23 | Jul |
| 63.4 | Vivien Bonner | W45 | (A F & D) | London (Col) | 3 | Sep |
| 64.5 | Brenda Elliott | W45 | (Cramlington) | Exeter | 6 | Aug |
| 65.3 | Caroline Oxton | W50 | (Parkside) | Reading | 1 | Oct |
| 70.62 | Josie Kimber | W50 | (Medway) | Buffalo, USA | 23 | Jul |
| 77.3 | Joyce Smith | W55 | (Shaftesbury B) | Enfield | 24 | Apr |
| 84.3 | Betty Steedman | W60 | (Musselburgh) | Jarrow | 29 | Jul |
| 82.6 | Monica Shone | W65 | (Altrincham & D) | Exeter | 6 | Aug |
| 99.7 | Josie Waller | W70 | (Teignbridge Tr) | Exeter | 18 | Jun |

## 800 Metres

| | | | | | |
|---|---|---|---|---|---|
| 2:10.37 | Sue Bevan | W35 (Essex L) | Aldershot | 23 | Jul |
| 2:10.9 | Janet Holt | W35 (Trafford Ac) | Glasgow | 6 | May |
| 2:15.6 | Clair Brook | W35 (Lisburn AC) | Antrim | 30 | Apr |
| 2:20.6 | Marianne Layden | W40 (Northampton Ph) | Solihull | 4 | Jun |
| 2:22.03 | Jackie Walpole | W40 (Exeter H) | Exeter | 6 | Aug |
| 2:19.25 | Barbara Blurton | W45 (Reigate Pr) | Buffalo, USA | 23 | Jul |
| 2:21.5 | Pat Gallagher | W45 (Westbury H) | Solihull | 4 | Jun |
| 2:23.0 | Caroline Oxton | W50 (Parkside) | Barn Elms | 10 | Sep |
| 2:52.8 | Pam Jones | W55 (Ilford) | London (LC) | 27 | Aug |
| 3:06.7 | Toni Borthwick | W60 (Trent Park Tr) | Enfield | 15 | May |
| 3:09.3 | Joselyn Ross | W65 (Garden City J) | Thurrock | 4 | Jun |
| 3:39.1 | Josie Waller | W70 (Teignbridge Tr) | Exeter | 18 | Jun |
| 4:12.06 | Grace Bulger | W75 (New Forest R) | Exeter | 6 | Aug |

## 1500 Metres

| | | | | | |
|---|---|---|---|---|---|
| 4:31.6 | Janet Holt | W35 (Trafford AC) | Glasgow | 6 | May |
| 4:36.3 | Jill Harrison | W35 (City of Bath) | Bath | 4 | Jun |
| 4:38.3 | Margaret Boleman | W35 (Sale AC) | Birmingham | 19 | Aug |
| 4:40.9 | Carol Sharp | W40 (Edinburgh WM) | Birmingham | 19 | Aug |
| 4:48.6 | Paula Fudge | W40 (Hounslow) | Watford | 7 | May |
| 4:45.97 | Pat Gallagher | W45 (Westbury H) | Buffalo, USA | 23 | Jul |
| 4:49.7 | Jannette Stevenson | W45 (Falkirk VH) | Coatbridge | 18 | Jun |
| 4:57.4 | Caroline Oxton | W50 (Parkside) | Welwyn GC | 30 | Jul |
| 5:28.2 | Joyce Smith | W55 (Shaftesbury B) | London (Col) | 3 | Sep |
| 5:57.52 | Myfanwy Loudon | W60 (Newport H) | Buffalo, USA | 23 | Jul |
| 6:16.6 | Joselyn Ross | W65 (Garden City J) | Thurrock | 4 | Jun |
| 7:19.8 | Josie Waller | W70 (Teignbridge Tr) | Exeter | 18 | Jun |
| 8:13.1 | Grace Bulger | W75 (New Forest R) | Exeter | 6 | Aug |

## 3000 Metres

| | | | | | |
|---|---|---|---|---|---|
| 9:40.58 | Jill Harrison | W35 (City of Bath) | Loughborough | 11 | Jun |
| 9:45.0 i | Teresa Dyer | W35 (Peterborough) | Birmingham | 12 | Feb |
| 9:47.26 i | Suzanne Morley | W35 (Brighton & H) | Birmingham | 26 | Feb |
| 10:03.3 | Bronwen Cardy-Wise | W40 (Bromsgrove & R) | Birmingham | 6 | Sep |
| 10:07.1 | Paula Fudge | W40 (Hounslow) | Walton | 20 | May |
| 10:11.0 | Pat Gallagher | W45 (Westbury H) | Millfield | 8 | May |
| 10:17.7 | Jannette Stevenson | W45 (Falkirk VH) | Coatbridge | 18 | Jun |
| 10:45.8 | Elaine Statham | W50 (Stoke) | Coventry | 13 | Aug |
| 11:16.6 | Myra Garrett | W50 (Bexley Borough) | London (CP) | 22 | Apr |
| 11:48.6 | Joyce Smith | W55 (Shaftesbury B) | London (Col) | 3 | Sep |
| 13:51.2 | Joselyn Ross | W65 (Garden City J) | Enfield | 15 | May |
| 14:53.6 | Josie Waller | W70 (Teignbridge Tr) | Exeter | 18 | Jun |
| 16:53.5 | Grace Bulger | W75 (New Forest R) | Exeter | 18 | Jun |

## 5000 Metres

| | | | | | |
|---|---|---|---|---|---|
| 16:30.85 | Jill Harrison | W35 (City of Bath) | Birmingham | 15 | Jul |
| 16:49.0 | Caroline Horne | W35 (Crawley) | Hexham | 4 | May |
| 17:27.4 | Teresa Dyer | W35 (Peterborough) | Wavertree | 2 | Jul |
| 17:15.9 | Paula Fudge | W40 (Hounslow) | Wirral | 11 | Jun |
| 18:24.5 | Judith Meeten | W40 (Northampton Ph) | Exeter | 6 | Aug |
| 18:33.6 | Denise Wakefield | W40 (Sale) | Bolton | 14 | May |
| 17:57.9 | Pat Gallagher | W45 (Westbury H) | Barry | 30 | Apr |
| 18:24.09 | Jane Davies | W45 (Epsom & Ewell) | Stoke | 10 | Sep |
| 18:41.78 | Elaine Statham | W50 (Stoke) | Wrexham | 25 | Jun |
| 19:13.2 | Dot Fellowes | W50 (Cannock & St) | Swansea | 11 | Jun |
| 20:53.2 | Joyce Smith | W55 (Shaftesbury B) | Watford | 26 | Jun |
| 21:45.85 | Myfanwy Loudon | W60 (Newport H) | Buffalo, USA | 23 | Jul |
| 25:02.38 | Betty Forster | W65 (Shaftesbury B) | Buffalo, USA | 23 | Jul |
| 28:30.9 | Grace Bulger | W75 (New Forest R) | Exeter | 6 | Aug |

## 10000 Metres

| | | | | | |
|---|---|---|---|---|---|
| 35:29.67 | Jill Harrison | W35 (City of Bath) | Bedford | 1 | Jul |
| 35:44.98 | Fiona Phillips | W35 (City of Bath) | Bedford | 1 | Jul |
| 39:45.1 | Sabrina Diggins | W40 (Porstmouth) | Exeter | 6 | Aug |
| 41:56.0 | Daphne Barclay | W45 (Wolds Vets) | Stretford | 17 | Sep |
| 38:51.71 | Elaine Statham | W50 (Stoke) | Buffalo, USA | 23 | Jul |
| 40:48.8 | Myra Garrett | W50 (Bexley Boro) | Exeter | 6 | Aug |
| 40:58.84 | Elizabeth Gilchrist | W50 (Scottish Vets) | Buffalo, USA | 23 | Jul |
| 44:33.0 | Mary Anstey | W55 (Garden City J) | Exeter | 6 | Aug |
| 44:57.13 | Myfanwy Loudon | W60 (Newport H) | Bufallo, USA | 23 | Jul |
| 52:43.41 | Betty Forster | W65 (Shaftesbury B) | Buffalo, USA | 23 | Jul |
| 58:48.8 | Grace Bulger | W75 (New Forest R) | Exeter | 6 | Aug |

## 80 Metres Hurdles

| | | | | | |
|---|---|---|---|---|---|
| 13.53 | Gilluan Hevingham | W40 (N Devon) | Exeter | 6 | Aug |
| 14.3 | Sue Burridge | W40 (Woking) | Thurrock | 4 | Jun |
| 12.9 | Jean Wills | W45 (Bournemouth) | Exeter | 18 | Jun |
| 14.48 | Emily McMahon | W45 (R Sutton C/Enf) | Exeter | 6 | Aug |
| 15.2 | Nanette Cross | W50 (Bromley V) | Enfield | 24 | Jun |
| 15.2 | Evaun Williams | W55 (Ex Ladies/Enf) | Thurrock | 4 | Jun |
| 15.7 | Carine Graham | W55 (Woking) | London (TB) | 28 | May |
| 17.9 | Betty Steedman | W60 (Musselburgh) | Sheffield | 10 | Sep |

## 100 Metres Hurdles

| | | | | | |
|---|---|---|---|---|---|
| 13.36 | Clova Court | W35 (Birchfield H) | Gateshead | 12 | Aug |
| 14.07 w | Jocelyn Harwood | W35 (NSP/Midd & C) | Gateshead | 17 | Jun |
| 16.6 | Sarah Owen | W40 (Newport H) | Newport | 17 | Jun |
| 17.4 | Gillian Hevingham | W40 (N Devon) | Watford | 2 | Sep |
| 19.4 | Janice Ferry | W45 (A F & D) | Redruth | 20 | May |
| 19.6 | Jean Wills | W45 (Bournemouth) | London (He) | 20 | May |
| 19.6 | Marjorie Hocknell | W50 (Riddings YAC) | Jarrow | 6 | Aug |

## 300 Metres Hurdles

| | | | | | |
|---|---|---|---|---|---|
| 53.3 | Marjorie Hocknell | W50 (Riddings YAC) | Grimsby | 15 | Jul |
| 55.86 | Nanette Cross | W50 (Bromley V) | Buffalo, USA | 16 | Jul |

## 400 Metres Hurdles

| | | | | | |
|---|---|---|---|---|---|
| 57.18 | Gowry Retchakan | W35 (Essex L) | Birmingham | 15 | Jul |
| 62.4 | Veronica Boden | W35 (Trafford) | Trafford | 6 | Aug |
| 65.5 | Dyanna Clarke | W35 (Thames VH) | Ilford | 30 | Apr |
| 69.8 | Jenny Pearson | W40 (Hallamshire H) | Peterborough | 7 | May |
| 71.3 | Jackie Walpole | W40 (Exeter H) | Exeter | 30 | Jul |
| 71.03 | Jean Wills | W45 (Bournemouth) | Buffalo, USA | 23 | Jul |
| 72.1 | Lynda Robson | W45 (Leamington) | Leamington Spa | 9 | Sep |
| 74.8 | Marjorie Hocknell | W50 (Riddings YAC) | Jarrow | 6 | Aug |

## 1500 Metres Steeplechase

| | | | | | |
|---|---|---|---|---|---|
| 6:56.2 | Siobhan Newman | W35 (Horsham BSH) | Crawley | 4 | Jul |
| 6:15.8 | Jane Davies | W45 (Epsom & Ewell) | Crawley | 9 | Jul |
| 6:57.5 | Janice Gumbley | W45 (Horsham BSH) | Crawley | 4 | Jul |

## 3000 Metres Steeplechase (2'6")

| | | | | | |
|---|---|---|---|---|---|
| 15:21.7 | Siobhan Newman | W35 (Horsham BSH) | Horsham | 20 | Aug |

## High Jump

| | | | | | |
|---|---|---|---|---|---|
| 1.72 | Jennifer Brown | W35 (Ashford) | Buffalo, USA | 23 | Jul |
| 1.65 | Louise Gittens | W35 (Southampton) | Enfield | 29 | Apr |
| 1.59 H | Manndy Laing | W35 (Liverpool H) | Sheffield | 10 | Sep |
| 1.45 | Pam Garvey | W40 (Corby) | Exeter | 6 | Aug |
| 1.45 | Gillian Hevingham | W40 (North Devon) | Buffalo, USA | 23 | Jul |
| 1.40 | Jenny Piercy | W40 (Epsom & Ewell) | Walton | 31 | May |
| 1.30 | Maria Williams | W45 (Rowntrees) | Leeds | 23 | Jul |

| 1.28 | Catherine Geddes | W45 (Kilbarchan) | Linwood | 24 Aug |
|---|---|---|---|---|
| 1.28 P | Emily McMahon | W45 (Royal SC) | Solihull | 13 Aug |
| 1.30 | Joanne Smallwood | W50 (Halesowen) | Warley | 23 Jul |
| 1.25 | Janet Phillips | W50 (Exeter H) | Exeter | 18 Jun |
| 1.23 | Carol Morris | W50 (Birchfield H) | Redditch | 4 May |
| 1.19 | Evaun Williams | W55 (Essex L) | Buffalo, USA | 23 Jul |
| 1.05 H | Betty Steedman | W60 (Musselburgh) | Sheffield | 10 Sep |
| 0.96 | Mary Wixey | W70 (MVAC) | Solihull | 4 Jun |

**Pole Vault**

| 2.10 | Bridget Wood | W35 (Ryston R) | Norwich | 14 May |
|---|---|---|---|---|
| 2.05 | Debbie Singleton | W35 (Walton) | Exeter | 6 Aug |
| 2.45 | Gillian Hevingham | W40 (North Devon) | Exeter | 6 Aug |
| 2.10 | Judi Stafford | W40 (Lincoln Well) | Lincoln | 23 Jul |
| 2.00 | Carole Eames | W45 (Bournemouth) | Southampton | 9 Apr |
| 1.70 | Julia Parslew | W45 (Ryston R) | Kings Lynn | 2 Aug |
| 1.50 | Christine Eades | W50 (Rhondda) | Wales | 9 May |
| 2.00 | Dorothy McLennan | W55 (Hounslow) | Watford | 7 May |

**Long Jump**

| 5.66 | Carol Zeniou | W35 (Hounslow) | London (PH) | 5 Jul |
|---|---|---|---|---|
| 5.39 | Carol Filer | W35 (Norfolk O) | Exeter | 6 Aug |
| 5.37 | Jennifer Brown | W35 (Ashford) | Bromley | 11 Jun |
| 4.77 | Rowena Richardson | W40 (Immingham) | Lincoln | 23 Jul |
| 4.70 | Margaret Daniels | W40 (Port F & D) | Crawley | 9 Jul |
| 4.78 | Emily McMahon | W45 (Royal SC) | Aldershot | 12 Aug |
| 4.60 | Brenda Elliott | W45 (Cramlington) | Jarrow | 23 Sep |
| 4.45 | Sylvia Wood | W50 (Linlithgow) | Jarrow | 29 Jul |
| 4.03 | Evaun Williams | W55 (Essex L) | Enfield | 15 May |
| 3.78 | Betty Steedman | W60 (Musselburgh) | Exeter | 6 Aug |
| 3.31 | Mary Wixey | W70 (MVAC) | Solihull | 4 Jun |

**Triple Jump**

| 11.36 | Jennifer Brown | W35 (Ashford) | London (CP) | 14 May |
|---|---|---|---|---|
| 10.29 | Linda Anderson | W35 (Salisbury & D) | Exeter | 18 Jun |
| 10.24 | Debbie Keenleyside | W35 (Dacorum & T) | Perivale | 30 Apr |
| 10.05 | Gwen Cunningham | W40 (Bexley Boro) | Hoo | 10 Sep |
| 9.84 | Helen Godsell | W40 (Bromley V) | London (Col) | 3 Sep |
| 9.67 | Jean Wills | W45 (Bournemouth) | Portsmouth | 25 Jun |
| 9.49 | Pat Oakes | W45 (Dartford H) | Bromley | 9 Apr |
| 9.00 | Sylvia Wood | W50 (Linlithgow) | Glasgow | 23 Apr |
| 8.61 | Christine Terry | W50 (Worthing & D) | Brighton | 6 May |
| 8.46 | Carina Graham | W55 (Woking) | Buffalo, USA | 23 Jul |
| 7.97 | Betty Steedman | W60 (Musselburgh) | Exeter | 6 Aug |
| 6.14 | Mary Wixey | W70 (MVAC) | Buffalo, USA | 23 Jul |

**Shot**

| 18.44 | Judith Oakes | W35 (Croydon H) | Kilkenny, IRE | 2 Sep |
|---|---|---|---|---|
| 14.08 | Clova Court | W35 (Birchfield H) | Birmingham | 20 May |
| 11.03 | Claire Cameron | W35 (City of Glasgow) | Greenock | 4 Jun |
| 12.31 | Bronwin Carter | W40 (Portsmouth) | Portsmouth | 20 May |
| 10.64 | Jacqueline Wright | W40 (Bracknell) | Bracknell | 22 Jul |
| 10.00 | S Herrington | W40 (Rugby & Dist) | Rugby | 29 Aug |
| 10.61 | Barbara Terry | W45 (Bromley V) | Exeter | 6 Aug |
| 9.23 | Romana Martin | W45 (Cambridge & C) | Braintree | 11 Jun |
| 11.50 | Barbara Terry | W50 (Bromley V) | Reading | 1 Oct |
| 9.75 | Margery Swinton | W50 (Moray Road R) | Exeter | 6 Aug |
| 9.62 | Liz Sissons | W50 (Epsom & Ewell) | London (TB) | 27 May |
| 11.86 | Evaun Williams | W55 (Essex L) | Buffalo, USA | 23 Jul |
| 7.60 | Averil Williams | W60 (Newport H) | Barry | 20 Sep |
| 9.09 | Jo Ogden | W65 (Thurrock H) | London (LC) | 27 Aug |
| 4.77 | Mary Wixey | W70 (MVAC) | Reading | 1 Oct |
| 4.27 | Mavis Williams | W80 (Worthing & D) | London (CP) | 5 Feb |

## Discus

| | | | | | | |
|---|---|---|---|---|---|---|
| 49.90 | Judith Oakes | W35 | (Croydon H) | Croydon | 13 | May |
| 39.42 | Claire Cameron | W35 | (City of Glasgow) | Wishaw | 13 | May |
| 36.42 | V Duffy | W35 | (Met Police) | London (BP) | 15 | May |
| 42.02 | Jacqueline Wright | W40 | (Bracknell) | Exeter | 6 | Aug |
| 38.80 | Bronwin Carter | W40 | (Portsmouth) | Portsmouth | 26 | Jun |
| 30.12 | Val Bovell | W45 | (Yeovil Oly) | Exeter | 18 | Jun |
| 29.12 | Barbara Terry | W45 | (Bromley V) | London (Col) | 3 | Sep |
| 27.48 | Joyce Rammell | W45 | (Dumfries) | Inverness | 10 | Jun |
| 24.44 | Margery Swinton | W50 | (Moray Road R) | Exeter | 6 | Aug |
| 23.82 | Vivian Branch | W50 | (Radley L) | London (Col) | 3 | Sep |
| 30.00 | Evaun Williams | W55 | (Essex L) | Buffalo, USA | 23 | Jul |
| 35.22 | Rosemary Chrimes | W60 | (Halesowen) | Warley | 23 | Jul |
| 19.88 | Jo Ogden | W65 | (Thurrock H) | Solihull | 3 | Sep |
| 12.74 | Mary Wixey | W70 | (MVAC) | Burton | 23 | Apr |
| 9.54 | Mavis Williams | W80 | (Worthing & D) | Exeter | 5 | Aug |

## Hammer

| | | | | | | |
|---|---|---|---|---|---|---|
| 41.90 | Jennifer Cunnane | W35 | (Wakefield H) | Middlesbrough | 9 | Apr |
| 34.92 | Beatrice Simpson | W35 | (Bromley V) | Crawley | 9 | Jul |
| 33.70 | Jenny Earle | W35 | (Basingstoke) | Basingstoke | 12 | Aug |
| 34.96 | Jennifer Clarke | W40 | (Peterborough) | Wakefield | 17 | Sep |
| 30.06 | Jan Colston | W40 | (Tonbridge) | Dartford | 13 | Aug |
| 33.12 | Lesley Shrosbree | W45 | (Harlow) | Reading | 1 | Oct |
| 32.92 | Rosemarie Alexander | W45 | (Bournemouth) | Buffalo, USA | 23 | Jul |
| 33.92 | Barbara Terry | W50 | (Bromley V) | Reading | 1 | Oct |
| 30.66 | Margery Swinton | W50 | (Moray Road R) | Mulheim, GER | 24 | Sep |
| 30.34 | Linda Fogg | W50 | (Shaftesbury B) | London (Col) | 3 | Sep |
| 44.78 | Evaun Williams | W55 | (Essex L) | Detroit, USA | 9 | Jul |
| 24.76 | Barbara Dunsford | W60 | (Belgrave H) | Reading | 1 | Oct |
| 25.06 | Jo Ogden | W65 | (Thurrock H) | Solihull | 3 | Sep |

## Javelin

| | | | | | | |
|---|---|---|---|---|---|---|
| 46.80 | Clova Court | W35 | (Birchfield H) | Derby | 23 | Jul |
| 35.84 | Manndy Laing | W35 | (Liverpool H) | Sheffield | 10 | Sep |
| 38.44 | Jean Lintern | W40 | (Crawley) | Crawley | 19 | Jul |
| 30.54 | Diana Pearce | W40 | (Harlow) | Harlow | 11 | Apr |
| 28.60 | Lesley Eldridge | W45 | (Hull Achilles) | York | 30 | Apr |
| 29.04 | Averil Green | W50 | (Eastbourne R) | Eastbourne | 31 | Jul |
| 37.02 | Evaun Williams | W55 | (Essex L) | Detroit, USA | 9 | Jul |
| 30.90 | Averil Williams | W60 | (Newport H) | Exeter | 6 | Aug |
| 28.00 | Jo Ogden | W65 | (Thurrock H) | London (LC) | 27 | Aug |
| 11.22 | Mary Wixey | W70 | (MVAC) | Reading | 1 | Oct |
| 10.12 | Mavis Williams | W80 | (Worthing & D) | Southend | 2 | Sep |

## Pentathlon

| | | | | | | |
|---|---|---|---|---|---|---|
| 3060 | Jennifer Brown | W35 | (Ashford) | London (CP) | 22 | Jan |
| 2917 | Danea Herron | W35 | (Finn Valley) | Sheffield | 5 | Mar |
| 2204 | Jane Thwaites | W35 | (Horsham BSH) | Crawley | 10 | Sep |
| 2623.58 | Susan Laws | W40 | (Derwentside) | Jarrow | 23 | Sep |
| 3307.86 | Brenda Elliott | W45 | (Cramlington) | Jarrow | 23 | Sep |
| 3161 | Emily McMahon | W45 | (Royal SC) | Solihull | 13 | Aug |
| 3137 | Jackie Charles | W50 | (VAC) | Sheffield | 5 | Mar |

## Heptathlon

| | | | | | | |
|---|---|---|---|---|---|---|
| 5208 | Manndy Laing | W35 | (Liverpool H) | Sheffield | 10 | Sep |
| 5153 | C Barrett | W35 | (Braintree) | Thurrock | 24 | Sep |
| 5062 | Jennifer Brown | W35 | (Ashford) | Buffalo, USA | 23 | Jul |
| 3628 | Gillian Hevingham | W40 | (North Devon) | Buffalo, USA | 23 | Jul |
| 3952 | Christine Cox | W45 | (Rigby & Dist) | Sheffield | 10 | Sep |
| 3751 | Maria Wilaiims | W45 | (Rowntrees) | Sheffield | 10 | Sep |
| 5388 | Evaun Williams | W55 | (Essex L) | Buffalo, USA | 23 | Jul |
| 4149 | Betty Steedman | W60 | (Musselburgh) | Sheffield | 10 | Sep |

# MENS INDEX

A BDY Thomas U15, Northampton :
PV - 3.10
ABERNETHY David J. V40 5.09.55, Barr & F :
DT - 43.32 (46.70-85), JT - 56.62 (63.86-86)
ACHIKE Onochie U23 31.01.75, Crawley :
100 - 10.96 (10.95-94), 200 - 22.15,
LJ - 7.34 (7.46-93),
TJ - 15.94w/15.91 (16.67w/16.53-94)
ACHURCH Simon U23 27.12.74, Peterbro :
JT - 60.16
ADAMS Brian V45 13.03.49, Leics WC :
3kW - 13:10.03 (12:02.2-76),
10kW - 46:50.0 (42:40.0-75),
20kW - 1:38:48.4t (1:27:46-75)
ADAMS Christopher U15 18.07.81, C of Stoke :
HTB - 48.94
ADAMS Francis 19.10.69, Thames Valley :
LJ - 6.97
ADAMS Nathan U15 14.04.82, Sheffield RWC :
3kW - 15:58.49, 3kWR - 15:30
ADAMS Nigel 17.07.62, Swansea :
10k - 31:19.65 (28:51.05-89)
ADAMS Simeon U13 1.07.84, Sheffield RWC :
2kW - 11:24.0
ADEPEGBA Sunny 6.06.71, Haringey :
200 - 21.4w/21.79 (21.5-90/21.53-91)
*AFILAKA Carl 13.07.68, Oxford City/TRI :*
*100 - 10.7/10.87*
AFILAKA Michael 16.11.71, N&E B/Staffs Un :
60 - 6.80i, 100 - 10.46w/10.63,
200 - 21.2/21.22 (21.09w-93/21.22-94)
AFILAKA Tunde, Thames Valley :
60 - 6.9i/6.93i
AGGARD T. U17, Hounslow :
400HY - 56.9
AGYEPONG Francis K. 16.06.65, Shaftes B:
TJ - 17.29wA/17.24w/17.18
AHERNE Christopher U17 21.12.79, Cardiff :
HTY - 53.34
AHMED Fayyaz 10.04.66, Shaftesbury Barnet :
HJ - 2.05 (2.21-86)
AHMED Idris U15 30.10.80, Hallamshire :
3k - 9:34.9
AIREY Martin 28.10.70, Brighton :
800 - 1:50.53
AITKEN Steven 8.07.66, SGA (Prof) :
SP - 14.14 (14.91-90)
AKESTER Neil U17 6.09.79, City of Hull :
400 - 50.47
AKINSANYA Oluwafemi 29.11.69, Peterbro :
LJ - 7.07w/7.00 (7.22-91), TJ - 16.03
AL-KOWARRI Ahmed U17 30.11.78, Aberd'n :
400 - 49.21
ALDWINKLE Matthew U23 23.08.74, Notts :
400 - 48.57 (48.5-94)
ALEXANDER Mark U13 17.09.82, Perth :
400 - 57.4
ALEXOPOULOS Dinos U20 2.12.76,
Yeovil Olympiads/Millfield Sch : SPJ - 16.17
ALLAN David Neil 17.10.70, Edinb SH/Inv :
HT - 60.12
ALLAN Graeme U15 24.09.80, Elgin :
60HB - 9.01i, 80HB - 11.76w/12.4,
SPB - 15.42, DTB - 45.48, HTB - 49.80
ALLAN Jason 17.09.72, Clydesdale :
HJ - 2.01 (2.05-93)

ALLAN Robert U17 4.11.78, Haringey :
200 - 22.62
ALLARD James U20 11.05.77, Birchfield :
60HJ - 8.16i,
110HJ - 15.2/15.49 (14.88w/15.2-94)
ALLEN Clarence 1.04.64, Herne Hill :
110H - 14.9/14.92 (14.8-92/14.82-94)
ALLEN George U15 19.10.80, Rowntrees :
TJ - 12.66
ALLEN Mark 23.09.66, Border :
100 - 10.87 (10.6-92/10.63w-93/10.74-94),
200 - 21.0w/21.10
ALLEN Sam U17 26.10.78, Rowntrees :
400HY - 56.9/57.14, OctY - 4982
ALLEN Stewart 1.02.70, Reading :
800 - 1:51.9
ALLISON Joseph 16.09.59, Newham & E B :
TJ - 15.05 (15.93w-86/15.86-85)
ALLISON Matthew U23 26.02.73, Leeds :
DT - 41.28, Dec - 6306 (6673-94)
ALLISTER David U15 22.09.80, Wirral :
PV - 3.30
*AMARA Prince U23 15.03.73, Woodf'd Gr/SLE :*
*800 - 1:51.23*
AMOS Matthew U17 20.11.78, Northampton :
1.5kSt - 4:25.72
ANDERSON Colin Lloyd 18.02.59, Team S/Army :
400H - 53.41 (51.85-90)
ANDERSON Keith 10.08.57, Bingley :
5k - 14:16.0 (14:09.00-94),
10kR - 29:23 (29:06-94), HMar - 1:04:38
ANDERSON Mark U20 5.11.77, City of Stoke :
110HJ - 15.16w/15.21, 400H - 54.60
ANGELL Steven 8.04.70, Old Gaytonians :
HT - 58.36
ANNAND A., Army :
Mar - 2:26:02
ANSELL Keith 30.03.62, Braintree :
SP - 14.66
ANSTISS Timothy J. 17.11.61, Hounslow :
PV - 4.30 (4.90-80)
ANTHONY T. U13, Verlea :
100 - 11.6, 200 - 24.1,
400 - 59.7, 80HC - 12.5
ANTOINE Leslie 16.12.65, Belgrave :
110H - 15.3/15.43 (14.97w-87/15.05-89)
APPLEBY Chris U15, Cornwall AC :
JTB - 48.82
APPS James U17 29.04.80, Blackheath :
JTY - 55.18
ARCHAMPONG James Quarshie U20 14.03.76,
Swansea : 60H - 8.03i (8.01i-94),
60HJ - 8.09i, 110HJ - 14.3w/14.44 (14.24-93),
110H - 14.53 (14.18-94)
ARCHER Clayton U20 29.05.76, Thames VH :
100 - 10.81, 200 - 21.54
ARIS Mike, :
24HrT - 213.133
ARMSTRONG Brett U20 9.09.76, Sandwell :
PV - 4.60
ARMSTRONG J. Simon 29.05.62, Bournem'th :
SP - 15.66 (16.52-90), DT - 44.86 (50.22-92)
ARMSTRONG Paul U17 20.10.79, Pitreavie :
OctY - 4350
ARMSTRONG Samuel U23 17.02.74, Nithsdale :
JT - 58.20

319

ASARE Maxwell 14.09.68, Skyrac :
60 - 6.96i, 100 - 10.7
ASHE Richard U23 5.10.74, Hillingdon :
800 - 1:52.3, 1500 - 3:42.9
ASHURST Andrew John 2.01.65, Sale :
PV - 5.20 (5.45i-92/5.40-88)
ASPDEN Richard U20 15.10.76, Belgrave :
HJ - 2.16
ASTON Peter R.G. V50 21.02.45, Woodf'd Gr :
HT - 46.38 (62.32-75)
ATKINS Matthew U20 23.06.77, Derby & Co :
JT - 64.68
ATKINSON Michael A. 6.03.58, Annadale Str :
SP - 13.48 (16.35-81)
ATKINSON Peter J. 13.12.65, Leeds :
1500 - 3:51.32
ATKINSON Steven U17 24.02.79, Middlesbro & C :
PV - 3.70, DecY - 5066
ATTWOOD Terry U17 8.09.78, St Albans :
DTY - 42.96
AUDSLEY Alistair 17.08.65, Manx :
100 - 10.87w/11.08, 200 - 22.08w (22.0-94)
AUGUSTUS K. U17, Hounslow :
200 - 22.5
AUSTIN James 9.08.65, Clydesdale :
3kSt - 9:12.2 (9:05.32-94)
AUSTIN Stuart U17 21.03.79, Blackheath :
800 - 1:57.38, 1500 - 4:05.5
AYRE Stephen C. 20.10.67, Morpeth :
DT - 48.56

BACK Stuart U20 12.05.77, Old Gaytonians :
HJ - 1.96
BACKLEY Stephen James 12.02.69, Camb H :
JT - 88.54 (91.46-92)
BAILEY David U23 19.10.73, Telford :
JT - 62.10
BAILEY Matthew U15 16.02.81, Barnsley :
800 - 2:01.73
BAILEY Stuart U20 6.08.78, Wigan :
800 - 1:54.9, 3kSt - 9:39.0
BAILLIE Christopher U15 21.04.81, Vict PAAC :
80HB - 11.44w/11.7/11.87, PenB - 2446
BAILLIE Ross U20 26.09.77, Victoria P AAC :
60 - 6.89i, 100 - 10.78w/10.96 (10.73w/10.89-94),
200 - 21.6w/21.7/21.75 (21.67i-94), 60H - 8.04i,
110HJ - 14.6w/14.8, 110H - 14.4w/14.54
BAIRD Laurence U20 14.12.77, Cleethorpes :
400 - 49.25i/49.25 (49.0-94)
BAKER Darran 30.03.67, Thames Valley :
HJ - 2.00 (2.15-92)
BAKER George U20 14.08.76, Newham & E B :
SP - 13.86, SPJ - 16.02
BAKER John U15 28.01.81, Blackheath :
1500 - 4:15.7
BAKER Peter U23 6.02.73, Portsmouth :
1500 - 3:51.6 (3:49.5-93)
BALDOCK Sean U20 3.12.76, Hastings :
400 - 48.79
BALDWIN Stefan M. 26.04.70, Thames Valley :
JT - 67.78 (72.92-93)
BALE Paul U20 20.12.76, Warwicks Sch :
JT - 56.72
BALL Andrew U13 13.05.83, Birchfield :
2kW - 11:20.0
BALL James R. 17.02.63, Steyning :
3kW - 13:32.4 (12:20.0-87),
20kW - 1:38:21 (1:28:46-87)

BALOGUN Anthony 7.02.66, Woodford Green :
800 - 1:50.8 (1:49.2-91/1:49.26-94)
BAMFORD Matthew 19.09.58, Hillingdon :
JT - 61.98
BANDA Rasheed U17 18.03.80, Eastb'ne Col :
LJ - 6.49
BANKS Peter G. 9.12.60, Blackburn :
Mar - 2:23:47, 3kSt - 9:23.8 (9:03.7-85)
BANNISTER Dominic 1.04.68, Shaftesbury B :
5k - 14:08.85
BANNISTER Simon U15 16.04.81, Ryston :
HJ - 1.76i/1.75
BARBER Michael W. U23 19.10.73, Bir/Staffs Un :
PV - 5.42
BARBER Nick U17 22.11.78, Hallamshire :
SPY - 15.76, DTY - 41.70, OctY - 4624
BARDEN Anthony J. 15.10.60, Basildon :
Mar - 2:24:21
BARDEN Spencer Christian U23 31.03.73, GEC :
1500 - 3:44.3, 3k - 8:00.46 (7:58.08-93),
5k - 13:57.63
BARGH Andrew U20 21.08.76, Team S/LSAC :
110H - 15.37w/15.5, 400H - 53.6/54.16
BARKER Leo U17 26.12.78, Diss :
100HY - 13.53, LJ - 7.00, TJ - 13.69,
SPY - 14.05io, OctY - 5423
BARKER Scott U20 22.07.77, Kettering :
DTJ - 43.20
BARLOW Alden, Doncaster :
24HrT - 221.920km
BARNARD Paul 27.07.72, Edinburgh/
Middlesbro & C/NESH : HT - 62.70
BARNES John U15 6.05.82, Hull Springhead :
DTB - 38.80, HTB - 49.44
BARNES Matthew John 12.01.68, Enfield :
1500 - 3:42.96 (3:38.31-93),
2kSt - 5:46.5, 3kSt - 8:53.9
BARNETSON David 1.07.71, Edin SH/Inv :
110H - 15.23, HJ - 2.17 (2.19-92)
BARRABLE Nick U23 8.06.74, Tonbridge :
3kW - 13:01.8
BARRETT Clint U20 21.11.77, Braintree :
DecJ - 5368
BARROS Demetrio 29.06.71, Hounslow :
JT - 64.66 (66.92-93)
BARROW Mark 30.06.68, Liverpool Pemb :
800 - 1:52.06 (1:52.04-92),
1500 - 3:51.9 (3:51.9-94)
BARTLETT Stuart G. 20.10.64, Thames VH :
JT - 58.44 (59.14-94)
BARTON Bruce 2.02.64, Belgrave :
3kSt - 9:24.43
BARTON Tim 3.10.70, Charnwood :
100 - 10.7 (10.99-94), 200 - 22.0 (22.0-94)
BARTSCH Matthew 12.12.64, Crawley :
200 - 22.0w/22.17w
(21.5-92/21.56w-93/21.68-94)
BASQUIL Conor U17 2.04.79, Enfield :
1.5kSt - 4:30.91
BASTILLE Gregory U23 25.04.73, Hounslow :
HT - 47.18 (49.24-94)
BATCHELOR Perry U23 11.12.75, Cov G :
110H - 15.2/15.38 (14.7w/14.81w/14.9/15.10-94)
BATESON Matthew 14.05.72, Old Gaytonians :
3kSt - 9:23.3
BATTY Christopher James U15 6.09.80, Invicta :
800 - 2:04.95

320

BAULCH James Steven U23 3.05.73, Cardiff :
  60 - 6.98i (6.94i-93), 100 - 10.51,
  200 - 20.86w/21.32 (20.84-94), 400 - 45.14
BEARD Gareth U17 28.02.79, Dudley & Stour:
  800 - 1:57.7
BEARD Keith 8.11.61, Leiden :
  JT - 67.02 (76.10-91)
BEASLEY Graham U20 24.10.77, Luton :
  100 - 10.8/10.99 (10.7/10.93-94),
  200 - 21.34 (21.3w/21.32w-94)
BEATTIE Jim U23 22.07.73, Lochgelly :
  400 - 47.73
BEATTIE William U13 22.10.82, Nithsdale :
  75HC - 12.41w
BEAUCHAMP William 9.09.70, Ealing,S & Mx :
  HT - 62.92
BEAUMONT Paul 27.03.63, Belgrave/Army :
  400H - 54.0 (51.23-89)
BEAUMONT Richard 2.05.71, Bicester RR :
  Mar - 2:29:00 (2:28:15-94)
BEAVERS A., Oxford Univ :
  3kSt - 9:22.4
BECKWITH Andrew U17 22.04.79, Invicta :
  1500 - 4:00.7, 3k - 8:50.40
BEDFORD Christopher 28.01.70, Wakefield :
  400 - 50.82
BEERLING Mark U20 16.03.76, Oxford City :
  5k - 15:05.74
BEGEN Thomas U17 14.04.79, Shettleston :
  100 - 10.88w/11.0/11.03,
  200 - 22.4/23.08, LJ - 6.50
BEHARIE Jonathan U15 21.09.80, Croydon :
  400 - 52.65
BEHARRELL Mark U15 10.01.81, City of Hull :
  PV - 3.30
BELL John U23 10.09.73, NSP/Loughbro St :
  400H - 53.88 (53.70-92)
BELL Keith U23 31.12.74, Chelmsford :
  Dec - 5054
BELL Martin 9.04.61, Annan/Splott C :
  3kW - 11:53.3, 10kW - 41:13.65,
  20kW - 1:27:05 (1:25:42-92)
BELL Matthew U20 2.06.78, Corby :
  HT - 54.00, HTJ - 57.14
BELL Michael U20 23.11.77, Coventry Godiva :
  400 - 48.51
BELL Simon 26.12.66, Cambridge Harriers :
  3kSt - 8:54.3
BELL Stuart 29.07.67, Chester Le Street :
  5k - 14:23.1, 10k - 29:45.6, 3kSt - 9:16.9
BELSHAM Matthew 11.10.71, Sale :
  PV - 5.30 (5.35-93)
BENN Andrew U20 2.09.77, Blackh'th/WLHS :
  HT - 53.56, HTJ - 60.22, JT - 60.80
BENN Thomas U17 20.04.80, Woodford Gr :
  60HY - 8.43i, 100HY - 13.34w/13.4/13.66,
  PV - 4.00
BENNETT Chris U23, :
  PV - 4.15
BENNETT Christopher U15 18.10.80, Soton C :
  200 - 23.5, 400 - 51.84
BENNETT Martin 14.10.67, Old Gaytonians :
  200 - 22.0/22.13 (21.7-93)
BENNETT Michael U15 22.11.80, Blackheath :
  HTB - 47.02
BENNETT Paul 9.08.71, Rotherham :
  800 - 1:51.8 (1:51.1-93),
  1500 - 3:47.9 (3:47.9-92)

BENNETT Richard U17 31.03.79, Bexley :
  HJ - 1.98
BENNETT Simon 16.10.72, N Devon :
  JT - 64.16
BENSON Mark 21.12.63, Leeds :
  800 - 1:52.7 (1:48.78-93),
  3k - 8:18.0, 5k - 14:36.0
BENT Colin 12.04.70, Shaftesbury B /RAF :
  HJ - 2.14
BENTHAM Kermitt E. 16.04.60, Thames VH :
  400 - 48.23 (46.57-87)
BENTHAM Nicolas Peter 7.12.70, Doncaster :
  800 - 1:50.1 (1:49.4-92),
  1k - 2:24.0i, 1500 - 3:49.1 (3:48.9-93)
BERGIN Steven 17.06.66, Gateshead :
  SP - 15.12 (16.09-89)
BERGQVIST Paul 17.08.72, Manx :
  400 - 48.5/49.19 (48.4un-93/49.08-91)
BERHRE Tsegay U15 15.01.81, Thames VH :
  3k - 9:37.43
BERNARD Darren 15.06.69, Herne Hill :
  400 - 49.0 (46.65-88)
BERRY Eric H. V40 23.04.54, Yeovil Oly :
  HT - 47.74/48.32un (62.00-74)
BERRY P., Andover :
  JT - 56.64
BERWICK Christopher V45 1.05.46, Leics WC :
  50kW - 4:39:27 (4:23:22-86)
BESWICK Christopher U23 9.10.75, E Ches :
  800 - 1:52.7
BESWICK Paul A. 5.12.68, GEC :
  PV - 4.60 (4.80ns-94/4.75-93)
BETTRIDGE Paul J. 27.02.57, Havering :
  Mar - 2:30:16 (2:21:15-92)
BETTS Edward G. 18.02.71, Queens Park :
  200 - 22.0w (22.0-94), 400 - 48.5/49.10 (47.9-94),
  400H - 51.24 (51.15-94)
BEVAN Nigel Charles 3.01.68, Belgrave :
  JT - 77.14 (81.70-92)
BEVAN Trystan U23 22.08.75, Swansea :
  400H - 55.41
BIGHAM David Bryce 4.07.71, Woodford Gr :
  110H - 15.1 (14.5w-91/14.59-92),
  JT - 59.22 (65.80-94)
BINNS Andrew U17 12.03.79, Blackpool :
  HJ - 1.97
BIRCHALL Matthew 11.01.71, Blackburn :
  LJ - 6.90 (7.09-94)
BIRCHALL Matthew John 1.11.71, Old G :
  400H - 54.02 (52.76-90)
BIRCHALL Rob 14.06.70, Peterborough :
  5k - 14:28.83 (14:16.1-94), 10k - 30:16.20
BIRD Christian U17 19.09.78, Reading :
  100HY - 13.7/13.92
BIRD Justin Paul 3.05.71, Morpeth :
  400 - 48.59 (47.68-94)
BIRSE Stephen U20 8.10.77, Middlesbro & C :
  JT - 57.92
BISHOP Gary 3.08.63, Croydon :
  Mar - 2:24:04
BISHOP Mark Andrew Paul 12.02.67, Havering :
  400 - 48.66 (46.49-89), 400H - 51.96 (51.28-89)
BLACK Chris V45 1.01.50, Edinburgh SH :
  HT - 59.18 (70.0-83)
BLACK David James U17 9.10.78, Cann & St:
  DTY - 47.42
BLACK Iain Russell 18.09.70, Edinburgh SH :
  PV - 4.45

BLACK Lee U17 26.11.78, Corby :
400 - 49.47, HJ - 1.90, OctY - 4873
BLACK Roger Anthony 31.03.66, Team Sol :
100 - 10.49 (10.4-87), 400 - 44.59 (44.59-86)
BLACKMAN Craig U17 3.04.79, Rowntrees :
800 - 1:57.65
BLACKMAN Gary U15 24.09.80, Old G :
1500 - 4:19.9, 3k - 9:37.4
BLACKMAN John U15 12.11.80, Rowntrees :
200 - 23.51
BLACKMORE Andrew U20 12.07.76, Telford :
800 - 1:50.7
BLAKE Chris U17 8.11.78, Sale :
100 - 11.0 (11.0-94), 200 - 21.84 (21.64w-94)
BLAKE Ian U13 9.05.83, Blackpool :
100 - 12.4
BLAKE John-Paul U17 2.08.79, Jersey :
LJ - 6.48
BLAKE Kevin 29.05.67, Cardiff :
5k - 14:29.1
BLAKELY Richard 19.05.72, Annadale Str :
3k - 8:21.5 (8:20.54-90), 5k - 14:29.60
BLANCHARD R. U17, Charnwood :
HJ - 1.90
BLIGHT Ross U20 28.05.77, Cardiff :
HT - 46.12 (47.62-94), HTJ - 52.60 (54.18-94)
BLOOMFIELD Ian V40 23.11.52, Chester L St:
Mar - 2:23:48 (2:17:14-93)
BOBB Samuel U23 29.08.75, Blackheath :
TJ - 14.46 (14.47w-94)
BODDAM-WHETHAM Charles U17 25.09.78,
Dacorum & Tring : 800 - 1:57.6
BOLT Christopher U15 21.09.80, Bracknell :
3k - 9:32.9
BONICH Daniel M. U17 22.11.78, Bexley :
60 - 7.0i/7.08i, 200 - 22.4
100 - 10.9w/10.93w/11.2/11.26 (11.1-94),
BONSALL Samuel U17 15.03.79, Crewe & N :
100HY - 14.04, OctY - 4612
BOON Andrew U17 7.10.78, Coventry Godiva :
100HY - 13.7/13.78,
BOOTH Jeremy 26.05.71, Croydon :
LJ - 6.96w/6.95, TJ - 14.13
BOOTH Stephen R. 21.10.71, Oxford C/Ach :
110H - 14.97, 400H - 55.5,
PV - 4.10, Dec - 6114
BOOTH Terry 19.10.66, Hounslow :
3k - 8:24.4, 5k - 14:32.41 (14:14.1-93)
BOOTHROYD Jason 26.11.69, Sale/Mich Un :
800 - 1:49.93 (1:49.7-91),
1500 - 3:44.63 (3:44.2-91), 1M - 4:06.73i
BORRETT D. U13, Great Yarmouth :
80HC - 12.1
BORSUMATO Anthony U23 13.12.73,
C of Stoke/Staffs Un : 400H - 51.99 (51.83-94)
BOSHER Brian, Darlington :
24HrT - 205.131km
BOUNDY Patrick U17 19.02.79, Hounslow :
JTY - 55.78
BOURNE Nigel 18.04.72, Queens Park :
100 - 10.7w, LJ - 7.17i/6.98
BOVELL Colin 9.03.72, Newham & Essex B :
110H - 14.48 (14.1/14.17-94)
BOWDITCH Kristen Robert U23 14.01.75, Bir :
3k - 8:04.66, 5k - 14:07.86
BOWEN Martin John P. 20.05.63, Cardiff :
100 - 10.6/10.79w/10.87

BOWERING Michael P. 19.05.63, Swindon :
Mar - 2:28:28 (2:24:34-89)
BOWERS K., :
Mar - 2:29:05
BOWLAND A. U13, Wilts Sch :
HJ - 1.55
BOWMAN Simon 11.09.71, Diss :
HT - 50.34
BOWN Simon Paul U23 21.11.74, Haringey :
HT - 58.28
BOWSKILL James U17 19.05.79, Notts :
1500 - 4:06.5, 3k - 8:57.3
BOX Toby 9.09.72, Sale :
60 - 6.87i, 100 - 10.31w/10.32 (10.07w-94),
200 - 20.78 (20.72-94)
BOYCE Theopese U20 11.12.76, Oadby & W :
3k - 8:34.7
BOYLE Scott U17 21.03.79, Livingston :
100 - 11.2/11.40w/11.46
BOYNE Frank 28.02.66, Aberdeen :
1500 - 3:52.0 (3:48.95-94),
3kSt - 9:11.5 (9:06.3-93)
BRABIN Andrew U15 19.10.80, Wirral :
1500 - 4:14.63
BRACE Steven 7.07.61, Bridgend :
10kR - 29:17 (29:04-91), 10MR - 48:24 (47:38-93),
HMar - 1:03:30 (1:02:29-90)
BRADLEY Colin 2.02.56, Trowbridge :
3kW - 13:20.79i/13:22.64 (12:54.8-86),
50kW - 4:51:57 (4:33:42-87)
BRADLEY Dominic U20 22.12.76, Stockport :
60HJ - 8.41i, 110HJ - 14.36w/14.54,
110H - 15.1/15.27
BRADSTOCK Arne Roald 24.04.62, Enfield :
JT - 75.64 (83.84-87)
BRADY Michael U15 21.02.81, Salford :
HTB - 45.88
BRADY Richard U17 20.09.78, Elswick :
1.5kSt - 4:26.53
BRAITHWAITE Darren 20.01.69, Haringey :
60 - 6.51i, 100 - 10.12,
150 - 15.09w (15.38-90), 200 - 20.47
BRAMBLE Marvin U20 10.06.77, Blackheath :
TJ - 15.23 (15.25w-93)
BRANNEN Anthony 16.09.68, City of Stoke :
60H - 8.05i (7.94i-93),
110H - 14.2/14.25w (14.35-89),
HJ - 2.05 (2.10i-93/2.07-88), PV - 4.90i/4.80,
LJ - 7.34, SP - 14.06, JT - 57.10, Dec - 7861
BRASHER Hugh 28.09.64, Hounslow :
3kSt - 8:54.59
BREAM Paul, Wallsend :
100kR - 7:45:15
BREND Peter A. U20 2.02.77, N Devon :
200 - 22.20, 400 - 48.67 (48.4/48.50-94)
BRENNAN David U15, Bolton :
1500 - 4:19.5
BRENNAN Steve 4.11.65, Manx H :
3kW - 12:56.7 (12:27.3-94),
20kW - 1:37:43 (1:35:38-93)
BRICE Patrick 8.02.69, Blackh'th/Camb Univ :
3k - 8:24.23, 3kSt - 8:55.05 (8:54.03-93)
BRIDGER Jeremy U23 23.09.75, Yeovil Oly:
400H - 54.8/55.62
BRIERLEY James U20 31.07.77, Telford :
HJ - 2.18i/2.17,
BRIFFETT Stephen U17 22.10.78, Highgate :
800 - 1:55.04, 1500 - 4:05.8

322

BRIGGS Martin Christopher 4.01.64,
C of Stoke/Birm U : 400H - 54.74 (49.86-84)
BRILUS Philip S. 29.12.68, Harlow :
110H - 15.5 (14.50-90)
BRISK Simon U20 5.07.77, Cheltenham :
DTJ - 41.10
BRISTOW Allister 27.04.72, Erne Valley :
Mar - 2:30:11
BRIZZELL Paul U20 3.10.76, Ballymena & A :
100 - 10.76, 200 - 21.50
BROADLEY Peter James 16.10.71, Notts :
800 - 1:52.6 (1:50.4-89)
BROCKLEBANK Robert J. U20 12.10.76,
Blackburn : HJ - 2.16
BROOKES Nigel, Brighton :
Mar - 2:30:03
BROOKING David 22.10.68, City of Plymouth :
110H - 15.34 (15.0-94)
BROOKS Stephen 8.06.70, Bing/Iowa St Un:
5k - 14:21.97i (13:52.54-94), 10k - 29:04.63
BROOME Edward 3.09.72, Blackpool/Ox Univ :
3kSt - 9:14.9
BROUGHTON Mark A. 23.10.63, Met. Police :
HT - 47.68 (54.28-93)
BROWN A. U15, Sale :
HJ - 1.80
BROWN Andrew U23 22.09.73, Blackheath :
DT - 41.50
BROWN Andrew U20 17.06.77, Edinburgh SH :
800 - 1:54.62
BROWN David 4.06.66, Thurrock :
JT - 58.16 (61.32-91)
BROWN Gareth 21.07.67, Falkirk :
800 - 1:49.55 (1:47.15-93),
1500 - 3:42.99 (3:42.66-94)
BROWN Gareth J. 10.05.68, Steyning :
3kW - 13:00.0 (12:36.91-87),
10kW - 46:20.6 (43:54.25-87),
20kW - 1:38:21 (1:30:15-89), 50kW - 4:28:44
BROWN Gareth U23 2.09.73, Swindon :
LJ - 6.92 (7.21w/6.98-92)
BROWN Jonathan M. 27.02.71, Sheffield :
3k - 7:54.81 (7:51.72-93),
5k - 13:37.83 (13:19.78-93),
10k - 28:08.31, 10kR - 27:20dh/28:48 (28:05-93)
BROWN Kevin 10.09.64, Belgrave :
SP - 14.66, DT - 59.50
BROWN Michael 6.05.62, Haringey :
TJ - 15.06w/14.83 (16.15-89)
BROWN Neil U20 6.04.78, Birchfield :
LJ - 6.80w (6.68-94)
BROWN Richard V45 18.11.46, Surrey WC :
100MW - 19:23:16 (16:50:28-93)
BROWN Robert U20 3.03.78, Elswick :
2kSt - 5:57.60, 3kSt - 9:28.4
BROWN Simon James 22.03.69, C of Stoke :
800 - 1:49.69
BROWN Steven U15 20.03.82, Southend :
PV - 3.35
BROWN Stuart 27.11.72, Deeside :
HJ - 2.05
BROWNE Adrian U20 14.07.78, Windsor S&E :
TJ - 13.94w/13.58 (13.92-94)
BROWNE Curtis U23 11.09.75, Birchfield :
100 - 10.8 (10.43w/10.6/10.66-94)
BRUCE Calum U23 28.02.75, Pitreavie :
HT - 52.54

BRUCE Daniel U20 29.09.76, Sandwell :
200 - 22.0/22.13w/22.56
BRUCE Michael U17 8.10.78, Edinburgh/Fife :
200 - 22.6w/22.62
BRUNT Daniel U20 23.04.76, Chesterfield :
SP - 13.29, SPJ - 14.35,
DTJ - 41.46 (43.00-94)
BRYAN James U15, Torfaen :
DTB - 41.04
BRYAN Justin 16.08.69, Torfaen :
DT - 41.80
BUCHANAN Andrew I. 12.09.70, AF&D :
PV - 4.20 (4.50-94)
BUCK Matthew U23 5.04.74, Woodford Green/
Brunel Univ : PV - 4.40 (4.50-93)
BUCKFIELD Nicholas U23 5.06.73, Crawley :
110H - 15.28, PV - 5.70
BUCKLEY Christopher T.P. 26.07.61, Westb :
Mar - 2:19:05 (2:15:48-91)
BUCKNALL Martyn 2.11.70, City of Stoke :
400 - 49.0
BUCKNER Thomas Christopher 16.04.63,
Havant : Mar - 2:21:40
BUDDEN Nicholas U23 17.11.75, Norfolk :
200 - 21.38, 400 - 47.5/47.76 (46.89-93)
BULL Andrew 26.06.69, Sheffield :
100 - 10.7/10.81w/10.94 (10.77w-92/10.93-88),
200 - 21.3 (21.61w-93/21.78-92)
BULL James U17 12.02.79, Ipswich :
SPY - 16.29
BULL Michael P. 6.06.70, Notts :
LJ - 6.85, Dec - 5805
BULLOCK Aaron U15 6.02.81, Cannock & St :
PV - 3.30
BULLOCK David U20 1.12.76, Here & W Sch :
DecJ - 5431 (5464-94)
BULLOCK Guy Ross U23 15.10.75, Wigan :
100 - 10.8,
200 - 21.25A/21.7 (21.80w/21.82-93),
400 - 46.41 (46.13-93)
BULLOCK Simon U15 22.11.80, Hereford :
400 - 52.36
BULMAN Neil Andrew U20 7.09.77, Mand/NESH :
HT - 45.44, HTJ - 50.80
BULSTRIDGE Michael U23 23.01.73, Birch :
5k - 14:34.2
BUNCE Keith St.John 5.04.66, Notts :
60H - 8.35i (8.1i/8.14i-88)
BURDEN Matthew U15 3.09.80, Yeovil Oly :
HJ - 1.80
BURKE Alan P. 23.05.65, Hounslow/IRE :
PV - 4.50 (5.00-89)
BURKE David    68, London Irish/IRE :
3k - 8:13.72 (8:06.66-94), 10kR - 29:05
BURKE John 18.05.70, London Irish/IRE :
1500 - 3:51.9, 3k - 8:02.84,
5k - 14:11.42 (13:56.31-93), 10kR - 29:23
BURKE Raymond Nicholas 11.11.69, Shaft B :
60 - 6.93i (6.71i-92),
100 - 10.4w/10.71w/10.81 (10.39-92),
200 - 21.88w (21.4-91/21.87-92)
BURMAN-ROY Sudip U20 15.01.78, Blackh'th :
SPJ - 14.15
BURNETT David U20 27.01.76, Shaftesbury B :
SP - 14.37i/13.26 (14.04-94),
SPJ - 14.18 (15.18-94), DTJ - 44.10
BURNS Ian T. U20 20.09.77, Durham Sch :
JT - 54.88

BURRAWAY Paul 30.11.68, Hounslow :
HJ - 2.08 (2.10-93)
BURROWS Darius U23 8.08.75, Birchfield :
1500 - 3:50.2 (3:48.9-94),
3k - 8:09.08i (8:01.26-94),
5k - 14:12.35 (14:11.27-94)
BURTON Simon U17 23.04.79, Notts :
1500 - 4:01.54, 3k - 8:48.8
BUSHELL Mark Anthony U20 22.10.76, Team S :
100 - 10.9, 110H - 14.7w/14.72w, PV - 4.30,
110HJ - 15.2/15.45w (14.64w/14.95-94),
LJ - 7.25, Dec - 6839, DecJ - 6457 (6622-94)
BUTLAND Mark U20, Carmarthen :
110HJ - 14.6db/15.94w,
BUTLER David U17 9.12.78, Charnwood :
LJ - 6.76
BUTLER Matthew U15 27.02.81, Havering :
200 - 23.24w/24.05
BUTTERFIELD Tim U15 2.01.81, :
TJ - 12.12
BUXTON Wayne 16.04.62, Bristol :
Mar - 2:27:39 (2:16:38-91)
BUZZA David 6.12.62, Cornwall AC :
HMar - 1:04:38 (1:03:13-89),
Mar - 2:26:39 (2:11:06-93)
BYRNE Jason 9.09.70, BH Mansfield/WLHS :
DT - 41.70 (50.12-91), HT - 69.44 (73.80-92)

C ADDY Neil U20 18.03.75, Newquay & P :
800 - 1:50.2, 1500 - 3:39.67,
1M - 3:59.6, 3k - 8:03.86
CADOGAN Gary A. 8.10.66, Haringey :
400H - 49.70 (49.07-94)
CADWALLADER Lee 17.01.69, Liverpool H :
800 - 1:47.8 (1:47.43-93),
1k - 2:18.61, 1500 - 3:43.39
CAINES Adrian U23 13.11.74, Sparkhill :
60H - 8.33i, 110H - 14.68w/14.88 (14.7/14.83-94)
CAIRNS Steven 3.11.67, Scottish Borders :
3kSt - 9:03.45
CALLAN Adrian 28.11.62, Shettleston :
3k - 8:19.9 (8:05.77-94),
5k - 14:05.58 (13:58.93-88),
10kR - 29:42 (29:30-92), 10MR - 47:35dh
CALLAWAY David J. 4.09.63, Haringey :
SP - 16.60 (17.55-93)
CALLENDER Clarence 16.11.61, Har/Army :
100 - 10.80 (10.27w/10.30-91)
CALLOW J. Allan V50 4.09.45, Manx H :
3kW - 13:35.4 (13:06.0-72),
10kW - 48:00.4 (46:44.0-73),
20kW - 1:39:29 (1:34:14-73)
CALVERT Ewan U23 28.11.73, TVH/A'deen/
Str'clyde Un : 800 - 1:49.06, 1500 - 3:46.83
CALVERT James U20 5.11.77, Tunbridge W :
2kSt - 6:05.0
CAMERON Rezlimond 18.05.60, Thames VH :
TJ - 15.68w/15.55 (16.32w-89/16.20-88)
CAMERON Trevor U20 25.11.76, Shaft Barn :
60 - 6.85i, 100 - 10.71 (10.29w/10.5/10.54-94),
200 - 21.60 (20.88w/21.18-94)
CAMPBELL Darren A. U23 12.09.73, Sale :
100 - 10.34 (10.28w-91)
CAMPBELL Donald U20 13.02.78, Peterbro :
LJ - 6.94
CAMPBELL Ian 6.09.71, Har/Dundee HH :
800 - 1:50.51i/1:50.73 (1:49.95-93),
1500 - 3:43.54i/3:47.31 (3:43.05i-94/3:43.64-93)

CAMPBELL Kenneth William 30.09.72, ESH :
60H - 8.00i (7.99i-94),
110H - 13.98 (13.86-94)
CAMPBELL P. I. Junior 13.02.70, Woodf'd Gr :
TJ - 13.91 (15.81w-89/15.50-86)
CANNES Daniel U17, R Sutton Coldfield :
200 - 22.6
CANNING Dale U20 12.06.78, Stockport :
800 - 1:52.0
CARD Gavin U20 11.05.78, Morpeth :
PV - 4.20
CARE Robert V45 8.04.47, Sandwell :
3kW - 13:11.84 (12:46.03-90)
CARELESS Robert U23 7.09.74, Telford :
HT - 54.28
CARMODY Noel 24.12.56, Cambridge H :
3kW - 12:45.05 (12:26.49-91),
10kW - 47:49.7 (44:45.63-91),
20kW - 1:37:57 (1:34:38-90)
CARNEY Daniel U17 25.12.78, Spenborough :
DecY - 5252, OctY - 4415
CARROLL Paul U20 25.01.78, Liverpool Pem :
DecJ - 5560
CARRUTH Jim, :
24HrT - 210.151km
CARSON Christopher U17 26.10.79, Lochgelly :
100 - 10.9w/10.99w/11.0/11.15,
200 - 22.2w/22.4/22.63w/23.02, 400 - 48.79
CARSWELL Adam U20 8.01.76, Exeter :
110HJ - 14.7/15.22w/15.38,
110H - 15.2w/15.40, JT - 55.76
CARTER Adrian R. 7.02.68, Thames Valley :
110H - 14.81 (14.72w/14.75-90)
CARTER Daniel U17 15.04.80, Harlow :
JTY - 58.96
CARTER Darren U17 29.10.78, Bournemouth :
100 - 11.0/11.57
CARTER Harley U20 28.06.78, Braintree :
JT - 52.62
CARTER Richard U15 3.02.81, City of Bath :
PV - 3.60
CARTER Simon U23 5.03.75, GEC/Reading U :
JT - 61.38 (61.54-93)
CARTHY Daniel U15 3.12.80, C of Plymouth :
1500 - 4:13.79
CARTWRIGHT Russell U20 13.10.77, Cov  G :
800 - 1:54.36, 1500 - 3:51.2, 3k - 8:30.5
CARTWRIGHT Tom U17 22.06.79, Cov G :
1500 - 4:04.1
CASCOE Benjamin U20 26.12.77, Belgrave :
JT - 55.50
CASEY Stephen 26.02.66, Woodford Green :
DT - 51.20 (58.64-91)
CASHELL Christopher 11.05.66, Team Solent :
400H - 53.0/53.16 (51.89-91)
CASTLE Andrew U17 8.12.79, Yeovil Oly :
SPY - 14.51, HTY - 51.20 '
CASTLE David 30.07.71, Tonbridge :
1500 - 3:50.7 (3:48.0-91)
CATTERMOLE Tim U20 17.08.77, :
JT - 55.48
CAUDERY Stuart 19.11.66, Cornwall AC :
PV - 4.10
CAULFIELD Quintan U17, Ballymena & A :
SPY - 14.92
CAVERS David 9.04.63, Teviotdale :
Mar - 2:23:32

CAWLEY Ian U17 21.11.78, Bournemouth :
60HY - 8.34i, 100HY - 13.7/13.84,
110HJ - 15.42w/15.44
CHAFFE Alex U15 5.12.80, Notts :
100 - 11.5, 200 - 23.09
CHALLENGER Ben U20 7.03.78, Charnwood :
HJ - 2.11
CHAMBERS Dwain Anthony U20 5.04.78, Har :
60 - 6.70i, 100 - 10.41, 200 - 21.37
CHAMPION Michael U23 3.01.75, Blackheath :
200 - 21.69 (21.4w/21.65w-94)
CHAPLIN Owen U20 2.12.77, Telford :
PV - 4.20i/4.05 (4.20-94), DecJ - 5563
CHAPMAN Darren U15 2.10.80, Old G :
80HB - 11.8w/11.89
CHAPMAN Keith U15 15.02.81, Wirral :
3k - 9:32.7
CHAPMAN Mark U20 28.12.76, Basildon :
400H - 56.8/56.95
CHARIJ Andrij, Basingstoke & MH :
HT - 47.52 (52.72-93)
CHARLES Andrew U17 14.01.79, Rich & T :
100HY - 13.45w/13.5/13.91
CHARLES Courtney 13.11.68, Thames Valley :
LJ - 7.44w/7.40 (7.54-94)
CHARLESWORTH Robert U17 25.03.79, Corby :
JTY - 57.74
CHASTON Justin 4.11.68, Belgrave :
1500 - 3:46.58, 5k - 13:51.86,
HMar - 1:03:06dh, 3kSt - 8:24.97 (8:23.90-94)
CHATBURN Craig U15 29.01.81, Halifax :
DTB - 37.86
CHEADLE Carl U15 6.09.80, Charnwood :
SPB - 13.67
CHEESEMAN Christopher 11.12.58,
Surrey WC/Crawley/Thames H & H :
10kW - 43:50.44 (43:05.11-93),
20kW - 1:29:55 (1:29:11-94)
CHIDLOW Glyn 21.10.71, Worcester/Ox Univ :
LJ - 7.28w/6.90 (7.25-94), Dec - 5220 (5362-90)
CHILES Garry 15.05.66, Norfolk :
PV - 4.10 (4.35-94)
CHILTON Alan 16.04.71, Handy Cross Jog's :
Mar - 2:24:26 (2:24:26-94)
CHINNICK Bruce 25.04.60, Westbury/RAF :
10k - 30:49.5 (30:09.5-90)
CHISHOLM Scott U20 20.10.77, Pitreavie :
400H - 54.98
CHRISTIE Linford 2.04.60, Thames Valley :
60 - 6.47i (6.43+-91),
100 - 9.97A/10.00 (9.87-93),
150 - 14.74w (14.97-94),
200 - 20.11 (20.09-88)
CHUKUKERE Enyinna U23 31.07.73,
Shaftesbury Barnet/West Virginia Un :
LJ - 7.57 (7.81w/7.64i-94)
CHURCH Michael U15 7.09.80, Newham & EB :
800 - 2:00.6, 1500 - 4:20.9
CHURCHILL Richard U20 29.09.77, Stainforth :
110HJ - 14.8/15.38, 110H - 15.57
CIARAVELLA Simon U23 24.11.73, Woodf'd Gr :
400 - 47.69 (47.33-93)
CLACK James U20 14.08.76, Portsmouth :
800 - 1:54.09
CLARE Jeffrey M. 21.03.65, Sale :
SP - 15.09 (15.76-87), DT - 52.32 (55.60-88)
CLARK David James 16.02.64, Edinburgh SH :
200 - 22.10db (20.75-90)

CLARK Ewan 4.04.69, Edinburgh/Pitreavie :
60 - 6.90i (6.85i-94)
CLARK Stephen 24.05.72, Enfield :
Dec - 5104
CLARK Trevor 29.04.56, Poole :
Mar - 2:24:10 (2:18:42-94)
CLARKE Andrew 10.08.70, Wigan :
JT - 61.14
CLARKE Jonathan 20.11.67, Swansea :
JT - 63.06 (68.74-86)
CLARKE Matthew U20 15.11.76, Daventry :
800 - 1:52.9 (1:52.4-94)
CLARKE Peter 9.07.65, Coventry Godiva :
400 - 48.5/49.30 (48.29-91)
CLARKE S. Ezra U23 9.12.74, Shaftesbury B :
TJ - 15.36i (15.46-94)
CLARKE Wayne A. R. U23 24.12.75, Peterbro :
SPJ - 13.86o, HT - 56.48 (57.24-94),
HTJ - 62.16o (62.60-94)
CLARKE Wesley 31.12.63, Ilford :
HT - 48.60 (48.88-94)
CLEMENTS A. U13, AF&D :
70HC - 12.2
CLERIHEW David U20 11.09.77, Edin SH :
LJ - 7.11w/7.06
CLIFT Lee U20 12.10.76, Crawley :
HTJ - 48.68
CLIFTON David U20 15.04.76, Birchfield :
400H - 56.38
CLINCH Mark U17 23.10.78, Sale :
HTY - 50.36
CLUSKEY Adrian U15 30.12.80, Blackheath :
SPY - 14.46i, SPB - 15.78, DTB - 44.82
COATS Edward U17 14.06.80, Guildford & G :
OctY - 4545
COCKER Jonathan 26.09.71, York :
50kW - 4:33:01
COHEN Scott 6.12.64, Leslie Deans RC :
Mar - 2:20:17
COLCLOUGH James U17 29.06.79, Stourport :
400 - 50.59
COLEMAN Andy U23 29.09.74, Enfield :
2kSt - 5:55.38, 3kSt - 9:17.84
COLLINS Liam U17 23.10.78, Gateshead :
60HY - 8.28i, 100HY - 13.44, 110HJ - 15.2
COLLINS Michael U17 12.11.78, Bolton :
LJ - 6.88
COLLINS Simon U15 23.11.80, City of Hull :
100 - 11.49w/11.75, 200 - 23.46w
COMBE Michael U17 24.12.78, Scottish Bord :
800 - 1:52.5
COMERFORD Nick 23.04.66, Cardiff :
1500 - 3:44.3, 3k - 8:00.54
CONDON Allyn U23 24.08.74, Sale :
60 - 6.84i, 100 - 10.47w/10.48 (10.37w-93),
200 - 21.00 (20.95-93)
CONDON David 11.04.72, Shaftesbury Barn :
SP - 15.65 (16.41-94)
CONDRON Ian W. 7.10.59, Lisburn/IRE :
Dec - 5957 (6343-89)
CONERNEY Michael 30.10.72, Braint/Camb U :
DT - 43.70 (44.28-93)
CONEY Shane U17, Annadale Striders :
1.5kSt - 4:33.4
CONLEY Kenneth 24.12.61, Border :
5k - 14:34.03
CONLON Greg U23 18.12.74, Bristol :
PV - 4.15i/4.10 (4.20-92)

325

CONNELLY David U20 6.02.76, Shettleston :
3kSt - 9:33.3 (9:17.53-94)
CONNIKIE Leon U15 6.01.81, Blackheath :
200 - 23.54, 400 - 51.11
CONWAY Adam U15 2.10.80, Southend :
3k - 9:39.2
COOK Austin James Gareth 20.02.69, Sut & D/
WLHS : SP - 14.01 (14.59-90),
DT - 47.70 (49.20-90), HT - 63.00 (67.32-91)
COOK Evan, :
Mar - 2:28:38
COOK Gavin 30.03.70, Thames Valley :
HT - 46.16 (46.62-93)
COOK Philip 7.05.69, Barry :
3kSt - 9:06.34 (8:55.6-93)
COOPER Darren 1.02.66, Peterborough/AUS :
110H - 14.02
COOPER Mark 3.09.62, Southampton City :
Mar - 2:25:47 (2:22:49-94)
COOPER Paul U20 4.12.76, Braintree :
JT - 65.34
COOPER Rufus U17 24.02.79, Kingston & P :
PV - 4.45
COPE Stuart U20, City of Stoke :
110HJ - 15.23w
COPELAND B. U13, London Schools :
70HC - 12.1
COPPIN Glen U13 16.01.83, Barking Sch :
400 - 58.7, 800 - 2:12.7, 1500 - 4:32.5
CORCORAN Fyn U20 17.03.78, Cornwall AC :
400H - 56.46, DecJ - 6180
CORDY Matthew U23 29.09.75, Portsmouth :
HJ - 1.98 (2.03-93)
CORR Kevin U17 17.04.79, Jarrow & Hebb :
800 - 1:56.4
CORRIGAN J. Paul 19.01.66, Gateshead :
SP - 15.49 (16.04-89), DT - 44.08
COSSELL Harvey U23 1.12.74, Invicta :
3kSt - 9:17.2
COSTELLO Denis M. 3.12.61, Belgrave :
TJ - 15.01 (15.66-83)
COTTER Christopher 3.02.72, Shaftesbury B :
LJ - 6.99i/6.93 (7.67w/7.47-93),
TJ - 14.68 (15.19-93)
COTTON Ben U20 10.03.78, March :
JT - 52.04
COUPLAND Steven C. 15.06.65, Sheffield :
100 - 10.7 (10.7-93),
200 - 21.3/21.72 (21.14-93),
400 - 47.8/48.10 (47.1-94/47.92-91)
COVENTON Dean 3.11.70, Enfield :
3kSt - 9:11.6
COWAN Lloyd 8.07.62, Shaftesbury Barnet :
200 - 21.85
    (21.3w-93/21.48w/21.7-86/21.71-93),
400 - 48.19 (47.42-86), 400H - 50.79,
110H - 13.7w/13.79w/13.83 (13.75-94)
COWAN Martin U15 16.11.80, Wilts Sch :
PenB - 2661
COWIE G. U15, :
80HB - 11.8
COX Jason U20 1.04.77, Sherbourne Sch :
100 - 10.9/11.25
CRAGGS Ray 9.07.63, RAF :
3kW - 13:19.9
CRAIG Ian 20.08.69, Border :
100 - 10.67 (10.4wdb/10.65w-93),
200 - 21.8/21.86 (21.56w-93)

CRAMPTON Peter 4.06.69, Spenborough :
200 - 21.84A (21.4w-91/21.5/21.57-87),
400 - 47.6/48.40i (46.03-87), 600 - 1:19.6,
110H - 15.6 (15.2-93), 400H - 49.58 (49.26-94)
CRAVEN Bruce 18.03.72, Sale :
400 - 48.3 (49.92i-94),
800 - 1:50.7
CRAWFORD Damien 22.08.68, Lond I/Sparta :
JT - 63.64 (70.34-91)
CREABY Christian U17 11.10.78, Leeds :
200 - 22.65w/22.76
CREEK Ian U15 20.09.80, Exeter :
JTB - 51.54
CREESE Robert U20 1.12.77, Thames Valley :
HJ - 2.04
CRESSWELL Andrew U17 4.04.80, Birchfield :
HJ - 1.91
CRICK Paul U15 9.10.80, Derby & Co :
200 - 23.67
CRIPPS Damon 9.10.70, Worcester :
HT - 50.76
CRITCHLEY Kim U23 15.07.73, Rowntrees :
1500 - 3:46.7, 1M - 4:00.15
CROAD Malcolm U23 27.10.73, Old Gayt/
Ox Un/WLHS : HT - 60.04 (61.22-92)
CROASDALE Mark 10.01.60, Lancaster & M :
10kR - 29:44, Mar - 2:21:19 (2:17:45-93)
CROLL Graeme 1.02.66, Cambuslang :
3k - 8:23.4 (8:07.6-90), 3kSt - 8:40.49,
5k - 14:05.3pace/14:17.3, 10k - 29:50.69
CROSLAND Adam U17 27.08.79, Longwood :
3k - 8:59.4
CROSS Derek V45 30.04.49, Verlea :
3kW - 13:14.65 (13:03.01-94),
10kW - 46:41.8 (46:33.6-94)
CROSS Stephen U20 12.02.77, Wirral :
JT - 55.44
CROSSLEY Andrew U17 22.05.79, Notts :
200 - 22.58w/23.14
CROSSLEY Paul U17 30.03.79, Luton :
400HY - 57.2/57.91
CROWTHER Eric U23 23.01.75, Sale :
1500 - 3:50.9
CUDDY Grant U20 6.01.77, Sale :
1500 - 3:54.9
CULLEN Keith John 13.06.72, Chelmsford :
1500 - 3:48.4 (3:43.12-92), 3k - 7:58.25,
10kR - 28:42 (28:36-92), 3kSt - 8:26.05
CULSHAW John 20.11.62, Tamworth :
Dec - 5310 (5314-92)
CUMMINS R. U15, West Yorks Sch :
3kW - 16:06.25
CURRAN Paul U20 5.04.77, North Down :
Dec - 5296w, DecJ - 5268
CURRIE Brian 7.10.62, Liverpool H :
10MR - 47:46sh (48:20-93)
CURRIE Byrne, RAF :
100 - 10.71
CURTIS Gary 21.11.61, Newham & Essex B :
HT - 50.42 (52.60-88)
CURTIS Neil U23 30.07.74, Corby :
HT - 53.90 (55.62-94)
CURTIS P., Army :
DT - 41.34
CURWEN Simon U17 26.10.78, Border :
3k - 8:56.1, 1.5kSt - 4:25.29
CUSACK Matthew U20 13.01.77, Doncaster :
SPJ - 13.81

326

CUTHILL David U20 18.01.78, Kilbarchan :
  DecJ - 5305
CZERNIK Richard 12.07.72, Dudley & Stourb :
  Dec - 5710 (6005-94)

D'ALMEIDA Gregory U15 16.11.80, Dac & T:
  100 - 11.59w/12.0/12.08
DAKIN Nicholas 13.11.63, N & EB/LSAC :
  110H - 15.10 (14.28-93)
DAKO Owusu U23 23.05.73, Sale :
  60 - 6.86i, 100 - 10.42, 200 - 20.57
DALE Gregg U15 2.10.80, City of Hull :
  400 - 53.9, 800 - 2:02.54
DALKINS Mark 9.09.71, City of Stoke :
  3kSt - 9:04.3
DALTON Timothy U17 18.01.79, Old Gayt:
  100HY - 13.8/14.10 (13.8/13.90w-94)
DALY Shane U23 21.03.73, Leeds/IRE :
  800 - 1:52.19i (1:50.4-93)
DALY Steven U17 29.12.79, Elan Valley :
  100 - 11.12w/11.19,
  200 - 22.51w/22.86 (22.26w/22.7-94)
DANGERFIELD Matthew, Dacorum & Tring :
  100 - 10.90w
DANIEL Nicholas U15 18.01.81, Belgrave :
  400 - 53.95
DANIELS Darren 2.09.70, Birchfield :
  5k - 14:24.7, 10k - 30:36.1
DANIELS Dean U20 1.02.76, Birchfield :
  DT - 40.90, DTJ - 42.78
DANSO Evans 29.11.72, Thames Valley :
  100 - 10.6w/10.8 (10.79-91)
DARBY Brian 14.10.72, Cov G/Loughbro St :
  400 - 48.2/48.84 (47.64-92)
DARLINGTON Landley Sean U20 19.01.77,
  Stamford & Deeping : JT - 60.06
DAVEY David U20 8.09.77, Barry :
  800 - 1:55.0
DAVEY Garard 21.08.68, Sale :
  3k - 8:07.86 (8:05.5-92)
DAVID Andrew 9.09.69, Cambridge Harriers :
  60H - 8.29i, 110H - 14.83
DAVIDSON Christopher U23 4.12.75, N & E B :
  100 - 10.8, 200 - 21.9, LJ - 7.33 (7.46w-94)
DAVIDSON Euan U23 8.12.73, Guildford & G :
  DT - 41.34
DAVIDSON Mark 15.11.68, TVH/Aberd'n :
  100 - 10.8w (10.50w/10.7-89),
  200 - 21.4w (21.07w/21.6-89/21.90i/22.11-90),
  400H - 51.94 (50.79-89)
DAVIES Ben U15 24.08.81, City of Bath :
  HJ - 1.81
DAVIES Chris U20 19.10.76, Telford :
  3k - 8:31.2, 5k - 15:01.03
DAVIES Daniel U20 2.02.76, Torfaen/LSAC :
  TJ - 14.04
DAVIES Gareth M. 11.05.71, Cardiff :
  LJ - 7.07 (7.62-94), TJ - 14.41 (14.73-94)
DAVIES J. U13, Barnet :
  200 - 25.5
DAVIES Kevin U20 11.01.78, Taunton :
  HTJ - 51.92, DecJ - 5276
DAVIES Mark Howard 10.01.71, Tonbridge :
  SP - 14.47 (15.56-92), DT - 46.94 (53.06-92)
DAVIES Matthew 23.07.71, Woodford Green :
  800 - 1:51.9, 1500 - 3:48.1 (3:48.0-93),
  1M - 4:09.6

DAVIES Matthew U17 16.09.78, Swansea :
  JT - 52.86, JTY - 58.12
DAVIES Peter 24.02.63, Haringey :
  1M - 4:08.0 (4:06.5-91)
DAVIES Philip 12.10.60, Wirral :
  DT - 41.08
DAVIES Stephen 4.02.58, Berry-H Mansfield :
  Mar - 2:27:00 (2:22:55-90)
DAVIES-HALE Paul 21.06.62, Cannock & St :
  10kR - 29:17 (28:17-85)
DAVIS Adam Gareth 19.11.72, Corby :
  PV - 4.60 (4.70-92), Dec - 5580
DAVIS Luke U17 1.01.80, Tipton :
  100 - 11.0/11.14, 200 - 22.40
DAVIS Mark U20 1.03.77, Corby :
  PV - 5.00
DAVIS Neal U20 11.10.77, Thurrock :
  PV - 4.15
DAVIS Richard U20 3.05.78, Bedford & Co :
  100 - 10.94w (10.9w/11.17-94)
DAVIS Scott U23 3.04.75, Coventry RWC :
  3kW - 13:30.89 (12:55.0-93)
DAVIS Timothy U20 25.01.78, Invicta :
  2kSt - 6:02.78
DAVIS Trevor 26.03.63, Windsor S & E/ANG :
  200 - 21.99 (21.41-90)
DAVOILE Ryan U17 29.09.78, Coventry G :
  800 - 1:52.64
DAVOREN Patrick 13.03.72, Brighton :
  1500 - 3:49.21, 1M - 4:04.6,
  3k - 8:15.94i, 5k - 14:16.0
DAWSON Richard 7.12.70, Highgate :
  400 - 48.9, 800 - 1:52.41
DE'ATH Matthew U17 27.10.78, Windsor S & E :
  800 - 1:55.04
DEACON David William 19.03.65, Morpeth :
  100 - 10.7/10.82,
  200 - 21.6w/21.7/21.86 (21.19w-94/21.24-93),
  300 - 33.88, 400 - 48.3 (47.10-93), LJ - 7.13
DEACON Gareth 8.08.66, Coventry Godiva :
  3k - 8:25.0
DEACON Jared Mark U23 15.10.75, Morpeth :
  100 - 10.8, 200 - 21.41w/21.5/21.66,
  300 - 33.12, 400 - 46.45
DEACON Michael U15 13.04.81, Leics WC :
  3kW - 15:46.25
DEARMAN Geoffrey U20 4.08.77, Hounslow :
  400 - 47.02
DEE William 18.12.61, Luton :
  3k - 8;23.5 (7:42.77-92)
DELL Gregory J. 20.11.64, Vale of Aylesbury :
  100kR - 7:03:05
DENHOLM Graeme U15 31.03.81, Edin SH :
  JTB - 50.24
DENMARK Robert N. 23.11.68, Basildon :
  1500 - 3:37.99, 3k - 7:47.80 (7:39.55-93),
  5k - 13:13.77 (13:10.24-92)
DENNY Stuart U15 28.04.81, N Shields Poly :
  DTB - 37.62, JTB - 49.30
DENSLEY Martin Richard U15 1.05.81,
  Ealing,Southall & Mx : PV - 3.50
DENT Richard U17 2.11.78, Wakefield :
  HJ - 2.03
DEVLIN Gareth U20 2.06.76, LoughbroSt :
  LJ - 6.91i/6.85 (6.86w-94)
DEVONISH Marlon U20 1.06.76, Coventry G :
  60 - 6.89i, 100 - 10.44w/10.5/10.55,
  200 - 20.88w/20.94, 400 - 48.5

327

DEVONSHIRE Adam U17 2.03.79, Bed & Co :
HT - 47.20, HTY - 59.90
DEVONSHIRE Stuart U20 19.09.76, Bed & Co :
HT - 46.14, HTJ - 51.10
DIAMOND Philip U23 15.10.74, Guernsey :
HJ - 2.06
DIBBLE Jason 15.02.71, Cannock & Stafford :
HT - 48.24 (49.68-94)
DICKENSON Derek Paul V45 4.12.49, Dac & T:
HT - 52.90 (73.20-76)
DICKENSON Jason 11.11.69, Army :
Dec - 5262
DICKINSON Barrie 17.09.67, Coventry G :
HT - 52.56
DICKSON Marlon U17 17.11.78, Belgrave :
60 - 7.07i, 100 - 10.9w/11.0/11.06w/11.11,
200 - 22.6w
DIXON Matthew U17 26.12.78, Wigan :
800 - 1:54.9, 1500 - 3:58.76, 3k - 8:55.3
DIXON N. U23      73, Southend :
DT - 41.24 (42.58-94)
DIXON Neil U15 16.09.80, Gateshead :
HJ - 1.87 LJ - 5.80
DOBBIE Mark U20 5.03.77, Aberdeen :
Dec - 5165w, DecJ - 5632
DOBBING Thomas F. U23 5.02.73, Blackpool/
RAF : JT - 61.14 (65.22-93)
DOBSON Martin U20 20.12.76, Shaft Barnet :
2kSt - 6:06.3
DOBSON Robert W. V50 4.11.42, Ilford :
50kW - 4:52:47 (4:07:23-79)
DOMI Papa U17, Cambridge Harriers :
100 - 11.0
DONALDSON Alasdair U20 21.06.77, Pitr :
400 - 48.7 (50.32-93), 800 - 1:50.20
DONKIN Bradley 6.12.71, Barton :
800 - 1:51.93
DONNELLY Dermot 23.09.70, Annadale Str :
3k - 8:09.75 (8:00.58-93),
5k - 13:54.02 (13:47.0-94),
10k - 29:33.8, 10kR - 29:24 (29:19-91)
DONOVAN Daniel 8.10.70, Crawley :
100 - 10.8, 200 - 21.9/21.94,
300 - 33.9 (33.7-94),
400 - 48.10 (47.8/47.87-94)
DOOMASIA Cyrus U23 31.03.73, Herne H/IND :
JT - 58.00 (59.52-94)
DORAN Anthony 22.10.72, Swansea :
HT - 46.02 (48.24-94)
DORGU Christopher 11.12.69, Hounslow :
110H - 14.6/14.81 (14.71-94)
DORSET Scott 10.04.69, Newham & Essex B :
100 - 10.8/10.96 (10.6/10.65-89),
200 - 21.7(21.4/21.88-89)
DOUGLAS Andrew J. 19.07.62, Edin SH/Army :
400H - 54.87 (53.5-91/53.59-92)
DOUGLAS Iain U20 4.01.77, Nithsdale/Border :
SPJ - 13.91
DOUGLAS Matthew U20 26.11.76, Milton K :
200 - 22.0 (22.58-93), 110HJ - 15.3,
400 - 48.2/48.61 (48.30-94), 400H - 51.73
DOUGLAS Nathan U13 19.06.83, Oxford City :
LJ - 5.37
DOUGLAS Quincy U23 7.09.75, :
200 - 21.82, 400 - 47.42
DOVELL Paul U20 5.05.77, Dorchester :
HJ - 2.05 (2.06-94)

DOWNES John 21.07.67, London Irish/IRE :
1500 - 3:48.7 (3:42.59-94),
3k - 8:00.24 (7:54.53-94),
5k - 14:12.59 (13:29.91-94), 10k - 30:08.36
DOWNES Shane, :
100kR - 6:55:12
DOWNIE Kevin 7.07.69, Border/Cambuslang :
3kSt - 9:23.2 (9:17.51-94)
DOWSETT James U15 10.11.80, Blackheath :
JTB - 47.24
DOWSETT Matthew U20 18.09.76, Walthamst :
DecJ - 5458
DOWSETT Nicholas J.E. U17 24.11.78, Wood Gr :
60HY - 8.41i, 100HY - 13.3/13.56,
LJ - 6.77, OctY - 4778
DRENNEN James 16.08.72, Bristol :
JT - 61.46 (68.38-91)
DRISCOLL Gareth U15 8.03.81, West Norfolk :
HTB - 43.22
DRONFIELD Elliot 26.10.72, Charnwood :
HJ - 2.00 (2.00-93)
DRURY Kevin U17 30.09.79, Oswestry :
100HY - 14.0/14.10, OctY - 4340
DRZEWIECKI Jan 29.11.57, Bracknell :
DT - 41.82 (44.40-91)
DUFFUS Andre U17 30.10.79, Haringey :
100 - 11.19
DUFFY Ian U20 1.12.77, Rossendale :
DecJ - 5069
DUGARD Daniel 21.06.65, Ilford :
LJ - 7.04 (7.15-89)
DUKE Adam U23 5.10.73, Thames VH/LSAC :
800 - 1:50.1 (1:48.8-92),
1500 - 3:45.39i/3:52.41 (3:45.3-92)
DUNSDON Chris U15 24.09.80, Hamps Sch :
TJ - 12.49
DUNSON J. Gregory 2.12.63, RAF/Shaft Barn:
400 - 48.52,
110H - 14.4/14.45 (14.23w-89/14.29-86),
400H - 51.8/52.03 (50.88-92),
HJ - 2.03 (2.06-85)
DUPUY Jason 31.01.71, Bexley :
800 - 1:51.3
DUVAL Spencer Gavin 5.01.70, Cannock & St :
3k - 8:05.67, 10kR - 29:10,
2kSt - 5:39.0 (5:33.09-92), 3kSt - 8:24.64
DYBALL Gareth U15 16.03.81, Woodford Gr :
HJ - 1.86
DYMOKE Peter L. 30.10.61, Livingston :
Mar - 2:24:57 (2:24:09-94)
DZIKOWSKI Ray 6.03.63, Woodford Green :
Mar - 2:27:47

EAGLE Gary 28.12.60, Westbury :
Mar - 2:29:36 (2:29:22-94)
EARLE Albert St.Clair 10.01.58, Wolves & B :
TJ - 14.19w/14.15 (15.14-79)
EARLE Robert B. 15.09.60, Haringey :
SP - 13.75 (14.87i-93/14.80-86),
DT - 44.06 (45.12-90), HT - 62.60
EASTLAKE David 2.07.63, Morpeth :
SP - 14.26i/13.60 (14.60-91)
EASTON Mark Jonathan 24.05.63, Surrey WC :
3kW - 12:15.45 (11:24.4-89),
10kW - 41:37.0 (41:14.3-89),
35kW - 2:45:58 (2:42:13-93), 50kW - 4:06:01
EAVES Kevin U17 16.03.79, Croydon :
LJ - 6.61

328

ECCLES Martin 16.01.57, :
100kR - 7:22:48
EDEN Tom U17 16.05.79, Trafford :
HTY - 52.86
EDGERTON Ross U15 13.09.80, IOW Sch :
HJ - 1.81
*EDMISTON Paul James 16.02.72, Bed&Co/AUS :*
*110H - 13.98w/14.14*
EDMONDS Andrew U17 17.09.78, Soton City :
100 - 11.1/11.13w, 200 - 22.31
EDMONDS P. U15, Oldham & Royton :
HJ - 1.80
EDMONDS Steve 15.05.69, Birchfield :
1500 - 3:49.63
EDMUNDS Cypren 20.06.70, Thames Valley :
60 - 6.91i, 100 - 10.59w/10.74 (10.7-94),
200 - 21.2w/21.31 (21.30w-94)
EDSALL Charles K. U23 2.05.74, Havant :
110H - 15.20 (15.1-94)
EDU Remi U17 14.12.78, Enfield :
200 - 22.5, 100HY - 13.7/13.98
EDWARDS Andrew 15.09.69, Belgrave :
400H - 53.73 (52.5/53.09-93)
, EDWARDS Dafydd U23 19.09.74, Cardiff :
HJ - 2.05i (2.10i-94/2.05-91)
EDWARDS Jonathan David 10.05.66, Gate:
100 - 10.7 (10.6w-89/10.63w-90/10.7/10.80-92),
TJ - 18.43w/18.29
EDWARDS Lee U23 14.09.75, Cardiff :
LJ - 6.99
EDWARDS Mark U23 2.12.74, Charn/LSAC :
SP - 15.60 (15.75-94), DT - 41.96 (43.02-92)
EDWARDS Michael 19.10.68, Belgrave :
PV - 5.20 (5.52-93),
LJ - 6.85 (7.13w-93/7.04-92), Dec - 6679
EDWARDS Noel 16.12.72, Leamington :
800 - 1:52.3 (1:51.70-91)
EDWARDS Paul 13.06.68, Cheltenham :
100 - 10.8
EDWARDS Richard Anthony 4.06.67, Crawley :
TJ - 14.87 (15.80-87)
EDWARDS Stephen U20 13.06.77, Carmarthen :
110HJ - 15.0 (14.8/15.10w-94)
EGAN James Nicholas U23 12.11.75, Skyrac :
100 - 10.64w/10.78 (10.78-94),
200 - 21.62w/21.8/21.90 (21.58-94)
EKOKU Abi 13.04.66, Belgrave :
DT - 52.96 (60.08-90)
ELDRIDGE Timothy U20 15.03.76, Shaft Barn:
JT - 55.62 (62.96-93)
ELIAS Matthew U17 25.04.79, Cardiff :
400HY - 56.36
ELKS Martin U17 26.01.80, City of Stoke :
400 - 50.53
ELLAMS Craig 24.11.72, City of Stoke :
HT - 57.46 (58.76-94)
ELLERSHAW Philip U20 9.02.76, Blackpool :
200 - 22.06
ELLIOTT Christopher John U23 29.05.75, Port/
Northumberland Un : 1500 - 3:49.4,
2kSt - 5:55.42 (5:51.00-94),
3kSt - 9:04.43 (8:59.57-94)
ELLIOTT Mark U20 3.04.78, Telford :
HTJ - 46.92
ELLIOTT Mensah U20 29.08.76, Blackheath :
110HJ - 15.15, DecJ - 5981
ELLIOTT Neil 10.04.71, Edinburgh/Helen :
SP - 14.42, DT - 41.68 (44.94-94)

ELLIOTT Steven U15 5.12.80, Bingley :
JTB - 49.26
ELLIS Alan, Sunderland :
TJ - 13.96
ELLIS David 4.09.59, Birchfield :
Mar - 2:30:11 (2:18:29-83)
ELLIS Ieuan T. 11.05.60, Elswick :
Mar - 2:25:09 (2:13:21-86)
ELLIS Joel U17 2.09.79, Sparkhill :
3k - 8:57.82
ELLIS-SMITH James 72, Reigate/Oklah St Un :
1M - 4:02.72i
ELSTONE Robert, Barnsley :
Mar - 2:30:40
EMBERTON Neil 11.09.72, Wrexham :
- 800 - 1:50.53
EMEAGI Chike U23 25.09.74, N & EB/Lond Un :
100 - 10.7
ENE Anthony 2.03.68, Cardiff :
60 - 6.86i
*ENGLISH Desmond 6.06.67, Havering/IRE :*
*800 - 1:51.2 (1:48.4-91),*
*1500 - 3:42.67 (3:41.39-94)*
ENGLISH Mark U15 2.02.81, Gateshead :
PV - 3.10
EROGBOGBO Tayo U23 8.03.75, Birch/LSAC :
TJ - 16.32
ESEGBONA Unuakpor H. 16.04.68, C of Stoke :
110H - 15.65w, LJ - 7.06, Dec - 6443
EVA Roland U17 6.09.78, Huntingdon :
100HY - 14.0/14.08
EVANS David U23 23.01.76, Birchfield :
JT - 55.82 (55.84-94)
EVANS Matthew U23 19.11.75, Telford :
PV - 4.55
EVANS Paul William 13.04.61, Belgrave :
3k - 7:56.17, 5k - 13:25.38,
10k - 27:49.54 (27:47.79-93), 10kR - 28:13,
HMar - 1:00:09sh?, Mar - 2:10:31
EVANS Sean U20 3.10.76, City of Plymouth :
JT - 59.64 (59.90-94)
EVERETT Daniel U15 30.01.81, Norfolk :
400 - 53.5/53.60, PenB - 2686
EXLEY Scott U20 9.02.78, Millfield Sch :
110HJ - 15.4, DecJ - 5639
EYNON Andrew 1.09.62, Swansea :
5k - 14:33.83, 3kSt - 9:08.9

F ABEN Stuart U20 28.02.75, Thames VH :
JT - 74.24
FAIRBROTHER Simon 28.03.68, Haringey :
800 - 1:49.66 (1:47.7-92),
1500 - 3:41.92 (3:38.64-92),
1M - 4:04.13 (3:56.83-90)
FAIRCLOUGH Lee 23.06.70, Team Solent :
100 - 10.78w/10.89 (10.7-93),
200 - 21.7/21.96 (21.5-93),
300 - 33.8 (33.6-94),
400 - 47.6/47.80 (47.6-92)
FALOLA Ayo 29.07.68, Woodford Green :
60 - 6.82i, 100 - 10.3w/10.50,
200 - 20.93w/21.20 (21.15-91), 110H - 14.89
FANNING Robert U17 31.10.78, Milton K :
400 - 49.86
FARAH Mohammed U13, Hounslow :
1500 - 4:43.9
FARQUHARSON Ruddy A. 26.03.61, Tel/RAF :
TJ - 14.95 (15.59w/15.57-85)

FARRELL David W. 29.06.64, Border :
3kSt - 9:12.34 (9:02.37-93)
FARRELL Kevin U20 31.10.77, Havering :
100 - 10.96, 200 - 21.99 (21.78A-94)
*FARRELLY John 4.12.67, London Irish/IRE :*
*SP - 14.90 (14.90-91), DT - 44.20 (47.52-89)*
FARRELLY Kieron U15 14.10.80, Blackheath :
1500 - 4:12.71
FARREN Robert 15.05.70, Sparta/IRE :
800 - 1:51.9 (1:51.50-92),
1500 - 3:45.1 (3:42.70-94),
1M - 4:02.5 (4:00.2-94), 3k - 8:04.69 (7:56.24-94),
5k - 14:00.2 (13:47.92-94)
FARROW Clive 24.04.70, Southend :
200 - 22.09, 400 - 48.45
FASINRO Ibrahim 'Tosi' 28.03.72, Haringey :
LJ - 6.95 (7.23-94),
TJ - 16.56 (17.30w/17.21-93)
FAULKNER Stewart 19.02.69, Birchfield :
LJ - 7.69 (8.15-90)
FENTON Malcolm L. 12.02.56, Newham & EB :
SP - 14.13i (14.56-85), HT - 61.62 (62.42-82)
FENWICK Sean, Tipton :
2kSt - 5:52.7, 3kSt - 9:10.2 (9:07.2-94)
FERGUS Jason R. U23 11.10.73, Brentwood :
60 - 6.68i, 200 - 21.5 (21.33-92),
100 - 10.46 (10.34w-94/10.4-93/10.44-92)
FERGUSON Martin M. 17.09.64, Edinburgh :
10k - 30:48.58 (30:43.6-89),
Mar - 2:26:45, 3kSt - 9:17.0
FERNS Austin U15 12.01.81, Hercules Wimb:
800 - 2:00.1,
FERRAND Adrian J. 5.02.68, Newham & EB :
110H - 15.52w (15.06-94), Dec - 6542 (6726-93)
FERRARO Michael U15 21.11.80, Deeside :
100 - 11.51, TJ - 12.39
FERRIN John 20.02.67, North Belfast :
Mar - 2:18:40
FIDLER Steven U15 18.10.80, Crawley :
PV - 3.40
FIDLER Terrence R. 13.10.71, Crawley :
110H - 15.3w/15.36 (15.1w-91/15.20-94),
PV - 4.40 (4.50-91), Dec - 6669 (6683-91)
FIELD Paul C. 24.06.67, Met. Police :
60 - 6.95i, 100 - 10.63w (10.8-91/10.90-92),
200 - 22.0, 400 - 48.46 (48.2-94/48.37-92),
60H - 8.30i, Dec - 7425w/7295,
110H - 14.68w/14.8/15.06 (14.61w/14.89-94),
PV - 4.10 (4.20-94), LJ - 7.31w/7.15 (7.19-94)
FINCH Rodney 5.08.67, Soton City/Army :
800 - 1:51.8 (1:51.1-94),
1500 - 3:42.92 (3:37.97-93),
3k - 8:10.2i (7:53.99i-94/7:59.33-93),
5k - 14:15.2 (14:03.27-93)
FINDLAY Mark U20 20.03.78, Blackheath :
100 - 10.55w/10.7/10.73,
200 - 21.36, LJ - 6.90 (7.13-94)
FINDLOW Richard David 4.12.66, Bradford :
5k - 14:01.45 (13:44.58-92),
10k - 29:32.67, 10kR - 29:42 (29:19-92)
FINNIE Stuart U17 14.12.78, Lisburn :
LJ - 6.99w/6.85
FISHER L. U17, Brentwood :
HJ - 1.94
FISHER Paul U17 17.05.79, Milton Keynes :
1500 - 4:02.5, 3k - 8:42.8
FITTALL Ross U17 4.09.79, Dursley :
1500 - 4:02.25

FITZGERALD Des 26.11.72, Pitreavie :
PV - 4.40 (4.50-94)
FITZSIMMONS James U23 20.04.74,
Stockport/Camb Un : 3kSt - 9:17.0
FLEMING Craig U13 29.01.83, Victoria PAAC :
75HC - 12.5/12.73, TJ - 10.37, PenC - 1866
FLEMING Peter Ross 5.01.61, Leslie Deans RC :
10MR - 47:38, HMar - 1:04:13 (1:02:52-93),
Mar - 2:13:35 (2:13:33-93)
FLEMING Rupert U20 15.11.76, :
110HJ - 15.2
FLETCHER Martyn 21.01.69, Birchfield :
SP - 15.59 (16.48-92)
FLINT Benjamin U17 16.09.78, Rotherham :
PV - 4.60
FLINT Christopher V50 6.12.44, London Vid :
100MW - 21:24:32 (20:17:28-89)
FLINT Mark A. 19.02.63, Telford/RAF :
10kR - 29:31 (28:38-94),
10MR - 47:56 (47:16-93),
HMar - 1:03:55 (1:01:56-93)
FLOYD Michael U20 26.09.76, Sale/NWHS :
HT - 57.72, HTJ - 63.94
FLYNN Julian T. 3.07.72, Birchfield :
LJ - 7.50 (7.52-92), TJ - 14.28 (15.32-93)
FOGG Nicholas U20 24.03.78, Shaftesbury B :
HTJ - 48.16
FOLEY Johnathan U17 24.10.78, Marlbro :
LJ - 6.61, OctY - 4495
FOOKS Andrew U23 26.04.75, Thames VH:
3kSt - 8:56.83
FORBES Brian U23 6.09.74, Mid Ulster :
400 - 48.92
FORD Nathan U15 17.09.80, Northants Sch :
TJ - 12.15
FORDER Martin John 7.08.70, GEC :
800 - 1:51.70 (1:48.51-92),
1500 - 3:47.02 (3:42.53-92)
FOREMAN Ben U13 18.03.83, Team Solent :
1500 - 4:42.8
FORESHEW Joe U20 2.05.77, Chichester :
3kSt - 9:44.1
FORREST Anthony U20 22.12.76, Milton K:
5k - 14:44.7
FOSTER Carl U23 24.10.75, Hallamshire :
400H - 54.2/54.58 (54.21-94)
FOSTER Steve U15, Lincs Sch :
SPB - 13.22
FOSTER William R.G. 9.08.58, Blackheath :
5k - 14:20.96 (13:59.29-88),
10k - 29:17.11, 10MR - 48:54,
HMar - 1:04:46, Mar - 2:15:49
FOWKES J. U15, Thurrock :
JTB - 46.24
FOWLER R. Melville 7.07.66, Inverness :
TJ - 14.30 (14.57-85)
FOX Morris 30.04.63, City of Stoke :
SP - 14.95, DT - 46.40
FRANCIS Alex U23 15.07.74, Newham & E B :
200 - 22.05w (22.11-94), 400 - 47.42
FRANCIS Mark U13 4.09.82, Birchfield :
100 - 12.14, 200 - 25.2
FRANCIS Mark U20 23.09.77, Sutton & D :
JT - 64.44
FRANCIS Nicholas U17 26.11.78, :
LJ - 6.58
FRANCIS Nick 29.08.71, Cambridge Harriers :
5k - 14:34.18

FRANCIS Peter U17 28.08.80, Blackheath :
TJ - 13.84
FRANCIS Steven U17 31.01.79, Newport :
100HY - 14.0w, PV - 4.40
FRANCIS Tony U13 6.07.83, AF&D :
JTC - 35.94
FRANKLIN Andrew U15 13.09.80, Sutton & D :
3k - 9:26.3
FRANKLIN John 1.03.66, Woodford Green :
110H - 15.2 (15.1w-90/15.13-91)
FRANKS David U20 21.04.78, Wigan :
HJ - 2.07
FRASER Peter U20 28.01.78, Aberdeen :
JT - 56.34
FRASER Scott U20 31.12.77, Inverness :
100 - 10.8w (10.70w/10.78-94)
FREARY Paul 3.04.68, Bolton :
1500 - 3:46.2 (3:43.3-91),
3k - 8:09.19 (8:07.84-90)
FREEMAN David U20 5.08.77, Solihull & S H :
2kSt - 6:06.38
FRICKER Simon David U23 14.07.75, Bournem'th :
SP - 14.62, DT - 45.74 (46.10-93)
FROST Andrew U15 17.04.81, Isle of Wight :
SPB - 13.11, HTB - 49.04
FUAT Fuat 20.09.71, Enfield :
JT - 58.60
FUGALLO Alexander 28.01.70, Highgate :
200 - 21.7/21.95i (21.20w-89/21.2/21.26-90),
400 - 47.88 (46.39-94)
FULLER Peter U20 30.04.78, Sutton & D :
HTJ - 48.06
FULLER William U20 19.10.76, Epsom & E :
SP - 15.64, SPJ - 16.96, DT - 41.18,
DTJ - 45.50, HT - 53.66, HTJ - 56.28
FULLER William J. V45 5.02.48, Epsom & E :
SP - 13.85 (17.87-72)
FURLONG Kevin 19.05.70, Manx H :
110H - 15.1/15.26

G AJJAR Kieran U20 25.09.76, Wakefield :
200 - 22.0/22.42 (22.03w/22.06-94)
GALBRAITH Edward U23 3.10.75, Basing & MH :
DecJ - 5251o (5712-94)
GALLAGHER Gary 7.06.71, GEC/Staffs Univ :
110H - 15.6/15.99 (15.0-94/15.20w-93/15.33-94)
GALLAGHER Michael 25.04.66, Border :
400 - 48.80 (48.3/48.31-94)
GANDA Thomas 9.10.72, North London/SLE :
100 - 10.50, 200 - 21.18w/21.27,
LJ - 7.63 (7.84-92)
GARBA Abu U20 6.05.76, :
TJ - 14.15i (14.38w/14.25-94)
GARDENER Jason U23 18.09.75, C of Bath :
60 - 6.73i (6.73i-94), 100 - 10.33 (10.25-94)
GARDNER Paul 5.08.69, Telford/RAF :
800 - 1:52.44 (1:51.5-91),
1500 - 3:45.64, 1M - 4:06.2
GARDNER Robert U17 23.12.78, Norfolk :
PV - 3.70
GARDNER Robin, Woodstock R :
100kR - 7:26:56
GARLAND Stephen U23 12.01.73, Liv Pemb/
Cambridge Univ : Dec - 6311
GARMSTON John J.P. 3.03.65, Wolves & B :
400H - 54.5/54.84 (52.31-88)
GARRETT Lee U17 2.09.78, Berry-H Mansfld:
800 - 1:57.7, 1500 - 3:59.5

GARRIDGE Stephen U15 31.12.81, Manx H :
3kW - 16:18.0
GASCOIGNE Stephen 20.12.66, Blackheath :
PV - 4.20 (4.70-88)
GASSON Chris U17 28.02.79, Eastbourne GS :
JTY - 53.48 (54.72-94)
GATES Nigel V40 18.05.53, Brighton :
5k - 14:28.62 (13:50.8-78)
GAUDEN Duncan J. 11.02.68, Telford :
Dec - 5751 (6244-94)
GAWTHORPE Richard U15 28.01.81, Der & Co :
LJ - 6.24w/6.03, PenB - 2816
GAY Chris U13 10.02.83, Blackheath :
3k - 10:23.0
GEE Simon U23 23.04.75, Liverpool H :
TJ - 14.13 (14.60-94)
GERCS John 7.06.69, Rugby :
800 - 1:49.56
GHENT Brendon U20 7.09.76, Coventry G :
100 - 10.97w
GHENT Gary U23 2.11.73, Coventry Godiva :
200 - 22.0
GIBSON Andrew U23 20.09.73, Wigan :
100 - 10.8 (10.8-92/10.84w-91), 200 - 21.50,
400 - 47.76i/48.1/48.26
GIDLEY Alistair 5.09.72, Old Gaytonians :
JT - 59.96 (62.88-93)
GIDLEY Ian 13.11.70, Sale :
HJ - 2.05 (2.05-93)
GIFFORD David U23 9.03.73, Cannock & St :
400H - 53.80 (53.34-94)
GILBERT Adam U15 24.02.81, Notts :
LJ - 5.89
GILBERT Gareth 24.08.72, Cardiff :
SP - 13.64, DT - 46.34
GILBERT Paul U15 21.06.81, Phoenix :
800 - 2:04.94
GILBY Clive Roger 24.02.66, Cambridge H :
800 - 1:47.33, 1500 - 3:46.9 (3:46.27-92)
GILBY Daniel P. 9.07.70, Cambridge Harriers :
PV - 4.50 (5.00-91), Dec - 5961
GILDING Paul U23 2.01.75, Brighton :
TJ - 14.60
GILHOOLY Tony U20 26.03.76, Cambuslang :
HJ - 2.02 (2.05-94)
GILL Andrew Robert 19.02.70, GEC :
110H - 15.0/15.46 (14.41w-89/14.9-90/14.92-88),
400H - 53.5/54.01 (52.78-91)
GILL Anthony U20 19.09.77, Bingley :
110HJ - 14.8/15.40, 110H - 15.66
GILL Jeffrey 15.09.71, Newquay & Par :
3kSt - 9:22.2 (9:34.0-90)
GILLARD Matthew U23 11.07.75, Wakefield :
200 - 22.0, Dec - 5817
GILLES William U23 15.02.73, Croydon :
110H - 15.47, Dec - 6601
GILLESPIE Ian 18.05.70, Birchfield :
1k - 2:24.6 (2:23.8-93),
1500 - 3:44.03 (3:40.72-93),
1M - 4:02.9(3:58.64-93), 3k - 8:00.9
GIRAUD Martin U20 16.11.77, Hercules Wim :
60 - 6.76i, 100 - 10.6w/10.78w/11.00 (10.7-94)
GIRVAN Richard U20 26.07.76, Annadale Str :
800 - 1:49.95
GISBEY David Edward 2.05.60, Edinburgh SH :
HT - 55.70
GITTINS Gareth U15, :
LJ - 5.80w

GOEDLUCK Philip Adrian Troy 10.09.67, Bel :
100 - 10.3w/10.43w/10.61 (10.48-94),
200 - 20.73w/21.20 (20.79-94)
GOFORTH James U15 7.12.80, Scarborough :
DTB - 42.66
GOLDING Julian U23 17.02.75, Blackheath :
100 - 10.30, 150 - 15.38w,
200 - 20.69w/20.7/20.75
GOLLEY Julian Quintin Patrick 12.09.71, TVH :
TJ - 16.18i/16.06 (17.06-94)
GOODALL Peter U17 7.05.79, Victoria PAAC :
HJ - 1.93i/1.90
GOODEY Greig U17 14.09.78, Basildon :
100HY - 13.7, 400HY - 55.96
GOODGER David U23 19.09.75, Newport :
400H - 53.8/54.09
GOODWIN Jon U20 22.09.76, C of Plymouth :
400H - 54.97, DecJ - 5568 (5715w-94)
GOOKEY Steven John 21.04.71, Rown/Notts Un :
60 - 6.87i (6.67i-91)
GORDDARD John 21.09.71, Beds& Co/AUS :
SP - 18.06
GORDON David 20.03.68, N& EB/LSAC :
PV - 4.70 (4.75-94/4.85Aun-93)
GORDON Dominic U15 7.01.81, Bristol :
100 - 11.20w/11.4/11.53, 200 - 23.16
GORDON Martyn U17 29.09.79, Mandale :
800 - 1:57.7
GORDON Peter V40 2.07.51, Haringey :
DT - 49.88 (61.62-91), HT - 46.06 (63.20-82)
GORDON Steven 9.04.67, Bedford & County :
LJ - 6.89w/6.81 (6.86-94)
GORHAM Paul U20 7.08.78, Thurrock :
HTJ - 53.24
GOSNALL Toby 21.04.71, Birchfield :
800 - 1:52.6
GOSS Steve 15.12.68, Shaftesbury Barnet :
3kSt - 9:17.50
GOUDIE Andrew U17 4.10.78, Bexley :
5kW - 25:47.96, 10kWR - 53:51
GOUDIE William U15 16.12.80, Wirral :
800 - 2:03.1
GOUGH S. 10.02.56, Royal Navy :
Mar - 2:27:09 (2:27:04-93)
GOULD Terence Anthony 12.06.65, WS&E/RAF :
400 - 48.55 (48.1/48.42-93)
GOWLAND Lionel V40 5.02.55, Preston :
Mar - 2:29:50 (2:28:12-90)
GRAFFIN Allen Gordon U20 20.12.77, Tonb :
1500 - 3:54.6, 3k - 8:30.34, 5k - 14:16.8
GRAFFIN Andrew Neill U20 20.12.77, Tonb :
800 - 1:53.91, 1500 - 3:48.9, 5k - 14:33.6
GRAHAM Andrew U15 1.09.80, Northampton :
DTB - 38.64
GRAHAM Anthony 15.10.63, Newport :
10k - 30:41.7 (30:18.9-92), Mar - 2:21:05
GRAHAM D., Ipswich :
PV - 4.30
GRAHAM Daniel U17 3.08.79, Liverpool H :
HJ - 2.05
GRAHAM Grant 27.12.72, Clydesdale :
800 - 1:49.55, 1500 - 3:43.2,
1M - 4:02.8, 3kSt - 9:14.31bsh
GRAHAM Paul U17 8.10.78, Blackheath :
HJ - 1.91
GRANGE Liam U13 18.08.83, Steyning :
2kW - 11:26.0 (11:13.4-94)

GRANT Andy 26.01.72, Herne Hill :
HJ - 2.00
GRANT Dalton 8.04.66, Haringey :
HJ - 2.35 (2.37i-94/2.36-91)
GRANT Keith U17 17.03.80, Pendle :
1.5kSt - 4:29.38
GRANT Mark 17.05.71, Thames Valley :
PV - 5.10
GRATTON Dave V40 25.10.55, Wakefield :
10k - 30:30.1 (30:05.51-92)
GRAY Daniel U15 23.10.80, Sale :
1500 - 4:21.3
GRAY Glenn 21.04.68, Thames Valley :
400 - 49.0 (48.26-91), 400H - 54.10
GRAY Marvin 18.12.71, Cardiff :
110H - 15.15, 400H - 53.7/54.06 (54.03-94)
GRAY Neil 30.08.65, Portsmouth :
SP - 16.28 (17.79lght-88/17.62-89)
GRAY Paul 25.05.69, Cardiff :
60H - 7.78i, 110H - 13.86 (13.53-94)
GRAY Wayne U15 7.11.80, Blackheath :
100 - 11.29w/11.3/11.45 (11.44-94),  200 - 23.68i,
80HB - 11.46, HJ - 1.97, PenB - 2868
GRAYS B., Huntingdon/USA :
SP - 15.44
GREALLY Michael 18.06.60, Pitreavie :
Mar - 2:28:13 (2:21:40-94)
GREAVES Damien David U20 19.09.77, N&EB :
110HJ - 14.0/14.40, 110H - 14.34
GREEN Adrian David 30.05.68, Woodford Gr :
3kSt - 8:56.46 (8:51.1-89)
GREEN Andrew Richard 14.12.62, Warrington :
HMar - 1:04:39 (1:02:48-93)
GREEN Clifton Paul U17 10.10.79, Medway :
JTY - 64.18
GREEN Mark 28.06.71, Hounslow :
400H - 53.1/55.72 (54.30-93)
GREEN Paul 7.04.72, East Cheshire :
3k - 8:23.7 (8:18.35-94)
GREEN Stephen Harold 18.02.71, Trafford :
800 - 1:48.9, 1k - 2:22.0 (2:21.95-94),
1500 - 3:42.4 (3:39.19-94),
3k - 8:03.82i/8:05.45
GREEN Stephen 28.07.70, Bingley :
3k - 8:19.5, 5k - 14:22.7 (14:17.2-94),
10k - 29:44.03, 10MR - 48:07,
HMar - 1:04:45
GREEN Thomas U13 6.05.83, Sheffield RWC :
2kW - 11:59.0
GREENHOW Richard U17 13.02.80, Border :
DTY - 40.42
GREENWOOD Tim U13 22.11.82, Oxford City :
80HC - 12.7, HJ - 1.66, JTC - 35.96
GREGORY Carl U20 17.08.77, Hounslow :
HT - 45.72 (48.60-94), HTJ - 53.68
GREGORY Geoffrey U23 8.06.74, Wolves & B :
PV - 4.20 (4.80-94)
GREGORY Jonathan 3.10.72, Rown/LSAC :
110H - 15.6 (15.68w-91)
GRIERSON Andrew U17 23.11.79, Reading :
HTY - 48.88
GRIFFIN David 5.12.63, Cardiff :
400 - 48.4, 400H - 52.07
GRIFFIN Mark U23 16.02.75, Walt/London Un :
800 - 1:52.3 (1:49.27-94)
GRIFFIN Neil V45 28.05.48, Windsor S & E :
DT - 44.38 (51.66-80)

GRIFFITHS David U23 22.12.74, C of Stoke :
PV - 4.20 (4.30-94)
GRIFFITHS M., Birmingham Univ. :
10k - 31:19.38
GRIFFITHS Malcolm, Bridgend :
100kR - 7:56:03
GRIFFITHS Tegid 19.04.60, Chester & Elles :
DT - 44.04 (48.36-89)
GRIME Ian 29.09.70, Newham & Essex B :
800 - 1:50.1 (1:49.10-94),
1500 - 3:42.73 (3:40.35-94),
1M - 4:07.0 (4:03.7-90),
3k - 8:16.5 (8:12.01-93),
5k - 14:35.58 (14:08.31-94),
10k - 31:01.15 (30:39.31-93)
GRINDLEY David 29.10.72, Wigan :
200 - 21.7 (20.89w-93/21.50-92),
400 - 46.15 (44.47-92)
GRINNELL Luke U17 21.03.79, Bristol :
100 - 10.96w/11.07
GRIPTON Paul U20 9.11.76, Bromsgrove & R :
60HJ - 8.28i, 110HJ - 14.41w/14.94 (14.91-94),
110H - 15.1/15.13 (15.1-94)
GRISS Edward U20 12.08.76, Gateshead :
DTJ - 45.52
GRITZ Ben U20 21.11.77, Old Gaytonians :
110HJ - 15.2
GROENEN Jonathan U15 12.09.80, Eastb R :
400 - 53.81, PenB - 2692
GROVES M. U13, Torfaen :
JTC - 38.70
GROVES Shaun U15 15.09.80, Torfaen :
JTB - 54.06
GUDGEON Alistair U17 26.10.79, Peterbro :
LJ - 6.83w/6.63
GUEGAN Michael Gerald 19.09.66, Team S :
800 - 1:52.04 (1:47.90-92)
GUILDER Alan J. 10.12.61, Blackheath :
3k - 8:23.6 (7:58.42-86),          •
Mar - 2:24:41 (2:21:46-93)
GUITE Craig U20 19.08.77, Rotherham :
PV - 4.40
GULLIVER Mark 11.02.72, Leeds :
HT - 51.24
GUTHRIE Alexander U17 6.07.79, Kilbarchan :
400 - 50.6/52.04
GUTTERIDGE Steven T. 5.07.71, Highgate :
PV - 4.45 (4.80-93)
GWYNNE Timothy J. 20.01.71, Birchfield :
400 - 48.91i
GYORFFY Terry 28.01.65, Basingstoke & MH :
PV - 4.20, JT - 57.04, Dec - 6648
GYPHION Justin U15 1.09.80, :
TJ - 12.01

H ACKETT Chris U13 1.03.83, Oxford City :
LJ - 5.21
HACKLEY Peter 19.02.71, Border :
800 - 1:50.10 (1:47.59-93),
1500 - 3:48.7 (3:48.5-93)
HACKNEY Roger Graham 2.09.57, AF&D/RAF :
3kSt - 9:16.8 (8:18.91-88)
HADLER John 18.08.69, Cambridge Harriers :
110H - 15.5w (14.8w/14.9-89/15.61-92)
HAINES Andrew 15.10.72, Crawley :
110H - 15.5 (15.1-92/15.13w/15.17-91)
HALE Steven U20 20.04.77, Sandwell :
DTJ - 42.94

HALES Matthew U17 6.10.79, Steyning :
3kW - 13:57.0, 3kWR - 14:16 (13:44o-94),
5kW - 23:52.4o/24:21.0, 5kWR - 23:24,
10kWR - 51:00
HALL Dominic 21.02.71, Highgate :
800 - 1:51.69 (1:50.9-91)
HALL Thomas U17 8.07.79, Salford :
1500 - 4:03.5
HALPIN Barry U17 20.07.79, Halifax :
200 - 22.6/22.90
HAMER Ian 15.04.61, Horwich :
Mar - 2:28:42
HAMER Nigel U20 1.01.76, Derby & Co :
200 - 21.8/21.92w (21.81-93)
HAMES Jeremy E. 17.11.70, Charnwood :
SP - 13.49 (13.95-94), DT - 43.86
HAMILTON Craig U15 10.05.81, N Yorks Sch :
1500 - 4:21.73
HAMILTON Ian 8.03.65, Medway :
5k - 14:24.83
HAMILTON Mark U15 18.11.80, Chesterfield :
SPB - 13.45
HAMILTON Nicholas U17 13.03.79, Blackh'th :
400 - 49.95
HAMMOND Lee U20 13.11.77, Coventry G :
JT - 54.60
HAMMOND Matthew 26.09.68, Scunthorpe :
HT - 46.14 (49.44-93)
HANLON Thomas 20.05.67, Leslie Deans RC :
3k - 7:56.71 (7:51.31-92),
3kSt - 8:24.37 (8:12.58-91)
HANNA David U23 13.12.75, Lincoln Well :
JT - 63.22
HANSEN Ben U15 12.10.80, Somerset Sch :
JTB - 48.86
HANSON C. U15, West Midland Sch :
TJ - 12.73w/12.68
HARDGRAVE William U15 17.09.80, Invicta :
DTB - 40.08
HARDWICK Richard U13 1.09.82, Wakefield :
3k - 10:32.7
HARDY Alan P. 4.09.58, Blackheath :
PV - 4.20 (4.50-92)
HARGRAVE Christopher U17 27.02.79, Bed&C :
60HY - 8.4i/8.45i, 100HY - 13.27w/13.34
HARGREAVES Aaron U17 5.12.78, Pendle :
1500 - 4:01.19, 3k - 8:45.1
HARGREAVES Mark 26.08.60, Bournemouth :
Mar - 2:25:36 (2:23:25-94)
HARKER Kenneth 25.02.71, Mandale :
1500 - 3:51.7 (3:49.6-94)
HARKINS Rodger R. 7.06.60, Shettleston :
TJ - 14.13w (15.02-84)
HARKNESS Ian 23.08.68, Old G/Camb Univ :
5k - 14:35.9 (14:21.1-89)
HARPER Ben U17 9.11.78, Braintree :
400 - 49.48, 800 - 1:57.0
HARPER Philip U15 18.11.80, Derby & Co :
1500 - 4:19.20
*HARPUR Ian 24.04.67, London Irish/IRE :*
*3k - 8:24.1*
HARRIES Kirk U23 7.08.74, Hillingdon :
60H - 8.3i (8.3i-94), 110H - 14.76
HARRIES Philip James Charles 7.04.66,
Der & Co/LSAC : 400H - 54.8 (50.01-88)
HARRIS Paul U23 16.09.73, Bicester RR :
Mar - 2:29:20

333

HARRIS Stephen 27.04.71, Phoenix :
10kR - 29:37, HMar - 1:04:08
HARRISON Alan 20.11.57, Southampton City :
400 - 48.97
HARRISON Ererton W. 8.04.66, Thames VH :
60H - 8.26i (8.10i-89),
110H - 14.67 (14.11-91), LJ - 6.90w (7.06-86)
HARRISON James 21.12.63, Blackheath/AUS :
10k - 29:36.58 (29:30.84-94),
10MR - 48:53, Mar - 2:21:30
HARRISON Josh U23 14.08.75, Birchfield :
JT - 56.72
HARRISON Paul U17 17.11.79, Southend :
PV - 3.60
HARRISON Stephen 19.12.72, Blackheath :
JT - 75.32
HART Andrew 13.09.69, Coventry Godiva :
800 - 1:48.2 (1:48.06-92),
1500 - 3:42.03, 1M - 4:01.8
HART Nathan U23 1.07.73, W S & E/Bris Un :
110H - 15.6 (15.4/15.66w-94)
HART Neal 15.04.68, Scottish Borders :
SP - 13.80, DT - 41.72
HARTLEY Adam 27.02.69, Leeds :
400H - 53.51 (53.15-94)
HARTLEY Mike, Cannock & Stafford :
100kR - 7:13:25
HARTMANN Henrik 7.09.72, Enfield :
400H - 55.52 (53.8/53.99-94)
HASSALL David 11.10.70, Sale :
JT - 56.20
HASSAN Eshref U17 7.12.79, Belgrave :
LJ - 6.85
HASSAN Malcolm U13, Sunderland :
1500 - 4:42.0
HATTON Darren U17 21.03.79, Medway :
LJ - 6.67, SPY - 14.69i,
DTY - 41.16, OctY - 4993
HAUGHIAN Samuel U17 9.07.79, Hounslow :
3k - 8:57.97
HAUGHTON Ben U15, Ballymena & Antrim :
JTB - 50.82
HAWKINS Christopher Michael 24.10.61, Bing :
3k - 8:16.62i (7:58.37i-88/8:03.6-87),
5k - 14:22.0 (14:17.92-92),
2kSt - 5:42.3 (5:31.59-90), 3kSt - 8:36.55
HAWKINS James U17 14.12.79, Medway :
HTY - 59.80
HAWORTH Alex, U20 12.04.78 :
HJ - 2.00
HAY Wayne U15 25.09.80, Reading :
LJ - 6.50w/6.30
HAYES Kerry D. 22.01.63, Milton Keynes :
3kSt - 9:15.70 (8:54.31-89)
HAYES Martin U17 31.08.79, Chesterfield :
SPY - 14.03i/12.54, DTY - 42.00, HTY - 54.10
HAYES Scott U23 4.01.73, Thames Valley :
SP - 15.98i/15.62, DT - 52.26
HAYFORD Kenneth N. 10.03.63, Camb H :
JT - 64.56 (69.90-87)
HAYMAN Tom U15 17.09.80, B-Hill Mansfield :
DTB - 38.22
HAYNES Peter 18.09.64, Basildon :
5k - 14:26.97 (14:05.05-94), Mar - 2:21:59
HAYNES Simon U23 12.08.74, Windsor S & E :
400 - 48.28
HAYWARD Andrew U23 26.10.74, Rowntrees :
JT - 60.38

HAYWARD Gregory 28.01.64, Peterbro/RAF :
JT - 56.80 (61.96-90)
HAYWARD Stephan U23 30.07.74, Edin/Sc Bord :
SP - 16.88, DT - 46.90 (47.76-94)
HEAD Paul 1.07.65, Newham & Essex B :
DT - 41.38 (44.12-89), HT - 68.88 (74.02-90)
HEALEY Ed V40    54, London Irish/IRE :
HT - 57.98 (66.96-79)
HEALY Graham 27.04.70, Havering :
400 - 48.74 (47.47-91)
HEALY Philip 1.10.70, Ballydrain :
800 - 1:51.8 (1:51.7-93),
1500 - 3:45.6 (3:43.8-93),
1M - 4:04.0 (4:02.01-93)
HEANLEY John U15 25.09.80, Windsor S & E :
800 - 2:00.64
HEARD Dwayne E. 2.02.64, Blackheath :
TJ - 14.99w/14.28 (15.63w-89/15.62-87)
HEASLEY B. U13, Mid Ulster :
200 - 25.7
HEATH Brett U23 6.01.75, Havering :
PV - 4.10 (4.20-94), Dec - 6193 (6579-94)
HEATH David J. 22.05.65, Blackheath :
800 - 1:52.6 (1:50.01-92),
1500 - 3:47.89 (3:41.0-89),
1M - 4:09.9 (3:59.36-89)
HEAVYSIDE John U15 19.11.80, Cumb Sch :
TJ - 12.76
HECHEVARRIA Eugene 30.12.63, Westbury :
TJ - 14.23 (15.05-94)
HEDMAN Graham U17 6.02.79, Braintree :
400 - 50.0/50.26
HEGGIE Jonathan U17 8.12.79, Hallamshire :
400HY - 57.9
HEGGIE Simon U20 12.01.76, Hallamshire :
400 - 48.55 (48.1/48.26-94)
HENDERSON James Alistair 28.03.69, ESH :
60 - 6.81i (6.66i-87), 100 - 10.79 (10.21-87)
HENDRY Martyn U23 10.04.75, Edinburgh :
110H - 15.4/15.56 (15.49-94)
HENNESSY Andrew U20 24.08.77, Wells :
800 - 1:54.4, 3k - 8:29.23
HENRY A. U15, :
80HB - 11.88
HENRY Corri U20 9.12.76, Notts :
200 - 21.78w/21.88
HENTHORN James U20 20.02.77, Carm :
100 - 10.41, 200 - 21.12
HERBERT John A.A. 20.04.62, Haringey :
LJ - 7.23w/7.19 (7.94w-82/7.74-85),
TJ - 16.50i/16.00w (17.41-85)
HERBERT Scott U23 12.02.74, Milton Keynes :
100 - 10.7w (10.6w-93),
200 - 21.7 (22.22w/22.35-90), 400 - 48.8
HERMANN Daniel U15 3.03.81, Pudsey & B :
800 - 2:02.6
HERRINGTON Gary 31.03.61, Rugby :
SP - 13.46 (13.96-88), DT - 56.32,
HT - 47.54 (48.34-88)
HEWSON Neil U15 4.09.80, Bolton :
400 - 52.79, TJ - 11.95
HEYWOOD Danny 27.05.71, Cardiff :
110H - 15.67w, 400H - 53.9/54.53
HIBBERD Matthew J. U23 23.06.73, TVH :
800 - 1:49.6 (1:49.2-92), 1k - 2:22.7,
1500 - 3:42.32 (3:41.73-94), 3k - 8:23.9
HIBBERT Paul N. 31.03.65, Birchfield :
400H - 51.33

334

HIBBINS Kevin U15 7.11.80, Grantham :
200 - 23.2, LJ - 6.74
HICKS Andrew U17 30.07.79, Banbury :
400HY - 57.14
HICKS Daniel U17 17.12.78, Hastings :
3k - 8:55.6
HICKS Maurice 1.01.70, Hounslow/Junc 10 :
DT - 42.38 (43.62-92), HT - 53.62 (53.70-92)
HILL Geoffrey 8.02.63, Swansea :
10k - 30:19.0 (29:54.3-88)
HILL Kevin U23 17.06.73, Wigan :
JT - 61.22 (66.60-94)
HILL Matthew U13, Blackheath :
800 - 2:18.49,
HILL Michael Christopher 22.10.64, Leeds :
JT - 84.14 (86.94-93)
HILL Robin U20 23.02.77, Hemsworth :
PV - 4.60
HILLIER James U20 3.04.78, Newport :
110HJ - 15.4/15.61w, 400H - 54.45
HILLIER Matthew U20 10.08.77, Belgrave :
3kSt - 9:47.21
HILSTON James U17 25.02.79, Belgrave :
100 - 11.0/11.06, 200 - 22.2/22.9w,
400 - 48.35, HJ - 1.90
HILTON Jonathan U23 11.01.74, Sale :
TJ - 15.03 (15.06-94)
HINDLEY Christopher U20 21.01.76, Worksop :
HJ - 2.06 (2.06-94),
Dec - 6127w/5197 (6514-94), DecJ - 6417
HINDS Elphinston 15.07.60, Thames Valley :
TJ - 14.32 (15.20w-85/14.82-91)
HOAD Paul 29.10.63, Enfield :
PV - 4.50 (5.01-86)
HOBBS Justin 12.03.69, Cardiff :
5k - 14:30.08 (13:45.53-94),
10k - 29:25.92 (28:17.00-94), 10kR - 28:35
HOBDELL Ian 07.07.68, Hounslow :
3kSt - 9:10.41
HOCKEY Jonathan U15 18.09.80, Essex Sch :
800 - 2:01.29
HODGE Andrew J. 18.12.68, Blackheath/
Cambridge University : HJ - 2.00 (2.10-93),
110H - 15.2w/15.56 (14.9-94/15.41w-92)
HODGKINSON Mark R. 20.07.72, Birchfield :
PV - 5.10
HODGSON Louis U20 29.12.76, Wakefield :
DTJ - 42.86
HODSON Ben U20 25.01.76, Old Gaytonians :
TJ - 14.27
HODSON James U17 28.09.78, Sale :
OctY - 4932
HOEY Michael 29.04.69, Bournemouth :
3kSt - 9:06.6
HOGG Alan U13 3.06.83, Steyning :
2kW - 10:34.0, 3kW - 16:10.0, 3kWR - 15:20
HOGSTON Philip U23 25.04.73, Blackheath :
1500 - 3:46.17, 5k - 14:05.66
HOLDER Graham P. 16.01.72, Bexley :
HT - 56.92 (57.07-94)
HOLDSWORTH Ian U20 12.01.78, Old Gayt :
PV - 4.10
HOLE Marcus 18.06.71, Exeter Univ :
110H - 15.5
HOLGATE Craig U20 21.09.76, Barrow & Fur :
DecJ - 5715
HOLGATE Martin C. 2.11.65, Woodford Gr :
400H - 54.2/54.51

HOLLEY Simon U17 2.09.78, Bedford & Co :
3k - 8:54.61
HOLLIDAY Ian U23 9.12.73, Gateshead :
HJ - 2.13
HOLLIER Steve U20 27.02.76, Wolves & B :
3kW - 12:44.48, 5kW - 21:51.0,
5kWR - 22:48+, 10kW - 45:20.42,
10kWR - 42:29
HOLLINGER Robert U15 11.10.80, Rotherham :
80HB - 11.07, SPB - 13.04, PenB - 2582
HOLLINGSWORTH Eric M. 6.12.62, Old Gayt :
110H - 15.0 (14.8db/15.25w/15.26-93),
PV - 4.60 (4.80-93), SP - 14.59 (15.27-93),
DT - 49.78 (50.12-92), Dec - 6393 (7748-93)
HOLLINGSWORTH Ivan U23 20.05.75, Gate :
1500 - 3:49.4
HOLLOWAY Alan J. 22.06.60, Charn/LSAC :
JT - 62.68 (67.62-89)
HOLLOWAY Gareth P. 2.02.70, Splott C :
3kW - 12:58.56i (12:12.36-92),
10kW - 46:44.96 (43:10.4-92)
HOLMES Jonathan U17 13.11.78, :
OctY - 4324
HOLMES Robert U15 2.11.80, Bristol :
JTB - 46.50
HOLMES Stephen U15 17.10.80, Blackheath :
800 - 2:04.8, 1500 - 4:13.52, 3k - 9:29.1
HOLT Andrew 23.02.64, Verlea :
Mar - 2:26:01 (2:24:26-93)
HOLT Peter U20 12.02.77, Hemsworth :
PV - 4.20 (4.30-93)
HOLT Richard 28.11.71, Blackh'th/Sheff Univ :
400H - 52.11
HOLTON Robert U17 8.09.78, B-Hill Mansfield :
HJ - 1.98
HOOPER Jonathan 22.07.64, Bridgend :
Mar - 2:24:27 (2:18:40-89)
HOOTON Robin U23 5.05.73, Oregon Univ. :
800 - 1:49.14
HOPE Steven 8.02.72, Tipton :
3k - 8:06.29, 5k - 14:32.54 (13:59.07-94)
HOPKINS Christopher U15 11.11.80, Spen :
PenB - 2656
HOPKINS Nicholas J. 28.08.66, Reigate :
3k - 8:11.86 (7:59.66-90), 5k - 14:05.08
HOPKINSON Mark U23 16.04.75, W S & E :
200 - 22.08i
HOPPER John 5.12.68, Newham & E B/LSAC :
HJ - 2.00 (2.15i-90/2.11-88)
HOQUE Nizamul U17 19.09.78, Blackheath :
400 - 48.66
HORAK Jiri U23 24.07.74, Hercules Wimb/CS :
HT - 52.22
HORNBY Jeff 17.01.66, Spenborough :
3k - 8:21.2, 5k - 14:24.2 (14:20.7-93),
10k - 29:59.5 (29:53.9-91)
HORNE P.D., SGA (Prof)/USA :
SP - 13.55
HORSBURGH Ian Joseph U20 10.01.78, Scot B :
400 - 49.39 (49.2/49.35-94)
HOUGH Robert S.D. 3.06.72, Sheffield :
1M - 4:01.4, 3kSt - 8:36.18
HOURIHAN Paul U20 7.11.76, Liverpool H :
Dec - 6481
HOWARD Carl U23 27.01.74, N & EB/BrunUn:
LJ - 7.51 (7.76-93), TJ - 15.97
HOWARD Damien U15 23.11.81, W Norfolk :
HTB - 41.62

335

HOWARD John U23 16.09.75, Annadale Str :
SPJ - 14.61o (14.12-94), DTJ - 42.36o
HOWARD Mark Denis 7.02.66, Crawley :
1500 - 3:51.5 (3:42.9-89), 10kR - 29:39
HOWARD Paul 19.10.66, Woodford Green :
PV - 4.10 (4.40-90), SP - 13.54 (13.63-92),
DT - 41.34 (43.06-90), JT - 61.26 (65.10-91),
Dec - 6479w (7094-92)
HOWARTH Duncan U17 20.02.79, Norfolk :
400HY - 56.13
HOWE Christopher W. 17.11.67, Woodford Gr/
LSAC : HT - 62.86 (63.74-90)
HOWE Glen U17 20.10.78, Sunderland :
400 - 50.7, 400HY - 56.5/57.97
HOWE Nicholas U15 15.02.81, Cannock & St :
TJ - 12.27
HOWLETT James U17 18.02.79, Peterbro :
HJ - 1.95
HOWSON Rick U13 9.02.83, :
400 - 58.87
HUBBARD Nicholas U20 17.04.76, Banbury :
LJ - 7.00w/6.93 (6.94-94)
HUDSPITH Ian 23.09.70, Morpeth :
3k - 8:03.9, 5k - 14:15.43,
10k - 29:58.09, HMar - 1:02:58
HUDSPITH Mark E. 19.01.69,*Morpeth :
HMar - 1:02:50dh?, Mar - 2:11:58
HUGGINS Mark 20.12.68, Leeds :
200 - 22.0
HUGGINS Marlon A. 11.02.71, Thames VH :
HJ - 2.00 (2.12i-89/2.11-94)
HUGHES Andy, RAF :
100 - 10.59
HUGHES Dean U17 22.09.78, Hounslow :
HTY - 55.02 (57.60-94)
HUGHES Gareth U23 22.10.73, Liverpool H :
110H - 15.34 (15.2-93/15.31-94)
HUGHES James U23 8.11.74, Cardiff :
60H - 8.14i, 110H - 14.37 (14.2-94)
HUGHES Kevin M. U23 30.04.73, Haringey :
PV - 5.30i/5.30
HUGHES Scott U17 20.11.78, Leigh :
800 - 1:56.1, 1.5kSt - 4:27.7
HULA Martin 2.01.66, Shaftesbury Barnet :
10k - 30:08.41
HULL Gregory 16.08.65, Leeds :
10k - 30:59.6, Mar - 2:26:34
HULME Delroy 14.09.72, City of Stoke :
TJ - 15.15 (15.50w-91/15.26-90)
HULSE G.Ewart W. 21.01.62, Colwyn Bay :
SP - 13.52 (14.09-93), DT - 42.08 (42.32-94),
HT - 51.48 (54.62-91)
HULSE Richard U17 22.09.78, Liverpool H :
PV - 4.00
HUMM Jason Alex 11.01.71, Cambridge H :
3kSt - 9:08.92 (9:07.60-94)
HUMPHREYS David James 10.10.69, Birch :
110H - 15.3/15.35 (14.30w-89/14.45-91)
HUNT Jamie U17 29.11.79, Norfolk :
SPY - 15.02
HUNT Martin, Ealing,Southall & Mx :
400 - 55.61
HUNT Paul U15 26.03.81, Bromsgrove & R :
3k - 9:37.79
HUNTER Richard 12.01.71, Belgrave :
110H - 14.8/14.99 (14.79w-89),
Dec - 5994w/5742 (6092-92)
HUNTER Roger U20 10.03.76, Skyrac :
110H - 15.33w, JT - 58.08, Dec - 6925

HUNTINGFORD Damian U20 11.06.77, GEC :
JT - 58.68 (59.18-94)
HUNTLEY Tendai U20 12.09.76, Blackheath :
LJ - 7.16w/7.11
HURRION James U23 11.11.73, Cov G/Ox Un :
JT - 63.90 (70.16r-91)
HURST Craig 30.12.70, City of Stoke :
200 - 22.08w (21.7-94/21.72w/21.81-92)
HURST Lee 29.07.72, Altrincham :
3k - 8:22.8, 3kSt - 8:54.01
HUSSAIN Bashir 20.12.64, Stockport :
3k - 8:12.78i (8:01.72-91),
5k - 14:12.04 (14:07.89-90),
10MR - 48:44 (48:28-91),
HMar - 1:04:13 (1:03:01-91), Mar - 2:26:56
HYDE Daniel U20 5.10.77, Torbay :
3k - 8:29.3
HYDE Felix U20 7.08.76, Old G/GHA :
SP - 17.38, SPJ - 18.67
HYDE Timothy 22.02.72, Windsor S & E :
3k - 8:22.1, 3kSt - 9:07.0
HYLAND Eamonn 23.07.60, Redhill/IRE :
10kR - 29:25, Mar - 2:18:48 (2:17:58-92)
HYLTON Mark U20 24.09.76, Windsor S & E :
100 - 10.8 (11.02un-93), 200 - 21.09,
300 - 33.0/33.70 (32.9-94), 400 - 45.83
HYNES Robin U20 22.04.77, Wigan :
LJ - 6.92

IBLE Keith 9.11.68, Shaftesbury Barnet :
TJ - 15.36
IDDON Chris U13 8.10.82, Bolton :
1500 - 4:44.1
IDESSANE Kheredine 1.12.69, Edinburgh SH :
800 - 1:49.95 (1:48.62-91),
1500 - 3:50.4 (3:48.06-91)
IDOWU Phillips U17 30.12.78, Belgrave :
TJ - 13.90
ILLIDGE Sam U20 4.02.77, Lincoln Well :
800 - 1:54.2
ILO Oluleke U20 25.06.78, Belgrave :
TJ - 14.10w/13.70
INGRAM David U17 19.01.80, Brighton :
PV - 3.80
INGRAM Geoff 31.01.68, RAF :
Dec - 5554 (5841-94)
INGRAM Ronnie U17 27.11.78, Trafford :
LJ - 6.53
INGRAM Stephen 22.09.70, Swansea :
LJ - 7.06 (7.91w/7.38-94)
IRVINE Gordon U17 29.11.78, Ipswich :
1.5kSt - 4:31.83
IRVING Anthony U23 30.04.75, Bord/E Kilb :
HT - 53.46
IRVING Jan U20 4.03.77, Wirral :
LJ - 7.13w/6.99 (7.02-94)
IRWIN David U17 18.12.78, Annadale Str :
SPY - 15.72

JACK Donley 7.11.66, Thames Valley :
200 - 21.4/21.84
JACKSON Carl U17 31.07.79, Trafford :
1.5kSt - 4:34.3
JACKSON Colin Ray 18.02.67, Brecon :
60 - 6.58i (6.49i-94), 100 - 10.63 (10.29-90),
60H - 7.39i (7.30i-94),
110H - 13.17 (12.8w-90/12.91-93)
JACKSON David U23 12.05.73, Rotherham :
100 - 10.72w/ (10.5wdb-89/10.53w/10.59-91)

336

JACKSON Gary 28.04.68, Birchfield :
PV - 4.60i (4.90-86)
JACKSON Iain U13 23.03.83, Harmeny :
PV - 2.25
JACKSON James 12.09.63, AF&D :
10k - 30:49.84
JACKSON P. U20, :
800 - 1:54.70
JACKSON Steven U15, Gateshead :
100 - 11.53
JACQUES Kevin 17.09.58, London Irish :
5k - 14:34.14 (13:52.94-82)
JAMES Gareth U20 16.08.77, Carmarthen :
LJ - 6.98
JAMES Kieron U15 22.09.80, W Midland Sch :
TJ - 12.49
JAMES Ronnie 14.12.64, Cornwall AC :
Mar - 2:26:35
JAMES Simon U20 21.01.77, Telford :
SPJ - 14.92
JAMES Simon R. U23 31.08.73, Wycombe :
400 - 48.5 (48.4-94/48.86-93)
JAMESON D., Brunel Univ :
100 - 10.8w
JAMIESON Paul U23 21.06.73, Liv Pemb :
200 - 21.7/22.20
JAMIESON Steven U17 4.02.79, Medway :
JTY - 63.74
JARRETT Anthony Alexander 13.08.68, Har :
100 - 10.47w (10.42w-87/10.45-94), 200 - 20.50,
60H - 7.42i, 110H - 13.04 (13.00-93)
JEFFERIES Adrian U17 12.04.79, Swindon :
TJ - 13.70 (13.77-94)
JEMI-ALADE Michael 13.10.64, Edin SH :
DT - 46.92 (52.38-87)
JENKINS Huw U20, Cardiff :
800 - 1:55.0
JENKINS William 13.07.71, Greenock Glen :
3kSt - 9:06.03 (9:00.8-93)
JENNINGS Gary 21.02.72, N & EB/LSAC :
400 - 46.95, 400H - 49.82
JENNINGS Neil U20 18.09.77, Mandale :
400 - 48.4/48.58
JEWERS William S. 27.09.62, Basingst & MH :
110H - 15.6 (14.8-86/15.22w/15.53-88),
HJ - 2.01 (2.14-86), LJ - 6.90 (7.26-86)
JOHN Eric 28.06.61, Verlea :
200 - 22.0w (21.46-83)
JOHN Jason 17.10.71, Newham & Essex B :
100 - 10.25 (10.08w/10.23-94),
200 - 20.74w/20.86 (20.51w-93)
JOHNSON A., Kent :
JT - 61.34
JOHNSON C. U13, :
JTC - 34.80
JOHNSON Dean U23 31.12.75, Hallamshire :
JT - 56.32 (60.50-93)
JOHNSON Paul 8.03.68, Birchfield :
LJ - 7.13i/7.13 (7.94i-89/7.87w-88/7.85-89)
JOHNSON Peter U23 25.09.75, Liverpool H :
JT - 57.00 (60.42-94)
JOHNSON Richard 13.10.71, Thames Valley :
100 - 10.8w/10.92 (10.6/10.74-94),
200 - 21.95w (21.5-90/21.62-94)
JOHNSON Russell U15 14.09.80, Blackheath :
100 - 11.3/11.44w (11.20w/11.54-94), 200 - 23.4
JOHNSTON Ben U17 8.11.78, Wirral :
PV - 3.60 (3.80-94)

JOHNSTON Ian 4.06.64, Enfield/Falkirk :
5k - 14:34.0
JOHNSTONE Daniel U15 10.01.81, Basildon :
80HB - 11.7/11.85
JONES A., Gloucester :
Mar - 2:28:31
JONES Alan U15 11.09.80, :
TJ - 11.96
JONES Andres U20 3.02.77, Carmarthen :
3k - 8:28.3, 5k - 14:36.35
JONES Colin U23 8.04.74, Eryri :
3k - 8:07.02, 10MR - 48:20
JONES David U15 4.10.80, Liverpool H :
HTB - 49.64
JONES Egryn 1.11.71, Swansea :
PV - 4.90
JONES Gareth 14.12.68, Cardiff :
HT - 57.50 (59.40-94)
JONES Gary 15.07.72, Wigan :
HJ - 2.10i/1.97 (2.06-91), LJ - 7.42
JONES Greg, Swansea :
200 - 22.15w
JONES Jonathan Garfield U23 14.09.74, Birm Un :
LJ - 6.90i (6.95-91)
JONES Martin John 21.04.67, Horwich :
3k - 8:21.12 (8:12.09-94),
5k - 14:19.0 (13:55.3-93),
10kR - 29:09 (28:24-94)
JONES Matthew U15 5.12.80, :
200 - 23.6/23.76
JONES Michael 23.07.63, Shaft B/WLHS :
HT - 70.48 (72.10-88)
JONES Paul U20 11.04.78, Wrexham :
PV - 4.10 (4.11-94), Dec - 5249w
JONES Peter 2.12.70, City of Hull :
1500 - 3:50.3 (3:47.3-94)
JONES Richard U15 14.05.81, Wirral :
800 - 2:04.75
JONES Robin Evans Hugh V40 1.11.55, Ranel :
Mar - 2:19:58 (2:09:24-82)
JONES Sean 21.03.69, Thames Valley/Army :
HT - 50.90 (54.88-92)
JONES Simon 23.02.65, Diss :
DT - 42.12 (44.72dh-94/44.44-86)
JONES Stephen H. V40 4.08.55, Newport :
10kR - 29:44 (27:59-84),
10MR - 48:22 (46:20un-79/46:49-89)
JONES Tim 15.09.57, :
Mar - 2:27:15 (2:25:44-90)
JOSEPH Courtney U17 25.12.78, Ealing,S & Mx :
100HY - 13.70
JOSEPH Darren U20 4.04.78, Solihull & S H :
HJ - 2.05i/2.05
JOSEPH Rafer E.L. 21.07.68, Dacorum & T :
SP - 13.68 (14.68i-94/14.01-87),
DT - 49.28 (50.66-94)
JOSEPHSON O. U13, Chiltern :
3k - 10:31.5
JOUSIFFE Warren U20 27.05.77, Hounslow :
PV - 4.60 (4.60-94)
JOYCE Brian 9.09.74, Bedford & Co :
60 - 6.8i (6.88i-93),
100 - 10.33w/10.5/10.52 (10.47-93)
JUBB Mike 20.06.70, Derby & Co :
3kSt - 8:56.02
JUDGE Andrew U23 24.05.75, Cov G/LSAC :
400H - 54.63

JUMP Ben Anderson 6.02.65, Aberdeen :
JT - 56.82 (57.70-92)

KABENGELE Darren U17 11.02.79, Leics C :
100HY - 14.10
KABISWA Samuel 28.10.66, Windsor S & E :
100 - 10.8 (10.8-94),
200 - 21.88 (21.7/21.82-93),
400 - 47.9/48.05 (47.5-94)
KARAYANNIS Constantine U17 9.01.79, S B :
SPY - 14.37, DTY - 41.48
KEARNEY Ronan, Deeside :
100 - 10.8
KEELEY Mark 4.01.72, Liverpool H :
3kSt - 9:22.9
KEITH Andrew 25.12.71, Hereford :
800 - 1:47.59 (1:47.56-92),
1500 - 3:39.17 (3:39.06-93),
1M - 3:57.96 (3:56.29i-94),
3k - 7:54.37 (7:49.83i-94), 5k - 13:48.13
KEITH Jonathon U15 5.11.80, Skyrac :
800 - 2:00.5, 1500 - 4:08.18
KELLER Simon U20 10.11.76, Newark :
SP - 14.40, SPJ - 15.39
KELLY Alexander U17 1.04.79, Exeter :
100HY - 14.0/14.62
KELLY Bryan U23 29.12.73, Liverpool H :
SP - 14.52 (15.75-93), DT - 46.64 (46.86-93)
KELLY Sean 8.11.72, Rowntrees :
800 - 1:49.9
KELSALL Alan U15 3.09.80, Newham & E B :
HTB - 49.00
KEMP Michael U17 23.12.79, Leics WC :
3kW - 16:00.0 (15:15.0-94), 3kWR - 14:19,
5kW - 26:04.6, 5kWR - 24:04, 10kWR - 49:14
KENDALL John 23.09.69, AF&D :
3k - 8:17.8 (8:09.1-91),
5k - 14:27.21 (14:16.45-93)
KENNARD Andrew 2.01.66, Walton :
400H - 53.1/53.59
KENNEDY Hugh, London Irish/IRE :
HT - 49.06
KENNY John David Patrick 17.12.70, Wood Gr :
100 - 10.6 (10.4w-90/10.64-93),
200 - 21.1w (21.1-90/21.14w-89/21.18-94)
KENNY Scott U17 20.02.80, Shettleston :
HJ - 1.94
KENNY S. U15 21.12.80, :
LJ - 5.81w/5.36
KEOGH Nigel 18.07.67, Blackheath/IRE :
400H - 54.59 (52.89-91)
KEOGHAN David U17 9.10.78, Bolton :
400HY - 56.8/57.38 (56.45-94)
KEOWN David U23 18.07.74, Roadhogs :
3kW - 12:46.05, 10kW - 48:26.0 (48:18.05-93)
KERR Eric 9.12.64, Luton :
HT - 54.58
KERR Glen U23 27.10.74, Bedford & County :
HT - 56.98
KERR Hugh U20 4.01.76, Har/Ayr Seaforth :
400 - 47.69i/47.75
KESKA Karl 7.05.72, Birchfield/Oregon Univ. :
1500 - 3:43.58, 10k - 30:27.19
KIDNER Ross U15 12.09.80, TVH/WLHS :
SPB - 14.49, HTY - 51.52,
HTB - 58.04/58.72un
KILGALLON Paul, Wirral :
Mar - 2:28:57

KILLEN Neal A. 10.04.59, Ald Serv/Rown:
SP - 13.48 (14.22-94), DT - 44.10
KILLICK Roger U20 20.11.76, Banbury :
JT - 56.24
KINDON James U20 18.06.76, Yeovil Oly :
DT - 42.46
KING Alistair Mark 16.09.62, Haringey :
Mar - 2:28:22 (2:22:51-94)
KING Allan 3.12.56, Roadhogs :
3kW - 13:42.8 (12:08.8-85)
KING Daniel U13 30.05.83, Colchester H :
2kW - 10:12.0, 3kW - 16:11.0, 3kWR - 15:34
KING Dominic U13 30.05.83, Colchester H :
2kW - 10:10.0, 3kW - 15:43.0, 3kWR - 15:20
KING Edward U23 26.11.75, Ballymena & A :
800 - 1:49.96 (1:48.93-94)
KING Kirk U15 18.09.80, Blackheath :
LJ - 6.61w/6.35
KING Philip U23 25.11.74, Coventry RWC :
3kW - 11:47.12i/11:49.64,
10kW - 42:28.0, 20kW - 1:29:07
KING Timothy John U20 10.12.77, Peterbro :
SPJ - 13.89i/13.74, DTJ - 41.92
KINGMAN Robert U23 21.02.73, N & EB/RAF :
PV - 5.00 (5.02-94)
KINNANE Matthew, Swansea :
3k - 8:23.9
KINSON Simon 3.12.70, Leamington :
5k - 14:35.8, Mar - 2:25:17
KIRK Neil U17 14.09.78, GEC :
800 - 1:53.42
KIRKHAM Christian U15 26.06.81, Ipswich :
TJ - 12.59
KIRKHAM Seth U23 9.09.75, Old Gaytonians :
JT - 59.79
KIRKPATRICK William U17 28.02.80, Lagan V :
DTB - 43.12o (39.84-94)
KIRKWOOD Brian V40 20.09.52, L Deans RC :
10MR - 48:08dh
KITNEY Timothy J. U17 26.04.80, Medway :
JTY - 57.02
KLOIBER Matthew 22.11.71, Belgrave :
800 - 1:50.8
KNELLER Steven 9.11.71, Birchfield :
400 - 48.70 (48.29-93)
KNIGHT Andrew G. 26.10.68, Cambridge H :
800 - 1:49.36 (1:48.38-94)
KNIGHT Andrew U23 11.11.73, Luton/LSAC :
100 - 10.6w/10.72 (10.7-93),
200 - 21.7/21.90 (21.4-93/21.62-94)
KNIGHT Steve 17.10.63, Cardiff :
10kR - 29:43
KNOTT Ashley U23 30.08.75, Birchfield :
DT - 47.48
KNOWLES Bradley U20 17.11.76, Birchfield :
110HJ - 15.4, HJ - 2.05i/2.00 (2.03-93)
KNOWLES Hayden U20 17.08.77, Wig/AUS :
SPJ - 13.89, DT - 44.52, DTJ - 48.48,
HT - 52.26, HTJ - 55.74
KNOWLES Leroy U17 26.09.78, Beds & Co :
LJ - 6.63, TJ - 13.60
KNOWLES Richard U23 12.11.75, Sol& S H :
400 - 48.28
KORJIE Haroun 17.02.72, Belgrave/SLE :
60 - 6.87i (6.77i-93), 100 - 10.63 (10.46-94),
200 - 21.89 (21.1w-94/21.3-93/21.31-94)
¶KRON Jonathon U23 16.02.73, W S & E/IRE :
100 - 10.7, LJ - 7.78

338

KRTEN Libor U23 26.02.73, Hercules W/CZE :
  SP - 14.43, DT - 45.92
KRUGER Alexander Eaton 18.11.63, Border :
  60H - 8.36i (8.32i-93), 110H - 14.76,
  HJ - 2.17 (2.20-88), PV - 4.90i/4.90,
  LJ - 7.35w/7.30 (7.57w-89/7.45-94),
  SP - 14.79i/14.60 (14.76-94),
  DT - 45.36, JT - 60.98, Dec - 8131
KRUSZEWSKI Andrew P. 7.04.59, Camb H :
  SP - 14.31 (15.21-90), DT - 49.16 (51.26-92)
KUBOTA Kengo 26.06.68, Edin/Strath Un/JAP :
  SP - 14.05, DT - 43.60 (44.74-94)
KUIPER Anthony U17 25.10.79, Liv Pemb :
  HJ - 1.92

L ACY Dave V50 9.09.44, Colchester H :
  Mar - 2:28:46, 100kR - 7:31:19
LADEJO Du'aine 14.02.71, Belgrave :
  400 - 45.74 (44.94-94)
LAFFLEY Stefan U20 10.09.77, Sale :
  400H - 56.8/57.63
LAING Robert H. 30.07.66, Liverpool H :
  110H - 15.4/15.44
      (14.7w/14.8/14.82w-91/14.90-92),
  PV - 4.20i/4.20 (4.60-88),
  JT - 61.20 (67.48-87)
LAJOIE Kevin U20, Guernsey :
  JT - 53.10
LALLEY Terry V45 12.11.49, Cardiff :
  HT - 47.44 (49.18-90)
LAMBETH Mark 3.09.72, Haringey :
  100 - 10.7, 200 - 21.4w/21.5/21.86,
  60H - 7.83i, 110H - 14.02
LANDON Marc U15 9.11.81, Corby :
  HTB - 48.48
LANE Nathaniel U20 10.04.76, Cardiff :
  5k - 14:57.36
LANGDON Stephen 1.01.58, Hercules Wimb:
  JT - 61.96 (63.52-93)
LANGLEY W. U15, Eastbourne GS :
  3k - 9:35.4
LANYON Simon U15 8.01.81, Devon Sch :
  LJ - 5.90
LASHORE Akinola U23 28.03.73, Serpentine :
  100 - 10.83 (10.8-94)
LATHAM Mark U20 13.01.76, City of Stoke/
  Staffs Univ : HJ - 2.07 (2.11-94)
LAUGHLIN Dale 28.12.66, Chelmsford :
  5k - 14:25.27 (13:43.29-91),
  10kR - 29:15 (28:55-93), HMar - 1:04:40
LAVELLE Keith U20 13.05.77, Telford :
  JT - 53.74
LAWNICZAK Christian 24.03.72, Peterbro :
  Dec - 5324 (5752-94)
LAWRENCE Hector U20 1.11.77, Haringey :
  DT - 42.74, DTJ - 43.72
LAWRENCE Mark 26.01.71, Leeds/Notts Univ :
  LJ - 6.97 (7.33-93), TJ - 13.99 (14.52-93)
LAWRENCE Steven U17, Swansea :
  3k - 8:52.59
LAWS Oliver U17 18.03.80, Wenlock O :
  3k - 8:52.7
LAWS Richard U23 8.10.75, Morpeth :
  HJ - 2.10
LAWSON David U17 12.05.79, Oswestry :
  200 - 22.5/22.65
LAY Graham U23 13.11.75, Scarborough :
  JT - 61.34 (63.14-94)

LEADER Steven 24.11.66, Enfield :
  110H - 15.5/15.71 (15.2-89/15.46-94),
  PV - 4.75i/4.70 (4.90-90),
  Dec - 6745 (7078-94)
LEAMAN Ian U17 14.10.78, Exeter :
  100 - 11.07, 200 - 22.21, SPY - 14.07
LEAMING Alan U20 2.11.76, Barrow & Furn :
  100 - 10.8 200 - 21.85w/22.10 (21.96-93)
LEAVER James U23 15.09.75, Bournemouth :
  HJ - 2.11, TJ - 15.11
LEBARI Suone U15 25.10.80, Liverpool H :
  400 - 53.21
LEE David James 16.09.65, Blackheath :
  1500 - 3:48.2 (3:45.9-89),
  3k - 8:13.44i/8:19.9 (8:09.94-88),
  2kSt - 5:38.0, 3kSt - 8:47.63 (8:31.22-92)
LEE Martyn A. V40 13.07.55, Enfield :
  Mar - 2:27:47 (2:27:12-90)
LEES Andrew U17 11.05.79, Edinburgh :
  100 - 10.9/11.05,
  200 - 21.9w/21.94w/22.2/22.47i
LEES Simon U17 19.11.79, Solihull & S H :
  1500 - 4:03.33, 1.5kSt - 4:24.80
LEGGATE Richard U23 20.07.74, Gateshead :
  110H - 14.91w/15.2/15.30
LEIGH Anthony 27.12.65, City of Stoke :
  200 - 22.0 (21.8-93/22.02w-94)
LEIPER J. Allan 23.07.60, AF&D :
  PV - 4.20i/4.20 (4.70-87),
  Dec - 5746 (6441-89)
LENNON-JONES Donald 9.05.68, N & EB :
  3kSt - 9:19.1 (9:06.4-89)
LEONARD Carl U23 19.01.73, Swansea :
  1500 - 3:45.07, 5k - 14:09.12
LEONARD Michael U20 28.05.77, Thurrock :
  DTJ - 45.76, DecJ - 5175
LEONCE Alec S. 19.04.62, RAF :
  LJ - 7.16 (7.55-86)
LERWILL Thomas U20 17.05.77, Braintree*:
  400 - 47.57, 800 - 1:50.49
LESLIE Matthew U20 17.06.76, Wirral :
  400H - 55.7/55.74 (55.6/55.67-94)
LETHBRIDGE Daniel U15 1.04.81, Crawley :
  DTB - 42.04
LETHBRIDGE Matthew U20 22.01.77, Craw :
  400H - 54.45
LEVY Myrone U15 12.02.81, Birchfield :
  100 - 11.43w/11.5, 200 - 23.41
LEVY Noel U23 22.06.75, Belgrave :
  400 - 48.9 (47.8-92/47.82-93),
  400H - 51.78 (50.70-94)
LEWIS Andrew 9.03.68, Highgate :
  100 - 10.89w/10.96 (10.7-91/10.80w/10.89-94),
  60H - 8.3i (8.23i-93), Dec - 5520un (7221-94)
  110H - 14.87w (14.67w/14.8/14.88-94),
  LJ - 7.24i/7.15w/7.09 (7.53w/7.39-94)
LEWIS Benjamin U15 6.03.81, Birchfield :
  100 - 11.30, 200 - 22.40
LEWIS Gareth U17 5.10.78, Torfaen :
  100HY - 13.90w/14.0/14.39, 400HY - 55.57
LEWIS James 8.03.69, Swansea/IRE :
  10kR - 29:45 (29:22-92)
LEWIS Junior 19.03.66, Verlea :
  TJ - 14.58
LEWIS M. U13, Cardiff :
  800 - 2:18.1
LEWIS Philip E. 12.01.70, Tonbridge/EdinUn :
  200 - 21.70w/22.15 (21.8-91), 400 - 47.8

339

LEWIS Robert U17 2.09.78, Bedford & Co :
400HY - 55.53
LEWIS Shane 22.08.72, Swansea :
JT - 58.38 (69.68-94)
LINDALL Marcus U23 23.01.75, :
200 - 21.99
LINDESAY Christopher U17 11.02.79, Wirral :
3k - 8:53.4
LINDLEY Ian V40 3.12.55, Bingley :
SP - 14.14 (17.87i/17.58-81)
LINDO Hopeton A. 25.08.70, Belgrave :
HJ - 2.10 (2.18-89)
LINSKEY Christian U17 14.06.80, Barnsley :
PV - 4.81
LISHMAN Gwynfor U15 1.12.80, Cockermouth :
HTB - 43.04
LISIEWICZ John 18.07.62, Morpeth/AUS :
5k - 14:33.51 (14:01.24-94), 10kR - 29:36
LITHERLAND Guy 13.11.68, Birchfield :
SP - 14.09 (15.83-88)
LITTLE Andrew 1.01.64, Shettleston :
10k - 31:06.87 (30:46.9-93)
LITTLE David U15 28.02.81, Border :
HTB - 48.22
LITTLE John V40 14.04.53, Border :
DT - 43.70, HT - 46.60 (47.06-89)
LITTLECHILD Danny U20 2.10.77, N & EB :
DT - 41.60
LIVINGSTONE Stuart U17 29.08.79, Edin SH :
HJ - 1.90
LLOYD Joseph U23 9.04.73, Swansea :
400 - 48.84 (48.2/48.27-94)
LLOYD Martin U17 18.06.80, Bexley :
HJ - 2.00
LLOYD Steven J. U23 20.03.74, Border :
DT - 43.32 (43.94-94)
LLOYD-BENNETT Graham U20 26.10.76, Tun W :
SPJ - 14.53
LOADER Joe U23 21.07.73, Bristol Un/High :
Mar - 2:26:07, 3kSt - 9:08.10
LOBO Jason 18.09.69, Blackburn :
800 - 1:48.14 (1:47.7-89), 1500 - 3:45.78
(3:44.14-93), 3k - 8:24.5 (8:17.80i-92)
LOCKER David Alan U23 28.03.75, C of Stoke :
800 - 1:51.3, 1500 - 3:49.66
LOCKLEY Brian V45 18.06.48, East Cheshire :
HT - 46.94 (51.52-68)
LONEY Craig U15 10.06.81, Elgin :
PenB - 2536
LONG Nicholas U17 1.02.79, Liverpool H :
100 - 11.00, 200 - 22.27w/22.6
LONSDALE Ian 8.09.71, Peterborough :
100 - 10.74 (10.5w-92/10.61w-91/10.74-90)
LOUGH Gareth 6.07.70, Annadale Str/LSAC :
800 - 1:48.03, 1500 - 3:34.76,
1M - 3:55.91, 3k - 7:49.45
LOUGHRAN Stuart U20 19.02.76, Swansea :
JT - 63.88
LOVE Alasdhair U20 29.07.77, Aberdeen :
400H - 56.6/57.22
LOVE David U13 17.12.82, Stewartry :
100 - 12.50w/12.76
LOVETT David U17 13.09.78, Southampton C :
SPY - 15.15, DTY - 43.70dh
LOW Charles U23 9.10.74, Newquay & Par :
3kSt - 9:18.3
LOW Chris U17 24.04.80, Arbroath :
60HY - 8.84i, 100HY - 14.0/14.01, OctY - 4712

LOWE Andrew U20 6.03.76, Trafford :
HJ - 2.07
LOWE Cliff U20 12.01.77, Stockport :
DecJ - 5493
LOWE Peter 4.07.65, Sheffield :
SP - 13.80
LOWLES Adam U20 29.01.77, Scot Borders :
100 - 10.9w (10.86w-93/11.01-94)
LOWTHIAN Ian U15 10.10.80, Liverpool H :
200 - 23.48w, 400 - 50.65
LUARD David U15 6.09.80, Yeovil Olympiads :
800 - 2:03.46
LUCAS Neil U17 2.10.78, Lisburn :
HJ - 1.95
LUMSDON Kevin U23 3.03.74, Morpeth :
60H - 8.09i, 110H - 14.33w/14.35 (14.20-94)
LUND Simon N. 22.12.65, Wigan Phoenix :
100kR - 6:56:02
LUNDMAN Jonathan U15 7.12.81, Braintree :
JTB - 49.98
LYNCH Andrew U23 28.06.74, Thames Valley :
HJ - 2.18
LYNCH Lawrence 1.11.67, Haringey :
400 - 48.13 (47.02-93), 400H - 50.62 (50.19-91)
LYONS Andrew 24.12.69, City of Hull :
10k - 29:04.87 (29:04.05-91)
LYSZYK Terry U13, Dorking & Mole V :
1500 - 4:42.2

M ACDONALD Angus 21.12.64, Pitreavie :
100 - 10.99
MACDONALD Duncan J. U23 30.03.74, TVH :
JT - 65.96
MACDONALD Mark W. 2.12.59, SGA (Prof) :
SP - 14.24 (15.98-90)
MACEY Dean U20 12.12.77, Castle Point :
110HJ - 15.08, 110H - 15.2/15.26,
HJ - 2.13, LJ - 6.85, JT - 61.30,
Dec - 6662, DecJ - 7134
MACEY Gary U15 25.10.80, Team Solent :
800 - 2:04.9, 1500 - 4:20.3
MACFADYEN John 1.08.72, ESH/Strathcl Un :
800 - 1:51.5 (1:50.46-92)
MACKE Patrick V40 18.06.55, Grantham :
100kR - 6:58:29 (6:52:39-89)
MACKENZIE Colin T. 30.06.63, Newham & EB :
JT - 79.90 (82.60r-91/82.38-93)
MACKENZIE John 23.08.65, Bel/Dundee HH :
LJ - 7.26i/7.15w (7.41w-94/7.32-93),
TJ - 16.07i/16.05w/15.77 (16.17-94)
MACKIE Ian U23 27.02.75, Pitreavie :
100 - 10.5/10.65 (10.50-94),
200 - 21.4/21.53 (20.91-94)
MACLENNAN Kevin U17 5.12.78, Black Isle :
100HY - 13.9/14.11w, TJ - 13.76w (13.34-93)
MADAR Abdi U15 25.11.81, Blackheath :
3k - 9:38.9
MADDEN Michael J. 13.09.65, Newquay & Par :
HT - 50.34 (55.92-93)
MADDEN Robert U17 25.10.78, East Kilbride :
1.5kSt - 4:34.4nwj/4:50.50
MADDOCKS Christopher Lloyd 28.03.57,
Plymouth City W :
10kW - 42:51.50 (41:06.57-87),
20kW - 1:26:35 (1:22:12-92),
30kW - 2:18:41 (2:11:09-88),
35kW - 2:43:18+ (2:36:19-91),
50kW - 3:53:14 (3:51:37-90)

340

MADEIRA-COLE Charles U20 29.11.77, Carm :
LJ - 7.01, TJ - 14.60
MAGEE Greg U17 27.09.78, Scottish Borders :
JTY - 55.32
MAINSTONE Keith U23 15.03.74, Horsham BS :
Dec - 5161
MAITLAND Peter U23 21.01.73, Swansea :
60 - 6.75i, 100 - 10.42,
200 - 20.96w/21.02 (20.96-94),
400 - 47.2/47.29
MALCOLM Anthony U20 15.02.76, Salisbury :
LJ - 7.21
MALCOLM Christian U17 3.06.79, Newport :
60 - 6.95i, 100 - 10.85, 200 - 21.41w/21.58
MALLON Chris 4.08.72, Richmond & Twick:
HT - 49.20
MALSEED Robert 16.09.71, Colchester H :
5k - 14:35.58, 10k - 31:04.69
MANDY Mark 19.11.72, Cannock & St/IRE :
HJ - 2.25
MANGLESHOT Lawrence Philip 28.05.63,
Woodford Green : 800 - 1:52.4 (1:50.4-85),
1500 - 3:49.57 (3:43.74-89)
MANN Richard U20 11.04.77, Solihull & S H :
800 - 1:54.8
MANNING Gareth 3.10.69, Dorchester :
800 - 1:52.04
MANNING N. U17, Oxford Sch :
PV - 3.60
MANSBRIDGE David C. 4.06.64, Telford :
Mar - 2:23:25 (2:22:23-94)
MANSFIELD Ian U23 27.11.74, Lincoln Well :
800 - 1:51.4
MARAR Leith 7.11.68, Belgrave :
SP - 14.04 (16.13-93), DT - 55.38
MARGIOTTA Stuart 19.11.69, GEC :
800 - 1:51.6, 1k - 2:23.2,
1500 - 3:44.26, 1M - 4:04.3
MARK Kevin U20 15.09.76, Ealing,S & Mx :
100 - 10.8/10.92 (10.38w-93/10.60-94),
200 - 21.8 (21.6w-94/21.7-93/21.97-92)
MARKS Gareth U20 31.05.77, Swansea :
DT - 44.68, DTJ - 51.38
MARLAND Chris U15 9.11.80, Deeside :
DTB - 38.88
MARRIOTT Alan D. 6.03.60, Oldham & Royton :
DT - 42.00
MARSDEN Ben U15 20.10.80, Braintree :
SPB - 13.16, DTB - 40.86
MARSH Brett U20 20.01.76, Newquay & Par :
HTJ - 49.40
MARSHALL Christopher U15 4.10.80, Wigan :
800 - 2:04.62
MARSHALL Guy ¶ 24.09.71, Hull Springhead :
SP - 16.00, DT - 41.28
MARTIN Eamonn Thomas 9.10.58, Basildon :
5k - 14:06.3 (13:17.84-89),
10kR - 29:31 (28:14-89), 10MR - 48:45,
HMar - 1:04:16 (1:02:52-93),
Mar - 2:11:18 (2:10:50-93)
MARTIN Paul U17 7.09.79, Hallamshire :
HJ - 1.90
MARTIN Wayne U20 12.08.76, Team Solent :
400 - 48.96 (48.5-94)
MARWOOD Simon U20 6.04.78, Mandale :
3kSt - 9:29.8
MASON Anthony U20 8.03.76, Haringey :
LJ - 7.11w/7.09 (7.24-94)

MASON Gavin U20 6.04.77, Belgrave :
400 - 49.1 (48.89-94), 800 - 1:52.85
MASON James Ryder 22.03.72, Belgrave :
SP - 16.74
MASON Keith U20 10.02.76, Cumnock :
400H - 56.8/57.22
MASON Kristian U17 17.09.78, Rowntrees :
LJ - 6.57
MASON Neil T. 10.02.71, SGA (Prof) :
SP - 14.06 (14.68-92)
MASON Robert U23 13.09.75, City of Stoke :
110H - 15.54
MASSEY Ian U20 9.09.76, Liverpool H :
HJ - 2.10
MATARAZZO Antonio U17 27.03.80, Chelt :
100 - 10.9 (11.43w-94), 200 - 21.90
MATE Anthony U23 15.12.74, Gateshead :
800 - 1:50.9, 1500 - 3:44.63
MATHIESON Duncan Graham 8.03.69,
C of Stoke/Aberdeen : 110H - 14.9w/15.42w
(14.81w-93/14.9-90/14.95-91), LJ - 7.62,
HJ - 2.02 (2.07-90), Dec - 7272 (7535-90)
MATHIESON Simon U17 20.01.79, Bristol :
400 - 49.49, DTY - 41.42
MATHIESON Stuart U15 5.02.81, Aberdeen :
400 - 53.1/55.25
MATTHEWS Richard U17 23.10.78, Corn AC :
1.5kSt - 4:29.51
MATTHEWS Simon 21.05.71, Kendal :
SP - 15.17i/14.54 (14.81-94)
MAULL Nigel U17 14.11.79, Leamington :
1.5kSt - 4:38.7
MAXWELL Ancell 17.01.69, Liverpool H :
100 - 10.92w
MAXWELL Joseph U15 23.12.80, W S & E :
80HB - 11.21
MAXWELL Stewart 29.06.58, Wirral/RAF :
JT - 57.90 (64.22-88)
MAY Ezekiel U15 20.03.81, :
LJ - 5.84
MAYNARD Darrell 21.08.61, Belgrave/Army :
400 - 48.6 (48.2-88/48.79-93),
800 - 1:50.47 (1:49.5a-88)
MAYO Thomas U20 2.05.77, Cannock & St :
1500 - 3:51.3
MAYOCK John Paul 26.10.70, Cannock & St :
800 - 1:49.7 (1:49.44-93), 1500 - 3:34.05,
1M - 3:51.89, 3k - 7:46.80i/7:47.28
MCADAMS Terry, Cannock & Stafford :
200 - 22.14
MCAREE Simon U23 28.12.75, Newham & EB :
60H - 8.37i (8.34i-94),
110H - 14.46 (14.43-94)
MCBRIDE Allan U17 31.12.79, Spango Valley :
100 - 11.1w/11.28w/11.38
MCBURNEY Paul 14.03.72, Newham & EB :
200 - 21.46 (20.81-94), 300 - 33.8,
400 - 46.68 (46.49-94)
MCCABE Fintan 27.03.72, Reading/IRE :
Dec - 6096
MCCAFFREY Liam U15, Preseli :
DTB - 38.64
MCCALLA Dave, Coventry Godiva/RAF :
TJ - 14.40
MCCALLUM Jon U23 19.11.75, Croydon :
1500 - 3:51.9
MCCAW Charles 21.01.72, Wood Gr/Ox Un :
400 - 47.30

341

MCCOLGAN Peter Conor 20.02.63, Haringey :
1500 - 3:50.3 (3:43.10-87),
1M - 4:05.6 (3:59.37-86)
MCCOURT Steven 6.05.71, Thames Valley :
100 - 10.7 (10.80w/10.82-94),
200 - 21.28 (21.03w-94), 400 - 48.9 (48.94-93)
MCCOY Bryan U23 31.12.75, Ballymena & A :
200 - 22.07, 400 - 48.80 (48.68-94)
MCCULLAGH Jamie U15 9.11.80, Kingst & P :
3k - 9:35.6
MCDADE Jason U17 3.04.80, Ipswich :
HJ - 1.90
MCDAID Damien U20 17.07.78, Cuchulainn :
JT - 56.94, JTY - 60.42o
*MCDERMOTT Dylan 1.12.70, Epsom & E/IRE :*
*PV - 4.70 (4.90i-92/4.85-90)*
MCDEVITT Peter 1.03.68, Shettleston :
800 - 1:52.6 (1:51.02-94)
MCDONAGH William 11.07.72, Leeds :
110H - 15.5 (15.37-94)
MCDONALD Colin 12.04.71, Edinburgh :
TJ - 14.20w
MCDONALD Denzil 11.10.65, Newham & EB :
SP - 15.90 (16.10-94), DT - 55.04
MCDONALD Michael John 24.08.65, B & A/
Border/Queen's Univ : TJ - 15.29 (15.78-94)
MCDONALD Richard U17 11.01.80, Perth :
400 - 49.8/50.18, TJ - 13.95w/13.60
MCEVOY Stephen 23.05.63, Met. Pol/WLHS :
HT - 54.00 (55.46-94)
MCFARLAND Ross U17 13.10.78, Vict PAAC :
HJ - 2.00, LJ - 6.92
MCGARRY Mark U20 16.02.77, Gateshead :
2kSt - 5:59.26, 3kSt - 9:38.8
MCGEOCH Michael I. V40 15.08.55, Les Cr:
Mar - 2:28:54 (2:17:58-83)
MCGINN Michael U23 13.12.75, Bournem'th :
HT - 46.16
MCGLYNN Trevor U20 6.06.78, Sparta :
110HJ - 14.9, 110H - 15.1/15.26
MCGOWAN Frank 23.08.70, Leslie Deans RC :
1500 - 3:50.8
MCGUIRE Ciaran U23 1.07.74, Coventry G :
3kSt - 9:21.35
MCHARDY Stephen U20 8.01.76, Birchfield :
200 - 22.0 (21.9w/22.10w-92/22.13-91,
400 - 47.53 (47.48-94)
*MCHUGH Terrance 22.08.63, Herne Hill/IRE :*
*SP - 15.35i/14.43 (15.07-93),*
*DT - 41.06 (42.02-93), JT - 79.06 (84.54-91)*
MCILROY Brian U13, Liverpool H :
800 - 2:16.27
MCILROY Gary 6.04.67, Epsom & Ewell :
Mar - 2:30:21 (2:24:49-94)
MCILWHAM John 29.02.72, Blackpool :
110H - 15.6, 400H - 54.0 (53.89-94)
MCINTOSH Leslie U15 25.02.81, Liverpool H :
HTB - 47.74
MCINTYRE Liam U20 22.09.76, Edinburgh SH :
SP - 14.16, SPJ - 15.72,
DT - 43.48, DTJ - 46.50
MCINTYRE Mark 14.10.70, Shaftesbury Barn :
100 - 10.3w/10.61w/10.77 (10.60-91),
200 - 21.50w/22.07 (21.3w-90/21.4/21.63-91)
MCKAY Kevin John 9.02.69, Sale :
800 - 1:48.0 (1:45.35-92),
1500 - 3:37.27 (3:35.94-92),
1M - 4:06.72 (3:53.64-94)

MCKAY Simon U13, Paddock Wood :
JTC - 35.32
MCKEAN Thomas 27.10.63, Har/Lanark & L :
800 - 1:47.46 (1:43.88-89)
MCKENZIE David Colin 3.09.70, Shaftesbury B :
200 - 21.3w/21.6 (21.5-94/21.54-90),
300 - 33.0, 400 - 45.96 (45.47-94)
MCKEOWN Kenneth U15 6.03.82, Ayr Seaforth :
80HB - 11.7w, HJ - 1.85
MCKERNAN Michael U17 28.11.78, Cov G :
TJ - 14.51w/14.27i/13.99 (14.16-94)
MCKINSON Kevin U15 6.09.80, Cambridge H :
HJ - 1.81, PenB - 2533
MCLEAN Colin U17 7.06.80, Cuchulainn :
3k - 8:50.5
MCLEAN Peter U15 5.10.80, Old Gaytonians :
LJ - 6.18w/5.79
MCLELLAN Neil U17 10.09.78, Steve& NH :
JTY - 53.40
MCLENNAN Stephen U17 17.11.78, Hounslow :
PV - 4.40
MCLEOD David 26.03.63, Morpeth :
PV - 4.45 (4.60-93)
MCLOUGHLIN Martin 23.12.58, Liv Pemb :
5k - 14:33.9, 10kR - 29:32 (28:45-88),
10MR - 47:51 (46:26un-87/47:02-93),
HMar - 1:04:25 (1:02:50un-89/1:02:57-88)
MCLOUGHLIN Wayne 27.03.66, Warrington :
JT - 58.10
MCMAHON I., Duncairn :
Mar - 2:22:16
MCMASTER Colin U17 15.01.80, Law & Dist :
HJ - 1.95
MCMENEMY Neil 6.04.67, Newham & EB/Cenl :
TJ - 14.74w/14.58 (15.13-94)
MCMILLAN Gregor William 4.04.70, Haringey :
400 - 48.80i/49.19 (47.41-92)
MCMILLAN Stewart 12.09.69, Edinburgh/Pitr :
SP - 13.76, JT - 59.42 (59.64-91)
MCMILLAN Stuart I. 14.05.67, Shetland :
TJ - 14.21w/14.17 (15.09-89)
MCMULLAN Ian U20 15.06.78, Lisburn :
SPJ - 14.07
MCMULLAN Ian U23 3.05.74, Met. Police :
DT - 43.86 (47.10-91)
MCMULLEN Carl U17 9.11.79, Warrington :
400H - 57.9, 400HY - 56.41
MCNABB Richard John U17 22.02.80, Roth :
400 - 48.34
MCNAMARA Paul U17 3.10.78, Luton :
HTY - 51.40
MCNICHOLAS Alan U23 10.12.74, Beds & Co :
HT - 57.44 (57.66-94)
MCPHAIL Malcolm 8.06.67, Har/Ayr Seaforth :
400 - 48.56i/49.7 (48.47-91)
MCRAE Leon U15 3.11.80, City of Bath :
80HB - 11.04, HJ - 1.76, PenB - 2822
MCSWEEN Trevor C. 27.10.66, Army :
HJ - 2.01
MCWILLIAMS F., :
Mar - 2:29:02
MEAD Darren 4.10.68, Belgrave :
3k - 8:01.0 (7:56.39-94),
5k - 14:14.89 (13:50.7-94),
10kR - 29:35 (29:31-94), 10MR - 48:30
MECHAM Robert U20 14.09.77, Steyning :
3kW - 13:20.07, 3kWR - 13:20,
5kW - 23:56.72, 10kWR - 50:58

MEDDER Benjamin U15 31.10.80, Croydon :
LJ - 6.30w/5.72
MELBER Stephen U17 26.02.79, Milton K :
JTY - 56.56
MELLOR Dean 25.11.71, Rotherham :
PV - 5.30
MELLUISH Christopher J. V50 15.07.44, Camb H :
HT - 46.52 (62.10-74)
MELVILLE-JACKSON James U23 24.01.74,
Windsor S & E/Loughborough Studnts :
400H - 54.6 (55.35-94)
MELVIN Gareth U15 11.12.80, Border :
1500 - 4:12.31, 3k - 9:19.47
MENHENNITT James U23 14.12.74, Guern/Bir :
JT - 60.92
MENSAH Andrew Peter 30.11.71, Haringey :
60 - 6.79i, 200 - 21.19 (21.14-94),
100 - 10.48w/10.51 (10.39w/10.49-94)
MENTON John 2.05.70, London Irish/IRE :
SP - 14.76, DT - 52.38 (52.96-93)
MENZIES Gordon U17 13.03.79, Kilbarchan :
100HY - 13.60, 400HY - 57.2/57.40
MERRICK Essop U23 24.05.74, Team Solent :
LJ - 6.92 (7.02-93)
MICHIE Craig U15 2.12.80, Fife :
800 - 2:03.70
MIDDLETON Barry U23 10.03.75, Aberd/Heriot W :
200 - 22.18w/22.40,
400 - 48.84i (49.40-94), 400H - 52.46
MIDDLETON Bryn U20 16.02.76, Cardiff :
60 - 6.96i, 100 - 10.7 (10.80w/10.90-94),
200 - 22.19i (21.77-94)
MIDDLETON Darren U15 14.11.80, Barnsley :
3k - 9:38.1
MIDDLETON Dominic 22.10.69,
Cannock & Stafford/East Mich Univ :
5k - 14:08.22 (13:49.16i-92)
MIDDLETON Graham 17.09.60, Cannock & St :
HT - 51.24 (55.00-82)
MILBURN James U15 17.07.81, Jarrow & H :
80HB - 11.8/11.85
MILES Mark Thomas U20 24.03.77, Sol& SH :
800 - 1:52.7rl?, 1500 - 3:48.1
MILES Paul U15 14.09.80, Birchfield :
PV - 3.45
MILES Paul U13 28.04.84, Leics WC :
2kW - 11:32.0
MILLARD Chris 19.07.66, Clevedon :
200 - 22.0/22.34
MILLER Adam U15 4.11.80, Cambridge & Col :
HTB - 43.08
MILLER Jonathon U15 10.06.81, Birchfield :
TJ - 13.18w/12.97
MILLER Mark 10.11.71, Enfield :
HT - 56.84
MILLS S., :
Mar - 2:29:34
MINNIKIN Steve 4.01.72, Doncaster :
HT - 60.56 (61.76-93)
MINNS Gavin U15 5.12.80, Holbeach :
HTB - 47.04
MITCHELL Andrew U20 30.07.76, Kilbarchan :
400 - 48.96, 400H - 56.3/57.81
MITCHELL Andy , Royal Navy :
HT - 47.30 (50.32-93)
MITCHELL Ian U20 10.03.76, Skyrac :
800 - 1:53.9, 1500 - 3:47.3

MITCHELL Stephen U20 1.09.77, Epsom & E :
400H - 56.16
MITCHELL Terrence 23.08.59, Fife :
Mar - 2:21:50 (2:17:56-92)
MITCHELL Wayne U23 25.12.74, Sale :
100 - 10.7/10.88, 200 - 21.98
MITCHINSON David U17 4.09.78, Swindon :
1.5kSt - 4:22.97
MOIR Gareth U15 17.12.80, Ipswich :
HJ - 1.80
MOK E., Birmingham Univ. :
PV - 4.20
MOLE Adam U23 31.08.75, North'ton/Brun Un :
400 - 48.64i (47.84-93), 600 - 1:19.4i
MOLLOY Thomas U23 25.03.73, Army :
Dec - 5000 (5102-94)
MONEY Daniel U20 7.10.76, Sale :
60 - 6.91i, 100 - 10.48w/10.60, 200 - 21.21
MONK Stuart U17 23.03.79, Loughton :
3kW - 12:50.67i/12:52.9, 5kW - 21:52.7,
5kWR - 22:16, 10kW - 47:36.60, 10kWR - 46:11
MOORE Colin 25.11.60, Bingley :
3k - 8:20.7 (8:04.60-90),
5k - 14:18.3 (13:33.95-90),
10k - 29:28.0 (28:13.13-90),
10kR - 29:42 (28:17-85),
HMar - 1:04:46 (1:02:22-85),
Mar - 2:15:02 (2:13:34-94)
MOORE David U17 25.04.79, Liverpool H :
1.5kSt - 4:39.89 (4:34.7-94)
MOORE James U15 4.11.80, Pitreavie :
100 - 11.59w
MOORE Neil 1.04.61, Barnsley :
Mar - 2:29:19 (2:28:28-94)
MOORE Stephen R. V45 17.12.47, Herts & W :
100kR - 7:12:15
MOORHOUSE Julian 13.11.71, Leeds :
3k - 8:04.9, 5k - 14:24.54
MORBY Paul James U17 15.01.79, So & SH :
800 - 1:56.6, 1500 - 4:02.6, 1.5kSt - 4:29.5
MORELAND John R. 13.09.58, Rugby :
DT - 51.76
MORGAN Derek N. 4.04.69, Bristol :
100 - 10.8 (10.6-93/10.77-89)
MORGAN Mark 19.08.72, Cardiff :
3k - 8:05.74 (8:00.50-94),
5k - 14:19.9 (13:59.46-94)
MORGAN Michael 30.07.66, Belgrave :
LJ - 7.22i (8.01wAUS/7.92AUS-86/7.75-94),
JT - 59.28 (61.62-94)
MORGAN Nathan U20 30.06.78, Leics Cor :
LJ - 7.43w/7.28i/7.28
MORGAN Noel U17 20.11.78, Trowbridge :
400 - 50.09
MORGAN-LEE Andrew 1.03.69, Soton City :
5k - 14:19.5, 10kR - 29:41,
2kSt - 5:46.9, 3kSt - 8:52.4
MORLEY Philip U15 8.12.80, Derbs Sch :
DTB - 38.60
MORLEY Roger U20 20.09.77, Lincoln Well :
800 - 1:52.59
MORRELL Anthony 3.05.62, Morpeth :
800 - 1:48.7 (1:44.59-88),
1500 - 3:44.75 (3:34.1+-90/3:35.60-89)
MORRIS James U17 2.12.79, Swansea :
LJ - 6.55w
MORRIS Paul U17 10.11.78, Birchfield :
400HY - 55.34

343

MORRIS William U23 18.08.73, Eastbourne R :
110H - 15.5 (15.4-92/15.48-93)
MORRIS Wyn 25.02.61, Shaftesbury Barnet :
TJ - 14.45 (15.28w-85/15.19-89)
MORRISON Brian U15 3.09.80, Birchfield :
LJ - 6.10
MORTIMER Chris U15 14.11.80, Wilts Sch :
TJ - 12.47
MORTLEY Martin Trevor U17 8.09.78, Med :
SPY - 14.29
MORTON Leslie 1.07.58, Sheffield RWC :
3kW - 12:43.57 (12:24.0-85),
10kW - 43:21.1 (43:03.4-92),
20kW - 1:33:37 (1:26:31sh-93/1:27:16-89),
35kW - 2:49:15 (2:37:27-91),
50kW - 4:01:36 (3:57:48-89)
MOSCROP Howard W. 16.12.57, Swindon :
400H - 53.9 (51.4-84/52.66-93)
MOSELEY Stephen J. 10.01.66, Cardiff :
1500 - 3:49.1 (3:47.1-94),
1M - 4:09.4 (4:06.9-93)
MOSES Alistair U20 5.07.78, Reigate :
800 - 1:54.8, 1500 - 3:54.16
MOSS Christopher U17 17.06.79, Blackheath :
800 - 1:54.49, 1500 - 4:02.01
MOSS Jonathan U17 24.09.78, Sale :
200 - 22.22
MOULTON David U15 7.09.81, S London :
400 - 53.7
MOWBRAY Philip U23 19.03.73, Edin Un/Edin :
1500 - 3:43.81 (3:41.63-94), 3k - 8:10.43,
5k - 14:08.08
MUIRHEAD James Cameron 26.01.71,
Liverpool H/Loughborough Studnts :
SP - 16.60, DT - 51.64 (51.82-94)
MULLEN Robert 8.08.64, Army :
JT - 62.02 (64.90-87)
MUNDEN Craig U20 24.12.76, Bournemouth :
DT - 40.42, DTJ - 42.76
MUNN D. U13, Ashford :
LJ - 5.55
MUNROE Gary 12.04.69, Newham & EB/RAF :
LJ - 7.20
MUNROE John 6.01.69, Thames Valley/RAF :
LJ - 7.65i/7.64
MURCH Kevin 11.11.58, Rugby :
JT - 58.78 (69.02-89)
MURDOCH Steven 16.04.61, Border :
10k - 30:19.1
MURPHY Ciaran 2.09.71, Sale :
800 - 1:50.83 (1:50.1-94), 1k - 2:24.6,
1500 - 3:43.42, 1M - 3:58.68
MURPHY David U17 16.09.78, Ballymena & A :
400HY - 56.8
MURPHY James U23 20.03.73, Corby :
SP - 15.54i/14.40 (15.04-94), DT - 55.52
MURPHY John U15 6.03.81, Leics WC :
3kW - 13:45.0, 3kWR - 14:11,
5kW - 24:03.6o, 5kWR - 23:25
MURPHY Lee U20 11.03.77, Medway :
400H - 54.93
MURRAY Alan 2.05.67, Kilmarnock :
400 - 48.5/48.57 (48.1-93/48.34-87)
MURRAY Gerard U20 13.02.78, Airdrie :
Dec - 5273w
MURRAY Sam U15 7.09.80, Belgrave :
400 - 52.64

MURRAY Thomas 18.05.61, Spango Valley :
5k - 14:28.0 (14:02.5-92),
10kR - 29:34 (29:18-88)
MURRAY-TAIT Ian U17 80, Ballymena & Antr :
HJ - 1.90
MYERS Nicholas U17 25.03.80, Birchfield :
LJ - 6.56
MYERSCOUGH Carl Andrew U17 21.10.79,
Blackpool : SP - 13.20,
SPY - 17.68, DTY - 52.76
MYLES Gary 3.02.63, Cannock & Stafford :
110H - 15.2w/15.28 (14.55-83)

N AGEL Gary Roderick 4.06.62, Valli :
5k - 14:22.5 (13:51.5-90)
NAISMITH David U17 15.12.79, Derby & Co :
·400 - 50.01
NAQUI Waqas U17 14.09.78, :
TJ - 13.44
NARTEY Michael U23 12.06.75, Blackheath :
100 - 10.81w (10.5w-92/10.67-91)
NASH Barry 4.09.71, Milton Keynes :
SP - 14.99
NASH Kevin U20 6.02.77, AF&D :
3k - 8:33.7 (8:28.6-94),
2kSt - 5:59.67, 3kSt - 9:07.22
NASH Robin 9.02.59, Westbury :
Mar - 2:25:11 (2:14:52-94)
NATHAM Simon D. 28.11.66, Bolton :
HT - 46.38 (50.84-88)
NEBLETT Gavin U17 27.12.79, Enfield :
HJ - 1.97
NEELY Ian U23 29.12.74, Ballymena & Antr :
400H - 54.17
NEPORT Darren U17 4.09.79, Enfield :
PV - 3.90
NERURKAR Richard David 6.01.64, Bingley :
10kR - 29:43 (28:25-94), 10MR - 46:19 (46:02-93),
HMar - 1:02:39 (1:01:33-92),
Mar - 2:11:03 (2:10:03-93)
NESBETH Michael U17 1.03.79, Croydon :
400HY - 57.0, TJ - 13.76
NEVIS John 24.12.69, Birchfield :
HT - 53.16 (56.10-93)
NEWMAN Lee Jon U23 1.05.73, Blackh'th/Bel :
SP - 18.46, DT - 53.52 (58.34-94)
NEWMARCH Alastair U17 28.11.78, Linc Well :
400HY - 55.58
NEWNES James 9.09.67, Salford :
10k - 30:54.9 (29:48.22-93)
NEWPORT Spencer John 5.10.66, Blackh'th :
1500 - 3:51.3 (3:43.46-87),
5k - 14:00.24 (13:56.82-92),
10k - 29:23.49, 3kSt - 8:45.3 (8:40.87-92)
NEWTON Adam U15 4.12.80, Windsor S & E :
100 - 11.37w/11.5/11.51, 200 - 23.3
NEWTON Keith 12.12.68, Woodford Green :
400H - 54.33
NEWTON Marc D. U17 15.03.80, Tamworth :
HJ - 1.91, LJ - 6.56, OctY - 5144
NEWTON Robert U15 10.05.81, B-H Mansfield :
80HB - 11.4w/11.79
NICHOLL David 16.09.69, Ballymena & Antr :
HT - 53.04
NICHOLL Michael 29.07.61, R Sutton Coldf'ld :
PV - 4.20 (4.60-93)
NICHOLLS Clinton Alan U17 16.02.79, Basild'n :
HJ - 2.00

344

NICHOLLS John S. 1.09.65, Sale :
SP - 15.48
NICHOLSON Martin 9.12.70, Birchfield :
60H - 8.13i (8.01i-93),
110H - 14.29 (13.8/14.14-94)
NICOLSON Christian U23 19.09.73, Team S :
1500 - 3:49.7, 3k - 8:05.0
NIELAND Nicholas 31.01.72, S B/Bris Univ. :
JT - 76.30
NOBLE Gareth U17 1.05.79, Old Gaytonians :
400 - 50.75
NOBLE Ian U20 2.04.77, Leeds :
PV - 4.20 (4.20-94)
NOLAN David 25.07.69, Belgrave/Army :
200 - 21.16 (22.0-94), 400 - 46.61
NOLAN Mike 15.07.67, Old G/Camb Univ :
3kSt - 9:19.2
NORMAN Anthony 5.07.63, Woking :
JT - 61.72
NORMAN Oliver U23 6.09.73, Crawley :
3kSt - 9:00.74
NORRISS Dominic 29.12.71, Hounslow :
HJ - 2.00i (2.00i/2.00-89)
NSUDOH Immanuel 8.04.72, Croydon :
LJ - 7.13
NUTTALL John Barry 11.01.67, Preston :
1500 - 3:42.66 (3:40.6-90), 3k - 7:48.59,
5k - 13:16.70, 10k - 28:07.43

O 'BRIEN Anthony 14.11.70, Liverpool H :
5k - 14:16.6, 10k - 30:32.2,
10kR - 29:21
O'BRIEN Barry U20 3.07.76, Middlesbro & C :
400 - 48.9/49.28
O'CONNELL Christopher A. 17.01.59, Leeds :
HT - 48.38 (52.98-87)
O'CONNOR Simon D. U23 3.09.73, Cann & St :
3kSt - 8:57.55
O'DELL Timothy 29.05.70, Woodford Green :
100 - 10.7/10.79, 200 - 21.31,
300 - 33.5, 400 - 46.34
O'DONNELL W., Bideford :
Mar - 2:30:30
O'DOWD Matthew U20 13.04.76, Swindon :
3k - 8:25.0, 5k - 14:20.2,
3kSt - 9:16.40 (9:10.83-94)
O'HANLON Sean U20 3.09.76, Dacorum & Tr :
JT - 57.86 (58.18-94)
O'KEEFE Patrick, Loughborough Studnts :
1500 - 3:49.5
O'LEARY David U17 3.08.80, Liverpool H :
100HY - 13.44
O'NEILL David U20 19.01.76, Peterborough :
PV - 4.40
O'RAWE Jamie U23 3.02.73, Southend :
3kW - 12:21.8, 10kW - 44:40.0, 20kW - 1:34:52
O'REILLY Brian U15 3.10.80, East Down :
1500 - 4:17.31
O'REILLY Michael 23.04.58, Highgate :
Mar - 2:24:53 (2:10:39-93)
O'REILLY Patrick 5.01.68, Crawley/IRE :
800 - 1:52.53 (1:51.5-94)
O'RIORDAN Donal T. 2.04.70, LSAC :
1500 - 3:51.90
O'SHEA John 13.04.67, Hounslow :
3k - 8:24.0 (8:18.7-93)
OAG Keith U20 11.11.77, Elgin :
DecJ - 5201

OAKES Jason U20 29.09.77, Gateshead :
JT - 60.26
ODWAR David U20 23.12.76, Oxford City :
JT - 56.48 (57.68-94)
OGBETA Mathias 19.06.68, Preston :
LJ - 7.26, TJ - 15.66
OHRLAND Stuart U23 6.09.75, Chelmsford :
HJ - 2.15 (2.17-94)
OJOK Geoffrey U17 19.05.79, Belgrave :
LJ - 6.83w/6.74
OKOTIE Mclean 31.07.69, Thames Valley :
60 - 6.9i/6.94i (6.9i-94),
100 - 10.79 (10.5/10.60-94)
OLDALE Richard 26.01.66, Sheffield RWC :
3kW - 12:55.70, 10kW - 46:15.2, 20kW - 1:34:21.6t
OLIVER Daniel U15 11.10.80, Devon Sch :
DTB - 40.98
OLIVER Michael J. V40 23.03.53, Brighton :
SP - 14.55 (15.67-91)
OLIVER Paulo U15 19.09.80, Cambridge & C :
800 - 2:03.91
OLUWA Bode U20 15.11.76, Herne Hill :
100 - 10.7/11.00w 200 - 22.20
OLWENU Philips U15 14.02.81, Ealing, S & Mx :
JTB - 58.74
OMONUA Samson U20 16.06.76, Haringey :
60 - 6.97i, 100 - 10.61w/10.87 (10.60w-93)
ONUORAH Onochie C. U23 16.10.73, Shaft B :
100 - 10.55, 200 - 22.0/22.07, LJ - 7.81w/7.58
ORR C. U13, Carlisle :
DTC - 33.14
*ORRELLE Jonathon U17 28.01.79, Ox C/ISR :*
*HJ - 1.91i, PV - 3.60, LJ - 6.50i,*
*SPY - 16.14iun, Dec - 5401w*
OSTAPOWYCZ Pawlo H. V40 1.07.52, Traff :
JT - 57.98 (60.38-93)
OSUIDE Stanley U23 30.11.74, Thames VH :
HJ - 2.05 (2.15-91)
OSWALD Tom U15 17.12.80, Gateshead :
200 - 23.39
OTENG Samuel U20 12.04.78, Shaftesbury B :
DecJ - 5561
OTTLEY David Charles V40 5.08.55, Telford :
JT - 65.02 (80.98-88)
OVINGTON Neil J. 26.01.63, Thames Valley :
10k - 31:19.0
OWEN Chris U17 9.07.79, Birchfield :
1500 - 4:06.1
OWEN John N. 28.10.64, Swansea :
HT - 52.96
OWEN Neil U23 18.10.73, Belgrave :
60H - 7.93i (7.86i-94), 110H - 13.60
OWEN Sion U17 6.03.79, Crewe & Nantwich :
800 - 1:55.27, OctY - 4665
OXBOROUGH Wayne 10.11.66, Thames H & H :
5k - 14:27.6, 10k - 30:39.38 (30:19.61-94),
10kR - 29:36
*OYEDIRAN Ademola 27.11.59, Herne H/NIG :*
*LJ - 7.26w/6.97 (7.13-86),*
*TJ - 15.57w/14.80 (15.91i/15.78-84)*

P AICE Matt U13, Windsor S & E :
HJ - 1.56, LJ - 5.16
¶PAINTER John J. T. 12.06.58, Norfolk :
SP - 13.73 (16.32i/16.09-89)
PAINTER Trevor 10.08.71, Wigan :
200 - 21.8 (21.8-94),
400 - 47.79A/48.07 (48.04-94)

345

PAISLEY Derek U23 1.12.73, Pitr/Edin Un :
400H - 53.8/53.82 (52.83-94)
PALMER Adrian M. 10.08.69, Cardiff :
HT - 62.48 (62.56-94)
PALMER Andrew U20 13.04.77, Soton City :
HJ - 2.00
PALMER Chris U13, Southend :
200 - 25.7
PALMER Colin 27.07.67, Medway/Aʀmy :
2kSt - 5:50.4, 3kSt - 9:11.0
PALMER James U20 21.04.78, Norfolk :
PV - 4.20
PALMER Karl 5.02.66, Swansea :
3kSt - 9:21.0 (9:00.8-92)
PALMER Keith A. 19.11.64, Southend :
200 - 22.17 (21.5-91/21.74-92),
400 - 48.99 (48.8-93/48.92-92)
PALMER Martin U20 5.04.77, Westbury :
5k - 15:04.72
PAMAH David 27.11.64, Belgrave :
800 - 1:52.7 (1:50.44-93)
PAMPHLETT Tim U15 18.02.81, GEC :
JTB - 52.10
PARK Dean U20 23.09.77, Newham & E B :
400 - 49.5 (49.15A-94), 400H - 55.16
PARK Iain U23 16.07.74, GEC/Falkirk :
DT - 41.40 (42.26-93), HT - 56.56
PARKER Andrew Jamie U23 20.11.74, S B :
800 - 1:52.5 (1:49.62-94)
PARKER Andrew U13 10.12.83, Wolves & B :
2kW - 11:21.0
PARKER David U17 28.02.80, Scarborough :
JT - 62.60, JTY - 68.32
PARKER John W. V40 31.10.54, Tipton :
Mar - 2:27:12 (2:23:26-92)
PARKER Jonathon U20 1.05.76, Birchfield :
400H - 53.80
PARKES Lee U20 23.12.76, Rotherham :
DecJ - 5411 (5149-94)
PARKIN Christopher U17 6.07.79, Notts :
1.5kSt - 4:33.1
PARKIN John U17 23.02.79, Colwyn Bay :
SPY - 14.15, DTY - 45.96, HTY - 50.74
PARKINSON Ian Philip U17 12.02.79, Wyc :
PV - 4.00
PARLEY Martin U20 26.07.78, Bristol :
PV - 4.30
PARR Stephen 18.03.59, Gateshead :
3kSt - 9:24.3 (8:52.8-90)
PARRY Philip John 4.10.65, Old Gaytonians :
JT - 67.28 (70.00-94)
PARSONS Gary, Cambridge & Colr'dge :
DT - 41.30 (42.08-93), HT - 47.14
PARSONS Geoffrey Peter 14.08.64,
London AC/Blue C : HJ - 2.24i/2.20 (2.31-94)
PARTINGTON Stephen W. 17.09.65, Manx H :
3kW - 11:33.4, 10kW - 41:14.61,
20kW - 1:26:32 (1:24:18-90)
PASSEY Adrian 2.09.64, Bromsgrove & R :
3k - 8:00.4+/8:16.7 (7:48.09-89), 5k - 13:22.73
PATE Martin U20 16.03.77, Victoria Pk AAC :
HJ - 2.00i/1.90 (2.01-93),
PATEL Shane U23 4.03.74, Cambridge H :
400 - 48.7
PATIENCE Matthew U15 22.12.81, Winch :
JTB - 47.48
PATIS Ryan U20 4.11.77, Medway :
400 - 48.80

PATRICK Adrian Leroy John U23 15.06.73,.
Windsor S & E : 200 - 20.62w/21.0/21.17,
300 - 33.6, 400 - 45.63
PAUL Jamie 17.07.70, Thames Valley :
100 - 10.6, 200 - 22.0 (21.9w-93/22.23-94)
PAUL Lenox 25.05.58, Belgrave/Army :
100 - 10.94 (10.25w-91/10.32-93)
PAVIS Jon 4.10.66, Rowntrees :
2kSt - 5:58.80, 3kSt - 9:23.10 (9:04.78-90)
PAVITT Simon U20 12.07.76, Braintree :
JT - 52.18 (54.44-94)
PAYNE-DWYER Russell H. 11.09.60, Birch :
HT - 52.68 (56.62-86)
PEACOCK James U20 29.09.77, Thurrock :
TJ - 15.04
PEACOCK Laurent U17 4.02.79, Exeter :
HJ - 1.90
PEACOCK Shane 5.03.63, Birchfield :
HT - 64.08 (71.60-90)
PEAKE John U17 14.02.79, Telford :
1.5kSt - 4:39.1
PEARCE Brian U15 9.12.80, Ashford :
60HB - 8.80i, 80HB - 11.86,
SPB - 13.55, PenB - 2626
PEARCE Duncan James 21.10.70, Sale :
PV - 4.80i/4.70 (4.80-92)
PEARSON Andrew 14.09.71, Longwood :
1500 - 3:47.5 (3:42.2-91),
3k - 8:08.7 (8:05.4-92),
5k - 14:18.84 (13:44.3-93), 10kR - 28:21
PEARSON J. U17, Telford :
JTY - 56.42
PEARSON John T. 30.04.66, Charn/WLHS :
HT - 63.50 (66.54-94)
PEARSON Kenneth W.G. 9.07.72, EdinSH :
Dec - 5864
PEARSON Stephen G. 13.09.59, Sale/NWHS :
HT - 62.96 (65.24-94)
PEDRICK Matthew U17 3.05.79, Cheltenham :
JTY - 56.24
PELESZOK Matthew U15 17.10.81, Shrewsb :
800 - 2:04.96, JTB - 48.00
PENGILLY Adam U20 14.10.77, Taunton :
DecJ - 5589
PENK Andrew U17 19.09.78, Wrexham :
HJ - 2.05, PV - 4.30
PENN Andrew S. 31.03.67, Coventry RWC :
3kW - 12:12.36 (11:39.54-91),
10kW - 46:02.0 (41:59.10-91),
20kW - 1:28:29 (1:23:34-92)
PENNEY Christopher J. 10.05.57, Stourport :
Mar - 2:20:39 (2:17:45-92)
PERIGO Phillip U17 25.09.78, Stainforth :
100 - 10.80, 200 - 21.5/21.69 (21.65w-94)
PERMAN Mark R. 6.01.68, Havering :
110H - 15.3 (15.06w-93/15.2-89/15.24-92),
Dec - 5705 (6606-93)
PERRY Kevin V45 7.12.48, Southend :
100MW - 21:41:37
PERRY Matthew Robin U20 15.02.78, Cardiff :
HJ - 2.01
PERRYMAN Guy St.D.M. 2.11.58, Reading :
SP - 14.91 (16.58-89)
PETERS Mark, 66 Bingley :
10kR - 29:12
PHILIP Colin U17 8.06.79, Edinburgh SH :
400HY - 56.50

346

PHILIP James U15 11.12.80, Luton :
TJ - 12.80
PHILIPS Andrew U17 9.04.79, Kendal :
800 - 1:57.5
PHILIPSON Morris U23 26.02.73, East Ches :
LJ - 6.90 (6.98-93)
PHILLIPS Matthew U20 22.09.77, Birchfield :
JT - 56.94
PHILLIPS Steven 17.03.72, Birchfield :
LJ - 7.77 (7.91-91), TJ - 14.95 (15.04-91)
PHILLIPS Tim U17 13.01.79, Verlea :
JTY - 57.06
PHILLIPS William U17 2.03.79, Havant :
HJ - 1.91
PHILLS Mark 26.07.64, Old Gaytonians :
100 - 10.5w/10.7 (10.55-91),
200 - 21.8/22.10 (21.29-93)
PHIPPS Nicholas D. V40 8.04.52, Woking :
SP - 14.02 (15.27-77)
PICKERING Shaun Desforges 14.11.61,
Haringey/ACC Amsterdam : SP - 18.94,
DT - 51.06 (54.38-89), HT - 62.14 (68.64-84)
PIERRE Henderson 29.10.63, Haringey :
HJ - 2.05 (2.20i-87/2.18-86), TJ - 14.28
PINNER Mark 12.05.64, Wolverhampton & B :
JT - 65.14 (65.74-93)
PIPER Richard U13, Eastbourne GS :
HJ - 1.60,
PITTAM Russell U15 12.10.80, Phoenix :
800 - 2:02.7, 1500 - 4:12.58, 3k - 9:20.8
PLANO Matthew U20 8.10.76, Trafford :
2kSt - 5:59.63, 3kSt - 9:25.0
PLANT Raymond 13.05.68, Newcastle :
2kSt - 5:51.97
PLASKETT Simon U17 9.04.79, Wycombe :
400 - 49.97
PLATT Christopher U17 25.09.78, Bolton :
TJ - 13.53
PLATTS Stephen J. 12.03.66, Morpeth :
5k - 14:33.34 (14:12.36-90)
PLEASANTS Peter 29.07.62, Barnsley :
Mar - 2:24:07
PLUMMER Daniel U15 4.01.81, Blackheath :
100 - 11.33, 200 - 23.12
POLLMEIER Klemmens 8.06.66, Bath Un/Bris :
PV - 4.55unc/4.30i/4.20
PONTING Mark U20 28.04.77, Cardiff :
400 - 48.02 (47.94-94)
POOLEY Anthony 14.01.64, St Edmunds P :
Mar - 2:24:56
POORE Stuart 30.12.72, Team Solent :
1500 - 3:46.7 (3:44.77-94)
POPE Robert E. 24.01.69, Shaftesbury B :
Dec - 6075 (6703-92)
PORTWAY John U17 13.10.78, Dartford :
HJ - 1.97
POTTER Martyn U17 16.02.80, Milton Keynes :
3k - 8:55.9/8:55.9
POVEY Soloman U17 8.02.80, Bournemouth :
100 - 11.1/11.28
POWELL Dalton 20.08.63, Belgrave :
100 - 10.90w/10.97 (10.7-91/10.88-92),
200 - 21.71w/22.0(21.1db/21.24w/21.26-92)
POWELL David U17 11.09.78, Richmond & Z:
400 - 50.86, DecJ - 5267,
DecY - 5618, OctY - 4897
POWELL Neil U20 5.03.77, Cardiff :
60 - 6.99i

POWELL Wayne 27.07.71, Stroud :
JT - 58.62 (59.36-93)
POWER Garry 1.09.62, Herne Hill/IRE :
DT - 45.98 (48.98-86)
POYNTER Benedict U15 23.09.80, Croydon :
JTB - 46.24 (47.70-94)
PRATT Stephen U20 14.06.76, Blackheath :
400H - 55.69
PRESTON Darren U23 19.12.74, Enf/Brun Un :
3kSt - 8:58.72
PRICE Glyn A. 12.09.65, Swansea :
PV - 4.70 (4.80-90)
PRICE Sean Myrion 4.01.63, Swansea :
800 - 1:51.3 (1:49.67-86)
PRITCHARD Chris U15 15.12.80, Grimsby :
PenB - 2535
PRITCHARD Jonathan U15 21.12.80, Burton :
400 - 53.62
PRITCHARD Nicholas 5.12.72, Cardiff :
PV - 4.60
PROCTOR Mark A. 15.01.63, N & EB/RAF :
SP - 19.37, DT - 52.86 (54.28-93),
HT - 51.80 (53.70-93)
PROPHETT Andrew U23 10.06.74, C of Stoke :
800 - 1:52.6
PROSSER Phil U17, Deeside :
PV - 3.85
PROVAN James U15 23.09.80, Verlea :
DTB - 38.46
PUCKRIN Alan 2.04.64, Greenock Glenpark :
3k - 8:12.0i (8:00.49i-89),
10k - 30:49.66 (29:32.29-94), 10kR - 29:34
PUGSLEY Justin 15.04.71, Haringey/LSAC :
5k - 14:23.01, 10k - 29:36.80
PUNCH James U17 19.12.79, Corby :
HTY - 55.92
PUNTAN Ian U17 6.04.79, GEC :
1.5kSt - 4:35.2
PURSER Mark 18.04.72, Croydon :
110H - 15.4 (15.02-91),
400H - 54.0/54.51 (52.26-93)
PURVES Grant U23 6.04.73, Edinburgh SH :
400 - 48.66 (48.40-94), 800 - 1:49.75

QUARRY James S. 15.11.72,
Old Gaytonians/Brunel Univ/Falkirk :
100 - 10.82, 60H - 8.1i (8.1i/8.15i-94),
110H - 14.23w/14.61 (14.10-94),
PV - 4.40i/4.30 (4.30-94),
LJ - 7.40w/6.88 (7.19-91), SP - 13.93
QUELCH Russell U17 9.09.78, AF&D :
400HY - 54.10
QUIGLEY Kevin U15 28.12.80, Law & Dist :
HJ - 1.78
QUINN Anthony U15 14.01.81, Annadale Str :
SPB - 14.92, DTB - 44.96
QUINN Robert 10.12.65, Kilbarchan :
3k - 8:16.1 (8:05.7-85), 5k - 14:00.91,
10k - 29:14.23
QUINT Jonathan U20 22.11.76, Norfolk :
800 - 1:53.50

RAFFERTY Joe U17 5.02.80, :
80HB - 11.72o
RALPH Paul 16.12.67, GEC :
LJ - 7.20w/7.19, TJ - 15.72w/15.67
RALPH Richard 14.07.71, Thames Valley :
200 - 21.5/22.24

347

RALSON David U20 22.02.77, Oxford City :
JT - 52.40, Dec - 5926w/5556 (5850-94),
DecJ - 6570
RAMSEY Richard 6.10.72, Annadale Striders :
PV - 4.25 (4.60-92)
RANDALL Matthew 28.04.70, Hastings :
LJ - 7.06w/6.96, TJ - 15.37
RATCLIFFE Ian U17 28.05.79, Bolton :
1.5kSt - 4:34.34
RATCLIFFE Trevor 9.03.64, Dacorum & Tring :
JT - 59.90 (64.38-88)
RATHBONE Daniel 9.04.69, Brighton :
Mar - 2:22:48 (2:18:35-93)
RAW David U15 1.02.81, Gateshead :
PV - 3.40
RAWLING Adrian U15 21.11.80, Newquay & P :
SPB - 14.10
RAWLING Nicky U15 28.12.80, Cleveland :
80HB - 11.7/12.09
RAWLINSON Christopher 19.05.72, Trafford :
400 - 48.9, 110H - 14.59,
400H - 50.90, Dec - 6291
RAWLINSON Geoffrey S. 2.08.57, Liv H :
Mar - 2:29:57 (2:26:21-89)
READLE David U17 10.02.80, Liverpool Pem :
SPY - 14.70
REDMAN Brian 25.10.68, Woodford Green :
SP - 13.86 (15.20i-92/14.92-90)
REED Bernard N. 18.10.56, Sale :
HT - 48.16 (49.14-93)
REED Paul 2.06.62, Morpeth :
SP - 16.68 (17.04-88), DT - 52.46 (54.50-94)
REED Stephen U17 7.09.78, North Yorks Sch :
SPY - 14.15
REES Dean U17, :
LJ - 6.42w/6.22
*REES Gareth 30.06.67, Oxford Univ/CAN :*
*SP - 13.41*
REESE Ben U20 29.03.76, Wirral :
800 - 1:51.4 (1:50.5-94), 1500 - 3:48.5
REEVE David U23 25.05.73, Bristol/Camb Un :
LJ - 6.93 (7.22-91),
TJ - 15.04 (15.38w/15.21-90)
REGIS John Paul Lyndon 13.10.66, Belgrave :
60 - 6.72i (6.71i-91),
100 - 10.32 (10.07w-90/10.15-93),
150 - 15.25w (14.93+-93/15.15-94),
200 - 20.26 (19.87A-94)
REID Alan 19.04.66, Peterhead :
10k - 30:37.0
REID Justin 26.09.69, Gateshead :
3kSt - 9:17.34 (8:55.61-92)
REID-HUGHES Geoffrey U15 14.10.81, Tun W :
SPB - 13.51
REILLY Brendan Anthony John 23.12.72,
Belgrave/Loughborough Studnts :
HJ - 2.27 (2.32i-94/2.31-92)
REILLY Darren 19.09.65, Liverpool Pembroke :
2kSt - 5:58.58, 3kSt - 9:16.6 (9:04.3-89)
REISS Michael 17.06.63, Highgate :
HT - 50.40 (50.60-94)
*RENAUD Pascal 20.04.70, Crawley/FRA :*
*60H - 8.3i (8.3i/8.38i-94),*
*110H - 14.95 (14.58-92)*
RENFREE Andrew U23 18.05.75, Newq & P :
1500 - 3:49.79
REY Michael 19.07.68, Windsor S & E :
200 - 21.7/22.03 (21.2w-91/21.23-90)

RICHARDS Edward U20 19.09.77, Oxford C :
PV - 4.40i/4.20
RICHARDS Gregory Roy 25.04.56, N London :
LJ - 7.02w/6.96 (7.65w/7.33-87),
SP - 13.65 (15.24-94), DT - 44.44 (50.66-91)
RICHARDS Henry U15 15.05.81, Charnwood :
100 - 11.56
RICHARDS Justin L. 25.01.71, Worthing :
PV - 4.20 (4.90-91)
RICHARDS Thomas U17 13.11.78, Oxford C :
PV - 4.10
RICHARDSON C. U17, Avonside :
400 - 51.0
RICHARDSON M. U13, Bedford & County :
JTÇ - 36.52
RICHARDSON Mark Austin 26.07.72, W S & E :
400 - 44.81
RICHMOND Stuart Anthony 11.04.69, GEC :
LJ - 6.92, TJ - 14.86
RICKETTS Delroy U23 17.07.74, Wolves & B :
TJ - 14.55 (15.48-92)
RICKETTS Derek, Hull Spartan :
24HrT - 204.833km
RICKETTS Kevin U20 29.06.76, Deeside :
Dec - 5491, DecJ - 5702
RIDLER Mark U17 20.07.79, Middlesbro & C :
100HY - 13.94, 400HY - 57.2
RIEPER Benjamin U23 20.12.73, Leigh :
1500 - 3:48.5, 3kSt - 9:00.16
RIGG John P. 3.06.67, Warrington :
800 - 1:50.7 (1:48.2-89)
RIMMER Neil 22.04.62, Sale :
3k - 8:16.1 (7:56.47-91),
5k - 14:32.88 (13:49.57-87)
RITCHIE Darren U23 14.02.75, Edin/Sc Bord :
LJ - 7.46
RITCHIE Don V50 6.07.44, Moray RR :
100kT - 7:07:29, 100kR - 7:09:49 (6:51:14-89)
RIXON Dale 8.07.66, Cardiff :
HMar - 1:04:38 (1:04:19-94)
ROACH Mark 11.04.65, Old Gaytonians :
HJ - 2.08 (2.10-85)
ROACHE Desmond U20 5.01.76, Clydesdale :
800 - 1:49.18, 1500 - 3:44.98,
1M - 4:08.2, 3k - 8:29.1
ROBB Aaron U20 1.11.76, Avonside :
HJ - 2.00
ROBB Bruce U20 27.07.77, Pitreavie :
SP - 15.03, SPJ - 16.18,
DT - 46.38, DTJ - 48.86
ROBB Curtis 7.06.72, Liverpool H/Sheff Univ :
800 - 1:46.34 (1:44.92-93)
ROBBINS Michael U20 14.03.76, Rotherham :
HJ - 2.17
ROBERSON Mark 13.03.67, Haringey :
JT - 78.44 (80.92-88)
ROBERTS Andrew U20 19.09.77, Wigan :
LJ - 7.03
ROBERTS Chris, Swindon :
HT - 47.64
ROBERTS Ian 15.06.68, Shaftesbury Barnet :
LJ - 7.10 (7.19w-92)
ROBERTS Mark S. 12.02.59, Potteries Mar :
Mar - 2:26:38 (2:19:19-92)
ROBERTS Paul 24.12.69, Cardiff/LSAC :
800 - 1:49.95 (1:49.48-93)
ROBERTS Peter 19.09.71, Swansea :
DT - 42.96 (44.52-90)

348

ROBERTSON David James U23 4.08.73,
Tonbridge : 1500 - 3:48.46 (3:40.90-92),
3k - 8:20.1 (8:09.66-92)
ROBERTSON Maximillian 27.12.63, Belgrave :
110H - 15.27 (14.14-86)
ROBERTSON-ADAMS Charles U20 5.12.77,
Telford : 110HJ - 15.2/15.61, 400H - 52.84
ROBINCOCKER Olu U23 27.11.75, Traff/SLE :
HJ - 2.00 (2.00-93), LJ - 7.14, TJ - 14.94
ROBINSON Brian U15 3.09.80, Birchfield :
TJ - 12.53
ROBINSON David U20 12.01.78, Sund/NESH :
HT - 47.64, HTJ - 52.62
ROBINSON Dean 25.06.70, Tipton :
PV - 4.20 (4.30-90)
ROBINSON Eifion U17, Carmarthen :
DTB - 42.28o
ROBINSON Ian 21.04.69, Preston/Iowa St Un :
3k - 8:12.02i (8:01.12i-92/8:04.3-94),
5k - 13:42.85, 10k - 28:34.84, 10kR - 29:37
ROBINSON James U20 27.08.76, Tipton :
PV - 4.20i (4.30i/4.30-94)
ROBINSON Keith V40 9.02.52, Havering :
HT - 51.20 (53.38-81)
ROBISON Christopher 16.03.61, Spango Val :
5k - 13:59.45 (13:54.66-84),
10k - 29:03.69 (28:39.35-86),
10kR - 29:35 (29:14-85)
ROBSON Philip U20 7.02.77, Reading :
200 - 22.13
ROCKHEAD Kevin U20 23.04.77, Beds & Co :
LJ - 6.99
RODEN Paul Anthony 18.04.65, Sale :
10kR - 29:41 (29:14-92),
HMar - 1:04:39 (1:03:19-93)
ROGAN Oliver U15 22.04.81, Bristol :
400 - 53.69
ROGERS Craig U14 02.76, Birchfield :
SP - 13.86, SPJ - 15.48
ROGERS Mark U17 14.03.79, Bexley :
1.5kSt - 4:37.2
ROGERS Nathan U15 11.11.80, Camb Sch :
TJ - 12.28
ROGERS Stephen A. 1.09.71, Liverpool Pem :
110H - 15.0/15.05w/15.42, PV - 4.60,
DT - 43.20, JT - 60.70, Dec - 7295
ROLAND Damian U20 15.01.77, Peterbro :
2kSt - 6:00.20, 3kSt - 9:48.58
ROLLINS Andrew U20 20.03.78, Wigan :
DT - 40.98, DTJ - 44.32
RONCIA M., Haringey :
HJ - 2.00
ROSATO Sebastian 19.11.72, GEC/Camb Un :
110H - 14.79w/14.97 (14.8db-93/14.8-94)
ROSCOE Martin Peter 19.09.64, Leeds :
5k - 14:31.24, 3kSt - 8:56.3 (8:53.2-89)
ROSE Nicholas H. V40 30.12.51, Bristol :
Mar - 2:22:32 (2:21:10-94)
ROSE Stefan U23 7.04.75, Team Solent :
200 - 21.6w, LJ - 7.00 (7.18-94)
ROSE Vincent 21.08.71, Thames Valley :
400 - 47.83 (47.29-94)
ROSS David 2.11.65, Scottish Borders :
5k - 14:35.6, 3kSt - 9:12.05 (9:04.16-92)
ROSSITER Martin R. 4.09.69, Hunt/Read Un :
TJ - 14.76
ROSSON Andrew U15 2.12.80, Broms& R :
1500 - 4:17.76

ROSSWESS Michael 11.06.65, Birchfield :
60 - 6.62i (6.54i-94),
100 - 10.29A/10.4w (10.07w-94/10.15-91),
200 - 20.88 (20.48w-90/20.51-88)
ROUND Keith U17 23.11.78, Chorley :
1.5kSt - 4:38.75
ROW Andrew U17 17.10.78, Gateshead :
100 - 10.86, 200 - 22.38 (22.19w/22.32-94)
ROWAN Paul 20.03.66, Willowfield :
10kR - 29:19
ROWBOTHAM Stephen 6.03.68, Rotherham :
LJ - 6.95 (7.12-94), Dec - 6637 (6792-94)
ROWE Ian U17 28.09.78, Team Solent :
TJ - 14.01w/13.86
ROWEN Daniel U17 30.12.79, Solihull & S H :
1.5kSt - 4:38.4
ROWLANDS Mark Stuart U20 18.04.78, Swan :
400H - 53.0/53.14,
400HY - 52.63o (53.30-94)
ROYDEN Barry Mark 15.12.66, Medway :
1500 - 3:51.8 (3:45.7-92),
5k - 14:11.17 (13:54.03-91),
HMar - 1:03:50 (1:02:25-94), Mar - 2:21:16
RUBENIS Richard U23 10.11.73, Telford :
60 - 6.90i, 100 - 10.6w/10.77w/10.8/10.90
(10.5w/10.7/10.77-94),
200 - 21.54w (21.6-94),
400 - 48.2/48.22 (47.4/47.76-94)
RUDD Lee U20 15.09.76, Cumbrian Sch :
DecJ - 5090 (5170-94)
RUDKIN Alan U17 5.11.78, Holbeach :
SPY - 16.64, DTY - 49.12,
JTY - 53.82, OctY - 5039
RULE Charles U17 22.05.80, Edinburgh :
PV - 3.60
RUMBOLD James U15 4.11.81, Bournemouth :
DTB - 39.96
RUSH Martin Gavin 25.12.64, Lakeland :
3kW - 13:27.4 (11:40.54i-93/11:49.85-84)
RUSH Simon U20 23.06.76, Woking :
400H - 55.10 (54.33-94),
PV - 4.20i/4.10 (4.30-94)
RUSHWORTH Brian 14.12.62, Sunderland :
10kR - 29:13 (29:04-88), 3kSt - 9:20.8,
HMar - 1:04:26 (1:03:35-90), Mar - 2:22:41
RUSSELL Alaister 17.06.68, Bord/Law & Dist :
5k - 14:26.7 (14:17.22-91), 10k - 29:52.16
RUSSELL Daryl U15 20.10.80, Woodford Gr :
PenB - 2878
RUSSELL Peter 7.05.60, RUC :
DT - 42.72
RUSSELL Robert U23 5.08.74, Sale :
SP - 14.23i/14.17 (14.24-94),
DT - 50.18 (52.14-93)
RUTHERFORD Tremayne 19.06.72, Cardiff :
60 - 6.74i, 200 - 22.18i (21.20-93),
100 - 10.5/10.61 (10.4w?/10.44-94)
RUTLAND Andrew U20 13.01.76, Sunderland :
DT - 42.24, DTJ - 45.82
RUTLAND Damon U23 10.07.75, Newq & Par :
HJ - 2.13

S ABNIS Dinkar U23 23.09.73, Aberdeen :
HJ - 1.98 (2.00-93),
LJ - 6.98w/6.95 (7.07i-94/7.06-93),
TJ - 14.05 (14.09-91)
SADLER Philip U20 22.04.77, Havering :
400 - 49.49

349

SAHANS Gurmukh U17 8.10.78, Hounslow :
OctY - 4827
SALAMI Raymond U23 11.04.74, Herne Hill :
200 - 21.9
SALLE Frederick Ebong 10.09.64, Belgrave :
60 - 6.89i, LJ - 7.95w/7.90i (8.10-94)
SALMON Lance U13, Manchester :
100 - 12.2
SALMON Thomas U17 12.04.79, Great Yarm :
1500 - 4:02.38
SALT Terry 6.11.65, :
800 - 1:52.21, 1k - 2:24.93
SALTER Lee U17 12.12.78, Exeter :
800 - 1:57.9
SAMMUT Steven 3.05.67, Team Solent :
HT - 57.20 (57.22-93)
SAMPSON Paul U20 12.07.77, Wakefield :
100 - 10.79
SAMUEL Lewis John Derek 12.02.66, Bel :
200 - 21.78w (21.1w?-91/21.48-90)
SAMUEL Rohan 30.01.66, Old Gaytonians :
100 - 10.7w/10.80w/10.8
(10.5w-89/10.58w-92/10.6/10.73-89),
200 - 21.9 (21.6-94/21.86-93)
SAMUELS Daniel U15 21.12.80, Elswick :
3k - 9:37.15
SANDERS Erik U15 31.10.80, North'land Sch :
SPB - 13.45, HTB - 43.68
SANDERSON David 6.05.71, Sale :
LJ - 6.96, TJ - 15.19w/15.11 (15.72w-93/15.29-92)
SANDY George 22.04.71, Hercules Wimb :
400H - 53.47
SANUSI Kahindi U20 17.01.77, :
200 - 21.9
SATCHWELL Anthony W. V40 3.02.53, Jers :
DT - 41.32 (53.54-73)
SAVAGE David 13.11.72, Sale :
400 - 47.99, 110H - 15.34, 400H - 51.39
SAWYER Anthony J. U17 29.04.80, Bucks Sch :
OctY - 4275
SAXON Sean 11.12.71, Telford :
110H - 15.5w
SCANLON Robert U23 13.04.74, Cov G/LSAC :
1500 - 3:46.45i (3:43.90-94), 3k - 8:11.0i
SCANTLEBURY Robert U20 9.11.76, Herc W :
400 - 48.7/48.78 (48.6-94)
SCHUSSEL Philip, Guildford & G/GER :
SP - 14.49
SCOTT Darren 7.03.69, Liverpool H :
100 - 10.70w/10.74, 200 - 21.3/21.35
SCOTT Richard U23 14.09.73, Exeter :
400H - 53.7/53.98
SCOTT Steven U17 5.06.79, Belgrave :
100HY - 13.8/13.86, 110HJ - 14.8
SCOTT Steven U17 29.05.79, Liverpool H :
SPY - 14.58
SCOTT-BOYLE Oladipo U23 17.06.74, Herc W :
100 - 10.8, 200 - 21.9
SCRIVENER Neil U15 18.09.80, Eastb'rne R :
PenB - 2535
SEAR Jonathon 3.04.64, Woodford Green :
3kSt - 9:04.64 (8:58.25-93)
SEAR Richard U17 21.08.79, Oxford City :
HJ - 1.90 (1.91-94)
SEPHTON Simon U17 27.09.78, Scunthorpe :
SPY - 14.62
SERRA Michael U20 1.07.77, Waverley :
110HJ - 15.36w/15.8, 400H - 56.5

SESAY Mark Gavin 13.12.72, Leeds/LSAC :
400 - 47.7 (48.19-90),
800 - 1:49.02 (1:48.30-90)
SESTON Tony U15 21.12.80, Ipswich :
80HB - 11.67, LJ - 5.95, PenB - 2559
SEXTON Michael U17 26.05.79, Haslemere :
HTY - 56.74
SHAH Arif U17 29.11.78, Leics Cor :
TJ - 14.03
SHALE Max U15 20.01.81, Oxford City :
JTB - 46.14 (46.56-94)
SHANKS R. Stephen 3.11.69, Border :
60 - 6.91i,
100 - 10.8/10.99 (10.7/10.80w-90/10.85-89),
200 - 21.7/21.72 (21.6/21.66w-91)
SHARP N., Stockport :
100 - 10.8
SHARPE David 8.07.67, Jarrow & Hebburn :
800 - 1:51.00 (1:43.98-92)
SHARPE Philip U15 6.03.81, Lancaster & Mor :
SPB - 13.71, JTB - 53.10
SHAW Davie, Liverpool Pembroke :
Mar - 2:29:22
SHAWCROSS James U17 12.02.79, Hallam :
200 - 22.69
SHEA Brett 17.04.71, Andover :
Dec - 5544
SHEFFIELD Jamie U20 26.06.78, Wrexham :
400H - 54.22
SHENAVA John U15 5.02.81, Falkirk :
400 - 52.79
SHENTON David U20 20.10.77, Gate/NESH :
HT - 46.94, HTJ - 51.56
SHEPHERD Alan 28.04.69, Morpeth :
Mar - 2:26:29
SHEPHERD Bruce David 20.03.67, Aber/Elgin :
SP - 13.75 (14.50-93), HT - 49.16 (52.30-94)
SHEPHERD Dominic U20 11.12.76, C of Stoke :
PV - 4.80 (4.90-94)
SHEPHERD John S. 23.12.61, Enfield :
LJ - 7.48w?/7.38 (7.89w-86/7.66-88)
SHEPPARD Kevin A. V45 9.06.48, Walton :
JT - 58.20 (60.70-89)
SHERBAN John Ian 30.07.64, S Barn/Falkirk :
1500 - 3:45.6,
5k - 13:46.76 (13:39.43-91)
SHEVYN Michael 12.12.71, Birchfield :
3k - 8:24.25 (8:16.2-92)
SHIPP James U20 10.11.77, Great Yarmouth :
100 - 10.9, 400 - 48.44
SHIRLEY Simon 3.08.66, Belgrave :
400 - 48.66 (48.0/48.32-88),
110H - 15.05 (14.7/14.82-94),
HJ - 2.01 (2.09-85), PV - 4.70 (4.70-88),
LJ - 7.31 (7.56w-88/7.55-86), SP - 14.59,
DT - 44.00 (44.68-91), JT - 62.06 (65.00-93),
Dec - 7822 (8036AUS-88/7980-94)
SHORT Lewis U15 26.10.80, Kilmarnock :
100 - 11.4
SHOWELL Gavin 29.09.72, Tamworth :
PV - 4.20i/4.20 (4.30-91),
Dec - 5251
SICHEL Willie, Orkney Islands :
100kR - 7:28:18
SIDDONS Craig U23 4.06.73, Sheffield :
3kSt - 9:24.5
SILEY Warren Gladstone U23 16.01.73, Traff :
PV - 4.80 (5.20-90)

SILVA Andre U15 18.11.80, Cardiff :
100 - 11.2w/11.29, 200 - 23.0w/23.41
SIMMONS D. U15, City of Stoke :
LJ - 5.97w/5.24
SIMMONS Steven U23 10.11.74, Havering :
200 - 21.7/21.71 (21.39-94)
SIMON Delroy U17 27.11.78, Old Gaytonians :
1.5kSt - 4:32.7
SIMON Robert, Carmarthen :
1M - 4:03.4
SIMPOLE Matthew U15 6.07.81, Enfield :
SPB - 13.04, DTB - 38.14
SIMPSON Ian Simon Fraser 3.08.66, Leeds :
LJ - 7.12 (8.04w/7.90-89)
SIMPSON Michael 6.01.70, Hounslow :
1500 - 3:51.7 (3:50.6-94),
5k - 14:22.79 (14:19.6-94)
SIMPSON Scott U17 21.07.79, Oxford City :
PV - 4.10
SIMSON Matthew 28.05.70, Thurrock :
SP - 18.68 (19.49-94), DT - 46.58
SINCLAIR Trevor 6.08.61, Birchfield :
LJ - 7.07 (7.56w/7.50i/7.47-84)
SINGER Richard U17 7.02.79, Banchory :
400 - 50.50, 60HY - 8.50i,
100HY - 13.9/14.10, 400HY - 55.37
SKEETE John U17 8.09.78, Blackheath :
60 - 7.01i, 100 - 10.74w/11.06,
200 - 21.78, 400 - 49.7
SKELDING Andrew J. 8.11.71, Dudley & Stour :
HJ - 2.00 (2.10-94)
SKELTON Matthew 8.11.72, Tonbridge :
1500 - 3:49.2, 3k - 8:17.3i/8:21.8 (8:18.7-91)
SKETCHLEY David U20 25.02.76, Team Sol :
JT - 59.84
SKEVIS George U17 12.10.79, Crawley :
DTY - 47.10, OctY - 4462
SKORNIA Richard U13, Devonia AC :
3k - 10:29.7
SLADE Garry 10.10.68, Cardiff :
LJ - 7.41w/7.24 (7.69w-88/7.68-92)
SLATER Damien U20 14.10.77, Beds & Co/WLHS :
HT - 45.48, HTJ - 51.18
SLEATH Justin E. 9.02.67, Bracknell :
200 - 21.7, 400 - 47.57 (46.99-91)
SLESSER M. U13, :
1M - 5:19.6
SLESSOR Daniel U17 5.10.78, Border :
HJ - 2.00,
SLOCOMBE Tim U20 15.11.77, Bournemouth :
400 - 48.86
SLOMAN Trevor 21.03.68, Enfield :
110H - 15.5/15.89 (15.1w-90/15.20-93),
PV - 4.20 (4.50-91),
Dec - 6258 (7076w-93/6905-91)
SLOWLEY Chris 16.02.63, Bristol :
5k - 14:33.9
SLOWLY Glyn F. 19.05.71, Exeter :
PV - 4.40 (4.70i-90/4.50-89)
SLYTHE Paul J. U23 5.09.74, GEC :
100 - 10.98, 200 - 21.7/21.78, 400 - 47.03
SMAHON Dean Carey 8.12.61, Lisburn/RUC :
JT - 66.00 (67.60-94)
SMAILES Andrew David 22.04.68, W & B/RAF :
110H - 15.0/15.07w/15.26
(14.6w-90/14.7/14.74-87)
SMALL Michael V40 31.03.54, Belgrave :
DT - 42.20 (44.14-88)

SMITH Adam U20 20.02.77, Annadale Str :
HJ - 2.10, TJ - 14.82
SMITH Andrew U17 10.01.80, Team Solent :
HJ - 1.90
SMITH Austen U17 26.09.79, Stroud :
100HY - 14.0/14.70
SMITH Brendan U20 20.07.77, Leigh :
1500 - 3:48.8, 3k - 8:20.6
SMITH C. Anthony 17.05.58, Shaftesbury B :
JT - 68.34 (69.94-91)
SMITH Christopher James U23 27.11.75,
Edinburgh/Arbroath : JT - 61.56
SMITH Christopher J. 23.12.58, Leics WC :
3kW - 13:19.0 (12.05.0-87),
10kW - 47:22.0 (43:15.0-87),
20kW - 1:39:52 (1:28:34-85)
SMITH Craig U15 1.03.81, Edinburgh :
SPB - 13.38, DTB - 39.92
SMITH Darrell Luke 10.04.67, Blackheath :
1500 - 3:50.0, 3k - 8:04.5 (8:00.02i-91),
5k - 14:16.8 (13:58.62-92)
SMITH David 21.06.62, City of Hull/NESH :
HT - 65.02 (77.30-85)
SMITH David U23 2.11.74, City of Hull/ERHS :
HT - 71.52
SMITH Dennis P. V45 26.01.49, :
Mar - 2:27:32
SMITH Gary 20.02.71, Shaftesbury Barnet :
110H - 14.9/15.63 (14.87w/15.00-91),
LJ - 7.15w/7.10 (7.35-93)
SMITH Glen E. 21.05.72, Solihull & S Heath :
SP - 13.53 (14.03-94), DT - 58.70 (59.78-94)
SMITH Iain James U23 12.05.73, Perth :
. Dec - 5981
SMITH Ian U15 7.01.81, Lincoln Well :
400 - 52.89, 800 - 2:02.6
SMITH James U20 2.08.77, :
110HJ - 15.4
SMITH Jason 20.05.68, Corby :
200 - 21.91w/22.01
SMITH Jeremy U23 16.08.74, Rotherham :
800 - 1:52.2
SMITH Kenneth M. 10.05.64, Sandwell :
HT - 48.80 (56.28-85)
SMITH Kevin 28.01.67, Sale :
10k - 30:29.1
SMITH Mark Richard 18.11.71, Woodford Gr :
100 - 10.55 (10.4w-90), 400 - 46.44A/46.60,
200 - 20.92w/21.00 (20.85w/20.87-90),
SMITH Matthew U23 26.12.74, Old G :
1500 - 3:48.8
SMITH Paul W. V40 12.08.54, Brecon/Les Cr :
Mar - 2:25:14 (2:21:24-91)
SMITH Phillip 26.05.64, Bridgend/Forres :
Mar - 2:25:47
SMITH Raymond L. 24.12.67, Old Gaytonians :
TJ - 14.18 (15.26-91)
SMITH Richard W. U15 17.01.81, Peterbro :
PV - 4.31, PenB - 2739
SMITH Robert Mark 3.11.66, Edinburgh SH :
SP - 14.01 (15.14i-90/15.06-91)
SMITH Stephen U17 13.02.80, Peterborough :
PV - 4.00i/4.00
SMITH Steven U15 4.12.80, Inverness :
LJ - 5.90w
SMITH Steven U23 29.03.73, Liverpool H :
HJ - 2.35 (2.38i-94/2.37-93),
LJ - 7.03 (7.65w-93/7.51-92)

SMITH Stuart U20 2.08.76, Coventry Godiva :
HJ - 2.05 (2.11-94)
SMITH Stuart U17 20.12.79, Grimsby :
100 - 11.1
SNADE Jonathan U20 31.03.77, Telford :
60HJ - 8.41i,
110HJ - 15.3 (14.50w/14.9/15.08-94)
SOALLA-BELL Anthony U20 3.10.76, Herne H :
SP - 14.05, SPJ - 15.38
SOLLITT Gary 13.01.72, Southampton City :
SP - 16.94
SOLLY Jonathon 28.06.63, Bingley :
5k - 13:56.96 (13:22.39-86),
10k - 28:58.29 (27:51.76-86),
10kR - 29:05 (28:03-86),
HMar - 1:03:32 (1:02:57-90)
SOUGRIN Neil 14.05.71, Enfield :
DT - 47.38 (47.82-94)
SOUTH James U23 4.01.75, Shaftesbury B :
SP - 14.00, DT - 47.08 (48.32-94)
SOUTHAM Carl U23 11.01.74, Charnwood :
400 - 48.41 (46.59-92)
SOUTHWARD Anthony 31.01.71, Stockport :
110H - 14.8w/15.10 (14.84w-94),
PV - 4.30, Dec - 7075
SOUTHWARD Robert U17 24.03.80, Wirral :
JTY - 54.62
SPAWFORTH Darren 1.08.69, Wakefield :
1500 - 3:48.2 (3:40.48-92)
SPEAKE William J. 24.01.71, Bilderston B :
Mar - 2:29:44 (2:26:49-94)
SPENCE William U15 29.12.80, Crewe & N :
SPB - 13.63
SPICER Matthew William 18.05.71, Bristol :
HT - 55.54 (58.42-89)
SPIKES Douglas U20 1.07.76, Ealing,S & Mx :
HT - 45.44 (47.12-94), HTJ - 47.40 (50.64-94)
SPILANE Paul U17 27.09.79, Leics WC :
3kW - 15:48.0, 3kWR - 14:53,
5kW - 26:13.20
SPINDLEY D. U15, G. Manchester Sch :
400 - 53.2
SPIVEY Philip 15.05.61, Belgrave/AUS :
HT - 63.46 (70.94-86)
SPRATLEY Nigel 1.04.70, Reading :
SP - 16.97 (17.96-94), DT - 45.00 (47.14-94)
SPRATLEY Stuart J. 18.07.72, Shaftesbury B :
HT - 53.30 (60.96-92)
SQUIRE Andrew U17 30.09.79, Cannock & St :
LJ - 6.44w/6.29, OctY - 4796
ST.HILLER W., RAF :
200 - 22.06
STAINES Gary Martin 3.07.63, Belgrave :
5k - 13:38.42 (13:14.28-90),
10k - 28:33.49 (27:48.73-91),
10kR - 28:34 (28:28-87),
10MR - 47:00 (46:11-93),
HMar - 1:02:38, Mar - 2:16:04
STAMP Terence 18.02.70, Newham & E B :
60 - 6.84i (6.84i-93), 100 - 10.47
STANFORD Steven U17 9.12.79, Liverpool H :
DTY - 41.88
STANLEY David U17 16.01.79, Basing & MH :
800 - 1:53.7, 1500 - 4:05.7
STANLEY-CLARKE Antony U15 10.10.80, Bel :
JTB - 49.06
STARBUCK Chris, Army :
Mar - 2:27:27 (2:26:21-93)

STARK Graeme 12.10.63, Rotherham :
SP - 14.43 (14.88i-94/14.70-85)
STARK Peter V40 9.12.53, Cardiff :
HT - 49.10 (55.96-79)
STARK William U20 11.03.77, Aberdeen :
LJ - 7.07w/7.06, TJ - 14.55
STARLING Brent U20 19.05.76, Rotherham :
JT - 55.24
STEBBINGS Simon 23.04.71, Luton/Okla St Un :
800 - 1:51.7 (1:49.91-93)
STEEL John A. 27.02.63, Edinburgh SH :
3kSt - 9:20.3 (8:54.86-88)
STEELE Martin Douglas 30.09.62, Longwood :
400 - 48.8 (47.4-90/48.65-93),
800 - 1:48.95i/1:49.15 (1:43.84-93)
STEERS Leonard 31.03.60, Liverpool H :
HT - 47.74 (49.32-92)
STEINLE Mark U23 22.11.74, Blackheath :
3k - 8:10.1, 5k - 14:16.88 (14:03.82-94),
10k - 29:07.33
STENNETT Kori U20 2.09.76, Cheltenham :
TJ - 14.64 (15.02-94)
STEPHENS Kevin 17.08.72, Bristol :
200 - 22.0
STEPHENSON Christian U23 22.07.74, Card :
1500 - 3:51.74
STEPHENSON J. U13, Irvine :
400 - 59.8
STERGIOU Alexander U17 27.09.78, Yeovil O :
HJ - 1.94
STERN Mark 22.05.72, Shaftesbury Barnet :
110H - 14.47 (14.11w/14.24-93)
STEVENS Richard U20 17.07.76, Herne Hill :
HJ - 2.00 (2.03-93)
STEVENSON Gary U17 12.09.79, Kilbarchan :
400HY - 57.3,
STEVENSON Samuel 20.12.63, Telford :
3kSt - 9:18.0 (9:04.6-94)
STEWART Alexander U15 30.09.80, C of Ply :
PV - 3.10
STEWART Eddie 15.12.56, Cambuslang :
10k - 30:43.0 (30:22.0-93), Mar - 2:23:40
STEWART Glen 7.12.70, Edinburgh SH :
800 - 1:51.4 (1:49.9-91),
1500 - 3:42.75 (3:40.17-94), 3k - 8:09.4i
STEWART Kris U17 11.04.80, Scottish Bord :
200 - 22.61, 400 - 49.8/50.16
STILL Matthew U17 1.12.79, Basingst & MH :
200 - 22.6/22.88
STIRRAT Kenneth A. 1.03.70, Falkirk :
3kSt - 9:15.5 (8:49.26-94)
STOKES Stuart U20 15.12.76, Bolton :
2kSt - 5:53.02, 3kSt - 9:05.84
STONE Darrell Richard 2.02.68, Steyning :
10kW - 41:10.11,
20kW - 1:24:49 (1:23:27sh-93), 35kW - 2:40:49
STONE Jason James U15 15.10.80, Houns :
HTB - 52.16
STOREY James U20 26.11.76, Enfield :
110HJ - 14.6 (15.40-94)
STRANG David Maxwell 13.12.68, Haringey :
800 - 1:46.02 (1:45.85-92),
1500 - 3:39.94 (3:36.53-94),
1M - 3:56.05 (3:54.30-94)
STREATHER Gavin Blair 14.04.71,
Woodford Green/Loughborough Studnts :
110H - 15.48w/15.5 (15.1/15.15-94),
400H - 54.60 (53.18-91)

STRINGER Martin U17 23.11.78, Blackheath :
JTY - 54.46
STUBBS Richard A.J. 6.06.66, Cardiff :
Dec - 5629 (5863w/5822-93)
STUCKEY Andy 24.04.72, Sandwell :
800 - 1:51.8
SUMMERS James A.E. 7.10.65, Royal Navy :
HT - 48.64 (58.86-87)
SUNSHINE Gavin S. U23 19.02.74, N & EB :
110H - 15.05w/15.6 (14.94-93),
400H - 55.2 (53.52-93), PV - 4.40 (4.70-92),
LJ - 7.04w (7.21-94), Dec - 6805 (7112-93)
SUSWAIN Tim U13 22.02.83, Team Solent :
200 - 25.7, 400 - 58.5, 800 - 2:13.0
SUTTON Matthew U15 8.09.81, Wolves & B :
HTB - 53.46
SWABY Nicholas U20 28.10.77, Birchfield :
100 - 10.8
SWAIN Anthony Michael U23 17.01.75,
Wakefield/ERHS : HT - 57.34
SWAIN Ashley U15 3.10.80, Team Solent :
PV - 3.50
SWART Tommie, Southampton City :
10kR - 29:24
SWEENEY Chris U15 26.05.81, Wirral :
HJ - 1.82
SWEENEY Christopher 3.03.66, Tipton :
10kR - 29:42 (29:22-92)
SWEENEY David 9.02.62, Sparta/Herne Hill :
SP - 13.80, DT - 46.72 (47.22-94)
SWEENEY Joseph L. 17.07.65, Windsor S & E :
LJ - 7.26w/7.08 (7.41-87),
TJ - 15.95w/15.60 (16.26-91)
SWEENEY Mark U20 26.02.77, Notts :
HJ - 1.98, DecJ - 5092
SWEETMAN D., Leics Cor :
110H - 15.4
SWIFT Michael 27.08.72, Blackpool/LSAC :
TJ - 14.18i/13.94 (14.87-94)
SWIFT-SMITH Justin U23 28.08.74, S Barnet :
800 - 1:50.14 (1:49.29-94)
SYMONDS Chris U23 21.11.73, Enfield :
2kSt - 5:52.6
SYMONDS Christopher M. 15.11.70, Craw/WLIHE :
SP - 14.90 (15.37-91), DT - 49.62 (50.46-92)
SYMONDS Matthew John 31.07.68, TVH :
SP - 15.59 (15.59-94), DT - 54.36,
HT - 46.42

TABARES Ruben U17 22.10.78, Blackh'th :
400 - 50.8, 100HY - 14.05w/14.67,
110HJ - 15.3, 400H - 56.2, 400HY - 54.52
*TADESSE Kassa U23 21.08.74, Bel/ETH :*
*5k - 14:23.0 (14:17.70-94),*
*HMar - 1:04:06 (1:03:54-94)*
TANSER Toby 21.07.68, Sparvagens :
3k - 8:08.26, 5k - 14:19.64 (13:58.59-94),
10k - 30:03.52 (29:46.24-94), Mar - 2:22:23
TAPPENDEN Mark U17, Invicta :
LJ - 6.57
TATHAM Alan U20 29.04.77, Derbs & C/LSAC :
800 - 1:52.6, 1500 - 3:48.4
TAYLOR Brian P.J.P. 13.08.70, Old Gayt :
60 - 6.79i (6.78i-93), 60H - 7.81i
TAYLOR C. U13 11.11.82, Hallam :
JTC - 37.06
*TAYLOR Callum 25.10.72, Belgrave/NZ :*
*400 - 47.49 (47.31-94)*

TAYLOR David 9.01.64, Blackheath :
3k - 8:05.02, 5k - 14:04.2,
10kR - 29:11, HMar - 1:03:31
TAYLOR Ian J. 2.07.67, Telford :
DT - 48.14 (49.44-93)
TAYLOR John 13.05.57, Leigh :
PV - 4.10 (4.20-91)
TAYLOR Jonathon U20 25.10.77, Wimborne :
JT - 52.16
TAYLOR Kenneth V45 24.10.48, Blackburn :
JT - 56.32 (64.36-89)
TAYLOR Kirk R. 30.05.68, Splott C :
3kW - 13:46.96 (12:30.5-89)
TAYLOR Paul Thomas 9.01.66, Border :
3k - 8:10.8 (7:53.38-93),
5k - 14:04.4 (13:45.31-89),
10kR - 28:41RL/28:57 (28:32-94)
TAYLOR Richard U23 5.12.73, Coventry G :
1500 - 3:51.2 (3:48.3-94), 3k - 8:23.6
TAYLOR Scott U20 28.07.78, Leics WC :
3kW - 14:53.6, 5kW - 24:16.7,
10kWR - 51:37
TAYLOR Steve 19.03.66, Manx H :
3kW - 12:42.9 (12:28.5-94),
10kW - 46:30.0 (44:38.2-92),
20kW - 1:36:17 (1:28:46-92)
TAYLOR Stuart 06.06.75, Old Gaytonians :
800 - 1:51.80
TEAPE Hugh D. 26.12.63, Enfield :
110H - 14.10 (13.44-92)
TEAPE Patrick 14.01.70, Enfield :
LJ - 7.17
TELFER Gary 10.01.65, Thames Valley :
400 - 48.91i (48.1/48.41-94),
110H - 15.2 (15.2-87/15.35-92), 400H - 51.29
TELFORD Craig U15 6.05.81, Border :
PV - 3.20
THACKERY Carl Edward 14.10.62, Hallam:
5k - 14:28.0 (13:42.98-87),
HMar - 1:03:28 (1:01:04-87)
THICKPENNY Robert U20 17.07.76, Peterbro :
PV - 4.70, DecJ - 5162
THOM Douglas 13.04.68, B & A/Scot Bord :
400H - 53.43
THOMAS Alex U17 31.12.79, Sandwell :
PV - 3.60
THOMAS Alun 16.03.57, Met. Police :
SP - 14.23
THOMAS Andrew U17 15.05.79, Liverpool H :
400 - 50.6, 800 - 1:55.06
THOMAS Barry V.S. 28.04.72, Sheffield :
100 - 10.88w/10.96, 60H - 8.36i (8.34i-93),
110H - 14.62w/14.88 (14.81-92),
HJ - 2.01 (2.05-92), PV - 4.90i/4.83 (5.00-92),
LJ - 7.15 (7.44-92), SP - 13.63, DT - 41.82,
JT - 60.30, Dec - 7766
THOMAS Graham U20 23.09.77, Carmarthen :
100 - 10.88w (11.1-94)
THOMAS Iwan U23 5.01.74, Newham & EB :
400 - 45.58
*THOMAS Josephus 11.07.68, WoodfGr/SLE :*
*60 - 6.84i (6.71i-94),*
*100 - 10.45 (10.43w-92), 200 - 20.93A/21.28*
*THOMAS Joslyn 11.07.71, Woodford Gr/SLE :*
*100 - 10.7A (10.4w/10.54-94),*
*200 - 21.92 (21.2/21.29-94)*
THOMAS Martin U17 21.09.78, Liverpool H :
400HY - 57.35

THOMAS Nicholas U17 4.04.79, Enfield :
TJ - 13.84
THOMAS Timothy U23 18.11.73, Swansea :
PV - 5.00 (5.20ns/5.10-94)
THOMPSON Alexander U20 5.05.78, Wells :
DTJ - 43.70
THOMPSON Chris U15 17.04.81, AF&D :
3k - 9:41.93
THOMPSON Jason 16.11.71, Dartford :
800 - 1:51.5 (1:51.4-94)
THOMPSON Jeremy U23 11.06.73, Portsm'th/
Warwick Un : 110H - 15.25 (15.0/15.02w-94)
THOMPSON Kenneth 28.02.71, Blackheath :
LJ - 7.11
THOMPSON Lee U20 21.10.76, Lincoln City :
400H - 54.55
THOMPSON Neville L. V40 28.03.55, S B :
SP - 14.63 (15.26i-88/15.15-87),
DT - 54.76 (55.68-93)
THOMPSON Paul 22.03.72, Birchfield :
400H - 53.56 (52.39-94)
THOMPSON Ross U15 7.12.81, Gateshead :
HTB - 50.44
THOMPSON Scot U15 10.08.81, Nairn :
SPB - 14.35, DTB - 46.18, JTB - 48.74
THOMSON Carl 8.04.65, Sarnia :
50kW - 4:38:10
THOMSON Charles 17.06.65, Cambuslang :
10k - 30:57.0 (30:29.6-91), 10MR - 48:10dh
THORN Darren M.M. 17.07.62, Cov RWC :
3kW - 13:48.4 (12:15.0-89)
THORNTON Andrew U20 29.11.77, Elswick :
LJ - 6.80w (6.87w-94)
THORNTON David U23 27.07.73, Hynd/LSAC :
800 - 1:51.0
THURGOOD Stuart U20 17.05.76, LSAC/N & EB :
HT - 52.56, HTJ - 51.94
THYER John U17 23.11.78, City of Plymouth :
SPY - 14.54, DTY - 41.58
TIBBETS Adam U17 14.12.78, Dudley & Stour :
100HY - 13.7/14.54
TIETZ Michael U20 14.09.77, Derby & Co :
100 - 10.8/10.82 (10.77w-94), 200 - 22.0
TILL Stephen, Basingstoke & MH :
24HrT - 215.954km (217.718-94)
TINKER R. U13, Hercules Wimbledon :
LJ - 5.23
TINWELL Mark U15 18.11.81, Sale/NWHS :
DTB - 37.68, JTB - 47.78
TOBIN Shaun 13.10.62, Swansea :
Mar - 2:23:57 (2:23:14-94)
TODD Damien 21.02.71, Royal Navy :
Dec - 5153
TOEMEN Erik U20 1.07.78, B-Hill Mansfield :
DecJ - 5449
TOLLETT Eric U15 29.04.81, Jarrow & H :
800 - 2:04.01
TOMKINS Ian 23.03.68, Haywards Heath :
Dec - 5027
TOMKINSON Tim 31.10.68, Sale/Army :
110H - 14.8/15.02
(14.5-92/14.74w-93/15.00-94)
TONNER James U23 3.06.75, Kilmarnock :
1500 - 3:51.8
TOONE Michael U20 25.09.76, Liverpool H :
HJ - 2.03
TORRY Paul U13 17.10.82, Ellon :
PenC - 1815

TOWNSEND Glen 23.04.64, Western (I.O.M.) :
DT - 42.24 (44.24-90)
TOWNSEND Neil 3.05.63, Herne Hill :
HT - 47.34
TRAYNER Peter U23 27.09.73, Ash/LSAC :
DT - 41.00
TREACY Brian Francis 29.07.71, Annadale Str :
800 - 1:49.89 (1:49.39-90),
1500 - 3:39.87 (3:38.93-94)
TREEN Kevin U20 1.02.76, Birchfield :
PV - 4.40 (4.50i-94/4.40-93)
TREU Robert 1.12.69, Guildford & G :
Dec - 6051
TRIGG Andrew B. 23.06.62, Trowbridge :
50kW - 4:49:40 (4:20:48-88)
TROMANS Glyn 17.03.69, Coventry Godiva :
800 - 1:52.0, 1500 - 3:44.8 (3:43.2-92),
3k - 7:59.27, 5k - 13:55.23
TROWER John 6.02.56, Telford :
JT - 57.14 (63.82-89)
TROY Martin U20 13.07.76, Luton :
400H - 56.1, JT - 54.98, DecJ - 6672
TULBA-MORRISON Phillip William U23 20.09.73,
Basingstoke & MH :
800 - 1:50.73, 1500 - 3:51.95
TULLETT Ian Roger 15.08.69, Belgrave :
PV - 5.30 (5.30i/5.30-92)
TULLETT Mark U17, Cardiff :
400HY - 57.2/58.15
TULLOCH Andrew George 1.04.67, W & B :
200 - 21.8 (21.2-90/21.60-93),
60H - 7.83i (7.76i-93),
110H - 13.62 (13.52-94)
TUNE David 29.10.70, Rotherham :
3k - 8:19.7 (8:14.58-93),
5k - 14:29.9 (14:09.49-94), 10k - 30:35.45
TUNSTALL Neil 3.01.62, Coventry Godiva :
400H - 55.3 (54.9-90)
TURNBULL Aidan U15 1.09.81, Houghton-l-Sp :
OctB - 3933
TURNBULL Gareth U17, Belfast Sch :
1500 - 3:56.67, 3k - 8:54.1i
TURNER Andrew 29.08.63, Crawley :
SP - 14.63i/14.57 (14.74-94), DT - 47.40,
HT - 51.20
TURNER Andrew U15 19.09.80, Notts :
60HB - 8.93i, 80HB - 11.5/11.63,
PV - 3.10, PenB - 2546
TURNER Clayton S. 9.01.68, Horsham BS :
SP - 13.89 (15.52-91)
TURNER Daniel U17 27.11.78, Havering :
HJ - 1.97
TURNER Douglas 2.12.66, Cardiff :
60 - 6.82i, 100 - 10.58, 200 - 20.68w/20.75
TURNER Garry U17 21.12.78, Notts :
60HY - 8.41i, 400HY - 56.9 (57.84-94),
100HY - 13.80w/14.1/14.16 (14.1-94)
TURNER Kelvin, Les Croupiers :
Mar - 2:28:58
TURNER Neil U20 17.05.77, Blackheath :
PV - 4.40i/4.40 (4.40-93)
TURNER Russell 1.06.68, Oxford City :
Dec - 5084
TURVILLE Steven U23 17.02.75, Basing & MH :
800 - 1:52.5
TWIGG Matthew 18.07.69, Peterbro/LSAC :
SP - 13.85 (14.92-94), DT - 44.26 (49.42-91)

354

TYLER Geoffrey A. V45 30.09.48, Sale :
DT - 41.60 (55.42-80)
TYLER John U23 6.03.74, C of Stoke/LSAC :
SP - 13.84 (15.38-93)
TYLEY Phillip Llewellyn 11.10.66, Tonbridge :
HT - 48.52
TYMMONS Tobens U17, Carmarthen :
1.5kSt - 4:35.10
TYNAN Stuart U15 3.10.80, Rhondda :
SPB - 14.38

UDECHUKU Emeka U17 10.07.79, Blackh :
SP - 15.72, SPJ - 16.62i/16.26,
SPY - 18.43, DT - 48.96, DTJ - 54.70,
DTY - 62.22, HTY - 48.18
UGONO Uvie U20 8.03.78, Herne Hill :
60 - 6.98i, 100 - 10.6w/10.64w/10.8/10.94,
200 - 21.38
ULYATT Kent 10.04.72, Norfolk :
200 - 21.46, 300 - 33.2, 400 - 46.31
UMPLEBY Andrew U15 31.10.80, Telford :
80HB - 11.85, HJ - 1.80
URQUHART Ronald John U20 14.11.77, Shett :
HT - 48.74, HTJ - 55.12
USHER Kevin 3.11.65, Hounslow :
3kSt - 9:19.9 (9:03.3-90)
UTTLEY Stephen J. 18.05.57, Ilford :
3kW - 13:47.3 (13:10.3-87)

VANHINSBERGH Tom U17 28.12.78, Craw :
HJ - 2.06
VAUX-HARVEY Matthew U20 30.03.76, Stour :
3k - 8:35.0, 5k - 14:38.10
VENESS Luke U23 5.12.73, Hastings :
800 - 1:51.5, 1500 - 3:51.2 (3:47.4un/3:50.55-94)
VERNON Stephen U15 17.10.80, Stockport :
3k - 9:40.82
VICKERY Christian U17 10.11.78, G & G/Junc 10 :
HTY - 51.14
VIDAL Nigel 18.11.72, Thames Valley :
100 - 10.8/10.87
(10.5wdb-89/10.66w-91/10.7w-90/10.74-91)
VIDGEN David U23 27.09.74, Oxford City :
110H - 15.1/15.31, Dec - 6542
VINT Richard U17 16.02.79, AF&D :
1.5kSt - 4:30.0
VIVIAN Peter J.P. 5.11.70, Thames VH/WLHS :
HT - 71.28

WADDINGTON Anthony U23 30.06.75, Read :
200 - 21.8 (22.10w/22.24-94)
WADE C. U13, Halifax :
JTB - 39.78
WAIN Andrew 2.06.65, Nene V H/Camm Un:
SP - 14.52
WALCOTT Andrew U23 11.01.75, Wolves & B :
100 - 10.60w/10.64, 200 - 21.28w/21.36
WALCOTT Mark U23 24.11.73, Wolves & B :
60 - 6.90i (6.82i-94),
200 - 21.89i (21.5/21.60-93)
WALKER Alvin 30.04.65, Mandale/Army :
LJ - 6.94 (7.36-94), TJ - 14.96, Dec - 5611
WALKER Ben T. U20 8.06.78, Dacorum & T :
DT - 43.68, DTJ - 44.84
WALKER Colin Frederick 29.10.62, Gates :
HMar - 1:03:23, Mar - 2:29:49
WALKER Darren U23 21.03.75, Crewe & N :
200 - 22.01w (21.4w-92/21.5/21.56w/21.59-93)

WALKER David U17 24.11.78, New Marske :
400HY - 57.2/58.03
WALKER Douglas U23 28.07.73, Edinburgh :
100 - 10.79 (10.54w-94/10.69-91),
200 - 20.53w/20.88 (20.71-94), 400 - 47.33i
WALKER Lee U20 17.08.77, Crawley :
PV - 4.20
WALKER Nicholas O. 24.02.64, Severn :
Dec - 5045 (5510-92)
WALKER Paul U23 2.12.73, Liv H/Edin Univ :
400 - 48.7 (49.12i-92),
800 - 1:49.71 (1:47.53-93)
WALKER Robin U20 8.02.78, Scunthorpe :
HTJ - 50.28
WALKER Simon U17 5.06.79, Aberdeen :
1.5kSt - 4:32.2
WALKER Stuart U17 22.09.78, Derby & Co :
JTY - 59.62
WALL Terry 12.06.70, Morpeth :
5k - 14:31.1, 10k - 30:37.7
WALLACE Carl U15 10.02.81, Cannock & St :
HJ - 1.78
WALLACE John 9.10.68, Morpeth :
HJ - 2.05 (2.16-90)
WALLACE Jonathan U17 1.01.79, Birchfield :
LJ - 6.62w, TJ - 14.76
WALLER Daniel U15 1.10.80, Hercules Wimb :
DTB - 38.60
WALLING Andrew U23 3.04.73, Sale :
800 - 1:50.6 (1:53.9-92),
WALMSLEY Dennis, Bourton RR :
Mar - 2:21:19
WALNE Nick U23 18.09.75, Newport/Camb Un:
LJ - 7.30w
WALSH Christopher U17 1.10.78, Mand/NESH :
HTJ - 48.76, HTY - 55.72
WALSH Liam U15 5.05.82, Deeside :
SPB - 13.76, DTB - 39.70, JTB - 50.42
WAN Pak Wai U15 1.09.80, Richmond & Zet :
80HB - 11.8w/12.0/14.48
WARCHALOWSKI Nicholas 10.11.71, ESH/SWE :
PV - 4.20i
WARD Darren U23 5.03.73, Grantham :
100 - 10.8 (11.03w-94)
WARD Jason U17 15.09.78, Hallamshire :
1.5kSt - 4:30.0
WARD Richard U15 5.05.82, Sutton & District :
3k - 9:37.0
WARDMAN James U15 26.10.80, Rich & Zet :
1500 - 4:21.63
WARISO Solomon Christopher 11.11.66, Har :
100 - 10.3/10.40w/10.43 (10.33-94),
150 - 15.25w, 200 - 20.50
WARMBY Mark U17 12.12.78, Longwood :
1.5kSt - 4:22.5
WARMINGTON Ben U17 20.03.79, North SP :
60HY - 8.46i, 100HY - 12.90w/13.2/13.27,
110HY - 14.16
WARREN Carl 28.09.69, Cannock & Stafford :
1500 - 3:47.72, 3k - 8:20.9 (8:09.29i-94),
5k - 14:34.1, 2kSt - 5:37.9, 3kSt - 8:40.74
WARREN Robert U15 17.07.81, Steyning :
3kW - 15:01.2, 3kWR - 15:12
WARRILLOW Paul 8.07.70, Team Solent :
110H - 15.1w/15.2/15.28
(14.9w/14.95w-90/15.0-93/15.04-91)
WASHINGTON Ivan 18.11.56, Sheffield :
DT - 44.62 (46.06-88)

WASSELL Simon 7.04.69, Rotherham :
400H - 54.3 (52.92-93), Dec - 6299
WATERMAN Peter U17 12.09.79, Blackheath :
SPY - 15.89, DTY - 42.00, HTY - 51.12
WATERS Andrew U17 11.10.79, Oxford City :
DTY - 42.78dh/42.32
WATERS Nick U17, Enfield :
PV - 3.91
WATERS Richard U13 30.11.82, Trafford :
1500 - 4:44.0, 3k - 10:30.7
WATERS Rupert 3.01.72, Sale :
800 - 1:50.3
WATSMAN David U13 20.10.82, Black Isle :
75HC - 12.6
WATSON Buster 19.11.57, Richmond & T :
JT - 58.04
WATSON Garth U23 20.04.73, East Cheshire :
800 - 1:50.2
WATSON Matthew U17 23.02.80, Bingley :
3k - 8:59.4
WATSON Peter U15 30.06.81, Oxford City :
HJ - 1.80, LJ - 6.25i/6.00, PenB - 2898
WATT Tim 19.09.66, Steyning :
50kW - 4:20:43
WATTS Kirk U17, Croydon :
1.5kSt - 4:37.8
WATTS Simon W. 30.03.61, East Hull :
Mar - 2:30:46 (2:29:48-94)
WEAVER Matthew U23 14.11.73, Old G/Ox Un :
PV - 4.85 (4.90-94)
WEBB Jamie U23 18.12.75, Belgrave :
PV - 4.25
WEBB Matthew 72, Oxford City :
HJ - 1.98 (2.00-94)
WEBB Paul U20 9.04.76, Wolverhampton & B :
400H - 55.9
WEDLAKE Andrew 30.11.71, Bournem'th/Prov Un :
5k - 14:31.34 (14:11.37-94), 10k - 30:01.20
WEIMANN Wayne 2.05.66, Huntingdon :
PV - 4.60 (4.65-85)
WEIR Peter 2.09.63, Birchfield :
SP - 16.07, DT - 46.54 (48.84-88)
WEIR Robert B. 4.02.61, Birchfield :
DT - 63.56, HT - 61.90 (75.08-82)
WELCH Mark U23 9.11.74, Army/Kettering :
JT - 56.60 (58.94-92)
WELLS Ian 18.02.62, Belgrave :
110H - 15.4w/15.5 (15.04-91),
400H - 53.34 (53.3-91)
WELLS Stuart U17 26.07.79, Havering :
LJ - 6.69
WELSH Graeme U23 8.10.75, Border :
100 - 10.7/10.99 (10.94w-93),
200 - 21.8/21.86
WEST Terence 19.11.68, Morpeth :
800 - 1:51.2 (1:48.2-92),
1500 - 3:47.31 (3:43.39i-94/3:47.1-92),
1M - 4:08.91
WESTON Andrew D. U23 4.12.73, Reading :
HJ - 2.05 (2.11-92), Dec - 6318
WESTON James 9.01.70, Cardiff :
100 - 10.92w, 400 - 47.9/48.21
WESTON Paul 6.10.67, Bristol :
TJ - 15.09 (15.46-92)
WETHERILL Andrew 6.12.57, Sutton-in-Ashf'ld :
Mar - 2:28:36 (2:27:23-94)
WHALEY Geoffrey 9.06.58, City of Plymouth :
HT - 50.58 (62.16-80)

WHALLEY Robert 11.02.68, C of Stoke/Staffs Un :
3k - 8:14.43i (8:09.72i-94)
WHEATCROFT Paul U15 22.11.80, Bolton :
LJ - 6.34w/6.10
WHEELER Craig U20 14.06.76, Trafford :
1500 - 3:54.8, 2kSt - 5:53.62 (5:53.5-94),
3kSt - 9:11.95 (9:10.50-94)
WHELDON Robin U15 7.12.80, C of Plymouth :
SPB - 15.00, HTB - 44.60
WHITBY Benedict U20 6.01.77, Hounslow :
2kSt - 5:59.67, 3kSt - 9:32.26
WHITE Adrian U20 10.09.76, Coventry G :
5k - 14:59.8
WHITE Adrian Paul U23 1.09.74, TVH/LSAC :
60 - 6.98i (6.92i-94), 100 - 10.40,
200 - 21.1/21.29 (21.21w-94)
WHITE Andrew U15 1.05.82, :
TJ - 12.00
WHITE Anthony U17 8.09.78, Hounslow :
HTY - 47.42
WHITE Craig Elliot 4.04.71, Sale :
400H - 54.58 (52.20-94)
WHITE Edward U23 16.11.73, Sale/Man Univ :
100 - 10.61, 200 - 21.12
WHITE Graham 28.03.59, Brighton :
35kW - 2:53:59 (2:48:50-94), 50kW - 4:14:59
WHITE Paul U20 17.11.76, :
LJ - 6.88
WHITE Simon U23 2.10.75, Kent Sch :
DecJ - 5296o
WHITE Steffan 21.12.72, Coventry Godiva :
1M - 4:04.3 (4:00.61-94),
3k - 8:09.79i/8:13.31 (8:01.90i-94/8:04.53-92)
WHITEHEAD Peter Kenneth 3.12.64, Skyrac :
10kR - 28:23, HMar - 1:02:33, Mar - 2:12:23
WHITEMAN Anthony 13.11.71, GEC/WLIHE :
800 - 1:49.60 (1:48.45-94), 1k - 2:23.0i,
1500 - 3:41.28i/3:43.4 (3:41.92-94),
1M - 3:59.44, 3k - 8:14.71i
WHITFIELD Matthew U20 23.01.76, Bingley :
3kSt - 9:35.2
WHITING Andrew U23 7.03.74, Reading :
JT - 56.44 (63.50-94)
WHITTLE Brian 26.04.64, Har/Ayr Seaforth :
400 - 47.01 (45.22-88)
WHITTLE Robert U15 14.06.81, Basing & MH :
3k - 9:34.6
WHORLOW Nigel U15 26.11.80, Belgrave :
3kW - 15:04.34, 3kWR - 15:08
WHYTE Stephen A. 14.03.64, Thames Valley :
SP - 16.95i/16.66 (17.78-89),
DT - 48.10 (50.40-94), HT - 61.02 (67.82-89)
WIECZOREK John 22.11.66, Accrington :
Mar - 2:25:31 (2:24:38-94)
WIGGINS John 1.07.71, Blackburn :
TJ - 14.16i/14.13 (14.34w-91/14.21-93)
WIGHT Graeme 3.06.65, Shettleston :
5k - 14:29.59 (14:18.2-94), 10MR - 47:54dh
WILD Jonathan U23 30.08.73, Sale/Okla St Un :
800 - 1:49.39, 1500 - 3:41.40, 1M - 3:59.79,
3k - 7:55.16, 5k - 13:49.15
WILDING Ian U23 3.03.75, C of Stoke/LSAC :
PV - 4.80 (5.00ex/4.85-94)
WILKES Carl U15 7.11.80, West Midland Sch :
HJ - 1.76, PenB - 2590
WILKIE Julian U20 18.03.76, Cirencester :
3k - 8:30.3

WILKINS Perris 12.11.68, Banbury :
DT - 53.62 (53.80-94)
WILKINSON Alex U15 10.10.80, Bingley :
200 - 23.23
WILKINSON Desmond F. 7.01.63, Luton :
110H - 15.6 (14.3-86/14.35w-84/14.49-86)
WILKINSON Jonathon 17.02.62, Spenbro :
JT - 62.34, Dec - 6077 (6259-94)
WILL Nigel Simon 18.10.67, Enfield :
100 - 10.8 (10.57w/10.66-89),
200 - 21.5 (20.7w-90/20.91-89),
400 - 47.04 (46.42-92)
WILLERS Edward U17 18.09.79, Braintree :
HJ - 2.00
WILLIAMS Anthony Richard 1.05.72, Sheff :
400 - 48.3 (47.65-93), 400H - 50.31
WILLIAMS Barrington Chester V40 11.09.55,
Wolverhampton & B :
LJ - 7.55i/7.50 (8.05i/8.01-89)
WILLIAMS Barry V45 5.03.47, Trafford :
HT - 49.58 (73.86-76)
*WILLIAMS Brett, Cambridge University/USA :*
*PV - 4.40 (4.95-94)*
WILLIAMS Edward 1.10.70, Thames Valley :
400 - 47.23 (46.84-94),
800 - 1:52.10 (1:51.00-94)
WILLIAMS Eric J.H. 6.05.56, Stockport :
Mar - 2:27:54 (2:16:56-84)
WILLIAMS Kevin 15.12.71, Cardiff :
60 - 6.71i, 100 - 10.50,
200 - 21.70 (21.47w-94)
WILLIAMS Paul U20 21.09.77, Charnwood :
SPJ - 14.24
WILLIAMS Rupert L. 17.03.64, Helen/R Navy :
100 - 10.8 (10.5w-85/10.7-89/10.74w/10.84-84)
WILLIAMS Simon U15 5.10.80, Basing & MH :
SPB - 14.57, DTB - 47.44, JTB - 48.12
WILLIAMS Simon Alexander 17.10.67, Enfield :
SP - 16.93 (19.44i-89/19.17-91),
DT - 58.20 (61.14-92)
WILLIAMS Terry 15.11.68, Shaftesbury B :
60 - 6.9i, 100 - 10.7/10.82 (10.17w/10.23-94)
WILLIAMSON Paul U23 16.06.74, Thames VH :
PV - 5.40i/5.40
WILLS Chris U20 18.05.76, Birchfield :
PV - 4.40i/4.30 (4.40-93)
WILSON David 7.09.68, Annadale Striders :
3k - 8:00.1, 10kR - 29:36 (28:53-93)
WILSON David 5.09.70, Tipton :
JT - 63.08 (64.86-88)
WILSON Ian U17 7.10.79, Coventry Godiva :
HJ - 1.95
WILSON Nana U17 14.01.79, Herne Hill :
100 - 11.1/11.19w/11.28
WILSON Peter 28.06.62, White Horse :
5k - 14:33.54 (14:24.5-94),
10k - 30:44.90 (30:10.1-86)
WILSON Trevor 20.03.62, Leeds :
Mar - 2:24:28 (2:19:49-93)
WILSON Vincent U23 1.04.73, Jarrow & H :
1500 - 3:51.2 (3:45.1-94)
WILTSHIRE Lee 26.07.62, Portsmouth :
SP - 16.10 (17.41-94)
WINCHCOMBE Nigel C. 10.12.59, Linc Well :
HT - 52.02 (59.18-88)
WING Jason 12.10.65, Hounslow :
LJ - 6.98 (7.22w/7.21-86)

WINROW Craig Nicholas 22.12.71, Wigan :
800 - 1:46.68 (1:46.54-94)
WINTER Neil Stephen U23 21.03.74, S B :
PV - 5.60
WISEMAN Mark, Army/Basingstoke & MH :
SP - 14.65 (14.66-94), DT - 48.84
WISMAYER Henry U15 26.11.80, :
TJ - 12.12
WITCHALLS Bruno U23 22.03.75, Dorking/LSAC :
800 - 1:49.48, 1500 - 3:41.51, 3k - 8:13.4
WITTON Gary U23 25.08.73, Brighton :
3kW - 12:24.29i/12:30.6,
5kW - 22:14.0, 10kW - 44:38.57
WNUK Guy U15 12.09.80, Croydon :
DTB - 37.52
WOAD Warren U17 16.03.80, Old Gaytonians :
SPY - 14.08
WODU Ejike U23 15.12.74, Blackheath :
60 - 6.87i, 100 - 10.7w/10.82 (10.38w/10.55-93),
WOLSTENCROFT Lee U15 19.07.81, Traff :
3k - 9:34.10
WOOD Anthony U23 30.03.74, City of Stoke :
LJ - 7.08i/7.07w/6.82 (7.40w-93/7.29-94)
WOOD James U20 9.07.77, Devon Sch :
110HJ - 15.3
WOOD James U15 5.02.81, Southend :
HJ - 1.81
WOODHOUSE Mark U23 1.11.75, Norf/LSAC :
100 - 10.4w?/10.68 (10.61w-93),
200 - 21.5w/21.6
WOODING Andrew U17 2.06.79, Colwyn Bay :
LJ - 6.79w/6.72
WOODS Alan P. V40 27.03.51, Birchfield :
HT - 46.98 (57.24-78)
WOODS Richard U13 4.09.82, Basildon :
800 - 2:18.2
WOODWARD Barry U15 20.11.80, B-H Mans :
800 - 2:00.61
WOODWARD Lyndon U15 22.11.80, Cann & St :
SPB - 13.90,
WOOLCOTT Nicholas D. 7.04.61, Haringey :
DT - 50.92 (55.34-88)
WORKMAN B. U13, Hamps Sch :
JTC - 34.24
WORKMAN Richard J. 31.05.71, East Ches:
200 - 22.0 (21.7/21.98-92)
WORRALL Robert U15 11.01.81, Trafford :
LJ - 6.33
WRAY Alan 6.01.71, Old Gaytonians :
800 - 1:52.58
WRIGHT Chris, Bracknell :
TJ - 14.10
WRIGHT Darren U17 7.09.79, Wrexham :
OctY - 4202
WRIGHT Finlay U15 23.12.80, Eton :
80HB - 11.41
WRIGHT Michael U20 15.09.77, Scarborough :
HJ - 1.98 (2.00-94)
WRIGHT Steven 12.02.71, Gate/Newc Univ :
1500 - 3:52.0, 5k - 14:35.52,
3kSt - 9:06.20 (8:52.50-94)
WURR Simon U20 7.01.77, Leamington :
2kSt - 6:03.86
WURR Timothy U17 1.03.79, Leamington :
HTJ - 47.38, HTY - 59.86
WYLLIE William U23 12.07.73, Bir/Birm Univ. :
110H - 15.3/15.57w (14.91-92)

**Y**APP Jonathan U23 1.02.75, Telford :
PV - 4.50 (4.50-94)
YATES Matthew Stewart 4.02.69, Belgrave :
800 - 1:47.98 (1:45.05-92),
1k - 2:18.26i (2:16.34-90),
1500 - 3:40.69 (3:34.00-91),
1M - 4:01.66 (3:52.75-93)
YATES Peter Derek 15.06.57, Blackheath :
JT - 65.90 (77.84-87)
YELLING Martin 7.02.72, Bedford & County :
1500 - 3:46.92, 1M - 4:10.0
YEWER Bradley U17 10.02.79, Newbury :
1500 - 4:07.0
YIANNACOU Andrew U20 18.08.78, Enfield :
JT - 55.58
YOUNG Andrew U20 20.06.77, Victoria P H :
800 - 1:51.9

YOUNG Dominic U15 2.06.81, Shaftesbury B :
800 - 2:04.36
YOUNG Kerrin U17 2.09.79, North Down :
400H - 57.9, 400HY - 56.62
YOUNG Martin 11.07.72, Roadhogs :
3kW - 12:20.38, 10kW - 43:53.97,
20kW - 1:30:28.6t (1:32:53-92)
YOUNG Neil U20 20.02.77, Lisburn :
PV - 4.85
YULE Thomas U17 13.09.78, Kilbarchan :
3k - 8:58.3
YUSUF Yacin U20 20.12.77, Croydon :
1500 - 3:53.0

**Z**AIDMAN Antony Adam 18.03.62, Enf :
SP - 16.05 (17.87i-83/17.22-81)
ZAREI James V50 12.01.44, Croydon :
100kR - 7:48:52 (7:18:18-89)

With the change of age group descriptions it is obvious that changes must be made to the names of the events. Whilst this is easy to organanize in the main lists, it is much more difficult with the index where a concise code is required. I have, therefore, decided to keep the previous descriptions of the events. This should not cause any confusion since the age group of each athlete is clearly shown in the new form eg U15 but some examples will clarify this.

A **J** after an event is used to designate an Under 20 event
eg 110HJ - 110 metres hurdles with 3'3" hurdles

A **Y** or an **I** is an Under 17 event (men and women)
eg 100HY - 100 metres hurdles with 3' 0" hurdles Heptl - Heptathlon with Under 17 implements

A **B** or a **G** is an Under 15 event (men and women)
eg JTB - 600 gram Javelin  SPG - 3.25kg Shot

A **C** or an **M** is an Under 13 event (men and women)
eg SPC - 3.25kg Shot  SPM - 2.72kg Shot

# WOMENS INDEX

ABBISS Susan V35 20.10.59, Ches Le St :
Mar - 2:55:14 (2:51:33-94)
ADAMS Claire 30.05.69, Bris (nee MORRISON) :
100H - 15.16 (14.8/15.14w-94), PV - 3.40i/3.30
ADAMS Gayle U17 5.04.79, Bristol :
3k - 10:34.2
ADAMS Leanda U17 7.12.79, City of Stoke :
80HI - 12.0w
AGYEPONG Jacqueline 5.01.69, Shaft Barnet :
60 - 7.43i (7.41i-89),
100 - 11.72w/12.1 (11.7-94/11.72w-88/11.81-93),
200 - 24.22i (24.1w-93/24.18-90),
60H - 8.01i, 100H - 12.90
AIREY Lisa U15 19.12.80, Solihull & S Heath :
2.5kW - 13:58.02, 3kW - 16:33.0
AKINBIYI Sarah U15 23.08.81, Tower Ham :
60H - 9.2io, 75HG - 11.18w/11.3/11.31
AKIWUMI Tuvola U17 15.10.79, Hercules Wim :
SP - 11.09
ALBERTS Emma U17 22.11.79, Gateshead :
1500 - 4:42.04 (4:36.4-94)
ALDER Elizabeth U15 20.11.80, Severn :
100 - 12.09, 200 - 25.4 (25.63w-94)
ALEXANDER Katie U23 28.04.74, Camb H :
PV - 3.10
ALLAHGREEN Diane U23 21.02.75, Liv H :
60 - 7.38i, 100 - 11.96w/12.0/12.10
(11.7-94/11.78w/11.88-93),
60H - 8.38i, 100H - 13.47w/13.53 (13.25-94)
ALLAN Fiona U23 6.11.75, Notts :
Hep - 3926 (4260w-94/4215-93)
ALLEN Angela, Keyham Plodders :
HMar - 1:18:28
ALLEN Avril E. V35, 1.08.59 Kimberley Str :
Mar - 3:00:09
ALLEN Carice U20 25.09.77, Telford :
HT - 39.80
ALLEN Claire U17 18.09.78, Copeland :
JT - 37.22
ALLEN Jenna U17 2.05.79, Charnwood :
JT - 40.16 (40.72-94)
ALLEN Sara 7.12.70, Sale :
SP - 12.65, DT - 42.90
ALLEN Sophie U13 7.09.82, Ipswich :
100 - 12.9, 200 - 26.8, LJ - 4.73
ALLEYNE Petrina U15 10.07.81, Reading :
100 - 12.3w/12.5
ALLSOPP Catherine U23 30.11.73, LSAC :
800 - 2:08.51i/2:12.02 (2:07.6-94),
1500 - 4:26.71, 1M - 4:48.72i
AMADI Onyema U23 28.06.73, Cardiff :
JT - 48.34 (49.04-94)
AMAKU Afi 6.05.70, Radley :
100 - 12.1
AMEDE Christine F. 7.08.63, Windsor S & E :
400 - 56.4 (55.35-90),
800 - 2:12.8 (2:09.4-92), 400H - 60.37
AMOS Katie U17 13.11.78, Thurrock :
JT - 44.56
ANDERSON Emma U17 19.06.79, Stoke :
60H - 9.01i, 80HI - 11.49, 300H - 46.2
ANDERSON Natalie U13 7.10.82, Tower Ham :
SPM - 9.11, DTM - 24.32
ANDERSON Pamela U20 16.10.76, Glasgow :
LJ - 5.62w/5.57i/5.51 (5.74-94),
TJ - 12.10

ANDERSON S., V35 :
10kR - 34:47
ANDERSON Shani U23 7.08.75, Shaft Barnet :
100 - 12.0/12.09w/12.26 (12.14-94),
200 - 24.7/24.76
ANDREWS Fiona U20 6.12.77, Cumnock :
400H - 65.6
ANDREWS Josephine U15 3.05.81, Notts Sch :
DT - 30.20
ANDREWS Nicola 11.06.70, Shaft Barnet :
800 - 2:10.87
ANDREWS Sharon Nivan 4.07.67, Essex L :
SP - 14.95i (15.80-93), DT - 53.18 (56.24-94)
ANDREWS Teresa U20 4.01.77, Preseli :
HJ - 1.75 (1.79-94), LJ - 5.61
ANDREWS Vicki 31.08.69, Wolves & B :
800 - 2:09.4
ANETO Stephanie U20 23.08.77, Essex L :
TJ - 11.47
ANIA Emma Candece U17 7.02.79, Shaft B :
60 - 7.80i, 100 - 12.17, 200 - 24.32
ANNING Clare U17 26.05.79, Cardiff :
60H - 9.17io (9.19i-94),
80HI - 11.9w/11.95w/12.0/12.19
APPLEBY Bonny E. V40 15.02.53, Cant H :
Mar - 2:58:50 (2:54:09-94)
ARCHER Claire U20 30.09.76, Mandale :
JT - 39.02
ARCHER R. U13, Morpeth :
200 - 27.7
ARCHIBALD Gemma U13 29.10.82, Pitreavie :
70HM - 11.70w
ARMISHAW Helen U15 4.10.80, Sale :
LJ - 5.32w/5.20
ARMITAGE Helen U13 13.12.82, Teesdale :
1500 - 5:03.3
ARMSTRONG Kirsty U17 14.05.80, Woking :
PV - 2.80
ARMSTRONG Susan U13 8.09.82, Stewartry :
100 - 13.1/13.73, 200 - 27.53
ARNOLD Helen U17 5.10.78, Portsmouth :
SP - 11.86 (12.16-94),
DT - 34.30 (34.32-94), HT - 46.98
ASGILL Julie V35 24.05.56, Trafford :
400 - 56.9
ASHBRIDGE Sarah U23 23.05.75, Copeland :
DT - 38.10
ASHBY Abigail U20 23.11.77, Rowntrees :
100H - 15.0/15.08, Hep - 4466
ASHBY Samantha 16.04.69, Spenbro :
(see BRETHERWICK)
ASHTON Suzanne U17 13.10.79, Kettering :
HJ - 1.65
ATAVWIGHO Susan U17 19.10.78, Invicta :
300 - 40.92
ATKINS Kerrie U15 8.04.81, Great Yarmouth :
JT - 31.04
ATKINS Nicola U13, Cannock & Stafford :
150 - 20.1, 70HM - 11.7
ATKINSON Rachel U23 26.05.73, Sale/Leeds Un :
TJ - 11.34i/11.33 (11.82-94)
ATUNUMUO Lucy U15 4.11.80, Hercules Wim :
LJ - 5.43
AUCOTT Jane Christine 10.10.68, Coventry G :
SP - 11.51 (12.99i-86/12.89-93),
DT - 42.92 (55.52-90)

AUGEE Esther 1.01.64, Essex L :
HT - 46.52 (56.76-93)
AUGEE Myrtle Sharon Mary 4.02.65, Bromley :
SP - 15.70 (19.03-90), DT - 49.44, HT - 46.64
AUSTIN Carly U13 16.05.83, Oxford City :
PenM - 1993
AXTEN Tracy 20.07.63, Hounslow :
SP - 14.90, DT - 53.62 (54.40-93),
HT - 37.84 (40.56-93)
AYERO J. U15, Middlesex Sch :
JT - 32.22
AYLING Amanda 4.04.65, Vale of Aylesbury :
HMar - 1:18:13

B ACKHOUSE Susan U17 6.12.78, Leeds :
DT - 39.72
BACKSHALL Samantha U17 6.10.79, Humb Sc :
JT - 35.70
BADEN Amy U17 30.05.79, Exeter :
Hepl - 3814 (3974-94)
BADEN Lucy U20 21.10.77, Exeter :
Hep - 3844
BAIGENT Sarah 22.12.71, Reading :
400H - 63.2/65.50 (62.5-90/62.92-94)
BAILEY Kate U17 14.09.78, Rugby :
80HI - 12.0w/12.12
BAILEY Kathryn 25.03.68, Havant :
3k - 9:52.1 (9:52.0-93), 5k - 17:19.1,
10kR - 34:07 (33:37-93), HMar - 1:14:07
BAILEY Kelli U17 8.09.79, Telford :
100 - 12.2/12.27w/12.37 (12.2-94)
BAILEY Serena U15 2.01.81, Essex L :
75HG - 11.14
BAILEY Wendy U17 31.01.80, Warrington :
3k - 10:23.2
BAIN Lynda V35 20.06.56, Aberdeen :
Mar - 3:06:49 (2:33:38-85)
BAIRD Kim V35 28.02.56, Dudley & Stourb :
3kW - 14:17.74, 5kW - 24:16.4,
10kWR - 49:39
BAKER Helen U17 5.02.79, Exeter :
TJ - 10.94, Hepl - 3832
BAKER Nicola U23 8.10.74, Gateshead :
HJ - 1.77
BAKER Samantha 14.04.72, Sale :
60H - 8.84i (8.42i-91),
100H - 14.7w (13.32dt-93/13.4w-90/13.43-93)
BALOGUN Jenny U20 23.02.77, AF&D :
200 - 25.10
BANNISTER Donna 27.12.72, Bromley :
100 - 12.07, 200 - 24.3w/24.4/24.76 (24.48-94)
BANNON Barbara 25.04.70, Cornwall AC :
PV - 2.60
BARCLAY Jaqueline 17.01.66, Glasgow :
SP - 11.31 (12.58-86), JT - 44.62 (50.38-84)
BARLING Helen U13 5.10.82, Oxford City :
70HM - 11.5, 75HG - 12.5
BARLOW Karen L. 15.11.67, Herne Hill :
Mar - 3:04:15
BARNES Catherine U20 28.09.77, Winch :
TJ - 11.49
BARNES Maureen A. 21.04.63, Bromley :
200 - 25.10w (24.6-84), 400 - 56.02 (54.5-84)
BARNETT Brenda, Buxton :
24HrT - 177.470km
BARNETT Lynne U23 12.08.74, Perth :
SP - 12.13 (12.83-93)

BARR Nicola 26.04.70, Edinburgh WM :
TJ - 11.05i (12.34-92)
BARR Samantha 14.08.70, Basildon :
(see PORTER)
BARTLETT Katherine U23 6.05.73, C of Hull :
100H - 14.6 (14.54-94),
400H - 61.2/61.56 (61.54-94)
BARTLETT Kelly U17 13.10.79, Dudley & St :
5kWR - 27:52
BATHO Louise U20 27.11.76, Thurrock :
100H - 15.0/15.06, SP - 11.58 (11.88-94),
Hep - 4635w/4626
BAXTER Morag 22.08.69, Glasgow
(see MCGOWAN) :
BEADLE Sarah U17 16.05.79, GEC :
60 - 7.96i
BEALES Emma Jay 7.12.71, Milton Keynes :
200 - 24.99, 400 - 56.9, 100H - 14.31,
HJ - 1.72 (1.76-92),
LJ - 5.89w/5.87 (6.20w?/5.99-92),
SP - 13.71 (14.53-92), DT - 54.68,
JT - 42.04 (42.48-93), Hep - 5609 (5632-93)
BECKINGSALE Elizabeth U17 20.03.80, Gres :
PV - 2.75
BEDDOW Helen 10.09.67, Rotherham :
PV - 2.40 (2.45-94)
BELL Lorraine U20 21.06.77, Motherwell :
200 - 24.69w/25.0/25.36 (24.99-94),
400 - 56.03
BEMROSE Antonia Marie U17 3.09.79, AF&D :
HJ - 1.73
BENNETT Carol U20 11.01.77, Hull Springhd :
SP - 12.76
BENNETT Christina Jayne U20 27.02.78, E & E :
SP - 13.24, DT - 38.12 (40.22-94), HT - 39.18
BENNETT Diana Faye U23 14.06.74, Eps & E :
800 - 2:12.77, 60H - 8.99i (8.9i-94),
100H - 14.74w/14.81 (14.47-94),
HJ - 1.73 (1.75-92), LJ - 5.86 (5.85-93),
JT - 38.48, Hep - 5220
BENNETT Joanne U23 1.09.73, LSAC :
100H - 14.9, TJ - 11.15
BENNETT Julia Margaret 26.03.70, E & E :
100H - 14.68w/14.74, 400H - 62.81 (62.2-94),
HJ - 1.87 (1.92i-90/1.89-94),
LJ - 6.02w/5.93 (6.12-94),
SP - 11.30, Hep - 5496
BENNETT Sarah U17 27.07.80, Birchfield :
3kW - 14:59.0 (14:56.4-93), 3kWR - 15:08,
5kW - 27:01.1, 5kWR - 26:05
BENNETT Yvette 2.07.65, Medway :
400H - 65.3
BENNINGTON Lisa U17 12.12.78, Grimsby :
300H - 46.10
BENTLEY Carli U15 29.01.81, Tower Hamlets :
LJ - 5.40
BENTLEY Sarah 21.05.67, City of Stoke :
800 - 2:08.2, 1500 - 4:22.51,
3k - 9:10.9mx/9:12.72,
5k - 15:53.86, 10kR - 34:39
BERMINGHAM Orla U23 7.10.75, Essex L :
200 - 24.8/24.86w (25.56-94), 60H - 8.54i,
100H - 13.8w/13.93 (13.87w-94),
400H - 63.3 (63.14-94)
BERRY Catherine U23 8.10.75, Kingston & P :
1500 - 4:27.74 (4:25.58-94)
BERRY Jayne N. 18.07.70, Cardiff :
SP - 14.35i (14.80-90)

BEVAN Susan F. V35 15.12.59, Essex L :
800 - 2:10.37 (2:01.93-91)
BEVERLEY Rachael U17 23.07.79, Mandale :
HT - 44.70
BISCOE Anna U17 13.09.79, Southend :
80HI - 12.0/12.18, HJ - 1.70, Hepl - 4073
BISHOP Tracy U17 1.05.79, Parkside :
100 - 12.2/12.57 (12.44w-94), 200 - 24.92
BLACK Caroline E. 19.05.72, Edinburgh WM :
LJ - 5.90i/5.73 (6.03w-91/6.00-92)
BLACK Gillian U17 27.10.79, Kilbarchan :
HJ - 1.65
BLACK Meredith, Serpentine :
Mar - 2:59:35
BLACK Sylvia V35 16.04.58, Birchfield :
3kW - 13:54.2i (13:42.10-90),
5kW - 24:52.95 (23:34.43-92),
5kWR - 23:32 (23:13-93), 10kW - 49:27.0,
10kWR - 50:10 (47:59-92)
BLACKBURN Caroline 6.08.71, WLIHE :
400H - 65.13
BLACKWOOD Kathryn U20 31.03.76, Dart :
TJ - 11.30 (11.80w-93/11.69-94)
BLAIR Victoria J. U15 20.11.80, Sale :
100 - 12.59w/12.66, LJ - 5.27
BLANCHARD Helen 11.07.72, City of Stoke :
100H - 15.1/15.29w (14.7-94/15.11w/15.15-90)
BLANK Paula U20 13.12.77, Verlea :
JT - 43.88
BLEASDALE Clare H. 6.07.71, Guildford & G :
200 - 24.9, 400 - 55.50 (55.0/55.44-94),
400H - 59.29 (58.04-94)
BLOOMFIELD Christine 12.02.68, Essex L :
100 - 11.98w/12.0/12.24 (11.59-93),
200 - 24.4/24.59i/24.79 (23.70-93)
BLOOMFIELD Tracey U17 13.09.79, G & G :
PV - 2.85
BODEN Veronica V. V35 23.12.58, Trafford :
400H - 62.4 (58.8-87/59.53-78)
BOLSOVER Maria Teresa U17 5.06.80, Hallam :
60 - 7.80i, 100 - 12.4 (12.47-94),
200 - 24.80 (24.58w-94),
300 - 38.95, 300H - 44.7
BOLTON Denise U20 1.02.77, Wigan :
200 - 25.15w (25.00-94),
100H - 14.27w/14.4/14.46 (14.04w/14.14-94),
400H - 63.0/63.35 (61.4/62.73-94), Hep - 4788
BONNER Angela U23 22.11.73, Cardiff :
HT - 46.64
BOOTH Joan 18.12.68, Edinburgh WM :
60 - 7.74i (7.6i-92/7.68i-87),
100 - 12.05w/12.1 (11.70w-93/11.90-94),
200 - 25.0 (24.39-86)
BOSNAK Fatmagul 23.01.69, Herne Hill/TUR :
3k - 9:57.6
BOTHAMS Valerie U23 19.03.75, Glasgow :
1500 - 4:28.2
BOUCHARD Sarah U23 23.10.74, Trafford :
800 - 2:11.4 (2:08.94-93)
BOULTON Catherine U20 2.11.77, Radley :
HJ - 1.70i/1.60 (1.76i/1.76-94)
BOULTON Jane V35 2.04.56, Crowborough :
Mar - 3:02:10
BOURNE Christina 24.09.69, Team Solent :
800 - 2:12.09
BOWEN Shelley-Anne U17 12.05.79, Reading :
60 - 7.8i/7.83i, 100 - 12.3/12.37 (12.31-93),
200 - 25.1/25.29

BOWER Sandra V35, Thetford :
Mar - 2:57:56
BOWRING Nicole U23 27.01.74, Tonbridge :
400 - 56.75
BOWYER Elizabeth U15 8.09.81, Wirral :
SPG - 10.74
BOWYER Sonya 18.09.72, Sale/LSAC :
800 - 2:01.67,
1500 - 4:22.1mx/4:24.79 (4:22.3-94)
BOYLE Viktoria U13 1.05.83, Rowntrees :
800 - 2:25.1
BRADBURY Sarah 25.02.73, AF&D :
3k - 9:49.78, 5k - 17:07.24, 10kR - 34:15
BRADDOCK Lynsey U20 14.10.77, Bracknell :
DT - 38.58 (39.02-94)
BRADFORD Joanne U13 22.03.83, Lancs & M :
800 - 2:23.7
BRADLEY Joanna U17 23.08.79, Ashford :
DT - 36.38/37.06dh
BRADLEY Lynne 21.05.67, Sheffield RWC :
3kW - 16:20.1, 5kW - 27:21.7,
10kW - 56:35.9, 10kWR - 57:29
BRADSHAW Noelle E. 18.12.63, Ports Fare :
SP - 12.26, DT - 37.76,
JT - 49.66 (52.40-93)
BRADSHAW Victoria U15 10.12.80, Ipswich :
JT - 31.20
BRADY Kelly U13 3.11.82, Trafford :
80 - 11.0
BRAHAM Alice U20 17.01.76, Park/Okla St Un :
1500 - 4:31.1,
3k - 9:33.49 (9:17.70i/9:26.31-94),
10kR - 34:42
BRAITHWAITE Kamila U15 26.01.81, Herc W :
800 - 2:18.9
BRANCH Lorraine V35 9.11.59, Chelmsford :
Mar - 3:01:18 (2:58:21-92)
BRANNAN Lesley U20 13.09.76, Wrexham :
SP - 12.10, HT - 44.22
BRAY Nicola U17 14.10.79, West Norfolk :
TJ - 10.52
BRAZIER Tanya U15 14.11.80, Steve & NH :
800 - 2:17.75, 1500 - 4:41.67
BRETHERWICK Samantha 16.04.69, Spenbro
(nee ASHBY) : 3k - 9:52.58
BREWER Nadia U17 14.04.80, Blackheath :
HJ - 1.64 (1.66-94)
BRIGGS Julie 13.03.69, Crawley :
3k - 9:56.9 (9:17.3-92)
BRIGGS Susan 26.03.67, Trafford :
60 - 7.79i, 100 - 11.94w/12.1
(11.6w-85/11.8-88/11.82w-89/12.00-93),
200 - 24.2/24.62w/24.74
(24.02i-92/24.1/24.17w-89/24.18-94),
300 - 39.1 (39.81-93), 400 - 57.4 (56.4-92)
BRIGHT Jane V45 24.03.50, Maidstone :
Mar - 3:02:36
BROOK Claire V35 13.03.60, Lisburn :
800 - 2:11.30 (2:07.63-91)
BROOKE Ruth U13 2.09.83, Reading :
75 - 10.2, 80 - 10.9, HJ - 1.43, LJ - 4.72
BROOKER Emma U17 26.10.78, Ipswich :
3k - 10:16.99
BROOKER Jessica U15 6.01.81, Exeter :
JT - 34.00
BROOKLAND Nicola 8.06.68, Westbury :
HMar - 1:17:59

BROOKS Ann 4.05.71, City of Hull :
60 - 7.69i, 100 - 11.91 (11.8w-94),
LJ - 6.16 (6.38w-94)
BROSCH Gabrielle 8.07.65, Milton Keynes :
HT - 34.24
BROW Kelly U17 24.09.78, Bingley :
TJ - 10.69w/10.38
BROWN Amanda U23 11.05.75, Stamford & D :
JT - 43.50
BROWN Beverley A. 9.05.65, Stubbington :
Mar - 3:05:56 (2:56:23-94)
BROWN Celia U20 22.01.77, Chelmsford :
400H - 65.03 (63.67-94)
BROWN Donna U15 1.05.81, City of Stoke :
1500 - 4:48.60
BROWN Emma U17 7.11.78, Sutton & District :
60H - 9.0i, 80HI - 11.9w (12.0-94),
300H - 45.9/46.45 (45.0-94)
BROWN Freida L. 6.05.63, Shaftesbury B :
Mar - 3:06:33
BROWN Jennifer A. V35 21.05.59, Ashford :
HJ - 1.72 (1.73-89), TJ - 11.36 (11.36-94),
Hep - 4303w/4279 (4803w-89/4727-94)
BROWN Karen Louise 31.08.68, Sale :
HT - 41.96 (47.10-93)
BROWN Lisa U20 16.03.76, Edinburgh WM :
HJ - 1.81, LJ - 5.57, TJ - 11.96w/11.91
BROWN Melanie 10.12.70, Norfolk :
400 - 57.4 (56.47-93)
BROWN Nicola U23 17.03.74, Tynedale :
3k - 9:58.21 (9:54.42-94), 10kR - 34:54
BROWN Sandra V45 1.04.49, Surrey WC :
24HrT - 199.278km, 5kWR - 25:51 (25:02-92),
50kW - 5:25:52 (4:56:27-94),
100MW - 21:37:21 (18:50:29-92)
BROWN Sarah A. 28.09.64, Steyning :
3kW - 14:42.0 (13:48.0-87),
5kW - 25:33.0 (24:00.0-91),
5kWR - 25:31 (23:57-87),
10kW - 52:25.0 (48:56.5-91),
10kWR - 54:08 (49:22-89),
20kW - 1:57:07 (1:51:38-94)
*BRUCE Jill U23 25.07.73, Dromore/IRE :*
*1500 - 4:20.18, 1M - 4:37.34,*
*3k - 9:22.6, 10kR - 33:59*
BRUCE Joanne U17 26.10.78, Woking :
JT - 41.22
BRUNNING Louise 6.03.72, Sutton & D/LSAC :
200 - 24.7, 400H - 57.30
BUCCIERRI Katrina U13 24.06.83, Hallam :
LJ - 4.92
BUCKLAND Natalie U15 19.02.82, Braintree :
SPG - 10.62, DT - 30.96
BUCKWELL Emily U15 25.09.80, Tonbridge :
PenG - 2710
BUDD Katie J. U20 3.01.76, Shaftesbury B :
100H - 14.5w/14.53w/14.58,
LJ - 5.70, Hep - 4620
BULL Sarah U23 4.06.75, Derby LAC :
800 - 2:11.1 (2:11.1-94)
BULLEN Kate 12.02.71, Birchfield :
200 - 25.21i (25.0-92), 400H - 64.11
BURKE Jacquie U20 12.09.76, Hull Springh :
SP - 12.53
*BURKE Olive C. 12.09.66, Croydon/IRE :*
*100H - 14.50*
BURLEIGH Antoinette V45 15.04.49, :
3k - 9:48.42 (9:34.9-94), HMar - 1:17:56

BURNETT Claire 17.10.72, City of Plymouth :
SP - 12.35, HT - 43.00
BURNHAM Sally U17 25.08.79, Hull Springh :
100 - 12.51
BURNS Gillian 12.07.64, Wirral :
SP - 11.74 (12.96-90)
BURNS-SALMOND Samantha U20 13.04.76,
City of Hull :
DT - 37.00 (37.54-94), HT - 49.48
BURROWS Catherine U20 11.02.76, Wigan :
LJ - 5.60w (5.60w-93/5.58-94),
TJ - 11.79w/11.72i/11.69
BURROWS Melanie U20 7.08.76, C of Plym :
JT - 38.02 (39.90-94)
BURTON Amy U20 24.06.77, Notts Sch :
DT - 36.18
BURTON Carly U15 14.10.80, Ashford :
DT - 34.32
BURTON Joanna U23 11.05.75, Dorchester :
JT - 47.28 (52.14-94)
BUSHBY Clare U20 7.09.76, North Shields P :
100H - 14.3w/14.37w/14.58
BUTLER Keeley U23 24.03.75, Coventry G :
200 - 24.54w/24.64 (24.4w/24.45-93)
BUTLER Natalie U17 25.11.78, Oxford City :
80HI - 11.88, TJ - 10.86io/10.81,
Hepl - 4170
BUTTLE Stephanie 27.03.72, Greenwich :
DT - 38.64 (43.90-89)
BUXTON Leanne U20 27.05.78, Brighton :
400H - 64.20, Hep - 4349

CADMAN Joanna 1.06.68, Edinburgh WM :
400H - 65.4 (60.7/61.06-93),
CAINES Vanessa U13 17.04.83, Steyning :
2kW - 10:56.0, 2.5kW - 13:59.36
CAINS Rhian U15 29.10.80, Telford :
200 - 25.39
CALDER Fiona 4.05.71, Glasgow :
100 - 12.14, 200 - 24.63
CALLAN Lisa U15 10.10.80, Glasgow :
100 - 12.47w, 200 - 25.64w
CALLANIN Elaine V35 13.09.60, Solihull & SH :
5kW - 24:09.66, 5kWR - 23:45,
10kW - 49:41.0, 10kWR - 50:05 (49:12-81),
20kW - 1:46:31 (1:45:11-93)
CALLAWAY Deborah A. 15.07.64, AF&D :
SP - 14.80 (14.88-93),
DT - 57.00, HT - 43.58
CALLOW Danaa L. 16.10.70, Sale
(nee MYHILL) : 60 - 7.46i,
100 - 11.7w/11.86w (11.58w/11.60-94)
CAMERON Claire V35 3.10.58, Glasgow :
DT - 39.42 (46.34-85)
CAMPBELL Katrina 8.03.72, Lisburn :
JT - 45.02
CAMPBELL Louise U17 22.02.79, Lagan Val :
HT - 37.96
CAMPBELL Michelle 24.02.69, Essex L :
100H - 13.08w/13.32 (13.26-90)
CAMPBELL Natasha U15 6.08.82, Medway :
JT - 30.86
CANWELL Elizabeth U17 25.12.78, Leeds :
800 - 2:16.8
CAPES Lucy U23 1.12.75, Trafford :
DT - 42.68 (44.18-94)
CARBERRY Helen U13 16.12.82, Liv Pemb :
80 - 11.0, 200 - 27.7un, LJ - 4.70

CARLESS Tammy U20 10.01.77, Tower Ham:
JT - 42.18
CARNEY Ruth 12.10.68, Lisburn :
1500 - 4:30.08
CARPENTER Alison J. V35 3.01.58,
Thames H & H : Mar - 3:06:47
CARPENTER Emma U15 16.05.82, Exeter :
SPG - 10.81, DT - 30.62
CARR Anne U20 1.05.76, City of Stoke :
Hep - 4526
CARSON Heather U17 18.07.79, East Ches :
1500 - 4:40.9,
3k - 10:09.7mx/10:13.4 (10:08.7-94)
CARSWELL Arlene J. V35, 14.12.55 Bracknell :
Mar - 3:02:35
CARTER Alexandra U17 1.04.80, Vale Royal :
1500 - 4:44.15
CARTER Alexis U15 23.10.81, Brom & R :
PenG - 2614
CARTER Bronwin A. V40 25.04.51, Port Fare :
SP - 12.31 (13.89-84), DT - 36.12 (41.08-84)
CARTER Lucy U20 7.03.78, Bedford & Co :
200 - 24.4/24.55
CARTHEW Lisa Jane 6.04.71, Swansea :
1500 - 4:32.69i (4:22.42-93)
CARVILLE Maria U23 8.12.73, Hillingdon :
800 - 2:08.73
CAVE Eleanor U23 23.01.73, Park/Oxford Un:
HJ - 1.66 (1.78-90)
CEESAY Amina U17 19.11.79, Newham & EB :
400H - 67.4
CEESAY Nusrat U15 18.03.81, Newham & EB :
PenG - 2600
CHAFFE Lucy U17 25.03.79, Essex L :
60 - 7.98i, 100 - 12.05,
200 - 24.51w/24.7/24.78,
300 - 39.47 (39.43-94), 400 - 56.4
CHALLONER Katie U17 18.09.78, Telford :
80HI - 11.96w, 300H - 45.34
CHAMBERLAIN Eleanor U17 17.04.79, Birch :
300H - 45.2/45.83
CHAMBERLAIN Rebecca U17 7.09.79,
Bournemouth : SP - 11.20
CHAMBERS Christine A. 4.03.69, Derby LAC :
100 - 12.26w (11.68w/11.8-92/11.84-87)
CHAMPION Fay 27.09.66, Yate :
HJ - 1.70, SP - 13.30, DT - 44.64
CHARLES Ayeesha U17 4.09.79, Oxford City :
60 - 7.82i (7.73i-94), 100 - 12.3/12.44 (12.2-94),
200 - 25.58i (24.90w/25.4-94), 300 - 41.3
CHARNOCK Catherine J. 3.05.75, Barr & F :
3kW - 14:28.25, 5kW - 25:22.67, 5kWR - 24:46
CHESNEY Sarah U23 3.03.73, Essex L :
60 - 7.7i/7.77i (7.65i-94)
CHEVERTON Dinah 24.03.65, Newport :
5k - 17:23.72
CHILD Amanda U15 28.11.81, Milton Keynes :
800 - 2:17.67
CHILDS Claire 8.10.72, Coventry RWC :
3kW - 15:35.9 (14:45.8-94), 5kWR - 25:22
CHILDS Ellie U13 26.05.83, Basildon :
600 - 1:42.26
CHIRNESIDE V. U13, :
SPM - 9.72
CHRISTIE Erica M. V35, 10.03.56 Vict PAAC :
Mar - 3:06:31
CHRISTIE Susan U17 7.03.79, Motherwell :
60 - 7.98i, 100 - 12.29w/12.44 (12.1w-94)

CHURCHLEY Elizabeth A. 17.07.66, Army :
Hep - 3896 (3948-92)
CLAPSON Emma 22.11.71, Bromley :
200 - 24.7/24.88w/24.92,
400 - 54.8/54.94 (54.25-88)
CLARENCE Emma Jane U17 2.12.78, Sale :
SP - 10.83 (10.96-94), DT - 34.68
CLARK Jean 5.10.68, Milton Keynes :
HT - 50.12
CLARK Joanna U23 11.02.73, AF&D :
200 - 24.6/24.72 (24.4-94), 400 - 54.99
CLARK Joanne U13 10.06.83, Lochgelly :
DTM - 24.32
CLARK Natalie U13 4.09.82, Hull Springhead :
HJ - 1.46
CLARK Nicola U20 14.04.77, Hull Springh :
TJ - 11.18i/11.17 (11.51-94)
CLARK Vicki U15 23.09.80, Invicta :
DT - 35.10
CLARKE Dyanna V35 27.02.58, Thames VH :
400 - 56.9/57.45 (52.98-79),
400H - 65.5 (62.9-94)
CLARKE Elizabeth M. V35 14.02.57, Les Cr :
Mar - 3:04:41 (2:53:29-91)
CLARKE Hazel U17 17.03.79, Copeland :
HJ - 1.70i/1.65 (1.67-94),
HepI - 4097 (4203-94)
CLARKE Jenny V40 19.10.52, Peterborough :
HT - 34.96 (36.08-94)
CLARKE Kim U15 30.04.81, Bedford & Co :
LJ - 5.36
CLARKE Rhian U20 19.04.77, Essex L :
PV - 3.50
CLASPER Fiona U17 16.10.79, Caithness :
300H - 45.9/46.17
CLAXTON Sarah U17 23.09.79, Colcr & T :
60 - 7.82i,
100 - 11.93w/12.0/12.22 (11.88w/12.19-94),
60H - 8.88i, 80HI - 11.5/11.57,
HJ - 1.65, LJ - 6.01
CLAYDON Emma Jayne U17 1.06.80, Med :
JT - 39.78
CLAYTON Bella U15 29.01.81, Bromley :
800 - 2:17.96
CLEMENTS Hayley D. 17.09.68, Dartford :
200 - 25.0 (23.4w-85/23.8/23.90-86)
CLEMENTS Lucy U20 20.07.78, Solihull & SH :
TJ - 11.31
CLIFF Jennifer U15 9.05.81, Peterborough :
1500 - 4:47.0
CLOKE Sarah U17 28.06.79, Exeter :
300H - 46.0
COATES Angela 2.04.67, Bingley :
800 - 2:12.08i (2:06.9-88)
COATES Nichola U15 24.03.82, Cramlington :
800 - 2:18.1, 1500 - 4:37.7
COBB Nicola 2.11.71, Windsor S & E :
JT - 39.22
COCHRANE-DYET Samantha U13 17.10.82,
AF&D :  800 - 2:22.8, 1500 - 4:57.5
COCKRAM Julia 1.01.68, Belgrave :
PV - 2.90i/2.80 (2.80-94)
CODD Danielle U17 17.02.79, Trafford :
PV - 2.60
COFFEY Shelley U20 22.10.76, Hyndburn :
HJ - 1.65
COHEN Paula 5.02.71, Trafford :
200 - 24.3 (23.64-92), 400 - 56.3 (54.02-94)

COLBOURNE Helen U15 28.08.81, Brom & R :
HJ - 1.60
COLEBROOK Christine 'Teena' V35 18.12.56,
Peterborough : 1500 - 4:29.09 (4:07.69-90)
COLEBY Julie V40 5.11.55, Durham :
10kR - 34:50 (34:35-94),
10MR - 56:53 (55:57-82),
Mar - 2:38:25 (2:35:53-84)
COLEMAN Hayley U13 24.05.83, Steyning :
2kW - 11:46.4
COLLERAN Joanne 1.09.72, Liverpool H :
800 - 2:11.3mx, 1500 - 4:32.0mx
COLLINS Danielle U17 8.12.79, Verlea :
TJ - 10.68
COLLINS Samantha U13 19.08.83, Sol & S H :
2kW - 11:34.0
COLLISON Gabrielle 10.02.66, Belgrave :
1500 - 4:27.4mx/4:29.3, 3k - 9:38.67,
5k - 16:45.43 (16:44.58-94), 10kR - 34:32
CONCANNON Claire U17 2.03.79, Hallam :
300 - 41.38
CONNELL Nicola 17.12.68, Scunthorpe :
JT - 38.54 (42.12-88)
COOK Lucy U23 11.09.75, Croydon :
JT - 42.46 (45.58-94)
COOKE Alanna Jane 11.01.70, Rotherham :
(see ROWBOTHAM)
COOKE Jacqueline U20 20.06.76, Rotherham :
100H - 14.9/15.09w (14.96w-93/15.14-94),
400H - 65.15, Hep - 4081
COOKSLEY Carol Ann 22.09.69, Coventry G :
SP - 14.23 (14.76i-91/14.71-90),
DT - 41.06 (44.70-89), HT - 39.08
COOPER Claire 4.01.72, City of Plymouth :
200 - 25.24
COOPER Louise J. U23, 25.08.75 Rossendale :
Mar - 2:58:16
COOPER Stephanie U13 16.09.82, Peterbro :
800 - 2:27.95, 1500 - 5:07.1
COOTE Joanne 10.02.68, Rowntrees :
DT - 36.68 (38.66-92), HT - 37.54 (39.06-94)
COOTES Sarah U17 3.11.78, Basildon :
300 - 40.22, 400 - 58.6
COPELAND Teresa Jayne 8.03.69, Medway
(nee SPRINGATE) : 60H - 8.9i (8.88i-91),
100H - 14.3/14.38 (14.03-93),
400H - 65.0 (61.92-93), LJ - 5.69 (5.96-90),
Hep - 4534 (5050-90)
CORLETT Sarah U17 28.05.79, Derwentside :
800 - 2:16.28, 3k - 10:34.4
CORNICK Michelle U20 21.09.76, Dorchester :
SP - 11.59
CORNWALL Karen 26.08.66, Valli :
10MR - 58:37, HMar - 1:16:38 (1:15:24-92),
Mar - 2:52:31 (2:41:58-92)
CORRAN Elizabeth V40 23.09.55, Manx H :
3kW - 14:11.1, 5kW - 25:13.03, 5kWR - 24:51,
10kW - 51:03.0, 10kWR - 51:34, 20kW - 1:55:10
COSTELLO Karen 21.10.68, Glasgow/Heriot W :
SP - 11.37 (12.64-94), JT - 48.82 (54.50-94)
COULSON Jackie D. 10.08.61, Unites Trades :
Mar - 2:59:30
COURT Clova V35 10.02.60, Birchfield :
60 - 7.63i (7.47i-94),
100 - 11.55w/11.69 (11.5w-90/11.6-87),
200 - 23.64 (23.57-90), 60H - 8.21i (8.12i-94),
100H - 13.19w/13.36 (13.04-94),
SP - 14.08 (14.23-93), JT - 46.80 (55.30-91)

COUSINS Dawn 16.03.68, Basildon :
100 - 12.0/12.13 (11.9-89/12.00-90),
200 - 24.40w/24.6/25.09 (24.1-89/24.49-91)
COWE Helen 7.09.66, Sale/Aberdeen :
SP - 13.78 (14.24-93), DT - 46.26 (48.64-94),
HT - 43.32 (43.52-93)
COX Maureen V45 7.09.50, Manx H :
5kWR - 27:19+, 10kWR - 56:08,
20kW - 1:58:22
COX Rachel U17 27.06.80, Birchfield :
DT - 33.60, HT - 37.92
COX Wendy U17 1.09.79, Gateshead :
100 - 12.4/12.44w/12.56, 200 - 24.66
COZENS Chloe U17 9.04.80, Bedford & Co :
60H - 9.15i, HJ - 1.75i/1.69, Hepl - 4378
CRANE Julie U20 26.09.76, Notts :
HJ - 1.81 (1.81-94)
CRESSWELL Lois U15 12.01.81, R S Coldfield :
200 - 25.48 (25.20w-94)
CRILLEY Kath V45 8.09.47, Surrey WC :
100MW - 23:05:21
CROCKER Linda U17 2.04.79, Huntingdon :
100H - 15.8w, 300H - 45.07, 400H - 66.1
CROFTS Andrea Donna 7.09.70, Roadhogs :
10kWR - 56:22 (49:55-90)
CROOT Selby U23 18.06.75, Dudley & Stour :
JT - 39.28
CROSBY Janine U17 17.01.79, Bingley :
DT - 33.16
CROSS M. Hazel 29.04.66, Lancs WC :
10kWR - 57:52 (55:02-92)
CROSSLAND Susan U20 3.03.77, Wigan :
PV - 2.75
CROTON Lyndsey U17 16.12.78, City of Hull :
300 - 41.18
CROUCH Karen U15, Croydon :
JT - 34.60
CROWTHER Nicola Jane 15.05.70, Cov G :
400 - 55.69i (53.76-94)
CROWTHER-PRICE Kimberley 19.01.66,
Middlesbro & C : 60H - 8.65i,
100H - 14.50 (14.22w-94), SP - 12.19,
Hep - 5017w (5297-86)
CRUICKSHANK Justina U20 27.09.77, Traff :
HJ - 1.67 (1.71-93), TJ - 11.30
CRUSE Julie 20.01.68, Croydon :
800 - 2:10.5
CUDDY Jane U15 25.08.81, Liverpool H :
LJ - 5.38
CUNNANE Cheryl U20 8.02.77, Wakefield :
HT - 43.52
CUNNANE Jennifer V35 23.02.57, Wakefield :
HT - 41.90
CURBISHLEY Allison U20 3.06.76, Edin WM :
400 - 54.28, 400H - 59.91 (59.04-93)
CURGENVEN Justine Elisabeth U23 5.11.73,
Cambridge University : JT - 38.58
CURTIS Laura U15 2.05.81, Hull Springhead :
PenG - 2973
CUTLER Aimee Louise U15 7.10.81, Torfaen :
LJ - 5.33
CUTTS E. U13, Somer :
70HM - 11.5

**D** AGNE Berhane U20 7.10.77, Ex L/ETH :
3k - 9:22.4, 5k - 16:17.5mx
DALES Ruth U15 29.10.80, Wakefield :
75HG - 11.74w/11.96

364

DAMM Sarah 12.09.70, Stoke :
200 - 25.18 (25.1-89), 400 - 56.4, 60H - 8.89i,
100H - 14.68w/14.78 (14.7w-89), 400H - 61.1,
LJ - 5.89 (5.93w-94), SP - 12.58i/12.44,
JT - 39.36, Hep - 5392
DANIEL Helen J. 24.10.63, Cambridge H :
400 - 57.2 (55.0-87), 800 - 2:05.96 (2:01.86-87),
1500 - 4:27.1mx (4:24.28-94)
DANIELS Nikki U15 25.08.82, City of Stoke :
800 - 2:15.86
DANSON Yvonne V35 22.05.59, Formby :
10kR - 33:30 (32:29-94), Mar - 2:30:53
DANVERS Natasha U20 19.09.77, Croydon :
60 - 7.7i, 200 - 25.1w (25.0-94),
60H - 8.42i, 100H - 13.45
DARGAN Leigh U15 31.03.81, Hastings :
SPG - 11.30
DAVEY Sarah U17 13.10.78, Worthing :
3k - 10:22.6
DAVIDSON Alison Y. 9.03.71, Hull Springh :
Mar - 3:05:08 (3:01:07-93)
DAVIDSON Linda 29.05.70, Aberdeen :
LJ - 5.94w/5.86 (5.95-92),
TJ - 11.11 (11.81-93)
DAVIES Alison 6.04.61, Woking :
100 - 11.77w/11.97 (11.9-93/11.93-94),
200 - 24.0/24.06 (23.87-93)
DAVIES Angela 21.10.70, Basing & MH/LSAC :
800 - 2:05.41 (2:03.67-94),
1500 - 4:12.8mx (4:09.29-94),
1M - 4:35.89 (4:31.83-94),
3k - 9:25.65i (9:14.1-94)
DAVIES Ceri U17 19.08.80, Telford :
3k - 10:32.51
DAVIES Charlotte U20 21.04.76, Peterbro :
DT - 40.12
DAVIES Diana Clare 7.05.61, Leics Cor :
HJ - 1.85 (1.95-82), LJ - 6.05 (6.32w/6.17-88)
DAVIES Emma U17 9.10.78, Andover :
400 - 58.2, 800 - 2:10.96, 1500 - 4:40.48
DAVIES Eryl V. V35 30.11.60, Bridgend :
Mar - 2:44:43 (2:43:26-87)
DAVIES Gael U17 5.02.79, Gloucester L :
100 - 12.3 (12.34w/12.42-94),
200 - 25.3/25.55i (25.51i-94), 300 - 40.58i,
80HI - 11.6w/11.62, 100H - 15.1,
300H - 43.83
DAVIES Hilary U23 9.02.75, Brecon :
JT - 39.48 (44.66-93)
DAVIES Jane V45 7.09.48, Epsom & Ewell :
1.5kSt - 6:15.8
DAVIES Samantha U17 20.09.79, Sol& S H :
60 - 7.97i, 100 - 12.24w/12.4, 200 - 24.69
DAVIS Coral 15.05.61, Croydon :
400 - 56.50 (55.4-88)
DAVIS Gahlie U17 3.05.79, Wimborne :
100 - 12.1/12.29, TJ - 11.09
DAVIS Joanne U23 20.09.73, Exeter :
1500 - 4:28.46 (4:23.36-94)
DAVIS Joanne U23 23.06.73, Swan
(nee SMITH) : JT - 40.64 (41.18-91)
DAVIS Julie U17 16.11.79, Lagan Valley :
60H - 9.18i (9.09i-94)
DAWKINS Carol A. V35 8.12.60, Team Solent :
400H - 65.6 (58.28-85)
DAWSON Catherine 9.03.66, Highgate :
800 - 2:09.12i (2:03.17-94),
400H - 65.7 (59.46-93)

DAY Victoria 19.06.72, Essex L :
200 - 24.45w/24.6, 400 - 54.08,
400H - 60.15 (59.72-94)
DAYKIN Mari-Anne L. U23 16.02.73, Tonb :
JT - 43.06 (46.08-93)
DE NOBREGA Emily U17 23.10.78, Herc Wim :
300 - 40.57, 400 - 57.8
DEACON Kelly U13 25.10.82, Phoenix :
600 - 1:44.9, 800 - 2:24.4, 1500 - 5:01.5
DEAR Joanne M. U23 8.06.75, Windsor S & E :
LJ - 5.96 (6.33-93)
DEJONGHE Odelle U13 17.03.83, Sol & S H :
HJ - 1.51o
DEMAINE Claire U17 6.09.78, Sale :
1500 - 4:39.4, 3k - 10:24.25
DENHAM Kate U17 18.03.80, Southampton C :
100 - 12.2/12.47, 200 - 24.69, 300 - 40.6
DENHAM Kerensa U23 8.03.74, Blackheath :
LJ - 5.61 (5.89-94), TJ - 11.63 (11.97-94)
DENNIS Leanne U17 30.12.79, Swansea :
300H - 45.4/45.68
DENNISON Andrea M. 22.04.63, Bradford :
Mar - 3:06:36 (3:06:19-94)
DENNISON Katie U17 8.06.80, City of Hull :
1500 - 4:41.37
DENT Angela U15 24.12.80, Scarborough :
800 - 2:18.9
DERBYSHIRE Heather U17 12.09.78, Traff :
JT - 41.28
DERBYSHIRE Nicola U20 8.08.76, Trafford :
DT - 37.74
DERHAM Zoe U15 24.11.80, Yate :
DT - 31.04
DEVERELL Bethan U20 23.08.76, Wrexham :
HT - 35.06
DHALIWAL Navdeep U20 30.11.77, Glasgow :
SP - 12.56, DT - 39.34 (40.08-94)
DICKINSON Leone U23 5.11.75, Bingley :
HJ - 1.67 (1.75-94)
DILLON Claire-Marie U23 1.03.73, B-H Mansf :
400 - 57.5 (57.2-93)
DILNOT Susan Mary 14.01.62, Soton City :
10MR - 58:46 (55:27-93),
HMar - 1:17:37 (1:12:41sh-89/1:14:43-94)
DIXON Sharon Jane 22.04.68, Parkside :
10k - 36:43.11 (35:08.23-94),
2KSTW - 7:37.20 (6:53.7-94)
DODD Alison U17 8.09.78, Derby LAC :
TJ - 10.57
DODSON Kay, :
24Hr - 166.845km
DOHERTY Kate U17 23.07.79, Cheltenham :
800 - 2:15.36, 1500 - 4:44.43
DONALD Elaine U23 30.04.74, Helensburgh :
400H - 64.04 (63.5-94)
DONALDSON Isobel 24.01.64, AF&D/WRAF :
400H - 63.1/64.19 (62.9-93),
LJ - 5.53 (5.76w/5.72-93),
JT - 40.30 (42.78-85), Hep - 4768 (5038-93)
DONE Cheryl 25.09.70, West'n (I.O.M.)/WRAF :
SP - 11.59i/11.03 (11.25-94)
DORAN Francesca U13 5.02.83, Bromley :
600 - 1:44.2
DORNAN Ali U13 13.10.82, Basildon :
HJ - 1.43
DOUBELL Elinor 27.09.71, AF&D :
800 - 2:12.5 (2:11.9-90),
1500 - 4:29.38 (4:27.16-90)

DOUGLAS L. Stephanie 22.01.69, Sale :
60 - 7.21i, 100 - 11.30 (11.27-91),
200 - 23.33w/23.50A/23.85i/23.91 (23.17-94)
DOUGLAS Laura U13 4.01.83, Wrexham :
SPM - 9.17
DOUGLAS Susan Mary U20 3.11.77, Lisburn :
100 - 12.1 (12.40-94)
DOWSETT Kathryn U17 24.11.78, Essex L :
LJ - 5.42 (5.50-92), Hepl - 4032
DOYLE Caroline U17 3.10.79, St Albans :
TJ - 10.61
DRAKE Julie Elizabeth 21.05.69, Brighton :
10kWR - 54:48 (45:59-93)
DRAKE Kathryn V35 25.05.60, Spenborough :
Mar - 3:06:52 (2:47:18-90)
DRAPER Lynne 10.05.67, Horsham BS :
100 - 12.1/12.29 (11.59w/11.6-88/11.72-87),
200 - 24.8 (23.8-86/23.87w-88/24.00-91),
LJ - 5.87
DREW Sally U13 23.11.82, City of Plymouth :
75 - 10.3, 200 - 27.36w/27.9,
LJ - 4.72 (4.84-94)
DREW Shelley Jean U23 8.08.73, Sutton & D/
Birmingham Univ. : DT - 55.70
DRUMMIE Susan 19.06.71, Belgrave :
PV - 3.10i/3.00
DRUMMOND Rebecca Louise U20 18.04.78, Stoke :
60 - 7.58i, 100 - 11.59 (11.50w-94), 200 - 24.9
DUANCE Lynne J. V45 28.12.46, Burnham :
Mar - 2:58:30
DUCK Emma U15 9.02.81, Southampton City :
75HG - 11.6
DUDGEON Sinead U20 9.07.76, Edin WM :
60 - 7.66i, 100 - 11.93 (11.8-94/11.88w-93),
200 - 24.17w/24.28 (23.9w/24.22-94),
400H - 61.34
DUFF Natalie 30.12.71, Lisburn/LSAC :
JT - 38.04 (41.84-93)
DUFFIELD Victoria U15 23.07.81, Durh Sch :
PenG - 2612
DUFFIN Irene M. V35 10.08.60, Shaft B :
SP - 12.95 (14.44-90),
DT - 38.04 (44.90-87), HT - 47.74
DUFFY Teresa 6.07.69, Essex L/IRE :
3k - 9:39.54 (9:12.87-91), 5k - 16:12.65,
10k - 34:55.76, 10kR - 34:04
DUFFY V. V35, Met. Police :
DT - 36.42
DUGDALE Catherine U23 29.11.74, :
3k - 9:56.3
DUKE Andrea U23 6.07.73, Mandale :
1500 - 4:33.07 (4:30.52-94),
3k - 9:34.11 (9:32.37-91), 5k - 16:41.0,
10kR - 34:17
DUNCAN Clare U17 22.08.79, Liverpool H :
1500 - 4:34.6, 3k - 10:12.45 (10:04.0-94)
DUNCAN Debra A. 13.02.69, Essex L :
400H - 64.19 (59.65-87)
DUNCAN Joanne 27.12.66, Essex L :
SP - 14.29
DUNCAN Tracey U17 16.05.79, Essex L :
300H - 43.88, 400H - 66.9
DUNKLEY Julie U17 11.09.79, Dartford :
SP - 12.02
DUNKLEY Michelle U20 26.01.78, Kettering :
HJ - 1.87, LJ - 5.68
DUNN Rachael U17 4.03.79, Gloucester L :
HT - 35.04

DURHAM Kellie U20 29.05.78, Sale :
HJ - 1.66 (1.71-93)
DUTCH Alison 25.05.65, Edinburgh WM :
HT - 35.18
DUTTON Jane U15 6.09.80, Wrexham :
75HG - 11.5/11.64
DYER Kate U17 12.07.79, Lincs Sch :
300H - 46.04, Hepl - 3826
DYER Teresa E. V35 29.09.59, Peterborough :
3k - 9:45.0i (9:15.0-92),
5k - 17:27.4 (15:58.8-93)
DYKES Linda U15 1.09.80, Liverpool H :
PV - 2.20i, SPG - 10.79

EARNSHAW Susan 13.10.70, Roth/Leeds P :
(see RAWLINSON)
EASTALL Sally R. 5.01.63, St Edmunds P :
10MR - 58:36 (56:30-92),
HMar - 1:17:19 (1:14:33-92)
EASTWOOD Laura U15 7.04.81, Deeside :
DT - 30.86
EASTWOOD Leanne U20 23.11.76, Wigan :
100 - 12.0w/12.2/12.22 (11.86w/11.9/12.00-93),
200 - 24.6/24.84w/25.02 (24.2w-94/24.26-93)
EATOUGH Hannah U17 14.08.79, Blackburn :
100 - 12.4/12.54
ECKERSLEY Jody U17 23.02.80, Thurrock :
3k - 10:34.5
EDEN Louise U20 11.12.77, Trafford :
100H - 15.0w/15.40,
LJ - 5.97w/5.94, TJ - 11.62
EDIS Clare U17 26.11.79, Grimsby :
PV - 2.20
EDWARDS Bethan U23 2.05.73, Cardiff :
60H - 8.72i (8.47i-92), 100H - 14.21 (13.57-92)
EDWARDS Claire U23 20.10.74, Wrexham :
400H - 62.5/62.82 (60.20-94)
EDWARDS Faithlyn U17 26.11.78, Essex L :
100 - 12.3/12.55, LJ - 5.47 (5.60-93)
EDWARDS Marcelle U20 9.01.78, Essex L :
HT - 39.98
EFOBI Uju Eugenie U23 10.10.74, Bromley :
60 - 7.6i/7.67i, 100 - 12.19, 60H - 8.6i/8.61i,
100H - 14.05, SP - 14.42 (15.21-94),
DT - 48.84, JT - 42.56
ELEY Joanne U23 12.01.74, Derby LAC :
HT - 42.58
ELLIOTT Alina U15 4.08.81, Yate :
SPG - 10.54
ELLIOTT Jacqueline U17 13.09.78, Elswick :
TJ - 10.81
ELLIOTT Lucy 9.03.66, Shaftesbury Barnet :
10kR - 33:45
ELLIS Clare U20 27.04.78, Solihull & S Heath :
3kW - 15:25.9 (15:20.86-93), 3kWR - 15:30,
5kW - 26:31.0 (26:19.78-94), 5kWR - 25:38
ELLIS Maggie 4.01.64, S London :
HJ - 1.67
ELMS Bonny U17 30.10.79, Newport :
PV - 2.50
ELPHICK Jennifer 24.11.66, Southampton C :
SP - 11.37 (14.01-90)
ELSON Sara Jo-Anne 8.05.70, Gateshead :
400H - 62.93 (58.19-92)
ENDACOTT Katherine U17 29.01.80, C of Ply :
100 - 12.24w/12.4/12.56, 200 - 24.72
ENDERSBY Susan V35 12.10.57, Barnsley :
Mar - 3:00:30 (2:49:03-94)

366

ENGLISH Una Marie Clare 14.08.70, Havering/
  Manchester Univ : 800 - 2:07.79 (2:03.5-92),
  1500 - 4:13.26 (4:11.82-92),
  3k - 9:10.6i/9:12.47 (9:10.0-92)
ENTWISTLE Claire U20 9.12.76, Wigan :
  800 - 2:11.2
ESSEX Joanne E. 16.04.63, Harlow :
  DT - 44.52 (50.06-89)
ESSEX Rebecca U13 16.11.82, Horsham BS :
  LJ - 4.66, PenM - 2022
EUSTACE Katharine U23 16.04.75, Bristol :
  400 - 55.92 (55.33-93)
EVANS Alison C. U23 13.12.73, Solihull & SH :
  HJ - 1.75i/1.65 (1.75-94)
EVANS Gail U17 23.07.80, Carmarthen :
  100 - 12.49, 200 - 25.35w
EVANS Joanne 3.10.68, Cardiff :
  SP - 11.62, DT - 37.34 (39.94-94)
EVANS Katherine V. U23 4.02.74, Birchfield :
  TJ - 12.20 (12.01-94)
EVANS Katherine U20 19.11.77, Coventry G :
  JT - 43.16
EVANS Lindsay U20 29.08.77, Ipswich :
  HJ - 1.76 (1.79-94)
EVANS Natalie U13 15.11.83, Wolves & B :
  2kW - 11:22.9
EVANS Non 27.02.67, Swansea :
  100H - 14.2/14.28
EVANS Sally U23 14.05.75, Tipton :
  200 - 24.9/24.98w (24.8w/25.17-94),
  400 - 57.09i/57.5
EVERETT Claire U17 25.06.79, Norfolk :
  TJ - 10.65, Hep - 4067 (4465-94),
  Hepl - 4366 (4489-94)
EVERETT Rebecca U17 10.03.80, Birchfield :
  3k - 10:33.12
EZEOGU Nina U13 11.10.82, Newham & E B :
  100 - 13.1, 200 - 27.4, LJ - 4.83

F ABEN Alison U20 7.02.77, Hunt :
  DT - 39.30
FACEY Denise 8.02.69, Hallamshire :
  400 - 56.01 (55.30-92),
  400H - 62.7 (61.1-91/61.96-94)
FAHERTY Michelle M. 10.08.68, Skyrac :
  800 - 2:05.3, 1k - 2:43.57 (2:41.76-93),
  1500 - 4:18.30 (4:15.37-93), 1M - 4:38.64
FAIRCLOUGH Joanne 24.12.71, Medway :
  3k - 9:38.69, 5k - 16:46.94
FAIRS Elizabeth U20 1.12.77, Hallamshire :
  100H - 14.1w/14.24w/14.26
FAIRWEATHER Lynne U17 15.01.80, Lassw :
  80HI - 11.56w/11.89
FAIRWEATHER Sheila U20 24.11.77, Glas :
  1500 - 4:28.67, 3k - 9:50.4
FALCONER Jane Olivia U23 20.09.74, Ex L/
  Camb Un : TJ - 11.77 (12.37w/12.10-93)
FALK Stacey U17 9.06.80, Gateshead :
  3k - 10:29.79
FALLON Gemma U13 4.01.83, Kilbarchan :
  HJ - 1.45
FARQUHARSON Claire U17 28.12.78,
  Horsham BS : HJ - 1.70
FARQUHARSON Samantha 15.12.69, Cardiff :
  60 - 7.49i (7.56i-94), 60H - 8.16i (8.11i-94),
  100H - 13.53 (12.9mf/13.08-94)
FARROW Wendy 25.12.71, Derby LAC :
  1500 - 4:28.6 (4:23.47-92)

FEARN Charlotte U15 26.11.80, Shaftesbury B :
  1500 - 4:50.1
FEE Helen U20 20.11.76, Shaftesbury Barnet :
  100 - 12.03
FEIGENBAUM Ronit 3.11.63, Highgate/ISR :
  400 - 56.8/57.11
FELLOWS Miranda U23 12.12.75, Malvern :
  TJ - 11.36
FELTON Rachel U17 27.06.79, Shaftesbury B :
  1500 - 4:39.1, 3k - 10:31.4
FENDER Becky U13, Wakefield :
  600 - 1:45.5
FENDLEY Amy U15 25.01.81, Worksop :
  PenG - 2690
FENSOME Sarah U17 28.09.79, Shaftesbury B :
  800 - 2:16.5
FERRIER Leigh 15.08.72, Sale :
  200 - 25.0 (24.68-93),
  400 - 56.1/57.17 (54.76-94)
FERRY Seonaid U15 19.11.81, Lochgelly :
  PenG - 2572
FICKEN Pam V50 25.07.41, Surrey WC :
  50kW - 5:55:29
FIELDS Michelle U23 15.05.73, Peterborough :
  JT - 48.30 (50.48-93)
FILCE Claudia Dawn 11.11.72, Charn/LSAC :
  HJ - 1.65 (1.67-93), PV - 3.00
FINDLAY/ADLAM Tania 8.11.70, Yate :
  200 - 25.0
FINDLAY-BADA Celia A. 19.06.62, Soton City :
  Mar - 3:04:46
FINDLAYSON Jacqui U17 27.01.80, Inv :
  HT - 32.64
FINIKIN Evette 25.09.63, Shaftesbury Barnet :
  LJ - 5.63 (6.29w/6.25i/6.14-89),
  TJ - 12.68i/12.39 (13.46-91), JT - 38.42
FISHER Jayne 2.11.70, Swansea :
  DT - 43.94 (45.46-93)
FISHER Kim V35 6.04.57, Pitreavie :
  Mar - 3:00:09
FLATHER Elaine F. 2.02.66, Soton RR :
  HMar - 1:18:10, Mar - 2:47:11
FLEET Lindsay U15 1.06.81, Bromley :
  200 - 25.05w/25.26
FLEETHAM Sarah U17 9.01.79, Braintree :
  TJ - 10.50
FLETCHER Lyndsey U20 18.09.76, Sale :
  100 - 12.1w/12.47, 200 - 25.1/25.21w/25.37
FLOCKHART Dawn 16.05.67, Edinburgh WM :
  60 - 7.78i,
  100 - 12.1w/12.20w/12.27 (11.7w-84/11.80-85),
  200 - 25i/24.81 (23.71-84), 400 - 54.4/55.14
FOLDS Rebecca U23 28.01.75, Exeter :
  LJ - 5.53 (5.73-93)
FORD Ann V40 30.03.52, Redhill :
  10MR - 58:27 (54:53-82),
  HMar - 1:18:45 (1:11:36-85)
FORD Katie U15 21.10.81, Sheffield RWC :
  2.5kW - 13:22.12, 3kW - 16:26.0
FORD-DUNN Elizabeth 13.05.71, Steyning :
  3kW - 16:10.0, 5kWR - 27:41
FORD-DUNN Helen U20 20.10.77, Steyning :
  3kW - 15:59.0 (15:45.4-93), 5kW - 27:33.0
FORD-DUNN Suzanne U23 25.04.73, Steyn :
  3kW - 15:38.0, 5kW - 27:04.40,
  5kWR - 26:43, 10kWR - 55:31
FORESTER Adele U20 27.03.76, Sunderland :
  LJ - 5.95w/5.90 (6.05-94)

FORREST Rachael U20 25.12.77, Birchfield :
HJ - 1.87
FORRESTER Amanda U17 29.09.78, Stoke :
60 - 7.92i, 100 - 12.08w/12.2/12.37,
200 - 25.0/25.16
FORRESTER Stephanie Emma 30.04.69,
Cambridge University : 3k - 9:51.1
FORSE Penelope A. V45 7.06.49, Stubb Grn :
Mar - 3:06:59 (2:55.37-90)
FORSTER Melissa U17 30.03.80, Morpeth :
300 - 41.40
FORSYTH Kate U17 5.06.79, North Shields P :
80HI - 11.65 (11.40w-94), 100H - 14.85
FOSTER Adele U20 16.11.76, Hull Springhead :
100 - 12.16
FOSTER Annette U17 7.05.80, Louth :
TJ - 10.59
FOSTER Elaine C. 21.07.63, Charn/LSAC :
3k - 9:31.31i (9:21.18-92),
5k - 17:09.9 (16:09.83-92),
10MR - 58:16 (57:47-94), HMar - 1:17:59
FOSTER Jenny U20 6.09.77, Sale :
JT - 38.60 (41.32-93)
FOSTER Laura U15 22.07.81, Halifax :
75HG - 11.61
FOSTER Rachel U20 1.09.76, Barnsley :
PV - 2.70
FOSTER Samantha U17 9.09.79, Basildon :
HJ - 1.72, Hepl - 4237
FOSTER Vickie 1.04.71, Salisbury :
SP - 13.18 (13.61-93),
DT - 43.60 (48.62-93), HT - 40.96
FOX Rachel U17 25.02.80, Barnsley :
PV - 2.30
FOX Rebecca U13, Ashford :
DTM - 25.30
FRANCE Deborah 16.10.65, Hull Achilles :
800 - 2:09.5 (2:06.9-90)
FRANCIS Elizabeth 22.12.63, Card :
(see FRANCIS)
FRANCIS Sarah U20 15.08.76, Scunthorpe :
PV - 2.60
FRANCIS Tammie U17 14.11.78, Bournem'th :
JT - 46.62
FRANKLIN Kate U17 16.07.80, Bristol :
HJ - 1.68
FRASER Donna Karen 7.11.72, Croydon :
100 - 11.9w/11.99w/12.07 (11.77w-91/11.88-93),
200 - 23.44w/23.47, 400 - 52.04
FRASER Ione U17 28.10.79, Thames Valley :
HJ - 1.66
FRASER Louise 10.10.70, Trafford :
100 - 11.61w/11.8 (11.6-90/11.88-89),
200 - 23.4/24.68 (23.41w-91/23.98i-92/24.13-91),
400 - 53.9 (53.55-92), 400H - 57.07 (56.26-92),
100H - 13.51w/13.6/13.71 (13.36-91)
FREEBAIRN Susan 22.08.65, Glasgow :
DT - 44.74 (46.70-94), HT - 37.30
FREEMAN Amanda U17 16.10.79, Beds & Co :
100 - 12.49w/12.62 (12.36w/12.4-94)
FREEMAN Danielle U17 11.02.80, Leeds :
LJ - 5.54, Hepl - 4507
FREEMAN Emily U15 24.11.80, Spenborough :
200 - 25.6/25.73
FREEMAN Laura U20 22.04.78, Coventry G :
HJ - 1.65
*FRONEBERGER Nicole U13 12.06.83, E,S&M/USA :*
*75 - 10.0, 100 - 12.6/13.22, 150 - 19.4*

FRY Sara 19.01.62, Met. Police/Lincoln Well :
JT - 38.06 (47.70-78)
FRYER Paula Tracy 14.07.69, Sale :
400 - 56.2/56.33 (54.7-92/55.34-94),
800 - 2:07.19 (1:59.76-91)
FUDGE Paula V40 30.03.52, Hounslow :
5k - 17:15.9 (15:14.51-81),
10MR - 58:18 (53:44-88),
HMar - 1:17:39 (1:11:37-88)
FULLER Jane K. U20 21.04.76, Parkside :
100H - 14.9, 400H - 62.7/63.20

**G** ABRIEL Linda 27.07.64, Coventry G :
400H - 63.8/64.38 (63.46-94)
GALLIGAN Joanne 18.12.71, Sale :
(see MORTIMER)
GANDY Dawn Suzanne 28.07.65, Team Sol :
400 - 56.4 (53.8/53.98-87),
800 - 2:06.29 (2:01.87-88)
GARDEN Catherine U17 4.09.78, Pitreavie :
SP - 11.94, DT - 42.20 (42.72-94), HT - 43.64
GARDEN Eleanor U20 20.11.76, Pitreavie :
SP - 11.69, DT - 40.82
GARDNER Ann 11.10.68, Corby :
SP - 11.22 (12.84-87), HT - 51.72 (54.02-93)
GASCOIGNE Amber U17 5.09.79, Wells :
800 - 2:16.0, 1500 - 4:41.2
GATRELL Eleanor U20 5.10.76, Woking :
SP - 13.37
GAUTIER Nicola U20 21.03.78, Hallamshire :
100H - 15.09, LJ - 5.55,
SP - 12.11, Hep - 4543
GAYTER Sharon, Mandale :
100kR - 8:12:03
GEAR Karen U17 30.09.79, N Devon :
100 - 12.57w (12.8-92), 200 - 25.34,
300 - 40.3/41.01, 400 - 58.59
GEE Michala U23 8.12.75, Rotherham :
100H - 15.1/15.12 (14.74w/14.8/15.08w?-93),
HJ - 1.66 (1.68i/1.67-94), LJ - 5.61,
Hep - 4449 (4625-94)
GENTLE Louise U17 4.09.78, Bedford & Co :
HJ - 1.70
GEORGE Alison 11.12.62, Cannock & Stafford :
SP - 11.63, HT - 34.38
GHOJEFA Elizabeth 24.02.69, Epsom & Ewell :
LJ - 6.27 (6.32w-94),
TJ - 12.49w/12.37 (12.64-93)
GIBBENS Elizabeth U20 5.04.77, Bromley :
HJ - 1.73, TJ - 12.42
GIBBONS Victoria U15 19.12.80, Llanelli :
DT - 31.92
GIBBS Lisa 9.01.69, Torfaen :
LJ - 5.62 (5.96-93), SP - 11.85 (12.54-94)
GIBSON Lynn M. 6.07.69, Ox C/WLIHE :
400 - 57.2 (56.5-92), 800 - 2:06.66 (2:02.34-92),
1500 - 4:16.2 (4:05.75-94)
GIBSON Sharon Angela 31.12.61, Notts :
SP - 12.76 (13.50-82), JT - 58.10 (62.32-87)
GILDING Nicola 16.05.72, Brighton :
TJ - 11.03 (11.20-94)
GILES Emily U15 31.10.80, Gateshead :
1500 - 4:42.74
GILES Nicola U13 30.09.82, Blackpool :
150 - 20.3
GILES Sally 6.04.62, Serpentine :
HT - 40.46

368

GILLHAM Michele U23 8.10.74, Tonbridge :
400H - 62.5/65.09
GITTENS Louise A. V35 9.03.60, T Solent :
HJ - 1.70i/1.70 (1.94-80)
GJELSETH Janice V35 16.09.60, Shettleston :
Mar - 2:58:00 (2:55:20-94)
GLOVER Joanne 6.10.71, Elswick :
LJ - 5.58
GODBEER Sarah U20 10.06.77, Exeter :
200 - 25.26, Hep - 3883 (4082-94)
GODDARDTracy Carol 29.11.69, Basing & MH :
(see JOSEPH)
GODDEN Fiona U13 17.12.82, Aberdeen :
100 - 13.20w/13.72, PenM - 1963
GOFF Charlotte U20 6.07.77, Colchester & T :
800 - 2:12.72 (2:12.45-94)
GOLDSMITH Sally 18.01.61, Edinburgh WM :
Mar - 2:39:06sh (2:38:39-94)
GOLLAN Sheila 18.07.64, Edinburgh WM :
3k - 9:59.2 (9:41.5-93)
GOMEZE Kelly U13, Croydon :
75 - 10.2
GOODMAN Kay U15 17.11.80, Peterborough :
PenG - 2860
GOODWIN Kim 16.05.70, City of Hull :
100 - 12.1w, 200 - 24.5/24.69 (24.4w-94),
400 - 54.64
GORDON Jackie 22.12.67, Birchfield :
SP - 11.43 (13.12-92)
GORDON Justine U17 10.05.80, Andover :
HJ - 1.65
GORE Caroline U13 29.03.83, Whitby Heath :
HJ - 1.48o/1.42, SPM - 9.31o
GOULD Bethan U13 23.02.83, City of Bath :
150 - 20.3, HJ - 1.42
GRADDEN Marilyn J. 26.01.61, Epsom & E :
Mar - 2:55:59
GRAHAM Dion Dainti-Ann U17 27.09.78,
Essex L/JAM : 200 - 24.4/24.69,
300 - 38.55, 400 - 58.4
GRANGER Katie U23 31.03.75, Exeter :
JT - 44.00 (50.32-93)
GRANT Jemma U17 17.09.78, Nairn :
JT - 36.20
GRANT Ros U15 18.06.81, AF&D :
800 - 2:18.23, 1500 - 4:49.9
GRANT Sue 10.05.69, Wakefield :
SP - 11.20
GRAVES Emma U17 18.05.79, Norfolk :
TJ - 11.20w/11.02
GRAY Amanda U17 22.03.79, Derby LAC :
200 - 25.2 (25.30-94), 80HI - 11.7,
300H - 44.42, Hepl - 4333
GRAY Josie U20 6.03.76, Birchfield :
1M - 4:50.21
GRAY Linda 23.03.71, Lincoln Well :
JT - 44.34 (45.68-94)
GREEN Francesca U17 10.02.80, Bromley :
800 - 2:15.2
GREEN Jill V50 10.10.41, :
50kW - 5:54:43, 100MW - 22:32:35
GREEN Sonya U17 6.03.80, Seaton :
100 - 12.3/12.57 (12.36w-94)
GREENSLADE Hannah U17 14.07.80,
Millfield Sch/Yate : LJ - 5.39
GREGORY\Louise U23 11.05.74, Sale :
400H - 62.2 (64.16-92)

GREGORY Vicky U15 16.03.81, Cornwall AC :
PenG - 2625
GREY Alison Helen U23 12.05.73, Glasgow :
SP - 15.36i/14.43 (15.85i/15.69-94),
DT - 45.94 (52.52-94)
GREY Leanne U20 6.02.78, Birchfield :
DT - 37.72 (41.28-94)
GRIFFIN Hayley U17 20.07.80, Milton Keynes :
800 - 2:15.8
GRIFFIN Helen U13, Sale :
150 - 20.1
GRIFFITH Michelle Amanda 6.10.71, W S & E :
LJ - 6.06 (6.12w-90), TJ - 14.03 (14.08-94)
GRIFFITHS Ann Margaret 20.08.65, Sale :
800 - 2:01.94 (1:59.81-94),
1k - 2:39.74 (2:39.29-90),
1500 - 4:14.74i (4:07.59-92)
GRIFFITHS Sarah B. U20 24.04.78, W S & E :
400H - 64.3
GRIFFITHS Shirley 23.06.72, Cramlington :
800 - 2:08.65,
1500 - 4:20.84i/4:33.01 (4:26.7-93),
3k - 9:30.73 (9:23.8-93), 5k - 16:23.0
GRIMSHAW Kate U17 26.10.79, North S P :
1500 - 4:42.8, 3k - 10:01.6
GRIMSTONE Jenny U17 30.04.79, Herc Wim :
JT - 38.30
GROGAN Jennifer U15 7.09.80, GEC :
800 - 2:15.8/2:18.86, PenG - 2677
GRONOW Joanne 29.11.72, Cardiff :
200 - 25.09
GROVES Jane U20 17.05.77, Vale Park :
800 - 2:10.80
GUILDFORD Gemma U13 28.09.82, Dartford :
75 - 10.3
GUISE Suzanne 3.02.62, Birchfield :
400 - 56.6 (53.40-86),
800 - 2:10.3 (2:05.87-91)
GUNNELL Sally Jane Janet 29.07.66, Ex L :
400 - 53.27 (51.04-94)
GUNNING Deborah 31.08.65, Andover :
800 - 2:08.0 (2:05.65-93),
1500 - 4:14.42 (4:12.69-90),
3k - 9:22.43 (9:12.12-94)

H AGGER Kim 2.12.61, Essex L :
HJ - 1.65 (1.90-86), LJ - 5.92 (6.70-86)
HAGGETT Lea M. 9.05.72, Croydon :
HJ - 1.90 (1.91-91), LJ - 5.81
HAIMES Charlotte U13 28.09.82, Wimborne :
75 - 10.3, 70HM - 11.4
HAIMES Kimberly U13 28.09.82, Wimborne :
150 - 19.9
HAINING Hayley 6.03.72, Nithsdale/Glas Un :
5k - 16:36.6, 10kR - 34:26
HAJIPAVLIS Alexandra U15 3.10.80, Sandwell :
SPG - 11.99, DT - 39.38
HALE Jane U23 4.01.74, Lagan Valley :
100H - 14.09 (13.85-93)
HALE Laura U17 21.01.80, Gloucester L :
800 - 2:16.2, 1500 - 4:36.98, 3k - 10:33.3
HALES Amy U15 16.03.82, Steyning :
2.5kW - 13:01.9, 3kW - 15:53.0,
3kWR - 15:52 (15:27-94)
HALL Andrea U20 28.01.77, Bedford & Co :
TJ - 11.14
HALL Cicely U17 12.10.78, Norfolk :
300H - 43.75, 400H - 64.05, Hepl - 3989

369

HALL Elizabeth U17 16.10.78, Solihull & S H :
60 - 7.82i
HALL Fiona U17 19.04.79, Hull Achilles :
300H - 46.8/47.41
HALL Layla U13 1.12.82, Shaftesbury Barnet :
600 - 1:45.3, 1500 - 5:01.9
HALL Nicola U17 14.12.79, Ipswich :
60H - 8.84i, 80HI - 11.40
HALL Sally 14.02.71, Birchfield :
5kWR - 27:40, 10kWR - 58:04
HALLETT Jodi U17 8.11.78, Bristol :
300H - 44.75, HJ - 1.65, Hepl - 4177
HALLIWELL Victoria U17 6.11.78, Wigan :
DT - 35.26
HAMILTON Sarah U13, Bristol :
100 - 13.2
HANCOX Carrie U17 8.08.80, Swindon :
300H - 46.39, TJ - 10.61
HANLEY Lydia U15 2.02.81, Liverpool H :
JT - 35.34
HANSEN Ashia 5.12.71, Essex L :
100 - 11.7 (11.81w-94),
200 - 24.57i (25.1-92),
LJ - 6.12w (6.27-94), TJ - 14.66
HANSON Lorraine I. 22.04.65, Birchfield :
400 - 52.47 (50.93-91)
HANSON Sarah 25.11.72, Birchfield :
LJ - 5.79
HARDING Lynn 10.08.61, Houghton-le-Spring :
Mar - 2:41:20 (2:31:45-89), 100kR - 7:53:23
HARDY Carole 31.12.66, Charnwood :
SP - 11.66 (12.76-89)
HARDY Rebecca J. 11.11.68, Highgate :
DT - 44.54
HARDY Simone U17 9.11.79, Kettering :
800 - 2:14.07, 1500 - 4:44.83
HARGRAVE Karen 23.09.65, :
1k - 2:48.11, 1500 - 4:15.83 (4:09.46-89),
3k - 9:25.14 (8:48.72-90), 5k - 16:26.65
HARKIN Julie U23 8.08.74, Rotherham :
400H - 64.1/66.23 (62.2/63.07-94)
HARNETT Jennifer U20 11.03.76, Medway :
800 - 2:10.8, 1500 - 4:31.99
HARNETT Jill U20 26.02.76, S London :
HT - 34.38
HARRIES Michelle 4.01.72, Essex L :
600 - 1:32.9, 800 - 2:07.80 (2:05.88-91),
1500 - 4:24.86 (4:19.9-93)
HARRIES Susan 9.09.70, Havering :
TJ - 11.49
HARRIS Dawn M. 22.06.69, Birch/Birm Un :
5k - 17:21.45
HARRIS Melissa U13 20.10.83, Oswestry :
PenM - 1932
HARRIS Michelle U17 26.10.79, Northampton :
1500 - 4:44.64
HARRIS Rachel U15 15.02.82, Liverpool H :
HJ - 1.67
HARRISON Debbie U17 13.11.78, RS Coldfield :
80HI - 11.88w/12.2,
LJ - 5.74w/5.54, Hepl - 4385
HARRISON Fiona U15 30.11.81, Barnsley :
100 - 12.55w/12.67, HJ - 1.60,
PV - 3.05, LJ - 5.45, PenG - 2661
HARRISON Jill V35 20.06.58, City of Bath :
3k - 9:40.58 (9:05.14-85),
5k - 16:30.85 (15:34.16-85),
10k - 35:29.67 (33:27.69-86), 10kR - 34:32

HARRISON Michelle U17 29.09.78, Derby LAC :
SP - 11.61
HARRISON Sarah U17 1.03.79, Cambridge H :
HT - 41.26
HARRISON Simone U20 2.09.77, Croydon :
400 - 56.80
HARROP Jane V35 25.07.60, Havant :
5k - 17:06.6, 10kR - 34:29
HART Siobhan U23 15.06.75, Guildford & G :
HT - 35.14 (36.06-94)
HARTIGAN Beverley Marie 10.06.67, Birch :
800 - 2:06.16 (2:00.39-88),
1500 - 4:11.96 (4:05.66-90), 10kR - 33:02,
3k - 9:17.19 (9:03.88i-90/9:10.4-92)
HARTLEY Sarah U15 4.05.81, Spenborough :
PV - 2.20
HARVEY Adrienne U13 2.12.82, Neath :
JTM - 27.24
HARVEY Amy U15, Colchester & T :
JT - 32.00
HARWOOD Jocelyn A. V35 21.11.57,
Middlesbro & C (nee KIRBY) :
100 - 12.29w (12.1-86/12.17-89),
200 - 25.0i (24.5/24.84-93),
100H - 14.07w/14.3/14.55 (13.79-89)
HASKELL Gaynor U20 11.08.76, AF&D :
SP - 12.27
HASLAM Claire M. 18.12.63, Shaftesbury B :
200 - 24.7/25.29 (24.4-91/24.79-92),
400 - 56.63
HASLER Suzanne U15 7.04.82, R S Coldfield :
800 - 2:16.30
HATHAWAY Emily U17 22.12.79, R S Coldfield :
800 - 2:13.48
HAWKINS Catherine U23 2.06.75, Parkside :
JT - 40.12
HAWSON Gabrielle U17 3.02.79, Jersey :
3k - 10:18.0
HAYLOCK Laura U17 20.02.80, Camb & C :
80HI - 12.0/12.65
HEAD Christine U17 18.12.79, Norfolk :
JT - 38.56, Hepl - 4200
HEALEY Margaret, Pitreavie :
Mar - 3:03:53
HEASMAN Heather 27.09.63, Horwich :
5k - 16:14.0,
10k - 34:18.68 (33:19.48-92),
10kR - 33:09 (32:31-94),
HMar - 1:15:51 (1:14:06-94)
HEGNEY Gillian U20 4.11.77, Glasgow :
60 - 7.72i (7.72i-94),
100 - 11.87w/12.0/12.08, 200 - 25.24
HENDERSON Laura U13 10.09.82, Aberdeen :
70HM - 11.57w/11.9, PenM - 2226
HENDRY Susan U20 30.06.76, Aberdeen :
400 - 56.24i/56.69 (55.96-94), 800 - 2:12.64
HENRY Corinne 15.04.72, Shaftesbury Barnet :
TJ - 13.01i (13.31-94)
HENSON Victoria U17 9.01.79, Peterborough :
80HI - 11.65, 100H - 15.7, LJ - 5.42
HENTON Sarah U23 4.05.73, Birch/Birm Un :
DT - 48.18
HEPHER Joyce Elena 11.02.64, Bromley :
LJ - 5.82 (6.80w/6.75-85)
HEPPLETHWAITE Louise U17 3.02.79, Traff :
JT - 37.22 (38.94-94)
HERRINGTON Lynsey U17 31.05.79, AF&D :
SP - 10.87, DT - 39.66/41.86dh

HESKETH Alison 29.04.63, Stockport :
400H - 65.1 (59.62-88)
HESLOP Justina Sara U17 3.03.79, Elswick :
1500 - 4:42.59 (4:35.24-94)
HESP Davinia U15 24.03.81, Rowntrees :
PenG - 2555
HEVINGHAM Gillian V40 24.06.54, N Devon :
PV - 2.45
HEWITT Jennifer U17 8.01.80, Medway :
DT - 35.56
HIGGINS Amanda U20 13.09.76, Telford :
100H - 15.0/15.28
HIGGINS Emma U13, Windsor S & E :
JTM - 29.40
HIGHAM Stephanie U13 26.12.83, Carlisle :
HJ - 1.43
HIGMAN Michelle U17 30.10.78, C of Plymouth :
DT - 34.32
HILL Alicia E. 10.12.67, Windsor S & E :
1500 - 4:33.0 (4:27.9-92)
HILL Amie U15 9.09.80, Oxford City :
DT - 36.64
HILL Cathy-Ann U20 4.05.77, Swindon :
SP - 11.84
HILL Clare U20 14.12.76, Sparta :
400 - 56.17
HILL Kathryn U15 13.12.80, V of Aylesbury :
100 - 12.40
HILLS Jennifer U15 25.03.81, Yeovil Oly :
HJ - 1.63
HIMSWORTH Jade U17 4.08.79, Holbeach :
400 - 59.0, 800 - 2:14.07 (2:12.57-94)
HOARE Jennifer U13 15.10.82, Hamps Sch :
70HM - 11.6
HODGE-DALLAWAY Naomi U15 1.06.81,
Tower Hamlets : 200 - 25.03w,
60H - 9.22i, 75HG - 11.01w/11.13
HODGSON Kathryn U17 30.03.80, Barnsley :
PV - 2.30
HODKINSON Kathryn U17 12.01.79, Sale :
3k - 10:29.2
HODSON Kirsty U13 6.03.83, Wakefield :
PenM - 2008
HOGAN Jackie U17 19.03.80, Scarborough :
1500 - 4:40.4, 3k - 10:11.9
HOGGARTH Donna U23 14.10.73, Preston :
100 - 11.6w/11.61w/11.83 (11.55w/11.61-92),
200 - 24.2 (24.06w-94/24.15-93)
HOLDEN Diana U23 12.02.75, Hounslow :
HT - 54.42
HOLDEN Genevieve U23 21.09.73, Oxford C :
400 - 57.5/57.64 (55.86-91), 400H - 64.7
HOLDEN Joanne 20.02.65, Shaftesbury Barnet :
3k - 9:40.12 (9:37.95-94),
5k - 16:37.16, 10k - 35:29.77
HOLDSWORTH Julie M. 22.07.61, Baildon :
Mar - 3:02:15
HOLLAND Kirsty U17 23.10.78, Livingston :
HT - 32.46
HOLLETT Sharon U17 26.12.78, Vict PAAC :
300 - 40.53 (40.10-94), 400 - 58.8
HOLLICK Lisa 1.01.70, Shaftesbury Barnet :
3k - 9:48.9 (9:27.67-91),
5k - 17:09.62 (16:40.12-91)
HOLLMAN Anne Marie U23 18.02.74,
Peterborough : 200 - 25.26w,
100H - 14.6/14.87 (14.1w/14.3/14.43w/14.51-92)
400H - 62.22 (61.56-93), HJ - 1.66 (1.69-91)

HOLLMAN Julie U20 16.02.77, Peterborough :
200 - 25.15, 100H - 15.08 (15.01w-94),
HJ - 1.70 (1.70-93), LJ - 5.97w/5.84 (5.99-94),
Hep - 4772 (4878-94)
HOLLOWAY Joanne U20 10.05.76, Hounslow :
SP - 11.44
HOLMAN Tara U15 13.10.80, Verlea :
JT - 34.02
HOLMES Carol 13.12.63, Notts :
3k - 9:57.6, 10kR - 34:08,
10MR - 56:44, HMar - 1:15:16
HOLMES Kelly 19.04.70, Ealing,S & Mx/Army :
200 - 25.29, 400 - 54.51,
600 - 1:26.0+, 800 - 1:56.21, 1k - 2:32.82,
1500 - 4:03.04 (4:01.41-94), 3k - 9:08.7
HOLROYD Shelley U23 17.05.73, Sale :
JT - 55.16 (60.10-93)
HOLT Janet M. V35 10.10.56, Trafford :
800 - 2:10.9 (2:05.9-89),
1500 - 4:31.6 (4:16.9-89), 10kR - 34:58 (33:40-93)
HOOD Maria U17 20.12.79, Bournemouth :
DT - 36.00
HOOKER Rachel U17 27.05.79, Bedford & Co :
100H - 14.95w/15.19
HOPE Jennifer 1.09.62, Wolverhampton & B :
DT - 40.64 (43.94-90)
HOPGOOD Rachel U20 2.06.78, Hallamshire :
SP - 11.93, DT - 48.04
HOPKINS Kathryn U20 6.11.77, Reading :
DT - 37.10
HORNBY Emma U23 12.12.73, Stourport :
PV - 3.10i/2.90
HORNE Caroline A. V35 7.11.56, Crawley :
3k - 9:54.4 (9:32.6-84),
5k - 16:49.0 (16:47.7-84),
10MR - 58:09 (55:58-85),
HMar - 1:17:30 (1:13:43-84),
Mar - 2:43:19 (2:37:26-85)
HORNER Katharine U20 6.01.78, Dorking :
PV - 3.00
HOROVITZ Gillian P. V40 7.06.55, AF&D :
Mar - 2:44:43 (2:36:52-92)
HORTON Amanda 18.05.71, Newport :
Hep - 3825
HORWILL Katherine U23 26.01.75, Dud & St :
3kW - 15:05.2 (14:41.0-93),
5kW - 25:27.72 (25:25.96-94),
5kWR - 25:00, 10kWR - 51:20
HOUGHTON Rachel U15 18.12.80, Sale :
LJ - 5.22, PenG - 2772
HOUNSLOW Anastasia U13, Guildford & G :
600 - 1:44.3
HOURIHAN Alyson J. V35 17.10.60, Cardiff :
SP - 11.29 (12.41-92), DT - 41.30 (43.58-92)
HOWARD Anna-Lisa U20 18.04.78, Norfolk :
SP - 12.37, JT - 38.96
HOWARD Gillian 14.04.69, Derby /Camb Un :
HJ - 1.76 (1.81i-92/1.80-90)
HOWARD Julie 24.09.66, City of Plymouth :
100 - 11.87w/12.0/12.15
(11.7w/11.9-88/12.00-93),
200 - 24.37w/24.6/24.72 (24.2w?-93)
HOWARD Tracey U15 11.02.81, Bournem'th :
JT - 31.74
HOWARTH Beverley U20 4.09.76, Blackburn :
HJ - 1.66 (1.73-93)
HOWARTH Mary, Steel City :
24HrT - 170.599

HOWELL Dionne U15 10.04.81, Southwark :
60 - 7.8i/7.81i, 100 - 12.2w/12.53,
200 - 25.5/25.61
HOWLEY Nina U20 22.01.78, Sheffield RWC :
3kW - 15:10.0, 3kWR - 15:40,
5kW - 25:41.4 (25:25.02-94),
5kWR - 26:18 (25:49-94),
10kW - 54:18.7, 10kWR - 55:24 (54:46-94)
HUBBARD Leigh M. U20 30.09.77, Banbury :
LJ - 5.61, TJ - 11.15
HUCKERBY Nikki U20 27.02.78, Birchfield :
3kW - 15:15.0, 3kWR - 15:22,
5kW - 26:03.46, 5kWR - 26:01,
10kWR - 54:56 (53:58-94)
HUDSON Michelle U13 11.11.82, Morpeth :
1500 - 5:06.4
HUGHES Anne-Marie 8.05.62, Shettleston :
Mar - 3:03:39
HUGHES Elizabeth U20 9.06.77, Bromley :
PV - 2.60
HUGHES Emma L. U15 15.09.80, Luton :
LJ - 5.62
HUGHES Rhian U17 11.05.79, Colwyn Bay :
JT - 38.76
HUGHES Sarah U23 14.03.75, Wrexham :
HT - 34.22 (36.62-94)
HULLEY Angela J. 8.02.62, Leeds :
5k - 16:38.04 (15:41.11-90),
10k - 34:05.42 (32:42.84-89),
10kR - 33:36 (33:21-94),
10MR - 56:27 (54:41-94),
HMar - 1:14:19 (1:12:25-90)
HUMBLE Amanda U17 15.08.79, North S P :
80HI - 12.0w/12.2 (12.0-94),
JT - 40.44, Hepl - 4250 (4475-94)
HUNT Tanya U13 14.09.83, Salisbury :
JTM - 30.16
HUNTE Abigail 12.05.71, Shaftesbury Barnet :
200 - 25.1, 400 - 54.9mx,
600 - 1:32.75i, 800 - 2:02.47
HUNTER Fiona U17 14.09.78, Arbroath :
LJ - 5.64w, TJ - 11.81db/11.21,
SP - 11.92io/11.11, JT - 35.46
HUNTER Jill 14.10.66, Valli :
3k - 9:02.30 (8:47.36-88),
5k - 15:28.46 (15:09.98-92),
10k - 32:22.93 (31:07.88-91),
10kR - 33:05 (31:42-89),
10MR - 53:45 (51:41-91)
HUNTER-ROWE Carolyn 25.01.64, Pud & B/
Knaves : Mar - 2:54:20 (2:40:28-94),
100kR - 7:40:18 (7:27:19-93)
HURST Jodie U20 21.06.77, City of Stoke :
HJ - 1.65, TJ - 11.38
HUSSON C. U13, Enfield :
600 - 1:45.6
HUTCHINGS Hayley U13 14.11.83, Steyning :
2kW - 11:40.3
HUTCHINSON Anya U20 16.07.77, Notts :
400H - 65.2/65.30 (64.76-94),
Hep - 3819 (3914-94)
HUTCHISON Fiona U20 18.01.77, Glasgow :
60 - 7.77i (7.69i-94),
100 - 12.16 (11.8w/12.04-94),
200 - 24.7/24.74 (24.3w/24.69-94)
HUTCHISON Nicola U17 1.02.79, Glasgow :
100 - 12.59w (12.3w/12.4/12.44-94),
LJ - 5.56 (5.58w/5.56-94)

HUTT Donna-Louise 6.06.72, Milton Keynes :
100H - 15.0 (14.4-91/14.64-92)
HYDE Zahara 12.01.63, Havant :
1500 - 4:26.5 (4:19.36-93),
3k - 9:17.97i/9:25.41 (9:05.49-91),
5k - 16:38.52 (16:36.0-94),
10k - 34:24.33 (33:23.25-94), 10kR - 33:46
HYNAN Julie U17 23.05.80, Liverpool H :
HJ - 1.70, PV - 2.40i
HYND Natalie U20 30.01.78, Pitreavie :
100 - 11.95w/12.00,
200 - 24.72w/25.00 (24.9-94)
HYSLOP Joanne U17 13.03.80, Coventry G :
HJ - 1.67

IANNONE Rosanna U17 15.06.79, Milton K :
3k - 10:26.9
IBLE Dionne 14.09.67, Shaftesbury Barnet :
100H - 14.6 (13.9w/14.1/14.23-87)
IDOWU Oluyinka 25.02.72, Essex L :
60 - 7.69i (7.62i-92),
60H - 8.5i (8.5i-91/8.67i-92),
100H - 13.76w/13.87 (13.62w-94/13.70-92),
HJ - 1.73 (1.76-89),
LJ - 6.54w/6.46i/6.35 (6.73-93),
SP - 14.19i/13.69, Hep - 5702
IGE Yewande U17 21.03.80, Sutton & District :
100H - 15.4, 300H - 44.65
IMPETT Lindsay U17 4.01.80, Wimborne :
100 - 12.2, 200 - 24.64,
300 - 40.09, 400 - 58.27
INGHAM Michelle U17 1.09.78, Bingley :
SP - 10.50, HT - 39.98
IRVING Ruth U23 20.07.74, Wirral/Camb Un :
100H - 15.2 (14.9-92/15.13-91),
LJ - 6.13 (6.28-94), TJ - 11.98

JACKSON Emily U15 16.10.80, Gateshead :
HJ - 1.60
JACKSON Lorna U23 9.01.74, Edinburgh WM :
SP - 12.38, JT - 55.48
JACOBS Kim Simmone Geraldine 5.09.66,
Shaftesbury Barnet :
100 - 11.34 (11.26w-84/11.31-88),
200 - 23.44 (23.01w-84/23.12-91)
JACQUES Stacey U20 24.06.77, Hallamshire :
400 - 55.85 (55.68-94)
JAMES Alison U17 9.03.79, Cheltenham :
HJ - 1.70
JAMES Anwen U15 17.02.81, Swansea :
DT - 31.54
JAMES Beth U17 12.02.79, Crickhowell :
HJ - 1.64
JAMISON Victoria U20 19.05.77, Lagan Val :
400 - 56.5 (57.47-93), 400H - 59.81,
100H - 15.0 (13.8dt-93/14.0/14.26-94)
JARVIE Nicola U13 11.09.82, Lanark & L T C :
100 - 12.89, 200 - 26.96w/27.90
JEGEDE Tolu U15 25.09.80, Newham & E B :
LJ - 5.26
JELLEY Claire U17 27.11.79, B-H Mansfield :
60 - 7.83i
JENKINS Andrea U23 4.10.75, Bedford & Co :
HT - 40.78
JENNER Jackie U20 25.10.76, Tonbridge :
100H - 14.84w/15.0/15.12, LJ - 5.52
JENNINGS Heather V35 10.07.60, Beaumont L :
10kR - 34:53, Mar - 2:58:11 (2:52:45-92)

372

JOHANSEN Michelle U13 1.02.84, Oxford C :
  LJ - 4.79
JOHN Davenia U20 29.12.77, Windsor S & E :
  LJ - 5.69w/5.51
JOHN Joanne E. U15 12.11.80, Ealing,S & Mx :
  DT - 35.44, JT - 31.82
JOHN Michelle U20 13.04.78, Swansea :
  400H - 65.8/66.93
JOHNS Karen U17 18.08.80, Shildon :
  800 - 2:12.28 (2:11.19-94)
JOHNSON Charmaine R. 4.06.63, W S & E :
  100H - 14.45w/14.77 (14.36-94),
  LJ - 5.63 (6.00w-90/5.92-92),
  SP - 13.63 (14.29-93), Hep - 4832w (5495-92)
JOHNSON Gemma Lynne U20 21.07.78, Notts :
  JT - 40.36
JOHNSON Gillian, 25.08.63 Dulwich R :
  Mar - 3:08:22
JOHNSON Jade U17 7.06.80, Herne Hill :
  60 - 7.84i, 100 - 12.2w/12.6/12.62,
  LJ - 6.24w/6.13
JOHNSON Julia U17 21.09.79, Invicta :
  TJ - 11.28
JOHNSON Sara 10.07.70, Carmarthen :
  400H - 65.10
JOHNSON Sarah U20 24.08.77, Swansea :
  DT - 36.12 (36.88-92)
JOHNSTONE Pamela U17 16.03.79, Edin WM :
  300 - 40.93, 80HI - 12.0w,
  300H - 44.2/44.47 (44.1-94), 400H - 62.5
JOINER Angela 14.02.69, Charnwood :
  1500 - 4:33.7, 5k - 16:54.98,
  10kR - 34:57, 10MR - 56:55
JONES Adele U20 23.09.77, Solihull & S H :
  HJ - 1.65 (1.72-93)
JONES Alison V35 11.08.59, Walton :
  1.5kSt - 6:35.6
JONES Dawn 16.02.70, Harlow :
  TJ - 11.05
JONES Elizabeth 25.04.61, Hailsham :
  Mar - 2:54:03
JONES Emma W. U20 9.07.77, Bournemouth :
  HT - 42.12
JONES Gemma U17 25.02.79, Torfaen :
  LJ - 5.47
JONES Jillian 23.12.69, Southampton City :
  800 - 2:09.05 (2:04.97-93),
  1500 - 4:24.55 (4:16.0-93)
JONES Katie U20 4.01.77, Trafford :
  100H - 15.20, 400H - 62.6/63.64 (62.6-94)
JONES Leanne U23 13.05.74, Rhondda :
  HT - 41.94
JONES Lindsay 24.10.71, Notts :
  TJ - 11.05
JONES Lindsey U20 8.09.77, Wakefield :
  HT - 39.10
JONES Lowri U13 22.07.83, Torfaen :
  100 - 13.2, 200 - 27.3
JONES Martha U17 31.07.80, Carmarthen :
  300H - 46.1/46.29
JONES Megan U20 10.07.76, Newport :
  100H - 15.0/15.15 (14.3-94/14.44w-93/14.58-94)
JONES Susan Eva U20 8.06.78, Wigan :
  100H - 14.45w/14.58 (14.3w/14.4/14.51-94),
  HJ - 1.81 (1.82-94), Hep - 4142
JONES Wendy C., 10.03.62 Ryston :
  Mar - 3:03:57

JORDAN Rachel 29.01.72, Birchfield :
  800 - 2:11.9 (2:10.54-94)
JOSEPH Tracy Carol 29.11.69, Basing & MH
  (nee GODDARD) :
  100 - 12.0/12.04 (11.8-87/11.81-94),
  200 - 24.34
    (23.64w-93/23.9w-92/24.1-89/24.16i-94),
  400 - 54.81i (53.23-91), 100H - 14.56,
  LJ - 5.74w/5.62, Hep - 4790
JOUSIFFE Karen U17 28.04.80, Hounslow :
  60H - 9.23i, 80HI - 12.0
JURY Kerry 19.11.68, Wigan :
  200 - 24.61 (24.57-94), 60H - 8.94i,
  100H - 14.4/14.45 (14.19w/14.32-94),
  HJ - 1.74, LJ - 5.71 (5.74-90),
  TJ - 11.51w/11.44 (11.72w-91/11.71-92),
  Hep - 5368

KAISER Kath M. V40 24.08.51, Valli :
  Mar - 2:58:56 (2:55:03-94)
KALU April U15 31.03.82, Sale :
  SPG - 12.16
KANE Kelly U23 28.10.74, Blackpool/IRE :
  SP - 11.67 (13.70-93)
KANE Minna U13 25.09.82, Stockport :
  600 - 1:45.0, 800 - 2:26.2
KAUFMAN Colette 30.09.63, Shaftesbury B :
  800 - 2:12.2 (2:08.6-92)
KAY Louise U20 1.12.77, Bolton :
  HT - 41.42 (42.14-94)
KAY Rachael U15 8.09.80, Wigan :
  100 - 12.1, 200 - 24.44, 60H - 8.99i,
  75HG - 11.5/11.56 (11.4-94), LJ - 5.20i,
  PenG - 2641
KEAST Susannah U20 28.03.77, Newquay & P :
  HT - 35.10
KEIGHTLEY Lauren U17 2.08.79, Bracknell :
  SP - 10.92, DT - 47.54/47.56dh
KELLAWAY Victoria U13 21.10.82, GEC :
  HJ - 1.45
KELLY Jennifer A. 20.06.70, Peterborough :
  100H - 14.48 (14.35-90), HJ - 1.65 (1.75-89),
  LJ - 5.90 (6.09-93),
  SP - 13.00 (14.88i-90/14.73-91),
  JT - 38.82 (42.44-92), Hep - 5338 (5826-94)
KELLY Siona U23 19.04.74, Sale :
  JT - 43.10 (43.46-94), Hep - 4096
KEMP Jennifer U17 18.02.80, Liverpool Pemb :
  JT - 42.06
KEMP Thomasin U17 5.03.80, Somerset Sch :
  1500 - 4:32.37
KENNARD Juliet U17 26.01.79, Marlborough :
  HJ - 1.64
KENNEDY Gillian R. V35, 16.01.56 Riddings :
  Mar - 2:54:50
KENNEDY Rachael U20 15.06.78, Hull Spring :
  100H - 15.0/15.34
KENNEY Deanne U17 8.09.78, Leics Cor :
  60H - 9.21i, 80HI - 11.7/11.88
KENNEY Lisa U13 17.02.83, Hull Springhead :
  JTM - 28.84
KENYON Janet V35 15.03.59, Horwich :
  10MR - 57:35
KEOUGH Linda 26.12.63, Basingstoke & MH
  ( see STAINES) :
KERAMBRUM Sylvia V. V35 5.11.58, London O :
  Mar - 3:03:51 (2:42:26-88)

KERBOAS Alison U15 21.05.81, Wigan :
   HJ - 1.70io/1.66, PenG - 3062
KERR Emma U20 15.10.77, Ayr Seaforth :
   HJ - 1.70
KERR Natalie V.S. U17 17.11.79, RS Coldfield :
   SP - 10.65i/10.61, DT - 41.94
KIDIMU Barbara U13 1.09.82, Bracknell :
   DTM - 25.94
KILBY Madeleine U17 16.01.80, Hounslow :
   100 - 12.4/12.57
KILGOUR Rebecca U23 18.10.75, Newton Ab :
   60 - 7.71i, 200 - 24.45w/24.52 (24.5-94)
KILNER Debbie 2.11.61, Aberdeen :
   3k - 9:58.8, 5k - 17:09.8,
   10k - 36:22.7, HMar - 1:18:17
KING Janine U23 18.02.73, Trafford :
   JT - 49.24 (49.50-94)
KING Lorna U13 22.01.83, Banbury :
   800 - 2:26.5, 1500 - 5:02.9
KING Rachel U20 11.05.76, Cardiff :
   60H - 8.90i, 100H - 13.99w/14.03
KING Sharon Marie 27.01.72, Sale :
   800 - 2:08.27, 1500 - 4:22.49 (4:21.18-92)
KINGSBOROUGH Ruth, 25.10.67 Overton :
   10MR - 58:10, Mar - 2:55:25
KIRBY Jocelyn A. V35 21.11.57,
   Middlesbro & C : (see HARWOOD)
KIRBY Rachel 18.05.69, Blackheath :
   TJ - 13.38i (13.64-94)
KIRKHAM Kelly U17 2.03.79, Hereford :
   DT - 35.04 (36.98-93)
KIRKPATRICK Julie 14.07.72, Lisburn :
   DT - 38.46 (44.18-92), HT - 48.56
KITNEY Emily U15 25.04.81, Medway :
   JT - 32.40
KITSON Mary J. 2.04.63, Hounslow :
   400 - 56.7 (55.19-88),
   800 - 2:03.8mx/2.06.36 (2:02.83-91)
KNEALE Karen 23.04.69, Manx H :
   3kW - 14:05.1, 5kWR - 24:21,
   10kW - 51:03.0,10kWR - 51:09
KOSTILEK Anna 16.11.65, Westbrook :
   3k - 9:41.6 (9:35.97-90),
   10kR - 34:46 (34:12-92)
KRIEL S., :
   Mar - 3:02:16

L ACKENBY Leah J. U23 18.09.74, Gate :
   100H - 14.3w/14.52 (14.3-94),
   HJ - 1.66 (1.71-94), Hep - 4918w/4846
LADROWSKI Nicola U17 13.07.79, C of Plym :
   TJ - 11.45w/10.63
LAING Manndy J. V35 7.11.59, Liverpool H :
   100H - 15.00 (13.71w-82/13.79-83),
   Hep - 4632 (5446-83)
LAING Wendy J. 29.12.62, Liverpool H :
   100H - 14.7w/14.72w/14.98
      (14.14w-93/14.2-81/14.35-86),
   400H - 64.1 (59.8-86/61.77-93)
LAMBOURN Angela J. 9.04.66, Northampton :
   SP - 12.76 (13.75-91), HT - 35.38 (36.92-92)
LANE Catherine U20 18.11.76, Dac & Tring :
   DT - 38.60, HT - 34.46
LANE Sarah U15 4.06.81, Torfaen :
   75HG - 11.3/11.81, LJ - 5.31w/4.82 (4.82-93)
LANE Sarah E. U13 24.11.82, Swansea :
   75 - 10.3, 100 - 13.0, 200 - 27.17, LJ - 4.78

LANG Andrea U15 6.03.82, Ayr Seaforth :
   100 - 12.49w/12.70
LANGDON Katherine U15 24.10.80, Bracknell :
   DT - 30.52
LANGFORD Lisa Martine 15.03.67, Wolves & B :
   3kW - 13:12.6mx/13:29.4+ (13:11.0-90),
   5kW - 22:20.03 (21:57.68-90),
   5kWR - 22:22 (22:01-89),
   10kWR - 46:00 (45:42-87)
LAPCZUK Nicola U13 16.11.82, Derby LAC :
   100 - 13.1, 150 - 19.8,
   200 - 27.07 (26.8-94), LJ - 4.91
LAPIDO Jane 24.08.69, Shaftesbury Barnet :
   400H - 62.36
LARBY Amanda 13.11.70, AF&D :
   3k - 9:57.8 (9:50.0-93)
LAST Suzanne F. 11.01.70, Medway :
   DT - 37.48 (37.80-91), HT - 44.72 (45.04-94)
LATIMER Joanna M. 30.01.71, Sale/Ox Un :
   800 - 2:08.33 (2:03.27-94)
LAVENDER Julie U23 9.11.75, Sunderland :
   HT - 49.86 (51.62-94)
LAVERS Lesley 6.08.68, Parkside :
   JT - 38.32 (40.18-90)
LAW Natalie U15 2.05.81, Belgrave :
   200 - 25.34
LAWFORD Rebecca U17 27.04.80, Sale :
   LJ - 5.42
LAWRENCE Victoria U23 9.06.73, Blackpool :
   800 - 2:04.42, 1k - 2:44.81, 1500 - 4:31.9
LAX Sian U17 4.08.79, Wenlock O :
   JT - 45.38
LAYZELL Alyson 16.12.66, Cheltenham :
   400 - 54.7, 800 - 2:07.06 (2:04.84-94),
   1500 - 4:25.80i
LEACH P., Sutton-in-Ashfield :
   Mar - 3:08:46
LEAK Jackie V35 19.10.60, Chiltern :
   HMar - 1:17:44
LEARMOUTH Jennifer U17 22.09.78, Dun HH :
   400 - 59.1
LEDGER Catherine U17 6.02.79, Ipswich :
   HJ - 1.64 (1.64-94)
LEE Dorothea U20 28.07.77, Yeovil Oly :
   800 - 2:08.8 (2:06.67-94)
LEE Helen U17 27.08.80, Rotherham :
   300 - 40.33
LEESON Joanne U17 28.07.79, Bedford & Co :
   HT - 33.86
LEGER Claudine U17 17.05.80, Havering :
   100 - 12.2/12.87
LEIGH Sandra C. 26.02.66, Stevenage & NH :
   400 - 55.08 (52.75-91), 400H - 63.9 (61.8-93)
LENNON Donna U17 8.12.78, Ballymena & A :
   100 - 12.56
LESLIE Wendy S. V35 3.10.56, Sandwell :
   Mar - 3:07:14
LESTRANGE Katy U17 17.09.79, Warrington :
   60H - 9.09i
LEVERMORE Janet 7.06.69, Birchfield :
   200 - 25.02i (24.2w?-86/24.6-89/24.88-94),
   400 - 55.4/56.99 (53.53-94),
   400H - 61.61 (59.11-91)
LEVY Margaret V40 8.09.52, Loftus :
   Mar - 3:08:43 (2:51:41-93)
LEWIS Ann V45 29.12.47, AF&D :
   3kW - 15:58.9, 5kW - 27:41.50 (27:40.35-94),
   5kWR - 27:27, 10kWR - 57:42

374

LEWIS Denise 27.08.72, Birchfield :
200 - 24.94 (24.80-94), 60H - 8.45i,
100H - 13.51 (13.47-94), HJ - 1.80 (1.81-94),
LJ - 6.67, SP - 13.58, JT - 49.76 (53.68-94),
Hep - 6299 (6325-94)
LEWIS Rebecca U20 31.12.77, Sale :
100H - 15.0/15.11,
LJ - 5.62w/5.31 (5.87w/5.73-94),
SP - 11.96, Hep - 4818
LEYSHON Anna U17 19.01.80, Swansea :
60H - 9.14i, 80HI - 11.8/11.94w/12.58
LILFORD Jane 28.11.70, Banbury :
HJ - 1.68 (1.78-89)
LILLEY Emma U20 2.05.76, Bingley :
JT - 44.08
LILLEY Nicola U17 17.02.80, Medway :
3k - 10:16.38
LINDSAY Emma 11.04.71, Edin WM/Lisburn :
200 - 24.8/24.86w/25.01 (24.18-94),
400 - 57.28 (56.8/57.09-93),
100H - 15.1w/15.20 (14.96-94),
400H - 65.8 (64.39-91), HJ - 1.70 (1.75-88),
LJ - 5.81w/5.71 (5.90i-93/5.89w-94/5.72-89),
SP - 11.29, Hep - 5108 (5353-94)
LINDSAY Sally U17 28.07.79, Kilbarchan :
300H - 46.77
LINTERN Jean V40 13.03.51, Crawley :
JT - 38.44 (51.56-72)
LISTER Helen U13 6.08.83, Sunderland :
1500 - 5:07.2
LISTER Rosanne 9.05.69, Havering :
DT - 48.64 (53.66-91), HT - 37.74
LISTON Bianca U20 28.05.78, Bromley :
100H - 14.7/14.81, LJ - 5.70
LITTLE Stephanie U15 5.11.81, Newport :
75HG - 11.7, PenG - 2606
LIVERTON Amanda Jayne 1.09.72, Exeter :
JT - 49.94 (57.84-90)
LIVESEY Katherine U17 15.12.79, Blackpool :
100 - 12.4w, 60H - 8.93i,
80HI - 11.9w/12.0/12.28,
HJ - 1.65i/1.64, LJ - 5.45, HepI - 4588
LLEWELLYN Stephanie 31.12.68, Shaft B :
200 - 24.2/24.38,
400 - 52.4/52.54
LLEWELLYN Wendy 30.05.63, Serpentine/NZ
(nee SUTHERLAND) :
3k - 9:51.03 (9:42.55-94),
5k - 16:56.45 (16:28.18-94),
10kR - 34:37, Mar - 2:40:35
LLOYD Hannah U17 14.11.78, Havant :
TJ - 10.91
LOCKHART Kathryn J., 6.06.61 Metros :
Mar - 3:07:36
LOCKWOOD Clare U17 7.10.79, Colwyn Bay :
JT - 35.84 (36.72-94)
LOMAS Anna U15 28.09.80, East Cheshire :
800 - 2:17.4, 1500 - 4:42.0
LONEY Jacqui U17 17.04.79, Elgin :
DT - 33.48
LONG Dana U20 1.10.76, Bournemouth :
HT - 34.00
LOPEZ Kelly U17 29.11.78, Essex L :
60 - 7.94i, 100 - 12.37, 200 - 25.3/25.98
LOVELAND Donna U20 28.06.78, Southend :
JT - 42.14
LOW Jane Kathryn V35 26.08.60, Glasgow :
400H - 59.9/60.31 (58.43-94)

LOWE Larissa 19.08.69, Reading :
PV - 2.90
LOWE Zoe A. 7.07.65, St Albans :
Mar - 2:49:28
LUCAS Amanda U13 23.05.83, Redhill :
600 - 1:43.9, 800 - 2:27.8, 1500 - 5:07.4
LUDLOW Jayne U17 7.01.79, Cardiff :
LJ - 5.41, TJ - 12.11 (12.14-94)
LUPTON Brenda V40 5.10.52, Sheffield RWC :
3kW - 14:56.61i/15:09.2 (14:42.9-91),
5kW - 25:50.7 (24:18.6-84),
5kWR - 25:50 (24:05-82),
10kW - 53:05.6 (50:10.2-84),
10kWR - 53:19 (50:22-83),
20kW - 1:53:14 (1:48:00-83)
LUPTON Victoria Anne 17.04.72, Sheff RWC :
3kW - 12:59.3, 5kW - 21:52.4,
5kWR - 23:12 (21:36-92), 10kW - 45:18.8,
10kWR - 46:40 (45:28sh-93/45:48-94),
20kW - 1:42:47
LYCETT Nicola U17 10.03.80, Newcastle (St) :
JT - 36.14 (37.20-94)
LYNCH Nnenna 3.07.71, Oxford Univ/USA :
1500 - 4:12.44, 2k - 5:58.17,
3k - 9:18.5 (9:09.46-92), 5k - 16:10.69
LYNCH Sally A. 6.11.64, Newport :
10MR - 58:24 (56:48-90)
LYNES Margaret Tracey 19.02.63, Essex L :
SP - 16.24 (16.57-94), DT - 42.44 (44.76-93)

M ACGREGOR Alice U13 3.10.82, Lanc & M :
800 - 2:26.8
MACKAY Nicola U20 26.08.78, Kettering :
JT - 44.20
MACKENZIE Margaret V35, 16.01.60 Border :
Mar - 3:04:38
MACKINTOSH Clare 2.04.71, Glasgow :
100H - 14.1w/14.24 (14.0w?-93/14.16w-94),
TJ - 11.24 (11.30-94)
MACLEOD Heather 12.03.72, Inverness :
DT - 37.74 (38.42-91)
MACLEOD Karen M. A. V35 24.04.58, Edin :
10kR - 33:49 (33:41-89),
10MR - 56:29 (53:42dh-93/54:34-92),
HMar - 1:11:44, Mar - 2:34:25 (2:33:16-94)
MACNEILL Fiona U17 8.09.79, IRE :
60 - 7.93i
MACPHEE Rhonda U20 30.04.76, GEC :
800 - 2:10.0, 1500 - 4:31.7
MACPHERSON Joan U15 18.09.80, Bas & MH :
SPG - 11.91, DT - 37.22
MADDISON Lynn 17.08.67, Colwyn Bay :
3k - 9:57.9mx (9:58.20-93)
MADDOX Keri 4.07.72, Cann & St/Staffs Univ :
200 - 24.8w
(24.1w-90/24.6-88/24.84i-91/25.08-89),
60H - 8.81i (8.47i-92),
100H - 13.36 (13.20w/13.24-93),
400H - 60.6 (59.49-94)
MADU Janet U13 3.02.83, Liverpool H :
600 - 1:43.0
MADUAKA Joice U23 30.09.73, Bromley :
100 - 11.74w/11.81, 200 - 23.81
MAHINDRU Alison 15.07.68, Glasgow :
400 - 56.1, 400H - 60.7/60.95
MAHONEY Joanne U20 22.10.76, Wirral :
400H - 60.73

375

MAILE Carolyn U13 5.04.83, Edinburgh WM :
  75 - 10.3, 150 - 19.9
MAIN Rachel 17.03.67, Brighton :
  TJ - 11.00 (11.10w-91/11.06-93)
MAIO Rosanna U13 28.03.83, Worthing :
  100 - 13.0, 150 - 20.1, 200 - 27.7, PenM - 1913
MAIR Angharad 30.03.61, Les Croupiers :
  5k - 17:24.00, Mar - 2:46:02
MAIS Chevette U13 22.09.82, GEC :
  75 - 10.3, 150 - 19.8
MAJOR Julie 19.08.70, Shaftesbury Barnet :
  HJ - 1.81 (1.85-94)
MAJOR Marie Ann U23 4.05.74, Basildon :
  100H - 14.84w (14.39w/14.4/14.72-93)
MAKEPEACE Rhona 7.08.62, Charnwood :
  3k - 9:50.1 (9:03.51-92)
MALCOLM Tina J. 8.09.67, Birchfield :
  LJ - 5.60w/5.53 (6.19-87)
MALE Samantha U20 11.04.76, AF&D :
  100H - 14.64w/14.96 (14.81-94),
  Hep - 4001 (4168w/4162-94)
MALLOWS Jayne 6.07.70, Coventry Godiva :
  400 - 56.4/57.49i (56.1-92/56.32-91)
MANN Christine U20 24.10.76, Arbroath :
  SP - 12.04
MANN D. U13, Kent Sch :
  70HM - 11.5
MANN Kelly U13 8.09.83, Solihull & S Heath :
  2kW - 10:09.0, 2.5kW - 12:57.66, 3kW - 15:41.0
MANN Michelle Louise U20 6.02.77, Preston :
  800 - 2:11.4, 1500 - 4:24.7mx/4:28.7,
  3k - 9:38.0mx/9:46.92
MANNING Caroline Louise U23 5.03.73, Wok :
  HT - 47.06
MANNING Chantell U15 4.09.80, Essex L :
  60 - 7.87i, 100 - 12.3/12.33
MANT Deborah U23 11.10.75, Bournemouth :
  100 - 12.26 (11.7w?/11.75w/11.88-93),
  200 - 24.80w/24.85 (23.96w/24.08-93)
MANTLE Sarina U15 19.01.81, Newham & EB :
  75HG - 11.6/11.82
MARCHANT Zina D. V45 30.09.50, C of Bath :
  HMar - 1:17:08 (1:13:38-90)
MARSHALL Gail 1.04.71, Glasgow Univ :
  PV - 2.80
MARSHALL Rebecca U15 13.09.80, Swindon :
  75HG - 11.50
MARTI Debora Jane 14.05.68, Bromley :
  HJ - 1.86i/1.85 (1.94i-91/1.93-92),
  LJ - 6.21w/5.98 (6.22w-85/6.19-92), TJ - 11.33
MARTIN Angela U15 26.11.80, Border :
  HJ - 1.63
MARTIN Fiona U17 17.09.79, Kilbarchan :
  100 - 12.54w/13.4/13.50
MARTIN Hayley U20 25.05.76, Camb H/Ox Un :
  JT - 43.06
MARTIN Helen U17 19.08.80, :
  80HI - 11.9
MARTIN Imogen Dee U23 13.02.74, Luton :
  DT - 37.82 (39.40-93), HT - 42.48
MARTIN J., Oxford Univ :
  2KSTW - 7:46.00
MARTIN Karen Lesley U23 24.11.74,
  Derby LAC/WRAF : SP - 11.73 (11.98-94),
  JT - 54.96 (55.72-92), Hep - 4050
MARTIN Laura U20 13.01.77, Horsham BS :
  400H - 65.4/67.17

MARTIN Rachel U17 9.09.78, West Coast :
  HJ - 1.74
MARTIN Tracy U17 4.04.80, Coventry Godiva :
  200 - 25.54 (25.46w-94)
MASSEY Anne M. U13 10.09.82, Liverpool H :
  80 - 11.0, 70HM - 11.17
MASSEY Eva U15 22.12.80, North Down :
  SPG - 10.82
MATUSZKIEWICZ Tracey U15 30.07.82,
  Brighton : PenG - 2553
MAUGHAN Andrea U15, :
  80 - 10.69
MAY Carolyn U23 15.10.74, Guildford & G :
  400H - 65.7 (65.4-94),
  HJ - 1.69 (1.76-91), LJ - 5.66
MAYFIELD Alison 12.05.69, Peterborough :
  100 - 12.1 (11.8-91/11.94-93),
  200 - 24.8w/24.9 (23.7-91/24.11-93),
  400 - 55.7
MAYHEAD Kirsty U20 17.02.78, Epsom & E :
  100H - 15.1/16.22
MCAULEY Lorraine U13 9.06.83, Irvine :
  800 - 2:25.5
MCBRINN Elaine 19.12.63, Shettleston :
  10MR - 57:33dh (58:16-94),
  HMar - 1:18:39 (1:17:42-94)
MCCABE Laura U17 24.01.80, Vale Royal :
  800 - 2:12.7
MCCALLUM Ruth U17 1.03.79, Black Isle :
  300H - 46.4/47.57
MCCAMMON Tammy U20 17.10.76, Hillingdon :
  LJ - 5.89i/5.64 (5.86-91)
MCCANDLESS Kate 22.06.70, Parkside/USA :
  3k - 9:07.29 (8:56.00-93), 5k - 15:34.11,
  10kR - 33:36, 10MR - 54:31
MCCANN Stephanie A. 26.10.65, Lisburn :
  200 - 24.28 (24.03w-90),
  400 - 53.5/54.31 (53.91-94),
  400H - 58.21 (58.09-94)
MCCARTHY Claire U17 6.11.79, Bournem'th :
  800 - 2:16.63
MCCLUNG Mary 19.02.71, Edinburgh WM :
  800 - 2:05.64
MCCOLGAN Elizabeth 24.05.64, Dundee HH :
  2k - 5:55.1+ (5:40.24-87),
  3k - 8:50.52 (8:34.80i-89/8:38.23-91),
  5k - 14:59.56, 10k - 31:40.14 (30:57.07-91),
  10kR - 32:06 (30:38-89),
  10MR - 53:12 (52:14-92),
  HMar - 1:09:49 (1:07:11-92),
  Mar - 2:30:32 (2:27:32-91)
MCCONNELL Alison U17 9.10.78, Parkside :
  400H - 65.0
MCCONNELL Lee U17 9.10.78, Gateshead :
  60 - 7.87i, 100 - 12.2/12.44 (12.19w-94),
  200 - 25.1/25.44 (24.0w/24.89w/24.9/24.94-94),
  300 - 39.49, HJ - 1.74i/1.71 (1.78-94)
MCCORMICK Angelique 29.04.69, Ipswich :
  JT - 45.76 (50.02-85)
MCCORMICK Suzanne U17 10.02.79, Lagan V :
  3k - 10:18.9
MCCORRY Julie U17 7.11.79, Ballymena & A :
  SP - 11.66
MCCREADIE Helen U23 10.05.75, Edin WM :
  DT - 41.32 (43.58-94), HT - 46.48
MCDONALD Donna U17 28.11.79, Glasgow :
  HJ - 1.64

MCDOUGALL Joanne U17 23.08.79, Southport :
200 - 25.3/26.29
MCEWAN Donna U20 17.01.78, Leamington :
DT - 40.70
MCEWEN Mairi U17 16.08.79, Victoria PAAC :
60 - 7.78i, 100 - 12.30w/12.39
MCGEORGE Sonia Marian 2.11.64, B&H/LSAC :
1500 - 4:17.22 (4:10.75-90),
3k - 9:48.9+ (8:51.33-90), 5k - 16:17.32
MCGILCHRIST Joanna U13 27.08.83, Arbroath :
JTM - 28.42
MCGILLIVARY Aileen 13.08.70, Edin WM :
60 - 7.36i, 100 - 11.62 (11.43w-93/11.54-92),
200 - 24.1/24.19 (23.29-93)
MCGIVERN Stacy U20 14.12.76, Camb & Col :
TJ - 11.64
MCGOLDRICK Lesley U17 12.09.79, Gate :
60H - 9.25i, 80HI - 11.71
MCGOVERN Nicola U17 26.11.79, Liverpool H :
HJ - 1.65
MCGOWAN Julia 12.05.59, Brighton & Hove :
Mar - 3:05:56 (2:36:31 - 86)
MCGOWAN Morag 22.08.69, Glasgow
(nee BAXTER) :
100 - 12.0w/12.08 (11.78w/11.97-93),
200 - 24.7w/24.8/25.02 (24.7w-89/24.71-93)
MCGOWAN Suzanne U20 13.04.78, Motherw :
200 - 24.79w/25.57 (24.9/24.99-93)
MCHUGH Anna U15 27.03.81, Kent Sch :
SPG - 11.59
MCILROY Debra U20 18.12.77, Richmond & Z :
HJ - 1.66 (1.70-93), JT - 38.32
MCINTOSH Dextene U20 27.08.78, Essex L :
100H - 15.0, 400H - 62.92
MCINTYRE Iona U13 14.03.83, Dundee HH :
800 - 2:24.39
MCKENZIE Eileen U23 6.10.75, Massey F :
10kR - 34:47 (34:04-91), 10MR - 58:46
*MCKENZIE Evadne U23 19.05.75,*
*Ealing,Southall & Mx/JAM : 60 - 7.57i,*
*100 - 12.0/12.10 (11.8/11.84w/12.02-94)*
MCKERNAN Jacqueline Lena 1.07.65, Lisb/LSAC :
SP - 12.91 (13.31i-91/13.20-92),
DT - 59.06 (60.72-93)
MCLAREN Margaret V35 21.04.57, Fife :
Mar - 3:07:17 (3:04:44-91)
MCLELLAN Shelley U13 21.03.83, Steve & NH :
SPM - 10.02
MCLEOD Geraldine Ann 24.09.71, Birchfield :
100 - 11.9/11.91 (11.2/11.51w-94/11.58-93),
200 - 24.2/24.43 (23.4-93/23.47-94)
MCLOUGHLIN Lauren U13 8.09.82, Newport :
200 - 27.6, 70HM - 11.5, PenM - 2127
MCNAIRNEY Susan U17 22.02.79, Irvine :
1500 - 4:44.92
MCNEILL Clare U13 10.10.82, Victoria PAAC :
70HM - 11.74w
MCPHAIL Ann 3.05.70, Glasgow Univ :
3k - 9:58.88, 5k - 17:28.6
MCPHAIL Fiona 23.06.71, Wigan/WRAF :
HJ - 1.75
MCPHERSON Vikki 1.06.71, Glas/Glas Univ :
10kR - 33:56 (33:05-92),
10MR - 53:57dh, HMar - 1:14:14
MCQUEEN Sophie U15 3.12.81, Cleethorpes :
HJ - 1.63
MEADOWS Jennifer U15 17.04.81, Wigan :
100 - 12.5, 200 - 25.3 (26.49-93), 800 - 2:14.88

MEEGAN Laura U13 22.04.83, Bingley :
80 - 11.0
MELLIS Kelly U17 4.12.79, Banbury :
DT - 41.96
MELVIN Hazel U23 19.11.73, Glasgow :
LJ - 5.59
MERCHANT Esther U20 9.01.76, Coventry G :
2KSTW - 7:51.32
MERRY Emma Louise U23 2.07.74, Cov G :
SP - 13.37 (13.62-93), DT - 50.58 (52.58-93)
MERRY Katharine U23 21.09.74, Birchfield :
100 - 11.47 (11.27w/11.34-94)
MERSH Joanne U23 19.10.74, Essex L :
400 - 56.7
MICHAELSON Lucie U13 18.04.83, S Livl :
1500 - 5:04.5
MIGHTY A. D. Natasha 21.12.70, Radley :
60H - 8.6i (8.49i-94)
MIJOVIC Catherine H. 11.04.61, Birchfield :
5k - 16:47.18, 10k - 36:16.29 (35:00.1-92),
10kR - 33:27, HMar - 1:13:43, Mar - 2:37:14
*MIKNEVICIUTE Dalia 5.09.70, Blackh'th/LIT :*
*HJ - 1.83i/1.80*
MILBURN Leanne U17 16.08.79, Copeland :
HepI - 3993
MILES Helen Louise 2.03.67, Cardiff :
60 - 7.70i (7.46i-91),
100 - 12.1 (11.4/11.41w/11.50-88),
200 - 25.1/25.44 (23.7w-88/23.81w/23.89-91)
MILES Lynne U17 14.06.79, Birchfield :
JT - 36.04
MILES Sarah U17 14.12.78, Newbury :
60 - 7.89i
Miller Caroline 16.09.72, Preston :
(see WARDEN)
MILLER Eve U17 1.12.79, Hertford & Ware :
300 - 41.3/41.62, 80HI - 12.0,
300H - 44.23, HepI - 3867
MILLER Karen A. 4.02.64, Crawley :
(see SHACKEL)
MITCHELL Elizabeth U17 13.10.79, Walth :
300H - 46.2/47.22
MITCHELL Jeina Sophia U23 21.01.75, Croy :
800 - 2:08.59i/2:09.62 (2:05.85-94)
MITCHELL Julie U23 3.10.74, Brighton :
1500 - 4:32.4
MITCHELL Virginia 29.01.63, Woking :
400H - 64.05
MIVELD Lian U20 8.09.76, Portsmouth :
100H - 15.0/15.37
MOCKLER Jennifer U15 28.04.82, Liverpool H :
1500 - 4:43.99
MOFFAT Basilie U20 8.04.78, Bingley :
HJ - 1.66
MOFFITT Alison J. 6.10.69, North Down :
SP - 11.30 (11.67-94), JT - 46.60 (47.54-93)
MONAGHAN Sylveen 25.08.72, Sale :
JT - 39.20 (46.46-91)
MONDS Debra U20 25.02.78, Wigan :
DT - 37.22
MONTADOR Karen U17 14.05.79, Central :
800 - 2:15.47, 1500 - 4:35.4mx/4:35.61
MOODY Carly U17 9.06.80, Braintree :
100 - 12.4/12.87
MOODY Hannah U17 26.07.79, Skyrac :
60 - 7.88i, TJ - 11.12i/10.90w/10.83
MOODY Karen 20.07.67, Cannock & Stafford :
JT - 42.60 (44.96un-87/44.66-84)

377

MOODY Kate U17 7.04.79, Cannock & Stafford :
300H - 46.2 (44.60-94)
MOORE Julie U23 5.12.73, Manx/LSAC :
200 - 25.0, 400 - 55.07
MOORE Sarah Louise U23 15.03.73, Bristol :
DT - 36.14 (38.84-94), HT - 53.00
MOOREKITE Janice D. V35 1.05.57, Invicta :
10MR - 58:40, Mar - 2:48:06
MORAN Faye U15 28.10.80, Rochdale :
JT - 31.58
MORETON Kelly U17 18.09.79, Newport :
100H - 15.6, HJ - 1.71,
Hep - 3943w, HepI - 4014
MORGAN Debbie U15 9.10.80, Torfaen :
100 - 12.5/12.53
MORGAN Kelly U17 17.06.80, Salisbury :
JT - 46.94
MORGAN Pamela 16.04.65, Liverpool H :
3k - 9:58.2
MORLEY Suzanne V35 11.10.57, Brighton :
3k - 9:47.26i (8:56.39-84)
MORRALL Leanne U17 7.07.79, Solihull & SH :
JT - 39.80
MORRIS Joanna U20 16.10.77, Newbury :
HJ - 1.67 (1.67-93), TJ - 11.59, Hep - 4209
MORRIS Kate U13 18.01.83, Dartford :
SPM - 9.81, DTM - 27.76
MORRIS Rachel 20.09.70, Shaftesbury Barnet :
DT - 39.52 (43.58-91)
MORRISON Catriona U20 11.01.77, Glasgow :
5k - 17:21.4
MORRISON Claire 30.05.69, Bristol :
(see ADAMS)
MORRISON Kirsty U23 28.10.75, Medway :
JT - 53.80 (59.36-93)
MORRISON Laurie U23 27.07.73,
Ealing,Southall & Mx/Army : JT - 39.40
MORTIMER Joanne 18.12.71, Sale
(nee GALLIGAN) : SP - 12.75 (13.18-92)
*MORTON Lesley 25.12.63, Westbury/NZ :*
*10kR - 33:42 (33:08-91)*
MOSS Jane U17 23.08.79, West Norfolk :
3k - 10:18.50
MOSS Julia U20 2.07.77, Chester Le Street :
400 - 57.0
MUNDEN Lisa U20 13.03.78, Bournemouth :
SP - 11.47, HT - 35.28
MUNRO Lynsay U20 1.02.77, Edinburgh WM :
JT - 41.92
MURPHY Catherine Ann U23 21.09.75, S B :
100 - 11.65w/11.78 (11.63w-94), 200 - 23.40
MURPHY Lindsey U13 26.06.83, Middlesbro & C :
80 - 10.77
MURRAY Pamela 13.01.67, Glasgow :
PV - 2.40 (2.50i/2.40-94)
MURRAY Sarah U17 24.04.79, Eastbourne R :
JT - 35.54
MURRAY Yvonne Carole Grace 4.10.64,
Motherwell : 800 - 2:12.06+ (2:00.80-87),
1500 - 4:05.61 (4:01.20-87),
2k - 5:46.3+ (5:26.93-94),
3k - 8:42.82 (8:29.02-88), 5k - 14:56.94,
10k - 32:16.76 (31:56.97-94)
MURRAY-JESSEE Alison 13.01.67, :
PV - 3.00un
MYERS Heather R. 5.12.64, AF&D :
400 - 57.0 (56.6-82), 100H - 15.1w (14.6-91),
400H - 59.9/60.12 (59.46-94)

MYHILL Danaa L. 16.10.70, Sale : (see CALLOW)

**N** ABOYA Maryann U15 16.09.80, S Lond :
SPG - 12.10
NASH Hayley L. 30.05.63, Newport :
5k - 16:56.98 (16:25.7-92),
10MR - 56:02 (55:32-94),
Mar - 2:39:59 (2:35:39-94)
NASH Sharon U23 5.05.74, GEC :
SP - 11.51 (12.67-93), DT - 38.62 (44.32-93),
HT - 36.72 (41.94-94)
NATHAN Nadya U13 3.11.82, Blackheath :
75 - 10.2, 80 - 10.9, 150 - 20.1
NAUGHER Abigail U17 26.02.80, Sunderland :
300 - 40.9/40.99
NAYLOR Christine V40 22.10.54, Arena :
Mar - 3:06:55 (3:04:31-92)
NAYLOR Donna U15 20.05.82, Birchfield :
100 - 12.3, LJ - 5.21
NEALL Alison U17 8.11.79, Croydon :
JT - 34.98 (37.86-94)
NEEF Melanie 26.05.70, Glasgow :
60 - 7.36i, 100 - 11.6w/11.70 (11.69w-88),
200 - 23.35, 400 - 51.18
NELSON Tatum U17 17.12.78, GEC :
100 - 11.92 (11.67w-93/11.78-94),
200 - 25.0 (24.35w/24.51-93)
NESBITT Sara U15 9.10.80, City of Plymouth :
SPG - 11.24i/10.87
NEVILLE Louise U15 18.09.80, Havering :
800 - 2:17.69
NEVIN Catherine E. V35, 12.11.55
Penny Lane Str. : Mar - 3:07:00
NEWCOMBE Rachel 25.02.67, Liverpool H :
400 - 55.89 (55.19-92)
NEWMAN Lucy U13 2.03.83, Horsham BS :
SPG - 8.97, SPM - 9.57, PenM - 2089
NEWMAN Maxine Claire 15.12.70, Coventry G :
800 - 2:09.5 (2:06.16-92),
1500 - 4:25.56 (4:10.07-92)
NEWMAN Wendy 31.08.71, Essex L :
JT - 44.96
NEWTON Jackie 28.08.64, Stockport :
10MR - 58:31, HMar - 1:17:46
NEWTON Lynne V45 19.05.47, Portsmouth :
3kW - 16:29.7
NEWTON Maria Angela 22.07.66, Ashford :
PV - 3.00i/2.80
NICCOLLS Jannette U20 7.09.76, Hercules W :
100 - 12.07, 200 - 24.8/24.96w (25.51-92)
NICHOLLS Emily U17 5.12.78, Westbury :
100 - 12.2/12.45w/12.53, 300 - 41.3
NICHOLLS Michelle U13 26.09.82, W S & E :
75 - 10.3, 80 - 10.7, 150 - 20.3
NICHOLLS Tamara U20 21.07.78, Basildon :
DT - 37.42 (38.86-94)
NICHOLLS Tasha U15 1.11.80, Basildon :
DT - 31.84
NICHOLS Claire U17 14.05.79, Woking :
300 - 40.33
NICHOLSON Sarah U13 30.06.83, Worthing :
DTM - 24.02
NICHOLSON Stephanie U20 28.06.76, C of Hull :
100H - 15.10 (14.96w-94), LJ - 5.52w
NICKLIN Debra U23 9.12.75, Colchester & T :
100H - 14.7 (14.84w-93)
NICKLIN Joanne 12.07.67, Colchester & T :
100H - 14.6, TJ - 11.25 (11.44-94)

NICOL Karen U20 1.11.77, Preston :
1500 - 4:33.8
NIGHTINGALE Julie U23 28.04.75, Eastb'rne GS :
JT - 42.80
NOBLE Susan 3.01.74, Pitreavie :
1500 - 4:43.46
NORMAN Hannah U15 1.06.81, Middlesbro & C :
HJ - 1.65
NORMAN Katrina U20 1.01.76, Walton :
400H - 60.15
NORTHEY Samantha U17 18.04.80, Dorset Sc :
3k - 10:33.7
NUGENT Donna 8.03.61, City of Hull/IRE :
100kR - 8:47:03
NUTTALL Diane U20 10.06.77, Braintree :
JT - 39.24
NUTTELL Amy U17 6.02.80, Holbeach :
80HI - 12.0/12.33, LJ - 5.45 (5.45-93),
Hepl - 4099
NYE Emma U20 17.07.77, Yate :
100H - 15.28
NYHAN Angela U20 13.04.78, Rowntrees :
LJ - 5.51, SP - 11.23, Hep - 4523

O'CONNOR Claire U23 24.09.74, Lisburn :
100 - 12.25, 200 - 24.75 (24.53-94)
O'CONNOR Gayle U17 24.08.79, Liverpool H :
HJ - 1.67
O'CONNOR Holly U13 9.12.83, St Helens :
600 - 1:42.2, 800 - 2:27.0
O'HARE Ellen U20 4.02.78, Cirencester :
800 - 2:09.35, 1500 - 4:28.1
O'MALLEY Jane U20 18.07.77, Hull Achilles :
100H - 14.8/15.17, 400H - 63.80,
Hep - 4220
O'SULLIVAN Clare U17 8.05.80, Sutton & D :
60H - 9.1i (9.1i-94), 80HI - 12.0/12.39
OAKES Judith Miriam V35 14.02.58, Croydon :
SP - 18.44 (19.36-88), DT - 50.56 (53.44-88)
OBOH Oteri U23 7.10.73, Herne Hill :
JT - 41.40 (48.30-92)
OGDEN Rachael U17 23.07.79, Rowntrees :
400 - 57.8, 800 - 2:08.78, 1500 - 4:40.0
OGOGO Leanne U13, Lowestoft :
LJ - 4.83
OKUSANYA Melissa U17 2.01.80, Derby LAC :
300 - 40.9/40.95
OKWUE Maurine U20 13.05.78, Thames VH :
TJ - 11.03
OKWUOSA Onome U13 2.08.83,
Ealing,Southall & Mx : SPG - 9.64
OLADAPO Georgina 15.05.67, Hounslow :
200 - 24.9 (23.65-85), 300 - 37.4+,
400 - 52.71
OLDFIELD Juliette U20 14.04.77, Birchfield :
1500 - 4:25.96
OLIVER Lindsey U20 12.03.78, Liverpool H :
HT - 37.00
ONIANWA Mary U15 20.01.81, Hercules Wim :
HJ - 1.63
ONIONS Gemma U15 6.03.81, Birchfield :
2.5kW - 13:31.89
ORE Wendy E. 23.05.66, Cardiff :
10kR - 34:44 (33:15-94)
ORFORD Beth U15 25.03.81, Coventry Godiva :
HJ - 1.64
ORRIDGE Sharon 7.03.66, Notts :
800 - 2:12.3

OSTERSBURG Karen 23.09.65, Birchfield :
SP - 11.24 (11.84-93)
OUTRAM Alison U20 14.06.77, Parkside :
3k - 9:59.2 (9:38.87-94)
OWEN Krissy U23 14.12.75, Eryri :
SP - 11.92i (12.88-94)
OWEN Suzanne U17 5.05.79, Chester & Elles :
800 - 2:16.94
OWEN Tracy A. 29.04.64, Arena :
Mar - 3:06:13 (3:03:32-94)
OWUSU Lesley U17 21.12.78, Windsor S & E :
60 - 7.75i, 100 - 12.1/12.20 (12.10-93),
200 - 24.2w/24.34w/24.41,
300 - 38.21, 400 - 54.57, 300H - 45.2
OXLEY Sarah U23 3.07.73, Birchfield :
60 - 7.69i (7.68i-94),
200 - 24.33w/24.38i (24.13w/24.6/24.65-94)
OYEYEMI Jean U15 24.08.81, Shaft B/NIG :
60 - 7.77i, 100 - 12.18 (11.86w-94)

PACE Anita 18.10.67, Hull Achilles :
400 - 57.3
PAGE Tracy 3.02.72, Braintree :
SP - 11.92 (12.59-88), JT - 39.18 (45.60-88)
PAINES Hannah U17 6.04.79, Cardiff :
60 - 7.90i (7.90i-94),
100 - 12.3/12.39 (12.36-94),
200 - 25.39w/25.70
PALKA Juliana U20 9.05.77, Glasgow :
400H - 64.6
PALMER Jane, 7.10.66 Sheffield :
10kR - 34:35
PALMER Karlene J. U15 23.10.80, W S & E :
60 - 7.83i, 100 - 12.2/12.43 (12.41w-94),
200 - 24.84
PALMER Leanne U17 22.03.80, Copeland :
100 - 12.4
PANKHURST Nicola U17 27.09.79, Crawley :
300 - 41.4/42.05, 400 - 59.1
PARKER Barbara A. V35 29.04.58, Jersey :
Mar - 3:02:19 (2:57:35-94)
PARKER Barbara U13 8.11.82, West Norfolk :
HJ - 1.43
PARKER Jacqueline T. 15.10.66, Team Sol :
300 - 38.73,
400 - 56.4/56.60 (54.07-89),
800 - 2:04.8mx/2:06.44 (2:03.78i-93),
100H - 13.9w/13.94w/14.32,
400H - 56.50 (56.15-91)
PARKER Jill U20 4.10.77, G. Manchester Sch :
Hep - 3866
PARKER Susan 24.03.70, Sale :
800 - 2:07.83 (2:05.50-93), 1k - 2:40.81,
1500 - 4:13.36 (4:12.3-93), 1M - 4:37.52,
3k - 9:18.92 (9:06.2-92)
PARKINSON Danielle U15 2.09.81, Rochdale :
HJ - 1.60
PARKINSON Hayley U23 5.12.75, Edin Univ :
800 - 2:11.60
PARRY Alison 19.06.66, Croydon :
800 - 2:11.29 (2:03.88-91)
PARRY Carys U15 24.07.81, Rhondda :
HT - 34.18
PARRY Hayley U23 17.02.73, Swansea :
400 - 57.3, 800 - 2:09.07,
1500 - 4:25.51, 1M - 4:48.88
PARRY Sheena U20 16.11.77, Rhondda :
HT - 42.66

379

PARSONS Katy U23 9.07.73, Team Sol
(nee SKETCHLEY) : 60H - 8.83i,
100H - 14.2/14.56 (14.15-92), Hep - 4219 (4509-92)
PARTINGTON Carolyn 27.06.66, Manx :
3kW - 13:13.3, 5kW - 22:41.19,
5kWR - 23:50+ (23:04-94), 10kWR - 46:26
PATRICK Elizabeth U20 29.08.77, Kingston & P :
TJ - 11.65
PATTINSON Helen U23 2.01.74, Preston :
800 - 2:11.0, 1500 - 4:27.7
PAUL Fiona U17 5.09.78, Edinburgh WM :
LJ - 5.56, TJ - 10.88
PAUZERS Clare 2.08.62, Herne H/London RR :
3k - 9:53.55, 10kR - 34:30, 10MR - 58:29
PAXTON Aileen U15 8.07.81, Motherwell :
JT - 35.04
PAYNE Charlene U13 7.10.83, Windsor S & E :
80 - 10.9
PAYNE Judith U17 7.07.80, Wakefield :
HJ - 1.65
PAYNE Kirsty U20 22.10.77, Birchfield :
60 - 7.78i, 100 - 12.16,
200 - 24.73w/25.00 (24.69w-94), TJ - 11.12
PAYNE Loni U13 17.12.82, Basingstoke & MH :
JTM - 27:52
PEACOCK Rachel U15 18.05.82, Wimborne :
LJ - 5.26, PenG - 2563
PEAKE Fiona U20 31.05.77, Woking :
PV - 2.80 (2.80i-94)
PEARCE Caroline U15 1.09.80, Huntingdon :
60H - 9.17io, 75HG - 11.50w/11.52,
LJ - 5.47, PenG - 3017
PEARSON Claire U17 23.09.78, Leics Cor :
60H - 8.84i (9.20i-94), 80HI - 11.44
PEARSON Helen U15 8.02.81, Newquay & P :
1500 - 4:41.82
PEARSON Jennifer Ann 3.07.62, Ashford :
400 - 56.81 (54.6-88),
100H - 15.0/15.29 (14.5-92/14.78-91/14.99w-94),
400H - 60.0/61.11 (57.41-88)
PEATFIELD Zoe U20 8.12.77, Stockport :
800 - 2:11.38
PEET Josephine 4.12.71, Guernsey/Brunel Un :
100H - 14.62w/14.7/14.73 (14.59-93),
LJ - 5.62 (5.74w?-93/5.64-88)
PENNET Catriona U13 10.10.83, Aberdeen :
70HM - 11.70w, PenM - 2016
PERCIVAL Deborah J. V35 22.04.58, Cant H :
10kR - 34:44 (34:18-94), Mar - 2:52:49
PERIDES Lynsay U17 24.05.79, Beds & Co :
PV - 2.60
PERKINS Candy 26.02.71, Ashford :
800 - 2:11.94
PERRETT Kirsty U20 17.03.76, Middlesbro & C :
HT - 38.30
PERRY Llyn U17 21.02.79, Braintree :
DT - 34.82, HT - 36.20, JT - 39.82
PHILLIPS Claire U23 13.03.75, Hastings :
DT - 36.46 (37.88-94)
PHILLIPS Fiona V35 8.03.60, City of Bath :
10k - 35:44.98, 10kR - 34:20, 10MR - 58:02
PHILLIPS Stephanie U17 25.10.78, Hastings :
LJ - 5.40, Hepl - 3962
PHYTHIAN Claire U23 7.02.73, Wigan :
100H - 14.17w/14.43 (14.30-94),
HJ - 1.76 (1.78-89), LJ - 5.88, Hep - 5455
PICTON Janette 4.03.63, Burnham :
Mar - 3:01:02 (2:54:42-94)

PIDGEON Elizabeth U20 27.04.77, Chelmsford :
JT - 41.00
PIERRE Michelle U23 30.09.73, Croydon :
200 - 24.8 (25.25-90), 400 - 54.05
PINEL Syreena U17 13.01.79, Leics Cor :
100 - 12.4/12.41, 200 - 25.0/25.03,
LJ - 5.41i (5.47-94)
PINFOLD Julie U17 18.07.79, Birchfield :
· DT - 33.24dh (33.44-94)
PITEL Edwige 4.06.67, Shaftesbury B/FRA :
1500 - 4:27.59 (4:24.95-93), 3k - 9:31.05,
5k - 16:22.25, 10kR - 34:30, HMar - 1:16:01
PLEAVIN Claire U13 25.04.83, Warrington :
PenM - 2015
POCOCK Nicola U17 9.05.79, AF&D :
60H - 9.26i, 300H - 44.64, 400H - 67.6
POPE Joanne 17.01.71, Brighton :
3kW - 15:32.97 (14:15.0-93),
5kWR - 26:48 (24:23-91)
PORAZINSKI Donna-Marie U15 29.01.81, Newp :
800 - 2:18.91i/2:19.92, PenG - 2654
PORTER Samantha 14.08.70, Basildon
(nee BARR) : 100 - 12.1 (12.0-91/12.37-94),
200 - 25.20w (24.9-94)
POTTER Helen U23 25.06.74, Trafford :
JT - 44.80 (45.06-93)
POTTER Sarah U23 28.10.75, Portsmouth :
HJ - 1.70
POWELL Kerry U15 28.02.82, Wilts Sch :
LJ - 5.20
PRATT Julie U17 20.03.79, Essex L :
100 - 12.4, 60H - 8.82i,
80HI - 11.32 (11.27w-94),
100H - 14.4/14.79w/14.84
PRICE Sharon U23 10.12.75, R S Coldfield :
60H - 8.94i, 100H - 14.4w/14.61 (14.43w-93)
PRIDMORE Rebecca U13 19.12.82, Leics WC :
3kWR - 15:51o
PRINGLE Maria U15 18.12.80, Copeland :
PenG - 2731
PRITCHARD Amanda U17 18.03.80, Cardiff :
300 - 40.50, 400 - 57.8,
800 - 2:12.9 (2:10.66-94)
PROCTER Lauren U13 9.09.82, Wimborne :
DTM - 24.30
PRYCE Elaine U23 4.10.73, Skyrac :
60 - 7.75i,
PRYER Helen U17 21.01.79, Camberley :
100 - 12.3/13.06, 200 - 25.01
PUCKERIDGE Jayne 23.10.71, Medway/LSAC :
800 - 2:12.03
PUGH Caroline U15 13.10.80, Kingston & P :
75HG - 11.7/11.94w/13.09
PURKISS Melanie U17 11.03.79, Team Solent :
60 - 7.8i, 100 - 12.25, 200 - 24.53
PURTON Alison 25.11.72, Birchfield :
100H - 14.9w/15.1 (14.40-92),
HJ - 1.70i/1.70 (1.76-89)

QUARTEY Tracey 16.12.71, Tower H :
DT - 36.06 (46.74dh/45.16-90)
QUIGLEY Lynne 19.02.69, Red Rose :
.Mar - 2:56:42
QUINN Pauline 2.08.70, Ballymena & Antrim :
800 - 2:11.8, 1500 - 4:29.56 (4:27.37-90)

380

R ADCLIFFE Paula J. U23 17.12.73,
Bedford & County :
800 - 2:05.22, 1500 - 4:06.84,
1M - 4:28.93, 2k - 5:46.1+ (5:39.20-93),
3k - 8:40.82 (8:40.40-93), 5k - 14:49.27
RADON Christina U17 12.07.79, Wycombe :
3k - 10:31.8
RAMMINGER Sarah Jane U23 1.10.75, Arbr :
LJ - 5.63w/5.58 (5.81-94),
TJ - 11.09i (11.47w/11.23-94),
Hep - 4293 (4517-94)
RAMWELL Lucy 16.08.67, Sale :
Mar - 2:53:04 (2:50:50-93)
RANKIN Adele 27.05.72, Oldham & Royton :
1500 - 4:29.92 (4:26.4-90)
RANKINE Lynsey U15 26.01.81, Cumbernauld :
HJ - 1.61
RANN Lucy U15 5.09.80, Isle of Wight :
SPG - 12.86, JT - 40.42, PenG - 2714
RASBUARY Danielle U23 15.01.74, Hull Ach :
TJ - 11.42
RATCLIFFE Karen 1.06.61, Cov RWC
(nee SMITH) : 3kW - 15:10.4 (14:02.29-93),
5kWR - 26:02 (24:03-94)
RATTIGAN Sinead U15 27.10.80, RS Coldfield :
100 - 12.53w/12.6/12.91
RAVEN Claire Heather 15.06.72, Cov G/LSAC :
400 - 54.4/55.06 (53.99-92), 800 - 2:08.37
RAVEN Sarah U13 22.11.82, Southend :
1500 - 4:58.3
RAWLING Kimberley U13 22.07.83, Newq & P :
DT - 24.90, DTM - 26.78
RAWLINSON Jennifer U13 30.11.82, GEC :
600 - 1:45.4
RAWLINSON Susan 13.10.70, Roth/Leeds P
(nee EARNSHAW) : 100 - 11.8 (11.8/11.89-94),
200 - 23.8w?/23.9 (23.5/23.80w/24.13-94),
400 - 53.4/53.69
REA Kelly U13 17.09.82, Springburn :
75 - 10.0, 80 - 11.0, 100 - 12.9,
150 - 19.2, 200 - 27.6
REA Tracy U17 19.01.79, Coventry Godiva :
SP - 11.46
READ Ann-Marie U23 24.05.75, Basing & MH :
DT - 36.08 (40.16-93)
READ Kimberley U13 31.12.82, Darlington :
1500 - 5:04.0
READER Catherine V40 19.10.54, Colch H :
3kW - 15:41.36 (15:07.1-91),
5kW - 27:16.04 (25:52.5-92),
5kWR - 26:36 (26:28-93),
10kW - 56:17.0 (52:43.3-92),
10kWR - 55:40 (52:45-91),
20kW - 1:53:28 (1:48:22-92)
READER Jennifer U20 23.12.77, Soton City :
HJ - 1.66
REDD Samantha U13, Brighton :
JTM - 27.26
REDDY Gisell U17 25.09.79, Haringey :
PV - 2.40
REDMOND Laura A. U15 19.04.81, Edin WM :
HJ - 1.61io, PenG - 2685
REDMOND Rachel U15 7.12.81, City of Stoke :
100 - 12.42, 200 - 25.39
REDMOND Rosemary U17 3.10.78,
Ealing,Southall & Mx : HT - 34.96 (36.82-94)
REEVE Sarah U13 16.12.82, Shaftesbury B :
600 - 1:44.5, 800 - 2:25.4

REEVES Katharine U23 2.03.73, Tonbridge :
400 - 56.49 (55.15-92)
REID Emma U15 5.01.81, Lochgelly :
75HG - 11.78, PenG - 2750
REID-HUGHES Frances U17 18.03.80, Tonb :
SP - 11.26, DT - 34.52
REINALDA Elona U20 31.03.76, Essex L :
100 - 11.90, 200 - 23.86
RETCHAKAN Gowry P. V35 21.06.60, Thurr :
100H - 14.6 (14.0-92/14.52w-89),
400H - 57.18 (54.63-92)
REYNOLDS Kay 15.09.67, Radley :
100H - 14.9 (14.1w/14.2-87/14.68w-90/14.77-87)
REYNOLDS Victoria U17 22.04.80, Blackpool :
LJ - 5.58w/5.42, TJ - 11.05w/10.50,
Hepl - 3891
RHIMES Sara V40, 12.09.54 Alton :
Mar - 3:03:58
RHODES Claire U13 25.01.83, Wakefield :
800 - 2:27.8
RHODES Vyvyan Anne U23 5.05.73, Hallam :
800 - 2:12.8, 400H - 58.85 (58.02-92)
RICE Lorna U17 10.01.79, Coventry Godiva :
300 - 41.22
RICH Emma U20 14.05.77, Yeovil Olympiads :
JT - 42.94
RICHARDS Angharad U20 9.12.76, Guild & G :
JT - 44.98 (46.20-93)
RICHARDS Anne-Marie 15.01.61, Cardiff :
5k - 17:22.5
RICHARDS Lara U13 7.03.83, Newport :
HJ - 1.45
RICHARDS Pauline 30.06.68, Birchfield :
200 - 24.92 (24.76-93),
400 - 54.4/55.33-93), 100H - 14.49,
LJ - 5.93, SP - 13.18, JT - 42.40,
Hep - 5417 (5420-94)
RICHARDSON Marcia M. 10.02.72,
Windsor S & E/WLIHE : 60 - 7.45i (7.36i-93),
100 - 11.51w/11.52 (11.39w-94/11.45-93),
200 - 23.53 (23.4-93)
RICHENS Nicola U17 26.10.79, Oxford City :
HJ - 1.65
RICHER Rosalind U23 5.10.74, Solihull & S H :
HJ - 1.65 (1.70-91)
RICHMOND Louise U15 15.12.81, Sol & SH :
2.5kW - 13:29.04, 3kW - 16:36.6,
3kWR - 15:39
RICHMOND Sarah U23 6.01.73, Pitr/Glas Un :
60H - 8.97i (8.7i-93/8.79i-91),
100H - 14.35 (14.02w/14.2/14.29-94)
RIDGLEY Becky U17 26.02.80, Team Solent :
PV - 2.90
RIDGLEY Clare Louise U20 11.09.77, Team S :
PV - 3.45
RIDLEY Jane 12.07.68, Shaftesbury Barnet :
400 - 56.7/57.29
RIDLEY Susan 'Anne' 7.05.65, Shaftesbury B :
3k - 9:52.7 (9:28.2-92),
5k - 17:14.3 (17:11.4-94)
RIDLEY Susan 25.10.65, Edinburgh WM :
1500 - 4:33.01 (4:30.6-93),
3k - 9:41.84 (9:27.94-93),
5k - 16:57.5 (16:51.80-94)
RIGG Suzanne 29.11.63, Warrington :
10kR - 34:55 (32:35-92),
10MR - 54:36 (53:42-93),
HMar - 1:14:37 (1:12:07-93), Mar - 2:34:21

RILEY Liz U23 31.05.74, Aberdeen Univ/USA :
10k - 35:12.14, HMar - 1:17:36
ROBERTS Catherine U13 27.09.82, Wigan :
600 - 1:42.5; 800 - 2:26.4
ROBERTS Nicola 22.01.70, Liverpool H :
HT - 35.62
ROBERTS Suzanne U17 19.12.78, Bingley :
HT - 34.72
ROBERTSON I. U13, Cheshire Sch :
HJ - 1.44
ROBIN Julie U20 16.01.77, Glasgow :
DT - 39.38 (45.10-94)
ROBINS Lorraine A. 13.05.70, Hounslow :
60 - 7.73i (7.5i-93/7.52i-94),
ROBINSON Eleanor M. V45 20.11.47, Border :
Mar - 2:51:36 (2:45:12-90),
100kR - 7:50:42, 24HrT - 213.504km
ROBINSON Gemma U17 30.12.78, Dartford :
300H - 46.49, TJ - 10.74
ROBINSON Lynne Elizabeth 21.06.69, Cov  G :
1500 - 4:27.2 (4:10.32-94), 10kR - 33:25
ROBINSON Tracey U15 28.09.81, Leics WC :
2.5kW - 13:58.7
ROBSON Debbie U20 12.07.76, Cannock & St :
100H - 14.91w/14.99
RODD Stacey U20 19.05.78, Barry :
100 - 12.26w/12.44 (12.31-93)
ROGER Kirsty U20 24.03.78, Inverness :
HJ - 1.65i
ROGERS Kate U17 14.02.79, Newark :
TJ - 10.54i (11.02-94), Hepl - 3894 (3971-94)
ROGERS Nina U17 19.09.78, Derby LAC :
300 - 40.8/40.99 (40.56-94)
ROGERS Rachel U15 20.11.80, Soton City :
200 - 25.5/25.60
ROKER Beverley 22.06.62, AF&D :
100H - 14.9/15.10 (14.1-91/14.40w-90/14.52-91)
ROLES Philippa U20 1.03.78, Swansea :
SP - 14.11, DT - 49.12, HT - 38.92
ROLES Rebecca U17 14.12.79, Swansea :
PV - 2.90, DT - 36.64
ROLFE Gemma U17 18.12.78, Windsor S & E :
HT - 39.84
ROLFE Nicola 19.08.69, Newbury :
JT - 42.82
RONALD Alison 20.01.67, Edinburgh WM :
PV - 2.75
ROSCOE Helen U17 4.12.79, Liverpool H :
60 - 7.90i, 100 - 12.34,
200 - 24.49, 300 - 40.09
ROSE Alison 27.09.67, Edinburgh WM :
10kR - 34:24 (34:03-94), Mar - 2:42:42
ROSE Dawn U17 25.01.79, Leamington :
60 - 7.63i, 100 - 12.2/12.25 (11.93w/12.2-94),
200 - 24.9/25.51i (25.84-94)
ROSS Lindsay U20 27.12.77, Nithsdale :
HT - 35.16
ROSS Michelle 31.01.72, City of Stoke :
3k - 9:45.46i/9:53.38 (9:44.62-93),
5k - 17:03.04
ROWBOTHAM Alanna Jane 11.01.70,
Roth (nee COOKE) : 200 - 24.3 (24.28-94),
400 - 56.0 (54.49-94), 400H - 60.0/60.43
ROWE Deborah 8.09.72, Coventry Godiva :
LJ - 5.77 (5.81w?-92/5.78-93), TJ - 12.44
ROWE Louise U17 8.11.78, Enfield :
1500 - 4:41.77

ROWLAND Katie 5.03.71, Birchfield :
JT - 41.00 (48.66-93)
ROWLANDS Leanne U17 16.09.79, Torfaen :
100 - 12.4/12.42
ROY Lesley Ann U15 3.01.82, Pitreavie :
SPG - 11.28, DT - 32.64
ROZE Anna U23 6.11.74, Shaftesbury Barnet :
400H - 61.31
RUDDOCK Ellena U20 23.02.76, Coventry G :
60 - 7.73i, 100 - 11.70,
200 - 25.23w (24.9w-93/25.0/25.44-94)
RUSHMERE Linda V35 14.11.59, Redhill :
HMar - 1:18:50 (1:14:31-94),
Mar - 2:45:26 (2:40:03-88)
RUSSELL Eve U13 27.09.82, C of Plymouth :
SPG - 8.53, SPM - 9.97,
JT - 31.28, JTM - 32.38
RUTHERFORD Susannah U17 26.02.79, Darl :
1500 - 4:44.2, 3k - 10:16.6
RUTLAND Emma U15 9.10.81, Blackpool :
1500 - 4:48.30
RYAN Catherine U17 4.02.80, Shrewsbury :
Hepl - 4068

S AGAR Sally U20 28.03.77, Barnsley :
100H - 14.76, 400H - 65.2/66.43
SAINT-SMITH Tasha 20.12.75, Enfield :
DT - 43.18 (44.68-94)
SALMON Georgina U17 1.11.79, Bristol :
800 - 2:16.8 (2:16.0-94),
1500 - 4:39.9
SALT Christa 17.06.64, Basel :
800 - 2:07.46, 1k - 2:47.22,
1500 - 4:26.18, 3k - 9:46.25i
SAMUELS Belinda U17 29.11.78, Birchfield :
Hepl - 4151,
LJ - 5.48i/5.48w/5.38 (5.57w/5.55-94)
SARGISON Hayley U13 15.09.82, Bracknell :
DTM - 24.04
SAUNDERS Kerry U20 28.03.77, Derby LAC :
HJ - 1.70 (1.70-94), TJ - 11.30
SAVAGE Marianne V45 26.01.49, Centurian :
100kR - 8:39:41
SAXELBY Jane 14.01.72, Notts :
100H - 15.0/15.01w
SAYERS Tina U15 19.07.81, City of Hull :
HJ - 1.60
SCHOFIELD Victoria 29.12.72, Rotherham :
200 - 24.95, 60H - 8.60i,
100H - 14.0w/14.2/14.24w/14.97 (14.06-94),
HJ - 1.78, LJ - 6.28,
SP - 11.41i/11.25 (11.84-94),
Hep - 5551 (5671-94)
SCHRAMM Louise 18.12.71, Epsom & Ewell :
PV - 3.30
SCOBEY Christina L. 1.06.66, London O/USA :
Mar - 2:46:24
SCOBIE Kirsten 13.11.67, Leeds :
3k - 9:39.3i (9:29.72-93)
SCOTT Jemma U13 14.03.83, Arbroath :
70HM - 11.73w, PenM - 2299
SCOTT Joanne U20 31.12.76, Elswick :
TJ - 11.40i/11.19w/11.09 (11.40-94)
SCOTT Karen U17 17.10.79, Ayr Seaforth :
60 - 7.87i, 100 - 12.19w/12.52
SEAGER Heather 4.04.68, Yeovil Olympiads :
SP - 11.44 (11.72-94), DT - 37.00 (38.72-92)

382

SEMENOVA Marina 12.07.64, Birchfield/RUS :
HT - 46.72
SEMUS Kate 18.01.70, Parkside :
DT - 38.38 (39.10-90)
SERGEANT J. U13, London Schools :
JTM - 26.72
SESTON Laura U17 9.02.79, Ipswich :
60 - 7.75i (7.62i-94),
100 - 11.93w/12.08 (11.84w/11.88-94),
200 - 25.3 (25.04i/25.3/25.34-94), 300 - 41.4
SHACKEL Karen A. 4.02.64, Crawley
(nee MILLER) : JT - 40.40 (50.12-87)
SHAW Lorraine A. 2.04.68, Gloucester L :
SP - 14.03 (14.21-94),
DT - 51.38 (55.04-94), HT - 64.90
SHAW Natalie U13 2.01.83, St Albans :
LJ - 4.67
SHEPHERD Victoria U17 26.01.80, Wakefield :
SP - 11.74
SHEPPARD Amanda 26.02.68, Halifax :
DT - 37.68
SHEPPARD Suzanne U17 24.09.78, Lisburn :
TJ - 10.89
SHIELDS Jane Elizabeth V35 23.08.60, Sheff :
3k - 9:25.5 (8:45.69-83),
5k - 15:54.80 (15:32.34-88),
10k - 33:46.07 (32:59.42-90), 10kR - 33:22
SHIPMAN Victoria U20 31.03.77, Derby LAC :
60 - 7.75i, 200 - 24.08
SHIRT Pauline U20 21.05.78, Hallamshire :
SP - 11.49i/10.80 (12.41-94)
SHOKAN Irene U15 7.03.81, Tower Hamlets :
HJ - 1.62
SHORT Nicola 30.10.69, Torfaen :
LJ - 5.68
SHORT Sallyanne 6.03.68, Torfaen :
100 - 11.57 (11.36w-89/11.39-92),
200 - 23.79 (23.19w-90/23.24-92), LJ - 5.67 (5.88-94)
SHORT Sarah U17 27.11.79, Essex L :
300H - 45.98
SHORTHALL Jeanette U15 9.09.80, Liv H :
1500 - 4:45.64
SHORTS Tracy 4.11.72, Edinburgh WM :
SP - 12.55, DT - 41.44, HT - 35.30, JT - 39.06
SHUM Cathy 30.05.61, Cannock & Staff/IRE :
5k - 16:58.0, 10k - 34:38.59,
10kR - 33:21, 10MR - 55:49,
HMar - 1:14:22 (1:12:48-94),
Mar - 2:43:10sh (2:38:14-93)
SIDDALL Naomi U23 2.04.75, Barn/Camb Un :
TJ - 11.60
SILVER Lorna U23 10.01.74, Dundee HH :
60H - 8.88i, 100H - 14.3w/15.23 (14.59-94),
400H - 60.4/60.63 (59.9/60.58-94)
SILVEY Helen U23 4.12.73, Enfield :
LJ - 5.59, TJ - 11.10
SIMMANS Sarah U17 29.11.78, Oldham & R :
JT - 39.94 (40.60-94)
SIMON Bianca U13 28.12.82, Belgrave :
150 - 19.9
SIMPSON Beatrice V35, Bromley :
HT - 34.92
SIMPSON Marian U20 2.11.77, Aberdeen :
HT - 39.40
SINCLAIR Fiona U20 14.02.77, Edin WM :
100 - 12.16w (12.50-94),
SINCLAIR Lorna U17 15.06.79, Edin WM :
100 - 12.48w

SKEETE Lesley-Ann 20.02.67, Trafford :
100H - 14.1 (13.01w/13.03-90)
SKEGGS Karen 26.10.69, Ashford :
LJ - 5.82 (6.29w/6.09-89),
TJ - 12.50 (12.93w/12.89-92),
SP - 11.73 (11.99-94)
SKETCHLEY Katy U23 9.07.73, Team Sol :
(see PARSONS)
SKINNER Rehanne U17 13.11.79, Scar :
JT - 35.60
SKINSLEY Helen U23 19.03.74, Bris/Warw Un :
JT - 38.52 (40.44-93)
SLATER Catriona U20 27.01.77, Chelmsford :
LJ - 5.70
SLATER Nicola Simone U20 11.01.77, Radley :
3k - 9:57.6 (9:21.20-94)
SLIMIN Caroline 27.08.65, Basingstoke & MH :
1500 - 4:25.37i (4:18.61-94),
10kR - 34:37 (34:27-94)
SLIMON Helen 18.02.71, Glasgow :
Mar - 3:06:23
SLOAN Kelly U17 18.09.78, Helensburgh :
DT - 33.82, JT - 35.08
SLOAN Patricia A., 22.03.66 Belle Vue :
Mar - 3:05:34
SLOANE Joanne U20 2.12.76, Coventry G :
400 - 54.59
SMALLWOOD Nicole U20 9.10.77, Halesowen :
HJ - 1.75
SMETHURST Natalie U20 31.03.77, Wigan :
200 - 25.1/25.63w/25.67
SMITH Carolyn 6.10.61, Dundee HH :
400H - 63.0/64.13 (62.95-94)
SMITH Claire U17 6.01.79, Chesterfield :
300 - 41.05
SMITH Diane V35 15.11.60, Hull Spartan :
HT - 41.14
SMITH Elaine U13 16.05.83, Middlesbro & C :
75 - 10.2, 80 - 10.85, LJ - 4.79
SMITH Gemma U23 16.01.75, Peterborough :
400H - 65.0
SMITH Janet 7.10.64, Windsor S & E :
HT - 44.92 (46.88-94)
SMITH Joanne U23 23.06.73, Swan :
(see DAVIS)
SMITH Joanne U17 22.11.78, Essex L :
SP - 10.80, DT - 34.90
SMITH Karen 1.06.61, Cov RWC :
(nee RATCLIFFE)
SMITH Karen U23 10.02.74, Sale :
DT - 41.36 (46.64-93)
SMITH Kelly U13, Preseli :
70HM - 11.5, HJ - 1.50
SMITH Laura U15 16.11.80, Hull Springhead :
HJ - 1.60, LJ - 5.22
SMITH Louise U20 11.07.77, Ipswich :
JT - 44.90
SMITH Megan U23 19.04.74, Edinburgh Univ :
5k - 17:23.8
SMITH Michelle Louise U20 1.01.78, Salisbury :
HJ - 1.65 (1.70-94)
SMITH Natasha U20 6.06.77, Hounslow :
SP - 13.56i/13.46, HT - 36.10 (37.28-92)
SMITH Phylis 29.09.65, Sale :
100 - 11.71w/11.9 (11.40w-90/11.60-87),
200 - 24.2w/24.6 (23.40-92), 400 - 52.5 (50.40-92)
SMITH Rachel U20 3.03.76, Oxford City :
Hep - 4154 (4242-94)

383

SMITH Rebecca U13 23.02.83, City of Stoke :
75 - 10.1, 100 - 13.10w/13.16,
150 - 19.2, 200 - 27.4w
SMITH Sophia U23 8.12.74, Hallamshire :
60 - 7.61i (7.5i/7.51i-94),
100 - 11.50w/11.69, 200 - 23.92 (23.57-93)
SMITHSON Claire U13 3.08.83, Brighton :
SPM - 9.40, DT - 29.58, DTM - 32.70
SMITHSON Kerry U20 13.09.76, Hyndburn :
800 - 2:10.5
SNAPE Rachel U15 21.12.80, Derby LAC :
HJ - 1.64
SNEDDON Esther U23 30.06.74, Central :
JT - 39.50 (40.12-94),
Hep - 4243 (4290w-94)
SNOOK Verity A. 13.11.70, AF&D :
3kW - 13:32.90 (13:27.9-94),
5kW - 23:38.85 (23:22.52-94),
5kWR - 22:58 (22:45+-94),
10kWR - 48:42 (46:06-94)
SOLLARS Loretta 29.10.63, Leeds :
3k - 9:58.1 (9:53.26-92)
SOPER Annabel 18.11.71, Croydon :
100 - 12.05 (11.5w/11.7/11.82-90),
200 - 24.89 (24.28w/24.5-87/24.57-94)
SOTHERTON Kelly Jade U20 13.11.76, Port :
100H - 14.54w/14.74, HJ - 1.68 (1.69-94),
LJ - 5.84, TJ - 11.54 (11.61w/11.56-94),
Hep - 4961
SOUTHGATE Deborah L. V35 2.02.56, Angels :
Mar - 3:04:37
SPACKMAN Karen 20.08.69, Bromley :
400H - 61.32
SPARK Jayne Clare 16.09.70, Altrincham :
3k - 9:32.5mx (9:06.7mx/9:22.5-93)
SPELLACY Jemma U13 27.11.82, Castle Pt :
SPM - 9.14, DTM - 27.14,
JT - 26.00, JTM - 26.00
SPENCER Joanne U13 1.11.82, Hounslow :
HJ - 1.43
SPINKS Stephanie U13 6.09.82, West Norfolk :
100 - 13.2, 200 - 27.1
SPRINGATE Teresa Jayne 8.03.69, Medway :
(see COPELAND)
SPRULES Lyn U23 11.09.75, Hounslow :
SP - 11.44, DT - 39.44 (40.72-93),
HT - 55.32 (55.44-94)
STACEY Joanne U17 23.09.79, Enfield :
HepI - 3816
STAINES Linda 26.12.63, Basingstoke & MH
(nee KEOUGH) :
200 - 24.72w/25.0 (23.1/23.51-89),
400 - 53.72 (50.98-91),
800 - 2:07.1 (2:01.82-93)
STANLEY Joanne U20 30.03.77, Elswick :
TJ - 11.16
STANTON Linda Mary U23 22.06.73, Roth :
PV - 3.72
STANWAY Gayle U20 29.10.77, Glasgow :
400H - 65.7/66.26
STAPLES Katharine 2.11.65, Essex L :
PV - 3.80i/3.80/3.90ex
STAPLETON Samantha U23 13.10.73, Sale :
PV - 2.80 (3.20-94)
STARES Hannah U17 13.11.78, Yate :
HepI - 3925
STEAD Caroline 14.09.71, Parkside :
LJ - 5.71, TJ - 12.15w/12.14 (12.17-94)

STEADMAN Marina V35 4.09.60, Bracknell :
HMar - 1:17:37 (1:13:29sh-87/1:13:43-89)
STEELE Emily U23 10.09.74, Birchfield :
JT - 40.92 (45.80-92)
STEELE Wendy E. 7.01.66, Edinburgh WM :
400 - 55.74 (54.84-92), 800 - 2:10.2/2:10.25
STEPHENS Tasmin U17 2.08.80, Lagan Val :
80HI - 12.0, 300H - 46.6
STERN Annette U20 9.09.76, Shaftesbury B :
100H - 15.0w/15.16
STERNE Victoria 12.10.68, Birchfield :
400 - 57.4, 800 - 2:06.1, 1500 - 4:27.92
STEVENS Annelies U20 16.05.78, Peterbro :
TJ - 11.52
STEVENS Barbara V35 2.05.56, Redhill :
Mar - 2:59:41
STEVENSON Lucy U23 30.01.73, Sale :
JT - 46.84 (52.00-92)
STEVENSON Sarah Anne Louise U23 31.12.73,
Birchfield : 400 - 55.9/56.26
STEWART Gillian U17 21.01.80, Edinburgh :
60H - 9.10i, 80HI - 11.89w/11.96
STILL Margaret 9.05.65, Wakefield :
100H - 15.1w (14.7/15.26-90),
400H - 60.8/62.12 (58.44-88), TJ - 11.62
STILL Sarah U23 24.09.75, Aberdeen :
Hep - 4157 (4643-94)
STOCKDALE Susan U13, Charnwood :
DTM - 24.68
STOREY Victoria U20 21.11.77, Sale :
JT - 39.86
STOTT Rachel U23 3.09.74, Cambridge Univ :
HT - 37.30
STOUT Keira U17 6.03.80, Braintree :
HJ - 1.67 (1.67-94)
STOUTE Jennifer Elaine 16.04.65, Essex L :
100 - 12.22 (11.63w/11.64-90),
200 - 23.90 (22.73-92),
400 - 54.5/55.36i (51.53-89)
STOWELL Rebecca U13 21.04.83, Oxford C :
DTM - 26.04
STRICKLETON Sarah U17 10.05.80, Wigan :
DT - 35.46
STRINGER Joanne U15 17.03.81, Bracknell :
75HG - 11.66
SUCH Jennifer U17 5.10.79, Chesterfield :
100 - 12.50
SUDDES Joanne U20 27.01.77, North S P :
60H - 8.96i, 100H - 14.64w/14.86 (14.85-94)
SULLIVAN Danielle U17 11.12.78, Cardiff :
80HI - 11.9w
SUMNALL Charlene U17 21.02.79, Corby :
DT - 35.34
SUTCLIFFE Elaine 6.04.70, Wakefield :
60 - 7.74i, 100 - 12.0 (11.8/11.94w/12.03-90),
200 - 24.3/24.65i/24.99 (24.48-94),
300 - 39.00i (38.7-94), 400 - 54.35
SUTHERLAND Carolynne U15 4.09.80, Edin WM :
75HG - 11.58,
SUTHERRLAND Wendy 30.05.63, Serp/NZ :
(see LLEWELLYN )
SUTTON Marian 7.10.63, Westbury :
5k - 17:06.0 (16:43.66-90),
10kR - 33:25 (32:55-94), 10MR - 55:06 (54:17-93),
HMar - 1:14:19 (1:11:42-93), Mar - 2:32:26
SWALLOW Jodie U15 23.06.81, Brentwood :
1500 - 4:41.22

384

SWANN Julie 15.07.62, Wolverhampton & B :
800 - 2:11.1 (2:07.94-94),
1500 - 4:28.77 (4:26.07i-94/4:27.0-93)
SWETMAN Gemma U15 28.09.80, Brighton :
PenG - 2869
SWIFT Claire U20 17.10.76, Liverpool H :
3k - 9:55.3 (9:55.09-94)
SWINBANK Caroline U23 16.06.75, Bristol :
400 - 57.06 (56.45-93)
SWINDELL Tracy 8.11.66, Thurrock :
10MR - 58:43, HMar - 1:18:18,
Mar - 2:48:20 (2:48:09-94)
SWITHENBANK Nicola, 10.12.63 Redhill :
HMar - 1:17:38
SWYER Kerry U13 2.12.82, Gateshead :
600 - 1:45.1, HJ - 1.47io/1.44
SYKES Julia U23 27.05.75, Hallamshire :
400H - 62.90 (61.68-94)
SYM Audrey 2.08.66, Glasgow :
10MR - 56:41dh, HMar - 1:17:26
SYMONDS Emma U20 5.06.77, Norfolk :
100 - 12.21w/12.62,
200 - 24.6/24.74w/24.97, 400 - 57.3
SYMONDS Joanne 19.02.68, Birchfield :
3k - 9:33.80i (9:20.20-93)
SYMONDS Sarah Louise U23 28.12.73, Radley :
DT - 44.82 (47.50-90), HT - 40.58

TAIT Natalie J. 24.08.72, Windsor S & E :
400 - 56.5, 800 - 2:02.69,
1k - 2:40.28, 1500 - 4:17.9
TALBOT Elizabeth U23 5.12.74, Bedford & Co:
800 - 2:12.5 (2:12.2-93), 1500 - 4:19.09,
3k - 9:29.8, 5k - 16:24.86
TALBOT Nicola 17.02.72, Telford :
SP - 11.46 (11.74-93), DT - 48.32 (54.24-93)
TAMIRAT Getenesh U20 11.07.77, Ex L/ETH :
3k - 9:40.3, 5k - 17:08.9mx
TAPPER Liz U20 2.06.78, Charnwood :
PV - 2.60
TASWELL Ann 31.05.71, Wells :
3k - 9:54.1,
TAYLOR Claire U20 6.08.76, Telford :
JT - 42.34 (48.00-92)
TAYLOR Emma U15 29.11.80, Walton :
HJ - 1.60
TAYLOR Gemma U13 18.09.82, North S P :
1500 - 5:03.0
TAYLOR Jane U17 18.02.80, City of Hull :
LJ - 5.48
TAYLOR Lynn Caroline 5.08.67, Woking :
400 - 57.4 (56.4-88), 800 - 2:07.9 (2:06.5-93)
TAYLOR Natalie U17 2.01.80, Girvan :
TJ - 10.76
TEALE Amy U13 30.12.82, North Shields P:
80 - 10.97, 75HG - 12.6
TEREK Ann 22.09.64, Lisburn :
800 - 2:10.81, 1500 - 4:23.1,
3k - 9:28.39, 5k - 16:54.47
TERRY Catherine U13 17.11.82, Southport :
1500 - 5:07.0
TERRY Sandra 28.04.69, Army :
DT - 36.52 (37.24-90)
THACKRAY Penny U23 18.08.74, Spenbro :
1500 - 4:29.3 (4:26.5-94),
3k - 9:36.1mx/9:46.89i (9:35.76-94)
THEOBALD Susan U13 4.03.83, Braintree :
JT - 25.40, JTM - 27.76
THIEME Helen U15 28.09.81, Sutton-in-Ashf :
PenG - 2755

THIRKLE Kelly Michelle 29.03.71, Sale :
HJ - 1.80i/1.76 (1.88i-92/1.85-91)
THIRWELL Tina M. U15 5.09.81, Sale :
PenG - 2705
THOMAS Clare U17 26.08.79, Swansea :
1500 - 4:44.32 (4:40.69-94), 3k - 10:14.0
THOMAS Elizabeth 22.12.63, Card
(nee FRANCIS) :
1500 - 4:33.0 (4:33.68-94), 1M - 4:52.58
THOMAS Kelly U15 9.01.81, Dartford :
100 - 12.4/12.59
THOMAS Kerry U13 5.12.82, Southport :
600 - 1:45.7, 1500 - 5:07.2
THOMAS Lisa U17 22.06.80, Shaftesbury B :
100 - 12.40 (12.24w-94)
THOMAS Michelle 16.10.71, Birchfield :
100 - 11.91 (11.9-91), 200 - 24.48
(24.2-94/24.29w-90/24.45-94),
400 - 54.31i (54.01-92)
THOMAS Paula 3.12.64, Trafford :
60 - 7.28i (7.23i-87),
100 - 11.33 (11.13w-88/11.15-94),
200 - 22.89 (22.69-94), LJ - 6.04 (6.07w-88)
THOMAS Petulia U13, Llanelli :
SPM - 9.49; DTM - 24.04
THOMAS Sonia U17 16.05.79, Wallsend :
1500 - 4:40.64, 3k - 10:24.9
THOMPSON Alison Kate U23 11.02.74, Sale :
100 - 12.16w (11.8w?-93/11.86db/11.88-94),
200 - 24.8/24.98 (24.3w/24.48w-93/24.58-92)
THOMPSON Jan Marie 9.03.70, Sale :
SP - 11.98 (12.93-89)
THOMPSON Lisa 12.07.62, Bromley :
400 - 57.22 (55.9-79),
800 - 2:07.44 (2:04.85-90)
THOMPSON Lisa U15 25.04.81, Colwyn Bay :
HJ - 1.66, PenG - 2927
THOMPSON Lisa U13 3.12.82, Nairn :
SPM - 10.40
THOMPSON Margaret V40 8.07.54, Potteries :
Mar - 3:08:36 (2:59:01-90)
THOMPSON Nikita U17 17.08.80, Birchfield :
80HI - 11.86, LJ - 5.60, Hepl - 3856
THOMSON Penny U17 10.04.80, Edin WM :
60 - 7.99i,
THOMSON Trudi V35 18.01.59, Pitreavie :
10kR - 34:59, HMar - 1:15:48, Mar - 2:38:23
THOMSON Wendy U23 24.06.75, Essex L :
DT - 37.42 (38.24-93)
THORN Joanna U15 19.02.81, Reading :
100 - 12.5
THORNE Alison 25.09.72, Windsor S & E :
400 - 55.7 (55.33-94)
THORNE Louretta U20 6.05.77, Wycombe :
200 - 24.49 (24.39-94),
400 - 55.25 (54.27-94)
THORNER Rosie 7.08.67, Bristol :
400 - 55.86
THORP Angela Caroline 7.12.72, Wigan :
100H - 13.62 (13.28-93)
THORPE Amanda 21.07.71, Hyndburn :
800 - 2:09.7 (2:09.5-94),
1500 - 4:12.9mx/4:25.92 (4:22.48-93),
3k - 9:40.08 (9:17.4mx-94/9:29.9-93)
THORPE Anna-Maria 15.07.71, Queens Park :
LJ - 5.51 (5.88-92)
THRIFT Joanna U13 14.09.82, Bracknell :
SPM - 9.16
THURSTON Kathy U20 2.01.76, Warrington :
400 - 57.50, 400H - 61.0/61.39

TIMMIS Irene 28.03.65, Southampton City :
SP - 11.36 (11.88-94)
TINDAL Jacqueline U17 21.01.79, Fife :
60H - 8.98i, 80HI - 11.69w/12.16 (12.04-94),
HJ - 1.66, SP - 11.50io/11.04, Hepl - 4409
TITTERINGTON Helen 24.10.69, Leics C/LSAC :
5k - 17:10.0 (15:40.14-89)
TODD Jennifer U17 23.10.78, Sale :
TJ - 10.58
TODD Sarah L. U17 3.11.79, Jarrow & H :
300 - 41.45
TONKS Sharon J. 18.04.70, Bromsgrove & R :
3kW - 14:38.5, 5kW - 26:07.85 (25:35.15-89),
5kWR - 25:04, 10kWR - 52:46 (52:39-94)
TOWN Anna U23 22.04.75, Verlea :
SP - 11.35 (11.90-92), HT - 35.60 (36.48-94)
TOWNSLEY Mary U17 20.10.78, Dundee HH :
JT - 35.68
TOZER Lynsey U23 6.12.75, Birchfield :
3kW - 14:29.00i (15:20.7-94),
5kWR - 26:01 (25:35-92),
10kWR - 54:31 (53:18-92)
TREMARCO Melissa U13 12.10.82, Whitby H :
PenM - 1924
TREMBLE Amanda U20 2.11.76, North S P :
800 - 2:11.0, 1500 - 4:22.70,
3k - 9:27.5, 5k - 16:50.4
TRIGGS Carmel U17 18.04.80, Elan Valley :
200 - 25.5/25.76w/26.02
TUGWELL Emily U20 26.05.78, Cornwall AC :
HJ - 1.65,
TUNALEY Sharon 2.09.68, Notts :
100 - 11.8/12.12 (11.5w-85/11.6-87/11.53w-86/
11.80-86), 200 - 23.6w?, 300 - 39.3, 400 - 53.58
TUOHY Teresa V35 1.06.59, London Oly/IRE :
Mar - 2:51:06 (2:50:33-92)
TURNBULL Jessica U23 4.07.75, Bury :
3k - 9:55.70, 5k - 16:57.5
TURNER Clare U15 23.09.80, Dartford :
75HG - 11.6/11.61
TURNER Lesley 1.08.66, Rowheath :
HMar - 1:18:20 (1:15:48-93),
Mar - 2:46:46 (2:41:09-93)
TURNER Lorna 11.05.72, Essex L :
HJ - 1.65 (1.65-94),
TJ - 12.40w/12.32 (12.94-94)
TURNER Natasha U23 8.11.74, Oxford City :
400H - 63.3/65.39 (61.9-94/65.02-93)
TWORT Becky U13 26.07.83, Reading :
JTM - 27.38

UNDERWOOD Diane R. V40 20.12.52, Cent :
HMar - 1:18:22 (1:16:33-90)
URBAIN Felicity U13 11.11.82, AF&D :
80 - 10.9

VAGGERS Melanie U15 16.06.82, C of Ply :
JT - 33.28, PenG - 2598
VANNET Lisa U23 8.11.74, Edinburgh WM :
200 - 24.93, 400 - 56.0/56.13 (56.11-94)
VAUGHAN Carys U15 15.09.81, Lincs Sch :
PenG - 2657
VAUGHAN-JONES Joanne U17 6.09.79,
Beds & Co : 300 - 40.9/41.95, 400 - 59.0
VEEVERS Sara U23 26.04.74, Pendle :
HJ - 1.70 (1.73-89)
VERNON Lyndsey U15 24.11.80, Liverpool H :
800 - 2:18.1

VEYSEY Sarah U23 4.03.75, Stroud :
400H - 63.0/63.34 (62.31-93)
VINCENT Lisa U23 23.09.74, Havering/War Un :
TJ - 11.23 (11.33-94)
VINEY Elaine 20.12.71, Peterborough :
200 - 24.87w/25.19 (24.2-90/24.78-91), 400 - 56.25
VINEY Gemma U13 7.01.83, Blackheath :
1500 - 4:54.8
VYFSCHAFT Jackie 15.12.64, Ballymena & A :
HJ - 1.70 (1.72i/1.71-82)

WADE Rebecca U17 11.06.80, C of Bath :
3k - 10:25.7
WAITE Amanda U20 1.02.78, Basildon :
100 - 12.25,
200 - 24.84w/25.1 (24.70w/24.8/25.09-94)
WAITE Camilla U17 24.05.80, Andover :
1500 - 4:39.02, 3k - 10:28.0
WALDO V. Ena 29.06.63, Birchfield :
100 - 12.00w/12.01 (11.55w/11.6/11.72-88),
200 - 24.40w (23.60w-88/23.8-87/23.82-88),
400 - 56.1 (55.1/55.20-88)
WALE Amanda 14.10.70, Wrexham :
Hep - 4076 (4302-94)
WALKER Cheryl U13 21.12.82, Cannock & St :
600 - 1:46.0
WALKER Elexi U13 28.10.82, Birchfield :
75 - 10.3, 150 - 19.8
WALKER Elizabeth U17 30.05.79, Barnsley :
100 - 12.3/12.67, 200 - 25.19 (24.99w-93)
WALKER Gail 7.12.71, Edinburgh WM :
100H - 14.56
WALKER Helen U15 12.10.80, Middlesbro & C :
PenG - 2579
WALKER Hilary C. V40 9.11.53, Serpentine :
Mar - 3:06:12 (2:59:00-89),
100kR - 8:26:28 (7:50:01-93)
WALKER Joanne U20 2.03.78, Kilmarnock :
JT - 47.14
WALKER Marcia 27.05.70, Shaftesbury Barn :
200 - 24.9 (24.36w-93/24.4-94/25.17-93),
TJ - 11.54
WALKER Melanie U17 29.04.79, Newbury :
SP - 11.61, JT - 35.86
WALL Kim U13, Braintree :
600 - 1:45.2
WALLACE Ailsa U20 12.03.77, Cardiff :
HJ - 1.70i/1.70 (1.73i/1.70-94)
WALLACE Alana, Ballymena & Antrim/IRE :
DT - 38.26
WALLACE Katie U17 19.09.78, Team Solent :
1500 - 4:40.09, 3k - 10:15.2 (10:10.8-94)
WALLACE Michelle 1.11.72, Notts :
DT - 38.62 (41.50-93)
WALLACE Rachel U23 7.11.74, Lincoln Well :
1500 - 4:30.43
WALLACE Sarah U23 31.05.73, Lincoln City :
3k - 9:58.78 (9:54.1-94)
WALLBANKS Carol U13 9.12.82, Workington :
JTM - 29.58
WALLEN Debbie U17 28.05.79, AF&D :
3kW - 16:10.62, 5kWR - 27:19, 10kWR - 55:59
WALSH Caroline U17 29.04.80, Shaftesbury B :
1500 - 4:44.4 (4:43.94-94)
WANSTALL Helen U15 13.11.80, Invicta :
HJ - 1.65
WARD Emma U15 2.01.82, City of Stoke :
800 - 2:14.0, 1500 - 4:37.16

386

WARD Jennifer U17 22.09.78, Glasgow :
800 - 2:14.1 (2:13.65-94),
1500 - 4:43.46i/4:43.6 (4:38.26-94)
WARDEN Caroline 16.09.72, Preston
(nee MILLER) : LJ - 5.61 (6.03w/5.85-93),
TJ - 11.74i/11.40 (12.31-94)
WARREN Sally U20 29.01.78, Steyning :
3kW - 15:40.6, 5kW - 26:49.87,
5kWR - 26:34, 10kWR - 56:15
WARRILOW Hayley U17 10.04.80, C of Stoke :
60H - 9.26i, LJ - 5.51w/5.49,
TJ - 10.77, Hepl - 4104
WATERS Elizabeth U20 19.02.77, Kettering :
400H - 64.4/65.87 (63.66-94)
WATSON Gillian 26.05.64, Sheffield RWC ;
3kW - 14:33.36i/14:46.0, 5kW - 25:00.79,
5kWR - 25:44 (25:33-93),
10kW - 54:06.6 (53:44.0-94),
10kWR - 53:17
WATSON Louise Carole 13.12.71, GEC/LSAC :
1500 - 4:28.9 (4:22.9-89),
3k - 9:18.1mx/9:25.90 (9:16.45-92),
5k - 15:57.06, 10k - 33:33.71
WATSON Natalie U13 29.01.83, Solihull & SH :
2.5kW - 13:51.9, 3kWR - 15:48o
WATSON Paula 5.09.70, Essex L :
LJ - 5.58 (5.85w-92/5.83-90)
WATSON Ruth U17 29.11.79, Cambridge & C :
100 - 12.3/12.51w/12.97,
200 - 24.9/24.99w/25.11, 300 - 39.68
WATT Fiona U23 29.01.73, Glasgow :
TJ - 12.15i/11.67
WATTS Katy U15 25.03.81, Basingstoke & MH :
JT - 32.52
WEALE Rebecca U20 7.02.78, Yeovil Oly :
HJ - 1.66
WEATHERILL Carolina 13.05.68, Shaft Barnet :
1500 - 4:27.6 (4:24.60-90), 3k - 9:23.1
WEBB Rachel U13 1.12.82, Bedford & County :
70HM - 11.4
WELBOURN Emma U17 14.02.79, C of Hull :
HT - 34.34
WELLSTEAD Sarah U17 22.10.79, Sutton & D :
TJ - 10.55
WEST Rebecca U23 9.09.74, Southampton C :
DT - 37.50 (40.04-94)
WESTON Claire U17 26.07.80, Broms & R :
100 - 12.4/12.56
WESTON Vicky U13 14.03.83, Team Solent :
LJ - 4.84
WHALLEY Michelle U15 1.10.80, Wigan :
800 - 2:15.6, 1500 - 4:39.95
WHEATCROFT Clare U17 15.12.78, Oxford C :
DT - 35.08
WHIGHAM Lisa U17 14.08.80, Victoria PAAC/
Kirkintilloch : 300H - 46.8
WHITBY Sharon U15 29.09.80, Crawley :
800 - 2:17.5
WHITCOMBE Andrea 8.06.71, Parkside :
1500 - 4:24.1 (4:14.56-90),
3k - 9:10.29 (8:58.59-91), 5k - 16:12.96
WHITE Claire U23 24.02.73, Rugby :
100H - 14.6/15.11w
WHITE Felicity U17 17.11.78, Shaftesbury B :
Hepl - 3867
WHITE Jacqueline 12.01.71, Tamworth :
LJ - 6.11w/5.97

WHITE Laura U17 5.09.79, Hyndburn :
HJ - 1.72, Hepl - 4069
WHITE Rebecca U17 5.06.80, Blackburn :
60 - 7.99i, 100 - 12.2/12.39w/12.48,
200 - 25.0/25.41w/25.42, 300 - 40.01,
400 - 58.6, LJ - 5.39, TJ - 11.36
WHITEHEAD Fiona 31.05.70, Croydon/WLIHE :
HT - 40.62 (52.84-93)
WHITEHEAD Hayley U17 14.05.79, B-H Mans :
1500 - 4:40.85
WHITEHEAD Louise U23 26.03.75, Liv Pemb :
100 - 12.1 (12.1-93), 300 - 39.50i,
200 - 24.27w/24.58 (24.1-93), 400 - 54.92
WHITFIELD Joanna U20 5.01.78, Bristol :
PV - 2.70i/2.70
WHITLEY Meryl 12.04.69, Chester Le Street :
5k - 17:30.7
WHITLOCK Janine U23 11.08.73, Spenbro :
200 - 24.7, 60H - 8.82i, 100H - 14.1/14.47,
PV - 3.60i/3.41, LJ - 5.54,
TJ - 11.03, Hep - 4161
WHITNEY Paula U17 21.03.79, Warrington :
1500 - 4:41.3, 3k - 10:32.0
WHITTAKER Louise U13 29.11.82, Sale :
600 - 1:43.11, 800 - 2:24.2, 1500 - 4:57.8
WHITTINGTON Mandy 1.08.64, Bicester RR :
Mar - 2:49:44
WHITTLE Elizabeth U23 23.06.75, Wigan :
DT - 36.90 (38.94-94), HT - 36.42 (37.96-94)
WHITTON Gemma U15 25.05.81, Leominster :
75HG - 11.78w
WILDE Linden 11.05.61, Sale :
3k - 9:37.6mx, 5k - 16:37.21
WILDING Amanda J. U17 3.05.79, Soton City :
400H - 66.41
WILDING Helen U20 25.10.76, Wirral :
SP - 13.88, DT - 42.90, HT - 39.24
WILHELMY Sarah U17 2.02.80, Southend :
60 - 7.54i, 100 - 11.83,
200 - 24.19 (23.99w-94),
300H - 44.97, LJ - 5.97i/5.86
WILKIN Paula U23 28.03.74, City of Hull :
100H - 14.3/14.43w (15.33-94)
WILKINS Frances U17 15.01.79, Birchfield :
SP - 10.74i (10.37-94), Hepl - 3881
WILKINS Melanie U23 18.01.73, AF&D :
60H - 8.66i (8.55i-92), 100H - 13.1/13.34
WILKINS Serena U20 7.08.78, Yate :
200 - 25.06
WILKINSON J. U20, :
HJ - 1.65
WILKINSON Michelle U23 1.01.73, Sale :
800 - 2:07.15 (2:06.3-90), 1k - 2:45.34
WILLIAMS Donna Maria U17 7.10.78, Sale :
SP - 12.34, DT - 42.18
WILLIAMS Elizabeth U20 2.06.77, Walton :
300 - 39.6, 400 - 55.47
WILLIAMS Evette U20 23.03.78, Dartford :
100 - 12.0/12.24w/12.33 (12.33-94),
200 - 23.95w/24.04
WILLIAMS Helen U20 2.06.77, Walton :
200 - 25.07
WILLIAMS Kate-Elin U20 18.04.77, Swansea :
400 - 56.7/56.71
WILLIAMS Kathryn U20 10.11.77, Swansea :
400H - 62.34
WILLIAMS Maureen 22.02.69, Thames Valley :
400 - 56.7/57.13

387

WILLIAMS Perri 2.06.66, London Irish/IRE :
  3kW - 13:25.99, 5kW - 23:32.31,
  5kWR - 23:19, 10kW - 48:54.0
WILLIAMS Ruth E. 18.03.70, Darlington :
  200 - 25.28w (24.78-91),
  LJ - 5.51 (5.76i/5.65-92)
WILLIAMS Sharon 20.05.70, Team Solent :
  100 - 11.53, 200 - 23.80w/23.9/23.91,
  400 - 55.8 (56.07-89)
WILLIAMS Sophie U17 29.03.80, Somer :
  100 - 12.4/12.91
WILLIAMS Susan U20 2.06.77, Walton :
  100 - 12.1 (12.0w-94/12.39-93),
  200 - 24.2/24.30 (24.11w/24.27-94),
  400H - 65.6
WILLIAMS Syretta U15 3.05.81, Birchfield :
  PenG - 2774
WILLIAMS Victoria U15 11.04.81, Clevedon :
  PenG - 2562
WILLIAMSON Kelly Louise U17 4.12.79, Derby :
  LJ - 5.58i/5.49w/5.46 (5.66w/5.48-94),
  TJ - 10.86
WILSON Amy U15 31.12.80, Ipswich :
  SPG - 13.11
WILSON Carley U15 6.12.81, Morpeth :
  800 - 2:15.49, 1500 - 4:48.5
WILSON Paula 20.11.69, Birchfield :
  PV - 3.50i/3.20 (3.45-94)
WILSON Rachel V35 13.03.56, Bristol :
  Mar - 3:02:03
WILSON Shelley U13 17.01.83, Blackpool :
  150 - 20.2
WILSON Zoe U20 28.08.76, Coventry Godiva :
  60 - 7.75i, 100 - 12.1/12.13,
  200 - 25.1/25.24w/26.03
WINCKLESS Sarah Katherine U23 18.10.73,
  Epsom & Ewell/Cambridge University :
  DT - 52.58 (53.16-94), HT - 35.30 (37.28-94)
WINSHIP Nicola U17 24.09.78, Enfield :
  TJ - 10.66
WINTER Michelle U17 18.06.79, Wigan :
  80HI - 11.8w/12.0/12.19w/12.23,
  Hep - 3871, Hepl - 4090
WISE Clare L. 22.08.69, AF&D :
  100H - 15.28 (14.9-94),
  400H - 62.5/63.19 (61.84-94)
WISE Hannah U23 8.10.74, Woking :
  HJ - 1.65 (1.68-92)
WISEMAN Rachel U17 25.09.79, Croydon :
  300 - 41.45
WOFFENDEN Laura 14.08.70, Leeds :
  5k - 17:23.5, 10kR - 34:55,
  HMar - 1:18:44
WOLDEMARIN Fransua, Essex L/ETH :
  3k - 9:26.8
WOOD Joanna 2.10.72, Wigan :
  DT - 39.72 (41.18-94)
WOOD Laura U17 31.10.78, Trafford :
  DT - 36:72, HT - 32.48
WOODFORD Rebecca U13 26.02.83, RS Coldf :
  LJ - 4.70
WOODGER Meryl 3.11.66, Reading :
  TJ - 11.07w
WOODLAND Paula U17 21.12.78, Radley :
  60H - 9.12i (8.90i-94),
  80HI - 11.7/12.12 (11.64w/11.68-94),
  300H - 46.4/46.74

WOODRUFF Mirandra U13 6.09.82, Sutton & D :
  100 - 13.0, 200 - 27.0
WOODS Kelly U23 28.05.75, Peterborough :
  200 - 24.98i/25.00w/25.42, 400 - 56.14
WOODS Michelle U17 2.08.80, Basildon :
  SP - 11.25, DT - 37.74,
  JT - 38.30
WOOLGAR Deborah 10.03.65, Worthing :
  100H - 15.1w (14.3w/14.38-89),
  LJ - 5.67 (5.81-86),
  TJ - 11.30 (11.43-94),
  SP - 13.53 (14.18-89),
  DT - 37.48 (40.92-91),
  JT - 38.82 (41.08-89),
  Hep - 4907 (5434w-90/5380-89)
WOOLRICH Sharon U20 1.05.76, Ports Fare :
  HJ - 1.70 (1.70-94)
WRAGG Emma U13 22.01.83, Hallamshire :
  LJ - 4.75
WRIGHT Alice U17 31.12.78, Rowntrees :
  300H - 45.69 (44.92-94)
WRIGHT Amanda 14.07.68, Shaftesbury Barn :
  10kR - 33:46 (33:05-92),
  10MR - 56:02 (55:29-91),
  HMar - 1:16:06 (1:15:15-94)
WRIGHT Dawn-Alice U20 20.01.76, Cov G :
  PV - 3.00i/3.00 (3.10-94)
WRIGHT Jackie V40 8.10.53, Bracknell :
  DT - 42.02 (49.58-75)
WRIGHT Lucy 17.11.69, Leeds :
  5k - 17:10.1 (16:58.5-93)
WRIGHT Melanie 5.04.64, Nuneaton :
  3kW - 13:59.58 (13:49.0-93),
  5kW - 24:04.57 (23:47.0-94),
  5kWR - 23:24, 10kW - 48:35.8,
  10kWR - 48:44 (47:40sh-93/48:18-92)
WRIGHT Michelle U23 26.04.74, Solihull & SH :
  DT - 43.72 (44.32-93)
WYETH Alison 26.05.64, Parkside :
  1500 - 4:06.58 (4:03.17-93),
  2k - 5:53.4+ (5:38.50-93),
  3k - 8:48.94 (8:38.42-93), 5k - 15:00.37
WYNTER-PINK Clover U20 29.11.77, Croydon :
  100H - 14.5w/14.81, HJ - 1.67, SP - 11.74,
  JT - 42.72 (44.20-93), Hep - 5143

YARWOOD Cathy 17.06.69, Bolton :
  400H - 63.0/63.74
YEARDLEY Laura U15 21.12.80, Hallamshire :
  LJ - 5.33
YELLING Hayley U23 3.01.74, Hounslow :
  3k - 9:46.89 (9:46.38-94), 5k - 16:55.9
YOUDEN Nicola U20 2.11.77, Kilmarnock :
  400 - 56.56
YOUDEN Sally U20 2.11.77, Kilmarnock :
  400 - 57.3, 400H - 65.50
YOUNG Cathy U15 14.03.82, Stamford & D :
  PenG - 2569
YOUNG Hayley U17 26.09.79, Stamford & D :
  HJ - 1.77, TJ - 11.06, Hepl - 4272
YOUNG Sarah 2.01.70, Salford :
  3k - 9:54.7mx, 10kR - 33:20

ZAWADA Sarah U15 9.04.82, AF&D :
  60 - 7.97i, 100 - 12.25,
  200 - 24.82w/24.94
ZENIOU Carol D. V35 30.11.56, N London :
  LJ - 5.66 (6.45-82)

388

# TSB RANKINGS

The TSB Calculation Formula is shown below. The same tables are used for both Senior and Junior Rankings, but the Senior Rankings are based on four results in the last year with extra points for Championship placing, whereas a single performance is used for the Juniors.

## HOW TO CALCULATE YOUR POINTS ON THE TSB RANKINGS

Your performance is expressed in seconds, metres or, in the case of multi-events, points divided by 100 (eg. Decathlon 6543pts = 65.43).

i)   Look at your performance and ensure it is in range for your event.

ii)  Subtract your performance from the base value in column A and square the result   (ie. multiply it by itself).
     Note for field events you will square a negative number giving you a positive result.

iii) Multiply the number obtained in ii) above by the event factor, in column B.

iv)  Take the result of iii) above and discard any resulting fractions.
     From the remaining whole number, subtract the offset in column C. This whole number is the TSB Rankings points.

For example :-

**MEN**
         100m in 11.50 secs, in range, so OK,
         17.5 minus 11.50  =  6.00,
         6.00  x  6.00  =  36.00,
         36.00  x  21.8  = 784.8
         784 minus 0 = 784 TSB Ranking points

**WOMEN**
         HJ at 1.98 m,
         -10.85 minus 1.98  = -12.83,
         -12.83 x -12.83 = 164.6089
         164.6089 x 37.65 = 6197.525
         6197.525 = 6197
         6197 - 5000 = 1197 TSB Ranking points

**WOMEN**

| EVENT | A<br>BASE | B<br>FACTOR | C<br>OFFSET | RANGE |
|-------|------|--------|--------|-------|
| 100 | 23.5 | 7.63 | 0 | 9.48 - 23.13 |
| 200 | 50.5 | 1.5 | 0 | 18.87 - 49.68 |
| 300 | 85 | 0.481 | 0 | 29.14 - 83.55 |
| 400 | 118 | 0.26 | 0 | 42.02 - 116.03 |
| 800 | 249 | 0.0693 | 0 | 101.87 - 245.20 |
| 1500 | 540 | 0.0134 | 0 | 205.32 - 531.36 |
| 1M | 580 | 0.0118 | 0 | 223.46-570.79 |
| 3k | 1280 | 0.00208 | 0 | 430.51 - 1258.07 |
| 5k | 2150 | 0.000762 | 0 | 746.96 - 2113.77 |
| 10K | 4530 | 0.000174 | 0 | 1593.89 - 4454.19 |
| 10M | 8020 | 0.00005 | 0 | 2542 - 7878 |
| HMAR | 10500 | 0.0000302 | 0 | 3452 - 10318 |
| MAR | 21600 | 0.0000074 | 0 | 7362 - 21232 |
| 75H | 21 | 10.4 | 0 | 8.99 - 20.68 |
| 80H | 24 | 6.4 | 0 | 8.69 - 23.60 |
| 100H | 31.4 | 3.43 | 0 | 10.49 - 32.0 |
| 300H | 98 | 0.332 | 0 | 30.78 - 100.45 |
| 400H | 140 | 0.163 | 0 | 44.07 - 143.50 |
| 10kW | 8160 | 0.0000381 | 0 | 1885 - 7997 |
|  |  |  |  |  |
| HJ | -10.85 | 37.65 | 5000 | 0.68 - 2.29 |
| PV | -42 | 2.9 | 4990 | 0.01 - 5.31 |
| LJ | -56 | 1.56 | 5000 | 0.62 - 8.55 |
| TJ | -100 | 0.472 | 5000 | 2.94 - 17.35 |
| SP | -490 | 0.0431 | 10000 | 0.01 - 26.55 |
| DT | -3507 | 0.00166 | 20000 | 0.02 - 91.88 |
| HT | -2900 | 0.00241 | 20000 | 0.02 - 86.90 |
| JT | -3605 | 0.00157 | 20000 | 0.02 - 95.58 |
| HEP | -2901 | 0.00241 | 20000 | 0.01 - 85.84 |
| HEPI | -2901 | 0.00241 | 19940 | 0.01 - 81.68 |
| PENG | -1200 | 0.0105 | 14990 | 0.01 - 53.19 |

## MEN

| EVENT | A<br>BASE | B<br>FACTOR | C<br>OFFSET | RANGE |
|---|---|---|---|---|
| 100 | 17.5 | 21.8 | 0 | 9.21 - 17.28 |
| 200 | 36 | 4.8 | 0 | 18.32 - 35.54 |
| 300 | 59 | 1.66 | 0 | 28.93 - 58.22 |
| 400 | 82 | 0.86 | 0 | 40.23 - 80.92 |
| 800 | 187 | 0.174 | 0 | 94.15 - 184.60 |
| 1500 | 395 | 0.0365 | 0 | 192.22 - 389.76 |
| 1M | 420 | 0.0334 | 0 | 208.07 - 414.52 |
| 3k | 870 | 0.00713 | 0 | 411.32 - 858.15 |
| 5k | 1500 | 0.00238 | 0 | 706.11 - 1479.50 |
| 10K | 3060 | 0.000612 | 0 | 1494.43 - 3019.57 |
| 10M | 5500 | 0.000155 | 0 | 2389 - 5419 |
| HMAR | 7200 | 0.000095 | 0 | 3226 - 7097 |
| MAR | 14700 | 0.0000248 | 0 | 6922 - 14499 |
| 1.5KST | 500 | 0.0167 | 0 | 200.29 - 492.26 |
| 2KST | 630 | 0.0125 | 0 | 283.58 - 621.05 |
| 3KST | 1060 | 0.00376 | 0 | 418.38 - 1043.69 |
| 80H | 21 | 8.6 | 0 | 7.79 - 20.65 |
| 100H | 24.8 | 7.2 | 0 | 10.37 - 24.42 |
| 110H | 29 | 4.86 | 0 | 11.43 - 28.54 |
| 400H | 104 | 0.39 | 0 | 41.98 - 102.39 |
| 20kW | 12000 | 0.0000231 | 0 | 3941 - 11791 |
| 50kW | 43200 | 0.00000137 | 0 | 10110 - 42345 |
| | | | | |
| HJ | -9.42 | 37.55 | 4000 | 0.91 - 2.68 |
| PV | -37 | 2.75 | 3850 | 0.43 - 7.11 |
| LJ | -50 | 1.82 | 5000 | 2.42 - 9.76 |
| TJ | -99.95 | 0.45 | 5000 | 5.47 - 20.24 |
| SP | -359 | 0.0775 | 9970 | 0.01 - 25.72 |
| SPB (4kg) | -359 | 0.0769 | 10000 | 1.63 - 27.72 |
| DT | -2380 | 0.00354 | 19950 | 0.02 - 81.58 |
| HT | -3000 | 0.00224 | 20030 | 0.02 - 100.26 |
| JT | -3095 | 0.00211 | 20130 | 0.02 - 106.76 |
| DEC | -3086 | 0.00211 | 20020 | 0.01 - 107.60 |
| OCT | -2250 | 0.00396 | 20000 | 0.01 - 80.09 |
| PEN | -1400 | 0.00772 | 14990 | 0.01 - 61.51 |

# TSB JUNIOR RANKINGS 1995

## Men Under 20

| | | | | | | | | |
|---|---|---|---|---|---|---|---|---|
| 1. | Mark Hylton | Berks | (400) | 1122 | 51. | Dominic Shepherd | Ches | (PV) | 971 |
| 2. | Dwain Chambers | Mx | (100) | 1094 | 52. | Michael Tietz | Derbs | (100) | 971 |
| 3. | Jamie Henthorn | | (100) | 1094 | 53. | Craig Wheeler | Gtr Man. | (3KST) | 969 |
| 4. | Marlon Devonish | West Mid | (200) | 1088 | 54. | Gareth Marks | Dyfed | (DTJ) | 968 |
| 5. | Damien Greaves | Essex | (110HJ) | 1056 | 55. | Bill Fuller | Surrey | (SPJ) | 966 |
| 6. | Des Roache | Scot | (800) | 1052 | 56. | James Storey | Herts | (110HJ) | 966 |
| 7. | Daniel Money | Derbs | (200) | 1049 | 57. | Mark Butland | Dyfed | (110HJ) | 966 |
| 8. | Geoff Dearman | Mx | (400) | 1049 | 58. | James Shipp | Norfolk | (400) | 965 |
| 9. | Richard Girvan• | Scot | (800) | 1032 | 59. | Marvin Bramble | Mx | (TJ) | 963 |
| 10. | Graham Beasley | Beds | (200) | 1031 | 60. | Allen Graffin | Kent | (5K) | 963 |
| 11. | Mark Findlay | Essex | (200) | 1028 | 61. | Roger Morley | Lincs | (800) | 962 |
| 12. | Mark Davis | Nothants | (PV) | 1026 | 62. | Nathan Morgan | Leics | (LJ) | 962 |
| 13. | James Archampong | | (110HJ) | 1026 | 63. | Charles R-Adams | Shrops | (400H) | 961 |
| 14. | Uvie Ugono | London | (200) | 1025 | 64. | Michael Bell | West Mid | (400) | 961 |
| 15. | Alasdair Donaldson | Scot | (800) | 1025 | 65. | Russell Cartwright | Leics | (1500) | 960 |
| 16. | James Brierley | Shrops | (HJ) | 1024 | 66. | Neil Jennings | Cleve | (400) | 960 |
| 17. | Mike Robbins | West Mid | (HJ) | 1024 | 67. | Tom Mayo | West Mid | (1500) | 959 |
| 18. | Steve McHardy | West Mid | (400) | 1019 | 68. | Simon Heggie | Notts | (400) | 959 |
| 19. | Richard Aspden | Surrey | (HJ) | 1017 | 69. | Corri Henry | Notts | (200) | 956 |
| 20. | Rob Brocklebank | Lancs | (HJ) | 1017 | 70. | Sam Omonua | Berks | (100) | 956 |
| 21. | Tom Lerwill | Essex | (800) | 1017 | 71. | Mark Bushell | Hants | (LJ) | 955 |
| 22. | Mark Rowlands | West Glam | (400HY) | 1015 | 72. | Gavin Mason | Surrey | (800) | 955 |
| 23. | Andrew Blackmore | Shrops | (800) | 1012 | 73. | Matthew Clarke | Nothants | (800) | 954 |
| 24. | Dominic Bradley | Ches | (110HJ) | 1010 | 74. | Peter Brend | Devon | (400) | 952 |
| 25. | Ross Baillie | Scot West | (110H) | 1010 | 75. | Matt O'Dowd | Wilts | (3KST) | 952 |
| 26. | Ian Mitchell | W. Yorks | (1500) | 1010 | 76. | Adam Carswell | Devon | (110HJ) | 951 |
| 27. | Paul Brizzell | | (200) | 1008 | 77. | Andrew Lowe | Gtr Man. | (HJ) | 950 |
| 28. | Hugh Kerr | Scot West | (400) | 1006 | 78. | David Franks | Gtr Man. | (HJ) | 950 |
| 29. | Matthew Douglas | Bucks | (400H) | 1005 | 79. | Mark Latham | Staffs | (HJ) | 950 |
| 30. | Mike Floyd | Gtr Man. | (HTJ) | 1005 | 80. | Anthony Malcolm | Wilts | (LJ) | 947 |
| 31. | Trevor Cameron | Mx | (100) | 1003 | 81. | Roger Hunter | W. Yorks | (DEC) | 946 |
| 32. | Clayton Archer | Mx | (200) | 1003 | 82. | Robert Scantlebury | Surrey | (400) | 946 |
| 33. | Mark Miles | Warks | (1500) | 1000 | 83. | Andrew Benn | Kent | (HTJ) | 946 |
| 34. | Alan Tatham | Derbs | (1500) | 996 | 84. | Ryan Patis | Kent ' | (400) | 945 |
| 35. | Ben Reese | Mersey | (1500) | 994 | 85. | Sean Baldock | Sussex | (400) | 945 |
| 36. | Dean Macey | Essex | (HJ) | 994 | 86. | Robert Thickpenny | Cambs | (PV) | 944 |
| 37. | Stuart Stokes | Gtr Man. | (3KST) | 993 | 87. | James Peacock | Essex | (TJ) | 943 |
| 38. | Brendan Smith | Gtr Man. | (1500) | 991 | 88. | Kevin Mark | Mx | (100) | 942 |
| 39. | Paul Gripton | Here &Wr | (110HJ) | 990 | 89. | Chris Hindley | Notts | (HJ) | 942 |
| 40. | Mark Ponting | Gwent | (400) | 990 | 90. | Carl Foster | S. Yorks | (400H) | 942 |
| 41. | Andrew Graffin | Kent | (1500) | 989 | 91. | Kevin Farrell | Essex | (200) | 941 |
| 42. | Kevin Nash | Surrey | (3KST) | 987 | 92. | Tim Slocombe | Dorset | (400) | 941 |
| 43. | Neil Young | | (PV) | 985 | 93. | Jon Quint | Norfolk | (800) | 939 |
| 44. | James Leaver | Dorset | (HJ) | 980 | 94. | Yacin Yusuf | Surrey | (1500) | 938 |
| 45. | Paul Sampson | W. Yorks | (100) | 980 | 95. | Richard Churchill | S. Yorks | (110HJ) | 937 |
| 46. | Ben Challenger | Leics | (HJ) | 980 | 96. | Anthony Gill | W. Yorks | (110HJ) | 937 |
| 47. | Andy Young | Scot West | (800) | 980 | 97. | Bryn Middleton | | (100) | 936 |
| 48. | Dale Canning | Gtr Man. | (800) | 977 | 98. | Wayne Martin | Wilts | (400) | 936 |
| 49. | Wayne Clarke | Lincs | (HTJ) | 976 | 99. | Andrew Mitchell | Scot West | (400) | 936 |
| 50. | Adam Smith | | (HJ) | 972 | 100. | Bode Oluwa | London | (100) | 936 |

# TSB JUNIOR RANKINGS 1995

## Men Under 17

| | | | | | | | | | |
|---|---|---|---|---|---|---|---|---|---|
| 1. | Emeka Udechuku | London | (DTY) | 1160 | 51. | Thomas Begen | Scot West | (100) | 911 |
| 2. | Leo Barker | Northants | (OCTY) | 1024 | 52. | Richard Singer | Scot East | (400HY) | 910 |
| 3. | Carl Myerscough | Lancs | (SPY) | 1009 | 53. | Andrew Squire | Staffs | (OCTY) | 910 |
| 4. | Christian Malcolm | Gwent | (200) | 997 | 54. | Clifton Green | Kent | (JTY) | 909 |
| 5. | Ben Warmington | Northumb | (100HY) | 996 | 55. | Andrew Charles | Mx | (100HY) | 909 |
| 6. | Phillip Perigo | S. Yorks | (200) | 982 | 56. | John Hepworth | Hants | (200) | 908 |
| 7. | Christian Linskey | S. Yorks | (PV) | 974 | 57. | Ben Harper | Essex | (400) | 906 |
| 8. | Marc Newton | Staffs | (OCTY) | 973 | 58. | Simon Mathieson | Avon | (400) | 906 |
| 9. | David Parker | N. Yorks | (JTY) | 971 | 59. | Courtney Joseph | Mx | (100HY) | 905 |
| 10. | James Hilston | Surrey | (400) | 971 | 60. | Robert Lewis | Beds | (400HY) | 904 |
| 11. | Richard McNabb | S. Yorks | (400) | 971 | 61. | Gareth Lewis | Gwent | (400HY) | 903 |
| 12. | John Skeete | Essex | (200) | 970 | 62. | Matthew Dixon | Lancs | (800) | 903 |
| 13. | Michael Combe | Scot East | (800) | 964 | 63. | Pete Waterman | Kent | (SPY) | 902 |
| 14. | Chris Blake | Gtr Man. | (200) | 962 | 64. | Alastair Newmarch | Lincs | (400HY) | 902 |
| 15. | Ryan Davoile | Warks | (800) | 961 | 65. | Richard Dent | W. Yorks | (HJ) | 902 |
| 16. | Russell Quelch | Hants | (400HY) | 961 | 66. | Steve Jamieson | Kent | (JTY) | 902 |
| 17. | Chris Hargrave | Northants | (100HY) | 961 | 67. | Stephen Briffett | London | (800) | 900 |
| 18. | Andrew Row | Northumb | (100) | 959 | 68. | Matthew De'Ath | Bucks | (800) | 900 |
| 19. | Antonio Matarazzo | Gloucs | (200) | 954 | 69. | Luke Grinnell | Avon | (100) | 900 |
| 20. | Alan Rudkin | Lincs | (OCTY) | 954 | 70. | Andrew Thomas | Mersey | (800) | 899 |
| 21. | Nizamul Hoque | London | (400) | 953 | 71. | Andy Edmonds | Hants | (200) | 899 |
| 22. | Darren Hatton | | (OCTY) | 946 | 72. | Nick Barber | S. Yorks | (SPY) | 895 |
| 23. | Liam Collins | Northumb | (100HY) | 945 | 73. | Sion Owen | Ches | (800) | 894 |
| 24. | Chris Carson | Scot East | (400) | 945 | 74. | Chris Low | Scot East | (OCTY) | 894 |
| 25. | David O'Leary | Mersey | (100HY) | 945 | 75. | Dave Irwin | | (SPY) | 892 |
| 26. | Sam Allen | Humber | (OCTY) | 944 | 76. | Andrew Boon | West Mid | (100HY) | 892 |
| 27. | Ruben Tabares | London | (400HY) | 944 | 77. | Marlon Dickson | London | (100) | 888 |
| 28. | Neil Kirk | Kent | (800) | 941 | 78. | Greig Goodey | Essex | (400HY) | 887 |
| 29. | James Hodson | Ches | (OCTY) | 935 | 79. | Luke Davis | West Mid | (200) | 887 |
| 30. | David Stanley | Hants | (800) | 934 | 80. | Ross McFarland | Scot West | (LJ) | 887 |
| 31. | Nick Dowsett | Essex | (100HY) | 929 | 81. | Robert Fanning | Bucks | (400) | 885 |
| 32. | David Powell | N. Yorks | (OCTY) | 928 | 82. | Lee Garrett | Notts | (1500) | 885 |
| 33. | James Bull | Suffolk | (SPY) | 926 | 83. | David Black | Staffs | (DTY) | 884 |
| 34. | Tom Benn | Essex | (100HY) | 926 | 84. | Ian Cawley | Hants | (100HY) | 883 |
| 35. | Lee Black | Northants | (OCTY) | 924 | 85. | Mark Warmby | W. Yorks | (1.5KST) | 882 |
| 36. | Ahmed Al-Kowarri | Scot | (400) | 922 | 86. | Kris Stewart | Scot East | (400) | 881 |
| 37. | Tom Vanhinsbergh | Sussex | (HJ) | 922 | 87. | Duncan Howarth | Nofolk | (400HY) | 881 |
| 38. | Andrew Lees | Scot East | (200) | 920 | 88. | Daniel Bonich | Kent | (100) | 880 |
| 39. | Gordon Menzies | Scot West | (100HY) | 920 | 89. | Edward Willers | Essex | (HJ) | 880 |
| 40. | Gareth Turnbull | | (1500) | 920 | 90. | Clint Nicholls | Essex | (HJ) | 880 |
| 41. | Nick Long | Mersey | (100) | 919 | 91. | Daniel Slessor | Cumbria | (HJ) | 880 |
| 42. | Ben Flint | S. Yorks | (PV) | 917 | 92. | Martin Lloyd | Kent | (HJ) | 880 |
| 43. | Andrew Penk | Clwyd | (HJ) | 916 | 93. | Steven Scott | London | (100HY) | 880 |
| 44. | Danny Graham | Mersey | (HJ) | 916 | 94. | Nick Hamilton | London | (400) | 880 |
| 45. | Gurmukh Sahans | | (OCTY) | 915 | 95. | Michael Collins | Lancs | (LJ) | 879 |
| 46. | Jonathan Wallace | West Mid | (TJ) | 914 | 96. | Simon Plaskett | Bucks | (400) | 879 |
| 47. | Chris Moss | Kent | (800) | 913 | 97. | George Skevis | Sussex | (DTY) | 878 |
| 48. | Paul Morris | West Mid | (400HY) | 912 | 98. | David Naismith | Derbs | (400) | 877 |
| 49. | Ian Leaman | Devon | (200) | 912 | 99. | Rufus Cooper | Mx | (PV) | 877 |
| 50. | Jonathan Moss | Ches | (200) | 911 | 100. | David Mitchinson | Wilts | (1.5KST) | 876 |

# TSB JUNIOR RANKINGS 1995

## Men Under 15

| | | | | | | | | |
|---|---|---|---|---|---|---|---|---|
| 1. | Ben Lewis | West Mid | (200) | 887 | 51. | Ken McKeown | Scot West (HJ) | 748 |
| 2. | Kevin Hibbins | Leics | (LJ) | 850 | 52. | Russell Pittam | Sussex (1500) | 748 |
| 3. | Ian Lowthian | Mersey | (400) | 842 | 53. | Lewis Short | Scot (100) | 747 |
| 4. | Andre Silva | S. Glam | (100) | 839 | 54. | Kieron Farrelly | Surrey (1500) | 746 |
| 5. | Richard Smith | Lincs | (PV) | 839 | 55. | Stuart Tynan | Mid Glam (SPB) | 746 |
| 6. | Ross Kidner | Bucks | (HTB) | 832 | 56. | Richard Gawthorpe | Derbs (PENB) | 745 |
| 7. | Wayne Gray | London | (HJ) | 831 | 57. | Tony Seston | Suffolk (80HB) | 744 |
| 8. | Adrian Cluskey | London | (SPB) | 829 | 58. | Jason Stone | Mx (HTB) | 740 |
| 9. | Leon McRae | Avon | (80HB) | 829 | 59. | Matthew Bailey | S. Yorks (800) | 740 |
| 10. | Daniel Plummer | Essex | (100) | 828 | 60. | Sam Murray | Kent (400) | 739 |
| 11. | Robert Hollinger | S. Yorks | (80HB) | 825 | 61. | Jonathan Beharie | Surrey (400) | 738 |
| 12. | Leon Connikie | Kent | (400) | 818 | 62. | Stephen Holmes | Kent (1500) | 736 |
| 13. | Graeme Allan | Scot North | (SPB) | 807 | 63. | Daniel Carthy | Devon (1500) | 734 |
| 14. | Joseph Maxwell | Berks | (80HB) | 806 | 64. | Shaun Groves | Gwent (JTB) | 734 |
| 15. | Dominic Gordon | Avon | (100) | 804 | 65. | Jonathon Miller | West Mid (TJ) | 731 |
| 16. | Philips Olwenu | Mx | (JTB) | 804 | 66. | Neil Hewson | Gtr Man. (400) | 731 |
| 17. | Simon Williams | Hants | (DTB) | 802 | 67. | John Shenava | Scot East (400) | 731 |
| 18. | Alex Chaffe | Derbs | (200) | 799 | 68. | Adrian Rawling | Cornwall (SPB) | 730 |
| 19. | Jonathon Keith | W. Yorks | (1500) | 798 | 69. | Simon Collins | Humber (100) | 729 |
| 20. | Robin Wheldon | Devon | (SPB) | 783 | 70. | Paul Crick | Derbs (200) | 729 |
| 21. | Alex Wilkinson | N. Yorks | (200) | 782 | 71. | Robert Newton | Notts (80HB) | 728 |
| 22. | Adam Newton | Berks | (100) | 781 | 72. | Chris Sweeney | Mersey (HJ) | 727 |
| 23. | Mike Ferraro | Clwyd | (100) | 781 | 73. | Ian Smith | Lincs (400) | 726 |
| 24. | Christopher Bennett | Hants | (400) | 779 | 74. | Richard Fowler | West Mid (3K) | 725 |
| 25. | Finlay Wright | Berks | (80HB) | 779 | 75. | Andrew Brabin | Mersey (1500) | 725 |
| 26. | Tony Quinn | | (SPB) | 778 | 76. | Morris Tolaram | (100) | 722 |
| 27. | Scot Thompson | Scot North | (DTB) | 778 | 77. | Gregg Dale | Humber (800) | 722 |
| 28. | Austin Ferns | London | (800) | 777 | 78. | Andrew Umpleby | Shrops (80HB) | 721 |
| 29. | Steven Jackson | | (100) | 775 | 79. | James Milburn | Northumb (80HB) | 721 |
| 30. | Russell Johnson | Essex | (100) | 773 | 80. | Daniel Johnstone | Essex (80HB) | 721 |
| 31. | Kirk King | Sussex | (LJ) | 770 | 81. | Jonathan Groenen | Sussex (PENB) | 721 |
| 32. | Henry Richards | Leics | (100) | 768 | 82. | Kevin McKinson | London (HJ) | 720 |
| 33. | Barry Woodward | Notts | (800) | 766 | 83. | Ross Edgerton | Hants (HJ) | 720 |
| 34. | Robert Worrall | Gtr Man. | (LJ) | 766 | 84. | James Wood | Essex (HJ) | 720 |
| 35. | Michael Church | | (800) | 766 | 85. | Ben Davies | Avon (HJ) | 720 |
| 36. | John Heanley | Berks | (800) | 765 | 86. | Danny Hermann | W. Yorks (800) | 720 |
| 37. | Tom Oswald | Northumb | (200) | 763 | 87. | Daniel Everett | Norfolk (PENB) | 720 |
| 38. | Neil Dixon | | (HJ) | 762 | 88. | Brian Pearce | Kent (80HB) | 719 |
| 39. | Matthew Sutton | Staffs | (HTB) | 761 | 89. | Paul Wheatcroft | Gtr Man. (LJ) | 719 |
| 40. | Peter Watson | Ox | (PENB) | 761 | 90. | Sheridan Williams | Warks (100) | 719 |
| 41. | Myrone Levy | West Mid | (200) | 760 | 91. | Brian Morrison | (LJ) | 719 |
| 42. | Wayne Hay | Berks | (LJ) | 759 | 92. | Philip Sharpe | Lancs (JTB) | 719 |
| 43. | Daryl Russell | Essex | (PENB) | 757 | 93. | Matthew Jones | Wilts (200) | 718 |
| 44. | Gareth Dyball | Essex | (HJ) | 754 | 94. | Chris Baillie | Scot West (80HB) | 718 |
| 45. | Matthew Butler | Essex | (200) | 754 | 95. | Lyndon Woodward | Staffs (SPB) | 718 |
| 46. | Simon Bullock | Here &Wr | (400) | 753 | 96. | A. Henry | (80HB) | 717 |
| 47. | Gareth Melvin | Cumbria | (1500) | 750 | 97. | Darren Chapman | Herts (80HB) | 715 |
| 48. | Jonathan Hockey | Essex | (800) | 750 | 98. | Martin Cowan | Wilts (PENB) | 715 |
| 49. | Andrew Turner | Notts | (80HB) | 749 | 99. | James Philip | Beds (TJ) | 714 |
| 50. | John Blackman | N. Yorks | (200) | 748 | 100. | Karl Robertson | Cumbria (200) | 714 |

# TSB JUNIOR RANKINGS 1995

## Women Under 20

| | | | | | | | | | | |
|---|---|---|---|---|---|---|---|---|---|---|
| 1. | Natasha Danvers | Kent | (100H) | 1104 | 51. | Nicole Smallwood | West Mid | (HJ) | 993 |
| 2. | Michelle Dunkley | Nothants | (HJ) | 1098 | 52. | Teresa Andrews | | (HJ) | 993 |
| 3. | Rachael Forrest | Shrops | (HJ) | 1098 | 53. | Josie Gray | | (1M) | 993 |
| 4. | Rebecca Drummond | Staffs | (100) | 1095 | 54. | Dorothea Lee | Dorset | (800) | 991 |
| 5. | Elona Reinalda | | (200) | 1076 | 55. | Rachel Hopgood | N. Yorks | (DT) | 990 |
| 6. | Ellena Ruddock | West Mid | (100) | 1076 | 56. | Helen Williams | Surrey | (200) | 989 |
| 7. | Evette Williams | Kent | (200) | 1063 | 57. | Serena Wilkins | Avon | (200) | 989 |
| 8. | Vicky Shipman | Derbs | (200) | 1060 | 58. | Jenny Balogun | Hants | (200) | 987 |
| 9. | Rhian Clarke | | (PV) | 1059 | 59. | Amanda Waite | Essex | (100) | 986 |
| 10. | Vicki Jamison | | (400H) | 1058 | 60. | Ellen O'Hare | Gloucs | (1500) | 986 |
| 11. | Allison Curbishley | Cleve | (400) | 1055 | 61. | Elizabeth Gibbens | Kent | (TJ) | 986 |
| 12. | Kate Norman | Surrey | (400H) | 1049 | 62. | Katie Jones | Gtr Man. | (400H) | 985 |
| 13. | Sinead Dudgeon | Scot East | (200) | 1046 | 63. | Stacey Rodd | S. Glam | (100) | 984 |
| 14. | Lisa Brown | Scot East | (HJ) | 1046 | 64. | Nicola Youden | Scot West | (400) | 983 |
| 15. | Susan Jones | Gtr Man. | (HJ) | 1046 | 65. | Jane Fuller | Bucks | (400H) | 983 |
| 16. | Julie Crane | Notts | (HJ) | 1046 | 66. | Julie Hollman | Lincs | (200) | 983 |
| 17. | Amanda Tremble | Northumb | (3K) | 1046 | 67. | Denise Bolton | Gtr Man. | (100H) | 983 |
| 18. | Jo Sloane | Here &Wr | (400) | 1045 | 68. | Suzanne McGowan | Scot West | (200) | 982 |
| 19. | Susan Williams | Surrey | (200) | 1044 | 69. | Sheila Fairweather | Scot West | (1500) | 982 |
| 20. | Clare Ridgley | Hants | (PV) | 1044 | 70. | Dextene McIntosh | Essex | (400H) | 981 |
| 21. | Clover Wynter-Pink | Surrey | (HEP) | 1036 | 71. | Kate-Elin Williams | | (400) | 979 |
| 22. | Jo Mahoney | Mersey | (400H) | 1035 | 72. | Simone Harrison | Surrey | (400) | 976 |
| 23. | Rachel King | | (100H) | 1034 | 73. | Emma Dengate | Surrey | (100) | 976 |
| 24. | Louretta Thorne | Bucks | (200) | 1030 | 74. | Sarah Godbeer | Devon | (200) | 975 |
| 25. | Alice Braham | Somerset | (3K) | 1028 | 75. | Rhonda MacPhee | Kent | (800) | 971 |
| 26. | Rebecca Kilgour | Devon | (200) | 1028 | 76. | Susan Mary Douglas | | (100) | 971 |
| 27. | Natalie Hynd | Scot East | (100) | 1026 | 77. | Lyndsey Fletcher | Gtr Man. | (100) | 971 |
| 28. | Lucy Carter | Beds | (200) | 1026 | 78. | Louise Sharps | Ches | (100) | 971 |
| 29. | Kathy Thurston | Ches | (400H) | 1024 | 79. | Rebecca Lewis | Ches | (HEP) | 971 |
| 30. | Helen Fee | Herts | (100) | 1021 | 80. | Natalie Smethurst | Gtr Man. | (200) | 970 |
| 31. | Elizabeth Williams | Surrey | (400) | 1017 | 81. | Clare Bushby | Northumb | (100H) | 969 |
| 32. | Jannette Niccolls | London | (100) | 1015 | 82. | Katie Budd | Surrey | (100H) | 969 |
| 33. | Michelle Mann | Lancs | (3K) | 1014 | 83. | Sharon Price | West Mid | (100H) | 966 |
| 34. | Gillian Hegney | Scot West | (100) | 1013 | 84. | Sarah-Louise Barker | London | (200) | 965 |
| 35. | Fiona Hutchison | Scot West | (200) | 1012 | 85. | Julia Moss | Ches | (400) | 965 |
| 36. | Philippa Roles | West Glam | (DT) | 1011 | 86. | Juliana Palka | Scot West | (200) | 964 |
| 37. | Liz Fairs | Derbs | (100H) | 1006 | 87. | Kerry Smithson | Lancs | (800) | 963 |
| 38. | Zoe Wilson | West Mid | (100) | 1005 | 88. | Louise Eden | Gtr Man. | (LJ) | 962 |
| 39. | Leanne Eastwood | Lancs | (200) | 1005 | 89. | Claire Swift | Mersey | (3K) | 962 |
| 40. | Stacey Jacques | West Mid | (400) | 1005 | 90. | Jennifer Impett | Dorset | (100) | 960 |
| 41. | Emma Symonds | Norfolk | (200) | 1005 | 91. | Jane O'Malley | Humber | (400H) | 960 |
| 42. | Lindsay Evans | Suffolk | (HJ) | 1002 | 92. | Gosha Rostek | Scot West | (200) | 959 |
| 43. | Juliette Oldfield | Nothants | (1500) | 1002 | 93. | Ellie Mardle | Devon | (200) | 958 |
| 44. | Lorraine Bell | Scot West | (400) | 1000 | 94. | Jenny Harnett | Kent | (800) | 958 |
| 45. | Kirsty Payne | Shrops | (100) | 1000 | 95. | Jane Groves | Ches | (800) | 958 |
| 46. | Kelly Sotherton | Hants | (HEP) | 1000 | 96. | S. Baker | London | (200) | 956 |
| 47. | Adele Foster | Humber | (100) | 1000 | 97. | Sally Youden | Scot West | (400) | 956 |
| 48. | Clare Hill | | (400) | 995 | 98. | Nicky Slater | Ox | (3K) | 955 |
| 49. | Kate Williams | Mid Glam | (400H) | 995 | 99. | Catriona Morrison | Scot | (5K) | 952 |
| 50. | Susan Hendry | Scot East | (400) | 993 | 100. | Kathryn Saunders | Berks | (400) | 952 |

# TSB JUNIOR RANKINGS 1995

## Women Under 17

| | | | | | | | | | |
|---|---|---|---|---|---|---|---|---|---|
| 1. | Lesley Owusu | Berks | (300) | 1062 | 51. | Lynne Fairweather | Scot East | (80HI) | 965 |
| 2. | Sarah Wilhelmy | Essex | (100) | 1054 | 52. | Tammie Francis | DORSET | (JT) | 964 |
| 3. | Julie Pratt | Essex | (80HI) | 1045 | 53. | Lee McConnell | Scot West | (200) | 963 |
| 4. | Lauren Keightley | Berks | (DT) | 1044 | 54. | Mairi McEwen | Scot West | (100) | 963 |
| 5. | Emma Ania | Mx | (200) | 1043 | 55. | Hannah Paines | S. Glam | (100) | 963 |
| 6. | Tatum Nelson | Kent | (100) | 1039 | 56. | Amanda Pritchard | | (300) | 963 |
| 7. | Nicola Hall | Suffolk | (80HI) | 1032 | 57. | Lisa Thomas | Mx | (100) | 962 |
| 8. | Helen Roscoe | Ches | (200) | 1030 | 58. | Sharon Hollett | Scot West | (300) | 962 |
| 9. | Maria Bolsover | S. Yorks | (300) | 1030 | 59. | Emily De Nobrega | London | (300) | 960 |
| 10. | Melanie Purkiss | Hants | (200) | 1027 | 60. | Leanne Rowlands | Gwent | (100) | 958 |
| 11. | Claire Pearson | Leics | (80HI) | 1025 | 61. | Nikita Thompson | | (80HI) | 958 |
| 12. | Lindsay Impett | Dorset | (200) | 1019 | 62. | Kelly Moreton | Gwent | (HJ) | 958 |
| 13. | Lucy Chaffe | Essex | (100) | 1018 | 63. | Joanne McDougall | Mersey | (200) | 956 |
| 14. | Wendy Cox | Durham | (200) | 1018 | 64. | Tracy Martin | West Mid | (200) | 956 |
| 15. | Emma Anderson | Staffs | (80HI) | 1017 | 65. | Ayeesha Charles | Ox | (100) | 955 |
| 16. | Samantha Davies | West Mid | (200) | 1016 | 66. | Susan Christie | Scot West | (100) | 955 |
| 17. | Kate Denham | Hants | (200) | 1016 | 67. | Tommy Kemp | Somerset | (1500) | 955 |
| 18. | Katherine Endacott | Devon | (200) | 1014 | 68. | Emma Davies | Hants | (800) | 955 |
| 19. | Laura Seston | Suffolk | (100) | 1013 | 69. | Deanne Kenney | Leics | (80HI) | 955 |
| 20. | Hayley Young | Lincs | (HJ) | 1011 | 70. | Claudine Leger | Essex | (100) | 955 |
| 21. | Jade Johnson | London | (LJ) | 1005 | 71. | Natalie Butler | Ox | (80HI) | 955 |
| 22. | Sarah Claxton | Essex | (80HI) | 1004 | 72. | Cicely Hall | Norfolk | (400H) | 954 |
| 23. | Tracy Bishop | Mx | (200) | 999 | 73. | Louise Gentle | Beds | (HJ) | 950 |
| 24. | Ruth Watson | Cambs | (300) | 998 | 74. | Claire Farquharson | Sussex | (HJ) | 950 |
| 25. | Gael Davies | Gloucs | (80HI) | 996 | 75. | Julie Hynan | Mersey | (HJ) | 950 |
| 26. | Helen Pryer | Surrey | (200) | 993 | 76. | Alison James | Gloucs | (HJ) | 950 |
| 27. | Syreena Pinel | Leics | (200) | 992 | 77. | Fiona Hunter | Scot East | (TJ) | 947 |
| 28. | Victoria Henson | Cambs | (80HI) | 992 | 78. | Gail Evans | Dyfed | (100) | 947 |
| 29. | Kate Forsyth | Northumb | (80HI) | 992 | 79. | Anna Leyshon | W. Glam | (80HI) | 946 |
| 30. | Rachael Ogden | N. Yorks | (800) | 991 | 80. | Jennifer Such | Derbs | (100) | 946 |
| 31. | Jayne Ludlow | | (TJ) | 989 | 81. | Susan Atavwigho | Kent | (300) | 945 |
| 32. | Pamela Johnstone | Scot East | (400H) | 988 | 82. | Sally Burnham | Humber | (100) | 944 |
| 33. | Dawn Rose | Warks | (100) | 986 | 83. | Clare Anning | S. Glam | (80HI) | 944 |
| 34. | Rebecca White | Lancs | (300) | 984 | 84. | Jackie Tindal | Scot East | (80HI) | 944 |
| 35. | Rachel Martin | Cumbria | (HJ) | 984 | 85. | Tracey Duncan | Mx | (300H) | 944 |
| 36. | Lesley McGoldrick | Durham | (80HI) | 982 | 86. | Melissa Okusanya | Derbs | (300) | 944 |
| 37. | Amanda Forrester | Staffs | (200) | 982 | 87. | Gillian Stewart | Scot East | (80HI) | 943 |
| 38. | Elizabeth Walker | S. Yorks | (200) | 980 | 88. | Karen Scott | Scot | (100) | 943 |
| 39. | Gahlie Davis | Dorset | (100) | 979 | 89. | Kate Grimshaw | Northumb | (3K) | 943 |
| 40. | Antonia Bemrose | Hants | (HJ) | 976 | 90. | Carmel Triggs | Mersey | (200) | 942 |
| 41. | Sarah Cootes | Essex | (300) | 975 | 91. | Abigail Naugher | Durham | (300) | 942 |
| 42. | Shelley-Anne Bowen | Berks | (200) | 973 | 92. | Nina Rogers | Staffs | (300) | 942 |
| 43. | Kelly Morgan | Wilts | (JT) | 971 | 93. | Emily Nicholls | Avon | (100) | 941 |
| 44. | Karen Gear | Devon | (200) | 970 | 94. | Chloe Cozens | Beds | (HJ) | 941 |
| 45. | Claire Nichols | Surrey | (300) | 970 | 95. | Claire Smith | Derbs | (300) | 940 |
| 46. | Helen Lee | Notts | (300) | 970 | 96. | Rebecca Clark | Leics | (200) | 940 |
| 47. | Sam Foster | Essex | (HJ) | 967 | 97. | Hannah Eatough | Lancs | (100) | 939 |
| 48. | Laura White | Lancs | (HJ) | 967 | 98. | Sian Lax | Shrops | (JT) | 938 |
| 49. | Kelly Lopez | Essex | (100) | 966 | 99. | Donna Lennon | NI | (100) | 936 |
| 50. | Kelli Bailey | Shrops | (100) | 966 | | | | | |

# TSB JUNIOR RANKINGS 1995

## Women Under 15

| | | | | | | | | |
|---|---|---|---|---|---|---|---|---|
| 1. | Rachael Kay | Gtr Man. | (200) | 1034 | 51. | Debbie Morgan | Gwent | (100) | 908 |
| 2. | Naomi Hodge-Dallaway | London | (75HG) | 1013 | 52. | Joanne Stringer | Berks | (75HG) | 907 |
| 3. | Libby Alder | Gloucs | (100) | 1012 | 53. | Helen Wanstall | Kent | (HJ) | 906 |
| 4. | Serena Bailey | Essex | (75HG) | 1011 | 54. | Rebecca King | Sussex | (200) | 903 |
| 5. | Karlene Palmer | Berks | (200) | 1005 | 55. | Joan MacPherson | Hants | (DT) | 903 |
| 6. | Sarah Zawada | Hants | (200) | 998 | 56. | Michelle Whalley | Mersey | (1500) | 902 |
| 7. | Sarah Akinbiyi | London | (75HG) | 976 | 57. | Beth Orford | Warks | (HJ) | 898 |
| 8. | Lindsay Fleet | Kent | (200) | 975 | 58. | Rachel Snape | Derbs | (HJ) | 898 |
| 9. | Chantell Manning | London | (100) | 973 | 59. | Syretta Williams | | (PENG) | 896 |
| 10. | Natalie Law | London | (200) | 970 | 60. | Rachel Houghton | Ches | (PENG) | 895 |
| 11. | Rhian Cains | Shrops | (200) | 966 | 61. | Melissa Anderson | Northumb | (100) | 894 |
| 12. | Rachel Redmond | Staffs | (200) | 966 | 62. | Sinead Rattigan | West Mid | (100) | 893 |
| 13. | Kate Hill | Bucks | (100) | 962 | 63. | Jodie Swallow | Essex | (1500) | 893 |
| 14. | Lois Cresswell | West Mid | (200) | 960 | 64. | Helen Thieme | Notts | (PENG) | 892 |
| 15. | Amy Wilson | Suffolk | (SPG) | 958 | 65. | Jennifer Meadows | Gtr Man. | (800) | 892 |
| 16. | Alison Kerboas | Gtr Man. | (PENG) | 952 | 66. | Emma Reid | Scot East | (PENG) | 891 |
| 17. | Rachel Rogers | Hants | (200) | 952 | 67. | Sarah Nash | Warks | (200) | 891 |
| 18. | Dionne Howell | Surrey | (200) | 951 | 68. | Tanya Brazier | Herts | (1500) | 890 |
| 19. | Alex Hajipavlis | West Mid | (DT) | 951 | 69. | Amie Hill | OX | (DT) | 890 |
| 20. | Emily Freeman | W. Yorks | (200) | 943 | 70. | Jennifer Hills | Somerset | (HJ) | 889 |
| 21. | Caroline Pearce | Cambs | (PENG) | 943 | 71. | Helen Pearson | Cornwall | (1500) | 889 |
| 22. | Lucy Rann | Hants | (SPG) | 940 | 72. | Mary Onianwa | London | (HJ) | 889 |
| 23. | Petrina Alleyne | Berks | (100) | 939 | 73. | Angela Martin | Cumbria | (HJ) | 889 |
| 24. | Becki Marshall | Wilts | (75HG) | 938 | 74. | Sophie McQueen | Humber | (HJ) | 889 |
| 25. | Emma Hughes | Beds | (200) | 937 | 75. | April Kalu | Gtr Man. | (SPG) | 888 |
| 26. | Laura Curtis | Humber | (PENG) | 935 | 76. | Clare Russell | Gtr Man. | (100) | 887 |
| 27. | Rebecca Martindale | Cumbria | (200) | 934 | 77. | Maria Pringle | Cumbria | (PENG) | 887 |
| 28. | Lisa Callan | Scot West | (200) | 933 | 78. | Heather Brooks | Gtr Man. | (200) | 885 |
| 29. | Kelly Thomas | Kent | (100) | 932 | 79. | Emily Buckwell | Kent | (PENG) | 883 |
| 30. | Sarah Lane | Gwent | (75HG) | 930 | 80. | Erica Burfoot | S. Glam | (200) | 883 |
| 31. | Claire Daniels | Hants | (200) | 928 | 81. | Maryann Naboya | Herts | (SPG) | 883 |
| 32. | Lisa Thompson | Gwynned | (PENG) | 926 | 82. | Emily Giles | Durham | (1500) | 883 |
| 33. | Rachel Harris | Mersey | (HJ) | 924 | 83. | Carley Wilson | Northumb | (800) | 882 |
| 34. | Fiona Harrison | S. Yorks | (PV) | 923 | 84. | Kimberley Canning | Scot West | (200) | 882 |
| 35. | Carolynne Sutherland | Scot East | (75HG) | 922 | 85. | Tina Thirwell | Gtr Man. | (PENG) | 882 |
| 36. | Emma Ward | Staffs | (1500) | 922 | 86. | Ellouise Francis | Wilts | (200) | 881 |
| 37. | Victoria Blair | Gtr Man. | (100) | 921 | 87. | Stefanie Oates | Gtr Man. | (200) | 880 |
| 38. | Kirsten Dyce | Scot West | (200) | 921 | 88. | Amy Fendley | Notts | (PENG) | 879 |
| 39. | Nichola Coates | Northumb | (1500) | 918 | 89. | Jennifer Grogan | Kent | (800) | 878 |
| 40. | Serena Woodhouse | Derbs | (100) | 918 | 90. | Rebecca Smith | Lincs | (100) | 878 |
| 41. | Laura Foster | S. Yorks | (75HG) | 916 | 91. | Laura Redmond | Scot East | (PENG) | 878 |
| 42. | Clare Turner | Kent | (75HG) | 916 | 92. | Devena Williams | West Mid | (100) | 878 |
| 43. | Andrea Lang | Scot West | (100) | 914 | 93. | Gemma Metherell | Somerset | (100) | 878 |
| 44. | Gemma Swetman | Sussex | (PENG) | 914 | 94. | Charlotte Todd | Scot East | (100) | 878 |
| 45. | Kay Goodman | Cambs | (PENG) | 913 | 95. | Charmaine Cameron | Staffs | (100) | 878 |
| 46. | Rebecca Lunn | Derbs | (200) | 913 | 96. | Hannah Norman | Scot East | (1500) | 878 |
| 47. | Jane Dutton | Ches | (75HG) | 911 | 97. | Nikki Daniels | Staffs | (800) | 877 |
| 48. | Emma Phillips | W. Yorks | (100) | 908 | 98. | Sarina Mantle | | (75HG) | 876 |
| 49. | Donna Naylor | West Mid | (200) | 908 | 99. | Kate Gilmore | Mersey | (100) | 875 |
| 50. | Jo Thorn | Avon | (100) | 908 | 100. | Sarah Venn | Lancs | (200) | 874 |

# AMENDMENTS TO BRITISH ATHLETICS 1995
From Peter Matthews, Ian Hodge and other members of NUTS

| | |
|---|---|
| **Results** | Page 75 3kSt result was from 1993! Correct result |
| | 1. Justin Chaston 8:28.28   2. Spencer Duval 8:28.33 |
| | 3. Colin Walker 8:29.65     4. Michael hawkins 8:39.39 |
| | 5. Robert Hough 8:40.09     6. Neil Smart 8:42.44 |
| | 7. David Lee 8:46.23        8. Carl Warren 8:47.00 |

**Merit**       **Mar** Moore 2:13:34; **HT** G Cook 3rd mark 62.88

**Men**
| | |
|---|---|
| **200** | 21.9 T White delete (see 21.6 White) |
| **400** | Hill (50.6) 15.12.77 |
| **10MRoad** | Harris (48:59) 27.04.71 |
| | add 49:05 Glyn Tromans 17.3.69 2 Coventry 19 Jun |
| **3kSt** | Eynon (9:24.46) 1.09.62 |
| **HJ** | Franks (1.91) 27.04.78 |
| **Marathon** | 2:23:15 Dennis Walmsley 19 Lisbon, POR 27 Nov |

**Women**
| | |
|---|---|
| **400** | delete Mills 54.81 |
| **3k et al** | Sally Goldsmith 18.1.61: 3k 9:48.25 Cesenatico, ITA 2 Oct |
| | 5k 16:28.38 Conegliano, ITA 22 May, 10k 35:17.12 Brescia, ITA |
| | 1 May (also **1993** 5k 17:02.56 S Bonifacio, ITA 23 May |
| | 10k 35:52.8 Ponzano Veneto, ITA 10 Apr, **1992** 5k 17:31.32 |
| | Cittadella, ITA 3 May, 10k 36:47.0 Verona, ITA 12 Apr) |
| | Yvonne Danson 22.5.59: 10kRoad 32:29 Kuatan, MAL 13 Nov |
| | & 32:54 1 Hong Kah South 29 May, 33:23 1 Singapore 17 Apr, |
| | Half Mar 1:12:32 1 Serembon, MAL 31 Jul |
| | (also **1993** 10kRoad 34:47 1 Singapore(?) 28 Mar, 10M 56:28 |
| | 1 Singapore (?) 19 Sep, Half Mar 1:14:38 Shah Alan, MAL 12 Dec) |
| **10kRoad** | Watson (33:58) Alaneda, USA 7 Aug |
| **Marathon** | 2:54:17  Gillian Beschloss 18.12.58 3 San Francisco, USA 31 Jul |
| **HJ** | 1.78 Rachel Forrest 1 Cheltenham 24 Sep (from 1.76) |
| **PV** | Alexander (3.00) 3.00 1 Nice, FRA 22 Jun |
| **LJ** | Idowu 6.26 4 Caorle, ITA 16 Jul |
| **JT** | 44.60 Helen Potter 2 Stretford 14 May |

| | |
|---|---|
| **Index** | DAVIS Trevor (100 - 10.3-91, 200 - 21.1-91) |
| | MURRAY Yvonne (5k - 15:50.54-84) |
| | TUNALEY Sharon (100 - 11.53w-86, 11.80/11.5w-85, 11.6-87 |
| | 200 - 23.8w-87, 23.94w-88, 24.2/24.26 -87) |

## Late amendments to British Athletics 1996
The following were recieved after printing of the lists
The marks in 2kSt and 3kSt are for Colin Palmer not Karl Palmer
Karl Palmer's best for 1995 is 9:21.0 Loughborough 24 May
100k better mark Willie Sichel 7:17:39 Winschoten, HOL 16 Sep

Many additions and corrections have been made to the index.

Any extra information for the index is always most welcome.